she trembled, though, oil fell from her lamp and severely burned Cupid's shoulder. He awoke, and finding that his wife had betrayed him, he fled.

In anguish at her faithlessness and at having hurt him and then lost him, Psyche vowed to show Cupid how much she loved him by spending the rest of her life searching for him. She prayed to all the gods for help, but none of them wanted to risk the wrath of Venus. Finally, in desperation, Psyche prayed to Venus herself.

Cupid had flown to his mother and asked her to treat his wound. When Venus heard that Cupid had married Psyche and that Psyche had betrayed her pledge to Cupid, Venus decided to punish Psyche severely. When Psyche begged for forgiveness from Venus, Venus belittled Psyche as faithless and plain and told her that her only hope for forgiveness was to perform certain tasks. The tasks were clearly impossible, but Psyche hoped that in her travels to complete the tasks she might find her lost love. First, Venus took some tiny seeds of wheat, poppy, and millet, mixed them, and dropped them in a single pile. She gave Psyche until nightfall to separate the seeds. Psyche despaired, but a colony of ants, showing compassion, sorted them for her. Venus returned, and seeing what had happened, became even angrier.

So Venus gave Psyche more impossible tasks, such as to fetch the golden wool of some fierce sheep and to obtain black water from the river Styx. Again, through the help of others, Psyche fulfilled her tasks. Finally Cupid, who was now healed, longed for her once again. He went to her, scolded her gently for her earlier faithlessness, and assured her that her search was over. He longed to reunite with her, so he approached Jupiter, king of the gods, and beseeched him to grant Psyche immortality. Jupiter consented and, before an assembly of gods, made Psyche a goddess and announced that Cupid and Psyche were formally married. Even Venus was joyous: Her son now had a suitable match. Moreover, with Psyche in the heavens rather than on Earth, people would no longer be distracted by Psyche's beauty and would worship Venus once again.

The curiosity of Psyche and her search — for both knowledge (of who Cupid was and what he looked like) and for love — are symbolic of our own spirit of inquiry as we go in search of the human mind. The story of Psyche exemplifies many of the phenomena that psychologists seek to study: curiosity, envy, love, compassion, altruism, and perseverance.

Most of all, the story of Psyche is a symbol of the one thing that we all have that can be studied but perhaps never fully understood, of the one thing that is given to us but can never be taken away — the human spirit. Despite tremendous obstacles, Psyche persisted in her search for what made her soul complete.

Love and Soul . . . had sought and,
after some trials, found each other;
and that union could never be broken.
(Hamilton, 1942, p. 100)

In Search of the

HUMAN MIND

This book is dedicated to my mother, who stood up for me when, during my seventh-grade science project, the school psychologist threatened to burn my copy of *Measuring Intelligence* if I ever brought it into school again.

In Search of the

HUMAN MIND

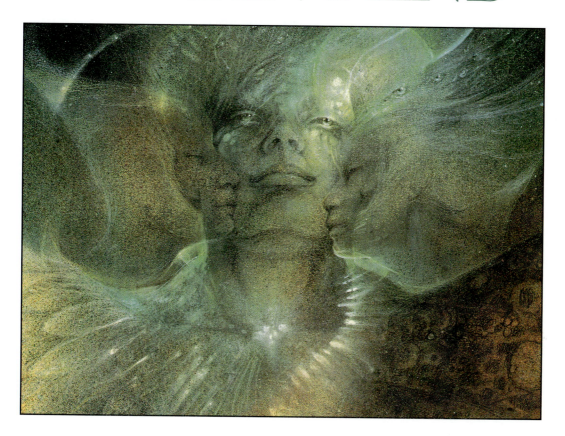

ROBERT J. STERNBERG

Yale University

HARCOURT BRACE COLLEGE PUBLISHERS

FORT WORTH PHILADELPHIA SAN DIEGO NEW YORK ORLANDO AUSTIN SAN ANTONIO
TORONTO MONTREAL LONDON SYDNEY TOKYO

Editor-in-chief	TED BUCHHOLZ
Acquisitions editor	CHRISTINA N. OLDHAM / EVE HOWARD
Senior developmental editor	SARAH HELYAR SMITH
Senior project editor	STEVE NORDER
Senior production manager	KENNETH A. DUNAWAY
Art director	BURL SLOAN
Electronic page layout	BILL MAIZE, DUO DESIGN GROUP
Photo permissions	SUE C. HOWARD
Literary permissions	JULIA STEWART
Editorial associate	SHARI HATCH
Cover illustrator	SUSAN SEDDON BOULET
Medical illustrator	HARWIN STUDIOS

Library of Congress Catalog Card Number: 94-79342

Address for Editorial Correspondence: Harcourt Brace College Publishers, 301 Commerce Street, Suite 3700, Fort Worth, TX 76102.

Address for Orders: Harcourt Brace & Company, 6277 Sea Harbor Drive, Orlando, FL 32887-6777. 1-800-782-4479, or 1-800-433-0001 (in Florida).

ISBN: 0-15-500342-9

Printed in the United States of America

6 7 8 9 0 1 2 3 4 048 9 8 7 6 5 4

ABOUT THE AUTHOR

Robert J. Sternberg is IBM Professor of Psychology and Education in the Department of Psychology at Yale University. He was graduated summa cum laude, Phi Beta Kappa, with a BA from Yale in 1972, receiving honors with exceptional distinction in psychology. He received the PhD in psychology in 1975 from Stanford University and an honorary doctorate from the Complutense University of Madrid in 1994.

Sternberg has won several scholarships and fellowships, including a National Merit Scholarship to attend Yale, where he won the Wohlenberg Prize; a National Science Foundation Fellowship to attend Stanford, where he received the Sidney Siegel Memorial Award; and a Guggenheim Fellowship while a faculty member at Yale. He also has won several other awards, including the Early Career and McCandless Awards of the American Psychological Association, the Outstanding Book and Research Review Awards of the American Educational Research Association, the Cattell Award of the Society of Multivariate Experimental Psychologists, and the International Award of the Association of Portuguese Psychologists. Sternberg is a Fellow of the American Psychological Association, American Psychological Society, and the American Association for the Advancement of Science.

Sternberg has been editor of the *Psychological Bulletin* and president of Divisions 1 (General Psychology) and 15 (Educational Psychology) of the American Psychological Association. He is the author of more than 400 books, book chapters, and articles, and has held more than $8 million in research grants and contracts.

About the Artists

Part One

Rebecca Ruegger notes, "Learning that Psyche had red hair, I wanted to portray that part of her physical being. I looked for an opportunity within the myth to illustrate this, and the talking reeds along the water's edge seemed to be the answer." She used watercolors on paper. Ruegger paints in a studio in her home on a small farm in Franklin, Tennessee.

Part Two

Trish Burgio writes, "I felt Psyche's constantly tumultuous environment is abstracted from her gentle personality." She used acrylics. Burgio paints and resides in Santa Monica, California.

Part Three

Terry Hoff explains, "My inspiration for the painting was to depict Psyche's searching for the elusive secrets common to the universal human experience." He used acrylics. Hoff has been a successful illustrator for 10 years. He works and resides in Pacifica, California.

Part Four

Kathleen Kinkopf writes, "I was naturally drawn to Psyche's struggle in the gathering of the golden fleece. The thought of the evil sheep seemed to be such a dichotomy. This is where I felt her goodness alone had protected her from evil." She used pastels. Kinkopf is a commercial illustrator and runs a gallery in Breckenridge, Colorado.

Part Five

Theresa Smith notes, "When I read the Psyche myth it became clear to me the fundamental attitudes that mothers portray toward their sons and their sons' objects of desire. Jealousy, betrayal, and revenge are insidious throughout the myth. All to end with the one aspect that is true to real life, that everyone just wants to be loved." She used oil pastels and colored pencils. Smith lives in Tucson, Arizona, where she maintains her freedom through her fine art, illustration, design, and computer animation.

Part Six

Arden von Haeger explains, "I tried to capture the scene when Psyche went to the summit of the rocky hill, alone, to await the winged serpent. There is the feeling of her dark despair and loneliness, only for her to be lifted, in the end, by the Zephyr winds into the arms of the god of love." He created the image with chalk pastels on German sandpaper. Von Haeger is a freelance illustrator based in Nashville, Tennessee.

PREFACE

In Search of the Human Mind is the product of a purpose and a passion: to teach students to understand and to think as psychologists do. It is the course I wish that I had taken when I studied Introductory Psychology.

Embracing equally the biological, cognitive, developmental, social, and clinical paradigms, the content is rigorous yet thoroughly readable. It is theory- and research-based, with pedagogical features that encourage students to apply the results of that research. The twenty chapters are organized into six parts, addressing the nature of psychology, basic biological and cognitive processes, higher cognitive processes, developmental processes, social psychological processes, and clinical processes. A statistical appendix demonstrates statistical methods by having students survey their classmates and analyze those data. A glossary fully defines key terms from the text, and a comprehensive reference list as well as detailed name and subject indexes complete the back matter.

This book focuses on three closely related themes: higher order thinking, the evolution of ideas, and integration. Through these themes, students come to understand psychology not as a static field but as a dynamic, evolving science. Students learn better and understand more because they understand the context of what they learn, not just a set of isolated facts.

HIGHER ORDER THINKING *In Search of the Human Mind* teaches students not only the facts and ideas they need to be psychologists but also how to think critically about these facts. This book's higher order thinking approach is much broader and far more useful than those of other textbooks. Whereas some books ask students to think analytically about isolated questions, *In Search of the Human Mind* asks students to think three ways—analytically, creatively, and practically—about not only a wide range of psychological issues but also how their own personal experiences relate to those issues.

The theory of pedagogy underlying the book derives from my own triarchic theory of human intelligence, but you need not accept this particular theory or any other to realize the value of students learning the facts and learning to think analytically, creatively, and practically with these facts. To be a psychologist—researcher, practitioner, or teacher—one needs to think about psychology in all three of these ways. Moreover, each student has a different, preferred style of learning and thinking about psychology. By teaching the facts and how to think about them in three different ways, you will find that, as a teacher, you will reach far more students than you ever have before. I know, because that is how I came to teach both my freshman undergraduates at Yale and the advanced-placement high school students who have come to the summer program at Yale that I designed according to this model. I have seen firsthand the difference this approach makes. In addition, class testing by Harcourt Brace showed that students preferred this book 2 to 1 over the market leader.

The textbook teaches students to think critically by providing two forms of prompting questions in each chapter: *In Search of . . .* questions, located at the beginning of major sections, ask students to think globally about the major issues of the chapter; and *triarchic questions*, scattered throughout the sections and at the end of each chapter and part, ask students to draw upon their own experiences and to think analytically, creatively, or practically about specific concepts. The text also models critical analyses of research and theories and highlights the critical processes that researchers go through as they refine their theories.

EVOLUTION OF IDEAS: DIALECTIC Critical thought is at the core of psychological research. For students to think about ideas as psychologists do, students need to understand how those ideas have come about. A key emphasis in this book, therefore, is on the evolution of ideas in psychology. *In Search of the Human Mind* emphasizes the dialectical progression of psychology: from one point of view, to an opposing view, to a synthesis of the two, which then becomes the basis for a new point of view to be opposed. The dialectical approach both enables students to understand the current theories in psychology and provides a framework for students to understand the shifts in emphasis over time among the biological, cognitive, developmental, social, and clinical paradigms.

INTEGRATION To support the universal perspective of dialectic, the text carefully integrates, generalizes, and applies the topics and theories of each chapter to all other related chapters. It encourages students to generalize their knowledge of psychology to other experiences by relating text material to other disciplines and by showing how those disciplines also progress through a dialectic. Because the field of psychology is embedded not only in its own historical antecedents but in other disciplines as well, the integrated approach allows psychology to come alive through numerous literary quotes, works of art, and examples from the natural sciences. In this way, students with interests in other disciplines as well as those whose primary interest is in psychology will see how psychology relates to the myriad ways of thinking about people and the world.

Students learn to think about psychology in a global perspective not only through the relation of key ideas to work in other disciplines, but also through the use of numerous multicultural and cross-cultural examples. My own research has looked at thinking both multiculturally—as when I have compared the conceptions of intelligence of different ethnic groups—and cross-culturally—as when I have studied effects of parasitic infections on the thinking of Jamaican schoolchildren. By studying problems beyond narrow groups of subjects, one learns to appreciate not just how complex these problems are, but how better they can be approached for solution. Just as problems need to be studied in their many contexts, so do people.

PEDAGOGY See the preface "To the Student" for illustrations and descriptions of the many pedagogical features, which include chapter outlines, triarchic questions, key terms, *Searchers* boxes, an extensive illustration program, a point-by-point chapter summary, and *Charting the Dialectic* part summaries.

DESIGN The design is an integral part of *In Search of the Human Mind*, reinforcing the book's many strong features. The design uses two primary symbols to unify the book: Psyche, the mythical soul and the symbol for psychology; and the dialectical tree. Psyche, whose image appears on the cover and whose myth is explained on the inside front cover, appears on each of the part openers. Each part image presents a different artist's interpretation of the myth of Psyche, the different interpretations themselves representing a form of dialectic. (See the artists' own comments about their interpretations in the "About the Artists" section, page vi.) Psyche's lamp is featured prominently in the broad *In Search of . . .*

questions in the chapters. The dialectical tree, on the inside back cover, illustrates the evolution of psychology from its roots to its present myriad branches. The tree image is echoed in each chapter and is highlighted in the dialectical discussions at the end of each part.

To continue the unified theme of critical thinking, the design also uses three secondary symbols, which represent the elements of the triarchic theory of intelligence. Rodin's *Thinker* symbolizes analytic thinking, an artist's palette symbolizes creative thinking, and a wheel symbolizes practical thinking. The symbols identify the type of each triarchic question both in the chapters and the parts.

ANCILLARY PACKAGE

In support of *In Search of the Human Mind*, the ancillary package builds on solid pedagogical theory to serve the needs of the Introductory Psychology student and instructor and to take full advantage of the latest in technology.

- The **Study Guide** by Bernard C. Beins (Ithaca College) is rigorously designed to mirror the features of the text. Each chapter lists specific goals and objectives, helps students review the material through fill-in-the-blank questions, reinforces terminology with matching exercises, and encourages students to synthesize the information through short-answer questions of varied rigor that reflect the triarchic theory. Finally, the Study Guide provides two practice tests per chapter.

As an APA fellow and secretary of Division Two, Teaching of Psychology, Bernard Beins is involved extensively with the issues regarding the Introductory Psychology course. He has published numerous articles and has given various presentations on the subject of enhancing the learning experience.

- The **Instructor's Manual** has been created by Edward P. Kardas (Southern Arkansas University). Its vast resources, designed to assist both new and experienced instructors, include hints on how to integrate critical thinking into the classroom, chapter goals and objectives that directly reflect those in the Study Guide, lecture suggestions and notes to enhance lectures, reading suggestions, demonstrations, video resources with a brief description of the content, as well as numerous exercises and handouts to encourage the student to think critically along the lines of the triarchic theory. A discussion of how to utilize the computer and Internet in teaching is unique to this manual.

Edward Kardas is chair of the APA Division Two taskforce on secondary and undergraduate psychology.

• The **Testbank** closely supports the theme of critical thinking from the textbook, the Study Guide, and the Instructor's Manual. Each chapter provides 180 convergent, multiple-choice items and 45 divergent, short-essay items. Two-thirds of the convergent items are conceptual (the remaining one-third are factual), and all are rated by difficulty and keyed to the section and the page in the textbook where the concept is discussed. The divergent items ask students to answer questions in essay format to bring out the triarchic forms of thinking. Answer guidelines give instructors key concepts to look for in the students' essays.

Closely reviewed by Robert Sternberg and Dennis Cogan (Texas Tech University), the testbank chapters were written by a panel of experienced instructors, including Stuart Korshavn (St. Norbert College), Terry Blumenthal (Wake Forest University), Paul Wellman (Texas A&M University), George Cicala (University of Delaware), Susan Davis (Loras College), Susan Lima (University of Wisconsin), Fran Spencer (Towson State University), Carolyn Mangelsdorf (University of Washington), Josephine Wilson (Wittenberg University), and Stephen Buggie (Presbyterian College).

Computerized versions of the testbank are available in DOS 3.5-inch, DOS 5.25-inch, Windows, and Macintosh versions. The testbank software, *EXAMaster+*™ offers three unique features to the instructor. *EasyTest* creates a test from a single screen in just a few easy steps. Instructors choose parameters, then either select questions from the database or let EasyTest randomly select them. *FullTest* offers a range of options that includes selecting, editing, adding, or linking questions or graphics; random selection of questions from a wide range of criteria; creating criteria; blocking questions; and printing up to 99 different versions of the same test and answer sheet. *EXAMRecord*™ records, curves, graphs, and prints out grades according to criteria the instructor selects. Grade distribution displays as a bar graph or plotted graph.

For the instructor without access to a computer or who has questions about the software, Harcourt Brace College Publishers (800-447-9457) offers two services. *RequesTest* provides a software specialist who will compile questions according to the instructor's criteria and mail or fax the test master within 48

hours. The *Software Support Hotline* is available to answer questions Monday through Friday, 9 a.m. to 4 p.m., Central time.

• The **Overhead Transparencies** come in two packages: 75 illustrations and tables, specially selected from *In Search of the Human Mind* by Paul Chara (Loras College), supplement the more than 200 transparencies in the Harcourt Brace Introductory Psychology Transparency package. Each acetate, with accompanying guide, is in full color.

Multimedia and Interactive Software

• **Harcourt Interactive,** *Psychology: The Core on CD-ROM,* prepared by John Mitterer (Brock University), is an innovative learning tool that allows students to explore and understand the realm of psychology in an interactive, multimedia environment. Mini-lectures, covering the key concepts in every chapter, include video footage, animation, and experiments, and are linked directly to the full text, which also appears on the CD-ROM. In addition, the CD-ROM allows students to test their mastery of the material via a series of test questions hyperlinked to the relevant sections of *In Search of the Human Mind.*

Mitterer, who has been praised for his authorship of Harcourt Brace's videodisc, *Dynamic Concepts in Psychology,* has coordinated the creation of the CD-ROM with the help of such experienced lecturers as Tom Brothen (University of Minnesota), Bill Buskist (Auburn University), Paula Goolkasian (University of North Carolina, Charlotte), Carolyn Meyer (Lake Sumter Community College), David Murphy (Waubonsee Community College), and Robert Patterson (Washington State University).

• *Dynamic Concepts in Psychology,* a highly successful videodisc developed by John Mitterer (Brock University), covers every major concept of Introductory Psychology. Media include animated sequences, video footage, still images, and demonstrations of well-known experiments. Adhesive bar codes facilitate quick access to images during lectures, and a modular format allows instructors to tailor the program to their course. Level III software gives instructors the ability to preprogram classroom presentations and to import material from other videodiscs (DOS, Macintosh).

• *Discovering Psychology,* a video series, is an Introductory Psychology course hosted by Philip Zimbardo, comprising 26 half-hour programs on 13 one-hour tapes. The *Teaching Modules* provide condensed versions of the programs, comprising 15 15-minute units. An Instructor's Guide provides descriptions and teaching suggestions. The program is available on videotape or videodisc.

- *LectureActive* software, which accompanies the videodiscs, enables instructors to create custom lectures swiftly and simply.

- *Infinite Voyage,* a videodisc series, incorporates on-location, interview, laboratory, and candid footage produced by WQED of Pittsburgh to provide compelling coverage of high-interest topics in psychology.

- *Harcourt Brace Quarterly: A Video News Magazine,* produced with CBS Television, brings current psychological applications from today's headlines into your classroom. One-hour videos are compiled from the *CBS Nightly News, CBS This Morning, 48 Hours,* and *Street Stories with Ed Bradley.* Instructors' Notes summarize each 2- to 5-minute segment. (Segments from *48 Hours* and *Street Stories* may be longer.)

- *The Brain* teaching modules compile key segments of the PBS series *The Brain* into 30 video modules of about 6 minutes each.

- *The Mind* video modules, developed by Frank Vattano (Colorado State University, Fort Collins) in cooperation with WNET of New York, offer selections from the PBS series *The Mind* to illustrate important concepts in Introductory Psychology.

- *Personal Discovery* provides a computerized series of self-description, self-exploration, and extended personal planning activities to help the student apply psychological principles to life (DOS, Macintosh).

- *The Psychology Experimenter* enables individuals or groups to create, design, modify, and conduct experiments. The resulting data can be saved, displayed, and printed (DOS).

- *Supershrink I and II,* developed by Joseph Lowman (University of North Carolina, Chapel Hill), introduces students to clinical interviewing techniques by allowing them to take the role of a helpline crisis volunteer with clients Victor (*Supershrink I*) and Jennifer (*Supershrink II*) (DOS).

- *PsychLearn* provides five experiments in which the student participates as subject (DOS, Macintosh).

- *BrainStack,* an interactive self-guided tour to the human cerebral cortex, includes a self-study quiz and an on-line index (Macintosh).

ACKNOWLEDGMENTS

I am indebted to colleagues who contributed many helpful ideas to the entire manuscript, both text and illustrations: Anne Beall, *Yale University* (test items); Talia Ben Zeev, *Yale University* (profile boxes); Richard Gerrig, *Yale University* (literature); Michael Gorman, *University of Virginia* (science); Walter Lonner, *Western Washington University* (cultural diversity); Colin Martindale, *University of Maine* (art); John Mitterer, *Brock University* (core topics); Cheryl A. Rickabaugh, *Redlands University* (development across the lifespan); Daniel Robinson, *Georgetown University* (philosophy); and Renuka Sethi, *California State University* (cultural diversity).

I am also grateful to colleagues who reviewed portions of the manuscript in its various drafts: Gordon A. Allen, *Miami University;* Joyce Y. Allen, *Eastern Illinois University;* Eileen Astor-Stetson, *Bloomsburg University;* Daryl Beale, *Cerritos College;* Charles M. Bourassa, *University of Alberta;* Nathan Brody, *Wesleyan University;* James F. Calhoun, *University of Georgia;* Leo M. Chalupa, *University of California, Davis;* Paul Chara, *Loras College;* Dennis Cogan, *Texas Tech University;* Edward H. Cornell, *University of Alberta;* Thaddeus M. Cowan, *Kansas State University;* George Diekhoff, *Midwestern State University;* Karen G. Duffy, *State University of New York, Geneseo;* Charles R. Early, *Roanoke College;* Gilles O. Einstein, *Furman University;* Fernanda Ferreira, *Michigan State University;* Katherine V. Fite, *University of Massachusetts, Amherst;* Donelson R. Forsyth, *Virginia Commonwealth University;* Linda D. Gerard, *Michigan State University;* Morton A. Gernsbacher, *University of Oregon;* Paula A. Goolkasian, *University of North Carolina, Charlotte;* Charles R. Grah, *Austin Peay State University;* Richard Griggs, *University of Florida, Gainesville;* Craig H. Jones, *Arkansas State University;* Seth C. Kalichman, *Loyola University, Chicago;* Daniel P. Keating, *Ontario Institute for Studies in Education;*

Mike Knight, *Central State University;* Lester Krames, *University of Toronto, Erindale;* V. K. Kumar, *West Chester University;* Marcy Lansman, *University of North Carolina, Chapel Hill;* Michael Levine, *University of Illinois, Chicago;* Paul E. Levy, *University of Akron;* Scott Maxwell, *University of Notre Dame;* Deborah R. McDonald, *New Mexico State University;* Timothy P. McNamara, *Vanderbilt University;* Anita Meehan, *Kutztown University of Pennsylvania;* Jim L. Mottin, *University of Guelph;* Gregory L. Murphy, *Brown University;* James M. Murphy, *Purdue University, Indiana University School of Medicine;* Thomas L. Nelson, *Illinois Central College;* John Nezlek, *College of William and Mary;* Michael Palij, *New York University;* Robert Patterson, *Washington State University;* Tamra Pearson D'Estrée, *University of Arizona, Tucson;* John B. Pittenger, *University of Arkansas, Little Rock;* James D. Roth, *University of Kansas;* Susan Schenk, *Texas A&M University;* William J. Struhar, *Sinclair Community College;* Lori L. Temple, *University of Nevada, Las Vegas;* Harry Tiemann, *Mesa State College;* Laura Thompson, *New Mexico State University;* Frank J. Vattano, *Colorado State University, Ft. Collins;* Frank Vitro, *Texas Woman's University;* Fred Whitford, *Montana State University;* Paul Whitney, *Washington State University;* Andrew Winston, *University of Guelph;* Edward Wisniewski, *University of Illinois, Urbana-Champaign;* John Wixted, *University of California, San Diego;* Lynn Zimba, *University of Iowa.*

Many people have contributed to the development of this book. I thank Tina Oldham, my acquisitions editor throughout most of the project, as well as Marc Boggs, who originally contracted the book, and Eve Howard who joined the project later. Sarah Helyar Smith, my developmental editor, helped shape the book throughout its progress; and Shari Hatch, my editorial associate, spent countless hours helping the book become what it is. Craig Johnson and Susan Kindel, marketing managers, deftly guided the book's introduction to the market. Steve Norder, project editor, has seen the book through its final phases of realization; Burl Sloan, art director, crafted the beautiful design; Sue C. Howard, photo researcher, creatively sought the photos; Julia Stewart secured the literary permissions; and Ken Dunaway, production manager, held the book to a very complex schedule. Others at Harcourt, especially Carl Tyson, Ted Buchholz, and Tom Williamson, have been supportive throughout.

I would like especially to thank my Introductory Psychology students for putting up with me over the years as I tried out the materials in class. My undergraduate advisor, Endel Tulving, and my graduate advisor, Gordon Bower, both profoundly affected how I think about psychology, as did Wendell Garner as a faculty mentor at Yale.

Finally, I thank my wife, Alejandra Campos; my children, Seth and Sara; and my group of collaborators at Yale for the support they have always shown me in my work.

RJS

STUDENT PREFACE
HOW TO USE THIS TEXTBOOK

To make your course more rewarding, we suggest that you review the following pages prepared especially for you. In them you will find examples and explanations of the organizational structure of *In Search of the Human Mind*. After reading the descriptions, you will be prepared to take full advantage of the learning tools that have been designed for you. By reviewing the organization before you enter the first chapter, you will have the advantage of having *seen the map* before you begin your search.

Part and Chapter Openers

Each **part opener** within *In Search of the Human Mind* shows a different artist's interpretation of the myth of Psyche and outlines the topics within that part.

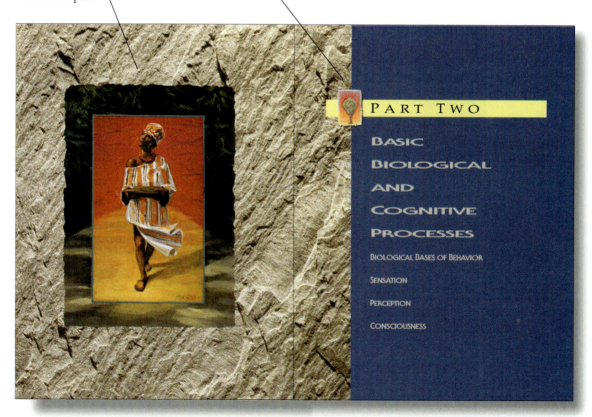

PART TWO

BASIC BIOLOGICAL AND COGNITIVE PROCESSES

BIOLOGICAL BASES OF BEHAVIOR

SENSATION

PERCEPTION

CONSCIOUSNESS

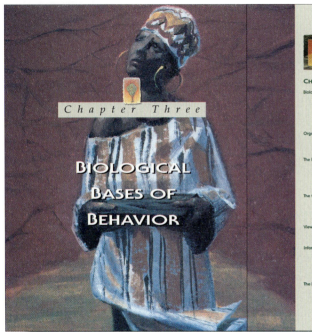

An annotated **chapter outline** opens each chapter, providing a brief introduction to the content of each major section and thus a general context for understanding the chapter.

A **vignette** opens each chapter, setting a mood or context and showing how the psychological principles of the chapter apply to everyday life. Here, an excerpt from *The Cask of Amontillado* by Edgar Allan Poe introduces Chapter 14's presentation of social psychology.

Higher Order Thinking

In Search of . . . questions, designated by Psyche's lamp, introduce major concepts in each chapter in a way that encourages you to explore how they relate to common experiences.

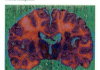

Triarchic questions scattered throughout the text encourage you to think about concepts and apply your own experiences in three ways. Questions identified by Rodin's *Thinker* ask you to think analytically, to analyze, compare and contrast, and evaluate facts and ideas. Questions identified by an artist's palette ask you to think creatively, to discover, invent, and design—to go beyond what you already know or do. And questions identified by a wheel ask you to think practically, to apply what you have learned and to think about how to use the information in your everyday life. (See these questions also at the end of each chapter.)

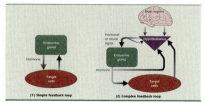

End of the Chapters and Parts

A **point-by-point summary,** organized by chapter sections, briefly reviews the material and the key terms within those sections.

Key terms, identified in boldface and defined in the text, are listed at the end of the chapter with a page number referring you to where the term appears in the chapter. These terms and more are defined further in the glossary at the back of the book.

At the end of each chapter also are some broader **triarchic questions** that will help you summarize the concepts of the chapter and understand them in a larger context. You will find three questions of each triarchic type, with some of the questions at times overlapping as to the type of questions they are.

When you reach the end of the part, you will find ***In Search of . . .*** questions and **Charting the Dialectic** summaries for each chapter. They will help you draw together the concepts you just have studied, whether in the individual chapters, in many of the preceding chapters, or in the part as a whole. The *In Search of . . .* section also includes a *Looking Ahead . . .* question to upcoming chapters, to help you build upon your current knowledge and prepare for the chapters to come. The "Charting the Dialectic" paragraphs synopsize the evolution of theories and ideas in each chapter—reviewing the original theory (the *thesis*), then the opposing theory (the *antithesis*), and finally the integrated theory (the *synthesis*). The Dialectical Tree on the back endpapers helps you map the progression of the major theories.

Illustrations

Seeing both a detailed anatomical illustration and a photograph of part of that anatomy gives you a deeper understanding of the **physiological functions.**

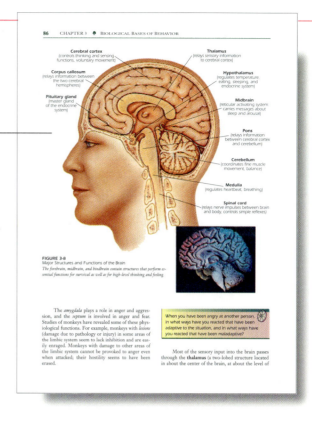

Tables provide a simple comparison of sometimes detailed or complex information.

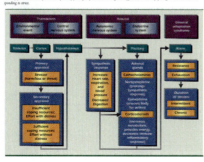

Charts visually simplify and clarify the more complex functions discussed in the text.

Photos

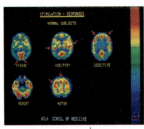

FIGURE 3-18
PET Scan Images
Images from PET scans show different metabolic processes in reaction to different activities and stimuli.

Now that we know a little about how to see the macrolevel anatomy and physiology of the brain, and we have some insight into what, how, and whether it is processing information, we can turn to the microlevel anatomy and physiology for processing information in the brain, and even throughout the entire nervous system.

What kinds of questions might we answer through PET scans that we cannot answer through CAT scans or MRI scans?

INFORMATION PROCESSING IN THE NERVOUS SYSTEM

IN SEARCH OF...

Does interpersonal communication serve as a helpful metaphor for the physiological communication processes that take place within the nervous system? Would a different metaphor be more appropriate?

Structural Components: Neurons and Glial Cells

Neurons

To understand how the entire nervous system processes information, we first need to examine the structure of the cells—*neurons*—and the bundles of neurons—*nerves*—that constitute the nervous system. Neurons are of three types, which serve three different kinds of functions: sensory neurons, motor neurons, and interneurons.

THREE FUNCTIONS OF NEURONS.   **Sensory neurons** receive information from the environment. They connect with *receptor cells* that detect physical or chemical changes in the sensory organs, including the skin, ears, tongue, eyes, nose, muscles, joints, and internal organs. Sensory neurons carry information away from the sensory receptor cells and *toward* the spinal cord or brain. **Motor neurons** carry information *away from* the spinal cord and the brain and toward the body parts that are supposed to respond to the information in some way. Both motor neurons and sensory neurons are part of the PNS. For example, motor and sensory neurons send information to and from the intestines (through the autonomic

---

Photographs showing psychological research and applications illustrate, for example, how biological functions affect behavior, how people can learn by observing, and how psychological principles and theories can explain behavior such as these children imitating the actions of an adult.

---

tion. Recall from Chapter 5 that when we habituate, we unconsciously tune out familiar stimuli, but that when we dishabituate, we tune in to novel stimuli. Although habituation and dishabituation are not reflexive, we do seem to be preprogrammed to respond differently to unfamiliar versus familiar stimuli. However, because both habituation and dishabituation can be subject to conscious control, they are more the result of learning than of preprogrammed behavior—and both phenomena certainly aid us in learning about new stimuli.

In many species of animals, even fairly complex behavior may be preprogrammed. These more complex preprogrammed behaviors, which involve more than a simple reflex, are **instinctive**. For example, the chinook salmon instinctively knows how to swim up river to reach its spawning ground. For another example, if a male stickleback (a kind of fish) swims too close to the nest of another male, the second male stickleback will warn and possibly attack the first male. The behavior pattern of the defender is automatic, and it is triggered by a sign stimulus—a red area on the belly of the male stickleback that develops during the mating season. In 1951, Niko Tinbergen, an **ethologist** (a scientist who studies comparative behavior across species and how it has evolved), demonstrated that the red spot, rather than any more generalized cue, triggered the instinctive response.

Some instincts involve a stimulus that prompts what may be a modest degree of learning. Ethologist Konrad Lorenz (1937, 1950) observed that newly hatched goslings will **imprint**—that is, form an immediate attachment—to the first moving object near them. The mother is usually the object of imprinting, which is adaptive because she is the source of sustenance and protection. However, in rare instances

when the mother is absent, the newborn will imprint to whatever else it is exposed to, including humans. Imprinting must occur during a **critical period,** a brief period of time in the animal's development during which the animal is preprogrammed for learning to take place.

Imprinting need not be visual. Goats imprint to olfactory stimuli, and salmon imprint to the odor of the stream in which they were hatched (Staddon & Ettinger, 1989). Imprinting is normally irreversible, but if an animal imprints to an unnatural object and a natural object replaces it some time later, the original imprinting may wear off (Staddon & Ettinger, 1989).

In summary, then, in imprinting, the animal is preprogrammed to seek out a particular stimulus, it learns to recognize that stimulus, and then it engages in a preprogrammed behavior in response to the stimulus.

Some psychologists argue that habituation and imprinting are actually simple forms of learning, whereas others contend that neither involves learning in any meaningful form. Give the reasons for and against considering habituation and/or imprinting to be simple forms of learning.

CLASSICAL CONDITIONING

It is beyond a doubt that all our knowledge begins with experience.

—*Immanuel Kant,* The Critique of Pure Reason

Ethologist Konrad Lorenz (left) studied how young birds imprint on the first moving objects they see after being hatched. The greylag goslings he studied imprinted on Lorenz, which prompted them to follow him wherever he went. Like Lorenz, Canadian ethologist Bill Lishman (right) had Canadian geese imprint on him. Unlike Lorenz, however, Lishman was able to accompany the goslings into the air.

---

such as French or Spanish, a computer-programming language, or even a word-processing language—we learn not only the specifics of that language, but also how best to learn new languages. Each subsequent language becomes easier, in part because of overlapping elements, but also in part because we have established a set of learning-to-learn techniques. Learning sets also may be used in many different learned behaviors. For example, in interpersonal relationships, we learn how we can learn more about people—what questions to ask them, what things to look for in their behavior, and so on. One of the things we learn about other people is how to behave in social interactions.

SOCIAL LEARNING

Wise men learn by others' mistakes, fools by their own.

—*Henry George Bohn*

When you follow in the path of your father, you learn to walk like him.

—*Ashanti proverb*

All of the research discussed so far has involved learning through classical or operant conditioning. In our everyday lives, however, not all of our learning derives from direct participation. Consider, for example, the effect on a child of seeing an older sibling punished for something that she herself did just the day before, or the effect on a drug addict of seeing a fellow addict die of an overdose of drugs.

Social learning occurs when we observe the behavior of others, as well as any environmental outcomes of the behavior we observe. Through social learning, we do not learn directly, but rather vicariously. Is there really any empirical evidence for **vicarious learning** (also called **observational learning**)?

Albert Bandura (1965, 1969) and his colleagues have performed numerous experiments demonstrating that vicarious social learning is an effective way of learning. In a typical study, preschool children were shown a film featuring an adult who punched, kicked, and threw things at a Bobo doll. The adult even hit the doll with a hammer. The given film ended in different ways, depending on the group to which a particular child viewer was assigned. In one group, the adult model was rewarded for the aggressive behavior; in a second group, the adult model was

punished; and in a third (control) group, the adult model was neither rewarded nor punished. When, after the film, the children were allowed to play with a Bobo doll, those children who had seen the adult

In numerous experiments, Albert Bandura has shown that children learn to imitate the behavior of others. By observing a movie of a woman behaving aggressively toward a Bobo doll (top), this boy and girl learned to punch the doll.

Relating to the World

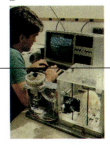

Examples of **art** demonstrate psychological concepts and themes. Here, the dialectical progression is recorded in paintings that reveal a shift in thinking over time.

The poetry of Ogden Nash is one example of a reference to **literature.** These references not only relate to the text's discussion but also incorporate learning from other disciplines.

Although the formal study of psychology is a Western tradition, many of the theories of psychology can be applied to peoples all over the world. Similarly, much of the wisdom of other cultures applies equally to Western culture. This book provides **cultural examples** in the text, in the illustrations, and in the quotations interspersed in the chapters.

Searchers . . . boxes profile individuals who have proposed important or influential theories, but who are above all good synthesizers. In their own words, these psychologists explain how they think critically, solve problems, build upon or react to given theories, and integrate their findings with other disciplines and subdisciplines. Consisting of interviews, the profiles are placed near references in the text to the individuals' works.

Study Aids for Students

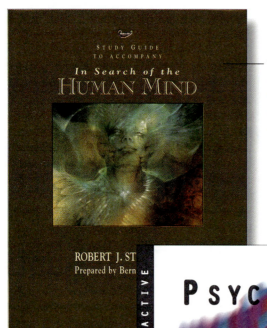

The **Study Guide** reflects the themes of the textbook and provides concentrated exercises for you to understand both the broader concepts and the narrower details of each chapter.

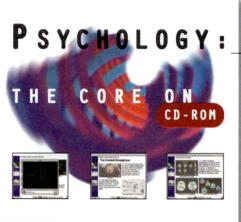

Harcourt Interactive, *Psychology: The Core on CD-ROM* gives you the opportunity to explore psychology through videos, animation, and experiments. Hyperlinked to the textbook, this multimedia product also lets you test your mastery of the material.

Contents in Brief

CONTENTS

Part Two
BASIC BIOLOGICAL AND COGNITIVE PROCESSES   71

3 BIOLOGICAL BASES OF BEHAVIOR   73

11 INTELLIGENCE   371

PART ONE

THE NATURE OF PSYCHOLOGY

WHAT IS PSYCHOLOGY?

THE ROOTS AND BRANCHES OF PSYCHOLOGY

Chapter One

What Is Psychology?

CHAPTER OUTLINE

PSYCHOLOGY DEFINED

IN SEARCH OF...

What do you think you will be studying in a course on psychology? What kinds of things do you believe psychologists are interested in?

Do you want to know what it means to be smart, to love someone, to be attractive to someone? Do you ever wonder how salespeople persuade you to buy things you do not want? How do some people resolve blatant contradictions between the beliefs they espouse and the way they behave (such as the belief of many prejudiced people that prejudice is wrong)? To study **psychology,** the study of the mind and of behavior, is to seek to understand how we think, learn, perceive, feel, act, interact with others, and even understand ourselves.

As a student of introductory psychology, you are now a *psychologist*—you study the mind and behavior.

You and your fellow psychologists (both amateurs and professionals) study such diverse phenomena as personality (How would we characterize ourselves, and what gives us our characteristics?), motivation (What prompts us to do what we do?), cognition (How do we think?), and deviant behavior (How and why do people you know behave in such strange ways?). In fact, if no one has yet found the answer to a question that interests you about how or why people think, feel, or act as they do, then the study of psychology will give you the perfect opportunity to answer it for yourself.

You and other psychologists may be found studying these phenomena in a variety of settings—the home, the school, the workplace, and almost anywhere else that humans live, work, and interact. Although people are the predominant focus of psychological theory and research, many psychologists study a broad array of other organisms, from single-celled creatures to mammals. These studies are sometimes ends in themselves and sometimes a way in which to investigate structures and phenomena that it would be impossible, impractical, or unethical to study in humans. For example, the study of animal physiology (such as the functioning of the eye or of nerve cells) and animal behavior (such as responses to various kinds of rewards) offers insights into possible corollaries in human physiology and behavior. As an amateur psychologist and student of behavior, you, too, may have noticed behavior in a pet or other animal that offered you insight into someone you know, although you may not have used scientifically rigorous methods to test your insights.

PSYCHOLOGY AS A SOCIAL SCIENCE

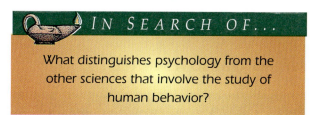

IN SEARCH OF...

What distinguishes psychology from the other sciences that involve the study of human behavior?

Psychology shares a focus on human behavior with other scientific disciplines, especially the other social sciences, such as sociology and anthropology. Actually, the borders among these fields are fuzzy, and the fields overlap considerably both in what they study and how they study it. Nonetheless, these disciplines offer slightly different emphases and perspectives. The focus of psychology is generally on the individual, whether alone or in interaction with others and the environment. Other social sciences view human behavior with other perspectives. For example, *sociologists* study larger aggregates of individuals, such as occupational, societal, economic, or ethnic groups. *Cultural anthropologists* seek to gain insight into various cultures; *physical anthropologists* study human evolution from simpler organisms; *political scientists* study human governance hierarchies and other systems and structures of human power relationships; and *economists* study systems of resource exchange, production, and consumption.

Even some non-social scientists study human behavior: For example, *geneticists* study the influence of heredity on behavior, and *physiologists* study physical and biochemical influences on behavior. Psychologists and other scientists view these various roads to understanding behavior as complementary, not as mutually exclusive. Indeed, psychologists also profit from the insights into human behavior offered by disciplines such as literature and art, on the one hand, and biology and computer science, on the other, to the extent that each seeks to understand behavior from a somewhat different vantage point.

Identify works of art or literature that seem to you to show an understanding of how people think, feel, and act. Explain briefly the reasons for your choices.

"ISN'T IT ALL OBVIOUS ANYWAY?"

IN SEARCH OF...

What nonobvious insights into psychology have you gained through your own observations of people?

Why study human behavior and the human mind? "Isn't it all obvious anyway?" asked one of my college friends. He could not understand why anyone would want to study psychology, because he saw psychologists as merely giving fancy labels to things everyone knows intuitively. Consider, for example, some research on love and close relationships, an area in which nearly all of us consider ourselves at least somewhat expert at observing and understanding behavior. You may have heard talk-show guests offer uninspired generalizations about love and how you can improve the love in your life. Such an earth-shatteringly original statement might be, "Two of the best predictors of happiness in a relationship are how you feel about your partner and how your partner feels about you." After reading that, you may wonder why psychologists even bother to study such obvious and commonsensical "facts" about human behavior. Surprisingly, this generalization shows just why psychologists *do* bother—because psychological research has proved that "obvious" statement to be wrong!

A colleague and I studied satisfaction in close relationships (Sternberg & Barnes, 1985). We found that how you feel about your partner is *not* a good predictor of satisfaction unless you take into account your expectations for the relationship. For example, you may love someone, but your idea of what constitutes satisfaction in a relationship may be so unrealistic that you are never satisfied with your actual interactions. Moreover, how your partner *actually* feels about you is not crucial to your happiness: What really matters is how you *think* he or she feels. Oddly enough, the connection between how your partner actually feels about you and how you imagine that your partner feels is not particularly strong. Thus,

Psychologists study various organisms, from human beings to other primates, snails, and even single-celled creatures.

contrary to talk-show guests' predictions, neither partner's feelings are a major predictor of happiness or satisfaction. A better predictor is the degree of difference between how you *perceive* your partner to feel about you and how you ideally *want* your partner to feel. The smaller the discrepancy, the better the chances for satisfaction in the relationship (see Chapter 14).

Apparently, not everything psychology has to teach us is self-evident. Also, just what is obvious? Proverbs show how contradictory the obvious can be. Suppose you are going away for the summer, leaving behind a boyfriend or girlfriend. Should you worry? No, for "absence makes the heart grow fonder." On the other hand, should you be confident that nothing will go wrong? Beware: "Out of sight, out of mind."

In addition, what seems unmistakably clear to those in one culture may not be at all clear to persons elsewhere. Consider the following anecdote:

Once upon a time, an anthropologist was telling an English folk-fable to a gathering of the Bemba of Rhodesia. She glowingly described "a young prince who climbed glass mountains, crossed chasms, and fought dragons, all to obtain the hand of a maiden he loved." The Bemba were plainly bewildered, but remained silent. Finally an old chief spoke up, voicing the feelings of all present in the simplest of questions: "Why not take another girl?" he asked.

—*M. M. Hunt*, The Natural History of Love

In sum, psychology does not just restate what is apparent to all. Some psychological findings are obvious and confirm what we already suspected, but many of them surprise us. In fact, psychologists, like other scientists, expect to find results that surprise them.

PSYCHOLOGY AS A SCIENCE

IN SEARCH OF...

What are some of the criteria you use to determine whether to rely on the information you receive? What criteria do you use for evaluating your own beliefs and opinions?

Scientists employ a particular set of methods for ascertaining, or at least striving to find, the truth—even if the truth contradicts what was expected. Scientists use these methods in their effort to ensure that scientific *data* (facts) and theories are (a) verifiable and accurately reported, (b) cumulative, (c) public, and (d) parsimonious. Of course, scientists cannot guarantee their data will have these characteristics—only that they seek to ensure these characteristics to the best of their abilities, given their frailties and their biases, as well as their cultural contexts (see Table 1-1).

Characteristics of Scientific Findings

Verifiable

Scientific findings are **verifiable**; there must be some means of confirming the findings. For example, if one scientist conducts an experiment and draws conclusions, other scientists must be able to **replicate** the experiment—to repeat the original methods and produce the same results obtained by the first scientist. For example, suppose you were to investigate why, in the middle of a test, you cannot remember something you studied earlier. Suppose also that you suspect anxiety about time constraints was the cause of this difficulty.

TABLE 1-1
Four Characteristics of Science
Scientists use various methods for obtaining data and formulating theories, which have these four characteristics.

Characteristics Prized by Scientists	Reason for Prizing the Characteristic
Verifiable	Researchers can evaluate well-designed and accurately reported research to verify whether the research outcomes are reliable and the conclusions are valid.
Cumulative	To move science forward, scientists build on past research.
Public	Carefully reviewed research published in scientific journals informs scientists about existing research, so that they may evaluate that research and build on it.
Parsimonious	Simpler explanations are easier to understand, easier to communicate, and easier to evaluate. When all else is equal, simpler is better.

To find out whether anxiety about time constraints is indeed the cause of being unable to think clearly while in a test situation, you must come up with a procedure that meets two criteria: reliability and validity. If your experimental procedure produces results that are **reliable,** you and others can count on your procedure to produce the same results time after time.

Reliability is necessary for evaluation, but it is not sufficient. For example, suppose that you read about a previous student's attempt to investigate the effects of anxiety about time constraints on test performance. Suppose that this researcher compared students' test performance in a room in which a clock loudly ticked the passage of time with performance in a room in which no clock was present. Even if the results of this procedure could be tested again and again and could reliably show that test-takers in the room without the clock performed better than did students in the room with the clock, the interpretation of those findings still might not be **valid**—that is, the investigation may not have shown what it was purported to show. An alternative explanation of the findings might be that the difference in test performance was due to test-takers' irritation with the noisy clock rather than to anxiety about time constraints. The results of the procedure might be deemed reliable, but the interpretation of those results might be considered invalid. Because of this alternative (plausible) interpretation of the findings, additional research would be needed in order to find out whether it was the anxiety about time constraints or some other factor that had caused the difference in test performance.

The preceding example shows the need for scientific findings to be *accurately reported*. Accurate reporting allows both the initial researcher and others to assess the reliability and the validity of the research results. Sloppy reporting or intentional distortion of research findings hinders scientific progress. If people carelessly reported results, disregarding accuracy, science would make slow progress because future researchers would be building on worthless (invalid, perhaps even unreliable) work.

"Woman in Kansas Gives Birth to
Two-Headed Twins!"
"Elvis Seen Disembarking from
Alien Spacecraft in Detroit!"

Stories that attract attention are not necessarily accurate. Unfortunately, inaccurate reporting of information has been a long-standing problem, as suggested by Mark Twain's response to a news story of his day, "The reports of my death are greatly exaggerated."

Cumulative

The need for verifiability and accurate reporting implies a second characteristic of scientific findings: The work of science is *cumulative*. Researchers cannot possibly do everything for themselves, so they depend, to a great extent, on the work of others. It is sometimes said that "there is nothing new under the sun," and in science, even the newest ideas build on the old.

Some ideas seem newer than others, though. Sometimes, there appear to be radical shifts in scientific research, as when a scientist rejects traditional approaches and blazes a new trail. These trailblazers are involved in **revolutionary science**, work that invents a new **paradigm** (theoretical system that provides an overarching model for organizing theories). Those who widen and extend existing paths are engaged in **normal science**—work that builds on a paradigm established by others (Kuhn, 1970). Even trailblazers must start somewhere, though; and so revolutionary science that invents a new paradigm builds on past work, perhaps using it as a basis for what *not* to do. When Albert Einstein revolutionized the way scientists view physics, he built on the foundation of Newtonian physics. Had Isaac Newton's previous work not existed, Einstein could never have formulated his general and special theories of relativity. Whether scientists embrace or reject the work of their intellectual ancestors, they profit from the earlier work. In designing your experiments for your hypothetical study of the factors affecting test performance, you would profit from your predecessors'

work. You would also benefit from reading widely about other research on attention, memory, thinking, the effects of emotions on performance, and the ways in which physiological stress affects thinking, among other things.

What are some revolutionary ideas in science, art, politics, or other areas? What made these ideas revolutionary? What ideas served as a basis for those revolutionary ideas?

Public

Science is *public*. Regardless of how many interesting research studies are conducted, the results do not fully benefit science and society until they become public, usually through *scientific journals* (periodicals that report research results to the scientific community).

Paradigms change in art just as in science. Pablo Picasso shifted through several different paradigms, such as from the realistic style (left, Portrait of Olga on an Armchair, *1917) to the expressionistic style (right,* Portrait of Jacqueline in Turkish Costume, *1955).*

Scientists are motivated to write about their results for at least three reasons: (1) to help them to clarify their findings through the writing process, (2) to discover what their peers think about their findings, and (3) to communicate their findings to others whose own work might profit from the results.

The process of writing has helped many scientists to interpret their own results and to clarify the directions their experiments were taking them. For example, while Antoine-Laurent Lavoisier was experimenting with oxygen, he toyed with various ideas when describing his experiments. During the writing process, he clarified his thoughts, which guided his subsequent experiments and interpretations. Similarly, Newton made discoveries about prisms and light while he wrote about his studies, and Hans Krebs unveiled the biochemistry of the ornithine cycle through writing about his investigations (Gorman, 1992).

Think about some of the things you have written—including school assignments, notes to friends, or even greetings on cards. How has writing helped you to clarify your thoughts and feelings? When might you try writing as a tool for clarifying your ideas and emotions?

The second reason for writing about research is to have the staff and peer reviewers of reputable scientific journals carefully scrutinize the relative scientific merits of articles submitted for publication. The reviewers—researchers in the relevant field—examine the merits of the ideas, the research testing these ideas, and the interpretations of the research presented in the article. Both the writer and the reader profit from the review process: The writer may learn from the evaluations and suggestions offered by colleagues, and the reader may benefit from the selection process in which only articles with the most compelling findings are published—usually only a fraction of the submitted articles.

How do you react when other people give you suggestions in response to the work you have done? Is there anything you could do to profit more from such suggestions?

The third reason for writing about research is that publication of compelling results permits readers to learn of research findings that might lead to further research or to relevant applications in the field of interest. Fellow scientists have the opportunity to read, pause, reread, reflect, mull over details, and carefully analyze the research, as well as to consider possible applications of the information. Once the scientific merits of the findings have been evaluated, reporters in the nonscientific news media may also consider broader publication of the findings, based on *news value*—the general appeal and popular interest of the findings. (Note that scientific value and news value often differ.)

This public aspect of science helped in the writing of this book and could help you in reading it. I used articles and books for investigating, documenting, and supporting the information in this book. For several reasons, wherever I use a particular work, I *cite* (mention the name of) the authors whose work I used. First, citations show that I can document my own statements and claims with previously published and accepted data—that I am building on the accumulated body of scientific knowledge. Second, citations publicly credit other researchers for their work. Third, citations identify for readers a source of further information. Whenever you see citations in this text and would like more information, you may look up the citations in the "References" section at the back of this textbook; these references can lead you to more information.

Parsimonious

It is vain to do with more what can be done with fewer.

—*William of Occam, c. 1285–1349*

Given the cumulative, ever-expanding, public body of scientific knowledge, it is easy to see why scientists seek to be *parsimonious:* When formulating their **hypotheses** (tentative proposals regarding expectations for research) and drawing conclusions from their data, scientists try to use relatively few words, while providing complete information. The purpose of scientific analysis is to discover and explain, or at the very least to describe systematically, some phenomenon or set of phenomena as simply as possible. Ideally, a scientific explanation is somehow more concise, more convenient, more accessible, and more comprehensible than what it explains. (A different English translation of "Occam's razor," originally written in Latin, uses fewer words but more syllables: "Entities should not be multiplied unnecessarily.")

Now that you have considered what science is, you are ready to consider what science is not.

Cite ten reasons you sometimes feel in a cheerful mood and sometimes do not. Can you think of a parsimonious explanation for your moods? Does your parsimonious explanation fully explain your moods? Why or why not?

Misconceptions About Science

In considering what science is not, it helps to bear in mind that scientists are also imperfect human beings. Hence, many of our misconceptions about science stem from believing that scientists can grasp as much as they can strive to reach. Although we try continually to reach ever farther outward and forward, we must also recognize when our research and our conclusions have exceeded our grasp.

Misconception 1: Science Is Always Correct

Scientific accounts are not always correct. In fact, they are often wrong, or at least incomplete. Today, we view many of the beliefs of nineteenth-century and even early twentieth-century psychology as quaint and curious. For example, many psychologists once believed that thinking is always accompanied by silent speech, known as *subvocalization* (Watson, 1930). Indeed, many early psychologists were unwilling to accept mental processes as a legitimate domain of inquiry at all. Today, most psychologists find this view to be of historical interest only. In the future, many of the views we hold dear today also will seem outdated and peculiar. To be of value, science must be dynamic and constantly evolving, as new theories continually supersede old ones.

Misconception 2: Science Is Always Conducted via an Idealized Method

Scientists in general, and psychologists in particular, rarely use the orderly, linear, simplistic scientific method they learned in school. Almost all scientists make false starts from time to time and have to reconceptualize *why* they are doing *what* they are doing, or even what they should do in the first place. Sometimes, they have to revise their original hypotheses or fine-tune their research procedures in order to get them to work. Sometimes, an experiment that starts off being about one thing ends up being about another.

For example, Percy LeBaron Spencer, in the mid-1940s, discovered that microwaves could be used for heating foods. Spencer happened to have a chocolate bar in his pocket while he was conducting experiments with microwaves for transmitting radio signals (Messadié, 1991c; Trager, 1992). Much to his dismay, he discovered that his candy had melted. This self-educated engineer (who never completed grammar school but patented more than 120 inventions) astutely recognized that the microwaves had caused the molecules in the candy bar to vibrate rapidly enough to heat it and cause it to melt (Flatow, 1993; Messadié, 1991c). To test his notion, he exposed a bag of popcorn kernels to the microwaves—Voilà! The first microwaved popcorn—and all the subsequent microwaved foods—resulted from Spencer's keen insight in recognizing a serendipitous discovery.

Many creative inventions were the results of serendipitous discoveries. What are some pleasantly surprising revelations that you have serendipitously discovered?

Misconception 3: Science Is Always Conducted with Perfect Objectivity

Scientists sometimes fail to reach their goal of being completely objective in deciding what to study, how to study it, and how to interpret the findings of their studies. Like their fellow humans, they can fall prey to errors in thinking. Consider the fallacy of **confirmation bias** (Wason & Johnson-Laird, 1972): People tend to seek to confirm rather than to deny their beliefs. For example, most people do not like hearing that what they believe is wrong. Moreover, they tend to seek out primarily information that supports their beliefs. Because of confirmation bias, we may unwittingly interpret or even distort new information so that it seems (in our minds) to be consistent with what we already think.

As noted, scientific evidence is often open to more than one interpretation, but confirmation bias occurs among scientists, too. When viewing new evidence, scientists tend to seek an interpretation of the evidence that best fits what they already believe (Kuhn, 1970). One way in which scientists counter this tendency is to seek specifically to **disconfirm** (prove wrong) their hypotheses. In fact, for this reason and other reasons, the philosophy and practice of modern science has been based on the idea that scientists should seek to disconfirm rather than to confirm what they believe (Popper, 1959).

Values—preconceptions regarding what is valuable—also affect the way in which research is conducted. What are some of your own core values? You may share some of these with society as a whole (e.g.,

NASA scientists failed to take steps to avoid confirmation bias, and the crew aboard the shuttle Challenger *suffered the tragic consequences of that error.*

"Do unto others as you would have others do unto you"), with your cultural or subcultural group (e.g., "The key to success is education"), with your family (e.g., "Show respect toward your parents"), your circle of friends (e.g., "Don't betray a friend's confidence"). Whatever your values are, and however widely you share them, your values will influence what topics you deem worthy of study, how you believe that these topics should be studied, and how you interpret the results of those studies. Fellow scientists are similarly influenced by their values in their choice of topics, methods of study, and evaluation of results.

As this chapter has shown, science itself has values: objectivity, tests of theories, accuracy, honesty, concise but illuminating public sharing of information, and openness to question and to verification. It would not be realistic—or perhaps even desirable—to aspire to have no values. A more realistic aspiration is to recognize our values and to try to keep them from coloring the way in which we study human behavior.

List ten characteristics you consider desirable in a friend. How might confirmation bias affect your ability to notice these characteristics in your friends but to fail to note those characteristics in persons you dislike?

Keep in mind also that the way scientists in general behave in their laboratories can largely be attributed to the postindustrial Euro-American tradition. A very large percentage of all psychologists who have ever lived was trained and educated in the laboratories and universities of the Western world. Although it is tempting to believe that we know the absolute truth, well-intentioned and brilliant scholars in other societies believe that *their* world views, and not the views that are unquestioningly accepted in the Western world, are more accurate representations of the way things are.

Misconception 4: Science Is Merely a Collection of Facts

One of the cultural values that can color our view of science is an emphasis on products (such as facts) above processes (such as the pursuit of knowledge and understanding). This emphasis leads to what may be the most important misconception about science—that science is merely a collection of facts. The foregoing discussion has shown that scientific research can lead to inaccurate conclusions reached by imperfect, sometimes biased researchers who use imprecise methods and are guided in part by culturally sanctioned values. Given the obvious fallibility of scientists, if science were only a collection of facts, perhaps we would abandon its pursuit.

Fortunately for all of us, a collection of facts does not a science make. Facts become part of the scientific enterprise only when they are presented in the context of a **theory**, a statement of some general principles explaining particular events. Theories are not merely opinions but are analyses of the relations among sets of facts. We need theories because science is not merely descriptive but also explanatory. Without theories, we still might be able to describe behavior, or at least to make some discrete observations about behavior, but we would not really understand it. In looking at human behavior, we would be able to investigate and find answers to *what* is happening, but not *why*, and possibly not even *how* it is happening.

Theories also play an important role in guiding observations and experimentation. For example, American physician Helen Taussig (known for her innovative treatment for infants with congenital heart defects) was alerted that hundreds of West German infants were being born with severely deformed limbs. She rushed to the scene and asked researchers there what they had observed. Many researchers suspected that the culprit was a drug, thalidomide, which pregnant mothers had taken to prevent nausea (and to induce sleep) during pregnancy. She soon issued a report describing the theory that ingestion of thalidomide during pregnancy was causing the birth defects. American researchers then specifically investigated the theory (Maccini, 1989). Fortunately, physician and pharmacologist Frances Kelsey, the Food and Drug Administration (FDA) official responsible for evaluating FDA applications to license drugs for release to the American public, became aware of this research; she then fought to prevent the thalidomide tragedy from reaching American infants (Truman, 1977). Thus, researchers formed a theory based on their observations, did further research to test the theory, and then applied their findings to benefit society.

To make information meaningful and scientifically useful in the long run, scientists must find ways in which to organize information in order to understand it. Theories provide such a framework for organizing information.

HOW DO SCIENTISTS THINK?

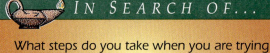

IN SEARCH OF...

What steps do you take when you are trying to solve the problems you confront? How does your own method compare with that used by scientists?

Thus far, we have described the characteristics of science, including some of its limitations. We have yet to discuss how scientists come up with ideas for study, how they think about the things they study, and how they study those things.

The Problem-Solving Cycle

Psychologists and other scientists, when faced with scientific problems, follow a seven-step process, referred to as the **problem-solving cycle** (Figure 1–1). Through this process, scientists must decide how to formulate and test their hypotheses about phenomena that intrigue them. Why does scientific problem solving occur in a cycle? Because in science, today's solutions frequently become tomorrow's new scientific problems.

For example, based on their extensive studies of young children, Barbel Inhelder and Jean Piaget (1958) concluded that children younger than 11 or 12 years of age could not understand analogies. Their views became widely accepted by both psychologists and educators, but it turns out that some of their conclusions were based on too little information. Some

of the distinctive characteristics of the tasks and situations that Inhelder and Piaget observed affected their interpretations. For example, sometimes children did not understand what was being asked of them in a testing situation. Thus, Inhelder and Piaget were led to believe that children were incapable of using analogies just because the children were not able to do so in the situations the two researchers observed.

Fortunately, other researchers continued to investigate children's understandings of analogies, building on Inhelder and Piaget's previous groundbreaking work. Some of these researchers learned that much younger children, even at the preschool level, can recognize analogies if they are given sufficient additional information and an appropriate context in which to recognize the analogies (e.g., Brown & Kane, 1988). That answer raised even more questions: What kinds of analogies can children see, and under what circumstances can they see them? Which children can see analogies? How obvious do the analogies have to be for very young children?

Solving one scientific problem or answering one question raises a host of other problems or questions. Consider now the steps of the problem-solving cycle: identifying the problem, defining the problem, formulating a strategy, organizing information, allocating resources, monitoring problem solving, and evaluating the process.

Identifying the Problem

"Is there any point to which you would wish to draw my attention?"
"To the curious incident of the dog in the nighttime."
"The dog did nothing in the night-time."
"That was the curious incident," remarked Sherlock Holmes.
    —Sir Arthur Conan Doyle, "Silver Blaze,"
            The Memoirs of Sherlock Holmes

The first step in problem solving is to identify the problem. You cannot study a problem unless you identify it as a problem. Also, some problems are more deserving of attention than are others. Harriet Zuckerman (1983) and other sociologists who study science have claimed that a major distinction between greater and lesser scientists is in their taste in problems: Greater scientists study more significant problems.

FIGURE 1-1
Problem-Solving Cycle
The process of solving problems occurs in a cycle because solutions to current problems often lead the way to seeking solutions to future problems.

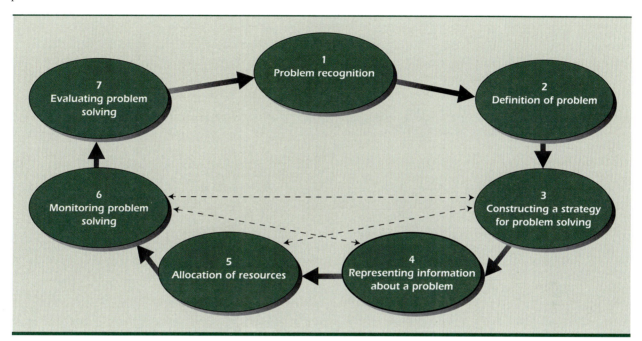

In some respects, problem identification is the most difficult part of the cycle, because it is the point at which the psychologist needs to generate ideas. For many student psychologists, problem identification is probably the most worrisome stage of problem solving: Students know that they can remember and analyze other people's ideas, at least to some degree. They are usually not as confident, however, about their ability to come up with their own new ideas.

No one way of coming up with ideas works for everyone. If you are having difficulty thinking of ideas for your own studies, try simply watching people, including yourself; you are bound to find puzzles that intrigue you regarding the way people act. You may also find ideas by trying some of the idea-generating techniques suggested by William McGuire (1983) (see Table 1-2).

Use some of McGuire's techniques to come up with ideas for a term project that addresses a puzzling psychological phenomenon. Which techniques seemed most helpful, and which seemed the least helpful for this particular problem?

One of the best ways to generate new ideas is to become broadly educated. Many of the best problem identifiers are people who bring ideas from one field to bear on another. For example, Sophie Germain was a pioneer in using mathematics to address physics problems in acoustics and in elasticity (Forbes, 1990). About a century later, Alexander Graham Bell was able to bring his knowledge of human speech from his work as a teacher of deaf students to his engineering work on telegraphy when he devised the voice-transmitting telephone.

More recently, Nobel Prize winning cognitive psychologist Herbert Simon dramatically influenced his field by introducing ideas he brought from computer science (such as comparing and contrasting how humans and computers solve problems). Other people have contributed ideas from far-flung disciplines to various areas of psychology, as well; for example, Margaret Floy Washburn brought her extensive knowledge of animal behavior to bear on questions of sensation and movement (Furumoto & Scarborough, 1986; Hilgard, 1987); Claude Shannon imported ideas regarding information theory from engineering theory; and George Miller used ideas from linguistics for his remarkable insights into memory.

What are some of your interests? How might your interests lead to your identification of scientific problems?

TABLE 1-2
Techniques for Generating Ideas
William McGuire suggested various techniques for generating ideas that may lead to the solution of a problem.

Technique	Description	Examples
Conduct intensive case studies	Observe the behavior of one or a few persons in great detail, and then contemplate what you do not understand in this behavior.	How and why does a successful musician or group of musicians become self-destructive, especially in regard to the use of alcohol and other drugs?
Account for paradoxical incidents	Attempt to explain things that do not seem to go together.	Why do some people smoke yet worry that smoking will kill them? Why do some people engage in unprotected sexual relations despite their fear of AIDS?
Explain practitioners' rules of thumb	Watch an expert do something and then attempt to explain how he or she did it.	How do some students just seem to know what to study and how to study it?
Extrapolate from similar problems that have already been solved	Consider the solution to a problem similar to the one of interest and think about whether the solution to the similar problem could be applied to the problem of interest.	To understand how to treat test anxiety, find out how people have solved other anxiety-related problems.
Introspect on your own experience in a comparable situation	Attempt to explain other people's behavior in a situation by asking how you have responded in similar situations.	When trying to understand interpersonal attraction, you might think about why you have felt attracted to particular people.
Role-play someone in the situation	Imagine or actually role-play a problem in order to understand a psychological phenomenon.	Instead of identifying with the anxious test-taker, imagine yourself in the position of having to evaluate students, to see how you might be able to come up with some alternatives to tests.
Reverse the direction of a commonsense hypothesis	Take an explanation that most people intuitively accept and consider the implications if the opposite were true.	What if students who do well on tests of reading comprehension could do almost as well without even reading the text passages before answering the questions?
Analyze a problem into its components	Take a problem that may in itself be too large and seek to solve a part of the problem.	To predict—or to influence—success in college, you might break down the big problem of how to be a successful student into small, manageable tasks or skills that you could investigate and master.

Defining the Problem

Once we identify the existence of a problem, we still have to figure out exactly what the problem is. In other words, we have to define the problem. When defining scientific problems, we use **operational definitions,** which describe as specifically as possible the precise elements and procedures involved in solving the research problem. Operational definitions allow researchers to communicate how they conducted an experiment and how they came to particular conclusions.

For example, Laurel Furumoto and Elizabeth Scarborough (1986) were interested in investigating the ways in which early women psychologists contributed to the field of psychology. How could they possibly even start to study such a broad, sweeping construct, though? They needed to find some way in which to pin down their study to a specific set of early women psychologists whose contributions they could study. Thus, they operationally defined the object of their study as the contributions to psychology made by "the 22 women who identified themselves as psychologists in the first edition of *American Men of Science*" (p. 35). The authors acknowledged that their study, by definition, did not include the work done by many other women who contributed significantly to the early development of psychology. Because these two researchers indicated their operational definition, other psychologists and historians who read about Furumoto and Scarborough's findings are able to interpret those findings in light of their definition.

One reason that operational definitions are so important in psychology is that psychology involves many **hypothetical constructs**—concepts that are not themselves directly measurable or observable but that give rise to measurable phenomena and patterns of data. For example, we infer the existence of the hypothetical construct of *intelligence*, based on test scores and on particular kinds of behavior. Such constructs are often the centerpieces of psychological theories.

Much of scientific research depends on how the problem is identified and defined. Unfortunately, many excellent students reach the halls of science ill prepared to identify and define problems. In school, many of us spend years learning how to solve problems: Typically, these problems are *given to us* by teachers, textbooks, or tests. This strategy of teaching students how to solve problems does not adequately prepare us for the scientific enterprise, an important part of which is first to identify and then to define—by and for ourselves—the problems to be solved. Otherwise, we may end up with the right answer—but to the wrong question.

What problems and questions do you wish you had been given a chance to explore when you were in elementary school?

Constructing a Strategy for Solving the Problem

Once you have determined what problem you wish to solve, you still need to figure out how you are going to solve it. In many psychological investigations the preferred strategy is to conduct experimental research, but other methods may be more effective for solving problems that do not lend themselves to experimental manipulations on the part of the investigator (alternative strategies are discussed in greater detail in a subsequent section of this chapter). There

is no single ideal strategy for addressing a problem. Instead, the optimal strategy depends on both the problem and the investigator's personal taste in problem-solving methods.

Consider, for example, a study of influence conducted by Robert Cialdini (1984). Cialdini starts by stating, "I can admit it now. All my life I've been a patsy. For as long as I can recall, I've been an easy mark for the pitches of peddlers, fund raisers, and operators of some sort or another" (p. 11). Cialdini's view of himself as a patsy got him interested in how people influence others, often persuading them to buy things they do not want, or to give to charities they do not really care about. Indeed, he says, "this long-standing status as sucker accounts for my interest in the study of compliance: Just what are the factors that cause one person to say yes to another person?" (p. 11). Such personal issues often lead to research interests. (What problems, peeves, or puzzles have been perplexing you?)

Cialdini decided on a strategy of *participant observation*, whereby the person studying a phenomenon both observes it and participates. For a three-year period, Cialdini answered newspaper ads for sales trainees in various advertising, public-relations, and fund-raising organizations. While feigning to be in training for sales, he learned the techniques that organizations used for persuading people to buy products and services that the people do not necessarily want. Cialdini's distinctive strategy provided the basis for his comprehensive model of influence.

When choosing from alternative strategies for solving a problem, you should consider the many possible different associated **variables** (aspects of the problem situation, which may differ or fluctuate from one setting to another, from one person to another, or from one problem to another). In addition, you should consider how to avoid *confounding variables*—that is, aspects of the problem situation that might confuse or make ambiguous the interpretation of the result by introducing variables other than the one in which you are interested.

Recall the hypothetical investigation in which the noisy clock presented a confounding variable. In this case, the study would have been subject to an *alternative explanation*—a different way of interpreting the results that accounts for the results in terms of the confounding variable. The resulting data would be subject to one or more alternative explanations, which would make the results of the study less definitive. To narrow down the possible explanations (by ruling out or ruling in alternative explanations of the data), you and others would still have to investigate further the various possible causes of the decrease in performance associated with the loudly ticking clock.

Representing Information to Examine the Problem

When you recognize and define problems, you need to perceive and organize the relevant information in your head. The process of finding alternative ways to understand and display information through various forms is known as **representation**. For example, illustrators, painters, photographers, and sculptors make visual representations of real or imagined people, places, events, experiences, emotions, and abstract ideas. Musical composers and choreographers represent images and experiences through sound and movement. Novelists, poets, and essayists do so through words.

You may think of representations as being lenses through which you view a situation or a problem. These lenses will affect your perspective differentially, depending on the lenses' thickness, color, clarity, and so on. In addition, the problem solver must use the lenses judiciously. For example, physicist Niels Bohr found it helpful to use the solar system as a metaphor for mentally representing the atom, in his theory of atomic structure (M. E. Gorman, personal communication, September 15, 1993). On the other hand, the metaphor is not a perfect match because planets do not suddenly jump orbits, thereby releasing energy. Bohr was able to use the metaphor flexibly, profiting from the representation where appropriate, and ignoring it where it was irrelevant. Had he used his mental model rigidly, his understanding of the atom would have been distorted.

Also, whereas some problem solvers are able to use a single model flexibly, others prefer to try representing the problem in various ways. For example, when Leonardo da Vinci wished to represent his ideas, he could do so by drawing, painting, sculpting, designing mechanical models, writing, and probably a few other means (see Figure 1-2). Few of us are quite so versatile. We can, however, try to come up with alternative ways of mentally representing the same information to see which mental representation best fits the information. In addition, how you represent information will affect not only how well you solve a problem, but also how you go about solving it, and probably also the sort of solution you reach. Once you have some ideas about which strategies you would like to use for tackling your problem, you can assess how to use the resources you have available to implement those strategies.

Allocating Resources

Even the most privileged among us rarely have unlimited resources to devote to a problem. Who has enough energy, time, money, staff, ideas, office and lab space, or equipment to do it all? Just as you must choose your problems carefully, you must also choose how many and what kinds of resources to devote to a given problem. Some problems are worth a lot of time and additional resources, whereas others are worth very little. Moreover, we need to know when to allocate which resources.

Studies show that expert problem solvers (and better students) tend to devote more of their mental resources to *global* (big-picture) planning than do novice problem solvers. Novices (and poorer students) tend to allocate more time to *local* (detail-oriented) planning than do experts (Larkin, McDermott, Simon, & Simon, 1980; Sternberg, 1981). For example, better students usually spend more time in the initial phase of problem solving—deciding how to solve the problem—and less time actually solving it than do poorer students (Bloom & Broder, 1950). By spending more time in advance deciding what to do,

FIGURE 1-2
Representations of the Problem
Leonardo da Vinci was able to represent problems in writing and in various other ways, such as through drawings, paintings, and sketches. Shown here is a sketch from his Studies of Infants.

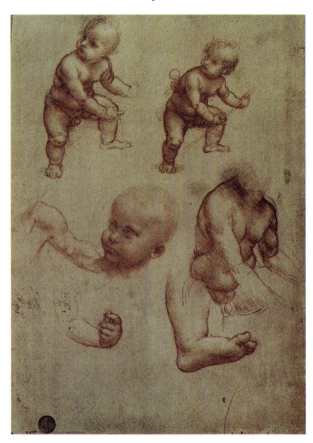

FIGURE 1-3
The Importance of Viewing More than One Perspective
In an Asian fable, blind men come across an elephant. Each man explores a different part of the elephant and describes what he perceives the animal to be. The men argue over which is the correct description, failing to see that the entire creature embraces all the aspects. Had the men been asked to determine the most effective use of the elephant, their conflicting—and limited—mental representations would have hampered their problem-solving abilities.

good students are less likely to fall prey to false starts, winding paths, and all kinds of errors. By allocating more of their mental resources to planning on a large scale, they are able to save time and energy and to avoid frustration. Similarly, in doing scientific research, it makes good sense to anticipate potential problems before you start. By thinking carefully at the outset, you are likely to avoid problems later on that could have been anticipated in advance.

In science, we need to know when to persevere and also when to quit. Many students, especially in the early stages of their careers, quit too soon, believing that because their experiments do not work initially, their hypotheses must be wrong. In fact, their hypotheses may be right, but other factors may be interfering: Sometimes, the subjects do not understand the instructions they are expected to follow, or the experimental designs contain irrelevant confounding factors that can be eliminated easily. One way for you to avoid major problems is to *pilot-test* (try out on a small scale) an experiment on a small number of subjects before doing the final experiment. Pilot experiments are a good allocation of resources because they help catch methodological errors and avoid wasting time later.

Monitoring Problem Solving

A prudent expenditure of time includes monitoring the process of solving the problem. As mentioned previously, the ideal we sometimes hold of the scien-

tific method is wrong because scientific pursuits rarely proceed in a strictly linear fashion. One of the reasons for this divergence from a linear path is that effective problem solvers always monitor their problem solving. They do not set out on a path to a solution and then wait until they have reached the end of the path to check where they are. Rather, they check up on themselves all along the way, to make sure that they are getting closer to their goal. If they are not, they reassess what they are doing, perhaps concluding that they made a false start, or that they got off track somewhere along the way.

Sometimes, researchers may even decide that the new track leads to a more interesting endpoint. Occasionally, researchers discover that the problem is different from what they had originally thought (necessitating a redefinition), but that the findings are nonetheless quite interesting. For example, biologists Nettie Stevens and T. H. Morgan "had specifically set out to study the effects of varying external conditions" (such as food and temperature) on male–female sex determination in insects (see Kass-Simon & Farnes, 1990, p. 225). Much to their dismay, the experiments yielded only negative results, but while Stevens was conducting the necessary tissue analysis for the experiments, she noticed (correctly) that the chromosome seemed to serve as the basis for determination of sex.

> How effectively do you monitor your own problem solving? How might you improve your monitoring skills?

Evaluating Problem Solving

Just as you need to monitor a problem while you are in the process of solving it, you need to evaluate your solution after you have finished. Some of the evaluation may occur right away; the rest may occur a bit later, or even much later. As suggested, very few scientific questions—particularly questions about how people behave—are ever resolved once and for all. Rather, we reach an answer that seems right at a given time, or that is the best or most nearly complete answer we are able to find at that time, only later to realize that the answer was incomplete or even incorrect. To a large extent, success in scientific problem solving depends on the researcher's ability to profit from feedback, both self-generated and from others.

Often, it is through the evaluation process that key scientific advances occur. When evaluating research, the original hypothesis may be contradicted, and an alternative, perhaps even opposing, hypothesis may be suggested—by the original researcher or by others who read about the research. When that hypothesis is tested and evaluated, it may turn out that some elements of the original hypothesis are valid, and that some elements of the opposing, alternative hypothesis are also valid, so the two views can be synthesized into a new, stronger, and more encompassing hypothesis.

Georg Hegel, a German philosopher, referred to this evolution of thought as a **dialectic**—an intellectual dialogue in which, first, thinkers strive to reach the truth by positing an initial **thesis** (statement of opinion); others soon propose an **antithesis** (an opinion that takes a somewhat different perspective and often contradicts the original thesis); and eventually, someone later suggests a **synthesis** (selective combination of the two) (1807/1931). This synthetic statement may then be considered a new thesis, for which there may then also arise an antithesis, and so on as the evolutionary process of developing thought continues. The dialectical process is not entirely linear, in that scientists may find new problems with long-established theses, and they may find that long-discarded theses have new relevance. This dialectical evolution of thought is a primary characteristic of science and helps contribute to the attainment of scientific goals. Just what are these goals?

THE GOALS OF PSYCHOLOGICAL RESEARCH AND PRACTICE

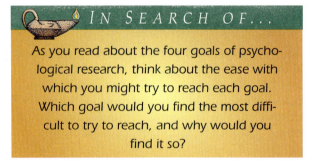

IN SEARCH OF...

As you read about the four goals of psychological research, think about the ease with which you might try to reach each goal. Which goal would you find the most difficult to try to reach, and why would you find it so?

Thus far, we have addressed the *what* and the *how* of scientific research. We still must discuss the *why*. Why do scientists do what they do? What are they trying to accomplish? In addition to the broad goal of advancing scientific thought, we generally distinguish among four main goals for science: description, explanation, prediction, and control. (See Table 1-3 for a summary of these goals.)

Description

In psychology, **description** refers simply to characterizing what and how people think, feel, or act in response to various kinds of situations. Before we can begin to explain or to predict people's behavior, we need to describe their behavior. At first, description might seem trivial. Why would scientists need to describe behavior that people could easily see for themselves? Indeed, descriptive research often starts with people watching, and then wondering.

Consider, for example, this event: In March of 1964, 38 mature adults in Queens, New York, watched or listened from their apartments as a maniacal murderer stalked and eventually stabbed a woman to death in three separate attacks over a half-hour period. No one intervened, no one made any attempt to help her, and no one even called the police until the woman was dead (at which point just one person called). The attack on the woman, Kitty Genovese, raised national headlines. When do bystanders intervene, and when do they just watch without doing anything? In order to understand why the bystanders behaved as they did, we needed research that would describe both the bystanders and the circumstances surrounding their behavior (Latané & Darley, 1970; see also Chapter 15). Once we have fully and accurately described the behavior (including the characteristics of the actors and of the surrounding context), we can try to explain why it happens.

Explanation

Explanation addresses why people think, feel, or act as they do. Were psychology only descriptive, people would almost certainly become disillusioned with it. Ideally, theories in psychology should be explanatory as well as descriptive, answering the *why* as well as the *what* and the *how* of psychological functioning. Bear in mind, however, that many of the explanations are not definitive. As psychologists learn more and gather more data, these explanations will be modified, contradicted, and perhaps replaced altogether by explanations that seem better to fit the new information.

Because of the rapid progress we see in psychology, it seems important to emphasize not only *facts*—research findings and what they show—but also how people in the field think and develop their ideas for explaining human behavior. What we know about phenomena changes. The content of an introductory psychology text of today does not much resemble that of an introductory psychology text of 30 years ago, nor will it resemble a text of the future; yet the thinking skills and techniques you learn today will be useful to you always.

TABLE 1-3
Four Primary Goals of Psychological Research
Psychologists seek to achieve one or more of the following goals by conducting research.

Goal	How Psychologists Try to Achieve It	Questions Psychologists Ask When Trying to Reach This Goal
Description	Try to characterize how people and other living beings think, feel, or act in various kinds of situations.	What happens? When and where does it happen? How does it happen?
Explanation	Try to understand why living beings think, feel, or act as they do.	Why does it happen?
Prediction	Attempt to predict behavior, based on available information about past performance.	What will happen next?
Control	Seek to influence behavior.	How can we influence this behavior or intervene in this situation?

Thinking critically and evaluatively is a skill that can be applied anytime, anywhere. Content is important, too: There is no such thing as contentless thought. Nonetheless, what is important in psychology, as well as in other fields of study, is not subject matter alone, but how to use it in research and in everyday life.

Prediction

Informative theory and research will enable you not only to describe and explain behavior, but also to predict it. **Prediction** can be very important in practice, as well as in theory. For example, suppose that you want to help someone to break an addiction. Your chances of helping the person will be improved if you know what to anticipate (see Chapter 6). Withdrawal from an addiction takes a somewhat predictable course, and if you know what to expect when, you can help the person to realize that the symptoms (such as the headaches, nervousness, hunger, digestive upsets, and nicotine cravings that accompany cessation of smoking) are not signs of ill health, but steps along the way to better health. You may even be able to help alleviate some of the symptoms if you can anticipate them in advance.

Predictive information can be a double-edged sword. It can help in predicting future behavior, but if overvalued, it can lead to erroneous judgments. Sometimes, it can even *affect* the outcomes it was originally supposed only to *predict*. Researchers tested this notion in one context by identifying particular students who the researchers told teachers were likely

to be "late bloomers"—students whose performance was likely to start picking up and improving (Rosenthal & Jacobson, 1968). Later on, the students who had been thus identified did indeed improve scholastically. However, the teachers had been deceived. In reality, the "late bloomers" had been selected at random—they were initially no different in measured abilities from any of the other students. Although the teachers could recall no differential treatment of the "late bloomers," the teachers' expectations of improvement clearly had an effect on their students. The results suggest that a prediction can become a *self-fulfilling prophecy:* The very fact of predicting something about someone can make that thing come true.

The Rosenthal-Jacobson study was not without its flaws (Elashoff & Snow, 1971), but the phenomenon of the self-fulfilling prophecy seems fairly common. Thus, we need to be careful about making predictions, especially pessimistic ones, about people's behavior, because those predictions may contribute to bringing about that very behavior.

Control

Psychotherapy is the use of psychological means to treat mental or emotional disorders and their related bodily problems. Many *therapeutic interventions*—active attempts to change maladaptive thoughts, attitudes, or actions—are directed toward the goal of bringing behavior and events under our control. Thus, the major goal of most psychotherapy is to allow clients to regain control in one or more domains

Robert Rosenthal and Leonore Jacobson named their study "Pygmalion in the Classroom," alluding to George Bernard Shaw's play Pygmalion, *about a man who trained an uneducated girl to become a cultured woman of society. This sculpture shows the mythical Pygmalion in love with his creation, Galatea.*

and thereby to improve their lives. For example, we want to help a depressed person to control depression, or an anxious person to control anxiety.

Control is also a major goal of interventions in *cognitive research*, which studies intellectual abilities. For example, a number of educational programs are designed to help students develop their thinking skills (Bransford & Stein, 1984; Detterman & Sternberg, 1993; Feuerstein, 1980; Lipman, 1982; Sternberg, 1986a). These programs are successful in that they help students to take better control of their intellectual functioning, and to develop and use their abilities more effectively.

In sum, psychological theory, research, and practice help us to describe, explain, predict, and control thoughts and actions. These goals are not mutually exclusive, and usually, we seek some combination of them in our work. The goals often interact, so that achieving one helps us to achieve another. In the time that psychology has been an academic discipline, it has made great strides toward achieving these ends.

RESEARCH METHODS IN PSYCHOLOGY

IN SEARCH OF...

As you read about the various research methods in psychology, think about which methods most appeal to you. Would you prefer interacting with a small number of individuals or a large number of persons? Would you prefer instead to collect data by observing people or by compiling data from surveys?

So far, this chapter has alluded to various methods that psychologists can use to study problems without systematically considering the range of these methods. This section shows some of the specific methods psychologists can bring to bear on the problems that interest them: (a) experiments; (b) tests, questionnaires, and surveys; (c) case studies; and (d) naturalistic observation. These research methods are summarized in Table 1-4.

Experiments

An **experiment**, in the strictest scientific sense, is an investigation that studies cause–effect relationships through the control of variables and the careful manipulation of one or more particular variables, to note their outcome effects on other variables. To understand the nature of experiments, we need to define some terms. There are basically two kinds of variables in any given experiment: (1) **independent variables**, which are individually *manipulated*, or carefully regulated, by the experimenter, while other aspects of the investigation are held constant (i.e., not subject to variation); and (2) **dependent variables**, the values of which depend on how one or more independent variables influence or affect the subject of the experiment. If you tell some student subjects that they will do extremely well on a task, but you do not tell the other students anything about how well they will do, the independent variable is the information that the students are given about their expected task performance (either they are or are not given information), and the dependent variable is how well both groups of students actually perform the task.

Experiments often involve two different types of **conditions**. In the first type of condition, the **experimental condition**, subjects are exposed to an experimental treatment. For example, they might be told that they will do extremely well on a task they are about to be given. The experimental condition is also described as the *treatment condition*. In the second condition, the **control condition**, the subjects do not receive the treatment. They might not be told anything about how they will do on a task they are about to be given. The goal of the experiment would then be to see whether the subjects who are told that they will succeed actually perform better on the task than do those who are told nothing.

Usually, two different groups of subjects are used for the experimental and the control conditions. When two or more groups of subjects are used, the subjects that receive the experimental treatment are the *experimental group*, and the subjects who are used as a comparison group are the *control group*. The control group may receive some alternative (and usually irrelevant) treatment or no treatment at all. A control group is included as a standard of comparison against which to judge the experimental group and also to control for irrelevant, confounding variables. Without a control group, it is usually hard to draw any conclusions at all. For example, if you told all of the subjects that they would do well on a task they were about to be given, you would have no way of isolating and hence of knowing the effect of telling them about their expected performance. To evaluate the effects of

TABLE 1-4
Research Methods
To achieve their goals, psychologists may use various methods of investigation.

Method	Description of Method	Form of Data Obtained	Advantages of Method	Disadvantages of Method
Experiments	Controlled investigations that study cause-and-effect relationships through the manipulation of variables	Quantitative ("hard data"; statistical, verifiable by replication)	1. Precise control of independent variables 2. Usually, large numbers of subjects allow results to be generalized	1. Usually, less intensive study of individual subjects 2. Sometimes, the ability to generalize to real-world behavior is limited
Tests, questionnaires, and surveys	Obtain samples regarding behavior, beliefs, and abilities at a particular time and place	Quantitative or qualitative ("soft data"; descriptive, practical)	1. Ease of administration 2. Ease of scoring and statistical analysis	1. May not be able to generalize results beyond a specific place, time, and test content 2. Discrepancies between real-life behavior and test behavior
Case studies	Intensive studies of single individuals, which draw general conclusions about behavior	Qualitative	Highly detailed information, including the historical context	1. Ability to generalize information is compromised by the small samples of people studied 2. Limitations on the reliability of the data
Naturalistic observations	Observations of real-life situations, as in classrooms, work settings, or homes	Qualitative	1. Wide applicability of results 2. Understanding of behavior in natural contexts	1. Loss of experimental control 2. Possibility that the presence of the observer may influence the observed behavior

telling subjects how well they would do on a task, you need a control group of subjects who are not told about their expected performance.

Thus far, we have defined *experiment* in the strictest sense and in terms of an example. However, we can broaden the use of the term *experiment* to apply to investigations not as highly controlled by the experimenter. More loosely speaking, an experiment studies the effect of some variables on other variables. Later in this chapter, we explore three ways in which to design experimental research, including the strict, narrow definition used here and two other types of experimental design.

Tests, Questionnaires, and Surveys

Early in the twentieth century, Alfred Binet, a French psychologist, was commissioned to develop a test to distinguish children who were genuinely mentally deficient from those who were capable of scholastic achievement but who had behavior problems that interfered with that achievement. A **test** is a procedure used to measure a factor or to assess an ability at a particular time and in a particular place; tests almost invariably key the responses as being either right or wrong, or at least as being better (more accurate, more appropriate, more creative, etc.) or worse. Test scores vary not only across people, but also for a given person, due to various factors that may affect performance at the time of testing, such as ill health or ambient noise. A person's score on a given test is an observed score. The **observed score** is just a sample of the person's behavior at a given time and place; it is a measure of neither the best nor the worst possible score that the person could obtain, nor is it even a measure of the average possible scores the person might obtain. Ideally, the observed score would be as close as possible to the **true score**—a hypothetical score that would be obtained if we could give the person the test an unlimited number of times and then average those scores. The hypothetical construct of the true score highlights the fact that tests are and always will be imperfect. Tests can indicate only approximately a person's true abilities, personality, or whatever else the tests are attempting to measure.

Tests are used in experimental situations, as well as in other kinds of studies. For example, an investigator might give a battery of mental-ability tests and then examine the data using **factor analysis**—a form of statistical analysis that allows the investigator to infer distinct **factors** (the underlying hypothetical constructs, elements, or structures that cause an effect). In tests of mental abilities, the factors discerned through statistical analysis are thought by some psychologists to reflect the underlying structure of related mental abilities, which then cause the scores on the intelligence tests. For example, a verbal-ability factor might be implicated in tests of vocabulary and reading comprehension.

Unlike tests, **surveys** and **questionnaires** virtually never have right or wrong answers; they are typically measures of beliefs and opinions rather than of abilities or knowledge. For example, you might use a questionnaire or a survey to determine college students' attitudes toward campus regulations regarding alcohol, or to gather their opinions regarding the usefulness of survey data or whether they mind responding to questionnaires. Questionnaires and surveys are notorious for lending themselves to multiple interpretations. During political campaigns, you probably have heard the identical survey data interpreted entirely differently by opposing candidates. Nonetheless, questionnaires and surveys are handy research tools.

> If you were to conduct a survey of students at your college, what would be the topic of your survey? What are three questions you might include in your survey?

Case Studies

In **case studies**, psychologists conduct intensive investigations of single individuals in order to draw general conclusions about behavior applying to these individuals and perhaps to others as well. Case studies are used in a variety of psychological pursuits. For example, in **clinical** work in which psychologists and psychiatrists deal directly with clients, case studies are essential for understanding problems that people face both individually and collectively.

One of the better-known writings in the field of marriage and family therapy (see Chapter 19, on psychotherapy) is on marital separation (Weiss, 1975). Called a *monograph*, because it was written about one topic in depth, the report drew almost exclusively on case-study observations. In Robert Weiss's analysis of why marriages fail, his style was to find commonalities in case studies that suggested reasons for failure. For example, a recurrent theme in some of the accounts of failed marriages was that the marriage was wrong from the start:

> The few months before the day we were married weren't that good. Differences already had come up and there were problems and we

weren't as happy as we were before. But the wheels of marriage had already started working and we were already buying silverware and dishes and it was too late. (Man, late twenties, p. 16)

Another recurrent theme was that each spouse wanted different things in life:

I was trying to find myself, and she wanted to have babies. Well, I did and I didn't. She would have been quite happy with ten children living in a little place. It was a clash of values. (Man, about thirty, p. 17)

Weiss wove together a large number of case studies to provide a coherent account of the causes and consequences of marital separation.

Some investigators, however, study just a single individual in great depth. One such investigator is Howard Gruber, world-renowned for his case study (1981) of Charles Darwin (the naturalist who proposed the theory of natural selection as a means of biological evolution). Gruber chose the case-study method because he believed that each creative person represents a unique configuration of talents, styles, and abilities. Therefore, as a researcher of creativity, he needed to study individuals in great detail in order to understand how they were creative (see Gruber & Davis, 1988). In his work on Darwin, Gruber concluded that creative people tend to have a lifetime "network of enterprises," a master plan consisting of many subplans. Gruber also concluded that insights, contrary to popular belief, tend not to be sudden. Instead, insights evolve over many years and often comprise numerous lesser insights that combine to form the major insight of the creative individual.

Naturalistic Observation

Naturalistic observation, also known as *field study*, involves going outside the laboratory or the clinical setting and into the community ("the field") to *observe* (listen to, watch, take note of) people engaged in the normal activities of their daily lives. It includes the participant observation done by Cialdini (1984), whose work on persuasion was described earlier in this chapter. An impressive naturalistic observation in the behavioral sciences is of language development in three communities in North Carolina (Heath, 1983, mentioned again in Chapter 13). Shirley Heath observed life in the three communities over a period of several years. Her work has provided rich and fine-grained insights about growing up that would be hard to obtain from laboratory experiments.

CAUSAL INFERENCE IN PSYCHOLOGICAL RESEARCH

IN SEARCH OF...

How do you form your beliefs about what may be causing particular phenomena?

The preceding section described four different methods of research that psychologists can use. As mentioned, both the problem studied and the personal stylistic preferences of the investigator often determine the researcher's choice of method. An important issue remains, however, which also influences the choice of research method. What kinds of circumstances enable investigators to draw conclusions about causality? In other words, what do we need in a research study in order to be able to conclude that "so-and-so" causes "such-and-such"?

A major goal of psychological research is to draw **causal inferences.** For example, we might ask whether a particular independent variable (e.g., whether people are told that they will do well on a task) is responsible for particular variation in a given dependent variable (e.g., number of items answered correctly on a mathematical problem-solving task).

It is not always possible, however, to detect a clear causal relationship between independent and dependent variables, for a variety of reasons. For one thing, our ability to draw causal inferences depends on how the research is designed. **Design** refers to how variables are chosen and interrelated, as well as to how subjects are assigned to groups. Next, we consider three of the major kinds of designs in psycho-

Jane Goodall uses naturalistic observation to study the behavior of chimpanzees.

logical research—experimental, quasi-experimental, and correlational—and the kinds and degrees of causal inference that can be drawn from each (see Table 1-5 for a summary of the similarities and differences among these designs).

Controlled Experimental Designs

In a true **controlled experimental design**, the experimenter manipulates or controls one or more independent variables in order to see the effect on the dependent variable or variables. To be sure the treatment (and not some other variables or even random variation) is producing the effect, the experimenter includes one or more control groups that do not receive the experimental treatment.

In a true controlled experimental design, subjects must be randomly assigned to the experimental and the control groups. This *random assignment* is important because it ensures that later differences between the results for each group are not due to prior differences in the subjects themselves. For example, if a test of learning were given early in the day, and the first 20 subjects who arrived were assigned to the treatment group and the second 20 subjects were assigned to the control group, we might suspect that differences between the two groups could be associated with promptness (early arrivers might be more diligent), with tiredness (early arrivers might still be tired), or with some other factor associated with whether the subjects arrived earlier or later. True controlled experimental designs are particularly use-

TABLE 1-5
Experimental Designs
Psychologists draw different conclusions from their research, depending on the type of research design they use for studying a given phenomenon

Type of Design	Definition	Advantages	Disadvantages
Experimental	Experimenter manipulates or controls one or more independent variables and observes the effects on the dependent variable or variables; subjects are randomly assigned to control or treatment conditions.	Permits causal inference regarding the treatment variable(s).	Might not apply to settings outside the laboratory; might not have used a sample that truly represents the entire population about which the experiment is designed to inform us. May involve ethical concerns.
Quasi-experimental	Has many of the features of an experimental design, but subjects are not randomly assigned to control versus treatment conditions; in some cases, there is no control group at all.	May be more convenient to implement in some situations; may be permissible where ethical considerations prohibit random assignment of subjects; may be conducted in a more naturalistic setting, which might permit more richly textured data. In the case of correlational data, the entire population (e.g., all voters) may sometimes be available for study.	Do not permit causal inferences regarding the treatment variable(s). Also may require the use of sample data that may not apply to the entire population.
Correlational	Researchers just observe the degree of association between two or more attributes that occur naturally. Researchers do not directly manipulate the variables themselves, and they do not randomly assign subjects to groups.		

ful in research because they enable us to draw causal inferences.

A problem in experimental research, however, is that we can never be certain that our inferences are correct because we can never be absolutely sure that a difference between group results is not due to chance—random fluctuations in the data—unless we test the entire population of people in whom we are interested. Unfortunately, it is rarely practical or even possible to test the whole population in which we are interested, so we have to settle for testing what we believe to be a **representative sample** (a subset of the population, carefully chosen to represent the proportionate diversity of the population as a whole) of people. We usually have no guarantee that our subjects do indeed accurately represent the entire population we would ideally like to test.

As you might imagine, some portions of the total population (e.g., college students) are more readily accessible to researchers, so they may be overrepresented in research. In addition, there may be other reasons why some people are under- or overrepresented in research samples. For example, women and persons of color are often understudied, and men, whites, and college students are often overrepresented in research.

It is quite common for cross-cultural researchers to use *samples of convenience* (also called "bunch" or "grab" samples) because of the immediate availability of such samples (Lonner & Berry, 1986). This strategy is not restricted to research across cultures; countless millions of students in U.S. colleges and universities have been included in such samples over the years. It is very common, for example, for researchers to solicit the participation of several hundred students from an introductory psychology class. Are such groups representative? If so, whom do they represent?

Because the whole population is not tested, we use **sample statistics** (numbers that characterize the sample we have tested) as estimates of **population parameters** (numbers that would characterize everyone we conceivably might test who fit our desired description). Actual population parameters are unknowable unless we have the whole population to test; as noted earlier, this situation is rare.

Because sample statistics are only estimates of the whole population parameters, they vary to some degree from one sample to another. When we test subjects, we are really interested in the results not only for those subjects in particular but also for the population as a whole from which the subjects were drawn (e.g., all humans, all mothers, or all college students). In general, researchers seek to include as

large a proportion of the population as possible in the research sample. Although constraints of time and other resources limit the sizes of the samples we can actually test, proportionately larger samples help to average out random sources of error.

Statistical analysis helps researchers to minimize errors in two ways: (1) by ensuring accurate and consistent *description* of a sample from a population (for example, the average annual salaries reported by 30-year-olds in the sample); (2) by providing a consistent basis for the *inference* of characteristics of an entire population, based on the characteristics of only a sample. For example, if the average annual salaries of college graduates in the sample were far greater than the annual salaries of nongraduates, we could infer that having graduated from college somehow enhances the potential to earn larger annual salaries. Clearly, it is easier to be certain of the accuracy of the descriptions than it is to be certain of the accuracy of the inferences.

To increase the accuracy of our inferences, we use specially devised *inferential statistics* (allowing us to draw reasoned conclusions based on the implications of the descriptive data). Inferential statistics can help us to decide whether the difference between a treatment group and a control group (or other group) is likely to be true of the population as a whole, or whether the difference is likely to be caused by chance fluctuations in the data. For example, when biologist Rachel Carson became aware that birds and other animals were dying (or otherwise showing evidence of pathology) wherever the pesticide DDT had

How representative is this sample of people? Psychologists try to obtain representative samples of a population. They statistically analyze data based on samples to obtain an indication of population parameters.

been used, she had to show that the casualties were, in fact, linked to the DDT and not attributable to co-incidental co-occurrence of the two events (the DDT and the pathology). In research, we use the concept of **statistical significance** to help us decide how likely it is that a result is *not* due to chance fluctuations. To determine whether a result is statistically significant, we measure the probability that an obtained result is *not* due to chance; if that probability reaches a particular preset point (usually 95% to 99%), we consider the result statistically significant. Rachel Carson successfully demonstrated that the relationship between DDT and the high rate of casualties had reached a level of statistical significance, and DDT was banned from the marketplace.

For example, if your analysis of your experiment revealed that there was a 95% chance that the results you found were *not* due to chance, leaving only a 5% probability that your results were a fluke of random circumstances, you could say that your results were statistically significant at the "0.05" level. The 0.05 level of statistical significance corresponds to a 5% chance that your results were a fluke. If your results showed a 0.01 level of significance, there would be only a 1% chance that your findings resulted from random circumstances. The smaller the probability of obtaining a result due to random fluctuations, the greater is the level of statistical significance for the result.

There are two important things to notice. First, although we can set our probability point as high as we want, we can never be absolutely certain that a difference is not due to chance. We can be 99% confident (with a 0.01 level of significance), but never 100% confident (with a 0.00 level). Second, we can never prove the **null hypothesis** (the hypothesis of *no* difference between groups) without a doubt; that is, we cannot prove that a particular variable has no effect or that there is no difference between two different groups of subjects or among two or more different conditions.

What statistical likelihood of rain would prompt you to carry an umbrella when leaving home? If you had heard that a particular kind of food might be carcinogenic or otherwise toxic, what level of statistical significance would prompt you to avoid that food? If you had heard that a particular kind of food was now no longer believed to be carcinogenic or otherwise toxic, what level of statistical significance would prompt you to begin eating that food? Why might you look for different levels of significance in each of these cases?

Quasi-Experimental Designs

Suppose that we wish to study the effect of a particular curriculum on students' learning. Ideally, we would establish two identical colleges to which we would randomly assign representative students, and which would have virtually identical instructors. In this setting, we would then offer two different curricula. However, this ideal, controlled experiment could never actually be done. Instead, we are likely to use a more convenient design: Students in one college serve as experimental subjects (they receive the independent variable, the new curriculum), whereas students in another similar college serve as control subjects (and do not receive the new curriculum). In this case, subjects are not randomly assigned to groups, and the design is therefore not a true controlled experimental design. Instead, it is considered a **quasi-experimental design:** It has many of the features of a controlled experimental design, but it does not ensure the random assignment of subjects to the treatment and the control groups. The study will still use the experimental method; variables are manipulated, and cause-effect relations are still being sought. Nonetheless, its design is less precise and less experimenter-controlled than is a true experimental design. For this reason, we cannot draw a definite causal conclusion from a quasi-experimental design.

In the curriculum study, for example, we cannot draw causal conclusions because it is possible that some of the difference in results between the college groups is due to preexisting differences in the kinds of students who attend the two colleges or in other aspects of the two college environments, and not to the experimental curriculum. There are statistical methods for trying to control for differences between groups after the fact. However, we can never be certain that we are controlling for all relevant differences, and so nonrandom assignment of subjects to groups precludes causal inferences.

Another form of quasi-experimental design involves a group that receives an experimental treatment, but in the absence of a control group. For example, a researcher might have students take a preliminary test (*pretest*) on their knowledge of social psychology, and then have an instructor teach a curriculum covering social psychology. Finally, the students would take a concluding test (*posttest*) similar in content to the pretest, the purpose of which would be to measure student achievement and curriculum effectiveness.

This quasi-experimental design is surprisingly common in research on various kinds of curricula. The prevalence of this kind of design is surprising because no one can conclude that the curriculum caused any of the gains that might be observed. Why not? For one thing, perhaps students matured from pretest to posttest, independently of the curriculum, and thus scored higher on the posttest because of their maturation. They also might have learned something about social psychology outside of class, between pretest and posttest, which helped them to improve. Perhaps even the very experience of taking the pretest enabled them to test better the second time around because the test information had become familiar, and they therefore knew what to expect in the test situation. A parallel control group that received the pretest and the posttest without the curriculum (or better, with an alternative curriculum on some other topic) would have countered these alternative explanations. Without the use of a control group, however, no clear conclusions can be drawn.

Although quasi-experimental designs are less scientifically desirable than controlled experimental designs, they are often unavoidable. In naturalistic observational settings that cannot be controlled by experimenters, we sometimes have to take what we are given or nothing at all. Sometimes, the limitations on research are ethical constraints. For example, if we wish to study the effects of long-term alcohol addiction on psychological health, we are ethically bound to accept in the alcoholic group those who already have chosen to drink excessively, and in the control group those who already have chosen not to do so. We cannot randomly assign people to one group or the other, and then insist that those assigned to the drinking group become chronic alcoholics! Thus, quasi-experimental designs are used when controlled experimental ones simply are not feasible or ethically appropriate.

> What are some psychological phenomena that should be studied, but cannot appropriately or feasibly be studied using controlled experimental designs?

Correlational Designs

Like quasi-experimental designs, correlational designs do not permit us to infer causation. In a pure **correlational design**, researchers merely observe the degree of association between two (or more) *attributes* (characteristics of the subjects, of the setting, or of the situation) that already occur naturally in the group(s) under study. In correlational designs, researchers do not directly manipulate the variables

themselves, and they do not randomly assign subjects to groups. Instead, researchers usually observe subjects in naturally preexisting groups, such as particular students in two or more classrooms, or particular employees in two or more work settings. As with quasi-experimental designs, a correlational study is less scientifically desirable than a strict controlled experimental investigation, but frequently, it is unavoidable.

When two attributes show some degree of statistical relationship to one another, they are *correlated*. **Correlation** is expressed as a number on a scale that ranges from -1 to 0 to 1, as follows:

-1 indicates a perfect **negative (inverse) correlation** (as A increases, B decreases, and vice versa). *Example*—amount of money saved in relation to amount of money spent

0 indicates no correlation at all. *Examples*—the frequency of eating pizza for dinner, in relation to undergraduate grade-point average

+1 indicates a perfect **positive correlation** (as A increases, so does B, and vice versa). *Examples*—getting high grades in all courses, in relation to having a high grade-point average (GPA); having money in a no-interest checking account, in relation to the amount deposited into the account

Numbers between 0 and +1 indicate some intermediate degree of positive correlation (e.g., 0.7, 0.23, 0.01); numbers between 0 and -1 indicate some intermediate degree of negative correlation (e.g., -0.03, -0.2, -0.75). Perfect correlations of -1 and 1 are extremely rare. Usually, if two things are correlated, it is in some intermediate degree, such as the correlation between number of years of education and future income. Figure 1-4 shows how correlations appear in graph form.

Note that for each kind of correlation (as shown in the examples), the direction of causality, if any causality exists at all, is not known. For example, we might give subjects a test of depression and a test of self-esteem in order to determine whether there is a connection between the two constructs. Both self-esteem and depression are preexisting variables over which experimenters have no control. Suppose that we find a *correlation* between self-esteem and depression. We might expect it to be negative (inverse) in some degree, and it is; those who have high self-esteem tend to be less depressed, and those with low self-esteem are more depressed. This correlation might mean that low self-esteem causes depression, or it might mean that depression causes low self-esteem, or it might even mean that both depression and low self-esteem depend on some third overarching variable, which we have not yet identified (e.g., rejection in childhood). To conclude, then, correlational designs are useful in spotting that relationships exist, but not in specifying exactly how they work or what might cause them.

What are some phenomena that are positively correlated? What are some that are negatively correlated? What are some that are correlated but are not causally related (i.e., some other factor affects the correlation of the two phenomena, but neither of the phenomena causes the other to occur?

One more important issue remains before we leave this introductory discussion of psychological research methods and practices: the issue of researcher ethics.

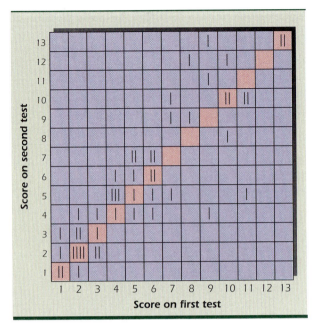

FIGURE 1-4
Graphic Representation of a Correlation
This graph shows positive correlation between a pair of variables.

ETHICAL ISSUES IN PSYCHOLOGICAL RESEARCH

IN SEARCH OF...

Is it ever right to lie to participants in a psychological experiment? Can we ever justify causing pain in an experiment? Is it somehow more justifiable to cause pain in squids, rats, or rabbits than in people?

The questions you just answered for yourself are the kinds of questions researchers face as they deal with the moral and ethical issues that arise in psychological research (as well as in medical and other research).

Deception

Research in psychology sometimes involves the deception of subjects. Sometimes, the deceptions are mild, such as not revealing to the subject the true purpose of an experiment until after it is over. For example, the deception involved in the Robert Rosenthal and Leonore Jacobson "Pygmalion in the classroom" study discussed earlier would probably be

considered benign. In some cases, however, psychologists have used extreme forms of deception, such as leading subjects to believe that they are delivering painful electric shocks to another person, when in fact they are not (Milgram, 1974).

Why is deception used at all? Typically, deception is a factor in an experiment when telling subjects the truth might seriously distort the results of the investigation, rendering them useless. For example, Stanley Milgram (1974) decided to use an extreme form of deception in order to study obedience. Milgram wanted to know whether people would follow the orders of an experimenter, regardless of how abhorrent they believed the orders to be.

Milgram was intrigued by the phenomenon of obedience because of the horrifying consequences of blind obedience by Nazis and other Germans preceding and during World War II.

The subjects in Milgram's experiments were told that the experiment involved testing the effects of punishment on learning. They were led to believe that they were administering increasingly intense electric shocks to other subjects, who behaved as if they were in increasing pain. In fact, however, the other "subjects" were not really subjects at all. Instead, they were the experimenter's **confederates**—a term applied to collaborators of the experimenter, who are hired to convince the subject of some aspect of the experiment. In the Milgram experiment, the confederates were not actually being harmed and were only pretending to feel pain.

As a result of this deception, many of those who believed themselves to be administering the shocks were in great psychological conflict; they wanted to obey the orders of the experimenter, but they were unhappy about causing apparent pain and distress to another person. On the other hand, the experiment would not have been possible if the subjects had known in advance that the apparent shocks would cause no pain whatsoever. In this case, the subjects would have had no reason to disobey orders, and the whole purpose of the experiment would have been lost (see Chapter 15 for more on Milgram's work).

When Milgram carried out this research, it was generally not required that researchers obtain advance approval of their plans in order to conduct a psychological investigation. Milgram's research sparked controversy about the use of deception and other ethical issues, and it contributed to the formation of institutional boards of review at universities and other research facilities. Today, virtually all institutions have a research-review process and require approval of investigations prior to their being carried out.

These boards are charged with protecting the rights of experimental subjects, and they use two key methods for making sure that subjects are protected. First, before subjects are asked to participate in a study, they are required to give *informed consent* to participating in the research; that is, the subjects are told what kinds of tasks they may be expected to perform and what kinds of situations they may expect

In Stanley Milgram's classic study of obedience, surprisingly, most subjects obeyed the instructions of the experimenter, even when they found the instructions objectionable.

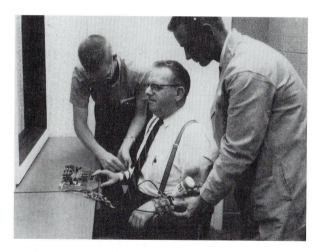

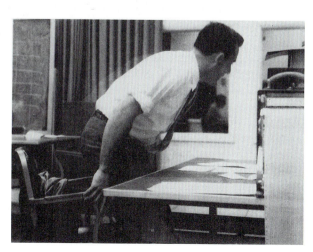

to encounter, with specific qualifications for use of deception (see Chapter 19 for more on informed consent). Second, after the research is completed, the subjects are fully *debriefed* about the research (told exactly the nature of the experiment, told about any deception that may have been involved, and given the reason for the deception). Most boards will allow minor deceptions if the value of the proposed research seems to justify the deception, and if the deceptions are fully explained afterward and are deemed necessary for the purpose of the experiment.

In what situations have you failed to be completely forthright in expressing your candid opinion of a situation? Why did you act as you did?

Physical or Psychological Pain

In the past, it was not uncommon for experiments to involve mild electric shocks to subjects. These shocks were slightly painful but not harmful. Occasionally, however, studies had potential for causing psychological damage. For example, many experiments are somehow stressful for participants, although how stressful they are often depends on the individual as much as on the experiment. What is difficult for one person may be relaxing for another and neutral for yet another. Still, researchers generally try to anticipate and minimize distress (unless distress itself is the construct under study), and institutional review boards will generally not permit studies that are likely to cause any long-lasting pain or harm. If participating in a study might cause short-term pain or stress, subjects must be fully informed in advance regarding possible consequences, via the informed-consent procedure. Moreover, informed consent requires that subjects be told that they are free to leave the experiment at any time without fear of any negative repercussions. Thus, if subjects thought that they could tolerate the conditions of an experiment beforehand but then find in the course of it that they cannot, they may leave at once.

The situation is murkier when animals—such as rats, pigeons, rabbits, dogs, or even simple multicelled organisms—are involved instead of people. Most institutions vigorously attempt to ensure that animals and their health are protected, and that the animals have all they require in terms of food, shelter, and freedom from harm or discomfort. At the same time, animals cannot sign informed-consent papers, and they sometimes have been exposed to painful or even harmful procedures. In such cases, review boards attempt to weigh the potential benefits of the research to humans against the potential harm to the animals. Furthermore, in recent years, government has increasingly regulated scientific research and the appropriate use of animals.

Questions regarding how to guard animal rights are not easily answered. No scrupulous researcher actively wishes to cause harm to animals. On the other hand, some of our most important discoveries in both medicine and psychology have come from research in which animals were sacrificed in order to advance our knowledge about and our ability to help humans. Review boards and policymakers attempt to weigh the costs and benefits involved in all research, whether it employs human or animal subjects. Still, the controversy over use of animal subjects is far from over.

Confidentiality

The large majority of experiments in psychology are conducted on an anonymous basis—participants' names are not associated with their data. Occasionally, however, complete anonymity is not possible. For example, if an experimenter wants to compare students' scores on some standardized test of ability in relation to their freshman grades in college, the experimenter needs to have some means of identifying individual students—to associate individuals with their test scores and with their grades—in order to correlate the scores and the grades. Even when research cannot be anonymous, however, experimenters go to great lengths to ensure that names of participants are known only to the investigator. The vast majority of experimenters do indeed meet the ethical standards that they promise to their subjects.

What are a few kinds of questions that you would answer differently if you believed your answers might not be kept confidential?

This chapter has considered many aspects of psychological research and practice at a general level. The next chapter considers the history and the geography—the roots and branches—of psychology, to answer the question: How has psychology evolved, and what are the various specializations in the field as it exists today?

SUMMARY

Psychology Defined as a Social Science   4

1. *Psychology* is the study of the mind and of behavior. Psychology is a *social science*. Psychologists seek to understand how organisms—primarily people—think, learn, perceive, feel, interact with others, and understand themselves.

"Isn't It All Obvious Anyway?"   5

2. Laypeople often feel concerned about psychology and psychologists, wondering whether what we learn from studying psychology is self-evident. However, many psychological results are *counterintuitive*—not at all what people expect.

Psychology as a Science   6

3. A scientific discipline has several characteristics: (a) ideas are accurately reported and can be *verified*, (b) work is *cumulative* with respect to past research, (c) researchers *report findings publicly* in scientific journals, and (d) theories are somewhat *parsimonious*, in that they reduce data to a manageable explanatory or descriptive framework.

4. It is important to recognize some misconceptions about science. Science (a) is not merely a collection of facts, (b) is not always correct, (c) does not always follow the orderly progression of steps students learned as "the scientific method," and (d) is not always completely objective and value-free because it is practiced by human beings.

How Do Scientists Think?   12

5. *Problem solving* is a thought process used by scientists. Typically, it occurs in a cycle, consisting of these steps: (a) *recognizing a problem*, (b) *defining the problem*, (c) *constructing a strategy* for problem solution, (d) *organizing information* to examine a problem, (e) *allocating resources*, (f) *monitoring problem solving*, and (g) *evaluating problem solving*. The evaluation of the solution often leads to the recognition of a new challenge and thus the repetition of the cycle. The cycle is not necessarily executed exactly in this order. Some problems are redefined as the process goes along, or new strategies are tried as old ones fail.

The Goals of Psychological Research and Practice   18

6. When addressing a problem, the goals of psychological research are (a) *description*, (b) *explanation*, (c) *prediction*, and (d) *control*. Some research, however, may address only one or two of these goals.

Research Methods in Psychology   20

7. Psychologists employ various research methods, such as (a) *experiments*; (b) *tests, questionnaires,* and *surveys*; (c) *case studies*; and (d) *naturalistic observation*.

8. An *experiment* is a carefully supervised investigation in which a researcher studies *cause-and-effect relations* through the manipulation of one or more *independent variables* in order to observe their effects on one or more *dependent variables*. Ideally, an experiment should include a *control group* to ensure that differences in results are due to the experimental treatment and not to irrelevant group differences.

Causal Inference in Psychological Research   23

9. Because we generally cannot conduct studies on whole populations, we use *sample statistics* (numbers that characterize the sample we have tested) as estimates of the *population parameters* (numbers that would characterize everyone we conceivably might test who would fit our desired criteria). The use of sample statistics is based on the assumption that the researcher has found a *representative random sample* of the population under study.

10. Although we are never able to prove the *null hypothesis* (which states that there is no difference between two groups under study), we can demonstrate that a particular difference has reached a level of *statistical significance*—that is, it is unlikely to have occurred due to random fluctuations of the data.

11. Psychological researchers try to draw *causal inference*, or conjectures about cause-and-effect relationships. *Experimental designs* are better suited to the drawing of such inferences than are *quasi-experimental* designs, which lack at least one

experimental characteristic, or than are *correlational* studies, which merely show associations.

Ethical Issues in Psychological Research   28

12. Scientists, including psychologists, must address questions of *ethical research procedures*. Most questions center on whether subjects—human or animal—are treated fairly. Research institutions today have standard policies that require *informed consent* by and *debriefing* of human subjects. Most institutions have also set up boards of review to study and approve proposed research; some government agencies also monitor research practices, especially as they pertain to animals.

KEY TERMS

antithesis 18

case studies 22

causal inferences 23

clinical 22

conditions 20

confederates 29

confirmation bias 10

control 20

control condition 21

controlled experimental design 24

correlation 27

correlational design 27

dependent variables 20

description 18

design 23

dialectic 18

disconfirm 10

experiment 20

experimental condition 20

explanation 18

factor analysis 22

factors 22

hypotheses 9

hypothetical constructs 15

independent variables 20

naturalistic observation 23

negative (inverse) correlation 27

normal science 8

null hypothesis 26

observed score 22

operational definitions 14

paradigm 8

population parameters 25

positive correlation 27

prediction 19

problem-solving cycle 12

psychology 4

psychotherapy 19

quasi-experimental design 26

questionnaires 22

reliable 7

replicate 6

representation 16

representative sample 25

revolutionary science 8

sample statistics 25

statistical significance 26

surveys 22

synthesis 18

test 22

theory 11

thesis 18

true score 22

valid 7

variables 15

verifiable 6

IN SEARCH OF THE HUMAN MIND: ANALYSES, CREATIVE EXPLORATIONS, AND PRACTICAL APPLICATIONS

1. What apparently obvious statements about human nature might you, as a psychological investigator, question?
2. What difficulties might you encounter if you were trying to conduct survey-based research?
3. For what kinds of psychological phenomena is *control* a suitable goal? What kinds of psychological phenomena would you like to control, either in yourself or in others? What kinds of psychological phenomena should be off-limits in terms of control? (If you answer "none" to any question, tell why you say so.)

4. Describe the steps you would take if you were systematically to observe members of a new and unfamiliar culture, with the goal of learning what their customs are and why they have those customs.

5. If you were in charge of the ethics committee deciding which experiments should be permitted, what questions about the experiments would you want to have answered?

6. If a psychologist from a distant planet were to observe television programs, what conclusions would the psychologist draw about our culture?

7. What challenging problem have you solved in your personal life? Compare the steps you took in solving your problem with the steps given in the problem-solving cycle.
   Which step of the problem-solving process was the most difficult? Why was that step so hard?

8. Think about an instance in which you and a friend or a family member resolved a serious disagreement. Describe the problem and its resolution in terms of a thesis (your view), an antithesis (your friend's view), and a synthesis (your resolution).
   What other dialectical developments might you anticipate related to this situation?

9. If you could engage in naturalistic observation of a psychological phenomenon that differs across cultures, what would you study and in what cultures would you study it? Why would this study interest you?

Chapter Two

The Roots and Branches of Psychology

Chapter Outline

Never hug and kiss them, never let them sit on your lap. If you must, kiss them once on the forehead when they say good night. Shake hands with them in the morning. Give them a pat on the head if they have made an extraordinarily good job of a difficult task. Try it out. In a week's time you will find how easy it is to be perfectly objective with your child and at the same time kindly. You will be utterly ashamed at the mawkish, sentimental way you have been handling it.

—*John Watson,* Psychological Care of Infant and Child

We have only to read behavioral psychologist John Watson's views to realize how much our beliefs about children and our standards for child care have changed. Few people today would follow Watson's advice, and many might find it scandalous. Nonetheless, when Watson presented his ideas about child rearing more than 60 years ago, they were not considered at all outrageous or even surprising.

What would you recommend as an alternative to Watson's advice?

The way we interpret contemporary ideas and determine what seems reasonable is shaped by our contemporary context of ideas and by the past ideas that have led up to the present ones. Today, we might consider many recent psychological ideas outrageous, other ideas proposed millennia ago to be reasonable, and still other intervening ideas to be surprising but appealing in some ways. This chapter attempts to provide both an historical and a contemporary context for many current perspectives in psychology.

THE DIALECTICAL PROGRESSION OF IDEAS

Those who cannot remember the past are condemned to repeat it.

—*George Santayana,* The Life of Reason, *Vol. 1*

Hegel was right when he said that we learn from history that men never learn anything from history.

—*George Bernard Shaw,* Heartbreak House

The first section of this chapter is based on the hope that you can learn a great deal from history and will not be condemned to repeat mistakes made by those who preceded you. Having this foundation allows you to do as other psychologists do—make your own original, innovative mistakes, from which you and others may learn. Many of the historical influences and perspectives that have served as the foundation for contemporary views are still at work in psychology today.

As you read this chapter, and this textbook, you will notice that much of psychological thinking proceeds in cycles, spiraling through the centuries of human thought. Often philosophers, psychologists, and others propose and believe strongly in one view for a while until a contrasting view comes to light; then the most attractive or reasonable elements in each are melded into a new view, which then gains acceptance. This new integrated view then serves as the springboard for a new contrasting view, and eventually yet another melding of views. As noted in Chapter 1, this process of evolving ideas through theses, antitheses, and syntheses was termed a *dialectic* by Georg Hegel (1770–1831), a German philosopher.

Dialectical progression depends on having a **critical tradition** that allows current beliefs (theses) to be challenged by alternative, contrasting, and sometimes even *radically* divergent views (antitheses), which may then lead to the origination of new ideas based on the old (syntheses). Western critical tradition is often traced back to the Greek philosopher Thales (624–545 B.C.), who invited his students to improve on his thinking, a stance not easy for any teacher to take. In addition, Thales did not hesitate to profit from knowledge accumulated in other parts of the world. He traveled around the Mediterranean and learned a great deal about astronomy, geometry, and other subjects from the ancient Egyptians. Today, when we criticize the ideas of our predecessors, we accept Thales's invitation to make progress by building upon or springing away from old ideas. Note that even when we reject outdated ideas, those ideas still move us forward, serving as valuable springboards for new ideas—the theses to our innovative antitheses.

A BRIEF INTELLECTUAL HISTORY: WESTERN ANTECEDENTS OF PSYCHOLOGY

IN SEARCH OF...

How does it profit us to learn more about our origins?

Where and when did the study of psychology begin? Arguably, historical records do not accurately trace the earliest human efforts to understand the ways in which we humans think, feel, and act. In fact, contemporary historians recognize that much of what we know—or think we know—about the past reflects the biases and prejudices of those who have written the accounts of history. All of us are shaped by the social context in which we live and view the world; we are guided in our thoughts by the thoughts of those persons who preceded us and those who surround us. Historians are not invulnerable to the influences of the society in which they are writing their historical records. For example, because the historical documents that have reached us have been written primarily by Europeans, these records tend to highlight the contributions of Europeans and to downplay or ignore altogether the contributions of Asians, Africans, and others.

In this chapter, we trace our roots only as far back as ancient Greece. Actually, however, many highly sophisticated civilizations predated European civilization by centuries, and many technological advances occurred outside of Europe millennia before Europeans either imported them or invented them independently. Some of these early civilizations made great strides in establishing agriculture and sophisticated political and economic systems while Europeans were roaming the countryside, only beginning to think about using stone tools. The rich, fertile soils of Africa and Asia produced an abundant harvest of developments in technology (e.g., agriculture and simple machines), science (e.g., medicine), literature (e.g., legends and a written alphabet), art (e.g., paintings and metalwork), and politics (e.g., hierarchical government and division of labor). Centuries later the seeds of such intellectual endeavor reached the northern shores of the Mediterranean, where they took root and grew. On the Greek isles, some of our earliest records of the attempt to understand human psychology may be found in literature, such as in the psychological insights orated by the blind poet Homer (ca. eighth century B.C.) in his epic poems about ancient Greece, the *Iliad* and the *Odyssey*.

The study of psychology derives its name from the ancient Greek myth of *Psyche*. Psyche's name was synonymous with the vital "breath of life"—the soul—believed to leave the body at death. The Greek term *thymos* was a motivational force generating feelings and actions; to this day, the Greek root *thym-* is used as a combinative form to mean "feelings and motivations." The Greek word *nous* (an organ responsible for the clear perception of truth) is an uncommon English word for the mind, particularly for highly reasoned or divinely reasoned mentation. Thus, according to the archaic Greeks, the body and the mind are somewhat distinct, although the mind, perhaps influenced by external causes, does cause activity of the body.

Ancient Classical Greece (600–300 B.C.)

Although literature offers us some insight into early views of human behavior, we usually trace the earliest roots of psychology to developments that followed the introduction of the critical tradition. In particular, psychology traces its roots to two different approaches to human behavior: **philosophy,** which seeks to understand the general nature of many aspects of the world, primarily through **introspection** (self-examination of inner ideas and experiences); and **physiology,** the scientific study of living matter and of life-sustaining functions, primarily through observation. Actually, in ancient Greece, the approaches of these two fields did not differ much. Both used the more philosophical approach of introspective contemplation and speculation as a means of seeking to understand the nature of the body and the mind—how each works and how they interact. In ancient Greece, many philosophers and physiologists believed that understanding could be reached without having or even pursuing supporting observations.

> Think about some important decisions you have made. How much of a role did your observations play in your decisions, and how much did your reasoning about options play a role?

As the fields of philosophy and physiology diverged, they continued to influence the way in which psychology was to develop. The following discussion intertwines several important philosophical precursors to modern psychological thought: whether the mind and body are separate entities; whether knowledge is innate or is acquired through experience; what contributes to learning and the acquisition of knowledge; and how speculation and theory development, on the one hand, and observation and data gathering, on the other, are used in seeking an understanding of the truth.

Before you read about these philosophical approaches, pause for a moment to consider how you now answer these questions: Are your mind and your body separate, or does your mind exist only in terms of the physiology of your brain? Are your personality, your skills, and your knowledge a part of who you were at birth, or are they shaped by the experiences you have? How do you think you find out about things or solve problems you have: by formulating hypotheses and then testing them, or by acting on the environment and then stepping back to look at what has happened? Of course, for each of these questions, your answer may lie somewhere between the two extremes posed here.

The ancient Greek physician (and philosopher) Hippocrates (ca. 460–377 B.C.), commonly known as the father of medicine, left his mark on the then overlapping fields of physiology and philosophy. What sharply distinguished him from archaic Greek philosophers and physicians was his unorthodox idea that disease was not a punishment sent by the gods. Hippocrates also used unorthodox methods—empirical observations—to study medicine. Contrary to the mode of the day, he studied animal anatomy and physiology directly, using both *dissection* (dividing cadavers into sections by separating one piece from another, usually with minimal cutting, for purposes of examination) and *vivisection* (operating on living organisms, as a means of study). He was not entirely empirical in his methods, however, often mistakenly assuming that what he had observed in animals could be generalized to apply to humans (Trager, 1992).

Hippocrates was particularly interested in discovering the source of the mind. He saw the mind as a separate, distinct entity that controlled the body. This belief that the body and the mind (or "spirit," or "soul") are qualitatively different is termed **mind-body dualism.** According to this view, the body is composed of physical substance, but the mind is not. Unlike his archaic Greek ancestors, Hippocrates proposed that the mind resides in the brain; Hippocrates induced this conclusion by observing that when either side of the head was injured, spasms were observed in the opposite side of the body (Robinson, 1986). Thus, Hippocrates held that the agent of control is within the body, not in external forces, whether gods or demons. He also presaged modern psychology by speculating that physiological malfunctions rather than demons cause mental illness, again turning away from divine intervention as a cause of human behavior.

Two younger contemporaries of Hippocrates also considered the location of the mind to be within the body: Plato (ca. 428–348 B.C.) agreed that the mind resides within the brain; his student Aristotle (384–322 B.C.) located the mind within the heart. These two philosophers profoundly affected modern thinking in psychology and many other fields. Of the many, far-reaching aspects of Platonic and Aristotelian philosophies, there are three key areas in which the dialectics between these two philosophers are particularly relevant to modern psychology: the relationship between mind and body, the use of observation versus introspection as a means for discovering truth, and the original source for our ideas.

Plato and Aristotle differed in their view of mind and body because of their differing views regarding the nature of reality. According to Plato, reality resides not in the concrete objects of which we are aware through our body's senses, but in the abstract forms that these objects represent. These

At the school of Athens, rationalist Plato disagreed with empiricist Aristotle regarding the path to knowledge. (Raphael Raffaello Sanzio, The School of Athens)

abstract forms exist in a timeless dimension of pure abstract thought. Thus, reality is not inherent in any particular chair we see or touch, but in the eternal abstract *idea* of a chair that exists in our minds. The objects that our bodies perceive are only transient and imperfect copies of these true, pure, abstract forms. In fact, Plato's reason for locating the mind in the head was based on his introspective reflections on these abstract forms, rather than on any observations of physiology or behavior. The head *must* contain the seat of the mind because the head resembles a sphere—a perfect abstract form. Thus, to Plato, body and mind are interactive and interdependent but are essentially different, with the mind superior to the body. We reach truth not via our senses but via our thoughts. Aristotle, in contrast, believed that reality lies *only* in the concrete world of objects that our bodies sense. To Aristotle, Plato's abstract forms—such as the idea of a chair—are only derivations of concrete objects.

Aristotle's concrete orientation set the stage for **monism,** a philosophy concerning the nature of the body and mind, based on the belief that reality is a unified whole, existing in a single plane. According to monism, the mind (or soul) does not exist in its own right but is merely an illusory by-product of anatomical and physiological activity. Thus, the study of the mind and the study of the body are one and the same. We can understand the mind only by understanding the body.

Their differing views regarding the nature of reality led Plato and Aristotle also to disagree about how to investigate their ideas. Aristotle's belief that reality is based on concrete objects led him to research methods based on the observation of concrete objects—and of actions on those objects. Thus, Aristotle (a naturalist and biologist, as well as a philosopher) was an **empiricist** (one who believes that we acquire knowledge via **empirical** evidence, obtained through experience and observation). The Aristotelian view is associated with empirical methods, by which we conduct research—in laboratories or in the field—on how people think and behave. Aristotelians tend to *induce* general principles or tendencies, based on observations of many specific instances of a phenomenon. For example, empiricists might induce principles of how to learn about psychology from observations of psychology students engaged in learning.

For Plato, however, empirical methods have little merit because true reality lies in the abstract forms, not in the imperfect copies of reality observable in the world outside our minds. Observations of these imperfect, nonreal objects and actions would thus be irrelevant to the pursuit of truth. Instead, Plato suggested a **rationalist** approach, using philosophical analysis in order to understand the world and people's relations to it. Plato's rationalism was consistent with his dualistic view of the nature of body and mind: We find knowledge only through using the mind, through reason and speculation about the ideal world, not about the corporeal world of the body. Rationalists, therefore, usually tend to *deduce* specific instances of a phenomenon, based on general principles. For example, rationalists might deduce from a set of general principles of learning that specific students in a specific psychology course would learn in the ways described by the general principles.

Aristotle's view, then, leads directly to empirical psychological research, whereas Plato's view foreshadows theorizing that might not be grounded in extensive empirical observation. Each approach has merit. Rationalist theories without any connection to observations have little validity, but mountains of observational data without an organizing theoretical framework have little use.

In addition to differing both in their views of the relationship between mind and body and in their methods for finding truth, Plato and Aristotle differed in their views about the origin of ideas. From where do ideas come? Aristotle believed that ideas are acquired from experience. Plato, on the other hand, believed that ideas are innate and need only be dug out from the sometimes hidden nooks and crannies of the mind. In the dialogue *Meno*, he claimed to show that the rules of geometry already resided within the mind of a slave boy, who needed only to be made aware of these innate ideas, not to be taught these ideas from the world outside of his mind. That is, through dialogue, Socrates (the protagonist in this and other Platonic dialogues) helped the boy bring into awareness his innate mental concepts of these pure forms. Today, many people still debate whether abilities and dispositions such as athletic skill or intelligence are innate or are acquired through interactions with the environment. The most plausible solution is that a synthesis of both experience and innate ability contribute to many aspects of personality, skill, and intelligence (see Chapters 3 and 11). Now

that you have read about the views of Plato and Aristotle, which philosopher do you agree with more regarding the issues of mind-body dualism versus monism, innate versus acquired knowledge, and rationalism versus empiricism?

> Describe a teaching method that would be effective if Plato was correct in assuming that knowledge is innate. Contrast that method with one that would be effective if Aristotle was correct in assuming that knowledge is acquired through experience.

The Early Christian Era (200–450 A.D.) and the Middle Ages (400–1300 A.D.)

The dialectics of monism versus dualism, empiricism versus rationalism, and acquired versus innate abilities continued in Europe throughout the early Christian era and the Middle Ages. These epochs were not, however, a golden age for empirical science. Even some rationalists did not thrive during this time. The basis of philosophical discourse was faith in a Christian God and in Scriptural accounts of phenomena. Neither empirical demonstrations nor rationalist arguments were considered valid or even permissible unless they illustrated what was already dictated to be true on the basis of religious faith and official doctrine. Whatever contradicted these beliefs was heretical and unacceptable—to the point where the freedom and even the life of the doubter were at risk.

Great Christian philosophers of this era, such as St. Augustine of Hippo (354–430 A.D.; bishop in Roman Africa), were much more interested in the afterlife than in life itself. They urged people to seek a desirable afterlife, rather than a desirable life. Unlike Plato, they were doctrinaire and not fully open to the critical tradition. However, they agreed with Plato that the main basis for thought was introspection, not observation. Like Plato, they considered the concrete, material objects and phenomena of the world to be of interest primarily for what they symbolically represented, not for any empirical value that might lead to knowledge.

> Can you think of any of your beliefs that you may cling to tenaciously, regardless of reasonable arguments or evidence to the contrary?

After centuries of medieval dogmatism, some thinkers tried to integrate empiricism and faith. St. Thomas Aquinas (1225–1274), a theologian and philosopher, was an avid student of and commentator on Aristotle and his works. He attempted to synthesize a sort of "Christian science," wherein empiricist philosophy was bounded by the dictates of Christian theology. According to Aquinas, reasoning was important and acceptable because reason would lead to God. Aquinas's acceptance of reason as a route to truth opened the way for those who followed him yet did not share his religious dogma.

According to Aquinas's precariously perched empirical-rational-religious approach, humans are at the juncture of two universes, the corporeal and the spiritual (similar to Plato's mind-body dualism). The goal for humans is to understand the life of the body through the life of the spirit. Science must therefore take a back seat to religion. As the Middle Ages drew to a close, particularly in the eleventh to thirteenth centuries, many changes heralded the arrival of the Renaissance: the first modern universities were founded, ancient Greek medical and natural-science texts were translated, and some experimental techniques were advanced.

> Imagine that you were living in pre-Renaissance Europe, and you were among the first students to study at one of the newly founded universities. What are some ways in which your college experience then would have differed from your present college experience?

The Renaissance (Rebirth) of Criticism (1300s to 1600s A.D.) and the Nascence (Birth) of Science

As critical thought was reborn throughout Europe, modern views of science were born. During the Renaissance, the established Roman Catholic Church remained a strong force both philosophically and politically, but the focus of philosophical thinking shifted from Christian doctrine's emphasis on God and the afterlife back to an interest in humankind and the here and now. Science as we know it began, and direct observation was established as the basis of knowledge.

During this period the intellectual movement known as humanism awoke after centuries of slumber. Renaissance **humanism** investigated the role of humans in the world, centering on humans "as the measure of all things." Humanists exalted the role of humans in nature, which contrasted with the previous exaltation of God. Humanism grew out of the rediscovery and revival of ancient classics of Greek and Roman philosophy, literature, mathematics, medicine, and the natural sciences, which had been

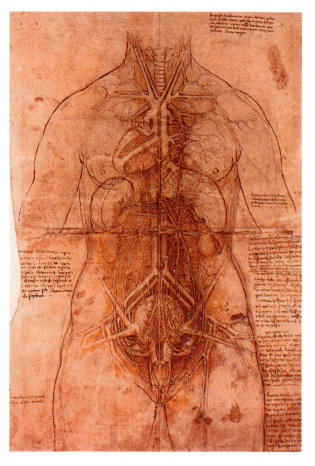

Leonardo da Vinci wrote in mirror writing, perhaps to avoid public scrutiny of his notebooks on biology, physiology, mathematics, and mechanics. Perhaps for similar reasons, he did not permit publication of his work on anatomy, based on his dissection of cadavers.

ignored, submerged, or even destroyed during the Middle Ages.

Revolutionary thinkers in mathematics and physics led the way toward empirical science as we know it today. Modern astronomy was heralded when Polish astronomer Nicolaus Copernicus (1473–1543) proposed his heliocentric theory, which argued that the sun and not the earth is at the center of our solar system. This theory contradicted both the traditional Ptolemaic geocentric theory and the then-official Church doctrine. Later in this era, Italian astronomer, mathematician, and physicist Galileo Galilei (1564–1642) was branded a heretic and placed under lifelong house arrest by the Roman Catholic Church. His unorthodox use of scientific observation rather than religious faith as the basis for his conclusions earned him suspicion and contributed to his arrest.

During the Renaissance, strict guidance by religious theory came under attack. Francis Bacon

(1561–1626) proposed an antithesis to the medieval point of view: Scientific study must be purely empirical—not guided by theory at all. Bacon believed that theories color our vision and get in the way of our perceiving the truth. He therefore asserted that studies of nature and of humankind must be wholly unbiased and **atheoretical** (not at all theory guided).

Many contemporary scientists seek to synthesize the two extreme views on the role of theory: Theory should guide and give meaning to our observations; yet our theories should be formed, modified, and perhaps even discarded as a result of our observations. The progress of psychology as a science depends on a continual interaction between theory and data.

The Beginnings of the Modern Period (1600s to 1800s)

Descartes and Locke (1600s to 1750)

The dialectic of theory versus data continued in the seventeenth century, when René Descartes (1596–1650) sharply disagreed with the glorification of the empirical methods espoused by Bacon and his intellectual predecessor Aristotle. Descartes agreed with Plato's rationalist belief that the introspective, reflective method is superior to empirical methods for

René Descartes (1596–1650)

René Descartes developed his ideas by watching the mechanical statues at the French Royal Gardens. The statues moved with apparent realism when visitors stepped on hidden switches. Descartes believed that the muscles of the human body functioned similarly, that we move because an external event impinges on our senses.

finding truth. *Cartesian* (from or about Descartes) rationalist philosophy contributed much to the modern philosophy of mind (a grandparent of psychology), and Descartes's views had numerous other implications for psychology.

Like Plato, Descartes (1662/1972) believed in both *mind-body dualism* (that the mind and the body are qualitatively different and separate) and innate (versus acquired) knowledge. According to Descartes, the dualistic nature of mind (nonmaterial, incorporeal, spiritual) and body (material) separates humans from animals. For humans, the mind and its powers are supreme: *Cogito ergo sum* (Latin, "I think, therefore I am"). According to Descartes, the mind has great influence over the body, but the body still has some effect on the mind. Thus, Descartes is considered both *mentalistic* (viewing the body as subordinate to the mind) and *interactionistic*, in that he held that there is a two-way interaction between mind and body.

On the other side of the dialectic, the British empiricist philosopher John Locke (1632–1704) be-

John Locke (1632–1704)

lieved that the interaction between mind and body is a symmetrical relationship between two aspects of the same unified phenomenon. The mind depends on sense experience processed by the body for its information, whereas the body depends on the mind to store for later use processed sense experience (1690/1961). Locke and other British empiricists also shared Aristotle's and Bacon's reverence for empirical observation. Locke's Aristotelian (and perhaps anti-Cartesian) valuing of empirical observation naturally accompanied his view that humans are born without knowledge—and must therefore seek knowledge through empirical observation. Locke's term for this view is *tabula rasa*, which means "blank slate" in Latin: Life and experience "write" knowledge upon us. Actually, according to Michael Gorman (personal communication, September 1993), Locke may not have intended the tabula rasa metaphor to be used quite so broadly as many have come to interpret it. More narrowly, he meant that we are born without the knowledge of specific ideas.

Mill and Kant (1750 to 1800)

Locke's philosophical successor was James Mill (1773–1836), who took British empiricism to its philosophical extreme. As a radical **associationist,** Mill believed that events occurring close to one another in time become associated in our minds, so that

they can later be recalled in tandem by memory. Mill suggested that the mind can be viewed in entirely mechanistic terms (1843). According to Mill, the laws of the physical universe can explain everything, including the activity of the mind. The idea of a separate mind or soul that exists independent of the body therefore is both unnecessary and wrong. This extreme version of monism is sometimes referred to as **reductionism,** because it reduces the role of the mind to the status of a mere cog in a larger physiological machine. The important thing is therefore the environment and how the sense organs of the body—eyes, ears, and so on—perceive it. In one form of reductionism, the individual responds mechanistically, with all knowledge starting at the level of sensations and working up to the mind, which is merely the next step in the "intellectual assembly line" (Schultz, 1981).

In the eighteenth century, the debates about both dualism versus monism and empiricism versus rationalism had peaked. German philosopher Immanuel Kant (1724–1804) began the process of dialectical synthesis for these questions. He redefined the mind-body question by asking how mind and body are related, rather than whether the mind is in control (1781/1987). Instead of phrasing the problem in terms of duality or unity, he proposed a set of *faculties* (mental powers): the senses, understanding, and reason. He said that the faculties, working in concert, control and provide a link between mind and body, integrating the two. Loosely speaking, Kant's *faculty of the senses* is closest to the idea of body, his *faculty of reason* parallels the concept of mind, and his *faculty of understanding* bridges the two. Faculties of mind also figured prominently in psychology when early twentieth-century psychologists tried to define and understand more clearly what the faculties of the mind might be. The debate still lives on today.

In terms of rationalism versus empiricism and whether knowledge is innate or is passively acquired through experience, Kant firmly declared that both rationalism and empiricism are needed to work together in the quest for truth. Kant called empirically acquired experiential knowledge **a posteriori** knowledge (from the Latin meaning "from afterward"); we gain this knowledge *after* we have experience. Most of us learn after a few poor grades, for example, that last-minute cramming for exams is not the most effective or healthful way to study.

On the other hand, Kant recognized that some knowledge ("general truth") exists regardless of individual experience. Kant referred to this "general truth" as **a priori** knowledge, from the Latin for "from beforehand"; such knowledge exists whether or not we become aware of it through our own experiences. A key example of a priori knowledge is our knowledge of time. We know a priori to link together our fleeting sensations over time into a seemingly continuous stream of experience. However, for us to observe any cause–effect relationship over time, we must have a posteriori knowledge of the related preceding and consequent events. According to Kant's synthesis, understanding requires both a posteriori, experience-based knowledge (thesis) and a priori, innate concepts (antithesis), such as knowledge of the concepts of time and causality, which permit us to profit from our experiences. In this way, understanding evolves both through nature (innate concepts) and through nurture (knowledge gained through experience).

> What are some things you know a priori? What are some things you know a posteriori? What is the relative importance you would assign to nature and to nurture, in regard to what you know?

Did Kant settle these debates once and for all? Certainly not. Questions probing the nature of thought and reality have not been and probably never will be settled for good. In fact, two influential books have appeared within the past decade that continue the dialectic about the mind-body issue. Cognitive philosopher Daniel Dennett's *Consciousness Explained* (1991) takes a reductionist view, saying that there is no mind without the physical body. Robert Penrose's *The Emperor's New Mind* (1989), on the other hand, allows for a consciousness not linked to the physical realm.

Scholars will always wrestle with aspects of these problems; that is the nature of intellectual inquiry. Kant did, however, effectively redefine many of the issues with which philosophers before him had grappled. Kant's enormous impact on philosophy interacted with nineteenth-century scientific exploration of the body and how it works (see Chapter 3) to produce profound influences on the eventual establishment of psychology as a discipline in the 1800s.

PSYCHOLOGICAL PERSPECTIVES: THE 1800S AND BEYOND

I N   S E A R C H   O F . . .

What relationships do you see among the modern fields of philosophy, medicine, and psychology?

The Merging of Philosophy and Physiology into Modern Psychology (1800s to 1900s)

Clearly, psychology has much in common with other disciplines. The issues that have faced and continue to face philosophers, physicians, and other scholars also confront psychologists. You have seen this confrontation in dialectics regarding the nature of mind and body and the sources of knowledge, and you will see it in the next chapter, on the biological bases of behavior.

So intertwined are the issues confronted by philosophers, physicians, and psychologists that in the 1800s (about the same time that Hegel proposed his idea of the dialectic), when psychology was starting out as a field, it was viewed by some as a branch of philosophy and by others as a branch of medicine. As psychology increasingly became a scientific discipline focused on the study of mind and behavior, nineteenth-century philosophy merged increasingly with the study of physiological issues pertaining to sensory perception. Gradually, the psychological branches of philosophy and of medicine diverged from the two parent disciplines and then merged to form the distinct, unified discipline of psychology. Today, although psychology, philosophy, and medicine are essentially discrete, they are not completely so, for many psychological questions remain rooted in both philosophy (such as the nature of the mind and its relation to the body) and medicine (such as the biological causes of behavior) (see also the fields of biological psychology and philosophical psychology, later in this chapter).

The Diverging Perspectives of Modern Psychology

Building on dialectics of the past, psychology has hosted a wide variety of intellectual perspectives on the human mind and how it should be studied. In order to understand psychology as a whole, you should be familiar with the schools of thought that have evolved in the field. Recall in the discussion of the problem-solving cycle in Chapter 1 that different people use varying perspectives (intellectual lenses) to organize information and to determine what is relevant when they approach a task or problem. The main early psychological perspectives (summarized in Table 2-1) are discussed in this section. As you read, notice how different perspectives build on and react to those perspectives that came before; the dialectical process that appeared throughout the history of psychology also threads through modern psychology, starting with approaches that focus on mental structures, and continuing with approaches that focus on mental functions, or on mental associations.

Structuralism, Functionalism, Pragmatism, and Associationism: Early Dialectics in Psychology

Structuralism

The goal of **structuralism,** generally considered to be the first major school of thought in psychology,

was to understand the *structure* (configuration of elements) of the mind (see Chapter 5) by analyzing it into its constituent components or contents. When structuralism was a dominant school of psychological thought, scientists in other fields were similarly analyzing materials into basic elements and then studying combinations of these basic elements—chemists were analyzing substances into their constituent chemical elements, biologists were analyzing the biochemical constituents of cells, physiologists were analyzing physiological structures, and so on.

TABLE 2-1
Early Psychological Perspectives

To this day, psychological research continues to reflect its roots in structuralism (focusing on physiological structures, and on specific abilities or skills) and in functionalism (focusing on the processes of thinking and feeling).

Perspective	Key Emphases	Key Methods of Acquiring Information	Key Thinkers Instrumental in Development of Perspective	Key Criticisms
Structuralism	The nature of consciousness; analysis of consciousness into its constituent components (elementary sensations)	Introspection (self-observation)	Wilhelm Wundt (German, 1832–1920); Edward Titchener (English-born German, 1867–1927)	Too many elementary sensations

Lack of means for understanding the processes of thought

Lack of application to the world outside the structuralist's laboratory

Rigid use of introspective techniques |
| Functionalism (and its offshoot, pragmatism) | Mental operations; practical uses of consciousness; the total relationship of the organism to its environment | Whatever works best | William James (American, 1842–1910); John Dewey (American, 1859–1952) | Too many definitions of the term *function*

Overly flexible use of too many different techniques, resulting in lack of experimental coherence

Overemphasis on applications of psychology; insufficient study of fundamental issues |
| Associationism | Mental connections between two events or between two ideas, which lead to forms of learning | Empirical strategies, applied to self-observation and to animal studies | Hermann Ebbinghaus (German, 1850–1909); Edward Lee Thorndike (American, 1874–1949); Ivan Pavlov (Russian, 1849–1936) | Overly simplistic; does not explain cognition, emotion, or many other psychological processes |

Although structuralism is no longer a dynamic force in psychology, it is important for having taken the first steps toward making psychology a systematic, empirical science and for establishing some of the dialectics of contemporary psychology—for example, the dialectic between molecular analysis of behavior, on the one hand (the position of structuralism), and global analysis, on the other.

An important progenitor of structuralism was German psychologist Wilhelm Wundt (1832–1920). Wundt was no great success in school, failing time and again and frequently finding himself subject to the ridicule of others. However, Wundt later showed that school performance does not always predict career success because he is considered to be among the most influential psychologists of all time.

Wundt believed that psychology should focus on immediate and direct, as opposed to *mediated* (interpreted), conscious experience. For example, suppose that you look at a green, grassy lawn. To Wundt, the concepts of *lawn* or even of *grass* would be irrelevant. Even your awareness of looking at a grassy lawn would not have particularly interested Wundt. These conceptually mediated experiences are too far removed from the mental elements of your experience, which you infer from the more important (to Wundt)

Wilhelm Wundt (1832–1920)

immediate experience of seeing narrow, vertical, spiky, green protrusions of varying lengths and widths, amassed closely together on a two-dimensional surface. It was to these elementary sensations that Wundt gave his attention.

For Wundt, the optimal method by which a person could be trained to analyze these sensory experiences is *introspection*, looking inward at pieces of information passing through consciousness—a form of self-observation. Today, we would call introspection subjective, but it did not seem so to the structuralists of the time.

Wundt's student, Edward Titchener (1867–1927), held views generally similar to Wundt's. Titchener (1910) believed that all consciousness could be reduced to three elementary states: *sensations*—the basic elements of perception (see Chapters 4 and 5); *images*—the pictures we form in our minds to characterize what we perceive (see Chapters 5 and 8); and *affections*—the constituents of emotions such as love and hate (see Chapter 16).

During most of his life, Titchener was a strict structuralist; he used structuralist principles in his teaching, research, and writings at Cornell University. Toward the end of his life, however, Titchener began to diverge from Wundt. He open-mindedly listened to alternative views (particularly the criticisms by functionalists, described in the following section), which suggested that structuralists had proposed too many sensations (see Table 2-1). Titchener eventually came to argue that psychology should study not merely the basic elements of sensation, but also the categories into which these sensations can be grouped (Hilgard, 1987).

Titchener's change of mind illustrates an important point about psychologists in particular and about scientists in general. Outstanding scientists do not necessarily adopt a particular viewpoint and then stick with it for the rest of their lives. The thinking of most scientists evolves; they reject or build on their earlier work (and the work of others) in the creation of what they hope will be their lasting contribution. Truly outstanding scientists are not immune to criticism and change; instead, they consider antitheses to their own theses, and they formulate their own syntheses, incorporating the alternative views into their own thinking. Early in his career, Titchener had been considered dogmatic, but he had the intellectual strength and fortitude to allow his thinking to evolve and change.

Think about some of the views you hold dear. (Some of your deeply held views might address questions such as, What behaviors are morally right? What work is important and valuable? What are im-

Edward Titchener (1867–1927)

portant things to strive to achieve or obtain?) How have some of your views changed over the years? When others challenge your views, what do they criticize about your views? Which of these criticisms are you now considering, and which might lead you to modify your views?

Functionalism: An Alternative to Structuralism

The roots of structuralism were in Germany, but its countermovement, **functionalism,** was rooted in America—the first U.S.-born movement in psychology. The key difference between structuralists and functionalists lay not in the answers they found, but in the fundamentally different questions they asked. Whereas structuralists asked, "What are the elementary contents [structures] of the human mind?" functionalists asked, "What do people *do,* and *why* do they do it?"

Another way of viewing the difference between structuralism and functionalism is to say that structuralists viewed the human or other organism as an object that passively receives sensations to analyze. Functionalists, in contrast, viewed humans and others

as more actively engaged in their sensations and actions. Some people have suggested that the American culture may have led to this more active view of psychology.

The functionalist addresses the broad question of how and why the mind works as it does by seeking functional relationships between specific earlier **stimulus** (something that prompts action) events and specific subsequent **response** (an action or reaction that is linked to a stimulus) behaviors. Psychologist and educator James Rowland Angell (1869–1949), whose criticism of structuralism was instrumental in swaying Titchener to change his views, suggested three fundamental precepts of functionalism (Angell, 1907): (1) the study of mental processes, (2) the study of the uses of consciousness, and (3) the study of the total relationship of the organism to its environment.

Even given these precepts, the functionalist school of thought never had the unity that structuralism had. Functionalists were unified by the kinds of questions they asked, but not necessarily by the answers they found or by the methods they used for finding those answers. We might even suggest that they were unified in believing that a diversity of methods could be used, as long as each method helped to answer the particular question being probed.

Functionalists' openness to diverse methodologies broadened the scope of psychological methods. Among the various approaches used by functionalists was animal experimentation, perhaps prompted by Charles Darwin's (1809–1882) revolutionary ideas on evolution. Darwin's work may also have been instrumental in the subsequent evolution of psychobiological psychology (discussed later in this chapter).

> What are the advantages and disadvantages of using various methods to study a phenomenon?

Pragmatism: An Outgrowth of Functionalism

There is a use for almost everything.

— *George Washington Carver, cited in* Voices of Struggle, Voices of Pride

Because functionalists believed in using whichever methods best answered the researcher's questions, it seems natural for functionalism to have led to pragmatism. **Pragmatists** believe that knowledge is validated by its usefulness: What can you *do* with it? Pragmatists are concerned not only with knowing what people do, but also with what we can do with our knowledge of what people do.

A leader in guiding functionalism toward pragmatism was William James (1842–1910)—physician, philosopher, psychologist, and brother of author Henry James. The chief functional contribution of William James to the field of psychology was a single book: his landmark *Principles of Psychology* (1890b). James proved that one truly influential work, as well as the reputation of its author, can help shape a field. Today, many regard James as among the greatest psychologists ever, although James himself seems to have rejected psychology later in his life.

James minced no words in his criticism of structuralism's detail-oriented approach, snidely commenting that structuralism's nit-picking approach "taxes patience to the utmost, and could hardly have arisen in a country whose natives could be bored" (p. 192). James is particularly well known for his pragmatic theorizing about consciousness, emphasizing that the function of consciousness is to enable people to adapt to the environment and to give them choices for operating within that environment.

William James (1842–1910)

Another of the early pragmatists has profoundly influenced my own evolution of thinking about psychology, as well as the thinking of many others. John Dewey (1859–1952), along with James Angell, is credited with laying out the formal defining principles for the philosophical school of functionalism. Dewey was important to psychology for his contribution to functionalism, as well as for his stimulation of new ideas in others. Dewey is remembered primarily, however, as a philosopher of education; his pragmatic functionalist approach to thinking and schooling heralded many of the current notions in educational psychology. Much of what educational psychologists say today reiterates what Dewey said early in the twentieth century.

Dewey (1910, 1913, 1922), ever the pragmatist, emphasized motivation in education. See whether his ideas make sense to you: If no one inspires you to learn, the chances are that you will not learn very well. To learn effectively, you need to see the point of your education—the practical use of it. One way to interest you in education is to give you more opportunity to select your own problems rather than always to tell you what problems to solve. Perhaps most important, you should learn by experimentation and by doing, rather than merely by being told *facts*, so that you can learn to think for yourself and to use information intelligently. Dewey also practiced what he preached: He opened an elementary school at Columbia University, which taught according to his precepts (Hilgard, 1987).

Dewey's practical applications of psychological principles were not universally well received. Many psychologists felt that true scientists should avoid diverting their attention from the study of underlying principles merely to address some immediate applications of those principles. Other scientists believed, and still do, that **basic research** (devoted to the study of underlying relationships and principles, which may not have any immediate, obvious, practical value) ultimately leads to many of the most practical applications. To this day, scientists disagree regarding how much of scientific research should be basic research and how much should be **applied research** (leading to clear, immediate, obvious applications). Ideally, we would have a balance between research that is basic and research that is applied.

In addition to the question of applied versus basic research, many of the dialectics that first emerged via functionalism and structuralism were fundamental to the development of psychology. In particular, functionalism expanded the scope of the fledgling academic discipline to comprise a range of techniques far wider than the structuralists ever would have permitted. Although functionalism, like structuralism, did not survive as an organized school of thought, its influence remains widespread in psychological specializations that stress both flexibility of research methods and practicality.

Associationism: An Integrative Synthesis

Associationism, like functionalism, was less a rigid school of psychology than an influential way of thinking. In general, the main concerns of associationism are the middle-level to higher-level mental processes, such as those of learning. **Associationism** examines how events or ideas can become associated with one another in the mind to result in a form of learning. This focus on rather high-level mental processes runs exactly counter to Wundt's insistence on studying elementary sensations.

For example, with repetition, concepts such as *thesis*, *antithesis*, and *synthesis* will become linked in your mind so often that they will become inextricably associated with one another. To put it another way, you will have learned that the dialectical process in-

"Evidently, your daughter strongly identifies certain apparel items with success, happiness, sex, and popularity. Consequently, I'm sorry to report, she's fallen in love with her pants."

John Dewey (1859–1952)

volves a thesis, an antithesis, and a synthesis. Learning and remembering thus depend on mental association.

Associationism itself has been associated with many other theoretical viewpoints. Its principles can be traced directly to Mill; even further back, we find Locke's view that the mind and the body are two aspects of the same unified phenomenon, a view rooted in Aristotle's ideas. Subsequent contemporary views were also founded on associationism (see behaviorism, described in the next section). Consequently, it is difficult to categorize associationism as belonging strictly to one era.

An influential associationist was the German experimenter Hermann Ebbinghaus (1850–1909), the first experimenter to apply associationist principles systematically. Ebbinghaus prided himself on using much more rigorous experimental techniques (counting his errors, recording his response times, etc.) than Wundt used during introspection. On the other hand, Ebbinghaus used himself as his only experimental *subject* (person, other organism, or other object of experimental study). In particular, Ebbinghaus used his self-observations to study and quantify the relationship between *rehearsal*—conscious repetition—and recollection of material.

Interestingly, Ebbinghaus had no university appointment, no formal laboratory, no formal mentor,

Hermann Ebbinghaus (1850–1909)

and none of the usual trappings of academe. He worked alone, yet he made a ground-breaking experimental discovery—that frequent repetition fixes mental associations more firmly in memory, and, by extension, that repetition aids in learning (see Chapter 8). Great contributions need not require academic positions or complicated equipment. Ebbinghaus's contribution to the study of memory spawned a wealth of memorization tactics, some of which your teachers may have encouraged you to use. In fact, to learn the information in this and subsequent chapters, what are some memory-enhancement strategies that you know how to use?

Psychologists' views about introspection have evolved since the days of Ebbinghaus and Wundt, but many controversies remain regarding its use. Some psychologists discount most self-observations as being fruitless for gathering empirical data because many of our thought processes are not available to our conscious minds (Nisbett & Wilson, 1977). Others consider self-observations valuable for generating hypotheses but useless in evaluating hypotheses. Still others view subjects' introspective self-analyses while they perform a task to be an invaluable source of confirmatory data (Ericsson & Simon, 1980). Even those who value self-observations as a tool for empirical study disagree regarding when to obtain the observational data. Some contend that if observations are obtained during the performance of a task, the very act of observing the task performance changes it. Others argue that inaccurate (or at least imperfect) recall interferes with self-observations obtained after the task performance has ended.

Ebbinghaus's ideas were elaborated by Edwin Guthrie (1886–1959), who observed animals instead of himself. Guthrie proposed that two observed events (a stimulus and a response) become associated through their close *temporal contiguity* (i.e., their occurring very close together in time). In other words, the stimulus and the response behaviors/events become associated because they continually occur at about the same time. In contrast, Edward Lee Thorndike (1874–1949) held that the role of "satisfaction," rather than of Guthrie's temporal contiguity, was the key to forming associations. Thorndike termed this principle the **law of effect** (1905): A stimulus will tend to produce a certain response (the *effect*) over time if an organism is rewarded (the *satisfaction*) for that response.

In considering the methods of Ebbinghaus, Guthrie, and Thorndike, we see that the associationists followed the functionalist-pragmatic tradition of using various methods in their research. In fact, Thorndike can be tied directly back to his functionalist mentor, William James. James even encouraged Thorndike to conduct his experiments on animals, offering his own house as the locale for some of Thorndike's earliest studies of animals learning to run through mazes. (The relationships and associations studied by Ebbinghaus, Guthrie, and Thorndike are described in greater detail in Chapter 7.)

TWENTIETH-CENTURY PERSPECTIVES ON PSYCHOLOGY

IN SEARCH OF...

As you watch the twentieth century draw to a close, what do you believe to have been the greatest intellectual, artistic, and scientific developments of this century? How are these developments tied to twentieth-century perspectives on psychology?

"Once it became clear to me that, by responding correctly to certain stimuli, I could get all the bananas I wanted, getting this job was a pushover."

Alternative Associations Between Stimulus and Response

Other researchers, who were contemporaries of Thorndike, used animal experiments to probe stimulus-response relationships in ways that differed from those of Thorndike and his fellow associationists. These researchers straddled the line between associationism and the emerging field of behaviorism (see Table 2-2). Some of these researchers, like Thorndike and other associationists, studied responses that were voluntary (though perhaps lacking any conscious thought, as in Thorndike's work), but others studied responses that were involuntarily triggered, in response to what appeared to be unrelated external stimuli.

Suppose, for example, that on every occasion that your instructor gives you a pop quiz (unexpected test), the instructor wears a red shirt, and on days when no pop quiz is given, your instructor never wears a red shirt. Suppose that you rarely do well on pop quizzes. If you then see your instructor wearing a red shirt, you may involuntarily experience a fear re-sponse to the stimulus of the red shirt. The formerly neutral stimulus of a red shirt is now associated with your response of feeling fearful of pop quizzes.

In Russia, Nobel Prize-winning physiologist Ivan Pavlov (1849–1936) studied involuntary learning behavior of this sort, beginning with his observation that dogs salivated in response to the sight of the lab technician who fed them before the dogs even saw whether the technician had food. To Pavlov, this response indicated a form of learning, termed **classically conditioned learning,** over which the dogs had no conscious control. In the dogs' minds, some type of involuntary learning was linking the technician with the food (Pavlov, 1955). (See Chapter 7 for more on Pavlov's landmark work, which paved the way for the development of behaviorism.)

Behaviorism

Behaviorism, an American school of psychology (see Chapter 7), may be considered an extreme version of associationism that focuses entirely on the association

TABLE 2-2
Modern Psychological Perspectives
The various psychological perspectives offer complementary insights into the human psyche.

Perspective	Key Emphases	Key Methods of Investigation	Key Developers of the Perspective	Key Criticisms
Behaviorism	Observable behavior	Experimental; shift of focus from human to animal subjects	John Watson (American, 1878–1958); B. F. Skinner (American, 1904–1990)	Doesn't address any internal causes of behavior; in its radical form, it even ignores thoughts and emotions entirely Doesn't allow for social (observational) learning Doesn't explain many aspects of human behavior, e.g., the acquisition and use of language or the enjoyment and appreciation of music or other arts
Gestalt psychology	Holistic concepts, not merely as additive sums of the parts, but as emergent phenomena in their own right	Experimentation and observation (less emphasis on control of discrete variables and more on observing holistic data)	Max Wertheimer (German-born American, 1880–1943); Kurt Koffka (German-born American, 1886–1941); Wolfgang Köhler (German-born American, 1887–1968)	Relative paucity of data to support the abundance of theory Lack of experimental control Lack of precise definitions and use of circular thinking
Cognitivism	Understanding how people think in order to understand human behavior; how knowledge is learned, structured, stored, and used	Experimentation and naturalistic observation, primarily of humans, as well as of other primates	Herbert Simon (American, 1916–); Ulric Neisser (American, 1928–)	Emotions, social interactions, and other aspects of human behavior are not investigated as enthusiastically as more obviously cognitive aspects of behavior Whenever naturalistic observations are involved, scientific rigor and control are reduced
Biological psychology	Biological interactions of the body and the mind, particularly the workings of the brain and nervous system	Experimentation; studies on humans, animals; neurophysiological and neurochemical examination of brains	Roger Sperry (American, 1920–); George Miller (American, 1920–)	Not all aspects of human behavior are now subject to investigation via biopsychological study Many aspects of human behavior may not now ethically be studied in humans, and animal investigations may not always generalize to humans

(Continued)

TABLE 2-2 *(Continued)*

Perspective	Key Emphases	Key Methods of Investigation	Key Developers of the Perspective	Key Criticisms
Psychodynamic psychology	Theory of personality development and psychotherapy; uncovering unconscious experience in personal development	Psychoanalysis, based on clinical case studies	Sigmund Freud (Austrian, 1856–1939)	Overemphasis on sexuality (which is less apropos now than during the Victorian era when Freud proposed his theory) Overreliance on case-study research Overly comprehensive; because there is no phenomenon that it cannot explain, it cannot be disconfirmed; hence, it is not easily subject to scientific investigation Overly theory driven
Humanistic psychology	Focus on free will and self-actualization of human potential; focus on conscious rather than unconscious experience	Clinical practice and case-study observations; holistic rather than analytic approach	Abraham Maslow (American, 1908–1970); Carl Rogers (American, 1902–1987)	Theories not particularly comprehensive Limited research base

between an observed stimulus and an observed response. Behaviorism was born as a reaction against the focus on personally subjective mental states found in both structuralism and functionalism. Instead, behaviorism asserts that the science of psychology should deal only with *observable* behavior. According to strict, extreme ("radical") behaviorists, any conjectures about internal thoughts and ways of thinking are nothing more than speculation, and although they might belong within the domain of philosophy, they certainly have no place in psychology. This behaviorist view originates in the philosophical tradition of **logical positivism,** which asserts that the only basis for knowledge is sensory perceptions; all else is idle conjecture.

What are at least two arguments in favor of logical positivism? What are two or more arguments against it?

Ivan Pavlov (1849–1936) is in his laboratory with his assistants and his dog.

Watson's Groundwork

The man usually acknowledged as the father of radical behaviorism is American psychologist John Watson (1878–1958) (whose advice on child rearing opened this chapter). Watson, like British empiricist

John Watson (1878–1958)

James Mill, had no use for internal mental contents or mechanisms. Still, although Watson disdained key aspects of functionalism, he was clearly influenced by the functionalists in his emphasis on what people do and what causes their actions. In fact, arguably, behaviorism depends more on the study of functions in behavior (linking external stimulus events to observable responses) than functionalism ever did. As an innovative thinker, Watson drew on the thoughts of others, both those who preceded him and his own contemporaries.

Behaviorism also differed from previous movements in psychology by shifting the emphasis of experimental research from human to animal subjects (although animal studies have been used since the days of Hippocrates). Historically, much behavioristic work has been conducted (and still is) with laboratory animals such as rats. Watson himself preferred animal subjects. He believed that with animal subjects it was easier to ensure behavioral control and to establish stimulus-response relationships while minimizing external interference. Indeed, the simpler the organism's emotional and physiological makeup, the less the researcher needs to worry about any of the interference that can plague psychological research with

humans as subjects. Many nonbehavioral psychologists wonder whether animal research can be *generalized* to humans (i.e., applied more generally to humans instead of just specifically to the animals that were studied). In response, some behaviorists would argue that the study of animal behavior is a legitimate pursuit in its own right, and all behaviorists would assert that we can learn useful principles that generalize to other species, including humans.

Hull's Synthesis with Pavlovian Conditioning

An American behavioral psychologist who tried to connect the involuntary learning studied by Pavlov with the voluntary learning studied by Watson and Thorndike was Clark Hull (1884–1952). Hull had always shown a predilection for synthesis; even his dissertation synthesized strict experimental psychology with theoretical analyses of thought processes, particularly in regard to the learning of concepts. Although Hull's work was virtually ignored for nearly a decade, during which he became quite discouraged (see Hilgard, 1987), his work on learning eventually became among the most widely cited works of his time. Hull's ideas also enriched the field of psychology with ideas from such diverse fields as physiology and evolutionary biology (see Robinson, 1986).

Above all, Hull was particularly influential for his belief that the laws of behavior could be *quantified*—expressed in terms of numerical quantities—as are laws in other scientific disciplines such as physics. Hull's (1952) final presentation of his theory of behavior contained numerous mathematical postulates and corollaries. Hull's interest in mathematical

Annie Sullivan used behavioral techniques with her gifted student Helen Keller, portrayed here in the film The Miracle Worker.

precision also led to his development of an early computational device, which he used in his psychological research and which used punch cards for statistical calculations.

Skinner's Radicalism

In modern times, radical behaviorism has seemed almost synonymous with one of its most radical proponents, B. F. Skinner. For Skinner, virtually all of human behavior, and not just learning, could be explained by stimulus-response relationships, which can be studied effectively by observing animal behaviors. Skinner applied the stimulus-response model to almost everything, from learning to language acquisition to problem solving, and even to the control of behavior in society. As a consequence, he was criticized for overgeneralizing the applicability of his data by making pronouncements about what would be good for society as a whole, based largely on data from learning in animals.

This deterministic view calls to mind the original radical conception of behaviorism, as proposed by Watson, which stated that any behavior can be shaped and controlled:

B. F. Skinner (1904–1990)

Give me a dozen healthy infants, well-formed, and my own specified world to bring them up in, and I'll guarantee to take any one at random and train him to become any type of specialist I might select—doctor, lawyer, artist, merchant-chief and yes, even beggarman and thief—regardless of his talents, penchants, tendencies, abilities, vocations, and race of his ancestors. (Watson, 1930, p. 104)

To illustrate the behavioral view, suppose that you were a behaviorist interested in understanding sexual attraction: Why are some people attractive—and attracted—to us, yet others are not? As a behaviorist, you would try to analyze the various stimulus-response contingencies involved in the characteristics of attraction. You would then observe each of these contingent responses, perhaps studying them in animals. You might start by looking at animals as low on the evolutionary scale as possible, given that the animals must be ones that reproduce sexually.

Suppose you were to design a course in psychology that was based on behavioristic principles. What might this course look like?

Can a paradigm such as behaviorism or functionalism be disproved? If so, how? If not, why not?

Many psychologists disagree with the behaviorist view (see Table 2-2). For example, in a debate between Watson and psychologist William McDougall (1871–1938), McDougall said:

I come into this hall and see a man on this platform scraping the guts of a cat with hairs from the tail of a horse; and, sitting silently in attitudes of rapt attention, are a thousand persons who presently break out into wild applause. How will the Behaviorist explain these strange incidents: How explain the fact that the vibrations emitted by the cat-gut stimulate all the thousand into absolute silence and quiescence; and the further fact that the cessation of the stimulus seems to be a stimulus to the most frantic activity? (Watson & McDougall, 1929, p. 63)

Despite many well-founded criticisms, behaviorism has had a great impact on the development of psychology as a rigorous science grounded in empirical evidence. The radical behavioristic approach does have flaws, but in evaluating behaviorism, we must remember three things: First, not all behaviorists follow the extreme stance of radical behaviorism; second, no approach is flawless; third, even critics must concede that the observed overt behavior of a subject is the object of study most accessible to observation.

Gestalt Psychology

Of the many critics of behaviorism, Gestalt psychologists may be among the most avid. According to **Gestalt psychology,** we best understand psychological phenomena when we view them as organized, structured wholes, not when we break them down into pieces. Actually, this movement was not only a reaction against the behaviorist tendency to break down behaviors into stimulus-response units, but also against the structuralist tendency to analyze mental processes into elementary sensations. The maxim "the whole is greater than the sum of its parts" aptly sums up the Gestalt perspective. The name of the approach comes from the German word "**Gestalt**" (now a legitimate English word), which does not have an exact synonym in English, although it is something close to "whole unitary form," "integral shape," or "fully integrated configuration" (Schultz, 1981). The movement originated in Germany, the fount of structuralism, and later spread to the United States, the fount of behaviorism, and to other countries.

Gestalt psychology is usually traced to the work of German psychologist Max Wertheimer (1880–1943), who collaborated with compatriots Kurt Koffka (1886–1941) and Wolfgang Köhler (1887–1968) to form a new school of psychology, with an emphasis on understanding "wholes" in their own right. The Gestaltists applied this framework to many areas in psychology. For example, they proposed that problem solving cannot be explained simply in terms of automatic responses to stimuli or to elementary sensations. Instead, new insights emerge in problem solving; people simply form entirely new ways to see problems.

To illustrate the Gestalt view, return to your investigation of understanding sexual attraction, this time as a Gestalt psychologist. Instead of analyzing the phenomenon into multiple discrete elements or characteristics, you might try to study it as a holistic process. You would be particularly interested in studying the "Aha!" experience (insight) when the attracted person feels attracted. However, the next step—designing your specific method and strategy for studying this phenomenon holistically—is probably a little more difficult for the Gestaltist than for the behaviorist.

What two images do you see in this Gestalt reversible figure?

What are two psychological phenomena that you have observed that must be seen as whole phenomena, not as the sums of intermingled parts, in order to understand the phenomena? Why are the wholes of these phenomena greater than the sums of their parts?

How might the contrast between structuralism and Gestaltism apply in a field other than psychology?

Given some of the criticisms of the Gestalt perspective (see Table 2-2), many psychologists now believe that the most fruitful approach to understanding psychological phenomena is to use both analysis and holistic strategies. Cognitivists are among the many who use both analytic and holistic strategies.

Cognitivism

Cognitivism is the belief that much of human behavior can be understood if we understand first how people think. The contemporary cognitivist examines the elementary structuralist contents of thought, the functionalist processes of thought, and the Gestaltist holistic results of thinking. The cognitivist, like the Gestaltist, may well conclude that indeed, the whole is greater than the sum of its parts. At the same time,

In Sunday on La Grande Jatte *(ca. 1885), Georges Seurat demonstrates the Gestalt principle of the whole being greater than the sum of its parts. See from the detail how the painting comprises only dots of paint.*

however, cognitive psychologists attempt to determine precisely which mental mechanisms and which elementary elements of thought make that conclusion true. Cognitivists would study the way in which we perceive the Gestalt of the chapter or of the Seurat painting, but they also would want to determine precisely how we perceive it as such.

Early cognitivists (e.g., Miller, Galanter, & Pribram, 1960) argued that traditional behavioristic accounts of behavior were inadequate precisely because they said nothing about—indeed, they ignored—how people think. Subsequent cognitivists Allen Newell and Herbert Simon (1972) proposed detailed models of human thinking and problem solving from the most basic levels to the most complex (such as playing chess). Ulric Neisser's (1928–) book *Cognitive Psychology* (1967) was especially critical in bringing cognitivism to prominence. Neisser defined *cognitive psychology* as the study of how people learn, structure, store, and use knowledge.

The cognitive approach has been applied in a variety of areas of psychology—everything from thinking to emotion to the treatment of various psychological syndromes, including depression. Cognitive psychologists use a variety of methods to pursue their goal of understanding human thought, such as the study of reaction times, the study of people's subjective reports as they solve problems, and computer simulations. As a cognitivist investigating sexual attraction, you might try to obtain people's self-reports about what they are thinking when they feel attrac-

tion toward someone. For example, you might ask them to describe the characteristics of persons to whom they feel attracted.

In the 1960s, cognitivism was just coming of age and behaviorism seemed to be on its way out. Today, cognitivism is popular, and many fields within psychology have adopted a cognitive perspective. This perspective, too, may someday fade in importance and yield to other perspectives. The dominant perspective of the future may be unimaginable today. Psychology is a dynamic science precisely because it is ever-evolving in its perspectives on the puzzles of human behavior.

What is a psychological phenomenon that you believe will become increasingly important as we enter a new millennium? Why do you believe that this phenomenon will become increasingly important?

Biological Psychology

One field that now yields exhilarating discoveries almost daily and that promises to offer much more excitement in the near future is **biological psychology,** which attempts to understand behavior by carefully studying anatomy and physiology, especially of the brain (*neurobiology*). Its roots go back to Hippocrates, who observed that the brain seems to control many other parts of the body. (Chapter 3 more elaborately traces these physiological roots of psychology from

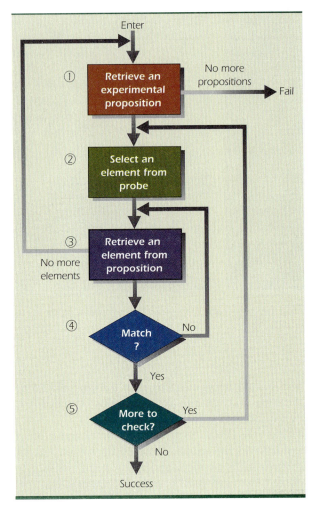

FIGURE 2-1
Computer-Based Model of Thinking
The study of computer models, such as of artificial intelligence, has helped psychologists think about thinking in different ways. Like most models, however, computer models can present only a limited view of the vast expanse of human cognition.

selection and evolution (1859), he sought to understand how behaviors such as facial expressions, mating rituals, or even emotions may have evolved from or be related to those in other species (see Chapters 13 and 16). A direct descendant of evolutionary theory is **behavioral genetics,** which attempts to account for behavior by attributing it to the influence of particular combinations of genes (see Chapter 3). A behavioral geneticist might attempt to explain, for example, the genetic elements contributing to intelligence, creativity, or mental illness.

Another psychobiological approach is to determine which specific regions of the brain are responsible for the origination, learning, or expression of particular behaviors, feelings, or kinds of thoughts. For example, Nobel Prize winning American researcher Roger Sperry (1920–) has tried to determine what kinds of thinking occur in each of the two halves of the brain. These and other insights into our minds and bodies—and the interactions between the two—fascinate scientists and laypeople alike. Thus,

FIGURE 2-2
The Left and Right Hemispheres of the Human Brain
Psychologists have begun to identify some of the specialized functions of various regions of the brain.

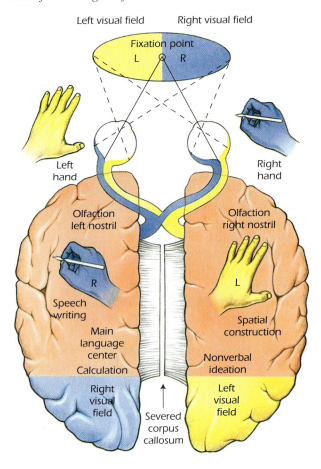

Hippocrates to the present.) The psychobiological approach also has philosophical roots in the monism of Locke and Mill (who built their ideas on Aristotle's views), for by definition, *psychobiology* assumes that the mind and the body are interrelated, and that the study of each one can yield information about the other.

The psychobiological perspective is less an organized school of thought grounded in a particular place and time than an affirmation of biological experimentation as the desired method of studying psychological problems. Thus, many influences on modern psychobiology have been adaptations from the biological sciences. As mentioned previously, naturalist Charles Darwin helped pave the way for the psychobiological perspective; in his theory of natural research that synthesizes the methods and the data from psychology and biology is likely to captivate us.

As a biological psychologist investigating sexual attraction, you might use sophisticated techniques and equipment to probe the living brains of your subjects. During these probes, you might measure your subjects' reactions to photographs of various individuals toward whom the subjects would report feeling varying degrees of attraction. You might also study biochemical factors in attraction; you could assess attraction responses in relation to your subjects' existing levels of chemicals in the brain or elsewhere in the body, or you could alter the levels of those chemicals and record any changes in attraction responses. For example, some drugs (such as cocaine) may initially heighten sexual desire, whereas their prolonged use generally leads to diminished sexual arousal (Wade & Cirese, 1991).

Psychodynamic Psychology

One of the most controversial, stimulating, and influential schools of psychology was based on the clinical practice of a *neurologist* (a physician who treats disorders of the brain and nervous system) who incorporated many ideas from biology into his psychological theories. The neurologist was Sigmund Freud (1856–1939), and his theory was psychodynamic psychology, the clinical practice of which was termed *psychoanalysis*. When many people think of psychology, they think of **psychodynamic theory,** a theory of human motivations and behavior, and of **psychoanalysis,** a form of psychological treatment based on that theory.

In his theory of psychoanalysis, Freud (1949a) proposed two levels of awareness of reality: the *conscious*, composed of mental states such as memories, of which we are aware, and the *unconscious*, composed of mental states of which we are unaware or to which we do not have access (see Chapter 6). According to Freud, the unconscious and conscious minds operate according to different governing principles. In addition, Freud proposed three mental structures, each of which operated according to different principles and served different functions. Freud also posited a multistage theory of development, which emphasized the important role of early childhood experiences in the development of later adult personality.

Thus, if you were a psychodynamic psychologist studying attraction, you might try to find the early childhood origins of the unconscious forces that determine feelings of attraction in adults. Early feelings of sexual attraction to a parent would probably be a prime target of your investigation. You would probably study just a few individuals intensively (the case-

Sigmund Freud (1856–1939)

study method), rather than a large number of subjects more superficially. You would try to analyze all the internal, unconscious dynamics affecting the feelings of attraction experienced by each subject.

The psychodynamic perspective is actually quite complex and has many dimensions, which are discussed in several other chapters (see discussions of Freud in Chapters 13, 17, 18, and 19). In addition, Freud's was not the only version of psychodynamic theory; several of his disciples rebelled, formulating their own versions of the theory. These newer psychodynamic theorists are often called "neo-Freudians," and their newer theories are discussed in Chapter 17. The forms of psychoanalytic treatment suggested by neo-Freudians are discussed in Chapter 19.

What progress we are making. In the Middle Ages they would have burned me. Now they are content with burning my books.

—Sigmund Freud's response in 1933, regarding the public burning of his books in Berlin; quoted in Who Said What When, *1991*

Despite the many valid criticisms of psychoanalysis (see Table 2-2), Freud contributed greatly to the development of psychological theory. His insights have shown us the rich material available in case-study research. Such research offers a valuable counterpoint to experimental research. Although most psychologists prize the rigor of the information yielded by experimental work, case-study work has merit. Freud also showed that some of the most innovative thinking profits from synthesizing the views of our intellectual predecessors with the knowledge we gain in applied practice.

Humanistic Psychology

During the 1950s, one of several responses to psychodynamic theory in America was the humanistic-psychology movement. In contrast to psychodynamic psychology, **humanistic psychology** emphasizes conscious rather than unconscious experience in personal development. Also, it stresses holistic Gestalt examination of psychological issues: A *holistic* approach to personality theory, for example, avoids dividing the personality into smaller elements, arguing that the essence of the construct would be lost; an *analytic* approach, however, aims to break down a construct such as personality into its constituent components, such as the elements Freud described (see Chapters 13, 17, 18, and 19). Finally, humanistic psychology emphasizes free will and the realization of our human potential. These hallmarks of the Renaissance-era humanistic movement (from which modern humanism takes its name) contrast with the more deterministic view of Freud, who seemed at times to believe that we are servants of our conflicting impulses and psychic motivators.

Abraham Maslow (1908–1970) proposed that all people possess an innate drive for *self-actualization* (1970). That is, they seek to *actualize* (make real through action) their potential as creatively as they can. Maslow believed that people differ in the extent to which they succeed in self-actualizing. Those who succeed have in common an objective view of reality; an acceptance of their nature, including both their strengths and their limitations; commitment to their work; a need for autonomy coupled with empathy for humankind; resistance to blind conformity; and a drive to be creative in their work and in their lives in general.

Carl Rogers (1902–1987) followed Maslow's emphasis on self-actualization, but Rogers stressed its dependence on the relationship between mother and child (1961a). He believed that if the mother meets the child's need for unconditional love, the child will probably later develop in a well-adjusted way. Rogers argued that we need this love, which he termed *unconditional positive regard*, in infancy and childhood, and that many of the problems we have later are due to the lack of it. (Humanistic psychology and its proponents are described in greater detail in Chapters 16, 17, 18, and 19.)

As a humanistic psychologist studying attraction, you might find it difficult to come up with a humanistic hypothesis for attraction that would be specific enough to enable you to test your hypothesis. Although it might be hypothesized that we feel most attracted to persons who have given us unconditional (or only moderately conditional) positive regard—or perhaps to persons who resemble such persons—this thesis would not provide a complete explanation of attraction.

Although humanistic psychology is less visible today than it was in the 1960s, it continues to influence our thinking, especially in its emphasis on personal values and goals.

Abraham Maslow (1908–1970)

Why do psychologists often lose interest in a paradigm in which they were formerly interested? What might contribute to this loss of interest?

In what ways is your own history helpful in understanding yourself and in formulating future plans? Analogously, how might the history of psychology help us understand the field and where it is going?

FIELDS WITHIN PSYCHOLOGY

IN SEARCH OF...

Which fields of psychology most interest you? What draws you to those fields?

As the various foregoing perspectives show, psychologists are unified by their interest in the study of mind and behavior, but they differ in the problems they study and in the approaches they use for studying these problems. In addition to having differing perspectives, psychologists choose from among a diversity of career specializations within psychology. What is the relationship between psychological perspectives and fields within psychology? They are related and complementary concepts. A psychological **perspective** centers on theory and beliefs, based on the philosophical strands described early in this chapter. For some perspectives (e.g., structuralism), a particular method or small set of methods may also be central to the perspective. Other perspectives (e.g., pragmatism) welcome a wide variety of methods.

A **field** of psychology, on the other hand, is grounded in the psychological topics of interest to the psychologists in that field. The very names of these topics suggest their scope: educational psychology, personality psychology, developmental psychology, social psychology, and so on. Certainly, investigators within some fields are believers in one or more perspectives that define the field. For example, biological psychologists take a biological viewpoint. Still, a given field can provide the grounds for a multitude of perspectives. For example, among *clinical psychologists,* those who treat clients with psychological problems, you will find psychoanalysts, behaviorists, cognitivists, and others.

Table 2-3 summarizes the specific work undertaken by psychologists in several fields. It is important

Carl Rogers (1902–1987)

to realize, however, that particular problems often cut across specialized fields. Specialists in various areas, using an assortment of problem-solving techniques, can study the same psychological question. To illustrate this diversity, Table 2-3 presents the quest to understand the nature of creativity as it is looked at from the view of the various fields of psychology highlighted in this book. A parallel to these overlapping perspectives exists in regard to addressing social problems: A problem such as homelessness can be combated differently by differing agencies, such as state, local, or federal governments; health organizations; public service agencies; individuals; and charitable organizations.

When reading about some of the fields and specialties within psychology, you may find yourself drawn to considering a career in psychology. Table 2-4 lists some of the specific career paths available to psychology majors and describes the typical duties, the education required, and the work settings for various fields.

In addition, new specialties within psychology are appearing almost every year, as psychology is applied to more and more other disciplines. Recent examples of this growth are health psychology and legal psychology. By the time you graduate from

TABLE 2-3
Fields of Psychology
The following fields show some of the possibilities for psychological practice and research.

Field of Psychology	Sample Problems and Questions	Methods
Psychobiology (also termed *biological* or *physiological psychology*) deals with the biological structures and processes underlying thought, feeling, motivation, and behavior (see Chapter 3).	• What portion of the brain is active when a person learns the meaning of a new word (see Chapters 7 and 8)? • What neurochemicals are active in the brain when a person feels depressed (see also Chapter 16)? • How do various kinds of drugs affect the brain and behavior (see Chapter 6)?	Psychobiologists differ greatly in the kinds of work they do, but they all rely heavily on the highly controlled experimental research method, often employing sophisticated technological equipment in the process. Some use single-celled creatures as subjects to study behavior in simple organisms. The goal is eventually to apply what they learn to humans. Other psychobiologists may study more complex organisms, including mammals. Those studying humans sometimes investigate patients with particular kinds of brain damage in order to understand what aspects of behavior are affected. Still others might conduct postmortem analyses of patients who have suffered from dementia, schizophrenia, or other pathology.
Cognitive psychology deals with how people perceive, learn, remember, and think about information (see also Chapters 5, 7–10, 12).	• How do people perceive depth (see Chapter 5)? • Why do people remember some facts but forget others (see Chapter 8)? • How do people think when they play chess or solve everyday problems (see Chapter 10?)	Cognitive psychologists use a variety of methods in their research. Many of them do controlled experiments, but they often combine experimentation with other techniques, such as computer simulation or mathematical models that predict or help to explain thought and behavior. Most cognitive psychologists do their research in a laboratory setting, but recently, more have gone out into the field, using naturalistic observation to help understand thought processes as they occur in everyday settings.
Developmental psychology is the study of how people develop over time through processes of maturation and learning (see Chapters 12 and 13).	• How much of the development of problem-solving skills is due to *physical maturation* (i.e., is preprogrammed into the organism), and how much is due to *learning* (i.e., is acquired through interaction with the environment)? • How do children form attachments to their parents? • How do people acquire an understanding of what others expect of them in social interactions?	Developmental psychologists use a wide variety of methods in their research. Some devise elaborate experiments, involving sophisticated equipment, to study responses to various kinds of stimulation. Others prefer intensive case studies or naturalistic observations (field studies) of infants, young children, or adolescents, to note how they develop socially, emotionally, cognitively, morally, or in other ways. Others engage in studies that are *longitudinal* (following the same people across a period of time) or *cross-sectional* (taking a representative sample of people of different ages), to follow development over the life span. In such studies, survey data are often used.
Social psychology is concerned with how people interact with each other, both as individuals and in groups (see Chap-	• Why and how can people be persuaded to conform to the expectations of others? • Why are people attracted to one another, and why do people like and even love one another? • Why are people sometimes generous and helpful, and why are they sometimes not?	Social psychologists use diverse methods in their research, ranging from experiments to surveys and questionnaires to naturalistic observation.

(Continued)

TABLE 2-3 *(Continued)*

Field of Psychology	Sample Problems and Questions	Methods
Personality psychology focuses on the personal dispositions that lead people to behave as they do, and also on how these dispositions interact with situations to affect behavior (see Chapter 17).	• Why are some people highly sociable, preferring the company of as many people as possible and thriving in social gatherings, whereas others seem to prefer solitude or just the company of a very few other people? • Why do some people seem nervous and tense, even in apparently safe settings, whereas other people are easygoing and relaxed? • What makes some people highly conscientious and others less so?	Personality theorists use a variety of methods to investigate personality. Some employ paper-and-pencil questionnaires, and others, *projective tests:* unstructured tests in which an experimenter shows a subject an ambiguous picture, for example, and asks him or her to interpret it freely. Still others have experimentally altered the conditions of the environment, perhaps by providing or removing free choice of activities, studying the reactions of different groups of people under these manipulations.
Clinical psychology deals with the understanding and treatment of abnormal behavior (see Chapters 18 and 19).	• What behavior is just a little out of the ordinary, and what behavior is truly maladaptively abnormal? • What factors contribute to such extreme psychological problems that a person loses touch with reality and with rational thought? • What causes people to engage in behaviors that they themselves consider inappropriate and even abnormal and would like to stop if they could?	Clinical psychologists seek to develop and use *taxonomies* (classification systems) of abnormal behavior, to understand its causes, and to find cures for it. They use a variety of methods in their research, including case studies, experimentation, and projective tests. Some clinical psychologists engage only in research, others only in diagnosing and treating patients, and still others in a combination of the two.

Note: Although the aforementioned fields of psychology are the main ones covered in this book, they are by no means the only ones. New specialties of psychology are constantly evolving as old ones fade, although specialties rarely die out altogether. Current examples:

Cross-cultural psychology extends the study of psychological topics to all cultures. Through it, mechanisms of mind and behavior can be compared in multiple cultures. Cross-cultural researchers endeavor to understand how culture and ethnicity affect human behavior.

Philosophical psychology deals with the philosophical presuppositions and contentions underlying psychological theory and research, attempting to define the nature of psychological theories.

Mathematical psychology deals with the application of quantitative models to the study of thought and behavior, such as predicting mathematically when learning should and should not occur.

Educational psychology uses psychology to improve and develop curricula, school administration, and classroom teaching practices.

Organizational psychology applies psychology to decision making about employees and hiring in institutional settings, such as workplaces and businesses.

Engineering psychology deals with human-machine systems and how instruments such as computers and automobile dashboards can be made more user-friendly.

Psycholinguistics investigates the ways in which humans learn and use language.

TABLE 2-4
Career Options for Psychologists
The study of psychology can prove valuable for any career path. Here are some of the options available to persons who pursue degrees in psychology.

Career	Typical Training	Job Description
Academic psychologist	PhD	Works in colleges and universities teaching and conducting research; advises students, assists in educational administration
Clinical psychologist	PhD or PsyD	Diagnoses and treats patients for psychological problems; teaches, trains, and conducts research in hospitals, clinics, colleges, or universities
Counseling psychologist	MA, EdD, or PhD	Counsels people about their problems, conflicts, or choices; often works in schools, offices, hospitals, or clinics
Engineering or human-factors psychologist	PhD	Works in industrial settings; designs machines and workplace environments to maximize productivity and safety; often works with engineers and designers
Industrial or organizational psychologist	MA or PhD	Works in business or industrial settings to help with hiring and firing, testing, interviewing, and placement; assists in developing more hospitable workplaces
Marketing psychologist	MA or PhD	Works in organizations or advertising firms to generate ads that will sell products; supervises testing of ads and determines consumer preferences
Military psychologist	PhD	Works in the armed forces to deal with the interface between psychology and military life; involved in testing, counseling, designing, and implementing new procedures and requirements
Psychometrician	MA or PhD	Creates psychological tests, including aptitude, achievement, personality, attitude, and vocational preference tests; collects and analyzes test data
School psychologist	MA, EdD, or PhD	Works in school settings to test and counsel students; identifies children with perceptual and learning disabilities, as well as gifted children
Consulting psychologist	MA, EdD, or PhD	Works for consulting firms on a special for-hire basis to perform any of the various aforementioned services

college, other specialties, as yet unheard of, may well have appeared. Psychology frequently draws on and contributes to other academic disciplines, which thereby continually stimulate and rejuvenate psychological thought. Just as psychological thought has evolved from diverse ideas in its past, it continues to develop through intersection and interaction with diverse sources of information in the present and will continue to develop in the future.

The next chapter, concerning the biological bases of behavior, looks at how psychology intersects with biology. In that chapter, we turn our focus to the body, the source of all biological and psychological activity. We examine how the nervous system works, as well as how the body's functioning affects and interacts with the functioning of the mind—which you may view as a separate entity from the body or as an alternative perspective on a single phenomenon.

SUMMARY

The Dialectical Progression of Ideas   36

1. By studying certain issues in *philosophy* and *physiology* over time, we can trace the history of the foundations of psychology. Some of the most important questions in the history of psychology are whether the mind and body are one or are two separate phenomena, whether *rationalist* or *empiricist* methods are the way to truth, whether knowledge is innate or acquired, and what constitutes learning.

2. A *dialectic* is a search for truth through the resolution of opposites; first, a *thesis* is proposed; then a countering *antithesis;* and eventually, a unifying *synthesis.* One such dialectic in psychology is about the role of theory in scientific research. Should research be wholly guided by theory, performed without regard to theory, or performed with both a theory in mind and a recognition that results may not fit into the proposed theoretical framework?

A Brief Intellectual History: Western Antecedents of Psychology   37

3. Psychology traces its roots back to archaic Greece. In fact, the word *psychology* (the study of the mind and behavior) is derived from the Greek word *psyche* (soul or breath of life). Other Greek concepts of personality were the *thymos* (the motivational force behind feelings and actions) and *nous* (the ability to perceive truth clearly).

4. The Greek physician Hippocrates (ca. 460–377 B.C.) believed that the source of the mind was in the brain. Hippocrates espoused an empirical approach to learning how the body works.

5. The work of the ancient Greek (ca. 428–322 B.C.) philosophers Plato and his student Aristotle aptly demonstrates the nature of dialectics. The issues raised in this work continue to be argued today. Plato emphasized the supreme power of the mind and thought, which made him a *rationalist*. Plato believed that knowledge is innate, that the search for truth can best be achieved through intellectual reflection, and that the mind and body are qualitatively different and separate *(dualism)*. Aristotle emphasized the world we can see and touch as the route to reality and truth, which made him an *empiricist*. In

contrast to Plato, Aristotle believed that knowledge is learned through interactions with and direct observation of the environment; he also presaged the view that the mind and body are essentially one *(monism)*.

6. The early Christian (200–400 A.D.) and medieval eras (400–1300 A.D.) were times in which many believed that the tenets of the early Christian church held the key to knowledge and truth. While the church fostered intellectual inquiry, it also dictated the boundaries of intellectual exploration.

7. During the Renaissance (1300s to 1600s), science as we know it was born. Thinkers began to depend less on faith and more on empirical observation for proof of theories. Francis Bacon, perhaps in reaction against the guidance by theory in medieval times, proposed that all science should proceed *only* from empirical observation; it should be completely free from the influence of any theory.

8. René Descartes, a rationalist philosopher, believed in mind-body dualism. In particular, he felt that the mind was the determiner of true existence—"Cogito ergo sum." In opposition, the British empiricist school of philosophers (1600–1850), including John Locke and James Mill, believed in the continuity and interdependence of mind and body.

9. Immanuel Kant sought to synthesize questions about mind-body dualism versus monism and innate versus acquired sources of knowledge. Kant's work in philosophy helped bring about the establishment of psychology as a discrete discipline, separate from philosophy and medicine.

Psychological Perspectives: The 1800s and Beyond   44

10. Over time, psychologists have approached their study of the mind and behavior from different perspectives or schools of thought. These perspectives, from functionalism through cognitivism, are often reactions to what has come before. Modern perspectives in psychology are, generally speaking, those that originated in the twentieth century. New theories continue to evolve dialectically.

11. Structuralism was the first real school of thought in psychology. *Structuralists* sought to analyze consciousness into its constituent components of elementary sensations, using the reflective self-observation technique of *introspection*.

12. *Functionalists*, in reaction to structuralism, sought to understand what people do and why. Many functionalists were *pragmatists*, who looked at the applications of knowledge to practice.

13. Scientists often disagree regarding how much of scientific research should be *basic research* (devoted to the study of underlying relationships and principles, which may not offer any immediate, obvious practical value) and how much should be *applied research* (leading to clear, immediate, obvious applications).

14. *Associationism* examines how events or ideas can become associated with one another in the mind to result in a form of learning.

Twentieth-Century Perspectives on Psychology   50

15. An offshoot of associationism, *behaviorism*, was a reaction to structuralism and is based on the belief that the science of psychology should deal only with observable behavior.

16. *Gestalt psychology* is based on the notion that the whole is often more meaningful than the sum of its parts; it developed partly as a reaction against the extreme analytic perspectives of structuralists and behaviorists.

17. *Cognitivism* is the belief that much of human behavior can be understood if we understand first how people think.

18. The basis of *psychodynamic psychology* is that many of the thoughts and feelings that motivate behavior are unconscious, and that there is a continual tension among internal mental structures.

19. *Biological psychology* studies the ways in which human anatomy and physiology (especially of the nervous system, including the brain) interact with human behavior.

20. *Humanistic psychology* studies how people consciously *actualize* (make real through action) their own great inner potential.

Fields Within Psychology   61

21. Under the umbrella of psychology are many different *fields* (career specializations); some of the main fields are psychobiology, cognitive psychology, social psychology, personality psychology, clinical psychology, and developmental psychology. Some fields (e.g., clinical psychology) provide ground for a variety of perspectives (cognitive, psychoanalytic, humanistic, etc.). New specialties are constantly evolving.

22. Psychologists in different specializations may study the same problem, but depending on the perspectives they use, they will organize information differently and use different research methods—in effect, approaching the same issue from different angles.

KEY TERMS

a posteriori 43

applied research 48

a priori 43

associationism 49

associationist 43

atheoretical 42

basic research 48

behavioral genetics 58

behaviorism 51

biological psychology 57

classically conditioned learning 51

cognitivism 56

critical tradition 37

empirical 39

empiricist 39

field 61

functionalism 47

Gestalt 56

Gestalt psychology 56

humanism 41

humanistic psychology 60

introspection 38

law of effect 50

logical positivism 53

mind-body dualism 38

monism 39

perspective 61

philosophy 38

physiology 38

pragmatist 47

psychoanalysis 59

psychodynamic theory 59

rationalist 40

reductionism 43

response 47

stimulus 47

structuralism 45

IN SEARCH OF THE HUMAN MIND:
ANALYSES, CREATIVE EXPLORATIONS, AND PRACTICAL APPLICATIONS

1. If you were to accept Thales's invitation to participate in the critical tradition, what perspectives and ideas in this book would you criticize? Critique at least two of the views that have been expressed in this book.
2. The study of animals to gain insight about humans dates back at least to Hippocrates and continues through contemporary behaviorists and medical researchers. What are your beliefs regarding the benefits and the drawbacks of such animal research?
3. Choose a nineteenth- and a twentieth-century school of thought. In what ways did the older one pave the way for the newer one? (List both similarities and differences.)

4. Imagine yourself as the slave child who interacted with Plato's Socrates. Describe your perspective regarding your dialogue with Socrates.
5. Quickly jot down a description of your sensations as you believe a structuralist would describe them introspectively. Write a poem (of any type—haiku, sonnet, free verse, etc.) based on your description. (You may prefer to go to a particularly appealing natural setting to do this.)
6. In *Walden Two*, B. F. Skinner describes a utopia in which behavioristic principles are applied to all aspects of life for people of all ages. Choose one of the schools of thought described in this chapter (even behaviorism, if you wish), and briefly describe a utopian community being governed by psychologists from that school of thought.

7. In your everyday life, you confront myriad new situations. Describe a situation in which your theory of the nature of the situation (which may be entirely idiosyncratic) guided your responses. Describe another situation in which your observations guided your responses. Compare and contrast the two situations. Which do you find to be most useful—theories or observations? (Explain your answer.)
8. What are some things that your psychology professor—or the author of this book—could do to apply Dewey's principles of education to your current psychology course? Give specific examples of how to apply Dewey's ideas.
9. If you could vote how Congress would appropriate $4 billion for scientific research, how much would you spend on applied research, and how much would you spend on basic research? Give a few examples of research projects you would like to see implemented.

In Search of the Human Mind . . . *Part One*

1. What is a particularly puzzling psychological phenomenon that you observe in your everyday experience? How would each of the various schools of psychological thought approach the study of this phenomenon?

2. How could you design an experiment to study a psychological phenomenon that especially puzzles you? Think about whether your experimental design is correlational, quasi-experimental, or controlled. How could you modify your experiment to use a different type of research design?

3. Compare the ways in which researchers from the various schools of psychological thought would follow each step of the problem-solving cycle to study a puzzling psychological phenomenon.

Looking Ahead . . .

4. Why are sensation, perception, and consciousness considered to be basic biological and cognitive processes? What makes these processes fundamental?

Charting the Dialectic

Chapter 1   WHAT IS PSYCHOLOGY?

Psychology is the study of the mind and of behavior. Some psychologists believe that the study of psychology should primarily confirm everyday intuitions, whereas others believe that psychology more fully serves its purpose when it generates counterintuitive findings. Psychology probably works best when it balances between the intuitive and counterintuitive. Psychology also requires a balance between theory and empirical observation: Although some scientists emphasize theory and others emphasize observation, ultimately, we need both to know how humans feel, think, and behave (observation) and why they do so (theory). Psychologists test their theories through observations based on a variety of research methods. Each of these methods has strengths and weaknesses, and ideally, we should use a variety of methods converging on the same conclusions to make the strongest case for what we wish to claim about the mind and behavior.

Chapter 2   THE ROOTS AND
BRANCHES OF PSYCHOLOGY

Although psychology is the study of the mind and of behavior, at some points in time psychologists have concentrated more on the mind (e.g., in the structuralist approach), whereas at other points in time they have concentrated more on behavior (e.g., the behavioristic approach). Here and elsewhere, scientists engage in a dialectic whereby one fairly extreme position (sometimes called a thesis) or its apparent opposite (the antithesis) gives way to an intermediate position that combines the best aspects of both extremes. For example, rationalists tend to believe more in a doctrine of innate ideas and empiricists tend to believe more in the role of the environment in the development of ideas. Yet many psychologists now believe our thoughts and behavior are the result of an interaction of innate aspects with aspects of the environment.

BASIC BIOLOGICAL AND COGNITIVE PROCESSES

Chapter Three

BIOLOGICAL BASES OF BEHAVIOR

Chapter Outline

"That's fantastic! Utterly fascinating!" I gasped out loud. The heavy tome had suddenly come to life. What had riveted my attention and set me wide awake was aphasia, a disorder of the brain. Damage in a specific part of the brain could rob you of language. Oh, you could move your lips and make sounds, but meaningful speech was suddenly gone. Worse yet, you were unable to read or even understand anything being said. Destroy a tiny area of brain tissue . . . and meaning suddenly vanished. I thought so diabolical an idea must belong to science fiction. But no. Here it was in my medical textbook.

—Richard Cytowic, The Man Who Tasted Shapes

The mind-body issue has long interested philosophers and scientists studying such subjects as physics, computer science, and psychology. Where is the mind located in the body, if at all? How do the mind and body interact? What happens to our bodies when we "lose our minds"? How are we able to think, speak, plan, reason, learn, remember, and feel emotion? What are the physical bases for our personalities and abilities? These questions all probe the relationship between psychology and biology, and some psychologists seek to answer such questions by studying the biological bases of behavior.

The brain is the last and greatest biological frontier . . . the most complex thing we have yet discovered in the universe.

—James Watson, biologist and codiscoverer of the structure of DNA

BIOLOGICAL HISTORY: EVOLUTION AND BEHAVIOR GENETICS

To understand the influence of biology on psychologists' thinking, we need to understand the influence of evolution on biologists' thinking. Because psychologists are interested in behavior, and biopsychologists are interested in the interaction of the body and behavior, evolution is a good place to start.

Evolutionary Theory

Evolutionary theory, which describes the way our bodies and behaviors change across many generations of individuals, is usually credited to English naturalist Charles Darwin (1809–1882). In his book *The Origin of Species* (1859), Darwin proposed that species have developed and changed through a mechanism of **nat-**

ural selection, known commonly as "survival of the fittest." In this view, species show a great deal of biological variation. At a given time, some members of a species will be able to cope with environmental conditions better than will others, and so they will have an advantage for survival and will multiply. Eventually, their progeny become more prevalent. They have been selected by nature for survival—hence, the term *natural selection*. Those types of individuals and species that are not as well able to cope will die off and perhaps become extinct.

> It may metaphorically be said that natural selection is daily and hourly scrutinising, throughout the world, the slightest variations; rejecting those that are bad, preserving and adding up all that are good; silently and insensibly working, *whenever and wherever opportunity offers*, at the improvement of each organic being in relation to its organic and inorganic conditions of life. We see nothing of these slow changes in progress, until the hand of time has marked the lapse of ages, and then so imperfect is our view into long-past geological ages, that we see only that the forms of life are now different from what they formerly were. (Charles Darwin, 1859, *The Origin of Species*, pp. 90–91)

For example, during the Industrial Revolution in late nineteenth-century England, a particular dark-colored moth became more prevalent than a related light-colored moth. Why? Industrial pollution had blackened the forests, improving the darker moth's camouflage against predators such as birds. The light-colored moth became too visible to predators to survive. Recently, however, with restrictions on air pollution, the light moth is making a comeback.

Thus, natural selection is a constantly shifting process, influenced by an organism's biology but also by the interaction of that biology with environmental demands.

How have Darwin's ideas about natural selection come to influence psychology and the study of behavior? As humans have evolved, an increasing percentage of our behavior has come under voluntary control by the brain; our actions are more self-directed and less instinctual than those of many other animals whose brains are less developed. Thus, biopsychologists study the nervous system to pinpoint its influence on our moods, feelings, drives, thought processes, and behavior. Others in fields related to psychology have also attempted to apply evolutionary principles of natural selection to human behavior, although using approaches very different from the biopsychological approach. (For information on these approaches, you may wish to look for references on social Darwinism, eugenics, and sociobiology.)

Evolutionary theory is important not only for the concept of natural selection, but also for its embodiment of the philosophy of *functionalism:* Just as early functionalists in psychology sought to understand *why* people behave as they do, functionalists who studied evolution sought to explain *why* organisms change and evolve as they do (see also the discussion of functionalism in Chapter 2). What purpose does a particular evolutionary change serve for the organism undergoing the change? From a functionalist standpoint, we seek to understand natural selection in terms of what enables some species to function and survive better than do others.

According to evolutionary theory as it was originally posed, the evolution of species through natural selection has been gradual. Recently, however, some

The response to survival during changing conditions can be seen in the natural selection of moths. When industrial pollution of the past century blackened the forests in England, the lighter-colored moths became more visible to predators, so their numbers dwindled. As pollution decreased in the last part of this century, the camouflage of the lighter-colored moths protected them once again.

theorists have proposed an alternative viewpoint: punctuated equilibrium. According to the viewpoint of *punctuated equilibrium*, species remain relatively stable for long periods of time, with such periods of stability punctuated by relatively brief periods (on an evolutionary scale) of rapid species development (e.g., Gould, 1981). Stephen Jay Gould and others agree with Darwin that natural selection is the key to evolution. They merely disagree with him regarding the timing of evolutionary processes.

When Darwin proposed his theory, he did not suggest a specific mechanism for change in the adapting organism. We now know that the mechanism for change is genetic **mutation,** a sudden structural change in a hereditary characteristic. The effects of evolution occur and appear in the **genes,** the physiological building blocks of hereditary transmission of traits. **Biological traits** are distinctive characteristics or behavior patterns that are genetically determined. We receive our genes, and hence our traits, from our parents at the time of our conception. Thus, we now turn to a consideration of **genetics,** the study of genes and heredity (and variations among individuals). We particularly focus on the marriage of psychology and genetics: *behavioral genetics.*

Genetics

Modern genetic theory dates back to the research of an Austrian monk and botanist, Gregor Mendel (1822–1884), who performed breeding experiments on common varieties of the garden pea. Mendel observed some interesting effects in the inheritance of attributes of the pea. For example, if true-breeding tall pea plants (ones that always produce tall offspring) are crossed with true-breeding dwarf pea plants (ones that always produce small offspring), the offspring of the tall and the dwarf plants will always be tall. Mendel referred to the stronger attribute that appeared in this first generation of offspring as the **dominant trait** (here, tallness). He called the weaker trait, which did not appear, **recessive trait** (here, dwarfism).

Next, if you interbreed all of the tall members of the first generation of offspring, the second generation of offspring will have both tall and short plants, in a ratio of about three tall plants to every one short plant. How can we account for this odd potpourri of results? Today, we know that these results are due to **genes,** the basic biological elements for hereditary transmission of traits in all life forms.

To make this example simple, suppose that the height of a plant is controlled by exactly two genes, one of which comes from each parent and forms each half of a gene pair. Both inherited genes may be for tallness, both may be for dwarfism, or one may be for tallness and one for dwarfism. If we represent tallness by T and dwarfism by d, then the possible gene combinations—the possible **genotypes**—for height in the plant are TT, Td, dT, or dd. Now we need to know just one principle: Whenever a dominant gene is paired with a recessive gene, even though both genes are present, the *observable result*—the **phenotype**—will be the dominant trait. Mendel determined that tallness was dominant because a plant with TT, Td, or dT gene combinations shows up as tall, whereas only a plant with a dd gene combination shows up as short.

Now we can account for Mendel's results in the varied heights of his pea plants in different generations. In the first generation, all offspring were hybrids, meaning that they contained mixed gene patterns (Td and dT). Because tallness (T) is the dominant trait, all offspring appeared tall. In the second generation of offspring, however, equal numbers of TT, Td, dT, and dd offspring existed. In this generation, three of the genotypes (TT, Td, dT) produce the phenotype of tall plants, and only one of the genotypes (dd) produces the phenotype of a short plant. (See Figure 3-1 for a chart of Mendel's results.)

In humans, the expression of a single genotype can give rise to a range of phenotypes, because the science of genetics is not as simple as what we have just seen. For example, a person's height is largely genetically controlled, but a range of actual phenotypic heights may be reached, depending on other factors such as nutrition, hormones (described in regard to the endocrine system, later in this chapter), and immune-system efficiency. Thus, even traits that are highly *heritable* (genetically based and passed from generation to generation) are not completely controlled by genetics. Genes do help to determine phenotypes, but not exclusively. The environment is also an important influence. In fact, this nature-versus-nurture question is an old one in psychology, and it still remains unanswered (see also Chapter 11).

What factors might result in phenotypes being different from genotypes? Be specific.

Chromosomes and Chromosomal Abnormalities

Genes are parts of **chromosomes,** rod-shaped bodies containing innumerable genes. Different species have different numbers of chromosomes, which come in pairs. Humans, for example, have 23 pairs of chromo-

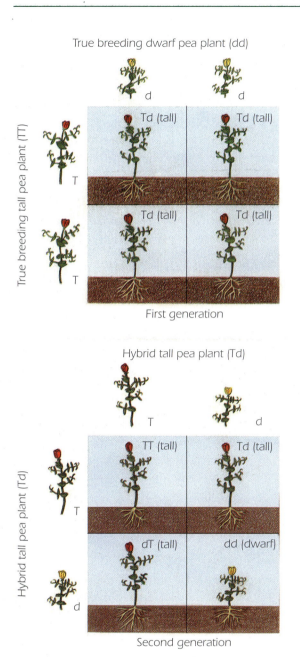

FIGURE 3-1
Genetic Chart of Pea Traits
By studying the characteristics of successive generations of peas, Gregor Mendel discovered the fundamental process of genetic inheritance.

blood type. In fact, an important part of each person's psychological self-image is *gender* (social and psychological identification of being male or female); self-perceptions of gender are predominantly influenced by *sex* (physiological distinction of being male or female, expressed in the body's physical development), as well as by social factors (see Chapter 13). Two specific chromosomes are crucial in determining sex: the X and Y chromosomes, which appear as the twenty-third pair in each set. Females receive an X chromosome from both parents. Their sex-chromosome pairing is thus XX. Males receive an X chromosome from their mothers and a Y chromosome from their fathers. Their sex-chromosome pairing is thus XY.

Selective Breeding

If we can breed for height in peas, we might expect that we can breed for other traits as well. Indeed, race horses often become breeding studs once they are retired, with their owners commanding high prices for granting the opportunity to mate mares with them. In fact, many sophisticated reproductive options (e.g., artificial insemination, in vitro fertilization, surrogacy) are currently in use among animal breeders. If we can breed racing ability, how about learning ability, emotionality, resistance to alcohol dependency, or

Humans have 23 pairs of chromosomes, including the pair that determines each person's sex.

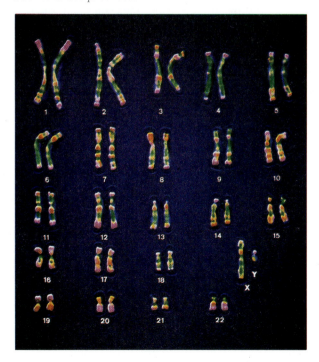

somes, for a total of 46 in all. Most of the cells of our bodies have each of these 23 pairs of chromosomes. One of each pair was received at conception from the mother, and one from the father, so half of each person's heredity can be traced to each parent.

Chromosomes are composed, in part, of genetic material: **deoxyribonucleic acid—DNA.** Chromosomes govern everything from our eye color to our even intelligence? In fact, all of these selective breeding experiments have been done; here, we focus on an experiment involving the breeding of rats for intelligence.

Various rats were tested for their ability to run a maze and then were bred in successive generations to be brighter or less bright, as assessed by their ability to run the maze (Tryon, 1940). Results were mixed. On the one hand, it was possible to breed maze-bright and maze-dull rats, as you can see in Figure 3-2. On the other hand, the rats' abilities turned out to be astonishingly specific. Even changes in the nature of the maze eliminated the significant difference in maze-running ability between groups.

Nature Versus Nurture

The best way to conduct a controlled experimental investigation of genetic influences on biological and psychological behavior is by using genetically identical twins. Among other characteristics, identical twins show similarities in intelligence, even if they have been raised separately in different environments.

This is not to say, however, that our genes inalterably determine everything about us. There is no question that our upbringing, our parents' personalities, our schooling, our physical surroundings—in short, our environments—greatly affect who we become. How much? No clear answer to this question is available.

An example of how nature and nurture may interact is in the expression of *handedness*, the preference a person shows for using the right hand, the left hand, or both, as in the case of ambidextrous individuals. There is substantial evidence in support of a genetic basis for handedness, but genetic factors alone cannot adequately account for variations in handedness across cultures (Berry et al., 1992). For example, although left-handedness apparently occurs in about 5% to 10% of individuals in populations that do not restrict the use of either hand, socialization processes in some societies use selective pressures to force the use of the right hand and not the left. In some of these more right-selective societies, the left hand is often used to achieve personal cleanliness and is therefore considered associated with dirtiness. Thus, cultural factors may influence rates of handedness. Nonetheless, even in cultures that exert pressure to change the use of hands, and in which the rates of left-handedness decline as a result, left-footedness may still hover around 10%, as may rates of left-eye dominance (Dawson, 1977).

The dialectic continues between those who argue for the effects of nature (genes) and those who argue for the effects of nurture (environment). Intelligence (see Chapter 11) and many other traits appear to be greatly affected by a highly complex and incompletely understood interaction of genetic and environmental factors. Much of how nature could affect our intelligence would depend on the organization of our nervous systems—the topic of the next section.

ORGANIZATION OF THE NERVOUS SYSTEM

IN SEARCH OF...

What kinds of mental models would aid you in comprehending the organization of the nervous system, as we now understand it?

Now that we know a little about how, in broad terms, our species' evolution and our own genes contribute to our traits and our behavior, we focus on how the systems of our bodies exert control over our behavior as well. We start with and highlight what is probably the most important system of the body for a biological psychologist: the **nervous system.**

The nervous system is the cornerstone of our ability to perceive, adapt to, and interact with the world around us. It is the means by which we receive, process, and then respond to messages from the environment and from inside our bodies. The discussion of the nervous system presented here takes the functional approach mentioned earlier: We are concerned

FIGURE 3-2
Selective Breeding in Rats
Successive generations of rats were bred for their ability to run particular mazes. However, this ability did not generalize to other aspects of intelligence—or even to other kinds of mazes. (After Thompson, 1954)

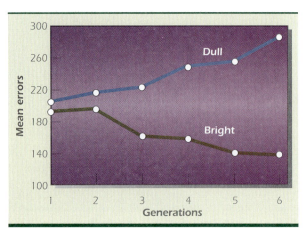

not only with what is there (the anatomical structures), but also with what those structures do and why (the physiological functions).

In describing the functions of our physiological communication systems, we often refer to various human-made inventions (e.g., phones, televisions, computers) as models for understanding the communication systems within our bodies. In fact, however, nothing created by humankind even approaches the complexity, subtlety, and sophistication of the systems of communication within our bodies.

Our nervous system begins as a mere neural tube (see Figure 3-7, later in this chapter). This generalized tube eventually develops into the spinal cord with a specialized extension, the brain stem. The back portion of the brain stem then develops the more specialized cerebellum (described later), and the front portion develops the cerebral hemispheres, which distinguish mammals from other animals (Kolb & Whishaw, 1990). The specialized structures of the human nervous system are described here next. Following this discussion, we examine in some detail the supreme organ of the nervous system—the brain—paying special attention to the cerebral cortex, which controls many of our thought processes. Finally, we consider how information moves through the nervous system. The overall structure of the nervous system is shown in the diagram in Figure 3-3.

FIGURE 3-3
Divisions of the Nervous System
The central nervous system (CNS), protected by bone, comprises the brain and spinal cord. The peripheral nervous system (PNS), not protected by bone, comprises the nerves of the autonomic and somatic systems. The autonomic system transmits messages between the brain and internal organs, and the somatic system transmits messages between the brain and the sensory and motor systems, which are linked to the skeletal muscles.

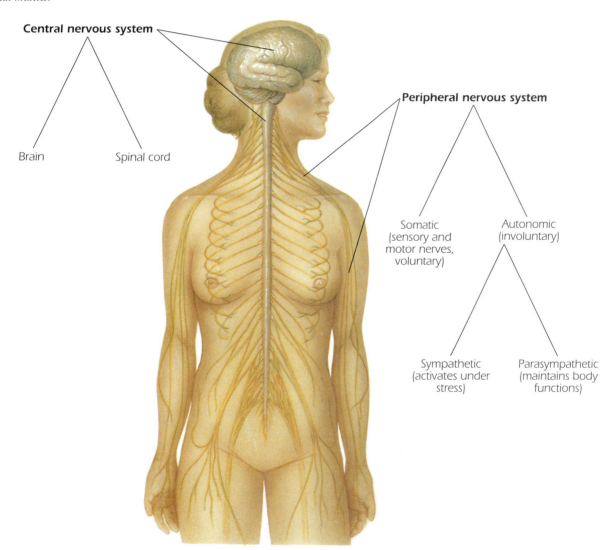

Central nervous system

Brain · Spinal cord

Peripheral nervous system

Somatic (sensory and motor nerves, voluntary) · Autonomic (involuntary)

Sympathetic (activates under stress) · Parasympathetic (maintains body functions)

The nervous system is divided into two main parts: the central nervous system and the peripheral nervous system. We turn first to the **central nervous system** (CNS), which consists of two parts: the brain and the spinal cord, both of which are encased in bone. In addition to being protected by bone, the brain and spinal cord are buffered from shocks and minor traumas (injuries) by a fluid that is secreted constantly in the brain. This **cerebrospinal fluid** circulates inside and around the brain and the spinal cord. Although the clear, colorless cerebrospinal fluid probably does not provide nourishment (which is provided by the rich blood supply going to the CNS), it may play a role in helping the CNS to get rid of waste products.

The Central Nervous System

The Brain and the Spinal Cord

The *brain*, protected by the skull, is the organ in our bodies that most directly controls our thoughts, emotions, and motivations. Textbook diagrams involving the brain and its interconnections must somewhat oversimplify structures in order to reveal their fundamental elements and relationships. Thus, such diagrams may not show all of the interconnections between the brain and other organs, or between the central and peripheral nervous systems, but the connections are there, and they are what makes the body work as wondrously well as it does.

If we start from your brain, we can follow a network of **neurons** (nerve cells) to your **spinal cord,** which gathers a series of interconnected neurons into **nerves** (bundles of fibers that extend from your brain down through the center of your back). The spinal cord is a roughly cylindrical bundle of nerves about the diameter of your little finger, enclosed within the protecting **vertebrae,** the backbones that form your *spinal column* (see Figure 3-4). Inside the spinal column, invisible from the outside of the body, the spinal cord bulges slightly in two places to accommodate large bundles of connecting nerves. One of the two bulges contains the nerve cells controlling the sensations in and the movement of the arms and hands, and the other bulge contains the nerve cells controlling the legs and feet. Because your arms, hands, legs, and feet are required almost constantly to do important work, their control requires many nerve cells. After the bulges, the cord then tapers gradually to a point in the lower portion of your back.

One function of the spinal cord is to collect information from the peripheral nervous system and transmit it to the brain, as well as to relay information back from the brain to the outlying nerves. The two-directional communication of the nervous system involves two different kinds of nerves and neurons: **Receptors** receive *sensory information* (e.g., sensations in the eyes, ears, and skin) from the outlying nerves of the body and transmit that information back up through the spinal cord to the brain. **Effectors** transmit *motor information* (e.g., movements of the large and small muscles) about how the body should act in response to the information it receives. Usually, this information comes from the brain.

Spinal Reflexes

The spinal cord plays a crucial role in routing sensory and motor information to and from the brain. Under some circumstances, however, the spinal cord transmits a message directly from receptor nerves to effector nerves, without routing the message through the brain until after the body has responded to the sensory information. The direct-connection responses are **reflexes** (see Figure 3-5), which offer much faster responses than do voluntary responses. For example, it takes only about 50 milliseconds from the time the patellar tendon in your knee is tapped until your calf and foot jerk forward, as compared with the many hundreds of milliseconds for you to move your knee in response to your being told to move it. Quick reflexes are adaptive because they allow the body to respond immediately to particular sensory information without taking the time to route the information through the brain. For example, when you feel pain, you reflexively withdraw from whatever causes you pain, without pausing to think, "Gosh, that hurts. I should probably move my body away from that." Not only do reflexes minimize pain, but they also minimize any damage that might result from whatever is causing the pain (e.g., fires or cuts). Thus, in both functional and evolutionary terms, our reflexes better enable us to survive.

The reflex response shows how the spinal cord has the power to act alone; yet it also demonstrates the brain's essential role in whether we consciously feel pain, pleasure, pressure, or temperature anywhere outside our heads. For example, suppose that a traumatic accident severed your spinal cord at the neck. You would be both paralyzed and without sensation below your neck, because your spinal cord would not be able to receive or send messages from or to your brain. This is not to say, however, that you could not move at all; your intact spinal reflexes would still jerk your hand away from a hot stove. You would never become consciously aware of pain, however, for your brain would not be able to get the sen-

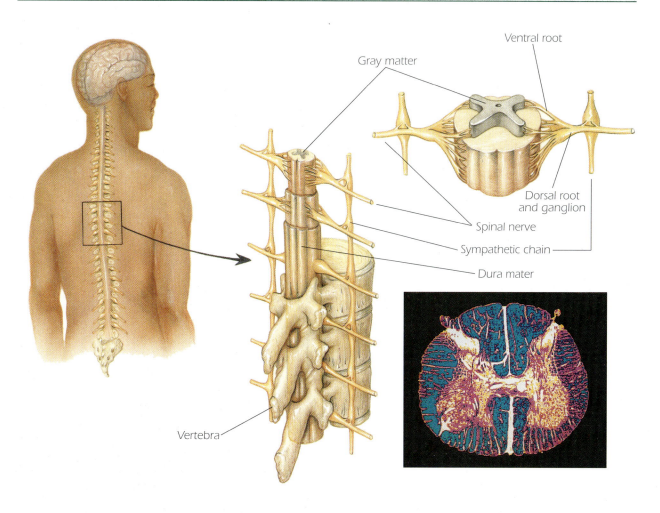

FIGURE 3-4
The Structure of the Spinal Column
The spinal cord and its connecting nerves are protected by dura mater and vertebrae.

sory information via your spinal cord. Nor could you intentionally move your hand away from any impending danger that your brain recognized. To recognize your bodily sensations or to move your body purposefully, your spinal cord must be able to communicate with your brain. This situation gives an interesting twist on the mind-body dilemma: When the brain is severed from the spinal cord, events that happen in the body below the severance do not happen in the body's mind.

In sum, the body is an exceptionally well-organized system, with lower levels in the hierarchy of command capable of responding without intervention of the brain when the immediate need arises, but with higher levels in the hierarchy essential for full physical interaction with and perception of the world around us.

Suppose that humans lacked spinal reflexes. What outcomes would you anticipate?

The Peripheral Nervous System

Below the level of the CNS is the **peripheral nervous system** (PNS), which comprises all of the nerve cells *except* those of the brain and the spinal cord. *Peripheral* has two meanings: "auxiliary," because the PNS assists the CNS; and "away from the center," because the peripheral nerves are external to the CNS. Note that the PNS even includes the nerves of the face and head that are not a part of the CNS. The primary function of the PNS is to relay information between the CNS and the receptors and effectors lying outside of the CNS. The PNS connects

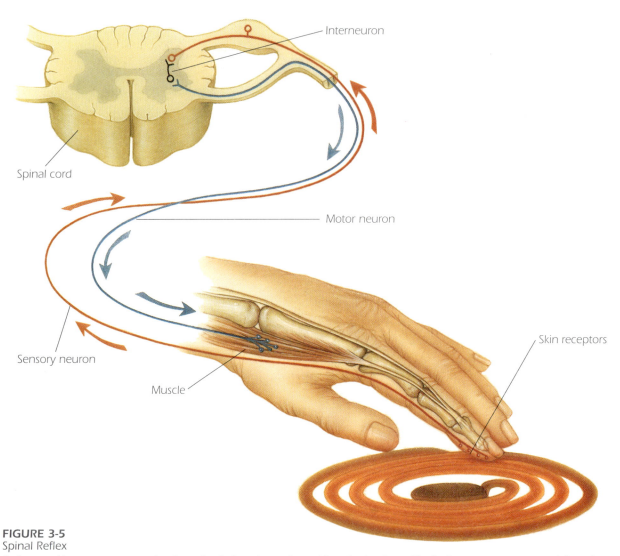

Interneuron

Spinal cord

Motor neuron

Sensory neuron

Muscle

Skin receptors

FIGURE 3-5
Spinal Reflex

Reflexes enable us to remove ourselves immediately from danger by avoiding the time it would take for a message to go to and from the brain. In this example, the interneuron in the spinal column intercepts the "extreme heat" message from the sensory neuron and directs the motor neurons to contract the hand muscles, thereby pulling the hand away from the burner.

with receptors in both our external sensory organs (e.g., skin, ears, eyes) and our internal body parts (e.g., stomach, muscles). It also connects with effectors in parts of the body that produce movement, speech, and so on. Most of the PNS nerves lack the surrounding protective bone that encases the brain (the skull) and spinal cord (the spinal column vertebrae), which leaves the PNS more vulnerable to injury than the CNS. Under most circumstances, however, injury to the PNS would be less devastating than injury to the CNS.

The PNS comprises two main parts: the somatic nervous system and the autonomic nervous system. The **somatic nervous system** is in charge of quick and conscious movements of our skeletal muscles. *Skeletal muscles* are those attached directly to our bones, and they allow us to walk, type, wave, swim—

in short, to move. The skeletal muscles are sometimes referred to as striated muscles because, under a microscope, they appear to have striations (stripes). In general, we have voluntary control over the muscles served by nerves from the somatic system; whenever we want to control them, we can. The somatic nervous system usually can respond quickly to whatever the CNS asks of it.

The **autonomic nervous system** controls movement of our *nonskeletal muscles*, which comprise the striated cardiac (heart) muscles and the *smooth muscles*, which lack the striations found in the muscles of the somatic system. The smooth muscles include those of the blood vessels and of the *viscera* (internal body organs), such as the muscles of the digestive tract. We have little and in some cases no voluntary control over these muscles. We are usually not even aware of their functioning. In fact, *autonomic* means "self-regulating"; this system does not need our conscious attention. To illustrate the two different systems, suppose that you are writing at a word processor. You are controlling the striated muscular movements of your hands and fingers as they press the keys, but you are not directing the smooth muscles of your stomach, which may be digesting your dinner. In general, the responses of the autonomic nervous system are more sustained and less rapid than those of the somatic nervous system.

The autonomic nervous system is itself further divided into two parts: the sympathetic nervous system and the parasympathetic nervous system (see Figure 3-6). Both systems are involved with your *metabolism* (the processes by which your body

FIGURE 3-6
The Autonomic Nervous System
Note how the two parts of the autonomic system, the sympathetic and parasympathetic systems, complement one another as they regulate the functions of the organs.

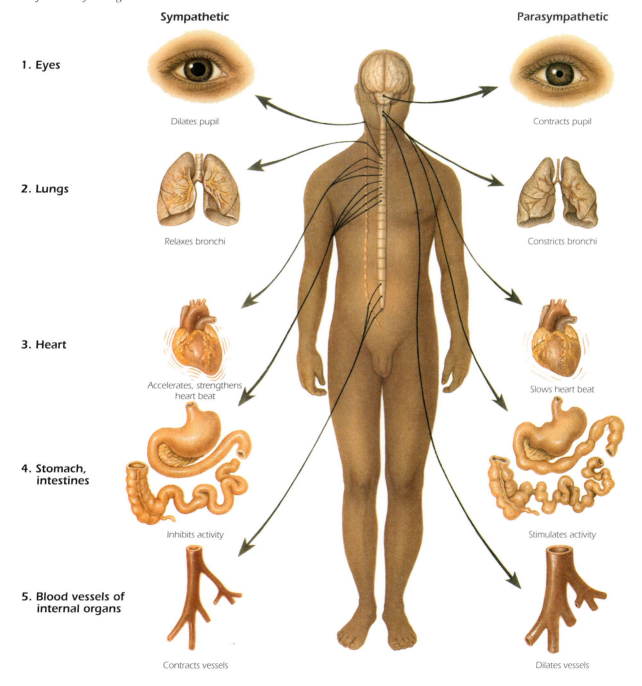

Sympathetic   **Parasympathetic**

1. Eyes
Dilates pupil   Contracts pupil

2. Lungs
Relaxes bronchi   Constricts bronchi

3. Heart
Accelerates, strengthens   Slows heart beat
heart beat

4. Stomach, intestines
Inhibits activity   Stimulates activity

5. Blood vessels of internal organs
Contracts vessels   Dilates vessels

captures, stores, and uses energy and material resources from food and eliminates the waste). The **sympathetic nervous system** is concerned primarily with *catabolism* (the metabolic processes that *use* the energy and other resources from the reserves stored in the body). The **parasympathetic nervous system** is concerned primarily with *anabolism* (the metabolic processes that *store* energy). (For more information on metabolism, see Chapter 20.)

The sympathetic and parasympathetic systems often work in tandem, as they do in determining our metabolism. In general, the sympathetic nervous system is activated by situations requiring arousal and alertness. At such times, this system increases heart rate and diverts blood flow to muscles, as needed for exercise or emergency. On the other hand, the parasympathetic nervous system becomes active when the body is conserving energy. It promotes the activity of the digestive system and also slows heart rate, thereby slowing the body and aiding in energy storage. Thus, the sympathetic and parasympathetic systems work in parallel, yet also in opposition to one another. If you have a heated argument right after dinner, your sympathetic system will be stirred up, readying you for a fight. Unfortunately, it will end up warring with your parasympathetic system, which will be trying to conserve body energy in order to digest your food. You may end up feeling drained, tired, and even sick to your stomach.

The interactions of our emotions with our physiological processes intrigue biological psychologists (see Chapter 20). While seeking insights into our minds, our experiences, and our physiological responses and functioning, these psychologists investigate how different branches of the nervous system interact, complement, and interfere with one another. In particular, psychologists are fascinated by the way in which the brain integrates, processes, and guides the complex interactions throughout the amazing network of the human nervous system.

THE BRAIN: STRUCTURE AND FUNCTION

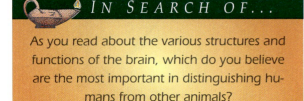

IN SEARCH OF...

As you read about the various structures and functions of the brain, which do you believe are the most important in distinguishing humans from other animals?

The brain is a wondrously complex organ. In these pages, we reveal its essential structure, given our present understanding of it. As you read on, bear in mind that many of the complexities have been simplified and many of the details we describe here may be reinterpreted as new information comes to light.

What does a brain actually look like? Figure 3-8 shows several views of a brain. Subsequent figures and schematic pictures (i.e., simplified diagrams) point out in more detail some of the main features of the brain.

The brain can be divided into three major regions: forebrain, midbrain, and hindbrain. These labels do not correspond exactly to their locations in an adult's or even a child's head, because the terms come from the front-to-back physical arrangement of these parts in a developing embryo's nervous system (which is formed from the neural tube): The **forebrain** is the farthest forward, toward what becomes the face; the **midbrain** is next in line; and the **hindbrain** is farthest from the forebrain, near the back of the neck. The remainder of the neural tube becomes the spinal cord (see Figure 3-7a). In development, the relative orientations change, such that the forebrain is almost a cap on top of the midbrain and hindbrain. Nonetheless, the terms are still used to designate areas of the fully developed brain. Figure 3-7b clearly shows the changing locations and relationships of the forebrain, the midbrain, and the hindbrain over the course of development of the brain, starting from an embryo a few weeks after conception and proceeding to a fetus of seven months. We now consider each of these major regions in turn, starting from the forebrain and working our way roughly downward and backward.

The Forebrain

The forebrain is the region located toward the top and front of the brain (see Table 3-1 and Figure 3-8). It comprises four parts: the cerebral cortex, the limbic system, the thalamus, and the hypothalamus. The cerebral cortex forms the outer layer of the cerebral hemispheres (the right and left spherical halves of the brain) and plays such a vital role in our thinking and other mental processes that it merits a special section, which follows the present discussion of the major structures and functions of the brain.

The **limbic system** is important to emotion, motivation, and learning. Animals such as fish and reptiles, which have relatively undeveloped limbic systems, respond to the environment almost exclusively by instinct. Mammals, especially humans, have relatively more developed limbic systems, which seem to allow us to suppress instinctive responses (such as

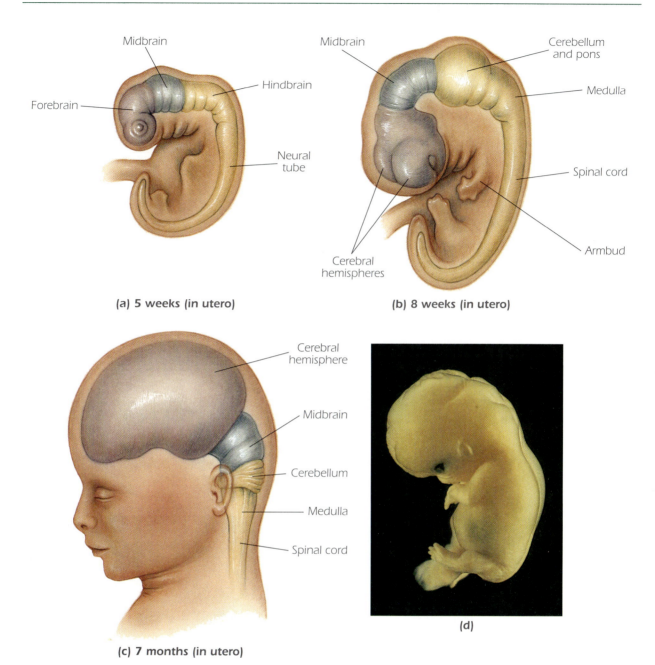

(a) 5 weeks (in utero)

(b) 8 weeks (in utero)

(c) 7 months (in utero)

(d)

FIGURE 3-7
Neural Development
Over the course of embryonic and fetal development, the brain becomes more highly specialized, and the locations and relative positions of the hindbrain, midbrain, and the forebrain change from conception to full term.

the impulse immediately to strike someone who accidentally causes us pain). Our limbic systems make us more able to adapt our behaviors flexibly in response to our changing environment.

The limbic system comprises three central interconnected cerebral structures: the hippocampus, the amygdala, and the septum. The **hippocampus** plays an essential role in memory formation. Persons who have suffered damage to or removal of the hip-

pocampus can still recall existing memories (for example, they can recognize old friends and places), but they are unable to form new memories (relative to the time of the brain damage). New information—new situations, people, and places—remain forever new. You could converse with such a person every day for a year, and each time you met you would be entirely unfamiliar to this person (Squire, 1987). (We return to the role of the hippocampus in Chapter 8.)

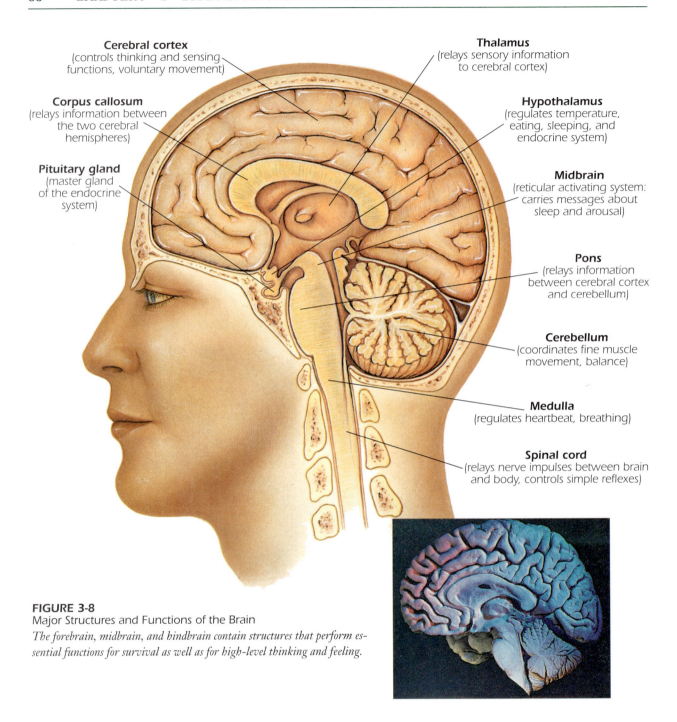

Cerebral cortex
(controls thinking and sensing functions, voluntary movement)

Corpus callosum
(relays information between the two cerebral hemispheres)

Pituitary gland
(master gland of the endocrine system)

Thalamus
(relays sensory information to cerebral cortex)

Hypothalamus
(regulates temperature, eating, sleeping, and endocrine system)

Midbrain
(reticular activating system: carries messages about sleep and arousal)

Pons
(relays information between cerebral cortex and cerebellum)

Cerebellum
(coordinates fine muscle movement, balance)

Medulla
(regulates heartbeat, breathing)

Spinal cord
(relays nerve impulses between brain and body, controls simple reflexes)

FIGURE 3-8
Major Structures and Functions of the Brain
The forebrain, midbrain, and hindbrain contain structures that perform essential functions for survival as well as for high-level thinking and feeling.

The *amygdala* plays a role in anger and aggression, and the *septum* is involved in anger and fear. Studies of monkeys have revealed some of these physiological functions. For example, monkeys with *lesions* (damage due to pathology or injury) in some areas of the limbic system seem to lack inhibition and are easily enraged. Monkeys with damage to other areas of the limbic system cannot be provoked to anger even when attacked; their hostility seems to have been erased.

When you have been angry at another person, in what ways have you reacted that have been adaptive to the situation, and in what ways have you reacted that have been maladaptive?

Most of the sensory input into the brain passes through the **thalamus** (a two-lobed structure located in about the center of the brain, at about the level of

TABLE 3-1

Region of the Brain	Major Structures Within the Regions	Functions of the Structures
Forebrain	**Cerebral cortex** (outer layer of the cerebral hemispheres)	Involved in receiving and processing sensory information, thinking, other cognitive processing, and planning and sending motor information
	Limbic system (hippocampus, amygdala, and septum)	Involved in learning, emotions, and motivation (particularly, the **hippocampus** influences learning and memory; the **amygdala**, anger and aggression; and the **septum**, anger and fear)
	Thalamus	Primary relay station for sensory information coming into the brain; transmits information to the correct regions of the cerebral cortex, through projection fibers that extend from the thalamus to specific regions of the cortex
	Hypothalamus	Controls the endocrine system (described later in this chapter); controls the autonomic nervous system, internal temperature regulation including appetite and thirst regulation, and other key functions; involved in regulation of behavior related to species survival: fighting, feeding, fleeing, and mating; plays a role in controlling consciousness (see reticular activating system); involved in emotions, pleasure, pain, and stress reactions
Midbrain	**Superior colliculi** (on top)	Involved in vision (especially visual reflexes)
	Inferior colliculi (below)	Involved in hearing
	Reticular activating system (also extends into the hindbrain)	Important in controlling consciousness (sleep, arousal), attention, cardiorespiratory function, and movement
	Gray matter, red nucleus, substantia nigra, ventral region	Important in controlling movement
Hindbrain	**Cerebellum**	Essential to balance, coordination, and muscle tone
	Pons (also contains part of the RAS)	Involved in consciousness (sleep/arousal); bridges neural transmissions from one part of the brain to another; involved with facial nerves
	Medulla oblongata	Serves as juncture at which nerves cross from one side of the body to opposite side of the brain; involved in cardiorespiratory function, digestion, and swallowing

the eyes, just beneath the cerebral cortex). The thalamus relays the incoming sensory information through its *projection fibers* (neurons that project from one part of the brain to another) to the appropriate region in the cortex. To accommodate all the different types of information that must be sorted out, the thalamus is divided into a number of *nuclei* (groups of nerve cells of similar function), which receive sensory information and project it to the cerebral cortex (see Table 3-2 for the names and roles of the various nuclei).

The thalamus also helps in the control of sleep and waking.

The small size of the **hypothalamus** (located at the base of the forebrain, beneath the thalamus) belies its important function: It controls water balance in the tissues and bloodstream as well as many other functions of the autonomic nervous system (see Table 3-1 and Chapter 16 for more information). The hypothalamus, which interacts with the limbic system, also regulates behavior related to species survival:

TABLE 3-2
Four Major Nuclei of the Thalamus[a]
Four key thalamic nuclei relay visual, auditory, somatosensory, and equilibrium-related information.

Name of Nucleus[b]	Receives Information from	Projects (Transmits Information) Primarily to	Functional Benefit
Lateral geniculate nucleus	The visual receptors, via optic nerves	The visual cortex	Permits us to see
Medial geniculate nucleus	The auditory receptors, via auditory nerves	The auditory cortex	Permits us to hear
Ventroposterior nucleus	The somatic nervous system	The primary somatosensory cortex	Permits us to sense pressure and pain
Ventrolateral nucleus	The cerebellum (in the hindbrain)	The primary motor cortex	Permits us to sense physical balance and equilibrium

[a] Other thalamic nuclei also play important roles.
[b] The names refer to the relative location of the nuclei within the thalamus: *lateral* = toward the right or left side of the medial nucleus; *ventral* = closer to the belly than to the top of the head; *posterior* = toward the back, behind; *ventroposterior* = bellyward and in the back; *ventrolateral* = bellyward and on the side.

fighting, feeding, fleeing, and mating. It makes sense, therefore, that the hypothalamus is also active in regulating emotions and reactions to stress. Mild electrical stimulation in particular areas of the hypothalamus causes pleasurable sensations, whereas stimulation in nearby areas causes sensations of pain. The hypothalamus also plays an important role in the endocrine (hormonal) system (discussed later in this chapter).

The Midbrain

The midbrain is more important in nonmammals than in mammals, because in nonmammals it is the main source of control for visual and auditory information. In mammals these functions are mostly taken over by the forebrain, but the midbrain does help to control eye movements and coordination. Table 3-1 lists several structures and functions of the midbrain, but by far the most indispensable of these is the **reticular activating system,** a network of neurons essential to the regulation of consciousness (sleep, wakefulness, arousal, and even attention, to some extent) as well as to such vital functions as heart rate and breathing.

The reticular activating system (RAS) actually extends into the hindbrain. Both the reticular activating system and the thalamus are essential to our having any conscious awareness of or control over our existence. Together, the thalamus and hypothalamus, the midbrain, and the hindbrain form the **brain stem,** which connects the brain to the spinal cord. As you may already know or presume, physicians make a determination of brain death based on the function of the brain stem.

The Hindbrain

The hindbrain comprises the medulla oblongata, the pons, and the cerebellum. The **medulla oblongata,** located where the spinal cord enters the skull and joins with the brain, is a part of the reticular activating system. It helps to keep us alive by entirely controlling the heart rate and largely controlling breathing, swallowing, and digestion. The medulla is also the place at which nerves from the right side of the body cross over to the left side of the brain, and nerves from the left side of the body cross over to the right side of the brain. (We examine the functional significance of this crossover shortly.)

The **pons** serves as a kind of relay station, containing nerve cells that pass signals from one part of the brain to another. The pons also contains a portion of the reticular activating system, as well as nerves serving parts of the head and face. The **cerebellum** controls bodily coordination, balance, and muscle tone. If the cerebellum is damaged, movement becomes jerky and disjointed.

Now that we have examined the forebrain, the midbrain, and the hindbrain, we move our study of the brain to a higher level. We turn to the cerebral hemispheres and the cerebral cortex (located in the forebrain), which together make up that essential part of the human brain that sets us apart from other members of the animal kingdom by allowing us a greater range of psychological functioning.

THE CEREBRAL HEMISPHERES AND THE CEREBRAL CORTEX

> ### IN SEARCH OF...
>
> Earlier, we mentioned that in mammals, particularly in humans, the limbic system is far more highly developed than it is in other animals. Nonetheless, most psychologists think of the cortex as the part of the brain that most significantly distinguishes humans from other species of animals. Why do we assign so much importance to the cortex?

The **cerebral cortex** is a 2-millimeter-deep layer on the surface of the brain. The cortex enfolds the brain, somewhat like the bark of a tree wraps around the trunk. In human beings, the cerebral cortex is highly *convoluted*, containing many folds. The purpose of these folds is to increase the surface area of the cortex; if the wrinkly human cortex were smoothed out, it would take up about 2 square feet. The cortex comprises 80% of the human brain (Kolb & Whishaw, 1990). The cerebral cortex is responsible for our being able to plan, coordinate thoughts and actions, perceive visual and sound patterns, use language, and in general, to think.

The surface of the cerebral cortex is grayish because it primarily contains the gray nerve cells that process the information that the brain receives and sends. The cerebral cortex is sometimes referred to as the *gray matter* of the brain. In contrast, the underlying *white matter* of the brain's interior comprises mostly white-colored nerve fibers, which conduct information. Both the white and the gray matter are essential to human intelligence.

The cerebral cortex is actually the outer layer of the two somewhat hemispherical halves of the brain, the **left** and **right cerebral hemispheres.** Although the two hemispheres look quite similar on visual inspection, they function quite differently. The left hemisphere is specialized for some kinds of activity, the right for other kinds. For example, receptors in the right eye, right ear, and right nostril generally send information through the medulla (in the hind-

brain) to areas in the left hemisphere of the brain, and the receptors on the left side generally transmit information to the right hemisphere. Similarly, the left hemisphere of the brain directs the motor responses on the right side of the body, and vice versa for the right hemisphere and left side of the body. Note that not all information transmission is **contralateral** (opposite side); some **ipsilateral** (same side) transmission occurs as well.

Despite this general tendency for contralateral specialization, the hemispheres do communicate with one another. The **corpus callosum,** a dense aggregate of nerve fibers, connects the two cerebral hemispheres, allowing transmission of information back and forth (see Figure 3-9). Once information has reached one hemisphere, the corpus callosum allows that information to travel across to the other hemisphere without difficulty.

How did psychologists find out that the two hemispheres have different responsibilities? Chapter 2 mentioned brain-hemisphere research in general terms; we now look more closely at the kinds of research that led to the discovery of specialized functioning in each hemisphere.

Hemispheric Specialization

A major figure in the study of hemispheric specialization was Paul Broca. At a meeting of the French Society of Anthropology in 1861, Broca noted that an *aphasic* patient (a person suffering from loss of speech as a result of brain damage) of his was shown later to have a lesion in the left cerebral hemisphere of the

FIGURE 3-9
Corpus Callosum
This dense network of fibers, shown from the base of the brain, provides a fundamental communication link between the two cerebral hemispheres.

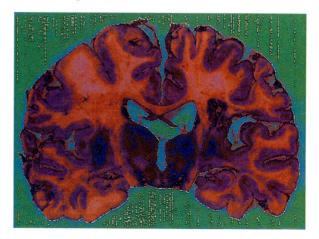

brain. Despite an initially cool response, Broca soon became a central figure in the heated controversy over whether functions, particularly speech, are indeed localized in particular areas of the brain, rather than generalized over the entire brain. By 1864, Broca was convinced that the left hemisphere of the brain is critical for speech, a view that others before him had proposed, and a view that has held up over time. In fact, the specific area Broca identified as contributing to speech is referred to as Broca's area (see Figure 3-8). (Curiously, although people with lesions in Broca's area cannot speak fluently, they can use their voices to sing or shout.) Another important early researcher, German neurologist Carl Wernicke (1848–1905), studied language-deficient patients who could speak, but whose speech made no sense. He also traced language ability to the left hemisphere, though to a different precise location, now known as Wernicke's area (see Figure 3-8).

Others continued in this tradition, studying problems such as *apraxia* (the inability to perform movements upon request) and *agnosia* (the inability to recognize familiar objects, often faces). In addition to Broca's and Wernicke's case-study research and postmortem examination of brains, other researchers (e.g., Penfield & Roberts, 1959) have used techniques such as stimulation by electrodes to map specific functions to particular areas of the brain. For example, following the stimulation of the speech area of the human brain, subjects experience temporary aphasia (loss of speech).

Despite these valuable early contributions, the individual most responsible for modern theory and research on hemispheric specialization is Nobel Prize-winning American psychologist Roger Sperry. Sperry (1964a, 1964b) argued that each hemisphere behaves in many respects like a separate brain. In a classic experiment that supports this contention, Sperry and his colleagues (Sperry, 1964a) severed the corpus callosum connecting the two hemispheres of a cat's brain. They then showed that information presented visually to one cerebral hemisphere of the cat was not recognizable to the other hemisphere.

Some of the most interesting information about how the human brain works, and especially about the respective roles of the hemispheres, has emerged from studies of humans with epilepsy in whom the corpus callosum has been severed. Surgically separating this neurological bridge prevents epileptic seizures from spreading from one hemisphere to the other, thereby greatly lessening their severity. However, this procedure also results in a loss of communication between the two hemispheres. It is as if the person had two separate specialized brains processing different information and performing separate functions.

People who have undergone such operations are termed **split-brain** patients. Although split-brain patients behave normally in many respects, in a few ways their behavior is bizarre. Instances have been reported of a person's left hand struggling against the right hand in order to accomplish a task such as putting on pants. A patient, angry at his wife, reached to strike her with his left hand while his right hand tried to protect her and stop his left one (Gazzaniga, 1970). Split-brain patients almost literally have two separate minds of their own.

Split-brain research reveals fascinating possibilities regarding the ways we think. Many in the field have argued that language is completely localized in the left hemisphere, and that *visuospatial* (involving vision and spatial orientation and perception) ability is localized in the right hemisphere (Farah, 1988a, 1988b; Gazzaniga, 1985; Zaidel, 1983). Jerre Levy (one of Sperry's students) and colleagues (Levy, Trevarthen, & Sperry, 1972) have probed the link between the cerebral hemispheres and visuospatial versus language-oriented tasks, using subjects who have undergone split-brain surgery.

In one kind of study, the subject is asked to focus his or her gaze on the center of a screen. Then a *chimeric face* (a face showing the left side of the face of one person and the right side of another) is flashed on the screen. The subject is asked to identify what he or she saw, either verbally or by pointing to one of several normal (not chimeric) faces.

Typically, split-brain patients are unaware that they saw conflicting information in the two halves of the picture. When asked to give an answer about what they saw in words, they say that they saw the right half of the picture. Bearing in mind the contralateral association between hemisphere and side of the body, it seems that the left hemisphere controls their verbal processing (speaking) of visual information. In contrast, when asked to use their fingers to point to what they saw, subjects chose the image from the left half of the picture. This finding indicates that the right hemisphere appears to control spatial processing (pointing) of visual information. Thus, the task that the subjects are asked to perform is crucial in determining what image the subject thinks was shown. Figure 3-10 provides a visual summary of this experiment.

Additional split-brain research supports the view that visuospatial processing occurs primarily in the right hemisphere (Gazzaniga & LeDoux, 1978; Gazzaniga, 1985) and language processing primarily in the left hemisphere, although some researchers

FIGURE 3-10
Chimeric Faces

Research on split-brain patients reveals that each hemisphere of the brain processes images and other information distinctively. (a) A composite photograph of two different faces is flashed before a split-brain subject. (b) When shown a group of photographs and asked to pick out a person shown in the composite, the subject will say it is the face from the right half of the composite. (c) However, if asked to point out which one the subject originally saw, she will indicate the picture from the left side of the composite. (After Levy, Trevarthen, & Sperry, 1972)

"Whom did you see?"
"It was Cher."
(b)

"Point to the person you saw."
(c)

Searchers . . .   *MICHAEL POSNER*

Michael Posner received his PhD in experimental psychology. He is Director of the Institute of Cognitive and Decision Studies and Professor of Psychology at the University of Oregon.

Q: *How did you become interested in psychology in general and in your area of work in particular?*

A: I entered psychology as a compromise between the two topics I studied as an undergraduate: physics and philosophy. I didn't even imagine then how appropriate they would turn out to be. I began to study human brain activity after experimental evidence suggested that measures of the speed of human performance (mental chronometry) were providing a unique functional model of the human brain.

Q: *What is your greatest asset as a psychologist?*

A: My generally average ability has given me insight into the design of tasks that most people can actually do, rather than those that can be performed only by a few.

Q: *How do you get your ideas or insights for research?*

A: My ideas generally come from thinking about the psychological and neuroscience literature and asking about the real issues to which this work might apply. In preparing classes, ideas for future research often come to me.

Q: *What obstacles have you experienced, and how have you overcome them?*

A: It would have been easier to carry out this work if I had been endowed with greater intelligence. My strategy is to work hard and hope for brilliant students.

Q: *What is your major contribution to psychology?*

A: I believe I have contributed to establishing stronger links between cognitive operations and localized brain activity than had been available previously. This has helped make it possible to conceive of joint cognitive and anatomical approaches to higher brain function.

Q: *What advice would you give to someone starting in the field of psychology?*

A: Don't pay too much attention to current fads. Know the techniques currently used, but ask questions you think worth answering.

Q: *What did you learn from your mentors?*

A: I learned from Paul Fitts that it was possible to develop simple empirical generalizations from careful and detailed experiments and from reading Broadbent that this sort of research could lead to important theoretical conceptions.

Q: *Apart from your life as an academic, how have you found psychology to be important to you?*

A: Psychology helps explain my own thoughts—and feelings. When I say something unusual, I look for the primed antecedents; when I feel angry, I look for what the underlying reasons might be.

Q: *How do you keep yourself academically challenged?*

A: This is such an exciting time for psychology with the new tools available for seeing human brain function that there is no difficulty finding challenges in understanding normal and pathological development.

Q: *What do you further hope to achieve?*

A: I am currently working to understand what brain developments underlie the human infant's achievement of self-regulation and how cultural devices influence that development.

---

hold that the right hemisphere may have some role in language processing. Michael Gazzaniga (1985) argues that the brain, especially the right hemisphere, is organized into relatively independent functioning units that work in parallel. According to Gazzaniga, the many discrete units of the mind operate relatively independently of the others, often outside of conscious awareness. While these various independent and often subconscious operations are taking place, the left hemisphere tries to assign interpretations to these operations. Even when the left hemisphere perceives that the individual is behaving in a way that

does not intrinsically make any particular sense, it still finds a way to assign some meaning to that behavior. In general, we resist the interpretation that our behavior is capricious; instead, we try to interpret the behavior in terms of some sensible hypothesis, even if there is none.

Some biopsychological researchers have also tried to determine whether the two hemispheres think in ways that differ from one another. Levy has found some evidence (1974) that the left hemisphere tends to process information *analytically* (piece by piece, usually in a sequence) and the right hemisphere to process it *holistically* (as a whole, all at once). At present, the specific distinctions between the right and left hemispheres are subject to alternative explanations of the findings. As always, alternative scientific interpretations of the same data make science both frustrating and exciting.

What adaptive purpose might hemispheric specialization serve?

Another way of viewing the research on the lateralization of the function of the two hemispheres may be found by studying persons who acquire languages other than spoken English. For example, work by Ursula Bellugi and colleagues (Bellugi et al., 1989; Corina et al., 1992a, 1992b; Haglund et al., 1993; Poizner et al., 1990) has shown that in native users of American Sign Language (ASL), the use of ASL is localized in the left hemisphere. However, like hearing speakers of English, when ASL signers use nonlinguistic gestures, such use seems to be localized in the right hemisphere. Similarly, their processing of nonlinguistic visuospatial information seems to be localized in the right hemisphere (Poizner et al., 1984). These findings support the view that the linguistic function of speech is localized in the left hemisphere, not the phonological nature of speech. It also appears that the visuospatial nature of nonlinguistic gestures determines their localization in the right hemisphere.

Cross-cultural research offers yet another way of looking at the localization of language as a meaningful system of communication, as contrasted with the distinctive visuospatial or sound-based symbols used for communication. In school, Japanese children study two forms of written language: *kanji*, which is based on Chinese ideographs and conveys an entire idea within each symbol; and *kana*, which is based on phonetic syllables and can be used for writing foreign words such as scientific terms. In the 1970s, Japanese researchers started wondering whether the pictorial versus the phonetic forms might be processed differently in the two hemispheres of the brain. Some concluded that Japanese children and adults process the phonetic-based kana entirely in the left hemisphere but the picture-based kanji in both the left and the right hemispheres (Shibazaki, 1983; Shimada & Otsuka, 1981; Sibitani, 1980; Tsunoda, 1979). It seems that to explore and understand the diverse abilities and functions of the human brain, researchers must study the rich diversity within the human community.

Lobes of the Cerebral Hemispheres and Cortex

Hemispheric specialization is only one way to view the various parts of the cortex. Another way to look at the cortex is to divide it into four *lobes*: frontal, parietal, temporal, and occipital (shown in Figure 3-14, at the conclusion of this section). These lobes are not distinct units but rather arbitrary anatomical regions, named for the bones of the skull lying directly over them. We are able to distinguish some local specializations among the lobes, but the lobes also interact. Roughly speaking, higher thought processes, such as abstract reasoning and motor processing, occur in the **frontal lobe,** *somatosensory* processing (sensations in the skin and muscles of the body) in the **parietal lobe,** auditory processing in the **temporal lobe,** and visual processing in the **occipital lobe.**

Sensory processing occurs in the **projection areas** where the nerves containing sensory information go to the thalamus, from which they are projected to the appropriate area in the relevant lobe. Similarly, the projection areas relay motor information downward through the spinal cord, via the PNS, to the appropriate muscles to direct their movement.

THE FAR SIDE   By GARY LARSON

"Whoa! That *was a good one! Try it, Hobbs—just poke his brain right where my finger is."*

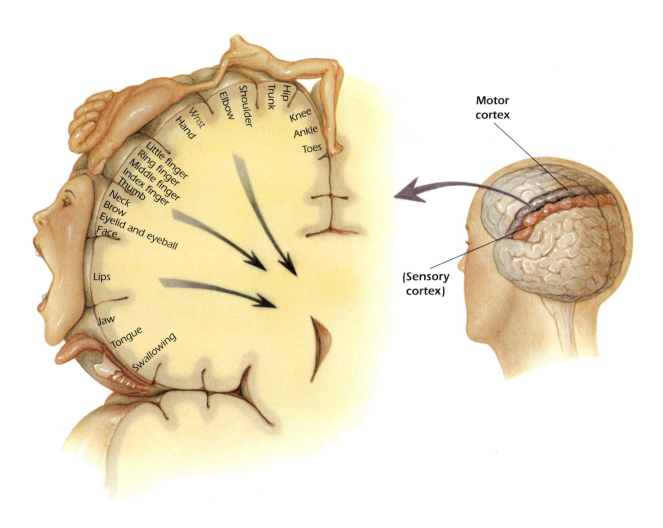

FIGURE 3-11
Homunculus of the Motor Cortex
The proportion of information received from the body's parts and sent to them can be mapped in the motor cortex of the frontal lobe.

Frontal Lobe

The frontal lobe is located toward the front of the head. It contains the **primary motor cortex,** which specializes in the planning, control, and execution of movement, particularly that involving any kind of delayed response. If your motor cortex were electrically stimulated, you would react by moving a corresponding body part, depending on where in the motor cortex your brain had been stimulated.

As with the hemispheres in general, control of the various kinds of body movements is located contralaterally on the primary motor cortex. A similar inverse mapping occurs from top to bottom, with the lower extremities of the body represented on the up-

per (toward the top of the head) side of the motor cortex, and the upper part of your body represented on the lower side of your motor cortex. Information going to neighboring parts of the body also comes from neighboring parts of the motor cortex. Thus, the motor cortex can be mapped to show where and in what proportions different parts of the body are represented in the brain. Such a map is often called a *homunculus,* which means "little person" (see Figure 3-11).

Parietal Lobe

The three other lobes are located farther away from the front of the head. These lobes specialize in vari-

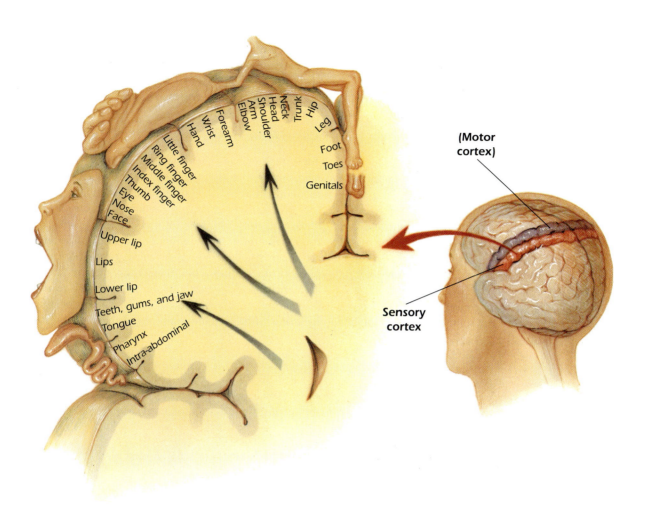

FIGURE 3-12
Homunculus of the Somatosensory Cortex
As with the motor homunculus, the proportion of sensory information received from the parts of the body can be mapped in the somatosensory cortex in the parietal lobe.

ous kinds of sensory and perceptual activity. For example, in the parietal lobe, the **primary somatosensory cortex** (located right behind the frontal lobe's primary motor cortex) receives information from the senses about pressure, texture, temperature, and pain. If your somatosensory cortex were electrically stimulated, you would probably report feeling as if you had been touched. As with the primary motor cortex in the frontal lobe, a homunculus of the somatosensory cortex maps the parts of the body from which it receives information (see Figure 3-12).

From looking at the motor and sensory homunculi, you can see that the relation of function to form applies in the development of the motor and somatosensory cortex regions: The more need we have

for use, sensitivity, and fine control in a particular body part, the larger the area of cortex generally devoted to that part. It appears that the brain has evolved such that its form relates to its function.

Temporal Lobe

The region of the cerebral cortex pertaining to hearing is located in the temporal lobe. This lobe performs complex auditory analysis, as is needed in understanding human speech or in listening to a symphony. The lobe is also specialized: Some parts are more sensitive to sounds of higher pitch, others to sounds of lower pitch. The auditory region, like the other regions we have discussed, is primarily contralateral, with processing on one side of the auditory cortex depending mostly on sensory information from the ear on the opposite side. However, both sides of the auditory area have at least some representation from each ear. If your auditory cortex were stimulated electrically, you would report having heard some sort of sound.

Occipital Lobe

The visual region of the cerebral cortex is primarily in the occipital lobe. Some nerve fibers carrying visual information travel ipsilaterally from the left eye to the left cerebral hemisphere and from the right eye to the right cerebral hemisphere; other fibers cross over the **optic chiasma** and go contralaterally to the opposite hemisphere (see Figure 3-13). In particular, nerve fibers go from the left side of the visual field for each eye to the right side of the visual cortex; complementarily, the nerves from the right side of each eye's

visual field go to the left side of the visual cortex. Electrical stimulation of the visual cortex results in the perception of random patterns of light, much like when you close your eyes and gently rub across your eyelids. (See Figure 3-14 for a summary of the cortical locations of the various lobes.)

Association Areas

The areas of the lobes that are not part of the somatosensory, motor, auditory, or visual cortices are **association areas,** which link the activity of the sensory and motor cortices. In humans, association areas make up roughly 75% of the cerebral cortex, although in most other animals the association areas are much smaller. When electrical stimulation is applied to association areas, there is no specific observable reaction. However, people with damage to their association areas often do not act, speak, or think normally. The specific abnormal behavior observed

FIGURE 3-13
Optic Nerves and Optic Chiasma
Some nerve fibers carry visual information ipsilaterally from each eye to each cerebral hemisphere; other fibers cross the optic chiasma and carry visual information contralaterally to the opposite hemisphere.

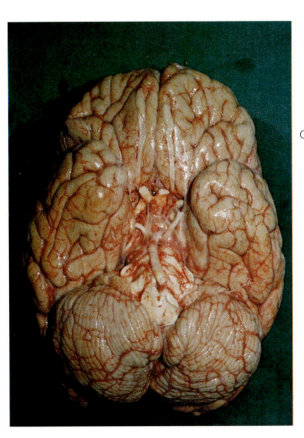

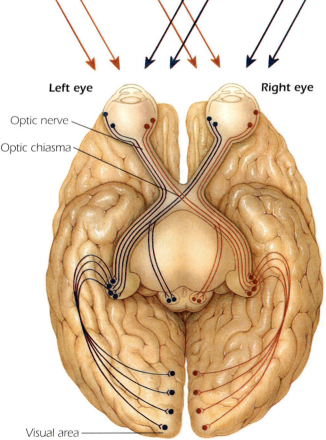

FIGURE 3-14
Lobes of the Cerebral Cortex
The cortex is divided into the frontal, parietal, temporal, and occipital lobes. The lobes have specific functions but also interact to perform complex processes.

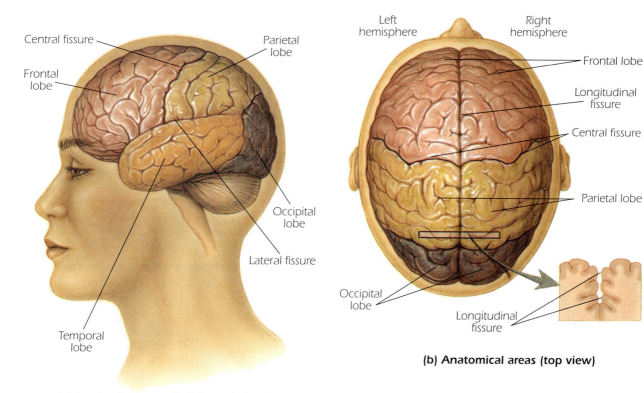

Central fissure

Frontal lobe

Parietal lobe

Occipital lobe

Lateral fissure

Temporal lobe

(a) Anatomical areas (left lateral view)

Left hemisphere

Right hemisphere

Frontal lobe

Longitudinal fissure

Central fissure

Parietal lobe

Occipital lobe

Longitudinal fissure

(b) Anatomical areas (top view)

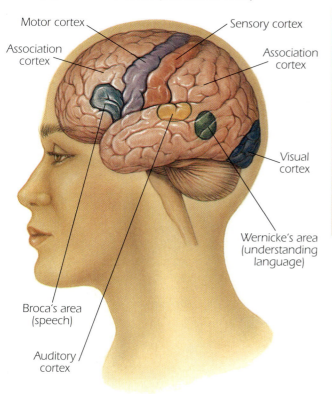

Motor cortex

Association cortex

Sensory cortex

Association cortex

Visual cortex

Wernicke's area (understanding language)

Broca's area (speech)

Auditory cortex

(c) Functional areas

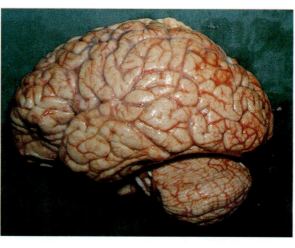

depends on the site of the damage. It seems that the association areas somehow integrate assorted pieces of information from the sensory cortices and send them on to the motor cortex, initiating purposeful behavior and expression of logical, reasoned thought.

The frontal association area in the frontal lobes seems to be crucial to problem solving, planning, judgment, and personality. In a situation calling for escape from danger, for example, people with damaged frontal lobes know that they ought to run away. Incomprehensibly, however, they may stand still, incapable of initiating flight. Broca's and Wernicke's speech areas, mentioned earlier in this chapter, are also located in association areas. Although the roles of association areas in thinking are not completely understood, these areas definitely seem to be places in the brain in which a variety of intellectual abilities are seated.

This paragraph concludes our discussion of the main *macroscopic* (big enough to be seen by the naked eye) structures of the brain and their primary functions. Given all the activities of the brain, it may not surprise you to learn that although the brain typically makes up only 2.5% (one-fortieth) of the weight of an adult human body, it uses about 20% (one-fifth) of the circulating blood, 20% of the available *glucose* (the blood sugar that supplies the body with energy), and 20% of the available oxygen. The following section describes some of the ways in which we have investigated the circulation, metabolism, structures, and functioning of the brain.

Imagine the brain of a highly adapted dinosaur living during the Paleolithic era. In what ways would you expect the dinosaur's brain to have differed from our own?

VIEWING THE STRUCTURE AND FUNCTIONING OF THE BRAIN

IN SEARCH OF...

Before you read about the various methods researchers use for investigating the structure and functioning of the brain, think about the kinds of questions that puzzle you about human behavior. Which methods might offer you the most insight into what happens in the brain to influence these puzzling behaviors?

Scientists have several means of studying the human brain. For centuries, investigators have been able to dissect a brain after a person has died (see Figures 3-8 and 3-9). Contemporary cytological, microscopic, electromicroscopic, and biochemical techniques allow scientists to study dissected portions of the brain at increasingly precise levels of detail. Broca would be delighted to know how much we are learning about the causes of diseases and psychological disorders of the brain as a result of these sophisticated studies of the microanatomy of the brain.

As valuable as such studies have been and continue to be, scientists are not content merely to study the state of dead brains. An organ characterized by constant dynamic activity seems to cry out for methods to study it *in vivo* (within living organisms). The methods available today far surpass early attempts to learn from electrical stimulation of the nervous system.

The electrical activity of the entire living brain can be measured by the tried and true method of using electrodes to obtain an **electroencephalogram**—an **EEG.** For EEGs, electrodes establish contact between the brain and a source that sums and records brain activity over large areas containing many neurons. Usually, electrodes are attached directly to the scalp; sometimes, however, microelectrodes are inserted into the brain. The former technique is used with humans, the latter with animals. In either case, the minute quantifiable fluctuations of electrical activity picked up by the electrodes are amplified, and an oscilloscope displays the amplified electrical activity as up or down fluctuations of waves. (Often, now, computer screens are used instead of oscilloscopes.) The graphic display of the electrical wave patterns in-

FIGURE 3-15
Electroencephalograms (EEGs)
EEGs record electrical activity and translate the data into wave patterns.

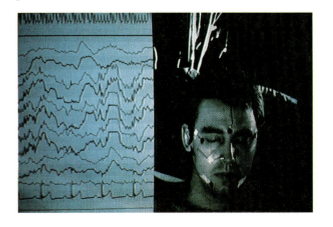

Searchers . . .   *B R E N D A   A .   M I L N E R*

Brenda A. Milner received a ScD in psychobiology. She is Dorothy J. Killam Professor at the Montreal Neurological Institute, McGill University.

Q: *How did you become interested in psychology?*

A: Well, it was a matter of good luck. I went to Cambridge University in mathematics, but I wanted to do something that was scientific as well as logical. I read Carl Murchison's handbook of psychology and found it interesting. As soon as I got in the lab, I was really very interested. I took to it like a duck to water. The psychology department at Cambridge was very experimental, but very biological in its orientation.

I moved to Montreal with my husband and pursued a degree at McGill. At this point, Don Hebb came to McGill with his book *The Organization of Behavior* in manuscript. I attended that first Hebb seminar, along with many other people that you know about. Hebb had spent a year or so at the Neurological Institute with Wilder Penfield, who was pioneering surgery for epilepsy. Hebb had extracted from Penfield the promise that if he ever came back to McGill, he would be allowed to send one student up to study Penfield's patients. And so he asked me if I would like to come up here to do my thesis. Again it was love at first sight. I have stayed here ever since.

Q: *What theories have influenced you the most?*

A: First of all, Bartlett's ideas about the notion that memory is not a reproductive, but a constructive process. I was also interested in perception in those days. Of course, the enormous influence on so many of us was Hebb, a towering figure.

Q: *What is your greatest asset as a psychologist?*

A: I'm very empirical; I'm not a theoretician. I think my asset is an enormous curiosity.

Q: *How do you get your ideas for research?*

A: I get them empirically. One of the things that has always helped my thinking enormously has been research with monkeys, the lesion work with monkeys. I was not, myself, working with monkeys, but I was intrigued by the role of the temporal cortex in vision.

Q: *What kind of obstacles, if any, have you experienced in your work?*

A: The only obstacles I had were very early in my life. I had very little money, and scholarships in England in the 1930s were few and far between. That was probably the only time in my life when being a woman was a handicap. I had to be very competitive. After that, the obstacles have been more like challenges that you meet along the way.

Q: *What is your major contribution to psychology?*

A: I suppose my major contribution has been the study of amnesia, the description of the syndromes. I showed that patients with left frontal lesions, although their verbal memory and other aspects of their verbal intelligence were fine, had a severe impairment in word fluency.

Q: *What advice would you give to someone starting in the field of psychology?*

A: I think experimental psychology is a very good discipline, so I would recommend a really good grounding in general experimental psychology. People should also know quite a bit about the brain—take a few CNS courses and not just read about neuroscience in a textbook. Know what the brain is.

Also, it is not going to be one exciting discovery after another. There is a lot of grind in science, and researchers have to work extremely hard and be very meticulous in their observations, because the results are only as good as the data.

Q: *How do you keep yourself academically challenged?*

A: It's not a problem because I'm living in an environment where all the time we work very closely with people in neuro-imaging. The Neurological Institute is a big center for interest in brain-behavior relations. Being in an institute like this with ties to the department of psychology is a very exciting environment.

Q: *What do you further hope to achieve?*

A: We are using PET and MRI scans to conduct experiments with normal, volunteer subjects, not patients. I am still working with patients, but also with normal subjects on cognitive activation during the performance of some tasks. It's an enormous challenge. It's in its infancy, this kind of thing.

---

dicates different levels and kinds of brain activity (see Figure 3-15).

The use of EEG measurement has been particularly helpful for the study of mental functioning, especially sleep, awareness, and brain disease. EEGs also have supported the notion of hemispheric localization discussed earlier. For example, more activity occurs in the left hemisphere during a verbal task, more in the right hemisphere during a spatial task (Kosslyn, 1988; Springer & Deutsch, 1985).

EEG measurement is problematic, however, because it is a *hash recording*. It measures the electrical activity of many different large areas in the brain at once, so it is hard to sort out exactly where particular wave forms are originating. For this reason, investigators have turned to the use of **evoked potentials** (EPs), which are measured by averaging wave forms on successive EEG recordings. In other words, an EP is an EEG recording in which at least some of the electrical interference has been averaged out of the data (see Figure 3-16). Evoked potentials have been used to map which parts of the brain are active and to what degree, in response to familiar and unfamiliar stimuli. It has been proposed that the more intelligent a person is, the less his or her brain is active when encountering familiar stimuli, and the more it is active when processing new and unusual stimuli (Haier et al., 1988, 1992; Schafer, 1982).

Despite many intriguing EEG and EP findings, the EEG and the EP provide only a limited understanding of various structures of the brain. We need some way of getting a picture of how a living, functioning person's brain is working. Fortunately, advances in technology have made it possible to observe the functioning of the brain with little discomfort to the patient. The photos and illustrations in this section show several of the many ways of viewing the brain.

For most of the twentieth century, *neuroscientists* (psychologists and other scientists interested in studying the nervous system) have been able to take various kinds of snapshots of the living brain. The first of these techniques uses *X rays*, a type of electromagnetic radiation capable of passing through solids, which yields a two-dimensional picture of the varying densities of the structures that have been scanned. Unfortunately, however, the density of most portions of the brain is roughly the same, so X-ray photos of the head are useful for showing skull fractures but little else that would be of concern to psychologists.

Angiograms are essentially X-ray pictures that have been enhanced by injecting special dyes into the blood vessels of the head, to provide some visual contrast. Angiograms are usually used to assess *vascular* diseases (diseases of the blood vessels, which may lead to strokes) and to locate particular kinds of brain tumors, but they can also indicate which parts of the brain are active when people perform different kinds of listening, speaking, or movement tasks (see Figure 3-17a). Thus, angiograms provide dynamic information about the living brain, although this information focuses mostly on the blood vessels.

As you might infer from the brain's extraordinarily great use of the nutrients and oxygen in the blood, any disturbance in the blood supply is dangerous. Impairment of the blood supply (due to clots, narrowed vessels, or hemorrhage) leads to stroke, which usually causes immediate changes in consciousness. If the blood supply is impaired for any length of time, the surrounding tissue begins to die. The potentially devastating implications of stroke depend on the duration of the stroke and the area of the brain affected.

FIGURE 3-16
Evoked Potential (EP)

An EP is a series of EEG recordings in which the variability of electrical interference has been averaged out of the data. The colored line here is averaged from the many recordings shown beneath it.

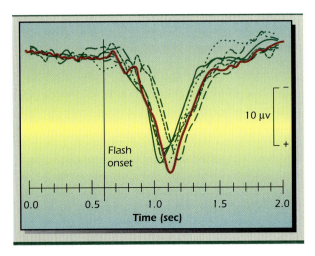

Louis Pasteur suffered a mild stroke at age 46 years, but he continued to make important contributions until additional strokes had disabled him by age 65. Both Vladimir Lenin and Woodrow Wilson suffered strokes at crucial moments in the history of their countries. At the Yalta conference, toward the end of World War II, Winston Churchill, Franklin Roosevelt, and Josef Stalin were all experiencing severely impaired blood flow in their brains as they considered how to divide the world into their respective spheres of influence. (Caplan, 1993)

When clinicians and researchers try to detect strokes or other physiological bases for disorders, they often use a more sophisticated X-ray-based technique for viewing the brain: the **computerized axial tomogram** *(CAT scan)*. The picture a CAT scan generates shows a cross-sectional slice of the brain (see Figure 3-17b). In this procedure, a patient lies on a

FIGURE 3-17
Images of the Brain

Researchers and physicians use various techniques to identify and diagnose the structures and processes of the brain. (a) A brain angiogram highlights the blood vessels of the brain. (b) CAT-scan images show a three-dimensional view of brain structures. (c) A rotating series of MRI scans shows a clearer three-dimensional picture of brain structures than CAT scans show. (d) PET scans permit the study of brain physiology.

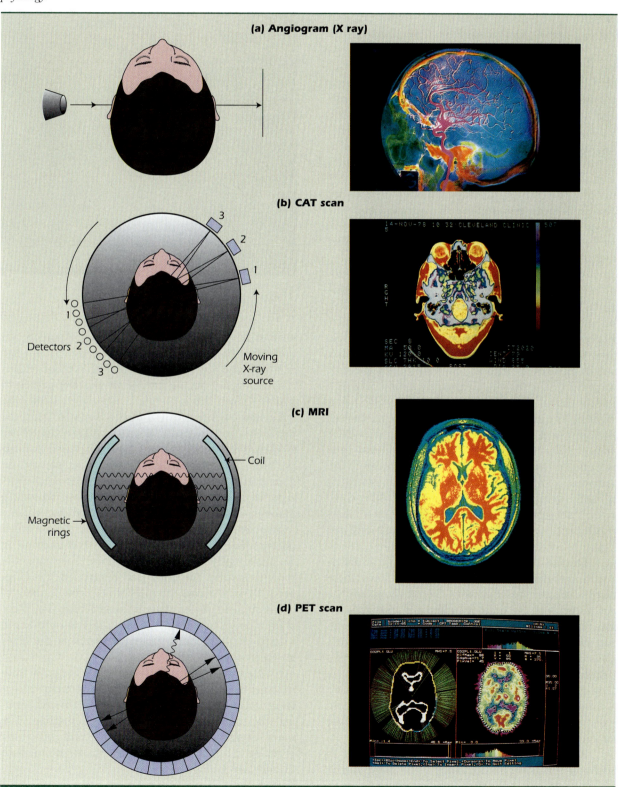

table with his or her head in the middle of a dough-nut-shaped ring that takes and analyzes X-ray pictures. The ring takes the pictures as it rotates 360 degrees around the patient's head. Thus, small amounts of X rays penetrate the head from many angles. Opposite the sources of the X rays in the ring are detectors recording the amount of X-ray radiation reaching them. This amount is determined by the density of tissue at various locations in the head—that is, the more dense the material through which the X rays must pass, the smaller the amount of X-ray radiation reaching the detectors. A computer then analyzes the amount of radiation reaching each of the detectors and thereby constructs a three-dimensional X-ray picture of a cross-section of the brain, which is far more revealing than would be obtained if the pictures were being taken from a single position only (see Figure 3-17b). CAT scans are often used to detect blood clots, tumors, or brain diseases, but they are also used by neuropsychologists to study how particular types and locations of brain damage affect people's behavior.

An even more sophisticated technique for revealing the structure of the brain is **magnetic resonance imaging** (*MRI*; also sometimes termed NMR, for nuclear magnetic resonance). The MRI scanner resembles a CAT scanner and reveals much of the same information, except that it uses no radiation, and its pictures are clearer and more detailed. With the patient lying down, an extremely strong magnetic field is passed through the part of the body being studied. The magnet changes the orbits of nuclear particles in the molecules of the body, and these changes (bursts of energy) are registered over time and analyzed by computer. Different molecules in the body react differently to the magnetic field as a result of their composition and environments. The computer then generates a highly precise, three-dimensional picture based on the molecular variations (see Figure 3-17c).

Despite the usefulness of the highly sophisticated snapshots offered by CAT and MRI scans, these images are static and anatomical. They show how the various parts of the brain look and are arranged, but they do not show how these parts of the brain function dynamically. In fact, X rays, CAT scans, and MRI scans cannot distinguish a dynamic living brain from a static dead one. Yet because moving pictures have been around since about the time that X rays were discovered, it is only natural that scientists would eventually devise a way to take moving pictures of the physiology of the brain.

A breakthrough in taking such pictures is **positron emission tomography** (*PET scan*), which

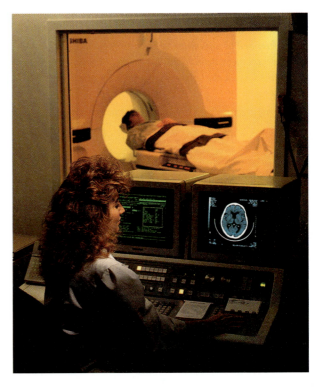

A lab technician gives a patient a CAT scan.

enables us to see the brain in action. A mildly radioactive form of glucose is injected into a patient and is absorbed by cells of the body. The amount of glucose absorption in the brain indicates the degree to which a given cell is metabolically active. While the irradiated glucose is going to the person's brain, the person's head is placed in a ring similar to that of the CAT scanner, and a beam of X rays is passed through the head. The radioactive substance is detected by the scanners. A computer then determines which portions of the brain have absorbed the most radioactive glucose, thereby determining the areas that are the most active. PET scans have been used to show which parts of the brain are active in such tasks as listening to music, playing computer games, speaking, and moving parts of the body (see Figure 3-17d). Thus, the PET scan shows the physiological functioning of the brain, not just its anatomical structure. The PET scan offers dynamic insights into the brain previously offered only by cruder techniques such as the EEG and the angiogram.

New technology for viewing the brain is even now being developed. One of the latest techniques is *optical imaging*, which uses fiber-optic light and a special camera attached to a surgical microscope. The many imaging techniques that are now becoming available are shedding new light on the brain, both literally and metaphorically.

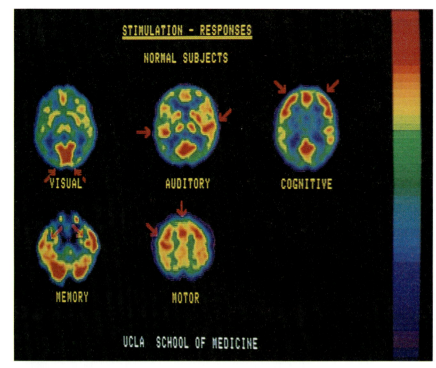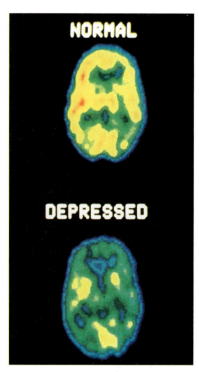

FIGURE 3-18
PET Scan Images
Images from PET scans show different metabolic processes in reaction to different activities and stimuli.

Now that we know a little about how to see the macrolevel anatomy and physiology of the brain, and we have some insight into what, how, and whether it is processing information, we can turn to the microlevel anatomy and physiology for processing information in the brain, and even throughout the entire nervous system.

> What kinds of questions might we answer through PET scans that we cannot answer through CAT scans or MRI scans?

INFORMATION PROCESSING IN THE NERVOUS SYSTEM

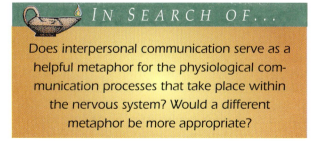

IN SEARCH OF...

Does interpersonal communication serve as a helpful metaphor for the physiological communication processes that take place within the nervous system? Would a different metaphor be more appropriate?

Structural Components: Neurons and Glial Cells

Neurons

To understand how the entire nervous system processes information, we first need to examine the structure of the cells—*neurons*—and the bundles of neurons—*nerves*—that constitute the nervous system. Neurons are of three types, which serve three different kinds of functions: sensory neurons, motor neurons, and interneurons.

THREE FUNCTIONS OF NEURONS. **Sensory neurons** receive information from the environment. They connect with *receptor cells* that detect physical or chemical changes in the sensory organs, including the skin, ears, tongue, eyes, nose, muscles, joints, and internal organs. Sensory neurons carry information away from the sensory receptor cells and *toward* the spinal cord or brain. **Motor neurons** carry information *away from* the spinal cord and the brain and toward the body parts that are supposed to respond to the information in some way. Both motor neurons and sensory neurons are part of the PNS. For example, motor and sensory neurons send information to and from the intestines (through the autonomic nervous system) or to and from the toe muscles (through the somatic nervous system).

Interneurons, as the name implies, serve as intermediaries between sensory and motor neurons. They receive signals from either sensory neurons or other interneurons, and they send signals either to other interneurons or to motor neurons. In complex organisms such as humans, the large majority of neurons are interneurons. In the spinal reflex discussed earlier in this chapter, an interneuron located in the spinal cord might act as an intermediary between the incoming sensory neuron, carrying the message, "Burning hand on stove!" and the outgoing motor neuron, carrying the message, "Move that hand!" Another interneuron sends the incoming message via the spinal cord to the brain, which interprets the incoming message as pain and more deliberately determines what to do about the situation.

PARTS OF THE NEURON.   Neurons vary in their structure, but almost all neurons have four basic parts, as shown in the assorted neurons of Figure 3-19: a soma (cell body), dendrites, an axon, and terminal buttons. We discuss each part in turn, as well as the important junction between neurons—the synapse.

The **soma,** which contains the *nucleus* (center portion, which performs metabolic and reproductive functions for the cell), is responsible for the life of the nerve cell. Together, the **dendrites** and the soma receive communications from other cells via distinctive receptors on their external membranes. The **axon** responds to the information received by the dendrites and soma; the axon can transmit the information through the neuron until it reaches a place where it can be transmitted to other neurons through the release of chemical substances. The axon is a long, thin tube, which can divide and branch many times at its *terminus* (end).

Axons are of two basic kinds, in approximately equal proportions in the human nervous system (see Figure 3-19). The key distinction between the two kinds of axons is the presence or absence of *myelin*, a white fatty substance. One kind of axon is *myelinated*, surrounded by a **myelin sheath,** which insulates and protects the axon from electrical interference by other neurons in the area. The myelin sheath also speeds up the conduction of information along the axon. In fact, transmission in myelinated axons can reach 100 meters per second (equal to about 224 miles per hour), or even more. Myelin is not distributed continuously along the axon, but rather in segments, which are broken up by **nodes of Ranvier**—small gaps in the myelin coating along the

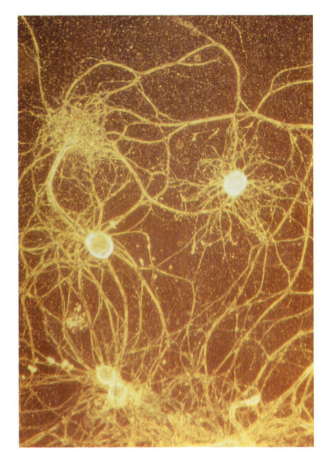

FIGURE 3-19
Neurons
The shape of a neuron is determined by its function. Each neuron, however, has the same structure: soma, dendrites, axon, and terminal buttons.

axon. The specific structure and role of these nodes is described more fully a little later in this chapter.

The second kind of axon lacks the myelin coat altogether. Typically, these axons are smaller and shorter than the myelinated ones, so they do not need the increased conduction velocity of a lengthy, myelinated axon. In unmyelinated axons, conduction is much slower, sometimes as relatively sluggish as 5 meters per second. (On the other hand, most of us would be lucky to be able to run that fast!)

The **terminal buttons** are small knobs found at the ends of the branches of an axon. The terminal buttons of the axon do not directly touch the dendrites of the next neuron. Rather, a very small gap, the **synapse,** exists between the terminal buttons of one neuron and the dendrites (or sometimes the soma) of the next neuron (see Figure 3-20). To send a message, the terminal buttons of the presynaptic neuron release a **neurotransmitter,** a chemical messenger, across the synaptic gap to the receptor sites of the receiving dendrites or soma of the postsynaptic neuron.

In sum, information transmission within a neuron usually starts at the dendrites, which receive a neurotransmitter from another neuron's axonic terminal buttons at the synapse. The information goes to the soma, is processed, and travels down the axon. Transmission in the neuron ends at the terminal buttons, which release a neurotransmitter into the synapse; the neurotransmitter then reaches one or more (usually more) neurons and continues the line of communication.

Now that you have an idea of the structure and function of neurons, it might help to give you an idea of their number and size. The number of neurons in the human nervous system is estimated at more than 100 billion (100,000,000,000). (If a team of scientists were to count 3 neurons per second, it would take them more than 1,000 years to count them all.) For the most part, these neurons are irreplaceable, at least in adults; once the neuron's soma dies, the neuron is gone forever. However, as long as the soma continues to live, the remaining stumps of damaged (e.g., cut) but living neurons can sometimes regenerate new ax-

ons, although this process is more successful in the PNS than in the CNS.

Neuronal size is more difficult to quantify in absolute terms. The soma of the neuron ranges in diameter from about 5 to about 100 microns (thousandths of a millimeter, or millionths of a meter). Dendrites, too, are relatively small, generally a few hundred microns in length. Axons, however, can vary considerably in length. Some axons are as short as a few hundred microns (in fact, some neurons in the eye and elsewhere have virtually indistinguishable axons), but the axons of some of the longer motor neurons can extend all the way from the head to the base of the spinal cord, and from the spinal cord to the fingers and the toes. In relative terms, visualize an orange attached to a long wire stretching the length of 240 football fields (roughly 14 miles); this metaphor roughly parallels the soma and axon of some of the long spinal neurons.

Glial Cells

Neurons are not the only kind of cell in the nervous system. Rather, they constitute about 10% of the cells

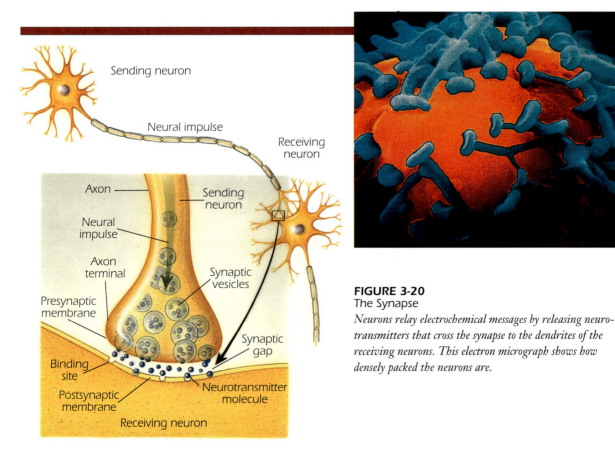

FIGURE 3-20
The Synapse
Neurons relay electrochemical messages by releasing neurotransmitters that cross the synapse to the dendrites of the receiving neurons. This electron micrograph shows how densely packed the neurons are.

in the CNS (Groves & Rebec, 1988). In the CNS, the neurons are supported by the all-purpose **glial cells** (also termed *neuroglia*). Glial cells, in part, function as a kind of glue to hold the CNS together, and more specifically, to hold the neurons in their proper places, keeping them at optimal distances from one another and from other structures in the body. Thus, glial cells help to ensure that signals do not get crossed. Some of the glial cells also assist in forming the myelin sheath; in fact, the nodes in the sheath are actually the gaps between glial cells.

Glial cells nourish the neurons of the CNS and also dispose of waste. They destroy and eliminate neurons that have died either through injury or age. The dead neurons are then often replaced with new glial cells. Destruction of glial cells, which can be caused by disease, can result in serious breakdowns in communication within the nervous system. Messages become scrambled as they cross through uncharted territory: The insulating myelin sheaths deteriorate, dead neurons and other waste accumulate and clutter the neural landscape, and inadequate nourishment impedes normal cell function and repair of damaged tissue.

Conduction of Information Within Neurons

Neuronal communication is basically of two kinds: intraneuronal and interneuronal. We consider communication within neurons first. Communication within the neuron is *electrochemical*—that is, interactions involving chemicals having positive or negative electrical charges. Each neuron contains *ions* (electrically charged chemical particles). If the concentrations of the various ions inside and outside the neuron always remained in a *static equilibrium* (a perfect balance, with no changes inside or outside the neuron), intraneuronal communication would never occur. In living organisms, however, change is constant. Ongoing electrical activity within the body stimulates changes in the concentrations of ions inside and outside the neuron, which in turn affects the functioning of the neuron.

Because of the tremendous amount of fluctuating electrical activity going on in our bodies every moment of our lives, our neurons must be somewhat selective in reacting to the electrical activity. If our neurons reacted to every slight fluctuation, utter chaos would result in a Byzantine tangle of electrical impulses slushing through mires of neurotransmitters sending incomprehensible messages. To avoid this pandemonium, electrical charges of most levels of intensity and frequency produce virtually no effect in the neuron at all. However, once a charge reaches or surpasses a certain level, the neuron's **threshold of excitation,** the neuron reacts quite differently (see Figure 3-21). At or above its threshold, an **action potential** is generated, and positively and negatively charged ions quickly flood across the neuronal membrane, changing the electrochemical balance inside and outside the neuron. The specific threshold of excitation that is required for a given neuron's action potential differs for the various neurons. When an action potential occurs, the neuron "fires."

It is the action potential that carries impulses through the axon, from one end to the other. Action potentials are *all or none*. Either the electrical charge is strong enough to generate an action potential, or it is not. Once the threshold is reached, the charge will travel all the way down the axon without losing strength.

You might compare the firing of a neuron to a sneeze. In order to generate a sneeze, the membranes of your nose must be tickled beyond a certain point by some outside irritant. If you are like most people, once that tickle threshold has been crossed, it is an all-or-none process—you will definitely sneeze, just as a neuron will definitely fire once its threshold level has been reached.

Now suppose that the neuron has just fired, and that another strong electrical charge has again reached the axon. Will the neuron fire? It will not. As long as the dynamic equilibrium of the ions inside and outside the neuron has not yet returned to normal after firing, the neuron cannot reach its action potential again. At this point—the **absolute refractory phase**—no matter how strong the stimulus is, the neuron cannot fire again. After the absolute refractory phase, some of the dynamic equilibrium of ions begins to return to normal, and the neuron reaches a **relative refractory phase,** in which the neuron can fire, but only in response to a stronger stimulus than would typically be necessary. Finally, after the dynamic equilibrium of ions has returned to normal, the neuron regains its usual sensitivity to electrochemical stimulation for reaching its action potential. Functionally, the refractory phases prevent the organism from overstimulation of individual neurons and from exhaustion of neural capacity as a whole.

Recall that myelin serves as an insulator and speeds up transmission of nerve impulses. In addition, conduction speed increases as the diameter of the axon increases. Motor neurons in control of supplying quick and constant power to arms and legs, for example, are generally thick and myelinated. On the other hand, neurons to the stomach muscles are mostly small in diameter and unmyelinated, because the digestive process usually does not require speed. Thus, form follows function.

Ironically, part of the reason myelin helps to speed up neural transmission is that there *are* gaps (nodes of Ranvier) in the myelin sheath. That is, electrochemical impulses save time by leaping across the myelin sheath, to be reconstructed anew at each uncoated node of Ranvier.

To summarize, transmission of information occurs within a neuron through the propagation of all-or-none action potentials along an axon. The potentials are set off by an electrical current at or beyond the neuron's threshold of excitation. This process sets in motion a complex electrochemical reaction that transmits the message down the neuron. Propagation of impulses is especially rapid in myelinated axons.

FIGURE 3-21
Action Potential

When electrochemical stimulation reaches a neuron's threshold of excitation, the neuron generates an action potential. During an action potential, ions swiftly cross the membrane of the neuron.

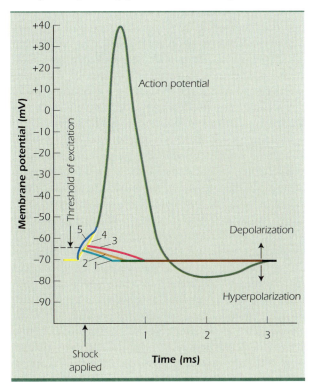

Communication Between Neurons

Up to now, we have discussed how chemical information is transmitted within a neuron (via chemicals sent from the soma to the axon and other chemicals picked up from the axon). Intraneuronal communication is essential for each neuron to work effectively, but the work of each individual neuron would be for naught if there were no way for neurons to communicate with one another.

We already know *where* (in the synapse) and *when* (whenever an action potential triggers release of a neurotransmitter) neurons communicate. We even know *what* (neurotransmitters) they use for communicating. We just need to know a little more about *how* they do so. Stated simply, here is how it works (see Figure 3-20):

1. One neuron ("Neuron A") releases a neurotransmitter from its terminal buttons.
2. The neurotransmitter crosses the synapse and reaches the receptors in the dendrites (or soma) of another neuron ("Neuron B").
3. The dendrites of Neuron B are stimulated by the neurotransmitters Neuron B receives from Neuron A until Neuron B reaches its own distinctive threshold of excitation.
4. At Neuron B's threshold of excitation, the Neuron B action potential travels down its axon.
5. When Neuron B's action potential reaches Neuron B's terminal buttons, Neuron B releases its own neurotransmitter into the next synapse (perhaps with Neuron C), and so on.

In practice, it is not really that simple. For one thing, at any given synapse, there are usually multiple, often hundreds, of connections among neurons, with dendritic trees branching out to receive messages from many axons (see Figure 3-20). Furthermore, on the receiving membranes of each postsynaptic neuron are numerous receptor sites for neurotransmitters. Neuroscientists have devised a useful, descriptive metaphor for the interaction of neurotransmitters and receptors. The distinctive molecular shape of a given receptor may be viewed as a keyhole, and the distinctive molecular shape of a given neurotransmitter may be viewed as a key (Restak, 1984). When the shape of the key matches the shape of the keyhole, the receptor responds.

Another complication of interneuronal communication is that differing receptor sites respond distinctively. Many receptors are *excited* by the neurotransmitters they contact in the synapse, thereby *increasing* the likelihood that the postsynaptic neurons will reach their threshold of excitation. Other receptors, however, are actually *inhibited* by the neurotransmitters they receive, thereby *decreasing* the probability that the postsynaptic neurons will reach their threshold of excitation.

That is, for a given neurotransmitter, certain receptor sites on some neurons may be excited, whereas certain other receptor sites on other neurons may be inhibited. Excitatory receptors on the postsynaptic neurons excite the neuron's response, and inhibitory receptors inhibit the neuron's response. To make matters even more complicated, although each neuron is equipped to release only one particular neurotransmitter, the terminal buttons of some neurons also release other chemical substances, called **neuromodulators,** which serve to enhance or to diminish the responsivity of the postsynaptic neuron, either by directly affecting the axon or by affecting the sensitivity of the receptor sites.

To summarize, myriad presynaptic neurons are releasing neurotransmitters and neuromodulators into the synapse. Some of the receptors of the postsynaptic neuron are being excited, and others are being inhibited. Furthermore, the degree of excitation or inhibition is being influenced by the actions of the neuromodulators, which either enhance or diminish the responsivity of the postsynaptic neurons. In order for the postsynaptic neuron to fire, the overall balance of excitatory and inhibitory responses must reach the neuron's threshold level of excitation. When you think about all that is involved in getting one neuron to fire, it seems a miracle that any of us can think at all. In fact, however, the time it takes for a given message to cross the synapse can be as little as half a millisecond, although it can take as long as a second or more.

Given the tremendous volume of neurotransmitters and neuromodulators spilling into each synapse, it makes sense that not all the chemical messengers released by axons can be neatly absorbed by the dendrites. What, then, happens to the unused transmitter chemicals? Fortunately, our bodies have two mechanisms for dealing with this problem.

The first and more common mechanism is **reuptake,** in which the terminal button of an axon reabsorbs (takes up again) the chemical transmitter that it released into the synapse. The next cell is thereby spared excessive stimulation, and the neuron that released the substance can store it for future use. The second, less common, mechanism is *enzymatic deactivation;* in this process, an *enzyme* (a protein that *catalyzes*—brings about—chemical reactions) breaks apart the neurotransmitter or neuromodulator, thereby making it inactive (deactivated).

Common Neurotransmitters and Neuromodulators

Although scientists already know of more than 50 chemical substances involved in neurotransmission, it seems likely that we have yet to identify all of them. Medical and psychological researchers are working to discover and understand these chemical substances and how they interact with drugs, foods, moods, abilities, and perceptions. Although we know quite a bit about the mechanics of impulse transmission in nerves, we still know relatively little about how the nervous system's chemical activity relates to psychological states. Despite the limits on present knowledge, however, we have gained some insight into how several of these substances affect our psychological functioning.

The key neurotransmitters, often termed the "classical neurotransmitters" because they were among the first neurotransmitters discovered, are acetylcholine, which is synthesized from the choline in our diet; dopamine, epinephrine, and norepinephrine, which are synthesized from dietary tyrosine; and serotonin, which is synthesized from dietary tryptophan.

In the brain, **acetylcholine**—*ACh*—excites the neuronal receptor sites. ACh has been found in the hippocampus (see the previous discussion of the forebrain), and it may therefore be involved in memory (Squire, 1987). Researchers are currently trying to find out whether ACh is somehow blocked from action in the brains of people with *Alzheimer's disease* (an illness that causes devastating losses of memory). ACh is also found in various sites throughout the body, where it can excite the PNS to cause contraction of the skeletal muscles, leading to movement, or it can inhibit the neurons in the muscles of the heart.

Dopamine (DA) seems to influence several important activities, including movement, attention, and learning. In *Parkinson's disease*, a particular group of neurons that produces dopamine degenerates; this degeneration is associated with tremors, rigidity of limbs, and difficulty in balance (James Murphy, personal communication, September 1993). Dopamine-producing neurons synthesize dopamine through enzyme actions: One enzyme adds a chemical ingredient to tyrosine, to form l-dopa, and then another enzyme removes a different chemical constituent from l-dopa, to form dopamine. Unfortunately, there is no easy way to get dopamine to the brain; but physicians have been able to give Parkinson's sufferers synthetic l-dopa, which is rapidly converted by the remaining dopamine-producing neurons to produce more dopamine. Although most receptors for dopamine are inhibitory, some of the receptors are excitatory. Unfortunately, it is possible to get too much of a good neurotransmitter: Schizophrenia appears to be associated with the release of too much dopamine. Similarly, overdoses of l-dopa in the treatment of Parkinson's disease can result in over-production of dopamine, which can lead to symptoms of schizophrenia. Two other substances that can serve as neurotransmitters are produced by further synthesis of tyrosine: norepinephrine and epinephrine, which appear to be involved in the regulation of alertness.

Serotonin (5-HT) appears to be related to arousal and sleep, as well as to regulation of mood, appetite, and sensitivity to pain. Although serotonin has an excitatory effect on a few receptor sites, it is usually an inhibitory neurotransmitter, and its behavioral outcomes are generally inhibitory. Among other actions, serotonin acts to inhibit dreaming. The mood-altering drug lysergic acid diethylamide (LSD) inhibits the actions of serotonin; LSD can accumulate in the brain and overstimulate nerve cells, leading to feelings of well-being but also to hallucinations—in effect, waking dreams. (The ways in which drugs disrupt neurotransmitter activity are discussed in more detail in Chapter 6.)

Other primary neurotransmitters are glutamate (glutamic acid), aspartate, and glycine. Also included in this group is gamma-aminobutyric acid (GABA), which is synthesized from glutamate by the simple removal of one chemical constituent. These neurotransmitters are particularly interesting because they appear to have both a specific neurotransmission effect, acting on specific neuronal receptor sites, and more general neuromodulating effects. For example, glutamate seems to have direct excitatory effects on the axons of postsynaptic neurons, thereby lowering the threshold of excitation, and GABA seems to have direct inhibitory effects on axons, thereby increasing the threshold of excitation. Imbalances in the amino-acid neurotransmitters have been linked to seizures, Huntington's chorea (an inherited neurological disorder), and the fatal effects of tetanus.

The preceding description—as complex as it may seem—drastically oversimplifies the intricacies of the neuronal communication that constantly takes place in our brains. Such complexities make it difficult to understand what is happening in the normal brain when we are thinking, feeling, and interacting with our environments. In addition to sharing our intellectual curiosity about these processes, many researchers feel compelled to understand the normal information processes of the brain in order to figure out what is going wrong in the brains of persons affected by neurological and psychological disorders. Perhaps if we can understand what has gone awry—what chemicals are out of balance—we can figure out how to put things back into balance by providing needed neurotransmitters or by inhibiting the effects of overabundant neurotransmitters.

Communication with the Bloodstream: The Blood–Brain Barrier

The ways in which neurotransmitters and other chemicals can affect the brain raise an intriguing question for biological psychologists: Is there any way for the brain to screen out undesirable substances, to protect itself from harm? The hard shell of our skull helps to minimize the harm from external assaults to our brains. For internal assaults that might come through our bloodstream, our physiology has come up with a somewhat more subtle barrier. Rather than having a single large vessel that carries blood directly to our brains, the blood that goes to our brains must pass through a network of tiny capillaries that screens out many substances, but that lets other substances pass through quite easily. For example, it screens out large water-soluble molecules, such as complex proteins and microorganisms, but it lets glucose and other small water-soluble molecules, as well as most fat-soluble molecules, pass through this **blood–brain barrier** rather easily.

In general, this system is reasonably effective in keeping most undesirable substances from reaching the brain, and it lets most desirable substances reach the brain quickly and easily. Like other mechanisms in the body, however, it is miraculously clever, but not perfect. The blood–brain barrier sometimes frustrates *psychopharmacologists* (psychologists interested in the ways in which drugs affect psychological processes) in their attempts to study the effects of drugs that do not readily pass through the barrier (see Chapter 6). In addition, if psychopharmacologists and others discover drugs that might minimize the devastation of brain disorders, they must then figure out how to transport these drugs past the blood–brain barrier.

The protective function of the blood–brain barrier also works both ways: Substances that should not reach the brain generally do not reach it, and substances in the brain that should not reach the body are prevented from doing so. In fact, one theory of the way in which people develop multiple sclerosis is that a virus damages the blood–brain barrier, thereby enabling protein constituents of myelin from the brain to enter the body's bloodstream. The body recognizes the protein as a foreign substance, and the immune system then forms antibodies against the myelin protein. This intrusion results in an *autoimmune reaction* (the body's defense system attacks the body itself) whereby the body attacks myelin in the CNS. As the myelin is destroyed, messages within the CNS become jumbled, resulting in sensory and motor disorders.

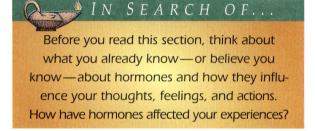

How might we use what we know about communication in the nervous system to enhance systems for people who need to communicate with one another?

THE ENDOCRINE SYSTEM

IN SEARCH OF...

Before you read this section, think about what you already know—or believe you know—about hormones and how they influence your thoughts, feelings, and actions. How have hormones affected your experiences?

Under most circumstances, the nervous system does an excellent job of communicating sensory information to our brains and motor information from our brains to our muscles. The nervous system is particularly effective in communicating specific informa-

tion speedily, so that we can respond immediately to our environments. Sometimes, however, our bodies use an alternative mode of communication. This other communication network is the **endocrine system** (secreting or releasing inside), which operates by means of **glands** (groups of cells that secrete a substance). (Actually, our bodies also have an *exocrine system*, by which some glands can secrete substances [e.g., tears or sweat] through *ducts* [physiological channels].) Endocrine glands release their chemical products directly into the bloodstream. The blood then carries the secreted substances to the target organ or organs.

Hormones and the Brain

The chemical substances secreted by endocrine-system glands are **hormones,** which foster the growth and proliferation of cells. In some cases, hormones affect the way a cell goes about its activities. Hormones perform their work either by interacting with receptors on the surfaces of target cells or by entering target cells directly and interacting with specialized receptor molecules inside the cells. Some parallels exist between neurotransmitters and hormones: Hormones are chemical substances operating within a communications network, which are secreted by one set of cells (i.e., the glands), and then communicate a message to another set of cells (i.e., the target organ or organs). Also, the specific actions of the chemicals

FIGURE 3-22
Negative-Feedback Loop
Through a negative-feedback loop, an endocrine gland monitors the levels of hormones in the bloodstream. If the monitoring processes yield negative responses (feedback), the hormone secretion continues.

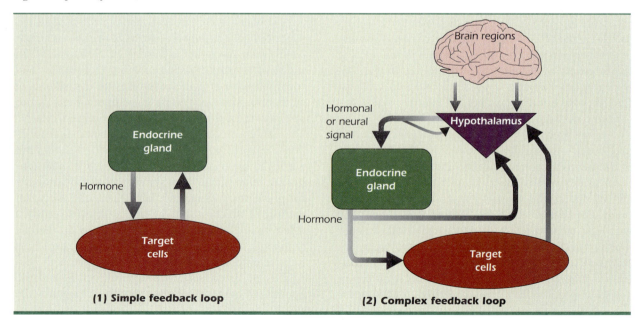

are largely determined by the nature of the receptors (e.g., in the digestive system or in the heart) that receive the chemicals. In fact, some substances function as neurotransmitters in the brain and as hormones in the bloodstream. When these substances act as hormones, however, the route to the target cells is quite a bit longer and quite a bit less direct than the cross-synaptic burst for neurotransmitters.

The whole endocrine system largely operates without our conscious control, and hormones are released reflexively. A stimulus from either inside or outside the body brings about a change in neural activity, which prompts secretion of one or more hormones. The body monitors the levels of a given hormone and the activities that the hormone affects through a *negative-feedback loop*, diagrammed in Figure 3-22. When the particular hormonal function has been accomplished or the hormone levels in the bloodstream have reached a desirable level, a message is sent to the brain (or more local command center), and the secretion is discontinued.

Next, we consider some of the major endocrine glands of the body (depicted, among other glands, in Figure 3-23).

FIGURE 3-23
Major Endocrine Glands of the Body
The adrenal glands, thyroid gland, and pituitary gland are among the most important of the endocrine glands, but other glands also carry out important physiological functions.

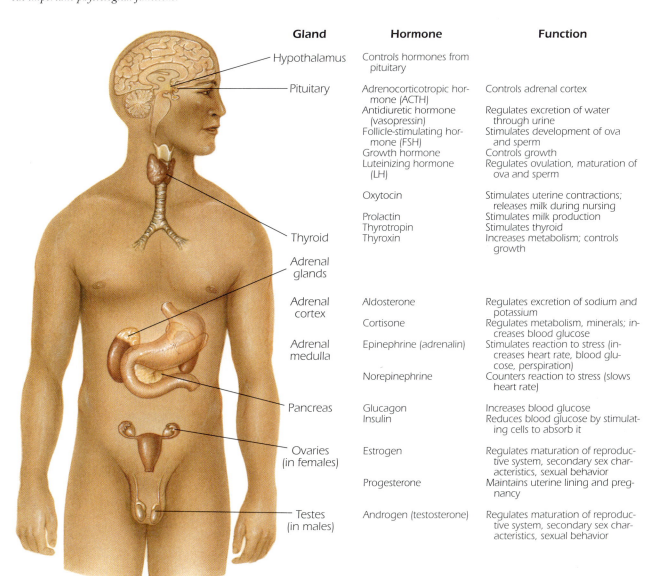

Gland	Hormone	Function
Hypothalamus	Controls hormones from pituitary	
Pituitary	Adrenocorticotropic hormone (ACTH)	Controls adrenal cortex
	Antidiuretic hormone (vasopressin)	Regulates excretion of water through urine
	Follicle-stimulating hormone (FSH)	Stimulates development of ova and sperm
	Growth hormone	Controls growth
	Luteinizing hormone (LH)	Regulates ovulation, maturation of ova and sperm
	Oxytocin	Stimulates uterine contractions; releases milk during nursing
	Prolactin	Stimulates milk production
	Thyrotropin	Stimulates thyroid
Thyroid	Thyroxin	Increases metabolism; controls growth
Adrenal glands		
Adrenal cortex	Aldosterone	Regulates excretion of sodium and potassium
	Cortisone	Regulates metabolism, minerals; increases blood glucose
Adrenal medulla	Epinephrine (adrenalin)	Stimulates reaction to stress (increases heart rate, blood glucose, perspiration)
	Norepinephrine	Counters reaction to stress (slows heart rate)
Pancreas	Glucagon	Increases blood glucose
	Insulin	Reduces blood glucose by stimulating cells to absorb it
Ovaries (in females)	Estrogen	Regulates maturation of reproductive system, secondary sex characteristics, sexual behavior
	Progesterone	Maintains uterine lining and pregnancy
Testes (in males)	Androgen (testosterone)	Regulates maturation of reproductive system, secondary sex characteristics, sexual behavior

Endocrine Glands

Adrenal Glands

There are two adrenal glands, which are located above the kidneys: the adrenal *medulla* (inner part of an anatomical structure) and the adrenal *cortex* (outer part). These glands are both important in mood, energy level, and reaction to stress. The **adrenal medulla** secretes two hormones: epinephrine and norepinephrine. When in the nervous system, epinephrine (also called "adrenaline") and norepinephrine (also called "noradrenaline") can serve as neurotransmitters, but they can also serve as hormones in the bloodstream. As a neurotransmitter, norepinephrine plays a more important role than epinephrine. For example, norepinephrine affects wakefulness. When the two substances function as hormones, both epinephrine and norepinephrine are intimately involved in sudden arousal reactions (such as increasing your heart rate and blood pressure and reducing the flow of blood to your digestive system), which can lead to a *fight-or-flight response:* When you feel a surge of energy in response to a crisis requiring confrontation or escape, the surge comes from adrenal arousal (see Chapters 16 and 20).

The *adrenal cortex* alone produces more than 50 different hormones, which perform various functions, many of which are vital to physiological survival, and many of which are crucial to our sexual differentiation and reproductive function. High doses of anabolic steroids—synthetic forms of the natural male sex hormones produced in the adrenal cortex—have been linked to extreme aggression, severe mood swings, and mental instability, as well as to sterility and other physiological damage or disease (Pope & Katz, 1988).

Thyroid Gland

The **thyroid gland,** located at the front of the throat, regulates the metabolic rate of cells. The hormone produced by the thyroid, *thyroxine,* increases metabolic rate. Overproduction of thyroxine leads to *hyperthyroidism,* associated with high blood pressure, weight loss, and muscular weakness. Not enough thyroxine causes *hypothyroidism,* associated with slowed metabolism and consequent weight gain and sluggishness. Often, when physicians are confronted by patients who feel fatigued or depressed, they check the patients' thyroid function before making a referral for psychological counseling.

Pituitary Gland

The **pituitary gland,** sometimes called the master gland, is of central importance to the endocrine system. It controls many other endocrine glands, which release their hormones in response to hormones released by the pituitary. The pituitary itself is controlled by the hypothalamus (in the forebrain). The pituitary gland (located above the mouth and underneath the hypothalamus, to which it is attached) releases hormones that both directly and indirectly affect other physiological functions.

The pituitary also provides a direct link from the endocrine system to the nervous system. When the nervous system signals a stressful situation to the brain, neurons in the hypothalamus stimulate it to act on the pituitary. In response, the pituitary secretes *adrenocorticotropic hormone (ACTH),* the primary stress hormone of our bodies. The bloodstream then carries ACTH to various other organs, most notably the

FIGURE 3-24
Action Loop
The physiological interaction of the pituitary gland and the hypothalamus provide a crucial link between the nervous system and the endocrine system.

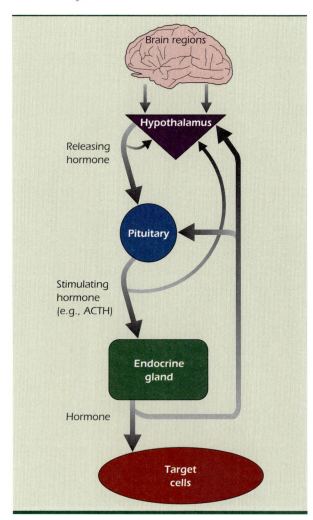

adrenal glands, which secrete, among other hormones, the fight-or-flight hormones of epinephrine and norepinephrine, mentioned earlier. This action loop is diagrammed in Figure 3-24. A summary listing the names of several endocrine glands, the hormones they secrete, and the effects of those hormones is shown in Figure 3-23.

Thus, the endocrine system provides a means of activating responses in the body via hormones in the bloodstream. The endocrine system is in some ways self-directing, but it is also subject to control by the nervous system via the hypothalamus. Nonetheless, both the endocrine system and the nervous system are an integral part of the fabulous network of the human body; both play important, but not yet fully understood, roles in defining the elusive relationship of the mind to the body. One role of the nervous system is in the transmission of sensory data, as discussed in the next chapter.

What are some examples of how hormones influence your behavior toward others?

SUMMARY

1. Biological psychology is the study of how biology affects behavior. Examination of the nervous and endocrine systems—in particular, the brain—helps psychologists answer questions about the interaction of mind and body.

Biological History: Evolution and Behavior Genetics   74

2. Darwin's view of *natural selection* holds that species tend to survive as a function of their ability to adapt to the environment, with less-adaptable species diminishing and, often, eventually disappearing.

3. A *mutation* occurs when the genetic message that would normally be passed on from parents to offspring is altered, resulting in a new organism with a genetic code not predictable from the genetic material of the parents.

4. *Punctuated equilibrium* refers to the view that evolutionary change proceeds in bursts rather than through smooth, gradual transitions.

5. *Genes* are the biological units that contribute to the hereditary transmission of traits. Genes are located on *chromosomes*, which come in pairs. Humans have 23 chromosome pairs, the twenty-third of which is responsible for determining male versus female sex.

6. A *genotype* is the genetic code for a trait. A *phenotype* is the actual visible expression of the trait in offspring. A given genotype may produce a variety of phenotypes.

Organization of the Nervous System   78

7. The nervous system is divided into two main parts: the *central nervous system*, consisting of the brain and the spinal cord, and the *peripheral nervous system*, consisting of the rest of the nervous system (e.g., the nerves in the face, legs, arms, and viscera).

8. *Receptors* are structures that receive something; receptor neurons receive sensory information (e.g., sensations in the eyes, ears, and skin) from the outlying nerves of the body and transmit that information back up through the spinal cord to the brain. *Effectors* transmit motor information (e.g., movements of the large and small muscles) from the spinal cord (and usually from the brain) about how the body should act in response to the information it receives.

9. A *reflex* is an automatic, involuntary response to stimulation that does not require input from the brain. The brain, however, assigns conscious meaning to stimuli.

10. The peripheral nervous system is divided into two parts: the *somatic nervous system*, which controls voluntary movement of skeletal muscles, and the *autonomic nervous system*, which controls the involuntary cardiac and smooth muscles.

11. The autonomic nervous system is divided into two parts: the *sympathetic nervous system* and the *parasympathetic nervous system*. The former is concerned primarily with expending energy, especially in situations requiring arousal and alertness. The latter is involved in storing energy.

The Brain: Structure and Function   84

12. In the *forebrain*, the *thalamus* serves as a relay station for input into the cerebral cortex. The *hypothalamus*, which controls the autonomic nervous system and the endocrine system, is

involved in activities such as regulation of temperature, eating, and drinking. The *limbic system*, also in the forebrain, is involved in emotion, motivation, and learning; in particular, the *hippocampus* is involved in memory.

13. The *midbrain* is involved in eye movements and coordination. Its relative importance is greater in animals of lesser brain complexity. The *reticular activating system*, which is responsible for arousal and sleep, extends from the midbrain to the hindbrain. The midbrain, the hindbrain, and part of the forebrain together compose the *brain stem*, which is vital to survival as an independent human being.

14. In the *hindbrain*, the *medulla oblongata* controls the heartbeat and largely controls breathing, swallowing, and digestion. The medulla oblongata also routes the sensory and motor neurons contralaterally from one side of the body to the opposite side of the brain. The *pons* contains nerve cells that pass signals from one part of the brain to another. The *cerebellum* controls bodily coordination.

The Cerebral Hemispheres and the Cerebral Cortex   89

15. The highly convoluted *cerebral cortex* surrounds the interior of the brain. It is the source of humans' ability to reason, think abstractly, and plan ahead.

16. The cerebral cortex covers the left and right hemispheres of the brain, which are connected by the *corpus callosum*. In general, each hemisphere contralaterally controls the opposite side of the body.

17. Based on extensive *split-brain* research, many investigators believe that the two hemispheres are *specialized* (perform different functions). In most people, the left hemisphere seems to control language; the right hemisphere seems to control aspects of spatial and visual processing. The two hemispheres may process information differently.

18. Another way to divide the brain is into four lobes. Roughly speaking, higher thought and motor processing occurs in the *frontal lobe*, sensory processing in the *parietal lobe*, auditory processing in the *temporal lobe*, and visual processing in the *occipital lobe*.

19. The *primary motor cortex*, in the frontal lobe, governs the planning, control, and execution of movement. The *primary somatosensory cortex*, in the parietal lobe, is responsible for the sensations in our muscles and skin.

20. *Association areas* are located in the lobes and appear to link the activity of the motor and sensory cortices.

Viewing the Structure and Functioning of the Brain   98

21. *Electroencephalograms (EEGs)* measure and record electrical activity in the brain. Because many different processes are measured at once through EEG techniques, wave forms are often averaged to increase the stability of the readings. Averaged wave forms are referred to as *evoked potentials (EPs)*.

22. X-ray pictures of the brain are taken by passing electromagnetic radiation through the tissues of the head. *Angiograms* are X-ray pictures taken after injection of special dyes that increase the visibility of specific structures, such as blood vessels.

23. A *computerized axial tomogram (CAT scan)* uses computer analysis of X-ray pictures taken from a variety of locations to construct a more revealing picture of the brain than is possible through X-ray pictures taken from a stationary device.

24. *Magnetic resonance imaging (MRI)* provides pictures of the brain by creating a very strong magnetic field that changes the orbits of nuclear particles, which emit energy bursts; these bursts are picked up by the scan.

25. *Positron emission tomography (PET scan)* enables psychologists, physicians, and other scientists to see the brain in action. A radioactive substance is injected, and its passage through various parts of the brain is traced by X rays.

Information Processing in the Nervous System   103

26. A *neuron* is an individual nerve cell. *Nerves* are bunches of neurons. There are three functional types of neurons. Some neurons are *sensory neurons*, by which the CNS receives information from the environment; others are *motor neurons*, which carry information away from the CNS toward the environment; and still others are *interneurons*, which transmit information between sensory and motor neurons.

27. The *soma* (cell body) of a neuron is responsible for the life of the nerve cell. The branchlike *dendrites* are the means by which neurons receive messages, either from bodily receptors or from other neurons. *Axons* are the means by which neurons transmit messages. Some axons are covered by segments of a white, fatty substance termed *myelin*, which increases the speed and

accuracy of transmitting information down the neuron. Axons often branch at their ends. *Terminal buttons* are knobs at the end of each branch of an axon; each of these buttons releases a chemical *neurotransmitter*. The small gap be tween the terminal buttons of one neuron and the dendrites of the next neuron is the *synapse*.

28. *Glial cells* serve as supportive structures for the neurons, holding them in place, isolating them from the rest of the body, and getting rid of dead neurons and other waste.

29. A rapid increase in the membrane potential (electrical charge) of a *neuron*, followed by a quick decrease, is an *action potential*. It provides the means by which intraneuronal communication takes place. Action potentials are *all or none*, occurring only if the electrical charge of the neuron has reached a *threshold of excitation*.

30. After a neuron fires, it goes through an *absolute refractory phase*, during which it absolutely cannot fire again, and a brief subsequent *relative refractory phase*, during which its susceptibility to firing is diminished.

31. The effects of neurotransmitters on the receptors located on the dendrites of postsynaptic neurons can be either *excitatory* (stimulating an increased likelihood of firing) or *inhibitory* (suppressing the likelihood of firing).

32. An excess of neurotransmitters at the synapse can be absorbed by *reuptake* back into the termi-nal buttons or by enzymatic deactivation, whereby the transmitter substance is chemically decomposed.

33. The classic neurotransmitters include *acetylcholine (ACh)*, *dopamine (DA)*, and *serotonin*. Newer neurotransmitters include glutamate and GABA.

34. The *blood–brain barrier* restricts the substances that may enter or leave the brain.

The Endocrine System   110

35. The *endocrine system* is a means by which *glands* can secrete their products directly into the bloodstream. The secretions of the endocrine system are *hormones*, and their release is regulated by a negative-feedback loop (which feeds information back to the gland regarding the level of a hormone in the bloodstream).

36. One of the major endocrine glands is the adrenal medulla, which secretes epinephrine and norepinephrine, both of which increase heart rate and blood pressure; both hormones also reduce the flow of blood to the digestive system.

37. The nervous and endocrine systems are, to some extent, parallel, in that both are communication systems, and both use chemical substances as messengers: neurotransmitters and hormones, respectively. The brain also has some control over the endocrine system, just as hormones can influence the brain.

KEY TERMS

absolute refractory phase   106
acetylcholine   108
action potential   106
adrenal medulla   112
angiogram   100
association areas   96
autonomic nervous system   82
axon   104
biological traits   76
blood–brain barrier   109
brain stem   88
central nervous system   80
cerebellum   88
cerebral cortex   89

cerebral hemispheres (left and right)   89
cerebrospinal fluid   80
chromosomes   76
computerized axial tomogram (CAT)   100
contralateral   89
corpus callosum   89
dendrites   104
deoxyribonucleic acid (DNA)   77
dominant trait   76
dopamine   108
effectors   80
electroencephalogram (EEG)   98

endocrine system   110
evoked potential (EP)   100
forebrain   84
frontal lobe   93
genes   76
genetics   76
genotypes   76
glands   110
glial cells   106
hindbrain   84
hippocampus   85
hormones   110
hypothalamus   87
interneurons   104

IN SEARCH OF THE HUMAN MIND:
ANALYSES, CREATIVE EXPLORATIONS, AND PRACTICAL APPLICATIONS

1. If it were possible to create a genetic breakthrough to enhance the adaptability of humans, what ethical issues would be involved in tinkering with humans' genetic material?
2. Compare and contrast the ways in which scientists respond to new information that casts doubt onto existing beliefs with the ways in which you respond to similar information about your own existing beliefs.
    How might you improve your ways of responding?
3. Psychologists often compare the prenatal development of the human brain to the brain's evolutionary development. In what ways does the individual development of a human compare to and contrast with the evolutionary development of humans?
4. The endocrine system uses a negative-feedback loop to regulate the secretion of hormones. Describe some other activity that is regulated by negative-feedback loops. (You can describe the activity of a biological system, a machine, a person, or anything else that comes to mind.)

5. If you were a master bioengineer and could create a genetic breakthrough to enhance the adaptability of humans (as suggested in Question 1), what change (or changes) would you make?
6. If you were designing the human brain, what, if anything, would you do differently in order to render humans more adaptive to their environments?
7. Imagine beings who evolved on another planet and who differed from humans in ways that led them never to have wars. What differences in brain structure might be associated with such a course of evolution?

8. Karl Spencer Lashley, a pioneering neuropsychologist in the study of brain localization, suffered from migraine headaches, the specific nature of which still puzzles neuropsychologists. Many scientists have personal reasons for their intense curiosity about particular psychological phenomena or special fields of study. What are aspects of human behavior that particularly puzzle you?
    Which areas of the brain might you wish to study to find out about that behavior? Why?

9. What are the circumstances in which you find it particularly difficult to think as clearly or as insightfully as you would like? If you were a biological psychologist trying to determine the physiological factors that contribute to these circumstances, how might you investigate these factors?

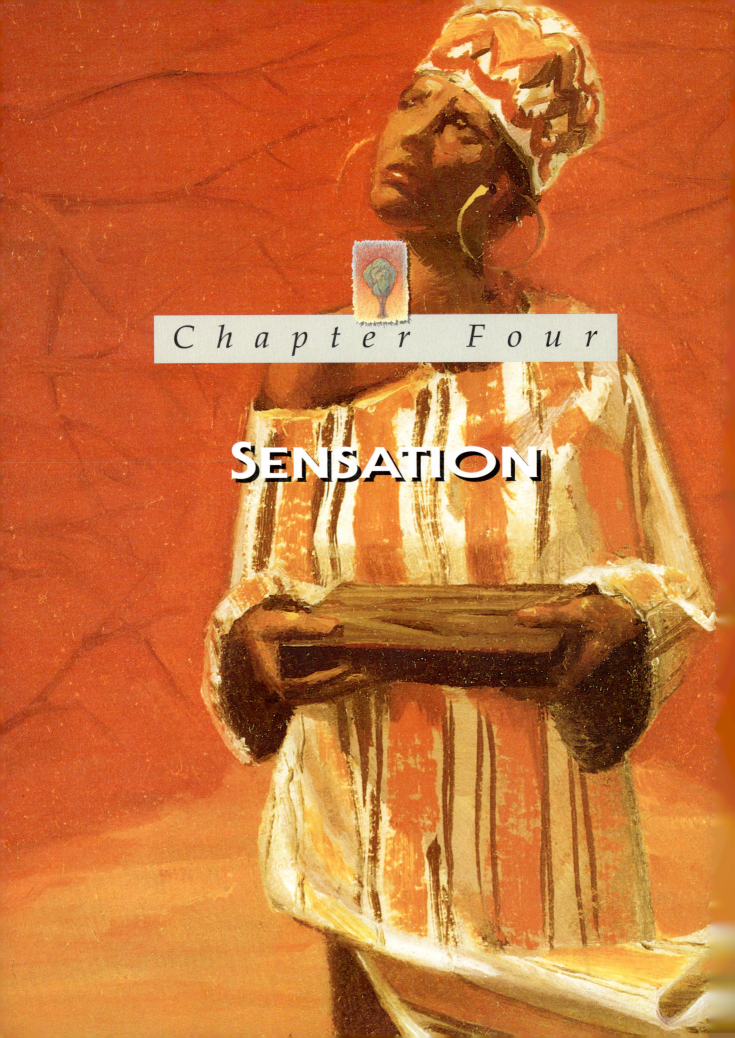

Chapter Four

SENSATION

Chapter Outline

Where am I?

She could see nothing. . . . It was not black, but . . . gray . . . like a night cloud reflecting the city lights of Moscow, featureless, but somehow textured. She could hear nothing, not the rumble of traffic, not the mechanical sounds of running water or slamming doors. . . . She turned her head, but the view remained the same, a gray blankness, like the inside of a cloud, or a ball of cotton, or—

She breathed. The air had no smell, no taste, neither moist nor dry, not even a temperature that she could discern. She spoke . . . but incredibly she heard nothing. . . .

Is this hell?

—*Tom Clancy*, The Cardinal of the Kremlin

Not hell, but sensory deprivation. In Tom Clancy's novel *The Cardinal of the Kremlin*, Svetlana Vaneyeva has been purposely deprived of all sensory stimulation to extract a confession from her. First she panics, later she hallucinates, and eventually she willingly confesses everything. Sensory deprivation can have such effects on people, but, interestingly, it is also used by some people for relaxation and stress reduction. The paradoxical effects of sensory deprivation illustrate both the importance of sensations from the world around us and the importance of occasionally being free of such sensations. Psychologists study sensation because our thoughts, feelings, and actions are largely a reaction to what our senses do—or do not—take in.

Generally speaking, psychologists define a **sensation** as a message that our brains receive from our senses. A **sense** is a physical system that collects information for the brain—either from the external world or from the internal world of the body—and then translates this information into a language that the brain can understand. As Chapter 3 showed, this neural language of the brain is primarily electrochemical. Thus, for example, you might collect information about a steaming, circular, flat,

tangy-smelling, red and white object via your eyes and nose, which then somehow translate this information and send it racing to your brain via sensory neurons. You would have yet to make sense of these sensations.

When your brain receives these various sensations, it then organizes, integrates, processes, and interprets the sensory information, so that you might say, "Ah! Pizza for dinner!" This high-level processing of information is *perception*, described in Chapter 5, which takes up roughly where sensation leaves off. Perception usually refers to the cognitive processes in the brain through which we interpret the messages our senses provide. Perception involves synthesizing and assigning meaning to sensations by taking into account our expectations, our prior experiences, and sometimes our culture. The boundary between sensation and perception is not clear-cut, however, for what we sense can also be affected by our prior experiences. When a background noise (e.g., a fan or other motor noise) is so common that we get used to its presence, for example, we may say that we "don't hear" it any more.

Many cross-cultural psychologists are intrigued by the extent to which the physiological structures and processes of the brain can be affected by culture. Although culture is known to have a profound effect on perception, there appears to be little variability in the various sensory domains that can be traced directly to culture (Poortinga, Kop, & van de Vijver, 1990). That is, the more closely a psychological phenomenon is tied to strictly physiological processes, the less variability we should expect to find among humans, regardless of culture. Conversely, the more closely the phenomenon is tied to the environment and to social processes, the more cultural (and, of course, environmental) variation we can expect to find. Thus, genetic (biological) factors appear to be far more important than cultural (nonbiological) factors in explaining sensory processes and structures, which constantly affect our lives and even our conversations.

References to the senses pervade our conversations. We may say, "I *see* what you mean," "I *smell* a rat," "This *feels* right," "That assignment leaves a bad *taste* in my mouth," or even "I *hear* music when he talks to me," even though in none of these cases do we literally see, smell, feel, taste, or hear with our senses. We also use the word *sensitive* to describe vulnerability to a wide variety of tangible and intangible stimuli; a person can be said to be sensitive to light—but also sensitive to slights. That such references have so permeated our language underscores their importance to us. Indeed, without our senses, we would be lost in a gray, quiet, pressureless, tasteless, odorless, neutral world.

This chapter describes how our senses provide us with the sensations of light, color, sound, taste, scent, pressure, temperature, pain, balance, and motion. Before we examine each sense individually, however, we explore two areas relevant to the study of all kinds of sensation: First, we investigate **psychophysics,** the study and measurement of the functioning of the senses; second, we probe some biological properties common to all our senses.

PSYCHOPHYSICS

Psychophysics attempts to measure the relationship between a form of *physical* stimulation and the *psychological* sensations it produces. A psychophysical experiment might measure the relationship between the rate at which a light flashes and your ability to detect individual flashes, or between the intensity of a sound and how loud you hear that sound to be. In effect, psychophysics addresses the interrelationship between mind and body.

Measurements of psychophysical relationships can be put to many practical uses in everyday life. When you have your vision checked, the eye doctor needs to determine how large the letters must be for you to see them clearly (see Figure 4-1). The audiologist who checks your hearing needs to determine how faint a tone you can hear. Psychophysics is also

FIGURE 4-1
The Snellen Vision Chart
This familiar psychophysical test assesses one aspect of visual sensation.

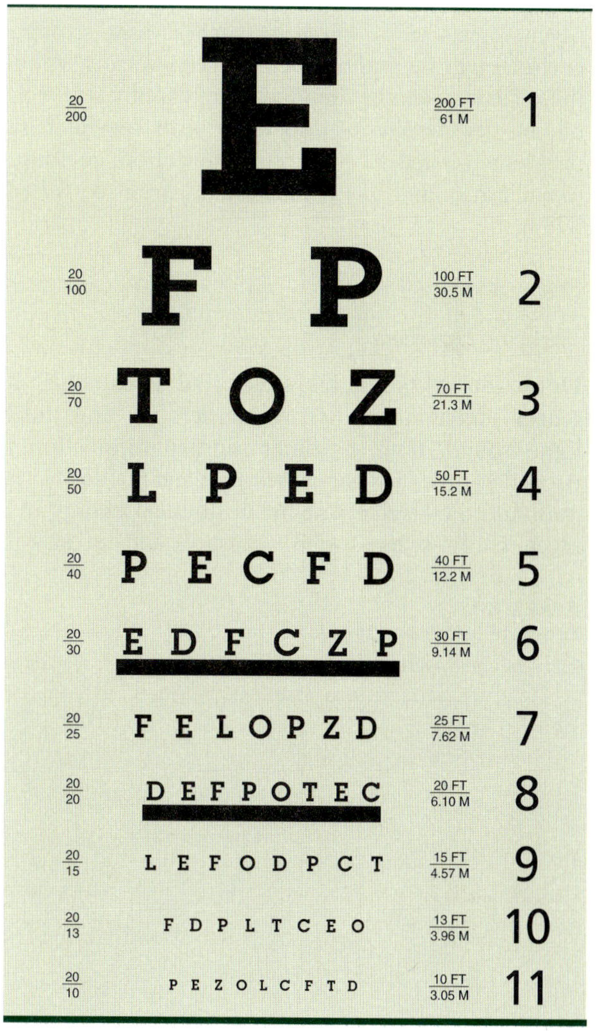

In Search of...

Early studies of intelligence assessed people's psychophysical abilities (such as auditory acuity) as measures of intelligence. How would you rate your own psychophysical abilities? Do you think your psychophysical abilities accurately reflect your intelligence? Why or why not?

Video game companies must take psychophysics into account when they design the complex functions of video games such as this. They must design the visual images on the screen to be optimally detectable.

relevant in human factors and engineering psychology, as in the design of instrument panels. How brightly should an automobile's dashboard gauges be illuminated in order to be visible but not distracting at night? In the development of products, consumer psychologists tackle questions such as how strong a perfume can be without being overpowering. All of these answers can be found with psychophysical techniques. Psychophysics also deals with several basic problems related to perception: detection, measurement error, and discrimination (Coren & Ward, 1989).

Detection

Absolute Threshold

Detection is the active sensing of a stimulus. In sensory-detection studies, researchers ask how much light, sound, taste, or other sensory stimulation is needed in order for our senses to detect it. Ideally, the minimum detectable amount of physical energy of a given kind—scent, sound, pressure, and so on—is

the **absolute threshold** for that kind of energy. We cannot sense the stimulus below the absolute-threshold level, and we can consistently sense the stimulus above that level. Table 4-1 shows some approximations of the absolute thresholds of different senses.

A simple way for an experimenter to determine an absolute threshold is to start with an extremely weak stimulus, such as a faint beep, and ask the person being assessed whether he or she can detect it. The beep should be so weak that detection is impossible. The experimenter then increases stimulus intensity until the subject hears the beep. The dividing line between when the subject can and cannot hear the stimulus is his or her absolute threshold for hearing that sort of sound. To account for differences among individuals, psychologists operationally define the absolute threshold as the level at which a stimulus is first detected 50% of the time (see Figure 4-2).

Signal-Detection Theory

A more systematic method of measuring detection allows for distortions of the measurement process. This method, *signal-detection theory*, provides both an important approach to psychophysics and ingenious insights into the processes of decision making.

According to **signal-detection theory** (SDT), four possible combinations of stimulus and response exist. Suppose you are asked to detect the flicker of a light. One possibility is that the **signal** (the stimulus; in this case, the flicker of the light) is present, and you detect it (your response); this pairing is a **hit**. Another possibility is a **miss**: The light flickers, but you do not detect it. A third possibility is a **false alarm**: The light doesn't flicker, but you think that you saw it flicker. The fourth possibility is a **correct rejection**: The light doesn't flicker, and you don't think that it does. These combinations of stimuli and responses are summarized in Table 4-2. Thus, like traditional psychophysical threshold measurement, SDT allows for hits and misses as well as for false alarms and cor-

TABLE 4-1
Absolute Sense Thresholds
Here are some approximations of the absolute thresholds for the senses. (After Galanter, 1962)

Sense	Minimum Stimulus
Vision	A candle flame seen at 30 miles on a dark, clear night
Hearing	The tick of a watch at 20 feet under quiet conditions
Taste	One teaspoon of sugar in 2 gallons of water
Smell	One drop of perfume diffused into the entire volume of six rooms
Touch	The wing of a fly falling on your cheek from a distance of 1 centimeter

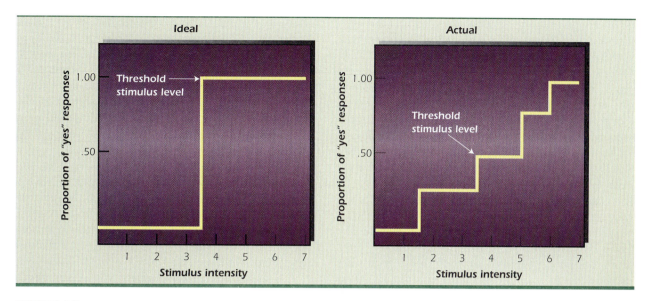

FIGURE 4-2
Ideal and Real Absolute Thresholds
Because it is virtually impossible to identify an ideal absolute threshold, psychologists define an absolute threshold as the level of stimulation that an individual can detect 50% of the time.

rect rejections (Green & Swets, 1966; Swets, Tanner, & Birdsall, 1961).

SDT is used not only in psychophysics, but also in the study of decision making, for it is, in part, a theory of the art of making choices. When we make decisions, we are influenced by moods, attitudes, likelihoods, settings, risks, benefits—all of which SDT considers. According to SDT, we do not merely *report* objectively whether we *do* or *do not* detect a signal, but we *decide*—taking into account the background noise, emotional context, and personal expectations—*how likely* it is that a sensation has been caused by a signal. For example, SDT can probably explain why we might experience false alarms, hits, misses, or correct rejections under differing circumstances. Have you

ever been at home alone at night, when your senses detected odd noises or shadows? Compare the sensations you would probably notice in such a situation with those sensations that you would probably experience were you walking down a main street in broad daylight. SDT would predict that your reports of sensations would be different in each situation.

> How could you use signal-detection theory to help decide whether to call someone up to go out with him or her?

Discrimination: Difference Threshold and the Just Noticeable Difference

Being able to detect a single stimulus is certainly crucial in many circumstances. Often, however, the problem is not how strong or intense a stimulus must be in order for a person to detect it, but rather how easily one stimulus can be distinguished from another. This psychophysics problem involves **discrimination**: the ability to ascertain the difference between one stimulus and another. For example, as a subject, you might listen to two tones or look at two color swatches and then be asked whether they are the same or different. In your everyday experience, you might be looking at a digital timepiece, trying to figure out whether you were seeing 1:11 or 1:17 (were the last two numerals alike [11] or different [17]?).

TABLE 4-2
Outcomes of a Signal Detection Experiment
Signal detection theory allows four possible combinations of stimulus and response thereby allowing psychologists to consider the expectations of the person sensing the stimulus.

Signal	Response	
	Yes	**No**
Present	Hit	Miss
Absent	False alarm	Correct rejection

The minimum amount of difference that can be detected between two stimuli is the *difference threshold*, or the **just noticeable difference (jnd)**. Just as our absolute thresholds for detecting stimuli vary, so do our responses to differences between stimuli; the resulting variation causes measurement error. For this reason, psychologists average data from multiple trials aimed at measuring difference thresholds. In practical terms, the operational definition of the jnd is the difference between two stimuli that can be detected 50% of the time.

In a typical jnd experiment, a researcher asks a participant to make many comparisons between pairs of a particular kind of stimulus that vary in one way only. For example, you could be asked to lay your hand on two otherwise identical metal pads that might differ in temperature; you would then have to say whether the two pads feel as though they are the same temperature, or different. The degree of difference that you could detect 50% of the time would be your jnd for temperature.

Sensory-difference thresholds are important in everyday life and even in some professions. A coffee taster must be able to taste and smell the differences among various blends, grinds, and roasts of bean; musicians must be able to hear whether their instruments are just a fraction of a note off-key. Human-factors and engineering psychologists use jnds to help determine aspects of product design. For example, the brightness dials on a television or the amplification dials on a stereo system depend conceptually on the jnd. Each notch on the dial must represent at least some jnd in brightness or loudness, or the dial is inefficient and ineffective.

There is no single jnd that applies to all senses equally. In addition to variations in jnds from person to person, the human species as a whole also varies in its responses to different types and magnitudes of sensory stimulation. For all senses, however, the jnd usually increases proportionately and consistently with increases in the magnitude of the stimulus. For example, if you were holding a 10-ounce bag of cherries, and the grocer added half an ounce more to your bag, you would notice the weight difference. If you were holding a 10-pound bag of cherries, however, and the grocer added a half-ounce more, you probably would not detect the weight difference. The reason that you would sense the extra half-ounce the first time but not the second is that as the stimulus intensity (here, the weight of the bag) increases, the amount of change needed to produce a jnd also increases. You need a greater proportion—probably at least a quarter of a pound—added to the 10-pound bag for you to sense the difference.

The fact that the change needed to cause a jnd increases proportionately with increases in the magnitude of the stimulus was first noticed in 1834 by Ernst Weber, a German physiologist. Weber noted that a jnd is not a constant fixed amount, but rather a constant proportion of the stimulus, and this conclusion is now known as **Weber's law.** Expressed as an equation, this law would be

$$\Delta I = KI,$$

where K is a *constant* (a numerical value that does not vary, such as pi), I is the intensity of the standard stimulus, and ΔI is the increase in intensity needed to produce a jnd. In other words, the greater the magnitude of the stimulus, the larger you need a difference to be to detect it as a difference.

The K needed for a given type of stimulus is termed the **Weber fraction;** the actual fraction varies for different sensory experiences. The Weber fraction for weights is about 0.02. For example, for a 10-pound bag, you would notice about a 2% difference, or as little as one-fifth pound. However, for a 50-pound bag, you would need a difference of 1 pound in order to detect a difference. Table 4-3 shows Weber fractions for a variety of different types of sensory stimulation. The smaller the fraction, the more sensitive we are to differences in that sensory *mode* (e.g., vision or hearing), and the higher the fraction, the less sensitive. For example, we are much better able to detect differences in amounts of electric shock (low

TABLE 4-3
Weber Fractions for Various Types of Stimuli
Because people show different degrees of sensitivity to distinct kinds of sensations, the Weber fractions for various kinds of stimuli differ. (After Teghtsoonian, 1971)

Type of Stimulus	Weber Fraction
Electric shock	.01
Heaviness	.02
Length	.03
Vibration (fingertip)	.04
Loudness	.05
Odor	.05
Brightness	.08
Taste (salt)	.2

Ernst Weber (1795–1878)

Weber fraction of 0.01) than we are differences in taste (high Weber fraction of 0.2).

Gustav Fechner, one of the first experimental psychologists and a founder of the science of psychophysics, used Weber's ideas to derive a law that relates the actual physical intensity of a stimulus (such as the brilliance of a light bulb) to the magnitude of the psychological experience (such as how bright we observe the light bulb to be) (1860/1966). **Fechner's law** suggests that as the intensity of the stimulus increases, it takes larger and larger differences in the physical stimuli (such as the volume of sound) to generate comparable differences in the corresponding psychological sensations (such as how loud we hear the sound to be). For example, the difference in speed between 25 miles per hour and 50 miles per hour seems greater to us than does the difference between 50 miles per hour and 75 miles per hour (which is one reason why we need speedometers!). Expressed as an equation, Fechner's law states that

$$S = W \log I,$$

where S is the magnitude of sensation elicited by a stimulus, I is the physical magnitude of the stimulus (as in Weber's law), and W is a constant (based on the value of the Weber fraction). Figure 4-3 shows the relation between the actual physical intensity of the

stimulus and the intensity of the sensation, as predicted by Fechner's law.

Fechner's law works better for some senses and stimuli than for others. For example, increases in the perceived intensity of electric shock require proportionately *less* increase in the actual electrical stimulation, not more, as Fechner's law would predict. The key aspect of Fechner's contribution was the observation that we humans cannot accurately and consistently sense absolute or even relative measures (although we do best in the range we normally encounter). For example, to double our psychological experience of visual intensity (brightness) requires about an eightfold increase in the physical intensity of a source of light. For loudness, we require a threefold increase in actual intensity in order to hear a twofold increase in volume. To compensate for insensitivity of our intrinsic physiological equipment, inventors have devised specialized sensing tools. For example, professional photographers use light meters, and professional sound engineers use sensitive audio equipment.

What advantages does signal-detection theory have over threshold theory?

Now that we have explored some of the techniques and theories psychologists use when assessing sensory functioning, we can find out what psychologists have discovered by using those techniques. The following section describes some of the common biological properties of the senses, many of which were

FIGURE 4-3
Fechner's Law
According to Gustav Fechner, as the physical intensity of a stimulus increases, we sense the differences in intensity less and less easily.

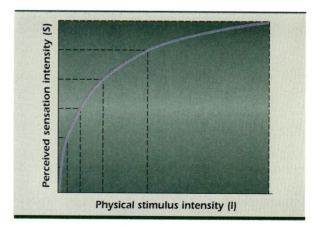

Gustav Fechner (1801–1887)

described, mentioned, or implied in Chapter 3. This chapter applies those properties specifically to the study of physical sensation.

BIOLOGICAL PROPERTIES COMMON TO ALL SENSES

 IN SEARCH OF...

In order to sense anything, our sense organs must change one form of energy into the electrochemical energy understood by our nervous systems. How are each of our sensory organs alike and different in the ways in which they transform energy?

Receptor Cells and Transduction

Our sensory organs are stimulated at their **receptor cells;** these cells are specialized to detect particular kinds of energy in the **receptive field** (area of the external world from which the cell receives messages) of each cell. Our visual system has receptors sensitive to light waves (visible electromagnetic radiation). Our

auditory (hearing), tactile (touch), kinesthetic (motion), and vestibular (balance) systems have various receptors for receiving special forms of energy (such as mechanical or electromagnetic energy) from the air, from other objects, or even from within our own bodies. Our gustatory (taste) and olfactory (smell) systems have receptors for chemicals from foods and other substances. Our senses have evolved to be receptive to and stimulated by these various forms of energy (e.g., mechanical, electromagnetic, or chemical).

When our sensory receptors (eyes, ears, etc.) are stimulated by a form of energy, they must relay that information to the brain. As we saw in Chapter 3, however, the brain and nervous system respond only to *electrochemical* energy. Our sensory receptors, therefore, **transduce** (convert) the incoming form of energy (mechanical, chemical, electromagnetic) into the electrochemical form of energy that is meaningful to our nervous system (see Figure 4-4). The neurons of our nervous system then carry (via our sensory neurons) those electrochemical messages to our brains for information processing.

Once transduction has occurred in the receptor cells, where do the impulses carrying the sensory information travel next? As shown in Figure 4-4, the impulses from all the senses except the nasal receptors go via the sensory neurons to the thalamus. The thalamus (located about in the middle of the head) relays incoming information to the parts of the cerebral cortex designed to process it. (Sensory neurons from the nasal receptors go more directly to the cerebral cortex.) Recall (from Chapter 3) the *contralateral shift,* in which the thalamus sends most of the sensory data from one side of the body to the appropriate area on the opposite hemisphere of the brain. (The information is still available to both sides of the brain, however, because the corpus callosum allows exchange of information between hemispheres.)

Recall also from Chapter 3 that regions of the cortex respond to specific parts of the body and its sensory organs. For example, the sensory homunculus shows that some parts of the body—such as the mouth and fingers—are overrepresented on the sensory cortex in relation to their actual size (see Figure 3-12). This overrepresentation occurs because those body parts have a high density of sensory receptors, which means they have a greater sensitivity in the corresponding body parts.

Sensory Coding

How can sensory receptors distinguish among assorted stimuli? A bright red floodlight does not look the same as a dim blue nightlight. The trill of a flute

(a) Visual cortex

(b) Auditory cortex

(c) Somatosensory cortex

(d) Motor cortex

FIGURE 4-4
How We Process Sensory Input
Our sensory receptors receive energy in one form (mechanical, chemical, or electromagnetic) and transduce it into the electrochemical form of energy of the nervous system. In this case, the runner's ears sense the mechanical energy of the fired starter's pistol and transduce it to a powerful electrochemical signal. The runner's auditory cortex receives the signal and identifies (perceives) it as the sound of the starter's pistol.

does not sound like the wail of an electric guitar. An onion's pungent odor is noticeably distinct from a violet's sweet scent. Clearly, each sense has a set of specialized receptors for transducing its own kind of stimulus energy. In addition, each set of receptors must use various ways to convey a range of information about individual stimuli. Otherwise we would not know a loving caress from a hostile punch; we would only know that we felt *something*. **Sensory coding** is how sensory receptors convey this range of information about stimuli. Receptors and neurons use an electrochemical language to signify shades of meaning in their messages.

A range of physical properties affects our psychological perception of a stimulus. Each sensory stimulus has both **intensity,** the amount of energy sensed (e.g., degree of spiciness); and **quality,** the nature of the stimulus (e.g., saltiness versus sweetness). For vision and hearing, we can measure the objective physical intensity in terms of **amplitude**—the height of the sound wave or the light wave if it is displayed

visually, such as on an oscilloscope. For light waves, the subjective experience of greater amplitude is increased brightness; for sound waves, it is increased loudness. For vision and for hearing, we also measure **wavelength,** the distance from the crest of one sound wave or light wave to the crest of the next wave. For light waves, the objective wavelength of a light wave is associated with the subjective experience of color. For sound waves, the objective wavelength is associated with the pitch—how high or low the tone seems to be.

Sensory neurons encode aspects of the physical properties of a stimulus via special *patterns* of neural firing that specifically identify those properties to the brain. One way to measure the firing patterns of individual neurons is **single-cell recording,** a recording of one nerve cell (neuron) in the brain. Single-cell recording lets researchers determine exactly which neurons are activated by exactly which kinds of stimuli. Once researchers know which neurons are active, they can then look for firing patterns.

In a single-cell recording experiment, an animal (e.g., a cat or a monkey) is anesthetized to eliminate any possible discomfort, as well as to reduce any movement and other interfering stimulation. The researcher determines a precise location for recording the activity of a single neuron and then places a microelectrode on that spot (see Figure 4-5). The electrode is attached to a computer, which collects and analyzes firing patterns and displays those patterns on an oscilloscope or a computer monitor. The animal is then exposed to various simple stimuli. An increase in the rate of neuronal firing in reaction to the presentation of each stimulus would mean that the neuron—or others connected to it—was responding to that stimulus.

Single-cell recording techniques have vastly increased our knowledge about how neurons perform sensory coding, especially regarding stimulus intensity. Two aspects of neuronal firing indicate stimulus intensity: the neuron's *rate of firing* (how many times it fires within a given period) and its *firing-pattern regularity*. The less intense the stimulus, the less frequently and the less regularly the neuron will fire; more intense stimuli prompt more frequent and more regular firing. This relation between the intensity of the stimulus and the rate and pattern of the neuronal firing makes sense intuitively because a more intense stimulus would more frequently and more regularly cause a neuron to reach its threshold of excitation,

FIGURE 4-5
Single Cell Recordings
A microelectrode implanted in a neuron of the anesthetized monkey's visual cortex records the neural impulses created in response to specific stimuli projected onto the screen—in this case the slanted line. This kind of research enables psychologists to identify how we sense stimuli, answering such questions as "Do specific cells respond only to specific stimuli?"

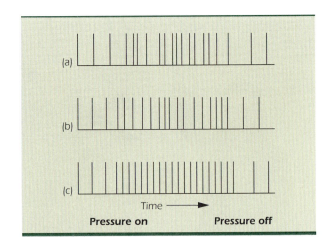

FIGURE 4-6
Neural Rates of Firing
Neurons fire at varying rates, according to the types of stimuli that prompt the neural activity.

stimulating its action potential. (See Figure 4-6 for an illustration of coding intensity.)

How neurons achieve sensory coding of stimulus quality is less clear. In some cases, specific receptor cells respond to specific aspects of quality (e.g., only one type of cell in the eye's retina responds to color). Qualitative sensory information may also be encoded in the rates and patterns of neural firing or perhaps in terms of the neural areas to which the information is sent. In addition, some sensory encoding may even occur at higher levels of processing, such as when the incoming sensory information is compared with prior sensory experience (Kolb & Whishaw, 1990). Psychologists and other scientists are still trying to decipher sensory coding.

Detection of Changes in Stimuli

One more attribute common to all the senses is how we detect changes in stimuli. As explained in the description of absolute and jnd thresholds, our senses are designed to detect *changes* in stimulus energy. When the stimulus energy changes, the receptor cells fire more vigorously, alerting the brain to the change. From a functional and evolutionary standpoint, this reaction makes sense: We need to pay attention to what is new and strange in order to determine whether it is—literally or figuratively—friend or foe. Our physiology seems to use two primary mechanisms for responding to changes in stimuli: adaptation and habituation. Adaptation, which is generally not subject to our conscious control, is described in this chapter. Habituation, which can be subject to conscious manipulation, is described in the chapter on perception.

Adaptation is a temporary physiological response to a change in the environment. Because it is generally not subject to conscious manipulation or control, it does not usually depend on previous experience with the given type of environmental change (e.g., changes in temperature or other changes in intensity). For example, without any conscious effort, our vision adapts to changes in light intensity (to darkness or to increased brightness). Similarly, our olfaction (smell) adapts to having a particular odor in the environment. A smell that is horrendous in the first minute may be barely detectable after a few minutes. You need no training or previous experience to make these adaptations, and you will make the adaptations just about exactly the same way the first time and every time thereafter. (There is some decrement in dark adaptation due to aging, however; it takes longer for dark adaptation to occur at age 70 than it does for it to occur at age 20.) The degree of adaptation required relates directly to the intensity of the stimulus in the environment, not to the number of times you were previously exposed to the stimulus or to the length of time between your last exposure and your present one. Furthermore, when the environment returns to its former state, your physiological mechanisms for adaptation return to their former states.

For example, if you have adapted to a stimulus, such as cold ocean water on your body, then you will eventually find that it does not seem as cold as it originally did. You have thus shifted to a new adaptation level (Helson, 1964). The **adaptation level** is the reference level of stimulation against which an individual may judge new stimuli. Once your body has adapted to the cold water, an ice cube will feel less cold to you than it would have before you went swimming; conversely, hot sand will feel hotter. However, as soon as you get out of the water and spend some time sunning on the sand, your body will adapt again to the change in temperature, reaching a new adaptation level for this warmer temperature. Regardless of how many times you repeat this process, or how long you wait between jumping into or out of the water, your body will go through approximately the same adaptation response that it went through the very first time you adapted to the change in temperature. Furthermore, you generally have little conscious control over how quickly your body adapts to the change in temperature.

How do environmental polluters use to their advantage people's ability to adapt to stimuli in their environment?

VISION

IN SEARCH OF...

How might you describe the experience of sight to someone who has never seen? In particular, how might you describe the cover of this book to someone who has never seen?

Have you ever awakened to pitch blackness? You get out of bed and stumble over the shoes you left out in the middle of the floor. The light switch on the wall—somehow, it's not there when you can't see it. You appreciate your vision then in a way that you cannot when you see well, and in a way that a blind person might like to be able to do. To understand how vision is possible, we need to know something about light, about the structure of the eye, and about how the eye interacts with light to enable us to see. We consider each of these topics in turn.

He found my hand, the hand with the pen. He closed his hand over my hand. "Go ahead, bub, draw," he said. "Draw. You'll see. I'll follow along with you. It'll be okay. Just begin now like I'm telling you. You'll see. Draw," the blind man said.

So I began. . . .

The blind man felt around over the paper. He moved the tips of his fingers over the paper, all over what I had drawn, and he nodded.

"Doing fine," the blind man said.

—Raymond Carver, "Cathedral"

The Nature of Light

Light is the form of electromagnetic energy that the receptors of our eyes are distinctively designed to receive. Our eyes detect only a very narrow band of the electromagnetic spectrum of radiation. The **electromagnetic spectrum** is a range of energy of varying wavelengths (see Figure 4-7), and human eyes are receptive only to the narrow wavelength range from about 350 to 750 *nanometers* (nm; billionths of a meter). Other species differ from humans in what they can see, so some animals can see electromagnetic radiation that is invisible to us. For example, humans cannot see wavelengths in the infrared or ultraviolet bands of the electromagnetic spectrum.

Anatomy of the Eye

Light beams enter the eye via the **cornea,** which bulges slightly to form a clear, dome-shaped window. The cornea serves as a curved exterior lens that gathers and focuses the entering light. The cornea is actually a specialized region of the *sclera* of the eye (the external rubbery layer that holds in the gelatinous substance of the eye). The entire sclera, and particularly the cornea, is very sensitive to touch. When a foreign substance comes in contact with the sclera, your body almost instantaneously initiates a series of protective responses, as you know from experiences with having had dust, lashes, or any other particles touch your eye.

Upon penetrating the cornea, the light beam passes through the **pupil,** a hole in the center of a circular muscle, the **iris.** (The iris reflects blue, green, or brown light beams back outward. In this way, the iris gives the eye its distinctive color.) When light is very bright, the iris reflexively causes the pupil to become constricted to limit the amount of light enter-

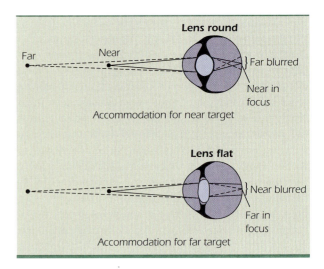

FIGURE 4-8
How the Eye Adjusts to Focus Visual Images
The cornea and lens refract light through the pupil to focus the light on the retina at the back of the eye.

FIGURE 4-7
Electromagnetic Spectrum
Within the wide range of the electromagnetic spectrum, humans can detect only a narrow band of wavelengths of light.

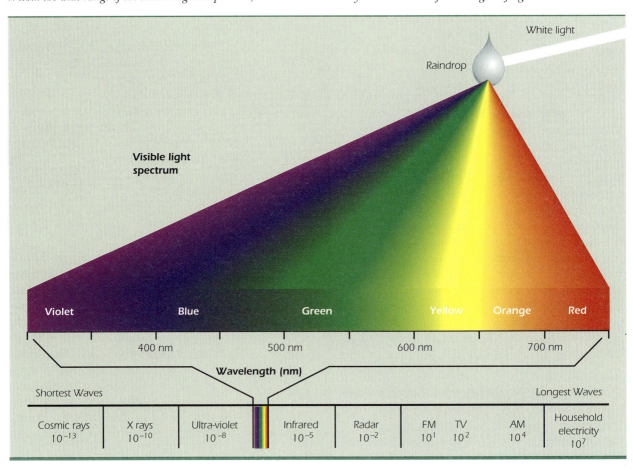

ing the eye. The pupil can reach a diameter of as little as 2 mm. When light is dim, the pupil becomes dilated to as much as 8 mm to collect more light. (The 4-fold increase in diameter is actually about a 48-fold increase in area, so the eyes are actually quite adaptive.) As we age, however, our pupils become less able to dilate; this decreased ability leads to more difficulty with vision in dim lighting. Slower pupillary reflexes also make it harder for older persons to adapt to rapid changes in light and dark (e.g., driving at night on a busy two-way street).

After entering the pupil, light bends as it passes through the curved interior **lens** of the eye. Because the curvature of the cornea does most of the gross **refraction** (bending of light), the lens does mostly fine tuning, adjusting its amount of curvature to get the focus just right. The process by which the lens changes its curvature to focus on objects at different distances is termed **accommodation.** Figure 4-8 shows how the changes in curvature of the cornea and the lens adjust the focus of objects at different distances; a flatter lens bends the light less and focuses more distant objects, whereas a more curved lens focuses closer objects more clearly.

The refracted light focuses on the **retina,** a network of neurons extending over most of the

FIGURE 4-9
Anatomy of the Eye
The light refracted through the cornea and lens onto the retina stimulates the sensory receptors in the retina. The receptors, the rods and cones, sense the wavelength (color) of the light and begin to transduce its electromagnetic energy to electrochemical energy. The optic nerve carries the neural impulses to the visual cortex.

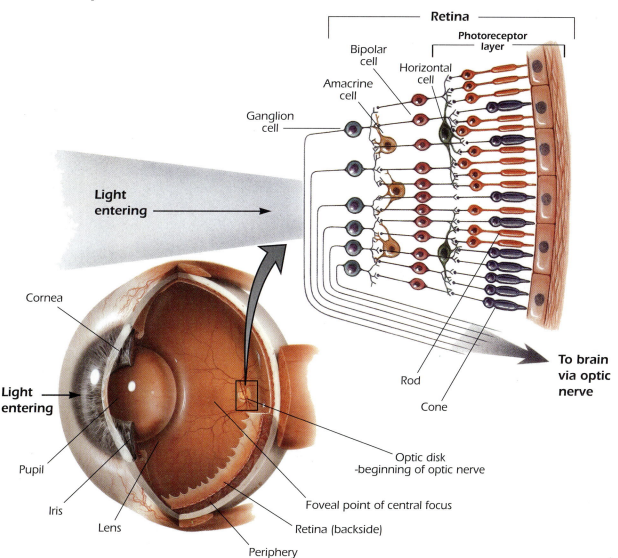

back of the interior of the eye. The retina is where electromagnetic light energy is transduced into neural electrochemical impulses. Even though the retina is only about as thick as a single page in this book, it nevertheless consists of three main layers of neural tissue, as shown in Figure 4-9.

The first layer of neuronal tissue—closest to the front, outward-facing surface of the eye—is the layer of **ganglion cells,** whose axons constitute the optic nerve. The second layer consists of three kinds of interneuron cells: **Amacrine cells** and **horizontal cells** make single connections among adjacent areas of the retina; and **bipolar cells** make dual connections forward and outward to the ganglion cells, as well as backward and inward to the third layer of retinal cells.

The third layer of the retina contains the **photoreceptors,** which transduce light energy into electrochemical energy. Ironically, the photoreceptor cells are the retinal cells farthest from the light source; light must pass through the other two layers first. There are two kinds of photoreceptors: The **rods** are long and thin, and the **cones** are short and thick. Each eye contains roughly 120 million rods and 8 million cones. Rods and cones differ not only in shape (see Figure 4-10), but also in their compositions, locations, and responses to light.

Within the rods and cones are **photopigments**—substances that absorb light. Cones contain three photopigments, whereas rods contain only one photopigment. The photopigments start the complex transduction process that transforms physical electromagnetic energy into an electrochemical neural impulse.

FIGURE 4-10
Photoreceptors

An electron microscope photo of photoreceptors shows the distinct shape and length of the rods (shown in yellow) and the cones (shown in blue).

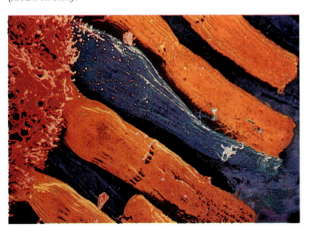

From the Eye to the Brain

The neurochemical messages processed by the rods and cones of the retina travel to the ganglion cells. Each cone in the **fovea**—a small, central, thin region of the retina—generally has its own ganglion cell, but the rods on the *periphery* (outer boundary area) of the retina share ganglion cells with other rods. Thus, each ganglion cell gathering information from the periphery gathers information from many rods, but each ganglion cell from the fovea gathers information from only one cone.

As noted earlier, the axons of the ganglion cells in the eye collectively form the optic nerve for that eye. The optic nerves of the two eyes join at the base of the brain, to form the optic chiasma (refer back to Figure 3-13). At this point, the ganglion cells from the inward (nasal) part of the retina cross through the chiasma and go to the opposite hemisphere. The ganglion cells from the outward (temporal) area of the retina go to the hemisphere on the same side of the body. To complicate matters even further, the lens of each eye naturally inverts the image of the world as it projects the image onto the retina, so that the message sent to your brain is literally upside-down and backward (see Figure 4-11).

After being routed via the optic chiasma, the ganglion cells then go to the thalamus. From the thalamus, neurons carry information to the primary visual cortex in the occipital lobe of the brain. The visual cortex contains several processing areas, each of which handles different kinds of visual information relating to intensity and quality, including color, location, depth, pattern, and form.

How We See: Rods and Cones— Duplex Retina Theory

The existence of two types of photoreceptors—rods and cones—led German biologist Max Schultze to propose the widely accepted **duplex retina theory.** The theory states that there are two separate visual systems. One system, responsible for vision in dim light, depends on the rods. The other, responsible for vision in brighter light, depends on the cones.

What evidence supports the existence of two separate visual systems? Evidence comes both from psychophysical tests and from people who lack either rods or cones. Although such people are rare, they can be found, and they were first studied by German physiologist J. A. von Kries. Von Kries (1895) found that people with no (or nonfunctioning) rods suffer from night (dim or no light) blindness. From twilight onward, and without artificial light, they cannot see.

FIGURE 4-11
Neural Pathways from the
Eye to the Brain

*From the photoreceptors in the retina,
the ganglion cells meet in the optic
nerve of each eye. The impulses from
each side of the eye then route via the
optic nerve through the optic chiasma
to the thalamus. The thalamus
organizes the visual information
and sends it to the visual cortex
in the occipital lobe.*

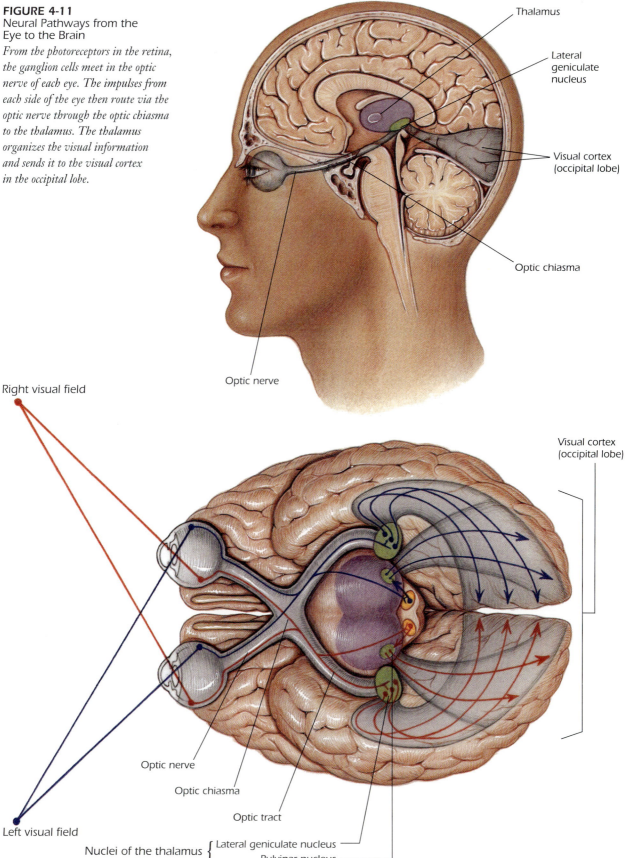

Thalamus

Lateral
geniculate
nucleus

Visual cortex
(occipital lobe)

Optic chiasma

Optic nerve

Right visual field

Visual cortex
(occipital lobe)

Optic nerve

Optic chiasma

Optic tract

Left visual field

Nuclei of the thalamus { Lateral geniculate nucleus
Pulvinar nucleus

FIGURE 4-12
Colorful Cones and Monochromatic Rods
During the day, in bright light, our cones enable us to see vivid colors. As the sun sets, limiting the amount of light, our rods enable us to see the same image but in monochromatic shades—that is, in shades of gray.

Individuals without functioning cones, in contrast, exhibit day (bright light) blindness. Whereas they can see relatively well when light is dim, they find normal sunlight or bright artificial light painful, and they have very poor visual **acuity** (keenness of the sensation) in such light. They are also completely color-blind, because the cones receive color, but the rods do not. It is for this reason that for all of us, in dim light, objects appear only in various shades of gray (see Figure 4-12). Our night vision is **achromatic** (lacking color).

The rods and the cones are unequally distributed in the eye, as shown in Figure 4-13. The cones are highly concentrated in the fovea, which makes it the area of clearest vision. In fact, when you look straight at an object, your eyes rotate so that the image falls directly onto the fovea. The visual receptive field of the fovea is approximately as big as the size of a grape if you hold it at arm's length. The rods, in contrast, are spread throughout the retina, except for two locations—the fovea and the blind spot.

The **blind spot** is where the optic nerve leaves the eye, pushing aside photoreceptors to exit the eye. Because you lack photoreceptors in the blind spot, you are unable to see any images that happen to be projected onto that spot. You are not normally aware

FIGURE 4-13
Retina of the Eye
In the fovea, the center of the retina, the concentration of cones is greater. In the periphery of the retina, the concentration of rods is greater. Why are these photoreceptors distributed as they are?

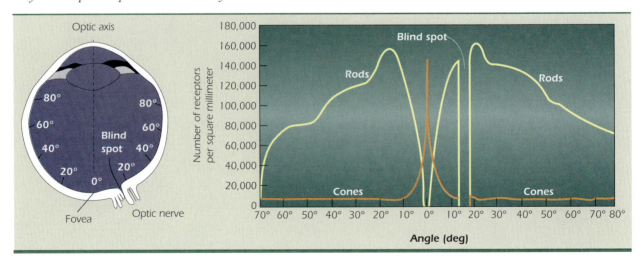

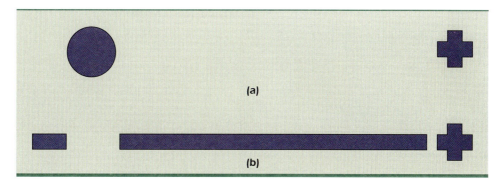

FIGURE 4-14
Blind Spot

To find your blind spot, hold this page about 12 inches from your face and close your right eye. Staring at the cross in the upper right corner, gradually move the page toward and away from your face until the circle on the left disappears. You can do the same to the cross and the bar, until the bar seems solid.

of the blind spot because the blind spot of one eye is in the normal visual field of the other eye, and your brain uses the complete information from each eye to compensate for the blind spot in the complementary eye (see Figure 4-14).

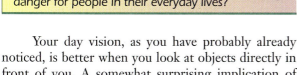

How does the existence of a blind spot create danger for people in their everyday lives?

Your day vision, as you have probably already noticed, is better when you look at objects directly in front of you. A somewhat surprising implication of the respective concentrations of rods and cones is that your rod-based night vision is better for objects in your peripheral vision than in your central line of vision (see Figure 4-15). Thus, at night, you can see a star more clearly if you look just to the side of it.

Brightness

Light has the physical dimensions of intensity and wavelength. It also has the corresponding psychological dimensions of brightness and color, which result

FIGURE 4-15
Visual Acuity

In dim light, look directly at these converging lines and mark with your finger where the lines begin to blur together. Then look slightly to the side and again mark where the lines begin to blur. Which condition showed greater acuity? Why?

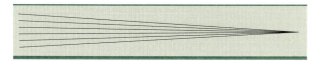

from how our bodies and minds process the physical information we take in through our receptors. The physically quantifiable amount of light that reaches our eyes from an object is termed the *retinal illuminance*. **Brightness,** however, refers not to an actual quantifiable light intensity, but to our *impression* of light intensity, based on lightwave amplitude. Brightness is thus a psychological rather than a physical quantity (see Figure 4-16). Our sensation of brightness is not directly related to the actual intensity of light reflected by an object. Rather, the relationship is curvilinear: An increase of one physical unit decreases in its impact as the intensity of the light increases. (We saw this principle earlier in the discussion of psychophysics.)

We sense brightness partly because of the physical structure of the eye—that is, perceived brightness depends in part on the retinal location of the image of a stimulus. The rods, because they are concentrated in the periphery of the retina, are more sensitive to brightness than are the cones, with the result that we are more sensitive to brightness in the periphery of our visual field than at its center. Habituation (see Chapter 5) and sensory adaptation also affect our sensation of brightness.

As mentioned previously, adaptation involves transitory environmental changes. When you walk from a dark room into bright sunlight, you probably have to squint, and you may even close your eyes for a moment. Your eyes are experiencing **light adaptation**—adjustment to the change in light intensity. Similarly, when you go from the bright outdoors into a dim or dark room, at first you will have difficulty seeing anything at all. It may take 30 minutes, or even more, for your eyes to adapt fully. Here, you are experiencing **dark adaptation**. Interestingly, in dark

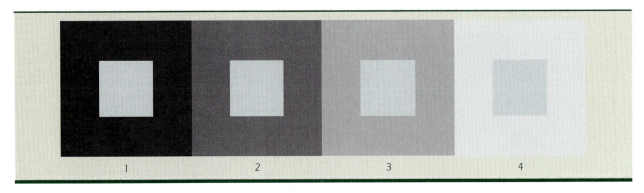

FIGURE 4-16
Brightness as a Psychological Phenomenon
Which gray area in the center appears to be brightest? Why?

adaptation, although your pupil area may increase by a factor of only as much as 16, your visual sensitivity to light may increase by a factor of as much as 100,000—quite a difference (Sekuler & Blake, 1985).

The time course of dark adaptation, as measured by absolute thresholds (see Figure 4-17a), does not progress uniformly. The curve shown in the figure represents the logarithm of the minimal light stimulus intensity you can see in the dark after spending varying amounts of time in the dark. Note the odd progression in the curve: First, the absolute threshold for sensing light decreases sharply, so you can see stimuli of less and less brightness relatively quickly. Then the curve starts to level off, and you do not continue to detect stimuli at increasing levels of dimness. After about 10 minutes in the dark, however,

the curve starts decreasing sharply again, and then it levels off again. Why the discontinuity after 10 minutes? What might generate this oddly shaped curve?

The appearance of a discontinuity in a curve often suggests that two or more processes underlie the function represented by the curve. As you may have guessed, the two mechanisms involve the cones and the rods. When you enter the dark room from a bright one, your cones are still active, but your rods are not yet working. The first part of the curve represents the action of the cones, which can help you in low light, but only up to a point. At this point, your low-light vision is at a temporary plateau of sensitivity—the first leveling-off place on the curve. As the time spent in darkness goes on, the rods become active. Once the rods kick in, your vision in darkness

FIGURE 4-17
Dark Adaptation Curve
After subjects have adapted to a bright light, they are placed in darkness and become increasingly sensitive to light. The sharp break in the curve at about 10 minutes is known as the rod-cone break.

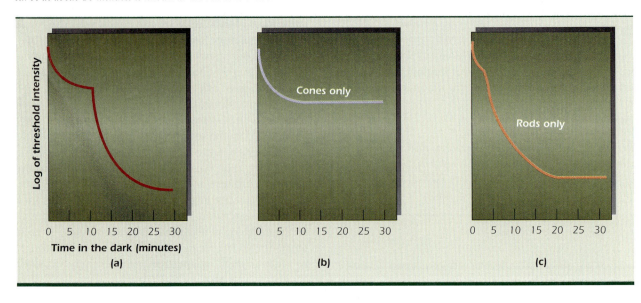

Searchers . . .   *NORMA GRAHAM*

Norma Graham received her PhD in experimental psychology. She is a Professor of Psychology at Columbia University.

Q: *How did you become interested in psychology, and in your area of work in particular?*

A: My family influenced me a great deal. My mother is an experimental psychologist and has done research all my life. Also, my father was a graduate student in psychology briefly before he went to medical school and ended up specializing in psychosomatic medicine. He, too, did research. At Stanford I majored in mathematics but realized that psychology didn't limit my choices. In psychology I could continue doing everything, from Dostoyevski through neuroscience and mathematics. So I applied to graduate programs in mathematical psychology. At Penn I learned that in the study of vision both neurophysiology and mathematics were heavily involved. I read *Mach Bands: Mathematical Models of Neural Networks* by Floyd Ratliff, and I was never the same after that. I just became hooked. I worked with Ratliff at Rockefeller that summer, and then I went back and did my postdoc with him four years later.

Q: *What ideas have influenced you the most?*

A: Well, Ratliff, through his mathematical modeling of neural networks. And then there's Jack Nachmias, who was my PhD advisor, and Dorothea Jameson and Leo Hurvich, also my teachers at Penn, and John Robson from Cambridge, England, who worked with Jack and then with me. They showed me the fun of framing ideas in rigorous terms that could be turned into mathematical models and the challenge of trying to test those models against the results of psychophysical and psychological experiments. Another person who certainly influenced me is Julian Hochberg here at Columbia. His understanding of the purpose of perception and the complexity of the task was very important to me as a graduate student and now as a fellow faculty member.

Q: *What is your greatest asset as a psychologist?*

A: Science progresses by people being different from one another, doing different things. One of the things that makes me different is the mathematics. I just have a lot of mathematical knowledge, and I use it. Another thing is simply the necessary quality of perseverance.

Q: *How do you get your ideas for research?*

A: My ideas don't burst out of nowhere. They come after a great deal of pondering about something, often from thinking about something that somebody else has done or said that's on a similar question.

These questions usually linger in my mind for years. Sometimes if what a person says seems to have intrinsic merit, then I think about whether there is an analogy to anything I'm worried about. I work away at things that seem to have promise, and I keep trying to compare them to other things. It's really like trying to apply a theorem that's been proved in some other context, except it's much more informal than that.

Q: *How do you decide whether to pursue an idea?*

A: This question has many factors that aren't a matter of cognitive structure. Often it's a matter of practicalities: Does a student need an idea for a research topic? Will NIH fund it? Does my computer currently have the capacity? Or if I mention an idea to Robson or Nachmias, are they bored by it or do they instantly see that it has possibilities? What seems important is to generate a number of ideas you can choose between. (If you keep looking for the earth-shaking best idea, you're never going to find it. However, also don't think that the first idea that comes to you is the best idea.) So I'm generally juggling a number of ideas.

Q: *What reasoning process do you follow to develop an idea into a workable hypothesis?*

A: Some of my ideas are hypotheses, but others are just about two different forms that a model could take. I think up mathematical models and I think up experiments, and I generate predictions from the model for the experiments that are worth doing.

Q: *What do you want students to learn from you?*

A: I encourage them to analyze, to look at their own behavior, and ask: "Do I really like this? Is this what I want to do, or should I do something else?" And to take direction over their own lives. To do research, you certainly have to take direction. You have to decide what question to pursue. I emphasize clearly thinking through the possible alternatives to the framework that you're currently embedded in.

Q: *What have you learned from your students?*

A: In teaching my introductory psychology students and in trying to answer their questions, I have gained so much more knowledge about the rest of psychology. They ask about the ways psychology interacts with their lives and their interests, and that gives me a new perspective on it. So I have learned to appreciate all the many contributions that psychology as a science has made.

Q: *What do you further hope to achieve?*

A: I would like to be able to continue doing research and teaching until I die. I'm still in the middle of whatever it is I'm doing.

improves markedly again. Thus, the two kinds of visual receptors generate the complex curve in Figure 4-17a. If we look at the individual curves for the cones and the rods, shown in Figure 4-17b and c, we can see that they account for the overall curve when they are combined.

Color

An area of psychological research about which there is considerable controversy is color vision. Unfortunately, some people do not see red or green; rather, they may see either or both of these colors as shades of gray, for they are either partially or fully colorblind. Before we address color-blindness and its causes, we should look at how a person with normal vision senses color. Check to determine whether you can see the shapes indicated in Figure 4-18.

If one says "Red" (the name of a color)
and there are 50 people listening
it can be expected that there will be 50 reds in
*   their minds.*
And one can be sure that all these reds will be very
*   different.*

—Josef Albers, "I. Color recollection—
visual memory"

Physical Properties of Light and Psychological Sensations of Color

Some of light's physical properties make colors appear, psychologically, the way they do to us. Wavelength produces the most basic quality for us: hue. **Hue** corresponds quite closely to what we call "color." Those of us with normal color vision see light waves of a variety of hues within the visible electromagnetic spectrum. The shortest wavelengths we can see are violet (≈ 400 nm), and the longest are reddish ($\approx 700+$ nm). Colors are not inherent in the objects we see as colored; they are not even inherent in the light reflected from objects. Rather, colors are a reaction of our nervous systems to particular wavelengths of the visible spectrum. The sensation of color, then, lies in the interaction between light and the nervous system. Color is an entirely subjective experience!

A second property of color, also determined by the spectral wavelength, is its saturation. **Saturation** refers to how vivid or rich the hue appears. A highly saturated hue will seem to be bursting with color, with no hint of paleness, whereas a weakly saturated one will seem washed out. The third property of color, *brightness*, was described earlier in terms of the way we see visible light. Brightness is caused by the amplitude of the light wave and refers to the amount of light that we see as emanating from the hue. (See Figure 4-19 for illustrations of these properties.)

FIGURE 4-18
Psychophysical Tests for Color Blindness
What shapes can you see when you look at these circles? These and other psychophysical tests are used to diagnose various kinds of red-green color blindness.

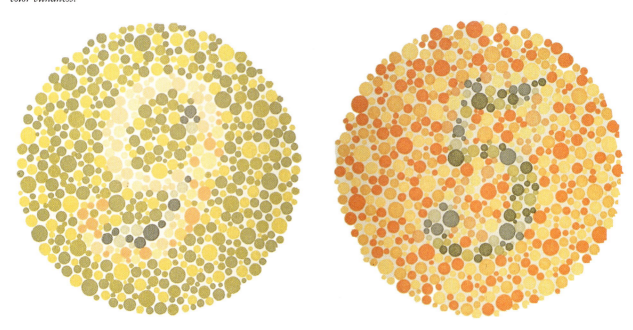

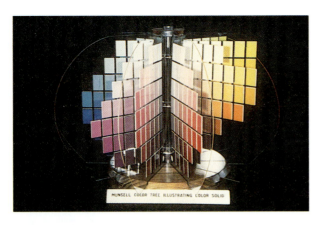

FIGURE 4-19
Color Solid

The color solid shows the three dimensions of color vision: hue (around the circumference), saturation (along the horizontal axis), and brightness (along the vertical axis).

Relationships Among Colors

We know that the colors we see correspond to spectrum intensities that increase from violet (the shortest visible wavelength) to red (the longest). Yet, psychologically, violet and red do not appear as different from each other as, say, violet and green, or red and green. Somehow, the way that we perceive colors to be related psychologically is not the way that they are related in terms of physical wavelengths on the spectrum (Figure 4-7).

Within the visible spectrum, we see approximately 150 hues, but most of the hues we see are not pure. **Purity** refers to the extent to which a hue cannot be broken down into a combination of other hues. It is by combining hues that we obtain the vast majority of the hues that we see; given that hues can also have brightness and saturation, we can discriminate more than 7 million colors of varying hue, intensity, and brightness. It turns out that hues can be mixed to produce other hues in two different ways.

Mixtures of Colors

Colors can be mixed either additively or subtractively, and the two processes work quite differently and result in different colors. When light waves of varying wavelengths are mixed, as when aiming spotlights of different colors toward one point, we obtain an **additive mixture.** Each light *adds* its wavelength to the color mixture, and the resulting sum of the wavelengths is what we see. Figure 4-20a shows what happens when red light, blue light, and green light are mixed in different combinations. The additive mixture of all three colors, or indeed, of all colors, of light will produce white light.

Unless you have worked as a lighting technician, you are probably more familiar with **subtractive mixture.** As we have seen, most colored objects do not generate light; they reflect it. That is, an apple appears red to us not because it generates red light, but because it absorbs all wavelengths other than red, subtracting those colors from our sight. It reflects only red light. Therefore, when light-reflecting colors (such as those found in paint pigments) are mixed, the pigments *absorb* (subtract from our vision) more wavelengths of light than each does individually. The more light that is subtracted, the darker the result looks. Figure 4-20b shows what happens when subtractively mixing together pigments that are yellow, *cyan* (greenish blue as a pigment, but deep blue when used as an additive color), and *magenta* (purplish red).

FIGURE 4-20
Color Mixtures

Additive color mixtures (a, left) combine lights; when all light colors are mixed together, the result is white. Subtractive color mixtures (b, right) combine pigments; when the three primary pigments are mixed together, the result is black.

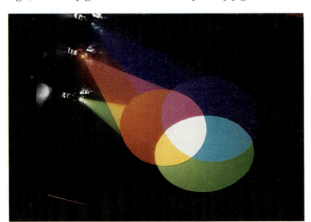

Theories of Color Vision

Psychologists who wish to propose a theory of color vision must address the question of how we can see more than 150 different hues and many thousands of colors that differ in saturation and brightness, as well as in hue (Coren & Ward, 1989). An easy answer would be that there is a different kind of receptor in the eye for each color we can see; this mechanism would require thousands of different receptors. Unfortunately, it seems highly unlikely that there would be one neural receptor in the eye for each color, any more than there would be a different neural receptor in the eye for each possible shape we can see. Such complexity is not impossible, but it does seem implausible.

A second possible mechanism draws on our understanding of the notion of **primary colors** (red, green, and blue), which can combine additively to form all other colors. If primary colors can generate all of the different hues, then perhaps different receptors are somehow attuned to each of the primary colors. Imagine, for example, that there are just three kinds of receptors, one especially sensitive to red, one to green, and one to blue. Each receptor is a different type of cone (each of which functions via photopigments). The idea, then, is that three different pigments exist, one of which is activated primarily on exposure to what we see as red, one to what we see as green, and one to what we see as blue. We see the full range of colors by the combination and the amount of activation of the pigments by which each of the three kinds of cones operates. Figure 4-21 shows how cones respond to different wavelengths of light. This theory was originally proposed (1901/1948) by Thomas Young and later revived (1909/1962) by Hermann von Helmholtz. Today, it is known as the Young–Helmholtz theory, or the **trichromatic theory** of color vision.

Support for the trichromatic theory can be found by studying people whose cones are defective. Most people who have such defects are only selectively color-blind. They can see some colors, but not others. The trichromatic theory suggests that people who are selectively color-blind will have trouble seeing red, or green, or blue, or combinations thereof. This prediction is, in fact, confirmed by empirical observations (Graham & Hsia, 1954). In addition, the genes that direct the cones to produce red-, green-, or blue-sensitive pigments have been found (Nathans, Thomas, & Hogness, 1986), thereby lending further support to the trichromatic approach. (Recall Figure 4-18 and see Figure 4-22 for how people with defective cones see color.)

The other major theory of color vision is the **opponent-process theory** of color vision, proposed

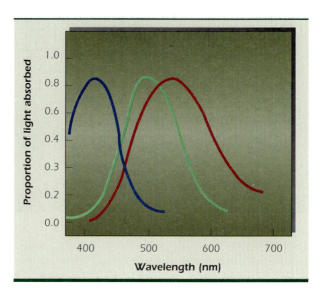

FIGURE 4-21
Trichromatic Theory
According to the trichromatic theory, our cones are particularly receptive to light of specific wavelengths: short, medium, and long. Light of short wavelength is blue, light of medium wavelength is green and yellow, and light of long wavelength is red. (After Wald & Brown, 1965)

originally (1878/1964) by psychophysiologist Ewald Hering and later formalized (1957) by Leo Hurvich and Dorothea Jameson. The opponent-process theory is based on the notion of opposing processes in human vision, each of which contrasts one color with another. It specifies two sets of two opposed colors—four colors altogether. Hurvich and Jameson also count black and white as a third opposing set of achromatic primaries that are perceived in much the same way as are the other opposing pairs.

The four opposed colors, according to the opponent-process theory, are blue and yellow, and red and green, as well as the black-white opponents. Hering noted that we virtually never combine the opposing primaries, referring, say, to a yellowish blue or a reddish green. Hering's suggestion was that an opponent color pair is handled by single neurons, the activity of which either increases or decreases, depending on which color in the pair is presented. For example, the activity of a red-green opponent-pair neuron would increase with exposure to red, and decrease with exposure to green. If you detected red at a particular point on your retina, you would be physiologically unable also to detect green at that same point, which explains why you cannot see greenish red. Red-green and yellow-blue neurons interact to produce sensations of other colors. (See Figure 4-23 for an illustration of how this process works.)

Searchers . . .   *DOROTHEA JAMESON*

Dorothea Jameson is University Professor Emeritus of Psychology and Visual Science at the University of Pennsylvania.

Q: *How did you become interested in psychology, and in your area of work in particular?*

A: As an undergraduate my general interest was in the natural sciences, and I discovered physiological psychology and psychophysics as a way to study human sensory mechanisms. I became intrigued by the many puzzles of brain function. The opportunity to carry out experiments on my own initiative and of my own design was challenging, and then an invitation to participate in ongoing research with Michael Zigler and Alfred Holway that continued throughout World War II really set my career path.

Q: *What theories have interested you the most?*

A: In the area of color vision, Helmholtz's views were the accepted paradigm, but his explanations of many perceived color phenomena seemed too *ad hoc* and unsatisfying. A serious study of the views of Ewald Hering, who attributed more significance to neurophysiological processes beyond the cones in the retina, convinced both Leo Hurvich (initially my research collaborator and later, spouse) and me that Hering's ideas offered a more viable and powerful basis for understanding visual function and perception. Also, some ideas of the Gestalt theorists, who emphasized fields of activity as opposed to mutually independent elements, seemed to be closer to the mark. However, the findings of our contemporaries who record directly from cells have been of greater importance to me than have global theorists.

Q: *What is your greatest asset as a psychologist?*

A: My primary intellectual asset is an eclectic curiosity and a stubborn need to disambiguate facile explanations and/or vague hypotheses. Also, I like designing experiments, designing and working with laboratory equipment, analyzing data, and unearthing the new questions embedded in each bite-size issue resolved.

Q: *How do you usually get your ideas for research?*

A: Most often from my last experiment or someone else's, sometimes from an experience in an art gallery, or a striking visual effect that I happen to see in a novel context.

Q: *What reasoning process do you follow to develop an idea into a workable hypothesis?*

A: I start with a question. Next I ask "How could I get the answer?" Then follows a tentative set of operations, and a set of possible outcomes and their implications for the answer. This is the stage at which alternative hypotheses get outlined, weak spots in the experimental operations are exposed, and revisions in the plans continue until diminishing returns set in. At some points in this process, it is helpful to see if a critical colleague can find some overlooked holes in the set of possible outcomes and/or implications. This is essentially the way I was trained and the way I have tried to train students.

Q: *What theoretical obstacles have you experienced?*

A: Early on, many influential color scientists were convinced that Leo Hurvich and I were on the wrong track in proposing that an opponent-process theory of color vision had greater explanatory value than the Helmholtzian theory. What was crucial for us was to have a deep understanding of their theoretical position and a respect for its strengths, as well as a detailed knowledge of the weaknesses that led us to reject the conventionally accepted view in favor of our alternative position.

Q: *What is your major contribution to psychology?*

A: The Distinguished Scientific Contribution Award from the American Psychological Association made jointly to Leo Hurvich and me in 1972 was for the experimental and theoretical work that provided a broadly inclusive and quantitative basis for an opponent-process theory of color vision. The citation for an honorary Doctor of Science degree from SUNY that I received in 1989 included in the citation a reference to my interest in relating the visual arts to color theory and perception. In teaching, I try to bridge the two-culture gap between science and humanities.

Q: *What do you want students to learn from you?*

A: Many how-to things: that everything takes longer than one would hope, that curiosity is the best motivator for good research, and that trying to solve problems is both hard work and fun. Also, that it is always worthwhile to find out who has already published your latest insight, acknowledge it, and then take it on from there.

Q: *What advice would you give to someone starting in psychology?*

A: As I see psychology in the 1990s, it partially overlaps a whole variety of disciplines. To work in any subarea of psychology means that one must master a good deal of specialized knowledge from other fields. This has been true to some extent, but it is more so now.

Q: *What do you further hope to achieve?*

A: For the near future, to finish a book I have had off and on the back burner for some time, and to get a satisfactory account of a pattern-color-motion phenomenon that interests me.

FIGURE 4-22
What Color-Blind People See
The vivid reds, oranges, yellows, and greens that normal-sighted people see become mud-colored or gray for color-blind people.

There is both psychological and physiological evidence to support the opponent-process theory. When people select what they think are the essential colors, they choose the four primaries postulated by the opponent-process theory. Furthermore, neurophysiological excitation of a red receptor does seem to inhibit the sensation of green, and vice versa. The same applies for blue and yellow (Hurvich & Jameson, 1957). Opponent-process theory also explains

and is explained by afterimages (see Figure 4-24). If you stare at a colored picture for a prolonged period and then look away at a white blank space, you will see an afterimage of the same picture in different colors. The colors of the afterimage are the opponent colors of opponent-process theory.

Eventually, the trichromatic and opponent-process theories probably will be synthesized into a new theory in the dialectic of theories of color vision. As of yet, however, no completely satisfactory fusion of the two theories has been found.

To summarize, color vision appears to be possible because of specialized receptors for red, green, and blue, as well as opponent processes involving as many as six color variables (red-green, blue-yellow, black-white). Individuals who are partially or fully color-blind either lack some of these receptors or have receptors that do not function normally. We do not have any final word on how people see colors, but whatever the system, it seems to use some finite set of colors to make possible vision for the myriad colors that we are capable of seeing.

Thus far, this chapter has focused on our visual sensations. Although most of us rely on vision as our primary means of sensing the world around us, our life experiences would be impoverished if we were deprived of our other sensations. Chief among our nonvisual senses is our sense of hearing.

FIGURE 4-23
Opponent-Process Theory
According to opponent-process theory, our color receptors are sensitive either to red-green pairs or to blue-yellow pairs. When we see a light of about 450 nm, the red-green pair will tip toward the red, and the blue-yellow pair will tip toward the blue. The combination of red and blue will produce what we see as violet. (After Hurvich & Jameson, 1957)

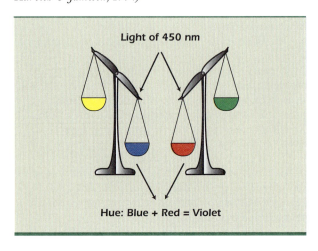

Light of 450 nm

Hue: Blue + Red = Violet

If you wanted to design a test of visual acuity that was as free from measurement error as possible, what would you do?

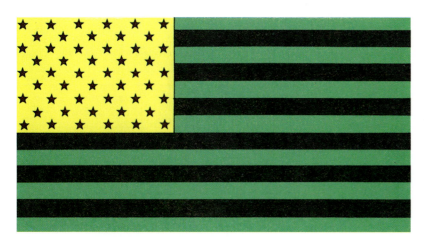

FIGURE 4-24
Afterimages
Stare at the center of this flag for about 30 seconds, then look at a blank white page. What do you see? How would the opponent-process theory explain the afterimage that you see?

HEARING

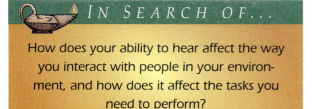

IN SEARCH OF...

How does your ability to hear affect the way you interact with people in your environment, and how does it affect the tasks you need to perform?

Imagine not being able to hear the crash of waves against the shore or the sound of your beloved's voice. Many of us consider hearing to be the second most important sense after vision. To understand hearing, you need to know about the structures and processes that permit us to hear: the nature of sound, the anatomy of the ear, and the distinctive interaction between sound and the ear.

The Nature of Sound

Physical Properties of Sound

Sound results from mechanical pressure on the air. When you pluck the string of a guitar or clap your hands together, you are pushing on air molecules. The disrupted air molecules momentarily collide with other air molecules, which then collide with still other air molecules, resulting in a three-dimensional wave of mechanical energy. The air particles themselves do not move much—it is the wave of pressure that covers the distance. Compare this effect to a line of cars waiting at a stoplight. Along comes a speeder who fails to stop in time, rear-ending the last car in line. That car then hits the car in front of it, and so

on. The mechanical pressure spreads in a wave forward through the line of cars, but the car that started the wave does not move much at all.

We are accustomed to thinking of sound as traveling though air, but it can also result from mechanical pressure being applied to another medium, such as water. Thus, if there is no medium, such as in an airless vacuum, there is no sound. For sound to occur, the air (or water) particles must have other particles through which the pressure wave can pass. Therefore, you can see light, but not hear sound, in a vacuum.

Sound also travels much more slowly than light, which is why you see a distant lightning bolt before you hear the thunder, even though they occur almost simultaneously. Also, unlike the speed of light, which is the same regardless of the medium through which light passes, the speed of sound depends on the density of the medium. Somewhat surprisingly, sound generally moves more quickly through more densely packed molecules. This phenomenon is not completely counterintuitive when you think about it in terms of the car-crash analogy. The more densely packed the cars, the more rapidly the wave of crashing cars proceeds. Sound travels approximately 340 meters per second (750 miles per hour) in air, or 1,360 meters per second (3,000 miles per hour) in water.

Corresponding Physical and Psychological Properties of Sound Waves

Sound waves have physical properties that affect how we sense them and process them psychologically. The first two are familiar: the amplitude and the wavelength. Sound amplitude (intensity) corresponds to our sensation of loudness: the higher the amplitude,

TABLE 4-4
Decibel Table
This table shows the intensities of some common sounds and indicates how dangerous to our receptors that certain levels of sound can become.

Decibel Level	Example	Dangerous Time Exposure
0	Lowest sound audible to human ear (threshold)	
30	Quiet library, soft whisper	
40	Quiet office, living room, bedroom away from traffic	
50	Light traffic at a distance, refrigerator, gentle breeze	
60	Air conditioner at 20 feet, conversation	
70	Busy traffic, noisy restaurant (constant exposure)	Critical level begins
80	Subway, heavy city traffic, alarm clock at 2 feet, factory noise	More than 8 hours
90	Truck traffic, noisy appliances, shop tools, lawnmower	Less than 8 hours
100	Chain saw, boiler shop, pneumatic drill	2 hours
120	Rock concert in front of speakers, sandblasting, thunderclap	Immediate danger
140	Gunshot blast, jet plane	Any exposure is dangerous
180	Spacecraft launch	Hearing loss inevitable

the louder the sound. The usual unit of measurement for the intensity of sound is the **decibel (dB)**. Zero decibels is the absolute threshold for normal human hearing. Table 4-4 shows the decibel levels of various common sounds.

Wavelength corresponds to our sensation of **pitch**—how high or low a tone sounds. Actually, for sound, we usually speak in terms of the **frequency** of the wave, conventionally measured as the number of *cycles* (crest-to-crest progressions of sound waves) per second, rather than in terms of wavelengths. A frequency of one cycle per second is called 1 **hertz (Hz),** after the German physicist Heinrich Hertz. Humans can generally hear sound waves in the range from about 20 to 20,000 Hz, whereas many other animals can hear sound waves of much higher frequencies. Frequency and wavelength are inversely related. This inverse relationship makes sense because a short wavelength would crest over and over again more frequently than would a long one, within the same space or time interval. Thus, a high-pitched sound has a high frequency and a short wavelength, and a low-pitched sound has a low-frequency sound and a long wavelength (see Figure 4-25). The absolute thresholds for hearing frequencies are depicted in Figure 4-26.

FIGURE 4-25
Properties of Sound Waves
What we sense of sound consists of waves of compressed air. Sound waves are measured in amplitude (what we sense as loudness) and frequency (what we sense as pitch).

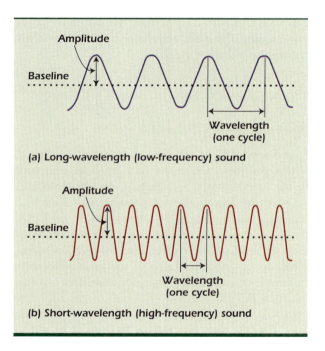

(a) Long-wavelength (low-frequency) sound

(b) Short-wavelength (high-frequency) sound

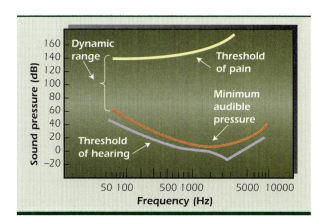

FIGURE 4-26
Absolute Thresholds for Hearing
Sound that is comfortably audible to humans ranges from about 50 to 100 decibels in amplitude and from about 20 to 20,000 hertz in frequency. For us to sense sounds above 20,000 hertz, they must have increasingly higher amplitude.

The third psychological dimension of sound is timbre (pronounced "tamber"). **Timbre** is the quality of sound; it allows us to tell the difference between an A flat played on a piano and an A flat played on a harmonica. It corresponds to the visual sensation of color saturation. When you play a note on a musical instrument, you generate a complex series of tones. The note itself is the **fundamental frequency,** but at the same time, the instrument produces **harmonics**—multiples higher than the fundamental frequency. Different musical instruments produce different harmonics, resulting in the distinctive sounds of the instruments. Not all sounds produce musical harmonics; sometimes, additional sound waves are generated, but these waves are not multiples of the fundamental frequency. When additional sound waves are irregular and unrelated, we hear **noise** (confusing, nonsensical, and often unpleasant sound). (Figure 4-27 shows the contrast between the poetry of harmonics and the random dispersal of noise.)

Anatomy of the Ear

When sound waves enter the ear, they pass through three regions: the outer ear, the middle ear, and the inner ear (see Figure 4-28a). Sound waves are collected by the **pinna,** the visible outer part of the ear. From the pinna, the sound waves move down the auditory canal toward the **eardrum** (also termed the *tympanum*), which vibrates with the sound waves. The higher the frequency of the sound, the faster the vibrations of the eardrum.

The eardrum vibrations pass into the middle ear, where a sequence of three tiny bones passes these vibrations to the inner ear. The three bones—the **malleus, incus,** and **stapes**—normally amplify the vibrations transmitted by the eardrum. Interestingly, though, for extremely intense sounds that could damage the inner ear, the angle of the stapes against the inner ear changes, decreasing the vibration and protecting the ear—another adaptive function of our physiology.

The stapes normally rests on the **oval window,** the first part of the inner ear. As Figure 4-28b shows, the oval window is at one end of the **cochlea,** the coiled and channeled main structure of the inner ear. Three fluid-filled canals run the entire length of the cochlea. The fluid-filled canals are separated by membranes, one of which is the **basilar membrane.** On the basilar membrane are thousands of **hair cells,** which are our auditory receptors. Specialized hairlike appendages (offshoots) of the hair cells are moved by the vibration of the stapes. The hair cells transduce the mechanical energy into electrochemical energy that is transmitted via the sensory neurons to the brain.

FIGURE 4-27
Sound Waves: Music Versus an Explosion
As you look at these two sets of sound waves, how would you explain the differences in our sensation of a single note played on a piano versus an explosion?

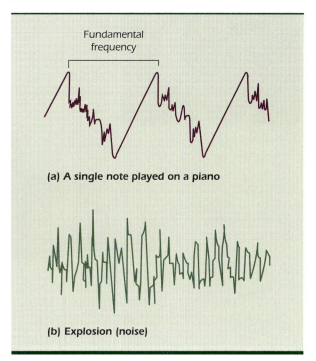

(a) A single note played on a piano

(b) Explosion (noise)

FIGURE 4-28
Anatomy of the Ear
The ear comprises three parts: the outer, middle, and inner ear. The inner ear includes the cochlea (see detail and photograph), which includes the auditory receptors as well as the vestibular system.

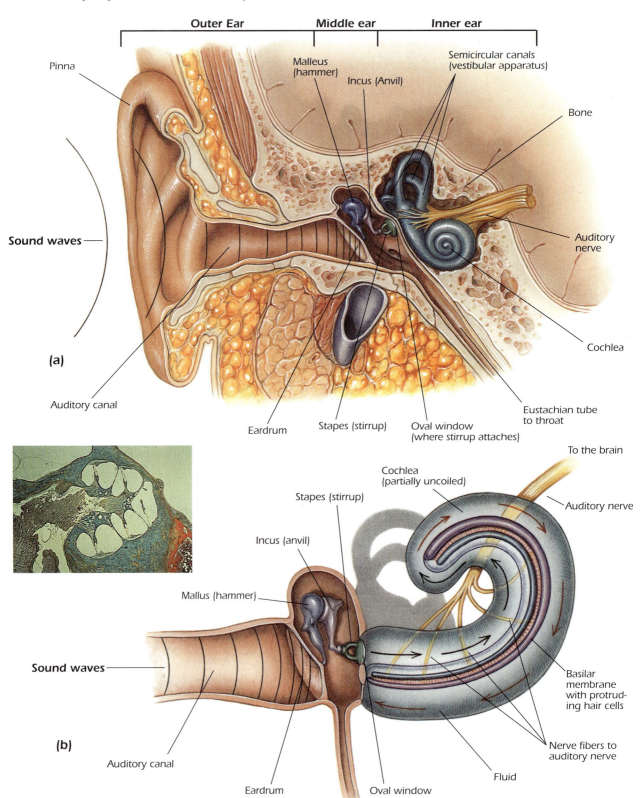

From the Ear to the Brain

The axons of the sensory neurons form the **acoustic nerve** (also called the auditory nerve; see Figures 4-28 and 4-29). As was the case for the axons of the optic nerve, some neurons have a one-to-one mapping to a minority of the receptors, and other neurons have a many-to-one (usually 10:1) mapping to other, more numerous receptors.

The specific route of information conveyed along the acoustic nerve is quite complex, involving relay stops first in the medulla oblongata and then in the midbrain. The information is finally relayed through the thalamus to the auditory cortex in the temporal lobes of the brain. The cortex seems to map out the relationships among frequencies of the auditory field in a way that very roughly approximates the way the visual cortex maps out spatial relationships in the visual field. Also, although the contralateral connections are the strongest ones, some information from both ears reaches both cerebral hemispheres. In the brain, the auditory cortex is connected to our areas for language perception and production.

How We Hear

Just as we can only see intermediate wavelengths on the full electromagnetic spectrum, we are most sensitive to sounds in the middle range of audible frequencies, roughly corresponding to the range of human voices. As you might expect from our discussions of psychophysics and evolutionary adaptability, we are especially sensitive to changes in sounds, such as

FIGURE 4-29
Neural Pathways from the Ear to the Brain
The auditory receptors on the basilar membrane of the cochlea join to form the auditory nerve, which routes through the medulla oblongata to the thalamus. The thalamus organizes the electrochemical impulses and sends them to regions of the auditory cortex in the temporal lobes.

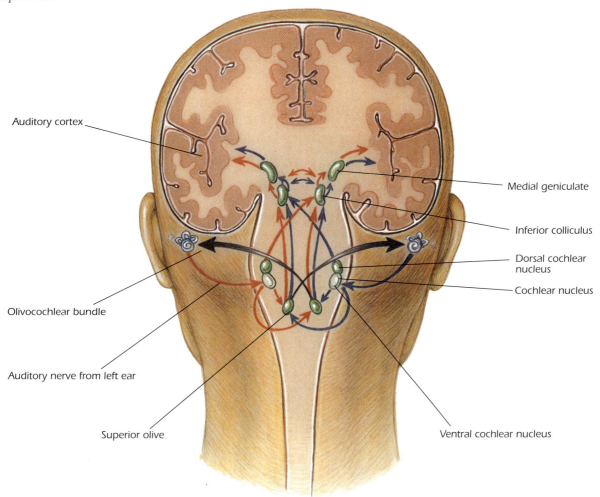

changes in pitch. Two major theories of how we sense pitch have been proposed: place theory and frequency theory.

Place Theory

Helmholtz, whose ideas on color have been seen in our discussion of vision, observed (1863/1930) that the basilar membrane in the inner ear is wider at one end than at the other. Imagine a harp: The longer strings generate lower pitches, whereas the shorter strings generate higher ones. Helmholtz thought that this same general principle might apply to the way people hear. **Place theory** posits that we hear each pitch as a function of the location in the basilar membrane that is stimulated. The hair cells at different places on the basilar membrane vibrate in response to different pitches, and in the process they excite different neurons. Each neuron is therefore sensitive to the specific frequencies that originally stimulated the basilar membrane. In fact, prolonged exposure to a very loud sound of a particular frequency damages the hair cells at a specific spot on the basilar membrane, causing hearing loss for sounds of that pitch.

Georg von Békésy did Nobel Prize–winning research (1960) that led him to similar conclusions. He cut tiny holes in the cochleas of guinea pigs and as pitches of different frequencies were played, he observed the guinea pigs' basilar membranes with a microscope. Low-frequency tones stimulated the hair cells at the wider end of the basilar membrane (farthest from the oval window), and high-frequency tones stimulated the cells at the narrower end (closest to the oval window). Unfortunately, not everything Békésy saw fit in perfectly with place theory. Low-frequency tones also stimulated the cells along the whole basilar membrane, and even tones of intermediate frequencies sometimes stimulated wide areas of the membrane.

Frequency Theory

Instead of relying on location to explain pitch, **frequency theory** suggests that the basilar membrane reproduces the vibrations that enter the ear, triggering neural impulses at the same frequency as the original sound wave (Wever, 1970). The pitch we sense is determined by the frequency of the impulses that enter the auditory nerve connecting the ear with the brain. A tone of 500 Hz produces 500 bursts of electrical responses per second in the auditory nerve, and so on.

Frequency theory handles well the broader stimulation associated with the sensation of low-frequency tones that place theory does not fully ex-

This electron micrograph shows healthy and scarred hair cells, which were damaged by prolonged exposure to loud noises.

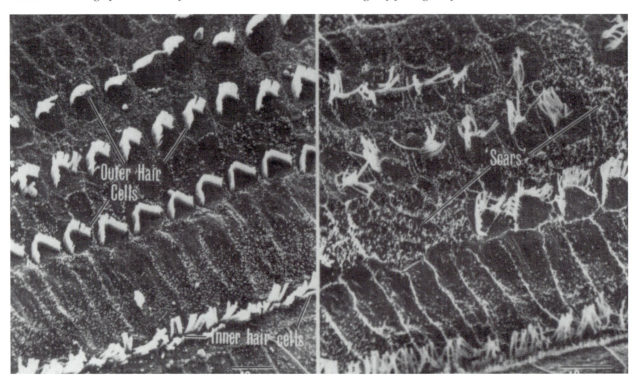

As many rock singers and attendees of rock concerts now attest, intense or prolonged exposure to music blasting from amplifiers can damage hearing.

process theories of color vision. Theories that incorporate elements of competing theories are popular ways of resolving problems because they use the best features of each of the competitors (Kalmar & Sternberg, 1988). The final word in theories of pitch has yet to be heard.

In what way could the place theory and the frequency theory of hearing both be partially correct?

Locating Sounds

How do we determine where sounds are coming from? The fact that we have two ears roughly six inches apart on opposite sides of the head is the key. When a sound comes from our right, it has less distance to travel to reach the right ear than the left ear. Granted, the time difference between arrival at the right and left ears can be minuscule, but it is enough for us to sense and process. In fact, we can detect time

plain. However, frequency theory cannot account for all of the phenomena associated with pitch at the high end of the frequency scale. The problem with frequency theory is that a single neuron can conduct a maximum of only about 1,000 impulses per second (corresponding to a 1,000 Hz sound), but humans can hear frequencies of up to 20,000 Hz. We are not capable of a high enough rate of neuronal conduction to mirror the vibrations of high-frequency pitches. So once again, one theory does not provide all the answers.

Keeping frequency theory alive is the **volley principle** (Wever, 1970), according to which neurons are able to cooperate. That is, neurons can fire not just singly, but in alternating groups. While one neuron is resting, a neighboring neuron can fire. This neighbor can cooperate similarly with other neurons, as well. Thus, although no one neuron can fire at a fast enough rate to simulate the vibrations of the higher frequencies, a group of neurons can. Think of a group of rifle-wielding sharpshooters, each of whom must reload after each shot. If the sharpshooters cooperate so that some of them fire while others reload, the group can fire volleys much faster than can any one sharpshooter alone.

Nonetheless, we must account for some findings that still support place theory. As a result, the current most widely accepted view on the hearing of pitch is **duplicity theory,** according to which both place and frequency play some role in hearing pitch. The details of duplicity theory have not yet been worked out, however. A similar dialectic occurred in vision research, with the trichromatic and opponent-

Georg von Békésy (1899–1972)

differences as brief as 10 microseconds (Durlach & Colburn, 1978). Another way we process location is by comparing the differences in the intensities of the sounds reaching our ears; the farther ear receives a sound of lesser intensity than the closer ear because our heads absorb some of the sound going to the farther ear. It seems that the *time-difference method* works best for low-frequency sounds, and the *intensity-difference method* works best for high-frequency sounds (see Figure 4-30).

What if a sound comes from a source equidistant from our ears, so that it arrives at both ears simultaneously? In such cases, we are easily confused. You have heard sounds for which you were not able immediately to pinpoint the location. In an attempt to locate the source, you probably (and almost unconsciously) rotated your head in order to receive two slightly different messages in your ears. Then, using either the time- or intensity-difference method, you located the source of the sound.

FIGURE 4-30
Determining the Source of a Sound
We locate the source of a sound by using two methods. We deduce that the sound is coming from the direction of the ear that either heard the sound first or sensed the greater volume.

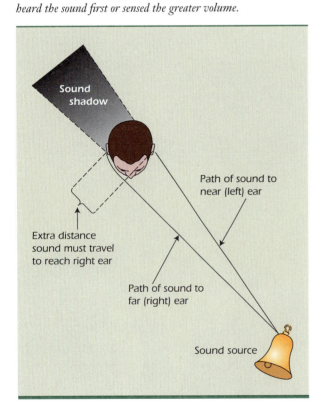

TASTE, SMELL, AND THE OTHER SENSES

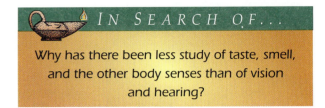

IN SEARCH OF...

Why has there been less study of taste, smell, and the other body senses than of vision and hearing?

Taste

We are able to see objects and hear events that occur at some distance from our bodies. To do so, we transduce the energy waves that we receive from those objects and events into the electrochemical energy of neural transmission. In contrast, to use our sense of taste, we must come into physical contact with the particular chemical makeup of the things we taste; in fact, what we taste has already entered our bodies. Just how does this highly intimate sensory system work? To answer this question, we explore the physical and psychological properties of taste, the anatomy of taste both in the tongue and in the nervous system, and the specific mechanisms of taste.

Physical and Psychological Properties in the Sense of Taste

For us to taste a stimulus, it must contain chemical molecules that can dissolve in saliva, and we must have sufficient saliva in our mouths to dissolve those chemicals. From these chemicals, we detect the four primary psychological qualities of saltiness, bitterness, sweetness, and sourness. Sweet tastes typically come from *organic molecules*, which contain varying amounts of carbon, hydrogen, and oxygen. Bitter-tasting substances tend to contain some amount of nitrogen; sour substances are usually acidic; and salty-tasting substances tend to have molecules that break down into electrically charged particles (ions) in water. Other tastes are produced by combinations of the four primary tastes, much as colors can be produced by a combination of the three primary colors. For example, a grapefruit is both sour and bitter and is also sometimes sweet.

Our sensitivity to taste changes as we age: Children are hypersensitive to taste, as you may have noticed if you have ever eaten with young children. The number of taste buds, however, decreases as we grow older, resulting in a decrease in our sensitivity to tastes. In addition, tobacco smoke and alcohol can kill taste buds prematurely.

Although most people's absolute thresholds for taste are fairly low, the jnd's for taste are rather high, with Weber fractions ranging from 0.1 to 1.0. These relatively high jnd thresholds mean that in order for us to perceive differences in intensities, we must add at least 10% more taste, and possibly 100% more, depending on the flavor! Taste is probably our least finely tuned sensory system.

Anatomy of the Tongue

As tasty substances enter the mouth, they land on the tongue, where they are detected by one or more of roughly 10,000 **taste buds,** clusters of taste receptor cells located inside the small visible protrusions on the tongue, the **papillae** (Figure 4-31). Taste buds are clustered all over the tongue and also in the back of the throat. In the center of each taste bud is a pore

through which chemicals from food and drink pass. Contact with these chemicals activates the taste buds, thereby beginning the transduction process. The receptors for taste (and for smell) transduce chemical energy into electrochemical energy; the taste receptors seem specially tailored to receive particular kinds of chemicals (e.g., salts or acids) and then send the message about the chemicals through the electrochemical system of neuronal conduction.

From the Tongue to the Brain

Three nerves are devoted to carrying information from the taste-bud receptors on different regions of the tongue to the medulla oblongata. From the medulla oblongata, the information is transmitted through the pons to the thalamus. In the thalamus, the information is routed to the somatosensory

FIGURE 4-31
Taste Buds
The taste buds on our tongues are the sensory receptors for taste and are located on the papillae, the small bumps that we can see on our tongues (see close-up of a papilla).

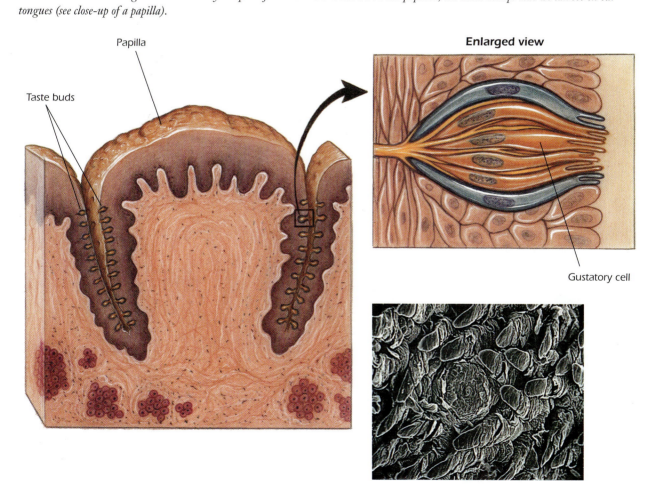

cortex, alongside the portion of the cortex where areas of the face are mapped, primarily in the parietal lobe and also in the temporal lobe (see Figure 4-32). Some of the gustatory (taste) information, however, gets sidetracked from the thalamus to the nearby hypothalamus and to parts of the limbic system.

How We Taste

What might account for our ability to distinguish the four primary tastes? The most widely accepted theory of taste (Pfaffman, 1974) posits that although the sensory receptors on the tongue do not each respond

FIGURE 4-32
Neural Pathway from the Tongue to the Brain
From the taste receptors on the tongue, three nerves carry electrochemical impulses to the medulla oblongata, which transmits most of the information through the pons to the thalamus. The thalamus organizes and then routes the impulses to the somatosensory cortex. Some of the information goes to the hypothalamus and to parts of the limbic system.

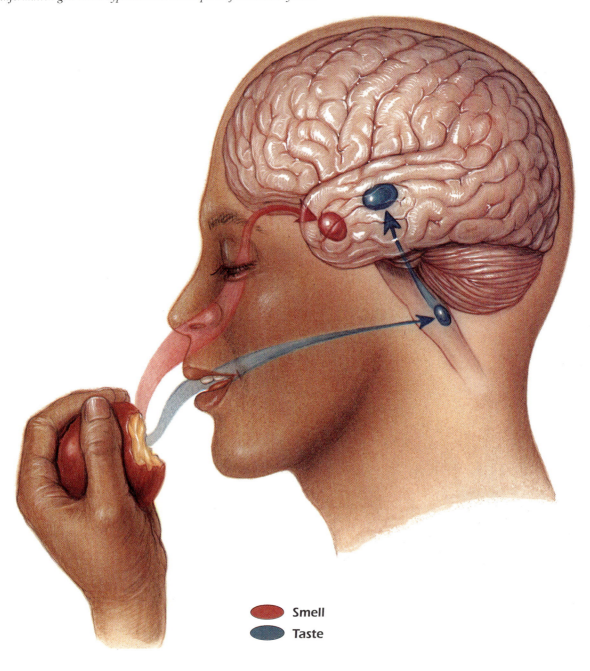

Smell
Taste

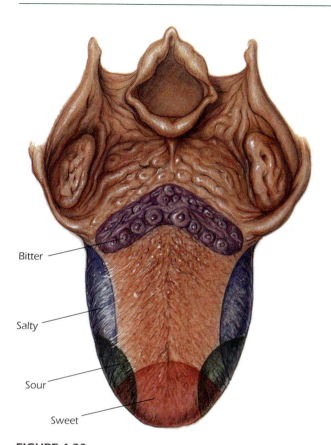

Bitter

Salty

Sour

Sweet

FIGURE 4-33
Tongue Sensitivity
Although all areas of the tongue have some sensitivity to all four primary tastes, the tongue can be mapped into zones of heightened sensitivity to each of the four primary tastes.

uniquely to a single taste, different receptors do respond more strongly to certain taste sensations than to others. Taste buds are also located in groups on the tongue according to their differential sensitivities (see Figure 4-33). Evidence suggests that four regions in the brain respond to the four tastes we sense (Yamamoto, Yuyama, & Kawamura, 1981a, 1981b). It appears that taste buds interact to produce the wide variety of tastes that we sense.

Thus far, we have indicated that taste embraces only four fundamental sensations. What about all the other nuances of taste we enjoy? Much of what we refer to as the distinctive taste of food is actually its smell (see Figure 4-34). Many of us discover the importance of smell when we have a bad cold: Our food seems virtually tasteless because our nasal passages are blocked. Thus, two foods that are equally sweet but that smell quite different (and hence are described casually as "tasting" different) may taste the same unless we can also smell them. The temperature of food can also affect our sensation of smell because heat tends to release aromas. For some of us, color and texture are also quite important to our enjoyment of food and drink.

Smell

As is the case with vision and hearing, humans depend on the sense of smell for survival and for information gathering, but not nearly as much as do other

FIGURE 4-34
The Importance of Smell to Perceived Taste
Many foods are much less easy to identify when they cannot be smelled.

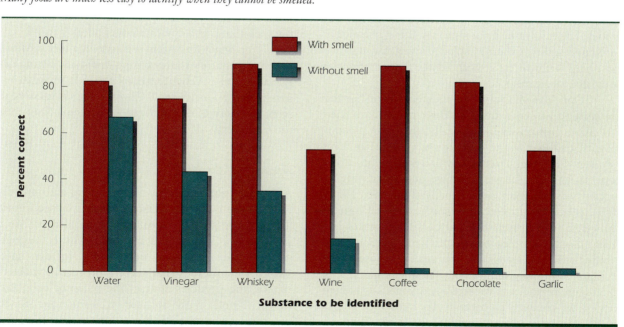

Your enjoyment of these foods depends largely on your sense of smell, in addition to their taste and appearance. Which looks as if it will taste better to you? Explain your reasons why, in psychophysiological terms.

animals. In fact, humans have only 10 million smell receptors, whereas dogs have about 200 million. Nonetheless, odors and fragrances interact powerfully with our emotions, instantaneously calling up memories of past times and places.

Physical and Psychological Properties in the Sense of Smell

The sense of smell, **olfaction,** enhances our ability to savor food, but also, of course, it functions on its own, independent of taste. Like taste, smell is a chemically activated sense. Airborne molecules that can dissolve in either water or fat are candidates for sensation by our olfactory system.

Once our olfactory system detects scent-bearing molecules, we sense the odor. Researchers have tried to define *primary smells* to parallel the basic psychological qualities of the other sense systems we have studied. One such attempt divided smells into flowery, foul, fruity, burnt, resinous, and spicy, leaving room for combinations of smells (Henning, 1915). The relationships and differences between smells, however, have proven very hard to define systematically. To get an idea of the problem, think of five things you enjoy smelling. Now, describe those smells without using any similes (i.e., "it smells like . . ."). For some reason, our vocabulary for smells is limited unless we compare or contrast one substance with a distinctive odor to another substance. Thus, although we know that smell is active in our psychological

functioning in the recall of memories, there is still no satisfactory way of characterizing what we sense when we detect a smell.

Absolute thresholds for smell are difficult to study because the nasal receptors are somewhat inaccessible. In addition, different substances have different thresholds for detection, as do the smell receptors of different people. In fact, some people are *odor-blind*—unable to detect one or more specific scents. It is also extremely difficult to control the concentrations of odors and to eliminate interference from body, clothing, and environmental odors.

The olfactory system seems to be more sensitive than the gustatory (taste) system in discriminating between stimuli. Weber fractions for jnd's in smell intensity can be as low as 0.05—that is, differences in scent intensity of only 5% can be detected about half the time (Cain, 1977).

Anatomy of the Nose

Airborne scent molecules are drawn up and into the nose by the force of a person's inhalation (see Figure 4-35). They pass up through the nasal cavity to a point below and behind the eyes, where they encounter the **olfactory epithelium** in the nasal *mucosa* (membranes that secrete protective mucus). There, the particles contact the receptor cells that detect smells and initiate transduction. Smell receptors are notable for being among the few kinds of neurons that can fully regenerate in adult mammals. It is a good thing they do because they die after 4 to 8 weeks.

From the Nose to the Brain

The receptors in the olfactory epithelium are also unique among sensory systems in that their axons actually penetrate the skull and combine directly to form each of the two olfactory nerves. Each of the olfactory nerves terminates at one of the two **olfactory bulbs,** where its neurons communicate with other neurons in complex arrangements. From the olfactory bulb, smell impulses primarily bypass the thalamus (unlike other sensory neurons) and go directly into the olfactory cortex in the temporal lobe or to the limbic system (especially the hypothalamus). The hypothalamus and the limbic system may be involved in whether we accept or reject a food, based on its smell.

How We Smell

We sense an odor when molecules are released from a substance and carried through the air into the nasal cavity and to the olfactory receptors in the olfactory epithelium. How, exactly, do those receptors work? Many of the specifics are not understood, although we do know that each smell receptor can respond to a number of different odors (Keverne, cited in Klivington, 1989). Because there is a constant turnover of smell receptors, it may be advantageous to have each receptor respond to more than one distinctive odor. Although the smell receptors do not respond to one odor alone, each receptor does seem to have a unique pattern of chemical responses to different odors. Given these findings, research has yielded two preliminary theories of smell, which are both prominent among psychologists today.

One proposition is the **lock-and-key theory** (Amoore, 1970), which states that we smell something when there is a special fit between the shape of a molecule that enters our noses and the shape of the olfactory receptors (see Figure 4-36). Different olfactory receptors are receptive to different-shaped molecules. When a given molecule fits a receptor, it is transduced into an electrochemical impulse. (Note that this mechanism strongly resembles that for the link between specific neurotransmitters and specific receptor sites; see Chapter 3.) Some suggest that our receptors also figure out how to form patterns for

FIGURE 4-35
Nasal Cavity
Airborne molecules are inhaled into the nasal cavity. Receptor cells in the olfactory epithelium transduce the chemical energy of smell into the electrochemical energy of the nervous system.

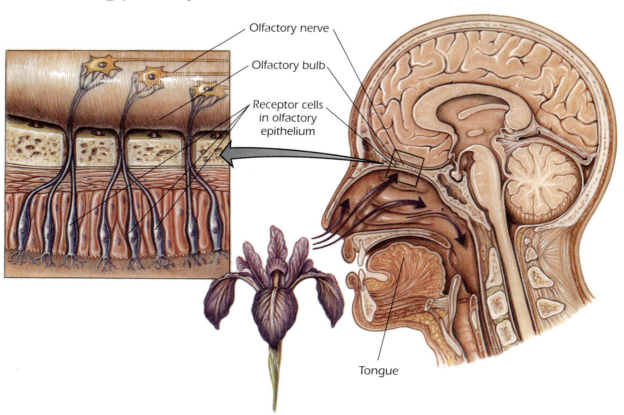

Olfactory nerve

Olfactory bulb

Receptor cells in olfactory epithelium

Tongue

new smells; this process may serve as a means by which we can create or adapt patterns for a diversity of smells (Keverne, cited in Klivington, 1989).

A second theory is the **vibration theory** (Wright, 1977, 1982), which postulates that the molecules of each distinctively smelled substance generate a specific vibration frequency. The characteristic vibration frequency of the molecule specifically affects the receptors by disrupting particular chemical bonds in the receptor cell membranes. When these bonds are ruptured, they release the energy stored in those bonds, which is transduced into the electrochemical energy of neural impulses. The distinctive pattern of ruptured bonds is transduced into a characteristic pattern of electrochemical activity, which the brain interprets as specific odors.

One of the most interesting topics in the study of smell is **pheromones,** chemical substances secreted by animals, which trigger specific kinds of reactions in other animals, usually of the same species. These reactions include mutual identification of parent and child, sexual signals, territorial-boundary markers, and both limits on and prompts toward ag-

FIGURE 4-36
Lock-and-Key Theory of Olfaction

According to lock-and-key theory, the characteristic molecular shapes of various odorous chemicals match the distinctive shapes of the receptor cells. When the two shapes match, the receptor cell begins to transduce the energy.

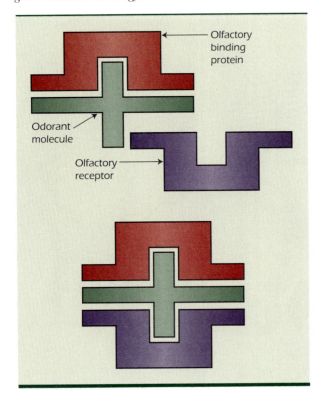

gression. The cortical mapping of smell information seems to fit an association with social and sexual behavior (Kolb & Whishaw, 1990). However, there is some disagreement as to whether pheromones operate in the human species.

Research shows that people react psychologically to smell. For example, evidence indicates that within the first few weeks of life, breast-fed infants can identify their mothers by smell. Women who have at least weekly contact with male underarm secretions (e.g., through intimate contact) appear to have more regularly timed menstrual cycles, and women who have regular contact with other women (or with their underarm secretions) tend to have synchronized menstrual cycles (Coren & Ward, 1989). The link between smell and sexual attraction is less clear, but women seem to find male odors more attractive than do other men. In any case, women seem more sensitive to odors (in absolute terms) and more responsive to odors (in terms of their self-reports and other behavior) than are men. In addition, smells have been known to evoke distant memories, including the emotions pertaining to the remembered events (see Chapter 3 for the neurological links between emotions and smells).

As with the other senses, there are wide individual differences in sensitivity to smells. Most people have lost most or all of their sense of smell at one time or another, as when their nasal passages are blocked by mucus, preventing any external access to the olfactory receptors. The sense of smell also decreases with age. Many people over age 70 years report a serious loss in their sensitivity to smells (Rabin & Cain, 1986), perhaps because as their nasal receptor cells die, the receptors are not regenerated as much or as quickly.

How would you go about devising a classification system for kinds of smells?

Skin Senses

Many talk-show hosts and perfume sellers suggest that smell plays a powerful role in our sexual and other interpersonal behavior. Although psychologists may question this conclusion about smell, few doubt that touch plays such a role. When infant monkeys are deprived of touch for days at a time, they show numerous physiological changes, as well as transitory behavioral aberrations. If the deprivation continues for extended periods of time, the monkeys demonstrate long-term effects, such as an apparent inability

The pain receptors in this boy's knee are alerting him to pay attention to the damaged tissue.

The pressure receptors in their skin enable these children to sense touching and being touched.

to demonstrate normal patterns of social interaction, particularly in regard to sexual behavior and parenting behavior (see Chapter 13 in regard to Harlow's studies on attachment).

Although researchers clearly would not introduce severe touch deprivation to human infants, some research indicates the importance of touch to humans. For instance, tactile stimulation seems to enhance the physiological stability of preterm infants and to promote their weight gain (a crucial factor in the health and vitality of such infants). Touch even seems important to the early development of visual perception (Bower, 1971). Some research on adults shows positive effects of touch as well. For example, touching or stroking a pet seems to lower heart rate.

Often, we call the sense of touch the fifth sense. The term "touch," however, insufficiently characterizes the various sensations of pressure, temperature, and pain. Thus, a better term may be the "skin senses"—formally termed the **haptic** senses—the

means by which we become sensitive to pressure, temperature, and pain stimulation directly on the skin.

Thus far, we have discussed the way in which our sensory systems respond to sensory information that reaches us from outside our bodies; these *exteroceptive* systems receive external stimulation. In addition, we have *interoceptive* systems, which receive internal stimulation from within our bodies, such as feeling flushed, feeling a bellyache, feeling dizzy, or feeling how our bodies are positioned in space. Some also refer to interoception as *proprioception* (receiving information about your own body).

Physical and Psychological Properties in the Skin Senses

Our skin can respond to a variety of external stimuli. The way we sense these physical stimuli results in a psychological interpretation of the sensation as pain, warmth, and so on. Objects pressed against the skin change the skin's shape, causing the sensation of pressure. When even a single tiny hair on our skin is displaced, we feel pressure from its movement. The temperature of an object against the skin results in a sensation of warmth or cold. Slight electrical stimulation of our skin usually results in a sensation of pressure and perhaps of temperature. Too much of any kind of stimulation generally results in pain.

Anatomy of the Skin

We can feel through our skin because its layers are permeated with sensory receptors (see Figure 4-37). Our various skin senses have different kinds of sensory receptors. Our specialized receptors for touch have distinctive globular ("corpuscular") swellings at their dendritic endings. These corpuscular cells are located at different levels of the skin and are sensitive to different types of touch (pin-point surface pressure, broad-region surface pressure, deep pressure, movement, and vibration). Suppose you were blindfolded and then touched by three different objects, each of which had a one-inch-square surface that was pressed against your skin: a cube of absorbent cotton, then a stiff brush, and then a polished metal cube. Even with the blindfold, you could probably tell the differences among them. If the brush or another object were vibrated, even if it were not moved otherwise, you would be able to detect the vibration, too. Our skin also contains specialized receptors for noticing when a hair follicle is bent, for noticing pain, and for noticing temperature. These noncorpuscular (i.e., lacking globular swellings) receptors are **free nerve endings.**

FIGURE 4-37
Skin Receptors

Our skin contains sensory receptors for pain, pressure, and temperature, each of which serves a different function and provides distinctive sensory information. (See the magnified photo.) As we saw in the discussion of reflex movement in Chapter 3, if the receptors detect a sudden, strong feeling of pain (or pressure or extreme temperature), the neural impulse normally sent to the brain may be rerouted at the spine to create a sudden muscular movement that removes the body from the source of the pain. If the strong pain continues, the neural impulses it creates go directly to the cerebral cortex; chronic pain is routed through the limbic system to the cortex.

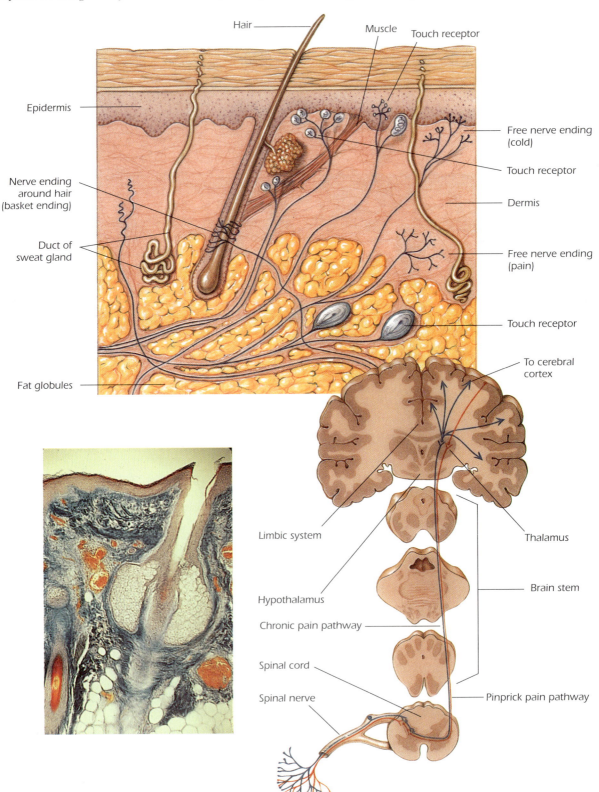

From the Skin to the Brain

From the skin, two different kinds of sensory neurons travel to the spinal cord, where they pass impulses to other neurons that travel to the brain (Coren & Ward, 1989). The sensory neurons are either fast-conducting myelinated neurons, which usually travel over relatively long distances to reach the spinal cord, or relatively slow-conducting unmyelinated neurons, which usually have to travel only short distances to reach the spinal cord. Once the sensory neurons reach the spinal cord, the two kinds of neurons take different routes, via two different kinds of nerves in the spinal cord.

The first kind of spinal-cord nerve collects the information from the myelinated neurons, ascends the spinal cord, crosses over to the other half of the brain at the medulla oblongata, goes to the thalamus, and then to the somatosensory cortex, where it is mapped as described in Chapter 3. This kind of nerve responds mostly to the sense of pressure and also to movement.

The second kind of spinal nerve collects information from the unmyelinated sensory neurons in the skin. In the spinal cord, these unmyelinated sensory receptor neurons can also make local connections with motor effector neurons to produce reflexive reactions. This second kind of nerve travels up the spinal cord and then divides into two bundles at the medulla oblongata. One bundle conveys information about diffuse, dull, or burning pain, and the other information about localized, sharp, or piercing pain. Both bundles cross over contralaterally, so that pain in the right side of the body is a function of activity in the left side of the brain, and vice versa. The nerve bundles stop at the thalamus and the limbic system, important for emotion and memory, and then go to the somatosensory cortex.

In addition to providing information about pain, the second kind of nerve carries information about temperature and pressure. Also, we sense pain, temperature, pressure, and movement with less precise localization than we do our sensations that travel via the faster route.

Pressure

The skin sense of pressure allows us to feel physical stimuli that contact the exterior of the body. We are able to sense heaviness, vibration, and location of pressure. Our absolute thresholds for pressure differ widely across various parts of the body. For example, the cheek is more sensitive than the palm of the hand (Weinstein, 1968). Absolute thresholds are usually tested by touching different locations on the skin with a small bristle or vibrating stimulus, using various amounts of force (see Figure 4-38).

Another means of testing skin sensitivity to pressure is to measure the two-point threshold, discovered by Weber. The **two-point threshold** is the point at which two touch stimuli cannot be distinguished and are felt as a single touch. In a way, this threshold is a form of jnd, although an additional variable—location on the body—is included in the measurement. Try it yourself; you will find that your lower face, hands, and feet are far more sensitive at discriminating two stimuli than are your back, calves, or upper arms (Weinstein, 1968; see Figure 4-39).

Temperature

Maintaining a consistent body temperature is essential to our survival, and two kinds of nerve fibers in the skin enable us to sense warmth and cold via their patterns of firing. **Cold fibers,** as you might imagine, respond to cooling of the skin by increasing their rate of firing relative to the rate at which they fire when at rest. **Warm fibers** respond to warming of the skin (in the range of 95–115 degrees Fahrenheit [35–46

FIGURE 4-38
Absolute Thresholds for Pressure
Different regions of the body have differing degrees of sensitivity to pressure. How would an evolutionary psychologist explain this varying amount of sensitivity?

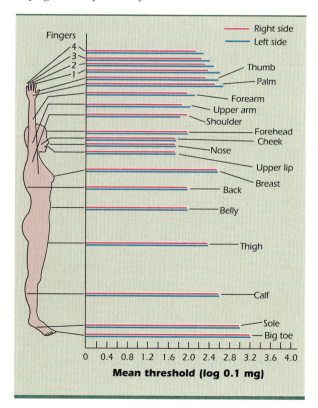

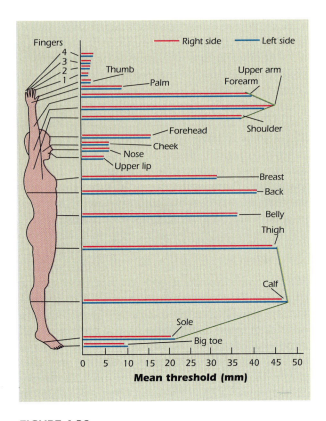

FIGURE 4-39
Two-Point Thresholds
Different regions of the body also have differing thresholds for sensing two close but distinctive points of contact. Again, how would an evolutionary psychologist explain this?

celsius]) analogously (Hensel, 1981). The two types of fibers are not equally distributed across the body. Even across a small patch of skin area, different portions may be differentially responsive to cold and warmth.

Because the two types of fibers are highly responsive to changes in temperature, what we sense as cold or warm depends on our adaptation level. When we start off cold, what we sense as warm may be quite a bit colder than what we sense as warm when we start off hot. Consequently, it is very difficult to quantify absolute thresholds in measurement of temperature, so research has focused largely on adaptation and, to a lesser extent, on jnds. When our skin is at a normal temperature, we can detect greater warmth of only 0.72 degrees Fahrenheit (0.4 celsius) and increased coolness of 0.27 degrees Fahrenheit (0.15 celsius) (Kenshalo, Nafe, & Brooks, 1961).

Intense stimulation, as well as any resulting damage to tissues, can lead to pain. It is important to recog-

nize, however, that factors that go beyond the individual's mere sensory physiology (e.g., cultural influences, personal expectations, and adaptation levels; see Chapter 20) seem to affect how much pain a person experiences. Although there may be external causes of pain, pain is generally considered an interoceptive phenomenon (i.e., the pain sensation itself is produced within the body.) When tissue is damaged, it releases a neurotransmitter, which starts an impulse on its way to the central nervous system.

Different parts of the body are differentially susceptible to pain. The back of the knee, for example, is much more susceptible than the sole of the foot. Moreover, people differ widely in their apparent sensitivity to pain. In extreme cases, some individuals feel no pain at all (see Sternbach, 1963). Although such insensitivity might seem to be an ideal state, many of these individuals die early deaths due to accidental injury. For instance, such persons might lose an enormous amount of blood before even noticing they had been injured, particularly in cases of internal bleeding. Pain is unpleasant, but it serves a functional, evolutionary purpose; it prompts us to remove ourselves from dangerous or stressful situations or to seek a quick remedy for injuries. Stomachache, earache, intestinal cramps, injured joints or bones, and other kinds and sources of proprioceptive pain alert us to internal assaults on our bodies, which may at least help us to avoid future insults to our systems, even if we cannot escape the immediate one.

Can cultural differences explain some variations in pain thresholds? A variety of needs, beliefs, expectations, and practices characteristic of one culture may serve either to raise or to lower thresholds in contrast with other cultures. For example, Asians report more pain than Caucasians and other groups in response to having their ears pierced (Thomas & Rose, 1991). (For more information on pain, its psychological consequences, social and demographic factors contributing to it, and therapeutic treatments of it, see Chapter 20.)

Pain is not the only proprioceptive sense that serves us. You probably do not remember when you learned to walk, but that moment was a triumphant one for your sense of kinesthesis and your vestibular sense (equilibrium). We are not typically conscious of the functioning of these senses, which help us to move, stand upright, and generally feel physically and spatially oriented. Our lack of awareness does not imply that these senses are unimportant, however. If you question the importance of the body senses, try spinning yourself around and around, as you probably did when you were a child, and then see whether you can walk a straight line.

Kinesthesis

Kinesthesis is the sense that helps us to ascertain our skeletal movements: Where are the various parts of our body in respect to one another, and how (if at all) are they moving? Kinesthetic receptors are in the muscles, tendons, joints, and skin. When these receptors detect changes in positions via pressure, they transduce this mechanical energy into neural energy, which codes information about the speed of the change, the angle of the bones, and the tension of the muscles. This information is sent up the spinal cord, where it eventually reaches the brain and is shifted contralaterally in the brain to the somatosensory cortex and to the cerebellum, which is responsible for automatic processes and motor coordination (see Chapter 3).

The kinesthetic receptors in this girl's skeletal muscles combine with her vestibular senses to make her aware of the swiftly changing positions of her body as she leaps through space.

Equilibrium: The Vestibular Sense

The vestibular sense—roughly speaking, the sense of balance or equilibrium—is determined by the orientation of the head relative to the source of gravity, as well as by the movement and acceleration of our bodies through space. We tend not to be aware of our vestibular sense unless it is overstimulated—perhaps on a bumpy airplane flight, or on a carnival ride that is a bit too wild. You probably know the results: dizziness and nausea.

The receptors for equilibrium are located in the inner ear (see Figure 4-40). The **vestibular system** comprises the vestibular sacs and semicircular canals, both of which contain a fluid that moves when the head rotates. The movement in turn causes the hair cells inside the sacs and canals to bend; this mechanical energy is then transduced into electrochemical impulses in the nerves. The impulses travel to the cerebellum and the cortex of the brain, carrying information about the rate of acceleration of the head, as well as about its direction of movement and its relative orientation. These portions of the ear are not used for hearing, although the information they collect is sent to the brain via a portion of the auditory nerve.

The vestibular system informs the visual system about how to control eye position to compensate for head movement. It also uses information from our eyes to assist in sensing motion and balance. In fact, input from the kinesthetic, vestibular, and visual systems converges in the cerebral cortex. Upon reflection, this complexity should come as no surprise to anyone who has suffered from motion sickness, which often results when the brain has to integrate incompatible information from those three systems. For example, picture yourself riding in a moving vehicle but

Part of the thrill of riding a roller coaster is feeling the rapidly changing sensations from our vestibular system.

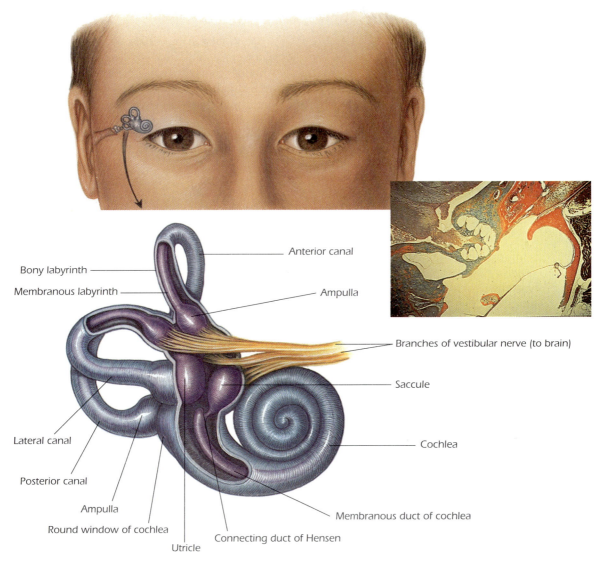

FIGURE 4-40
Vestibular System

Movement of fluid in the semicircular canals in the inner ear enables us to sense shifts in the orientation of our head in relation to gravity.

being unable to see outside (much as a young child might be in a car or a below-deck passenger might be on a boat). What you would see (the inside of the vehicle) would not be moving, but your body would still feel vestibular and kinesthetic movements. As you might guess, we generally feel better when our visual information agrees with our vestibular and kinesthetic information than when it disagrees.

If you were to design an automobile that would minimize the likelihood of occupants experiencing motion sickness, what design features would you include?

Vestibular sensations are welcomed by more than just sensation-seekers who crave speed and motion. The countless rocking chairs that have been used for ages attest to the lulling effects of vestibular stimulation. Perhaps even you have gone for a drive or for a walk when troubled and seeking to be soothed.

We are tremendously lucky to have the resources of our sensory systems available to us. When they are damaged, or lacking, life as we know it is radically different. Our senses are our gateways to thoughts, feelings, and ideas—our bridges from the external world, through our bodies, to our minds. Once we have gathered sensations into our minds, we must make some sense out of them—which calls for perception, the topic of the following chapter.

SUMMARY

Psychophysics 121

1. A *sensation* is a message that the brain receives from a sense. A *sense* is a physical system that collects information for the brain and transduces it from one form of energy into the brain's electrochemical energy.
2. *Psychophysics* is the study of the relationship between physical stimulation and its psychological effects.
3. *Detection* refers to the ability to sense a stimulus. The minimal amount of physical energy of a given kind that can be sensed (detected) 50% of the time is operationally defined as the *absolute threshold*.
4. *Signal-detection theory* (SDT) analyzes responses in terms of *hits* (true positive responses), *false alarms* (false positives), *correct rejections* (true negatives), and *misses* (false negatives). SDT is also used for explaining how we determine the likelihood that a sensation is caused by a particular signal.
5. *Discrimination* involves ascertaining the distinction between one stimulus and another. The *just noticeable difference (jnd)* is the minimum amount of difference that can be detected between two stimuli 50% of the time. The jnd provides a way of measuring the difference threshold.
6. *Weber's law* states that a *jnd* is a constant proportion of the stimulus; the *Weber fraction* is a measure of the ratio of change in stimulus intensity to intensity.
7. *Fechner's law* suggests that as stimulus intensity increases, it takes larger and larger differences between stimuli to generate comparable differences between psychological sensations.

Biological Properties Common to All Senses 126

8. All of the senses share particular biological properties, such as psychophysical thresholds, *transduction*, *sensory coding*, and *adaptation*.
9. Each sense has specialized sensory *receptor cells*, which take in a particular form of energy and transduce it so that sensory neurons can transmit the sensed information to the brain.
10. Impulses from most sensory receptors go via the sensory neurons to the thalamus, which then relays information to the cerebral cortex.
11. The contralateral shift enables sensory neurons from the left side of the body to cross over to the right hemisphere of the brain, and vice versa.
12. Through sensory coding, sensory receptors convey a range of information, such as *intensity (amplitude)* and *quality* (e.g., *wavelength*) of a stimulus. Sensory neurons encode these physical aspects through neural firing, which can be measured by *single-cell recording*. Stimulus intensity is coded by rate of firing and firing-pattern regularity.
13. When our senses detect changes in energy, receptor cells fire vigorously to alert the brain. *Adaptation* is the temporary physiological response to a change in the environment; it varies according to the intensity of the change in the stimulus.

Vision 129

14. We can see because the receptors of our eyes receive and transduce the electromagnetic radiant energy of a very small portion of the electromagnetic spectrum of light.
15. The black round opening in the center of the *iris* is the *pupil*, which becomes dilated or contracted, in response to the amount of light entering it.
16. The *lens* of the eye refracts light and focuses it on the retina, enabling us to see objects clearly at varying distances from us.
17. The *retina* transduces the electromagnetic radiant energy in light into electrochemical impulses.
18. The *duplex retina theory* of vision posits two separate visual systems, one of which is used primarily for vision in the dark (*rods*), and the other of which is used primarily for vision in light (*cones*).
19. *Brightness* refers to our impression of light intensity; it is a psychological, rather than a physical, phenomenon.
20. Three properties of color are *hue*, which is what we usually refer to as "color"; *saturation*, which is the vividness or richness of a color; and *brightness*, reflected from the color.
21. The *trichromatic theory* of color vision posits that we see color through the actions and interactions of cone receptors for three primary colors—red, green, and blue.
22. The *opponent-process theory* of color vision states that we see color through the opposing actions of cells in the thalamus for red versus green and blue versus yellow.

Hearing 143

23. The *cochlea*, the main structure of the inner ear, has within it the *basilar membrane*. The *hair cells* of the basilar membrane transduce the mechanical energy of sound waves into electrochemical energy that can be processed by the brain.
24. According to *place theory*, we hear each pitch as a function of the location that is stimulated in the inner ear.
25. According to *frequency theory*, the vibrations in the inner ear reproduce the vibrations of the sounds that enter the ear. According to the *volley*

principle, neurons cooperate in reproducing these vibrations.

26. *Duplicity theory* holds that both place and frequency contribute to hearing.

27. There are two methods for locating the source of a sound: The *time-difference method* works best for low-frequency sounds, and the *intensity-difference method* works best for high-frequency sounds.

Taste, Smell, and the Other Senses 150

28. We are able to taste because of interactions between chemical substances and *taste buds*, sensory receptors on our tongues. According to a widely accepted theory of taste, the various sensory receptors in the tongue are differentially sensitive to various combinations of the four primary tastes: sweet, sour, bitter, and salty.

29. We are able to smell because of interactions between chemical substances and sensory receptors in our nasal cavities. According to *lock-and-key theory*, we smell something when there is a special fit between the shape of a molecule that enters our noses and the olfactory receptors there. According to *vibration theory*, smell results from a unique vibratory pattern for the various molecules we can smell.

30. Some skin-sense nerves respond to the sense of pressure and movement; others convey two kinds of pain information (one dull, the other sharp), as well as temperature and pressure information.

31. The *two-point threshold* measures skin sensitivity to pressure in different locations.

32. *Cold* and *warm nerve fibers* in the skin enable us to sense temperature through their patterns of firing. Our response to temperature depends on our existing adaptation level.

33. Pain results when damaged tissue stimulates release of a neurotransmitter, which sends an impulse to the central nervous system. Different parts of the body have differing sensitivity to pain. People also differ in their sensitivity to pain.

34. *Kinesthesis* is the sense whereby we ascertain whether we are moving or stationary, where our various body parts are, and how (if at all) the parts are moving. The receptors for kinesthesis are in the muscles, tendons, joints, and skin.

35. Receptors of the *vestibular system*, located in the inner ear, allow us to maintain our balance, also termed equilibrium. Inputs from the vestibular, kinesthetic, and visual systems converge in the cerebral cortex.

KEY TERMS

absolute threshold 122
accommodation 131
achromatic 134
acoustic nerve 147
acuity 134
adaptation 129
adaptation level 129
additive mixture 139
amacrine cells 132
amplitude 127
basilar membrane 145
bipolar cells 132
blind spot 134
brightness 135
cochlea 145
cold fibers 159
cones 132
cornea 130
correct rejection 122
dark adaptation 135
decibel (dB) 144
detection 122
discrimination 123
duplex retina theory 132
duplicity theory 149
eardrum 145

electromagnetic spectrum 129
false alarm 122
Fechner's law 125
fovea 132
free nerve endings 157
frequency 144
frequency theory 148
fundamental frequency 145
ganglion cells 132
hair cells 145
haptic 157
harmonics 145
hertz (Hz) 144
hit 122
horizontal cells 132
hue 138
incus 145
intensity 127
iris 130
just noticeable difference (jnd) 124
kinesthesis 161
lens 131
light adaptation 135
lock-and-key theory 155
malleus 145
miss 122

noise 145
olfaction 154
olfactory bulbs 155
olfactory epithelium 154
opponent-process theory 140
oval window 145
papillae 151
pheromones 156
photopigments 132
photoreceptors 132
pinna 145
pitch 144
place theory 148
primary colors 140
psychophysics 121
pupil 130
purity 139
quality 127
receptive field 126
receptor cells 126
refraction 131
retina 131
rods 132
saturation 138
sensation 120
sense 120

IN SEARCH OF THE HUMAN MIND:
ANALYSES, CREATIVE EXPLORATIONS, AND PRACTICAL APPLICATIONS

1. Try eating your next meal (or a snack) while keeping your eyes closed. Briefly describe how the other senses work together in helping you to enjoy the task of eating.
2. Why do you suppose that being rocked, held, patted, or caressed seems to soothe distressed humans of all ages, with all kinds of problems—from crying infants and emotionally disturbed children to burned-out parents and anxious great-grandparents?
3. In what ways have you noticed that smells affect the way you feel about particular people, particular kinds of food, and particular situations or settings?

4. Earlier in this chapter, you were asked how you might describe the cover of this textbook to someone who has never seen. Now, think about how you would describe it to someone who cannot now see but who was formerly able to see. Compare the ease of performing the two tasks.
5. A rare minority of individuals are *synesthetic*—they respond to one type of sensory stimulus (e.g., a sound or a color) with more than one sensory response (e.g., sensing a particular color when exposed to a given sound). For synesthetes, this cross-modal experience is involuntary, but nonsynesthetes can consciously choose to link sensory modalities. Close your eyes and listen to a piece of instrumental music. What visual images do the musical sounds evoke in you? How would you expect the experience of a synesthete to differ?
6. A neurological patient who had completely lost his sense of smell—and had lost much of his enjoyment of life's sensory pleasures as a result—suddenly seemed to regain his sense of smell. Testing suggested that he had not regained sensory function, but that his brain was reconstructing smells from memory. What are the smells you would be most likely to reconstruct if you had lost your sense of smell?

7. If you had to memorize a long list of terms and definitions, would you be better off trying to remember them by seeing them (e.g., reading printed flashcards) or by hearing them (e.g., having someone drill you by saying the words aloud)? Do you seem to be able to remember material better if it is presented visually (e.g., in a book) or auditorily (e.g., in a lecture)? How do you tailor your studying to your sensory preferences?
8. Many people earn their living based on keen development of at least one of their senses. List at least two examples of professionals who depend on each of the senses described in this chapter.
9. For many of the tragic industrial accidents that have occurred (e.g., the Three Mile Island or Chernobyl nuclear accidents), industrial psychologists have assigned some of the blame to poor design of elements of the environment, such as equipment. Some industrial psychologists have noted that people in jobs such as air-traffic control are often expected to sense sights or sounds or other sensations that are not easy to notice. What is something in your own environment that is poorly designed and which could be made safer, easier to use, or more practical to use? What changes would you make?

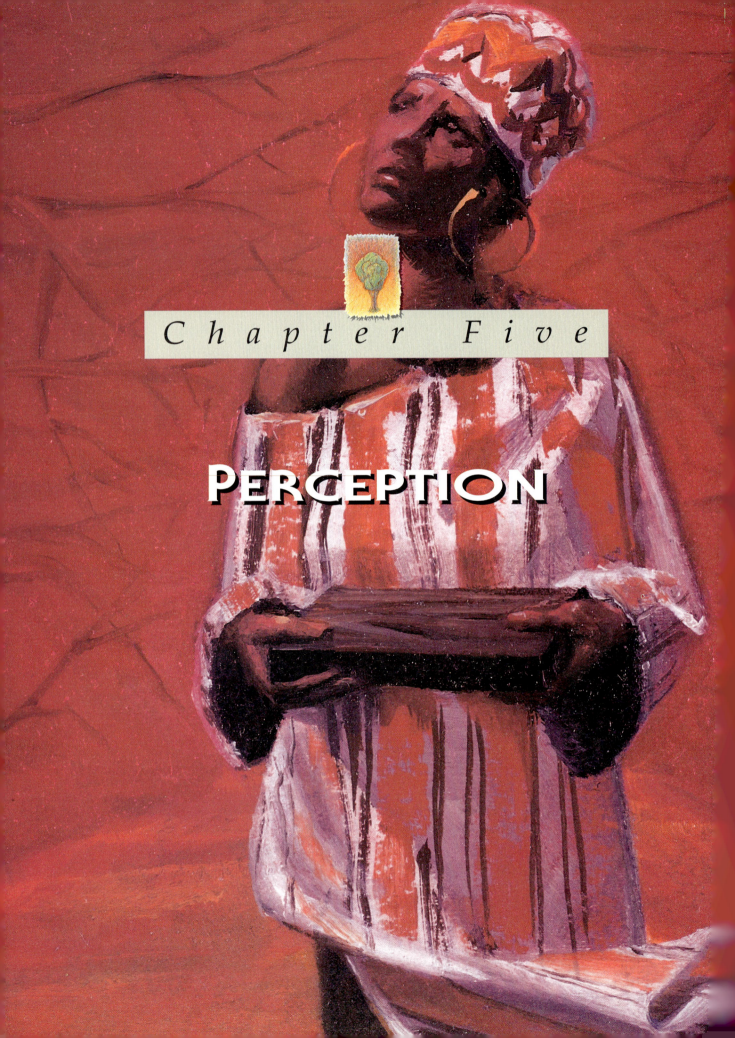

Chapter Five

PERCEPTION

CHAPTER OUTLINE

There was the hint of a smile on his face. He also appeared to have decided that the examination was over and started to look around for his hat. He reached out his hand and took hold of his wife's head, tried to lift it off, to put it on. He had apparently mistaken his wife for a hat! His wife looked as if she was used to such things.

—*Oliver Sacks*, The Man Who Mistook His Wife for a Hat

The preceding passage sounds as though it might come from fiction—perhaps even science fiction. Unfortunately, it comes from an actual case study of a patient, not from the ramblings of a naïve sci-fi writer. The description of this patient illustrates a problem in **perception,** the set of processes by which we recognize, organize, and make sense of the sensations we receive from environmental stimuli.

Perception encompasses many psychological phenomena. For example, have you ever been told that you cannot see something that is right under your nose? Have you ever listened to your favorite song over and over, trying to decipher the lyrics? These examples show that sometimes we do not perceive what we know exists. At other times, however, we perceive things that do not exist. For example, in Figure 5-1, notice that there appear to be two triangles: one right side up and the other upside down. The right side-up one seems to leap out at you, and probably looks lighter and brighter than what surrounds it. It isn't. In fact, if you look closely, you will discover that it does not even exist. It is an **optical illusion,** an image that prompts a distortion in visual perception.

Consider also the Maurits C. Escher illustration, *Belvedere*, shown in Figure 5-2. How many illusions can you find? Each of these examples highlights the complexity of perception.

In general, how well a person perceives and even what a person perceives are related to specific patterns of human adaptation and experience (Berry, 1976). For instance, on average, nomadic people who live in small bands and who must hunt daily (e.g., among many native peoples of Alaska) have sharper and more differentiated visual perception than do people who live in sedentary agricultural communities (Witkin & Berry, 1975; Witkin & Goodenough, 1981).

Optical illusions are normal distortions in perception, but some people have genuine deficits in perception. Some people have severe deficits in their ability to perceive sensory information; these people are said to suffer from **agnosia** (see Chapter 3). Many kinds of agnosias exist, the most well-known of which are visual. People with visual agnosia have normal sensations of whatever sights are in front of them but cannot recognize these sights. In other words, their problem is at the perceptual, not the sensory level.

FIGURE 5-1
Perceived Shapes
What shapes do you see here? Why do you perceive them?

FIGURE 5-2
Belvedere
Dutch artist M. C. Escher (1898–1972) enjoyed playing with optical illusions, making the impossible seem possible. What optical illusions does he employ here? (Copyright © M. C. Escher Heirs, c/o Gordon Art Baarn, Holland)

The cause of their problem usually can be traced to lesions in the brain.

Illusions result from perceptual operations on sensory input. Indeed, perception is inextricably tied to sensation—vision, hearing, and the other senses—yet it also is considered a distinct field of psychological study. This chapter explores how we use our knowledge and understanding of the world to decipher and assign meaning to our sensations.

THEORIES OF PERCEPTION

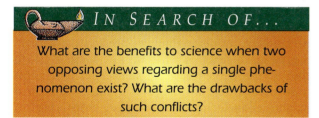

IN SEARCH OF...

What are the benefits to science when two opposing views regarding a single phenomenon exist? What are the drawbacks of such conflicts?

Humans have been pondering perception for millennia, as indicated by the optical illusions used in the construction of the Parthenon (Figure 5-3). Currently, two major theories of perception exist: constructive perception and direct perception. These theories are usually presented in opposition to each other, although sometimes they simply deal with different aspects of the same phenomenon. Few theories really deal with an entire phenomenon, and as we have seen repeatedly, differing theories may actually complement each other.

Constructive Perception

Constructive perception, the traditional view, is often traced to the German physicist and physiologist Hermann von Helmholtz (1821–1894). In Helmholtz's view (1909/1962), the focus of study should be basic sensations. Only when Helmholtz could not figure out a sensory explanation did he suggest any involvement of unconscious inferences or other higher-order processes. Thus, Helmholtz was led to study perception only when sensation offered no adequate explanation of psychological phenomena.

More recently, cognitivist Irvin Rock (1983) has elaborated on Helmholtz's conception of constructive perception. In **constructive perception,** the perceiver constructs (builds up) the perceived stimulus,

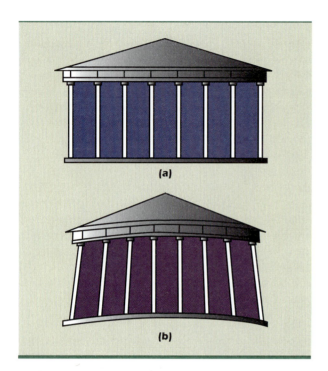

FIGURE 5-3
The Parthenon

Ictinus and Callicrates, designers of the Parthenon, were keenly aware of optical illusions—that is, how the immense façade would appear to people standing at its base. To make the façade look rectilinear (a), they raised the center of the base to offset the illusion (b).

using sensory information as the foundation for the structure. This viewpoint is also known as *intelligent perception* because it holds that higher order thinking plays an important role in perception. According to this view, patterns of stimulation would basically be about as meaningful as the arrangement of grains of sand on a beach were it not for the thinking processes we use to make sense of them.

For example, picture yourself driving down a road you've never traveled before. As you approach a blind intersection, you see an octagonal red sign with white lettering, bearing the letters "ST_P." An over-

grown vine obscures the sign between the "T" and the "P." Chances are, you would construct from your sensations a perception of a stop sign, and you would respond appropriately.

According to the theory of constructive perception, we perceive what we really are looking at because we perform **unconscious inference**—that is, by using more than one source of information, we make unconscious judgments. At first, *sensory information* (in this case, from the retina) implies that the sign shows a meaningless assortment of oddly spaced consonants. However, your *prior learning* tells you that a sign of this shape and color, posted at an intersection of roadways, and containing these three letters in this sequence, probably means that you should stop thinking about the odd letters and start slamming on the brakes. The critical point to remember about this theory is that successful perception requires intelligence and thought, in combination with experience.

Direct Perception

In contrast to the constructivist view, the **direct-perception** perspective holds that the array of information in our sensory receptors—including the sensory context—is all we need to perceive anything. In other words, we do not need anything else, such as prior knowledge or thought processes, to mediate between our sensory experiences and our perceptions. We need to consider only the stimulus object on the retina, or basilar membrane, or taste bud, and so on.

This view was championed by psychologist James J. Gibson. It clearly contrasts with Helmholtz and Rock's ideas because Gibson claimed that we need *not* apply higher level intelligent processes in order to perceive. Instead, like Plato, he believed that we are born with everything we need to know in order to make sense of what we see. Gibson (1979) thought that in the real world sufficient contextual information is usually available to make perceptual judgments, including those regarding shapes. He believed that we use this contextual information directly; in essence, we are prewired to respond to it. Such contextual information might not exist in a laboratory experiment, but it is likely to exist in a real-world setting. Gibson's model is sometimes referred to as an *ecological model* because of Gibson's concern with perception as it occurs in the everyday world (the ecological environment) rather than in laboratory situations.

More recently, David Marr (1982) proposed a theory of visual perception that shares Gibson's emphasis on the information available in the sensory pattern of stimulation. Marr proposed that information from the retina can be organized through the use of two kinds of features: contours and regions of similarity. **Contour** features differentiate one kind of surface from another. For example, one kind of contour represents a convex surface, as would be found on a rounded ball of clay, and another kind of contour represents a concave surface, as would be found if someone bashed in the ball of clay and left a sizable indentation. **Regions of similarity** are areas largely undifferentiated from each other. Marr showed how a model of perception could be specified in such detail that it could be simulated by a computer; hence, his approach is considered a *computational model*.

Compare and contrast the theories of direct perception and constructive perception.

Synthesizing the Two Theories

The Helmholtz–Rock position on perception seems to contradict the Gibson–Marr position. The first view is largely empiricist; the second is largely rationalist. The first view emphasizes the importance of prior knowledge in combination with information in the sensory receptors; this sensory information is presumed to be relatively simple and ambiguous. The second view, by contrast, emphasizes the completeness of the information in the receptors themselves. In their more extreme forms, the viewpoints are incompatible, but in more moderate forms, they are not. Sensory information may be more instrumental (i.e., more complex, less ambiguous, and more important to perception) in interpreting experiences than the constructive (Helmholtz–Rock) position hypothe-

sizes, and yet less instrumental than the direct (Gibson–Marr) position suggests. It seems likely that we use a combination of information from the sensory receptors and our past knowledge to make sense of what we perceive. Your perception of "upside-down" in Figure 5-4 probably requires both direct perception (the immediate shapes of the letters) and constructive perception (based on our knowledge of the words and their meanings).

VISION: DEPTH PERCEPTION

IN SEARCH OF...

Before you read this section, look at the engraving by William Hogarth in Figure 5-5. List the perceptual cues in Hogarth's picture that are consistent with other such cues, and those that are not consistent with other cues. (For example, notice some oddities about the sign hanging in front of the building.)

FIGURE 5-5
False Perspective
At first, the engraving of English artist William Hogarth (1697–1764) seems realistic, but closer inspection reveals conflicting perceptual cues. As Hogarth explained, "Whoever makes a design, without the knowledge of perspective, will be liable to such absurdities as are shown in this print."

FIGURE 5-4
Direct and Constructive Perception
Images such as Scott Kim's "upside-down" challenge us to use both our direct perception and our constructive perception.

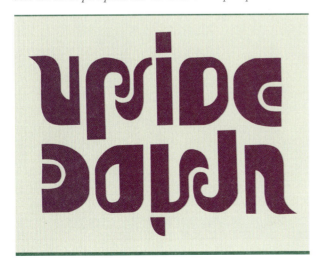

As you move, you constantly look around and visually orient yourself in three-dimensional space. As you look forward into the distance, you look into the third dimension of **depth** (distance from a surface, usually using your own body as that reference surface). Whenever you transport your body, reach for or manipulate objects, or otherwise position yourself in your three-dimensional world, you must make judgments regarding depth.

You even make judgments regarding depth and distances that extend beyond the range of your body's reach. When you drive, you judge depth to assess the distance from you of an approaching automobile. When you decide to call out to a friend walking down the street, you determine how loudly to call according to how far away you perceive your friend to be. If you decide to jump into water, you use depth cues to ascertain whether you are about to land with a thud in shallow water or to plunge freely into deep water.

Refer back to Escher's *Belvedere* (Figure 5-2). One of the confusing aspects of this figure (as well as of other impossible figures by artists such as Escher) is that we perceive contradictory depth cues from different sections of the picture. Small segments of these impossible figures look reasonable to us because there is no inconsistency in their individual depth cues (Hochberg, 1978). However, when we try to make sense of the figure as a whole, the depth cues of the various segments appear to conflict.

Generally, depth cues are either monocular (one-eyed) or binocular (two-eyed). We consider each of these kinds of cues in turn.

Monocular Depth Cues

One way of judging depth is through **monocular depth cues,** which can be represented in just two dimensions, as in a picture. These depth cues are referred to as "monocular" because one eye is sufficient to perceive them, in contrast to those depth cues (considered later) that require two eyes to be perceived. Refer to Figure 5-6, which beautifully illustrates the following monocular depth cues.

Relative size is the perception that things farther away (such as the rear tiles on the floor) are smaller; the farther away an object is, the smaller its image is on the retina.

In this terrible agitation of mind I could not forbear thinking of Lilliput, whose inhabitants looked upon me as the greatest prodigy that ever appeared in the world: where I was able to draw an imperial fleet

in my hand, and perform those other actions which will be recorded for ever in the chronicles of that empire. . . . Undoubtedly philosophers are in the right when they tell us, that nothing is great or little otherwise than by comparison.

—*Jonathan Swift*, Gulliver's Travels

Texture gradient is a change in both the relative sizes of objects and the *densities* in the distribution of objects (i.e., distances among particles, components, or objects, such as the grating on the window to the right of the corridor) when viewed at different distances.

Interposition occurs when an object perceived to be closer partially blocks the view of an object perceived to be farther away. That is, the blocking object

FIGURE 5-6
Monocular Depth Cues in Art
The Annunciation, *by Venetian artist Carlo Crivelli (1430–1494), illustrates several monocular depth cues: texture gradients, relative size, interposition, linear perspective, and location in the picture plane.*

(e.g., the peacock) is perceived to be in front of the blocked object (e.g., the frieze on the wall).

Linear perspective helps us make judgments about distance based on the perception that parallel lines (such as the lines along the sides of the walls) converge as they move farther into the distance. In some pictures, the lines extend all the way toward the horizon, where we can see the so-called vanishing point. At the **vanishing point,** the lines appear to converge, to become indistinguishable, and then to disappear entirely at the horizon.

Location in the picture plane indicates depth, in that objects farther from us are higher in the picture plane under most circumstances (such as the location of the people at the rear of the corridor, compared with the woman kneeling in the cubicle to the right of the corridor). The exceptional circumstances that violate this general rule apply to objects that appear above the horizon line; in this exceptional case, rather than higher objects appearing farther, higher objects appear to be closer. (Try noticing this phenomenon for yourself, either by looking out the window or by drawing a horizon and then drawing two birds—one higher and one lower in the picture plane—then notice which bird appears to be closer to you.)

Glance back at Hogarth's *False Perspective* (Figure 5-5) and at your list of perceptual cues and miscues. How many cues did you miss before that you can find now? In addition to the preceding five monocular depth cues, two monocular depth cues are not shown clearly in either Carlo Crivelli's painting or Hogarth's engraving. These are aerial perspective and motion parallax.

Aerial perspective observes the relative distribution of moisture and dust particles in the atmosphere as a means of judging distance. Objects close to us are relatively unaffected by these particles and so appear clear. But at increasing distances larger numbers of these particles make objects appear hazier and less distinct. The effect of aerial perspective is particularly dramatic on foggy, smoggy, or otherwise hazy days, when objects can appear farther away than they actually are because of the unusually high concentration of water droplets or dust particles in the air. On a particularly clear day, objects may appear closer than they actually are, due to the near-absence of such particles. (Hogarth's engraving shows this effect somewhat, in that the building in the foreground appears more clearly textured than does the building in the background. See also Figure 5-16, in which Renoir has illustrated aerial perspective.)

Motion parallax is the apparent difference in the speed and direction of objects when seen from a moving viewpoint. Because motion parallax is the result of movement, it cannot be shown in a two-dimensional, static picture. You have observed the phenomenon before, however. Imagine going for a ride and watching the passing scenery through a side window. Parallax is created by motion as you move from one point to another and apprehend stationary distant objects from changing points of view. If you look through the window and fixate on one given point in the scene, objects closer to you than that point will appear to be moving in the direction opposite to your direction, while objects beyond the fixation point will appear to be moving in the same direction as you are. You thereby obtain a depth cue by ascertaining which objects are moving in which direction. Moreover, the objects that are closer to you appear to be moving (toward you or with you) more quickly.

Motion parallax is more visually complex than the other monocular cues because it requires movement and therefore cannot be used to judge depth in a stationary image, such as a picture. Another level of complexity involves binocular depth cues, which are based on disparities in perception between the two eyes. Table 5-1 summarizes some of the monocular and binocular cues used in perceiving depth.

> Which of the monocular depth cues seems to be the most important to depth perception? Why?

Binocular Depth Cues

Binocular depth cues capitalize on the fact that each eye views a scene from a slightly different angle; this disparity of viewing angles provides information about depth. The term for three-dimensional perception of the world through the use of binocular (two-eyed) vision is **stereopsis.** With stereo sound, you hear slightly different sounds coming to each ear, and you fuse those sounds to form realistic auditory perceptions. With stereopsis, you receive slightly different visual images in each eye, and you fuse those two images to form realistic visual perceptions. You rely on this fusion of the images from each eye to give you a coherent visual representation of what you are viewing. Not all parts of a visual image actually fuse, although you are not normally aware of seeing two images. (Under extraordinary circumstances—after a concussive blow to the head, for example—your eyes may go out of alignment, and you may become uncomfortably aware of *diplopia*, or double vision.)

TABLE 5-1
Monocular and Binocular Cues for Depth Perception
Various perceptual cues help us perceive the three-dimensional world. We can observe some of these cues with only one eye and others with both eyes.

Cues for Depth Perception	Appears Closer	Appears Farther Away
Monocular Depth Cues		
Texture gradients	Larger grains, farther apart	Smaller grains, closer together
Relative size	Bigger	Smaller
Interposition	Partially obscures other object	Is partially obscured by other object
Linear perspective	Apparently parallel lines seem to diverge	Apparently parallel lines seem to converge
Aerial perspective	Images seem crisper, more clearly delineated	Images seem fuzzier, less clearly delineated
Location in the picture plane	Above the horizon, objects are higher in the picture plane; below the horizon, objects are lower in the picture plane	Above the horizon, objects are lower in the picture plane; below the horizon, objects are higher in the picture plane
Motion parallax	Objects closer to you than the fixation point appear to be moving in the direction opposite to your direction	Objects beyond the fixation point appear to be moving in the same direction as you
Binocular Depth Cues		
Binocular convergence	Eyes feel a tug inward toward nose	Eyes relax outward toward ears
Binocular disparity	Huge discrepancy between image seen by left eye and image seen by right eye	Minuscule discrepancy between image seen by left eye and image seen by right eye

Binocular Convergence

Because your two eyes are in slightly different places on your head, when you rotate your eyes so that an image of an object that is in front of you falls directly on each fovea (see Chapter 4), each eye must turn inward slightly to register the same image. The closer the object you are trying to see, the more your eyes must turn inward, as illustrated by Figure 5-7b. Our brains receive neural information from the eye muscles about the convergence of the eyes, and they assume that the more the eyes converge, the closer the perceived object must be.

Binocular Disparity

Because the two eyes are in different places, each has a slightly different view of the world (see Figure 5-7a). Because of this **binocular disparity** (slight discrepancy in the viewpoint of each eye), the brain must integrate two slightly different sets of information from each of the optic nerves to make decisions about depth, as well as about height and width.

The closer an object is to us, the greater the disparity is between each eye's view of the object. You can test these differing perspectives by holding your finger about an inch from the tip of your nose. Look at it first with one eye covered, then with the other eye covered. Your finger will appear to jump back and forth. Now do the same for an object 20 feet away, then 100 yards away. The apparent jumping, which indicates the amount of binocular disparity, will decrease with distance. If something is askew in our depth perception, we are seriously impaired in our ability to function in a three-dimensional world. Another aspect of vision seems to be at least as important as depth perception and appears to be far less complex than depth perception does at first glance: form perception.

FIGURE 5-7
Binocular Convergence and Disparity
To focus on an object, our eyes converge—that is, they adjust to have the image fall on each retina. Because our eyes are separated, they see a slightly different angle of the object. This disparity in the view from each eye is greater for objects that are closer to us. Our brains use the convergence and disparity information as depth cues.

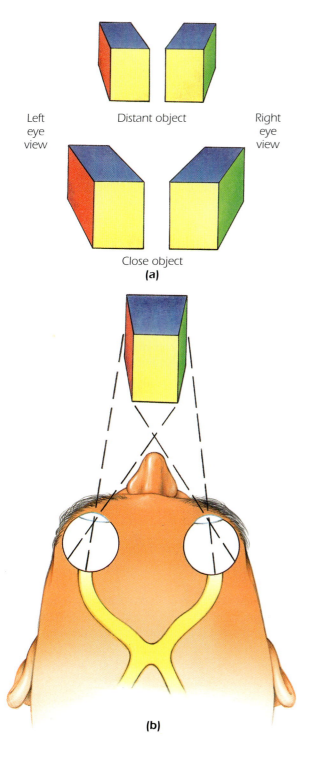

Left eye view   Distant object   Right eye view

Close object
(a)

(b)

What tasks would require the use of binocular depth cues? How might a person with only one eye compensate for the lack of binocular depth cues?

VISION: FORM PERCEPTION

IN SEARCH OF...

Imagine you are magically transported to an alien world, in which you recognize nothing (much as newborns arrive in our strange world). How would you react? How would you learn to orient yourself and to function in this alien world?

Our discussion of form perception is divided into two main parts: (1) how we recognize forms, and (2) how we recognize forms that fall into patterns, such as letters and numbers.

Theories of Form Recognition

Two of the main attributes of form are size and shape. How, exactly, do we perceive size and shape? Let's consider the Gestalt and the feature-detector approaches to form perception.

Gestalt Psychology

The **Gestalt approach** is based on the notion that the whole is greater than the sum of its individual parts (see Chapter 2). Gestalt principles are particularly relevant to understanding how we perceive an assembly of forms.

When you walk into a familiar room, you perceive that some things stand out (e.g., faces in photographs or posters) and that others fade into the background (e.g., undecorated walls and floors). A **figure** is any object perceived as being highlighted, almost always against, or in contrast to, some kind of receding, unhighlighted (back)**ground.**

Figure 5-8 illustrates the **figure-ground** concept. It shows **reversible figures,** in which each of a given pair of adjacent or even interconnecting figures can be seen as either figure or ground. In one, you can see a white vase against a black background; in the other, two silhouetted faces peer at each other against the ground of a white screen. Note, however,

FIGURE 5-8
A Gestalt Gift

Is this a light vase against a dark ground or the light-silhouetted profiles of Queen Elizabeth II and Prince Philip against the background? The vase was a gift to the queen on her silver jubilee.

that it is impossible to see both sets of objects simultaneously. Although you may switch rapidly back and forth between the vase and the figures, you cannot see them both at the same time. Table 5-2 summarizes and defines a few of the Gestalt principles of form perception, including figure-ground perception: **proximity, similarity, closure, continuity,** and **symmetry** (see also Figure 5-9).

The Gestalt principles of form perception are remarkably simple, yet they characterize much of our perceptual organization. It is important to realize, however, that these principles are descriptive rather than explanatory. Merely labeling a phenomenon does not, in itself, account for how the phenomenon occurs. One contemporary approach to form perception better explains how we perceive forms.

If Gestalt principles of form perception do not explain the mechanism of form perception, why are they considered valuable to the understanding of form perception?

A more recent approach attempts to link the perception of form to the functioning of neurons in the brain. This psychophysiological method, the **feature-detector approach,** is based on the pioneering work of Nobel laureates David Hubel and Torsten Wiesel (1979). Using single-cell recording techniques with animals, these researchers carefully traced the route of the neurons from the receptors in the retina, through the ganglion cells and the thalamic nucleus cells, to the visual cortex (see Chapter 4). Their research showed that specific neurons of the visual cortex respond to varying stimuli that are presented to the specific retinal regions connected to these neurons. Each individual cortical neuron, therefore, can be mapped to a specific *receptive field* on the retina, with a disproportionately large amount of the visual cortex devoted to neurons mapped to receptive fields in the foveal region of the retina.

Surprisingly, most of the cells in the cortex do not respond simply to spots of light, but rather to "specifically oriented line segments" (Hubel & Wiesel, 1979, p. 9). What's more, these cells vary in the degree of complexity of the stimuli to which they respond. In general, the size of the receptive field increases—as does the complexity of the stimulus required to prompt a response—as the stimulus proceeds through the visual system to higher levels in the cortex. More specifically, Hubel and Wiesel isolated three kinds of visual cortex neurons (see Figure 5-10): (1) a layer of relatively primitive cells that receive direct input from the geniculate nucleus of the thalamus and that operate similarly to those subcortical cells, (2) "simple cells," and (3) "complex cells."

The primitive cells chiefly relay information to the appropriate simple cells. **Simple cells** receive input from the more primitive cortical cells and then fire in response to lines in the receptive field. These cells seem to be the most excited by lines oriented at a particular optimal angle. To stimulate a response, the lines must fall within about a 15-degree range of the optimal angle. The specific optimal angle of stimulation differs from one cell to another. A particular cell might also preferentially respond to particular light-dark boundaries, to particular bright lines on dark backgrounds, or to particular dark lines on bright backgrounds; even the thickness of the lines may affect whether the cell responds to the stimulus. Hubel and Wiesel call the various lines *features*, and so the neurons that detect and respond to them are called *feature detectors.*

Hubel and Wiesel (1979) have guessed that groups of these simple cells feed into **complex cells.**

FIGURE 5-9
Gestalt Principles of Visual Perception
The Gestalt principles of figure-ground, proximity, similarity, continuity, closure, and symmetry aid in our perception.

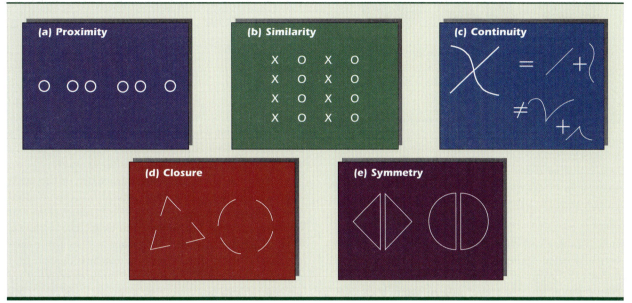

TABLE 5-2
Gestalt Principles of Form Perception

Gestalt Principles	Principle	Figure Illustrating the Principle
Figure-ground	When perceiving a visual field, some objects (figures) seem prominent, and other aspects of the field recede into the background (ground).	Figure 5-8 shows a figure-ground vase, in which one way of perceiving the figure brings one perspective or object to the fore, and another way of perceiving the figure brings a different object or perspective to the fore and relegates the former foreground to the background.
Proximity	When we perceive an assortment of objects, we tend to see objects that are close to each other as forming a group.	Figure 5-9a shows six circles, which we tend to see as forming groups rather than six separate circles.
Similarity	We group objects on the basis of their similarity.	Figure 5-9b shows four rows of letters. We see alternating rows of *X*s and *O*s.
Continuity	We tend to perceive smoothly flowing or continuous forms rather than disrupted or discontinuous ones.	Figure 5-9c shows crossed lines, which we perceive as a straight line bisecting a curved line, rather than disjointed angles.
Closure	We tend perceptually to close up, or complete, objects that are not, in fact, complete.	Figure 5-9d shows only disjointed, jumbled line segments, which we close up in order to see a triangle and a circle.
Symmetry	We tend to perceive forms that comprise mirror images about their center, based on limited sensory information	Figure 5-9e shows a diamond and a circle each split into two symmetrical parts.

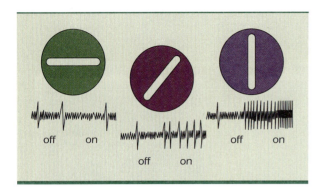

FIGURE 5-10
Feature Detectors
David Hubel and Torsten Wiesel discovered that cells in our visual cortex become activated only when they detect the sensation of line segments or particular orientations. (Recall Figure 4-5)

Each complex cell then fires in response to lines of particular orientations anywhere in the receptive field of that cell's group of simple cells. Complex cells may receive input from one eye only or from both eyes (Hubel & Wiesel, 1979), and they appear insensitive to the particular type of light-dark contrasts of a line segment, as long as the segment is oriented appropriately. Some complex cells fire in response only to line segments of particular orientations and precise lengths in the receptive field.

Based on Hubel and Wiesel's work, other feature detectors have been found that respond to corners and angles (DeValois & DeValois, 1980; Shapley & Lennie, 1985). In some areas of the cortex, highly sophisticated complex cells (called "hypercomplex cells" by some researchers) fire maximally only in response to very specific shapes (e.g., a hand or a face). Interestingly, the size of the form does not seem to affect how frequently these cells will respond (Kolb & Whishaw, 1990).

> How might you visually depict the functional interrelationships among the primitive cells, the simple cells, the complex cells, and even the hypercomplex cells? Label the visual elements showing these interrelationships.

Pattern Recognition

The forms we perceive fall into *patterns* of various kinds. One of the more interesting problems that psychologists have tried to address is how people recognize such patterns as letters, numbers, or faces. The problem is tricky. Although it is possible to specify in a reasonably complete way the features of a letter or

number, it is exceedingly difficult to specify completely the features of a face. What you may take for granted—for example, the ability to recognize the face of your friend—is not something everyone does easily.

Theoretical Approaches to Pattern Recognition

How do you know the letter *A* when you see it? You may be thinking, it is an *A* because it *looks* like an *A*. What makes it look like an *A*, though, instead of an *H*? Just how difficult it is to answer this question becomes apparent when you look at Figure 5-11. What subjectively feels like a simple process of pattern recognition is almost certainly quite complex.

How do we connect what we sense in the environment to what we have stored in our minds? Gestalt psychologists (Köhler, 1940) referred to this question as the **Hoffding function** (the function that links what is sensed with what is stored in memory), in honor of the nineteenth-century Danish psychologist Harald Hoffding, who questioned whether perception can be reduced to a simple association between what is seen and what is remembered. The problem posed by this question is shown in Figure 5-11, where two identical perceptual forms evoke different letter names. What explanations account for how we make the connection between what we perceive and what we know?

TEMPLATE-MATCHING APPROACHES.   A theory posits that we have stored in our minds **templates** (prototypes, best examples) that represent each of the patterns we might potentially recognize. We recognize a pattern by matching it to the template that best fits what we see (Selfridge & Neisser, 1960). We see examples of *template matching* in our everyday lives. Fingerprints are matched in this way, and machines rapidly process imprinted numerals on checks by comparing them to templates. However, the theory of template matching has some obvious

FIGURE 5-11
Pattern Recognition
When you read these words, you probably see a capital H and a capital A in the middle of each respective word. Look more closely at them, though. Do any features differentiate the two letters? If not, why did you perceive them as different? (After Selfridge, 1955)

Searchers . . . *WENDELL GARNER*

Wendell Garner received his PhD in experimental psychology. He is Professor Emeritus in the Psychology Department at Yale University.

Q: *How did you become interested in psychology in general and in your area of work in particular?*

A: I took my first psychology course in my junior year of college, from Paul Whitely, and I became hooked on psychology as a career. It was a fascinating, quantitatively oriented course, and perception simply fascinated me the most. Then this fascination was enhanced by my working in the research laboratories at Harvard University during World War II, since most of the research I did was perceptual in nature.

Q: *What theories have influenced you the most?*

A: Information theory certainly influenced much of my research; it helped me get solutions to problems I was already working on. I don't feel that my research has been much influenced by any single person in the specific sense. In the broader sense, Paul Whitely was trained as a Functionalist, and the willingness of functionalism to accept any kind of problem certainly has been a principle in my own research.

Q: *What is your greatest asset as a psychologist?*

A: The ability to be analytic about a problem without preconceived ideas about what should come out of the research. I can let the data talk to me.

Q: *What distinguishes a great psychologist from just a good psychologist?*

A: A good psychologist knows how to use the ideas and tools of the profession effectively. A really great psychologist introduces the ideas and even the tools.

Q: *How do you usually get your ideas for research?*

A: I get my research ideas to a large extent from personal observation. Some came from applied work I have done. A lot of ideas have come simply from reading the literature in my field and noting incongruities, which made it clear that we did not understand it.

Q: *How do you decide whether to pursue an idea?*

A: Whether I pursue a research project depends on whether I have the resources to pursue it now, or whether I can translate the idea into a viable research project. Rarely do I drop a good problem. Rather, I put it on the back burner until the right conditions occur to pursue it. My record for keeping an idea on the back burner is seven years.

Q: *What is your major contribution to psychology?*

A: Emphasizing the importance of the concept of perceptual structure. It has not only helped me solve problems, but has also had considerable influence on others in fields as far removed from perception as developmental and social psychology.

Q: *What do you want students to learn from you?*

A: I want my students to learn to think clearly, analytically, and objectively about their research.

Q: *What advice would you give to someone starting in psychology?*

A: Be sure that the ideas you choose to work on are intellectually stimulating. But also be sure that you are going to enjoy the nitty-gritty of doing research in the field you have chosen, because if you don't enjoy what is such a large part of the research process, you will burn out.

Q: *What did you learn from your mentors?*

A: I learned, largely from Paul Whitely, to be tolerant of all schools of psychology and to accept all methods. Pragmatism is my personal philosophy of science.

Q: *How do you keep yourself academically challenged?*

A: I don't have to keep myself academically challenged. My work and other people constantly challenge me.

Q: *What do you want people to remember about you?*

A: I want to be remembered as innovative and analytically clear, and as having done research of long-term, if not permanent, significance. My first book, *Applied Experimental Psychology*, and my most important book, *Uncertainty and Structure as Psychological Concepts*, were both in print for 20 years. That longevity is more important to me than greater but momentary success. Some research articles I published in the late 1940s are still cited in the literature and have been represented as classics. That is very satisfying!

---

difficulties, as suggested by its inability to explain our perception of the words in Figure 5-11.

FEATURE-MATCHING APPROACHES.   Plausible explanations, which fit the Hubel and Wiesel findings, are **feature-matching** theories, according to which we attempt to match features of a pattern to features stored in memory. One such feature-matching model is Oliver Selfridge's (1959) "pandemonium" model, based on the notion that metaphorical "demons" with specific duties receive and analyze the features of a stimulus, as shown in Figure 5-12.

Compare Selfridge's model with Hubel and Wiesel's description of the hierarchically arranged visual system. Selfridge's model describes "image demons" (much like the subcortical parts of the visual system), which pass on a retinal image to "feature demons." The feature demons behave like the simple and the complex cells described by Hubel and Wiesel. Selfridge did not specify exactly what such features might be, but Hubel and Wiesel's feature detectors respond to such features as orientation of lines, angles of intersecting lines, shapes, and so on.

At this point, the parallel ends, because Hubel and Wiesel left it to future research to trace the higher levels of cortical processing. Selfridge's model continues, suggesting that at a higher level are "cognitive [thinking] demons," which "shout out" possible

FIGURE 5-12
Pandemonium

According to the feature-matching model, we recognize patterns by matching observed features already stored in memory. We recognize the patterns for which we have found the greatest number of matches. (After Selfridge, 1955)

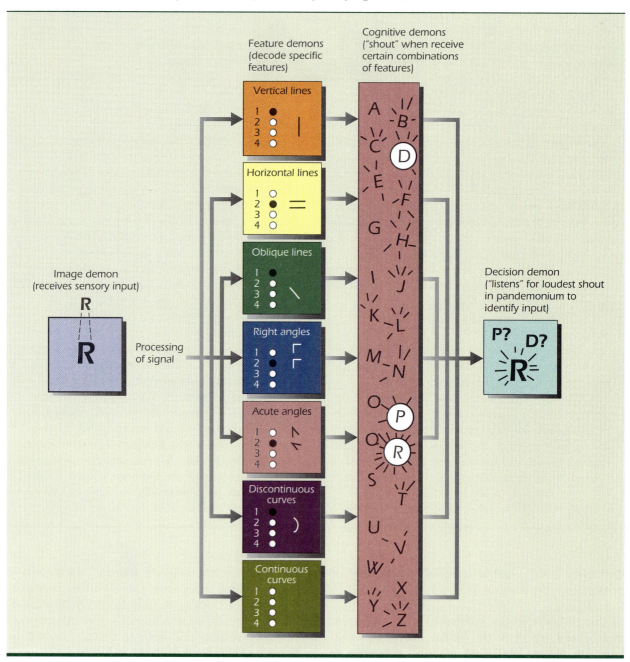

patterns stored in memory that conform to one or more of the features processed by the feature demons. A "decision demon" listens to the pandemonium of the shouting cognitive demons and decides what has been seen, based on which demon is shouting the most frequently (i.e., which has the most matching features).

Although Selfridge's pandemonium model specifies neither exactly what the elementary features are, nor how to go about determining what they might be, Hubel and Wiesel supplied some of the missing information, based on how the brain really works. However, no one would argue that lines of various lengths and orientations can account for the richness of all our visual perception. Irving Biederman (1987) has proposed a more comprehensive set of elementary components: *geons*, which are variations of the shape of a cylinder. Figure 5-13 shows how a small number of geons can be used to build up basic shapes, and then basic objects. A small set of geons comprising as few as 36 elements can generate myriad three-geon objects. Other theorists have taken a similar tack (e.g., Guzman, 1971; Marr, 1982). Thus, it seems within our grasp to construct a feature-matching theory that specifies the simple features that together compose complex objects; as of yet, however, no theory is definitive.

Problems for Theories of Matching in Pattern Perception

Neither template nor feature theories can account fully for some remaining difficult problems. We consider here context effects. Current models still do not fully explain **context effects**, as demonstrated when we perceived "THE CAT" correctly even though what we perceived as two different letters are actually physically identical.

Context effects can be demonstrated experimentally. In one study, people were asked to identify objects after they had viewed them in either an appropriate or an inappropriate context (Palmer, 1975). For example, subjects might have seen a scene of a kitchen followed by stimuli such as a loaf of bread, a mailbox, and a drum. Objects that were appropriate to the established context, such as the loaf of bread in this example, were more rapidly recognized than were objects inappropriate to the established context.

Perhaps even more striking is a context effect known as the **word-superiority effect,** which means that letters are more easily read when they are embedded in words than when they are presented either in isolation or with letters that do not form words. The first report of this effect dates back to James

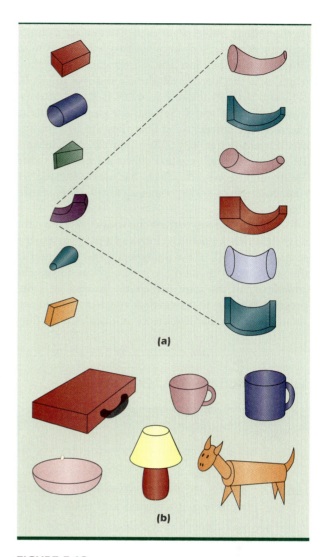

FIGURE 5-13
Geons

Irving Biederman amplified feature-matching theory by proposing a set of elementary shapes (a) that can be combined to become more sophisticated objects (b). (After Biederman, 1987)

McKeen Cattell, who observed that it takes people substantially longer to read unrelated letters than to read letters that form a word (1886). Further demonstrations of the effect were offered by Gerald Reicher (1969) and Daniel Wheeler (1970), so it is sometimes called the "Reicher–Wheeler effect." In a typical word-superiority effect experiment, subjects are very briefly presented with either a word or a single letter (Reicher, 1969; Wheeler, 1970). The presentation is so brief that subjects are almost unaware they have seen the stimulus. The test stimulus is then followed by a **visual mask** (a pattern of "visual noise," which wipes out any visual afterimage that might remain on the retina). Subjects are then given either a choice between two words or between two letters and must choose which they just saw. For example, if the test stimulus is the word *BAR*, the alternatives might be *BAR* and *TAR*. If the test stimulus is *B*, the alternatives might be *B* and *T*. Subjects are more accurate in choosing the correct word than they are in choosing the correct letter (e.g., Johnston & McClelland, 1973). Interestingly, context effects are not limited to letters and words. Research has demonstrated an analogous effect with geometric forms (Pomerantz, 1981).

To summarize, current theories concerning the ways in which we perceive forms and patterns explain some, but not all, of the phenomena we encounter in the study of form and pattern perception. Given the complexity of the form-perception process, it is impressive that we understand as much as we do, although a comprehensive theory still eludes our grasp.

VISION: MOTION PERCEPTION

IN SEARCH OF...

What are some of the many ways that you move (e.g., while standing or sitting, while running or walking, while driving a car, or while riding as a passenger)? How do your perceptions of motion differ under those different conditions?

To put motion perception into context, we must first note that not all psychologists agree there really is such a thing as motion perception. According to some psychologists, we do not perceive actual motion; all we see is an object first in one place, then in another. On this view, then, motion perception is nothing more than a subconscious inference drawn from observing two static states.

Stroboscopic Motion

Through the study of stroboscopic motion, Gestalt psychologists found evidence inconsistent with the idea that motion is only inferred. **Stroboscopic motion** (termed "apparent motion" in the descriptions of Gestalt psychology in Chapter 2) is the appearance of motion produced by a *stroboscope*—an instrument that intermittently flashes an alternating pair of lights against a dark background. If the lights are flashed at

an appropriate distance apart and at appropriately timed intervals (within milliseconds), it appears that a solitary light has moved. If the time interval is too short, the lights appear to flash simultaneously; if the interval is too long, the lights appear to flash in succession, and the observer does not sense the apparent motion. Given just the right timing, the experience of apparent motion indicates that the viewer actually perceives motion and does not just make an inference from two static states (Wertheimer, 1912).

Movies and cartoons use the principle of stroboscopic motion. Similarly, movies are merely rapidly displayed sequences of individual *frames* (single still pictures), shown at the rate of 24 frames per second. We see the same effect in signs that appear to be flowing cascades of moving lights. The apparently flowing lights are merely rapid linear sequences of individual bulbs flashing on and off.

Induced Movement and Apparent Stability

In stroboscopic movement, we see motion where there is none. Sometimes, however, what appears to be motionless is moving and what appears to be moving is standing still. In the earlier description of motion parallax, we noted an example of **induced movement:** When we are passengers looking out the side windows of a moving vehicle, we perceive the scenery, not ourselves, to be moving. Similarly, we may *perceive* the moon as moving through the clouds as we walk along, although we *know* that the clouds are actually moving, not the moon. What determines the appearance of movement in related objects?

Typically, when we perceive an object as being framed by another object, and then either one or both objects move, we perceive the framed object as appearing to move. To use the terminology introduced earlier, the perceived figure (framed object) moves; the perceived ground (frame) remains still. Thus, the scenery framed by a train or bus window seems to be moving in relation to the (seemingly stationary) interior of the vehicle. (Note that this perception does not occur when we look out the front windshield of a car because the view of the moving objects encompasses a larger proportion of our visual field, diminishing the frame effect.) Similarly, when we see the figure of the moon framed against a background of sky and clouds, the figure of the moon appears to be moving within the background of sky and clouds. This effect has been replicated in the laboratory. In one experiment, subjects in a dark room saw a luminous dot surrounded by a luminous frame (Duncker, 1929). When the experimenter moved the frame, the subjects thought that the dot moved.

When we view a rapidly changing series of still photos from a strip of movie film or animated cartoon frames, we perceive a seamless stream of movement, rather than a series of still images. For example, observe carefully the changes in the mouth and right hand of the figure on the left, as well as the position of the crescent on the figure on the right.

Causality

The preceding perceptions have involved determining either (a) whether a single object is moving or (b) which one of two objects is moving. Sometimes, however, the perceptual problem involves determining the interrelationship of the movements of two moving objects. We know that some movements that occur sequentially are related causally. For example, when a moving object bumps into another, the moving object causes the bumped object to move. Sometimes, however, events that occur sequentially and appear to be causally related are actually causally unrelated. They just happened to occur in sequence. This point was familiar to David Hume, a philosopher, who observed that we can only infer causality; we cannot directly perceive it. Still, perceptual psychologists have studied what perceptions lead us to infer causality in the events we perceive.

For example, imagine being in an airplane, viewing a miniature (to you) line of taxicabs pulling up to the curb at the airport. You would observe taxis pulling up to the curb behind one another as other taxis pulled out. Perceptually, if one taxi pulled in and seemed briefly to touch another taxi just at the moment that the other taxi pulled out, it would appear as though the taxi pulling in had nudged the other taxi out. Even though your mind would know otherwise, if the timing of the movements were just right, you would misperceive the causality of movement; that is, you would perceive that one taxi had caused the other to move, even when that clearly was not the case.

A number of variables, including the relative speed of the two taxis and the length of time they are in contact, affect the perception of causality. For example, if the taxi pulling up to the curb were moving faster than the taxi pulling away, and the two taxis were to touch for a short amount of time, the first taxi

would seem to be *launching* the movement of the second taxi. However, if the first taxi were moving more slowly than the second one, and they were to touch for a longer time, the first one would seem to be *releasing* or triggering some latent energy stored in the second one. These effects were actually found in a study of subjects who were watching squares—not taxicabs—which appeared to cause one another to move (Michotte, 1963) (see Figure 5-14).

> In your opinion, do the findings regarding the perception of causality better support the direct-perception theory or the constructive-perception theory of perception? Explain your reasoning.

FIGURE 5-14
Causality of Motion
Even though the dark and colored squares are stationary on this page, we perceive the dark square as having caused the colored square to move. (After Krech & Crutchfield, 1958)

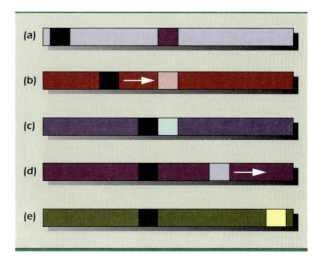

VISION: PERCEPTUAL CONSTANCIES

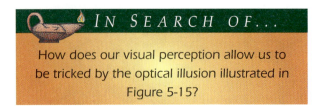

IN SEARCH OF...

How does our visual perception allow us to be tricked by the optical illusion illustrated in Figure 5-15?

Picture yourself walking across campus to your psychology class. Suppose that a student is standing just outside the door as you approach. As you get closer to the door, the amount of retinal space devoted to the student increases. Yet, despite this clear sensory evidence that the student is becoming larger, you know that the student has remained the same size. Why is that?

Your classmate's apparent consistency in size is an example of perceptual constancy. **Perceptual constancy** occurs when our perception of an object remains the same even when our immediate sensation of the object changes. The immediate sensation of the object is the internal **proximal stimulus,** as registered by the sensory receptors on the retina. The external **distal stimulus** is the object as it exists in the world. We know from experience that the physical characteristics of the external distal stimulus are probably not changing, and this belief affects our interpretation of the proximal stimulus. Thus, the perception remains constant even though the sensation changes. Of the several kinds of perceptual constancies, we consider here some of the main ones: size, shape, and lightness and color constancies.

Size Constancy

Size constancy is the perception that an object maintains the same size despite changes in the size of the proximal stimulus. The size of an image on the retina directly depends on the distance of that object from the eye. That is, the same object at two different distances projects different-sized images on the retina. Size constancy is illustrated nicely by *Le Moulin de la Galette,* a painting by French Impressionist Pierre-Auguste Renoir (1841–1919), shown in Figure 5-16. The characters in the background are much smaller than the ones in the foreground, but we are not led to believe that the background characters are midgets, or the foreground characters, giants. Rather, we perceive all of the characters as being about the same size because of size constancy.

How do we experience size constancy? According to the constructivist point of view, we know from years of experience that people do not, in fact, grow larger as they approach us, and we use this knowledge to guide our perception, if unconsciously. Those who criticize the constructivist view argue that this view offers only an ex post facto explanation, which does not permit us unambiguously to predict how people might respond in a novel situation, such as a distorted room (see Figure 5-15).

A classic example of how experience helps us interpret perceptions comes from C. Turnbull's (1961) ethnographic account of the pygmies of the Iturbi forest. Turnbull told of a pygmy who once accompanied him out of the forest. At one point, the two saw some cows grazing in the distance. Although most pygmies frequently have seen cows at close range in

FIGURE 5-15
Perceptual Constancy
When we view the boy and dog through a hole in the wall, we perceive impossible relative sizes. When we see a sketch of the room, however, we see that its shape actually is quite distorted. (Photos © Norman Snyder 1985)

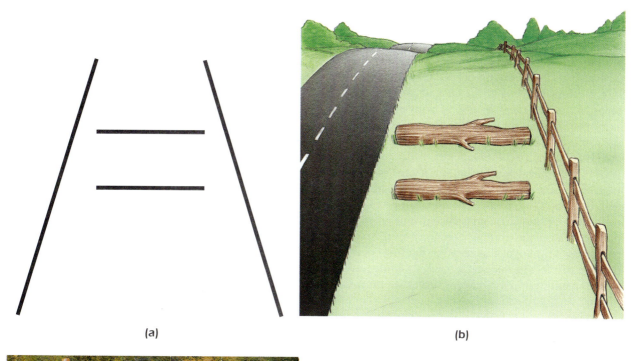

(a)   (b)

FIGURE 5-16
Ponzo Illusion

Which log is larger? Measure them. The principle of size constancy leads us to believe that the log farther from us is larger. French impressionist Pierre-Auguste Renoir's Le Moulin de la Galette *relies on our perception of size constancy to know that the people in the background are similar in size to those in the foreground.*

the forest, few have ever seen cows at a distance. Much to Turnbull's surprise, his travel companion thought that he was looking at ants.

Michael Cole and Sylvia Scribner (1974) provide a similar anecdotal example of the breakdown of size constancy in a 10-year-old Kpelle child. The island-dwelling Kpelle are quite familiar with boats, but they generally see the boats only at close range. The child was with Cole and Scribner in a tall hotel high on a hilltop overlooking a harbor when the psychologists pointed to some ocean tankers in the distant harbor and told the child that many men travel to sea on the tankers. The child expressed amazement that so many men would be brave enough to go out to sea in such small boats.

Some striking illusions can be achieved when our perceptual apparatus is fooled by the very same information that usually helps us to experience size constancy. For example, in Figures 5-16a and b we perceive the top line and the top log as being longer than the bottom line and the bottom log, respectively, even though the top and bottom figures are identical in length. We do so because in the real three-dimensional world, the top line and log *would* be larger. This effect, called the **Ponzo illusion,** stems from the depth cue provided by the converging lines.

Another illusion, which you may have seen elsewhere, is the **Müller-Lyer illusion,** illustrated in Figure 5-17. In this illusion, too, we tend to view two equally long line segments as being of different lengths. In particular, the vertical line segments in panels *a* and *c* appear shorter than the line segments in panels *b* and *d*, even though all the line segments are the same length. Psychologists are not yet certain why such a simple illusion occurs. One explanation is that the diagonal lines at the ends of the vertical segments in panels *a* and *b* serve as implicit depth cues similar to the ones we would see in our perceptions of the exterior and interior of a building (Coren & Girgus, 1978; Gregory, 1966).

The Müller-Lyer illusion was a key basis for advancing the *carpentered-world hypothesis* (Segall, Campbell, & Herskovits, 1966). The term *carpentered world* describes our world of constructed buildings, comprising right angles and horizontal, vertical, and parallel lines. This angular perception does not occur in cultures that live in a noncarpentered, rounded world, where rectilinear relationships are the exception, rather than the rule.

We see one of the most striking and unexplained size illusions regularly: the *moon illusion* (see Figure 5-18). When we see the moon on the horizon, it appears to be larger than when we see it high in the sky. Obviously, the moon does not alter size as a function of its location in the sky, nor does it change distance.

A possible explanation of the moon illusion is the *relative-size hypothesis* (Restle, 1970). The perceived size of an object depends partly on its context, including its visual frame of reference. According to this view, the moon appears smaller when it is overhead because it is surrounded by a large empty visual space. It appears larger on the horizon because there is little or no space between the moon and the horizon line. A related illusion is the comparison of the

center circle in the pair of circle patterns in Figure 5-18. Guess which center circle is larger, and then measure the diameter of each.

How might a set designer use the phenomenon of size constancy for designing a theater or movie set? Give specific examples.

Shape Constancy

Shape constancy refers to how we perceive an object to remain the same even though its orientation—that is, the shape of its retinal image—changes. For example, in Figure 5-19, you see a rectangular door and door frame, showing the door as closed, slightly opened, or more fully opened. Of course, the door does not seem to take on a different shape in each panel. It would be most odd, indeed, if we perceived a door to be changing shapes as we opened it. Yet, the shape of the image of the door on the retina *does* change as we open the door. If you look at the figure mindfully, you will see that the drawn shape of the door is different in each panel.

Lightness and Color Constancies

Lightness constancy refers to our perception that an object is evenly illuminated, despite differences in the actual amount of light reaching our eyes. In fact, we are remarkably capable of compensating for differences in the actual amount of light that is reflected at a given moment. For example, observe how Michelangelo da Caravaggio used lightness constancy to advantage in his painting *The Calling of St.*

FIGURE 5-17
Müller-Lyer Illusion
Which of the line segments (a or b, c or d) is longer? Measure them. The principle of depth constancy may lead us to perceive the inward-facing angles as being larger, as if they represent the "far" corner of the room instead of the "near" corner of the wall.

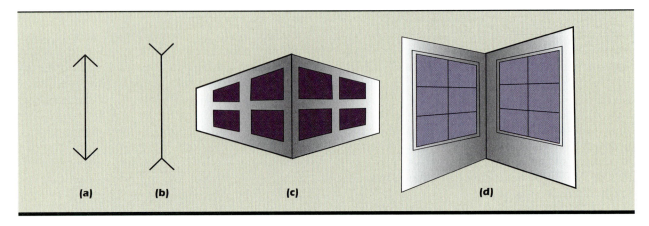

FIGURE 5-19
Shape Constancy

When we look at a door, we perceive it always to have the same shape, even though our sensations of the shape change as the door opens and closes. (After Gibson, 1950)

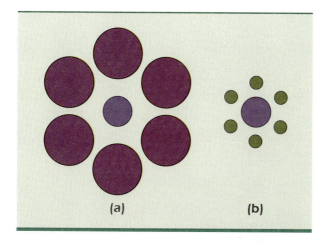

FIGURE 5-18
Size Constancy and the Moon Illusion

Which of these inner circles (a or b) is larger? Measure them. The size of the outer circles makes us perceive the inner circles to be of different sizes. Similarly, although the moon is no closer to the earth when viewed at the horizon than when viewed overhead, its nearness to the horizon often makes it seem to be much larger than when it is overhead.

Matthew, shown in Figure 5-20. The wall in the background is illuminated by a brilliant ray of light, as are the faces of some of the figures in the painting. Nonetheless, we see the wall as black and the faces as white, despite the fact that the shades on the wall are varied.

Color constancy functions similarly to the other forms of perceptual constancy. Even when our senses tell us that a hue (color) is changing, due to changes in the hue of the light shining on the object, we perceive the hue as being constant. For example, suppose we are drawing still-life sketches of a basket of fruit, when suddenly the entire art studio is flooded with intense blue light. Despite the changes in the lighting, the fruits in the basket would appear to retain their original colors. Our senses would tell us that the fruits had changed color in the blue light, but we would continue to perceive a green lime, a yellow banana, an orange orange, and so on, just as we had perceived them in the white light. Thus, we continue to perceive the fruits in a constant way across changes in lighting.

How might a sculptor, a designer of stained-glass windows, or another artist working in a medium other than paint manipulate the phenomena of shape, light, and color constancy to create distinctive visual effects?

An entirely different way of viewing perception is to consider evolutionary theory. That is, how does perceptual constancy aid us in surviving as a species? We are indeed more fit as a species because of the way our brains work to create the constancies described here. In fact, our species would not survive long in this world if we were unable to experience perceptual constancies. You could not even have found this book on your desk—let alone opened the book and positioned it for reading—if you were incapable of perceptual constancy.

What are some of the pluses and the minuses of having perceptual constancies? If you could redesign your perceptual system, how might you modify your perception of visual constancies? Explain your response.

We are subject to occasional misperceptions because our brains constantly take perceptual shortcuts to make sense of the constant barrage of perplexing sensory information. If our brains were to assess and consider carefully each incoming sensation, attempting methodically and analytically to make sense of our perceptual world, we would be incapable of comprehending anything. Instead, our brains have devised clever shortcuts to avoid having to think through the perception of every minute sensory detail. Although the cognitive compensations that result in perceptual

FIGURE 5-20
Lightness and Color Constancy
The Calling of St. Matthew *by Italian artist Michelangelo da Caravaggio (1573–1610) uses the principles of lightness and color constancy to manipulate our perception of the people and the room. We perceive his use of highlighting and shadowing as changes in illumination, not as changes in the perceived lightness of the room.*

constancies can lead to occasional illusions, the world would be thoroughly chaotic and nonsensical without them. Under most circumstances, the few illusions that trick you have little harmful effect on your daily life. On the other hand, our survival depends on creating perceptual constancies in the face of retinal inconstancies.

This chapter describes several ways in which our expectations affect our perceptions. How do illustrators, commercial artists, and other artists make use of your expectations in the array of artworks that you see in your visual environment?

AUDITION: SPEECH PERCEPTION

IN SEARCH OF...

What are the situations that enhance your speech perception, and what situations impair it? Why do these situations have differing effects?

Although psychologists have studied visual perception more than any other form of perception, they have also studied auditory perception fairly extensively. In this discussion of auditory perception, we consider the perception of speech.

Recall that there are two fundamental theories of visual perception: direct perception and constructive perception. Similarly, there are two basic paradigms for theories of speech perception. **Passive theories** of speech perception are similar to the direct-perception theory of vision, in that speech perception depends exclusively on filtering and feature-detection mechanisms at the sensory level. **Active theories** of speech perception are similar to the constructive-perception theory of vision, in that speech perception actively involves cognitive aspects of the listener's expectations, context, memory, and attention.

According to passive theories, specialized neurons detect particular aspects of a speech signal, just as specialized neurons detect particular aspects of a visual signal (as demonstrated by Hubel and Wiesel). Passive theories postulate that there are stages of neural processing; in one stage, speech sounds are analyzed into their components (phonemes), and in another stage, these components are analyzed for patterns (e.g., Massaro, 1987). The two stages may occur either serially or in parallel, depending on the specific theory.

In contrast to passive theories, active theories of speech perception posit more active involvement and cognition on the part of the listener. An early but still influential active theory is the **motor theory** of speech perception (Liberman, Cooper, Shankweiler, & Studdert-Kennedy, 1967; Liberman & Mattingly, 1985). According to this theory, speech perception depends on both what we hear a speaker articulate and what we infer as the intention of the speaker.

According to the motor theory, it is difficult for many Americans whose native language is English to hear the difference between the /r/ and /rr/ phones (or distinctive speech sounds) in everyday Spanish-language contexts, because English does not distinguish the two. Thus, we may have to rely on the context to figure out whether a speaker is saying "pero" ("but") or "perro" ("dog").

Another theory that emphasizes active processing is the **phonetic-refinement theory** (Pisoni, Nusbaum, Luce, & Slowiaczek, 1985), which states that we identify words by successively *refining* (paring down by removing extraneous elements) the choices of possible words that the heard word might be, based on the sounds of the words (phonetics). According to this theory, an initial sound establishes the set of possible words from which we may choose the correct word. We then successively eliminate words from the set of possible words, on the basis of subsequent features of the word, as well as by considering context and other expectations. You may have observed this phenomenon yourself even on a conscious level. Have you ever been watching a movie or listening to a lecture in which you heard only garbled sounds for some of the words, and for which you then took a few moments to figure out what the speaker must have said? To *decide* what you heard, you may have gone through a conscious process of phonetic refinement.

What active theories have in common, and what distinguishes them from passive theories, is that they all require decision-making processes based on initial feature detection or template matching. Thus, the speech we hear may differ from the sound that actually reaches our ears because cognitive and contextual factors influence our perception of the physiological signal. For example, if you are a passenger in a car and the driver asks you to "get out the mup," slightly garbling the last syllable, you may not even notice the garbled sound as you reach for a map. On the other hand, if you are standing in the kitchen with someone who drops a carton of milk and says, "Get out the mup!" you'll probably perceive a request for a mop, not a map. Additional contextual cues may include inflection, gesturing, and other nonverbal cues from the speaker.

HABITUATION

IN SEARCH OF...

When you are studying, you probably become accustomed to various aspects of your environment. Under what circumstances (in both your external environment and your own inner thoughts and motivations) do you stop being accustomed to your environment?

In the phenomenon of **habituation,** we become accustomed to a stimulus and gradually notice it less and less. The counterpart to habituation is **dishabituation,** in which a change (sometimes even a very slight change) in a familiar stimulus prompts us to start noticing the stimulus again. Any aspects of the stimulus that seem different or novel (unfamiliar) make habituation less likely or prompt dishabituation. For example, suppose that a radio is playing instrumental music while you are studying your psychology textbook. At first, the sound may distract you, but after a while, you may become habituated to the sound and scarcely notice it. If the intensity (loudness) of the sound were to change, however, you would immediately become dishabituated to the sound you are hearing; the sound that had become familiar and had been filtered out of your conscious awareness would then have become unfamiliar and thereby have entered your awareness.

We usually exert no effort whatsoever to become habituated to sensations of our environment. Nonetheless, although we usually do not consciously control habituation, we *can* do so. In this way, habituation differs from the phenomenon of sensory adaptation (described in Chapter 4). Whereas you can exert some conscious control over whether you notice something which you have become habituated to, you have no conscious control over sensory adaptation. For example, you cannot consciously force yourself to smell an odor to which your senses have become adapted. Nor can you consciously force your pupils to adapt—or not to adapt—to differing degrees of brightness or darkness. In contrast, you can consciously control habituation; for example, if someone were to ask you, "Who's the lead guitarist playing that song?" you might once again notice background music.

Psychologists can observe habituation occurring at the physiological level (see Chapter 3). For example, when an unchanging visual stimulus remains in our visual field for a long time, our neural activity in response to that stimulus decreases. Other physiological activity (e.g., heart rate) can be measured to detect arousal in response to perceived novelty or lack of arousal in response to perceived familiarity. In fact, psychologists in many fields use these indications of habituation to study a wide array of psychological phenomena in persons who cannot provide verbal reports of their responses (e.g., infants or comatose patients). The physiological indicators of habituation tell the researcher whether the person notices the stimulus at all, as well as what changes the person notices in the stimulus.

Psychologists have used habituation to study visual discrimination in infants, among other phenomena. First, researchers habituate the infant to a particular visual pattern; then they introduce a visual pattern that differs only slightly from the one to which the infant has become habituated. If the infant shows habituation to the new as well as the old pattern, the researchers may conclude that the infant is unable to discriminate between the old pattern and the new one. However, if the infant appears *not* to be habituated to the new pattern, the researchers may conclude that the infant is able to discriminate between the old pattern and the new one.

Habituation allows us to filter our sensations effortlessly, permitting some sensations to enter our conscious awareness and screening out others. Thus, habituation offers another example of a mental process that usually takes place without any conscious effort and yet that greatly facilitates our ability to understand, think about, and interact with our environment. It is almost impossible to comprehend how we would function in our highly stimulating environments if we could not habituate to familiar stimuli. Imagine trying to listen to a lecture if you could not habituate to the sounds of your own breathing, the rustling of papers and books, or the muffled noises of your fellow students. Because we can habituate unconsciously to familiar stimuli, we are much more easily able to manipulate consciously the attention we give to the stimuli that interest us.

> How might you create an environment that would maximize your ability to habituate to the stimuli in that environment? Be specific. How might you create an environment that would maximize the likelihood that you would dishabituate to many stimuli in the environment? When might you want to try to create one or the other type of environment?

ATTENTION

IN SEARCH OF...

> When you have a particular goal you want to achieve (such as studying psychology), how do you monitor your attention, and what do you do to keep your attention focused on your goal instead of being distracted?

Another crucial aid to our perception and understanding of ourselves and our environments is our ability to pay close attention to what interests us and to disregard what does not. The highly complex phenomena of perception would be a great deal more complex if we were unable to limit our experience of stimuli in the environment through our attention. **Attention** is the link between the enormous amount of information that assails our senses and the limited amount of information that we actually perceive. As you read these words, you are paying attention to the words (figure) on the text page and disregarding all the other visual sensations (ground) reaching your retina. If you paid attention to all the sensory information available to you at any one time, you would never be able to concentrate on the important and ignore the unimportant. As you read this page, you may be vaguely aware of the ways your skin is being touched by your clothes, of the ambient sounds surrounding you, or even of some internal cues such as hunger or fatigue. What allows you to dismiss most of this sensory information and to concentrate on reading? Pay attention and find out.

Selective Attention

Suppose you are at a banquet. It is just your luck to be seated next to this year's winner of the "Most Boring Conversationalist" award. As you are talking to this blatherer, who happens to be on your right, you become aware of the conversation of the two diners sitting on your left. Their exchange is much more interesting, so you find yourself trying to keep up the semblance of a conversation with the bore on your right while tuning in to the dialogue on your left.

This vignette describes a naturalistic experiment in **selective attention,** in which you attempt to track one message and to ignore another. This very phenomenon inspired the research of E. Colin Cherry (1953), who was interested in how we follow one conversation in the face of the distraction of other conversations. Cherry referred to this phenomenon as the **cocktail party phenomenon,** based on his observation that cocktail parties provide an excellent setting for observing selective attention.

Cherry did not actually study conversations at cocktail parties, but rather conversations in a more carefully controlled experimental setting. He used *shadowing*, in which each of the ears listens to a different message, and the subject is required to repeat back the message going to one of the ears as soon as possible after hearing it. In other words, the subject is to follow one message (think of a detective "shadowing" a suspect) but ignore the other. This form of presentation is often referred to as *dichotic presentation*, meaning that each ear receives a different message. When the two ears receive the same message, it is referred to as *binaural presentation*.

Cherry's work prompted additional work in this area. For example, Anne Treisman (1964a, 1964b) noted that subjects shadowing the message presented to one ear heard almost nothing of the message presented to the other ear. They were not, however, totally ignorant of the other message. They could hear,

for example, if the voice in the unattended ear was replaced by a tone or if a man's voice was replaced by a woman's. Moreover, if the unattended message was identical to the attended one, all subjects noticed it, even if one of the messages was temporally out of synchronization with the other. When this delay effect was studied systematically, subjects typically recognized the two messages to be the same when the shadowed message was either as much as 4.5 seconds ahead of the unattended one, or as far as 1.5 seconds behind the unattended one (Treisman, 1964a, 1964b). In other words, it is easier to recognize the unattended message when it follows, rather than precedes, the attended one. Treisman also observed that, when fluently bilingual subjects were studied, some of them noticed the identity of messages if the unattended message was the translated version of the attended one.

Before you read about psychologists' theories of selective attention, think about your own present understanding of attention. What do you think explains why you attend to some things and not to others? Why do you think that you sometimes find it difficult to choose how to focus your attention?

Theories of Selective Attention

Various theories have been proposed to account for how we can attend selectively to inputs from the environment. These theories differ primarily in terms of whether or not they propose that we somehow filter and thus sort out the stimuli to which we pay attention. If the theories do propose a filter, disagreements arise over when filtering occurs and what it affects.

Filter Theories

An early theory of selective attention, proposed by Donald Broadbent, suggested that we filter information right after it is registered at the sensory level (Broadbent, 1958). Subsequent research, however, indicated that Broadbent's model must be wrong. For example, subjects will generally hear one particular stimulus in the unattended ear, regardless of when it occurs: the sound of their own names (Moray, 1959). If we are able to recognize our own names in this way, some higher level processing of the information must reach the supposedly unattended ear. If such processing were not occurring, subjects would not recognize

Searchers . . .

ANNE TREISMAN

Anne Treisman received her PhD in psychology. She is Professor of Psychology at Princeton University.

Q: *How did you become interested in psychology in general and in your area of work in particular?*

A: I have always been interested in psychology, in the sense of trying to understand human minds. I started out studying it in a different way by reading French and Italian literature at Cambridge University. When I switched to psychology, I knew no science at all, but found it fascinating. Psychology was just beginning the transition from what seemed the straitjacket of Behaviorist S-R theories to the new horizons opened by the idea of the mind as an information-processing system.

Q: *What theories have influenced you the most?*

A: Richard Gregory's idea of perception as hypothesis testing and Donald Broadbent's view of the mind as an information-processing system were the strongest early influences. Signal detection theory had a big influence on my thinking. Ulric Neisser's book on cognitive psychology reinforced my interest in perception and cognition generally, and opened more new horizons, as did the excitement and challenge of Noam Chomsky's claims that language was impossible to explain within a Behaviorist framework. The links between neurophysiology and perception have been important in my thinking since Hubel and Wiesel first published their findings of feature detectors, and a stream of new discoveries in that field have continued to amaze and intrigue me.

Q: *What reasoning process have you followed to develop an idea into a workable hypothesis?*

A: The idea that conjoining features could pose a problem for the perceptual system came to me as I puzzled over the findings suggesting that vision depended on specialized modules for different aspects of the stimulus, such as color, size, motion, shape. I drew stimuli with colored pens on paper and tried them out on my three children sitting on the lawn. Luckily they showed exactly the effects I predicted, so I set up the experiments in the lab and found that undergraduates did the same.

Q: *What obstacles have you experienced?*

A: Some of my ideas haven't worked out, so I've tried another version or dropped them. Some of the ideas have been proved wrong or incomplete by other researchers, but that is typical of science.

Q: *What is your major contribution to psychology?*

A: In selective listening, the modification of Broadbent's filter theory to show that attention is not an all-or-nothing gate but an "attenuation" of unwanted information. And the hypothesis that visual attention plays a role in feature integration.

Q: *What do you want students to learn from you?*

A: How to generate and test hypotheses, and how to enjoy the excitement of collecting and analyzing data that tell us something new about the mind. I encourage them to plan, to think, and especially to write.

Q: *What advice would you give to someone starting in psychology?*

A: They should be convinced that they want to do research in psychology and are excited by it. I would also encourage them to get a solid grounding in the tools and neighboring disciplines that will help them, such as computer science and programming, neuroscience, and statistics.

Q: *What did you learn from your mentors?*

A: To enjoy the process of empirical discovery and to appreciate innovative ideas and elegant empirical tests.

Q: *What have you learned from your students?*

A: That individuals learn differently and have different talents and interests. I hope they have improved my teaching a little.

Q: *How has psychology influenced you?*

A: I think it colors my understanding of many everyday interactions with other people. It also gives me an empirical approach to solving problems and a respect for data as opposed to speculation.

Q: *How do you keep yourself academically challenged?*

A: I don't take any active steps to keep academically challenged. The job and the students do that.

---

the familiar sounds. That is, if the incoming information were being filtered out at the level of sensation, we would never perceive it in order to recognize it.

This kind of finding led some investigators to adopt a theory that places the filter later in the perceptual process, after some conceptual analysis of input has taken place (Deutsch & Deutsch, 1963; Norman, 1968). This later filtering would allow sub-

jects to recognize information entering the unattended ear (such as the sound of the listener's name).

An alternative to both of these theories suggests that a filter may take the form of a signal-attenuating mechanism rather than of a signal-blocking mechanism (Treisman, 1964b). According to this view, information is not totally blocked out at any level; rather, it is weakened. The filter lets through some information, but not other information. What gets through is determined by a series of tests that decides whether the information is more likely to be important (such as our names) or more likely to be unimportant (such as idle prattle).

Attentional Resource Theories

More recent theories have moved away from the notion of filters and toward the notion of attentional resources. The idea is that people have a fixed amount of attention, which they can choose to allocate according to what the task requires. Our attention has a single pool of resources that can be divided up, say, among multiple tasks (Kahneman, 1973). For example, suppose that you were dividing your total attention among the acts of talking to a friend, reading your textbook, and drawing a doodle in the margin of your textbook. Thus, the amount of attention you could devote to each task would depend on how you allocated your single pool of attentional resources to each task. In this model, allocating attention to one task always takes away attention from all other tasks.

However, it now appears that such a model is an oversimplification because people are much better at dividing their attention when competing tasks are in different perceptual modalities (e. g., one task requiring seeing, the other, hearing). At least some attentional resources may be specific to the modality in which a task is presented. Thus, it is more likely that two visual tasks will interfere with each other than it is that a visual task will interfere with an auditory one. Competition for resources also can occur as a result of overlap in the content type. For example, words heard on a radio are more likely to interfere with your reading of words than is instrumental music heard on the radio.

> Compare your own tentative theory of selective attention (which you described previously) with the filter and the resource theories of attention. Which theories most closely match?

Vigilance and Search Phenomena

Selective attention is not the only phenomenon studied by scientists interested in attention. Two other attentional phenomena are of especially great practical importance: vigilance and search. **Vigilance** refers to a person's ability to attend to a field of stimulation over a prolonged period—such as watching for something that might occur at an unknown time.

Typically, the phenomenon is studied in settings where a given stimulus occurs only rarely, but must be attended to as soon as it does occur. For example, a lifeguard at a busy beach must be ever-vigilant to potential drownings, which occur infrequently. If you have ever flown in an airplane, you also realize the practical importance of having your air-traffic controller be highly vigilant.

Decreases in vigilance occur primarily because of an increase in doubtfulness about perceived observations, not because of decreased sensitivity (Broadbent & Gregory, 1965). In other words, subjects become less willing to report the phenomenon when they believe they observe it but are not sure. Training can help to increase vigilance (Fisk & Schneider, 1981), but in tasks requiring sustained vigilance, there may be no substitute for frequent rest periods.

Whereas vigilance involves passively waiting for an event to occur, **search** refers to a scan of the environment for particular features—actively looking for something when you are not sure where it will appear. Trying to locate a particular shop in a crowded shopping center—or a particular term in a crowded textbook—is an example of search. When we are

For some jobs, vigilance is a matter of life and death.

searching for something, we usually encounter a number of *distractors* at the same time. For instance, when searching in the shopping center, we may see several distracting shop signs and storefronts that look something like the shop we hope to find. Distractors cause more trouble under some conditions than under others. When we know of some distinctive feature (e.g., a purple neon sign or a large pink elephant in the store window) that we can look for, we simply scan the environment for that feature. In that case, distractors play little role in slowing our search. When the target shop has no one unique or distinctive feature, the only way we can find the shop is to look for a particular *conjunction* (joint appearance) of features distinguishing the store. In this case, the distractors of the other store names slow us down because we must read each name and compare it with the target shop's name.

In sum, the psychological study of attention has included, among other phenomena, selective attention, vigilance, and search. Current models of selective attention emphasize that we bring to bear multiple attentional resources, using more than one sensory modality, on tasks that require divided attention. Models of vigilance underscore decreases in confidence for reporting a phenomenon over time. Models of search highlight feature searches, conjunction searches, and the avoidance of distractors.

The whole of perception is indeed much more than the sum of its parts. As Gestalt psychologists pointed out nearly a century ago, the perceptual system functions wonderfully as an intact whole. As subsequent chapters show, the perceptual system described here influences many of our thoughts, feelings, and actions. Although many aspects of perception occur at an unconscious level, other aspects are subject to conscious manipulation. Just what constitutes consciousness—and what mental processes occur in different states of consciousness—is the subject of the next chapter.

SUMMARY

Theories of Perception   169

1. *Perception* is the set of processes by which we recognize, organize, and make sense of stimuli in our environment.

2. The viewpoint of *constructive* (or *intelligent*) *perception* asserts that the perceiver essentially constructs or builds up the perceived stimulus, using sensory information (such as from the retina) as merely the foundation of the perceptual experience.

3. The alternative viewpoint, *direct perception*, asserts that all the information we need in order to perceive is in the sensory input (such as from the retina) that we receive.

Vision: Depth Perception   171

4. Depth perception is made possible in part by *monocular depth cues*, which can be noted by just a single eye. Examples of monocular depth cues are *relative size, texture gradients, interposition, linear perspective, location in the picture plane, aerial perspective,* and *motion parallax.* Artists manipulate many of these cues to create illusions of depth on two-dimensional surfaces.

5. *Binocular depth cues*, those used by the two eyes in conjunction, also facilitate space perception.

Binocular convergence cues depend on the degree to which our two eyes must turn inward toward each other as objects get closer to us. *Binocular disparity* cues capitalize on the fact that each of the two eyes receives a slightly different image of the viewed object.

Vision: Form Perception   175

6. Alternative approaches to form perception are the Gestalt approach and the feature-detector approach.

7. According to the *Gestalt approach*, the whole is more than the sum of its parts. *Gestalt principles of form perception*—such as *figure-ground, proximity, similarity, closure, continuity,* and *symmetry*—characterize how we perceptually group together various objects and parts of objects.

8. According to the *feature-detector approach* to form perception, various cortical neurons can be linked to specific receptive fields on the retina. Differing cortical neurons respond to different kinds of forms, such as line segments or edges in various spatial orientations. Visual perception seems to depend on three levels of complexity in the cortical neurons; each succes-

sive level of complexity seems to be further removed from the incoming information received by the sensory receptors.

9. Two of the main theoretical approaches to pattern perception are *template matching*, according to which we recognize a pattern by matching it to a corresponding form (prototype) in our minds, and *feature matching*, according to which we recognize a pattern by comparing the features or aspects of the pattern to features stored in our memories.

10. Neither template-based nor feature-based models of pattern perception, however, can fully account for *context effects*, or influences of the situation in which perception occurs.

Vision: Motion Perception   182

11. *Stroboscopic motion* is the appearance of motion produced by the precisely timed intermittent and alternating flashing of two lights positioned at precise locations against a dark background.

12. *Induced movement* occurs when what appears to be moving is actually motionless. Motion parallax and other phenomena can produce this perception.

13. When particular visual events occur in close sequential proximity to one another, they can give the appearance of causality. That is, a visual event may appear to cause a subsequent event to occur.

Vision: Perceptual Constancies   184

14. *Perceptual constancies* result when our perceptions of objects tend to remain constant even as the stimuli registered by the sensory apparatus change. Examples are size, shape, lightness, and color constancies. Two size-constancy illusions are the *Ponzo illusion* and the *Müller-Lyer illusion*, both of which may be related to the way in which we interpret monocular depth cues. Shape constancy, too, may be tied to our interpretation of depth cues (e.g., in the observation that parallel lines appear to converge as they recede into the distance). Lightness and color constancy appear to be affected by context cues.

Audition: Speech Perception   188

15. *Passive theories of speech perception* hold that speech perception involves relatively little work on the part of the listener, whereas *active theories* maintain that speech perception involves substantial work, such as inferring speech sounds from contextual cues.

Habituation   189

16. In the phenomenon of *habituation*, we become accustomed to a stimulus and gradually notice it less and less. The counterpart to habituation is *dishabituation*, in which a change (sometimes even a very slight change) in a familiar stimulus prompts us to start noticing the stimulus again.

Attention   190

17. People use *selective attention* to track one message and simultaneously ignore others (such as in the *cocktail party phenomenon* or in shadowing).

18. Two existing theories of *selective attention* are filter theories, according to which information is selectively blocked out or attenuated as it passes from one level of processing to the next, and attentional resource theories, according to which people have a fixed amount of attentional resources (perhaps modulated by sensory modalities) that they allocate according to the perceived requirements of a given task.

19. In addition to selective attention, psychologists study other phenomena of attention. For example, *vigilance* refers to a person's ability to attend to a field of stimulation over a prolonged period of time, usually with the stimulus to be detected occurring only infrequently. Whereas vigilance involves passively waiting for an event to occur, *search* involves actively seeking out a stimulus.

KEY TERMS

IN SEARCH OF THE HUMAN MIND:
ANALYSES, CREATIVE EXPLORATIONS, AND PRACTICAL APPLICATIONS

1. Compare and contrast direct (or passive) and constructive (or active) theories of perception as they might be applied to smell, taste, or the haptic senses.
2. What are the main limitations of template-matching theories of visual perception?
3. How might psychologists modify either template-matching or feature-matching theories to account for context effects in form perception? Choose one of the theories and suggest a modification that might allow for the effects of context on the visual perception of forms.

4. This chapter contains many examples of perceptual illusions. Based on what you have learned, design an illusion. Try showing someone your illusion to test whether it works. Explain why your illusion did or did not work.
5. Create a drawing, painting, collage, or other illustration that highlights at least four of the six depth cues that can be shown in a static two-dimensional figure.
6. Make up the plot of a movie that uses some feature of perception (binocular convergence or disparity, optical illusions, etc.) as the basis for a plot point. (An example might be a murder mystery with an eyewitness account that is based on some kind of perceptual illusion.)

7. Hubel and Wiesel have noted that their discoveries and their research were possible because of the technologies available to them. What current technology do you find not only pleasant but even important to your ability to perform a task you do often? How would your life be different without that technology? (It does not have to be a complex or "high-tech" item.)

8. This chapter included quite a few examples of art. What are a few of your favorite works of art? What aspects of visual perception are called into play when you observe these works of art?

9. In what circumstances do you need to be vigilant? What factors can enhance your ability to be vigilant when you need to be? What factors can enhance your ability to search for something you need to find? Compare and contrast the factors that are helpful for each task.

C h a p t e r   S i x

CONSCIOUSNESS

CHAPTER OUTLINE

Milkman slipped into Sweet's bed and slept the night in her perfect arms. It was a warm dreamy sleep all about flying, sailing high over the earth. But not with arms stretched out like airplane wings, nor shot forward like Superman in a horizontal dive, but floating, cruising, in the relaxed position of a man flying on a couch reading a newspaper. Part of his flight was over the dark sea, but it didn't frighten him because he knew he could not fall. He was alone in the sky, but somebody was applauding him, watching him and applauding. He couldn't see who it was.

When he awoke the next morning and set about seeing to the repair of his car, he couldn't shake the dream, and didn't really want to. In Solomon's store he found Omar and Solomon shaking sacks of okra into peck baskets and he still felt the sense of lightness and power that flying had given him.

—*Toni Morrison*, Song of Solomon

Nobel Prize–winner Toni Morrison frequently explores consciousness from a literary perspective. In the preceding excerpt, the protagonist in her novel illustrates the way in which an altered state of consciousness, such as dreaming, can affect waking experiences. Psychologists, too, observe that our conscious awareness of the world and even of ourselves often changes from moment to moment, influenced both by our sensations of the world around us and by our inner thoughts and feelings.

Consciousness is the complex process of evaluating our environment and then filtering that information through our minds. American psychologist William James (mentioned in Chapter 2) saw consciousness as the state of mind in which we compare various possibilities for what we might be perceiving and then select or reject those possibilities (1890/1970). He described this awareness as an ongoing process: "Consciousness . . . does not appear to itself chopped up in bits. . . . In talking of it hereafter, let us call it the stream of thought." I view consciousness as the mental reality we create in order to adapt to the world in which we live.

The history of the world is none other than the progress of the consciousness of freedom.

—*Georg Hegel*, Philosophy of History

PHILOSOPHICAL ANTECEDENTS

To be conscious that we are perceiving or thinking is to be conscious of our own existence.

—*Aristotle*, Nicomachean Ethics

Philosophers have long considered consciousness and its relationship to personal identity. John Locke (1632–1704) (see Chapter 2) and David Hume (1711–1776) held opposite views about whether consciousness gives us a continuous personal identity—whether it makes us who we are. Both men, British empiricist philosophers, agreed that the only true source of knowledge comes from observable experience.

For Locke, only our consciousness establishes our personal identity; only our consciousness makes us unique:

> Consciousness . . . unites existences and actions, very remote in time into the same person, as well as it does the existences and actions of the immediately preceding moment: so that whatever has the consciousness of present and past actions, is the same person to whom they both belong. (quoted in Perry & Bratman, 1986, p. 410)

Locke argued that in order to know about and to form a personal identity, we must have consciousness.

Interestingly, Locke's view seems to have some physiological basis. Most of our body cells continually die and regenerate, so the physiological substance of which we are composed is, quite literally, constantly changing. Intriguingly, there is a distinctive exception to this rule: Beyond a certain point in childhood (about the time when our earliest memories begin), the cells we use to achieve consciousness do *not* regularly die and are *not* replaced. These brain cells are therefore more enduringly part of us than are most other body cells. The stability of these cells may permit us to maintain our consciousness of our personal identity and to preserve our integrity as distinct individuals despite the changes in the rest of our cells.

Hume argued against Locke's views, asserting instead that our sense of self is illusory. According to Hume, "the identity, which we attribute to the [human] mind . . . , is only a fictitious one" (quoted in Perry & Bratman, 1986, p. 422). Hume argued that what we perceive as identity is only a very close relationship among a very rapid succession of mental and physical states. We create the links of continuity across these states through our imaginations. We do not actually experience consciousness directly. Indeed, for Hume, all causal connections are created through our imaginations.

For Hume, identity is a convenient fiction, but not something that we can empirically establish through any of our senses. Consciousness cannot truly give us a sense of personal identity, unless we choose to create such a sense out of our imaginations.

Are you inclined to agree more with Locke's view of consciousness or with Hume's view? Explain why.

LEVELS OF CONSCIOUSNESS

Most people live . . . in a very restricted circle of their potential being. They make use of a very small portion of their possible consciousness.

—*William James (emphasis in original),*
The Letters of William James

Beyond establishing a personal identity, consciousness serves two main purposes: monitoring and controlling (Kihlstrom, 1984). **Monitoring** refers to our keeping track of ourselves and our environment, so that we maintain awareness of ourselves in relationship to our environment. **Controlling** refers to our planning what we are going to do, based on the information we receive from monitoring. These two functions seem to operate, in one way or another, at various levels of consciousness. Normally, we see ourselves as being at a fully conscious level of awareness. However, various lower levels of consciousness exist as well, classified as either preconscious or subconscious.

Give an example of a situation in which the monitoring function of consciousness would be more important to you than the controlling function. Cite a situation in which the controlling function would be relatively more important to you.

The Preconscious Level

The **preconscious level** of consciousness comprises information that could become conscious readily, but that is not continuously available at the conscious level. For example, if prompted, you could remember what your bedroom looks like, but obviously, you are not always thinking about your bedroom. Also stored at the preconscious level are *automatic behaviors* (those requiring no conscious decisions regarding which muscles to move or which actions to take, such as dialing a familiar telephone number or driving a car to a familiar place via empty roads).

Searchers . . .   JOHN F. KIHLSTROM

John Kihlstrom is Professor of Psychology at Yale University.

Q: How did you become interested in psychology in general and in your area of work in particular?

A: I've always been interested in psychology. The idea that the psychologist at school could assess intelligence, predict success in school, help people learn, and help organize environments to facilitate learning, impressed me greatly. But I wasn't sure what kind of psychology I wanted to pursue. At Colgate I was advised by theologian M. Holmes Hartshorne, who was interested in the connections between psychology, existentialist philosophy, and theology. I really got caught up in it. I went to Penn to do hypnosis research with Martin Orne and his lab group. I had been introduced to hypnosis at Colgate by William Edmonston, who was a hypnosis researcher and specialized in psychophysiology with a Pavlovian approach—about as far from existentialism as you could get. But the hypnosis bug bit me, and I quickly developed an interest in altered states of consciousness.

I have finally connected hypnosis with existentialism. Being aware of ourselves and defining ourselves are closely connected. It may seem like a tenuous connection to other people, but it's very real to me.

Q: Whose ideas have influenced you the most?

A: I have been profoundly influenced by my graduate advisor, Martin Orne. Orne's central interest is the objective study of subjective experience—what consciousness is all about. Jack Hilgard revived Janet's concept of dissociation, which has played a central role in my work on the unconscious, and I have long been interested in Endel Tulving's concept of episodic memory. Reid Hastie showed me how to develop and test formal models about the representation and processing of social knowledge. Also, talking with Nancy Cantor about applying social-cognitive principles to personality resulted in our social intelligence approach to personality. Daniel Schacter introduced me to the theoretical possibilities created by the study of brain-damaged patients, and I have found his concept of implicit memory important for my own work.

Q: What is your greatest asset as a psychologist?

A: My style of open inquiry. I have theoretical preferences, but I'm not doctrinaire. I build and maintain bridges between clinical and experimental psychology, between cognitive and social psychology, between the present and the past. Also, I like to write, and I like to teach, especially undergraduates who are just getting introduced to the field.

Q: How do you usually get your ideas for research?

A: I read, attend conferences and seminars, and do committee work that takes me out of my own re-

search. So I get ideas by taking what I've learned and pushing it in the direction of what I'm interested in.

Q: How do you decide whether to pursue an idea?

A: Research is resource-limited; a lot depends on whether I have the time and energy to do the work myself. Often the idea has to wait until a collaborator comes around, usually a student, whom I can interest in it. I keep ideas on the back burner, simmering slowly, waiting for the right person to come along and help me cook, or for the right opportunity to finish the dish myself.

Q: What obstacles have you experienced?

A: Getting people to take hypnosis research seriously. Some people think it's beyond the pale, others think it's just fakery and self-delusion, and still others are simply wary of studying one unknown with another. I have overcome these obstacles by connecting hypnosis with larger issues, like memory or the unconscious. Once people see the connections to their own interests, they become more tolerant of ideas that initially seem to be outside the mainstream.

Q: What is your major contribution to psychology?

A: In terms of theory, I have contributed to reviving the problem of the unconscious and keeping it alive. In terms of service to the field, I've helped psychology continue as a coherent, unified discipline.

Q: What do you want students to learn from you?

A: That the mind can be studied, and human behavior understood, by applying the methods of natural science. While this knowledge can be applied to the task of making our lives better, I also want them to learn to value knowledge for its own sake. Whatever their specialties, they should respect their colleagues in other subfields in psychology and be open to what they can learn from those fields. Work in a spirit of open inquiry.

Q: What advice would you give to someone starting in the field of psychology?

A: Choose problems that interest you intrinsically. As you develop your research program, follow your nose. Teach the introductory course regularly.

Q: What have you learned from your students?

A: Students, especially in the introductory course, sometimes ask the most provocative questions, like "Can H.M., the amnesic patient, fall in love?" Meditating on a question like that can take me in a whole new direction in my work.

Q: How do you keep yourself academically challenged?

A: I work on interesting, complex problems, problems that don't have easy answers. And I work with colleagues who ask difficult questions about my work. With that combination of intrinsic and extrinsic factors, it's no problem to keep myself challenged.

What automatic behaviors have you learned? What are the advantages of having these behaviors be automatic? When might it be disadvantageous that these behaviors are automatic?

I remembered what it was like to be a boy, and to turn a simple, rather meaningless act into a skill through constant and endless repetition. I remembered throwing rocks at a streetlamp on summer evenings, my friends and I, for hours and hours.

—*David Mamet,* Some Freaks

Perhaps our most common experience of preconsciousness is the *tip-of-the-tongue phenomenon,* which occurs when we are trying to remember something we already know but cannot quite retrieve. This phenomenon indicates that particular preconscious information, although not fully accessible, is still available in conscious thinking. (The ability to retrieve information stored in memory is described more fully in Chapter 8.)

Researchers have demonstrated preconscious processing (Marcel, 1983). Subjects were shown words for just 10 milliseconds, after which the word was replaced by a visual mask. The rate of presentation was so rapid that observers were generally unaware that they had even seen a word. When subjects were shown a second word for a longer period of time, this new word was recognized more quickly if it was related to the first word than if it was unrelated. Some kind of recognition of the rapidly presented word must have taken place—the recognition was clearly preconscious. This *subliminal perception,* a kind of preconscious processing, suggests that people have the ability to detect information without being aware they are doing so.

To summarize, automatic behaviors, tip-of-the-tongue phenomena, subliminal perception, and other forms of preconscious knowledge are outside the view of our conscious minds, but they are available to our conscious minds under many circumstances.

The Subconscious Level

Unlike knowledge stored at the preconscious level, information stored at the unconscious level is not easily accessible. The terms *subconscious* and *unconscious* are sometimes used interchangeably, and sometimes in slightly different ways so that **unconscious** refers to a less accessible level of consciousness than does **subconscious.** For our purposes, we make no distinction. In general, however, the term *unconscious* is usually preferred by followers of Sigmund Freud, the founder of psychoanalysis (see Chapter 17). Freud believed that many of our most important memories and impulses are unconscious but nonetheless have a profound effect on our behavior.

According to Freud, material that we find too difficult to handle at a conscious level is often *repressed*—that is, never admitted past the unconscious level. Although these difficult memories and desires are not conscious, their effects can be seen through careful observation. For example, Freud believed that many of the slips of the tongue we make actually indicate unconscious processing. Thus, if we were introduced to a potential business rival, and said, "I'm glad to beat you," when we intended to say, "I'm glad to meet you," Freud would have interpreted the slip as being psychologically significant. This sort of verbal error is still sometimes called a "Freudian slip" (see Figure 6-1).

Classical Freudian theory can be neither proved nor disproved because it focuses on variables affecting the unconscious mind that cannot be isolated. Thus, there is little direct empirical support for Freud's theories of the mind. Nonetheless, Freud's theories of the levels of consciousness were ground-breaking when first proposed, and they continue to be highly influential. Another aspect of consciousness that fascinated Freud was altered states of consciousness.

In an altered state of consciousness, awareness is somehow changed from our normal, waking state. Each state of consciousness involves qualitative changes, which include the differing degrees of alertness and awareness associated with each state.

Altered states of consciousness have several common characteristics (Martindale, 1981). First, cognitive processes may be more shallow or uncritical than usual. For example, during sleep, you accept unrealistic dream events as being real, although you

FIGURE 6-1
Freudian Slips
A Freudian slip waiting to happen

would never accept those events as realistic while awake. Second, perceptions of self and of the world may change from what they are during wakefulness. Under the influence of hallucinogenic drugs, for example, objects may appear to take on bizarre forms, or objects that do not exist may be clearly perceived. Third, normal inhibitions and the level of control over behavior may weaken. People under the influence of alcohol, for example, may do things they normally would not do in a sober state.

The most common altered state of consciousness is sleep, to which we now turn.

SLEEP AND DREAMS

Weary with toil, I haste me to my bed,
The dear repose for limbs with travel tired,
But then begins a journey with my head
To work my mind when body's work expired;
For then my thoughts, from far where I abide,
Intend a zealous pilgrimage to thee,
And keep my drooping eyelids open wide,
Looking on darkness which the blind do see;
    Lo, thus, by day my limbs, by night my mind,
    For thee, and for myself, no quiet find.

—*William Shakespeare, "Sonnet XXVII"*

Why Do We Sleep?

Despite centuries of inquiry, scientists have yet to reach a consensus about exactly why people need to sleep. Although it has been suggested that sleep served to keep our evolutionary ancestors safely out of harm's way during the nighttime hours when predators roamed the landscape, a more widely accepted view is that we sleep to restore depleted resources and to dissipate accumulated wastes. In other words, a restorative theory of sleep posits that there may be chemical causes of sleep.

Chemical Causes of Sleep

One way that psychologists study the restorative theory of why people sleep is to search specifically for sleep-causing chemicals produced in our bodies. Several substances seem to be associated with sleep, although none of them has been shown conclusively to cause sleep. One experiment was designed to see whether chemicals in the brains of sleep-deprived goats would induce sleep in rats (Pappenheimer,

Koski, Fencl, Karnovsky, & Krueger, 1975). One group of goats was deprived of sleep for several days, while a control group was allowed to sleep normally. Then cerebrospinal fluid (see Chapter 3) from each group of goats was injected into rats. Rats injected with fluid from the first group of goats slept more than did rats who received fluid from the control group. What was in the sleep-deprived goats' cerebrospinal fluid that caused the rats to sleep more? It was a small peptide made up of five amino acids, including muramic acid. This finding was surprising because muramic acid was already known to stimulate an organism's immune-system defenses against foreign substances, making researchers wonder why this acid would also cause sleep.

Another sleep-producing compound, SPS (sleep-promoting substance), has been isolated (Inoue, Uchizono, & Nagasaki, 1982), but its chemical structure is not yet known. Yet a third sleep-producing substance, DSIP (delta-sleep-inducing peptide), has been isolated as well (Schroeder-Helmert, 1985).

Although some chemicals that *can* cause sleep have indeed been found, the assumption in this work—that sleep actually *is* induced chemically—has not been proved. Researchers have thus sought other ways to study why we sleep, such as studying the effects of not sleeping.

Sleep Deprivation

In sleep deprivation experiments (e.g. Borbely, 1986; Dement, 1976), subjects usually have few problems after the first sleepless night, and they appear to be relaxed and cheerful. They have more difficulty staying awake during the second night, however, and usually are severely tired by 3 A.M. of the second day. If they are given long test problems to solve, they will fall asleep but will often deny having done so.

By the third day, the subjects appear tense. They become increasingly apathetic and are irritable when disturbed. Although they may follow the instructions of the experimenter, they do so with little energy. Their moods swing wildly. By the third night, they are unable to stay awake without special intervention. By this time, periods of *microsleep* are observed: Subjects stop what they are doing for periods of several seconds and stare into space. During these periods, their EEGs (electroencephalograms; see Chapter 3) show brain-wave patterns typical of sleep. Subjects may start to experience **illusions** (distorted perceptions of objects) as well as **hallucinations** (perceptions of nonexistent objects). They may also experience auditory hallucinations, such as hearing voices in the sound of running water.

Things really start to fall apart after 4 days. Subjects typically become paranoid, sometimes believing the experimenters are plotting against them. It is possible to keep sleep-deprived subjects awake for longer than 4 days, but clearly prolonged sleep deprivation is serious business and of questionable ethical justification. Surprisingly, however, there is no documentary evidence of anyone dying or becoming seriously and chronically ill solely from lack of sleep.

> What practical benefits may result from the study of sleep deprivation?

Circadian Rhythms

The familiar cycle of sleep and wakefulness occurs, in one form or another, in all animals. Usually, newborn humans alternate frequently between sleep and wakefulness, for a total of about 17 hours of sleep per day. Within the first 6 months, however, their sleep patterns change to about two short naps and one long stretch of sleep at night, for a total of about 13 hours per day. By 5 to 7 years of age, most of us have adopted what is basically an adult pattern of sleep (Berger, 1980), in which we sleep about 8 hours each night and remain awake about 16 hours each day. Regardless of the average, the actual range of sleep needed varies widely across individuals, with some people requiring as little as an hour of sleep each day and others requiring 10 to 12 hours of sleep per day.

Studies of long sleepers (people who regularly sleep more than 9.5 hours per day) and short sleepers (who regularly sleep less than 4.4 hours per day) show no differences in their average relative health (Kolb & Whishaw, 1990).

A cross-cultural study has suggested that there may be differences in sleep patterns across cultures. Using questionnaires, John M. Taub (1971) found that the average duration of sleep for a sample of nearly 300 Mexicans exceeded the duration typically reported for persons in the United States. Taub also reported a greater incidence of sleep disturbance for Mexicans more than 50 years of age.

Despite individual and cultural differences, the usual sleeping–waking pattern for most people roughly corresponds to our planet's cycle of darkness and light. Humans experience physiological changes that can be measured according to this daily rhythm, such as a lowering of body temperature at night, as well as changes in various hormone levels. The term for these cyclical daily changes is **circadian rhythm.**

Several investigators have studied circadian rhythms (see Hobson, 1989; Wever, 1979). Subjects in one study were placed in a specially built underground living environment in which they were deprived of all cues normally used for telling the time of day—the rising and setting of the sun, clocks, scheduled activities, and so on (Wever, 1979). For one month, subjects were told that they could create their own schedules. They could sleep whenever they wished, but they were discouraged from napping.

French geologist Michel Siffre (left) was shielded from all time cues in this underground cavern (below) for six months. When people have no external time cues, their natural circadian rhythms shift from a 24-hour day to a 25-hour day. When they return to a normal environment, their circadian rhythms return to a 24-hour day, cued by clocks and the daily cycle of the sun.

The results were striking and have since been replicated many times. As subjects acclimated to an environment without time cues, their subjective days became longer, averaging about 25 hours. Subjects showed stable individual rhythms, although the rhythms differed somewhat from subject to subject. When returned to the normal environment, however, the subjects reestablished a 24-hour cycle.

Anything that changes our circadian rhythm can interfere with sleep. Many of us have experienced *jet lag*, which is a disturbance in circadian rhythm caused by altering the light–dark cycle too rapidly or too slowly when we travel through time zones. Even if you have never flown out of your own time zone, you may have experienced a mild case of jet lag if you have changed to and from daylight savings time. Think about how you feel that first Monday morning after setting your clocks forward an hour.

Stages of Sleep

When studying circadian rhythms and other aspects of our sleeping–waking cycles, psychologists often examine people's brain-wave patterns, using electroencephalograms (EEGs). EEG recordings of the brain activity of sleeping people have shown that sleep occurs in stages common to almost everyone. During relaxed wakefulness, we exhibit an *alpha-wave* EEG pattern, as shown in Figure 6-2. As we doze, the alpha-wave rhythm of the EEG gives way to smaller, more rapid, irregular waves. This pattern characterizes *Stage 1* sleep, which represents a transitional state between wakefulness and sleep. If we are brought back to full consciousness from Stage 1 sleep, we may

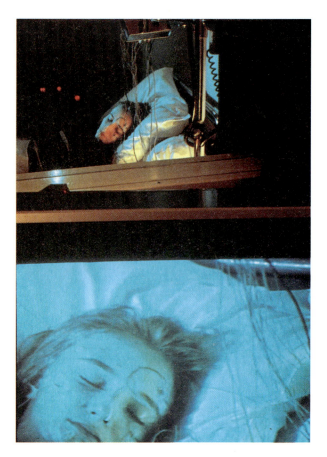

Sleep researchers monitor the patterns of brain-wave activity throughout the sleep cycles of their subjects.

Athletes who travel to competitions in different time zones, such as this diver competing in the 1992 Barcelona Olympics, must adjust their sleep schedules carefully to stay in peak performance.

observe that our thoughts during this period did not make much sense, even though we may have felt fully or almost fully awake.

In *Stage 2*, the stage in which we spend more than half of our sleeping time, the EEG pattern changes again. Larger EEG waves appear, and they overlap with *sleep spindles* (bursts of rapid EEG waves) and occasionally with *K-complexes* (large, slow waves). Muscle tension is markedly lower in Stage 2 than in the waking state.

In the next stage, the EEG pattern changes to *delta waves*, which are larger and slower than alpha waves. Delta waves characterize *delta sleep* (deep sleep), which comprises both Stages 3 and 4. The distinction between Stages 3 and 4 is the proportion of delta waves. When delta waves represent 20–50% of the EEG waves, the sleeper is in *Stage 3*; when delta waves represent more than 50% of the EEG waves, the sleeper is in *Stage 4*.

These first four stages of sleep make up **N-REM sleep** (non–rapid eye movement sleep). During these four stages, as the name "N-REM" im-

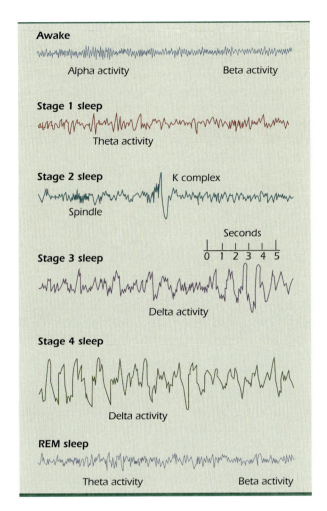

FIGURE 6-2
EEG Patterns Showing the Stages of Sleep

These EEG patterns illustrate changes in brain waves, which reflect changes in consciousness during REM sleep and during the four stages of N-REM sleep. (a) Alpha waves typify relaxed wakefulness. (b) More rapid, irregular brain waves typify stage 1 of N-REM sleep. (c) During Stage 2, large, slow waves are occasionally interrupted by bursts of rapid brain waves. (d) During Stages 3 and 4, extremely large, slow brain waves predominate. (e) During REM sleep, the brain waves look very much like those of the awake brain.

plies, our eyes are not moving very much. During the next stage, however, our eyes roll around in their sockets (Kleitman, 1963). If sleepers are awakened during this eye-rolling stage of sleep, they usually report being in the midst of a dream (Dement & Kleitman, 1957). The distinctive kind of sleep that characterizes the fifth sleep stage has become known as **REM sleep,** for rapid eye movement sleep. REM sleep is the stage of sleep most often—although not exclusively—associated with dreaming. Dreaming may also occur during N-REM sleep.

EEG patterns become extremely active during REM sleep, which begins about an hour after Stage 1. The EEG of REM sleep somewhat resembles the EEG of the awake brain (see Figure 6-2), although REM sleep is so deep it is usually difficult to wake a person from it. Because this stage of sleep is both the most profound in terms of people's rousability and the most like wakefulness in terms of people's EEG patterns, REM sleep is sometimes called "paradoxical sleep."

The stages of N-REM and REM sleep alternate throughout the night, roughly in 90-minute cycles. As the night progresses, the duration and sequence of the sleep stages may vary, as shown in Figure 6-3.

Sleep Disorders

Although scientists do not know why people need to sleep, ample evidence indicates that lack of sleep (insomnia) can wreak havoc on a person's life. Likewise, sudden uncontrollable sleep (narcolepsy), breathing difficulties during sleep (sleep apnea), and sleepwalking (somnambulism) can cause problems.

Insomnia, a sometimes debilitating condition that afflicts millions, varies in intensity and duration. As with other sleep disorders, insomnia is more common among women and the elderly (Borbely, 1986). Various types of insomnia include difficulty falling asleep, waking up during the night and being unable to go back to sleep, or waking up too early in the morning. Although almost everybody has trouble falling asleep occasionally, in one survey, 6% of adult subjects said that they had sought medical attention because of sleeplessness (Borbely, 1986). Somewhat

FIGURE 6-3
Sequences of States and Stages of Sleep

The sequence of REM and N-REM stages of sleep cycles alternates throughout the night. The REM stages are identified in color at the top of stage 1. (After Hartmann, 1968)

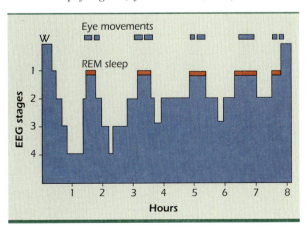

surprisingly, most people who suffer from insomnia usually sleep for at least a few hours, although they may not even be aware of having slept. Laboratory studies have also shown that insomniacs usually overestimate the amount of time it takes them to fall asleep.

People may experience temporary insomnia because of stress, or prolonged bouts of insomnia because of poor sleeping habits. Sleeping pills may help temporarily, but their side effects are troublesome, and they often eventually exacerbate the insomnia.

Prescription sleeping pills interfere with the natural sleep cycle, usually decreasing REM sleep. Moreover, sedatives often continue to work during the day, impairing cognitive and motor functions while the sedative user is awake. Sedatives are also habit-forming, and people who rely on them may find it hard to sleep without taking medicine. (We discuss sedatives and other drugs later in this chapter.) For all of these reasons, physicians often recommend that their patients take the steps listed in Table 6-1 to avoid medicine (Borbely, 1986).

TABLE 6-1
How to Get a Good Night's Sleep
The following recommendations have been suggested by numerous experts in the field of sleep research. (After Atkinson et al., 1993)

Regular Sleep Schedule

Establish a regular schedule of going to bed and getting up. Set your alarm for a specific time every morning, and get up at that time no matter how little you may have slept. Be consistent about naps. Take a nap every afternoon or not at all; when you take a nap only occasionally, you probably will not sleep well that night. Waking up late on weekends can also disrupt your sleep cycle.

Alcohol and Caffeine

Having a stiff drink of alcohol before going to bed may help put you to sleep, but it disturbs the sleep cycle and can cause you to wake up early the next day. In addition, stay away from caffeinated drinks like coffee or cola for several hours before bedtime. Caffeine works as a stimulant even on those people who claim they are not affected by it, and the body needs four to five hours to halve the amount of caffeine in the bloodstream at any one time. If you must drink something before bedtime, try milk; evidence supports the folklore that a glass of warm milk at bedtime induces sleep.

Eating Before Bedtime

Don't eat heavily before going to bed, because your digestive system will have to do several hours of work. If you must eat something before bedtime, have a light snack.

Exercise

Regular exercise will help you sleep better, but don't engage in a strenuous workout just before going to bed.

Sleeping Pills

Be careful about using sleeping pills. All of the various kinds tend to disrupt the sleep cycle, and long-term use inevitably leads to insomnia. Even on nights before exams, avoid using a sleeping pill. One bad night of sleep tends not to affect performance the next day, whereas a hangover from a sleeping pill may.

Relax

Avoid stressful thoughts before bedtime and engage in soothing activities that help you relax. Try to follow the same routine every night before going to bed; it might involve taking a warm bath or listening to soft music for a few minutes. Find a room temperature at which you are comfortable and maintain it throughout the night.

When All Fails

If you are in bed and have trouble falling asleep, don't get up. Stay in bed and try to relax. But if that fails and you become tense, then get up for a brief time and do something restful that reduces anxiety. Doing push-ups or some other form of exercise to wear yourself out is not a good idea.

In contrast, persons with **narcolepsy** (which affects about 1 or 2 people in 1,000; Borbely, 1986) experience an uncontrollable urge to fall asleep periodically during the day. The loss of consciousness can occur when a person is driving or otherwise engaged in activities where sudden sleep might be hazardous. Narcolepsy may seem to be the opposite of insomnia. Actually, narcolepsy is more accurately described as a disorder of the waking state, although narcoleptics frequently experience disturbed nighttime sleep as well. About 10 or 15 minutes after losing consciousness, narcoleptics generally awaken feeling refreshed. Narcoleptics usually fall into REM sleep immediately; a person with normal sleep patterns rarely (if ever) does so. This observation has led some scientists to suggest that, for narcoleptics, REM sleep may be insufficiently differentiated from the waking state. Although the cause of narcolepsy is unknown, the disorder seems to run in families, which suggests that it may be inherited. Fortunately, medication can usually control the symptoms of this disorder.

Another disorder with unknown etiology and possible hereditary involvement is **sleep apnea,** a breathing disturbance in which an individual repeatedly stops breathing during sleep. These attacks can occur hundreds of times per night; the episodes usually last only a few seconds, but they may last as long as two minutes in severe cases. There are two major kinds of sleep apnea. During episodes of *obstructive apnea*, the upper airway becomes blocked, and the sufferer cannot inhale. When breathing restarts, it is usually accompanied by a loud, snoring noise. In *central apnea*, the sleeper seems to forget to breathe for short periods of time. People with this disorder are likely to feel drowsy during the day, but more seriously, they may suffer oxygen deprivation while asleep. Sleep apnea most often afflicts overweight men over 40 years of age; it also seems to be associated with alcohol consumption. Sleep apnea is also found frequently in prematurely born infants, for whom the disorder may be life threatening if the infants' breathing patterns are not closely monitored. It has been suggested that there may be some link between sudden infant death syndrome (SIDS) and sleep apnea. Infants generally outgrow the disorder, but the disorder is difficult to treat in adults, although weight loss sometimes helps.

Somnambulism (sleepwalking) combines aspects of waking and sleeping, with the sleepwalker able to see, walk, and perhaps even talk, but usually unable to remember the sleepwalking episodes. For many years, scientists believed that sleepwalkers were merely acting out their dreams. In fact, however, sleepwalking usually begins during Stage 3 or Stage 4 of N-REM sleep, when dreaming is rare. If the sleep-walking episode is short, sleepwalkers may stay in the deep sleep of Stages 3 and 4; if the episode is lengthy, EEG patterns begin to resemble either those of Stage 1 of N-REM sleep or those of the waking state.

Sleepwalking varies in severity. Some people may experience episodes in which they simply sit up in bed, mutter a few words, and then lie down again. Other people may get out of bed, get dressed, walk around, and even leave their homes. Although sleepwalkers' eyes are open (usually with a rigid facial expression), and they can see, their perception is often impaired, and they can injure themselves by mistaking one thing for another, such as a window for a door.

Most sleepwalkers do not remember their episodes of sleepwalking when they awaken the next morning, and they may even be surprised to find themselves asleep in some place other than their beds. Scientists have not found a cause or a cure for sleepwalking, although sleepwalking is known to be more common in children than in adults, and it usually disappears as children grow older.

Dreams

People have always been fascinated with dreams. Dreams have been used to predict the outcomes of battles and have caused people to change religions. Indeed, dreams fill our heads with fantastic ideas—sometimes pleasant, sometimes frightening. Author Robert Louis Stevenson, in *Memories and Portraits* (1887, p. 167), aptly described both the absurdity of dreams and the power of dreams to prompt us to creative insights.

> Behold! at once the little people [who create dreams] begin to bestir themselves in the same quest, and labour all night long, and all night long set before [the dreamer] truncheons of

"Wait! Don't! It can be dangerous to wake them!"

tales upon their lighted theatre . . . , and at last a jubilant leap to wakefulness, with the cry, "I have it, that'll do!" upon [the dreamer's] lips.

Many have experienced breakthrough insights or other creative ideas while dreaming or in a dreamlike state of mind. What is it about dreaming that may facilitate such breakthroughs?

All of us have dreams every night, whether or not we remember them (Ornstein, 1986). Dreams often occur in the form of strange fantasies that we accept as true while we sleep, yet would dismiss as fantastic if we were awake. Why do we dream? Consider several theories.

Perhaps the best-known theory of dreaming was proposed by Sigmund Freud (1900/1954). According to Freud, dreams allow us to express unconscious wishes in a disguised way. Freud called dreams the "royal road to the unconscious" because they are one of the few ways we have of allowing the contents of the unconscious to be expressed. However, he also postulated that the contents of the unconscious would be so threatening if expressed directly and clearly that we might awaken every time we dreamed. Thus, according to Freud, we dream in symbols that both express and disguise our unconscious wishes. Because these wishes are disguised, they do not shock us into wakefulness.

Other theorists, however, have suggested that sometimes the disguises of dream content are rather thin (Dement, 1976). For example, the dreams of subjects deprived of liquids were studied, and a number of the dreams were found to involve liquid consumption (p. 69): "Just as the bell went off, somebody raised a glass and said something about a toast. I don't think I had a glass."

Another view of the causes of dreams is the **activation-synthesis hypothesis** (McCarley & Hobson, 1981), which states that dreaming represents a person's subjective awareness and interpretation of neural activity during sleep. According to Robert W. McCarley and J. Allan Hobson, our acceptance of bizarre occurrences in dreams is caused by changes in brain physiology. That is, just as our brains organize sensory information during wakefulness, our brains also organize sensory information during sleep. Thus, the brain may interpret the blockage of motor commands that occurs during dreaming as a sensation of our being chased. Our sleeping brains may interpret neural activity in the vestibular system (which controls balance; see Chapter 4) as the sensation of floating, flying, or falling.

Like other Surrealist artists, René Magritte attempted to portray the workings of the subconscious mind through his art, as shown here in La Grande Famille.

Compare the theories of dreaming, indicating the theory you find most credible, as well as the reasons you find it credible.

Although the biological purpose of dreaming may someday be discovered, it is unlikely that scientists will ever devise a definitive model of dream interpretation. Dreams are highly personal, and to say that you could prove why people dream what they dream, you would have to be able to predict the content of a specific dream at a specific time (Hobson, 1989). Such prediction is not likely to occur, however. Because dreams are personal, many people can and do freely interpret their own dreams within the context of their current lives and past memories, drawing whatever conclusions seem appropriate to them.

No discussion of dreaming would be complete without mentioning **daydreaming**—a state of consciousness somewhere between waking and sleeping. In normal wakefulness, we shift our concentration

Daydreaming can help us to creatively contemplate the information we have been studying.

between external events and internal thoughts, with more emphasis on the external. When we daydream, we shift our focus to the internal and often become unaware of the external. Although daydreaming can be disruptive—as anyone knows who has ever been questioned while daydreaming in class—it can also be helpful in setting and reaching goals because it generates thoughts that are more creative and less restrained than those of a completely alert waking state. Another state of mind often associated with creative, unrestrained thought is the state of consciousness that results from hypnosis.

HYPNOSIS

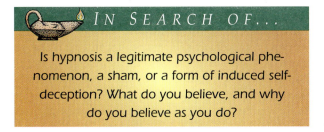

IN SEARCH OF...

Is hypnosis a legitimate psychological phenomenon, a sham, or a form of induced self-deception? What do you believe, and why do you believe as you do?

Hypnosis is an altered state of consciousness that bears some resemblance to sleep. A person undergoing hypnosis is usually deeply relaxed and extremely sensitive to suggestion. For example, hypnotized people may imagine that they see or hear things when they are prompted to do so (Bowers, 1976). Subjects may also receive a **posthypnotic suggestion,** in which they are given instructions during hypnosis that they implement after having wakened

from the hypnotic state; subjects often have no recollection of having been given the instructions or even of having been hypnotized (Ruch, 1975). They also may not sense things that they otherwise would sense; for example, a person may not feel pain when dipping an arm into very cold water. Hypnotized persons also may be induced to remember things they had seemingly forgotten.

Despite what has been found about the hypnotized state, many psychologists wonder whether hypnotism is a genuine psychological phenomenon. Historically, even the man credited with introducing hypnotism as a psychological phenomenon did not recognize the phenomenon as hypnotism, and he certainly did not credit hypnotism as the means by which he cured his patients of their nervous disorders.

Brief History of Hypnosis

Franz Anton Mesmer (1734–1815), an Austrian physician, believed that psychological illnesses were caused by magnetic imbalances. To achieve a cure, he manipulated what he called "animal magnetism" (which differed from but was related to physical magnetism). He believed that he used the animal magnetism emanating from his hands to redistribute the "universal magnetic fluid" in the disturbed person's body (see Figure 6-4).

Remarkably, these mysterious treatments did prove to be successful with some patients, but the government of France, where he was practicing, remained skeptical, partly because of Mesmer's showmanlike manner. In 1784, Louis XVI appointed a commission to investigate the relative merits of magnetism, as well as the peculiar ways in which Mesmer treated and sometimes cured his patients. The commission concluded that animal magnetism was not a legitimate phenomenon. They further concluded that Mesmer's results were due to *experimenter effects*, or *demand characteristics*. That is, the apparent cure was a result of Mesmer's (the experimenter's) interaction with his patients (the subjects), rather than a result of the treatment itself. According to the commission, the subjects (Mesmer's patients) were only behaving as if cured, or as if they believed they were cured, to comply with the demands of the experimenter (Mesmer). (A similar phenomenon, the placebo effect, is described in Chapter 16.)

When Mesmer's technique was discredited, was hypnotism therefore discredited as well? No. If scientists discredit one or even several demonstrations of a phenomenon, they cannot on this basis conclusively decide that the entire phenomenon is therefore a fraud. A given demonstration of a phenomenon may

FIGURE 6-4
Mesmerism

Franz Anton Mesmer, one of the first to experiment with hypnotism, believed that animal magnetism could cure illnesses. His patients would sit around the "magnetized" tub, wrap themselves with cord, and hold onto bent iron bars. "Magnetizers," Mesmer's helpers, would rub the patient's afflicted part to hasten the cure.

be false, but other demonstrations may be true. In fact, although Mesmer was disgraced by the findings of the commission, the phenomenon we now know as hypnotism was at one time called *mesmerism* in his honor. We still sometimes refer to some spellbinding experiences as being "mesmerizing."

Since Mesmer's time, scientists have continued to investigate hypnotism. One way to determine whether hypnotism is genuine is to use the **simulating paradigm** (Orne, 1959), a technique in which one group of subjects is hypnotized and another group (a control group) is not. The subjects in the unhypnotized group are then asked to behave as though they were hypnotized. Experimenters must then try to decide whether the behavior of the hypnotized group is distinguishable from the behavior of the control group.

As it turns out, simulators are able to mimic some, but not all, of the behavior of hypnotized subjects (Gray, Bowers, & Fenz, 1970). Also, hypnotized

subjects in simulation experiments provide very different reports of their subjective experiences. Simulating subjects report themselves as actively faking, whereas hypnotized subjects report the behavior as more or less just happening to them. Moreover, simulating subjects try to figure out what the hypnotist expects from them, whereas hypnotized subjects claim to be uninfluenced by the experimenter's expectations of them (Orne, 1959).

How would you design an experiment to differentiate simulators from truly hypnotized subjects?

Theories of Hypnosis

If we accept the phenomenon of hypnosis as genuine, we still need to determine exactly what goes on during hypnosis. We discuss here only the more credible theories. One such theory holds that hypnosis is a

Searchers . . . ERNEST HILGARD

Ernest "Jack" Hilgard is Emeritus Professor of Psychology at Stanford University.

Q: *Why did you become interested in psychology in general, and in your area of work in particular?*

A: Well, in my case it's a little complex. It was a synthesis between my training as a chemical engineer and my courses at the Yale Divinity School. Both of those experiences were valuable to me. But I lost an interest in chemistry, and I was not really deeply religious. Psychology combined both the scientific approach and the human interest that had motivated me right along. So without much undergraduate work in psychology at all (I had had one course, I think) I settled on graduate study at Yale.

To tell you what psychology was like at that time, about the late 1920s, Edward Titchener was still alive at Cornell, and he was, of course, the man who had mostly influenced Edwin Boring. John B. Watson had really just come to prominence in developing his behaviorism. B. F. Skinner was about to do his graduate work the same time I was. We were the same age, so he wasn't on the scene yet. And William McDougall, who was probably the most distinguished British psychologist, attracted a good deal of attention. He was best known for his instinct theories, but what brought him the most attention was his interest in social psychology, which hadn't had much of a play. I was never particularly impressed by any one of them. I got interested in both William James and in Sigmund Freud. And then a little later, Gestalt psychology was coming along, so we had some choices to make. Because of my non-psychological background, it seemed to me wise to choose something that sounded like hard-boiled psychology, so I studied conditioned reflexes for my doctoral dissertation. I had to prove, to myself, that I was an experimental psychologist.

Clark Hull brought hypnotism to Yale, but I didn't do anything with it then because it was kind of a marginal field, and I was still feeling I had to identify myself with the central trend in psychology. But it sowed a seed that I picked up years later after I was better established in psychology and felt I wouldn't ruin my reputation doing hypnosis.

Q: *What is your greatest asset as a psychologist?*

A: One thing is a curiosity about all aspects of psychology, so none of it's really foreign to me. It's important to keep that curiosity alive so the work stays relevant. The second thing is tolerance, so that as I look around for the work that people are doing who may be quarreling with me, I find there's something to be learned from each of the fields. I was never a disciple of Fred Skinner, but we were always good friends, and I felt there were things to be learned from him.

Q: *How do you usually get your ideas?*

A: I begin with a commonsense question that I want to answer. In the case of the conditioned response, the question that puzzled me was: Is all that gets conditioned really reflex? How do you answer that question? Well, you had to have some criteria of what's a reflex and what isn't. And so I handled that pretty much in terms of the latency of the responses. It turned out that the conditioned responses had a latency much more like voluntary responses than like knee-jerks or pupilary responses or the things that were really reflex. The outcome was that all that gets conditioned is not reflex.

Q: *What is your major contribution to psychology and why?*

A: A critical functionalism. I chose critically the things that seemed like good ideas from other points of view. My students were pretty much imbued with that, and so the best of them all turned out with a breadth of interest.

Q: *What advice would you give to someone starting in the field of psychology?*

A: It's a great advantage to have mathematical and statistical ability. Also, see yourself as part of both biological and social science. It depends partly on your own interest, but if you are interested in the biological side, you'd better get enough chemistry to work your way up to biochemistry and so on. It's hard to take those background things as a graduate student if you don't have some preparation. Or in social science, you ought to take some economics and sociology or anthropology, whatever you find congenial, because they are all closely interrelated.

Q: *How has psychology been important to you?*

A: It's become an integral part of my life, as teacher and researcher.

Q: *How do keep yourself academically challenged?*

A: I've been retired since 1969, but I still have an office at the university. I read the reviews in *Contemporary Psychology*, and I note the new books that are coming out. I can't really keep up with all of it, but I talk to my colleagues. I keep my curiosity alive. I'm not doing much with these things, but I like to know what's going on. I participated in the centennial celebration of the APA.

Q: *What would you like people to remember your work for?*

A: Well, I guess my approach to the problems of psychology, as illustrated in my textbooks, books on learning theory; making hypnosis a respectable part of scientific psychology; and my historical writings.

form of deep relaxation (Edmonston, 1981). This theory builds on the idea of hypnosis as a form of sleep, as suggested by Ivan Pavlov (see Chapter 7 for more on Pavlov). We know that EEG patterns obtained during hypnosis are different from EEG patterns during sleep, however. Nevertheless, there may still be a close connection between hypnosis and the deep relaxation that sometimes precedes or resembles sleep.

A second theory suggests that hypnosis is an *epiphenomenon* (a phenomenon that exists only as a secondary outcome of another phenomenon). According to this view, hypnosis is a form of role playing in response to experimenter demands (the demand characteristics mentioned earlier). In attempting to fulfill the role set out by the experimenter, the subject acts in particular ways. This view differs from the more cynical view of the conscious simulator. The subject in this situation is believed to become so genuinely caught up in the role that he or she unwittingly enacts that role for a brief period of time.

Perhaps the most widely accepted view among scientists who believe that hypnosis is a genuine phe-

nomenon is the **neodissociative theory.** According to this view, people are capable of experiencing a *dissociation* (separation) of one part of their minds from another. In effect, when subjects are hypnotized, their consciousness splits. One part of them responds to the hypnotist's commands, while another part becomes a hidden observer, monitoring everything that is going on, including some things of which the hypnotized subject may not even be consciously aware (Hilgard, 1977).

For example, studies of pain relief through hypnosis have found that while subjects respond to a hypnotist's suggestion that they feel no pain, they are also able to describe how the pain feels. In other experiments, subjects can be made to write down messages while unaware that they are doing so, because they are actively engaged in another task (see Kihlstrom, 1985; Knox, Crutchfield, & Hilgard, 1975; Zamansky & Bartis, 1985). Thus, it seems that part of the subject's consciousness is un-self-consciously involved in the hypnosis, while another part observes and thereby knows, at some level, what is taking place.

People differ in their susceptibility to hypnosis (Hilgard, 1965), with some people readily becoming deeply hypnotized, others less so, and still others appearing invulnerable to hypnotism. Unsurprisingly, hypnosis is more successful as a clinical treatment with highly hypnotizable subjects. Today, hypnosis is used in clinical settings to control smoking and to treat a variety of health-related problems, such as asthma, high blood pressure, and migraine headaches. The effects of hypnosis, however, appear to be temporary. For this reason, hypnotism generally is used in conjunction with other therapeutic techniques. Still, hypnosis appears to have an effect that goes beyond other treatment techniques, whether in relieving pain or in changing behavior.

To conclude this discussion, the results are inconclusive. Psychologists have not reached consensus regarding what hypnosis is, or even whether it is a genuine phenomenon. Persuasive evidence suggests that hypnosis is more than a crass simulation.

Hypnotists are able to induce a state of deep relaxation in susceptible subjects. Here, Ernest Hilgard conducts an experiment to determine the effects of hypnosis.

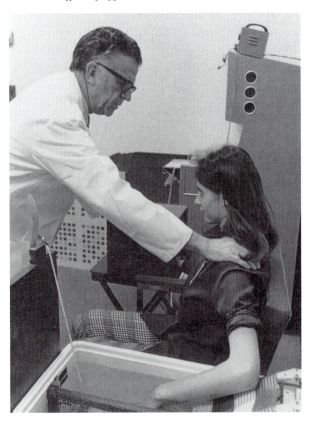

MEDITATION AND ALTERED STATES

IN SEARCH OF...

Why might certain productive ideas come to a person who is meditating that do not occur to the person when he or she is not in a meditative state?

Meditation is a set of techniques used to alter consciousness by "a shift away from the active, outward-oriented, linear mode and toward the receptive and quiescent mode, and often, a shift from an external focus of attention to an internal one" (Ornstein, 1977, p. 159). Some of the different kinds of meditation are described here.

Kinds of Meditation

In **concentrative meditation,** the meditator focuses on an object or thought and attempts to remove all else from consciousness. Concentrative meditation is performed in various ways. In **Zen,** the classical Buddhist form of concentrative meditation, meditators go through a graded series of steps as they advance from novice to expert. The exact set of steps depends on the particular form of Zen. Initially, the meditator might be instructed to sit peacefully in the lotus (cross-legged) position (the customary position for Zen meditation) and to count breaths from 1 to 10, then repeat the count again and again. On the other hand, meditators might be asked to focus on the whole process of breathing—to think about the movement of the air as it reaches the nose, permeates the lungs, remains in the lungs, and then is finally expelled. The idea is to focus on a simple, repetitive, and rhythmic activity.

At another time, the meditator might be asked to contemplate the answer to a *koan*—a riddle or paradox, such as "What is the sound of one hand clapping?" or "What is the size of the real you?" These questions have no logical answers, which is just the point. You can think about the questions time and again without coming to a conclusion.

Another form of concentrative meditation is **yoga,** which, like Zen, comes in various forms. Yoga is a form of exercise, but the exercises are actually a part of a larger scheme, the center of which is meditation. Practitioners sometimes use yoga to control involuntary processes of the autonomic nervous system (see Chapter 3), such as blood flow, heart rate, and digestive activity. In yoga, meditation often involves the use of a *mantram* (plural: *mantra*), a set of words that typically have some kind of meaning but that mainly serve as a focus of awareness. The meditator repeats the words of the mantram over and over again, either aloud or silently, focusing on these words and excluding everything else from consciousness as much as possible. Transcendental meditation (TM) is a form of mantram yoga.

Opening-up meditation, a second general form of meditation, is in some respects the opposite of concentrative meditation. In opening-up medita-

Miroku (538–642 A.D.) sculpted this Buddha of the Future, shown sitting in meditative contemplation at the Koryu-ji Temple in Kyoto, Japan.

tion, a person integrates meditation with—rather than separating it from—everyday life and seeks to expand awareness of everyday events. Yoga can take an opening-up form, as well as a concentrative one. In one form of opening-up yoga, you learn to observe yourself as though you were another person. In another form of opening-up meditation, you perform everyday actions slightly differently from the customary way, in order to become more aware of the routine of your life.

Effects of Meditation

What happens during meditation, and what value, if any, is there in the various forms of meditation? In general, respiration, heart rate, blood pressure, and muscle tension decrease (Shapiro & Giber, 1978; Wallace & Benson, 1972). Some evidence indicates that meditation can help patients with bronchial asthma (Honsberger & Wilson, 1973) and that it can decrease blood pressure in patients who are hypertensive (Benson, 1977). It may reduce insomnia in some people (Woolfolk et al., 1976) and some symptoms of psychiatric syndromes in others (Glueck & Stroebel, 1975). EEG studies suggest that concentrative meditation tends to produce a concentration of alpha waves, the type of brain wave associated with a state of relaxation and the beginning stages of sleep (Ornstein, 1977). Thus, concentrative meditation seems to relax people, which is of value in its own right. In addition, many practitioners of meditation believe that it enhances their overall consciousness and moves them toward a more enlightened state of consciousness. However, the effects of meditation may not all be positive. Too much meditation may cause dizziness, depression, confusion, and anxiety (Otis, 1984)—symptoms also associated with many drug-induced alterations in consciousness.

DRUG-INDUCED ALTERATIONS IN CONSCIOUSNESS

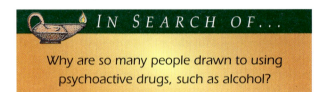

I N   S E A R C H   O F . . .

Why are so many people drawn to using psychoactive drugs, such as alcohol?

TABLE 6-2
Four Basic Categories of Drugs

Psychoactive drugs can be sorted into four basic categories, each of which produces distinctive psychoactive effects.

Category	Effect	Drugs in This Class
Narcotics	Produce numbness or stupor, relieve pain	Opium and its natural derivatives: morphine and codeine Synthetic derivative of opium: heroin Opioids (synthetic narcotics): meperidine (Demerol®), propoxyphene (Darvon®), oxycodone (Percodan®), methadone

CNS depressants ("downers")	Slow (depress) the operation of the central nervous system	Alcohol
		Sedative-hypnotics
		    Barbiturates: secobarbital (Seconal®), phenobarbital (Dilantin®),
		    Tranquilizers (benzodiazepines): chlorpromazine (Thorazine®), chlordiazepoxide (Librium®), diazepam (Valium®), alprazolam (Xanax®)
		
		Methaqualone (Quaalude®)
		
		Chloral hydrate

CNS stimulants ("uppers")	Excite (stimulate) the operation of the central nervous system	Caffeine (found in coffee, teas, cola drinks, chocolate) Amphetamines: amphetamine (Benzedrine®, "bennies"), dextroamphetamine (Dexedrine®), methamphetamine (Methedrine®) Cocaine Nicotine (in tobacco)
Hallucinogens (psychedelics, psychotomimetics)	Induce alterations of consciousness	LSD Mescaline Marijuana Hashish Phencyclidine (PCP)

Drugs introduced into the body may destroy bacteria, ease pain, or alter consciousness. In this chapter, we are concerned only with **psychoactive** drugs, which achieve a **psychopharmacological** effect—that is, drugs that affect behavior, mood, and consciousness. Psychoactive drugs can be classified into four basic categories (Seymour & Smith, 1987): narcotics, central nervous system depressants, central nervous system stimulants, and hallucinogens. (See Table 6-2 for a summary of drugs in each category.) We consider each of these four kinds of drugs in turn, starting with the potent analgesics (pain relievers) known as narcotics.

Narcotics

Historical Background

Narcotic, from the Greek term for "numbness," originally referred only to *opium* and drugs derived from opium, such as codeine and heroin. Narcotics can be either naturally or synthetically derived (see Table 6-2). Narcotics derived from the opium poppy bulb are **opiates.** Drugs that have similar chemical structures and effects but are synthetically derived are **opioids.** When used illegally, opiates and opioids are usually injected intravenously, smoked, or inhaled. When used medically, they are either ingested orally or injected intravenously. Today, the term *narcotic* generally encompasses drugs that produce some degree of numbness or stupor and lead to addiction. The numbness is generally perceived as a feeling of well-being or as analgesia.

Drug Actions

Narcotics are highly addictive and are usually either regulated by prescription or banned outright. Narcotics are sometimes prescribed for very brief periods to cure postsurgical pain, and, in very low doses, to relieve diarrhea. They have a constipating effect because narcotics also depress other physiological systems, including metabolic processes.

Narcotics primarily affect the functioning of the brain and of the bowel. They bring about pain relief, relaxation, and sleepiness. They also help to suppress coughs (hence their use in the form of *codeine* prescription cough medicines) and can stimulate vomiting. Users typically notice impairment in their ability to concentrate and experience a sense of mental fuzziness or cloudiness. For these reasons, driving under the influence of narcotics is extremely dangerous, and doing cognitively intensive work (such as studying) while affected by them is likely to be unproductive.

Side effects of narcotics include contraction of the pupils of the eyes, sweating, nausea, and depressed breathing.

Another danger of narcotic use over time is the possibility of an eventual **overdose** (ingestion of a life-threatening or lethal dose of drugs). Narcotics users develop **tolerance** to the drug effects, prompting them to seek increasing amounts of the drug to achieve the same desired effect. Actually, most narcotics users find that the euphoria they experienced when using the drug initially disappears after prolonged use. Rather, they must continue to use drugs in order to keep from feeling ill from withdrawal of the drugs.

Neural biochemistry explains the actions and effects of narcotics. Like many other drugs, narcotics mimic neurotransmitters in the way they act at synapses (see Chapter 3 and Figure 6-5). The molecular composition of opiates resembles that of endorphins, which are *endogenous morphines*, the body's naturally produced painkilling neurotransmitters (see also Chapter 20). Initial use of narcotics prompts pain relief and some of the euphoria that normally accompanies the natural release of endorphins. Prolonged use of narcotics apparently causes a drop in the body's natural production of particular endorphins.

As a drug replaces the body's natural painkillers, drug dependence increases and tolerance develops because more narcotic is needed to do the job that the body gradually ceases to perform. **Withdrawal symptoms,** the result of decreased dosage or discontinuation of a drug, occur as the body finds itself with fewer of its own natural painkillers, as well as fewer of the drug-induced ones. Typical narcotic withdrawal symptoms are chills, sweating, intense stomach cramps, diarrhea, headache, and repeated vomiting—similar to a really horrible case of intestinal flu.

FIGURE 6-5
Molecular Similarity of Opiates and Endorphins
Opiates and endorphins have very similar structures, which is why narcotics easily fit the receptor sites for endorphins.

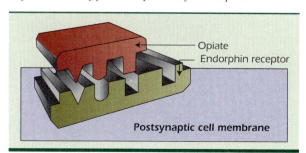

Treatment of Dependency

The form of treatment for narcotic dependence differs for *acute toxicity* (the damage done from a particular overdose) versus *chronic toxicity* (the damage done by long-term drug addiction). Acute toxicity is usually treated with naloxone. Naloxone (as well as a related drug, naltrexone) occupies opiate receptors in the brain better than the opiates themselves occupy those sites; thus, it blocks all effects of narcotics (see Figure 6-6). In fact, naloxone has such a strong affinity for the endorphin receptors in the brain that it actually replaces existing narcotics and moves into those receptors as well. Naloxone is not addictive, however, because even though it binds to receptors, it does not activate them. Although naloxone can be a life-saving drug for someone who has overdosed on opiates, its effects are short-lived, making it a poor long-term treatment for drug addiction.

FIGURE 6-6
Molecular Similarity of Opiates and Naloxone
The nonnarcotic drug naloxone fits the receptor sites for endorphins so well that it can push out opiates and block them from re-entering those sites. Hence, naloxone can be used as an effective temporary treatment for narcotic overdose, although its effects are short-lived.

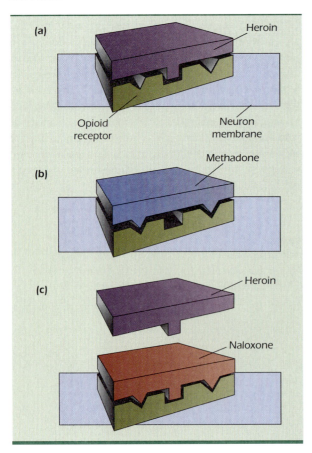

Maintenance and detoxification are the primary methods of treating chronic toxicity caused by prolonged drug addiction. *Maintenance* controls an addict's use of the drug. In a maintenance program, the addict is still given the drug or a substitute, but in a controlled manner. The goal is to substitute a more controllable, less lethal, addiction—a goal considered controversial by many. *Detoxification* seeks to break the addiction both by weaning an addict off the drug to break the habit and by restoring good health habits. In narcotic detoxification, methadone is substituted for the narcotic (typically, heroin), and then gradually decreasing dosages are administered to the patient until he or she is drug-free.

Central Nervous System Depressants

General Drug Actions

Central nervous system (CNS) depressants include alcohol and the sedative-hypnotics. Depressants, like narcotics, are "downers" that slow the operation of the CNS. Alcohol is readily available for purchase in the United States to people of age 21 or over. Sedative-hypnotics are usually prescribed or taken in low doses to reduce anxiety and in higher doses to combat insomnia. CNS depressants can be ingested orally or injected.

In general, CNS depressants usually elevate mood, reduce anxiety and guilt, and relax normal inhibitions. However, people **intoxicated** (stupefied by the effects of toxins) with depressants may also find themselves susceptible to sudden shifts in mood, so that their relaxation and euphoria quickly give way to *increased* anxiety and irritability. High doses of depressants can cause slow reflexes, unsteady gait, slurred speech, and impaired judgment. Overdoses can slow physiological responses so much that they cause death.

Alcohol

Alcohol is the most well-known and widely used CNS depressant. The natural result of the fermentation of fruits and grains, alcohol is so widely promoted and consumed that people tend to ignore the fact that it is an addictive psychoactive drug.

Alcohol's effects vary with the amount consumed, rate of consumption, and an individual's body weight, tolerance, and metabolism. Someone who sips a drink over the course of an evening is less likely to become intoxicated than someone who gulps it, and a 300-pound person is typically less affected than a 100-pound person by the same amount of alcohol.

However, a frequent drinker usually builds up a tolerance (similar to narcotics tolerance), and this tolerance can lead to increased consumption.

At blood-level concentrations of 0.03 to 0.05%, people often feel relaxed, uninhibited, and have a general sense of well-being. At a blood-alcohol level of 0.10%, sensorimotor functioning is markedly impaired. Many states consider people to be legally drunk at this level. People may exhibit slurred speech, and grow angry, sullen, or morose. At a concentration of 0.20%, people show grave dysfunction. With concentrations of 0.40% or more, there is a serious risk of death.

Most dosages of alcohol decrease the effectiveness of the neurotransmitter *dopamine* (see Chapter 3), thereby reducing motor abilities and attention. Alcohol also appears to interfere with the activities of other neurotransmitters (Groves & Rebec, 1988). At first, alcohol often appears to increase people's level of arousal, apparently because it first depresses the

Although party-goers often drink alcohol to relax and reduce inhibitions, prolonged or excessive drinking can cause stupor, damage to the brain and nervous system, and sometimes death. Is this person having fun yet?

effects of synapses that release inhibitory neurotransmitters in the brain. Because the inhibiting neurotransmitters are depressed, they do not inhibit neurotransmission as much. Thus, even though synaptic activity is being depressed, people initially may feel more excited because inhibitory activity is slowed. Soon, however, alcohol depresses the effects of excitatory synapses as well, causing a general decrease in sensorimotor functioning.

Alcoholism, now widely regarded as a disease, is one of the most common afflictions in the United States. Alcoholics are unable to abstain from alcohol and cannot control their drinking once they start. Roughly two-thirds of adults in the United States report that they use alcohol. An estimated 10% of these people have problems related to alcohol use, and 5% of them are alcoholics, with physical as well as psychological dependence. Probably at least 10 million adults in the United States suffer from alcohol dependence (Seymour & Smith, 1987), and an estimated 90% of all assaults, 50% to 60% of all murders, and more than 50% of the rapes and of the sexual attacks on children are alcohol related.

Chronic alcoholics may sustain permanent damage to the nervous system, pancreas, liver, and brain cells. Heavy drinking can also lead to suppression of the immune system, nutritional deficits, and general failure to be careful about health matters. These problems can eventually lead to many other unfortunate consequences, including increased risk of cancer (Herity et al., 1982; Heuch et al., 1983). For these and other reasons, alcoholics generally have their life expectancy cut short by an average of 10 to 12 years. Alcoholics also may experience blackouts, loss of memory, cardiac arrest, psychosis, and alcohol-induced death. Alcohol use by pregnant women, even in moderate amounts, can result in *fetal alcohol syndrome*, which may produce tragic permanent mental retardation, as well as facial deformities, in the children who must endure this toxic prenatal environment.

The National Institute on Alcohol Abuse and Alcoholism has developed a list of seven questions for self-diagnosis of alcoholism (see Table 6-3). An affirmative answer to even one question may suggest that alcohol is a problem, and affirmative answers to several questions should be taken as an indication that you may be an alcoholic. Most of these questions boil down to a central issue: Is your use of alcohol creating problems in other areas of your life?

Heavy drinkers experience withdrawal symptoms when they stop drinking alcohol. For the withdrawal from chronic (long-term) intoxication, symptoms are severe, including the possibility of

TABLE 6-3
Are You an Alcoholic?

If you answer yes to any of these questions, developed by the National Institute on Alcohol Abuse and Alcoholism, alcohol may be a problem in your life. If you answer yes to several of the questions, you may be an alcoholic.

If you can answer yes to even one of these questions, consider seeking advice about your use of alcohol.

1. Has someone close to you sometimes expressed concern about your drinking?
2. When faced with a problem, do you often turn to alcohol for relief?
3. Are you sometimes unable to meet home or work responsibilities because of drinking?
4. Have you ever required medical attention as a result of drinking?
5. Have you ever experienced a blackout—a total loss of memory while still awake—when drinking?
6. Have you ever come in conflict with the law in connection with your drinking?
7. Have you often failed to keep the promises you have made to yourself about controlling or cutting out your drinking?

severe convulsions, hallucinations, tremors, agitation, and even death (Seymour & Smith, 1987). Chronic alcoholism can be treated through medical intervention, through a counseling program such as Alcoholics Anonymous, or through a combination of treatments.

For the withdrawal from acute intoxication, typical symptoms are headache, loss of appetite, nausea, and shakiness—in short, a hangover. Detoxification for a hangover is simply a matter of time. As time passes, the body will metabolize the alcohol, and the symptoms will dissipate. Drinking a lot of nonalcoholic liquids can help, as can moderate exercise. Drinking coffee does not reduce the effects of alcohol. Instead, it creates a wide-awake, stimulated drunk. Drinking more alcohol to reduce the effect of a hangover does little good, and it can lead to increased alcohol dependence.

Sedative-Hypnotics

Sedative-hypnotics are depressant drugs used to calm anxiety and relieve insomnia (see Table 6-2; see also Chapter 19). The most widely used sedative-hypnotics are classified as **barbiturates.**

When used properly, barbiturates are effective sedative-hypnotics. In low doses, barbiturates do calm the user. Higher dosages inhibit neurons in arousal centers in the brain, causing sleep. Still higher dosages, however, can cause respiratory failure. As is true of nearly all psychoactive drugs, their addictive properties encourage rampant abuse; chronic use leads to increased tolerance, so that the user takes more and more of the drug to achieve the same effect. Increased dosages can misfire in several ways, how-

ever. For one thing, the user may fall asleep or be groggy in situations demanding full attention, which can lead to accidental injury or even death. For another, the user may ingest a lethal dosage in a desperate attempt to fall asleep.

Following the development of tranquilizers (benzodiazepines, listed in Table 6-2), physicians shifted away from prescribing barbiturates as sedatives and moved toward prescribing them primarily as sleep inducers. **Tranquilizers** are antianxiety drugs considered to be safer than barbiturates. They effectively relieve the symptoms of psychological stress without causing drowsiness, they are effective at low dosages, and they do not interfere as much with the respiratory system. Tranquilizers, too, can be addictive, yet they are the second most commonly prescribed drugs in the United States (Seymour & Smith, 1987). Clearly, the potential for abuse exists.

Treatment of Abuse

Treatment for addiction or overdose varies according to the sedative–hypnotic drug, but both a psychological and a physiological dependence must be addressed. Chronic toxicity may be treated through a counseling and support program, or, in the case of barbiturates, through maintenance via gradual phenobarbital substitution. Whereas withdrawal from narcotic drugs is extremely uncomfortable but usually not life threatening, withdrawal from sedative-hypnotic drugs can be both painful and life-threatening. Withdrawal symptoms can include anxiety, tremors, nightmares, insomnia, anorexia, nausea, vomiting, fever, seizures, and delirium (Seymour & Smith, 1987).

Central Nervous System Stimulants

Physiological and Psychological Effects

Stimulants, like the other drugs we have considered, have been around for centuries. **CNS stimulants** excite the central nervous system, either by stimulating the heart or by inhibiting the actions of natural compounds that depress brain activity (in other words, they act as "double-negatives" on brain stimulation). Common CNS stimulants include caffeine, amphetamines, cocaine, and nicotine (found in tobacco) (see Table 6-2). In the short term, CNS stimulants can increase the user's stamina and alertness, stave off hunger pains, and create a sense of euphoria. In stronger doses, the drugs can cause anxiety and irritability. Societally, illegal stimulants, most notably cocaine, have overtaken narcotics as the greatest drug problem in the United States.

Caffeine is probably the mildest stimulant, and it creates fewer problems than the other drugs in this category. Caffeine is found in a number of drinks that come close to being "national drinks"—coffee in the United States, tea in the United Kingdom, *guarana* in Brazil, *mate* in Argentina. Chocolate and cola drinks are also sources of caffeine. A 6-ounce cup of coffee contains between 100 and 150 milligrams of caffeine. Tea and cola contain considerably less.

Caffeine increases neural activity, stimulating tension in the heart and skeletal muscles. Caffeine stimulates the CNS partly by suppressing the effects of *adenosine*, a naturally occurring depressant (inhibitory chemical) in the brain. High doses of caffeine can cause anxiety, nervousness, irritability, tremulousness, muscle twitching, insomnia, rapid heart beat, hyperventilation, increased urination, and gastrointestinal disturbances. Very high levels of caffeine also can increase blood pressure and possibly contribute to coronary heart disease (Lane & Williams, 1987; Shapiro, Lane, & Henry, 1986), although it appears that caffeine is dangerous for most people only in very large amounts. Thus, whereas someone who drinks seven or eight cups of coffee a day is likely to be at risk, someone who drinks a cup or two of coffee a day is *not*.

Caffeine is addictive. Caffeine addiction is not a major societal problem, but the indications of addiction are similar to those of other, more destructive drugs. These indications include compulsive behavior, loss of control, and continued drug use despite adverse consequences (Seymour & Smith, 1987). Symptoms of withdrawal from caffeine include lethargy, irritability, difficulties in working, constipation, and headache.

Amphetamines are synthetic stimulants that are usually either ingested or injected. Amphetamines increase body temperature, heart rate, and endurance. They are sometimes used by people whose jobs require long hours and sustained attention and are also used in some diet pills to reduce appetite. In the brain, amphetamines stimulate the release of neurotransmitters such as *norepinephrine* and *dopamine* (see Chapter 3) into brain synapses, creating a euphoric "high" and increasing alertness. Amphetamines may further increase the levels of these neurotransmitters by preventing their reuptake from the synaptic gaps (Groves & Rebec, 1976). The resulting higher-than-normal concentrations of these neurotransmitters lead to increased arousal and motor activity. At very high levels, amphetamines also affect transmission of *serotonin*. When taken over long periods of time, the levels of serotonin and other neurotransmitters in the brain may start to decrease, thereby producing damage to the neural communication system within the brain.

As is true of many other drugs, prolonged use of amphetamines creates tolerance and a resulting need for higher doses. In sufficiently large doses, amphetamines can produce odd behavior, such as repetitive searching and examining, prolonged staring at objects, chewing, and moving an object back and forth (Groves & Rebec, 1988). Overdoses produce intoxication, paranoia, confusion, hallucinations, and death due to respiratory failure or wild fluctuations in body temperature. Withdrawal symptoms include extreme fatigue and depression. Intermittent use of amphetamines also seems to produce the paradoxical phenomenon of **sensitization,** in which the rare or occasional user actually demonstrates heightened sensitivity to low doses of the drug.

Compare the phenomena of sensitization, withdrawal, and addiction. How might physicians in drug-treatment programs use their knowledge of these phenomena when treating newborns who appear to show symptoms of drug use?

Cocaine, the most powerful known natural stimulant, was used in religious ceremonies by the Incas in pre-Columbian times. For centuries, South Americans have chewed the leaves of the coca plant to increase their physical stamina in their rugged, harsh environment. Cocaine, commonly known as "coke," is highly addictive, especially when smoked in the form of "crack." Physiologically, cocaine increases body temperature and constricts peripheral blood vessels. It also produces spurious feelings of increased mental ability, and it can produce great excitement and, if consumed in sufficient quantity, hallucinations and seizures. Like amphetamines, cocaine appears to increase the transmission of *norepinephrine* and *dopamine* across synapses, and to inhibit the reuptake of both these neurotransmitters and of *serotonin*, resulting in the heightened arousal and motor activity associated with amphetamines. Initially, at least, cocaine also seems to stimulate acute sexual arousal, but prolonged use diminishes sexual arousability and performance (Wade & Cirese, 1991). Prolonged use also leads to difficulties in neural transmission similar to those associated with prolonged amphetamine use.

Recovering cocaine addicts crave the drug intensely. Their prolonged use has diminished their natural brain-stimulant mechanisms, so they feel great anxiety, a loss of control, depression, and lethargy. Education about its dangers and support groups are, for now, the best methods of overcoming cocaine addiction.

Tobacco is legally available in a variety of forms, although stop-smoking campaigns, widespread publicity about the health dangers, and reports of the harmful effects of *secondary smoke* (inhaling smoke that is exhaled by smokers or otherwise released into the air by burning tobacco) have led to increasingly restrictive laws prohibiting smoking in public places.

The tobacco leaf is grown throughout the world and is usually smoked, but it is also often chewed. *Nicotine*, the stimulant substance in tobacco, is absorbed through the respiratory tract, as well as the oral and nasal mucosa and the gastrointestinal tract. Most of the inhaled nicotine is absorbed by the lungs. Nicotine activates nicotinic receptors located on nerve cells and on skeletal muscles. These receptors use *acetylcholine*, and their activation thereby increases the neurotransmission of acetylcholine.

Tobacco has complex effects on the body. It can act as both a stimulant and a depressant, increasing respiration, heart rate, and blood pressure, but decreasing appetite. Intoxication is characterized by euphoria, light-headedness, giddiness, dizziness, and a tingling sensation in the extremities (Seymour & Smith, 1987). Tolerance and dependence develop relatively quickly, so that the intoxication effect is typically experienced only by new initiates to smoking. People who habitually use tobacco usually stabilize at some point that becomes a maintenance dosage for them.

Tobacco is now believed to be among the most addictive substances in existence, and 9 out of 10 people who start smoking become addicted (as compared to 1 in 6 people who try crack cocaine and 1 in 10 people who experiment with alcohol). Smoking by pregnant women has been linked both to premature birth and to unusually low birth weight, grave risk factors for newborns. Most of the long-term adverse effects of tobacco occur after prolonged use. They include heart disease, cancers of various sorts (especially lung and mouth cancer), gum disease, eating disorders, emphysema, gastrointestinal disease, and brittleness of bones. Secondary smoke has been linked with many of these ailments as well. Nicotine is highly poisonous and is even used as a potent insecticide. Tobacco smoke also contains a number of potentially harmful by-products in addition to nicotine, including tar, carbon monoxide, and hydrogen cyanide. During the 1980s, 5 million people are believed to have died because of tobacco use, compared with 1 million who died from alcohol-related causes, and 350,000 who died from other addictions. Actually, nearly all of the stimulant drugs discussed here can cause death if taken in sufficient quantities.

Treatment of Stimulant Abuse

The most common treatment for drug addiction is individual or group psychotherapy. Drug-substitution therapy is generally not used except in the case of nicotine. For acute nicotine withdrawal, nicotine gum and epidermal patches appear to be effective when

Nicotine is one of the most highly addictive substances known. Because so many methods to stop smoking are readily available, the opportunities and support for people who wish to quit smoking are greater than ever.

used in combination with some other form of therapy. Without additional supportive treatment, users run the risk of becoming addicted to the substitute. In any case, stimulant abusers need to become drug free, develop a lifestyle that will enable them to stay drug free, understand what got them addicted in the first place, and find ways to stay off drugs. Organizations dedicated to helping people get off drugs include Narcotics Anonymous and Cocaine Anonymous. Numerous stop-smoking programs (such as those offered by the American Lung Association) use a wide array of techniques, including hypnosis, acupuncture, *aversion therapy* (overdosing people with smoke or nicotine to render it repulsive), group support, and education (see Chapter 19 for more information on these treatments).

Acute toxicity from stimulants must be treated medically. The exact treatment depends on the drug that was taken. For example, massive amphetamine overdose may call for inducing bowel movements in conscious subjects and for stomach pumping in individuals who have lost consciousness. Overdoses of cocaine may be treated with tranquilizers and may require hospitalization.

Hallucinogens

Hallucinogenic drugs (also known as "psychedelics" or "psychotomimetics") alter consciousness by inducing hallucinations and affecting the way the users perceive both their inner worlds and their external environments. *Hallucinations* are experiences of sensory stimulation in the absence of any actual corresponding external sensory input. Some clinicians hold that these drugs mimic the effects produced by psychosis (hence the term *psychotomimetic*), but others suggest that these hallucinations differ in kind from those produced by psychosis. Mescaline, LSD, and marijuana are examples of hallucinogenic drugs (see Table 6-2).

People react in very different ways to hallucinogenic drugs, and their reactions appear to be determined partly by situational factors. Physiologically, most hallucinogenic drugs work by interfering with the transmission of *serotonin* in the brain (Jacobs, 1987). Serotonin-releasing neuronal systems begin in the brain stem (see Chapter 3) and progress to nearly all parts of the brain; the fact that hallucinations can seem so real on so many different sensory levels may be connected to this widespread cerebral interference. Some suggest that a way to think of this mechanism is that serotonin normally blocks us from dreaming when we are awake, so the inhibition of serotonin during wakefulness allows the hallucinations associ-

ated with dreams to occur. This interference is not characteristic of marijuana, mescaline, or phencyclidine (PCP), however, whose mechanisms of action are still uncertain, although stimulation of norepinephrine neurotransmission may be a factor.

The hallucinogenic effects of *lysergic acid diethylamide (LSD)* (first synthesized in 1938) were discovered in 1943, when a chemist working for Sandoz Pharmaceuticals in Switzerland accidentally ingested some. LSD typically causes physical symptoms such as dizziness, creeping or tingling of the skin, nausea, and tremors; perceptual symptoms such as hallucinations and an altered sense of time; affective (emotional) symptoms such as rapid mood swings, ranging from severe depression to extreme agitation and anxiety; and cognitive symptoms, such as the feeling of having learned things not possible to have been learned without the drug (Groves & Rebec, 1988; Jacobs & Trulson, 1979).

Yet, LSD can also cause people to become anxious at their inability to control the drug experience or "trip." The most dangerous time in a bad reaction to LSD occurs during hallucinations. Users may try to flee the hallucinations, which can put them into physical danger. Even LSD users who enjoy the experience can be at risk; people have jumped out of windows, thinking they could fly! Also, on occasion, users have forgotten that they have ingested LSD or have been given the drug without their knowledge. In such instances, users may panic, thinking that the hallucinations will last forever.

The most commonly used hallucinogen, *marijuana*, is produced from the dried leaves and flowers of the cannabis plant. *Hashish* is a stronger form of marijuana, made from the concentrated resin that can be derived from the plant's flowers. Most users of marijuana or hashish either smoke or ingest the drug.

"Tell me more about these hallucinations. . . ."

HABERFELD

People under the influence of marijuana typically experience a flow of disconnected ideas and altered perceptions of space and time. Some people become extremely talkative, others inarticulate. Users may experience intense food cravings and may become impulsive. Very high doses can even lead to hallucinations.

Even moderate use of marijuana appears to lead to impairment in some short-term learning and memory processes (Darley et al., 1973). There is disagreement about the long-term effects of marijuana use. Some investigators claim that it damages nerve cells and the reproductive system; other researchers have failed to replicate such findings (Rubin & Comitas, 1974). Because marijuana is usually smoked, however, daily use has been conclusively shown to contribute to mouth and lung cancer.

Phencyclidine (PCP) is popular among young adolescents in some communities because of its modest price and easy accessibility. PCP somehow profoundly alters the relationship between the body's physical experiences and the mind's perceptual experiences, causing extreme cognitive and perceptual distortions. Its effects work particularly on receptors that play a role in learning, and its potential for causing serious cognitive deficits is great.

Acute overdoses of hallucinogens are normally treated by having a therapist attempt to talk to the user in order to reduce anxiety reactions and to make the user feel as comfortable as possible ("talking the user down"). Tranquilizers are also sometimes used, with a final alternative being antipsychotic drugs. Chronic use of hallucinogens can lead to prolonged psychotic reactions, severe and sometimes life-threatening depression, a worsening of preexisting psychiatric problems, and flashbacks of past drug experiences without further ingestion of the drug (Seymour & Smith, 1987). Scientists do not understand how flashbacks occur because they have not yet found any physiological mechanism that can account for them.

With all the problems associated with drug use, you may wonder why anybody uses drugs. The answers are as varied as are people themselves. Some people take drugs to experiment, feeling confident that they are personally immune to addiction or that they will not get addicted in the short amount of time that they plan to take the drugs. Others feel so unhappy in their daily lives that the risks seem worth it. Whatever the reasons for taking psychoactive drugs, the harmful outcomes generally outweigh any perceived benefits, particularly in the case of addictive drugs such as alcohol, tobacco, and cocaine.

Before we conclude this chapter, we consider two more topics related to consciousness.

EXTRASENSORY PERCEPTION

IN SEARCH OF...

What do you believe causes people to believe they have experienced a form of extrasensory perception?

It is difficult for psychologists to know where to place *extrasensory perception (ESP)* in the field of psychology, or even whether to relate it to psychology—or to any science—at all. ESP belongs to the realm of **parapsychology,** a branch of psychology concerned with phenomena that are unexplainable using known psychological principles. Some psychologists are convinced that such phenomena (including ESP) exist, but many others are equally convinced that they do not exist. If ESP does exist, it is probably an altered state of consciousness, because it seems unlikely that we would experience it in a normal waking state.

There are four alleged types of ESP: precognition, clairvoyance, telepathy, and psychokinesis. **Precognition** refers to perception of a future event. A fortune-teller who claims to see the future uses precognition. **Clairvoyance** is the perception of objects or events for which there is no apparent stimulation of the known senses. For example, a clairvoyant might claim to be able to determine a randomly selected number that was placed in a sealed envelope. **Telepathy,** probably the most commonly claimed form of ESP, is the direct transfer of thoughts from one person to another without any visible form of expression. **Psychokinesis** is the ability to move objects by thought alone, as in trying to bend metal objects via mental concentration.

The Amazing Randi, a magician, has made a career of exposing many fraudulent claims of ESP phenomena. Why would a magician be particularly suited to the task of exposing these fraudulent claims?

You may wonder whether I believe in ESP. I just don't know. Scientific studies have not convinced me of its existence. My own view is that we need to remain open-minded and to reserve judgment.

How would you design an experiment to test an ESP phenomenon?

NEAR-DEATH EXPERIENCES

IN SEARCH OF...

To what do you attribute people's accounts of their near-death experiences?

I have saved for last one of the strangest and most intriguing phenomena in the psychology of consciousness, the **near-death experience,** which occurs occasionally in people who come extremely close to death. In some cases, they are thought to be dead before it is realized that they are not completely gone. During this time, some people undergo unusual psychological experiences.

A variety of researchers have reviewed accounts of people claiming to have had near-death experiences (e.g., Blackmore, 1993; Serdahely, 1990; Zaleski, 1987). Near-death experiences have been reported in writings throughout history and in the lore of cultures as disparate as those of the ancient Greeks, Buddhists, and North American Indians. A large number of people, of differing ages and cultural backgrounds, report common near-death sensations. They often feel peace or intense joy. Some feel that they have left their bodies or have looked at their own bodies from the outside. They often report traveling through a dark tunnel and seeing a brilliant light at the end of it. Some speak of reunions with deceased friends or relatives, and others report contact with a being who encourages them to return to life. Some report rapidly reviewing many or all of the events of their lives.

Not all of the people who have the near-death experience are equally likely to experience all of these phenomena. The frequency and intensity of these experiences tend to be greatest for people who are ill, lowest for people who have attempted suicide, and in between for accident victims. Interestingly, few people have reported any negative experiences (Ring, 1980).

Why do people have this common core of near-death experiences? Nobody really knows a definitive answer to this question. No demographic trends (e.g., age, gender, socioeconomic status, marital status, religion, or degree of religiousness) have been found in studies of near-death experiences (Greyson, 1990; Roberts & Owen, 1988), nor does familiarity with the phenomenon increase the likelihood of a person's experiencing it (Ring, 1980). On the contrary, people who have heard about the phenomenon seem somewhat *less* likely to experience it. Some biopsychologists explain near-death experiences in terms of

Persons who have undergone near-death experiences frequently report seeing an image of a dark tunnel with a bright light at the end. This perceptual phenomenon may be linked to the physiological experience of having an inadequate supply of oxygen to the brain.

biochemical reactions in the body and brain, such as *hypoxia* (inadequate supply of oxygen) in the brain, which would account for the commonality of content despite the diverse diseases, traumas, and disorders that may have caused the experience.

Perhaps the most interesting thing to come out of near-death-experience research is that people who have such experiences typically say that their lives have changed for the better. They are more appreciative of what they have, less afraid of death, and more determined to live life to the fullest. These are lessons all of us can learn, even without having a near-death experience.

SUMMARY

Philosophical Antecedents   200

1. *Consciousness* is a stream of thought or awareness—the state of mind by which we compare possibilities for what we might perceive, and then select some of these possibilities and reject others.

2. Some of the functions of consciousness are to aid in our species' survival, to sift important from unimportant information, and to facilitate memory and planning.

3. Debates about the nature of consciousness extend back in the philosophical literature. John Locke believed that consciousness is essential to establishing a sense of personal identity, whereas David Hume believed that personal identity is an illusion.

Levels of Consciousness   201

4. Consciousness occurs on multiple levels. The *preconscious* level is immediately prior to or just outside of consciousness. The *unconscious* level is deeper, and we normally can gain access to it only with great difficulty or via dreams.

5. Subliminal perception occurs below the level of full consciousness.

Sleep and Dreams   204

6. Scientists have isolated several chemical sleep substances in our bodies, although it has not been proved that any of these is fully responsible for our normal sleep.

7. If people are subjected to sleep deprivation for several days, they show increasingly severe maladaptive symptoms. By the fourth day of deprivation, they often show signs of psychopathology, such as paranoid delusions of persecution.

8. In the absence of typical environmental cues, people seem to show a *circadian* (daily) *rhythm* of about 25 hours.

9. There are two basic kinds of sleep—*REM sleep* and *non-REM* (N-REM) *sleep.* The former is characterized by rapid eye movements and is usually accompanied by dreaming. N-REM sleep is customarily divided into an iterative series of four stages of successively deeper sleep and is seldom accompanied by dreaming.

10. *Insomnia* is a condition in which an individual has trouble falling asleep, wakes up during the night, or wakes up too early in the morning. *Narcolepsy* is a syndrome characterized by the strong impulse to sleep during the day or when it is otherwise undesirable to do so, as well as at night. Narcoleptics may fall asleep during an activity that would keep most people awake. *Sleep apnea* is a syndrome in which oxygen intake is temporarily impaired during sleep. *Somnambulism* (sleepwalking) most often occurs in children. Contrary to popular belief, somnambulists are typically not dreaming while they are engaging in wakeful-seeming behaviors in their sleep.

11. Several different theories of dreaming have been proposed. According to Freud, dreams express the hidden wishes of the unconscious. According to McCarley and Hobson's activation-synthesis theory, dreams represent our subjective interpretation of nocturnal brain activity.

Hypnosis   211

12. *Hypnosis* is an altered state of consciousness in which a person becomes extremely sensitive to, and often compliant with, the communications of the hypnotist. The hypnotized person will accept distortions of reality that would not be accepted in the normal waking state of consciousness.

13. Some psychologists question whether hypnotism is a genuine psychological phenomenon; they suggest instead that it is an epiphenomenon, in which subjects respond to demand characteristics, pleasing the hypnotist by doing what he or she says to do.

14. A *posthypnotic suggestion* is a means by which hypnotized subjects can be asked to do something—typically something that they would not normally do or that they might have difficulty doing—after the hypnotic trance is removed. Generally, hypnotized subjects will not engage in behaviors that violate their usual norms of behavior, however, either during the trance or as a result of posthypnotic suggestion.

15. Various theories of hypnosis have been proposed. One theory views it as a form of deep relaxation. Another theory views hypnosis as genuine involvement in a play-acted role. A third views it as a form of split consciousness; that is, there is a hidden observer in the person who observes what is going on, as though from the outside, at the same time that the person responds to hypnotic suggestions.

Meditation and Altered States   214

16. *Meditation* is a set of techniques to alter the state of consciousness by shifting away from an active, linear mode of thinking toward a more receptive and quiescent mode. Meditation generally decreases respiration, heart rate, blood pressure, and muscle tension.

17. Two main kinds of meditation are *concentrative*, in which the meditator focuses on an object or thought and attempts to remove all else from consciousness, and *opening-up*, in which the meditator attempts to integrate meditation with, rather than to separate it from, other activities.

Drug-Induced Alterations in Consciousness   216

18. The state of consciousness can be altered by four kinds of *drugs:* narcotics, CNS (central nervous system) depressants, CNS stimulants, and hallucinogens.

19. *Narcotics*, including natural *opiates* and synthetic *opioids*, produce some degree of numbness or stupor and often a feeling of well-being or freedom from pain.

20. *Depressants*, including alcohol and sedative-hypnotic drugs, slow the operation of the central nervous system. In contrast, *stimulants*—including *caffeine*, *nicotine*, *cocaine*, and *amphetamines*—speed up the operation of the central nervous system.

21. *Hallucinogens*—including LSD and marijuana—produce distorted perceptions of reality.

Extrasensory Perception   224

22. Some psychologists accept extrasensory perception (ESP) as a genuine phenomenon, but most do not. Included among parapsychological phenomena are *precognition* (perception of future events), *clairvoyance* (perception of objects or events for which there is no apparent stimulation to the known senses), *telepathy* (direct transfer of thoughts from one person to another), and *psychokinesis* (moving objects via thought).

Near-Death Experiences   225

23. Reports of *near-death experiences* seem to have several commonalities: feelings of peace and emotional well-being, separation from the body, entrance into a dark tunnel, a bright light, and entering into the light. These commonalities may be due to oxygen deprivation in the brain.

KEY TERMS

activation-synthesis hypothesis   210

amphetamines   221

barbiturates   220

caffeine   221

central nervous system (CNS) depressants   218

circadian rhythm   205

clairvoyance   224

CNS stimulants   221

cocaine   221

concentrative meditation   215

consciousness   200

controlling   201

daydreaming   210

hallucinations   204

hallucinogenic   223

hypnosis   211

illusions   204

insomnia   207

intoxicated   218

meditation   215

monitoring   201

narcolepsy   209

narcotic   217

near-death experience   225

neodissociative theory   214

N-REM sleep   206

opening-up meditation   215

opiates   217

opioids   217

overdose   217

parapsychology   224

posthypnotic suggestion   211

precognition   224

preconscious level   201

psychoactive   217

psychokinesis   224

psychopharmacological   217

REM sleep   207

sedative-hypnotics   220

sensitization   221

simulating paradigm   212

sleep apnea   209

somnambulism   209

subconscious   203

telepathy   224

tobacco   222

tolerance   217

tranquilizers   220

unconscious   203

withdrawal symptoms   217

yoga   215

Zen   215

IN SEARCH OF THE HUMAN MIND:
ANALYSES, CREATIVE EXPLORATIONS, AND PRACTICAL APPLICATIONS

1. Compare the views of consciousness held by Locke and Hume.
2. What are your normal sleep patterns? How do you react when your normal patterns are interrupted? How do your experiences compare with the experiences of subjects in sleep-deprivation research?
3. Do you believe in any form of ESP? Why or why not?

4. Freud suggested an entire array of dream imagery that he believed to have symbolic value. Think of a recent dream you have had, or make up a fanciful dream. If you were to analyze the symbolic meanings for the objects and events in your dream, what would you say your dream meant?
5. If you were to have a near-death experience, what aspects of your life would you appreciate more fully? What, if anything, might you do differently from what you are doing now? Could you follow through on any of the preceding ideas now, without having to experience a near-death experience?
6. Propose your own theory of hypnotism.

7. When do you experience the tip-of-the-tongue phenomenon? What seems to help you to grasp the elusive word or idea? What seems to hinder you?
8. How should society regulate the sale, purchase, possession, and use of psychoactive drugs? How should society respond to individuals who abuse such drugs but who do not directly harm others with their drug use?
9. What factors do you believe lead people to abuse psychoactive drugs? What do you believe can be done to help people to avoid becoming involved in the abuse of these drugs?

In Search of the Human Mind . . . *Part Two*

1. How do the processes of sensation, perception, and consciousness interrelate? How does each one affect the others?

2. Design a series of PET (positron emission tomography) studies that would help us better understand some aspect of sensation, perception, or consciousness.

3. How would people from different cultures experience sensation, perception, and consciousness differently? Which of these aspects of our psychological processing would be most subject to cultural influences?

Looking Ahead . . .

4. Why are sensation, perception, and consciousness considered to be basic cognitive processes for the higher cognitive processes of learning, memory, thinking, and intelligence? How do the processes of learning, memory, thinking, and intelligence build on the more foundational processes?

Charting the Dialectic

Chapter 3   BIOLOGICAL BASES OF BEHAVIOR

Biological psychology studies the interaction between biology, on the one hand, and our thoughts, feelings, and behavior, on the other. Biological psychologists have sought to isolate those portions of the brain responsible for various types of behavior, and have found that although it is sometimes possible to isolate the portions of the brain so responsible, at the same time the brain shows tremendous flexibility in what it can do. For example, people with lesions to one portion of the brain often recover some or even all of their functioning that is temporarily lost through activity that is picked up in another portion of the brain.

The human brain can be studied either in its own right or as the product of evolutionary adaptations that render the brain a remarkable structure for facilitating the survival of the species. Ideally, study of the brain combines an intensive analysis of what it can do, as well as an analysis of how it performs in the context of evolutionary adaptation in general and of current-day demands on the human organism in particular.

Chapter 4   SENSATION

A sensation is a message received by the brain from the senses. Theories of sensation show the same kind of dialectical development common in the evolution of psychological thought. For example, the opponent-process theory of color vision was proposed to remedy defects in the trichromatic theory, but neither theory fully accounted for how we can see color. Subsequent theorists therefore tried to combine the two theories and to go beyond them so as to account for phenomena that neither theory by itself could explain. Similarly, neither place theory nor frequency theory fully accounts for how we hear, and so more recent theories have attempted to combine the best elements of both theories. New theories of how we sense information continue to be proposed, but even when these new theories diverge from old ones, they tend to adopt some of the features of the old ones, so that the present is constantly drawing upon the past in the development of psychological understanding.

Chapter 5   PERCEPTION

Theories of perception show the dialectic common to most fields of psychology. The theory of constructive perception, first advanced in the nineteenth century, holds that although sensory information is the foundation for perception, higher order thinking also plays a key role. Patterns of stimulation would not make sense to us were it not for the thinking processes that render these patterns meaningful. In contrast, the theory of direct perception holds that all the information you need to make sense of what you perceive comes through sensory receptors. For vision, therefore, the retina has encoded all information needed for the perception of the environment. Attempts have been made to achieve a meaningful integration of these two positions, creating a synthesis for the original thesis (constructive perception) and antithesis (direct perception). The dialectical operation can be seen in other areas of perception as well—in pattern recognition, for instance. Feature-matching theories, for example, can be contrasted with template-matching theories; here, again, attempts have been made to integrate the two points of view. Thus, research has proceeded in the dialectical fashion common to psychology.

Chapter 6   CONSCIOUSNESS

One of the principal dialectics in the study of consciousness had its origins roughly three hundred years ago, when John Locke argued that in order to know about and form a personal identity, we must have consciousness. Memory provides the key to the maintenance of a stable sense of identity through time. David Hume, in contrast, argued that our sense of identity is illusory. According to Hume, we have only various perceptions, and fool ourselves into believing that they constitute a stable personal identity. Today, many psychologists agree with Locke that memory gives us one basis for a continuing sense of personal identity, while recognizing that people can lose this sense of identity through various disorders, such as the loss of memory that comes with amnesia. As another example of the dialectic, we can consider theories of dreaming. Whereas Sigmund Freud suggested that we should pay considerable attention to our dreams because they provide a royal road to the unconscious, other investigators view dreams as potentially informative about our psychological state, but not with quite the level of rich symbolism that Freud suggested. Our understanding of dreams, as of other phenomena, advances as we proceed in our thinking along the dialectical path.

PART THREE

HIGHER COGNITIVE PROCESSES

LEARNING

MEMORY

LANGUAGE

THINKING

INTELLIGENCE

Chapter Seven

LEARNING

CHAPTER OUTLINE

"But I'm hungry!"

She [the narrator's mother] was ironing and she paused and looked at me with tears in her eyes.

"Where's your father?" she asked me.

I stared in bewilderment. . . . [I]t had never occurred to me that his absence would mean that there would be no food.

"I don't know," I said. . . .

As the days slid past the image of my father became associated with my pangs of hunger, and whenever I felt hunger I thought of him with a deep biological bitterness.

—*Richard Wright*, Black Boy

Personally, I'm always ready to learn, although I do not always like being taught.

—*Winston Churchill*

Psychologists generally define **learning** as any relatively permanent change in the behavior, thoughts, and feelings of an organism—human or other animal—that results from experience. Given this definition, it appears that young Richard Wright has learned to associate his physiological feelings of hunger with his emotional responses toward his father.

PREPROGRAMMED BEHAVIOR: REFLEXES, INSTINCTS, AND IMPRINTING

IN SEARCH OF...

What aspects of human behavior are not learned?

Not everything we need to know is learned. We know some things because of programming that ap-

pears to be built into us. One kind of preprogrammed response is the *reflex* (see Chapter 3). We do not have to think about whether to blink when something gets in our eyes or whether to flinch when we touch something painful. Reflexes are adaptive for survival; we would be subject to myriad perils if we had to decide consciously whether and when to blink, to flinch, or to react reflexively in other ways.

In humans and animals, a specialized kind of reflex seems to facilitate our ability to learn from our environments: the orienting reflex. The **orienting reflex** is a series of responses prompted by a sudden change in the environment, such as a flash of light or an abrupt loud noise. We look up or turn toward the source, perhaps to see if we are in danger. In addition, brainwave patterns change, our pupils dilate, and other physiological changes occur that enable us to respond to the sudden stimulus.

Many cognitive psychologists are particularly interested in the orienting reflex. Why would this reflexive behavior interest cognitive psychologists, who are generally interested only in higher level thought processes?

A related form of preprogrammed behavior is often considered a simple form of learning: habituation. Recall from Chapter 5 that when we habituate, we unconsciously tune out familiar stimuli, but that when we dishabituate, we tune in to novel stimuli. Although habituation and dishabituation are not reflexive, we do seem to be preprogrammed to respond differently to unfamiliar versus familiar stimuli. However, because both habituation and dishabituation can be subject to conscious control, they are more the result of learning than of preprogrammed behavior—and both phenomena certainly aid us in learning about new stimuli.

In many species of animals, even fairly complex behavior may be preprogrammed. These more complex programmed behaviors, which involve more than a simple reflex, are **instinctive.** For example, the chinook salmon instinctively knows how to swim up river to reach its spawning ground. For another example, if a male stickleback (a kind of fish) swims too close to the nest of another male, the second male stickleback will warn and possibly attack the first male. The behavior pattern of the defender is automatic, and it is triggered by a sign stimulus—a red area on the belly of the male stickleback that develops during the mating season. In 1951, Niko Tinbergen, an **ethologist** (a scientist who studies comparative behavior across species and how it has evolved), demonstrated that the red spot, rather than any more generalized cue, triggered the instinctive response.

Some instincts involve a stimulus that prompts what may be a modest degree of learning. Ethologist Konrad Lorenz (1937, 1950) observed that newly hatched goslings will **imprint**—that is, form an immediate attachment—to the first moving object near them. The mother is usually the object of imprinting, which is adaptive because she is the source of sustenance and protection. However, in rare instances when the mother is absent, the newborn will imprint to whatever else it is exposed to, including humans. Imprinting must occur during a **critical period,** a brief period of time in the animal's development during which the animal is preprogrammed for learning to take place.

Imprinting need not be visual. Goats imprint to olfactory stimuli, and salmon imprint to the odor of the stream in which they were hatched (Staddon & Ettinger, 1989). Imprinting is normally irreversible, but if an animal imprints to an unnatural object and a natural object replaces it some time later, the original imprinting may wear off (Staddon & Ettinger, 1989).

In summary, then, in imprinting, the animal is preprogrammed to seek out a particular stimulus, it learns to recognize that stimulus, and then it engages in a preprogrammed behavior in response to the stimulus.

> Some psychologists argue that habituation and imprinting are actually simple forms of learning, whereas others contend that neither involves learning in any meaningful form. Give the reasons for and against considering habituation and/or imprinting to be simple forms of learning.

CLASSICAL CONDITIONING

It is beyond a doubt that all our knowledge begins with experience.

—*Immanuel Kant,* The Critique of Pure Reason

Ethologist Konrad Lorenz (left) studied how young birds imprint on the first moving objects they see after being hatched. The greylag goslings he studied imprinted on Lorenz, which prompted them to follow him wherever he went. Like Lorenz, Canadian ethologist Bill Lishman (right) had Canadian goslings imprint on him. Unlike Lorenz, however, Lishman was able to accompany the goslings into the air.

Does the sight of particular foods turn your stomach? Does the sound of barking or growling dogs make your heart pound? Each of these common responses results from **classical conditioning,** the learning process whereby an originally neutral stimulus (such as the food or the dogs) becomes associated with a particular physiological or emotional response that the stimulus did not originally produce.

The Discovery of Classical Conditioning

The mechanisms of classical conditioning were originally studied by Ivan Pavlov (1849–1936), who acci-

dentally noticed a phenomenon of learning while he was studying digestive processes in dogs. A meticulous investigator, Pavlov conscientiously avoided letting extraneous factors interfere with his research on digestion. However, one particularly annoying factor continually hampered his work. He had devised a means of collecting dogs' salivations in a container in which he measured the amount of saliva the dog produced when it smelled food (meat powder, in this case). (See Figure 7-1.) The dogs would start salivating even *before* they smelled the powder, in response to the sight of the lab technician, or even to the sound of the lab technician's footsteps. At first, Pavlov

FIGURE 7-1
Pavlov's Apparatus
Ivan Pavlov used specialized equipment to measure the amount of saliva that dogs produced when they smelled food. During this work, he noticed that the dogs started to salivate even before they smelled the food. This observation led him to figure out the principles of classical conditioning.

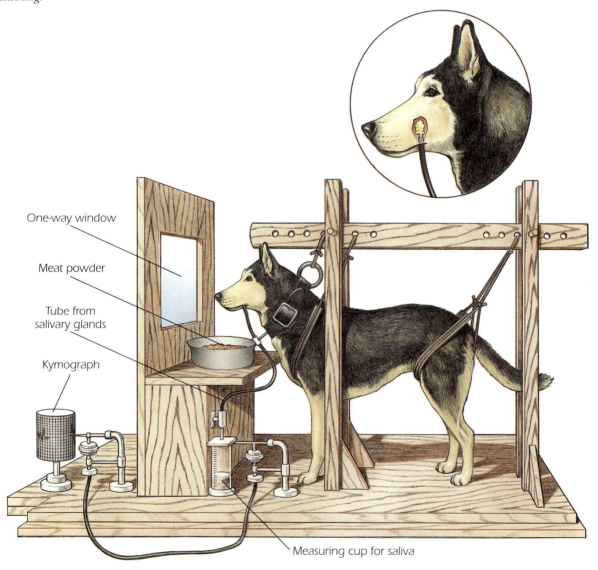

One-way window

Meat powder

Tube from
salivary glands

Kymograph

Measuring cup for saliva

tried to invent ways to keep this irritating phenomenon from interfering with his important research on digestion.

Happily for psychology, however, Pavlov was open to new discoveries and was able to see the startling implications that any number of other scientists doing the same research might well have let pass. As Louis Pasteur once said, "Chance favors only the prepared mind."

In your opinion, what would have happened if Pavlov hadn't become intrigued by the puzzling phenomenon he observed? How much of the development of scientific thought occurs because a unique individual caused that development to occur in a particular way, and how much occurs because the timing and circumstances were ripe for someone, somewhere, to discover a particular insight? Give supporting examples for your view.

Pavlov realized that some kind of associative learning must have taken place. The response (the salivation) that was originally elicited by the food was now being elicited by stimuli associated with the food. This form of learning has come to be called *classical conditioning*, or *Pavlovian conditioning*. Having made his serendipitous discovery, Pavlov set out to study classical conditioning systematically. First, he needed to show that dogs would naturally and spontaneously salivate at the sight or other sensation of food but would not naturally salivate in response to a non-food stimulus, such as a buzzer. His experiment indeed confirmed that a dog would salivate in response to meat powder being placed on its tongue, but that it would not salivate in response to the sound of the buzzer alone.

Alexander Graham Bell was astute in noting the potential benefit of a puzzling event. While Bell was refining the telegraph, a steel reed on his

FIGURE 7-2
Pavlov's Classic Experiment
Before the experiment, the sound (CS) yielded no response from the dog, whereas the food (UCS) made the dog salivate (UCR). During the experiment, Pavlov paired the sound (CS) with the food (UCS) to prompt the dog to salivate (UCR). After many repetitions, the sound (CS alone) prompted the dog to salivate (CR).

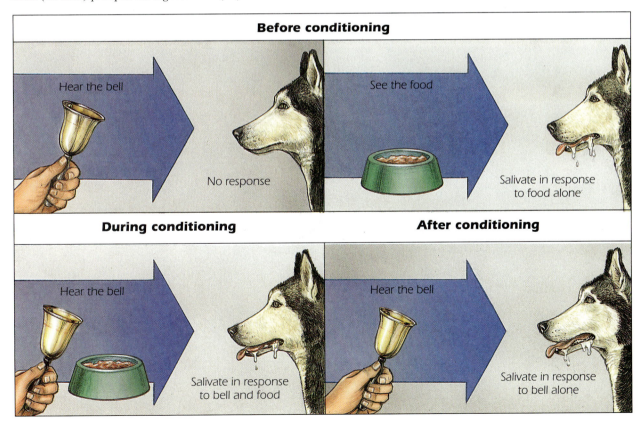

apparatus got stuck and sent both the fundamental tone of the reed, which he had intended to send, and the overtones of the fundamental tone, which he had not intended to transmit. Many inventors would have dismissed the puzzling outcome, fixed the reed, and returned to perfecting the initial invention. Bell, instead, realized that the fluctuating, multitonal human voice might be transmitted across long distances. Bell then turned his attention to the phenomenon that generated the outcome, and invented the telephone (Gorman, 1992).

Once the original pattern of stimuli and responses was established, Pavlov started the second phase of the experiment. He sounded the buzzer and then immediately placed the meat powder on the dog's tongue. After he repeated this procedure a number of times, he sounded the buzzer without the meat powder following it. The dog still salivated. It had been conditioned to respond to the buzzer (originally a neutral stimulus) through the pairing of the buzzer with the food. (Figure 7-2 illustrates this experiment.)

The Components of Classical Conditioning

Although the content of the stimuli and responses used in classical conditioning can vary, the basic structure of the paradigm does not. If you were to create a classical conditioning experiment, you would proceed as follows:

1. Start with a stimulus (e.g., meat powder) that elicits a physiological or emotional response—that is, determine the **unconditioned stimulus (UCS).**
2. Note your subject's automatic physiological response (e.g., salivation)—the **unconditioned response (UCR)**—to this stimulus.
3. Choose a stimulus (e.g., buzzer) that is originally neutral but that will later elicit the desired response. This originally neutral stimulus is the **conditioned stimulus (CS).**
4. Pair your CS and your UCS, so that the CS and the UCS become associated. Eventually, you obtain from this CS a **conditioned response (CR)** (e.g., salivation), which is essentially identical to the UCR, except that it is elicited from the CS rather than from the UCS.

After using a buzzer in his first experiments, Pavlov went on to investigate whether other sound cues, and even cues to other senses, such as sight and touch, could be manipulated systematically to prompt associative learning in his dogs. His creative exploration of alternative stimuli illustrates the scientific method at work.

Create an experiment that would classically condition a particular physiological or emotional response in association with an otherwise neutral stimulus. You may design the experiment for a human or for an animal.

Timing and Classical Conditioning

Stand-up comics, actors, musicians, ventriloquists, dancers, and magicians appreciate the value of timing. Psychologists involved in classical conditioning, too, have observed the importance of timing (see Figure 7-3).

Panel A of Figure 7-3 shows the standard classical conditioning paradigm, with the onset of the CS almost immediately preceding the onset of the UCS. Panel B shows **delay conditioning,** which introduces a long delay between the onset of the CS and the onset of the UCS. **Trace conditioning** is similar to delay conditioning, except that the CS is terminated for a while before the UCS begins. What is the result of delay or trace conditioning? Initially, conditioning results are similar to those for the standard paradigm. Eventually, however, the animal learns that there will be a long delay from the onset of the CS to the onset of the UCS, with the result that the CR does not appear until the CS has been in effect for some length of time.

Panel C shows an even more obvious example of conditioning responsive to time intervals—**temporal conditioning.** In this procedure, there is no CS at all. Rather, the time interval between UCS presentations is fixed, so that the animal learns that the UCS—say, food—will occur at a given, fixed time. The result is that the animal begins to show a CR right before the presentation of the UCS. In effect, it has learned that when a certain amount of time has passed, the food will be presented.

Panel D shows **simultaneous conditioning,** in which the CS and the UCS occur simultaneously. Simultaneous conditioning typically produces minimal conditioning or none at all (except under some special circumstances beyond the scope of the present discussion). Finally, Panel E shows **backward conditioning,** in which the initiation of the CS follows rather than precedes the initiation of the UCS. Backward conditioning, too, typically produces minimal or no learning. Thus, for conditioning to occur, it appears that the CS either must precede the UCS or must be the passage of time itself. Neither simultaneous nor backward conditioning typically produce learning.

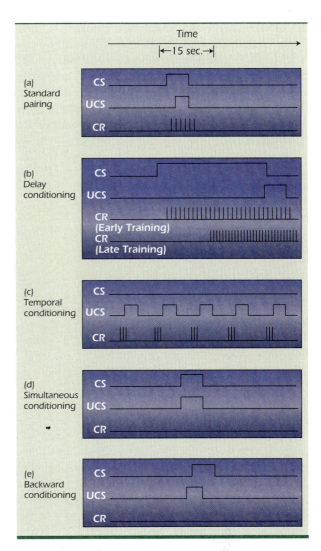

FIGURE 7-3
Some Common Pavlovian Conditioning Procedures
Various classical conditioning procedures yield differing outcomes.

Give an example of each of the preceding types of classical-conditioning experiments, using human subjects.

The obvious question here is, Why is there typically no learning in simultaneous (and backward) conditioning, given that the CS is paired with the UCS just as in the other paradigms? An Ivory Coast proverb suggests that it is because "Two flavors confuse the palate." Psychologists suggest that the reason for the lack of conditioning appears to be the phenomenon of **overshadowing,** whereby one stimulus dominates, or "overshadows," the other. In an experiment involving simultaneous conditioning, because the information in the sound of the buzzer is completely redundant with the meat powder, there is no need to form an association between the buzzer and the meat powder. In effect, the buzzer can be ignored, and as a result, no association is formed. Thus, when one stimulus overshadows or dominates another, the dominated (overshadowed) stimulus fails to serve as a conditioner.

Why Does Conditioning Occur? A Cognitive Explanation

Psychologists—and most other scientists—are rarely satisfied with merely noting their observations of phenomena. Many of the most intriguing investigations attempt to discover why particular phenomena occur. Several explanations have been proposed to explain why classical conditioning takes place.

An obvious explanation is **temporal contiguity**—that is, the mere closeness in time between the CS and the UCS is sufficient to explain conditioning. However, although simple contiguity is necessary for learning—if too long a time period passes between the offset of the CS and the onset of the UCS, conditioning will not take place—it is by no means sufficient for learning to take place.

A now-classic study by Robert Rescorla (1967) suggests that what is needed for conditioning to take place is **contingency** (the dependence of one or more actions or events on either the occurrence of an event or the presence of a stimulus), not just temporal contiguity. Rescorla designed an experiment to test the notion that contingency analysis underlies classical conditioning. In the experiment, the CS was a tone, and the UCS was a painful shock. Rescorla conducted the experiment with four different groups of dogs. In all four groups, he was looking to see whether the physiological and emotional (in this case, fear) responses of pain (UCRs) would become associated with the tone (thereby becoming CRs). The four conditions were as follows:

1. *Condition A*—The dogs received the standard pairing of the CS with the UCS. In other words, shock consistently followed the presentation of a tone. The prediction was that classical conditioning would take place, as usual.
2. *Condition B*—The dogs received the same number of CSs and UCSs as in Condition A, except that they were explicitly unlinked; that is, the CS was disassociated from the UCS—they were never presented together. In other words, the CS (tone) predicted the *absence* of the UCS (shock).

3. *Condition C* (a control group)—The dogs again received the same number of CSs and UCSs, but now, there was a random association between the UCS and the CS: Sometimes, the CS (the tone) predicted the UCS (the shock), whereas at other times, it did not. Any pairings that occurred were strictly by chance, so the CS was a worthless predictor of the UCS.
4. *Condition D*—The CS and the UCS were again paired only at random, with one exception. Whenever the random pairing indicated delivery of the UCS (shock) more than 30 seconds after the most recent CS (tone), the UCS was canceled. Thus, the UCS never occurred more than 30 seconds after the CS. Therefore, although the number of accidental pairings between the UCS and the CS would be the same in Group D as in Group C, the shock was more likely to occur within 30 seconds following the tone than to occur in the absence of the tone. Thus, the animals should learn to associate shock with the tone because there is a contingency, albeit an imperfect one.

The results of Rescorla's experiment confirmed the contingency point of view. Fear conditioning took place in Conditions A and D, where there was a positive contingency between the tone and the shock. No conditioning took place in Group C, because although the tone and the shock were sometimes paired, the pairing was random and hence not contingent. In Group B, the tone actually became an inhibitor of fear. The dogs learned to associate the tone with safety. Thus, they learned a *negative contingency*, whereby the CS (a tone) would predict the absence of the UCS (a shock).

Give an example of a real-life experience in which people learn a negative contingency.

In his experiment, Rescorla showed that contingency rather than contiguity seems to establish classical conditioning. He suggested that the mechanism underlying classical conditioning is more cognitive—that is, more sophisticated and thoughtful in terms of the functioning of the mind—than would seem possible for such a simple form of learning. According to Rescorla, humans and other animals try to make sense of the stimuli in their environments that affect them. The initial presentation of the UCS is unexpected and is therefore surprising. This element of surprise sets the stage for optimal learning in order to make subsequent presentations of the UCS more predictable and thus less surprising—thereby making the environment more comprehensible. When a CS contingently predicts the occurrence of the UCS, learning occurs easily and rapidly.

In sum, humans and other animals learn not simply because two stimuli happen to occur together in time, but also because the first stimulus predicts the second. Temporal proximity alone, where one stimulus does not predict the other, will not establish systematic learning.

Influences on Rate of Conditioning

Rescorla was not content simply to establish the importance of contingency for classical conditioning. Pavlov had long established that classical conditioning takes place over a series of learning trials, not all at once (although exceptions to this rule are described later in this chapter). Rescorla and his colleague, Allan Wagner, built on the suggested mechanism of contingency and observed the process of learning over successive learning trials. They then proposed a quantitative theory to specify precisely the rate at which learning would take place (Rescorla & Wagner, 1972; Wagner & Rescorla, 1972).

The two researchers found that learning tends to increase at a rate that actually *slows down* as the amount of learning increases. The reason for this slowing of the rate of learning is that as learning progresses, the relative unpredictability of the UCS declines. As the UCS becomes more predictable, the need to notice the contingent relationship between the UCS and the CS declines. In this pattern of **negative acceleration,** the amount of increase is smaller and smaller with successive trials. The more learning that has taken place, the slower the pace of subsequent learning is.

According to this theory, if we were to plot graphically the trials linking the UCS and the CS (as shown in the idealized learning curve of Figure 7-4), the curve would start rising quickly, but as it went up, the curve would level off and eventually reach an **asymptote,** the place on the curve showing maximum stability, where the degree of learning levels off.

Rescorla and Wagner further noted that success of conditioning depends on at least two variables: the salience of the stimuli and the maximum level of conditioning that can be achieved for a given UCS. As the *salience*—degree of conspicuousness, obviousness—increases, so does the rate of learning. For example, a strong *emetic* (chemical that causes vomiting) is likely to be a very salient UCS, whereas a barely

noticeable electric shock is likely to be much less salient and to result in a slower *rate* of learning. In addition, according to the theory, different UCSs support different maximum levels of conditioning. A strong emetic is likely to lead to a higher stable level of learning than is a very weak shock. Thus, the second variable is the particular *maximum* stable level of learning (the distinctive asymptote of the learning curve) that can be achieved for a given CS–UCS pairing. If we were to plot curves graphing the trials linking the UCS and the CS for different stimuli, each stimulus would have a distinctive curve. Some of these curves would yield higher asymptotes than others.

Basic Phenomena of Classical Conditioning

Phases of Classical Conditioning

Although the *rate* of learning may *decrease* over learning trials, the *probability* of learning—that is, the likelihood of the occurrence of a CR—*increases* over learning trials. The phase of learning during which the probability increases for the occurrence of a CR is the **acquisition** phase. Eventually, as shown in the work by Rescorla and others, the CR reaches its asymptote—its most stable probability of occurrence.

Suppose that the CS were to continue to be presented, but in the absence of the UCS. For example, a buzzer that previously had preceded shock

FIGURE 7-4
Idealized Learning Curve
According to Robert Rescorla, the rate of learning slows down as the amount of learning increases, until eventually learning peaks at a stable level.

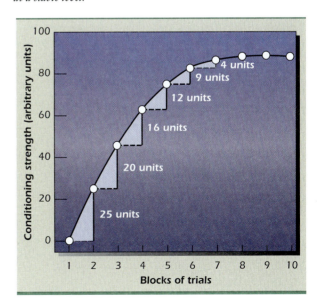

would no longer precede shock. Gradually, the probability of the CR occurring would decline until it reached negligible levels. This phase of learning is the **extinction** phase; the probability of the CR decreases over time, eventually approaching zero. The curve and asymptote for extinction would show a decrease in the number of responses over time with the response level eventually reaching zero.

The term *extinction* may be somewhat misleading, however. A casual observer of an extinguished CR might assume that because the CR was extinguished, it was gone forever, as if the CR had never existed at all. That is not quite the case. The CR may be extinguished, but the memory of the learning has not been completely erased, and the behavior is still possible to elicit. In fact, an interesting phenomenon occurs after an individual is given a series of extinction trials and is then allowed to rest; surprisingly, a resumption of experimental trials after the rest period will result in a higher level of responding than has occurred just before it. This phenomenon is **spontaneous recovery.** The individual seems to recover some level of responding spontaneously during the rest period, even though the CS has been absent during this period.

Note that in spontaneous recovery, the CS is presented again, *without* the UCS. Spontaneous recovery is not quite the same as **savings,** which occurs when the CS is presented again *in the presence of* the UCS. In conditioning involving savings, when the CS is paired with the UCS, perhaps only briefly, the CR returns to levels approaching those at the asymptote (stable peak of the learning curve) of the acquisition phase. Table 7-1 illustrates these phases.

Levels of Classical Conditioning

Up to now, we have discussed only what is sometimes referred to as **first-order conditioning,** whereby a CS is linked with a UCS. Suppose, however, that we have conditioned a fear response to the sound of a tone. Now suppose that we pair the flash of a light with the tone: Right before the tone, a light illuminates. In this case, we might observe the CR (the emotion of fear) to the second CS, which is already linked to the first CS. When a second CS is linked to

TABLE 7-1
Phases of Classical Conditioning
Once a learner acquires a CR, if the CS and the UCS are uncoupled, the CR may be extinguished. Even if the CR is extinguished, however, the learner may still experience spontaneous recovery or savings of the CR.

Phase	Explanation	Example
Acquisition	The probability of a CR increases as the CS is paired with the UCS.	Each time your phone has rung, it has been your new beloved, calling to tell you how delightful this evening will be. Your heart flutters joyously in response. As the morning progresses, your heart starts to flutter just on hearing the phone ring.
Extinction	The probability of a CR decreases as the CS and the UCS are uncoupled, with only one or the other being presented at any one time.	Your phone continues to ring, but your beloved is in a meeting, so now your calls are from a salesperson, a wrong-number caller, and several people who want you to do things you do not want to do. Your heart stops fluttering at the sound of the phone's ring.
Spontaneous recovery	After a brief period of rest, following extinction, the CS spontaneously prompts the CR.	Your phone service is temporarily out of order. After service is restored, your heart flutters at the first ring.
Savings	When the CS is paired with the UCS again, even briefly, the CR returns to levels approaching those at the peak of the acquisition phase.	Your beloved's meeting ends, and your phone begins ringing again with frequent calls from your beloved. Once again, your heart flutters when you hear the phone ring.

a first one, the resulting conditioning is *second-order conditioning*. In theory, we can have conditioning proceed up to any level of **higher order conditioning,** although conditioning beyond the first order tends to be rather unstable and relatively more susceptible to extinction than is first-order conditioning.

> Describe how an experimenter could modify Pavlov's experiment to produce second-order conditioning in Pavlov's dogs.

Features of Classical Conditioning

He who is bitten by the snake fears the lizard.

—*Bugandan proverb*

A man who has been tossed by a buffalo, when he sees a black ox, thinks it's another buffalo.

—*Kenyan proverb*

As these proverbs suggest, conditioning occurs not only in association with the exact CS, but also with stimuli that are similar to it. For example, slightly changing the frequency (pitch) of a tone that is a CS will have only a barely perceptible effect on the CR, if any at all. However, the more the frequency of the tone is changed, the less the tone will elicit the CR. **Stimulus generalization** is the mechanism whereby stimuli similar to the original CS can elicit the CR.

The mechanism whereby the CR becomes less probable as the new stimulus increasingly differs from the old one is **stimulus discrimination.** The individual distinguishes between the new and the old stimuli, and the greater the discrimination the individual makes, the lower the probability of eliciting the CR.

For example, the proverbial Bugandan who fears lizards, which somewhat resemble snakes, would be less likely to feel afraid of a long, thin but furry mammal, such as a weasel or a mink, and would be highly unlikely to fear pigs, elephants, or buffaloes. However, the fabled Kenyan who fears both the buffalo and the black ox might feel mildly anxious at the sight of a pig or an elephant but would be fearless at the sight of a snake, a lizard, or a weasel. Thus, for the snake-shy Bugandan, the fine gradations of discrimination center on the stimulus's similarity to the snake; for the buffalo-fearing Kenyan, being able to discriminate among animals that resemble the buffalo determines his likelihood of experiencing fear.

The Qualitative Relationship Between the Stimulus and the Response

Up to now, we have described conditioned and unconditioned stimuli that bear only an arbitrary relationship to each other—for example, a tone and an electric shock. Does the relationship between the nature of the CS and the UCS ever make any difference? Apparently, it does, although this relationship was not appreciated until the 1960s. In fact, the discovery of a relationship we now consider "obvious" was not at all obvious prior to its discovery.

In an experiment by John Garcia and Robert Koelling (1966), whenever a group of experimental rats licked a drinking spout, the rats tasted some flavored solution, heard a clicking sound, and saw a flash of light. That is, whenever the rats licked the spout, they sensed three conditioned stimuli: the taste of flavored solution, the sound of a click, and the sight of a flash of light. Subsequent to licking the spout, some of the rats were mildly poisoned (causing them to vomit), whereas other rats were shocked. After a number of learning trials for both the poisoned rats and the shocked rats, a new procedure was introduced: The CS of the flavoring was separated from the combined CS using the sound and the light. Thus, for each group of rats, on one day, when the rats licked the spout, the rats tasted the flavored solution without seeing the light or hearing the noise. On another day, when the rats licked the spout, they saw the light and heard the noise, but tasted only regular tap water instead of the flavored solution.

The critical finding was that for the rats who were exposed to poison as the UCS, taste was a more effective CS than was the combination of light and

This woman's disgusted expression may indicate that she suffers from the Garcia effect as a result of a previous sickening experience with that kind of food. What foods have you become conditioned against eating?

Searchers . . .   *JOHN GARCIA*

John Garcia is Professor Emeritus of Psychology, Psychiatry, and Biobehavioral Science at the University of California, Los Angeles.

Q: *How did you become interested in psychology?*

A: I have been interested in medical science since childhood. I decided on psychological research after reading Sigmund Freud's *Psychopathology of Everyday Life* and Woodworth's introductory text. I think psychology is the most fundamental science.

Q: *What theories have influenced you the most?*

A: Positively, I was influenced by Charles Darwin's *Origin of Species* and Edward Tolman's ideas of cognitive maps. (I was Tolman's T.A.) Negatively, I was offended by B. F. Skinner's overextension of Edward Lee Thorndike's efficient, but limited, paradigm and world view of animal behavior.

Q: *What is your greatest asset as a psychologist?*

A: I was ever a curious student of animal (including human) behavior, albeit forever puzzled by what I observed.

Q: *What distinguishes a really great psychologist from just a good psychologist?*

A: A great psychologist must be a keen observer of a wide spectrum of behavior and able to provide explanations rooted in the mind-brain of his subjects, phrased in evolutionary and ecological terms.

Q: *How do you get your ideas for research?*

A: I get my ideas from closely observing animals. Being born to a Hispanic farm-worker family and growing up in rural areas rich in domestic and wild animal species gave me an appreciation for comparative culture and the diversity of animal behavior. I prefer to read old books rather than current research reports. I prefer to talk with students and plain folks rather than listen to experimenters and philosophers of science. My ideas in my early work came when Bob Koelling and I noticed the disgust reactions of rats to water from plastic bottles which had been available to them during long periods of exposure to low-level X rays. We suspected that the X rays had induced nausea causing a taste aversion and that the gut was the site of action. By pairing saccharin flavor with X rays we demonstrated a conditioned taste aversion.

Q: *How do you decide whether to pursue an idea?*

A: Once I have an idea for research I consult the literature. If my idea opens up a new line of investigation and explanation, I pursue it; if not, I drop it.

Q: *How have you developed an idea into a workable hypothesis?*

A: When we stumbled onto the X-ray-induced taste aversion effect and observed that the rats did not struggle to escape the deadly X-ray chamber, I knew that the rat naturally associated taste with nausea but not with external cues and signals. It was then a simple matter to pair either a bright-noisy signal or a sweet taste with nausea or with the pain of foot-shock. Rats quickly learned either noise-pain or taste-nausea but not noise-nausea or taste-pain.

Q: *What is your major contribution to psychology?*

A: My contributions stemmed from studying responses to X rays, a form of learning then unknown in psychology. Animals can smell X rays. Taste and nausea are associated over spans of hours. After tasting, animals rendered unconscious during nausea will nevertheless acquire the aversion. Cognition is not enough; unconscious learning modifies the incentives for which we strive.

Q: *What do you want students to learn from you?*

A: My students must focus on the big issues in conditioning and learning. I expect them to explain behavior by referring to brain mechanisms. I talk and listen to my students as I do with my colleagues. I insist they write in plain English and shun psychological jargon. I do try to make ideas, regardless of sophistication or source, the arbiters of discussion. (Edward Tolman, a consummate gentleman and psychologist, was my role model.)

Q: *What advice would you give to someone starting in the field of psychology?*

A: Observe, observe, test, and observe again! Do not be blinded by preconceptions and theories.

Q: *What have you learned from your students?*

A: Not to use them as another pair of hands. Once they learned to handle the animals, to use the equipment, and the general strategy of research, I backed off and let them work. Then I listened to their specific advice on how experimental tactics should be changed to meet our research goals.

Q: *Apart from your life as an academic, how have you found psychology to be important to you?*

A: Since childhood I have been "a psychologist"—most people are, for better or worse. Going to college and becoming a professor merely gave me the official trappings.

Q: *How do you keep yourself academically challenged?*

A: I remain curious about behavior and life. I lecture and write occasionally. I'm retired, but I'm not dead—yet.

Q: *What do you further hope to achieve or contribute?*

A: I will continue to work to expunge the nature-nurture division as it exists in some areas of psychology, specifically the notion that genetic endowment and environmental influences are uncorrelated and can be parceled into additive components. The organism is inseparable from its environmental niche. Its genetic endowment is acquired from the environment by natural selection—by survival and death. Its habits are also acquired inductively from the same environment by trial and error. At every stage of development the organism requires and acquires environmental information. A major portion of our genetic endowment is given over to this function. Whenever we stop learning and remembering, we are, for all practical purposes, dead.

Modality of CS	Modality of UCS	Classical-Conditioning Response
Taste	Vomiting and other signs of poisoning	Easily paired; apparent predisposition to classical conditioning
Light and noise click	Vomiting and other signs of poisoning	Not easily paired; apparent resistance to classical conditioning
Taste	Electric shock	Not easily paired; apparent resistance to classical conditioning
Light and noise click	Electric shock	Easily paired; apparent predisposition to classical conditioning

FIGURE 7-5
Sickening Tastes and Shocking Sights and Sounds
John Garcia and Robert Koelling surprised the scientific community when they found that some pairs of stimuli and responses were more easily formed than were others. Taste was a more effective CS for learning a CR to poisoning, and a pairing of bright light and noises was a more effective CS for learning a CR to electric shock.

noise. In contrast, when electric shock was the UCS, the bright, noisy water was a more effective CS than was the flavored solution. In other words, there was a natural association between taste and poison, on the one hand, and between electric shock and the combination of the light and sound, on the other (see Figure 7-5). In addition, the most effective timing of the stimulus is influenced by the type of physiological response (see Table 7-2; e.g., the timing of digestive processes vs. the timing of other responses).

> What stimulus-response pairs do you believe would effectively lead to strong associations? Describe a situation (either a contrived experiment or an everyday occurrence) in which one of these stimulus-response pairs might actually lead to a conditioned association.

How Fast Can Learning Occur?

Garcia and Koelling's finding of an association between the CS and the UCS surprised the scientific community, given the then-prevalent view that the choice of CS was arbitrary. Garcia had yet another surprise for fellow psychologists that was even more counterintuitive to the prevailing perspective: Conditioning could occur after only a single learning trial. Garcia found that rats demonstrated a CR to the flavored solution after just one exposure to it if they were subsequently poisoned. Because his finding so strongly conflicted with the prevailing views at that

time, Garcia had a great deal of difficulty getting his research published. People just did not believe—and did not want to believe—Garcia's results, precisely because his results differed sharply from what they thought they knew about learning.

Applications of Classical Conditioning Theory

We have discussed classical conditioning theory primarily in the context of experiments with animals, but

TABLE 7-2
Classical Times
Because differing physiological responses occur at different rates, the timing of the most effective stimulus for each type of response also varies.

Physiological Response	Response Times
Motoric responses (e.g., eye blinks)	1 second
Visceral autonomic responses (e.g., heart rate and salivation)	5–15 seconds
Fear and other emotion-linked responses	seconds to minutes
Digestive processes (e.g., reaction to emetic or to mild poisoning)	up to hours

They were dead maybe?

the principles of classical conditioning are very relevant to the lives of humans as well. Consider just a few of these applications: fear and other conditioned emotional reactions, neuroses, and addictions. An understanding of these phenomena already has led to some treatments and may lead to others.

> *"I can feel the anxiety I had before doing a monologue now as I talk about it," [Woody Allen] continued, a little discomfited. "I remember sitting backstage so many times with Keaton in Vegas and as soon as we heard Edie Adams going into a certain song, it meant she had one more before I was introduced. I'd start to get tense. It's just Pavlovian. . . . "*
>
> —*Eric Lax,* Woody Allen

Conditioned Emotional Responses

Fear (e.g., of a particular object) and *anxiety* (a more generalized feeling about a situation or experience) are both emotions that we can become conditioned to feel. Classical conditioning also accounts for many of our other emotional responses. Most of these **conditioned emotional responses** (sometimes called CERs) are linked to distinctive physiological feelings. For example, most of us have experienced the *Garcia effect*, in which we avoid eating a particular food because of a past unpleasant association; the mere sight or smell or even mention of it disgusts us, making our stomachs queasy.

CERs need not be negative. For example, as you see your loved one approach, you may feel joyful, tingling from head to toe, due to previous pleasurable experiences with that individual. Television advertisers are experts in classically conditioning our positive emotions. They know how to use classical conditioning to appeal to our appetites for food and for sexual gratification, leading us to associate satisfaction with new cars, perfumes, cosmetics, and foods of every shape, texture, and color. Just what are you expected to learn about a product by sensing the high-pitched acceleration of a flashy red car as a sexy driver zips around a narrow road on a mountainous cliff overlooking the ocean? Partly because of their potent physiological associations, emotional responses appear to be very susceptible to classical conditioning (see Chapter 16 for more on the physiological aspects of emotions).

The *process* of becoming conditioned to experience particular emotions appears to be universal. However, the *content* of the conditioning can vary widely across both individuals and cultures. For in-

stance, although many U.S. students and instructors have learned to feel annoyed when other people talk during lectures (i.e., total silence means rapt attention), students and educators elsewhere may respond differently. In India it is fairly common for students to talk among themselves during lectures. The Indian professor typically interprets classroom chatter as affirmation that he or she is stimulating students to talk about the topic. In fact, for many Indian instructors, silence in the classroom may be a classically conditioned stimulus that might arouse in the instructor a fear that the students may have lost interest in the lecture (W. Lonner, personal communication, December 1993).

Neuroses

In addition to discovering and investigating classical conditioning in dogs, Pavlov explored how dogs reacted to an unusual *discrimination-learning procedure*, in which subjects learned to recognize the differences between at least two stimuli. At the start of the procedure, one neutral stimulus was linked to an unconditioned stimulus, whereas another neutral stimulus was not. In one experiment, a picture of a circle was followed by food, whereas a picture of an ellipse was not (Pavlov, 1928). Pavlov then changed the conditioned stimuli slightly. Through repeated trials, Pavlov changed the stimuli, gradually making the circle more like the ellipse and the ellipse still more like the circle. Eventually, the two stimuli became virtually indistinguishable. Pavlov observed that the dogs subjected to this conditioning procedure became extremely agitated, barking and howling and attempting to escape from the situation. Pavlov referred to this conditioning procedure as having induced an **experimental neurosis**—what at first seems like a clear choice becomes less and less clear, leading to conflict on the part of the learner.

It is possible that some neuroses or disorders (maladjustments in living) develop as a result of a classical conditioning procedure similar to the one Pavlov used in his laboratory. Pavlov's idea that his discoveries regarding experimental neurosis in animals apply to humans is not as widely accepted as are his discoveries about classical conditioning overall; still, it is easy to see how such neuroses might develop.

Sometimes, it is very difficult to tell which stimuli are associated with which responses. For example, some people make us feel both excited with passion and frustrated with anger. Some situations strike fear in our hearts, yet thrill us with the possibility of tremendous rewards. In each of these cases, it is not clear whether the relevant stimulus is aversive or delightful, with the result that we find ourselves agitated when exposed to it. Like Pavlov's dogs, we may be experiencing a neurosis induced through classical conditioning.

Addictions

Addictions—persistent, habitual, or compulsive physiological or at least psychological dependencies on psychoactive drugs, such as alcohol—are extremely complex, which is one reason why they are so hard to break (see Chapter 6). At least in part, addictions appear to be classically conditioned. Consider, for example, the consumption of alcoholic beverages. Many people find the state of intoxication induced by the alcohol to be pleasant, so that this state (or the emotion associated with the anticipation of it) becomes the UCS. The CS would be the taste of the alcohol, or possibly even the sight of the bottle of alcohol or a location in which it is consumed, which may evoke pleasant feelings of anticipation. Through this conditioning, many people learn to associate the alcohol-related stimuli with what they consider to be the pleasant sense of intoxication that follows. Thus, we view addictions as being at least partly classically conditioned.

Classical conditioning also has important implications for treating addictions. Simply to stop drinking—or to stop smoking, to consider another addiction—will not break the addiction (Schwartz, 1989). Extinction does not result from simple discontinuation of the CS. Rather, the addict has to break the pairing of the CS with the UCS. Effective procedures for overcoming addictions break this association (see Chapter 19).

One way of breaking addictions is through the procedure of **counterconditioning,** in which the positive association between a given UCS and a given CS is replaced with a negative one by substituting a new UCS, which has a different UCR. For example, some specific drugs can cause violently aversive reactions to the consumption of alcohol (or of tobacco). The idea is that the addict is thereby counterconditioned to avoid rather than to seek out the addictive substance. A less aggressive procedure is to elicit extinction simply by removing the desirable properties of the addictive substance. Thus, the recovering addict might start drinking nonalcoholic beer or smoking cigarettes with little or no nicotine. In such cases, the idea is to achieve extinction by removing the association between the CS and the UCS. Regardless of the procedure, the strategy involves using principles of learning to fight the addiction.

How could you countercondition yourself to reduce the potency of a conditioned response that you wanted to minimize or eliminate altogether? Be specific.

Clearly, classical conditioning offers many practical applications. An entirely different type of conditioning also offers a vast array of practical applications. This alternative means of associative learning—operant conditioning—holds similar potential for improving people's lives when understood and applied appropriately.

OPERANT CONDITIONING

He who learns and runs away will live *to learn another day.*

—*Edward Lee Thorndike (emphasis in original)*

Imagine a hungry cat in the puzzle box shown in Figure 7-6. The door to the *puzzle box* is held tightly shut by a simple latch, which opens easily when its fastening device (located inside the cage) is triggered (e.g., by a button, a loop, or a string). The cat inside the cage can see a delicious-looking piece of fish in a dish just outside the cage. The cat first tries

FIGURE 7-6
Thorndike's Puzzle Box
Edward Lee Thorndike's puzzle box demonstrates operant conditioning—that is, how an animal (including a human) can learn a behavior by interacting with its environment. In this case, a cat put in the box learns how to release the latch, which will enable it to get out of the box and eat the fish placed nearby.

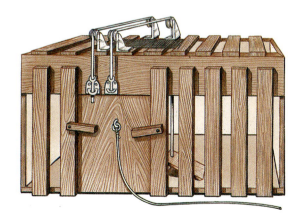

to reach the fish by extending its paws through the slats; then it starts scratching, bumping, and jumping around the cage. Eventually, it accidentally releases the latch, simply through trial and error. When the latch gives way, the door to the cage opens, and the cat runs to get the fish. Later, the cat is placed again in the cage, and the whole procedure is repeated. This time, the scratching and jumping around do not last very long. As Edward Lee Thorndike explained, "After many trials, the cat will, when put in the box, immediately claw the button or loop in a definite way" (1898, p. 13) to release the latch, thereby opening the cage, to get the fish.

Now imagine another situation. You want to go to a particular movie with a friend. Your friend wants to go dancing. Your voices get more impassioned as you argue for the movie and your friend for the dancing, and you are getting nowhere. Finally, you give in, saying that the friendship is worth a lot more to you than going to the movie. Your friend looks you straight in the eye and—to your surprise—suggests that you go to the movie after all. The next time you disagree about what to do, you argue again, but for a shorter time. You give in for the sake of the friendship, and again your friend goes along with your preference. The next time, there is no argument. You immediately indicate the value of the friendship; your friend has taught you a way to get what you want—oddly enough, through not arguing rather than through arguing.

Law of Effect

It is a process of selection among reactions . . . by eliminating the unsuitable reaction directly by discomfort, and also by positively selecting the suitable one by pleasure. . . . It is of tremendous usefulness.

—*Edward Lee Thorndike*

Both of these examples—the hungry cat and the nonconfrontational friend—involve operant conditioning. Just as the study of classical conditioning is usually considered to have originated with Pavlov, the study of operant conditioning is usually viewed as originating with Thorndike. Through the experiments with the cat in the puzzle box, Thorndike (1898, 1911) discovered the basic paradigm of **operant conditioning** (also termed *instrumental conditioning*), which is learning produced by the active behavior (an *operant*) of an animal (such as a human) interacting with an environment.

Thorndike proposed a mechanism to account for operant conditioning, which he termed the **law of effect.** That is, much of behavior constitutes random, trial-and-error exploration of the environment. Occasionally, our actions result in a reward—an outcome with pleasurable consequences. At other times, our actions result in a punishment—an outcome with aversive consequences. The law of effect states that those actions that are rewarded will tend to be strengthened and thus will be more likely to occur in the future, whereas actions that are punished will tend to be weakened and thus will be less likely to occur in the future.

The main difference between classical and operant conditioning is in the role of the individual. In classical conditioning, the individual is largely passive. The experimenter or the environment controls the reinforcement schedule—for example, by repeatedly pairing a CS with a UCS. In operant conditioning, the individual is largely active. The individual operates on the environment to create reinforcement. In classical conditioning, the crucial relationship for conditioning is between the CS and the UCS; in operant conditioning, the crucial relationship is between an environmental response and the behavioral stimulus that it creates.

Experimental Analysis of Behavior

Possibly the most influential of modern behaviorists was B. F. Skinner, who developed the theory and methods for what he called the "experimental analysis of behavior." For Skinner, the **experimental analysis of behavior** meant that all behavior should be studied and analyzed into specific stimulus-response contingencies; Skinner particularly prized observation of animal behavior as a means of understanding behavior in humans, as well. Boxes in which conditioning

"Remember, every time he gives you a pellet, reinforce that behavior by pulling the lever." (© 1994 Joe Dator and the Cartoon Bank, Inc.)

experiments are conducted are often termed **Skinner boxes,** in Skinner's honor.

Skinner believed that the principles of conditioning could be applied widely in life. What mattered to him were the reinforcement contingencies that produce various patterns of behavior, regardless of what might go on inside the head. Notice that by defining the problem of understanding human behavior totally in terms of stimulus–response contingencies, Skinner essentially created a mission for the field of psychology different from the mission that people typically follow now.

The cattle [are] as good as the pasture in which [they graze].

—*Ethiopian proverb*

Operant conditioning is of great importance in our lives, literally from the day we are born. Parents

A researcher collects data from the behaviors demonstrated by the rat in the Skinner box. To B. F. Skinner, every aspect of human behavior that is worthy of investigation can be probed by studying learning in animals. Do you agree with this theory? Why or why not?

These children are learning some skills and information about things in their environment. Perhaps more importantly, however, they are learning that when they work hard and try to gain skill and knowledge, they gain both smiles of approval and companionship from their parents.

reward some actions and punish others, exploiting the laws of operant conditioning to socialize their children. In this way, parents hope to strengthen their children's adaptive behavior and to weaken the children's maladaptive behavior. The same mechanisms are used in school. Some kinds of behavior are rewarded by nods, approbation, good grades, and so on, whereas other kinds of behavior result in isolation from other students, trips to the principal's office, and so on.

Kinds of Reinforcement

In the study of operant conditioning, the term **operant** refers to a *response* that has some effect on the world. Asking for help, drinking a glass of water, threatening to hurt someone, kissing your lover—all of these are operants. Operant conditioning results in either an increase or a decrease in the probability that these operant behaviors will be performed again.

A **reinforcer** is a *stimulus* that increases the probability that the operant associated with it (which usually has occurred immediately or almost immediately before the reinforcing stimulus) will happen again. Reinforcers can be either positive or negative.

A **positive reinforcer** is a reward (pleasant stimulus) that follows an operant and strengthens the associated response. Examples of positive reinforcers (for most of us) are a smile or compliment from a teacher following a correct answer, or a candy bar released by a vending machine after we put in the required change. When a positive reinforcer occurs soon after an operant response, we refer to the pairing of the positive reinforcer with the response as **positive reinforcement.**

A **negative reinforcer** is the removal or cessation of an unpleasant stimulus, for example, physical or psychological pain or discomfort (such as would be elicited by confinement in an extremely hot room). **Negative reinforcement** refers to the removal of an unpleasant stimulus that results in an increased probability of response. Table 7-3 shows several examples of negative reinforcement.

Punishment

Do not call to a dog with a whip in your hand.

—*Zulu proverb*

Punishment is a stimulus that *decreases* the probability of a response, through either the application of an unpleasant stimulus or the removal of a pleasant one. (In contrast, negative reinforcement *increases* the likelihood of a response by removing or reducing the level of an unpleasant stimulus.) Examples of punishment include being hit, humiliated, or laughed at; being restricted from an enjoyable activity such as television viewing or social interactions with friends; receiving a failing grade in a course or a negative evaluation from a work supervisor.

In general, punishment is less effective in achieving behavioral change than is positive reinforcement. In addition, punishment may lead to several unintended consequences (Bongiovanni, 1977).

First, a person may find a way to circumvent the punishment without reducing or otherwise changing the operant behavior. Second, punishment can increase the likelihood of aggressive behavior on the part of the person being punished. That is, the person being punished may imitate the punishing behavior in other interactions. The stereotypical example of this pattern is when the boss yells at the parent, the parent goes home and screams at the child, the child wails at the dog, and the dog snarls at the cat. Third, the punished person may be injured. Punishment becomes child abuse when the child is damaged, physically or psychologically—an unfortunately common occurrence. Fourth, sufficiently severe punishment may result in extreme fear of the punishing person and context, rendering the punished individual incapable of changing the behavior that is being punished. For example, screaming at a child who scored poorly on a test because of test anxiety is more likely to increase than to reduce the child's anxiety. Fifth, even if behav-

TABLE 7-3
Examples of Negative Reinforcement
What stimuli do you find so unpleasant that you would like to be able to remove them?

Unpleasant Stimulus	Operant Behavior	Negative Reinforcer
An intense noise	Cover your ears with your hands	Relief from noise
Traumatic injury, discomfort, or disease	Give first aid; seek a physician	Relief from pain or discomfort
Bright sunlight	Wear sunglasses	Relief from overly intense light
Snow, rain, or wind	Wear protective clothing (snowsuits, raincoats, and windbreakers)	Protection from discomfort
The sight of gore or violence	Close eyes	Reduction of negative emotions
Rotten or other bad-tasting food	Spit out the food	Relief from or reduction of discomfort or other noxious stimulus

ioral change is achieved, the change may damage the punished person's self-esteem. This cost may be greater in the long run than was the cost of the operant behavior that prompted the punishment.

> Describe a situation in which a child might find a way to avoid punishment without changing the undesirable behavior that was being punished. How could you nevertheless modify the child's behavior, perhaps by using positive reinforcement?

To correct errant behavior, punishment works best under the following circumstances (Park & Walters, 1967; Walters & Grusec, 1977). The punisher should

1. Make alternative responses available to replace those that are being punished. A Kenyan proverb suggests the intuitive wisdom of this strategy: "When you take a knife away from a child, give him a piece of wood instead."
2. Complement the punishment technique by using positive reinforcement to foster the desired alternative operant behavior.
3. Make sure that the individual being punished knows exactly what behavior is being punished and why.
4. Implement the punishment immediately after the undesirable operant behavior.
5. Administer a punishment that is sufficiently intense to stop the undesirable behavior, but no greater and of no longer duration than necessary.
6. Try to ensure that it is impossible to escape punishment if the operant behavior is demonstrated.
7. Prefer the use of *penalties*—removal of pleasant stimuli—to the use of physical or emotional pain as a punisher.
8. Take advantage of the natural predilection to escape from and to avoid punishment; use punishment in situations in which the desired alternative operant behavior involves escape-seeking or avoidance (e.g., teaching a child to seek escape from dangerous places or to avoid dangerous objects).

The use of punishment as a means of encouraging escape-seeking or avoidance is **aversive conditioning,** which has as its goal **avoidance learning,** whereby an individual learns to stay away from something. For example, rats can learn to avoid a particular behavior (such as scratching at a door latch) by being aversively conditioned (such as through shocks) to avoid that behavior. Note that the aversive conditioning that leads to avoidance learning may also lead to some classical conditioning, in that the object or situation that the individual is being conditioned to avoid may also serve as a conditioned stimulus for a fear response. For example, in the case of rats that learn to avoid scratching at a latch, the rats also may learn to feel fearful of the latch or even of the area near the latch. Operant conditioning through the use of punishment leads to the behavioral outcome of avoidance, and the classical conditioning that may accompany it leads to an emotional and physiological response of fear. Thus, the two forms of learning may interact complementarily to strengthen the outcome.

Discriminating Between Reinforcement and Punishment

To summarize, reinforcement *increases* the probability of some future response; punishment *decreases* it. Reinforcement can involve the presentation of a rewarding stimulus (positive reinforcement) or the removal of an aversive stimulus (negative reinforcement), just as punishment can involve the presentation of an aversive stimulus or the removal of a rewarding one (penalty). In other words, both forms of reinforcement (positive or negative) teach the person what to do, whereas punishment teaches the learner what *not* to do. Table 7-4 summarizes these differences.

What Makes a Stimulus a Reinforcer?

Thus far, we have discussed reinforcement without explicitly discussing what makes a stimulus reinforcing, both in general and in particular circumstances.

The Premack Principle

In 1959, David Premack offered children a choice of two activities: playing with a pinball machine or eating candy. Not surprisingly, some children preferred one activity, others the alternative activity. What was more interesting was that, for children who preferred eating candy, the rate of playing with the pinball machine could be increased by using candy as a reinforcer; for the children who preferred playing with the pinball machine, the amount of candy eaten could be increased by using pinball-machine playing as a reinforcer. Thus, the more preferred activity served to reinforce the less preferred one, whichever may have been the more or less preferred activity for a given child.

This research led to what is termed the **Premack principle:** More preferred activities reinforce less preferred ones. According to Premack, all individuals have a reinforcement hierarchy, so that (a)

TABLE 7-4
Summary of Operant Conditioning

For a given operant behavior, reinforcement increases the probability of its future recurrence, whereas punishment reduces the likelihood that it will be repeated in the future. How might you use these principles to shape the behavior of persons in your environment?

Operant-Conditioning Technique	Stimulus Introduced in the Environment as an Outcome of Operant Behavior	Effect of Stimulus on Operant Behavior
Positive reinforcement	*Positive reinforcer*—pleasant stimulus	Strengthens and increases the likelihood of the operant behavior
Negative reinforcement	*Negative reinforcer*—relief from unpleasant stimulus	Strengthens and increases the likelihood of the operant behavior
Punishment	*Punishment*—unpleasant stimulus *Penalty*—removal of pleasant stimulus	Weakens and decreases the likelihood of the operant behavior

reinforcers higher in the hierarchy are more likely to trigger operant behaviors than are reinforcers lower in the hierarchy, and (b) activities higher in the hierarchy reinforce those lower in the hierarchy. Using this principle, we can reinforce someone's operant behavior by offering as a reward something the person prefers more than the activity we wish to reinforce.

Primary and Secondary Reinforcers

It is not always easy to design operant conditioning to provide **primary reinforcers**—such as food, sexual pleasure, and other immediately satisfying or enjoyable rewards. As you may recall from the earlier discussion of the levels of classical conditioning, second-order conditioning sometimes develops, based on first-order conditioning. Similarly, **secondary reinforcers**—such as money, good grades, high-status objects, and other less immediately satisfying, tangible rewards—may gain reinforcing value through association with primary reinforcers. Thus, when a primary reinforcer is not immediately available or is inconvenient to administer, and primary gratification must be delayed, secondary reinforcers can fill the gap.

A common type of secondary reinforcer used extensively in designing operant conditioning is the *token*, a tangible object that has no intrinsic worth but that can be exchanged for something of worth to the person whose behavior is subject to operant conditioning. *Token economies*, or systems in which token-based reinforcement is systematically used to change behavior, have shown some success in facilitating language development and behavioral control in autistic persons, who are otherwise out of touch with their environments (Lovaas, 1968, 1977). Researchers and clinicians have become interested in using similar reward systems with normal children. A danger of such systems, however, is that they will undermine children's natural interest in performing the behaviors that are being rewarded (Lepper, Greene, & Nisbett, 1973; see also Chapter 16).

What might be some advantages and disadvantages of using a token economy in a prison setting?

Physiological Considerations in Reinforcement

Just how primary is primary reinforcement? Most of the reinforcers we consider, and the large majority of reinforcers that have been studied in the laboratory, are either objects or activities. However, research suggests that the brain itself offers even more fundamental reinforcement. Reinforcement can come through direct stimulation of specific regions of the brain. About four decades ago, James Olds and Peter Milner (1954) were investigating rat brains via the use of microelectrodes. (Recall that when electrically activated, these devices stimulate the area of the brain in which they are implanted; see Chapter 3.) During their studies of mammal brains, Olds and Milner implanted an electrode in an area of the brain near the hypothalamus. Much to the surprise of these investigators, the animals sought the electrical stimulation. When the rats were given a chance to press a bar that would produce stimulation to this same area of the brain, the rats pressed at phenomenal rates, in excess of 2,000 times per hour for as long as 15 to 20 hours. Indeed, the rats kept pressing until they collapsed through sheer exhaustion. Subsequent research has shown that similar behavior can be generated in other species. Moreover, whereas the stimulation in this research was pleasurable, stimulation in other areas of the brain can be aversive and thus punishing. In short, it is possible to produce learning not only through reactions to external objects and activities, but also through reactions to direct internal stimulation of the brain.

> What speculations might you make regarding human behavior, based on the findings in rats by Olds and Milner? What ideas for research could be explored, based on your speculations?

The physiological processes of learning continue to be a dynamic area of psychological research. Other physiological factors internal to the individual also influence learning (see Table 7-5).

The Gradient of Reinforcement: Effects of Delays

Another important consideration in operant conditioning is the **gradient of reinforcement**—that is, the longer we wait to reinforce a given operant, the weaker the effect of the reinforcement will be. This principle is important both for establishing and for suppressing behavior. For example, one of the difficulties people face when trying to stop smoking is that the positive reinforcement for smoking comes soon after lighting up the cigarette, whereas the punishment is not certain and, in any case, is usually per-

ceived as occurring far in the future. Similarly, in the age of AIDS, couples know that they should use condoms for protection against the deadly disease, and yet many couples continue not to use them. For these couples, the immediate reinforcements of not using condoms (e.g., not wishing to interrupt the flow of sexual communion) take psychological precedence, at the moment, over the perception of a less immediate and less predictable danger. For all that we know about the dangers of smoking and unprotected intercourse, even very intelligent people engage in these dangerous behaviors because reinforcement principles can be so strong that they overpower the effects of rational thinking.

The effectiveness of reinforcement generally declines very rapidly with the passage of time because the link between the reinforcement and the behavior it reinforces rapidly becomes less clear. The father who tells the child that she will be sorry for her misbehavior when her mother comes home is reducing the effect of the punishment by having the child wait for hours. Similarly, it would be ineffective to reward children for desirable behavior long after the behavior occurs; immediate reinforcement would produce far more potent results. The principle applies to all species.

> How could either high school counselors or the parents of adolescents benefit from knowing about the psychological principle of gradients of reinforcement? How could they use such knowledge to help adolescents avoid the perils of unprotected sexual intercourse or of cigarette smoking? Give specific suggestions.

TABLE 7-5
Physiological Consideration in Learning

Physiological Considerations	Examples
Behavioral predispositions	It is much easier to train a seal to perform stunts such as leaping into and out of the water than to train a kangaroo to do so.
Maturational considerations	It is easier to toilet-train a 30-month-old child than an 18-month-old because the 30-month-old is maturationally ready for bowel and bladder control.
Trauma and acute physiological factors	An injured leg might hamper the ability to jump over a hurdle. Also, fatigue and other temporary physiological conditions affect performance and the conditioning experience. The effects of physiological need (e.g., hunger) on the salience of stimuli (e.g., food) are well known.

Successive Approximations: The Shaping of Behavior

She who does not yet know how to walk cannot climb a ladder.

—Ethiopian proverb

Sometimes, of course, we wish to create a behavior, not suppress one. If the behavior is likely to occur by chance, as was the case for the cat who learned to escape from the puzzle box, we have only to wait for its occurrence and then to reinforce it immediately and powerfully. However, not all behaviors we seek are likely to occur by chance (e.g., washing the dishes or the laundry). Particularly when a behavior is complex, how can we create behavior when we cannot realistically expect it to occur by chance? We **shape** behavior through the method of **successive approximations.** This method is used for training animals in circuses, in aquatic shows, and the like. To implement this method, you first reward a very crude approximation of the behavior of interest. Once that rather rudimentary behavior has been established, you begin to look for a somewhat closer approximation to the desired behavior, and you reward only those closer approximations. You continue with this procedure until the desired behavior is reached.

Parents use the method of shaping on their children all the time. For example, when toilet training a child, parents may choose first to reward just a small degree of control, such as when and where the child defecates. They may teach the child to be aware of when he or she needs to defecate, and to go to the toilet when the need is felt. Next, they may reward the child for occasionally making it to the toilet on time, even if the child misses frequently. Finally, after the frequency of hits far exceeds that of misses, the parents may reward only regular successful trips to the toilet.

Design an operant-conditioning program for training an animal (such as a monkey) to perform a specific self-help task (such as feeding or self-grooming) for a person who cannot perform the task independently, due to physical limitations.

Sometimes, a person can change his or her behavior without any apparent intervention from anyone else. Such change is **autoshaping.** The individual sets up a system of reinforcements that results in gradual behavioral change. For example, if you wanted to increase your amount of exercise, you might generate a system of rewards by which at first

Often, when we think of trained animals, we think of amazing stunts performed in circuses or other shows. More commonly, trained animals perform much more important—and perhaps even heroic—work, such as enabling their owners to perform daily tasks or to hike the entire Appalachian Trail.

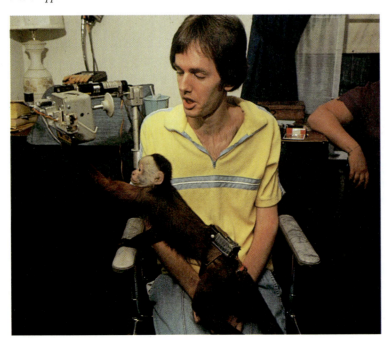

you reward yourself for small increases in the amount of exercise per week. Then you would gradually increase the amount of exercise you require of yourself in order to get the reward.

Schedules of Reinforcement

Children and other persons who behave in an exemplary fashion are not always rewarded, and people who misbehave are not always punished. When we think of reinforcement, we need to think of it as a phenomenon that can be administered on various kinds of **schedules of reinforcement**—that is, patterns by which the reinforcements follow the operants.

Up to now, we have assumed **continuous reinforcement,** whereby a reinforcement always follows a particular operant behavior. One example of continuous reinforcement is biofeedback, which uses equipment and technical assistance to provide continuous reinforcing feedback on a person's biological processes (e.g., blood pressure, muscle tension, or pulse rate) to help the person regulate these processes. A continuous schedule of reinforcement is fairly easy to establish in a laboratory but is actually quite rare in everyday life. In normal everyday life, we are much more likely to encounter a schedule of **partial reinforcement** (also termed *intermittent reinforcement*), whereby a given operant will be reinforced sometimes, but not at other times. Partial reinforcement schedules are of two types: ratio schedules and interval schedules. In a **ratio schedule,** a proportion (ratio) of potentially reinforceable operant responses is reinforced, regardless of the amount of time that has passed. In an **interval schedule,** reinforcement occurs after a certain amount of time has passed, regardless of how many operant responses have taken place during that time, as long as at least one response has occurred during the interval.

Ratio Schedules

Ratio schedules are of two basic types: fixed ratios and variable ratios. In a **fixed-ratio reinforcement** schedule, reinforcements always occur after a certain number of responses. Many factory workers and cottage-industry artisans get *piecework wages*, meaning that they get paid a flat rate for completing a set number of tasks or crafting a set number of products. In a **variable-ratio reinforcement** schedule, reinforcements occur, *on average*, after a certain number of responses, but the specific number of responses preceding reinforcement changes from one reinforcement to the next.

Design a fixed- or variable-ratio program that would condition someone (such as your roommate) to engage in a particular behavior (such as returning dishes to the sink and rinsing them or putting dirty laundry in a hamper) more frequently.

Interval Schedules

Just as there are fixed- and variable-ratio schedules, there are fixed- and variable-interval reinforcement schedules. In a **fixed-interval reinforcement** schedule, reinforcement always occurs after a certain amount of time has passed. Note that the reinforcement occurs regardless of the number of responses made, as long as at least one desired response (or avoidance of the undesired response) is made. Many aspects of our lives are tied to fixed-interval reinforcements. In most salaried and wage-based jobs, workers are reinforced with paychecks at regular intervals. Similarly, you may study your school assignments in anticipation of fixed-interval reinforcement—such as high grades on final examinations. In a **variable-interval reinforcement** schedule, reinforcement occurs, *on average*, after a certain amount of time has passed, but the specific amount of time between reinforcements changes from one reinforcement to the next.

Comparison and Contrast of Reinforcement Schedules

What effects can we expect from the four different kinds of partial-reinforcement schedules? How do they compare with each other and with a continuous-reinforcement schedule? Perhaps the most important point is that partial reinforcement is generally more effective than continuous reinforcement at maintaining a long-term change in behavior. If we want to establish or maintain a behavior, we will be more successful if we partially reinforce it. This result seems paradoxical. Why should partial reinforcement be more effective than continuous reinforcement in maintaining behavior? With continuous reinforcement, cessation of reinforcement is obvious and easy to recognize. For example, when people notice that a vending machine (which supplies continuous reinforcement for depositing money) has stopped dispensing the items being purchased, individual purchasers stop depositing their quarters into the machine almost immediately. With partial reinforcement, it is often difficult to distinguish the cessation of reinforcement from merely a prolonged interval within a partial-reinforcement schedule. For example, people often do not immediately stop putting their quarters into a slot machine for gambling even when the machine has not provided any reinforcement for quite a while.

Figure 7-7 shows the patterns of behavior that tend to be produced by the various schedules of reinforcement. Note that the patterns of behavior produced by the various schedules are different. Although the rate of extinction is greater for continuous reinforcement, the onset of the operant behavior is also faster for this schedule; that is, on this schedule, behavior starts quickly and stops quickly. For the intermittent-reinforcement schedules, ratio schedules generally produce more operant behavior than do interval schedules; that is, fixed-ratio schedules produce higher rates of operant behavior than do fixed-interval schedules, just as variable-ratio schedules produce higher rates than do variable-interval schedules. Note that for the fixed schedules, for a period of time after each reinforcement the operant ceases. Variable schedules maintain a more constant rate of responding.

In everyday life, reinforcement schedules may be complex, with the ratio or interval of reinforcement changing with the time and the circumstances. Moreover, what starts out as one kind of schedule may change to another (e.g., variable ratio to variable interval).

Learned Helplessness

Some types of conditioning, particularly of punishment, may lead to a far more serious consequence: the phenomenon of learned helplessness. **Learned helplessness** is passive behavior caused by the recognition that there is no way to escape a painful stimulus. In a classic experiment, Martin Seligman and S. F. Maier (Seligman, 1975; Seligman & Maier, 1967) placed dogs in a chamber where they received painful (but not harmful) electric shocks. The dogs were unable to escape the shock. Later, the chamber was divided into two parts, so the dogs could escape the shock simply by jumping over a barrier that separated the first, electrified part of the chamber from the second, nonelectrified part. However, because the dogs had previously learned that they could not escape, they made no effort to escape; instead, they just whined.

In contrast, consider the behavior of a second group of dogs, who did not have the previous experience of being unable to escape. These dogs were placed in the cage, and the shock was turned on. At first, the dogs ran around frantically. Then eventually they saw the barrier and jumped it, escaping the shock. On subsequent trials, when the shock was

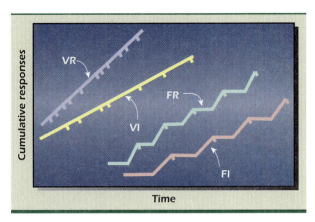

FIGURE 7-7
Typical Patterns of Responding to Reinforcement
Each of the four kinds of reinforcement schedules leads to a different characteristic pattern of response. In general, variable schedules lead to more stable patterns of response (as shown by straight lines) than do fixed schedules (as shown by zig-zag lines), and ratio schedules produce higher levels of response than do interval schedules.

turned on, they quickly jumped the barrier, minimizing the time that they experienced pain. Thus, the first group of dogs' feelings of helplessness rendered them unable to learn.

Alas, humans are not invulnerable to the effects of learned helplessness, which appears to be a fairly pervasive phenomenon in everyday life. We try something; we fail. Maybe we try again and fail again. Soon we have learned that we cannot perform that task or master that skill; as a result, we never try again. The child who fails in school, the adult who fails on the job, the lover who fails to sustain a lasting romantic relationship—all of these people are susceptible to learned helplessness. Our past conditioning may tell us that we cannot succeed. Some people stop accepting one new challenge after another because they feel sure that they cannot cope with these challenges. Right now, you may be feeling greatly challenged by the similarities and differences between classical and operant conditioning. At this point, it may be helpful to summarize briefly the features of each, as shown in Table 7-6.

ADDITIONAL CONSIDERATIONS FOR LEARNING

The Learning-Performance Distinction: Latent Learning

Up to this point, we have described conditioning in terms of the observable changes that occur as a result of learning. However, what we learn is not always im-

TABLE 7-6
Comparison of Classical and Operant Conditioning
Both classical and operant conditioning are processes of association by which individuals learn behavior, but the two processes differ in several key ways.

Characteristics	Classical (or Pavlovian)	Operant (or Instrumental)
Key relationship	Environment's CS and Environment's UCS	Organism's response and Environment's stimulus (reinforcement or punishment)
Organism's role	Passively (emotionally or physiologically) responds to stimuli (CS or UCS)	Actively operates on environment
Sequence of events	Initiation of conditioning: CS → UCS → UCR	Operant response → Reinforcer → Increase response
	Peak of acquisition phase: CS → CR	Operant response → Punishment → Decrease response
Schedules of conditioning	Standard classical conditioning, delay conditioning, trace conditioning, temporal conditioning	Continuous reinforcement, variable ratios, fixed ratios, fixed intervals, and variable intervals of reinforcement
Extinction techniques	Uncouple the CS from the UCS, repeatedly presenting the CS in the absence of the UCS	Uncouple the operant response from the stimulus reinforcer or punishment; repeatedly fail to reinforce or to punish the operant behavior

mediately evident. In 1930—long before other researchers acknowledged internal mechanisms that affect conditioning—Edward Tolman and C. H. Honzik performed an elegant experiment to illustrate a way in which performance may not be a clear reflection of learning. The investigators were interested in the ability of rats to learn a maze, such as that shown in Figure 7-8. Rats were divided into three groups:

Group 1. The rats had to learn the maze, and their reward for getting from the start box to the end box was food. Eventually, these rats learned to run the maze without making any wrong turns or following blind alleys.

Group 2. The rats were also placed in the maze, but they received no reinforcement for successfully getting to the end box. Although their performance improved over time, they continued to make more errors than did the reinforced group. These results are hardly surprising; we would expect the rewarded group to have more incentive to learn.

Group 3. The rats received no reward for ten days of learning trials. On the eleventh day, however, food was placed in the end box. With just one reinforcement, the learning of these rats improved dramatically, so that they ran the maze about as well as the rats in Group 1.

The Tolman and Honzik experiment shows the effects of **latent learning**—learning that is not reflected in performance. It seems that the unrewarded rats learned the route, even though it was not reflected in their performance. Once they were given a reward, they displayed their learning, as shown by the fact that just one rewarded trial enormously boosted their performance.

What, exactly, were the rats learning in Tolman and Honzik's experiment? It seems unlikely that they were learning simply "turn right here, turn left there," and so on. Rather, Tolman argued that the rats were learning a **cognitive map**—an internal representation of the maze. Through this argument,

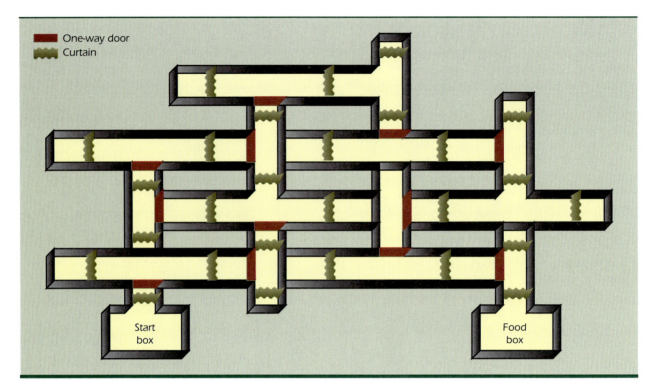

One-way door
Curtain

Start box

Food box

FIGURE 7-8
Latent Learning
In Edward Tolman and C. H. Honzik's experiment, the rats learned to form a mental map of the maze shown here, although they did not show their learning until they were rewarded for doing so.

Tolman became one of the earliest cognitive theorists, arguing for the importance not only of behavior, but also of the mental representations that give rise to the behavior.

> A map is one kind of internal representation. What are a few other kinds of mental representations that you use yourself or that you believe other people use?

Learning to Learn

Sometimes, what we learn is not a particular, specific internal representation, but rather a **learning set,** a generalized internal representation that facilitates learning. In a series of experiments, Harry Harlow (1949) first taught monkeys to make a simple choice between two alternatives. The monkeys were to look for food hidden under either of two boxes: a square box or a round box. Each time the monkey learned which box hid the food, a new pair of boxes was introduced—for example, triangular boxes differing in color. Note that each new set of stimuli was just as hard to learn as the previous set. The critical result

was that as the animals gained more experience with the type of task, their rate of learning increased. Obviously, the animals were not going into new versions of the task with more information about which box hid the food. Rather, they were establishing a learning set, also known as *learning to learn*. Again, it would seem that the animals had formed some kind of internalized general representation of the kind of task, which they could then use to their advantage in discriminating new pairs of stimuli.

Learning-to-learn phenomena are relevant even more in human than in monkey affairs. Each time we learn a new language—whether a national language

HEY PAL, YOU SEEN A CLUMP OF CHEESE AROUND HERE? I'M BEING TIMED.

such as French or Spanish, a computer-programming language, or even a word-processing language—we learn not only the specifics of that language, but also how best to learn new languages. Each subsequent language becomes easier, in part because of overlapping elements, but also in part because we have established a set of learning-to-learn techniques. Learning sets also may be used in many different learned behaviors. For example, in interpersonal relationships, we learn how we can learn more about people—what questions to ask them, what things to look for in their behavior, and so on. One of the things we learn about other people is how to behave in social interactions.

SOCIAL LEARNING

Wise men learn by others' mistakes, fools by their own.

—*Henry George Bohn*

When you follow in the path of your father, you learn to walk like him.

—*Ashanti proverb*

All of the research discussed so far has involved learning through classical or operant conditioning. In our everyday lives, however, not all of our learning derives from direct participation. Consider, for example, the effect on a child of seeing an older sibling punished for something that she herself did just the day before, or the effect on a drug addict of seeing a fellow addict die of an overdose of drugs.

Social learning occurs when we observe the behavior of others, as well as any environmental outcomes of the behavior we observe. Through social learning, we do not learn directly, but rather vicariously. Is there really any empirical evidence for **vicarious learning** (also called **observational learning**)?

Albert Bandura (1965, 1969) and his colleagues have performed numerous experiments demonstrating that vicarious social learning is an effective way of learning. In a typical study, preschool children were shown a film featuring an adult who punched, kicked, and threw things at a Bobo doll. The adult even hit the doll with a hammer. The given film ended in different ways, depending on the group to which a particular child viewer was assigned. In one group, the adult model was rewarded for the aggressive behavior; in a second group, the adult model was

punished; and in a third (control) group, the adult model was neither rewarded nor punished. When, after the film, the children were allowed to play with a Bobo doll, those children who had seen the adult

In numerous experiments, Albert Bandura has shown that children learn to imitate the behavior of others. By observing a movie of a woman behaving aggressively toward a Bobo doll (top), this boy and girl learned to punch the doll.

model rewarded for aggressive behavior were more likely than the controls to behave aggressively with the doll, whereas those who had observed the adult model punished were less likely than the controls to behave aggressively with the doll. Clearly, observational learning had taken place.

Other studies show that reinforcement contingencies are not needed for social learning to take place. In another experiment (Bandura, Ross, & Ross, 1963), preschool children watched an adult model either sit quietly next to the Bobo doll or attack it. No rewards or punishments went to the adult. When children were later left alone with the doll, those who had observed aggressive behavior were more likely to behave aggressively.

What conditions are necessary for observational learning to occur? There appear to be four of them (Bandura, 1977b):

1. *Attention* to the behavior on which the learning might be based;
2. *Retention* of the observed scene when the opportunity arises later to exploit the learning;
3. *Motivation* to reproduce the observed behavior; and
4. *Potential reproduction* of the behavior—in other words, you need to be able to do what you saw being done.

Also, generalization and discrimination play important roles in the effectiveness of learning and in the applicability of learning to a particular context. For example, several factors enhance the salience of a model, although these factors are not necessary for social learning to take place: (a) The model stands out in contrast to other competing models; (b) the model is liked and respected by the observer (or by others in the environment); (c) the observer perceives a similarity between herself or himself and the model; (d) the model's behavior is reinforced.

Observational learning is not limited to scenes with Bobo dolls, of course. Many children as well as adults spend countless hours in front of televisions watching violent behavior. Considerable evidence supports the contention that exposure to violent activity on television leads to aggressive behavior (e.g., Friedrich-Cofer & Huston, 1986; Huesmann, Lagerspetz, & Eron, 1984; Parke et al., 1977).

Observational learning is important not only in identifying behavior typically considered to be undesirable, such as highly aggressive behavior, but also in identifying and establishing who we are. For example, gender identification and gender-role development clearly rely heavily on observational learning; children's observations of same-sex parents, as well as of same-sex peers are particularly influential (with much of gender identification having occurred by age two or three years; S. K. Thompson, 1975).

Clearly, social learning is important to many aspects of our identity development. Sometimes, social learning seems to guide us to limit ourselves in terms of the options we feel that we have available. What are some specific ways in which parents can help their children to broaden their horizons through social learning?

In sum, observational learning is important to both children and adults. We are not always aware of its occurrence, but it is always consequential for us—whether beneficial or harmful. Those of us who are loath to practice what we preach especially need to be aware: Children are more likely to learn and remember by imitating what we practice than by listening to what we preach. The many factors that influence our later recollection of what we observe are the subject of the next chapter.

SUMMARY

Preprogrammed Behavior: Reflexes, Instincts, and Imprinting   236

1. An organism (including a human) *learns* when it makes a relatively permanent change in its behavior, thoughts, or feelings as a result of experience.
2. *Reflexes*, *instincts*, and *imprinting* are behaviors that are mainly preprogrammed but can be in-

fluenced by learning. Imprinting is the most susceptible to learning.

Classical Conditioning   237

3. Pavlov identified *classical conditioning* when he was trying to conduct experiments on digestion. After noting that his dog drooled when it anticipated some meat powder, he realized that he

could condition or teach the dog to have the same reaction to a sound, something that it would not do otherwise.

4. *Classical conditioning* teaches an organism to pair a neutral stimulus with a stimulus that produces an unconditioned physiological or emotional response.

5. The dog's drooling for the meat powder was the *unconditioned response (UCR)*, the meat powder was the *unconditioned stimulus (UCS)*, the buzzer (an originally neutral stimulus) became the *conditioned stimulus (CS)*, and the drooling (originally the UCR) in response to the buzzer became the *conditioned response (CR)*.

6. In the standard classical conditioning paradigm, the CS precedes the onset of the UCS by a brief interval of time. Other timing arrangements include *delay conditioning, trace conditioning, temporal conditioning, simultaneous conditioning*, and *backward conditioning*.

7. *Temporal contiguity* appears not to be sufficient for classical conditioning to occur; rather, a *contingency* must be established between the stimulus and the response if conditioning is to occur.

8. If we plotted the rate of learning, the curve would rise quickly but then level off at the *asymptote*. The rate of learning shows a *negative acceleration* over time.

9. The probability of learning is highest in the *acquisition* phase. If the UCS is not presented in conjunction with the CS, the learned response is *extinguished*. However, the learned behavior will spontaneously recover if the CS is presented once again. If the UCS is presented once again with the CS, then *savings* will occur and the CR will be almost as strong as during the *asymptote*.

10. In *first-order conditioning*, a CS is linked to a UCS. In *second-order conditioning*, a second CS is linked to the first CS, and so on analogously for *higher orders of conditioning*.

11. When we show a CR to a stimulus that is similar to the CS, we use *stimulus generalization*. However, when the new stimulus increasingly differs from the CS, to the point where we are unlikely to show the CR, we use *stimulus discrimination*.

12. We seem to be predisposed toward making some associations and not others. For example, for rats who were exposed to poison as the UCS, taste was a more effective CS than the combination of light and noise as the CS.

13. Classical conditioning applies to more than just animal experimentation. Many of our *conditioned emotional responses*—such as fear, anxiety, or even joy—are linked to distinctive physiological feel-

ings. When we experience conflicting stimuli, we may experience a neurosis. *Addictions* also appear to be partly classically conditioned, although they can be broken by *counterconditioning*.

Operant Conditioning   249

14. *Operant conditioning* is learning produced by the active behavior (an *operant*) of an individual. According to the *law of effect*, operant actions that are rewarded will tend to be strengthened and thus will be more likely to occur in the future, whereas operant actions that are punished will tend to be weakened and thus will be less likely to occur in the future.

15. B. F. Skinner believed that all behavior should be studied and analyzed into specific stimulus-response contingencies.

16. A *reinforcer* is a stimulus that increases the probability that the operant associated with it will happen again. A *positive reinforcer* is a reward that strengthens an associated response; *positive reinforcement* pairs the positive reinforcer with an operant. A *negative reinforcer*, which also strengthens an associated response, is relief from or a reduction in an unpleasant stimulus; *negative reinforcement* pairs an operant with the discontinuation of an unpleasant stimulus.

17. *Punishment* is a stimulus that decreases the probability of a response. It differs from negative reinforcement, which increases the probability of a response. Punishment should be administered carefully because it can lead to many unintended consequences.

18. *Avoidance learning* occurs when an individual learns to stay away from something. Under some circumstances, avoidance learning can occur after just a single trial of *aversive conditioning*.

19. According to the *Premack principle*, more-preferred activities can serve to reinforce less-preferred activities.

20. When *primary reinforcers* (e. g., food, sexual pleasure) are not available, *secondary reinforcers* (e.g., money, gifts, good grades) can provide reinforcement if they are associated with primary reinforcers.

21. Reinforcement can be administered directly to the brain. Reinforcement to some areas of the brains of animals can cause them to seek repeated stimulation until they drop from exhaustion.

22. The *gradient of reinforcement* refers to the fact that the longer the time interval is between the

operant behavior and the reinforcement, the weaker the effect of the reinforcement will be.

23. When *shaping* behavior, such as training an animal or changing a person's behavior, the method of *successive approximations* reinforces operant behaviors that are successively closer to the desired behavior. Sometimes a person can change to the desired behavior through *autoshaping*, without intervention by anyone else.

24. In operant conditioning, behavior can be *reinforced continuously* or *partially*. Partial reinforcement has four forms: *fixed-ratio schedule*, *variable-ratio schedule*, *fixed-interval schedule*, and *variable-interval schedule*.

25. Animals or people display *learned helplessness* when they feel there is no way to escape a painful or aversive stimulus. The experimental demonstration of this phenomenon was the dogs who learned that they could not escape the electric shocks. People display this behavior when they have repeated failures.

Additional Considerations for Learning   258

26. We do not always display in our behavior what we have learned; this nonobservable learning is termed *latent learning*. Edward Tolman showed that mental representations, such as a *cognitive map*, are the foundation for behavior. An internalized general representation that makes learning a particular task easier is a *learning set*.

Social Learning   261

27. When we watch the behaviors of others and the outcomes of those behaviors, we learn those behaviors vicariously; we engage in *social learning*. A classic example of this kind of social learning is shown in Bandura's experiment with children who watched and mimicked aggressive behavior with a Bobo doll.

28. Learning by observation is important because it helps us identify desired behaviors and establish our identities.

KEY TERMS

acquisition 243
addictions 249
asymptote 243
autoshaping 256
aversive conditioning 253
avoidance learning 253
backward conditioning 241
classical conditioning 238
cognitive map 259
conditioned emotional responses 248
conditioned response (CR) 240
conditioned stimulus (CS) 240
contingency 242
continuous reinforcement 257
counterconditioning 249
critical period 237
delay conditioning 241
ethologist 237
experimental analysis of behavior 250
experimental neurosis 248
extinction 244
first-order conditioning 244

fixed-interval reinforcement 257
fixed-ratio reinforcement 257
gradient of reinforcement 255
higher order conditioning 245
imprint 237
instinctive 237
interval schedule 257
latent learning 259
law of effect 250
learned helplessness 258
learning 236
learning set 260
negative acceleration 243
negative reinforcement 252
negative reinforcer 252
observational learning 261
operant 251
operant conditioning 250
orienting reflex 236
overshadowing 241
partial reinforcement 257
positive reinforcement 252
positive reinforcer 252
Premack principle 253

primary reinforcers 254
punishment 252
ratio schedule 257
reinforcer 252
savings 244
schedules of reinforcement 257
secondary reinforcers 254
shape 256
simultaneous conditioning 241
Skinner boxes 251
social learning 261
spontaneous recovery 244
stimulus discrimination 245
stimulus generalization 245
successive approximations 256
temporal conditioning 241
temporal contiguity 242
trace conditioning 241
unconditioned response (UCR) 240
unconditioned stimulus (UCS) 240
variable-interval reinforcement 257
variable-ratio reinforcement 257
vicarious learning 261

IN SEARCH OF THE HUMAN MIND:
ANALYSES, CREATIVE EXPLORATIONS, AND PRACTICAL APPLICATIONS

1. B. F. Skinner was originally an English major; Ivan Pavlov was originally a Nobel Prize winning physiologist. What do you think might have attracted them to the study of psychology in general and to the study of conditioning in particular?
2. In what kinds of situations would preprogrammed behavior be advantageous? Why would learned behavior be less advantageous in these situations?
3. What are the main similarities and differences between classical and operant conditioning?

4. Prescribe a counterconditioning program for a specific phobia, neurosis, or addiction.
5. What is something (a skill, a task, or an achievement) that you think is worthwhile, but that you feel a sense of learned helplessness about successfully accomplishing?

How could you design a conditioning program for yourself to overcome your learned helplessness?
6. Suppose you were a storyteller or a movie maker. How might you use classical conditioning to influence your audience's emotions? (Use a real story or movie plot for your example.)

7. Suppose you wanted people to buy a particular real or imaginary product. How could you use some of the principles of conditioning to encourage people to buy this product?
8. What are some examples of learning to learn that apply to your study of psychology (or to the topics of other college courses)? What have you already learned about how to learn new information?
9. Given the powerful effects of social learning, how might the medium of television be used as a medium for *lowering* the rate of violent crimes in our society? State your proposal in terms of a brief main statement and some supporting statements.

In light of your answer and the importance of reducing the rate of violent crimes, what are some opposing views that might be stated as antitheses to the control of television programming? What might be a possible synthesis view regarding this issue?

Chapter Eight

Memory

Chapter Outline

A psychology professor arrived in a small town where he was scheduled to give a talk on memory to the faculty and students in the psychology department of a college. The professor was exhausted because this was the last in a long string of engagements, and he knew he was incapable of giving a good talk at this point. As he was riding in a taxi to his destination, he had an idea. He offered his taxi driver $50 if the driver would give the talk for him. He didn't know anyone at the college, and he assured his driver that because the talk was completely written out, the driver didn't need to know anything at all about memory. All he had to do was deliver the talk. Moreover, the psychologist assured the driver he would be in the audience, so the driver could always rely on him to bail him out in case things got tough. Business had been slow, so the taxi driver decided that it was worth going through with the deal for $50. He gave the talk, and it went flawlessly. Then the question-and-answer period started, and the taxi driver couldn't answer even the first, simple question about memory asked by a member of the audience. He knew the answer was in the talk he had given, but he had been so busy concentrating on delivering the talk that he couldn't remember a thing he had said. Thinking quickly, the driver looked the questioner straight in the eye, and responded: "Why, that question is so easy, even my taxi driver could answer it, and he just happens to be in the audience."

The story of the psychology professor and the taxicab driver illustrates two basic points about human memory. First, we can deliver a set of lines, but unless we process these words in a way that renders them memorable, we may remember nothing of what we have said (or have read). We address this issue in the section on long-term memory. Second, when we cannot remember, we can often rely on external memory aids to help us out. In this case, the speaker used the memory of the professor who had been invited to give the talk in the first place. More often, we use what are called "mnemonic devices," which we address in this chapter. In addition, we consider the answers to several important questions about memory: What, exactly, is memory? How does memory work? Are there different kinds of memory, and if so, what are they? How is each kind of memory organized? How are different kinds of memories related? How can we measure memory, and how can we improve it? To answer these questions, we first explore what memory is, by noting what happens when memory is deficient and contrasting low with exceptionally high levels of memory.

WHAT IS MEMORY?

IN SEARCH OF...

How does memory affect the way we think and feel about ourselves and our surrounding environment?

As a process, **memory** refers to the dynamic mechanisms associated with the retention and retrieval of information about past experience (Crowder, 1976). We draw upon our memory of the past to help us understand the present. We usually take for granted the ability to remember, much as we do the air we breathe. However, just as we become more aware of the importance of air when we do not have enough to breathe, we are less likely to take memory for granted when we observe people with serious memory deficiencies.

That sacred Closet when you sweep—
Entitled "Memory"—
Select a reverential Broom—
And do it silently. . . .

—*Emily Dickinson*, Poem 1273

Memory Deficiencies: Amnesia

One of the most famous cases of **amnesia** (severe loss of memory) is the case of H. M., reported by William Scoville and Brenda Milner (1957; Milner, Corkin, & Teuber, 1968). Following an experimental surgical treatment for uncontrollable epilepsy, H. M. suffered severe **anterograde amnesia**—he had great difficulty remembering events that occurred from the time of the surgery onward. However, he had full recollection of events that had occurred before his operation. Although his postsurgical intelligence test score was 112, which is above average, his score on the memory test was 67, which is much below average (see Chapter 11). Moreover, shortly after taking a test from the memory scale, he could not remember that he had taken it. Had he been given the test again, it would have been as though he were taking it for the first time. H. M. once remarked on his situation: "Every day is alone in itself, whatever enjoyment I've had, and whatever sorrow I've had" (Scoville & Milner, 1957, p. 217). H. M. all but lost his ability to form new memories, so he lived suspended in an eternal present in which he was unable to create any memories of the time following his operation.

Without [memory] all life and thought [are] an unrelated succession. As gravity holds matter from flying off into space, so memory gives stability to knowledge; it is the cohesion which keeps things from falling into a lump, or flowing in waves.

—*Ralph Waldo Emerson*,
Natural History of Intellect

Another type of memory loss is **retrograde amnesia,** in which an individual loses his or her memory for events that occurred prior to a trauma that induced the memory loss. W. Ritchie Russell and P. W. Nathan (1946) reported a case of severe retrograde amnesia following a physical trauma: A 22-year-old greens keeper suffered serious memory loss following a motorcycle accident. By 10 weeks after the accident, however, he had recovered his memory for most events, starting with the events in the most distant past and gradually progressing up to more recent events. Eventually, he was able to recall everything that had happened up to a few minutes prior to the accident. As is often the case, the events that occurred immediately before the trauma were never recalled.

Compare anterograde and retrograde amnesia, relating how each form would affect your own life if you were to fall victim to it.

Yet another form of amnesia is one that most of us experience: **infantile amnesia,** the inability to recall events that happened when we were very young (see Spear, 1979). Generally, we can remember little or nothing that has happened to us before the age of about 5 years, and it is extremely rare for someone to recall any memories before the age of 3 years. The reports of childhood memories usually involve memories of significant events (e.g., the birth of a sibling or the death of a parent) (see Fivush & Hamond, 1991). The accuracy of childhood memories has since come into question, however. In fact, many psychologists (e.g., Stephen Ceci, personal communication, 1993) question the accuracy of children's recollections of events, even shortly after these events occurred. (The unreliability of our memories for events is discussed more fully later in this chapter.)

Outstanding Memory: Mnemonists

The flip side of the memory coin is the **mnemonist,** a person who relies on a special technique, such as imagery, for greatly improving his or her memory. The mnemonist's ability shows us what we might long to have, especially when, as students, we wish we had photographic memories for material we need to remember when taking exams.

Perhaps the most famous of mnemonists was a man called "S.," who was described by Alexander Luria, a celebrated Russian psychologist. Luria (1968) reported that one day a man employed as a newspaper reporter appeared in his laboratory and asked to have his memory tested. Luria tested him and discovered that the man's memory appeared to have virtually no limits. S. could reproduce series of words of any length whatsoever, regardless of how long before the words had been presented to him. Luria studied S. over a period of 30 years and found that even when his retention was measured 15 or 16 years after a session in which S. had learned words, S. could still reproduce the words. S. eventually became a professional entertainer, dazzling audiences with his ability to recall whatever was asked of him.

What was S.'s trick? How did he remember so much? Apparently, he relied heavily on the mnemonic of visual imagery. He converted material that he needed to remember into visual images. For example, he reported that when asked to remember the word "green," he visualized a green flowerpot, whereas for the word "red," he would visualize a man in a red shirt coming toward him. Even numbers called up images. For example, "1" was a proud, well-built man, and so on. However, S.'s heavy reliance on imagery created difficulty for him when he tried to understand abstract concepts, such as *infinity* or *nothing*, which did not lend themselves well to visual images.

A mnemonist studied by K. Anders Ericsson, William Chase, and Steve Faloon (1980), S. F., remembered long strings of numbers by segmenting them into groups of three or four digits each, and encoding them as running times for different races. An experienced long-distance runner himself, S. F. was familiar with the times that would be plausible for different races. S. F. did not enter the laboratory a mnemonist; rather, he was selected to represent the average college student in intelligence and memory ability. S. F.'s original memory for a string of numbers was about seven digits, average for a college student. After 200 practice sessions distributed over a period of 2 years, S. F. had increased his memory for digits more than tenfold and could recall up to about 80 digits. His memory was severely impaired, however, when the experimenters purposely gave him sequences of digits that could not be translated into running times. The work with S. F. by Ericsson and his colleagues suggests that a person with a fairly typical level of memory ability can be converted into one with quite an extraordinary memory, at least in some domains, with a great amount of concerted practice.

Exceptional mnemonists offer some insight into the processes of memory. For example, mnemonists generally translate arbitrary, abstract, meaningless information into more meaningful or sensorily concrete information. In the next section, we consider how to use mnemonic devices to improve our own memory abilities. These devices rely on similar kinds of trans-lations that add meaning to otherwise meaningless information. Although most people will never perform at the level of these extraordinary mnemonists, we can all improve our memories by using mnemonics.

MNEMONIC DEVICES

There are . . . two kinds of memory: The natural memory is that memory which is imbedded in our minds, born simultaneously with thought. The artificial memory is that memory which is strengthened by a kind of training and system of discipline.

—*Cicero*, Ad Herennium

The memory performance of mnemonists is quite rare, but you can use several similar mnemonic devices to improve your learning of new material. **Mnemonic devices** are a variety of specific techniques to help you memorize lists of words and vocabulary items. Because these methods add meaning or imagery to an otherwise arbitrary listing, using them is usually much easier than rote memorization. Table 8-1 describes and illustrates each of the following mnemonic devices: **categorical clustering, interactive images** among the words in a list, a **pegword system,** the **method of loci, acronyms, acrostics,** and **keywords.** These mnemonic devices prove particularly valuable for many memory tasks. Cognitive psychologists who study memory use a variety of such tasks in their studies. These tasks are the subject of the next section.

TASKS USED FOR MEASURING MEMORY

IN SEARCH OF...

As you read about the following tasks that measure memory, think about how they might have real-world applications. What things have you done that required some of the same memory skills as those being measured in these tasks?

In studying memory, both in exceptional persons such as mnemonists and amnesics and in persons with normal memories, researchers have devised vari-

TABLE 8-1
Mnemonic Devices

Of the many mnemonic devices available, the ones described here rely on organization of information into meaningful chunks—such as categorical clustering, acronyms, *and* acrostics; *or on visual images—such as* interactive images, *a* pegword system, *the* method of loci, *and the* keyword system.

Technique	Description	Example
Categorical clustering	Organize a list of items into a set of categories.	If you need to remember to buy apples, milk, grapes, yogurt, Swiss cheese, and grapefruit, try to memorize the items by categories: *fruits*—apples, grapes, grapefruit; *dairy products*—milk, yogurt, Swiss cheese.
Interactive images	Create interactive images that link the isolated words in a list.	If you need to remember a list of unrelated words such as aardvark, table, pencil, and book generate *interactive images*. Imagine an *aardvark* sitting on a *table* holding a *pencil* in its claws and writing in a *book*.
Pegword system	Associate each new word with a word on a previously memorized list, and form an interactive image between the two words.	One such list is from a nursery rhyme: One is a bun, two is a shoe, three is a tree, four is a door, five is a hive.
Method of loci	Visualize walking around an area with distinctive landmarks that you know well, and link the landmarks to items to be remembered.	Mentally walk past each of the landmarks and visualize an interactive image between a new word and a landmark. Envision an *aardvark* digging at the roots of a tree, a *table* sitting on the sidewalk, a *pencil*-shaped statue in the center of a fountain. To remember the list, you take your mental walk and pick up the words you have linked to each of the landmarks along the walk.
Acronym	Form a word or expression whose letters stand for a certain other word or concept (e.g., U.S.A., IQ, and laser).	To remember the names of these mnemonic devices, use the acronym I AM PACK: **I**nteractive images, **A**cronyms, **M**ethod of loci, **P**egwords, **A**crostics, **C**ategories, and **K**eywords.
Acrostic	Form a sentence rather than a single word to help you remember the new words.	To memorize the notes on lines of the treble clef, music students learn that "**E**very **G**ood **B**oy **D**oes **F**ine."
Keyword system	Form an interactive image that links the sound and meaning of a foreign word with the sound and meaning of a familiar word.	To learn that the French word for *butter* is *beurre*, you might note that beurre sounds like "bear." Next, you would associate the keyword bear with butter in an image or sentence, such as a bear eating a stick of butter. Later, bear would provide a retrieval cue for beurre.

ous tasks that require subjects to remember arbitrary information (e.g., numerals) in different ways. Because this chapter includes many references to these tasks, it is useful to have an *advance organizer*—a basis for organizing the information to be given—so that you will know how memory is studied. The tasks involve recall versus recognition memory, implicit versus explicit memory, and declarative versus procedural memory.

Recall Versus Recognition Tasks

If you were given a task requiring **recall,** you would be asked to produce a fact, a word, or other item from memory. Fill-in-the-blank tests require that you recall items from memory. However, if you were given a task requiring **recognition,** you would have to select or identify an item as being one that you learned previously. Multiple-choice and true-false tests involve recognition. The types of recall tasks used in experiments are serial recall, free recall, and paired-associates recall.

A simple way to assess recall is through a **serial-recall** task, in which you are presented with a list of items, and your job is to repeat the items in the exact order you heard or read them. Occasionally, subjects are asked to repeat the list they heard, but backward, as on the Wechsler intelligence scales (see Chapter 11). Serial recall can be done with other kinds of stimuli besides digits, of course. Frequently, researchers use words or *nonsense syllables*, which are pronounceable but do not spell meaningful words, such as "DAX" or "JAF."

In **free recall,** as in serial recall, you are presented with a list of items and must repeat that list. In free recall, however, you can repeat the items in any order you prefer.

In **paired-associates recall,** you are presented with a list of pairs that may or may not be related. Later, you are tested by being given the first item in each pair. Your job is to repeat the item with which it was paired. For example, if you learn the list of pairs: "TIME–CITY, MIST–HOME, SWITCH–PAPER, CREDIT–DAY, FIST–CLOUD, NUMBER–BRANCH," when you are later given the stimulus "SWITCH," you will be expected to say "PAPER."

In each of these tasks, you need to produce an item from memory. In a **recognition task,** however, the experimenter produces an item, and your job is to indicate whether it is one that you have learned in the context of the experiment. For example, if you receive the list *time, city, mist, home, switch,* you may be asked later if the word *switch* appeared on the list.

Recognition memory is usually much better than recall (although there are some exceptions, which are discussed later). For example, Lionel Standing, Jerry Conezio, and Ralph Haber (1970) found that subjects could recognize close to 2,000 pictures in a recognition-memory task.

Recall from Chapter 7 the discussion of the relationship between learning and performance. Your performance on a memory task would often seem to indicate different levels of learning, depending on whether you were asked to recall or simply to recognize what you had learned. (For this reason, you may prefer multiple-choice over fill-in-the-blank questions when you are less confident of your knowledge in a particular subject.) Some believe that recognition memory requires *receptive* knowledge and that recall memory requires *expressive* knowledge. Differences between receptive and expressive knowledge also are observed in areas other than simple memory tasks. Chapter 9 notes how our receptive knowledge of language exceeds our expressive knowledge of it. Chapters 10, 11, and 12 describe other learning-performance distinctions as they relate to other aspects of thinking, intelligence, and cognitive development.

Implicit Versus Explicit Memory Tasks

Each of the preceding tasks involves **explicit memory,** in which subjects are asked to make a conscious recollection—to recall or recognize words from a particular prior list. Psychologists also find it useful to understand phenomena of **implicit memory** (Graf & Schachter, 1985), which involves unconscious recollection of information. Every day, you engage in many tasks that involve your unconscious recollection of information. Even as you read this book, you are unconsciously remembering the meanings of particlar words, some of the psychological concepts you read about in earlier chapters, and even how to read. In the laboratory, experimenters sometimes study implicit memory by studying people's performance on word-completion tasks, which involve implicit memory. In a word-completion task, the subject is presented with a word fragment, such as the first three letters of a word, and is asked to complete it with the first word that comes to mind.

For example, suppose that you were asked to supply the missing five letters to fill these blanks and form a word: imp_ _ _ _ _. Because you had recently seen the word *implicit*, you would be more likely to provide the five letters l-i-c-i-t for the blanks than would someone who had not recently been exposed to the word. In general, subjects perform better when the word is one they have seen on a recently presented list, even though they have not been explicitly instructed to remember words from that list. In fact, even amnesia victims, who perform extremely poorly on most memory tasks, show normal or almost

Searchers . . .   *ENDEL TULVING*

Endel Tulving is Tanenbaum Chair of Cognitive Neuroscience at the Rotman Research Institute of Baycrest Center, Ontario. He is also Professor Emeritus at the University of Toronto.

Q: *How did you become interested in psychology?*

A: I decided in high school that psychology was the only science that had some unsolved problems in it. I always liked problems and puzzles.

Q: *What ideas have influenced you the most?*

A: I've been rather eclectic. I liked the Gestalt view of things; when I was introduced to it as an undergraduate, it made sense to me. Later on, when information processing ideas and information theory appeared on the scene, I thought that was pretty neat too. George Miller was doing very interesting work. I was influenced by Smitty Stevens, too, in terms of his general attitude toward science—very professional and very profound.

Q: *How do you usually get your ideas for research?*

A: They just occur. I listen to, see, or read something, and immediately it makes contact with something that I already know. It's like a piece of a jigsaw puzzle fitting into what is already there, but it's automatic and, essentially, nonconscious.

Q: *How do you decide whether to pursue an idea?*

A: Well, I go purely by intuition. I decide whether it is important or interesting, in which case I drop everything and start pursuing it. Or I say, well it's interesting but not interesting enough to displace what I'm doing now, so I write it down, put it into my idea file, or suggest it to somebody else.

Q: *What obstacles have you experienced, and what strategies have you used to overcome them?*

A: Nothing profound. I mean, theoretical obstacles are those having to do with our ignorance about how nature works. You live with the uncertainty of nature, or things that we do not yet understand, and our current limitations. I wouldn't call it an obstacle. It's simply normal life, a normal state of affairs. Practical obstacles are essentially lack of time. Nothing other than that.

Q: *What is your major contribution to psychology?*

A: I am one of the people who have tried to work out methods of studying the interaction between storage and retrieval processes. Also, I have been busy for the last 25 years with the concept of multiple memory systems, dividing long-term memory into episodic and semantic forms.

Q: *What do you want your students to learn?*

A: I want them to be skeptical and keep an open mind about anything they hear. Be independent in their thinking, too. Try to create, not follow, fads, if they can. Don't give up. Mostly, work very hard, and think common sense. Don't trace after irrelevancies and trivia. Always try to establish what the substance of a problem is, and stick with that.

Q: *What did you learn from your mentors?*

A: Dedication. They worked very hard, and I was impressed by that. Also, doing research, thinking scientifically, writing papers, giving lectures, or talking about things that you're interested in are high-level skills. And there's just no way that one can expect to be able to acquire the skill just in a year or two. It takes many, many years. One should not be frustrated at the beginning; it's just practice, practice, practice and hard work.

Q: *Apart from your life as an academic, how have you found psychology to be important?*

A: Not psychology, as such, but the scientific method that is embodied in psychology. I try to treat any problem like a scientific problem. First of all, I define it as clearly, precisely, and concisely as I can. Exactly what is the problem? Then I ask, Is there any relevant evidence out there? If so, what is it? Why do I think it's relevant?

Q: *How do you keep yourself academically challenged?*

A: I always look for new things to do, look into a new field that I know nothing about and see what I can make of it. Right now, I'm into PET scans. I know a little bit more now than I knew last year. And I'll know, again, a little bit more a year from now.

Q: *What would you like people to remember about you?*

A: If I'm dead, I don't care one bit. But I'd be a liar if I said I don't care what people think of my work [while I'm still alive]. I care very much. I want them to listen to it and argue with me. Agree with me or point out my errors so they can do better thinking or find a better way.

---

normal performance on word-completion tasks (Baddeley, 1989). When asked whether they have previously seen the word they just completed, however, they are unlikely to remember the specific experience of having seen the word.

Procedural Versus Declarative Knowledge

Amnesia victims also show paradoxical performance in tasks that involve **procedural knowledge** (knowing-how—skills, such as how to ride a bicycle) versus those that involve **declarative knowledge** (knowing-that—factual information, such as the terms in a psychology textbook). For example, amnesia victims may perform extremely poorly on traditional memory tasks requiring recall or recognition memory of declarative knowledge. However, they may demonstrate improvement in performance due to learning—remembered practice—when engaged in tasks that require procedural knowledge, such as solving puzzles, learning to read mirror writing, or mastering motor skills (Baddeley, 1989).

Psychologists study amnesia patients in part to gain insight into memory function in general. One of the general insights gained by studying amnesia victims who perform tasks involving procedural memory and implicit memory (e.g., on word-completion tasks) is that the ability to reflect consciously on prior experience, which is required for tasks involving explicit memory of declarative knowledge, seems to differ from the ability to demonstrate remembered learning in an apparently automatic way, without conscious recollection of the learning (Baddeley, 1989).

What is the value of having implicit memory? Wouldn't it be better if we could remember everything explicitly? Explain why implicit memory is or is not distinctly beneficial.

TYPES OF MEMORY

IN SEARCH OF...

What processes and structures underlie both the extraordinary memory deficits of H. M. and other amnesics and the exceptional memories of S. and other mnemonists? How do psychologists conceptualize these psychological processes and structures?

To understand why amnesics have extraordinary difficulties with memory and why mnemonists do not,

Learning to tie shoes and to ride a bicycle requires the encoding, storage, and retrieval of procedural knowledge. Prior to storing this knowledge, both the girl and the boy must work hard to try to remember how to move their muscles in the right ways at the right times. With a little rehearsal, however, both children will master these skills so well that they will be able to remember them the rest of their lives.

it is necessary to understand different types of memory, as well as how information is placed into, retained in, and later extracted from memory.

In previous chapters, we have seen how different psychologists interpret identical data in different ways. Memory is an area in which what we know can be interpreted in more than one way. The core differences among the alternative views center on the metaphor used for conceptualizing memory (Roediger, 1980). Metaphors often serve an important function in organizing ideas, aiding researchers to conceptualize a phenomenon well enough to investigate it. As the research progresses, the metaphor may be modified to accommodate new data, or other researchers may propose alternative metaphors. The prevailing metaphor in psychology was originally proposed by Richard Atkinson and Richard Shiffrin (1968), who conceptualized memory in terms of three memory stores: (1) a brief, fleeting sensory memory; (2) a somewhat larger but still very limited store of actively conscious memory; and (3) a store of information that is of virtually limitless capacity, which requires effective retrieval to bring it into active memory. This model is not the only way to conceptualize memory, but variants of the Atkinson-Shiffrin model are still commonly used by psychologists.

How might a given metaphor or model help scientists understand phenomena more clearly? How might such a model limit their understanding of phenomena?

Three Memory Stores

Memory theorists often distinguish among three different memory stores: (1) the **sensory store,** which stores relatively limited amounts of information for very brief periods of time; (2) the **short-term store,** or short-term memory (STM), which stores information for somewhat longer periods of time but is also of relatively limited capacity; and (3) the **long-term store,** or long-term memory (LTM), which has a large capacity and is capable of storing information for very long periods of time, perhaps even indefinitely. These three stores are not distinct physiological structures; rather, they are hypothetical constructs embracing sets of processes. Figure 8-1 shows a simple information-processing model of these stores, which typifies models proposed in the 1960s and 1970s (e.g., Atkinson & Shiffrin, 1971).

What aspect of your own memory do you find puzzling? How would the study of this phenomenon fit into the Atkinson-Shiffrin model?

Three Operations: Encoding, Storage, and Retrieval

All three stores process information similarly; they encode, store, and retrieve it. Each operation represents a stage in memory processing. **Encoding** refers to how we transform a physical, sensory input into a kind of representation that can be placed into

FIGURE 8-1
The Three-Stores View
In Richard Atkinson and Richard Shiffrin's model of memory, information flows from sensory to short-term to long-term memory stores. Their metaphor for memory long served as the basis for research on memory processes. (After Atkinson & Shiffrin, 1971)

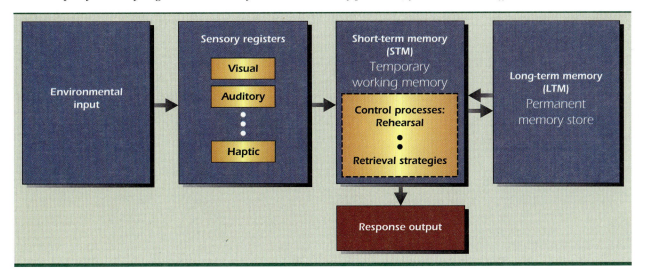

memory. **Storage** refers to how we retain encoded information in memory. **Retrieval** refers to how we gain access to information in a memory store. Encoding, storage, and retrieval are sequential stages, whereby we first take in information, then hold it for a while, and later pull it out. However, the processes interact with each other and are interdependent.

The three stages of memory can be illustrated with reference to the object pictured in Figure 8-2. Suppose that you see a photo of this animal while you are leafing through a magazine. You are in a hurry and do not have time to read the accompanying article. You do not know what the animal is and, as a result, find the creature difficult to fathom. Later, you go back to the magazine and learn that the animal is a large African mammal that feeds on ants and termites: an *aardvark*. You have heard of this animal before but have never actually seen one, either in life or in a picture. Now, knowing what the animal is, you find yourself encoding features in the picture, such as the animal's powerful claws, large ears, and heavy tail. You also encode the animal's name, as well as an image of what it looks like. Although you do not make any particular effort to remember what an aardvark looks like, the visual information has been stored in your memory because the verbal label has made it meaningful to you. Several years later, on a visit to a zoo, you see an animal and immediately recognize it as an aardvark. You have retrieved from memory the representation you stored earlier without even being fully aware you were doing so.

The example of the aardvark illustrates an interesting property of memory—namely, that having a verbal label (such as a name) to attach to something can often help us make sense of that something, even though it is, indeed, only a label. In this case, the verbal label helped us organize information about an animal shown in a picture. Verbal labels also can help us encode, store, and retrieve information that is presented in text. Consider, for example, the following passage from an experiment by John Bransford and Marcia Johnson (1972; cited in Bransford, 1979, pp. 134–135):

> The procedure is actually quite simple. First you arrange items into different groups. Of course one pile may be sufficient depending on how much there is to do. If you have to go somewhere else due to lack of facilities that is the next step; otherwise, you are pretty well set. It is important not to overdo things. That is, it is better to do too few things at once than too many. In the short run this may not seem important but complications can easily arise. A mistake can be expensive as well. At first, the whole procedure will seem complicated. Soon, however, it will become just another facet of life. It is difficult to foresee any end to the necessity for this task in the immediate future, but then, one can never tell. After the procedure is completed one arranges the materials into different groups again. Then they can be put into their appropriate places. Eventually they will be used once more and the whole cycle will then have to be repeated. However, that is part of life.

Bransford and Johnson's subjects had a great deal of difficulty understanding this passage and recalling the steps involved. It is difficult to encode the information and therefore to store and retrieve it. However, a verbal label can facilitate encoding, and hence storage and retrieval. Subjects do much better with the passage if given its title, "Washing Clothes." The verbal label helps us to encode, and therefore to remember, a passage that otherwise seems incomprehensible. Now that we have mapped out an overview of memory processes and of the three memory stores, we can more deeply probe each memory store, starting with the sensory store.

FIGURE 8-2

THE SENSORY STORE

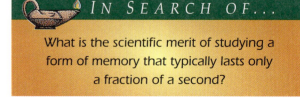

IN SEARCH OF...

What is the scientific merit of studying a form of memory that typically lasts only a fraction of a second?

Icons capture an entire idea in a single image. What ideas are being conveyed by these icons?

The sensory store, which is the initial repository of much information that eventually enters the short- and long-term stores, may take two forms: the iconic store and the echoic store.

Excellent evidence (Sperling, 1960) indicates the existence of a discrete visual sensory register, or **iconic store** (so called because information is believed to be stored in the form of *icons*, visual images that represent something).

If you have ever "written" your name with a lighted sparkler on the Fourth of July, you have experienced the persistence of a visual memory; that is, you briefly "see" your name, even though the sparkler leaves no physical trace. This *visual persistence* is an example of the type of information held in the iconic store.

Visual information appears to enter our memory system through an iconic store that holds the visual information for very short periods of time. In the normal course of events, this information may be either transferred to another store or erased if other information is superimposed on it before there is sufficient time for the transfer of the information to another memory store.

Until recently, many psychologists were fairly convinced of the existence of an auditory **echoic store** roughly analogous to the iconic one (Darwin, Turvey, & Crowder, 1972). The echoic store was believed to do for hearing what the iconic store does for vision. However, there is now some question as to whether such a store exists, and if so, as to what form it takes (Greene & Crowder, 1984; Spoehr & Corin, 1978).

THE SHORT-TERM STORE

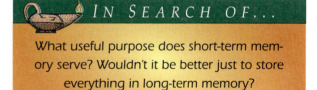

IN SEARCH OF...

What useful purpose does short-term memory serve? Wouldn't it be better just to store everything in long-term memory?

Our short-term memory stores hold information for matters of seconds and, occasionally, up to a minute or two. When you look up a phone number in the phone book and try to remember it long enough to dial, you are using the short-term store. Why do we forget such simple information so easily, and how can we keep ourselves from forgetting it? In discussing the short-term store, we consider next the encoding, storage, and retrieval of information.

Encoding of Information

When you encode information into short-term memory, what kind of code do you use? A landmark experiment by R. Conrad (1964) successfully addressed this question. Conrad presented subjects visually with several series of six letters at the rate of 0.75 seconds per letter. The letters used in the various lists were B, C, F, M, N, P, S, T, V, and X. Subjects had to write down each list of six letters, in the order given, immediately after the letters were presented. Conrad was interested particularly in the kinds of recall errors subjects made. The pattern of errors was clear. Despite the fact that letters were presented *visually*, errors tended to be based on *acoustic confusability*. In other words, instead of recalling the letters they were supposed to recall, subjects substituted letters that sounded like the correct letters. Thus, they were likely to confuse F for S, T for C, B for V, P for B, and so on. In an experiment based on acoustically similar and dissimilar words versus semantically similar and dissimilar words, Alan Baddeley (1966) clinched the argument that short-term storage relies primarily on an acoustic rather than a *semantic code* (one based on word meaning).

Storage and Forgetting

Why does information retained in the short-term store not remain there indefinitely? How do we keep it in, and how do we lose it? We consider in turn what we know about the answers to each of these questions.

How We Retain Information

Although psychologists may disagree about how we forget information from the short-term store, they have reached fairly widespread consensus as to how we retain it. The key technique we use for keeping information in storage is **rehearsal,** which is the re-

Short-term memory is fickle and fleeting. The man in the center booth just looked up a phone number, dialed the number, got a busy signal, and then had to look up the number again because within the few seconds it took him to dial and wait for someone to answer, he forgot the number. Has that ever happened to you?

peated recitation of an item. (Rehearsal is also involved in transferring information into long-term memory, which we discuss later in this chapter.)

Rehearsal comes naturally to almost all of us as adults—so much so that we may take for granted that we have always done it. We have not. The major difference between the memory of younger and older children (as well as adults) is not in basic mechanisms, but in learned strategies, such as rehearsal (Flavell & Wellman, 1977). In particular, younger children lack *metamemory* skills—that is, knowledge and understanding of their own memory abilities. Metamemory and other aspects of *metacognition* (thoughts involving the use of strategies and skills to enhance our thought processes) are discussed further in Chapters 10, 11, 12. The various mnemonic devices, described earlier in this chapter, also may be viewed as metamemory strategies. Older children understand that to retain words in the short-term store they need to rehearse; younger children do not understand this fact. Another consideration is that for rehearsal to be effective, the person must be actively engaged in the process of trying to encode and store the information; mere repeated exposure to words does not constitute rehearsal (Tulving, 1966).

How We Forget Information

Why do we forget a phone number or the names of people at a party after a brief period of time? Several theories have been proposed as to why we forget information from the short-term store. The two most well-known theories are *interference theory* and *decay theory*. **Interference** refers to competing information causing us to forget something; **decay** refers simply to the passage of time causing us to forget.

INTERFERENCE THEORY.   One of the most famous experimental paradigms is called the Brown-Peterson paradigm, after its originators, John Brown (1958) and Lloyd Peterson and Margaret Peterson (1959). Their work is an example of *independent discovery*, whereby two scientists or groups of scientists make the same discovery independently and roughly at the same time (Merton, 1973). Both the Brown and the Peterson and Peterson studies were taken as evidence for the existence of a short-term store and also for the **interference theory** of forgetting, according to which forgetting occurs because new information interferes with, and ultimately displaces, old information in the short-term store. Consider the experiment of Peterson and Peterson (1959).

The Petersons asked their subjects to recall *trigrams* (strings of three letters) at intervals of 3, 6, 9,

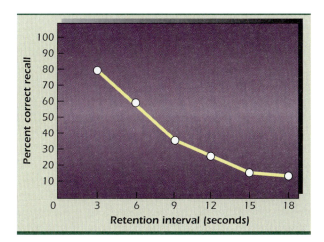

FIGURE 8-3
Percentage of Recall from Short-Term Memory
In the study by Lloyd Peterson and Margaret Peterson, subjects were unable to use rehearsal to keep information in short-term memory. As a consequence, their ability to recall three consonants (a trigram) rapidly declined as the delay between presentation and recall increased from 3 to 18 seconds. Some have suggested that retroactive interference may have caused the rapid decline in recall.

12, 15, or 18 seconds after the presentation of the last letter. The Petersons used only consonants, so that the trigrams would not be easily pronounceable—for example, "K B F." Figure 8-3 shows percentages of correct recalls after the various intervals of time. Why does recall decline so rapidly? Because after the oral presentation of each trigram, the Petersons asked their subjects to count backward by threes from a three-digit number spoken immediately after the trigram. The purpose of having the subjects count backward was to prevent them from rehearsing during the *retention interval*—the time between the presentation of the last letter and the start of the recall phase of the experimental trial. Clearly, the trigram is almost completely forgotten after just 18 seconds if subjects are not allowed to rehearse it.

At least two kinds of interference figure prominently in memory theory and research: retroactive interference and proactive interference. **Retroactive interference** (or retroactive inhibition) is caused by activity occurring *after* we learn something, but before we are asked to recall that thing. The interference in the Brown-Peterson task appears to be retroactive because counting backward by threes occurs after learning of the trigram; it interferes with our ability to remember information that we learned previously.

Proactive interference (or proactive inhibition) occurs when the interfering material *precedes*

the to-be-remembered material. Does proactive interference actually operate in forgetting of material stored in the short-term store? A study conducted by Geoffrey Keppel and Benton Underwood (1962) suggests that it does. Indeed, Keppel and Underwood argued that forgetting in the Brown-Peterson paradigm is due to proactive rather than to retroactive interference.

This interpretation may seem counterintuitive at first, but suppose that interference in the Brown-Peterson paradigm was indeed proactive—that is, the trigrams learned earlier interfered with subjects' ability to remember later trigrams. Then we would make two predictions based on two characteristics of proactive interference. First, level of retention should be lower to the extent that the number of syllables previously tested is higher. In other words, the more prior material learned, the greater the extent of the interference. Keppel and Underwood indeed found that there was almost no forgetting when the subjects did not have any previous syllables to remember; further, as the number of trigrams tested increased, the subjects' ability to recall the trigrams decreased (see Figure 8-4). Second, the increase in forgetting as a function of the number of syllables previously learned should be greater for longer retention intervals than for shorter ones. This was found to be the case. The degree to which the subjects forgot as a function of the number of items previously tested was greater

FIGURE 8-4
Proactive Interference and Short-Term Memory
Geoffrey Keppel and Benton Underwood demonstrated that proactive interference also affects recall, as shown by the decline in recall after increasing numbers of trigrams were presented. The effect of proactive interference increased over increasingly long retention intervals.

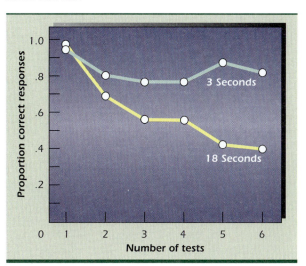

at the 18-second retention interval than at the 3-second retention interval. The Keppel and Underwood study, therefore, clearly suggests that proactive interference is operating in the Brown-Peterson paradigm.

Subsequent experiments, however, have suggested that retroactive interference may also play a part in forgetting (e.g., Reitman, 1971; Shiffrin, 1973; Waugh & Norman, 1965). This sequence of events illustrates that few issues are conclusively resolved.

This sequence also brings to mind the dialectical progression discussed in previous chapters. Like other kinds of knowledge, psychological theory and research often proceed in this fashion (see Kalmar & Sternberg, 1988). Hence, proactive and retroactive interference (thesis and antithesis) are now viewed as complementary phenomena (synthesis). To take this process one step further, an antithesis to interference theory itself is decay theory.

> Give an example of a task (comprising several steps) that would involve both proactive and retroactive interference. Explain how the two types of interference would serve in complementary roles.

DECAY THEORY.   **Decay theory** asserts that information is forgotten because of the gradual disappearance, rather than displacement, of the trace. Thus, whereas interference theory views one piece of information as knocking out another, decay theory views the original piece of information as gradually disappearing unless something is done to keep it intact.

Decay theory is exceedingly difficult to test because it is difficult to prevent subjects from intentionally or even inadvertently rehearsing—and thereby maintaining in memory the given information. However, if subjects are prevented from rehearsing, the possibility of interference arises: The task used to prevent rehearsal may interfere retroactively with the original memory (Reitman, 1971, 1974). Try, for example, not to think of white elephants as you read the next page. When instructed not to think about them, it is actually quite difficult not to, even if you try to follow the instructions.

> Is memory decay a real psychological phenomenon? How can researchers rule out the effects of retroactive interference, while also ruling out the effects of unconscious or at least unintentional rehearsal?

To conclude, evidence exists for both interference and decay in the short-term store. The evidence for decay is not airtight, but it is certainly suggestive. The evidence of interference is rather strong, but at present, it is unclear as to the extent to which the interference is retroactive, proactive, or both.

The Capacity of the Short-Term Store

How much information can we hold in the short-term store? How would we even know how much information can be held? In a classic paper, George Miller (1956) noted that our short-term memory capacity appears to be about 7 items, plus or minus 2. An item can be something simple such as a digit, or something more complex, such as a word. If we **chunk** together a string of, say, 20 letters or numbers into 7 meaningful items, we can remember them, whereas we could not remember 20 items and repeat them immediately. For example, we could not hold in short-term memory this string of 21 numbers: 101001000100001000100. However, if we chunked it into larger units, such as 10, 100, 1000, 10000, 1000, and 100, we would be able to reproduce easily the 21 numerals as six items.

Of course, as the preceding discussion has suggested, our seven-item capacity can be limited still further by any delay or any interference in recall. Cognitive psychologists have sought a way to measure the degree to which delay and interference may limit this seven-item capacity. One method for estimating the capacity of the short-term store under delay or interference conditions involves inferences from a **serial-position curve,** which represents the probability of recall of a given word, given its *serial position* (order of presentation) in a list.

Suppose you are presented with a list of words and are asked to recall them. You might even try it on yourself. Say the following list of words once to yourself, and then, immediately thereafter, try to recall all the words in any order, without looking back at them: table, cloud, book, tree, shirt, cat, light, bench, chalk. If you are like most people, you will find that your recall of words is best for items at and near the end of the list, second best for items near the beginning of the list, and poorest for items in the middle of the list. An idealized serial-position curve is shown in Figure 8-5.

Superior recall of words at and near the end of the list is a **recency effect.** Superior recall of words at and near the beginning of the list is a **primacy effect.** Recall of words from the beginning and middle of the list is due primarily to the effects of the long-term store, considered later in this chapter, and recall of words from the end of the list is due primarily to the

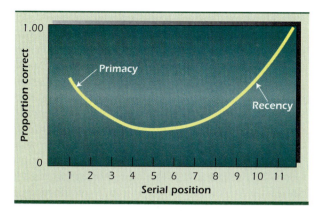

FIGURE 8-5
Idealized Serial-Position Curve
Most people recall items at the end of a list (greatest recall) and at the beginning of a list (second-greatest recall) much more easily than items in the middle of a list (least recall).

effects of the short-term store. The recency effect is due to the subjects' dumping out the contents of their short-term store just as soon as they are given the signal to recall. The serial-position curve, incidentally, makes sense in terms of interference theory. Words at the end of the list are subject to proactive but not to retroactive interference; words at the beginning of the list are subject to retroactive but not to proactive interference; and words in the middle of the list are subject to both. Thus, recall would be expected to be poorest in the middle of the list, as indeed it is.

Another way of broadening our understanding of short-term memory is to consider also the cultural contexts within which people are immersed. For example, Rumjahn Hoosain and others have shown that Hong Kong undergraduates have a mean digit span (number of numerals that can be stored in short-term memory) of 9.9, a little over 2 digits more than the span reported for speakers of several Western languages. Before we infer any far-reaching conclusions regarding the arithmetic abilities of Asians, however, it may be important to consider an artifact of the Chinese language. Readers can read numerals more quickly in Mandarin than in German, for example, and speakers can pronounce numbers in Cantonese more rapidly than in English (Bond, 1986; Hoosain & Salili, 1987). The linguistic differences may affect encoding.

Retrieval

No Passenger was known to flee—
That lodged a night in memory—
That wily—subterranean Inn
Contrives that none go out again—

—Emily Dickinson, Poem 1406

Once we encode and store information in the short-term store, how do we retrieve that information? A classic series of experiments on this issue was done by Saul Sternberg (1966). The phenomenon he studied is short-term **memory scanning,** whereby we check the contents of our short-term memories.

Sternberg's basic paradigm was simple. He gave subjects a short list containing from one to six digits that he expected subjects to be able to hold in short-term storage. After a brief pause, a test digit was flashed on a screen, and subjects had to say whether this digit had appeared in the set they had been asked to memorize.

The idea of an information-processing model is to specify the stages of processing a subject must go through from start to finish when undertaking a task such as the one Sternberg proposed. Psychologists studying retrieval from the short-term memory store wondered whether items are retrieved all at once (parallel processing) or sequentially (serial processing). If we retrieve the items serially, the question then arises, do we retrieve all of the items, regardless of the task, or do we stop retrieving items as soon as an item seems to accomplish the task?

Parallel processing refers to multiple operations being done simultaneously, so that the items stored in short-term memory would be retrieved all at once, not one at a time. The prediction in Line A of Figure 8-6 shows what would happen if parallel processing were being used in Sternberg's task involving the recall of digits. Response times should be the same, regardless of the size of the positive set, because all comparisons are being done at once. In other words, it is no more time consuming to retrieve four digits than two, because in each case, all digits are being accessed at once.

Serial processing refers to operations being done one after another; on the digit-recall task, the digits would be retrieved in succession, rather than all at once. According to the serial model, it should take longer to retrieve four digits than to retrieve two digits (as shown in Line B of Figure 8-6). Nonetheless, it will not necessarily take twice as long to do so because some processes (e.g., starting the retrieval process and making the overt response) take a constant amount of time, regardless of how many digits are retrieved.

If information processing is serial, then there are two ways to gain access to the stimuli: exhaustive or self-terminating processing. **Exhaustive serial processing** implies that the subject always checks the test digit against *all* digits in the positive set, even if a match is found partway through the list. Exhaustive processing would predict the pattern of data shown in Line C of Figure 8-6. Note that positive responses all

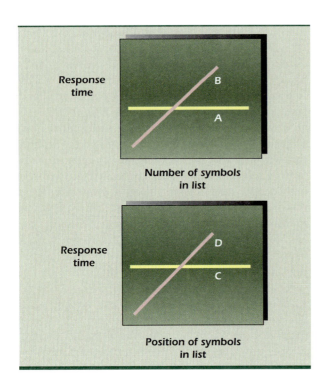

FIGURE 8-6
Retrieval from Short-Term Memory
Saul Sternberg's memory-scanning task suggested that retrieval probably occurs through exhaustive serial processing (Lines B and C).

take the same amount of time, regardless of the serial position of a positive test probe. In other words, in an exhaustive search, you will take the same amount of time to find a digit, regardless of where in the list it is located.

Self-terminating serial processing implies that the subject checks the test digit against only those digits that are needed in order to make a response. Line D shows that response time now increases linearly as a function of where a test digit is located in the positive set. The later the serial position, the longer the response time.

When Sternberg actually looked at the data, the pattern was crystal clear. The data looked like the data in Lines B and C of Figure 8-6. Response times increased linearly with set size but were the same regardless of serial position. Later, Sternberg (1969) replicated this pattern of data. Moreover, the statistical means for the positive and negative responses were essentially the same, further supporting the exhaustive model. Sternberg (1966) found that comparisons took roughly 38 milliseconds (0.038 seconds) apiece.

It is always delightful when a set of data comes out as cleanly and as unequivocally as Saul Sternberg's

did. However, few psychological questions are decided unequivocally, and this set of findings is no exception. For example, James Townsend (1971) and other investigators have proposed alternative interpretations of Sternberg's data, one of which shows a way to use parallel processing and self-terminating strategies to explain the data. For example, a parallel model could yield set-length effects such as Sternberg obtained if we imagined a parallel model analogous to a horse race, in which the slowest horse determines how long the race takes. The more horses (or items in Sternberg's task), the longer the race (memory scan) will take.

The key is that although Sternberg did not take into account all of the possible explanations for his data or all the results that might be obtained for various possible kinds of stimuli, the value of his work is judged in guiding future research. By this criterion, Sternberg's paradigm has been among the most important in all of psychology. No initial study or even set of studies is going to reveal all of the limits of a phenomenon.

Just as psychologists view short-term memory processes from alternative perspectives, they also view long-term memory from more than one viewpoint. The view presented next is the more traditional perspective, and the research on long-term memory is presented in light of this viewpoint. Later in this chapter, however, an alternative way to view long-term memory is also presented.

THE LONG-TERM STORE

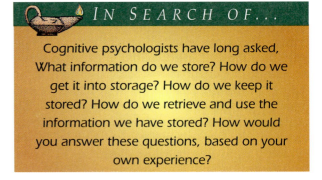

I N   S E A R C H   O F . . .

Cognitive psychologists have long asked, What information do we store? How do we get it into storage? How do we keep it stored? How do we retrieve and use the information we have stored? How would you answer these questions, based on your own experience?

When we talk about memory in our everyday interactions, we are usually talking about the long-term store, which is where we keep memories that stay with us over long periods of time, sometimes indefinitely. How does information get from the short-term store to the long-term store? One method is through rehearsal of information. Another is by

Once we have stored information in long-term memory, that information can be recalled again many years later. Through long-term memory, this grandfather can vividly describe many of his childhood experiences to his grandson, such as the hardships he faced when he had to walk 10 miles uphill to school.

deliberately attending to information to understand it. Perhaps an even more important way that we accomplish this transfer is by making connections or associations between the new information and what we already know and understand, by integrating the new data into our existing stored information.

Encoding of Information

Forms of Encoding

Information in the long-term store seems to be primarily *semantically encoded*—that is, encoded by the meanings of words. However, we can also hold visual and acoustic information in the long-term store.

One way to show semantic encoding is to use test words that bear a semantic relationship to other test words. Weston Bousfield (1953), for example, had subjects learn a list of 60 words that included 15 animals, 15 professions, 15 vegetables, and 15 names of people. The words were presented in a random order, so that members of the various categories were thoroughly intermixed. After subjects heard the words, they were asked to recall the items in any order they wished. Bousfield then analyzed the order of output of the recalled words. The subjects recalled successive words from the same category more frequently than would be expected by chance. It thus appears that subjects were remembering words by grouping them into categories.

Encoding of information also can be achieved visually. Nancy Frost (1972), for example, presented subjects with 16 drawings of objects, including 4

items of clothing, 4 animals, 4 vehicles, and 4 items of furniture. Frost manipulated not only the semantic category, but also the visual category. The drawings differed in visual orientation, with four angled to the left, four angled to the right, four horizontal, and four vertical. Items were presented in random order, and subjects had to recall them freely. Subjects' output orders showed effects of both semantic and visual categories, suggesting that subjects were encoding visual as well as semantic information.

Even acoustic information can be encoded in the long-term store (Nelson & Rothbart, 1972). The picture that emerges from these data, therefore, is one of considerable flexibility in the way we store information. Under what circumstances do we use each form of encoding?

Circumstances of Encoding

Allan Paivio (1971, 1986) believes that we store memories both verbally and visually in ways that are complementary. The form of representation used depends on both the form of presentation (verbal or nonverbal) and the imagery value of the stimuli to be remembered. Some words are highly concrete and also high in imagery value, such as *bluejay*, *lemon*, *radio*, and *pencil*. They lend themselves to visual representation, even if presented verbally. In contrast, words such as *truth*, *kindness*, and *joy* are less likely to be stored visually, simply because we have no images that we more or less uniformly associate with these words. (Recall Luria's mnemonist, S., had difficulty remembering such concepts, given his orientation toward visual encoding.)

According to John Anderson and Gordon Bower, these children may be encoding these pictures at a propositional level, not as specific images or as specific verbal statements about these images.

What about the meaning underlying a relationship among concepts? John Anderson and Gordon Bower (1973) posed a **propositional** view in which both images and verbal statements are stored in terms of their *deep meanings*—that is, as propositions, not as specific images or statements. Herbert Clark and William Chase (1972) proposed a fairly simple model of how both the verbal form of the statement and pictorial form could be encoded into propositional form. Colin MacLeod, Earl Hunt, and Nancy Mathews (1978) obtained persuasive evidence suggesting that subjects can use either a propositional or an imaginal representation.

Stephen Kosslyn has done a number of experiments to demonstrate the use of imaginal representations in memory. In one of the more interesting experiments (Kosslyn, Ball, & Reiser, 1978), subjects were shown a map of an imaginary island, which you can see in Figure 8-7. Subjects studied the map until they could reproduce it accurately from memory, placing the locations of each of the six objects in the map no more than a quarter of an inch from their correct locations. Once the memorization phase of the experiment was completed, the critical phase began.

FIGURE 8-8
Image Size
Stephen Kosslyn's subjects tested the limits of their mental imagery by picturing the rabbit with the honeybee and then imagining the rabbit with the elephant. When picturing the rabbit and the bee, subjects had to zoom in to see details of the honeybee. When picturing the rabbit and the elephant, the image of the elephant overflowed their mental image space as they imagined approaching it.

FIGURE 8-7
Image-Based Encoding in Long-Term Memory
This map of an imaginary island shows six objects, such as a hut, a tree, and a lake. Subjects learned to draw such maps from memory, accurately placing each of the six objects within 1/4 inch of their correct locations.

Subjects were instructed that, upon hearing the name of an object read to them, they should picture the map, mentally scan directly to the mentioned object, and press a key as soon as they arrived at the location of the named object. This procedure was repeated a number of times, with the subjects mentally moving between various pairs of objects on successive trials. The experimenter kept track of response times on each trial—how long it took. There was an almost perfect linear relation between the distance between successive pairs of objects in the mental map and the amount of time it took subjects to press the button. In other words, subjects seem to have encoded the map in the form of an image and actually to have scanned that image as needed.

Kosslyn (Kosslyn & Koenig, 1992) has also found some intriguing effects of image size. Look at the rabbit and the honeybee in Figure 8-8. Now close your eyes and picture them both in your mind. Now imagine only the honeybee and determine the color of its head. Do you notice yourself having to take time to zoom in to "see" the detailed features of the honeybee? Now look at the rabbit and the elephant and picture them both in your mind. Now close your eyes and look only at the elephant. Imagine walking toward the elephant, watching it as it gets closer to

Searchers . . .   *GORDON BOWER*

Gordon Bower is Professor of Psychology at Stanford University.

Q: *How did you become interested in psychology in general and in your area of work in particular?*

A: I was impressed by a high school teacher who was very interested in the social sciences and in psychiatry. I found the whole area fascinating to hear and talk about. By the time I was a freshman in college, I had gone through much of Freud's collected works. In my junior year I became convinced that what was needed in psychology was more experimental method and a bit less clinical intuition. I dropped my idea of becoming a psychoanalyst or psychiatrist and decided to get a PhD in experimental psychology. I also became very interested in philosophy of science and methodology.

Q: *Whose ideas have influenced you the most?*

A: During my graduate career I worked with Neal Miller and Frank Logan, who was a very dedicated Hullian (following Clark Hull). Frank and Neal were immensely impressive intellects to me, and still are. I was fortunate to have been exposed to the work of Bill Estes, Bob Bush, and Fred Mosteller. Estes and Bush gave me a heavy dose of mathematical models in psychology. Estes and I long ago started a dialogue that has continued to this day. Bill, I would say, has been my continuing intellectual colleague. I get tremendous inspiration from listening and talking to him. I learned from him both rigor and what constitutes an interesting explanation of a phenomenon.

Q: *What is your greatest asset as a psychologist?*

A: My persistence at working. I don't have any particular sources of insights, although I try to read widely, especially in artificial intelligence. I just tend to work long hours.

Q: *How do you get your ideas for research?*

A: Taking someone else's ideas and making variations on them or taking findings in one research area and applying them to analogous situations in another area.

Q: *What obstacles have you experienced and how have you overcome them?*

A: Hitting a dry spell in ideas or in motivation, or wondering why I'm bothering with a project that is doing

nothing for the human race. But there are various things I can do to get out of it. One way is to think about the students; another is to read autobiographies of scientists, who all speak of dry spells; it's nice to know that other people have been through it.

Q: *What do you want students to learn from you?*

A: How to make experimental arguments. How to sharpen an idea or decide what is a researchable idea and to produce an experimental test of it. I try to teach them that science is largely a social enterprise, as well as an intellectual one—that is, it is important to get to know the people who are working on topics similar to yours, and treat them as friends and colleagues regardless of where they are.

Q: *What have you learned from your students?*

A: To give intellectual guidance along with moral and psychological support when it's needed and to stand out of the way when it's not. Also, I try to teach students to discriminate between what's a valid criticism, and what isn't.

Q: *What advice would you give to someone starting out in the field of psychology?*

A: The life of a research professor at a research university is one of the best jobs in the world you can have. It's an interesting life and you can change what you do at a drop of a hat. And you get to work with very bright, energetic, and curious people. So it is a great life. I would strongly recommend it to anybody who is thinking about going into it.

Q: *What do you further hope to achieve or contribute?*

A: I am doing research on the way people construct mental models of situations described in texts. This is the age-old question of what knowledge people extract from text and how they do so. I'm continuing research on this fascinating process. I'm also heading a large task force on review of basic behavioral sciences at the National Institute of Mental Health. John Kihlstrom and I are putting together a report to influence policy makers in Washington, D.C., to increase or at least not drastically cut funding of psychosocial and behavior research. The field as a whole should benefit from the report. Other than that I'll just keep on doing day-by-day experimental work and try to get a few things published.

you. Do you find there comes a point when you can no longer see all of the elephant? Most people find that the image of the elephant will appear to overflow the size of their image space.

People also may use mental images to store geographical information in memory (Stevens &

Coupe, 1978). For example, many people have stored in memory a rough map of the United States. Which city is further west: Reno, Nevada, or San Diego, California? Most people believe San Diego to be west of Reno. Their map looks something like that in Panel A of Figure 8-9. Actually, however, Reno is

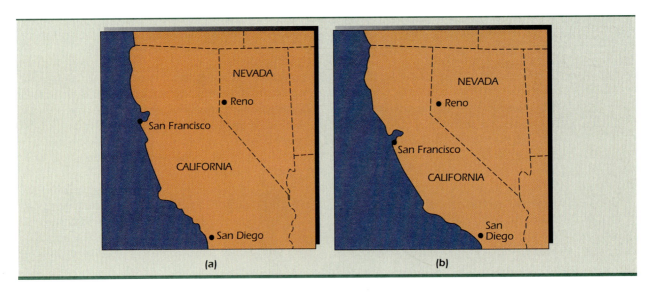

FIGURE 8-9
Accuracy of Images Stored in Memory
Maps locating Reno, Nevada, and San Diego, California: Most people believe San Diego to be west of Reno, so their mental map looks something like the map in Panel A. Actually, however, Reno is west of San Diego, as shown in the correct map in Panel B.

west of San Diego, as shown in the correct map in Panel B of the figure. The kinds of errors people make in this task suggest the use of imaginary representations.

As these studies show, we seem to encode information in memory by using both propositional and imaginal representations. *Dual-trace theory* captures this dual representation, although other theories explain it in different ways. The question we presently need to address is when we use which representation.

Design an experiment that would test whether propositional or imaginal representations were being used for a particular task or in a particular situation.

Storage and Forgetting

We rely heavily on our long-term store, in which we keep the information we need to function in our daily lives. We have seen how we encode information, but how do we store it?

Rehearsal

In the discussion of short-term memory, we saw that rehearsal clearly helps maintain information in memory. Rehearsal also seems to facilitate the transfer of information from short-term to long-term memory. For example, suppose you have to study vocabulary words for a French test. You have 240 vocabulary words to learn, and you can allocate 4 hours to study. You could budget your time in several ways. One would be to study each word once for 1 minute. Another would be to study each word twice for 30 seconds each time. Actually, it does not matter which strategy you use. According to the **total-time hypothesis,** which is accepted in at least a limited form by many researchers, the amount of learning depends on the amount of time spent studying the material, more or less without regard to how that time is divided up into trials in any one session. (How you distribute your time across a series of sessions, however, is another matter, which we discuss later in this section.)

How you rehearse the information, though, influences how effectively you retain it. You could simply repeat the items over and over again, or you could elaborate the items in a way that makes them more meaningful to you. That is, you could relate the items to what you already know or connect them to one another and thereby make them more memorable. (Recall the effects of chunking, in which a person can chunk many smaller units of information into larger units of integrated information in order to remember the information more easily.) One way to elaborate information is to organize it.

Organization of Information: Semantic and Episodic Memory

In what form do we organize information in memory? Probably the most illuminating studies addressing this question have looked at information in **semantic memory** (general world knowledge—our memory for facts that are not unique to us and that are not recalled in any particular temporal context) (Tulving, 1972). Semantic memory is distinguished from **episodic memory** (personally experienced events or episodes), which is the kind of memory we use when we learn meaningless lists of words, or when we need to recall something that occurred to us at a particular time or in a particular context. For example, if I need to remember that I saw Hector Hinklemeyer in the lunchroom yesterday, I must draw on an episodic memory; however, if I need to remember the name of the person I now see in the lunchroom again today ("Hector Hinklemeyer"), I must draw on a semantic memory. There is no particular time tag associated with the name of that individual as being Hector, but there is a time tag associated with my having seen him at lunch yesterday. It is not clear that semantic and episodic memory are two distinct systems, although they do appear to function, at times, in different ways. (Later, this chapter describes research on conscious patients undergoing brain surgery that provides physiological evidence suggesting the distinctive storage of episodic memories.)

Design an experiment that would test your semantic memory. Contrast that experiment with one that would test your episodic memory.

Semantic memory operates on **concepts**—ideas to which a person may attach various characteristics and with which the person may connect various other ideas. People mentally organize concepts in

For most Americans, photos of the U.S. Capitol and other monuments in Washington, D.C., prompt recollections from semantic memory—such as facts about the government.

For many people, the mention of a first kiss, a first date, and many other firsts will evoke specific recollections from episodic memory.

some way, and memory processing can be understood more readily by envisioning an organizational structure of memory. Psychologists often use the term **schema** to describe a cognitive framework for organizing associated concepts (information and ideas), based on previous experiences. For example, a schema for having lunch might associate all the things you have personally experienced regarding lunch, as well as what you have learned from other people and from other information sources regarding lunch.

Describe your schema for something highly concrete, such as shoes. Describe your schema for something more abstract, such as parenting or criminal justice. Compare the two descriptions, as well as your ease in performing each task.

Interference in the Long-Term Store

We have seen that interference affects short-term memory; it also plays an important role in long-term memory. Recall that *retroactive interference* is caused by activity occurring *after* trying to store something in memory, but before trying to retrieve that thing from memory. In contrast, *proactive interference* occurs when the interfering material occurs *before* the learning of the material.

In other situations, however, prior learning can cause **positive transfer**—that is, greater ease of learning and remembering the new material. For example, the prior experience of learning to drive an automatic-shift car may offer positive transfer when learning to drive a standard-shift car; most of the skills and knowledge of the former aid in learning the latter. Often, prior learning helps in some ways and hurts in others.

Massed Versus Distributed Learning

Many factors affect our ability to store or to forget information, such as rehearsal, organization of information, and both retroactive and proactive interference. Another factor affecting our storage or forgetting of information is the temporal pacing of learning. Harry Bahrick and Elizabeth Phelps (1987) found an important principle of memory while studying people's long-term recall of Spanish vocabulary words learned 8 years earlier. People tend to learn better when they acquire knowledge via **distributed learning** (i.e., learning that is spaced over time) rather than via **massed learning** (i.e., learning that is crammed together all at once). The greater the distribution of learning trials over time, the more that people remember. This principle is important to remember in studying. You will recall more, on the average, if you distribute your learning of subject matter, rather than trying to mass or cram it all into a short period of time. Even after 8 years (a great deal longer than most experiments in psychology), subjects showed significant recall of Spanish vocabulary. The remarkable duration of long-term memory found in this study suggests the following question: How much information can we hold in the long-term store, and how long does the information last?

What might cause a student to use massed learning, rather than distributed learning? How could you create a situation that would make it more likely for a student to use distributed rather than massed learning?

The Capacity of the Long-Term Store

We can quickly dispose of the question regarding the capacity of our long-term storage because the answer is that we do not know, nor do we know how we would find out. Although we can design experiments

to tax the limits of the short-term store, we do not know how to tax the limits of the long-term store and thereby find out its capacity. Some theorists have suggested that the capacity of the long-term store is infinite, at least in practical terms (Hintzman, 1978). Of course, some believe differently. Sherlock Holmes once commented to Dr. Watson that the reason he, Holmes, did not know some of the most basic facts about the world was that he believed that if he used up his memory on such basic facts, he would not have available to him the memory he needed for his work in detecting crimes. It turns out that the question of how long information lasts in the long-term store is not very easily answerable either because, at present, we have no proof that there is an absolute outer limit to how long information can be stored.

Researchers have found evidence in support of the durability of long-term memories. An interesting study on memory for names and faces was conducted by Harry Bahrick, Phyllis Bahrick, and Roy Wittlinger (1975). They tested subjects' memories for names and photographs of their high school classmates. Even after 25 years, subjects tended to recognize names as belonging to classmates rather than to outsiders, and recognition memory for matching names to graduation photos was quite high. As you might expect, recall of names showed a higher rate of forgetting. Even these experimental studies do not yield unequivocal results, however, because of a confounding in experimental design between storage and retrieval, the next topic we consider.

Retrieval

But this mysterious power that binds our life together has its own vagaries and interruptions. It sometimes occurs that Memory has a personality of its own, and volunteers or refuses its information at its will, not at mine.

—Ralph Waldo Emerson,
Natural History of Intellect

Nothing may ever be lost from long-term memory. If that is true, then why do we sometimes have trouble remembering? It is important to distinguish between **availability** (whether information is permanently stored in long-term memory) and **accessibility** (the degree to which we can gain access to stored information). Memory performance depends on the accessibility of the information to be remembered.

Studies of retrieval from the long-term store are often dated back to Hermann Ebbinghaus (1902, 1913/1964), who tested his own memory using nonsense syllables. The idea of using such syllables was that they would have no meaning attached to them, which should have made it possible to study pure recall phenomena without the influence of prior associations and meanings. There are two problems with this logic, however. The first is that people sometimes make up their own associations. The second is that, arguably, we should be interested in how people learn material of the kind they actually need to recall in their everyday lives, not material that they will never have any occasion to learn.

Frederick Bartlett (1932), recognizing the need to study memory retrieval for connected texts and not just nonsense syllables, had subjects learn a text and then recall it. He also was interested in whether memory for material is affected by previous (e.g., culturally based) understandings. Bartlett had his sub-

jects in Britain learn what was to them a strange and difficult-to-understand North American Indian legend called "The War of the Ghosts." The text is depicted in its entirety in Figure 8-10. He found that subjects distorted their recall to make the story more understandable. In other words, their prior knowledge and expectations had a substantial effect on their recall. Bartlett suggested that people bring into a memory task their already existing schemas, which affect the way they recall what they learn.

Today, we know that prior knowledge has an enormous effect on memory. That effect seems to explain why adults generally perform better on memory tests than do children. Intriguingly, a test on which children perform better actually supports this view. Michelene Chi and Randi Koeske (1983) found that children can remember material better than adults if

FIGURE 8-10
Bartlett's Legend

Quickly read the following legend, then turn over the page and write all that you can recall from the legend. Turn back to the legend, and compare what you wrote with what the legend describes.

(a) Original Indian myth

The War of the Ghosts

One night two young men from Egulac went down to the river to hunt seals, and while they were there it became foggy and calm. Then they heard war-cries, and they thought: "Maybe this is a war-party." They escaped to the shore, and hid behind a log. Now canoes came up, and they heard the noise of paddles, and saw one canoe coming up to them. There were five men in the canoe, and they said:

"What do you think? We wish to take you along. We are going up the river to make war on the people."

One of the young men said, " I have no arrows."

"Arrows are in the canoe," they said.

"I will not go along. I might be killed. My relatives do not know where I have gone. But you," he said, turning to the other, "may go with them."

So one of the young men went, but the other returned home.

And the warriors went on up the river to a town on the other side of Kalama. The people came down to the water, and they began to fight, and many were killed. But presently the young man heard one of the warriors say: "Quick, let us go home; that Indian has been hit." Now he thought: "Oh, they are ghosts." He did not feel sick, but they said he had been shot.

So the canoes went back to Egulac, and the young man went ashore to his house, and made a fire. And he told everybody and said: "Behold I accompanied the ghosts, and we went to fight. Many of our fellows were killed, and many of those who attacked us were killed. They said I was hit, and I did not feel sick."

He told it all, and then he became quiet. When the sun rose he fell down. Something black came out of his mouth. His face became contorted. The people jumped up and cried.

He was dead.

(b) Typical recall by a student in England

The War of the Ghosts

Two men from Edulac went fishing. While thus occupied by the river they heard a noise in the distance.

"It sounds like a cry," said one, and presently there appeared some in canoes who invited them to join the party of their adventure. One of the young men refused to go, on the ground of family ties, but the other offered to go.

"But there are no arrows," he said.

"The arrows are in the boat," was the reply.

He thereupon took his place, while his friend returned home. The party paddled up the river to Kaloma, and began to land on the banks of the river. The enemy came rushing upon them, and some sharp fighting ensued. Presently someone was injured, and the cry was raised that the enemy were ghosts.

The party returned down the stream, and the young man arrived home feeling none the worse for his experience. The next morning at dawn he endeavoured to recount his adventures. While he was talking something black issued from his mouth. Suddenly he uttered a cry and fell down. His friends gathered round him.

But he was dead.

Searchers . . . *ELIZABETH LOFTUS*

Elizabeth Loftus is Professor of Psychology at the University of Washington.

Q: *How did you become interested in psychology in general and in your area of work in particular?*

A: I started as a mathematics major, but I took a psychology class and I absolutely loved the material. So I began taking more and more psychology courses. By the time I was done with my undergraduate education, I had a double major in mathematics and psychology. I went to graduate school to study mathematical psychology.

Q: *What ideas have influenced you the most?*

A: Those ideas that challenge conventional wisdom. I recently heard a very interesting talk by Jonathan Brown, following up on work he had done with Shelley Taylor. Supposedly the healthiest people, the mentally healthiest people, are the ones who have the best sense of reality and are in touch with reality. But their work seems to show that a little bit of illusion and a little bit of false reality are actually good for you.

Q: *How do you get your ideas for research?*

A: Lately, my ideas often come from things that I see in court cases. The whole line of repression, and the reality of repressed memories, has come about as a result of my being an expert witness in the trial of a woman who accused her father of killing her best friend when she was 8 years old. She had repressed the memory for 20 years. Because of my involvement in that case, I started looking into the literature on repression and repressed memories, trying to find some evidence that the mind really works this way. There is no cogent scientific support for that, and so, for the last two years, I've been doing almost nothing but work on repressed memories.

Q: *How do you decide whether to pursue an idea?*

A: It depends; one criterion has to do with whether or not an idea is closely related to other things that I'm doing, so it isn't spreading me too thin. Another is, can I find a graduate student or a collaborator who might be interested in pursuing it with me? Or is it going to be something that requires a lot of equipment, and lots of resources that I don't have available?

Q: *What obstacles have you experienced?*

A: In the midst of having a field of work that is so rewarding and so exciting, it's necessary to seek grant funding. It's a continuing process, and it's forever a headache. These are bureaucratic obstacles to getting your work done.

Q: *What is your major contribution to psychology?*

A: My research on memory distortion is something that I'm most proud of. This has both theoretical and practical significance. And it's nice to be involved in work that looks in two directions. Because of its immediate and obvious practical implications, it's something that is very interesting to students, so I think that this line of work has gotten students excited about the area of cognitive psychology.

Q: *What do you want your students to learn?*

A: An enthusiasm and an excitement for the subject matter and for the whole process of discovering insights about the workings of memory.

Q: *What advice would you give to someone starting in the field of psychology?*

A: You need a real appreciation of the scientific method, and how you come up with a hypothesis and then gather meaningful information that might either support or refute that hypothesis, and of what really constitutes good evidence.

Q: *What have you learned from your students?*

A: Well, the students bring me examples, and they ask questions and sometimes I can't answer those questions, and it makes me want to figure out how to answer them. The students have come up with some great ideas that I hadn't thought about.

Q: *Apart from you life as an academic, how have you found psychology to be important?*

A: My life is so full of things that are related in one way or another to psychology. If I'm not in class teaching psychology or writing psychology or reading psychology, I might be testifying in some court case.

Q: *What do you further hope to contribute?*

A: Well, since I only started this new line of work on repressed memories a couple of years ago, or the potential creation of memories that are false about childhood events, I've got a lot of work cut out for me for the next few years, just in this general domain.

the children are more familiar than the adults with the domain—in this study, the domain of dinosaurs.

Schemas provide an internal context that affects memory retrieval, yet external contexts may also affect our ability to recall information. We appear to be better able to recall information when we are in the same context as we were when we learned the material. In one experiment, 16 underwater divers were asked to learn a list of 40 unrelated words, either while they were on shore or while they were 20 feet beneath the surface (Godden & Baddeley, 1975). Later, the divers were asked to recall the words either when in the same environment as where they had learned them, or in the other environment. Recall was better when it occurred in the same place as the learning. More recently (Butler & Rovee-Collier, 1989), researchers have found that even infants demonstrate context effects on memory. When given an opportunity to kick a mobile in the same context in which they first learned to kick it or in a different context, they kicked more strongly in the same context.

Even our moods and states of consciousness may provide a context for encoding and later retrieving memories. That is, those things that we encode during a particular mood or state of consciousness we may retrieve more readily when we are in the same state again (Baddeley, 1989; Bower, 1983). For example, some (e.g., Baddeley, 1989) have suggested that a factor in maintaining depression may be that the depressed person can more readily retrieve memories of previous sad experiences, which may further the con-

tinuance of the depression. If psychologists or others can intervene to prevent this vicious cycle, the person may begin to feel happier, leading to retrieval of happier memories, thus further relieving the depression, and so on. Perhaps the folk wisdom to "think happy thoughts" is not entirely unfounded.

Cue Effectiveness and Encoding Specificity

In addition to using categorical clustering, how else can people increase their recall of information? Research has confirmed the importance of making cues meaningful to the individual. Timo Mantyla (1986) found that when subjects made up their own retrieval cues, they were able to remember, almost without errors, lists of 500 and 600 words. For each word on a list, subjects were asked to generate another word (the cue) that, to them, was an appropriate description or property of the target word. Later, they were given a list of their cue words and were asked to recall the target word. Mantyla found that cues were most helpful when they were both *compatible* with the

When Simon Rodia built the Watts Towers in East Los Angeles (c. 1921–1954), he assembled them from fragments of realistic objects, according to his own preexisting ideas. Similarly, we construct our memories from fragments of realistic events, according to our own preexisting schemas.

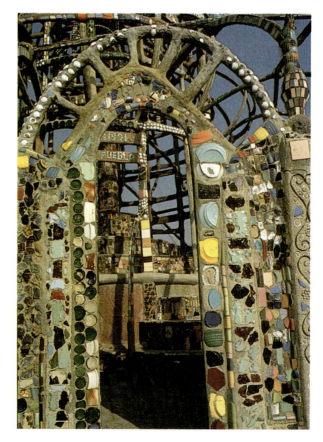

target word, and *distinctive*, in that they would not tend to generate a large number of related words. For example, if you are given the word *coat*, then *jacket* might be both compatible and distinctive as a cue; however, if you came up with the word *wool* as a cue, it might make you think of a number of words, such as *fabric* and *sheep*, that were not the target word.

The results of the various experiments on retrieval suggest that how items are encoded has a strong effect on how and how well items are retrieved. Endel Tulving and Donald Thomson (1973) have referred to this relation as **encoding specificity**—that is, what is recalled depends on what is encoded. To summarize, retrieval interacts strongly with encoding. If you study for a test and want to recall the information well at the time of testing, organize the information you are studying in a way that will help you to recall it.

The Constructive Nature of Memory

It appears that we recall meaningful information more readily than meaningless information, and that sometimes we even create the meaning that we later recall. In fact, it appears that memory is not just **reconstructive,** in that we use only what we have just encountered to help us recall; it is also **constructive,** in that prior experience affects how we recall things and what we actually recall. In other words, we try to fit our memories into our existing schemas.

Some cross-cultural work (Tripathi, 1979) illustrates the importance of schemas as a framework for constructive memory. For example, Indian children were asked to read several stories from *The Panchatantra*, a collection of ancient Hindi fables and folktales. The stories contain quaint names and unusual settings that are unfamiliar to contemporary Indian schoolchildren. Subsequently, the children were asked to recall the stories. Over time, the children added words and sentences not originally presented in the stories, and their reconstructions generally modified the stories from unfamiliar to more familiar forms, as well as from complex to simple forms.

The jurors in this courtroom are counting on the reconstructive memory of this eyewitness account. However, hard evidence shows that eyewitness accounts are often built using constructive memory, *based partly on what actually happened and partly on what the individual assembles from various fragments of recollections.*

Some of the strongest evidence for the constructive nature of memory has been obtained by those who have studied the validity of eyewitness testimony. In one such study, Elizabeth Loftus, David Miller, and Helen Burns (1978) showed subjects a series of 30 slides in which a red Datsun drove down a street, stopped at a stop sign, turned right, and then knocked down a pedestrian crossing at a crosswalk. As soon as they finished seeing the slides, subjects had to answer a series of 20 questions about the accident. One of the questions contained information that was either consistent or inconsistent with what they had been shown. Half of the subjects were asked: "Did another car pass the red Datsun while it was stopped at the stop sign?" The other half of the subjects received the same question, except with the word "yield" replacing the word "stop." In other words, the information in the question given this second group was inconsistent with what the subjects had seen.

Later, after *interpolated* (inserted) activity, all subjects were shown two slides and asked which they had seen. One had a stop sign, the other a yield sign. Accuracy on this task was 34% better for subjects who had received the consistent question (stop sign question) than for subjects who had received the inconsistent question (yield sign question). This experiment and others (e.g., Loftus, 1975, 1977) have shown people's great susceptibility to distortion in eyewitness accounts. Although this distortion may be due to phenomena other than just constructive memory, it does show that we can easily be led to construct a memory that differs from what really happened.

Recall a situation in which you and at least one other person shared the same experience, yet each remembers the experience differently. That is, each of you recalls different sights and sounds, different sequences of events, or different statements as having been said. How do you account for these differences?

For young soldiers and their families, the start of the Gulf War may very well be stored as a vivid flashbulb memory.

Given the workings of constructive memory, how might you now explain the differing experiences you and your friend had previously "shared"?

When we are recalling a given experience, we often associate the degree to which the remembered experience seems vivid and richly detailed with the degree to which we are accurately remembering the experience. Ulric Neisser (1982) and others have questioned that association. Apparently, we cannot distinguish constructive from reconstructive memory, based on the vividness of our recall.

A factor that seems to enhance the likelihood that we will recall a particular experience (over other experiences) is the emotional intensity of that experience. Unfortunately, however, such intensity does not ensure the accuracy of our recall. An oft-studied form of vivid memory is the **flashbulb memory**—a memory of an event so emotionally powerful that the person remembers the event as vividly as if it were indelibly preserved on film (Brown & Kulik, 1977). Memories of the assassination of President John F. Kennedy, as well as memories of the attack on Pearl Harbor or even of the explosion of the space shuttle *Challenger*, have been studied as examples of common flashbulb memories. Surprisingly, although people feel certain of their memories of the events, and the vividness and detailed texture of their memories seem to support their accuracy, it turns out that these re-membered events are often recalled inaccurately.

Thus far, we have discussed several ways that psychologists disagree about some of the specific mechanisms of memory, within the context of the three-store model of memory. Next, we consider whether there is a plausible alternative way to view what we know about memory.

ALTERNATIVE PERSPECTIVES, ALTERNATIVE METAPHORS

IN SEARCH OF...

In this section, we view some alternative ways of conceptualizing memory. Which of the various alternative conceptualizations seems to you to explain best the way that you see your own memory working? Why?

Working Memory and Parallel Processing

Some psychologists (e.g., Baddeley, 1990a, 1990b; Cantor & Engle, in press; Daneman & Tardif, 1987; Engle, 1994; Engle, Carullo, & Collins, 1992) view short-term and long-term memory from a different perspective. Table 8-2 contrasts the traditional Atkinson-Shiffrin model with this alternative perspective. You may note the semantic distinctions, the differences in metaphorical representation, and the differences in emphasis for each view. The key feature of the alternative view is the emphasis on **working memory,** which is regarded as a specialized part of long-term memory. Within working memory is short-term memory, which is the small reservoir of information of which we are consciously aware at any given moment. From this perspective, working memory holds only the most recently activated portion of long-term memory, and it moves these activated elements into and out of short-term memory.

This view implies that working memory contains simultaneously activated (parallel) yet perhaps widely distributed portions of long-term memory. Thus, the new metaphor also broadens the debate between serial and parallel processes in memory function, encompassing more than just its ramifications for short-term memory. Based partly on the use of computer models (simulations of memory, an aspect of artificial intelligence) of memory processes, many cognitive psychologists now prefer a *parallel-processing model* to describe many phenomena of memory, particularly in terms of working memory as the activated portion of long-term memory.

Levels of Processing: An Alternative Framework for Understanding Memory

An even more radical departure from the three-stores view of memory is the **levels-of-processing framework,** originally proposed by Fergus Craik and

TABLE 8-2
Traditional Versus Nontraditional Views of Memory
The traditional three-stores view differs from a contemporary alternative view in terms of the choice of terms, of metaphors, and of emphasis.

	Traditional Three-Stores View	**Alternative View of Memory**[a]
Terminology	*Working memory* is another name for short-term memory, which is distinct from long-term memory.	*Working memory* (active memory) is the part of long-term memory that comprises all the knowledge of facts and procedures that has been recently activated in memory, including the brief, fleeting short-term memory and its contents.
Relationships of stores	Short-term memory is distinct from long-term memory, perhaps either alongside it or hierarchically linked to it.	Short-term memory, working memory, and long-term memory are concentric spheres, in which working memory contains only the most recently activated portion of long-term memory, and short-term memory contains only a very small, fleeting portion of working memory.
Movement of information	Information moves directly from long-term memory to short-term memory, and then back, never in both locations at once.	Information remains within long-term memory; when activated, information moves into long-term memory's specialized working memory, which would actively move information into and out of the short-term memory store contained within it.
Emphasis	Distinction between long- and short-term memory.	Role of activation in moving information into working memory and the role of working memory in memory processes.

[a] Examples of studies proposing this view: Cantor & Engle, in press; Engle, 1994; Engle, Cantor, & Carullo, 1992.

Robert Lockhart (1972), which postulates that memory does not comprise any specific number of separate stores. Rather, storage varies along a continuous dimension in terms of depth of encoding. In other words, there are theoretically an infinite number of levels of processing at which items can be encoded, with no distinct boundaries between one level and the next.

This framework has an immediate, practical application. In studying, the more elaborately and diversely you encode material, the more readily you are likely to recall it later. Just looking at material again and again in the same way is likely to be less productive for learning the material than is asking yourself meaningful questions about the material and finding more than one way in which to learn it.

Alan Baddeley (1990a, 1990b) has suggested a further refinement, which synthesizes the three-stores, parallel processing, and levels-of-processing views. Essentially, he views the levels-of-processing framework as an extension of, rather than a replacement for, the modified three-stores model of memory. In particular, he suggests that working memory comprises a *central executive*, which coordinates attentional activities (moving items in and out of short-term memory); a *visuospatial sketchpad*, which holds visual images; an *articulatory loop*, which holds inner

speech for acoustic rehearsal; and probably a number of other "subsidiary slave systems" (Baddeley, 1989, p. 36). Baddeley's visuospatial sketchpad might be used for Craik's physical level of processing, and Baddeley's articulatory loop might be used for Craik's acoustic level of processing. Additional kinds and levels of processing remain to be defined. Thus, in the future, this synthesis may serve as a thesis on which further theory development may be based.

Alternative Conceptualizations of Semantic Memory

In addition to having differing views regarding the structure of memory in general, psychologists have come up with a few ways to conceptualize the structure of semantic memory in particular. Each of these conceptualizations includes the notion of concepts and schemas, but the conceptualizations differ in terms of the ways they view concepts as being associated within schemas. In 1969, Allan Collins and Ross Quillian conducted a landmark study suggesting a hierarchical structure of semantic memory. The subjects were given statements such as "A robin is a bird" and "A robin is an animal," and were asked to verify whether the statements were true. Collins and Quillian concluded that a hierarchical network representa-

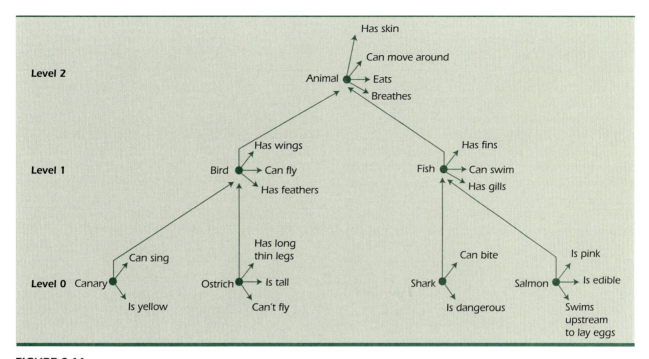

FIGURE 8-11
Hierarchical System of Categories
According to this model, memories are represented and stored in the form of a hierarchical tree diagram.

tion such as the one shown in Figure 8-11 adequately accounted for the response times in their study. According to this model, storage takes the form of a hierarchical tree diagram.

NEUROPSYCHOLOGY OF MEMORY

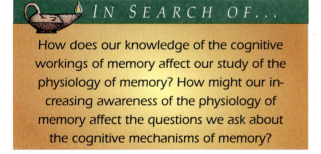

IN SEARCH OF...

How does our knowledge of the cognitive workings of memory affect our study of the physiology of memory? How might our increasing awareness of the physiology of memory affect the questions we ask about the cognitive mechanisms of memory?

Psychologists have been able to locate many cerebral structures involved in memory, such as the hippocampus and other nearby structures, but the physiological structure may not be such that we will find locations of specific ideas, thoughts, or events. Studies of amnesia victims, such as those mentioned at the outset of this chapter, have revealed much about the way memory depends on effective functioning of particular structures of the brain. Memory is volatile and may be disturbed by a blow to the head, a

disturbance in consciousness, or any number of other injuries to or pathologies of the brain. Thus, although some structures of the brain clearly play a vital role in memory (Squire, 1987), and disturbances or lesions in these areas cause severe deficits in memory formation, we cannot say that memory—or even part of memory—resides in these structures. Nonetheless, studies of brain-injured patients are informative, offering distinctive insights not previously observed in normal subjects. (Recall the previous mention of insights into declarative vs. procedural knowledge, gained through the study of amnesia victims.) In addition, although studies of brain-injured subjects do not necessarily provide conclusive evidence regarding localization of function, such studies may still indicate that a particular structure at least participates in a given function.

For example, some studies show preliminary findings regarding the specific structures involved in various kinds of memory, such as procedural versus declarative memory. In particular, procedural knowledge seems to depend on the basal ganglia (Mishkin & Petri, 1984). However, the hippocampus seems to play a crucial role in complex learning (McCormick & Thompson, 1984), particularly in regard to the encoding of declarative information (Kolb & Whishaw, 1990; Zola-Morgan & Squire, 1990). The hippocampus also appears to be involved in the consolidation of encoded information in the long-term store, perhaps as a means of cross-referencing information stored in different parts of the brain (Squire, Cohen, & Nadel, 1984). In addition, the cerebral cortex appears to play a minor but important role in long-term memory, particularly declarative knowledge (Zola-Morgan & Squire, 1990). Another form of memory is the classically conditioned response, in which the cerebellum seems to play a key role (Thompson, 1987).

In addition to these preliminary insights into whatever macrolevel structures of memory may exist, we are beginning to understand the microlevel structure of memory. For example, we know that repeated stimulation of particular neural pathways tends to strengthen the likelihood of firing; that is, at a particular synapse, there appear to be physiological changes in the dendrites of the receiving neuron, making the neuron more likely to reach the threshold for firing again.

Studies of brain-injured patients may lead to insights regarding the macrolevel structures of the brain. How might psychologists investigate the microlevel structures and processes of memory? (Refer to Chapter 3, as needed, to recall some of the basic techniques for studying these structures. Be specific in noting how such techniques could be applied to the study of memory.)

We also know that some neurotransmitters disrupt memory storage, and other neurotransmitters enhance memory storage. Both serotonin and acetylcholine seem to enhance neural transmission associated with memory, and noradrenaline may also do so. High concentrations of acetylcholine have been found in the hippocampus of normal persons (Squire, 1987), but low concentrations are found in victims of Alzheimer's disease—a disorder causing severe memory loss. In fact, Alzheimer's patients show severe loss of the brain tissue that secretes acetylcholine. Despite intensive research in this area, scientists have yet to pin down the specific causes of Alzheimer's disease. Researchers have been better able to track down the cause of another form of memory dysfunction, alcohol consumption, which disrupts the activity of serotonin, thereby impairing the formation of memories (Weingartner et al., 1983).

This chapter has shown that although we have learned a great deal about how memory works, much remains unknown. As researchers engage in increasingly sophisticated studies of the cognitive and physiological mechanisms of memory, we will understand memory much more profoundly. We are also rapidly approaching the day when we can use physiological means to help people who have pathological deficits of memory. Perhaps we will even be able to expand our normal memory capacities through neuropsychological intervention. For now, however, we must be content to use mnemonic devices and other external aids to enhance our memories.

One of the key ways we remember information is the use of language. Language aids memory by offering us external aids such as written lists, and by making isolated bits of information meaningful, through the organization of the information and through the use of mnemonic devices, such as acrostics and acronyms. The many facets and uses of language form the topic of the next chapter.

SUMMARY

What Is Memory?   268

1. *Memory* is the set of dynamic mechanisms for storing the information we have from past experiences.
2. Severe loss of memory is referred to as *amnesia*. *Anterograde amnesia* refers to difficulty in remembering events occurring after the time of trauma, whereas *retrograde amnesia* refers to severe difficulty in remembering events occurring before the time of trauma. *Infantile amnesia* is our inability to remember events that occurred to us before about age 5.
3. A *mnemonist* relies on special techniques, such as imagery, for greatly improving his or her memory; anyone can use these techniques.

Mnemonic Devices   270

4. *Mnemonic devices* are used to improve recall. Examples of such devices include categorical *clustering*, *interactive imagery*, *acronyms*, *acrostics*, and *keywords*.

Tasks Used for Measuring Memory   270

5. Four of the main kinds of tasks used to study memory are (1) *serial recall*, in which a person needs to remember items according to the order in which they are presented; (2) *free recall*, in which the person can remember items in any order; (3) *paired-associates recall*, in which a person needs to remember the second member of

two paired words; and (4) *recognition*, in which a person must indicate whether a presented word is one that has been learned previously. In addition, memory researchers study *explicit memory*, in which subjects are asked to make a conscious recollection, as well as *implicit memory*, in which task performance is assisted by a recollection of which we are not conscious. They also study *procedural knowledge* ("knowing how"—skills, such as how to ride a bicycle) versus *declarative knowledge* ("knowing that"—factual information, such as the terms in a psychology textbook).

Types of Memory   274

6. Memory is often conceived of as involving three stores: (1) a *sensory store*, capable of holding relatively limited amounts of information for very brief periods of time; (2) a *short-term store*, capable of holding small amounts of information for somewhat longer periods of time; and (3) a *long-term store*, capable of storing large amounts of information virtually indefinitely.

7. Three operations that occur in all three of the suggested memory stores are (1) *encoding*, by which information is placed into the store; (2) *storage*, by which information is maintained in the store; and (3) *retrieval*, by which information is pulled into consciousness from the store.

The Sensory Store   276

8. The *iconic store* refers to visual sensory memory, whereas the *echoic store* refers to auditory sensory memory. Of the two, the iconic store seems better supported by existing evidence.

The Short-Term Store   277

9. Encoding of information in the short-term store appears to be largely, although not exclusively, acoustic, as shown by the susceptibility of information in the short-term store to acoustic confusability—that is, errors based on sounds of words.

10. We retain information mainly by *rehearsing* it. Two of the main theories of forgetting are (1) *interference theory*, which hypothesizes that information is forgotten when a new memory trace competes with an old one; and (2) *decay theory*, which postulates that information is lost when it remains unused for a long period of time. These theories apply to both short-term and long-term memory.

11. Interference theory distinguishes between (a) *retroactive interference*, caused by activity occurring *after* we learn the stimulus material to be recalled; and (b) *proactive interference*, caused by activity occurring *before* we learn the stimulus material to be recalled.

12. The capacity of the short-term store is about 7 ± 2 items. We often *chunk* bits of information if they are lengthy or complex. The *serial-position curve* shows our level of learning as a function of where a particular item appears in a list. The curve typically shows elevated recall at the beginning (*primacy effect*) and the end (*recency effect*) of a list, although experimental conditions can be constructed to reduce or eliminate these effects.

13. Processing of information in the short-term store may be in the form of either (a) *parallel processing*, which refers to multiple operations occurring simultaneously; or (b) *serial processing*, which refers to just a single operation occurring at a given time.

14. Serial processing can be characterized as either (a) *exhaustive*, implying that a person always checks all information on a list; or (b) *self-terminating*, implying that a person checks only that information on a list that is necessary for a particular comparison to be made.

The Long-Term Store   282

15. Information in the long-term store appears to be encoded primarily in a *semantic* form, so that confusions tend to be in terms of meanings rather than in terms of the sounds of words.

16. Theorists disagree as to whether all information in the long-term store is encoded in terms of *propositions* (the meaning underlying a particular relationship among concepts or things) or in terms of both propositions and images (mental pictures).

17. How we *rehearse* information influences how well we retain it. If we elaborate the items—that is, if we relate them or connect them to something we already know—then we are far more likely to remember them.

18. Some theorists distinguish between (a) *semantic memory*, our memory for facts not recalled in any particular temporal context; and (b) *episodic memory*, our memory for facts having some kind of temporal tag associated with them.

Our memory for the meaning of a word is normally semantic; we do not remember when or where we learned that meaning. In contrast, our memory for the words on a list to be learned is normally episodic; we are likely only to recall words from some list just learned and not from other lists that may be in the long-term store.

19. We tend to remember better when we acquire knowledge through *distributed learning* (learning that is spaced over time), rather than through *massed learning* (learning that occurs within a short period of time). To learn material gradually over the term of a course would be an example of distributed learning, whereas to cram for an examination would be an example of massed learning. Tee Hee... Why are YOU reading the summaries?

20. *Encoding specificity* refers to the fact that what is recalled depends largely on what is encoded: How information is encoded at the time of learning will greatly affect how it is later recalled. The context and the category of information also influence how we encode information.

21. Memory appears to be not only *reconstructive* (a direct reproduction of what was learned), but also *constructive* (influenced by attitudes and past knowledge).

Alternative Perspectives, Alternative Metaphors   293

22. *Working memory* usually is defined as being part of long-term memory and also comprises short-term memory; from this perspective, working memory holds only the most recently activated portion of long-term memory, and it moves these activated elements into and out of short-term memory. Instead of this view, some psychologists define working memory as being the same as short-term memory.

23. The *levels-of-processing framework* suggests that memory may not comprise separate stores, but rather a continuum of successively greater depths at which information can be processed.

Neuropsychology of Memory   295

24. Although they have yet to identify particular locations for particular memories, researchers have been able to learn a great deal about the specific structures of the brain that are involved in memory. In addition, researchers are investigating the biochemistry of neural processes involved in memory, such as the role of some specific neurotransmitters (e.g., serotonin and acetylcholine) and hormones.

KEY TERMS

accessibility 288
acronyms 270
acrostics 270
amnesia 269
anterograde amnesia 269
availability 288
categorical clustering 270
chunk 280
concepts 287
constructive 290
decay 278
decay theory 280
declarative knowledge 274
distributed learning 288
echoic store 277
encoding 275
encoding specificity 292
episodic memory 287
exhaustive serial processing 281
explicit memory 272
flashbulb memory 292
free recall 272
iconic store 277

implicit memory 272
infantile amnesia 269
interactive images 270
interference 278
interference theory 278
keywords 270
levels-of-processing framework 293
long-term store 275
massed learning 288
memory 268
memory scanning 281
method of loci 270
mnemonic devices 270
mnemonist 269
paired-associates recall 272
parallel processing 281
pegword system 270
positive transfer 288
primacy effect 280
proactive interference 279
procedural knowledge 273

proposition 284
recall 272
recency effect 280
recognition 272
recognition task 272
reconstructive 290
rehearsal 278
retrieval 276
retroactive interference 279
retrograde amnesia 269
schema 287
self-terminating serial processing 282
semantic memory 287
sensory store 275
serial-position curve 280
serial processing 281
serial recall 272
short-term store 275
storage 276
total-time hypothesis 286
working memory 293

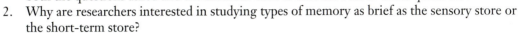

IN SEARCH OF THE HUMAN MIND:
ANALYSES, CREATIVE EXPLORATIONS, AND PRACTICAL APPLICATIONS

1. How did the Atkinson-Shiffrin model shape the study of memory? How did the model shape both the questions asked and the methods used to find answers to those questions?
2. Why are researchers interested in studying types of memory as brief as the sensory store or the short-term store?
   How would such information really have any practical use?
3. It is often said that Alzheimer's patients eventually lose their personalities and their distinctive identities when they lose their memories.
   How does your memory serve as the basis for your unique personality and identity?

4. Test for yourself a variation of Bransford and Johnson's research on encoding. Write a brief description of a common task (such as washing dishes), carefully omitting any concrete nouns (such as *plates* or *spoons*) that would identify the task. Ask someone to read the description you wrote, and then ask the person to recall the steps you described. (Check off the steps if the person gives an oral account; another alternative is to have the person write the account.) Now, tell the person the title of your description, and ask the person to recall the steps again. (If you wanted to rule out the possibility that the person simply recalled the information the second time around, have a second person do the same task, but do not give the person the label for the second recitation of the steps.)
5. How could researchers design an experiment to distinguish the effects of encoding, of storage, and of retrieval of categorical information?
6. Describe one means by which a researcher could study the relation between perception and memory.

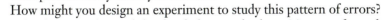

7. How do we get information into and out of the short-term store?
   What makes it more likely that we will forget or remember particular information temporarily being kept in the short-term store?
8. Cognitive psychologists frequently study patterns of errors when they investigate how a particular cognitive process works. What is a pattern of errors that you notice in the memory tasks performed by those you observe?
   How might you design an experiment to study this pattern of errors?
9. What have you learned that has led you to both positive transfer and negative transfer when you were learning something else? Explain the effects of each, and tell whether you believe that the net outcome was negative or positive.

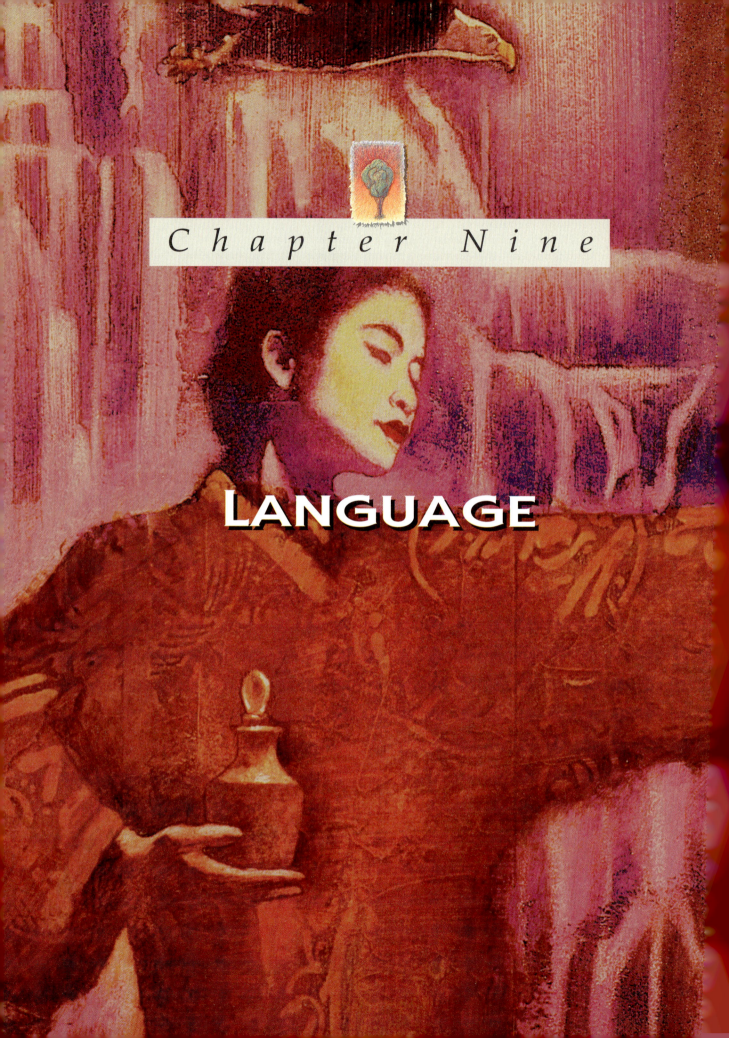

Chapter Nine

LANGUAGE

Chapter Outline

In Through the Looking Glass, *Alice talks with Humpty Dumpty, who points out that there is only one day in a year when people receive birthday presents, as opposed to 364 when they can receive unbirthday presents. He remarks:*

"There's glory for you!"

"I don't know what you mean by 'glory,'" Alice said.

Humpty Dumpty smiled contemptuously. "Of course you don't—till I tell you. I meant 'there's a nice knockdown argument for you.'"

"But 'glory' doesn't mean 'a nice knockdown argument,'" Alice objected.

"When I use a word," Humpty Dumpty said in rather a scornful tone, "it means just what I choose it to mean—neither more nor less."

"The question is," said Alice, "whether you *can* make words mean so many different things."

"The question is," said Humpty Dumpty, "which is to be master— that's all."

—Lewis Carroll, 1872, pp. 229–230

For language to be meaningful, words and other features of language must have meanings at least somewhat common to us all. **Language**—the use of an organized means of combining words in order to communicate—makes it possible for us to communicate in the first place.

GENERAL PROPERTIES OF LANGUAGE

IN SEARCH OF...

Think about your native language; then think about what you would have to learn to acquire another language. What are the important properties of language? Now, compare your intuitive descriptions with the properties described by psychologists.

What are the distinctive properties of language? The answer to this question, as to so many questions in psychology, depends on whom you ask. Nonethe-

less, some consensus exists regarding six properties that many psychologists would accept as distinctive of language (e.g., Brown, 1965; Clark & Clark, 1977; Glucksberg & Danks, 1975).

First, language is *communicative*. Despite being the most obvious feature of language, it is the most important one. The notion that I can write what I am thinking and feeling so that you may read and understand my thoughts and feelings is truly amazing.

Second, and perhaps more astounding, language is *arbitrary*. We communicate through a shared system of **arbitrary symbolic reference** to things, ideas, processes, relationships, and descriptions. A particular combination of letters or sounds may be meaningful to us, but the particular symbols do not themselves lead to the meaning of the word; with the rare exceptions of *onomatopoeia*, in which the word sounds like what it describes (e.g., *buzz*, *hiss*, and *hum*), the sound combination is arbitrary.

Third, language is *meaningfully structured*, which makes possible this shared system of communication. Particular patterns of sounds and of letters form meaningful words, and particular patterns of words form meaningful sentences, paragraphs, and discourse.

Fourth, language has *multiplicity of structure.* Any meaningful utterance can be analyzed at more than one level. That is, particular patterns of words can have more than one meaning (e.g., a sign seen in a New York drugstore: "We dispense with accuracy" [Lederer, 1987, p. 63]), and a particular basic idea can be expressed by more than one pattern of words (e.g., "The student chewed the pencil" is fundamentally the same as "The pencil was chewed by the student").

Fifth, language is *productive.* We can use language to produce an infinite number of unique sentences and other meaningful combinations of words. Language is inherently creative, precisely because it would never be possible for any of us to have previously heard all the sentences we are capable of producing. Moreover, any language has the potential to express any idea that can be expressed in any other language, although the ease, clarity, and succinctness of expression of a particular idea may vary greatly from one language to the next.

Finally, language is *dynamic;* it constantly evolves. New words, phrases, and meanings make their way into common usage every day.

Although many differences exist among them, languages also share properties. Moreover, for communication purposes, languages are largely interchangeable. Later in this chapter, we consider several universal aspects of language as they apply to the relation between thought and language. For now, we consider how psycholinguists and other linguists describe language, and then observe some universal aspects of how we humans acquire our primary language.

> What additional properties of language have you observed? Which of the listed properties had not occurred to you?

DESCRIPTION OF LANGUAGE IN ITS OWN WORDS

IN SEARCH OF...

Jargon (specialized terminology) is used to describe elements in and aspects of many fields. Psycholinguistics, too, has a jargon for the study of language. Why do people develop jargon? What are the benefits and the drawbacks of using jargon?

Chapter 5 described the way we perceive speech; in this chapter, we broaden our view of speech to encompass speech production. Recall from Chapter 5 that the smallest distinguishable unit of all possible human speech sounds is the *phone,* of which there are more than 100. No known language uses all of the possible phones, however. Each distinct language uses only a subset of these possibilities; the particular speech sounds the users of a particular language can identify are *phonemes.* In English, phonemes are generally identifiable as vowel or consonant sounds.

For example, in English, the difference between the /p/ and the /b/ sound is an important distinction. We distinguish between "they bit the buns from the bin" and "they pit the puns from the pin" (an example of a well-structured, meaningless sentence). On the other hand, we pay little regard to other phonemes. Put your open hand about one inch from your lips and say aloud (using your normal speech, not trying to add any sounds you don't normally pronounce) "Put the paper cup to your lip." If you are like most English speakers, you should have felt a tiny puff of air when you pronounced the /p^h/ in *Put* and *paper* and no puffs of air when you pronounced the /p/ in *cup* or *lip.* The study of the particular phonemes of a language is *phonemics,* and the study of how to produce or combine speech sounds or to represent them with written symbols is *phonetics.* (See Figure 9-1 for a diagram of a human vocal tract, indicating where some speech sounds are produced.)

Chapter 5 also introduced the term *morpheme,* the smallest unit of sound that denotes meaning within a particular language. English courses may have introduced you to two forms of morphemes: (1) *root words,* to which we add (2) **affixes**—both **suffixes,** which follow the root word, and **prefixes,** which precede the root word. Linguists analyze the structure of morphemes and words in a way that goes beyond the analysis of roots and affixes. Linguists refer to words that convey the bulk of meaning as **content morphemes.** Morphemes that add detail and nuance to the meaning of content morphemes or that help content morphemes to fit the grammatical context are **function morphemes** (e.g., the suffix *-ist,* the prefix *de-,* the conjunction *and,* the article *the*). A subset of function morphemes are **inflections,** the common suffixes we add to words to fit the grammatical context. For example, most American kindergartners know to add special suffixes to indicate the following:

Verb tense—You *study* often; you *studied* yesterday; and you *are studying* now.

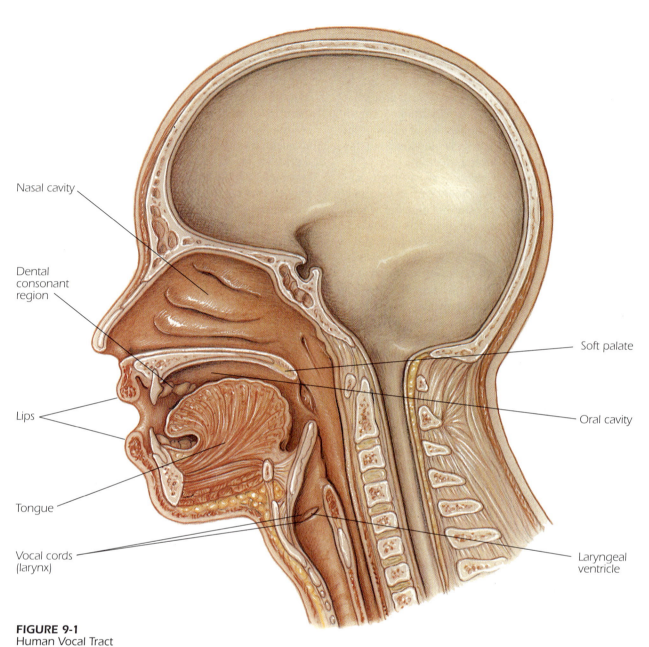

FIGURE 9-1
Human Vocal Tract

The human vocal tract allows us to produce a diversity of speech sounds, many of which cannot be produced by other animals.

Verb and noun number—The professor assigns homework; the teaching assistants assign homework.

Noun possession—The student's textbook is fascinating.

Adjective comparison—The wiser of the two professors taught the wisest of the three students.

Linguists use the term **lexicon** to describe the entire set of morphemes in a given language or in a given person's linguistic repertoire. The average English-speaking high school graduate has a lexicon of about 60,000 root morphemes, and most college students have lexicons about twice that large (Miller, 1990). By combining morphemes, most adult English speakers have a **vocabulary** (repertoire of words) of hundreds of thousands of words. For example, by attaching just a few morphemes to the root content morpheme *study*, we have *student, studious, studied, studying,* and *studies.* One reason English has more words than any other language is the relative ease with which its vocabulary can be expanded by combining existing morphemes in novel ways. Some suggest that a part of William Shakespeare's genius lay in his proclivity for creating new words by combining existing morphemes. He is alleged to have coined more than 1,700 words (8.5% of his written vocabulary) as well as countless expressions—including the word *countless* itself (Lederer, 1991). (For example, other words attributed to Shakespeare include *accommodation, assassination, critical, dexterously, eyesore, horrid, initiated, pedant,* and *premeditated.*)

For linguists, the next level of analysis after the analysis of phonemes, morphemes, and lexicon is *syntax,* which refers to the way users of a particular language put words together in sentences. A sentence comprises at least two parts: (1) a **noun phrase,** which contains at least one noun (usually, the subject of the sentence, including all the relevant descriptors of the subject) and (2) a **verb phrase,** which contains at least one verb and sometimes that on which the

verb acts. The verb phrase also may be termed the **predicate,** because it affirms or states something about the subject, usually an action or a property of the subject. Linguists consider the study of syntax to be fundamental to understanding the structure of language, and the syntactical structure of language is specifically addressed later in this chapter.

The final level of analysis is that of **discourse,** which encompasses language use at levels beyond the sentence, such as in conversation, or in paragraphs, articles, or entire books. Although the present chapter does not discuss discourse analysis per se, it does discuss some discourse-relevant aspects of language in regard to reading and writing, and in regard to broad aspects of language use. (Table 9-1 summarizes these aspects of language.) Just how does an individual acquire the ability to speak or write volumes of discourse? The following section describes this process.

TABLE 9-1
Summary Description of Language
All human languages can be analyzed at many levels.

Language Input		Language Output
	Phonemes (distinctive subset of all possible phones)	. . ./t/ + /ā/ + /k/ + /s/ . . .
↓	Morphemes (from the distinctive lexicon of morphemes)	. . . take (content morpheme) + s (plural function morpheme) . . .
D e c o d i n g	Words (from the distinctive vocabulary of words)	It + takes + a + heap + of + sense + to + write + good + nonsense.
	Phrases Noun phrases (NP: a noun and its descriptors) Verb phrases (VP: a verb and what- ever it acts on)	NP = It + VP = takes a heap of sense to write good nonsense.
	Sentences (based on the language's syntax—syntactical structure)	It takes a heap of sense to write good nonsense.
↓	Discourse	"It takes a heap of sense to write good nonsense," was first written by Mark Twain (Lederer, 1991, p. 131).
Comprehend Language		**Produce Language**

LANGUAGE ACQUISITION

IN SEARCH OF...

Many specialists in the field of language acquisition distinguish between "language acquisition" (the unconscious process of coming to understand and speak a given language) and "language learning" (the conscious process of trying to learn the usage rules and vocabulary of a given language). Which process do you believe to be more important to the ability to comprehend and to express your native language? How might the processes be different for becoming fluent in a second language, if the processes differ at all?

Stages of Language Acquisition

All people seem to acquire their primary language in the same sequence and in just about the same way. Within the first years of life, we progress from listening and responding to language to being able to produce it ourselves. Humans progress through the following stages: (1) prenatal responsivity to human voices; (2) postnatal cooing, which comprises all possible phones; (3) babbling, which comprises only the distinct phonemes that characterize the primary language of the infant; (4) one-word utterances; (5) two-word utterances; (6) telegraphic speech; and (7) basic adult sentence structure (present by about age four).

As you read about the stages of language acquisition, be thinking about your own views of how language acquisition may be affected by nature and nurture. Which do you think plays the more important role in each of these stages? Why?

Some suggest that language acquisition begins before birth. Fetuses can hear their mothers' voices in the watery prenatal environment, and within days after birth, newborns show clear preferences for their mothers' voices over the voices of other women (DeCasper & Fifer, 1980). They also seem to prefer hearing their mother read stories they heard her read in utero to stories she never read aloud before their birth (DeCasper & Spence, 1986). However, they show no clear preferences for their fathers' voices over those of other men (DeCasper & Prescott, 1983).

The results of these studies seem to show that newborns already have gained some familiarity with their mothers' voices and so are becoming prepared to pay attention after birth to her voice.

After birth, in addition to responding preferentially to their mothers' voices, newborns seem to respond motorically—to move—in synchrony with the speech of the caregivers who are interacting with them directly (Field, 1978; Martin, 1981; Schaffer, 1977; Snow, 1977; Stern, 1977). Further, the emotional expression of infants responds to and matches that of their caregivers (Fogel, 1992). Infants also produce sounds of their own; most obviously, the communicative aspect of crying—whether intentional or not—works quite well to get babies attention or food, or to signal distress in general. In terms of language acquisition, however, it is the cooing of infants that most intrigues linguists. **Cooing** is the infant's oral expression that explores the production of all the possible phones humans can produce. The cooing of infants around the world, including deaf infants, is practically identical.

During the cooing stage, hearing infants can also discriminate among all phones, not just among the phonemes characteristic of their own language. For example, during the cooing stage, both Japanese and American infants can discriminate the /l/ from the /r/ phone (Eimas, 1985). However, as infants move into the next stage (babbling), they gradually lose this ability to distinguish the phones, and by one year of age, Japanese infants—for whom the distinction does not make a phonemic difference—can no longer make this discrimination (Eimas, 1985).

At the babbling stage, deaf infants no longer vocalize, and the sounds produced by hearing infants change. **Babbling** is the infant's preferential production of only those distinct phonemes characteristic of the infant's own language. Thus, although the cooing of infants around the world is essentially the same, infant babbling distinctively characterizes the language the infant is acquiring. As suggested, the ability of the infant to perceive, as well as to produce, nonphonemic phones recedes during this stage.

Eventually, that first magnificent word is uttered, followed shortly by one or two more and soon after yet a few more. The infant uses these one-word utterances—termed *holophrases*—to convey intentions, desires, and demands. Usually, the words are nouns describing familiar objects that the child observes (e.g., car, book, ball, baby, nose) or wants (e.g., Mama, Dada, juice, cookie). By 18 months of age, children typically have vocabularies of 3 to 100 words

(Siegler, 1986). Because the young child's vocabulary cannot yet encompass all the child wishes to describe, the child quite deftly overextends the meaning of words in his or her existing lexicon to cover things and ideas for which a new word is lacking. For example, the general term for any man may be "Dada"—which can be quite distressing to a new father in a public setting—and the general term for any kind of four-legged animal may be "doggie." The term for this adaptation is **overextension error.**

Why do overextension errors occur? A **feature hypothesis** suggests that children form definitions that include too few features (Clark, 1973). Thus, a child might refer to a cat as a dog because of a mental rule that if an animal has the feature of four legs, it is a "doggie." An alternative **functional hypothesis** (Nelson, 1973) suggests that children first learn to use words that describe important functions or purposes: Lamps give light, and blankets make us warm. Overextension errors are due to functional confusions. A dog and a cat both do similar things and serve the same purposes as pets, so a child is likely to confuse them. Although the functional hypothesis has usually been viewed as an alternative to the feature hypothesis, it seems entirely possible that both mechanisms are at work in children's overextensions. As is often the case, perhaps neither position is completely right, and the truth as best we can know it is a synthesis of both views.

Gradually, by about two and one half years of age, children begin to combine single words to produce two-word utterances. Thus begins an understanding of syntax. These early syntactical communi-

When children are acquiring language, they frequently overextend the meanings of the words in their limited vocabulary. For example, these two young children may call all four-legged animals "doggie" after hearing the older child call this four-legged animal "doggie."

cations lead to speech that seems more like telegrams than conversation because articles, prepositions, and other function morphemes are usually left out. Hence, linguists refer to these next utterances with rudimentary syntax as **telegraphic speech.** In fact, the term, "telegraphic speech," can be used to describe three-word utterances and even slightly longer ones if they have these same characteristic omissions of some function morphemes. Vocabulary expands rapidly, more than tripling from about 300 words at about age 2 to about 1,000 at about age 3. Almost incredibly, by age 4 children acquire the foundations of adult syntax and language structure. By age 5 most children also can understand and produce quite complex and uncommon sentence constructions, and by age 10 children's language is fundamentally the same as that of adults.

Theoretical Explanations of Language Acquisition

Recall from Chapter 2 that philosophers have long debated whether nature or nurture molds who we are and what we do. This debate continually resurfaces in new forms, particularly in regard to language acquisition.

Nurture Alone

Few psychologists (if any) have asserted that language is entirely a result of nature. Both the diversity of languages in the world and the observations of children acquiring language appear to dispute this possibility. In contrast, some researchers and theoreticians have suggested that children acquire language largely because of the environment to which they are exposed. Two mechanisms for this phenomenon have been proposed: imitation and conditioning.

IMITATION.   One proposed mechanism for acquiring language is imitation. Even amateur observers notice that children's speech patterns and vocabulary reflect those of persons in their environment. In fact, parents of very young children seem to go to great lengths to make it easy for children to attend to and to understand what they are saying. Almost without thinking, parents and other adults tend to use a higher pitch than usual, to exaggerate the *vocal inflection* of their speech (i.e., raising and lowering pitch and volume more extremely than normal), and to use simpler sentence constructions when speaking with infants and young children. This distinctive form of adult speech has been termed *motherese*, but it is also perhaps more accurately termed **child-directed speech.** Through child-directed speech, adults seem to go out of their way to make language interesting and comprehensible to infants and other young children.

Indeed, infants do seem to prefer listening to child-directed speech more than to other forms of adult speech (Fernald, 1985). These exaggerations seem to gain and hold infants' attention, signal to the infants when to take turns in vocalizing, and communicate affect (emotion-related information). Across cultures, parents seem to use this specialized form of speech, further tailoring it to particular circumstances: using rising intonations to gain attention; falling intonations to comfort; and brief, discontinuous, rapid-fire explosions of speech to warn against prohibited behavior (Fernald et al., 1989).

Parents even seem to model the correct format for verbal interactions. Early caregiver-child verbal interactions are characterized by *verbal turn-taking*, in which the caregiver says something and then uses vocal inflection to cue the infant to respond; the infant babbles, sneezes, burps, or otherwise makes some audible response; the caregiver accepts whatever noises the infant makes as valid communicative utterances and replies; the infant further responds to the cue; and so on for as long as they both show interest in continuing. Parents also seem to work hard to understand children's early utterances, in which one or two words might be used for conveying an entire array of concepts. As the child grows older and more sophisticated and acquires more language, parents gradually provide less linguistic support and demand increasingly sophisticated utterances from the child. It is as if they initially provide a scaffolding from which the child can construct an edifice of language, and as the child's language develops, the parents gradually remove the scaffolding.

The mechanism of imitation is quite appealing in its simplicity; unfortunately, it does not explain many aspects of language acquisition. For example, if imitation is the primary mechanism, why do children universally begin by producing one-word utterances, then two-word and other telegraphic utterances, and later complete sentences? Why not start out with complete sentences? In addition, the inherent productivity of language suggests that we produce speech we have never heard before. Shakespeare may have been more productive than most of us, but all of us are quite innovative in the production of language.

The most compelling argument against imitation alone is the phenomenon of **overregularization,** which occurs when young children have acquired an understanding of how a language usually works and apply its general rules to exceptional cases. For example, instead of imitating their parents' sentence, "The

mice fell down the hole, and they ran home," the young child might overregularize the irregular forms and say, "The mouses falled down the hole, and they runned home." An alternative explanation of language acquisition is thus needed.

CONDITIONING. The proposed alternative mechanism of conditioning is also exquisitely simple: Children hear utterances and associate those utterances with particular objects and events in their environment. They then produce those utterances and are rewarded by their parents and others for having spoken. Initially, their utterances are not perfect, but through successive approximations, they come to speak just as well as native adult speakers of their language. The progression from babbling to one-word utterances to more complex speech would seem to support the notion that children begin with simple associations, and their utterances gradually increase in complexity and in the degree to which they approximate adult speech.

As with imitation, the simplicity of the proposed conditioning mechanism does not suffice to explain actual language acquisition. For one thing, parents are much more likely to respond to the *veridical content* of the child's speech—that is, whether the statement is true or false—than to the relative pronunciational or grammatical correctness of the speech (Brown, Cazden, & Bellugi, 1969). In addition, even if parents did respond to the grammatical correctness of children's speech, their responses might explain why children eventually stop overregularizing their speech but not why they ever begin doing so. Perhaps the most compelling contradiction relates to productivity: the observation that children constantly employ novel utterances, for which they have never previously been rewarded and which they never heard uttered before. Children consistently apply the words and language structures they already know to novel situations and contexts for which they have never before received reinforcement. Clearly, some other process or predisposition must be involved in children's acquisition of language.

> How might researchers design an experiment (or a series of experiments) to assess the roles of imitation and of conditioning in children's language acquisition?

Nature, Too

If neither nature nor nurture alone adequately explains all aspects of language acquisition, just how might nature facilitate nurture in the process? Noted linguist Noam Chomsky proposed (1965, 1972) that humans have an innate **language-acquisition device (LAD),** which facilitates language acquisition. That is, we humans seem to be mentally prewired or biologically preconfigured to be ready to acquire language.

Given the complex neuropsychology of other aspects of human perception and thought, it is not unreasonable to consider that we may be neuropsychologically predisposed to acquire language. Several observations of humans support this notion. For one thing, human speech perception is quite remarkable. In addition to noting our rapid phonemic specialization (mentioned in regard to babbling), recall from Chapter 5 our amazing ability to discern from a continuous flow of auditory stimuli the distinct places where one word ends and another word begins. Note also that all children within a broad normal range of abilities and environments seem to acquire language at an incredibly rapid rate. In fact, deaf children acquire sign language in about the same way and at about the same rate as hearing children acquire spoken language. If you have ever struggled to acquire a second language, you can appreciate the relative ease and speed with which young children acquire their first language. What's more, children seem to have a knack for acquiring an understanding of the many rules of language structure and can apply those rules to new vocabulary and new contexts.

As we have seen, almost all children seem to acquire these aspects of language in roughly the same progression and at about the same time. Yet the linguistic environment clearly plays a role in the language-acquisition process. In fact, there seem to be **critical periods**—times of rapid development, during which a particular ability must be developed if it is ever to develop adequately—for acquiring these understandings of language. During such periods, the environment plays a crucial role. For example, the cooing and babbling stages seem to be a critical period for acquiring a native speaker's discrimination and production of the distinctive phonemes of a particular language; during this critical period, the child's linguistic context must provide those distinctive phonemes.

There seems to be a critical period for acquiring a native understanding of a language's syntax, too. Perhaps the greatest support for this view comes from studies of adult users of American Sign Language (ASL). Among adults who have signed ASL for 30 years or more, researchers could discernibly differentiate among those who acquired ASL before age 4, between ages 4 and 6, and after age 12. Despite 30 years of signing, those who acquired ASL later in childhood showed less profound understanding of the distinctive syntax of ASL (Meier, 1991; Newport, 1990). Studies of linguistically isolated children seem to provide additional support for the notion of the interaction of both physiological maturation and environmental support. Of the rare children who have been linguistically isolated, those who are rescued at younger ages seem to acquire more sophisticated language structures than do those who are rescued when they are older.

Thus it seems that neither nature nor nurture alone determines language acquisition. An alternative postulate, **hypothesis testing,** suggests an integration of nature and nurture: Children acquire language by mentally forming tentative hypotheses regarding language and then testing these hypotheses in the environment. It has been suggested (Slobin, 1971, 1985) that the way in which they implement this process follows several operating principles. In forming

This interpreter is translating spoken English into American Sign Language, which has a distinctive vocabulary and grammatical structure.

Searchers . . .   *ELISSA NEWPORT*

Elissa Newport is George Eastman Professor of Psychology at the University of Rochester.

Q: *How did you become interested in psychology in general and in your area in particular?*

A: When I was an undergraduate, I became very interested in learning theory. Then in graduate school I took a physiological psych class, which read a paper by Eric Lenneberg on the biological basis of language. That paper got me particularly interested in language acquisition issues. I started taking linguistics courses from Lila Gleitman, who became my advisor, and cognitive psychology courses from Henry Gleitman. So I focused on language.

Q: *What ideas or whose theories have influenced you?*

A: Well, certainly Noam Chomsky's. His view of language has had a very big impact on the way that I have come to think about language. And also Eric Lenneberg, who had a biological view of language; some of the developmental psychobiology literature, done by lots of people; and then individuals who have personally influenced me, Lila and Henry Gleitman.

Q: *What is your greatest asset as a psychologist?*

A: A continuing interest in the unsolved big questions and a continuing breadth of interests. I always try to keep up with other fields, like developmental psychobiology and linguistics, by sitting in on lots of other people's courses. Staying abreast of other fields keeps me thinking about connections.

Q: *What distinguishes a really great psychologist from just a good one?*

A: What makes someone really great is the ability to keep their eye on the major questions, the enduring questions about behavior, and not get sucked into small issues that may arise from an experiment.

Q: *How do you get your ideas or insights for research?*

A: Often, it's actually that some phenomenon that I notice in the world, or in my subjects, is really pertinent to some question I hadn't meant to be studying. I do a lot of work on sign language acquisition. At the same time, I'm married to a deaf person, and I spend a lot of time with deaf adults, and sometimes deaf children.

When I was first learning to sign, I noticed that I could always tell who was a native signer and who wasn't.

Then I realized that the differences between them may have been about critical periods. Lenneberg had suggested there was a critical period for learning language. But it has been very difficult to figure out how to study that question. So I realized, we had an experiment on our hands here that addressed that question because of natural variations in the community.

Q: *What is your major contribution to psychology?*

A: I hope I haven't made it yet. Of what I've done thus far, my most important contribution has to do with sign language. I think bringing sign language research to bear on some of the enduring questions about language and language acquisition is a contribution that I hope will stick.

Q: *What advice would you give to someone starting in the field of psychology?*

A: Keep hold of what seems interesting and important, and don't get into a mode where you try to grind out as many experiments as you can. Also, try to work with the very best and most interesting people. Think about whose work you've found really compelling and interesting, and then try to work with that person.

Q: *Apart from your life as an academic, how have you found psychology to be important?*

A: Well, the fact that I work on sign language and I work in the deaf community, makes a big connection between what I do as an academic and what issues I'm interested in outside of academics. It's one of the few fields I can think of where what we've learned as academics is really pertinent to people's lives.

Q: *How do you keep yourself academically challenged?*

A: In addition to taking a lot of courses, I also change topics or subtopics every five years. I find myself wanting to study something new. If I keep working on exactly the same topic I start feeling like I'm getting down to the little boring experiments.

Q: *What do you want people to remember about your work?*

A: I hope that some of the things I studied will outlast current theorizing or current views of things. I try to study things that I think would be pertinent to any kind of theory we're ever going to build.

hypotheses, young children look for and attend to (1) patterns of changes in the forms of words; (2) morphemic inflections that signal changes in meaning, especially suffixes; and (3) sequences of morphemes, including both the sequences of affixes and roots and the sequences of words in sentences.

In addition, children learn to avoid exceptions to the general patterns they observe and to avoid interrupting or rearranging the noun phrase and the verb phrase in sentences. Because children seem to follow these same general patterns of hypothesis testing, regardless of the language they acquire or of the context in which they acquire it, some psychologists believe that children must be naturally predisposed to hypothesis testing. Although not all linguists support the hypothesis-testing view, the phenomena of over-regularization (using and sometimes overapplying rules) and of language productivity (creating novel utterances based on some kind of understanding of how to do so) seem to support it.

Elissa Newport (1990) adds a slightly different twist to this view, suggesting that while children are acquiring language, they do *not* pay attention to all aspects of language. Instead, children focus on the perceptually most salient aspects of language, which happen to be the most meaningful aspects in most cases. Although her studies have focused on deaf children's acquisition of ASL, it is thought that this phenomenon applies to spoken language as well.

Language Acquisition in Nonhuman Species

Yet another argument in favor of the combined roles of nature and nurture in language acquisition comes from studies of language acquisition in nonhuman species. The philosopher René Descartes suggested that language is what qualitatively distinguishes human beings from other species. However, this point is debatable, and we now consider the evidence both favoring and opposing it.

Before we get into the particulars of language in nonhuman species, we should underscore again the distinction between communication and language. Few would doubt that nonhuman animals communicate in one way or another. What is at issue is whether they do so through what reasonably can be called a language. *Language* is the specific use of an organized means of combining words in order to communicate. *Communication* more broadly encompasses not only the exchange of thoughts and feelings through language, but also nonverbal communication such as through gestures, glances, distancing, and other contextual cues. Studies of animal communication illustrate the distinction between language and communication.

Primates—especially chimpanzees—offer our most promising insights into nonhuman language. Perhaps the most internationally well-known investigator of chimpanzees in the wild has been Jane Goodall. She has studied many aspects of chimp be-

havior, including chimps' vocalizations, many of which she considers to be clearly communicative, although not necessarily indicative of language. For example, chimps have a specific cry indicating that they are about to be attacked and another vocalization calling together their fellow chimps. Nonetheless, their repertoire of communicative vocalizations seems to be small, nonproductive, limited in structure, lacking in multiplicity of structure, and relatively nonarbitrary. It does not satisfy our criteria for a language.

Initial attempts to teach language directly to chimpanzees failed. Early investigators (Hayes, 1951; Kellogg & Kellogg, 1933) attempted to teach chimpanzees to communicate vocally, and failed rather miserably. R. Allen Gardner and Beatrice Gardner (1969) suggested that a better way to teach language to chimpanzees might be through the use of ASL. By using sign language, the Gardners were able to teach their chimp, Washoe, rudimentary language skills (Brown, 1973), although her development certainly never went beyond the stages of infant language. Subsequently, David Premack (1971) had even greater

Although primates definitely communicate in their natural environments, they do not spontaneously use language. Attempts to teach nonhuman primates to use language have been successful to varying degrees.

success with his chimpanzee, Sarah, who picked up a vocabulary of more than 100 words of various parts of speech and who showed at least rudimentary linguistic skills.

A less positive view of the linguistic capabilities of chimpanzees has been taken by Herbert Terrace (1979), who raised a chimp named Nim Chimpsky, a takeoff on the name of the eminent linguist Noam Chomsky. Over the course of several years, Nim made more than 19,000 multiple-sign utterances in a slightly modified version of ASL. Most of his utterances consisted of two-word combinations.

Terrace's careful analysis of these utterances, however, revealed that the large majority of them were repetitions of what Nim had seen. Terrace concluded that despite what appeared to be impressive accomplishments, Nim did not show even the rudiments of syntactic expression: The chimp could produce single- or even multiple-word utterances, but not in a syntactically organized way. For example, Nim would alternate signing, "Give Nim banana," "Banana give Nim," and "Banana Nim give," showing no preference for the grammatically correct form. Moreover, when Terrace studied films showing other chimpanzees supposedly producing language, he came to the same conclusion for them that he had reached for Nim. His position, then, is that although chimpanzees can understand and produce utterances, they do not have linguistic competence in the same sense that even very young humans do. They lack structure and particularly multiplicity of structure.

> Sometimes, well-intentioned researchers unwittingly attribute more meaning to utterances than is actually being communicated. In addition, researchers may unintentionally cue and then reinforce given "signs" of communication. How can researchers avoid such practices, which might overestimate the communicative abilities of their nonhuman subjects?

Susan Savage-Rumbaugh, Kelly McDonald, Rose Sevcik, William Hopkins, and Elizabeth Rubert (1986) have found the best evidence yet in favor of language use among chimpanzees. Their pygmy chimpanzees have spontaneously combined the visual symbols of an artificial language the researchers taught them (by manipulating visual symbols such as red triangles, blue squares, etc.). They even appear to understand some of the language spoken to them. One pygmy chimp in particular (Greenfield & Savage-Rumbaugh, 1990) seems to possess remarkable skill, even demonstrating a primitive grasp of language structure. It may be that the difference in

results is due to the particular kind of chimp tested or to the procedures used. At this point, we cannot be sure.

Our best guess, then, is that at least some chimpanzees can be taught the rudiments of language. Hence, we humans may not be able to point to language as the distinguishing feature between us and other species. Although our fundamental ability to use language may not qualitatively differentiate us from all other species of animals, it seems almost certain that the language facility of humans far exceeds that of other species we have studied. Chomsky (1991) has stated the key question regarding nonhuman language quite eloquently:

> If an animal had a capacity as biologically advantageous as language but somehow hadn't used it until now, it would be an evolutionary miracle, like finding an island of humans who could be taught to fly.

SEMANTICS: THE STUDY OF MEANING

> ### IN SEARCH OF...
>
> What are a few ways in which you find or figure out the meanings of words?

Language is very difficult to put into words.

— *Voltaire*

You probably do not remember the moment that words first came alive to you, but your parents surely do. In fact, one of the greatest joys of being a parent is to watch a child's amazing discovery that words have meanings. **Semantics** is the study of the meanings of words.

Theories of Meaning

Linguists, philosophers, and psychologists have long contemplated just what "meaning" means and have proposed several theories over the years. Two theories, componential (or definitional) theory and prototype theory, have appealed to psychologists.

Componential theory, also termed *definitional theory,* claims that meaning can be understood by disassembling words into a set of meaning components (Katz, 1972; Katz & Fodor, 1963). In other words,

Searchers . . .

George Miller is James S. McDonnell Distinguished University Professor of Psychology Emeritus at Princeton University.

Q: *What is your major contribution to psychology?*

A: Introducing the importance of language in psychology. You cannot have a decent psychology of human beings that doesn't include the psychology of language.

Q: *What did you learn from your mentors?*

A: Smitty Stevens and Edwin Boring told me to be careful about writing. Boring told me that if I spent an hour focusing on what exactly I wanted to say in an article, I could save readers five minutes in understanding. Over time, that would be hours and hours of time saved. They were always extremely careful about saying what they meant. The other thing I learned from Smitty and fellow graduate students was psychophysical methods. I still think along the lines I learned to think in terms of designing psychophysical experiments.

Q: *How do you usually get your ideas or insights for research?*

A: Most of my ideas come from reading broadly and borrowing ideas from one field to use in another. I've wandered through statistics and linguistics, probability theory, information theory, computer science, artificial intelligence, and computer simulation. I keep my eyes open and have certain problems that I worry about. I say to students, "The grass grows in the cracks between fields." That's where things really grow.

Q: *Apart from your life as an academic, how has psychology been important to you?*

A: I've always wondered about that. We used to have a family joke, how to get kids to bed. I said I would use psychology on them, by which I meant I had a baseball bat behind the door with the word "psychology" on it. And I would chase them upstairs with the baseball bat! The way I look at the world is influenced by the fact that I think the mind and the mental representations that I and other people that I'm working with have, are important.

Q: *How do you keep yourself academically challenged?*

A: A lot of people seem to depend on me to keep going. It would be easy for me now, being emeritus, and having accomplished as much as I've liked to, to just retire and play golf. But I've got an awfully good group working with me, and I think I would just get bored to death if I didn't have these people to interact with. So, the situation I am in is challenging. I could retire, but I wouldn't know what to do if I did.

Q: *What would you like people to remember about you and your work?*

A: I hope they think that reintroducing the mind into experimental psychology was a worthwhile thing to do.

Q: *What do you further hope to achieve or contribute?*

A: Marvin Minsky said it best: "We are least aware of what our minds do best." One of the things that our minds are extremely good at is what the linguists call disambiguation. That is, if you look up any common word in the dictionary, you'll find five or six different meanings for it. If you try to program computers to process language, the hard thing is to tell the computer which of the five or six meanings is the one that is intended in a given content. And that's necessary for any kind of language understanding or machine translation. Even a good spelling checker could be improved if it understood. But people are so good at it. If I say to you, "He nailed the board across the window," it doesn't occur to you that board has any meaning other than a piece of wood. But if I say to you, "He nailed the board for corruption," it doesn't occur to you that board could have any meaning other than a group of people in some position of authority. You do that totally unconsciously. You select the correct meaning so fast that the ambiguity of it really doesn't enter consciousness, most of the time.

So, what we're trying to do now is to build a computer simulation that will be able to recognize the correct meaning. We have lots and lots of good ideas, and they work about 80 percent of the time. I see it in the larger context, sort of a test tube example of something we do all the time. All of our social and cultural understanding involves taking into account the context. Not just of a word in a sentence, but also of a behavior in a given context.

each component is an essential element of the concept; together, the properties uniquely define the concept. These components may be viewed as **defining features** because they constitute the definition of a word, according to the componential point of view.

Consider, for example, the word *bachelor*. A bachelor can be viewed as comprising three components: male, unmarried, and adult. Because the components are each singly necessary, even the absence of one component makes the word inapplicable. Thus, an unmarried male who is not an adult would not be a bachelor.

The **prototype theory** suggests that meaning is derived not from the defining features of a word, but from the **characteristic features** that describe the prototypical model of the word. What is a *characteristic feature?* Whereas a defining feature is possessed by every instance of a concept, a characteristic feature need not be; instead, many or most instances would possess a characteristic feature. Thus, the ability to fly is typical of birds, but it is not a defining feature of a bird. An ostrich seems less birdlike than a robin, in part because it cannot fly. Similarly, a typical game may be enjoyable, but it need not be so. Indeed, when people are asked to list the features of a word that is a category, such as *fruit* or *furniture*, the majority of features they list are characteristic rather than defining (Rosch & Mervis, 1975). According to the prototype view, an object (or idea) will be classified as an instance of a category if it is sufficiently similar to the prototype. Exactly what is meant by similarity to a prototype can be a complex issue, and there are actually different theories of how this similarity should be measured (Smith & Medin, 1981). For our purposes, we view similarity in terms of the number of features shared between an object and the prototype.

Actually, some (e.g., Ross & Spalding, 1994) suggest that instead of using a single prototype for deriving the meaning of a concept, we use several **exemplars**—several alternative typical representatives of the class. For example, in considering birds, we might think of not only the prototypical songbird, which is small, flies, builds nests, sings, and so on, but also exemplars for birds of prey, for large flightless birds, for medium-sized water fowl, and so on. Brian Ross and Thomas Spalding suggest that if we have multiple exemplars, when we see an instance of a bird, we can more flexibly match this instance to an appropriate exemplar than to a single prototype.

SYNTAX: THE STUDY OF STRUCTURE

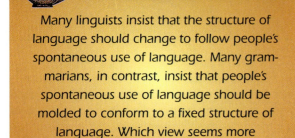

IN SEARCH OF...

Many linguists insist that the structure of language should change to follow people's spontaneous use of language. Many grammarians, in contrast, insist that people's spontaneous use of language should be molded to conform to a fixed structure of language. Which view seems more appropriate to you? Why?

An important part of the psychology of language is the study of linguistic structure—specifically **syntax,** which is the systematic way in which words can be combined and sequenced to make meaningful phrases and sentences (Carroll, 1986). Syntax begins with the study of the grammar of phrases and sentences.

Although you have heard the word *grammar* used to refer to how people *ought* to structure their sentences, psycholinguists use **grammar** to refer to the study of language patterns. Regular patterns relate to the functions and relationships of words in a sentence, extending as broadly as the level of discourse and as narrowly as the pronunciation and meaning of individual words.

In your English courses, you may have been introduced to **prescriptive grammar,** which prescribes the "correct" ways to structure the use of written and spoken language. Of greater interest to psycholinguists is **descriptive grammar,** in which an attempt is made to describe the structure, functions, and relationships of words in language. In particular, linguists are interested in syntax because of the importance of sentence structure to language function.

Phrase-structure grammars analyze sentences according to the order in which words appear. Also termed *surface-structure grammars*, these grammars deal with syntax at a surface level of analysis. This level is concerned only with the superficial sequence of words, regardless of differences or similarities of meaning.

Basically, any sentence in the English language can be analyzed according to a phrase-structure grammar. Sentences in other languages can be analyzed according to phrase-structure grammars relevant to those languages.

Despite the wide applicability of phrase-structure grammars, their value for understanding syntax has been questioned. Chomsky (1957) revolutionized the study of syntax by convincingly arguing that phrase-structure grammars are inadequate to convey fully the structures of sentences, let alone the broader aspects of language beyond the sentence level. Consider an example that illustrates Chomsky's points:

1. Susie greedily ate the hungry crocodile.
2. The hungry crocodile was eaten greedily by Susie.

Oddly enough, a phrase-structure grammar would not show any particular relation at all between sentences 1 and 2. Indeed, phrase-structure analyses of each pair of sentences would look almost completely different. Yet the two sentences in each pair differ only in voice, with the first sentence expressed in the active voice and the second in the passive voice.

According to transformational grammar, the underlying meaning of the two sentences is the same, so the structural difference between the two sentences centers on *attitude*—that is, the stance that the speaker is taking toward the events or items being described. Recall from Chapter 8 the mention of propositions, illustrating that the same meaning can be derived through alternative means of representation. The preceding two sentences represent the same proposition.

Chomsky proposed that sentences can be analyzed both at a surface-structure level, as is done with phrase-structure grammars, and at a **deep-structure level,** which takes into account the meanings we derive from the sentence structures. He posited a way to derive surface structures from deep structures, and to interrelate different surface structures. Chomsky's grammar is termed **transformational grammar** because the operations used for generating surface structures from deep structures are referred to as *transformations.*

PRAGMATICS AND SOCIOLINGUISTICS: LANGUAGE IN CONTEXT

IN SEARCH OF...

How do you change the ways in which you express your thoughts to suit your linguistic context (e.g., with friends vs. with a job interviewer)?

Traditionally, linguistic studies have focused on how people understand language at the phoneme, morpheme, word, and sentence levels, giving little attention to the broader range of discourse. Psycholinguistic research has followed suit. In recent decades, however, students of language have become increasingly interested in **pragmatics,** the study of how people use language, and *sociolinguistics*, the study of how people use language in the context of social interaction.

Some sociolinguists study the ways in which people use nonlinguistic elements in conversational contexts. For example, sociolinguists and psycholinguists interested in observing your language use in context would be interested in your use of gestures and vocal inflections, as well as your use of *proxemics* (relative distancing and positioning of you and your fellow conversants). Under most circumstances (perhaps first or blind dates to the contrary), you change your contextual cues for language without giving these changes much thought. Similarly, you usually

We often use gestures to enhance our verbal communication. Sometimes, our gestures, such as finger-pointing and lip-biting, communicate more effectively than do our words.

un-self-consciously change your language patterns to fit different contexts.

To get an idea of how you change your own use of language in different contexts, suppose that you and your friend are meeting right after work. Something comes up, and you must call your friend to change the time or place for your meeting. When you call your friend at work, your friend's supervisor answers and offers to take a message. Exactly what would you say to your friend's supervisor to ensure that your friend will know about the change in time or location? Suppose, instead, that the 2-year-old son of your friend's supervisor answers. Exactly what would you say in this situation? Finally, suppose that your friend answers directly. How has your language for each context been modified, even though your purpose in all three contexts was the same?

Speech Acts

Another key aspect of the way in which you use language depends on what purpose you plan to achieve with language. In the preceding example, you were using language to try to ensure that your friend would meet you at the new location and time. When you speak, what kinds of things can you accomplish?

In the living room he pulled on the same pants he'd draped over the sofa the night before. "You eat?"

Like most of his questions, this one caused me to hesitate. Did I eat? Had I eaten? Did he want to know if I was hungry? Whether I usually ate breakfast? Whether eating was customary with me, as with other mortals? I took a stab.

"Sure," I said.

"What?"

I blinked. "What?"
"What did you eat?"
"Nothing. I meant I'm hungry," I said.

—*Richard Russo*, The Risk Pool

John Searle (1975a), a philosopher, has proposed a theory of **speech acts** that addresses the question of what can be accomplished with speech. According to Searle, all speech acts fall into five basic categories, based on the purpose of the acts: **repre-**

TABLE 9-2
Speech Acts
The five basic categories of speech acts encompass the various tasks that can be accomplished through speech (or other modes of using language).

Speech Act	Description	Example
Representative	A speech act by which a person conveys a belief that a given proposition is true	If I say that "The Marquis de Sade was a sadist," I am conveying my belief that the marquis enjoyed seeing others feel pain. I can use various sources of information to support my belief, including the fact that the word "sadist" derives from this marquis. Nonetheless, the statement is nothing more than a statement of belief. Similarly, I can make a statement that is more directly verifiable, such as "As you can see here on this thermometer, the temperature outside is 31 degrees Fahrenheit." We can put in various qualifiers to show our degree of certainty, but we are still stating a belief, which may or may not be verifiable.
Directive	An attempt by a speaker to get a listener to do something, such as supplying the answer to a question	I can ask my son to help me shovel snow in various ways, some of which are more direct than others, such as "Please help me shovel the snow," or "It sure would be nice if you were to help me shovel the snow." The different surface forms are all attempts to get him to help me. Some directives are quite indirect. If I ask, "Has it stopped raining yet?" I am still uttering a directive, in this case seeking information rather than physical assistance. In fact, almost any sentence structured as a question probably serves a directive function.
Commissive	A commitment by the speaker to engage in some future course of action	If my son responds, "I'm busy now, but I'll help you shovel the snow later," he is uttering a commissive, in that he is pledging his future help. If my daughter then says, "I'll help you," she, too, is uttering a commissive, because she is pledging her assistance now. Promises, pledges, contracts, guarantees, assurances, and the like all constitute commissives.
Expressive	A statement regarding the speaker's psychological state	If I tell my son later, "I'm really upset that you didn't come through in helping me shovel the snow," that would be an expressive. If my son says, "I'm sorry I didn't get around to helping you out," he would be uttering an expressive. If my daughter says, "Daddy, I'm glad I was able to help out," she is uttering an expressive.
Declaration (also termed *performative*)	A speech act by which the very act of making a statement brings about an intended new state of affairs	When the cleric says, "I now pronounce you husband and wife," the speech act is a declaration, because once the speech act is accomplished, the marriage rite is completed. Instead, suppose that you are called into your boss's office and told that you are responsible for the company losing $50,000, and then your boss says, "You're fired." The speech act results in your being in a new state—that is, unemployed. You might then tell your boss, "That's fine, because I wrote you a letter yesterday saying that the money was lost because of your glaring incompetence, not mine, and I resign." You are again making a declaration.

sentatives, **directives, commissives, expressives, declarations** (also termed **performatives**). Table 9-2 defines and illustrates these categories. The appealing thing about Searle's taxonomy is that it classifies almost any statement that might be made. It shows exhaustively, at least at one level, the different kinds of things speech can accomplish.

Sometimes, speech acts are indirect, meaning that we accomplish our goals through speaking obliquely. One way of communicating obliquely is by **indirect requests,** through which we make a request without doing so straightforwardly (Gordon & Lakoff, 1971; Searle, 1975b). (See Table 9-3 for examples of indirect requests.)

Conversational Postulates

In speaking to each other, we implicitly set up a cooperative enterprise. Indeed, if we do not cooperate with each other when we speak, we often end up talking past rather than to each other, and we do not communicate what we intended. H. P. Grice (1967) has proposed that conversations thrive on the basis of a **cooperative principle,** by which we seek to communicate in ways that make it easy for our listener to understand what we mean. According to Grice, successful conversations follow four maxims: the *maxim of quantity*, the *maxim of quality*, the *maxim of relation*, and the *maxim of manner* (see Table 9-4).

Scripts

Maxims and turn-taking strategies may help to guide us through almost any conversational context. In some situations, however, in order to communicate effectively, the parties to the communication must have a shared understanding about the situation being discussed. For such situations, some suggest that we may use scripts to help us fill in the gaps that often appear in actual conversations. Roger Schank and Robert Abelson (1977, p. 41) define a **script** as "a predetermined, stereotyped sequence of actions that defines a well-known situation."

Various empirical studies have tested the validity of the script notion. For instance, Gordon Bower, John Black, and Terrence Turner (1979) presented their subjects with various brief stories describing common situations. The subjects were then asked either to recall as much as they could of each of the stories or to discern which of several sentences had been included in the stories. The critical result was that subjects showed a significant tendency to recall elements and sentences that were not actually in the stories, but that were parts of the scripts that the stories represented. That is, scripts seem to guide what people recall and recognize (see also Chapter 8, regarding the influence of prior knowledge on memory tasks).

In a conversational context, being able to draw from the same script (i.e., share similar schemas re-

TABLE 9-3
Indirect Speech Acts
One way of using speech is to communicate obliquely, rather than directly.

Type of Indirect Speech Act	Example of an Indirect Request for Information
Abilities	If you say, "Can you tell me where the restroom is?" to a waitress at a restaurant, and she says, "Yes, of course I can," the chances are she missed the point. The question about her ability to tell you the location of the restroom was an indirect request for her to tell you exactly where the restroom is.
Desire	"I would be grateful if you told me where the restroom is." Your statements of thanks in advance are really ways of getting someone to do what you want.
Future action	"Would you tell me where the restroom is?" Your question seeks a future action from your conversational partner—to say where the restroom is (and not just that, yes, the partner could tell you if he or she wished).
Reasons	You need not spell out the reasons to imply that there are good reasons to comply with the request. For example, you might imply that you have such reasons for the waitress to tell you where the restroom is: "I need to know where the restroom is."

TABLE 9-4
Conversational Postulates
In order to maximize the communication that occurs during conversation, speakers generally follow four maxims.

Postulate	Maxim	Example
Maxim of quantity	Make your contribution to a conversation as informative as required, but no more informative than is appropriate	If someone asks you the temperature outside, and you reply, "It's 31.297868086298 degrees out there," you are violating the maxim of quantity because you are giving more information than was probably wanted.
Maxim of quality	Your contribution to a conversation should be truthful; you are expected to say what you believe to be the case	Clearly, there are awkward circumstances in which each of us is unsure of just how much honesty is being requested, such as for the response to, "Honey, how do I look?" Under most circumstances, however, communication depends on an assumption that both parties to the communication are being truthful.
Maxim of relation	You should make your contributions to a conversation relevant to the aims of the conversation	Almost any large meeting I attend seems to have someone who violates this maxim. This someone inevitably goes into long digressions that have nothing to do with the purpose of the meeting and that hold up the meeting. That reminds me of a story a friend once told me about a meeting he once attended, where. . . .
Maxim of manner	You should try to avoid obscure expressions, vague utterances, and purposeful obfuscation of your point	Nobel-prize winning physicist Richard Feynman (1985) described how he once read a paper by a well-known sociologist, and he found that he could not make heads or tails of it. One sentence went something like this: "The individual member of the social community often receives information via visual, symbolic channels" (p. 281). Feynman concluded, in essence, that the sociologist was violating the maxim of manner when Feynman realized that the sentence meant, "People read."

garding a particular scenario) allows us to economize on what we say, omitting details known to all those who know the script. When we share a script, our conversational partners can fill in the gaps based on knowledge about the script. Shared scripts clearly make conversation much more comprehensible and more interesting. We would bore one another to tears and have little time to discuss what interests us if we had to provide all the minute details of common experiences. Often, the conversations between long-married couples or long-time friends are completely incomprehensible to others due to the huge amount of detail omitted because of elaborate shared scripts for the situations being discussed. When one or more parties to a conversation are not conversing from the same script, however, communication breaks down.

> Make up a script for a common experience, such as going to see a doctor. Be sure to include all the relevant features of the script. How might someone else's script be different from yours if the person writing the script were a different age, a different gender, from a different culture, or otherwise viewing the experience differently? Give an example of at least one different point of view.

Slips of the Tongue

Until now, this chapter has focused on how people use—or at least attempt to use—language correctly. It is only fair, in a discussion of pragmatics, to talk about how people use language incorrectly. One of the most obvious errors is **slips of the tongue**—inadvertent semantic or *articulatory* (the production of language sounds) mistakes in what we say. Among the first psychologists to study slips of the tongue was Sigmund Freud. In fact, his description of this phenomenon led us to term particular instances of such errors *Freudian slips*, which are those slips that seem to reveal hidden (repressed) motivations and sentiments. For example, a businessperson might encounter a business rival and say, "I'm glad to beat you," instead of saying, "I'm glad to meet you."

In contrast to the psychoanalytic view, psycholinguists and other cognitive psychologists are intrigued by slips of the tongue because of what the errors may tell us about how language is produced. In speaking, we have a mental plan for what we are going to say. Sometimes, however, this plan is disrupted when our articulatory mechanism does not cooperate with our cognitive one. Slips of the tongue may be taken to indicate that we have a language of thought that differs from the language through which we express our thoughts (Fodor, 1975). We have the idea right, but its expression comes out wrong. Sometimes, we are not even aware of the slip until it is pointed out to us, because in the language of the mind, whatever it may be, the idea is right, even though the expression is inadvertently wrong.

Victoria Fromkin (1973) has classified the various kinds of slips that people tend to make in their conversations:

1. *Anticipation*—using a vocal sound before it is appropriate in the sentence because it corresponds to a sound that will be needed later in the utterance: In describing the death of a mutual acquaintance, a colleague of mine once referred to the acquaintance as having "fought the farm," rather than as having "bought the farm," the intended colloquialism to describe someone's death.
2. *Perseveration*—using a sound that was appropriate earlier in the sentence but is not appropriate later on: In a fit of rage I once had in my recent youth, I guaranteed someone that I would "cream that castard!"
3. *Substitution*—substituting one word for another: A friend once warned me to do something "after it is too late," rather than "before it is too late."
4. *Reversal*—reversing the initial sounds of two words: I once ordered "keaches and pream" at an ice cream store. Sometimes, reversals can be fortuitously opportune, creating **spoonerisms**, in which the reversal of initial sounds makes

two entirely different words. The term is named after the Reverend William Spooner, who was famous for reversals. One of his choicest slips was "You have hissed all my mystery lectures."

Although these and other kinds of slips of the tongue can be classified in a neat list, different kinds of slips appear to occur at different hierarchical levels of linguistic processing—that is, at the acoustical level of phonemes, the semantic level of morphemes, or even higher levels. For example, a substitution is a semantic error, whereas a reversal is probably primarily a phonemic, articulatory error. Although we do not know how many levels of processing are needed to produce speech, the presence of various kinds of errors suggests that there may be at least several such levels. Data from studies of speech errors may help us better understand normal language processing. As you might have guessed, many slips of the tongue provide insights not only into how people use language, but also into how people think. The interaction of language and thought is the topic of the next section.

LANGUAGE AND THOUGHT

> IN SEARCH OF...
>
> How does your linguistic context (the language you hear, read, speak, and write) affect what you think and how you think?

One of the most interesting areas in the study of language is the relationship between language and thought. For one thing, this relationship pervades the study of language such that almost everything written about language implies that thought and language interact. The language we hear and read shapes our thoughts, and our thoughts shape what we say and write. Of the many ways in which to study this relationship, cognitive psychologists and psycholinguists are particularly intrigued by studies comparing and contrasting users of differing languages and users of differing dialects. Such studies form the basis of this section.

"This rain is very strong," I said in Chinyanja. The word I used for rain, mpemera, was very precise. It meant the sweeping rain driven into the veranda by the wind.

—Paul Theroux, My Secret History

Linguistic Relativity and Linguistic Universals

Different languages use different lexicons and syntactical structures that reflect the physical and cultural environments in which the languages arose and developed. For example, the Garo of Burma distinguish among many different kinds of rice, which is understandable, because they are a rice-growing culture. Nomadic Arabs have more than 20 different words for camels. These peoples clearly conceptualize rice and camels more specifically and in more complex ways than do people outside their cultural groups. The question is, as a result of these linguistic differences, do the Garo think about rice differently from the way we do? Also, do the Arabs think about camels differently from the way we do?

The syntactical structures of languages differ, too. Almost all languages permit some way in which to communicate actions, agents of actions, and objects of actions (Gerrig & Banaji, 1994). What differs across languages is the range of grammatical inflections and other markings that speakers are obliged to include as key elements of a sentence. For example, in describing past actions in English, we indicate whether an action took place in the past by so indicating in the verb form (e.g., walk*ed*). In Spanish and German, the verb further must indicate whether the agent of action was singular or plural and is being referred to in the first, second, or third person. In Turkish, the verb form must indicate past action, singular or plural, and the person, and it must indicate whether the action was witnessed or experienced directly by the speaker or was only experienced indirectly. Do these differences and other differences in obligatory syntactical structures influence—perhaps even constrain—the users of these languages to think about things differently because of the language they use while thinking?

Two interrelated propositions relevant to this question are linguistic determinism and linguistic relativity. **Linguistic determinism** asserts that the structure of our language shapes our thoughts; in fact, the actual cognitive systems in which we think about things are determined by the language we use to describe these things. **Linguistic relativity** takes a less deterministic view, asserting that the speakers of different languages have differing cognitive systems, and that these different cognitive systems influence the ways in which people speaking the various languages think about the world. Thus, according to the relativity view, the Garo would think about rice differently from the way we do. For example, the Garo would develop more cognitive categories for rice than would

an English-speaking counterpart. When the Garo contemplated rice, they would purportedly view it differently—and perhaps with greater complexity of thought—than would English speakers, who have only a few words for rice. Thus, language would shape thought.

The linguistic relativity hypothesis is sometimes referred to as the Sapir-Whorf hypothesis, after the two men who most assertively propagated it. Edward Sapir (1941/1964) said that "we see and hear and otherwise experience very largely as we do because the language habits of our community predispose certain choices of interpretation" (p. 69). Benjamin Lee Whorf (1956) said it even more strongly:

> We dissect nature along lines laid down by our native languages. The categories and types that we isolate from the world of phenomena we do not find there because they stare every observer in the face; on the contrary, the world is presented in a kaleidoscopic flux of impressions which has to be organized by our minds—and this means largely by the linguistic systems in our minds. (p. 213)

The Sapir-Whorf hypothesis has been one of the most widely mentioned ideas in all of the social and behavioral sciences (Lonner, 1989). However, some of its implications appear to have reached mythological proportions. For example, many social scientists have warmly accepted and gladly propagated the notion that Eskimos have multitudinous words for the single English word *snow*. In direct refutation of the myth, anthropologist Laura Martin (1986) has asserted unequivocally that Eskimos do *not* have numerous words for snow. According to G. K. Pullum (1991), "no one who knows anything about Eskimo (or more accurately, about the Inuit and Yupik families of related languages spoken from Siberia to Greenland) has ever said they do" (p. 160). Martin, who has done more than anyone else to debunk the myth, understands why her colleagues might consider the myth charming, but she has been quite "disappointed in the reaction of her colleagues when she pointed out the fallacy; most, she says, took the position that true or not 'it's still a great example'" ("The Melting of a Mighty Myth," 1991).

Thus, it appears that we must exercise caution in our interpretation of linguistic relativity when we observe nouns such as *rice* and *camel*. In fact, such relativity becomes even more interesting when we go beyond the names we assign to various phenomena in our environment. For example, Spanish has two forms of the verb *to be*—*ser* and *estar*. However, they are used in different contexts. In general, *ser* is used for permanent or at least long-term states of being. For example, I might say, "Soy profesor," which uses the first-person singular form of *ser* to communicate that I am a professor. *Estar* is used for temporary states of being. I would say "Estoy escribiendo," using the first-person singular form of *estar*, to express that I am temporarily engaged in writing. The psychological question is whether native Spanish speakers have a more differentiated sense of the temporary and the permanent than would native English speakers who would use the same verb form to express both senses of *to be*. Thus far, based on the existing literature in linguistic relativity and cross-cultural analyses, this question can be answered with unequivocal certainty: We don't know.

Some research addresses **linguistic universals**—constant patterns across languages of various cultures—and relativity. Much of this research has used color names. At first glance, these words seem to be an ideal focus of research because they provide an especially convenient way of testing the hypothesis. People in every culture can be expected to be exposed, at least potentially, to pretty much the same range of colors. Yet it turns out that different languages name colors quite differently.

Do different languages divide up the color spectrum arbitrarily, or is there some systematic pattern across languages in color naming? This question has been addressed by two anthropologists, Brent Berlin and Paul Kay (1969; Kay, 1975), who investigated color terms in a large number of languages. Berlin and Kay unearthed two apparent linguistic universals about color naming across languages. First, all the languages surveyed take their basic color terms from a set of just 11 color names: black, white, red, yellow, green, blue, brown, purple, pink, orange, and gray. Languages ranged from using all 11 color names, as in English, to using just two of the names. Second, when only some of the color names are used, the naming of colors falls into a hierarchy of five levels: (1) black, white; (2) red; (3) yellow, green, blue; (4) brown; and (5) purple, pink, orange, gray. Thus, if a language names only two colors, they will be black and white. If it names three colors, they will be black, white, and red. A fourth color would be taken from the set of yellow, green, and blue, and so on until all 11 colors have been labeled.

Berlin and Kay also found evidence indicating that there exist certain *focal colors*, or colors that best represent each of the basic color terms in the language, regardless of the number of labels used in the language. (Other psycholinguists might call these colors "exemplars" or "prototypes.") Berlin and Kay worked with a set of 320 small square color chips,

which represented close to the full range of colors that people see. They asked the speakers of the various languages to point to the chip that best represented each of the color terms in their language. Berlin and Kay found that what people selected as the best red or green or other color was essentially the same, regardless of the language being spoken. Eleanor Rosch (1973) obtained similar findings and drew similar conclusions after studying the Dani tribe of New Guinea. The Dani have only two color terms, yet Rosch (who had previously published under the name "Heider") and others (Heider & Olivier, 1972) found that the Dani were able not only to identify selectively the focal colors but also even to remember focal colors more accurately than nonfocal colors.

Subsequent research (e.g., Garro, 1986; Lucy & Schweder, 1979, 1988) has questioned these findings, however, based on confounding variables. It turns out that Berlin and Kay had unwittingly used color chips that made the focal colors more salient than the nonfocal colors. Nonetheless, subsequent research on the use of color names by Kay and Willet Kempton (1984) indicated that (a) there are some linguistic universals with regard to the way in which people seem to think about color, (b) thought influences language, and (c) language appears to influence thought under some circumstances but not others.

Do you think that the researchers were wise to choose people's use of color words as an aspect of language that would facilitate their study of the cross-cultural interactions between language and thought? Why or why not?

Some people believe that persons who are not native to a given culture cannot effectively study that culture. What are the arguments for and against having non-natives study various aspects of a culture?

Thus, the findings to date on color naming suggest that some universal cognitive functions, which are important for human cultures, are not constrained by the limitations of a particular language. However, in the study of linguistic relativity, as in most areas of psychology, issues are rarely clear-cut. The absence of relativity in one domain does not necessarily imply its absence in another domain. It seems logical that language can influence thought in some ways and in some circumstances. However, it seems clear also that linguistic determinism, whereby language determines differences in thought among members of various cultures, is almost certainly inconsistent with the available evidence.

Curt Hoffman, Ivy Lau, and David Johnson (1986) came up with an intriguing experiment designed to assess the possible effects of linguistic relativity. In Chinese, a single term, *sh ì gù*, specifically describes a person who is "worldly, experienced, socially skillful, devoted to his or her family, and somewhat reserved" (p. 1098). English clearly has no comparable single term to embrace these diverse characteristics. Hoffman and colleagues composed text passages in English and in Chinese describing various characters, including the *sh ì gù* character. The researchers then asked subjects who were bilingual in Chinese and English to read the passages either in Chinese or in English and then to rate various statements about the characters, in terms of the likelihood that the statements would be true of the characters. Their results seemed to support the notion of linguistic relativity, in that the subjects were more likely to rate the various statements in accord with the *sh ì gù* stereotype when they had read the passages in Chinese than when they had read the passages in English. Similarly, when subjects were asked to write their own impressions of the characters, their descriptions conformed more closely to the *sh ì gù* stereotype if they had previously read the passages in Chinese. These authors do not suggest that it would be impossible for English speakers to comprehend the *sh ì gù* stereotype, but rather that having that stereotype readily accessible facilitates its mental manipulation.

Bilingualism

The research by Hoffman and colleagues brings up questions that have fascinated psycholinguists: If a person can speak and think in two languages, does the person think differently in each language? In fact, do **bilinguals**—people who can speak two languages—think differently from **monolinguals**—people who can speak only one language? (*Multilinguals* speak at least two and possibly more languages.) What differences, if any, emanate from the availability of two languages versus just one? It appears that some bilinguals (particularly those who are highly fluent in each language and who come from middle-class backgrounds) profit from having more than one language (Hakuta, 1986). However, others (particularly those who have less fluency in either language and for whom the second language incompletely replaces the first) suffer ill effects of bilingualism.

Matching the silence I started hearing in public was a new quiet at home. The family's quiet was partly

due to the fact that, as we children learned more and more English, we shared fewer and fewer words with our parents. Sentences needed to be spoken slowly when a child addressed his mother or father. (Often the parent wouldn't understand.) The child would need to repeat himself. (Still the parent misunderstood.) The young boy, frustrated, would end up saying, 'Never mind'—the subject was closed.

—Richard Rodriguez, Hunger of Memory

James Cummins (1976) has suggested that we must distinguish between what might be called additive versus subtractive bilingualism. In **additive bilingualism,** a second language is taught in addition to a relatively well-developed first language. In **subtractive bilingualism,** elements of a second language replace elements of the first language. Cummins believes that the additive form results in increased cognitive functioning, whereas the subtractive form results in decreased functioning. In particular, there may be something of a threshold effect: Individuals may need to be at a certain relatively high level of competence in both languages for a positive effect of bilingualism to be found. Children from backgrounds with lower socioeconomic status (SES) appear to be more likely to be subtractive bilinguals than are children from the middle SES; their SES may be linked to the cause of their being hindered rather than helped by their bilingualism.

Whether bilingualism is additive or subtractive may affect the way in which the two languages are

These bilingual men are communicating through a shared language. Do bilinguals have differing conceptual structures for each language, or do they have a similar conceptual structure for both languages? Studies of the brain give some support to each view, and a synthesis of the two views may be more accurate than either view alone.

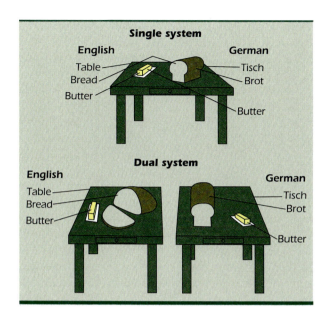

FIGURE 9-2
The Dual- Versus the Single-System Conceptualizations of Bilingualism
The dual-system conceptualization of bilingualism hypothesizes that each language is represented in a separate cognitive system. The single-system conceptualization hypothesizes that both languages are represented in a unified cognitive system.

represented in the bilingual's mind. The **dual-system hypothesis** suggests that the two languages are represented somehow in separate systems of the mind (Paradis, 1981). For instance, French language information might be stored in a physically different part of the brain than English language information. Alternatively, the **single-system hypothesis** suggests that the two languages are represented in just one system. Figure 9-2 shows schematically the difference in the two points of view.

One way to address this question is through the study of bilinguals who have experienced brain damage. Unfortunately, the results of clinical studies of brain-injured bilinguals have not allowed researchers to draw clear conclusions. A more conclusive kind of study was conducted by George Ojemann and Harry Whitaker (1978), who mapped the region of the cerebral cortex relevant to language use in two of their bilingual patients being treated for epilepsy. Mild electrical stimulation was applied to the cortex of each patient. Electrical stimulation tends to inhibit activity where it is applied, leading to reduced ability to name objects for which the memories are stored at the location being stimulated. The results for both patients were the same and may help explain the contradictions in the literature. Some areas of the brain showed equal impairments for object-naming in both

languages, but other areas of the brain showed differential impairment for one or the other language. The results also suggested that the weaker language was more diffusely represented across the cortex than was the stronger language. In other words, asking the question of whether two languages are represented singly or separately may be asking the wrong question. The results of this study suggest that some aspects of the two languages may be represented singly, and other aspects may be represented separately.

Another way to study the question of single versus dual representation is to look at a cognitive rather than an anatomical level of analysis. Paul Kolers (1966a) took this approach. He presented bilinguals with lists of words to learn. Some words were in one of their languages, and other words were in the other language. We know that repeating words in a list increases the probability that the repeated word will be remembered. Kolers found that this beneficial effect carried over to presentations in either language. Hearing a repetition was equally helpful whether the repetition was in the same language or in the other language. This result is consistent with a single-system view.

In another study, Kolers (1966b) had subjects read passages that were either all in English, all in French, or in a mixture of French and English. Bilinguals took no longer to read the mixed-language passages silently than they took to read the single-language passages. Moreover, their comprehension was equal in the two languages. If, however, subjects were asked to read the passages orally, they read the single-language passages more quickly than they read the mixed-language passages. These results, therefore, are consistent with the studies of the brain suggesting that there may be both shared and separate aspects to bilingual language representation. This phenomenon may be another one in which a synthesis of two competing theories offers a better explanation of the data than does either theory by itself.

To summarize, two languages seem to share some, but not all, aspects of mental representation. Learning a second language is more likely to be a plus if the person learning the second language is in an environment in which the learning of the second language adds to rather than subtracts from the learning of the first language. Moreover, for beneficial effects to appear, the second language must be learned rather well. The approach usually taken in schools, whereby students may receive as little as two or three years of second-language instruction spread out over a few class periods a week, probably will not be sufficient for the beneficial effects of bilingualism to appear.

LANGUAGE AND THE BRAIN

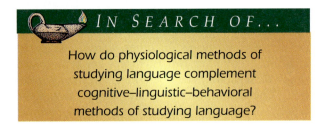

IN SEARCH OF...

How do physiological methods of studying language complement cognitive–linguistic–behavioral methods of studying language?

Recall from Chapters 2 and 3 that some of our earliest insights into brain localization related to an association between specific language deficits and specific organic damage to the brain, as first discovered by Paul Broca and Carl Wernicke. Broca's aphasia and Wernicke's aphasia are particularly well-documented instances in which brain lesions affect linguistic functions (see Chapter 3). Through studies of brain-injured patients, researchers have learned a great deal about the relations between particular areas of the brain (the areas of lesions observed in patients) and particular linguistic functions (the observed deficits in the brain-injured patients). For example, we can broadly generalize that many linguistic functions are primarily located in the areas identified by Broca and Wernicke, although it is now believed that damage to Wernicke's area, in the posterior of the cortex, entails more grim consequences for linguistic function than does damage to Broca's area, closer to the front of the brain (Kolb & Whishaw, 1990). Also, lesion studies have shown that linguistic function is governed by a much larger area of the posterior cortex than just the area identified by Wernicke, and that other areas of the cortex also play a role, such as other association-cortex areas in the left hemisphere, and a portion of the left temporal cortex, as well as some subcortical structures.

From her studies of brain-injured men and women, Doreen Kimura (1987) has observed some intriguing sex differences in terms of the ways in which linguistic function appears to be localized in the brain. The men she studied seemed to show more left-hemisphere dominance for linguistic function than the women showed; women showed more bilateral, symmetrical patterns of linguistic function. Further, the brain locations associated with aphasia seemed to differ for men and women. Most aphasic women showed lesions in the anterior region, although some aphasic women showed lesions in the temporal region. In contrast, aphasic men showed a more varied pattern of lesions, and aphasic men were more likely to show lesions in posterior regions rather than in anterior regions. One interpretation of

Kimura's findings is that the role of the posterior region in linguistic function may be different for women than it is for men; another interpretation is that because women show less lateralization of linguistic function, women may be better able to compensate for any possible loss of function due to lesions in the left posterior hemisphere through functional offsets in the right posterior hemisphere. The possibility that there also may be subcortical sex differences in linguistic function further complicates the ease of interpreting Kimura's findings. (See Chapter 14 for a discussion of communication differences between men and women.)

Sex differences are not the only individual differences that have interested Kimura. She has also studied hemispheric processing of language in persons who use sign language rather than speech to communicate (Kimura, 1983) and found that the locations of lesions that would be expected to disrupt speech also disrupt signing. Further, the hemispheric pattern of lesions associated with signing deficits is the same pattern shown with speech deficits. (That is, all right-handers with signing deficits show left-hemisphere lesions, as do most left-handers, but some left-handers with signing deficits show right-hemisphere lesions.) This finding supports the view that the brain processes both signing and speech similarly, in terms of their linguistic function, and it refutes the view that signing involves spatial processing or some other nonlinguistic form of cognitive processing.

Although lesion studies are valuable, researchers also investigate brain localization of linguistic function via other methods, such as by evaluating the effects on linguistic function that follow electrical stimulation of the brain (e.g., Ojemann, 1982; Ojemann & Mateer, 1979). Through stimulation studies, researchers have found that stimulation of particular points in the brain seems to yield discrete effects on particular linguistic functions (such as the naming of objects) across repeated, successive trials. However, across individuals, these particular localizations of function vary widely.

Using electrical-stimulation techniques, George Ojemann has found that although females generally have superior verbal skills to males, males have a proportionately larger (more diffusely dispersed) language area in their brains. Ojemann has somewhat counterintuitively inferred that the size of the language area in the brain may be inversely related to the ability to use language. This interpretation seems further bolstered by Ojemann's findings with bilinguals, mentioned earlier, regarding the diffuse distribution of the nondominant language versus the more concentrated localization of the dominant language.

> What are the benefits of using more than one psychophysiological method to study a psychological phenomenon?

Yet another avenue of research involves the study of the metabolic activity of the brain and the flow of blood in the brain during the performance of various verbal tasks. For example, preliminary metabolic and blood-flow studies of the brain (e.g., Petersen, Fox, Posner, Mintun, & Raichle, 1988) have indicated that more areas of the brain are involved in linguistic function than we would have determined without having these studies available.

> What specific language tasks might lend themselves to metabolic or blood-flow studies? Give an example of a semantic task, a syntactic task, and a pragmatic or sociolinguistic task (which involves the social context of language use).

The various methods of studying the brain support the view that for all right-handed individuals and most left-handed persons, the left hemisphere of the brain seems clearly implicated in syntactical aspects of linguistic processing, and it is clearly essential to speech. The left hemisphere also seems to be essential to the ability to write, whereas the right hemisphere seems capable of quite a bit of auditory comprehension, particularly in terms of semantic processing, as well as some reading comprehension. The right hemisphere also seems to be important in several of the subtle nuances of linguistic comprehension and expression, such as understanding and expressing vocal inflection and gesture, as well as comprehending metaphors and other nonliteral aspects of language (e.g., jokes and sarcasm) (Kolb & Whishaw, 1990).

> How would you design an experiment to study the relationships between cross-cultural differences among language users (or another individual difference that interests you) and the ways in which people process language in their brains?

Much of this chapter has revealed the many ways in which language and thought interact. The following chapter focuses on thinking, but it also further reveals the interconnectedness of the ways in which we use language and the ways in which we think.

SUMMARY

General Properties of Language   302

1. *Language* is the use of an organized means of combining words in order to communicate.
2. There are at least six properties of language: (1) Language permits us to communicate with one or more persons who share our language. (2) Language creates an arbitrary relationship between a symbol and its referent—an idea, a thing, a process, a relationship, or a description. (3) Language has a structure; only particularly patterned arrangements of symbols have meaning. Different arrangements yield different meanings. (4) The structure of language can be analyzed at more than one level (e.g., phonemic and morphemic). (5) Despite having the limits of a structure, language users can produce novel utterances; the possibilities for creating new utterances are virtually limitless. (6) Languages constantly evolve.

Description of Language in Its Own Words   303

3. As mentioned in Chapter 5, the smallest seman-tically meaningful unit in a language is a *morpheme*. Morphemes may be either roots or *affixes* (*prefixes* or *suffixes*), which may be either *content morphemes* (conveying the bulk of the word's meaning) or *function morphemes* (augmenting the meaning of the word).

Language Acquisition   306

4. Humans seem to progress through the following stages in acquiring language: (a) prenatal responsivity to human voices; (b) postnatal *cooing*, which comprises all possible phones; (c) *babbling*, which comprises only the distinct phonemes that characterize the primary language of the infant; (d) one-word utterances; (e) two-word utterances; (f) *telegraphic speech*; (g) basic adult sentence structure (present by about age four).
5. During language acquisition, children engage in *overextension errors*, in which they extend the meaning of a word to encompass more concepts than the word is intended to encompass.
6. Neither nature alone nor nurture alone can account for human language acquisition. The

mechanism of *hypothesis testing* suggests an integration of nature and nurture: Children acquire language by mentally forming tentative hypotheses regarding language and then testing these hypotheses in the environment. They are guided in the formation of these hypotheses by an innate *language-acquisition device (LAD)*, which facilitates language acquisition.

7. Animals can clearly communicate with each other, although currently debate exists over whether this communication constitutes animal language—that is, communication exhibiting all the properties of language shown in human language.

Semantics: The Study of Meaning   312

8. *Semantics* is the study of meaning.
9. Several alternative theories of meaning exist. The two main alternatives are the *componential theory* (meaning can be understood in terms of components, or basic elements, of a word) and the *prototypic theory* (meaning inheres in "best examples" of a concept).

Syntax: The Study of Structure   314

10. *Syntax* is the study of linguistic structure at the sentence level.
11. Alternative kinds of grammars have been proposed to understand the structure of sentences: (a) *Phrase-structure grammars* analyze sentences in terms of the order in which words appear in phrases and sentences; and (b) *transformational grammars* analyze sentences in terms of deep (propositional meaning) structures that underlie surface (word-sequence) structures.

Pragmatics and Sociolinguistics: Language in Context   315

12. *Pragmatics* is the study of how language is used.
13. *Speech acts* refer to what can be accomplished with speech. Speech acts comprise *representatives, directives, commissives, expressives,* and *declarations.*
14. An *indirect request* is a way of asking for something without doing so straightforwardly. Indi-rect requests may refer to abilities, desires, future actions, and reasons.

15. Conversational postulates provide a means for establishing language as a cooperative enterprise. The conversational postulates comprise several maxims, including the maxims of quantity, quality, relation, and manner.
16. Sociolinguists, who study the relationship between social behavior and language, have observed that people engage in various strategies to signal turn-taking in conversations.
17. In order to communicate effectively, parties must have a shared understanding about the situation being discussed; these shared understandings are termed *scripts.*
18. *Slips of the tongue* refer to inadvertent semantic or articulatory errors in things we say. Four kinds of slips are anticipations, perseverations, reversals (including *spoonerisms*), and substitutions.

Language and Thought   319

19. *Linguistic determinism* asserts that linguistic structure shapes cognitive structure.
20. *Linguistic relativity* asserts that cognitive differences resulting from a given language cause people speaking that language to perceive the world uniquely.
21. *Bilinguals* are people who speak two languages.
22. *Additive bilingualism* occurs when a second language is taught in addition to a relatively well-developed first language, whereas *subtractive bilingualism* occurs when a second language essentially replaces a first language.
23. Theorists differ in their views as to whether bilinguals store two or more languages separately (*dual-system hypothesis*) or together (*single-system hypothesis*). It is possible that some aspects of multiple languages are stored separately, others, unitarily.

Language and the Brain   324

24. Several linguistic functions in the brain have been localized, largely from observations on what happens when a particular area of the brain is injured or is electrically stimulated.

KEY TERMS

IN SEARCH OF THE HUMAN MIND:
ANALYSES, CREATIVE EXPLORATIONS, AND PRACTICAL APPLICATIONS

1. Can semantics and syntax be studied in isolation from each other? Why or why not?
2. Many language lovers enjoy the dynamic quality of language and relish each new nuance of meaning and change of form that arises. In contrast, many feel that to cherish a language is to preserve it exactly as it is at present—or even exactly as it was at some time in the past. Give the pros and cons of both welcoming and resisting change in language.
3. Assuming that some animals can be taught rudimentary language, what distinguishes humans from other animals? What characteristics of human language are unlikely in even the most sophisticated animals who have been taught language?

4. Is there a way psychologists ethically can investigate the critical periods for language acquisition in children? Is so, how? If not, why not?
5. Other than the study of color words, what set of words or other aspect of language would lend itself to the study of cross-cultural interactions between language and thought? Why would that set of words or aspect of language facilitate such cross-cultural study?
6. What steps can non-natives take when studying another culture in order to understand the breadth and depth of that culture with minimal hindrance from their own biases?

7. How might con artists take advantage of people's predilection for using prototypes when trying to con people? How can people avoid being conned by such artists?
8. What are some everyday examples of each kind of speech act? What are some highly unusual examples of each kind of speech act?
9. What are some situations in which you might violate each of the conversational maxims?

Chapter Ten

Thinking

ABOUT WIPING A ROACH-Y CUP ON THIS BOOK? GO RIGHT AHEAD (I DID!)

Right Here (I DID!)

CHAPTER OUTLINE

Prior to the final ratification of the North American free-trade agreement, a plane with Canadian registry crashed, carrying 32 natives of Canada, 44 natives of the United States, 4 naturalized Canadian citizens, 8 naturalized U.S. citizens, and 6 foreign travelers who were carrying their valid passports, as well as 1 foreign traveler with an invalid passport. The plane originated in Montreal, was headed to New York, and was to proceed on to Mexico City. On which side of the border should the survivors be buried?

Which would aid you more in solving the preceding problem: a calculator or a law book? Perhaps you would do better to reframe the question: If you had survived the crash, on which side of the border would you want to be buried?

Descartes was one of the few who think, therefore they are.
Because those who don't think, but are anyhow, out-number them by far.

—Ogden Nash, "Lines Fraught with Naught but Thought"

Thinking involves the representation and processing of information in the mind. One way in which we view thought is to consider **critical thinking,** in which we consciously direct our mental processes to find a thoughtful solution to a problem, as opposed to noncritical thinking, in which we routinely follow customary thought patterns, without consciously directing how we think. Psychologists have observed that critical thinking may be directed to **analysis** (breaking down wholes into components) or to **synthesis** (putting components together into wholes). Critical thought may also involve **divergent thinking** (generating many ideas) or **convergent thinking** (focusing in on one idea). Analysis and synthesis can be complementary processes, as can divergent and convergent thinking (see Table 10-1).

Psychologists also sometimes categorize thinking in terms of four domains of inquiry: problem solving, judgment and decision making, reasoning, and creativity. Although these four domains overlap somewhat in everyday thinking, the goal of thinking in each domain is different. The goal of **problem solving** is to move from a problem situation (e.g., not having enough money to buy a car) to a solution, overcoming obstacles along the way. The goal of **judgment and decision making** is to select from among choices or to evaluate opportunities (e.g., choosing the car that would please you the most for the amount of money you have). The goal of **reasoning** is to draw conclusions from evidence (e.g., reading consumer-oriented statistics to find out the reliability, economy, and safety of various cars). The goal of *creativity* is to produce something original and valuable (e.g., a fuel-efficient engine design, a distinctive marketing idea for the car, or a story to tell your parents as to why you need a car). Accordingly, this chapter is divided into four parts, each of which corresponds to one of these four domains of inquiry.

PROBLEM SOLVING

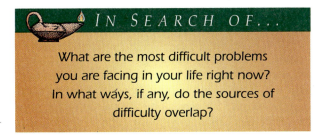

IN SEARCH OF...

What are the most difficult problems you are facing in your life right now? In what ways, if any, do the sources of difficulty overlap?

The Problem-Solving Cycle Revisited

We engage in problem solving when we need to overcome obstacles in order to answer a question or achieve a goal. If we have an answer immediately available in memory, we either do not have a problem or have a problem without knowing it (if the answer is unsatisfactory). If we do not have an answer, we then have posed a problem to be solved. Before getting into other aspects of problem solving, it seems wise to review briefly the seven-step problem-solving cycle described in Chapter 1: (1) identify the problem; (2) define the problem; (3) formulate a strategy;

As Auguste Rodin's The Thinker *illustrates, throughout the ages and across cultures people have pondered the fundamental questions. Psychologists have sought to understand not only the answers to these universal questions but also the processes people undergo while thinking about these and other questions.*

TABLE 10-1
Kinds of Critical Thinking
Critical thinking can be viewed both in terms of analysis and synthesis and in terms of divergent thinking and convergent thinking.

Kind of Thinking	Description	Example
Analysis	Breaking down large, complex concepts or processes into smaller, simpler forms	Suppose that you were asked to write a term paper. You might break down the whole big project into the smaller steps: (1) choose a topic, (2) research the topic, (3) write a first draft, (4) revise, etc.
Synthesis	Combining or integrating two or more concepts or processes into a more complex form	In writing a psychology term paper, you might combine some examples from your literature or your history class showing how poor judgment affected various literary or historical figures and then integrate the examples with psychological theories of decision making and judgment.
Divergent thinking	Generating a diverse assortment of possible alternative solutions to a problem	To discover topic ideas for a term paper, you might try to come up with as many ideas as possible in order to find interesting research topics that can be investigated and reported within a single semester.
Convergent thinking	Proceeding from various possible alternatives to converge on a single, best answer	From the many ideas you generated, you might try to converge on a single research topic that you would find interesting, one with plenty of available references and specific enough to complete, given your available time to do the needed research for the given topic.

(4) represent and organize the information; (5) allocate resources; (6) monitor the problem-solving process; and (7) evaluate the solution. Recall also that the earlier description of the problem-solving cycle underscored the importance of flexibility in following the various steps of the cycle. Successful problem solving may occasionally involve tolerating some ambiguity regarding how best to proceed. Rarely can we solve problems by following some ideal or optimal problem-solving cycle.

In fact, cognitive psychologists often categorize problems according to whether the problems have clear paths to a solution. Problems with clear solution paths are sometimes termed **well-structured problems** (e.g., "How do you find the area of a parallelogram?"); those without clear solution paths are termed **ill-structured problems** (e.g., "How do you succeed in the career of your choice?"). Of course, in the real world of problems, these two categories may represent more a continuum of clarity in problem solving than two discrete classes with an unambiguous boundary between the two. Nonetheless, the categories are useful in understanding how people solve problems. We next consider each of these kinds of problems in turn.

Well-Structured Problems

On tests in school, your teachers have asked you to tackle countless well-structured problems in specific content areas (math, history, geography, and so on); these problems had clear paths—if not necessarily easy paths—to their solutions. For example, the path to finding the answer to "What is the square root of 4,575,321?" is clear, if not easy. Cognitive psychologists study thinking as it applies to a variety of kinds of problems. One class of problem of particular interest is **move problems,** so termed because they require a series of moves to reach a final goal state.

Perhaps the most well-known of the move problems is one involving two antagonistic parties, whom we call book-burners and book-lovers in our example:

> Three book-burners and three book-wielding book-lovers are on a river bank. The book-burners and book-lovers need to cross over to the other side of the river. They have for this purpose a small rowboat that will hold just two people (and several books). There is one problem, however. If the number of book-burners on either river bank exceeds the number of book-lovers, the book-burners will burn the books of the book-lovers on that bank. How can all six people get across to the other side of the

river in a way that guarantees that they all arrive there with the books intact?

This problem is represented pictorially in Figure 10-1. Try to solve the problem before reading on.

The solution to the problem is shown in Figure 10-2. The solution contains several features worth noting. First, the problem can be solved in a minimum of 11 steps, including the first and last steps. Second, the solution is essentially *linear* in nature—there is just one valid move (connecting two points with a line segment) at most steps of problem solution. At all but two steps along the solution path, only one error (i.e., nonoptimal move) can be made without violating the rules of the move problem: to go directly backward in the solution. In other words, only two possible legal moves exist: undoing the previous move or making the only possible next move. At two steps, there are two possible forward-moving responses, but both of these lead toward the correct an-

FIGURE 10-1
Book Burners and Book Lovers Problem
How can all six people get across to the other side of the river in a way that guarantees they all arrive there with the books intact? (See the text for a description of this problem.) Psychologists use this and other puzzles to study how people solve well-structured problems.

swer. Thus, again, the only possible error is to return to a previous state in the solution of the problem.

A second kind of error is to make an illegal move—that is, a move that is not permitted according to the terms of the problem. For example, a move that resulted in having more than two individuals in the boat would be illegal. You might wonder, given the essentially linear nature of the solution path, why or how people would have any trouble at all solving this kind of problem. The main errors people seem to make, according to those who have studied the problem, are (a) inadvertently moving backward, (b) making illegal moves, and (c) not realizing the nature of the next legal move (Greeno, 1974; Simon & Reed, 1976; Thomas, 1974).

Heuristics and Algorithms

People seeking to solve the book-lovers and book-burners problem, and others like it, rely on a set of **heuristics**—informal, intuitive, speculative strategies, which sometimes work and sometimes do not—for solving the problems. For example, you might try several different routes to your early morning class in order to find the fastest one, so that you can sleep as late as possible. Here you would be employing a simple *trial-and-error heuristic.* Heuristics are often contrasted with **algorithms,** which are paths to a solution that, if followed, guarantee an accurate solution to the problem for which they are used. Algorithms generally involve successive, somewhat mechanical iterations of a particular strategy until the correct solution is reached. For example, an algorithm for solving a cryptogram—a puzzle involving secret writing—would be to try to substitute each letter of the alphabet for each cryptic letter in the cryptogram. (Can you figure out the following cryptogram? "YJOD OD S VTUQYPHTSZ.") Algorithms guarantee a solution to a problem—a clear advantage—whereas heuristics do not. (An algorithm for the preceding cryptogram would have led you to decipher, "This is a cryptogram.")

"... *Circumstances, and a certain bias of mind, have led me to take an interest in such riddles [cryptograms], and it may well be doubted whether human ingenuity can construct an enigma of the kind which human ingenuity may not, by proper application, resolve....*"

—declared by Legrand, a cryptographer depicted in Edgar Allan Poe's "The Gold Bug"

Why would anyone ever use a heuristic, which does *not* guarantee a solution, instead of an algorithm, which does guarantee a solution? For one thing, often there is no obvious algorithm for solving a problem. For example, in chess, it is usually not obvious to us

FIGURE 10-2
Solution to Book Burners and Book Lovers Problem
What can you learn about your own methods of solving problems by seeing how you approached this particular problem?

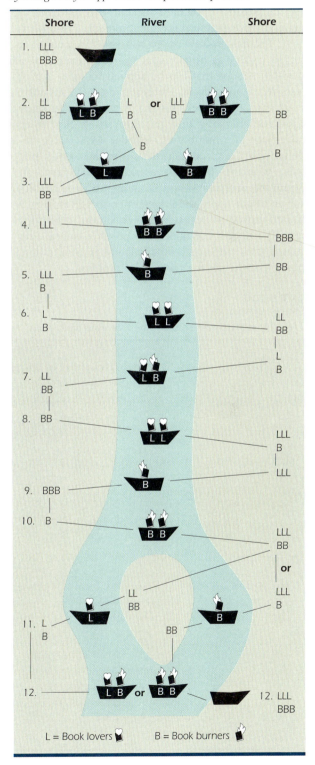

L = Book lovers   B = Book burners

what algorithm, if any, would guarantee our winning the game. Later in this chapter, we discuss judgment and decision making, for which we may be able to apply heuristics in some situations, but for which it is rare to find a surefire algorithm. For another thing, it may be that an available algorithm would take so long to execute that it just is not practical to do so. For example, an algorithm for cracking a safe would be to try all possible combinations, but this algorithm is generally not practical for the safecracker in a hurry!

Problem solvers apply heuristics in what is referred to as a **problem space**—the universe of all possible actions that can be applied to solve a problem. Allen Newell and Herbert Simon (1972) postulated that all problem solving takes place by search activities occurring in a problem space. Search can take place in a number of different ways. Table 10-2 defines four different heuristics—**means–ends analysis, working forward, working backward,** and **generate and test**—and illustrates how a problem solver might apply these heuristics to the aforementioned move problem (Greeno & Simon, 1988). Figure 10-3 shows a rudimentary problem space, illustrating that there may be any number of additional possible strategies for a particular problem.

> What are some problem-solving strategies that you use? Would your strategies be considered algorithms or heuristics?

Many problems can be solved in more than one way. Often, the way in which we view a problem is shaped by our cultural contexts. For example, suppose that you want to sail from one island to another. If you are a native Westerner, you will probably plan to use your charts and navigational equipment. However, some natives of particular islands in the South Pacific would probably scoff at such technicalities, and they might be puzzled by the idea of "going to" another island. Instead, these natives use the concept of the "moving island" to navigate vast expanses of ocean (Gladwin, 1970). That is, in their view, each island is adrift, floating along in the ocean. To get from one floating island to another, they don't "go" anywhere in the usual sense. Rather, they sit in their small boats, watch the changes in the currents and the color of the water, and then "catch" the island as *it* drifts by. As this alternative view of figuring out how to get from one island to another suggests, many problems may be solved in various ways, and some of

TABLE 10-2
Four Heuristics

These four heuristics can be used to solve the move problem illustrated in Figures 10-1 and 10-2.

Heuristic	Definition of Heuristic	Example of Heuristic, Applied to the Move Problem
Means–ends analysis	The problem solver analyzes the problem by viewing the end—the goal being sought—and then tries to decrease the distance between the current position in the problem space and the end goal in that space.	An example of this strategy would be to try to get as many people on the far bank and as few people on the near bank as possible.
Working forward	The problem solver starts at the beginning and tries to solve the problem from the start to the finish.	An example of this strategy would be to evaluate the situation carefully with the six people on one bank and then to try to move them step by step to the opposite bank.
Working backward	The problem solver starts at the end and tries to work backward from there.	The problem solver would start with the final state—having all missionaries and all cannibals on the far bank—and try to work back to the beginning state.
Generate and test	The problem solver simply generates alternative courses of action, not necessarily in a systematic way, and then notices in turn whether each course of action works.	This method works fairly well for the move problem, because at most steps in the process there is only one allowable forward move, and there are never more than two possibilities, both of which will eventually lead to the solution.

FIGURE 10-3
Problem Space

A problem space contains all the possible strategies leading from the problem to the solution. This problem space shows the heuristics described in Table 10-2 that might be used in solving the move problem in Figures 10-1 and 10-2.

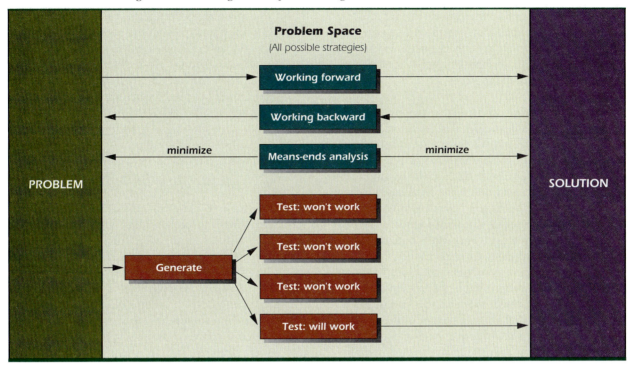

Isomorphic Problems

The book-lovers and book-burners problem has also been presented in terms of cannibals and missionaries, in which cannibals might eat missionaries, or in terms of hobbits and orcs, where orcs might eat hobbits. These alternative forms of presentation bring us to another point about problems. Sometimes, two problems are **isomorphic**—their formal structure is the same; only their content differs. Sometimes, as in the case of the book-burners and book-lovers problem, the missionaries and cannibals problem, and the hobbits and orcs problem, the isomorphism is obvious. Similarly, you can readily detect the isomorphism of many games that involve constructing words from jumbled or scrambled letters.

In discussions of cognition, a dichotomy often arises between the structural form of something and its informational content. In problem solving, the actual informational content of the problem can be seen

these methods may seem more obvious to us than others. When the apparently obvious means of solving a problem does not seem to be working, it may be valuable to try to view the problem from a different perspective.

as a surface characteristic that either helps or hinders your ability to see the underlying deep-structural form of the problem. Thus, the ability to see isomorphism in two problems can be impaired when the content (or the context) of the problems differs sharply. For example, most of us have solved isomorphic problems involving leverage, such as prying open a bottle by using a bottle opener rather than our fingernails or a small coin. Nonetheless, unless we stop to think about it, most of us fail to notice the isomorphism of these problems with other problems in which leverage might help us (e.g., using a long-handled shovel to dig into a hard surface).

Why are some problems easier to solve than are their isomorphisms? Kenneth Kotovsky, John Hayes, and Herbert Simon (1985a) have concluded that a major consideration is how a problem is represented. The following problems illustrate some of the difficulties created by the way in which a problem is represented.

Problem Solving: A Brief Practicum

Before reading on, treat yourself to a little quiz (Sternberg, 1986a). Be sure to try each of the following three problems before you read about their solutions.

1. Figure 10-4 shows a picture of nine dots arrayed three by three. Your task is to connect all nine dots with a set of line segments. You must never lift your pencil off the page, you must not go through a dot more than once, and you must not use more than four straight line segments. See whether you can connect the nine dots with a series of line segments without ever taking your pencil off the page.

2. Figure 10-5 shows a picture of a monk climbing a mountain. The monk wishes to pursue study and contemplation in a retreat at the top of the mountain. The monk starts climbing the mountain at 7:00 A.M. and arrives at the top of the mountain at 5:00 P.M. on the same day. During the course of his ascent, he travels at variable speeds, and he takes a break for lunch. He spends the evening in study and contemplation. The next day, the monk starts his descent at 7:00 A.M. again, along the same route. Normally, his descent would be faster than his ascent, but because he is tired and afraid of tripping and hurting himself, he descends the mountain slowly, not arriving at the bottom until 5:00 P.M. of the day after he started his ascent. Must there be a point on the mountain that the monk passes at exactly the same time of day on the two successive days of his ascent and descent? Why or why not?

3. A woman was putting some finishing touches on her house and realized she needed something she did not have. She went to the hardware store and asked the clerk, "How much will 150 cost me?" The clerk in the hardware store answered, "They are 75 cents apiece, so 150 will cost you $2.25." What did the woman buy?

Ill-Structured Problems

The Nature of Insight

Each of these three problems is an ill-structured problem. These three particular ill-structured problems are termed **insight problems,** because in order to solve each one, you need to see the problem in a novel way—different from the way you would probably see it at first, and different from the way you would probably solve problems in general. **Insight** is a distinctive and sometimes seemingly sudden understanding of a problem or of a strategy that aids in solving the problem. Insight often involves reconceptualizing a problem or a strategy for its solution in a

FIGURE 10-4
The Nine-Dot Problem

How can you connect all nine dots without lifting your pencil from the paper and using just four straight lines? Psychologists study how people use insight to solve this and other ill-structured problems.

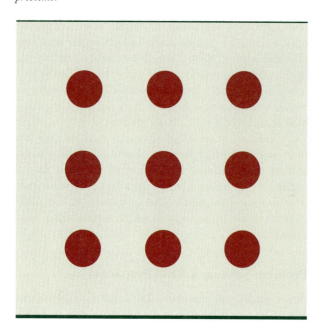

FIGURE 10-5
The Monk-on-the-Mountain Problem

Must there be a point on the mountain that the monk passes at exactly the same time of day on the two successive days of his ascent and descent? Why or why not? To solve this problem, you may find it helpful to view it from another perspective.

totally new way. Frequently, the insight emerges through the detection and combination of relevant old and new information to gain a novel view of the problem or of its solution. Insight can be involved in solving well-structured problems, but it is more often associated with the rocky and twisting path to solution that characterizes ill-structured problems. Although insights may feel sudden, they are often the result of much prior thought and hard work, without which the insight would never have occurred.

To understand insightful problem solving, it is useful to know the solutions to the preceding three insight problems. The solution to Problem 1, the nine-dot problem, is shown in Figure 10-6. Most people find the problem extremely difficult to solve, and many never solve it. One hindrance is the common assumption that the lines must be kept within the confines of the square implicitly formed by the nine dots. Most people do not allow their solution to extend beyond the boundaries of the dots, even though the problem does not present this constraint. However, the problem cannot be solved with four lines restricted to the interior of the figure. Thus, some people make the problem insoluble by unnecessarily limiting their options. They err at Step 2 of the problem-solving cycle (defining the problem), after which they never recover. This problem provides a typical example of how a nonoptimal definition of a problem can reduce, and in this case, possibly even eliminate, the chances of finding a solution to the problem. Unfortunately, you, I, and other people misdefine problems much of the time. Each of us must learn to free ourselves of self-created constraints to problem solving that are not inherent in the actual problem.

With respect to Problem 2, the monk *must* pass through exactly the same point (or altitude) on the mountain, wherever on the mountain it may be, at corresponding times on the days of his ascent and descent. The solution shown in Figure 10-7 illustrates why. The problem becomes much easier to conceptualize if you *redefine the problem:* Rather than imagining the same monk climbing the mountain one day and going down the mountain the next day, imagine two different monks—one ascending and the other descending the mountain on the same day. This reconceptualization does not change the nature of the problem or its solution; the reconceptualization is isomorphic to the problem posed, but it makes it easier to find the solution. Given the redefined problem, with two monks, you can see that the paths of ascent and descent of the two monks would necessarily pass each other. Obviously, their meeting must be in a given place at a given time. The redefinition of the

problem simply makes it easier to see how it must be the case that at some point the original monk will be at a given point at a given time of day on the two consecutive days.

The monk problem is not insoluble in its original form. The argument that the monk's paths of ascent and descent must reach a given point at a given time on the two consecutive days can be made without the suggested reconceptualization of the problem. However, as with the nine-dots problem, redefining the problem makes the problem much easier to solve.

With regard to Problem 3, the woman might have been buying house numbers. Her house number is 150, so she needs three numerals, for a total cost of $2.25. From this point of view, this problem can be solved only if it is recognized that the "150" in the problem may refer to the three separate digits, rather than to the number 150. "House numbers" is not the only possible answer. For example, the woman might have been buying boxes of nails, whereby one box (of 50 nails) would cost 75 cents, and 150 nails (three boxes) would cost $2.25. With the solution involving nails, the problem can be solved only if we realize that the units have changed from nails to boxes of nails. Whether the problem is defined as one of house numbers or of nails (or something else bought in quantity), the terms of the problem are not what they originally appear to be. Sometimes, problems that appear to be about one thing really turn out to be about another, as was the case here.

> What is a problem that you have faced that required you to have insight to solve the problem? Describe the way in which you experienced the insight. What were the circumstances that led to the insight?

Psychological Perspectives on Insight

Insight problems such as the preceding ones have intrigued psychologists—including associationists and behaviorists—for decades. The first psychologists to explore such problems in great depth, however, were Gestalt psychologists (see Chapter 2). According to the Gestaltists, insight problems require problem solvers to go beyond associations among various parts in order to perceive the problem as a whole. Gestalt psychologist Max Wertheimer distinguished between **productive thinking** (Wertheimer, 1945/1959), which involves insights that go beyond the bounds of existing associations, and **reproductive thinking,** which is based on existing associations involving what is already known. According to

FIGURE 10-6
Solution to Nine-Dot Problem
How did your approach to solving this problem differ from your approach to solving the move problem (book lovers/book burners problem)?

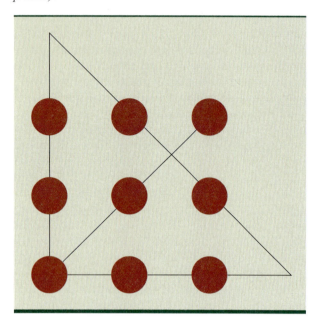

FIGURE 10-7
Solution to Monk-on-the-Mountain Problem
How did you reframe the problem in a way that aided you in solving it?

Wertheimer, insightful (productive) thinking differs fundamentally from associationistic (reproductive) thinking; it does not just extend associationistic thinking to novel kinds of problems. In solving the preceding insight problems, you had to break away from your existing associations and see each problem in an entirely new light. Productive thinking also can be applied to well-structured problems, as shown in Figures 10-8 and 10-10. (Before looking at Figure 10-10, try to solve the problem in Figure 10-8.)

Wertheimer's Gestaltist colleague, Wolfgang Köhler (1927), studied insight by observing a chimpanzee confined in a cage with two sticks (see Figure 10-9). Outside the cage, out of his reach and out of the reach of either stick, was a banana. After trying to grab the banana with his hand and each stick, the chimp took to tinkering with the sticks. Suddenly, he realized that the sticks could be attached to one another to form a new tool: one long pole that he could then use to roll the banana into range. In Köhler's view, the chimp's behavior illustrated insight and showed that insight is a special process, involving thinking that differs from normal information processing.

Gestalt psychologists provided and described many other examples of insight and speculated on a few ways in which insight might occur: It might result from (a) extended unconscious leaps in thinking,

(b) greatly accelerated mental processing, or (c) some kind of short-circuiting of normal reasoning processes (see Perkins, 1981). Unfortunately, the Gestaltists did not provide convincing evidence for any of these views, nor did they specify just what insight is. Therefore, we need to consider alternative views as well.

THE NOTHING-SPECIAL VIEW. According to the nothing-special view, insight is merely an extension of ordinary perceiving, recognizing, learning, and conceiving (Langley, Simon, Bradshaw, & Zytkow, 1986;

FIGURE 10-8
Area of Parallelogram Problem
What is the area of this parallelogram? According to Gestaltist Max Wertheimer, you will need to engage in productive thinking, not reproductive thinking, to solve it.

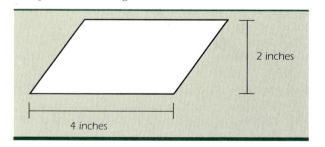

2 inches

4 inches

Perkins, 1981; Weisberg, 1986). Those who hold the nothing-special view suggest that Gestalt psychologists failed to pin down insight because no special thinking process called "insight" exists. Insights are merely significant products of ordinary thinking processes. What distinguishes the insights of extraordinary individuals from those of ordinary persons is that outstanding thinkers choose the problems they contemplate based on their extensive expertise in an important domain. For example, Rosalind Franklin had an insight regarding the structure of DNA—the notion that DNA was formed by a two-stranded helix—which served as a basis for James Watson and Francis Crick's model (Weisberg, 1992).

THE THREE-PROCESS VIEW.   Yet another view of insight has been proposed by Janet Davidson and myself (Davidson & Sternberg, 1984). According to this view, insights are of three kinds, involving three different processes: selective encoding, selective combination, and selective comparison. We agree with the nothing-special theorists to some extent, in that the three processes that we suggest as underlying the three kinds of insights also can be used mundanely and noninsightfully. However, we also agree with the Gestalt psychologists in proposing that there is something special about insight—that when the three processes are applied insightfully, the processes go beyond the boundaries of conventional thinking and involve constructing or reconstructing a problem in a new way.

Selective-encoding insights involve distinguishing relevant from irrelevant information. Recall from earlier chapters that *encoding* involves representing information in memory. We are all barraged with much more information than we can possibly handle. Thus, each of us must select the information that is important for our purposes, and we must filter out the unimportant or irrelevant information. Selective encoding is the process by which this filtering is done. For example, when you are writing a term paper, you must selectively encode which points to emphasize, which to play down, and which to leave out.

Consider, too, the ways in which scientists have used selective encoding. Recall from Chapter 1 how Percy LeBaron Spencer discovered the use of microwaves for heating and from Chapter 7 how Ivan Pavlov discovered classical conditioning. Both scientists could have ignored the apparently trivial phenomena that obstructed their intended primary goals in research. Instead, they had the insight to see the importance of the phenomena they observed: Spencer's observation of the melted candy in his pocket, and Pavlov's observation of the anticipatory salivation of dogs prior to being given food.

Selective-comparison insights involve novel perceptions of how new information relates to old information. The creative use of analogies is a form of selective comparison. When solving important problems, we almost always need to call on our existing knowledge and to compare that information with our new knowledge of the current problem. Insights of selective comparison are the basis for this relating of the new to the old. A famous example of a selective-comparison insight is Friedrich August von Kekulé's account of his discovery of the ring-shaped structure

FIGURE 10-9
A Demonstration of Insight by a Chimpanzee
In another of Wolfgang Köhler's experiments the chimp demonstrated insightful problem solving to retrieve the bananas hanging from the top of the enclosure. According to Gestaltists, insightful problem solving is a special process that differs from ordinary information processing.

FIGURE 10-10
Solution to Area of Parallelogram Problem
To solve the problem proposed by Wertheimer, you may have to re-
frame the problem, as suggested by the lines shown in this figure.
Once the problem is reframed, you can see that it is isomorphic to
finding the area of a rectangle. (After Wertheimer, 1945/1959).

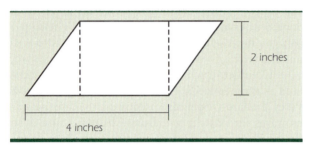

of benzene. Kekulé had been struggling to determine the structure of benzene. When he dozed off into sleep, he dreamed, "the atoms were gamboling before my eyes . . . long rows, . . . all twining and twisting in snakelike motion. But look! What was that? One of the snakes had seized hold of its own tail, and the form whirled mockingly before my eyes. As if by a flash of lightning I awoke" (quoted in Rothenberg, 1979, pp. 395–396). Kekulé realized that the image of the snake biting its tail formed the geometric shape for the structure of benzene—a ring. You don't have to be a brilliant scientist to have selective-comparison insights. For example, a college student might gain a deeper insight into a literary character by comparing the character's motivations and behaviors to some of the motivations described in a psychology class.

Selective-combination insights involve taking selectively encoded and compared snippets of relevant information and combining that information in a novel, productive way. Often, it is not enough for us just to identify analytically the important information for solving a problem; we must also figure out how to synthesize the information. Consider a famous example of a selective-combination insight: the formulation of the theory of evolution. The naturalistic observational information that formed the basis for Charles Darwin to formulate his theory had been available to him and to others for a long time. What had initially eluded Darwin and his contemporaries was how to integrate this information to account for the observed changes in species. When Darwin finally saw how to combine the available information, he formulated his theory of natural selection.

Similarly, you may experience selective-combination insights when you can combine the information you have gained in several courses. For example, suppose that you were writing a term paper for your psychology course regarding fetal alcohol syndrome as a possible cause of learning disabilities in school-aged children. You might integrate the data you found on the demographics of alcoholism, from a sociology course; the information about the effects of alcohol on the brain, from a physiology course; the information on critical periods of development, from a child-development course; the cognitive and perceptual requirements for reading, from an educational-psychology course; and so on. The distinctive way in which you would integrate these diverse ideas would require a selective-combination insight.

FIGURE 10-11
Examples of Selective Encoding
Excellent examples of selective encoding include Claude Lorrain's keen awareness of the natural beauty of landscapes in Il Tramonto
("The Sunset") (left) and Paul Cézanne's observations of diffuse, warm light in Mont Saint-Victoire seen from Les Lauves *(right).*
Each artist selected the key relevant visual elements from the vast array of visual information.

TABLE 10-3
The Water-Jar Problems
What is the most effective way of measuring out the correct amount of water using jars A, B, and C? (After Luchins, 1942)

Problem No.	Jars Available for Use			Required Amount (Cups)
	A	**B**	**C**	
1	29	3		20
2	21	127	3	100
3	14	163	25	99
4	18	43	10	5
5	9	42	6	21
6	20	59	4	31
7	23	49	3	20
8	15	39	3	18
9	28	76	3	25
10	18	48	4	22
11	14	36	8	6

Insights can startle us with their brilliance but still be wrong. Many of the great insights of history have seemed right at the time but were later proved wrong. No matter how convinced we may be of the validity of our own or someone else's insights, we need to be open to the possibility that the insights may later seem to be incorrect. On the other hand, we should not casually dismiss our insights just because they seem improbable at first glance.

Hindrances to Problem Solving

Mental Sets and Fixation

Many insight problems are hard to solve because problem solvers tend to bring to the new problem a particular **mental set**—a frame of mind involving an existing predisposition to think of a problem or a situation in a particular way. When problem solvers have a mental set (sometimes called "entrenchment"), they fixate on a strategy that normally works in solving many problems, but that does not work in solving this particular problem. For example, in the nine-dot problem, we may fixate on strategies that involve drawing lines within the dots; in the monk problem, we may fixate on trying to envision one monk making two successive trips; in the house-numbers problem, we may fixate on strategies involving 150 items.

Abraham Luchins (1942) exquisitely demonstrated the phenomenon of mental set in what he called "water-jar" problems. In these problems, subjects are asked how to measure out a certain amount of water, using three different jars, with each jar holding a different amount of water. Table 10-3 shows the problems used by Luchins. You need to use the three jars to obtain the required amounts of water (measured in numbers of cups) in the last column. Columns A, B, and C show the capacity of each jar. The first problem, for example, requires you to get 20 cups of water from just two of the jars, a 29-cup one (Jar A) and a 3-cup one (Jar B). Easy: Just fill Jar A and then empty out 9 cups from this jar by taking out 3 cups three times, using Jar B. Problem 2 is not too hard either. Fill Jar B with 127 cups, then empty out 21 cups using Jar A, and then empty out 6 cups, using Jar C twice. Now try the rest of the problems yourself.

If you are like many people solving these problems, you will have found a formula that works for all of the remaining problems: You fill up Jar B, then pour out of it the amount of water you can put into Jar A, and then twice pour out of it the amount of water you can put into Jar C. The formula, therefore, is B − A − 2C (Figure 10-12). However, Problems 7 through 11 can be solved in a much simpler way, using just two of the jars. For example, Problem 7 can be solved by A − C, Problem 8 by A + C, and so on. People who are given Problems 1 through 6 to solve generally continue to use the B − A − 2C formula in solving Problems 7 through 11. However, people who go from Problem 2 immediately to Problem 7 generally see the simpler formula: They have no established mental set that interferes with their seeing things in a new and simpler way.

FIGURE 10-12
Luchins's Water-Jar Solution
This figure shows an algorithm for solving the water jar problems shown in Table 10-3. Although the algorithm solves each of the problems given, is there an easier way to solve some of them? (After Luchins, 1942)

Functional Fixedness

A particular type of mental set involves **functional fixedness,** which is the inability to see that something that is known to have a particular use may also be used for performing other functions. Functional fixedness prevents us from using old tools in novel ways to solve new problems. Becoming free of functional fixedness is what first allowed people to use a reshaped coat hanger to get into a locked car, and it is what first allowed thieves to pick simple spring door locks with a credit card. It is also what might allow you to think of an introductory psychology textbook as a resource for criminal ideas!

Functional fixedness may be influenced by cultural context in a way that might surprise some Westerners. Some early writers hypothesized that there are higher and lower levels of mental development across cultures, and that these levels influence the depth or quality of cognitive processes. French anthropologist Claude Levi-Strauss (1966; see also Cole & Scribner, 1974) has rejected this highly ethnocentric hypothesis. Instead, he maintains that the human mind works in essentially the same way across cultures and across time. The only difference between the thought systems employed by persons in nonindustrialized versus industrialized, highly specialized societies might be in the strategies people use. Levi-Strauss has noted that scientific thinkers and problem solvers in nonindustrialized societies are generally *bricoleurs* (jacks-of-all-trades). A *bricoleur* has a bag of tools that can be used to fix all sorts of things, whereas the focused expert of an industrialized society might be effective only in thinking about and solving problems within a narrow area of expertise. One extension of this line of thinking is that persons who live in less specialized, nonindustrialized societies may be less subject to functional fixedness than their more specialized, industrialized counterparts.

Negative Transfer

Often, when people have particular mental sets that prompt them to fixate on one aspect of a problem to the exclusion of other possible relevant ones, they are carrying knowledge and strategies for solving one kind of problem over to a different kind of problem. Cognitive psychologists use the term *transfer* to describe the broader phenomenon of any carryover of knowledge or skills from one problem situation to another. Transfer can be either positive or negative. **Positive transfer** (described in the next section) occurs when the solution of an earlier problem facilitates solving a new problem, whereas **negative transfer** occurs when the experience of solving an earlier problem impedes the solution of a later one.

Consider, for example, the negative transfer that may occur when going from high school to college. Some students find that they can get fairly good grades in high school without working very hard. They then go to college and transfer their less-than-diligent work habits to the college setting. For many such students, the transfer proves to be negative: Their easygoing attitude toward studying or their poor work habits may have gotten them through high school, but those same attitudes and habits do not get them through college.

> Many books have been written describing ways in which to avoid the negative transfer of mental sets. Such books often suggest doing something that specifically unsettles your existing views. What are some really wacky, unsettling things you could do to jar yourself free from your mental sets?

Aids to Problem Solving

If mental sets can impede problem solving, what might facilitate it? Among other things, cognitive psychologists have noticed four positive influences on problem solving: positive transfer, searching for analogies, cuing, and incubation. Do not become fixed on only these strategies, however. Myriad other aids to problem solving await your discovery.

Positive Transfer

As mentioned previously, transfer can be either positive or negative. Positive transfer occurs when the solution of an earlier problem facilitates the solution of a new problem. Recall from the previous section that poor work habits in one setting—such as high school—might negatively transfer to a new setting—such as college. On the other hand, if you developed industrious work habits in high school or in an after-school job, you might experience positive transfer to the college setting. In any case, the knowledge and academic skills (such as reading textbooks and writing term papers) you gained in high school would positively transfer to the college setting. Thus, when you go from one setting to another, you not only have to look for what transfers positively from the first setting to the second, but also for what does not transfer to your advantage. When it is not fairly obvious how to transfer knowledge or skill from one setting to another, to do so requires a selective-comparison insight, because old information must be applied to a new setting in a novel way.

TRANSFER OF ANALOGIES.   Mary Gick and Keith Holyoak (1980, 1983) have designed some elegant studies of positive transfer involving analogies. Understanding of their results requires your familiarity with a problem first used by Karl Duncker (1945), often called the "radiation problem."

> Imagine that you are a doctor treating a patient with a malignant stomach tumor. You can't operate on the patient because of the severity of the cancer, but unless you destroy the tumor somehow, the patient will die. You could use X rays to destroy the tumor. If the X rays are of sufficiently high intensity, then the tumor will be destroyed. Unfortunately, the intensity of X rays needed to destroy the tumor will also destroy healthy tissue through which the rays must pass. X rays of lesser intensity will spare the healthy tissue but will be insufficiently powerful to destroy the tumor. Your problem is to figure out a procedure that will destroy the tumor without also destroying the healthy tissue surrounding the tumor.

This problem is particularly tricky because X rays would penetrate any material that might be used to attempt to guide the rays to the correct location. Furthermore, no known substances or devices can be given to the patient to prevent harm from the intense concentration of radiation.

Duncker had in mind a particular insightful solution as the optimal one for this problem. This solution involves dispersion. The idea is to direct weak X rays toward the tumor from a number of different points outside the body. No single set of X rays would be strong enough to destroy either the healthy tissue or the tumor. However, the rays would be aimed so that they would all converge at one spot within the body—namely, at the site of the tumor. This idea is actually used today in some X-ray treatments, except that a rotating source of X rays is used for dispersing the rays. Figure 10-13 shows the solution pictorially.

Prior to presenting Duncker's radiation problem, Gick and Holyoak would present another problem, called the "military problem" (Holyoak, 1984, p. 205):

> A general wishes to capture a fortress located in the center of a country. There are many roads radiating outward from the fortress. All have been mined so that although small groups of men can pass over the roads safely, any large force will detonate the mines. A full-scale direct attack is therefore impossible. The general's solution is to divide his army into small groups, send each group to the head of a different road,

FIGURE 10-13
The X-Ray Problem
Karl Duncker's X-ray problem requires an insightful solution: issue several weak X rays from different directions that converge on a single point, in this case the tumor. Duncker and other psychologists study whether insight into one problem involving convergence from radial locations allows for the positive transfer of insight to other problems involving radial convergence. (After Duncker, 1945)

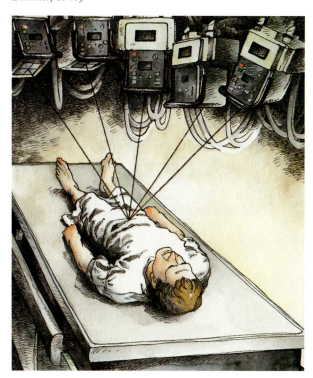

and have the groups converge simultaneously on the fortress.

Table 10-4 shows the correspondence between the radiation and the military problems, which turns out to be quite close, although not perfect. The question is whether being shown a radial-convergence solution to the military problem helped subjects in solving the radiation problem. What did the investigators find? If subjects received the military problem with the convergence solution, and then were given a hint to apply it in some way to the radiation problem, about 75% of the subjects reached the correct solution to the radiation problem; in comparison, fewer than 10% of the subjects who did not receive the military story first but instead received no prior story or only an irrelevant one reached the correct solution.

Gick and Holyoak found that the usefulness of the military problem as an analogue to the radiation problem depended on the induced mental set with which the problem solver approached the problems. If subjects were asked to memorize the military story under the guise that it was a story-recall experiment and then were given the radiation problem to solve, only 30% of subjects produced the convergence solution to the radiation problem. Gick and Holyoak also found that positive transfer improved if two analogous problems were given in advance of the radiation problem rather than just one. Gick and Holyoak expanded these findings to encompass problems other than the radiation problem.

Perhaps the most crucial aspect of these studies is that people have trouble noticing the analogy unless they are explicitly told to look for it. Davidson and Sternberg (1984) found similar results in studies of mathematical insight problems such as the house-numbers example. Thus, in order to find analogies, we generally have to be looking for them.

INTENTIONAL TRANSFER: SEARCHING FOR ANALOGIES.   In looking for analogies, we need to be careful not to be misled by associations between two things that are analogically irrelevant. For example, Georgia Nigro and I studied children's solutions to verbal analogies of the form "A is to B as C is to X," where the children were given multiple-choice options for X. We found that children will often choose as a solution a completion that is associatively close but analogically incorrect. (In representing analogies, a single colon [:] indicates the "is to" expression and a double colon [::] is used to indicate the "as" expression.) For example, in the analogy

TABLE 10-4
Correspondence between the Radiation and the Military Problems
What are the commonalities between the two problems, and what is an elemental strategy that can be derived by comparing the two problems? (After Gick & Holyoak, 1983)

Military Problem
    Initial State
        Goal: Use army to capture fortress
        Resources: Sufficiently large army
        Constraint: Unable to send entire army along one road
    Solution Plan: Send small groups along multiple roads simultaneously
    Outcome: Fortress captured by army
Radiation Problem
    Initial State
        Goal: Use rays to destroy tumor
        Resources: Sufficiently powerful rays
        Constraint: Unable to administer high-intensity rays from one direction
    Solution Plan: Administer low-intensity rays from multiple directions simultaneously
    Outcome: Tumor destroyed by rays
Convergence Schema
    Initial State
        Goal: Use force to overcome a central target
        Resources: Sufficiently great force
        Constraint: Unable to apply full force along one path
    Solution Plan: Apply weak forces along multiple paths simultaneously
    Outcome: Central target overcome by force

LAWYER : CLIENT :: DOCTOR : (A. NURSE, B. PATIENT, C. MEDICINE, D. DIAGNOSIS),

children might choose option A because NURSE is more strongly associated with DOCTOR than is the correct answer, PATIENT (Sternberg & Nigro, 1980). Thomas Achenbach (1970), the first to notice the associative effect, actually constructed a test of reasoning for children based on the premise that less able children would use associative thinking more often than would more able children.

Psychologists often ponder the way in which people are influenced both by the form of something (e.g., the A:B::C:D form of analogies) and by its informational content (e.g., characteristics of professionals). In regard to analogies, cognitive psychologists view the underlying form of the analogies to be more important than the superficial content of the terms of the analogies. For example, Dedre Gentner (1983) has argued that analogies between problems involve mappings of relationships between problems, and that the actual content attributes of the problems are irrelevant. In other words, what matters in analogies is not the similarity of the content, but how closely their structural systems of relationships match. Because we are accustomed to considering the importance of the content, however, we find it difficult to push the content to the background and bring form (structural relationships) to the foreground. Thus, what makes the analogy between the military problem and the radiation problem hard for people is that although the problems match closely in terms of relationships, their content is very different. The differing content impedes positive transfer.

Gentner terms the opposite phenomenon—in which people see false analogies because of similarity of content—**transparency.** For example, we might see the political situations in two Latin American countries as being similar because both are Latin American, rather than because the situations themselves are actually similar. In making analogies, we need to be sure we are focusing on the relationships between the two terms being compared, not just on their surface content attributes. Similarly, when comparing two people's personalities, it is easy to let surface similarities in appearance or speech deceive us into believing that the people are necessarily similar in personality. Because two people have a similar accent or appearance, it does not mean that their behavior will be similar.

Incubation

We make errors of transparency when we inappropriately transfer knowledge about one situation to a different situation that appears to be similar in content. One way of minimizing this negative transfer is **incubation**—simply putting the problem aside for a while. For example, if you find that you are unable to solve a problem, and none of the strategies you can think of seem to work, try just setting the problem aside for a while to incubate. During incubation, you do not consciously think about the problem. Still, the problem may be processed subconsciously, much as Kekulé subconsciously worked on his problem when he was not consciously trying to solve it. Some investigators of problem solving have even asserted that incubation is an essential stage of the problem-solving process (e.g., Cattell, 1971; Helmholtz, 1896; Poincaré, 1913).

Several possible mechanisms for the beneficial effects of incubation have been proposed. Among them are:

1. When we no longer keep something in active memory, we let go of some of the unimportant details and keep only the more meaningful aspects in memory. From these aspects, we are then free to reconstruct anew, with fewer of the limitations of the earlier mental set (e.g., B. F. Anderson, 1975).
2. As time passes, more recent memories become better integrated with existing memories (e.g., J. R. Anderson, 1985). During this reintegration, some associations of an irrelevant mental set may weaken.
3. As time passes, new stimuli—both internal and external—may activate new perspectives on the problem, weakening the effects of the mental set (e.g., Bastik, 1982; Yanis & Meyer, 1987).
4. When problem solvers are in a low state of cortical arousal (e.g., in the shower, in bed, taking a walk), attention span—and perhaps working-memory capacity—increases, and increasingly remote cues can be perceived and held in the memory simultaneously. The person may relaxedly toy with cues that might otherwise be perceived as irrelevant or distracting when the person is in a high state of cortical arousal (e.g., while trying actively to solve the problem) (Luria, 1973/1984).

Craig Kaplan and Janet Davidson (1989) have reviewed the literature on incubation and found that the benefits of incubation can be enhanced in two ways: (1) invest enough time in the problem initially, perhaps explore all aspects of the problem and investigate several possible avenues of solving it, and (2) allow sufficient time for incubation to permit negative transfer to weaken somewhat. A drawback of incubation is that it takes time. If you have a deadline for problem solution, you must begin solving the problem early enough to meet the deadline, and include the time you will need for incubation.

For example, when you write a paper for a course and you find that you just cannot seem to organize the paper effectively, it may help just to let the problem incubate for a while. A few days later, you may find that what seemed like an insoluble problem is now more easily solved. Using this strategy means, of course, that you need to start thinking about the paper enough in advance of the deadline so that you have time for incubation.

Expertise: Knowledge and Problem Solving

Thus far, this chapter has discussed various strategies for solving problems. Why are some people better problem solvers than are other people? In particular, why can experts solve problems in their field more expertly than can novices? What do experts know that makes the problem-solving process more effective for them than for novices in a field?

William Chase and Herbert Simon (1973) set out to find out what experts know and do by determining what distinguishes expert from novice chess players. In one of their studies, Chase and Simon had expert and novice players briefly view a display of a chess board with the chess pieces on it and then recall the positions of the chess pieces on the board. In general, the experts did quite a bit better than did the novices—but only if the positions of the chess pieces on the board made sense in terms of an actual game of chess. If the pieces were randomly distributed around the board, experts recalled the positions of the pieces no better than did the novices.

The work of Chase and Simon, combined with earlier work by Adrian de Groot (1965), suggested that what differentiated the experts from the novices was their use of *knowledge*. Both chess tasks—whether with a random array of pieces or with a meaningful arrangement of pieces—required the expert to have stored and then to retrieve information about the chess board. According to these investigators, the key difference between groups was that chess experts (but not novices) could call on their knowledge of tens of thousands of board positions, each of which they could remember as integrated, organized chunks of information. For a random pattern of pieces on the board, however, the knowledge of the experts offered them no advantage over the novices. Like the novices, they had to try to memorize the distinctive interrelations among the many discrete pieces and positions.

After the Chase and Simon work, a number of other investigators conducted extensive studies of large numbers of experts in different domains (e.g., see Chi, Glaser, & Farr, 1988). Although several characteristics were found to distinguish experts from novices, what most clearly differentiated the two groups was the amount of existing knowledge, and how well the existing information was organized. For example, Jill Larkin and her colleagues found that experts in physics differ from novices primarily in their knowledge base and in the resulting ability that this knowledge base gives them to represent physics problems effectively (Larkin, McDermott, Simon, & Simon, 1980).

Micheline Chi and her colleagues (e.g., Chi, Feltovich, & Glaser, 1981), further studying performance in physics, found that when people were asked to sort physics problems into groups of problems that "belonged together," experts tended to sort problems by the underlying principles of physics involved, whereas novices tended to sort the problems in terms of surface features of the problems, such as whether the problems involved pulleys. Alan Lesgold and his colleagues studied radiologists and found several other differences between experts and novices (Lesgold, 1988; Lesgold et al., 1988). For example, they found that experts tend to spend more time than do novices in representing problems, and that experts are better at using new evidence than are novices.

In a way, the preceding studies support the nothing-special view of expertise, in that the experts' knowledge—not extraordinary mental processes—provides the basis for their insights. On the other hand, the superior performance of experts also makes sense if we think in terms of the three-process view of insight. Experts can more readily selectively encode relevant information that fits with the vast existing knowledge they already have stored in memory. When the experts are presented with new information or with new problems, they can selectively combine the new information in far more ways than can novices, because the experts have more existing information with which to make such combinations. Finally, experts can also draw on a much larger repertoire of possibilities for selective-comparison insights into problem solving.

In part, what experts gain from their experience is a large set of virtually automatic procedures that novices lack. The term **automaticity** refers to the way in which experts have mastered many procedures and heuristics of their area of expertise to such a degree that the manipulation of these procedures is virtually automatic (see also Chapter 8, regarding expertise and the organization of increasingly complex chunks of information). When asked to play a card game that had a change in surface structure (the suits were given nonsense names such as "fricks" for clubs),

Searchers . . .   *HERBERT SIMON*

Dr. Simon received his PhD in political science from the University of Chicago and is Richard King Mellon University Professor of Computer Science and Psychology at Carnegie Mellon University.

Q: *How did you become interested in psychology?*

A: My career began in the field of public administration, with a special interest in how managers make decisions in organizations. Pursuing this interest brought me to social psychology (organizational behavior) and cognitive psychology (theory of problem solving) in order to provide a foundation for a theory of organizations and decision making.

Q: *What theories have influenced you the most?*

A: In my early psychology reading, I found William James and Edward C. Tolman more helpful than the then-prevailing behaviorists. I also studied the European work on problem solving: Wertheimer, Selz, and Duncker. Things began to come together when I encountered early computers and saw their potential for simulating human thought processes.

Q: *What is your greatest personal asset as a psychologist?*
A: Curiosity.

Q: *How do you develop ideas for research?*

A: The ideas come from looking for surprises and anomalies in my and others' research findings. Other ideas come from fixing my mind on important unsolved problems that come to my attention.

Q: *Which of your ideas has been particularly innovative?*

A: My most important idea (developed in collaboration with Allen Newell) is that human problem solving is a process of selective search using means-ends analysis, and that it could be simulated by computer.

Q: *What obstacles have you experienced in your work and how have you overcome them?*

A: Stupidity, lack of time, and occasionally lack of money or computing power. Mostly the first two, which I don't know how to overcome, except that stupidity can be reduced by finding smart colleagues.

Q: *What do you want students who work with you to learn?*

A: I want students to learn how to do important research by doing it, including the skills of working with others, without being intimidated or mistaking science for politics, or vice versa.

Q: *What advice would you give to someone starting in the field of psychology?*

A: Find one or two problems that you really want to solve and see if you can take some steps toward solving them. Recognize that you will need at least ten years (including your past work) of intensive immersion in the field and its literature to do anything major. And don't try to work at anything you don't basically enjoy.

Q: *What have you learned from your own students?*

A: That interaction can keep you mentally alive well beyond the usual onset of senescence.

Q: *So apart from your life as an academic, how have you found psychology to be important?*

A: I'm not sure I have a life apart from my academic life. It is a part of everything I do, and fortunately I can share much of it with my wife and children.

---

expert card players could easily adapt to the new terms (Frensch & Sternberg, 1989). Unfortunately, however, experts may gain expertise at the expense of being open to alternatives. Experts may risk losing some degree of flexibility, so that they have more trouble than novices when a fundamental change is made in the nature of the task. For example, expert bridge players may have more difficulty than do novices when adjusting to changes in the basic rules of the game. The disadvantage of expertise can be overcome, however. For example, in the Frensch–Sternberg research, the expert bridge players soon caught on to a basic change in the rules and thus outperformed the novices. Nonetheless, there can be costs—at least initially— as well as benefits of expertise, particularly if the experts resist adapting to changing circumstances.

Whereas problem solving involves inventing or discovering strategies in order to answer a complex question, other forms of thinking may involve simply (but not necessarily easily) choosing among alternatives or evaluating opportunities. The next section deals with how we make these choices and judgments.

What are some procedures or tasks that you can perform automatically, without having to think about each step in the process? In what situations might your automaticity of these procedures be problematic? How?

JUDGMENT AND DECISION MAKING

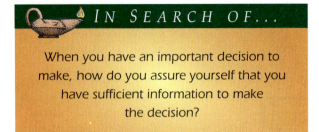

IN SEARCH OF...

When you have an important decision to make, how do you assure yourself that you have sufficient information to make the decision?

In the course of our everyday lives, we are constantly making judgments and decisions. One of the most important decisions you may have made is that of whether and where to go to college. Once in college, you need to choose the courses you will take and, eventually, your major field of study. You make decisions about friends, about how to relate to your parents, and about how to spend money. How do you go about making these decisions?

How do you go about making important decisions? How do your decision-making processes differ, if at all, when you are making less important decisions?

Decision Theory

The earliest models of decision theory assumed that decision makers operate in ideal circumstances and make optimal decisions. Although we may now see these assumptions as unrealistic, a great deal of economic research has been and still is based on this model. Subsequent models of decision making have recognized that we humans may not make ideal decisions, but these models have asserted that we nevertheless strive to make optimal decisions. For example, according to **utility maximization theory,** the goal of human action is to seek pleasure and to avoid pain. Therefore, in making decisions, people will seek to maximize pleasure (referred to as *positive utility*) and to minimize pain (referred to as *negative utility*). Utility-maximization theorists suggest that we can predict what people will do by assuming that they will seek the highest possible utility—in other words, whatever decision maximizes pleasure and minimizes pain. Suppose, for example, that you are deciding whether to call someone to ask the person out for an evening. You are afraid to call because you may be turned down, and you are not really certain you will have a good time. These factors can be viewed as negative utilities. On the other hand, you have hopes that maybe the evening will actually turn out to be really

fun, despite your doubts. Moreover, perhaps the evening together will be the beginning of a new, long-term relationship. These factors provide positive utilities. Whether you call will depend on whether the positive utilities outweigh the negative ones in your mind.

Although it is certainly appealing to come up with objective, mathematical models for decision making, in practice, it is very difficult to assign objective utilities to decisions, and models based on such assignments are likely to produce inaccurate representations of reality. As a result, cognitive psychologists interested in decision theory introduced **subjective-utility theory,** which acknowledges that utilities for a given action may be different from one person to another, depending on each person's system of values. Although subjective-utility theory takes into account the many subjective variables that arise when people are involved, it soon became apparent that decisions are more complex even than this modified theory implies, as shown in work that has been done on game theory.

Game Theory

Game theory suggests that many decisions, especially those involving more than one person, have gamelike aspects. Sometimes, the gamelike properties of a decision are simple. For example, in a game of chess or of checkers, one person wins and the other loses. Such a game is termed a **zero-sum game,** because a positive outcome for the winner is balanced by a negative outcome for the loser—positive plus negative equals zero. Some games are more complex than are chess or checkers, however.

One such complex game is the *prisoner's dilemma* (Luce & Raiffa, 1957).

> Suppose that two men have been arrested and are charged with pulling off a bank heist. Each man is found to have an unregistered firearm at the time of arrest. The police do not have conclusive evidence that the two men actually robbed the bank. The police need a confession from at least one of the men so that the district attorney can win the case. The district attorney hatches a Machiavellian plan in order to wring out a confession from at least one prisoner.
>
> She separates the two prisoners, preventing them from communicating with each other. The district attorney tells each of the accused that what happens to him will depend not only on what he does, but also on what the other prisoner does. If neither prisoner confesses, the district attorney will be unable to prove the

bank-robbery charge, but she will prosecute both of them on the charge of illegal possession of a firearm, and each prisoner will be jailed for one year. The district attorney informs the prisoners that if they both confess, she will recommend an intermediate-length term for each of them: 10 years in prison. In addition, however, the district attorney offers each prisoner immunity from prosecution if he is the only one to confess. In this case, the prisoner who confesses will go scot-free, whereas the prisoner who does not confess will be slapped with the maximum possible sentence—20 years.

Table 10-5 represents the **payoff matrix**—the individual consequences for each decision maker regarding each of the various decisions.

The prisoner's dilemma presents a complicated situation for the prisoners. The greatest individual payoff is for being the only one to pull a double-cross, thereby enabling oneself to go scot-free. However, if both prisoners double-cross each other, they will both go to jail for a decade. The greatest loss is for being the only one *not* to double-cross the other, and thereby having to spend the maximum term in prison. The best deal for the two partners together is for each prisoner to remain silent—a potentially costly strategy if one partner is less altruistic than the other.

Subjective-utility theory does not do a good job of explaining how to make decisions in the prisoner's dilemma and similar dilemmas because the decision maker cannot identify the subjective utilities without knowing the decision of the other party, but there is no way of knowing the other party's decision before making one's own decision.

Game theory suggests various strategies a person can use in a gamelike situation such as the prisoner's dilemma. According to the **minimax loss rule,** you make a choice that *mini*mizes your *max*imum loss. Using this rule, the prisoner in the prisoner's dilemma will confess because he wants to minimize the possibility of going to jail for 20 years, the maximum loss. Another strategy is the **maximin gain rule,** according to which you *maxi*mize your *mini*mum gain; for example, you might stay with a dull job at a modest salary (a rather minimal gain) rather than taking a chance on starting a new business you might thoroughly enjoy. Staying with your old job maximizes your minimum gain, whereas opening the new business might maximize your potential maximum gain but does not maximize your potential minimum gain. For the **maximax gain rule,** the strategy is to *maxi*mize the *maxi*mum gain. For example, an investor using the maximax strategy is likely to invest in highly risky stocks in order to maximize potential gain, at the possible cost of losing all her money. She is also a good candidate for buying lottery tickets: The maximum gain is huge, but the chances of getting it, remote. (The minimax-loss strategist would never follow such a risky approach.)

Which of the three game-theory rules seems best to suit your style of decision making? Which one seems least suitable to you? Why do you think you prefer the style you chose?

Satisficing

All of the various game rules are based on the notion that decision makers have unlimited rationality and use it in making their decisions. They decide what criterion to maximize or minimize and then make the optimal decision for doing so. Even in the 1950s, however, some psychologists were beginning to recognize that we humans do not always make ideal decisions, that we usually include subjective

TABLE 10-5

Payoff Matrix for Prisoner's Dilemma

It is not always possible to predict the outcome of your own behavior without also considering the behavior of other persons. We must often make decisions based on our best guesses about possible outcomes, without being sure of a definite, predictable outcome.

Prisoners' Dilemma		Prisoner A	
Prisoner B	Payoff matrix	Confess	Not confess
	Confess	Both get 10 years	A = 20 years B = 0 years
	Not confess	A = 0 years B = 20 years	Both get 1 year

considerations in our decisions, and that we are not entirely and boundlessly rational in making decisions.

The most well-known challenge came from Herbert Simon (1957), who went on to win the Nobel Prize in economics. Simon did not suggest that we humans are irrational, but rather that we exhibit **bounded rationality**—we are rational, but within limits. Simon suggested one of the most typical decision-making strategies: satisficing. In **satisficing,** we do *not* consider all possible options and then carefully compute which of the entire universe of options will maximize our gains and minimize our losses. Rather, we consider options one by one, and then we select an option as soon as we find one that is satisfactory—just good enough. Thus, we will consider the minimum possible number of options to arrive at a decision that we believe will satisfy our minimum requirements. For example, you may use satisficing when considering research topics for a term project or paper; of the countless possible topics, you may consider a few, and then settle on the first satisfactory or even pretty good topic you think of, without continuing your exploration.

The trend that led from fully rational models of decision making to models of bounded rationality involved the increasing recognition that people are not perfect decision makers. We make decisions in less than ideal circumstances, given inadequate or incomplete information, and using limited objectivity and rationality. Often, we are even willing to settle for the first acceptable option that becomes available, fully aware that other options may be better. What additional human frailties have researchers discovered in the study of decision making?

Heuristics and Biases

In the 1970s, Amos Tversky and Daniel Kahneman found even more evidence of the boundaries of human rationality. Tversky, Kahneman, and their colleagues have investigated several heuristics and biases we often use when making decisions and other judgments; some of these heuristics and biases—such as representativeness, availability, and some of the other phenomena involving judgment—are described in the following section.

Representativeness

Before you read a definition of representativeness, try out the following problem (Kahneman & Tversky, 1971):

> All the families having exactly six children in a particular city were surveyed. In 72 of the

families, the exact order of births of boys (B) and girls (G) was G B G B B G.

What is your estimate of the number of families surveyed in which the exact order of births was B G B B B B?

Most people judging the number of families with the B G B B B B birth pattern estimate the number to be less than 72. Actually, the best estimate of the number of families with this birth order is 72, the same as for the G B G B B G birth order. The expected number for the second pattern would be the same because the gender for each birth is independent (at least, theoretically) of the gender for every other birth, and for any one birth, the chances of a boy (or a girl) are one out of two. Thus, any particular pattern of births is equally likely, even B B B B B B or G G G G G G.

Why do people believe some birth orders to be more likely than others? Kahneman and Tversky suggest that it is because they use the heuristic of **representativeness,** in which we judge the probability of an uncertain event according to (a) how obviously it is similar to or representative of the population from which it is derived, and (b) the degree to which it reflects the salient features of the process by which it is generated (such as randomness). For example, people believe that the first birth order is more likely because first, it is more representative of the number of females and males in the population, and because second, it looks more random than does the second birth order. In fact, of course, either birth order is equally likely to occur by chance. Similarly, if asked to judge the probability of flips of a coin yielding the sequence—H T H H T H—people will judge it as higher than they will if asked to judge the sequence—H H H H T H. Thus, if you expect a sequence to be random, you tend to view as more likely to occur a sequence that "looks random." Indeed, people often comment that the ordering of numbers in a table of random numbers "doesn't look random," because people underestimate the number of runs of the same number that will appear wholly by chance.

In order fully to understand the representativeness heuristic, it helps to understand the concept of **base rate**—the prevalence of an event or characteristic within its population of events or characteristics. People often ignore base-rate information, even though it is important to effective judgment and decision making. In many occupations, the use of base-rate information and the representativeness heuristic are essential for adequate job performance. For example, if a doctor were told that a 10-year-old girl is suffering chest pains, the doctor would be much less

Searchers . . .   DANIEL KAHNEMAN

Dr. Kahneman is Eugene Higgins Professor of Psychology and professor of public affairs at the Woodrow Wilson School of Public and International Affairs at Princeton University.

Q: *How did you become involved with thinking and heuristics?*

A: Well, by an accident, actually. I was teaching a graduate course in applied psychology, and I invited Amos Tversky to tell us about applications in his area, which was judgment and decision making. My area, at the time, was mainly perception and attention. I thought, from my vantage point, some of the things that he described seemed very implausible. We discussed things over lunch, and actually came up with the heuristics and biases idea very quickly.

Q: *What theories have influenced you the most?*

A: There is a permanent imprint on my thinking from being exposed as an undergraduate to Kurt Lewin. I keep coming back to ideas from Kurt Lewin. The other major intellectual influence on my life, obviously, is Amos Tversky because we have interacted over many years.

Q: *Is there a common denominator among great psychologists?*

A: One very obvious characteristic is that they work very, very hard. At the same time, they have an ability to see opportunities and exploit them, so they respond opportunistically when they find a twist or a new idea. It's the combination of persistence and opportunistic behavior.

Q: *What experiences have prompted some of your ideas?*

A: Most of them have come to me through personal observation of incidents in my life.

Q: *How do you decide whether to pursue an idea?*

A: That's a very complex decision. The criterion is really aesthetic—how interesting it would be if we managed to do it. If it's an elegant idea, it will have high priority. And if it's an elegant idea, it will often be simple to do, too, or at least conceptually simple.

Q: *What is your major contribution to psychology?*

A: Unquestionably, the work that Amos Tversky and I have done. To a large extent, I think, we opened up an area. We applied a cognitive analysis to the notions of heuristics and biases. What made the work influential was the vivid examples and the style of demonstration. So, the contribution is in part stylistic and in part bringing cognitive analysis to a field that didn't have it before.

Q: *What advice would you give to an undergraduate in psychology?*

A: Realize that the questions you have when you begin as an undergraduate may not have easy answers. Part of what you are going to learn in psychology is to reformulate the questions so they can be answered within the scientific method.

Q: *What have you learned from your students?*

A: A lot of the work on judgment and on judgmental biases and on probabilistic thinking came from teaching statistics. I asked myself why some things are very easy and other things hard, both for myself and for my students. I tried to understand the source of their difficulty. That turned out to have a big impact on all my subsequent work on probabilistic judgment.

Q: *What do you further hope to achieve?*

A: I'm very interested in the development of psychology that is relevant to policy and to human affairs. There's a lot of policy making where psychology could have an input. I would be interested in developing measures of human misery and happiness in their various forms. This is too big an agenda, and I probably won't get it done. But in the process of trying, I may hit upon something.

---

likely to worry about an incipient heart attack than if told that a 50-year-old man has the identical symptom. Why? Because the base rate of heart attacks is much higher in 50-year-old men than in 10-year-old girls.

Fewer than 1 in 250,000 plane flights has even the most minor of accidents; fewer than 1 in 1.6 million scheduled flights ends in fatalities (Krantz, 1992); the odds were 1 in 2.2 million of being killed in an airplane crash in 1988 (Shook & Shook, 1991). Although the chances of dying during any given car trip (however brief) are low, more than 1 in 125 Americans will die in a car-related accident (Krantz, 1992). Drivers who are 18-year-old, intoxicated, unseat-belted males are 1,000 times more likely to die in a car crash than are 40-year-old, sober, seat-belted men or women drivers (Shook & Shook, 1991).

Which of these accidents has the higher base rate? How does the availability of some information (and the unavailability of other information) influence our perceptions and decisions?

Availability

Why is it that so many more people are afraid of flying in airplanes than of riding in cars, despite the fact that the probability of being injured or dying in a car crash is much higher than that of being injured or dying in a plane crash? One reason is the **availability heuristic** (Tversky & Kahneman, 1973), according to which people make judgments on the basis of how easily they are able to call to mind what they perceive as relevant instances of a phenomenon. Newspapers give much more play to plane crashes than to car crashes, and it is usually easier to call to mind grim instances of plane crashes than of car crashes. Hence, people tend to fear riding in planes more than they fear riding in cars.

> Are there more words in the English language that begin with the letter *R*, or are there more words that have *R* as their third letter?

> What would you estimate to be the product of $8 \times 7 \times 6 \times 5 \times 4 \times 3 \times 2 \times 1$?

Tversky and Kahneman (1973) found that most people could more easily think of words beginning with R than they could of words having R as their third letter. (There are actually more English words with R as the third letter.) Tversky and Kahneman also studied the availability heuristic by giving their subjects 5 seconds to estimate the product of either of two sets of eight numbers: $8 \times 7 \times 6 \times 5 \times 4 \times 3 \times 2 \times 1$ or $1 \times 2 \times 3 \times 4 \times 5 \times 6 \times 7 \times 8$. The median (middle) estimate for the first sequence was

2250. For the second sequence, the median estimate was 512. (The actual product is 40,320!) The two products are the same, as they must be because the numbers are exactly the same (applying the commutative law of multiplication). Nonetheless, people provide a higher estimate for the first sequence because their computation of the first few digits multiplied by each other renders a higher estimate more available for the first string of numbers than for the second.

> Why do you think that even the higher of the two estimates so dramatically underestimates the actual product of the numbers?

Sometimes, availability and representativeness work together to lead to a less than optimal conclusion. Take, for example, the following true story, which is similar to a story used in the research of Tversky and Kahneman.

A high school senior has thoroughly checked out two colleges. Call them College A and College B. He has looked in guide books and spoken to people who are well acquainted with each college. On the basis of all the available information, College A looks better. Yet, when he visits, he likes his host at College B more than his host at College A, and the class he attends at College B is more interesting than the one he attends at College A. Moreover, on the day he visits College B, the weather is excellent, whereas on the day he visits College A, the weather is terrible. He even gets paint on his raincoat at College A. He finds it hard not to prefer College B. The actual visits to the colleges seem more representative in their information about the colleges than does second-hand information, and the information from the visits is also more readily available. Yet, College A is probably the better choice because it is almost certainly a mistake to judge two colleges on the basis of a single host, a single class, and the weather on the day of the visit.

This very set of events happened to me. I chose College A in spite of it all, and I'm happy I did.

It is important to realize that heuristics such as representativeness and availability do not always lead to wrong judgments. Indeed, we use them because they are so often right. For example, in buying a computer, you may decide to buy from a company for which the company name is readily available in memory, based on the view that you are taking a bigger risk in buying from a company that is relatively unknown. The known company does not necessarily make a better computer, but because the computer is a large purchase, you may not want to take the risk of buying from an unknown manufacturer.

Other Judgment Phenomena

There are other oddities in people's judgments. One is **overconfidence**—an individual's overvaluation of her or his own personal skills, knowledge, or judgment. Baruch Fischhoff, Paul Slovic, and Sarah Lichtenstein (1977) gave people 200 two-alternative statements, such as "Absinthe is (a) a liqueur, (b) a precious stone." People were asked to choose the correct answer and to give the probability that their answer was correct. People were strangely overconfident. For example, when people were 100% confident of their answers, they were right only 80% of the time! (*Absinthe* is a licorice-flavored liqueur.) Kahneman and Tversky (1979) asked people questions such as "I feel 98 percent certain that the number of nuclear plants operating in the world in 1980 was more than ___ but less than ___." Nearly one third of the time, the correct answer to questions such as these (exactly 189 at that time) was outside the range that people gave. Due to overconfidence, people often do things that are dangerous or bad for them. One example of overconfidence is the belief of many smokers that although lung cancer and heart disease may strike other people, they themselves are

not likely to be struck by these diseases. It is not clear why we tend to be overconfident in our judgments; one simple explanation is that we prefer not to think about being wrong (Fischhoff, 1988).

Right now, flip to the key terms at the end of this chapter. Quickly estimate the percentage of these terms that you believe you already know and understand. Now, jot down your own definitions for every other term in the list (not selecting just the half you more easily grasp). Compare your definitions with those in the glossary. How accurately had you estimated your own accuracy?

Another common error is **gambler's fallacy,** which refers to the belief that just by the nature of things, eventually, a person's luck is bound to change. Thus, the gambler who loses in five successive bets may believe that a win is more likely the sixth time. In truth, of course, the gambler is no more likely to win on the sixth bet than on the first—or on the 1,001st! Of course, luck *can* change. Often, however, it changes only when we make our own luck!

Another frequent error of judgment is the **fallacy of composition.** We commit this fallacy when we believe that what is true of the parts of a whole must necessarily be true of the whole as well. Often, when a whole comprises many parts, the quality of the integration of those parts strongly influences the quality of the whole. For example, all-star baseball teams, ballet companies composed of prima donnas, and blue-ribbon panels may end up being ineffective because the members, despite their stellar individual abilities and credentials, find themselves unable to work together.

Much of the work on judgment and decision making has focused on the errors people make. As Jonathan Cohen (1981) has pointed out, however, people do act rationally in many instances. (For example, you have made the rational decision to read the textbook in order to do well on the examinations in your psychology course—as well as to learn about psychology.) Nonetheless, the research of Tversky and Kahneman, as well as of others, shows that however rational we may be, our rationality is limited. It is as much a part of being human not to be rational at times as it is to be rational at other times.

What are some heuristics that people use in decision making that are not listed in this book? Describe them.

REASONING

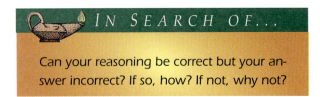

IN SEARCH OF...

Can your reasoning be correct but your answer incorrect? If so, how? If not, why not?

We have seen that judgment and decision making involve evaluating opportunities and selecting one choice above any others. A more formal kind of thinking, familiar to students in logic courses, is reasoning. Reasoning pertains to the process of drawing conclusions from evidence (Wason & Johnson-Laird, 1972). It is often divided into two types—deductive and inductive reasoning. **Deductive reasoning** is the process of reasoning from one or more general **premises**—statements on which an argument is based—regarding what is known, to reach a logically certain, specific conclusion. In contrast, **inductive reasoning** is the process of reasoning from specific facts or observations to reach a general conclusion that may explain the facts; in inductive reasoning, it is not possible to reach a logically certain conclusion—only a particularly well-founded or probable conclusion.

Deductive Reasoning

Deductive reasoning proceeds from a set of general premises to a specific, logically certain conclusion. It is the process of reasoning from what is already known to reach a new conclusion. One specific type of problem often used to illustrate deductive reasoning is the syllogism. **Syllogisms** are deductive arguments that involve drawing conclusions from two premises. Two key types of syllogisms—linear syllogisms and categorical syllogisms—are described in detail in this chapter, but other types of syllogisms are also used in deductive reasoning.

Linear Syllogisms

In a **linear syllogism,** each of the two premises describes a particular relationship between two items, at least one of which is common to both premises. Logicians designate the common term as the *middle term* (which is used once in each premise), the first term of the first premise as the *subject*, and the second term of the second premise as the *predicate*. Suppose, for example, that you are presented with the following problem:

You are smarter than your best friend.
Your best friend is smarter than your roommate.
Which of you is the smartest?

The two premises each describe a relationship between two items; Table 10-6 shows the terms of each premise and the relationship of the terms in each premise. The deductive-reasoning task for the linear syllogism is to determine a relationship between two items not already occurring in the same premise. In the preceding linear syllogism, the problem solver needs to infer that you are smarter than your roommate in order to realize that you are the smartest of the three.

When a linear syllogism is **deductively valid,** its conclusion follows logically from the premises. In the preceding linear syllogism, we can deduce with complete certainty that you are the smartest of the three individuals. Your roommate or your best friend may, however, point out an area of weakness in your conclusion. Even a conclusion that is deductively valid may not be objectively true if the premises are not true.

Three basic kinds of models have been proposed for how people solve linear syllogisms. The first kind of model, a spatial model, posits that people imagine a linear array representing the relations among terms (DeSoto, London, & Handel, 1965; Huttenlocher, 1968). In the example, you might imagine yourself at the top, your best friend in the middle, and your roommate at the bottom of the linear array. The second kind of model is propositional, according to which people interrelate the terms of the linear syllogism via propositions such as TALLER (you, your best friend) (Clark, 1969). The third kind of model is a mixture model, according to which people use both spatial and propositional representations in solving the linear syllogisms (Sternberg, 1980). There is some evidence that people differ in their stategies, with the majority using a mixture strategy, but others using either purely spatial or purely propositional strategies (Sternberg & Weil, 1980).

Categorical Syllogisms

Probably the best-known kind of syllogism is the categorical syllogism. Like other kinds of syllogisms, **categorical syllogisms** comprise two premises and a conclusion; in the case of the categorical syllogism, the premise states something about the categories to which the terms belong. In fact, each term represents all, some, or no members of a particular class or category. As with other syllogisms, each premise contains two terms, one of which must be the middle term, common to both premises. The first and the second

TABLE 10-6
Linear Syllogisms
This table illustrates the components of and the relationships within the linear syllogism, "You are smarter than your best friend. Your best friend is smarter than your roommate. Which of you is the smartest?"

	First Term (Item)	Relationship	Second Term (Item)
Premise A	You	are smarter than	Your best friend
Premise B	Your best friend	is smarter than	Your roommate
Conclusion: Who is smartest?	_____	is/are the smartest of the three.	

terms in each premise are linked through the categorical membership of the terms—that is, one term is a member of the class indicated by the other term. However the premises are worded, they state that some (or all or none) of the members of the category of the first term are (or are not) members of the category of the second term. To determine whether the conclusion follows logically from the premises, the reasoner must determine the category memberships of the terms. An example of a categorical syllogism would be

All psychology students are pianists.
All pianists are athletes.
Therefore, all psychology students are athletes.

To illustrate class membership and to make it easier to figure out whether a particular conclusion is logically sound, logicians often use *Venn diagrams*—diagrams using circles (and sometimes ovals) to represent sets. As Figure 10-14 shows, the conclusion for this syllogism does in fact follow logically from the premises, but the conclusion is false because the premises are false. For the preceding categorical syllogism, the subject is "psychology students," the middle term is "pianists," and the predicate is "athletes." In both premises, we asserted that all members of the category of the first term were members of the category of the second term.

Statements of the form "All A are B" are sometimes referred to as **universal affirmatives,** because they make a positive (affirmative) statement about *all* members of a class (universal). In addition, there are three other kinds of possible statements in a categorical syllogism: **universal negative** statements (e.g., "No psychology students are flutists"); **particular affirmative** statements (e.g., "Some psychology students are left-handed"); and **particular negative** statements (e.g., "Some psychology students are not physicists"). These are summarized in Table 10-7.

Various theories have been proposed as to how people solve categorical syllogisms. According to the atmosphere theory, different elements within a syllogism (such as negative versus affirmative premises or particular versus universal premises) create an atmosphere that determines the conclusion (negative/affirmative, particular/universal) people will draw. Another theory has focused attention on the *conversion* of premises, in which the terms of a given premise are reversed, and the reversed form of the premise is believed to be just as valid as the original form. Although some premises are indeed reversible (such as universal negatives—e.g., "No students are axe murderers" < = > "No axe murderers are students"), many premises are not (e.g., "All ostriches are birds" < ≠ > "All birds are ostriches"). Phil Johnson-Laird and Mark Steedman (1978) have proposed a more recent theory, which is probably the most comprehensive theory of syllogistic reasoning that we have. This theory is based on the notion that people solve syllogisms using mental models; that is, they manipulate in their minds actual exemplars of elements of the syllogisms, trying to find what the correct solution should be.

Make up one categorical syllogism for each of the four types. Try reversing the syllogisms you created. Show the syllogisms and the reversals to two other people. Observe their reactions, particularly noting whether they detected the logical fallacies. Describe their reasoning.

Other Forms of Deductive Reasoning

There are also other forms of deductive reasoning. For example, **conditional syllogisms** are syllogisms

FIGURE 10-14
Venn Diagram of a Syllogism
Logicians often use Venn diagrams to illustrate the relations among the terms of a logical syllogism. This diagram shows that the conclusion "All psychology students are athletes" follows logically from the two premises of the syllogism "All psychology students are pianists" and "All pianists are athletes." Does the validity of the logic ensure that the conclusion is true?

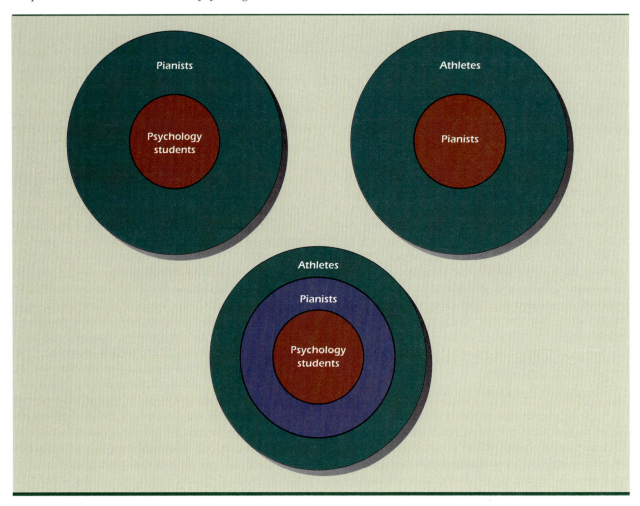

that use the form, "If A, then B. A (or 'not A'). Therefore, B (or 'not B')." An example would be, "If Jill studies hard, she will pass her psychology exam. Jill studies hard. Therefore, Jill will pass her psychology exam." It appears that the way in which people solve conditional syllogisms is similar to the way that they solve categorical syllogisms (see, e.g., Guyote & Sternberg, 1981).

Deductive-reasoning problems need not consist of just two premises. For example, mathematical and logical proofs are deductive in character and can have many steps as well.

Not all studies of deductive reasoning have focused entirely on formal logical syllogisms. Patricia Cheng and Keith Holyoak (1985) have investigated how people use deductive reasoning in realistic situa-

tions. They propose that, rather than using either formal inference rules or just memories of our own experiences, we employ pragmatic reasoning schemas. **Pragmatic reasoning schemas** are general organizing principles—rules—related to particular kinds of goals, such as permissions, obligations, or causations; these schemas are sometimes referred to as *pragmatic rules.* In a situation in which our previous experience or existing knowledge is not sufficient to tell us what we want to know, we may rely on pragmatic-reasoning schemas to help us deduce what might reasonably be true. Particular situations or contexts activate particular schemas. For example, suppose that you are walking across campus and see someone who looks extremely young on campus; then you see the person walk to a car, unlock it, get in, and drive away. This observation would activate your *permission schema* for driving, "If you are to be permitted to drive, then you must be at least 16 years old." You might then deduce that the person you saw is at least 16 years old.

In problems involving pragmatic reasoning schemas and other forms of deductive reasoning, there is at least a possibility of finding the logically valid answer. In inductive reasoning, considered next, the reasoner cannot reach a logically certain conclusion; she or he can only hope to determine the strength, or probability, of a conclusion.

"Alas, Adso, you have too much faith in syllogisms! What we have, once again, is simply the question. . . . "
I was upset. I had always believed logic was a

universal weapon, and now I realized how its validity depended on the way it was employed.

—*Umberto Eco*, The Name of the Rose

Inductive Reasoning

Suppose that you are not given a neat set of premises from which you can draw a conclusion. Instead, you are given a set of observations. For example, suppose that you notice that all of the persons enrolled in your introductory psychology course are on the dean's list (or honor roll). From these observations, you could inductively reason that all students who enroll in introductory psychology are excellent students (or at least earn the grades to give that impression!). However, unless you can observe the grade-point averages of all persons who ever have or ever will take introductory psychology, you will be unable to prove your

TABLE 10-7
Categorical Syllogisms: Types of Premises
Of the four types of categorical syllogisms, only the universal negative categorical syllogism is reversible.

Type of Premise	Form of Premise Statement	Description	Examples	Reversibility[a]
Universal affirmative	All A are B.	The premise positively (affirmatively) states that *all* members of the first class (universal) are members of the second class.	All men are males.	All men ≠ All males are males. are men. Nonreversible All A are B. ≠ All B are A.
Universal negative	No A are B. (Alternative: All A are *not* B.)	The premise states that none of the members of the first class are members of the second class.	No men are females. *or* All men are not females.	No men = No females are females. are men. Reversible No A are B. = No B are A.
Particular affirmative	Some A are B.	The premise states that some of the members of the first class are members of the second class.	Some females are women.	Some females ≠ Some women are women. are females. Nonreversible Some A are B. ≠ Some B are A.
Particular negative	Some A are not B.	The premise states that some members of the first class are not members of the second class.	Some females are not women.	Some females ≠ Some women. are not women. are not females. Nonreversible Some A ≠ Some B are not B. are not A.

[a] Note that in formal logic, the word *some* means "some and possibly all." In common parlance, *some* means "some and not all." Thus, in formal logic, the particular affirmative would also be reversible. For our purposes, it is not.

conclusion. Further, a single poor student who happened to enroll in an introductory psychology course would disprove your conclusion. Still, after many observations, you might conclude that you had made enough observations to make an inductive inference.

In this situation and in many others requiring reasoning, you were not given clearly stated premises or obvious, certain relationships between the elements, by which you would be able to deduce a sure-fire conclusion. In this type of situation, you simply cannot deduce a logically valid conclusion. An alternative kind of reasoning is needed. Inductive reasoning involves reasoning from specific facts or observations to a general conclusion that may explain the facts. For example, when Sherlock Holmes gathers clues (many specific observations) and develops a scenario (a general unifying theme) of what probably happened at the scene of a crime, he is engaging in inductive reasoning.

"I had," said he, "come to an entirely erroneous conclusion, which shows, my dear Watson, how dangerous it always is to reason from insufficient data. The presence of the gypsies, and the use of the word 'band,' which was used by the poor girl, no doubt, to explain the appearance which she had caught a hurried glimpse of by the light of her match, were sufficient to put me upon an entirely wrong scent. I can only claim the merit that I instantly reconsidered my position when, however, it became clear to me that whatever danger threatened an occupant of the room could not come either from the window or the door. My attention was speedily drawn . . . to this ventilator, and to the bell rope which hung down to the bed. The discovery that this was a dummy, and that the bed was clamped to the floor, instantly gave rise to the suspicion that the rope was there as a bridge for something passing through the hole, and coming to the bed. The idea of a snake instantly occurred to me, and when I coupled it with my knowledge that the Doctor was furnished with a supply of creatures from India, I felt that I was probably on the right track. . . ."

—Sir Arthur Conan Doyle, "The Adventure of the Speckled Band"

A key feature of inductive reasoning, which forms the basis of the empirical method, is that we cannot reasonably leap from saying, "All observed instances of X are Y" to "Therefore, all X are Y." For example, suppose that a child has seen many different kinds of birds flying in the sky. She may reasonably conclude, "All birds fly." However, when she visits the zoo and encounters penguins and ostriches for the first time, she can see that her inductive conclusion is false. Like other empiricists, she can thereby find that her inductive conclusions, based on many observations, can be disproved by just one contradictory observation. Furthermore, regardless of the number of observations or the soundness of the reasoning, no inductively based conclusions can be proved; such conclusions can only be supported, to a greater or lesser degree, by available evidence. Thus, the inductive reasoner must state any conclusions about a hypothesis in terms of likelihoods, such as "There is a good chance of rain tomorrow," or "There is a 99% probability that these findings are not a result of random variability."

John Holland and his colleagues (Holland, Holyoak, Nisbett, & Thagard, 1986) have proposed a broad framework for understanding inductive reasoning. Their framework integrates theories and studies from philosophy, psychology, and computer science. Their main question was: How can a cognitive system (such as a human mind) process stored knowledge in relation to the information observed in the environment, in a way that allows the individual to interact effectively and to benefit from experience? These investigators noted that people seem to synthesize their experiences to form various general, flexible rules regarding their observations. Holland and colleagues noted also that people use these rules to construct mental models (representations) of their environments. These rule-based mental models allow the individual to make at least tentative predictions regarding what to expect in a given situation. The individual can then use these predictions as a basis for interacting in the environment. Through interactions with the environment, the individual can learn exceptions to the rules, modify old rules, or even form new rules.

For example, suppose that in Jason's mental model of a college campus, he originally formulated a rule that "people on college campuses are either students or professors." Later, after Jason had a few encounters with administrative personnel, librarians, service personnel, and others on campus who are neither students nor professors, he realized that his rule had to be modified. He then modifies his rule to be "people on college campuses are students, professors, or paid staff members."

To conclude our discussion of reasoning, it seems that despite our occasional lapses and distortions, we often reason pretty well. Still, even the most enlightened reasoning cannot create something from what appears to be nothing. To do that, we need creativity.

CREATIVITY

IN SEARCH OF...

Some researchers who study creativity believe that creativity is a special process, achieved by the serendipitous co-occurrence of a tremendously creative individual and a context in which the creative idea is nurtured to fruition. Others seem to suggest that creativity is a rather ordinary process that results from a lot of hard work and dedication on the part of the creative individual. What is your view?

When Realism was the reigning school of art, Édouard Manet (1832–1883) violated the accepted forms and forged the path for Impressionism. Initially, his work was adamantly rejected by critics and the public. Gradually, however, other artists joined Manet in his exploration of light-illumined arrangements of eye-pleasing colors, and Impressionism gained favor and eventually became the celebrated form of art, which some chose to follow (such as Parisians Paul Cézanne and Georges Seurat) and against which others decided to rebel.

Miles away from Paris, Vincent van Gogh (1853–1890) delved into color much more lustily than Impressionism would permit. He wrote to his brother Theo, "I should not be surprised if the Impressionists soon find fault with my way of working" (de la Croix, Tansey, & Kirkpatrick, 1991, p. 936). On the other side of the world, Van Gogh's contemporary, Paul Gauguin (1848–1903) wrote, "The Impressionists study color exclusively, but without freedom, always shackled. . . . They heed only the eye and neglect the mysterious centers of thought, so falling into merely scientific reasoning" (de la Croix, Tansey, & Kirkpatrick, 1991, p. 937). Thus, Van Gogh and Gauguin each shocked the art community with their distinctive explorations: Van Gogh through vibrant colors and rich textures and Gauguin through paintings of warm, sensual Tahitian women. Manet's revolutionary art had become the established form against which others revolted (de la Croix, Tansey, & Kirkpatrick, 1991).

Gauguin rebuked the Impressionists as being overly scientific in their methods, but scientific methods do not prevent creativity. In fact, many suggest that Leonardo da Vinci's (1452–1519) remarkable artistic creativity is based on his scientific attention to the details of nature. Full-time scientists, too, have many creators in their ranks. Nicolaus Copernicus (1473–1543) revolutionized astronomy by shifting from a geocentric to a heliocentric view of the solar system. Albert Einstein (1879–1955), while working

FIGURE 10-15
The Dialectic and Art

Adolphe-William Bouguereau's L'Innocence *(left) is an example of the academic Realistic school of art against which Édouard Manet rebelled. Manet's innovations included a flattening of the picture plane through the lack of shading to indicate form, the lack of shadows, and large areas of solid color, as shown in his* The Dead Toreador *(middle). Highly creative individuals often show a revolutionary movement away from both tradition (Realism) and the contemporary mode (Impressionism), as in Vincent van Gogh's* Landscape with Cypress and Star *(right).*

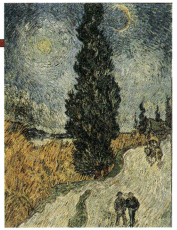

in a patents office and hoping for an appointment as a university professor, created his theory of relativity, which changed long-held theories of mass, energy, and light.

How can we possibly define creativity as a single construct that unifies the work of Van Gogh and of Einstein? Although there may be about as many narrow definitions of creativity as there are people who think about creativity (see Figure 10-16), most would broadly define **creativity** as the process of producing something that is both original and worthwhile. The *something* could be a theory, a dance, a chemical, a process or procedure, or almost anything else.

> What are five of the most creative ideas, inventions, artful masterpieces, or discoveries about which you are aware? What makes these things creative? What made it possible to create these things?

Just what does it mean for that something to be *original*? Almost everything we do is based on the ideas and the work of those who have come before us. Still, we recognize that composers, choreographers, poets, and other artists create original somethings, even if they learn from the techniques, styles, and subjects of their predecessors and contemporaries. Can scientists and other nonartists create anything original? When Copernicus proposed his heliocentric view of our solar system, he based his idea on the work of his predecessors and his contemporaries, as well as on his own observations. What makes his work creative? He analyzed and then synthesized the existing information in a novel, uncommon, and perhaps even surprising way. Through his creative endeavor, he fundamentally altered the way in which we see our planet in relation to the universe.

That Copernicus's creation was worthwhile seems doubtless now, but during his lifetime, many doubted its worth. Sometimes, people do not appreciate the value of the creative work until long after the creator dies. This is not so counterintuitive as it might seem: By definition, creative work violates conventions, scorns norms, and scoffs traditions. It may take a while for colleagues and contemporaries to see that the unconventional, abnormal, or nontraditional may have great value. Even after quite some time, a creative product may not be considered valuable by everyone. For example, almost anyone would recognize Charles Darwin's theory and Richard Wagner's operatic compositions as original, but not everyone deems evolutionary theory or Wagner's operas as being worthwhile. What makes something worthwhile is that it is significant, useful, or valuable in some way, to some segment of the population or some field of endeavor.

What does it take to create something original and worthwhile? What are creative people like? Almost everyone would agree that creative individuals show *creative productivity*. Creative people produce inventions, insightful discoveries, artistic products, revolutionary paradigms, or other creative products that are both original and worthwhile. Conventional wis-

FIGURE 10-16
Artistic Definitions of Creativity
(After Torrance, 1988)

CREATIVITY IS...

DIGGING DEEPER

CREATIVITY IS...

LOOKING TWICE

CREATIVITY IS...

LISTENING FOR SMELLS

CREATIVITY IS...

~~TALKING~~ LISTENING TO A CAT

CROSSING OUT MISTAKES

dom suggests that highly creative individuals also have creative life-styles, characterized by flexibility, nonstereotyped behaviors, and nonconforming attitudes. What characteristics do psychologists notice in creative individuals?

Describe four aspects of what you think might characterize a creative life-style.

Although we have yet to develop a method for detecting highly creative individuals at a glance, psychologists have found that highly creative individuals seem to share a few intrinsic characteristics. Psychologists who take a *psychometric* approach, such as Joy Guilford (1950), have emphasized performance on tasks involving specific aspects of creativity, such as **divergent production,** which involves the ability to generate a diverse assortment of appropriate responses. Similarly, Paul Torrance (1988) asserted that creative individuals score high on tests of creativity; on such tests (including his own *Torrance Tests of Creative Thinking*, 1974, 1984), high scores reflect diverse, numerous, appropriate responses to open-ended questions—such as to think of all the possible ways in which to use a paperclip or a ball-point pen.

Other psychological researchers, such as Robert Weisberg (1988) and Pat Langley and Randolph Jones (1988), have focused on a broader range of information processing, such as problem solving and insight. Recall that Weisberg holds the nothing-special view of creative insight: What distinguishes remarkably creative individuals from less remarkable persons is their expertise as acquired from experience, and their commitment to the creative endeavor. Highly creative individuals work long and hard studying the work of their predecessors and their contemporaries in order to become expert in their fields; they then use what they know to create innovations. Langley and Jones focus on creativity as it is manifested in scientific insight; these researchers suggest that specific cognitive processes account for much of scientific insight. For example, insight may occur through memory processes such as spreading activation; that is, one remembered idea may activate related memories, and this activation of ideas may spread across many related memories; one or more of these activated memories may then provide the needed insight (see Chapter 8). Insight may also occur through thinking processes such as analogical reasoning (mentioned earlier), in which an analogy to a related situation may provide insight into the present situation.

Other psychologists, such as Frank Barron (1988), would add that personality factors are also important to creativity. For example, Barron (p. 95) has underscored the importance of personal style, such as "openness to new ways of seeing, intuition, alertness to opportunity, a liking for complexity as a challenge to find simplicity, independence of judgment that questions assumptions, willingness to take risks, unconventionality of thought that allows odd connections to be made, keen attention, and a drive to find pattern and meaning—these, coupled with the motive and the courage to create." Barron also has mentioned the role of personal philosophy in creativity, suggesting that flexible beliefs and broad, accepting attitudes toward other cultures, other races, and other religious creeds enhance creativity.

An individual's personal philosophy also may be affected by changes in development across the life span. It seems that differing forms of literary creativity surface at different ages. For instance, a survey of 420 literary creators both across cultures and across vast expanses of time supports the notion that people write more creative poetry during their youth, but better prose when they are older (Simonton, 1975). These data suggest that powerful poetry draws on the idealism, romanticism, passionate love, and whimsical moods that often comes with youth. On the other hand, it appears that outstanding prose (such as epic novels) requires the depth, wisdom, and understanding that age provides.

Teresa Amabile and others (e.g., Hennessey & Amabile, 1988) have still further expanded our understanding of creativity. They have noted the importance of motivation. Amabile and others differentiate *intrinsic* (internal to the individual) from *extrinsic* (external to the individual) motivation; for example, intrinsic motivators might include sheer enjoyment of the creative process or personal desire to solve a problem, whereas extrinsic motivators might include a desire for fame or fortune. According to Amabile, the former is essential to creativity, but the latter may actually impede creativity under many circumstances. (See Chapter 16 for more on the issue of motivation and the role of intrinsic versus extrinsic motivators.)

In addition to these intrinsic characteristics of creative individuals, some researchers focus on the importance of external factors that influence creativity. For example, according to Mihaly Csikszentmihalyi (1988, p. 325), "we cannot study creativity by isolating individuals and their works from the social and historical milieu in which their actions are carried out. . . . (W)hat we call creative is never the result of individual action alone." Csikszentmihalyi urges us to consider both the existing knowledge in an area of

One of the common characteristics of creative people is their diversity. Pictured here are physicist Albert Einstein (top left), artists Salvador Dali (top right) and Georgia O'Keeffe (bottom left), and authors Alice Walker (bottom middle) and Amy Tan (bottom right).

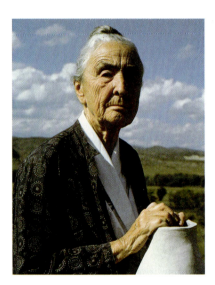

creative endeavor (the *domain*, such as particle physics or painting) and the social organization of the people involved in or surrounding a particular creative endeavor (the *field*, such as schools, museums, or even the society as a whole). Dean Simonton (1988) goes beyond the immediate social, intellectual, and cultural context to embrace the entire sweep of history. In Simonton's view, multiple internal and external factors contribute to highly creative work. Thus, a highly creative individual must be the right person, exploring the right ideas, in the right social, cultural, and historical setting. For example, as Csikszentmihalyi (1988) points out, the great Renaissance artist Filippo Brunelleschi might never have become an artist at all if he had not been choosing a career during the decades when his home city of Florence was enjoying a surge of artistic patronage and appreciation.

These contextual considerations may be the reason why so few women gained recognition in art

and science in earlier times. Until the latter half of the nineteenth century, few women were encouraged—or even permitted—to nurture their intellects; most young women were expected to prepare to nurture others instead. Even women who were permitted to gain an education or to develop their talents were discouraged later from using them. For example, Felix Mendelssohn's older sister, Fanny, was sometimes viewed as being a finer musician and composer than her brother—or was considered at least comparable in talent. Yet her family, including her younger brother, would not permit her to publish her compositions under her own name and would not allow her to perform in public (Forbes, 1990). Once society allowed women to be productive outside of the family, outstanding women came to the fore, such as Maya Angelou (literature), Nelly Bly (journalism), the Brontë sisters (literature), Rachel Carson (biology), Marie Curie (physics and chemistry), Emily Dickinson (literature), Rosalind Franklin (DNA structure), Sophie Germain (mathematics and physics), Frida Kahlo (fine arts), Margaret Mead (anthropology), Toni Morrison (literature), Gertrude Stein (literature), Helen Taussig (medicine), Sojourner Truth (poetry and politics), Alice Walker (literature), Virginia Woolf (literature), and countless others.

> Many psychologists point to the societal context as a factor limiting the creative productivity of women, at least in earlier eras. What do you think are some of the experiences, constraints, actions, feelings, and thoughts that might have limited women's creative productivity? Be as specific as possible.

Sternberg and Todd Lubart (1991a, 1991b) have synthesized several of these approaches by suggesting that multiple individual and environmental factors must converge for creativity to occur. That is, in addition to having a suitable environmental context, the creative individual must possess adequate knowledge, intellectual processes, personality variables, and motivation, as well as an intellectual style to facilitate creativity. Persons with a creative intellectual style like to see the big picture in their work (not just focusing on details). For example, revolutionary scientists such as David Hubel and Torsten Wiesel changed entirely our view of how we perceive what we see. Creative intellects also tend to prefer relative novelty (as opposed to tradition or convention). Finally, creative intellects tend to prefer generating ideas, and not just evaluating or implementing the ideas generated by others. For example, artist Georgia O'Keeffe explored the novel idea of painting a representation of musical sounds.

The theory of Sternberg and Lubart is termed the *investment theory of creativity* because the theme unifying the various factors is that the creative individual buys low and sells high. That is, the creative individual focuses attention on an idea that is undervalued by contemporaries ("buys low"), then develops that idea into a meaningful, significant creative contribution. Once the creator has convinced other people of the worth of his or her idea, this creator moves on to the next idea ("sells high").

> Before you read suggestions offered by experts, think about what you believe helps you to be particularly creative. What would you recommend to someone who was trying to be more creative?

Although some researchers believe that only a few rare persons can be creative, most believe that anyone can become more creative by working to become so. Quite a few also believe that many more of us could become exceptionally creative if we wished to become so. For example, you could increase your own creativity by taking these steps:

1. Become extremely highly motivated to be creative in a particular field of endeavor. Under most circumstances, however, you should avoid allowing others to entice you with extrinsic motivators related to an outcome of the creative work. In general, your motivation must be intrinsically related to the creative work itself.

2. Show some nonconformity, as necessary to promote your creative work—audaciously question and possibly violate rules, conventions, and norms that inhibit your creative work. Realize, though, that some rules and conventions can be useful. On the other hand, maintain rigorous standards of excellence in your performance and your work habits, and demonstrate fervent self-discipline as it relates to your creative work.

3. Deeply believe in the value and importance of your creative work; do not let others discourage you or dissuade you from pursuing your work. On the other hand, you should constantly monitor and criticize your own work, seeking always to improve it.

4. Carefully choose the problems or subjects on which you will focus your creative attention (remembering the importance of problem selection and definition, as mentioned previously); find problems that appeal to your own sense of aesthetics. Creative people thus often generate ideas that are undervalued, underappreciated, and even scorned by their contemporaries—that is, ideas that are initially considered ugly and unappealing by others.

5. Use the processes, such as seeing analogies, that characterize insight, as well as divergent-thinking processes (mentioned previously). At the same time, realize that creative work always takes tradition into account, even if it is to disagree with it.

6. Choose associates who will encourage you to take risks, go against convention, try new ideas and methods, and flout tradition.

7. Acquire as much of the available knowledge as possible in your chosen field of endeavor. In this way, you can avoid reinventing the wheel or producing the same old stuff being produced by others in your field. Find the intriguing gaps in the existing information. At the same time, you

TABLE 10-8
Key Issues in Creativity
Psychologists who study creativity often disagree not only about their responses to the key issues in creativity research, but also about what they believe the key issues to be. Nonetheless, the following key issues seem to surface repeatedly in the literature on creativity.

Topics	One Perspective	A Contrasting Perspective	A Synthesis of the Two Perspectives
Method for studying creativity	Directly study creatively productive individuals.[c, d, e]	Use psychometric tests of creativity as a means of understanding creative individuals. [a, m, n]	Review the existing research based on each method, formulate a model of creativity, and investigate the ways in which the model explains creative behavior.[l]
Role of insight	Creativity depends on insight, usually elaborating on an initial insight.[c, m]	Brief flashes of insight have little importance for creative processes.[e, k, p]	The consensus is that flashes of insight play a small but necessary role in creativity.[d, h, l, n]
Role of chance versus mindful planning	Creative products are outcomes of random variations at the stage of generating or selecting creative ideas.[c, g, h, k, m]	Creative processes involve an active search for gaps in existing knowledge, problem finding, or consciously attempting to break through the existing boundaries and limitations in the particular field of endeavor or domain of the creative process.[a, h, d, e, i, l, o]	Creative processes may be seen as initiating from a previous failure to find explanations for phenomena or to incorporate new ideas into existing knowledge[a, c, d, j, k, n, p] or from a general drive toward self-organization through the reduction of chaos.[a, c, e, k, m, n]
Domain (field of endeavor) specificity versus generality of creative processes	Creative processes apply generally, across domains.[a, c, e, f, i, j, k, l, m, n, o, p]	Specific creative processes apply to specific domains.[b, d, g, h]	Even those who propose that creativity is domain specific agree that some characteristics cross domains in describing creativity. Similarly, those who advocate the domain-generality view acknowledge that some aspects of the creative process in a particular domain may be distinctive to that domain.
Domain specificity of creative individuals	The reason for domain-specific creativity is that the creative individual has inborn sensitivities to particular types of information or modes of operation or has a unique combination of what may be called "intelligences."	The reason for domain-specific creativity is that the creative individual has highly practiced skills in a particular domain, has been in an environment that has nurtured creativity in a particular domain, or has some other noninnate reason to develop special creative abilities in a specific domain.	It is generally agreed that creative individuals are creative within limited domains and that a large part of the reason for creative productivity within specific domains has to do with using existing knowledge in a domain as a base for creating new ideas.[r] At least some knowledge facilitates creativity largely because the creative person can identify novel ideas and can find gaps in domain knowledge. There is no consensus as to whether it is nature or nurture or both that play the key role in knowledge acquisition.

(Continued)

TABLE 10-8 *(Continued)*

Topics	One Perspective	A Contrasting Perspective	A Synthesis of the Two Perspectives
Unique, distinctive, or nothing special	Creativity occurs only in some special, distinctive individuals at rare moments in history.[a, b, e, f] For a product to be deemed creative, it must be unique.[s]	Creativity can occur in anyone, and creative processes can be trained and perfected.[h, j, m, n] There is nothing special about the individual or the individual's unique context.[i] For a product to be deemed creative, it must be distinctively novel, but not necessarily unique in that no one else could ever have arrived at a similar conception.[t]	Creative products are uncommon and are distinctive but are not necessarily unique (e.g., Newton's and Leibniz's discovery of the calculus). Creative individuals exhibit distinctive characteristics and mental processes, which may result from a confluence of optimal intrinsic cognitive abilities, personality and motivational proclivities, and environmental influences, including home, domain of interest, and broader culture.
Role of the unconscious	Creativity depends on unconscious and semiconscious processes and on bringing unconscious elements into conscious awareness.[c, n]	The role of the unconscious is irrelevant to discussions of creativity.	Unconscious processes and elements are important to creativity but are not the essence of creative thought processes.
Neuropsychology of creativity[q]	Some suggest that the right hemisphere is more important than the left during creative thought processes.[u]	Others disagree.[v] Both hemispheres appear to be equally involved during dreaming, so the left hemisphere appears to be just as important as the right during at least this free-form, loosely structured mental process.[w]	Each hemisphere seems to process information somewhat differently, but both hemispheres are important to thinking and to different aspects of creative thought. Both verbal and nonverbal, logicomathematical and visuospatial processes are essential to creative thought. Perhaps a more important neuropsychological factor in terms of creative insights may be level of cortical arousal (recall the mention of how low cortical arousal during periods of incubation may promote insight).[q] A more important location for creativity may be the prefrontal lobe of both hemispheres, in which planful activity takes place.[q]

Source. Sternberg, R. J., (Ed.). (1988a). The nature of creativity. New York: Cambridge University Press. [a]Barron, 1988. [b]Csikszentmihalyi, 1988. [c]Feldman, 1988. [d]Gardner, 1988. [e]Gruber & Davis, 1988.
[f]Hennessey & Amabile, 1988. [g]Johnson-Laird, 1988. [h]Langley & Jones, 1988. [i]Perkins, 1988. [j]Schank, 1988. [k]Simonton, 1988. [l]Sternberg, 1988a. [m]Taylor, 1988. [n]Torrance, 1988. [o]Walberg, 1988.
[p]Weisberg.
[q]Ochse, 1990, pp. 200–201, 227–228, 249.
[r]See Sternberg & Lubart, 1993, p. 13.
[s]See also Dennis, 1955, & Moles, 1968; regarding musicians; cited in Ochse, 1990, p. 56.
[t]See also Zuckerman, 1977, regarding Nobel Prize winners; cited in Ochse, 1990, pp. 52–53.
[u]E.g., Ehrenwald, 1984, cited in Ochse, p. 228.
[v]E.g., Corballis, 1980, cited in Ochse, p. 228.
[w]Lavie & Tzischinsky, 1985, cited in Ochse, p. 228.

must find a way to avoid the rigidity that can accompany a large knowledge base—the anticreative phenomena of mental sets and negative transfer. One way in which to gain as much knowledge as you need, yet to avoid mental sets, might be to investigate various phenomena that interest you, so that you do not get bogged down in the current dogma and conventional thinking characterizing the study of just a single phenomenon.

8. Commit yourself deeply to your creative endeavor.

There is some consensus that each of the preceding suggestions may play a role in creative productivity. However, many psychologists and other researchers might dispute one or more of these factors, and many creative individuals deviate from this general pattern. In fact, we might say that as a group, creative people are characterized by their deviations.

There are many other issues in the study of creativity about which psychologists have not reached consensus. Because the scope of this introductory chapter cannot encompass the breadth and depth of these issues, Table 10-8 briefly highlights some of the controversial issues in this field.

One additional factor seems consistently to show a relationship to creativity: above-average intelligence. Surprisingly, beyond a given level of intelligence, further increases in intelligence do not necessarily correlate with increases in creativity. Thus, to be creative, an individual must be bright but not necessarily brilliant. In the next chapter, we discuss the nature of intelligence.

How might you use one of the strategies described in this chapter to improve your personal problem solving?

SUMMARY

Problem Solving   331

1. *Problem solving* involves mental work to overcome obstacles that stand in the way of answering a question.
2. Problems with well-defined paths to solution are referred to as *well-structured*.
3. *Ill-structured problems* are problems for which there is no clear, readily available path to solution.
4. *Heuristics* are informal, intuitive, speculative strategies for solving problems, which sometimes work and sometimes do not. Among the various heuristics that people use in solving problems are means–ends analysis, working forward, working backward, and generate and test. Heuristics are often contrasted with *algorithms*, which are paths to a solution that, if followed, guarantee an accurate solution to the problem for which they are used.
5. There are several alternative views of how insightful problem solving takes place: (a) According to the *Gestalt view*, our overall thinking in problem solving comprises more than the sum of its parts; (b) according to the *nothing-special view*, insightful problem solving is no different from any other kind of problem solving; and (c) according to the *three-process view*, insight involves a special use of three processes: selective encoding, selective combination, and selective comparison.
6. *Mental set* refers to the inappropriate use of a strategy that has worked in the past but that does not work for a particular problem that needs to be solved in the present. A particular type of mental set is *functional fixedness*, which involves the inability to see that something that is known to have a particular use may also be used for performing other functions.
7. *Transfer,* which may be either positive or negative, refers to the carry-over of learning or problem-solving skills from one problem or kind of problem to another.
8. *Incubation*, which follows a period of intensive work on a problem, involves laying a problem to rest for a while and then returning to it, so that subconscious work can continue on the problem while consciously the problem is being ignored.

9. A *problem space* is the universe of all possible moves that can be applied to solve a problem.

10. Experts differ from novices in both the *amount* and the *organization of knowledge* that they bring to bear on problem solving in the domain of their expertise.

Judgment and Decision Making 348

11. *Utility maximization theory* assumes that the goal of human action is to seek pleasure and to avoid pain. A refined form of this theory is *subjective utility theory*, which acknowledges that utilities cannot always be objectified.

12. *Game theory* assumes that many decisions, especially ones involving more than one person, have characteristics of games. People can use several strategies in making decisions, based on game theory, such as the *minimax loss rule*, which involves minimizing a maximum loss, or the *maximin gain rule*, which involves maximizing a minimum gain.

13. *Satisficing* involves selecting the first acceptable alternative that comes to mind.

14. A person using the *representativeness heuristic* judges the probability of an uncertain event by the degree to which that event is essentially similar to the population from which it derives, and by the degree to which it reflects the salient features of the processes by which it is generated.

15. A person using the *availability heuristic* makes judgments on the basis of how easily he or she is able to call to mind what are perceived as relevant instances of a phenomenon.

16. People often exhibit *overconfidence*, judging that the probability of their correctness in reaching a solution to a problem is substantially higher than it actually is.

17. *Gambler's fallacy* refers to the belief that a person's luck is bound to change, just by the nature of things.

18. The *fallacy of composition* refers to our belief that what is true of the parts of a whole must necessarily be true of the whole as well.

Reasoning 354

19. *Reasoning* refers to the process of drawing conclusions from evidence.

20. *Deductive reasoning* is involved when a person seeks to determine whether one or more logically certain conclusions can be drawn from a set of premises. Two examples of deductive-reasoning problems are linear and categorical syllogisms.

21. *Inductive reasoning* involves reasoning from specific facts or observations to reach a general conclusion that may explain the specific facts. Such reasoning is used when it is not possible to draw a logically certain conclusion from a set of premises.

Creativity 359

22. *Creativity* involves producing something that is both original and worthwhile.

23. Factors that characterize highly creative individuals are (a) extremely high motivation to be creative in a particular field of endeavor (e.g., for the sheer enjoyment of the creative process); (b) both nonconformity in questioning any conventions that might inhibit the creative work and dedication in maintaining standards of excellence and self-discipline related to the creative work; (c) deep belief in the value of the creative work, as well as willingness to criticize and improve the work; (d) careful choice of the problems or subjects on which to focus creative attention; (e) thought processes characterized by both insight and divergent-thinking; (f) associates who encourage risk taking; (g) extensive knowledge of the relevant domain; and (h) profound commitment to the creative endeavor.

KEY TERMS

algorithms 333

analysis 330

automaticity 346

availability heuristic 352

base rate 350

bounded rationality 350

categorical syllogisms 354

conditional syllogisms 355

convergent thinking 330

creativity 360

critical thinking 330

deductive reasoning 354

deductively valid 354

divergent production 361

divergent thinking 330

IN SEARCH OF THE HUMAN MIND:
ANALYSES, CREATIVE EXPLORATIONS, AND PRACTICAL APPLICATIONS

1. Who is a highly creative person (now living or a historical figure) whom you admire? What are the factors that you believe helped to make that person highly creative?
2. How do advertisers (and other propagandists) use invalid reasoning to influence people? Give some specific examples of ads you have seen or experiences you have had with salespersons or other persuaders.
3. Under what circumstances do you satisfice when you are making a decision? Why do you do it under those circumstances and not under some others?

4. Review the problems used as the brief practicum on problem solving (the nine-dot problem, the monk-on-the-mountain problem, and the house-numbers problem). Invent an isomorph to one of these problems (or to one of the other problems described in this chapter).
5. What might be a simple test of creativity that would involve a minimum of equipment and a modest amount of time for the participants?
6. If you were the head of a problem-solving team, and your team members seemed to be running into a block in their approach to the problem being addressed, what would you have the team members do to get around the block?

7. Think of a problem that you face in a field in which you have quite a bit of expertise. (For example, is there a hobby or a school subject about which you know quite a bit?) What could you do to avoid having your expertise hamper your effectiveness due to mental set?

8. What is a particularly challenging ill-structured problem that you now face (or have recently faced)? What strategies do you find (or did you find) most helpful in confronting this problem?

9. What are some heuristics you use for figuring out what things to study for an upcoming examination?

Chapter Eleven

INTELLIGENCE

CHAPTER OUTLINE

Two sophomores are hiking in the woods. One of them "aced" her freshman-year courses, getting straight A's. Her college entrance test scores were phenomenal, and she was admitted to college with a special scholarship reserved for the brightest entering students. The other student barely made it through her freshman year. Her college entrance test scores were marginal, and she just squeaked by in even getting into college. Nonetheless, people say of her that she is shrewd and clever—her teachers call her "street-smart." As the friends are hiking, they encounter a huge, ferocious, obviously hungry grizzly bear. Its next meal has just come into sight, and they are it. The first student calculates that the grizzly bear will overtake them in 27.3 seconds. At that point, she panics, realizing there is no escape. She faces her friend, the fear of death in her eyes. To her amazement, she observes that her friend is not scared at all. To the contrary, her friend is quickly but calmly taking off her hiking boots and putting on jogging shoes. "What do you think you're doing?" the first hiker says to her companion: "You'll never be able to outrun that grizzly bear." "That's true," says the companion, "but all I have to do is outrun you."

Both students in this obviously fictional story are intelligent, but it is clear that they are intelligent in different ways. Indeed, the story raises the issue of just what it means to be intelligent, because although the first student would typically be labeled so, it is the second student who would come out of the crisis alive. The preceding exemplifies the following definition: **Intelligence** is goal-directed adaptive behavior. Actually, there are perhaps as many definitions of intelligence as there are intelligence researchers and theoreticians. In fact, much of intelligence research is dedicated to trying to answer such questions as What is intelligence? and How can we even find out what it is?

TRADITIONS IN THE STUDY OF INTELLIGENCE

 IN SEARCH OF...

Stop for a moment to think about how you would assess yourself and your associates in terms of intelligence. When making these assessments, which seems more important to you: psychophysical abilities (such as sensory acuity and motor responses) or judgment abilities?

To understand current thinking about intelligence, we must go back to the late nineteenth and early twentieth centuries to peek at the work of two intellectual giants: Francis Galton and Alfred Binet. These men started two largely opposing traditions for measuring, and to some extent understanding, intelligence: Galton the psychophysical tradition, Binet the judgmental. Galton and Binet did not agree about much, but they did agree about one thing—that it was possible scientifically to understand and to measure intelligence.

The Tradition of Francis Galton: Psychophysical Performance

The publication of Charles Darwin's *The Origin of Species* (1859) profoundly affected many areas of scientific endeavor (see Chapter 3). One of these was the investigation of human intelligence and its development. Darwin suggested that human capabilities are in some sense continuous with those of lower animals and, hence, can be understood through scientific investigations like those conducted on animals. By studying individual human development, he argued, we might better understand the evolution of the human species, and vice versa.

Darwin's cousin, Sir Francis Galton, was probably the first to explore the implications of Darwin's book for the study of intelligence. Galton's (1883) theory of the "human faculty"—intelligence—and its development proposed two general qualities that distinguished the more gifted from the less so: energy (the capacity for labor) and sensitivity to physical stimuli.

James McKean Cattell brought many of Galton's ideas from England to the United States. As head of the psychology laboratory at Columbia University, Cattell was in a good position to publicize the psychophysical approach to the theory and measurement of intelligence. Cattell (1890) proposed a series of 50 psychophysical tests, such as *dynamometer pressure* (greatest possible squeeze strength of a hand), rate of arm movement over a distance of 50 cm, the threshold for distance on the skin by which two points need to be separated for them to be felt separately, and the span of letters that could be recalled from memory. Underlying all of these tests was the assumption that these psychophysical tests measure mental ability.

The death blow for the Galtonian tradition, at least in its original form, was administered by one of Cattell's own students, Clark Wissler. Wissler (1901) investigated 21 psychophysical tests. His hypothesis was that if the same people did well (or poorly) on large numbers of the tests, then the tests revealed some general construct of intelligence. Wissler's results were disappointing, however. He found the tests generally to be unrelated, and concluded that his results "lead us to doubt the existence of such a thing as general ability" (p. 55). Despite these disappointing findings, psychologists did not give up hope of finding a construct of general intelligence; an alternative approach to its discovery was beginning to lead to greater success.

The Tradition of Alfred Binet: Judgment

In 1904, the Minister of Public Instruction in Paris named a commission to find a means to differentiate truly mentally "defective" children from those who were not succeeding in school for other reasons. The commission was to ensure that no child suspected of retardation be placed in a special class without first being given an examination "from which it could be certified that because of the state of his intelligence, he was unable to profit, in an average measure, from the instruction given in the ordinary schools" (Binet & Simon, 1916, p. 9). Alfred Binet and his collaborator, Theodosius Simon, devised tests to meet this placement need. Thus, unlike theory and research in the tradition of Galton and Cattell, which grew out of pure scientific concerns, theory and research in the tradition of Binet grew out of practical educational concerns.

Binet and Simon's conception of intelligence and of how to measure it differed substantially from that of Galton and Cattell, whose tests they referred to as "wasted time." To Binet and Simon (1916), the core of intelligence is "judgment, otherwise called good sense, practical sense, initiative, the faculty of adapting one's self to circumstances. To judge well, to comprehend well, to reason well, these are the essential activities of intelligence" (pp. 42–43).

Do you agree or disagree with Binet and Simon's definition of intelligence? Why? Give an example that supports your view.

Binet cited the example of Helen Keller as someone of known extraordinary intelligence whose scores on psychophysical tests would be notably inferior and yet who could be expected to perform at a very high level on tests of judgment. A physically handicapped individual could do well on Binet's tests, but not on Galton's tests. In contrast, someone with extraordinary sensory acuity—for example, with terrific sight or hearing—might do well on Galton's tests but poorly on Binet's. To Binet, intelligent thought depended on mental judgment, not on sensory acuity.

For Binet, intelligent thought comprises three distinct elements: direction, adaptation, and criticism. As you read about these three elements, think about how you are intelligently using these elements yourself at this moment. *Direction* involves knowing what has to be done and how to do it. *Adaptation* refers to customizing a strategy for performing a task, then monitoring and adapting that strategy while implementing it. *Criticism* is the ability to critique your own thoughts and actions. In addition to using these elements while you study psychology, you might also use them for intelligently writing a term paper: First, you would figure out what you needed to do to write the paper; next, you would devise a coherent strategy for getting the paper written, and you would monitor the process of writing the paper; finally, once you had finished writing the first draft of the paper, you would evaluate the quality of your ideas and your writing.

How might you apply Binet's three elements of intelligence to a particular difficult problem or complex task?

Mental Age and the Intelligence Quotient

To this day, schools usually segregate children according to their *chronological age*. In conjunction with his theory of intelligence based on judgment, Binet suggested that we might assess children's intelligence

Antaeus, a giant and murderous wrestler, derived his tremendous strength from being in contact with the earth. To slay Antaeus, Hercules used both judgement—realizing that he needed to keep Antaeus from contacting the earth—and strength—lifting Antaeus off the ground. Whereas Francis Galton would have viewed both Antaeus and Hercules as being intelligent due to their psychophysical ability, Alfred Binet would have viewed only Hercules as being intelligent, due to his superior judgment.

based on their **mental age**—their level of intelligence compared to an "average" person of the same chronological age. If, for example, a person performs on a test at a level comparable to that of an average 12-year-old, the person's mental age will be 12, regardless of the person's chronological age. Suppose, for example, that José is 10 years old, but his performance on a test of intelligence is equal to that of the average 12-year-old. Then his mental age would be 12. Mental age also conveniently suggests an appropriate school placement for a child according to mental, rather than chronological, age.

William Stern, a German psychologist, noted that the use of mental age alone is less useful when comparing mental ages within a group of children of differing chronological ages. Stern (1992) suggested instead that we measure intelligence by using an **intelligence quotient** (IQ): a ratio of mental age (MA) divided by chronological age (CA), multiplied by 100. This ratio can be expressed mathematically as follows:

$$IQ = \frac{MA}{CA} \times 100$$

Thus, if Anita's mental age of 5 equals her chronological age of 5, then her intelligence is average, and her IQ is 100, because (5/5)(100) = 100. People whose mental age equals their chronological age always have IQs of 100 because the numerator of the equation equals the denominator, giving a quotient of 1. If Bill's mental age of 4 is only half of his chronological age of 8, then his IQ is 50, because the quotient is ½, and half of 100 is 50. Subsequent investigators have suggested further modifications of the IQ, so Stern's conception of expressing intelligence in terms of a ratio of mental age to chronological age is now termed a **ratio IQ.**

Unfortunately, the concept of mental age proved to be a weak link in the measurement of intelligence, even when used for calculating a ratio IQ. First, increases in measured mental age slow down at about the age of 16 years. Think about what you knew and how you thought when you were 8 years old, and compare that with your knowledge and thought processes when you were 12 years old. Quite a difference! Now think about someone who is 30 years old and how you imagine that person's knowledge and thought processes will be at age 45 years. You probably do not picture as much of a difference in this case, even though the difference in age is more than twice as great. Thus, it might make sense to say that an 8-year-old who performs at the level of a 12-year-old has an IQ of 150, but it makes no sense at all to say that a 30-year-old who performs at the level of a 45-year-old has an IQ of 150, because the performance of a typical 45-year-old usually differs only minimally from that of a typical 30-year-old. Indeed, in older age, scores on some kinds of mental tests actually start to decrease. Thus, it seems less than effective to base the calculation of intelligence on mental age across the life span.

What is a cognitive or academic task that the average 8-year-old could perform but the average 6-year-old could not? What is a cognitive or academic task the average 12-year-old could perform easily, but not the average 8-year-old? What is a cognitive task the average 16-year-old could perform easily, but not the average 12-year-old?

Score Distributions

NORMAL DISTRIBUTIONS.   Subsequent measurements of IQ have turned away from the construct of mental age across the life span and have focused instead on the way in which intelligence is believed to be distributed within the human population at a given age or range of ages. In measurements of large human populations, we find that the measurement values often show a roughly normal distribution. In a **normal distribution,** most people show measurements around the **median** (the middle value) of the distribution (100), with measured values rapidly declining in number on either side of the median and then tailing off more slowly as scores get more extreme. Also in a normal distribution, the median is approximately the same as both the **mean** (the average score, computed by adding all the scores and then dividing by the number of scores) and the **mode** (the most frequent score). Like other measurements of large populations, IQ scores at a given age or range of ages show a roughly normal distribution. Figure 11-1 shows a picture of a normal distribution as it applies to IQ.

PERCENTILES.   Graphs of normal distributions are valuable in helping us to visualize the distribution of measurements within a given population. For individual scores, however, it is less helpful to try to describe the score in terms of a graph than in terms of a **percentile**—the proportion of people whose scores fall below a given score, multiplied by 100. For example, if 50% of the people who take a test receive scores less than 25, then the percentile equivalent of the score of 25 is 50. In this case, 25 would be the **raw score**—the actual number of items answered correctly on the test—and 50 would be the percentile. If Rosa's score is 30, and 75% of the people taking the test scored below her score, then her percentile would be 75. Percentiles allow for relatively easy comparison of an individual's score with the scores of others in the population. As Figure 11-1 shows, percentiles can also be calculated for IQ. A person who scores 105 on an IQ test has scored better than 63% of the population and therefore has a percentile of 63. More commonly, however, the raw scores obtained on intelligence tests are translated into more comprehensible form by using a different means of comparison.

DEVIATION IQS.   Commonly, scores for many psychological tests—including intelligence tests—are calculated such that the norm or median score is 100. In a normal distribution of IQ scores for a large population, roughly two-thirds of the scores are computed to fall between 85 and 115, and about 95% of the scores fall between 70 and 130. In contrast to ratio IQs, which are based on an actual quotient (mental age divided by chronological age), **deviation IQs,** based on deviations from the average score, are not, strictly speaking, IQs, because no quotient is involved.

What are the comparative advantages and disadvantages of using percentiles rather than deviation IQs for reporting the test scores of individuals?

FIGURE 11-1
Normal Distribution of IQs

Normal distributions can be applied to almost any measurement of large populations. Most college students have IQ scores above the middle score. Does that mean that most college students are smarter than most people who never attended college? Why or why not?

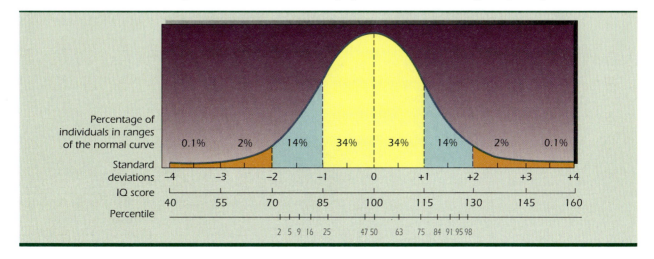

FIGURE 11-2
The Stanford-Binet Intelligence Scales

The sample questions used throughout this chapter are not actual questions from any of the scales. They are intended only to illustrate the types of questions that might appear in each of the main content areas of the tests. How would you respond to these questions? What do your responses indicate about your intelligence?

Content area	Explanation of tasks/questions	Example of a possible task/question
Verbal reasoning		
Vocabulary	Define the meaning of a word	What does the word **diligent** mean?
Comprehension	Show an understanding of why the world works as it does	Why do people sometimes borrow money?
Absurdities	Identify the odd or absurd feature of a picture	(Point out that ice hockey players do not ice-skate on lakes into which swimmers in bathing suits are diving.)
Verbal relations	Tell how three of four items are similar to one another yet different from the fourth item	(Note that an apple, a banana, and an orange can be eaten, but a cup or mug cannot be.)
Quantitative reasoning		
Number series	Complete a series of numbers	Given the numbers 1, 3, 5, 7, 9, what number would you expect to come next?
Quantitative	Solve simple arithmetical-word problems	If María has six apples, and she wants to divide them evenly among herself and her two best friends, how many apples will she give to each friend?
Figural/abstract reasoning		
Pattern analysis	Figure out a puzzle in which the test-taker must combine pieces representing parts of geometric shapes, fitting them together to form a particular geometric shape	Fit together these pieces, to form a (geometric shape). 
Short-term memory		
Memory for sentences	Listen to a sentence; then repeat it back exactly as the examiner said it	Repeat this sentence back to me: "Harrison went to sleep late and awoke early the next morning."
Memory for digits	Listen to a series of digits (numbers); then repeat the numbers either forward or backward	Repeat these numbers backward: "9, 1, 3, 6."
Memory for objects	Watch the examiner point to a series of objects in a picture; then point to the same objects in exactly the same sequence as the examiner	(Point to the carrot, then the hoe, then the flower, then the scarecrow, then the baseball.) 

These items are used for administering the Stanford-Binet Intelligence Scales.

The Stanford-Binet Intelligence Scales

The preceding progression of methods for comparing relative intelligence was reflected in the actual progression of intelligence tests. For example, Binet and Simon's original intelligence test calculated mental age alone, but the next major developer of intelligence tests—Lewis Terman, a professor of psychology at Stanford University—used ratio IQs for comparing intelligence across different individuals. Terman rewrote Binet and Simon's test in English, added some of his own ideas for items, and restructured the scoring to be in terms of ratio IQs instead of mental age, thereby constructing the earliest version of what has come to be called the *Stanford-Binet Intelligence Scales* (Terman & Merrill, 1937, 1973; see Figure 11-2).

For years, the Stanford-Binet test was the standard for intelligence tests, and it is still widely used. More recently, however, psychologists have begun using scales that avoid the construct of mental age entirely and focus instead on the degree to which individual scores deviate from the normal distribution of scores for persons of that age or in that age range. David Wechsler created scales that have become the preeminent intelligence scales of this type.

The Wechsler Scales

The scores on the Wechsler intelligence scales, including the *Wechsler Adult Intelligence Scale–Revised (WAIS-R)*, the third edition of the *Wechsler Intelligence Scale for Children (WISC-III)*, and the *Wechsler Preschool and Primary Scale of Intelligence (WPPSI)*, are expressed as deviation IQs. The Wechsler tests yield three scores: a verbal score, a performance score, and an overall score. The *verbal score* is based on tests such as vocabulary and *verbal similarities*, in which the test-

taker has to say how two things are similar. The *performance score* is based on tests such as *picture completion*, which requires identification of a missing part in a picture of an object, and *picture arrangement*, which requires rearrangement of a scrambled set of cartoonlike pictures into an order that tells a coherent story. The *overall score* is a combination of the verbal and the performance scores. Figure 11-3 shows the types of items from each of the Wechsler adult-scale subtests, which you may wish to compare with those of the Stanford-Binet.

Wechsler, like Binet, had a conception of intelligence that went beyond what his own test measured. Although Wechsler clearly believed in the worth of attempting to measure intelligence, he did not limit his conception of intelligence to test scores. To Wechsler (1974), intelligence affects our everyday life. We use our intelligence not just in taking tests and in doing homework, but also in relating to people, in doing our jobs effectively, and in managing our lives in general.

On both the WAIS-R *(for adults) and the* Wechsler Intelligence Scale for Children (WISC-III), *test-takers are asked to arrange simple cartoonlike pictures into a logical time sequence that tells a story. In the* WISC-III, *the sequences involve fewer pictures and simpler stories than the sequences in the* WAIS-R.

FIGURE 11-3
The Wechsler Adult Intelligence Scale—Revised (WAIS-R)
The Wechsler scales are based on deviation IQs. Based on the content areas and the kinds of questions shown here, how does the Wechsler differ from the Stanford-Binet?

Content area	Explanation of tasks/questions	Example of a possible task/question
Verbal scale		
Comprehension	Answer questions of social knowledge	What does it mean when people say, "A stitch in time saves nine"? Why are convicted criminals put into prison?
Vocabulary	Define the meaning of a word	What does **persistent** mean? What does **archaeology** mean?
Information	Supply generally known information	Who is Chelsea Clinton? What are six New England states?
Similarities	Explain how two things or concepts are similar	In what ways are an ostrich and a penguin alike? In what ways are a lamp and a heater alike?
Arithmetic	Solve simple arithmetical-word problems	If Paul has $14.43, and he buys two sandwiches, which cost $5.23 each, how much change will he receive?
Digit span	Listen to a series of digits (numbers), then repeat the numbers either forward or backward or both	Repeat these numbers backward: "9, 1, 8, 3, 6."
Performance Scale		
Object assembly	Put together a puzzle by combining pieces to form a particular common object	Put together these pieces to make something. 
Block design	Use patterned blocks to form a design that looks identical to a design shown by the examiner	Assemble these blocks to make this design. 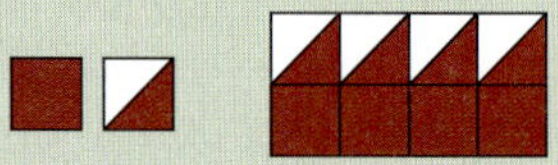
Picture completion	Tell what is missing from each picture	What is missing from this picture? 
Picture arrangement	Put a set of cartoonlike pictures into a chronological order, so they tell a coherent story	Arrange these pictures in an order that tells a story, and then tell what is happening in the story. 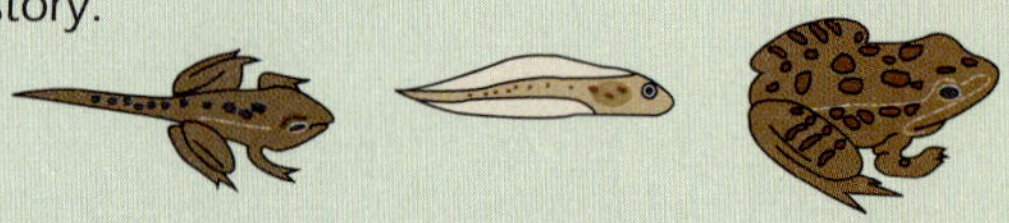
Digit symbol	When given a key matching particular symbols to particular numerals, copy a sequence of symbols, transcribing from symbols to numerals, using the key	Look carefully at the key. In the blanks, write the correct numeral for the symbol above each blank.

Additional Tests Related to Intelligence Testing

Galton and Binet, and later Terman and Wechsler, were enormously influential in starting a tradition of testing for intelligence. Today hundreds of intelligence tests are in everyday use. Some of them, like the Stanford-Binet and the Wechsler, are administered to people individually by highly trained psychologists. Others are group tests, which can be administered to large numbers of people at once by someone without extensive training.

Not all tests of cognitive performance assess intelligence. For example, some cognitively oriented tests measure **aptitudes**—people's ability to learn in a specific area of endeavor, such as musical aptitudes, athletic aptitudes, or fine eye–hand-coordination aptitudes—which may or may not involve intelligence. Table 11-1 describes the content of items from one of the mostly widely used aptitude tests, the *Differential Aptitude Tests* (1982).

> If you were to develop a test of important aptitudes, which aptitudes might you try to assess? How would you assess them?

You are probably quite familiar with another widely used test that includes content often considered to reflect intelligence: the *Scholastic Assessment Test (SAT)*. The *SAT* contains items such as those shown in Table 11-2. Formerly titled the *Scholastic Aptitude Test*, the *SAT* was renamed to acknowledge that it measures both aptitude and **achievement**—what an individual has already accomplished or learned to date in a given area of endeavor.

Designing a suitable test of intelligence requires a lot of careful planning and trial-and-error testing. The following section of this chapter describes some of the **psychometric**—psychological measurement—properties of psychological tests and some of the ways in which test developers work to create the most suitable tests possible.

TABLE 11-1
The Differential Aptitude Tests
Compare the types of questions and content areas in this test with those in either of the intelligence tests described in this chapter. What fundamental distinctions underlie the observable differences between this test and the two intelligence tests?

Content Area	Explanation of Task/Question
Verbal reasoning	Choose a pair of words that best completes an analogy
Numerical ability	Choose the answer to arithmetic problems (includes fractions, decimals, and square roots)
Abstract reasoning	Choose the figure that best completes a series of figures
Clerical speed and accuracy	Choose the letter and/or numeral combination that matches the one underlined
Mechanical reasoning	Answer questions about physical problems presented in pictures
Space relations	Choose the figure that can be made from the pattern shown (given the outside of the figure, make it into a three-dimensional shape)
Spelling	Decide whether a word is correctly spelled
Language usage	Find the error in sentences (punctuation, grammar, or capitalization errors)

PSYCHOMETRIC PROPERTIES OF INTELLIGENCE TESTS

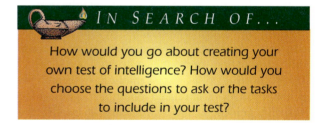

IN SEARCH OF...

How would you go about creating your own test of intelligence? How would you choose the questions to ask or the tasks to include in your test?

Bases for Tests: Theories and Observations

The first step in test construction is to decide what is to be measured and how. There are two fundamental approaches to designing tests: (1) develop a theory of the construct to be measured—intelligence, in this case—and then design a test based on that theory; and (2) make a series of observations of people who succeed in a particular context—such as school—and design questions to separate the people who are most likely to succeed from those who are least likely to succeed.

If test developers were to use either extreme, problems might arise. (Recall from the discussion in Chapter 2 that there is a long history for the dialectic of basing our understanding of psychology on theory versus on empirical observations.) Most professional test developers—including those who

TABLE 11-2
The Scholastic Assessment Test
In the early 1990s, the full name of the SAT was changed from Scholastic Aptitude Test *to* Scholastic Assessment Test, *in recognition that the test assessed not only aptitude, but also achievement. Which of the following questions or types of questions more clearly assess achievement, and which more clearly test aptitude?*

Content Area	Explanation of Task/Question	Example Task/Question
Verbal		
Vocabulary	Show knowledge of words and their definitions	Choose the word or set of words that best fits into the whole sentence Choose the pair of words with the same relationship as a given pair (analogies).
Comprehension	Demonstrate understanding of a text passage	Correctly answer multiple-choice questions reflecting understanding of a text passage.
Quantitative		
Quantitative skills	Make calculations involving geometry, algebra, fractions, arithmetic, exponential numbers, etc.	Choose the correct answer from among several possible answers.

design intelligence tests—use both theory and observations in designing their tests. For example, when Binet was composing his test of intelligence, he asked teachers what kinds of questions would be answered correctly by students who succeeded in school yet answered incorrectly by students who failed. Had this compilation been the only means by which Binet constructed his test, it might have seemed like a hodgepodge of unrelated questions. Thus, Binet was also guided by his own theory of intelligence, although he primarily based his test on his observations. Recently, however, test construction has been more closely guided by theories of intelligence.

Quality Control in Test Design

Many steps are involved in test construction and evaluation in order to ensure that tests provide high-quality measurement. Test developers seek to achieve four key aspects of quality control:

1. **Validity,** which indicates that the test measures what it purports to measure;
2. **Reliability,** which indicates that the test consistently measures whatever it is that it actually measures;
3. **Standardization,** which ensures that the conditions for taking the test are the same for all test-takers; and

4. **Norms,** which translate raw scores into scaled equivalents that reflect the relative levels of performance of various test-takers.

Several different kinds of validity exist. **Construct-related validity** is the extent to which a test measures the construct it is supposed to measure. That is, a test designer tries to design a test that reflects a given theory. **Predictive validity** predicts some kind of performance substantially after the test was taken. For example, the *SAT* is designed to predict freshman grades in college. The higher the relation between the test scores and the student's performance in college, the more predictively valid the test is said to be. **Concurrent validity** assesses the test and the performance at the same time. If students take aptitude and achievement tests at the same time, and then the aptitude test is used to estimate the achievement test scores, the procedure for validation would assess concurrent validity. **Content validity** is the extent to which the content of a test actually measures the knowledge or skills the test is supposed to measure. If a general mathematics achievement test includes only algebra, the test would not be content-valid. Finally, **face validity** is the extent to which test-takers judge the content of the test to measure all the knowledge or skills that the test is supposed to measure. For instance, students who do better on term projects and papers than on in-class exams might not consider the *SAT* to be face valid in assessing their aptitude for performing well in college.

Whereas validity assesses how well a test measures what it is supposed to measure, reliability assesses how consistently the test measures whatever it is that it actually measures. A test can be perfectly reliable, and yet totally invalid if it consistently measures something that is irrelevant to what the test is supposed to measure. For example, it would be possible to develop a highly reliable measure of the length of college applicants' index fingers, but we would not expect any significant validity of this measure in predicting performance in college. Both reliability and validity are important in test construction.

There are four main kinds of reliabilities. **Test-retest reliability** is the degree of relationship (correlation) between test scores when people take a test and then take exactly the same test some time later. (Of course, the problem with this kind of reliability is that if people take exactly the same test twice, their performance on the second test may be enhanced merely because they are already familiar with the material.) **Alternate-forms reliability** is the correlation between test scores when people take one form of a test and then later take an alternate, parallel form of the same test. (Alternate-forms reliability is often used instead of test-retest reliability.) **Internal-consistency reliability** is the extent to which all items on the test measure the same thing. Finally, **inter-rater reliability** is the extent to which two or more evaluators of a given response would rate the response in the same way. For example, when the College Board includes an essay on their English Composition achievement test, they will typically have more than one person score the quality of the test. The inter-rater reliability here is the correlation between the ratings of the various people evaluating the essay.

What is an example of a test or a test question that would be reliable but not valid in measuring intelligence? (For example, a reliable but invalid question might be, "How tall are you?") What is an example of a test or a test question that might not even be reliable, without considering its validity?

Most tests are standardized prior to being administered. To ensure that the conditions for taking the test are the same for all test-takers, environmental distractors (such as interruptions) should be kept to a minimum, the instructions prior to the start of the test and during the test should be uniform, the amount of time available for making responses should be identical for all test-takers, the materials available should be consistent across test sessions, and almost every other aspect of the test-taking experience should be as consistent as possible for all test-takers.

Part of the standardization procedure ensures that those who administer the tests do so consistently, including the same wording, the same emotionality of expression (as little as possible), and so on, thereby minimizing the possibility of environmental influences affecting the scores. For group tests administered with paper and pencil, the requirements for standardization are relatively simple, in that interpersonal contact is kept to a minimum. For individual tests, administered by a trained psychologist to an individual test-taker, the test developers must create rigorous standardized *test protocols*—procedures for implementing the tests. The developers may also require that the psychologists who administer the tests receive specialized training to ensure that the test is implemented according to the standardized protocols.

A test that has been standardized can be administered to an enormous number of individuals, which then makes it possible to determine scaled scores based on the scores across large numbers of test-takers. Test developers can use any scale they choose. The IQ, for example, is a standard score that centers around a median of 100, so that the raw scores on various subscales are translated into standardized equivalents centered around 100, thus facilitating comparisons among individuals. (See Figure 11-4, comparing the normal distributions for the *SAT* and for the *WAIS*.) The College Board uses a different standard scale, with an average of 500 and a standard deviation of 100. The range is from a low of 200 to a high of 800.

What is the advantage of scoring the SAT on a scale different from the IQ scale used for scoring WAIS?

EXPERTS' DEFINITIONS OF INTELLIGENCE

IN SEARCH OF...

How do you define intelligence?

In 1921, 14 famous psychologists made explicit their implicit views on the nature of intelligence (see "Intelligence and its measurement: A symposium," 1921). Although their responses varied, two common themes ran through many of their responses: Intelligence is (1) the capacity to learn from experience, and

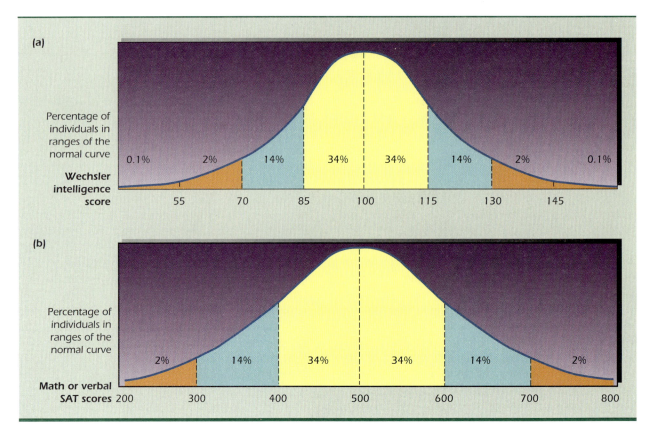

FIGURE 11-4
Normal Distributions of Scores on the WAIS and the SAT

Both the WAIS and the SAT are given to large numbers of individuals, so normal distributions of scores may be obtained. For both tests, raw scores are translated into standard (normative) scores, with a mean value of 100 for the WAIS and of 500 for the SAT. The WAIS and the SAT are administered to different populations, and hence an IQ of 100 does not correspond to an SAT score of 500. On the WAIS, only 16% of the test-takers score above 115. Should decisions regarding college admission, employment, or other opportunities be based on using tests such as these for screening applicants?

(2) the ability to adapt to the surrounding environment. These common themes are important. Capacity to learn from experience implies, for example, that smart people are not invulnerable to mistakes: Rather, smart people learn from their mistakes, and they do not keep making the same ones again and again. Adaptation to the environment means that being smart goes beyond getting high scores on tests or good grades in school: It includes how you handle a job, how you get along with other people, and how you manage your life in general.

Sixty-five years after the initial journal symposium, 24 different experts were asked to give their views on the nature of intelligence (Sternberg & Detterman, 1986). Once again, the experts noted the themes of learning from experience and adapting to the environment. However, contemporary experts also put more emphasis than did earlier ones on the role of *metacognition*—people's understanding and control of their own thinking processes (such as during problem solving, reasoning, and decision mak-

ing). Contemporary experts also more heavily emphasized the role of culture, pointing out that what is considered intelligent in one culture may be considered stupid in another. In fact, the subsequent discussion of explicit theories of intelligence specifically addresses the issues of metacognition and the role of culture.

THEORIES OF THE NATURE OF INTELLIGENCE

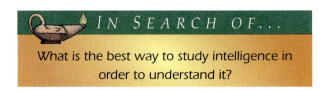

IN SEARCH OF...

What is the best way to study intelligence in order to understand it?

In the study of intelligence and many other psychological phenomena, the questions scientists have asked have largely determined their answers. We must go yet one step further and wonder, "Why that question?" Consider some of the kinds of questions psychologists have asked about intelligence, and the ways in which they have chosen to answer those questions.

Psychometric Models: Intelligence as a Measurement-Based Map of the Mind

The view of intelligence as a map of the mind extends back at least to the 1800s, when phrenology was in vogue. During the first half of the twentieth century, the model of intelligence as something to be mapped dominated theory and research. The psychologist studying intelligence in this way was both an explorer and a cartographer, seeking to chart the innermost regions of the mind. Like any other explorers, psychologists who studied intelligence needed tools; in the case of research on intelligence, the indispensable tool appeared to be **factor analysis,** a statistical method and model for separating a construct—intelligence, in this case—into a number of distinct hypothetical abilities that the researchers believed to form the basis of individual differences in test performance. The specific factors derived, of course, still would depend on the specific questions being asked and the tasks being evaluated.

Factor analysis is based on studies of correlation. In research on intelligence, a factor analysis might involve these steps: (1) Give a large number of people various tests of ability, (2) determine the correlations among all those tests, and (3) statistically manipulate those correlations to simplify them into a handful of factors that seem to summarize people's performance on the tests. The investigators in this area generally agreed on and followed this procedure, yet the resulting factorial structure of intelligence differed among theorists. Among the many competing theories, the main ones were probably those of Spearman, Thurstone, Guilford, Cattell, and Vernon. Figure 11-5 visually contrasts four of these theories.

The "g" Factor

Charles Spearman is usually credited with inventing factor analysis. Using factor-analytic studies, he concluded (1927) that intelligence could be understood in terms of both a single general factor (*g*) that pervaded performance on all tests of mental ability and a set of specific factors (*s*), each of which was involved in performance on only a single type of mental-ability test (e.g., arithmetic computations). In Spearman's view, the specific factors were of only casual interest, due to the narrow applicability of these factors. The general factor, however, provided the key to under-standing intelligence. Spearman believed that *g* was derived from individual differences in mental energy.

Primary Mental Abilities

In contrast to Spearman, Louis Thurstone concluded (1938) that the core of intelligence resided not in one single factor but in seven such factors, which he referred to as *primary mental abilities*. According to Thurstone, the primary mental abilities are (1) *verbal comprehension*, measured by vocabulary tests; (2) *verbal fluency*, measured by tests requiring the test-taker to think of as many words as possible that begin with a given letter, in a limited amount of time; (3) *inductive reasoning*, measured by tests such as analogies and number-series completion tasks; (4) *spatial visualization*, measured by tests requiring mental rotation of pictures of objects; (5) *number*, measured by computation and simple mathematical problem-solving tests; (6) *memory*, measured by picture and word-recall tests; and (7) *perceptual speed*, measured by tests that require the test-taker to recognize small differences in pictures, or to cross out the *a*'s in strings of various letters.

The Structure of Intellect

At the opposite extreme from Spearman's single *g*-factor model was J. P. Guilford's (1967) **structure-of-intellect (SOI)** model, which includes more than 120 factors of the mind. According to Guilford, intelligence can be understood in terms of a cube that represents the intersection of three dimensions: operations, contents, and products. According to Guilford, *operations* are simply mental processes, such as memory, cognition (defined by Guilford as under-standing), convergent production (reaching a single "correct" answer to a problem that requires a unique response, such as a word problem in arithmetic), divergent production (generating multiple answers to a problem that has many possible answers, such as "Think of as many words as you can that have *c* as a third letter"), and evaluation (making judgments, such as determining whether a particular statement is fact or opinion, is based on reasoned thought or on emotion or prejudice). *Contents* are the kinds of terms that appear in a problem, such as semantic (words), symbolic (e.g., numbers), behavioral (what other people do), auditory (sounds), and visual (pictures). *Products* are the kinds of responses required, such as units (single words, numbers, or pictures), classes (hierarchies), relations (John is *taller than* Mary), and more sophisticated responses such as systems, transformations, and implications. In a recent version of the theory, Guilford (1982) proposed as many as 150 factors (see Figure 11-5).

Some psychologists believed that the number of factors made the structure-of-intellect model complex and unwieldy (Eysenck, 1967). They also raised serious questions about the methodology used to extract the various factors. Other researchers analyzed and interpreted Guilford's data and reached conclusions different from Guilford's. John Horn and John Knapp (1973), for example, found that with Guilford's statistical methodology, Guilford's own

data could be made to support random theories as well as these data supported his own theory. Perhaps Guilford's most valuable contribution was to suggest that we consider various kinds of mental operations, contents, and products in our views and our assessments of intelligence.

Hierarchical Models

A more parsimonious way of handling a number of factors of the mind is through a hierarchical model of

FIGURE 11-5
Comparisons Among Some of the Psychometric Models of Intelligence
Although Spearman (a), Thurstone (b), Guilford (c), and Vernon (d) all used factor analysis to determine the factors underlying intelligence, they all reached different conclusions regarding the structure of intelligence. Which model most simply, yet comprehensively, describes the structure of intelligence as you understand it? How do particular models of intelligence shape our understanding of intelligence?

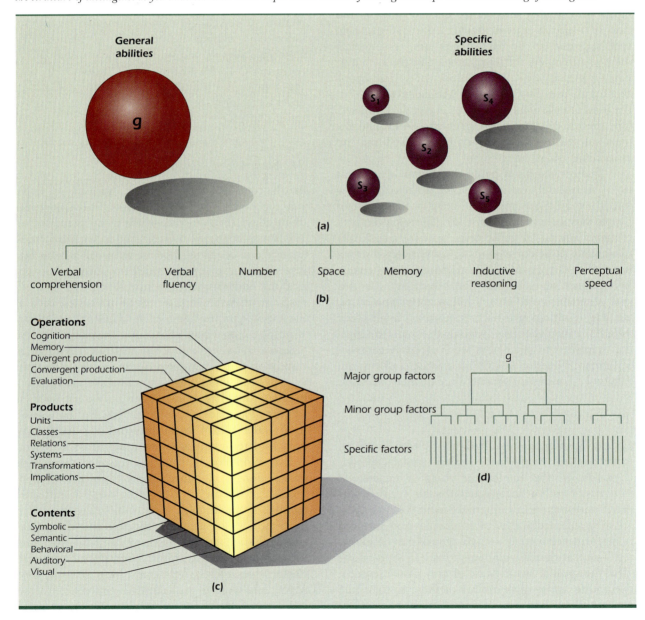

intelligence. One such model, developed by Raymond Cattell (1971), proposes that general intelligence comprises two major subfactors: fluid ability and crystallized ability. **Fluid intelligence** requires understanding of abstract and often novel relations, as required in inductive reasoning tests such as analogies and series completions. **Crystallized intelligence** represents the accumulation of knowledge and is measured, for example, by vocabulary tests and general-information tests. Subsumed within these two major subfactors are other, more specific factors. A similar view was proposed by Philip Vernon (1971), who made a general division between practical–mechanical and verbal–educational abilities.

> Compare two of the psychometric models of intelligence, emphasizing the strengths and weaknesses of each. What is an aspect of intelligent behavior that is explained well or is explained poorly by either or both of the theories?

Critique of the Psychometric Model

Models of intelligence represent theoreticians' attempts to simplify and understand the underpinnings of intelligence. A model that perfectly represented intelligence would retain all its complexities and dynamics—and it would be as incomprehensible as that which it attempted to model. Thus, all models have limitations in the degree to which they succeed in balancing the need to represent intelligence accurately with the need to make the model comprehensible. Given that all models have limitations, we must choose those models that have the fewest limitations, or that have the least bothersome limitations. The most troubling limitation of the psychometric model is that it does not say much about the mental processes of intelligence.

Computational Models: Intelligence as a Computer Program

> What do highly intelligent people do better than less intelligent people? What, if anything, might less intelligent people do better than more intelligent people?

Unlike the psychometric model, which maps the structures of human intelligence, the computational model strongly emphasizes the *processes* underlying intelligent behavior. In particular, theorists using this model are interested in studying how people engage in **information processing**—that is, how people mentally manipulate what they learn and know about the world. The ways in which information-processing investigators study intelligence differ primarily in terms of the complexity of the processes being studied. Among the main advocates of this approach have been Earl Hunt, Herbert Simon, and myself. Each of us has considered both the speed and the accuracy of information processing to be important factors in intelligence. (A subsequent discussion indicates that the emphasis on speed may be a function of our cultural values.)

Lexical-Access Speed

Earl Hunt (1978) has suggested that intelligence be measured in terms of speed. He has been particularly interested in verbal intelligence, so he has focused on **lexical-access speed**—the speed with which we can retrieve information about words (e.g., letter names) stored in our long-term memories. To measure this speed, Hunt has proposed using a letter-matching, reaction-time task (Posner & Mitchell, 1967).

For example, suppose that you are one of Hunt's subjects. You would be shown pairs of letters such as "A A," "A a," or "A b." For each pair, you would be asked to indicate whether they constitute a match in name (e.g., "A a" match in name of letter of the alphabet but "A b" do not). You would also be given a simpler task, in which you would be asked to indicate whether the letters match physically (e.g., "A A" are physically identical, whereas "A a" are not). Hunt would be particularly interested in discerning the difference between your speed for the first set of tasks, involving name matching, and your speed for the second set, involving matching of physical characteristics. Hunt would consider the difference in your reaction time for each task to indicate a measure of your speed of lexical access. Thus, he *subtracts* from his equation the elementary reaction time. For Hunt, the response time in indicating that "A A" is a physical match is unimportant. What interests him is a more complex reaction time—that for recognizing names of letters. He and his colleagues have found that students with lower verbal ability take longer to decode, or to gain access to lexical information, than do students with higher verbal ability.

The Componential Theory and Complex Tasks

In 1977, I used exclusively cognitive approaches for studying information processing in more complex tasks, such as analogies, series problems (e.g., completing a numerical or figural series), and syllogisms (Sternberg, 1977, 1984; see Chapter 10). My goal was to find out just what it was that made some people more intelligent processors of information than others. My idea was to take the kinds of tasks used on conventional intelligence tests and to isolate the **components** of intelligence—the mental processes and strategies used in performing these tasks, such as translating sensory input into a mental representation, transforming one conceptual representation into another, or translating a conceptual representation into a motor output (Sternberg, 1982). **Componential analysis** breaks down people's reaction times and error rates on these tasks according to the processes that make up the tasks. As a result of this analysis, it seems that people solve analogies and similar tasks by using several component processes, among which are (1) encoding the terms of the problem; (2) inferring relations between at least some of the terms; (3) mapping the inferred relations to other terms, which would be presumed to show similar relations; and (4) applying the previously inferred relations to the new situations.

Consider the analogy LAWYER : CLIENT :: DOCTOR : (a. PATIENT b. MEDICINE). To solve this analogy, you need to *encode* each term of the problem, which includes perceiving the term and retrieving information about it from memory. You then *infer* the relationship between lawyer and client—that the former provides professional services to the latter. You would then *map* the relationship in the first half of the analogy to the second half of the analogy, noting that it will involve that same relationship. Finally, you would *apply* that inferred relationship to generate the final term of the analogy, leading to the appropriate response of PATIENT. (Figure 11-6 shows how componential analysis would be applied to

With stunning perspicacity, the legendary Sherlock Holmes carefully encodes all aspects of the problem he encounters and then formulates a strategy for solving the problem.

an analogy problem, A is to B as C is to D, where D is the solution.) Studying these components of information processing tells us more than measuring mental speed alone.

When measuring speed alone, I have found significant correlations between speed in executing these processes and performance on other, traditional intelligence tests. However, a more intriguing discovery is that subjects who are more intelligent—that is, score higher on traditional intelligence tests—take *longer* to encode the terms of the problem than do less intelligent subjects, but they make up for the extra time by taking less time to perform the remaining components of the task. In general, more-intelligent subjects take longer during *global planning*—encoding the problem and formulating a general strategy for attacking the problem (or set of problems)—but they take less time for *local planning*—forming and implementing strategies for the details of the task (Sternberg, 1981). The advantage of spending more time on global planning is the increased likelihood that the overall strategy will be correct. Thus, brighter people may take longer to do something than will less bright people when it is advantageous to take more time. For example, the brighter person might spend more time researching and planning for writing a term paper, but less time actually writing it. This same differential in time allocation has been shown in other tasks, as well (e.g., in playing chess and in solving physics problems; see Sternberg, 1979, 1985a); that is, more intelligent people seem to spend more time planning for and encoding the problems they face, but less time engaging in the other components of task performance.

> If you were assigned a research project to complete over the course of one term, how would you apportion your time for global versus local planning? How might you improve your time-management strategies for working on a term-length project?

Complex Problem Solving

Herbert Simon has studied the intelligent information processing of people engaged in solving complex problems such as chess problems and logical derivations (Newell & Simon, 1972; Simon, 1976). For example, a simple, brief task might require the subject to view an arithmetic or geometric series, figure out the rule underlying the progression, and guess what numeral or geometric figure might come next; more complex tasks might include some ill-structured problem-solving tasks, such as those tasks mentioned

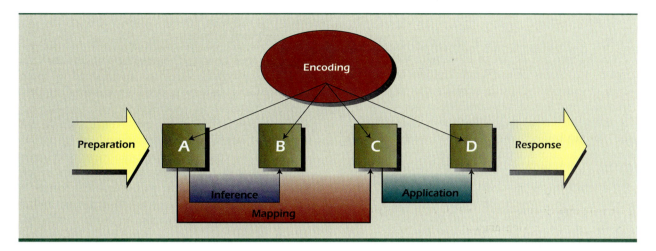

FIGURE 11-6
Componential Analysis of an Analogy Problem
In solving an analogy problem, the problem solver must first encode the problem, A is to B as C is to D. The problem solver must then infer the relationship between A and B. Next, he or she must map the relationship between A and B to the relationship between C and an ideal solution to the analogy. Finally, the problem solver must apply the relationship to choose which of the given solutions is the correct solution to problem.

in Chapter 10 (e.g., the move problems or the water-jugs problems) (see Estes, 1982). In his work with Allen Newell and others, Simon created computer simulations that would solve these complex problems. The idea was to understand intelligence through highly complex problem solving, where solution times may be measured in minutes, rather than seconds. Simon was particularly interested in the limits imposed by working memory and by the ways in which more intelligent people organize and sequence the processes by which they solve problems. Just as more artificially intelligent computer programs can be designed to handle various procedures more efficiently, more intelligent humans should be able to coordinate their handling of mental procedures more efficiently.

Critique of the Computational Model

The computational model says a lot more about mental processes than does the psychometric model. At the same time, most computational theories say less about the structure of abilities than do psychometric theories. (Recall from the discussion in Chapter 2 that the debate over the importance of structure versus function is long-lived.)

Biological Models: Intelligence as a Physiological Phenomenon

Biological approaches seek to understand intelligence by directly studying the brain rather than by studying

primarily products or processes of behavior. As previous chapters have suggested, early studies (e.g., those by Karl Lashley and others) seeking to find biological indices of intelligence and other aspects of mental processes were a resounding failure, despite great effort. As tools for studying the brain have become more sophisticated, however, we are beginning to see the possibility of finding physiological indications of intelligence. Some (e.g., Matarazzo, 1992) believe that we will have clinically useful psychophysiological indices of intelligence very early in the next millennium, although widely applicable indices will be much longer in coming. For now, some of the current studies offer some appealing possibilities.

Electrical Evidence

For example, P. T. Barrett and Hans Eysenck (1992) have found that complex patterns of electrical activity in the brain, which are prompted by specific stimuli, correlate with scores on IQ tests (see Chapter 3 for a discussion of evoked potentials, EEGs, and so on). Also, several studies (e.g., McGarry-Roberts, Stelmack, & Campbell, 1992; Reed & Jensen, 1992; Vernon & Mori, 1992) suggest that the speed of conduction of neural impulses correlates with intelligence, as measured by IQ tests. Additional replication studies are still needed to confirm these findings. Some investigators (e.g., Vernon & Mori, 1992) suggest that this research supports a view that intelligence is based on neural efficiency.

Metabolic Evidence

Additional support for neural efficiency as a measure of intelligence can be found by using a different approach to studies of the brain: studies of how the brain metabolizes *glucose* (a simple sugar required for brain activity) during mental activities (see Chapter 3, regarding brain-imaging techniques). Richard Haier and his colleagues (1992) cite several other researchers to support their own findings that higher intelligence correlates with reduced levels of glucose metabolism during problem-solving tasks—that is, smarter brains consume less sugar (and hence expend less effort) than do less-smart brains doing the same task. Further, Haier and colleagues found that cerebral efficiency increases as a result of learning in a relatively complex task involving visuospatial manipulations (such as in the computer game *Tetris*). As a result of practice, more intelligent subjects show not only lower cerebral glucose metabolism overall, but also more specifically localized metabolism of glucose. In most areas of their brains, smarter subjects show less glucose metabolism, but in selected areas of their brains (thought to be important to the task at hand), they show higher levels of glucose metabolism. Thus, more-intelligent subjects may have learned how to use their brains more efficiently. These findings are only preliminary, but they have intuitive appeal, particularly because they apply to more complex cognitive processes.

How do the data on the physiology of intelligence relate to other physiological data, such as data on the physiology of memory?

Critique of the Biological Model

Most psychologists accept the data being documented by physiologists and others regarding the physiological and cognitive structures and processes of intelligence. What they question is whether we can truly study a brain or its contents and processes in isolation, without also considering the entire human being, the interactions of that human being, and the entire environmental context within which the brain acts intelligently. Such researchers and theorists would urge us to take a more anthropological view of intelligence.

If you could study the physiology of the brain as it operates during intelligent behavior in a real-world context, what would you study, and what might you expect to find? (Refer to physiological data elsewhere in this book to support your hypotheses.)

Anthropological Models: Intelligence as a Cultural Invention

We have seen how psychometric, computational, and biological psychologists view intelligence as something residing inside the head. In contrast, **contextualist** theorists of intelligence use an external, anthropological model of intelligence, which presumes that intelligence cannot be understood outside its real-world context. In fact, they view intelligence as so inextricably linked to culture that they believe intelligence is something that a culture creates to define the nature of adaptive performance and to account for why some people perform better than others on the tasks that the culture happens to value. Psychologists who endorse this model study how intelligence relates to the external world in which the model is being applied and evaluated. Before exploring some of the anthropological theories, it may help to see just what prompted psychologists to believe that culture might play a role in how we define and assess intelligence.

Cultural Influences on Perceived Intelligence

People in different cultures may have quite different ideas of what it means to be smart. One of the more interesting cross-cultural studies of intelligence was performed by Michael Cole and his colleagues (Cole, Gay, Glick, & Sharp, 1971), who asked adult members of the Kpelle tribe in Africa to sort terms. In Western culture, when adults are given a sorting task on an intelligence test, more intelligent people will typically sort hierarchically. For example, they may sort names of different kinds of fish together, and then the word "fish" over that, with the name "animal" over "fish" and "birds," and so on. Less intelligent people will typically sort functionally. They might sort "fish" with "eat," for example, because we eat fish, or "clothes" with "wear," because we wear clothes. The Kpelle sorted functionally—even after investigators unsuccessfully tried to get the Kpelle spontaneously to sort hierarchically.

Finally, in desperation, one of the experimenters directly asked the Kpelle to sort hierarchically. When asked to sort in this way, the Kpelle had no trouble at all sorting hierarchically. They had been able to sort this way all along; they just had not done it because they viewed it as foolish—and they probably considered the questioners rather unintelligent for asking such foolish questions. Why would they view functional sorting as intelligent? Simple. In ordinary life, we normally think functionally. When we think of a fish, we think of catching or eating it; when we think of clothes, we think of wearing them. However, in

Searchers . . .   *EDMUND GORDON*

Edmund Gordon is John M. Musser Professor of Psychology Emeritus at Yale University and Distinguished Professor of Educational Psychology at the City University of New York.

Q: *How did you become interested in psychology and in your area of work in particular?*

A: I came out of my adolescence interested in the human services. I became a minister and gravitated toward the counseling ministry. I began to realize, however, that I needed to know a great deal more about human behavior, so I went back to school to study psychology. I was originally trained in health psychology, development, and child guidance. The first ten years of my career I spent in clinical work. My wife and I organized a health and mental health clinic in Harlem. I began to realize, however, that even though psychology claimed to know a great deal about behavioral change, it was technique-driven, rather than theory-driven—at least to us guidance counselors and therapists. I found myself dealing more with the learning problems of the kids, and that led me back to school to study developmental psychology and, ultimately, cognitive.

Q: *What theories have influenced you the most?*

A: Interactionism, situationalism, comparative development. Early in my career, Kurt Lewin's work and perspective on the nature of human behavior greatly influenced me. I was particularly impressed by Donald Hebb, more for his theoretical than his empirical work.

Q: *What is your greatest asset as a psychologist?*

A: I think I'm probably better at perspective taking, conceptual synthesis, critical interpretation.

Q: *How do you get your ideas for research?*

A: Mostly out of practical experience and reading. When I run into real-life problems, I try to figure out what they mean. I don't have a high tolerance for ambiguity, so when I see something, I need a way of explaining it. If I can't identify some mechanisms that explain how a thing works, or some notions of what it means, I'm uncomfortable. And that drives my research ideas.

Q: *How do you decide whether to pursue an idea?*

A: I am a humanist: I believe in social justice, and I view most of the events and problems of the world from the perspective of what human ends are served or frustrated.

Q: *How have you developed an idea into a workable hypothesis?*

A: Well, for a long time, particularly for minority and low-status populations, the social science literature focused on their deficits—how they differ from the majority population, the differences always being viewed negatively. But there were people who, according to the traditional standards, never should have succeeded. Somehow, these people had gone on to high levels of success. I got fascinated by that problem. And the work I am trying to complete right now is on people who defy negative predictions for success. I took a small population and studied them intensively using life history analysis. I didn't want to know just the correlates; I wanted to be able to explain how these lives came to be successful.

Q: *What obstacles have you experienced?*

A: In the early part of my career, the opportunities for research grants seemed to be limited. But by the middle of my career—the beginning of the War on Poverty—the stuff I was doing became popular. Many more resources became available for it. Another, more important obstacle is theoretical and conceptual. I am more of a relativist than a positivist, and that creates a disadvantage. It is much easier to design research, and to interpret it, if you are looking for definite answers. When you begin to view the problem as a kind of moving target, susceptible to the changing context in which it operates, then designing that kind of work is very difficult. Because I have tended to view problems in that multi-contextual, multi-perspectivist frame, I have found designing really careful work to be very difficult.

Q: *What is your major contribution to psychology?*

A: I am more of an applied psychologist than a generator of knowledge in psychology. I was among the group that helped design and put in place Head Start. Several of us picked up the idea, put it together, and applied it. I also helped to write the Elementary and Secondary Education Acts of 1965, Title I. Also, some years ago, people used to say I was ahead of my time, talking about the importance of environmental and cultural phenomena before many other people in the field were taking them seriously. Those notions have come to be respectable now and are embraced by a lot of mainline psychologists.

Q: *What do you want students to learn from you?*

A: First, I place humane values highest in what I try to communicate to students. No matter what we achieve or end up doing, if it doesn't contribute to the common cause of humanity, then it is of lesser value. Second, I try to teach students how to think. I expose students to a variety of views of a problem and help them as they think through the process. Third, I help them develop critical interpretation of data, to know what data mean in different contexts, what their consequences are. Beyond that, I help kids expand their command of knowledge and techniques.

Q: *What advice would you give to someone starting in the field of psychology?*

A: If students are serious about psychology, they need to know the many ways people have thought about the field, and what ideas have driven the field.

Q: *What did you learn from your mentors?*

A: That there are few if any problems in this world that you can't solve if you are willing to put your mind to them and work on them. That the human mind is a marvelous tool, and you can do something with it.

Western schooling, we learn what is expected of us on tests. The Kpelle did not have Western schooling and had not been exposed to intelligence testing. As a result, they solved the problems the way Western adults might do so in their everyday lives, but not on an intelligence test.

The Kpelle people are not the only ones who might question Western understandings of intelligence. The work by British psychologist Robert Serpell in Zambia further illustrates the importance of considering culture when trying to define or to measure intelligence. According to Serpell (1994), the language, legacies, needs, and beliefs of a society combine to form a culturally appropriate conception

When Michael Cole and other researchers asked Kpelle adults to sort items intelligently, the Kpelle sorted the items according to the functional uses of the items. When asked to sort items as a foolish person would sort them, Kpelle adults sorted the items hierarchically, according to attribute categories. In contrast, a majority of Western researchers generally consider hierarchical sorting to reflect greater intelligence than does functional sorting. What conclusions might Kpelle researchers have drawn regarding the intelligence of Westerners if they had administered intelligence tests to a group of Westerners? What should we infer regarding cultural definitions of intelligence?

of intelligence, which may be equivalent to the Western concept in some regards but not in others. A focal point of Serpell's work concerns the Chi-Chewa concept of *nzelu*, which is similar to the Western concept of intelligence, but which differs from it in ways that should not be ignored. Whereas the Western concept of intelligence has a cognitive orientation, *nzelu* appears to comprise the dimensions of wisdom, cleverness, and responsibility within the Zambian cultural context. Thus, as compared with Western children, Zambian schoolchildren learn to value a much broader notion of intelligence and may be expected to demonstrate a broader range of behaviors that would be deemed intelligent within their culture (Serpell, 1993).

A study by Seymour Sarason and John Doris (1979) provides a closer-to-home example regarding the effects of cultural differences on intelligence, particularly on intelligence tests. These researchers tracked the IQs of an immigrant population: Italian Americans. Less than a century ago, first-generation Italian-American children showed a median IQ of 87 (low average; range 76–100), even when nonverbal measures were used and when so-called mainstream American attitudes were considered. Some social commentators and intelligence researchers of the day pointed to heredity and other nonenvironmental factors as the basis for the low IQs—much as they do today for other minority groups.

For example, a leading researcher of the day, Henry Goddard, pronounced that 79% of immigrant Italians were "feeble-minded" (he also asserted that about 80% of immigrant Hungarians and Russians were similarly unendowed with intelligence) (Eysenck & Kamin, 1981). Goddard (1917) also asserted that moral decadence was associated with this deficit in intelligence; he recommended that the intelligence tests he used be administered to all immigrants and that all those he deemed substandard be selectively excluded from entering the United States. Stephen Ceci (1991) notes that subsequent generations of Italian-American students who take IQ tests today show slightly above-average IQs; other immigrant groups that Goddard had denigrated show similar "amazing" increases. Even the most fervent hereditarians would be unlikely to attribute such remarkable gains in so few generations to heredity. Cultural assimilation, including integrated education, seems a much more plausible explanation.

How do you explain the apparent phenomenal increases over time in measured intelligence among some immigrant groups?

Early in the twentieth century, some experts on intelligence attempted to bar many European immigrants from entering the United States because these immigrants scored poorly on group intelligence tests. Subsequent generations of Americans descended from these immigrants have IQs slightly above the national average. If IQ scores are not used as immigration criteria, what criteria should be used to determine who will be allowed to enter and remain legally in this country?

Whenever I brought a book to the job, I wrapped it in newspaper—a habit that was to persist in other cities and under other circumstances. But some of the white men pried into my packages when I was absent and they questioned me.

"Boy, what are you reading those books for?"
"Oh, I don't know, sir."
"That's deep stuff you're reading, boy."
"I'm just killing time, sir."
"You'll addle your brains if you don't watch out."

Richard Wright, Black Boy

The preceding arguments may make it clear why it is so difficult to come up with a test that everyone would consider **culture-fair**—equally appropriate and fair for members of all cultures. If members of different cultures have different ideas of what it means to be intelligent, then the very behaviors that may be considered intelligent in one culture may be viewed as unintelligent in another. Consider, for example, the concept of mental quickness. In mainstream U.S. culture, quickness is usually associated with intelligence. To say someone is "quick" is to say that the person is intelligent, and indeed, most group tests of intelligence are quite strictly timed, as I have found out the hard way myself when I have failed to finish all the items on some of them. Indeed, there can be no doubt that sometimes it is important to be fast. When you are taking a timed test, you have to be fast. When you have not yet started writing a paper that is due tomorrow, it is definitely smart to be quick. If you are an air-traffic controller, you had better be fast if you value the lives of the passengers on the airplanes you are monitoring.

In many cultures of the world, however, quickness is not at a premium. In these cultures, people may believe that more intelligent people do not rush into things. Indeed, Thurstone (a leading psychometric theoretician of intelligence) (1924) once defined intelligence as the ability to withhold an instinctive response. In other words, the smart person is someone who does not rush into action but thinks first. Even in our own culture, no one will view you as brilliant if you decide on a marital partner, a job, or a place to live in the 20 to 30 seconds you might normally have to solve an intelligence-test problem.

> Design a task that a reasonably intelligent 10-year-old American child would be able to perform easily, but that an intelligent adult who lived in a remote area, untouched by industrialization or urbanization (such as the Amazon forest) would not. Design a task that a 10-year-old in a remote, unindustrialized region might easily perform, but that an intelligent American adult would probably find difficult.

Relative Degrees of Cultural Relativism

The extent to which psychologists have underscored the importance of context has varied widely. John Berry (1974) has taken an extreme view of **cultural relativism,** arguing that indigenous notions of cognitive competence should be the sole basis for any valid description and assessment of psychological phenomena such as intelligence. Accordingly, the Western concept of intelligence has no universal merit, according to Berry, for intelligence is different in each culture. To Berry, the goal of the psychologist should be to understand what constitutes intelligence in the culture at hand.

Almost everyone would like to construct only culture-fair tests. However, the preceding discussion shows why it is so difficult to come up with a test that everyone would consider culture-fair. If members of different cultures have different ideas of what it means to be intelligent, then the very behaviors that may be considered intelligent in one culture may be viewed as unintelligent in another. Unfortunately, at present and for the foreseeable future, there exist no perfectly culture-fair tests of intelligence. Even among the tests devised to date, performance on those tests that have been labeled as "culture-fair" seems to be influenced by cultural factors, such as years of schooling and academic achievements (e.g., Ceci, 1991).

Although the development of culture-fair tests may be an unrealistic goal, it is possible to provide **culture-relevant** tests, which employ skills and knowledge that relate to the cultural experiences of the test-takers despite definitions of intelligence that may differ from those of the test-takers. Just how do culture-relevant intelligence tests measure intelligence? Culture-relevant tests assume a given culturally based definition of intelligence, involving, say, memory and other aspects of information processing, but they use content and procedures that are relatively culture-relevant in measuring intelligence according to their underlying definition of it.

Designing culture-relevant tests requires creativity and effort but is probably not impossible. For example, a study by Daniel Wagner (1978) investigated memory abilities (one aspect of intelligence as Western culture defines it) in American and Moroccan cultures. Wagner found that level of recall depended on the content that was being remembered, with culture-relevant content being remembered more effectively than nonrelevant content (e.g., Moroccan rug merchants were better able to recall complex visual patterns on black-and-white photos of Oriental rugs). Wagner further suggested that when tests are not designed to minimize the effects of cultural differences, the key to culture-specific differences in memory may be the knowledge and use of metamemory strategies (involving people's knowledge about their memories, e.g., mnemonic devices), rather than actual structural differences in memory (e.g., memory span and rates of forgetting). In short, making a test culturally relevant appears to involve much more than just removing specific linguistic barriers to understanding.

Stephen Ceci (Ceci & Roazzi, 1994) has found similar context effects in children's and adults' performance on a variety of tasks. Ceci suggests that the *social context* (e.g., whether a task is considered masculine or feminine), the *mental context* (e.g., whether a visuospatial task involves buying a home or burgling it), and the *physical context* (e.g., whether a task is presented at the beach or in a laboratory) all affect performance. For example, 14-year-old boys performed poorly on a task when it was couched as a cupcake-baking task but performed well when it was framed as a battery-charging task (Ceci & Bronfenbrenner, 1985). Brazilian maids had no difficulty with proportional reasoning when hypothetically purchasing food but had great difficulty with it when hypothetically purchasing medicinal herbs (Schliemann & Magalhües, 1990). Brazilian children whose poverty had forced them to become street vendors showed no difficulty in performing complex arithmetic computations when selling things but had great difficulty performing similar calculations in a classroom (Carraher, Carraher, & Schliemann, 1985).

Critique of the Anthropological Model

Two key criticisms have been aimed at the contextual approach. First, contextualists do not provide well-elaborated theories of context and the influence of context. Second, even if we acknowledge that much of intelligence may be governed by context, something must be happening in the individuals' heads to influence the individuals to demonstrate intelligence within that context. Few contextualists say much about what happens in the head in terms of internal structures and processes, even within given contexts. In response to the criticism targeting both the internal (psychometric, computational, and physiological) models of intelligence and the external (anthropological) models of intelligence, some theorists have attempted explicitly to deal with intelligence in terms of its relationship to both the internal and the external worlds of the individual. Those systems theorists have tried to combine the best elements of the various kinds of models we have just described.

The Systems Model of Intelligence

Two contemporary theorists have proposed theories of intelligence that attempt to be fairly encompassing in dealing with both the internal and the external worlds. These theories view intelligence as a complex system.

Multiple Intelligences

Howard Gardner (1983, 1993) has proposed a **theory of multiple intelligences,** in which intelligence is not just a single, unitary construct. However, instead of speaking of multiple abilities that together consti-

tute intelligence, as have other theorists, such as Thurstone, Gardner speaks of seven distinct intelligences that are relatively independent of each other (see Table 11-3). Each is a separate system of functioning, although these systems can interact to produce what we see as intelligent performance.

> Look at Gardner's list of intelligences, and evaluate your own intelligences, rank ordering and giving examples of your strengths (or weaknesses) in each.

In some respects, Gardner's theory sounds psychometric because it specifies several abilities that are construed to reflect intelligence of some sort. However, Gardner views each ability as a separate intelligence, not just as a part of a single whole. Moreover, a crucial difference between Gardner's theory and factorial theories is in the sources of evidence for identifying the seven intelligences. Gardner used converging operations, gathering evidence from multiple sources and types of data, such as the distinctive effects of localized brain damage on specific kinds of intelligences, distinctive patterns of development in each kind of intelligence across the life span, evidence from exceptional individuals (from both

TABLE 11-3
Gardner's Seven Intelligences
On which of Howard Gardner's seven intelligences do you show the greatest ability? In what contexts can you use your intelligences most effectively? (After Gardner, 1983, 1993)

Type of Intelligence	Tasks Reflecting This Type of Intelligence
Linguistic intelligence	Used in reading a book; writing a paper, a novel, or a poem; and understanding spoken words
Logical-mathematical intelligence	Used in solving math problems, in balancing a checkbook, in doing a mathematical proof, and in logical reasoning
Spatial intelligence	Used in getting from one place to another, in reading a map, and in packing suitcases in the trunk of a car so that they all fit into a compact space
Musical intelligence	Used in singing a song, composing a sonata, playing a trumpet, or even appreciating the structure of a piece of music
Bodily-kinesthetic intelligence	Used in dancing, playing basketball, running a mile, or throwing a javelin
Interpersonal intelligence	Used in relating to other people, such as when we try to understand another person's behavior, motives, or emotions
Intrapersonal intelligence	Used in understanding ourselves—the basis for understanding who we are, what makes us tick, and how we can change ourselves, given the existing constraints on our abilities and our interests

Searchers . . .   HOWARD GARDNER

Howard Gardner is Professor of Education at Harvard University Graduate School of Education, codirector of Harvard Project Zero, and Adjunct Research Professor of Neurology at Boston University School of Medicine.

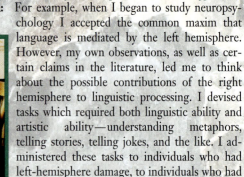

Q: *How did you become interested your area of work?*

A: As a youngster I was particularly interested in music but eventually decided to pursue a non-artistic career. When I attended Harvard College I became interested in sociology and psychology. I had the opportunity to work with Erik Erikson, and I decided to pursue graduate work in clinical psychology. After finishing college, I took a job with Jerome Bruner, the cognitive psychologist, and I discovered that cognition, rather than personality, motivation, or clinical work, was my deep interest. Bruner introduced me to the writings of Jean Piaget, and these excited me in a way that nothing had before. I decided I wanted to be a developmental psychologist. However, I was dismayed to find that neither Piaget nor other developmentalists had any professional interest in music or other art forms.

The philosopher Nelson Goodman was beginning a research project at Harvard in the area of "the arts as knowing": Project Zero. As a research assistant on the project, I combined an interest in the arts with the rigor of philosophical thinking and the methods of the experimental developmental psychologist. As my first empirical work, I studied the development of artistic abilities in children. Project Zero continues today, and we are still pursuing the issue of how artistic abilities and talents develop.

Q: *Whose ideas have influenced you the most?*

A: Erikson, Bruner, Piaget, and Goodman had the biggest influence on me. I did a postdoctoral fellowship at the Harvard Medical School and the Boston University Aphasia Research Center with Norman Geschwind, and that stint convinced me of the importance of a neuroscientific approach to cognition. Also, I became interested in intelligence and critical of standard psychometric approaches to intelligence—approaches which assume that there is a single thing called intelligence and that it can be adequately measured by paper-and-pencil instruments.

Q: *What is your greatest asset as a psychologist?*

A: Because of a curiosity about various disciplines, ranging from philosophy to the arts, I can bring a broad perspective to bear on issues of behavior and thought.

Q: *How do you get your ideas for research?*

A: Sometimes an idea grows out of my own personal experience. At other times I will read an assertion in the literature that contradicts my own experience. At still other times I will note an apparent contradiction between two assertions and will then create an experiment that adjudicates between these positions.

Q: *How have you developed an idea into a hypothesis?*

A: For example, when I began to study neuropsychology I accepted the common maxim that language is mediated by the left hemisphere. However, my own observations, as well as certain claims in the literature, led me to think about the possible contributions of the right hemisphere to linguistic processing. I devised tasks which required both linguistic ability and artistic ability—understanding metaphors, telling stories, telling jokes, and the like. I administered these tasks to individuals who had left-hemisphere damage, to individuals who had right-hemisphere damage, and to various control groups. I was able to identify which aspects of linguistic sophistication are mediated by the left (or dominant) hemisphere and which are under control of the right hemisphere.

Q: *What is your major contribution to psychology?*

A: I hope that I have broadened the sense of psychologists about what can be studied and how it can be approached; that human cognitive development culminates in artistic thinking as well as in scientific thinking; that the notion of a single intelligence is simplistic—there exist a variety of human intelligences; that creativity can and should be studied in a multi-disciplinary perspective; and that psychologists should combine knowledge from different domains and disciplines.

Q: *What advice would you give to someone starting in the field of psychology?*

A: Know something besides psychology. Know the arts, literature, philosophy. Get additional scientific leverage by studying neuroscience, cognitive science, or anthropology. Most of the breakthroughs in psychology have come from individuals with roots in other disciplines.

Q: *What did you learn from your mentors?*

A: The importance of breadth of knowledge, a sense of a question worth spending time on, and the crucial role of clear communication in plain English. They valued good scholarship and good communication rather than the pursuit of a question that is in vogue.

Q: *What have you learned from your students?*

A: Students question things that I have taken for granted. I am so devoted to a developmental approach and to a focus on cognition that I often fail to appreciate the assumptions built into those disciplinary preferences and the need at least occasionally to challenge them.

Q: *How do you keep yourself academically challenged?*

A: I have projects that will keep me busy for at least the next century! If that were not enough, my students, my children, and my peers keep me on my toes. I have just begun a study of the nature of effective leadership and how it might be cultivated, and so I am deeply immersed in reading history, biography, sociobiology, and political science.

ends of the spectrum), and evolutionary history. Thus, the base of evidence used by Gardner goes well beyond the factor analysis of various psychometric tests.

> In thinking about your own intelligences, how fully integrated do you believe them to be? How much do you perceive each type of intelligence to depend on any of the others?

Gardner's view of the mind is modular. *Modularity theorists* believe that different abilities—such as Gardner's intelligences—can be isolated as emanating from distinct portions or modules of the brain. Thus, a major task of existing and future research on intelligence would be to isolate the portions of the brain responsible for each of the intelligences. Gardner has speculated as to at least some of these locales, but hard evidence for the existence of these separate intelligences has yet to be produced.

The Triarchic Theory

Whereas Gardner emphasizes the separateness of the various aspects of intelligence, I tend to emphasize the extent to which they work together in my **triarchic theory of human intelligence** (Sternberg, 1985a, 1988b). According to the triarchic theory, intelligence comprises three aspects: dealing with the relation of intelligence (a) to the internal world, (b) to experience, and (c) to the external world. Figure 11-7 illustrates the parts of the theory and their interrelations.

HOW INTELLIGENCE RELATES TO THE INTERNAL WORLD. This part of the triarchic theory emphasizes the processing of information, which can be viewed in terms of three different kinds of components: (1) *metacomponents*—executive processes (i.e., metacognition) used to plan, monitor, and evaluate problem solving; (2) *performance components*—lower order processes used for implementing the commands of the metacomponents; and (3) *knowledge-acquisition components*—the processes used for learning how to solve the problems in the first place. The components are highly interdependent.

Suppose you were asked to write a term paper. You would use metacomponents to decide on a topic, plan the paper, monitor the writing, and evaluate how well your finished product succeeds in accomplishing your goals. You would use knowledge-acquisition components for research to learn about the topic. You would also use performance components for the actual writing. (Recall that greater intelligence is associated with spending more time on metacomponents such as global planning of an overall strategy than on performance components such as implementation of the details of the task.) In practice, the three kinds of components do not function in isolation. Before actually writing the paper, you would first have to decide on a topic and then do some research. Similarly, your plans for writing the paper might change as you gather new information. It may turn out there just is not enough information on particular aspects of the chosen topic, forcing you to shift your emphasis. Your plans also may change if particular aspects of the writing go more smoothly than do others.

> How might you apply Sternberg's three components of information processing to the task of studying for your psychology examination?

HOW INTELLIGENCE RELATES TO EXPERIENCE. The triarchic theory also considers how prior experience may interact with all three kinds of information-processing components. That is, each of us faces tasks and situations with which we have varying levels of experience, ranging from a completely novel task, with which we have no previous experience, to a completely familiar task, with which we have vast, extensive experience. As a task becomes increasingly familiar, many aspects of the task may become *automatic* (see Chapter 10, regarding

[Handwritten note: Hmm... Whose name is on the cover of this book? Biased Much? And not even a Datar... shameless]

FIGURE 11-7
Sternberg's Triarchic Theory of Intelligence
According to Robert Sternberg, intelligence comprises analytic, creative, and practical abilities. In analytical thinking, we try to solve familiar problems by using strategies that manipulate the elements of a problem or the relationships among the elements (e.g., comparing, analyzing). In creative thinking, we try to solve new kinds of problems that require us to think about the problem and its elements in a new way (e.g., inventing, designing). In practical thinking, we try to solve problems that apply what we know to everyday contexts (e.g., applying, using).

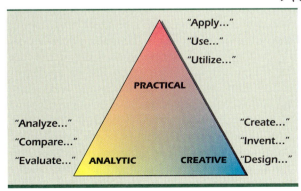

automaticity), requiring little conscious effort for determining what step to take next and how to implement that next step. A novel task makes demands on intelligence different from those of a task for which automatic procedures have been developed. According to the triarchic theory, relatively novel tasks—such as visiting a foreign country, mastering a new subject, or acquiring a foreign language—demand more of a person's intelligence. The most intellectually stimulating tasks are those that are challenging and demanding but not overwhelming. (Chapter 12 discusses a related construct, posited by Lev Vygotsky.)

> What is a novel task that you now face, one you find challenging, but not overwhelming? How could you modify the task to make it more challenging or less challenging?

HOW INTELLIGENCE RELATES TO THE EXTERNAL WORLD.   The triarchic theory also proposes that the various components of intelligence are applied to experience in order to serve three functions in real-world contexts: adapting ourselves to our existing environments, shaping our existing environments to create new environments, and selecting new environments. You use adaptation when you learn the ropes in a new environment and try to figure out how to succeed in it. For example, when you first start college, you probably try to figure out the explicit and implicit rules of college life and how you can use these rules to succeed in the new environment. You also shape your environment, such as deciding what courses to take and what activities to pursue. You may even try to shape the behavior of those around you. Finally, if you are unable either to adapt yourself or to shape your environment to suit you, you might consider selecting another environment—transferring to another college.

According to the triarchic theory, people may apply their intelligence to many different kinds of problems. For example, some people may be more intelligent in the face of abstract, academic problems, whereas others may be more intelligent in the face of concrete, practical problems. The theory does not define an intelligent person as someone who necessarily excels in all aspects of intelligence. Rather, intelligent persons know their own strengths and weaknesses and find ways to capitalize on their strengths and either compensate for or remediate their weaknesses. For example, a person strong in psychology but not in physics might choose as a physics project the creation of a physics aptitude test (which I did when I took physics!). The point is to make the most of your strengths and to find ways to improve upon or at least to live comfortably with your weaknesses.

> What is one of your key strengths in terms of intelligence? What is one of your key weaknesses? How might you use your strength to compensate for your weakness?

Critique of and Conclusions Regarding the Systems Model

The theories of Gardner and Sternberg are somewhat broader than conventional theories of intelligence, and they include aspects that other theorists, especially earlier ones, would not view as intelligence. In fact, the systems model is broader than any of the psychometric, computational, physiological, or anthropological ones. Some would say that the breadth of the systems theories is a problem because it is difficult to disconfirm theories that are so broad. A sound theory should be specific enough that it could be clearly disproved, if evidence against it were to be found. Perhaps systems theories are so general that they could incorporate almost anything under, say, "adaptation to the environment." Nonetheless, the trend in the coming years seems to be toward broader, rather than narrower, conceptions of intelligence, and toward appreciation of abilities that previously either were ignored or were relegated to secondary status. Systems theories may be a step in the right direction, but plenty of room exists for the theories of the future, which may combine the specificity of the computational models with the breadth of the systems models.

EXTREMES OF INTELLIGENCE

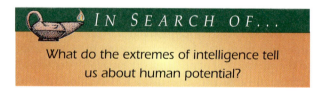

IN SEARCH OF...

What do the extremes of intelligence tell us about human potential?

Every theory of intelligence must deal with the issue of extremes. Although most people fall within the broad middle range of intellectual abilities, there are, of course, people at both the upper and the lower extremes. Different theorists conceive of the extremes in different ways. People at the upper extreme are usually labeled as *intellectually gifted*, whereas those at the lower extreme are often labeled as *mentally retarded*. We consider next each of the two extremes.

Intellectual Giftedness

Psychologists differ in terms of how they define the intellectually gifted. Some use an exclusively IQ-based criterion. For example, many programs for the gifted screen largely on the basis of intelligence tests, taking children in perhaps the top 1% (IQ roughly equal to 135 or above) or 2% (IQ roughly equal to 132 or above) for their programs. Others also supplement the assessment of IQ as the basis of giftedness with other criteria, such as school or career achievements or other measures of gifted performance.

Probably the most well-known studies of giftedness were conducted by Lewis Terman. Terman conducted a **longitudinal study,** which followed particular gifted individuals over the course of their life spans (Terman, 1925; Terman & Oden, 1959). The study has continued even after Terman's death. In his sample of the gifted, Terman included children from California under age 11 with IQs over 140, as well as children in the 11- to 14-year age bracket with slightly lower IQs. The mean IQ of the 643 subjects selected was 151; only 22 of these subjects had IQs lower than 140.

The accomplishments in later life of the selected group were extraordinary by any criterion. By 1959, there were 70 listings among the group in *American Men of Science* and three memberships in the highly prestigious National Academy of Sciences. In addition, 31 men were listed in *Who's Who in America*, and 10 appeared in the *Directory of American Scholars.* There were numerous highly successful businessmen as well as individuals who were successful in all of the professions.

The sex bias in these references is obvious. Most of the women became housewives, so it is impossible to make any meaningful comparison between the men (none of whom were reported to have become househusbands) and the women.

Many factors other than IQ could have contributed to the success of Terman's sample, among the most important of which is familial socioeconomic status and the final educational level achieved by these individuals. Thus, as with all correlational data, it would be difficult to assign a causal role to IQ in accounting for the accomplishments of the successful individuals in the study.

How do you account for the differing achievements of men and of women in Terman's sample? Be specific.

Today, many, if not most, psychologists look to more than IQ for the identification of the intellectu-

ally gifted. (See Sternberg & Davidson, 1986, for a variety of theories of giftedness.) For example, Joseph Renzulli (1986) believes that high commitment to tasks (motivation) and creativity are important to giftedness, in addition to above-average (although not necessarily outstanding) intelligence. John Feldhusen (1986) additionally looks for high self-concept, knowledge, and specialized talents. Janet Davidson (1986) emphasizes the importance of insight abilities, and I (Sternberg, 1986d) propose that gifted people are generally persons who are good at something—sometimes just one thing—but find a way of capitalizing on that something to make the most of their capabilities. All of these theorists are in agreement that there is more to giftedness than a high IQ. Indeed, I argue that people can be creatively or practically gifted, and not even show up as particularly distinguished at all on an IQ test.

What do you consider to be the key characteristics of intellectually gifted individuals?

In sum, the tendency today is to look beyond IQ to identify intellectually gifted individuals. There are many ways to be gifted, and scores on conventional intelligence tests represent only one of these ways. Indeed, some of the most gifted adult contributors to society, such as Albert Einstein or Thomas Edison, were not top performers either on tests or in school during their early years. Einstein did not even speak until he was 3 years old, and many other remarkably gifted persons have even shown particular characteristics that some have regarded as indicating mental retardation. We might then wonder how we can identify truly retarded intellect.

Mental Retardation

Mental retardation refers to low levels of intelligence. Simple enough. Much less simple is determining how we conceive of mental retardation, and whom we label as being mentally retarded. Different viewpoints lead to different conclusions.

The Role of Adaptive Competence

The American Association on Mental Retardation includes within its definition of mental retardation two components: low IQ and low *adaptive competence*, the latter of which refers to how a person gets along in the world. In other words, to be labeled as retarded, an individual not only would have to perform poorly on an intelligence test, but also would have to show

According to Howard Gardner's theory of intelligence, this young gymnast is showing gifted levels of bodily kinesthetic intelligence.

problems adapting to the environment. A child whose performance was normal in every way except for low IQ would not, by this definition, be classified as mentally retarded. Table 11-4 illustrates some of the ways in which particular IQ scores have been related to particular adaptive life skills.

It is not always easy to assess adaptive competence, however, as the following example (Edgerton, 1967) shows. A retarded man (who had scored low on tests of intelligence) was unable to tell time—an indication of some kind of cognitive deficit. However, the man employed a clever compensatory strategy: He wore a nonfunctional watch, so that whenever he wanted to know the time, he could stop, look at his watch, pretend to notice that his watch did not work, and then ask a nearby stranger (who would have observed his behavior) to tell him the correct time. How should we assess this man's adaptive competence—in terms of his strategy for determining the time or in terms of his inability to tell time by looking at a watch?

Cognitive Bases of Mental Retardation

Edward Zigler (1982) believes that some mentally retarded children simply develop mentally at a slower rate than children with normal intelligence. Most investigators, however, seek not only to look at quantitative differences in rates of development but also at qualitative differences in performance. A key qualitative difference centers on metacognitive skill. There is fairly widespread agreement that mentally retarded individuals have difficulty with the executive processes of cognition, such as planning, monitoring, and evaluating their strategies for task performance (Campione, Brown, & Ferrara, 1982).

We use these metacognitive processes (a) to plan how to solve problems, such as figuring out what to study; (b) to monitor how well we are doing at solving the problems, such as checking ourselves to ensure that we understood what we have just studied; and (c) to evaluate how well our existing strategies have succeeding in accomplishing the tasks we have set for ourselves, such as grasping a set of concepts, as a result of our studies. Even when retarded persons have been taught specific metacognitive skills for tackling specific tasks, they do not transfer those skills to any tasks other than the specific one for which they learned the skills. Nonretarded persons demonstrate much better ability to transfer strategies from one task to another. For example, recall from Chapter 8 that retarded children do not spontaneously rehearse lists of words they are asked to memorize (Brown, Campione, Bray, & Wilcox, 1973); even when such children are trained to memorize a given kind of list, they do not transfer that strategy to memorizing other kinds of lists (Butterfield, Wambold, & Belmont, 1973).

> Suppose you are a teacher of mentally retarded children. How might you design a program to help your students use some metacognitive strategies?

Hereditary and Environmental Impairments of Intelligence

Both hereditary and environmental factors may contribute to retardation. A child exposed to an impoverished environment or denied opportunities for even basic instruction in the home might display retardation. Even fetal environmental influences may cause permanent retardation—for example, retardation resulting from a mother's inadequate nutrition or ingestion of toxins such as alcohol during the individual's prenatal development. Even a brief trauma, such as

TABLE 11-4
Levels of Mental Retardation
Contemporary views of mental retardation de-emphasize IQ scores and more strongly underscore the ability of the individual to show the skills needed for adapting to the requirements of self-care and societal expectations.

Degree of Retardation	Range of IQ Scores	Adaptive Life Skills
Mild (~85% of retarded persons; about 2% of general population)	50–70	May acquire and demonstrate mastery of academic skills at or below the sixth-grade level, particularly if given special education. Likely to acquire various social and vocation-related skills, given adequate training and appropriate environment. Given appropriate environmental support and assistance (especially during times of stress), may achieve independent living and occupational success.
Moderate (~10% of retarded persons; 0.1% of the general population)	35–55	Have considerable difficulty in school, but may acquire and demonstrate mastery of academic tasks at or below the fourth-grade level if given special education. Given appropriate very structured environmental support and supervision, may be able to engage in unskilled or possibly highly routinized semiskilled vocational activities that contribute to self-support. Able to engage in many personal self-maintenance activities. A sheltered home and work environment, in which supervision and guidance are readily available, often works well.
Severe (~4% of retarded persons; <0.003% of the general population)	20–40	May learn to talk or at least to communicate in some manner. Unlikely to profit from vocational training, but given adequate full supervision and highly structured environmental support, may be able to perform simple tasks required for personal self-maintenance (including toileting) and possibly even some limited vocational activity. Some custodial services may be required, in addition to a carefully controlled environment.
Profound (<2% of retarded persons)	Below 25	Limited motor development and little or no speech. Generally unresponsive to training, but may be trained to participate in some self-maintenance activities (not including toileting). Constant supervision and assistance in performing fundamental self-maintenance within a custodial setting are required.

from a car accident or a fall, can injure the brain, causing mental retardation.

Although we do not understand well the subtle influences of heredity on intelligence at present, we do know of several genetic syndromes that clearly cause mental retardation (see Chapter 3 for more on heredity). For example, one of the more common genetic causes of mental retardation is *Down's Syndrome*, once called "mongolism." This syndrome results from the presence of extra chromosomal material on one of the chromosomes. The extra material disrupts the normal biochemical messages and results in retardation and other features of this syndrome.

Sometimes, hereditary factors interact with environmental ones to produce mental retardation. Although we cannot yet prevent the inheritance of these diseases, we can try to block the environmental contribution to the retardation. For example, we now know how to minimize the likelihood of mental retardation in *phenylketonuria (PKU)*, a rare hereditary disease that results in mental retardation if environmental intervention is not imposed. Essentially, children with this disease do not produce an enzyme needed for properly metabolizing the amino acid phenylalanine. As a result, if PKU is not quickly discovered after birth, and the infant consumes foods containing complete proteins or other sources of phenylalanine, by-products of the incomplete metabolism of this amino acid will accumulate in the bloodstream. These by-products will cause progressively more severe brain damage and permanent retardation. In PKU, the interactive roles of nature and nurture are clear, and we can specify clearly these roles. Most of us, however, can distinguish less clearly the specific influences of nature and nurture on the development of our intelligence.

HERITABILITY OF INTELLIGENCE

> ### IN SEARCH OF...
>
> What causes individual differences in intelligence? To what extent are different people born with differing levels of intelligence? To what extent do differences in children's environments as they grow up affect their intelligence?

Today, the large majority of psychologists and *behavior geneticists*—people who specialize in the effects of genes on behavior—believe that differences in intelligence result from a combination of hereditary and environmental factors. The ancient nature-nurture controversy continues in regard to intelligence.

The contribution of heredity to intelligence is often expressed in terms of a **heritability coefficient,** a number on a scale from 0 to 1 that expresses the proportion of the variation among individuals that is alleged to be due to heredity. A coefficient of 0 would mean that heredity has no influence on variation among people, and a coefficient of 1 would mean that nothing but heredity has any influence. It is important to remember that the coefficient indicates *variation* in measured intelligence. The more similar people are in terms of the gene pool from which they come, the lower the heritability coefficient will tend to be; the more similar the environments from which people come, the higher the heritability coefficient will tend to be (see Herrnstein, 1973).

Current estimates of the heritability coefficient of intelligence are based almost exclusively on performance on standard tests of intelligence. The estimates can be no better than the tests, and we have already seen that the tests define intelligence somewhat narrowly. How can we estimate the heritability of intelligence (at least that portion of it measured by the conventional tests)? Several methods have been used. The main ones are studies of separated identical twins, studies of identical versus fraternal twins, and studies of adopted children.

Separated Identical Twins

Identical twins have identical genes. No one knows exactly why identical twinning occurs, but we do know that identical twins result when a sperm fertilizes an egg, and then the newly formed embryo splits in two, resulting in two embryos with identical genes. Suppose that a set of twins is born, and then one of the twins is immediately whisked away to a new environment, chosen at random, so that no relationship exists between the environments in which the two twins are raised. The two twins would have identical genes, but any similarity between their environments would be due only to chance. If we then created a number of such twin pairs, we would be able to estimate the hereditary contribution to intelligence by correlating the measured intelligence of each individual with that of his or her identical twin. The twins would have in common all their heredity but none of their environment (except any aspects that might be similar due to chance). In fact, some circumstances have created instances in which twins have been separated at birth and then raised separately. In studies of twins reared apart (e.g., Bouchard & McGue, 1981; Juel-Nielsen, 1965; Newman, Freeman, & Holzinger, 1937; Shields, 1962), the various estimates tend to fall within roughly the same heritability-coefficient range of 0.6 to 0.8.

These relatively high figures become less impressive, however, when the studies are examined more carefully. In many cases, the twins were not actually separated at birth, but at some point afterward, giving the twins a common environment for at least some time before separation. In other cases, it becomes clear that the supposedly random assortment of environments was anything but random. Placement authorities tend to place twins in environments relatively similar to those the twins had left. These tendencies may inflate the apparent contribution of heredity to variation in measured intelligence, because variation that is actually environmental is included in the correlation that is supposed to represent only the effect of heredity.

Identical Versus Fraternal Twins

Another way to estimate heritability is to compare the correlation of IQs for identical versus fraternal twins. The idea is that whereas twins share identical genes, fraternal twins share only the same genes as would any brother or sister. On average, they share only 50% of their genes. To the extent that the identical and fraternal twin pairs share similar environments

These identical twins were separated at birth and were not re-united until they were 31 years old, when the two firefighters met and discovered striking similarities in their personal habits and interests. Studies of twins reared apart reveal a great deal about how much of our intelligence is due to our nature and how much is due to our nurture.

due to age, we should not get environmental differences due merely to variations in age among sibling pairs. According to a review by Thomas Bouchard and Matthew McGue (1981), the average correlation between IQs of fraternal twins is 0.61, compared with 0.86 for identical twins reared together.

These data suggest an environmental contribution to IQ of $0.86 - 0.61$, or 0.25, leaving us with a heritability coefficient of $1.00 - 0.25$, or 0.75, again suggesting a high level of heritability. Unfortunately, however, these data are affected by the fact that fraternal twins do *not* share environments to the same extent that identical ones do, particularly if the fraternal twins are not same-sexed twins. Parents tend to treat identical twins more nearly alike than they do fraternal ones, even to the extent of having them dress the same way. Moreover, the twins themselves are likely to respond differently if they are identical, perhaps seeking out more apparent identity with their twin. Thus, once again, the contribution of environment may be underestimated.

Adoption

Yet another way to examine hereditary versus environmental contributions to intelligence is by comparing the correlation between the IQs of adopted children, on the one hand, and those of their biological and adoptive parents, on the other. To the extent that heredity matters, the higher correlation should be with the intelligence of the biological rather than

the adoptive parents; to the extent that environment matters, the higher correlation should be that with the intelligence of the adoptive rather than the biological parents. In some families, it is also possible to compare the IQs of the adopted children to the IQs of either biological or adoptive siblings.

When we review the uncertain, mixed results of adoption studies, we must conclude that we still do not know how heritable intelligence is. Many psychologists, who have typically studied intelligence as measured by IQ, believe it to be about 0.5. However, there probably is no one heritability. Indeed, changes in distributions of genes or environments can change the estimates, and those distributions may differ with age. Moreover, even if a trait shows a high heritability, we could not say that the trait cannot be developed. For example, the heritability of height is very high—about 0.9—yet we know that over the past several generations, heights have been increasing. We can thus see how better environments can lead to growth, physical as well as intellectual. This possibility of making the most of our intelligence brings us to the last topic of the chapter: improving intelligence.

IMPROVING INTELLIGENCE: EFFECTIVE, INEFFECTIVE, AND QUESTIONABLE STRATEGIES

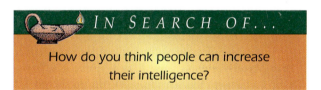

IN SEARCH OF...

How do you think people can increase their intelligence?

At one time, it was believed that intelligence is *fixed*, and that we are stuck forever with whatever level of intelligence we have at birth. Today, many researchers believe that intelligence is *malleable*, that it can be shaped and even increased through various kinds of interventions (Detterman & Sternberg, 1982). For example, the Head Start program was initiated in the 1960s as a way of providing preschoolers with an edge on intellectual abilities and accomplishments when they started school. Long-term follow-ups have indicated that by midadolescence, children who participated in the program were more than a grade ahead of matched controls who were not in the program (Lazar & Darlington, 1982; Zigler & Berman, 1983). Children in the program also scored higher on a variety of tests of scholastic achievement, were less likely to need remedial attention, and were

Searchers . . .   *SANDRA SCARR*

Sandra Scarr is Commonwealth Professor of Psychology at the University of Virginia.

Q: *How did you become interested in psychology in general and in your area of work in particular?*

A: I was interested in psychology as an adolescent because I was always curious about what made people the way they are. I became especially interested in genetic differences in behavior when I was in college and I was told that there weren't any. At that time, in the late '50s, the social sciences were committed to the view that all differences among people were environmental. So being perverse, I decided that there was more here than met the eye.

Q: *What theories, or whose ideas, have influenced you the most?*

A: Well, clearly Darwin and Dobzhansky, the great geneticist.

Q: *What distinguishes a great psychologist from just a good psychologist?*

A: Creativity and courage. There's a certain kind of venturesomeness and courage that go into pursuing what seem to other people to be unlikely avenues of inquiry. Or, to have the courage of one's convictions about something being worthwhile.

Q: *How do you get your ideas or insights for research?*

A: From observing my children.

Q: *How do you decide whether to pursue an idea?*

A: Well, I've always liked to look for opportunities to do hypothesis-testing research, to be able to actually answer a question. And sometimes, I've had questions for which I have not been able to figure out what kind of study to do that would be more than just merely descriptive. So, for example, I've always been interested in gender differences. You know, how boys and girls are so different in some ways in their developmental patterns and their behaviors, especially at certain points in development. Why are they so different? But I've never been able to think of a kind of quasi-experimental design that would allow me to answer that question.

Q: *What do you want your students to learn?*

A: I would like them to learn to be honest and rigorous scientists, to care about the research they do, and to enjoy it.

Q: *What advice would you give to someone starting in the field of psychology?*

A: Learn how to evaluate evidence and to be a critical consumer of research. Learn how to think statistically about probabilities, because so many students don't understand statistical probability and distributions.

Q: *What did you learn from your mentors?*

A: I learned to be a rigorous scientist, to care about hypothesis testing, to know that intellectual give-and-take, and even battles, can be fun and not personal. That you can have some of the best arguments with people and still be good friends.

Q: *What have you learned from your students?*

A: That being considerate and nurturing is better than playing God.

Q: *Apart from your life as an academic, how have you found psychology to be important?*

A: It has helped as a parent and in various policy arenas, knowing something about research. I've been asked to testify in Congress about child care and have given a policy seminar to Congressional members on child care in the United States. And I have been an expert witness in cases having to do with lead exposure in children. I've testified in two adoption cases.

Q: *How do you keep yourself academically challenged?*

A: Oh, that doesn't seem to be a problem. There always seem to be things that I don't know that I'd like to know.

Q: *What would you like people to remember about you and your work?*

A: That I was very tough-minded and tender-hearted.

---

less likely to show behavioral problems. Although such measures are not truly measures of intelligence, they show strong positive correlations with intelligence tests. A number of newer programs have also shown some success in environments outside of the family home (e.g., Adams, 1986; Feuerstein, 1980).

Support for the importance of home environment was found by Robert Bradley and Bettye Caldwell (1984) in regard to the development of intelligence in young children. These researchers found that several factors in the early (preschool) home environment may be linked to high IQ scores: emotional and verbal *responsivity* of the primary caregiver and the caregiver's *involvement* with the child, *avoidance of restriction* and punishment, *organization* of the physical environment and activity schedule, provision of appropriate play *materials*, and opportunities for *variety* in daily stimulation. Further, Bradley and

Caldwell found that these factors more effectively predicted IQ scores than did socioeconomic status or family-structure variables. Note, however, that the Bradley-Caldwell study pertained to preschool children, and children's IQ scores do not begin to predict adult IQ scores well until about age 4. Moreover, before age 7, the scores are not very stable (Bloom, 1964).

> Some people fervently believe that taxpayers would benefit from spending money to educate parents regarding how to provide optimal environments for the intellectual stimulation of their children. Do you agree or disagree with their views? Why?

Altogether, abundant evidence now indicates that environment, motivation, and training can profoundly affect intellectual skills. Heredity may set some kind of upper limit on how intelligent a person can become. However, we now know that for any attribute that is partly genetic, there is a **reaction range**—that is, the attribute can be expressed in various ways within broad limits of possibilities. Thus, each person's intelligence can be developed further within this broad range of potential intelligence. We have no reason to believe that people now reach the upper limits in the development of their intellectual skills. To the contrary, the evidence suggests that we can do quite a bit to help people become more intelligent.

SUMMARY

Traditions in the Study of Intelligence   372

1. Two traditions in the study of intelligence are those of Francis Galton and of Alfred Binet. The tradition of Galton emphasizes *psychophysical acuity*, whereas that of Binet emphasizes *judgment*.

2. *Mental age* refers to a person's level of intelligence, as compared with the "average" person of a given chronological age. Because of conceptual and statistical problems, the mental-age construct is rarely used in testing today.

3. The *intelligence quotient* (IQ) originally represented the ratio of mental age to chronological age, multiplied by 100. It was intended to provide a measure of a person's intelligence, relative to his or her agemates.

4. A *percentile* refers to the proportion of people whose scores fall below a given level of performance, multiplied by 100. Thus, a percentile of 75 on a test would refer to a score at or above the score of 75% of the other persons taking the same test.

5. Today, IQs are typically computed so as to have a median (middle score) of 100 and a standard deviation (which measures dispersion of scores) of 15 or 16. IQs computed in this way are *deviation* IQs.

6. Two of the most widely used individually administered intelligence tests are the *Stanford-Binet Intelligence Scales* and the *Wechsler Adult Intelligence Scale–Revised* (as well as the third edition of the *Wechsler Intelligence Scale for Children*).

Psychometric Properties of Intelligence Tests   379

7. Test validity is of several kinds. *Construct validity* is the extent to which a test measures the construct it is supposed to measure. *Predictive validity* is the extent to which a test predicts some kind of performance measured long after the test was taken. *Concurrent validity* is the extent to which a test measures some kind of performance measured at about the same time that the test was taken. *Content validity* refers to the extent to which experts judge the content of a test to represent the universe of material that it is supposed to sample. *Face validity* is the same judgment made by the people who take the test or by other laypersons.

8. Test reliability is also of several kinds. *Test-retest reliability* refers to the degree of relation between two administrations of the same test. *Alternate-forms reliability* refers to the degree of relation between two administrations of parallel forms of a test. *Internal-consistency reliability* is the extent to which a test measures a single (homogeneous) construct. *Inter-rater reliability* refers to the extent to which two or more raters

of a given product or set of products rate the same products the same way.

9. *Test standardization* refers to the process whereby the administration of the test in a given way ensures that the conditions for taking the test are the same for all test-takers. *Norms* are standardized scores representing a translation of raw scores into scaled equivalents that reflect the relative performance of individual test-takers, thereby permitting comparison.

Experts' Definitions of Intelligence   381

10. Two common themes that run through the definitions of intelligence proposed by many experts are *the capacity to learn from experience* and *the ability to adapt to the environment*.

Theories of the Nature of Intelligence   382

11. One approach to intelligence, *psychometric*, is to understand it in terms of *factor analysis*, a statistical technique that seeks to identify latent sources of individual differences in performance on tests. Some of the principal factor models of the mind are the two-factor model of Spearman, the primary-mental-abilities model of Thurstone, the structure-of-intellect model of Guilford, and the hierarchical models of Cattell and Vernon, among others.

12. An alternative approach to intelligence, computational, is to understand it in terms of *information processing*—the mental manipulation of symbols. Information-processing theorists have sought to understand intelligence in terms of constructs such as speed of lexical access and the components of reasoning and problem solving.

13. A third approach is the biological model, which uses increasingly sophisticated means of viewing the brain while the brain is engaged in intelligent behaviors.

14. A fourth approach to understanding intelligence (based on an anthropological model) is a *contextual approach*, according to which intelligence is viewed as wholly or partly determined by cultural values. Contextual theorists differ in the extent to which they believe that the meaning of intelligence differs from one culture to another.

15. What is considered to be intelligent behavior is, to some extent, *culturally relative*. The same behavior that is considered to be intelligent in one culture may be considered to be unintelligent in another culture.

16. It is difficult, perhaps impossible, to create a test of intelligence that is *culture-fair*—that is, equally fair for members of different cultures—

because members of different cultures have different conceptions of what constitutes intelligent behavior.

17. A fifth approach to understanding intelligence is based on a *systems model*. Gardner's *theory of multiple intelligences* specifies that intelligence is not a unitary construct, but rather that there are multiple intelligences, each relatively independent of the others. Sternberg's *triarchic theory of human intelligence* conceives of intelligence in terms of information-processing components, which are applied to experience to serve the functions of adaptation to the environment, shaping of the environment, and selection of new environments.

Extremes of Intelligence   396

18. *Intellectual giftedness* refers to a very high level of intelligence and is often believed to involve more than just IQ—for example, high creativity and high motivation.

19. The American Association on Mental Retardation includes within its definition of mental retardation two components: *low IQ* and *low adaptive competence*, the latter of which refers to how a person gets along in the world.

20. Mental retardation appears to be caused by both hereditary and environmental factors, often in interaction.

21. *Down's Syndrome* results from the presence of extra chromosomal material, and it usually results in some degree of mental retardation.

Heritability of Intelligence   400

22. The *heritability of intelligence* refers to the proportion of variation across individuals in their scores on intelligence tests that is inherited within a given population. Heritability can differ both across populations and within populations, across different times and places.

23. Heritability can be estimated in several ways. Three of the most common are through the study of *separated identical twins*, by comparisons of *identical versus fraternal twins*, and by *adoption studies* that compare IQs of adopted versus biological siblings raised by a given set of parents to both the biological and the adoptive parents.

Improving Intelligence: Effective, Ineffective, and Questionable Strategies   401

24. Intellectual skills can be taught. Thus, intelligence is malleable rather than fixed.

KEY TERMS

achievement 379
alternate-forms reliability 381
aptitudes 379
componential analysis 386
components 386
concurrent validity 380
construct-related validity 380
content validity 380
contextualists 388
crystallized intelligence 385
cultural relativism 392
culture-fair 391
culture-relevant 392
deviation IQs 375
face validity 380
factor analysis 383

fluid intelligence 385
heritability coefficient 400
information processing 385
intelligence 372
intelligence quotient 374
internal-consistency reliability 381
inter-rater reliability 381
lexical-access speed 385
longitudinal study 397
mean 375
median 375
mental age 374
mental retardation 397
mode 375
normal distribution 375
norms 380

percentile 375
predictive validity 380
psychometric 379
ratio IQ 374
raw score 375
reaction range 403
reliability 380
standardization 380
structure-of-intellect (SOI) 383
test-retest reliability 381
theory of multiple intelligences 393
triarchic theory of human intelligence 395
validity 380

IN SEARCH OF THE HUMAN MIND: ANALYSES, CREATIVE EXPLORATIONS, AND PRACTICAL APPLICATIONS

1. Does it make sense to speak of "overachievers"? Why or why not?
2. What would be the benefits of knowing the relative contributions of nature and of nurture to intelligence? What might be some drawbacks—or at least possible misuses—of such knowledge?
3. To what extent are people's achievements—including your own—an accurate reflection of their aptitudes? What other factors beside aptitudes affect achievement?

4. Create a test question that assesses a particular skill or topic of knowledge. Tailor that question to the following persons: (a) a 13-year-old homeless boy who supports himself by whatever means he finds available, (b) a 20-year-old member of a college sorority, (c) a 40-year-old attorney, and (d) a 70-year-old retired plumber.
5. Many museums now include specifically child-oriented experiences and exhibits. Think of an exhibit at a museum you have visited or have heard about. How might you enhance the learning experience of a 10-year-old to help the child profit from the exhibit?
6. If neither school performance nor existing tests of intelligence accurately predict or reflect intellectual giftedness, how should educators foster the intellectual gifts of their students? Give at least one concrete suggestion.

7. Are there things you could do to increase your own abilities? If so, what?
8. Are there aspects of your abilities that you could better utilize? If so, how might you better utilize them?
9. If you were to select a job for yourself, solely on the basis of your abilities, what would that job be?

1. How do the processes of perception, learning, memory, thinking, language, and intelligence interrelate? How does each one affect the others?

2. Suppose that you have available to you the full range of modern methods for studying the brain and the nervous system. Design an experiment that would help us better to understand the physiological processes that underlie learning, memory, language, thinking, or intelligence.

3. What metacognitive and metamemory strategies could you implement to enhance your study of psychology and other fields of endeavor?

Looking Ahead . . .

4. How do you think the processes of learning, memory, thinking, and intelligence change over the course of the human life span?

Charting the Dialectic

Chapter 7   LEARNING

The study of learning illustrates the dialectical evolution of ideas. Early in the century, learning theorists debated the respective roles of contiguity and reinforcement in learning, eventually recognizing that both played an important role. Early learning models stressing the importance of reinforcement were largely behaviorist, giving little or no role to cognitive processes. Theorists such as Tolman, however, argued for the importance of cognitive processing. Eventually, Rescorla and Wagner showed how a largely cognitive model could account for many conditioning phenomena. These models developed rather separately from work on people's social interactions with each other. In more recent years, however, a synthesis has emerged between what had originally developed as two separate areas. This synthesis reflects the study of phenomena such as learned helplessness and social learning.

Chapter 8   MEMORY

Various kinds of models of memory have emerged. The traditional model of Atkinson and Shiffrin that emerged during the 1960s postulated separate memory stores, such as short-term memory and long-term memory, each performing rather distinct functions. Then, in the 1970s, an antithetical model arose: Craik and Lockhart suggested that there are no separate stores at all, but rather various levels of processing along a single continuum. A synthesis of these two kinds of models by Baddeley became popular by the 1980s, which suggested that working memory (similar in many of its characteristics to short-term memory) actually may be that part of long-term memory that is activated at a given time.

Chapter 9 LANGUAGE

Theorists of language have debated many issues, from the nature of language itself to the origins of language in humans. With regard to the latter, theorists early in the century proposed various models by which language could be understood as wholly environmentally conditioned. Later theorists, such as Chomsky, proposed an opposing view, according to which an innate language acquisition device, present at birth, was responsible for the acquisition of language. Today, many theorists view language as developing from an interaction of genetic and environmental factors. As another example of the dialectic in operation, early theorists proposed a model of meaning according to which concepts could be decomposed into a set of defining features— for example, all bachelors are unmarried, adult males. Later theorists suggested, on the contrary, that concepts are better understood through characteristic features that combine to form prototypes: The more characteristic features a word has, the more it corresponds to the prototype. Thus, a robin would be a more prototypical bird than a penguin. Today, many theorists believe in a synthesis according to which many concepts, such as that of "odd number," can have both defining and characteristic features in combination.

Chapter 10 THINKING

A number of dialectics have arisen in the evolution of our understanding of thinking. For example, Gestalt psychologists viewed insight as a special process that bypassed conventional thought processes and that could not be understood through normal experimental procedures of investigation. Some information-processing psychologists, in contrast, have suggested that there is nothing special about insight processes at all: Only the product of thinking is different. More recently, still other psychologists have suggested that insight processes are special in certain respects, but that they can be understood using the same techniques of investigation as can be normal thought processes. In the field of decision making, early theorists suggested models of thinking that postulated a fully logical decision maker. Later psychologists suggested that thinking was far from rational. Today, most theorists recognize that people combine rational thinking, at some times, with thinking that at other times can be quite irrational.

Chapter 11 INTELLIGENCE

The study of intelligence has evolved dialectically. Early in the century, theorists concentrated on the structure of abilities, creating models that specified underlying factors of the mind. Cognitive psychologists in the 1970s turned to an emphasis on the processes of abilities. Most recently, theorists have tried to combine these two emphases to understand both the mental structures and processes underlying abilities. In another vein, early emphases on the hereditary origins of abilities later gave way to a very strong environmental emphasis. Today, most theorists recognize the importance of the interaction between heredity and environment in the development of abilities.

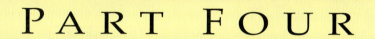

PART FOUR

DEVELOPMENTAL PROCESSES

COGNITIVE AND PHYSICAL DEVELOPMENT

SOCIAL DEVELOPMENT

Chapter Twelve

Cognitive and Physical Development

CHAPTER OUTLINE

My first recollection of life is one that my mother insisted I could not possibly have. . . . Be sure that children know far more than we give them credit for; I hear fond parents praising their precious darlings, and I wince, noting how the darlings are drinking in every word. Always in my childhood I would think: "How silly these grownups are! And how easy to outwit!"

What can we find out about people by observing the ways children develop into adults? What can you tell about the adult quoted above, based on his childhood recollections? The quotation is by writer Upton Sinclair.

Developmental psychologists are intrigued by changes that occur across the life span; these psychologists study the differences and similarities among people of different ages. In particular, psychologists who study cognitive development want to know how and why people think and behave differently at different times in their lives.

At first glance, it might seem differences across the life span are simply due to cognitive **growth**—quantitative simple increases in which we start out knowing and thinking just a little and end up knowing and thinking a great deal more. If this were the case—given that Chapters 8 through 11 have fully defined the many aspects of cognition, including memory processes, language processes, problem solving, judgment and decision making, reasoning, creativity, and intelligence—we would not need a separate chapter devoted to cognitive development. However, development involves much more than growth. **Development** also encompasses qualitative

changes (e.g., changes in complexity) that accompany the simple increases of growth.

Developmental psychologists also study social development, which we describe in the next chapter, the first of a trio of chapters on social psychology. For now, however, we focus on cognitive development following the series of chapters on cognitive psychology. Actually, much of social development depends on various cognitive developments.

How might various aspects of cognitive development affect an individual's social development?

In this chapter, we first discuss some of the basic issues in **cognitive development,** the study of how mental skills build and change with increasing physiological maturity and experience. Then we present some theories of how cognition develops and consider the growth of cognition in specific domains, such as perception and reasoning. Finally, we look briefly at the development of adult cognition and at the principles that unify the field of cognitive development.

THE NEURAL ASPECTS OF COGNITIVE DEVELOPMENT

One view of cognitive development considers the physiological development of the brain and neural apparatus. Recall from Chapter 3 (Figure 3-7) the physiological development of the prenatal brain. The neural networks of the brain become increasingly complex during the first two years after birth. After that time, the rate of neural growth and development declines dramatically. In fact, 90% of neural growth is complete by age 6 years. At birth, the brain stem is almost fully developed, but the cerebral cortex is still largely immature. The areas of the brain to develop most rapidly after birth are the sensory and motor cortexes, and subsequently, the association areas relating to problem solving, reasoning, memory, and language development. This pattern of neural development parallels the cognitive development detailed in this chapter.

Another area of physiological investigation has yielded some intriguing findings. A study (Thatcher, Walker, & Giudice, 1987) of the EEG patterns of 577 people ranging in age from 2 months to early adulthood shows the different patterns for each of the two cerebral hemispheres. In the right hemisphere, there appear to be continuous, gradual changes in EEG patterns associated with age. In the left hemisphere, however, there appear to be abrupt shifts in the EEG patterns, at least up through the time of early adulthood (see Figure 12-1). (See also Chapter 3 for more on EEGs and other aspects of physiological psychology over the course of the life span.)

BASIC QUESTIONS IN THE STUDY OF COGNITIVE DEVELOPMENT

> ### IN SEARCH OF...
>
> Five questions stand out in the field of cognitive development: (1) What cognitive-processing capabilities does the newborn have? (2) At what ages do infants, children, and adults first demonstrate various kinds of thought and behavior? (3) What causes progressive, developmental changes in cognition, and what causes individual differences in these developments? What are the relative roles of maturation (nature) and learning (nurture) in cognitive development? (4) To what extent is development stagelike and discontinuous, and to what extent is it smooth and continuous—an uninterrupted, gradual progression? (5) To what extent is development domain general, and to what extent is it domain specific?

The last three questions above have often been the subject of great controversy among developmental psychologists. Often, they have been phrased in ways that suggest an either–or answer, such as "Which is more important: nature or nurture?" (see Sternberg, 1989a; Sternberg & Okagaki, 1989). When phrased as either–or questions, they seem to require a single, definitive answer. Unfortunately, development—like so many other aspects of psychology—is not that simple. Simplistic questions tend to promote simplistic answers. (Remember the problem-solving cycle described in Chapter 1 and repeated in Chapter 10. *The questions we ask and the ways we define problems, in general, determine how we go about seeking answers—and whether we will find them.*) If we are to understand human development, we must phrase these questions in ways that encourage us to find realistic—and therefore probably complex—answers. As you read about the theories described in this chapter, mull over the ways that each of the theories answers

FIGURE 12-1
Developmental Changes in EEG Patterns
This graph of developmental changes in EEG patterns shows increasing electrical activity in both cerebral hemispheres. Note, however, that whereas the course of development in the left hemisphere is discontinuous, showing bursts and plateaus, the course of development in the right hemisphere is continuous. (After Thatcher, Walker, & Giudice, 1987)

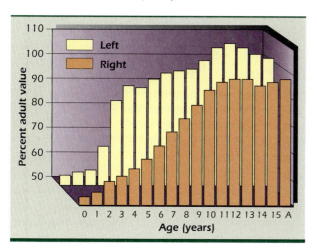

these questions. Toward the end of the chapter, we compare and contrast the various theoretical responses.

The Respective Roles of Maturation and Learning

Two main concepts in cognitive development are maturation and learning. **Maturation** is any relatively permanent change in thought or behavior that occurs as a result of the internally (biologically) prompted processes of aging, without regard to personal experiences. **Learning** is any relatively permanent change in thought or behavior as a result of experience (see Chapter 7). Maturation is preprogrammed; it will happen regardless of the environment. For example, the infant's sucking reflex appears and then disappears at preprogrammed ages, almost entirely without regard to the influences of the environment. In contrast, learning will take place only if the individual has particular experiences. For example, recognizing your own name when it is spoken occurs from a very early age and is almost exclusively a function of learning.

Fundamentally, the subject of maturation versus learning is the age-old philosophical and psychologi-

This young woman's amazing innate musical talent (her nature) might never have been discovered if she had been raised in a home in which music was not an important part of her environment (her nurture).

cal debate over nature (heredity) versus nurture (environment). Today, almost all psychologists believe that both maturation and learning influence cognitive development, as interactive processes. We may be born with a particular genetic capacity (e.g., to play a musical instrument), but the extent to which our performance develops to meet this capacity will depend to a large extent on the environment (e.g., whether we are given an opportunity to play an instrument or even to be exposed to various forms of music). One environment might bring out cognitive skills that another might not. A child with extraordinary musical talent might never discover this talent if raised in a nonmusical home.

The concept of **canalization** characterizes the extent to which an ability develops without respect to environment (Waddington, 1956). An ability is highly *canalized*—or channeled—if it will develop almost independently of environmental circumstances. It is weakly canalized if its development depends heavily on environmental factors. The more canalized an ability is, the deeper it lies in its channel, where it is less accessible to the influences of the outside world. Basic memory abilities, as required in recalling a list of words, appear to be highly canalized (see Jensen, 1980; Perlmutter & Lange, 1978), whereas interpersonal skills (e.g., the ability to persuade others or to negotiate effectively) are less so (see Gardner, 1983).

What cognitive abilities would you expect to be highly canalized? What other abilities would you expect to be weakly canalized?

Another controversy regarding development similarly depends on the way we interpret the data we find: Does development occur in a series of discrete stages, or does it occur in a single, continuous progression that gradually unfolds?

Continuity Versus Discontinuity in Cognitive Development

First, exactly what is a stage? C. J. Brainerd (1978) proposed two major criteria. The first criterion is that sets of behaviors (stages) occur in an invariable sequence (see also Beilin, 1971; Kurtines & Greif, 1974). For example, in terms of physical development, children almost always can crawl on their bellies before they can creep on hands and knees, and they can do both before they can walk. Recall, too, the progressive sequence of language acquisition, described in Chapter 9. Hence, children seem to acquire these behaviors in an invariably sequenced progression.

The second criterion is that each stage must be associated with a unique set of qualitatively distinct **cognitive structures**—specific mental abilities. Thus, when children are in particular stages, they can think and reason only in particular ways, and they develop the ability to think and reason in those ways only when in that stage and not before. For example, according to prominent developmental theorist Jean Piaget, young children are unable to think in terms of *conserving matter* (i.e., noticing that the quantity of something remains the same, despite transformations in its appearance).

Given these criteria (the invariable sequence and the set of qualitatively distinct cognitive structures), does development actually exhibit stagelike properties? As with so many questions in psychology, the answer depends on whom you ask. Piaget (1969, 1972) deeply believed in the discontinuously phased nature of development. Interestingly, after proposing his criteria for stages, Brainerd (1978) remained unconvinced that development is discontinuous. In Brainerd's view, too many findings do not meet his criteria for classifying development into discrete stages. Some theories of cognitive development (such as Piaget's) posit stages, but others (such as learning theories) do not. Moreover, even those theorists who propose discontinuous stages of development recognize that the stages are rarely clear-cut. For example, Piaget (1972) conceded that achievements within a given stage do not appear to occur for every task in every domain all at once. For example, children seem to be able to *conserve number* (recognize countable items as the same in number despite changes in their appearance) before they can *conserve volume* (recognize volume as the same, despite changes in appearance). They can also conserve volume before they can conserve weight (recognize that the weight is the same, despite changes in appearance).

Domain Generality Versus Domain Specificity in Development

Why can children conserve number *before* they can conserve weight? In contrast, why do children seem to develop the ability to walk at about the same time that they utter their first couple of words? Why do some abilities seem to develop at about the same time and others seem always to develop sequentially, never simultaneously? These questions have prompted some psychologists to focus on **domain generality,** which implies that development occurs more or less simultaneously in multiple areas (e.g., walking and

talking). Other psychologists, however, have more keenly emphasized **domain specificity,** which implies that development may be confined to particular cognitive areas at a given time (e.g., the development of the concept of conservation of weight).

Throughout the first half of the twentieth century, theories of cognitive development emphasized domain generality. Some contemporary researchers continue to study domain-general processes of development. For example, many information-processing theorists point to several ways in which children's information processing becomes increasingly sophisticated, such as in the children's ability to encode, combine, and compare information across domains.

Since the 1970s, however, theorists have placed more emphasis on domain specificity. Much of this emphasis can be traced back to studies of chess masters, which showed that the experts recall chessboard positions better than chess novices only if the positions they need to remember make sense in terms of their prior experience (Chase & Simon, 1973; de Groot, 1965) (see Chapters 8 and 10). Masters have better memories only within their domain of expertise, and then only if what they need to remember fits their schema for that domain.

This finding has been replicated not only with experts and novices, but also with adults and children. Countless experiments have shown that adults remember better than do children (see Keil, 1989). However, the domain in which memory is tested can affect this finding. Recall the research on memory and domain specificity mentioned in Chapter 8, in which child experts on dinosaurs performed better than adults at remembering dinosaur names (Chi & Koeske, 1983). The children's memory is not better overall, but it is superior in their domains of expertise (see Figure 12-2). Thus, children's conceptual development appears to be largely (although not entirely) domain specific.

We probably pose an unanswerable question if we ask whether development is domain general or domain specific. It appears to be both. Those who argue for domain generality have to account for why development is not uniform across content domains within a given stage. On the other hand, those who argue for domain specificity are hard pressed to account for obvious uniformities in children's development, starting with those we observe at birth.

> What is a content domain in which you would expect development to show domain specificity? How could you design an experiment to test your hypothesis?

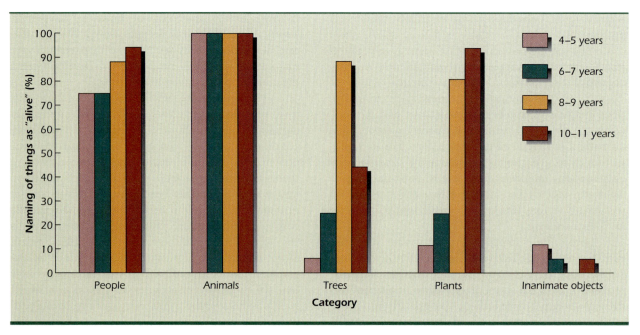

FIGURE 12-2
The Domain of Biological Knowledge
Development influences children's biological knowledge. Between ages 4 and 11, children's knowledge of the animal world becomes restructured, as novices reorganize their knowledge when they become experts. When D.D. Richards and Robert Siegler asked children to name things that are alive, the responses depended on the children's level of development. For instance, although even younger children realize that eating, breathing, and reproduction apply to all animals, not until they get a little older do many understand that people are animals, too. (After data from Richards & Siegler, 1984)

Capabilities of the Newborn

Our views regarding the capabilities of the **neonate,** or newborn, have changed radically over time. Recall from Chapter 2 that Aristotle and, later, John Locke (a seventeenth-century English philosopher) believed that the mind of the infant is a *tabula rasa*, a blank slate, on which the infant's experiences will be written. More recently, William James (1890b) surmised that the infant starts from scratch: "The baby, assailed by eyes, ears, nose, skin, and entrails at once, feels that all is one great blooming, buzzing confusion" (p. 4). In contrast to these proponents of the role of nurture (environmental learning), Plato argued that learning brings into consciousness what we already know (see Chapter 2). In the eighteenth century Jean-Jacques Rousseau advocated the *nativist* position— that our nature dictates our course of development.

Just what can newborns do? To start with, although newborns are very near-sighted they can see, contrary to former belief. For roughly the first month of life, the infant's eye has virtually no ability to accommodate to distances that vary from about 19 centimeters in distance. Those images that are closer or farther than the optimal 19 centimeters appear to be blurred (Teller & Movshon, 1986). Thus, infants can-

not see small objects well, but they can see large ones close up. During early infancy, the eye's lens reaches approximately normal flexibility with respect to accommodation, but with age, the lens again starts to lose some of its flexibility, so that many older people

Is this infant seeing "one great blooming, buzzing confusion," or is this infant already starting to scan the environment to find the most interesting sights? The more sophisticated we become in our observations of infants, the more we are amazed by their capabilities.

have difficulty accommodating their vision to near objects (Weale, 1986).

Psychologists who study infants have deduced that infants seem to have a set of inborn rules that guides their scanning of the environment (Haith, 1979). For example, infants seem to have a general rule to scan the environment broadly, but to stop scanning and explore in depth if they see an edge, which is more likely than an uninterrupted surface to contain interesting information.

Infants also have a preference for looking at particular kinds of objects; these objects are characterized by a high degree of complexity (e.g., preferring many somewhat narrow stripes to a few wide ones), many visual contours (e.g., preferring edges and patterns to solid regions of color), curved contours (rather than straight ones), high contrast between light and dark (e.g., preferring black and white to gray), and frequent movements (see Banks & Salapatek, 1983). Quite conveniently, every parent has available a highly stimulating object that perfectly matches these criteria: a human face. In one study, infants as young as 4 days of age were shown three different patterns—a standard face, a face with its features scrambled, or a bull's-eye pattern (Fantz, 1958, 1961). (See Figure 12-3) The babies showed a small but consistent preference for the sensible face over the scrambled one, and a much larger preference for both faces over the bull's-eye. Some researchers have suggested that infants' preference for faces might be some built-in biological imperative, but others question this notion. In addition, newborns can distinguish red, yellow, and green from gray, but they cannot distinguish blue from gray or yellow from green (Maurer & Adams, 1987). By 3 months of age, however, infants can distinguish essentially the same colors that adults can discern (Teller & Bornstein, 1987).

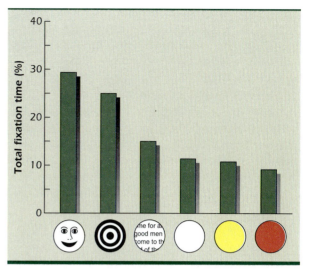

FIGURE 12-3
Newborns' Visual Preferences
Newborns from the ages of 10 hours to 5 days old showed a preference for the disk with the black and white face on it over the other simpler black and white as well as colored disks. (After Fantz, 1961)

Given infants' preferences for frequent movements, the appeal of mobiles is obvious. Bearing in mind other preferences of infants, draw or describe other toys that would be appropriate for young infants—or even design a mobile with particularly interesting objects for young infants.

Recall from Chapter 9 that fetuses can hear, although the amniotic fluid may impede their hearing. Within just a few days after birth, however, any residual amniotic fluid has drained or evaporated from their ear canals, and infants can hear voices and distinguish musical notes just one tone apart. Recall, too, that neonates preferentially attend to the human voice, particularly the child-directed speech ("moth-

erese") that characterizes the way in which adults communicate with infants. Newborns particularly respond also to the "clicks, kisses, and clucks" often used by their caregivers (Blass, 1990). Newborns even respond to their caregivers by appearing to dance in synchrony to their caregivers' vocalizations and movements (e.g., Field, 1978; Martin, 1981; Stern, 1977). Some researchers have found that newborns seem also to have almost a reflexive response for imitating a caregiver's smile, pout, open-mouthed expression of surprise, or tongue protrusion (e.g., Bower, 1989; Field, 1989; Meltzoff & Moore, 1989; Reissland, 1988). It appears that newborns seem custom-designed to elicit and encourage the attention—perhaps even the love—of their caregivers.

Infants can also detect smells. Breast-fed 6-day-olds seem to prefer the smell of their own mothers' milk, and breast-fed 3-month-olds seem to prefer the body smells of their own mothers (MacFarlane, 1975; Russell, 1976). Infants also prefer odors that adults consider pleasant (e.g., the scent of honey) to ones we would consider offensive (e.g., rotten eggs, vinegar, or ammonia) (Maurer & Maurer, 1988; Rieser, Yonas, & Wilkner, 1976; Steiner, 1979). Neonates also are predisposed to prefer sweet tastes over sour or bitter tastes (Crook, 1987; Steiner, 1979); on the other hand, they will still drink unpleasant-tasting solutions, so parents cannot depend on infants to resist drinking potentially toxic solutions.

The sense of touch is so highly developed in infants that it deserves special attention in regard to

Newborns seem to have an inborn knack for imitating some of the facial expressions of their caregivers (e.g., a smile, pout, open-mouthed expression of surprise, or tongue protrusion). This grinning infant and mother share closely matched facial expressions. How do interchanges such as this one affect their feelings toward each other?

infant attachment (discussed in Chapter 13). By 1 month of age, infants seem able to integrate sensations perceived through touch (e.g., a bumpy or a smooth pacifier) with visual sensations (later being shown both kinds of pacifiers and showing a preference for looking at the one sucked on previously; Meltzoff & Borton, 1979). In addition, infants' sensitivity to touch can be studied by investigating their reflexes.

In normal infants, many reflexes are present at or before birth (e.g., rooting—see Table 12-1). Some reflexes stay with us throughout life (e.g., the papillary reflex), and others disappear soon after birth (e.g., the stepping reflex). Most reflexes are only of passing interest because their presence indicates only

that the infant falls within the broad range of normal responses. Table 12-1 shows some of the key reflexes that physicians and psychologists look for in normal infants. Deviations from the broad normal range may indicate some form of damage to the central nervous system, which means that more careful investigation is necessary.

Look over the list of reflexes to see whether you notice a pattern. Many reflexes seem to provide neonates with the means to nourish themselves: attracting the attention of caregivers (crying), turning toward a source of food (rooting), securely attaching themselves to the food source (grasping the clothing, hair, or fur of the caregiver), taking in the food (sucking and swallowing), and eliminating waste (vomiting, urinating, defecating). Other reflexes enable newborns to protect themselves (eye-blinking, sneezing, pupil-contracting, startling, and withdrawing from pain or other aversive stimuli). Also, full-term, normal infants reflexively gasp their first breath almost immediately after birth (their hearts have been beating reflexively for months). In addition, some reflexes seem to lay down the nervous-system pathways for key behaviors that later come under conscious, voluntary control (e.g., palmar, stepping, placing).

Psychologists and physicians have long been aware of most of these reflexes, so they do not stimulate much interest in psychologists. One particular reflex does, however: the **orienting reflex,** in which infants (and others) reflexively orient themselves to sudden changes in the environment. The orienting reflex never disappears; when a bright light flashes, we pay attention to it reflexively.

This apparent preference for novelty has led some researchers to propose the *moderate-discrepancy hypothesis,* according to which infants prefer stimuli that are moderately discrepant (different) from what they already know (McCall, Kennedy, & Appelbaum, 1977). This preference explains why infants learn about things only when they are ready to learn about them. They do not waste their time attending to completely familiar things, or to things so new that they are overwhelming. Indeed, it may be that infants who prefer some degree of novelty are more intelligent than are those who do not (Bornstein & Sigman, 1986; Lewis & Brooks-Gunn, 1981). Joseph Fagan (1984, 1985; Fagan & Montie, 1988) and Marc Bornstein (1989) have found that infants who show stronger preferences for novelty at ages 2 to 6 months are more likely to have high scores on intelligence tests at ages 2 to 7 years. Other researchers (e.g., Humphreys & Davey, 1988; Kagan, 1989; McCall, 1989) would advise that we not leap to conclusions at this point. For one thing, recall from Chapter 11 that

TABLE 12-1
Reflexes Present in Newborns

Infants come well equipped with the reflexes they need for basic physiological survival; for eliciting help, affection, and care giving from their parents; and for subsequent development of conscious control over their bodies.

Reflex	Stimulus for Reflex	Infant's Response	Adaptive Function
Rooting (birth to around 1 year)	Gentle touch on infant's cheek	Turns toward the source of the stroking	Turns the infant's head toward the nipple for feeding
Sucking (present at birth)	Insertion of a nipple or finger into the infant's mouth	Sucks on the object inserted	Draws out the fluid from a nipple
Swallowing (present at birth)	Putting fluid on the back of the infant's mouth (e.g., through a nipple)	Swallows the fluid	Ingests breast milk
Vomiting (present at birth)	Too much fluid in the digestive tract	Vomits	Eliminates excess fluid
Eliminating (present at birth)	Feed the infant and wait for the outcome	Urinates and defecates	Removes waste products from infant
Crying (present at birth)	Hunger	Cries	Gets the attention of a caregiver; lays down the neural pathways for more subtle psychological reasons for crying
Breathing (starts at full-term birth)	Birth or pat on back	Inhales and exhales	Oxygenates the blood
Eyeblink (present at birth)	Puff of air or bright light in eye	Closes eyes	Protects eye from foreign matter
Pupillary contraction (present at birth)	Bright light in eye	Pupil contracts	Protects eye from too strong a light source
Withdrawal (present at birth)	An aversive stimulus, such as pin-prick	Flexes the legs, cries, and also may flex the arms or twist the body, depending on the location of the stimulus	Protects the infant from the stimulus and gets the attention of the caregiver to offer further protection
Palmar (present within weeks after birth)	Pressing an object (e.g., a finger) against the palm of the infant's hand	Grasps the object	May serve an immediate protective function and lays down the neural pathways for later voluntary control
Stepping (present shortly after birth)	Holding the infant upright so feet press against a solid surface	Makes heel-to-toe, alternate-foot stepping movements	Lays down the neural pathways for later voluntary control

intelligence tests administered prior to age 7 years usually do not show stable correlations with adult intelligence tests. What cognitive developments occur between infancy and age 7—and beyond—that could cause these critical changes in what we view as intelligent behavior?

Bearing in mind the orienting reflex and the moderate-discrepancy hypothesis, how might you advise new parents of infants to provide an optimally (neither excessively nor deficiently) stimulating environment?

Ages of Acquisition of Cognitive Skills

During much of the twentieth century, the fundamental goal of developmental psychology has been to answer the question, "When can which children accomplish what skills?" An exclusive focus on this question limits our understanding of development to a discussion of "who does what when," which is a bit like viewing history merely as the study of dates, or geography merely as the study of locations. Developmental psychologists must seek a more integrated, insightful view of development than a mere listing of age-sequenced events.

Yet the preoccupation with the who-does-what-when question is easy to understand. First, because the study of adult cognition has been viewed as the discovery of what adults can do intellectually, the study of childhood cognition might well be viewed as the discovery of what children can do intellectually—and when. Second, in order for us to assess when there are serious problems in children's development, we need to know the normal progression of developmental milestones and the normal age ranges for these milestones. Third, researchers and theorists need data about the basic accomplishments of different ages in order to construct theories of what underlies such achievements (see Table 12-2).

In addition, psychologists with an interest in cognitive processes are not alone in their interest in development. The development of various other abilities also has been studied. For example, Nancy Bayley's *Bayley Scales of Infant Development* (1968) specify the ages at which various physical, **motor** (involving movements of the muscles) tasks are usually accomplished (see Figure 12-4). Some psychologists have even devoted their careers to specifying what skills (e.g., walking) and task performances (e.g., using thumb and forefinger to grasp a cube or other small object) can be expected to develop when. Perhaps the most notable of these was Arnold Gesell (1928; Gesell & Ilg, 1949), who meticulously specified a calendar of expected childhood accomplishments in a number of domains (e.g., motor skills and language achievements).

As with the development of most reflexes, the ages at which children develop particular motor skills bear little relation to their cognitive development or their future intelligence, *unless* the development of these skills falls far outside the normal range. For example, if particular 6-month-olds cannot lift their heads at the shoulders, 18-month-olds cannot crawl, or 4-year-olds cannot walk—and these children have no known motoric reason for this impairment—they may have serious impairments of the nervous system. Such impairments can have grave implications for children's cognitive development. In addition, although particular motor accomplishments do not directly correlate with particular cognitive changes, they do alter the way the child can interact with the environment, and these interactions may facilitate cognitive development.

Imagine yourself as an infant or young child, and describe your view of and experiences in the world before and after achieving one of the psychomotor developmental milestones. How would your opportunities for thinking about and interacting with your environment change?

Of the five questions posed at the outset of this chapter, the second one has prompted the most speculation and the most research: At what ages do infants, children, and adults demonstrate various kinds of thought and behavior? Despite many disagreements, most developmental psychologists would agree that the key to understanding cognitive development is not the identification of the specific ages at which children acquire particular cognitive capabilities, but rather the understanding of the developmental progression and unfolding of these abilities. They would urge you to notice the sequential process of building an edifice of cognition, rather than the date on which a particular brick was laid.

THEORIES OF COGNITIVE DEVELOPMENT

IN SEARCH OF...

After weighing the strengths and weaknesses of each of the following theories of cognitive development, think about which one seems most sensible. Why is this particular theory most reasonable to you?

No single theory has yet explained all aspects of cognitive development. The theories included here represent psychological theorists' best attempts to explain how human cognition develops. We now turn to the cognitive-development work of Jean Piaget and the "neo-Piagetians," Lev Vygotsky, and the information-processing theorists. After looking at these theorists' work, we briefly summarize how each would respond to the questions that opened this chapter. (For a brief summary of how each of the theories describes the characteristic progression of cognitive development, see Table 12-2. For an advance peek at how the various theorists might respond to the questions, see Table 12-3, at the conclusion of the theories section.)

TABLE 12-2
Characteristic Progression of Cognitive Development
The various theories of cognitive development offer complementary information regarding how cognitive development progresses from birth through adolescence.

Theorists	Birth to 1 Yr.	1 to 2 Yrs.	2 to 4 Yrs.	4 to 6 Yrs.	6 to 8 Yrs.	8 to 10 Yrs.	10 to 12 Yrs.	12 to 16 Yrs.
Bayley, Gesell, various psychometricians	Sensorimotor alertness and abilities; social imitation and then verbal and motor imitation		Persistence; verbal labeling, comprehension, fluency, and syntax	Abstract reasoning ability emerges. Cognitive abilities increase (e.g., manipulation of language, emergence of reading and writing skills, as well as quantitative skills).				
Piaget	Sensorimotor: builds on reflexive actions and acts to maintain or repeat interesting sensations (major accomplishment: object permanence)		Preoperational: intentional experimentation on physical objects, increasing thoughtful planning and internal representations of physical objects; has trouble decentering to consider more than one characteristic at a time (major accomplishment: language and conceptual development)		Concrete operations: increasingly sophisticated mental manipulations of the internal representations of concrete objects; can decenter to consider more than one characteristic at a time (major accomplishment: conservation of quantity)			Formal operations: abstract thought and logical reasoning (major accomplishment: systematic abstract reasoning)
Fifth-stage theorists	Sensorimotor (see Piaget)		Preoperational (see Piaget)		Concrete operations (see Piaget)			Formal operations (see Piaget)[a]
Vygotsky	Increasing internalization and increasing abilities within the zone of proximal development							
Information-processing theorists	Increasingly sophisticated encoding, combination, knowledge acquisition, self-monitoring, feedback. Increasing ability to distinguish appearances from reality, increasing verbal fluency and comprehension, increasing grasp of quantity. Increasing knowledge of, control over, and capacity in memory; increasing ability mentally to manipulate objects in space. Increasing control over strategies for solving problems; increasing ability to reason deductively, inductively, and analogically.							

[a] Fifth-stage theorists propose a stage of cognitive development that follows the period of formal operations. This fifth stage would be considered a stage of postformal thinking, characterized by the ability to handle ambiguities and contradictions in solving problems.

FIGURE 12-4
Landmarks of Motor Development

Although the ages at which infants achieve various psychomotor tasks may differ across individuals, the sequence of achievements hardly varies.

	Motor Behavior	Hand-Eye Coordination
	1 Month • Prefers to lie on back • Cannot hold head erect; head sags forward • Hands usually tightly fisted	• Looks at object held directly in line of vision • Grasps reflexively if object is placed in hand • Eyes begin to coordinate
	2–3 Months • When lying on stomach, can lift head 45° and extend legs • Head-bobbing gradually disappears; may hold head erect	• Follows objects visually within limited range • Looks at object but can grasp only by reflex
	4 Months • Can roll from back to side • When lying on stomach, can lift head 90°, arms and legs lift and extend • Can sit propped up for 10–15 minutes	• Follows objects with eyes through an arc of 180° • When presented with object, may touch or grasp it • Brings any object grasped to mouth
	5–6 Months • Can roll from back to stomach • May "bounce" when held standing	• Grasps small block using palmar grasp; little use of thumb or forefingers • Scratches at tiny objects but cannot pick them up • May hold own bottle with one or two hands
	7–8 Months • When lying on back, can lift feet to mouth • Can sit erect for a few minutes • May crawl • Can stand supporting full body weight on feet—if held up	• Can grasp a small block, or may transfer block from hand to hand • Likes banging objects to make noise
	9–10 Months • Creeps on hands and knees • Can sit indefinitely • Can pull self to standing position and may "cruise" by moving feet • By 10 months may be able to sit down from standing position	• Pokes at objects with forefinger • Can play pat-a-cake • May uncover toy he or she has seen hidden
	11 Months • Pulls self actively to feet and "cruises" along table or crib • May stand momentarily without support • Can walk if one hand is held; may take a few steps alone	• Can grasp small objects in a pincer grasp; can grasp larger objects using thumb opposition • May try to stack two blocks
	12 Months • Can get up without help and may take several steps alone • Can creep upstairs on hands and knees • May squat or stoop without losing balance • Can throw ball	• Helps turn pages of book • Can stack two blocks • Can find toy under box, cup, or cloth • Enjoys putting objects into containers and taking them out

The Cognitive Developmental Theory of Jean Piaget

It would be hard to overestimate the importance of Swiss psychologist Jean Piaget to developmental research. His theory is generally considered the most comprehensive theory of cognitive development. Although aspects of Piaget's theory have been questioned and in some cases have been disconfirmed, the theory is still enormously influential. Indeed, the contribution of his theory, like that of others, is shown more by its influence on further theory and research than by its precise accuracy.

Piaget first entered the field of cognitive development when, working as a graduate student in Alfred Binet's psychometric laboratory (see Binet, Chapter 11), he became intrigued with children's wrong answers to intelligence-test items. Piaget reasoned that researchers could learn as much about children's intellectual development from examining their incorrect answers to test items as from examining their correct answers. Through his repeated observations of children, including observations of his own children, and especially through investigation of their errors in reasoning, Piaget concluded that coherent logical systems underlie children's thought. These systems, he believed, differ in kind from those that adults use. If we are to understand development, we must identify these systems and their distinctive characteristics. In this section, we first consider some of Piaget's general principles of development and then look at the stages of development he proposed.

General Principles of Piaget's Developmental Theory

INTELLIGENCE. Piaget believed that the function of intelligence is to aid in adaptation to the environment. He rejected the delineation proposed by the Gestaltists (see Chapters 2 and 5) and others between "intelligent acts," which require insight or thought, and "nonintelligent acts," which are habits and reflexes (see Sternberg & Powell, 1983). Instead, Piaget preferred to think of a continuum of increasingly complex responses to the environment (Piaget, 1972). He further proposed that both intelligence and its manifestations become differentiated with age.

EQUILIBRATION. Although Piaget employed observation, much of his research was also a logical and philosophical exploration of how knowledge develops from primitive to sophisticated forms. He believed that development occurs in stages that evolve via

Jean Piaget (1896–1980) learned a great deal about how children think by observing his own children and by paying detailed attention to what appeared to be errors in their reasoning.

equilibration, in which children seek a balance (equilibrium) between what they encounter in their environments and what cognitive processes and structures they bring to the encounter, as well as among the cognitive capabilities themselves. Equilibration involves two processes: assimilation and accommodation. In some situations, the child's existing mode of thought and existing *schemas* (mental frameworks) are adequate for confronting and adapting to the challenges of the environment; the child is thus in a state of equilibrium.

At other times, however, information that does not fit with the child's existing schemas creates cognitive disequilibrium. The imbalance comes from shortcomings in thinking as the child encounters new challenges, and disequilibrium is more likely to occur during periods of stage transition. The child consequently attempts to restore equilibrium through **assimilation**—incorporating the new information into the child's existing schemas. Piaget would suggest that the child modifies existing schemas through **accommodation**—changing the existing schemas to fit the relevant new information about the environment. Together, the processes of assimilation and accommodation result in a more sophisticated level of thought than was previously possible. In addition, these processes result in the reestablishment of equilibrium and in offering the individual higher levels of adaptability.

Piaget's Stages of Development

According to Piaget, the equilibrative processes of assimilation and accommodation account for all of the changes associated with cognitive development. Although Piaget posited that these processes go on throughout childhood as we continually adapt to our environment, he also considered development to involve discrete, discontinuous stages. In particular, Piaget (1969, 1972) divided cognitive development into four main stages: the sensorimotor, the preoperational, the concrete-operational, and the formal-operational.

THE SENSORIMOTOR STAGE.   The first stage of development, the **sensorimotor stage,** involves the growth of sensory (input) and motor (output) abilities during infancy—roughly from birth to age 2. In the first month after birth, the infant responds primarily reflexively, such as through the reflexive schemas for sucking, grasping, orienting toward noises and other novel stimuli, and so on. According to Piaget, infants gradually modify these reflexive schemas to purposeful action as they adapt to their environments. During the next few months, infants repeat interesting effects they produce, such as a gurgling noise.

From ages 4 through 12 months, new actions involve repetitive behavior, but now the outcomes also may involve objects other than the child's own body (the "secondary" aspect of the reactions). For example, the infant might play with a ball or a mobile and watch what it does, again and again. Still, even these actions are largely a means of capitalizing on interesting events that happen by chance.

From 12 to 18 months, however, the infant actively searches for novel ways of relating to objects. The infant no longer waits for interesting things to happen by chance but rather makes them happen. Although the child repeats actions, he or she may modify them to achieve some desired effect, as in getting a mobile to swing in a certain preferred way. During this time, infants also actively experiment with the objects in their environments, just to see what *might* happen.

> Piaget had many insights into child development while observing his own three children. What are the potential advantages and disadvantages to this means of gaining insight into psychological processes?

Throughout these early phases of cognitive development, infant cognition seems to focus only on what the infants can immediately perceive through their senses. They do not conceive of anything that is not immediately perceptible to them. According to Piaget, infants do not have a sense of **object permanence,** by which objects continue to exist even when imperceptible to the infant. For example, before about 9 months of age, infants who observe an object being hidden from view will not seek the object once it is hidden from view. If a 4-month-old were to watch you hide a rattle beneath a blanket, the 4-month-old would not try to find the rattle beneath the blanket, whereas a 9-month-old would (Figure 12-5).

FIGURE 12-5
Object Permanence
Before about 9 months of age, infants do not yet realize that objects continue to exist even when they cannot be seen or heard. To this infant, once the turquoise monkey is out of sight, it no longer exists, so the infant loses all interest in it. An older infant would try to pursue the monkey behind the barrier.

To have a sense of object permanence requires some internal, mental representation of an object even when the object is not seen, heard, or otherwise perceived. By 18 to 24 months of age, in fact, children begin to show signs of **representational thought**—internal representations of external stimuli. In this ending of the sensorimotor stage, which is a transition to the preoperational stage, the child starts to be able to think about objects and people who are not necessarily immediately perceptible.

> Why did Piaget emphasize the importance of object permanence and internal mental representations? Why are they important?

As children grow older, they become less **egocentric**—that is, less focused on themselves. Note that egocentrism is a cognitive characteristic, not a personality trait. For example, early mental representations involve only the child, but later ones begin to involve other objects. Piaget viewed this early trend as indicative of a broader trend for children of all ages to become increasingly aware of the outer world and of how others perceive that world. (Egocentrism in interpersonal interactions is discussed in Chapter 13.)

THE PREOPERATIONAL STAGE.   In the **preoperational stage,** from roughly 2 to 7 years of age, the child begins actively to develop the internal mental representations that started at the end of the sensorimotor stage. With representational thought comes verbal communication. However, the communication is largely egocentric. A conversation may seem to have no coherence at all. Children say what is on their minds, pretty much without regard to what anyone else has said. As children develop, however, they increasingly take into account what others have said when forming their own comments and replies.

Many developmental changes occur during the preoperational stage. Children's active, intentional experimentation with language and with objects in their environments results in tremendous increases in conceptual and language development. These developments help to pave the way for the next stage of cognitive development.

THE CONCRETE-OPERATIONAL STAGE.   In the stage of **concrete operations,** from roughly ages 7 until 12 years, children become able to manipulate mentally the internal representations they formed during the preoperational period. They now not only have thoughts and memories of objects, but they also can perform mental operations on these thoughts and memories. However, they can do so only in regard to

concrete objects (e.g., thoughts and memories of cars, food, toys, and other tangible things).

Perhaps the most dramatic evidence of the change from preoperational thought to the representational thought of the concrete-operational stage is seen in Piaget's classic experiments (1952, 1954, 1969) on conservation, mentioned earlier in this chapter. Initially, children rely on their immediate perceptions of how things appear to be; gradually, they begin to formulate internal rules regarding how the world works; and eventually, they use these internal rules to guide their reasoning, rather than appearances alone.

Perhaps the most well-known Piagetian conservation experiment uses two beakers, demonstrating *conservation of liquid quantity* (Figure 12-6). The experimenter shows the child two short, stout beakers with liquid in them. The experimenter has the child verify that the two beakers contain the same amounts of liquid. Then, as the child watches, the experimenter pours the liquid from one beaker into a third beaker, which is taller and thinner than the other two. In the new beaker, the liquid in the narrower tube rises to a higher level than in the other still-full shorter beaker. When asked whether the amounts of liquid in the two full beakers are the same or different, the preoperational child says that there is now more liquid in the taller, thinner beaker because the liquid in that beaker reaches a perceptibly higher point. The preoperational child does not conceive that the amount is conserved despite the change in appearance. The concrete-operational child, on the other hand, says that the beakers contain the same amount of liquid, based on the child's internal schemas regarding the conservation of matter.

What can the concrete-operational child do that the preoperational child cannot? The concrete-operational child can manipulate internal images, mentally conserving the notion of amount and concluding that despite different physical appearances, the quantities are identical. Moreover, concrete-operational thinking is *reversible*. If the experimenter poured the liquid back into the small beaker, the concrete-operational child would still recognize it as the same amount. Note, however, that the operations are concrete—that is, the mental operations act on mental representations of actual physical events. The final stage of cognitive development, according to Piaget, involves going beyond these concrete operations and applying the same principles to abstract concepts.

Although children in the stage of concrete operations can readily grasp the principle of conservation when it is applied to concrete objects, they may encounter more difficulty when trying to manipulate mathematical concepts that are more abstract. The

FIGURE 12-6
Conservation of Liquid Quantity

This young boy is participating in the classic Piagetian task in which the researcher measures out equal quantities of liquid into two identical short stout beakers, then pours from one of the beakers into a tall thin beaker. Still in the preoperational stage, this boy cannot yet conserve liquid quantity, so he does not recognize that the quantity is conserved, despite superficial changes in the appearance of the amount. In the final photo, he asserts that the tall thin beaker contains more liquid than the short stout beaker. Once this boy reaches the stage of concrete operations, he will readily conserve.

following excerpt from Norton Juster's children's classic, *The Phantom Tollbooth*, illustrates some of the difficulties a young child might experience when trying to conserve distances (length) as measured in various units of measurement:

Up ahead, the road divided into three [and] an enormous road sign, pointing in all three directions, stated clearly:

DIGITOPOLIS

5	Miles
1,600	Rods
8,800	Yards
26,400	Feet
316,800	Inches
633,600	Half inches

"Let's travel by miles," advised the Humbug; "it's shorter."
"Let's travel by half inches," suggested Milo; "it's quicker."

THE FORMAL-OPERATIONAL STAGE.   The **formal-operational stage,** from roughly 11 or 12 years of age onward, involves mental operations on abstractions and symbols that may not have any physical and concrete forms. Moreover, children begin to understand some things that they have not directly experienced themselves (Inhelder & Piaget, 1958). During the stage of concrete operations, children begin to be able to see the perspective of others if the alternative perspective can be concretely manipulated. During formal operations, however, children are finally fully able to take perspectives other than their own even when they are not working with concrete objects. Furthermore, those in the formal-operations stage purposefully seek to create a systematic mental representation of situations they confront.

According to Piaget (1972), during the formal-operational stage, people first become able to conceive of **second-order relations**—that is, relations between relations. For example, in the stage of formal operations, children realize that not only do they have parents (first-order relationships) but that all children have parents (second-order relationships—I am to my parents as other children are to their parents). Eventually, they become able to see second-order relations in the mathematical domain as well, such as being able to draw a parallel between the inverse relations of addition and subtraction, on the one hand, and multiplication and division, on the other.

They can now see not only how two individual objects are related, but also how two sets of objects are related (as in reasoning by analogy). (See Table 12-2 for a summary of Piaget's stages.)

In sum, Piaget's theory of cognitive development involves stages that occur in a fixed order and are irreversible: Once a child enters into a new stage, he or she never regresses. Other theorists would disagree with this view; among other things, observations of some elderly persons seem to discredit the view that regression never occurs. To Piaget, however, stages occur at roughly the same ages for different children, and each stage builds on the preceding stage.

Evaluation of Piaget's Theory

Piaget contributed enormously to our understanding of cognitive development. His work continues to have great impact on psychology. His major contribution was in prompting us to view children in a new light and to ponder the way children think. As a scientist, Piaget knew his work would not be an endpoint of investigation, but rather a beginning of an entire field of investigation. Others who have followed him have profited from his work and his insights, although their investigations have led them to question many of his specific conclusions and even some of his observations. To give you a fuller perspective on Piaget's place in the field of developmental psychology, we must consider a few of the major criticisms of Piaget's theory.

First, as suggested earlier, many developmental theorists question Piaget's fundamental assumption that development occurs in discontinuous stages. Many believe that development is at least partly continuous (e.g., Brainerd, 1978). Second, theorists have questioned Piaget's view of what causes difficulty for children in particular tasks (as discussed further later in this chapter). Third, theorists have questioned the accuracy of Piaget's estimates of the ages at which particular accomplishments can first be made. In general, the trend has been toward demonstrating that children can do things at ages earlier than Piaget had thought (see, e.g., Baillargeon, 1987; R. Gelman & Baillargeon, 1983). Fourth, at the other end of the spectrum, some adolescents and adults do not show formal-operational thinking under all circumstances (Neimark, 1975). In fact, most of us demonstrate a wide range of performance, so that what we may be optimally capable of doing may often differ from what we actually do most of the time. Theorists who emphasize context in cognitive development believe that we humans are not as scientific as Piaget would

have us believe, and that there is more to cognition than scientific or logical thinking.

A fifth criticism of Piaget has been that his work largely centered on children in Western cultures, so it is difficult to know whether his findings would apply to children in non-Western cultures. Several cross-cultural studies have indicated that although the sequence of the early Piagetian stages seems to be confirmed by cross-cultural research, the specific age ranges hypothesized for many of the stages may vary across cultures. For example, in a review of more than 50 studies (Werner, 1972), infants in non-Western societies (e.g., in sub-Saharan Africa and in some Asian and Latin American countries) generally demonstrated psychomotor accomplishments at earlier ages than did infants in Western societies.

Cross-cultural research shows that children may pass thorough the Piagetian stages of cognitive development at different ages, perhaps due to variations in environment. Nonetheless, some researchers believe that all children pass through the same sequence of stages and show the same patterns of cognitive development, as shown by the cross-cultural similarity of many children's games (e.g., jumping rope or acting out the rhythmic patterns of chants).

Most cross-cultural psychologists attribute the disparities in achievement to environmental, experiential differences, rather than to hereditary differences. In addition, some researchers have questioned the universality of Piaget's later stages. For example, in some non-Western cultures, neither adolescents nor adults seem to demonstrate the cognitive characteristics of Piaget's stage of formal operations, and some adults do not even demonstrate mastery of the relatively symbolic aspects of the Piagetian stage of concrete operations (see Dasen & Heron, 1981). In 1972, Piaget modified his own theory to acknowledge that the stage of formal operations may be more a product of an individual's domain-specific expertise, based on experience, rather than on the maturational processes of cognitive development.

Neo-Piagetian Theorists

Neo-Piagetian theories are based on a broad understanding of Piaget's theory of cognitive development. These theorists do not fully accept Piaget's theory, but have decided to modify and build upon the theory rather than reject it. Although each neo-Piagetian is different, most (a) accept Piaget's broad notion of developmental stages of cognitive development; (b) concentrate on the scientific or logical aspects of cognitive development (often observing children engage in much the same tasks as those used by Piaget); and (c) retain some ties with the notion that cognitive development occurs through equilibration. Of the many neo-Piagetian theorists, we briefly consider here only a few, namely, those proposing a fifth stage of development beyond formal operations.

Fifth-stage theorists do not posit an entirely different theory of cognitive development; instead, they build on Piaget's four stages by suggesting a fifth stage of development. Patricia Arlin (1975) proposes that a fifth stage of cognitive development is **problem finding.** In this stage, individuals master the tasks of figuring out exactly what problems face them and deciding which ones are most important to solve.

Several theorists have suggested that logical reasoning beyond Piagetian formal operations might proceed to a fifth stage of **dialectical thinking.** It recognizes that in much of life, there is no one final,

Some neo-Piagetians propose a fifth stage of cognitive development, in which individuals recognize that many real-life situations pose multiple problems and opportunities, for which there will not be one clear answer. Often, what is needed is to consider various alternatives and then to choose what seems to be the best option for the situation, recognizing that other possibilities may have offered other benefits. In deciding which route to take, these hikers must figure out which route offers them the best combination of advantages, realizing that they may miss some appealing landmarks or other benefits along the route not traveled.

correct answer, but rather a progression of beliefs whereby we first propose some kind of thesis, then later see its antithesis, and finally effect some kind of synthesis between the two, which then serves as the new thesis for the continuing evolution of thought. Psychologists such as Deirdre Kramer (1990), Gisela Labouvie-Vief (1980, 1990), Juan Pascual-Leone (1984, 1990), and Klaus Riegel (1973) assert that after the stage of formal operations, we reach a stage of **postformal thinking,** in which we recognize the constant unfolding and evolution of thought—the dialectic originally proposed by philosopher Georg Hegel. Postformal thought allows adults to manipulate mentally the vagaries and inconsistencies of everyday situations, in which simple, unambiguous answers rarely are available. Through postformal thinking, we can consider and choose among alternatives, recognizing that other alternatives may offer benefits not obtainable from the chosen one.

> What evidence do you see regarding a fifth stage of cognitive development? Do you see evidence of developmental differences between older adults and young adolescents? Give specific examples from your observations of people that would support or refute the notion of a fifth stage of cognitive development.

The Cognitive Developmental Theory of Lev Vygotsky

Cognitive developmental theorist Lev Vygotsky died tragically of tuberculosis at age 38. Despite his early demise, Vygotsky's stature in developmental psychology is comparable to that of Piaget. The importance of this Russian psychologist has increased in recent years. Whereas Piaget dominated developmental psychology in the 1960s and 1970s, Vygotsky was rediscovered in the late 1970s and 1980s, and continues to be influential. Although Vygotsky had many fertile ideas, two of them are particularly important for us to consider here: internalization and the zone of proximal development.

Internalization

In Piaget's theory, cognitive development proceeds largely "from the inside out" through maturation. Environments can foster or impede development, but Piaget emphasizes the biological and hence the maturational aspect of development. In contrast to Piaget's inside-out approach, Vygotsky (1962, 1978) emphasizes the role of the environment in children's intellectual development. He posits that development

Many of the ideas about how children think that were proposed by cognitive-developmental theorist Lev Vygotsky (1896–1934) have been important not only to psychologists but also to educators.

proceeds largely from the outside in, through **internalization**—the absorption of knowledge from context. Thus, social rather than biological influences are key in Vygotsky's theory.

Every day, at home, in school, and on the street, children listen to what people say and how they say it, and watch what people do and why they do it. Then they internalize what they see, making it their own. They re-create within themselves the kinds of conversations and other interactions they see in their world. According to Vygotsky, then, much of a child's learning occurs through his or her interactions within the environment, which largely determine what the child internalizes.

The Zone of Proximal Development

Vygotsky's (1962, 1978) second major contribution to educational and developmental psychology is his construct of the **zone of proximal development** (ZPD) (sometimes termed the *zone of potential development*). The ZPD is the range of ability between a child's observable level of ability and the child's latent capacity, which is not directly obvious. When we observe children, what we typically observe is the ability that they have developed through the interaction of heredity and environment. To a large extent, however, we are truly interested in what children are capable of doing—what their potential would be if they were freed from the confines of an environment that is never truly optimal. Before Vygotsky, people were unsure of how to measure this latent capacity.

Vygotsky argued that we need to reconsider not only how we think about children's cognitive abilities, but also how we measure them. Typically, we test children in a **static assessment environment,** in which an examiner asks questions and expects the child to answer them. Whether the child responds correctly or incorrectly, the examiner moves to the next question or task on the list of items in the test. Vygotsky recommended instead that we move to a **dynamic assessment environment,** in which the interaction between child and examiner does not end when the child responds, especially not if the child responds incorrectly. In dynamic assessment, when the child gives a wrong answer, the examiner gives the child a sequence of guided and graded hints to facilitate problem solving. In other words, the examiner serves as both teacher and tester. The examiner is particularly interested in the child's ability to use hints. The ability to use hints is the basis for measuring the ZPD because this ability indicates the extent to which the child can expand beyond her or his observable abilities at the time of testing. Several tests have been created to measure the ZPD (e.g., Brown & French, 1979; Campione, 1989; Campione & Brown, 1990), the most well-known of which is Reuven Feuerstein's *Learning Potential Assessment Device* (1979).

The ZPD is one of the more exciting concepts in cognitive-developmental psychology, because it enables us to probe beyond a child's observed performance. Moreover, the combination of testing and teaching appeals to many psychologists and educators. Educators, psychologists, and other researchers have been captivated by Vygotsky's notion that we can extend and facilitate children's development of cognitive abilities.

> Design a problem-solving task for which you could provide a series of graded hints to help a child solve the problem within the child's ZPD.

Extensions of Vygotsky

Feuerstein (1980) has extended Vygotsky's work by highlighting the role of parents in facilitating their children's learning through *mediated learning experiences* (MLE; see Chapter 11). Through such experi-

ences, an adult may introduce a child to an interesting environment (such as a museum) or task (such as how to cook) and then enhance the child's ability to learn by interpreting the experience through language the child understands.

An alternative to MLE is *direct instruction,* in which the adult directly tells the child specific information that the child is to learn. In particular, direct instruction may be used to help children acquire *tacit knowledge* (Polanyi, 1976; Wagner & Sternberg, 1985), which is information that is not explicitly stated, but that may be helpful to know in order to thrive in an environment. Among other things, students benefit from being explicitly taught to understand their own learning styles, to build on their own existing knowledge base, to use memory and problem-solving strategies, to search for key ideas in text, to represent conceptual information comprehensibly, to participate appropriately in class discussions, and so on. As shown by the studies of MLE and direct instruction of tacit knowledge, Vygotsky's ideas have prompted both additional practical applications and further investigations regarding our fundamental understandings of how cognition develops.

The power of Piaget and Vygotsky lay in their interest in probing beneath the surface to try to understand why children behave and respond as they do. As is true of almost any significant contribution to science, the ideas of Vygotsky and of Piaget are measured more by how much they prompt us to extend our knowledge than by how perfectly they have represented a complete, final understanding of a concept. Perhaps the most we can ask of a theory is to be worthy of further exploration.

Information-Processing Theories of Cognitive Development

Information-processing theorists seek to understand cognitive development in terms of how people of different ages process information (i.e., decode, encode, transfer, combine, store, and retrieve information), particularly when solving challenging mental problems. Information-processing theorists make no claim to providing as comprehensive an explanation of cognitive development as did Piaget, but they do consider the entire range of mental processes that persons of all ages use to manipulate information. Any mental activity that involves noticing, taking in, mentally manipulating, storing, combining, retrieving, or acting on information falls within the purview of information-processing theory.

When we turn the focus of information-processing theory to the topic of cognitive development, we ask, how do our processes, strategies, or ways of representing and organizing information change over time, if at all? If there are changes, what might cause the changes? These and related questions form the basis for the information-processing approach to cognitive development.

Information-processing theorists, as noted earlier in this chapter, take one of two fundamental approaches to studying information processing: a primarily domain-general or a primarily domain-specific approach. Theorists believing in domain generality try to describe how we mentally process information. They want to show how general principles of information processing apply and are used across a variety of cognitive functions, from learning new words to reading maps to solving calculus problems. Theorists believing in domain specificity focus on explaining processes within one specific realm—what happens when people read, for example. In this section, we first look at domain-general types of theories, and we examine general information-processing models of cognitive development. Then we turn to domain-specific research and theories, where we look at more specific domains in which information processing develops.

A Domain-General Theory of the Development of Information Processing

Of the various general information-processing theories of cognitive development, only a few describe specific mechanisms by which development occurs. Here, we consider briefly one general information-processing view that proposes specific mechanisms of development. This theory posits processes that both children and adults use when developing their intellectual skills throughout their lives.

The theory emphasizes two processes for dealing with new information: encoding and combination (Siegler, 1984). **Encoding**, as we have seen in the memory and language chapters, essentially means mentally taking in and making sense of the features of the world. As children age, they can encode more fully many features of their environment, and they organize their encodings more effectively. As you might guess, **combination** means putting together encoded pieces of information. As children grow older and gain more experience, they are better able to see relations among the pieces of information they have taken in, and they therefore combine information more effectively. In regard to memory, recall that the use of chunking effectively combines separate small chunks of information into larger chunks, which can then be remembered more easily. Thus, as we effectively combine small chunks of data into increasingly large chunks, we are better able to keep

them in memory and thereby to manipulate that information in other ways.

> In what specific ways do you seek feedback and implement changes in response to feedback when writing term papers and reports? What specific strategies for self-monitoring do you use when studying for tests?

The theory of Robert Siegler attempts to depict human intellectual development in terms of the general mechanisms for processing information that change as a person grows older. These mechanisms apply across all domains of information processing. As mentioned, however, other information-processing theorists intensively study abilities within particular domains. Next, we consider some of these specific intellectual domains in which cognitive development occurs.

Development of Information Processing in Specific Domains

We can understand the domains that information-processing theorists study by tracking how humans process information. First, we notice or *perceive* particular stimuli or other information in our environments. Then, we relate the new information to the information we already have stored in *memory*. Next, we figure out how to process the information, based on the form in which we receive the information—that is, *verbal* (words and similar conceptual information), *quantitative* (numbers and operations on numbers), or *visuospatial* (figures, shapes, forms, positions, locations, rotations, perspectives, and any other information about objects in space). Finally, we use the information to *solve problems* and to make judgments and decisions (e.g., through *deductive* or *inductive reasoning*).

PERCEPTUAL SKILLS. Even in infancy, children show remarkable skill at perceiving the world around them. To learn about the world, infants need to know where and how to pay attention to stimuli. They seem to be surprisingly competent in doing so. Various explanations have been suggested for how they attend so effectively to the important changes in the environment, such as the rules for scanning and the orienting reflex, mentioned earlier in this chapter. The cause of these perceptual preferences is not entirely clear. What is clear is that infants' perceptual abilities are well developed at birth.

Furthermore, these perceptual abilities develop rapidly to enable babies to learn a great deal about

Searchers . . .   *JOHN FLAVELL*

John Flavell is Professor of Psychology at Stanford University.

Q: *How did you become interested in psychology in general and in your area of work in particular?*

A: In college I was first a pre-med major, and then I took an introductory psych course in my sophomore or junior year and really liked it. I went on to get a clinical psych degree, but in a place, Clark University, that was strong on developmental as well. I was a clinical psychologist for a while, then taught both clinical and developmental, and gradually just did developmental.

Q: *What theories, or whose ideas, have influenced you the most?*

A: Principally Heinz Werner, who was my teacher at Clark. He is an Old World developmental psychologist, kind of a Piaget type. Then, of course, Jean Piaget himself: I read his work extensively and wrote a book about him. Also James Jenkins, a cognitive psychologist now at Florida, introduced me to Noam Chomsky, psycholinguistics, and cognitive psychology.

Q: *What is your greatest asset as a psychologist?*

A: Intuition. I have an originality and creativity for certain kinds of things.

Q: *What distinguishes a great psychologist from just a good psychologist?*

A: Certainly vision. Having some picture of how things could go that's different from what other people have. Chomsky is a wonderful example. And certainly originality, being a pioneer.

Q: *How do you get your ideas for research?*

A: I'm not always sure where they come from. Almost always they grow out of previous work. I also spend quite a lot of time thinking, with just a pad and pencil, mulling over things. Also talking with my research colleagues, Frances Green and Ellie Flavell. If an idea feels right and is something that people really haven't followed before, then I'll tend to pursue it. The three of us often have a lot of research ideas we could be pursuing, and we decide one is more important than another.

Q: *What is your major contribution to psychology?*

A: There are two of them. One, which is indirect, is that I helped make Piaget available to people. My biography of him helped get people interested in his work. The other one has to do with one or another form of understanding in children, the development of knowledge about the mind, basically. Early on, it was on role taking; later it became meta-memory, meta-cognition; now, the theory of mind development is the current vogue. And I worked on all three of those. They're really the same thing, just different research traditions and different ways of looking at them.

Q: *What do you want your students to learn?*

A: To really stretch their thinking, to spend time thinking and not just reading and doing what someone else has done. I convey enthusiasm for research and try to get them to be enthusiastic too. I would like to be a model that they will emulate, in that they will be considerate and available to their students, as I try to be.

Q: *How do you keep yourself academically challenged?*

A: By doing the things that I've been doing. I like teaching. I like doing research. I like working with students and other colleagues on research. I enjoy going to talks about things I haven't known before.

Q: *What would you like people to remember about you and your work?*

A: Well, that I was no genius, but I certainly contributed something to our understanding of cognitive development.

Q: *What do you further hope to achieve?*

A: I plan to continue to do research on the theory of mind development until it seems to be unprofitable or seems to be not panning out, and doesn't any longer seem to be where I want to be.

---

the world. For example, in one study, children as young as 4 months were shown two movies (Spelke, 1976). In one, a woman was playing and saying "peek-a-boo." In the other film, the child saw a hand holding a stick and rhythmically striking a wooden block. The catch was that the baby was shown the film either with its corresponding sound track, or with the other movie's sound track. Infants spent more time looking at the picture if the sound corresponded to it. In other words, even at 4 months, children can match visual and auditory stimuli.

Information-processing researchers also have been interested in the perceptual skills of older children, such as their perceptions of appearance and reality. For example, children of 4 and 5 years of age were shown imitation objects such as a sponge that looked exactly like a rock (Flavell, Flavell, & Green, 1983). The researchers encouraged the children to become thoroughly familiar with the objects. Children then had to answer questions about the objects. Afterward, the children were asked to view the objects through a blue plastic sheet and to make color judgments about the objects; they also were asked to make size judgments while viewing the objects through a magnifying glass. The children were fully aware that they were viewing the objects through these intermediaries.

The children's errors formed an interesting pattern. They made two fundamental kinds of errors. On the one hand, when asked to report the reality (the way the object actually was), the children would sometimes report the appearance (the way the object looked). Conversely, when asked to report the appearance of the objects, they would sometimes report the reality. In other words, they did not yet clearly perceive the distinction between appearance and reality.

MEMORY.   As you might expect, memory is better in older children than in younger children (see Kail, 1984). The differences in gross memory capacity are obvious, but factors other than physiological ones may also play a role in children's performance on memory tasks. For example, recall from Chapter 8 that the way we organize information plays a powerful role in memory. In particular, we know that when we are knowledgeable about an area, and we can collect many small bits of information into larger chunks, we can more easily recall the information.

Although many information-processing theorists and other researchers have been interested in the effects of content knowledge on cognitive development, some of the most fascinating work has focused more on the strategies children use in regard to memory. One particular line of memory-development research has sparked great interest: **metamemory**—knowing about and controlling our own memory (Flavell, 1976, 1981; Flavell & Wellman, 1977). For example, young children seriously overestimate their ability to recall information, and they rarely spontaneously use rehearsal strategies when asked to recall items. That is, young children seem not to know about many memory-enhancing strategies. In addition, even when they do know about strategies, they do not always use them. For example, even when trained to use rehearsal strategies in one task, most do not transfer the use of that strategy to other tasks (Flavell & Wellman, 1977). (Recall from Chapter 8 that mentally retarded children show a similar lack of transfer.) Thus, it appears that young children lack not only the knowledge of strategies but also the inclination to use them when they do know about them. Children improve in metamemory skills with age, al-

though generally, metamemory is not a particularly good predictor of memory skills (Flavell, 1985; Flavell & Wellman, 1977).

Cross-cultural comparisons of Western and non-Western children support the thesis that culture, experience, and environmental demands affect the use of memory-enhancing strategies. For example, Western children, who generally have more formal schooling than non-Western children do, are given much more practice using rehearsal strategies for remembering isolated bits of information. In contrast, Guatemalan children and Australian aboriginal children generally have many more opportunities to become adept at using memory-enhancing strategies that rely on spatial location and arrangements of objects (Kearins, 1981; Rogoff, 1986).

VERBAL COMPREHENSION AND FLUENCY. Chapter 9 described language acquisition in detail, so we only summarize it briefly here. Recall that **verbal comprehension** is the ability to comprehend written and spoken materials, such as words, sentences, and paragraphs; and **verbal fluency** is the ability to produce such materials. In general, children's ability to process information efficiently (comprehend) increases with age (e.g., Hunt, Lunneberg, & Lewis, 1975; Keating & Bobbitt, 1978). Older children also demonstrate greater verbal fluency than do younger children (e.g., Sincoff & Sternberg, 1988). In addition to the increases in verbal comprehension and fluency abilities that develop with age, we can best understand development by looking not simply at a child's age, but also at the strategy a child of a given age uses to comprehend or generate verbal material. Much of what develops is not just verbal ability but also the ability to generate useful strategies, such as comprehension monitoring.

An interesting aspect of research on strategies of verbal comprehension has been research on **comprehension monitoring** (Markman, 1977, 1979). Consider a typical experiment. Children between the ages of 8 and 11 years heard passages containing contradictory information. This description of how to make the dessert Baked Alaska is an example:

> To make it they put the ice cream in a very hot oven. The ice cream in Baked Alaska melts when it gets that hot. Then they take the ice cream out of the oven and serve it right away. When they make Baked Alaska, the ice cream stays firm and does not melt. (Markman, 1979, p. 656)

Note that the passage contains a blatant internal contradiction, saying both that the ice cream melts and that it does not. Almost half of the young

Searchers . . .   *ROCHEL GELMAN*

Rochel Gelman is Professor of Psychology and Chair of the Developmental area at the University of California, Los Angeles.

Q: *How did you become interested in psychology and in your area in particular?*

A: I liked my first year undergraduate course and so entered the honors program in psychology at the University of Toronto.

Q: *What is your greatest asset as a psychologist?*

A: To build a systematic line of work and to stick with it. Another important one is to watch kids closely and to ask about abilities in a different way, to let them show me something and then go after it.

Q: *What distinguishes a really great psychologist from just a good one?*

A: I think the great psychologists are those who both pick a problem that has lasting significance and stick to it; as well as being able to develop the idea with a cumulative data base, a coherent theory, and be responsive to what's happening, so they end up with a more coherent account of a phenomenon of the mind.

Q: *How do you decide whether to pursue an idea?*

A: Ideas come when I write, mainly because I see holes both in what I'm writing and in experimental data that I have. That is a very salient way for me to decide to do an experiment. So is reading because it leads me to think about things. Finally, I run a lab with graduate students who are all thinking about the same kinds of issues. It is a guarantee of new ideas.

Q: *What is your major contribution to psychology?*

A: I think the major contribution has been to turn attention from description of young children in negative terms to positive terms. To focus on what they are capable of doing as well as what their limits are. Related to that is a theoretical perspective that focuses on domain-specific knowledge, first principles, skeletal understanding, which recognizes the tendencies of kids to take from their environment.

Q: *What do you want students to learn from you?*

A: I want them to be independent, to be known for their own contributions. I want them to be ethical researchers and committed teachers. I want them to think of themselves as researchers as well as scholars. I also want them in turn to train students who become contributors to the field, and that has clearly happened. I consider that a major accomplishment.

Q: *What advice would you give to someone starting in the field of psychology?*

A: Never hesitate to knock on somebody's door. So few undergraduates do so. If you are really interested in an individual's work, the odds are high that you'll get attention and eventually work with them in the lab if you want. The other thing I really work on is getting them to write coherent pieces.

Q: *What did you learn from your mentors?*

A: To be available for conversations, be in my office with the door open, having fixed meetings every week with each student, or using e-mail. Encourage people never to be embarrassed to ask.

Q: *What would you like people to remember about you and your work?*

A: That I started a line of inquiry that has a rather surprising conclusion: that people can do a reasonable amount of arithmetic with or without schooling.

Q: *What do you further hope to achieve?*

A: Helping set up curricula that will enhance literacy in mathematics and science. For example, in Los Angeles students have to take a certain amount of math and science to be on any good career path. Yet the school systems tend to be set up to minimize their chances. Students who don't speak English have had to take English courses before they took science. Well that slows down the rate they can get into science courses. So we have put a science curriculum into their English classes, based on principles of cognitive development. They can now move into science more quickly, and so far it looks like that's what's happening.

---

children who saw this passage did not notice the contradiction at all. Even when they were warned in advance about problems with the story, many of the youngest children still did not detect the inconsistency. Thus, young children are not very successful at comprehension monitoring, even when cued to be aware of inconsistencies in the text they read.

QUANTITATIVE SKILLS.   Several lines of cognitive-development research have studied the quantitative skills of young children. One line of research has dealt with simple number understanding (as shown by counting) and arithmetic computation. The ability to count objects—and thereby to conserve number—is one of the earliest indications of children's quantitative skills and their conceptions of number. Five principles may underlie children's ability to count, particularly how to count and what to count (R. Gelman & C. R. Gallistel, 1978). The first three deal with the "how" of counting, the fourth with the "what," and the last combines both. Rochel Gelman and C. R. Gallistel (1978) consider Piagetian descriptions of the numerical abilities of young children to have generally underestimated those abilities. They conclude that many 2- and 3-year-olds may not be able to count more than three or four items, but nevertheless, they can differentiate when making judgments about unknown quantities. For example, toddlers may not be able to count to 100, but they know that 100 cookies are more than 20 cookies. Thus, even very young children have some rudimentary counting abilities, not considered in Piagetian accounts.

VISUOSPATIAL SKILLS.   We now shift our focus from principles of algebra (and rules for arithmetic computation of quantities) to understandings that form the basis for geometry. Underlying such understanding is **spatial visualization**—our ability to orient ourselves in our surroundings, or the ability mentally to manipulate images of objects. Although several studies have examined spatial visualization in children (e.g., Huttenlocher & Presson, 1973; Marmor, 1975, 1977), just one typical example of this research is summarized here.

Subjects in grades 3, 4, and 6, and in college judged whether pairs of stimuli were identical or were mirror-image reversals of each other (Kail, Pellegrino & Carter, 1980). One stimulus in each pair was presented in an upright position and the other was rotated from the standard upright position. The pairs comprising each stimulus item were either alphanumeric symbols—such as 4, 5, F, and G—or unfamiliar abstract geometric forms. Robert Kail and his colleagues found that the speed of mental rotation increases with age and with the degree of familiarity of the objects. Thus, older subjects can mentally rotate more quickly, and all subjects can rotate familiar objects more quickly than they can rotate unfamiliar ones.

The findings raised several questions, two of which particularly intrigued researchers. First, why might the rate of mental rotation increase with age? The researchers suggested that younger children must rotate the entire stimulus, whereas older children rotate stimuli more analytically, so that they rotate each component separately and may need only to rotate a part of the stimulus. Thus, the change in cognitive development may involve more than a sim-

ple change in processing speed. Second, why did subjects encode and rotate the unusual geometric forms more slowly than the familiar, alphanumeric ones? The difference might be due to the activation of an already existing, easily accessible pattern in memory for the familiar characters, in contrast to the requirement that the subjects form a new memory pattern for the unfamiliar stimuli. (Recall from Chapter 8 that most information-processing theorists view memory as a network of information; various nodes on a given network can then be activated through the spreading activation of related information.)

PROBLEM SOLVING.   Many psychologists have worked on problem solving in children. Here, we focus on one particularly interesting line of research, on balance-scale problems (Siegler, 1976, 1978). In the balance-scale task, children see a balance scale with four equally spaced pegs on each side. The arms of the balance scale can fall down to the left or right or they can remain even, depending on the distribution of weights. The child's task is to predict which (if either) side of the balance scale will descend if a lever that holds the scale motionless is released.

Siegler (1976) combined Barbel Inhelder and Piaget's (1958) analysis of the problem with his own to formulate four rules to govern the solution of balance-scale problems. At first, children consider only the number of weights, not the distance from the fulcrum, in their predictions. Gradually, children use more complex rules as they grow older, with more complex rules defined as those that take into account more information than is present in the problem situation (e.g., discerning a relationship between the distance from the fulcrum and the weight).

DEDUCTIVE REASONING.   Recall from Chapter 10 that in *deductive reasoning*, the premises of a problem contain the information needed to arrive at a logically correct solution, and the reasoning must proceed from the general to the specific to deduce the answer logically. An important kind of deduction is *transitive inference*, which involves a chain of reasoning in which the reasoner must infer the relation between two objects that are not explicitly linked, based on the relations between objects that are explicitly linked. For example, "María is taller than Sandra. Sandra is taller than Roxanne. Who is tallest?" is a transitive-inference problem.

The developmental research on transitive inference has focused on two key questions: (1) When does the ability to make transitive inferences first appear? (2) How do children of different ages actually make transitive inferences, and what contexts would increase the likelihood of their doing so? If we can gain insight into the developmental progression of transitive inference, we may better understand how children come to reason deductively.

Originally, Piaget (1928, 1955) proposed that children cannot make transitive inferences until the stage of concrete operations at about the age of 8 years. In fact, transitivity has often been used by Piagetian psychologists as a test to determine whether children have yet reached the stage of concrete operations.

In contrast to the Piagetian view, some information-processing theorists have proposed that limitations on memory, not on reasoning, explain the failure of preoperational children to solve transitive-inference problems. For example, Peter Bryant and Tom Trabasso (1971) showed that it is possible to train children who are identified as preoperational to solve transitive-inference problems by showing them how to use memory-enhancing strategies.

INDUCTIVE REASONING.   Recall from Chapter 10 that *inductive reasoning* does not lead to a single, logically certain solution to a problem, but only to solutions that have different levels of plausibility. In inductive reasoning, the reasoner induces general principles, based on specific observations.

Susan Gelman (1985; S. Gelman & Markman, 1987) has noted that children even as young as 3 years of age seem to induce some general principles from specific observations, particularly those principles that pertain to categories for animals. For example (S. Gelman & Kremer, 1991), preschoolers were able to induce principles that correctly attribute the cause of phenomena (such as growth) to natural processes rather than to human intervention. Preschoolers also were able to reason correctly that a blackbird was more likely to behave like a flamingo than like a bat because blackbirds and flamingos are both birds (S. Gelman & Markman, 1987). Note that in this example, preschoolers are going against their perception that blackbirds look more like bats than like flamingos, basing their judgment instead on the fact that they are both birds (although the effect is admittedly strongest when the term *bird* is also used in regard to both the flamingo and the blackbird).

To summarize these findings, it appears that once again, early developmental psychologists may have underestimated the cognitive capabilities of young children. In addition, a supportive context for induction can greatly enhance children's ability to induce appropriate principles (Keil, 1989). Nonetheless, there does appear to be a developmental trend toward increasing sophistication in inducing general principles from specific information and toward in-

creasing reliance on more subtle features of the information on which such inductions are based.

Considering the Four Perspectives

The preceding theories of cognitive development (Piagetian, neo-Piagetian, Vygotskyan, and information-processing theories) are all influential in psychology. They are not mutually exclusive, however; some have been pursued simultaneously, some have evolved as reactions to others, and some are offshoots of others. Table 12-3 summarizes some of the ways these theories relate to one another. These theories of cognitive development, and of other important issues in psychology, all contribute to the ongoing dialectical process of understanding how and why we humans think, feel, and behave as we do.

COGNITIVE DEVELOPMENT IN ADULTHOOD

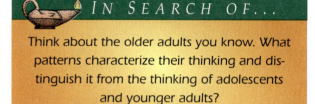

IN SEARCH OF...

Think about the older adults you know. What patterns characterize their thinking and distinguish it from the thinking of adolescents and younger adults?

Thus far, this chapter has focused primarily on cognitive development in children. The field of psychological development, however, does not stop at adolescence. Many psychologists study **life-span development**—the changes in abilities that occur over a lifetime. Before we close this chapter, we look at adult and life-span cognitive development.

Neurological Changes

In addition to the good news associated with our increasing cognitive capabilities, one developmental trend in our physiology brings bad news. Between our peak of neural growth (in early adulthood) and about age 80 years, we lose about 5% of our brain weight. Nonetheless, our continually increasing neural connections (as long as we remain mentally active) help to compensate for our cell loss (Coleman & Flood, 1986).

Patterns of Growth and Decline

Is cognitive growth never-ending? Do scores on cognitive-abilities tests continue to increase indefinitely?

TABLE 12-3
Summary of Theories of Cognitive Development
How do the theories presented in this chapter address the issues of nature versus nurture, continuity versus discontinuity, domain generality versus domain specificity, and the nature of the developmental process?

Theory	Nature or Nurture?	Continuous or Discontinuous (Stages)?	Domain General or Domain Specific?	Process By Which Development Occurs?
Piaget	Biological maturation is crucial; environment plays a secondary but important role	Four stages	Development largely occurs simultaneously across domains, although some domains may show change slightly ahead of others	Equilibrative processes of assimilation and accommodation
Neo-Piagetians	May emphasize role of the environment somewhat more than Piaget did	May add a fifth stage; may question the ages for particular stages suggested by Piaget	Same as Piaget (i.e., development largely occurs simultaneously across domains, although some domains may show change slightly ahead of others)	Same as Piaget
Vygotsky	Social and physical environment plays a crucial role; maturational readiness may provide the broad parameters (zone of proximal development) within which the social environment determines development	Continuous	The zone of proximal development may apply to many domains, but the environment may provide sufficient support for development only in specific domains, thus affecting development	Internalization that results from interactions between the individual and the environment, occurring within the individual's zone of proximal development
Information-processing theorists	Nature provides the physiological structures and functions (e.g., memory capacity), and nurture provides the environmental supports that allow the individual to make the most of the existing structures and functions	Continuous	Some theorists have been interested in processes that generalize across all domains; others have focused their research and theories on specific domains	Internal changes in cognitive processing, as a result of physiological maturation, environmental events, and the individual's own shaping of cognitive processes

Available data suggest they may not. Recall from Chapter 11 the difference between *fluid intelligence*—the ability to perform mental operations, such as the manipulation of abstract symbols, as in mathematics—and *crystallized intelligence*—specific knowledge tied to a particular cultural and historical milieu. Although crystallized intelligence is higher for older adults than for younger adults, fluid intelligence is higher for younger adults than for older ones (Horn & Cattell, 1966). In general, crystallized cognitive abilities seem to increase throughout the life span, whereas fluid cognitive abilities seem to increase until the 20s or 30s and slowly decrease thereafter. The rate and extent of decline vary widely.

Other cognitive abilities also seem to decline. For example, performance on many information-processing tasks appears to be slower, particularly on complex tasks (Bashore, Osman, & Hefley, 1989; Cerella, 1985; Poon, 1987; Schaie, 1989). Similarly, for older adults, performance on some problem-solving tasks appears not to be as effective (Denny, 1980), although even brief training appears to improve their scores on problem-solving tasks (Willis, 1985).

The evidence of intellectual decline has come under question, however (Schaie, 1974). For one thing, not all cognitive abilities decline; for example, some investigators (Schaie & Willis, 1986) have found that particular learning abilities seem to increase, and other investigators (Graf, 1990; Labouvie-Vief & Schell, 1982; Perlmutter, 1983) have found that the ability to learn and remember meaningful skills and information shows little decline. Also, even in a single domain, such as memory, decreases in one kind of performance may not imply decreases in another. For example, although short-term memory performance seems to decline (Hultsch & Dixon, 1990; West, 1986), long-term memory (Bahrick et al., 1975) and recognition memory (Schonfield & Robertson, 1966) remain quite good.

Our views of memory and aging also may be confounded because when we hear about the devastating memory losses associated with aging, such as those associated with Alzheimer's disease, we may tend to think that such cases are widespread among the elderly. In fact, they are uncommon even among the most elderly of us (see Figure 12-7). In fact, the elderly population as a whole shows much more diversity of abilities than does the population of young adults.

Another reason for questioning the evidence regarding decline is that most of it has come from **cross-sectional studies**, which look simultaneously at independent samples of people of varying ages. In contrast, **longitudinal studies,** which look at a single sample of people as they age, tend not to show comparable evidence of decline (e.g., Bayley & Oden, 1955).

It is hard to say that one or the other kind of study is more likely to be an accurate indication of ability because each type of study has limitations. Cross-sectional studies are susceptible to **cohort effects,** which are the effects of a particular group of subjects having lived through a particular time in history. It would be difficult to compare the cognitive performance of current 80-year-olds to current 30-year-olds, for example, because the two cohorts of individuals have lived in very different eras, with different educational systems, opportunities, and values.

For instance, many of those who grew up during the Great Depression had to drop out of school to support their families, regardless of their school performance. Thus, differences among cohorts may reflect not ability differences, but cultural and historical differences in terms of their opportunities.

On the other hand, longitudinal studies are not perfect either. Longitudinal studies are susceptible to dropout; over time, people inevitably will disappear from the study sample. Some move away; others decide that they no longer want to participate. Still others die. Unfortunately, the selection process for dropping out is not entirely random, so neither those who drop out nor those who remain are a random sample of the group as a whole. For example, in a study of abilities, perhaps those with lower abilities will be less likely to continue in the study because they feel embarrassed or otherwise unmotivated to continue. Perhaps people who die young or who

When the members of this group work together, the younger members may show more fluid intelligence, *rapidly performing mental manipulations on information, whereas the older members may show more* crystallized intelligence, *bringing to bear more specific knowledge related to the content of their work.*

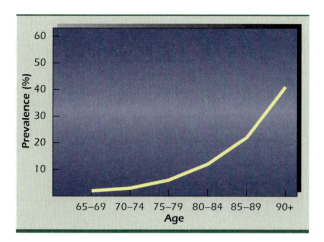

FIGURE 12-7
Prevalence of Dementia
Studies conducted in Japan, Australia, New Zealand, United Kingdom, Sweden, and Denmark show that the actual rate of dementia does not meet our preconceptions of memory loss among the elderly until people reach very late adulthood. (After data from Preston, 1986)

move frequently and thus disappear are cognitively different from those who live longer or whose lives are more stable. Today, many scholars believe that both cross-sectional and longitudinal designs are necessary, separately or in combination, to draw more accurate conclusions about cognitive development.

Although the debate continues about intellectual decline with age, positions have converged somewhat. For example, three basic principles of cognitive development in adulthood have been suggested (Dixon & Baltes, 1986). First, although fluid abilities and other aspects of information processing may decline in late adulthood, this decline is balanced by stabilization and even advancement of well-practiced and pragmatic aspects of mental functioning (crystallized abilities). Thus, when adults lose some of their speed and physiology-related efficiency of information processing, they often compensate with other knowledge- and expertise-based information-processing skills (see Salthouse & Somberg, 1982). Second, despite the age-related decline in information processing, sufficient reserve capacity allows at least temporary increases in performance, especially if the older adult is motivated to perform well. Third, other investigators (Baltes & Willis, 1979) have further argued that at all times throughout the life span, there is considerable **plasticity**—modifiability—of abilities. None of us is stuck at a particular level of performance: Each of us can improve.

Many researchers have come to believe that not only does adult cognition not decline, it actually continues to develop and improve. Recall, for example, the characteristics of postformal thought described in regard to some of the Piagetian fifth-stage theorists. Those who support the notion of postformal thought indicate several ways in which older adults may show a kind of thinking that differs qualitatively from the thinking of adolescents and perhaps even of young adults. Although older adults generally do not demonstrate the same speed of information processing shown in younger adults, they may show instead the benefits of taking time to consider alternatives and to reflect on experience before making judgments—a skill often termed as *wisdom*.

Wisdom and Aging

In recent years, life-span developmental psychologists have become particularly interested in the development of wisdom in adulthood (see Sternberg, 1990). Most theorists have argued that wisdom increases with age, although there are exceptions (Meacham, 1990). Psychologists' definitions of wisdom have been diverse. Some (Baltes & Smith, 1990) define **wisdom** as "exceptional insight into human development and life matters, exceptionally good judgment, advice, and commentary about difficult life problems" (p. 95). Another psychologist (Sternberg, 1985b) has found six factors in people's conceptions of wisdom: reasoning ability, sagacity (shrewdness), learning from ideas and from the environment, judgment, expeditious use of information, and perspicacity (intensely keen awareness, perception, and insight). It is also important in wisdom to know what you do not know (Meacham, 1983, 1990). Whatever the definition, the study of wisdom represents an exciting new direction

Members of the U.S. Supreme Court are expected to show wisdom, which sometimes is described in part as knowing what you do not know. Would younger justices have the wisdom to know what they do not know?

for discovering what abilities may be developed during later adulthood at the same time that fluid abilities or the mechanical aspects of information processing may be flagging.

CONCLUSIONS

> *IN SEARCH OF...*
>
> What general principles of cognitive development can be extracted and synthesized from the collective observations and theories noted by developmental psychologists?

This chapter has described a number of different theories and approaches for studying cognitive development. After viewing these diverse approaches, can we find any unifying principles that transcend the particular theory or method being used? In other words, regardless of the particular theoretical approach—whether Piagetian, Vygotskyan, or information processing—what basic principles crosscut the study of cognitive development and tie it together?

As we review the data, we find some possible answers (Sternberg & Powell, 1983). First, over the course of development, we seem to gain more sophisticated control over our own thinking and learning. As we grow older, we become capable of more complex interactions between thought and behavior. Second, we engage in more thorough information processing with age. Older children encode more information from problems than do younger children, and they are therefore more likely to solve problems correctly. Third, we become increasingly able to comprehend ideas of successively greater complexity over the course of development. Finally, over time we develop increasing flexibility in our uses of strategies or other information. As we grow older, we become less bound to using information in just a single context, and we learn how to apply it in more and more contexts. We may even gain greater wisdom—insight into ourselves and the world around us.

The fact that these conclusions are confirmed by a wide variety of theoretical and experimental approaches strengthens them. The next chapter, on social development, offers an even greater diversity of perspectives. Will the diverse perspectives on social development similarly yield a harvest of conclusions regarding human development?

SUMMARY

The Neural Aspects of Cognitive Development   413

1. Neural networks of the brain have the greatest growth during the first six years of a child's life. The brain areas to develop most rapidly are the sensory and motor cortexes followed by the association areas relating to problem solving, reasoning, memory, and language development. Studies suggest, however, that development throughout the brain is not uniform. EEG patterns indicate that while the right cerebral hemisphere undergoes continuous, gradual changes, the left hemisphere shifts abruptly.

Basic Questions in the Study of Cognitive Development   413

2. *Learning* refers to any relatively permanent change in thought or behavior as a result of experience; *maturation* refers to any relatively permanent change in thought or behavior that

occurs simply as a result of aging, without regard to particular experiences.

3. Today, almost all psychologists believe that both maturation and learning play a role in cognitive development and, moreover, that the two processes interact.

4. An ability is highly *canalized* if it will develop almost without respect to environmental circumstances and weakly canalized if it is highly sensitive to environmental factors.

5. Various criteria have been proposed for demonstrating that cognitive development occurs in discontinuous stages, such as that development occurs in an invariant sequence and that each stage involves a distinctive set of thinking skills.

6. Much of children's conceptual development appears to be *domain specific*—occurring at different rates in different domains—although some appears to be *domain general*—occurring in all domains at about the same rate.

7. Infants possess many more physical and per-

ceptual capacities than was once believed to be the case.

Theories of Cognitive Development   *420*

8. Jean Piaget proposed that cognitive development occurs largely through two processes of *equilibration*: *assimilation*, whereby the child incorporates new information into the child's existing cognitive schemas, and *accommodation*, whereby the child attempts to change his or her cognitive schemas to fit relevant aspects of the new environment.

9. Piaget posited four stages of cognitive development: the *sensorimotor stage*, in roughly the first two years of life; the *preoperational stage*, from roughly 2 years to 7 years of age; the *concrete-operational stage*, from roughly 7 years of age to 12 years of age; and the *formal-operational stage*, from 11 or 12 years onward.

10. As children grow older, they become less *egocentric*—that is, less focused on themselves and more able to see things from the perspective of others.

11. At the end of the sensorimotor stage, children start to develop *internal representations*—thoughts about people and objects that the child cannot see, hear, or otherwise perceive.

12. Children start to show conservation in the concrete-operational stage; they can recognize that two quantities remain the same, despite transformations on them that may change their appearance.

13. Despite the valuable contribution of Piaget's theory to our understanding of cognitive development, most scholars now believe that it inadequately estimates the ages at which children first become able to perform various tasks.

14. Some theorists have posited a fifth stage beyond Piaget's original four. Such a *postformal* stage might involve *problem finding* (rather than problem solving); the ability to perceive very complex, higher order relations; or a tendency toward dialectical thinking. In *dialectical thinking*, beliefs tend to incorporate disparate, sometimes seemingly contradictory elements, with the recognition that many problems have no one right answer.

15. Lev Vygotsky's theory of cognitive development stresses the importance of (a) *internalization*, whereby we incorporate into ourselves the knowledge we gain from social contexts, and (b) the *zone of proximal development*, which is the range of ability between a child's existing undeveloped potential ability and the child's observed ability.

16. Reuven Feuerstein has emphasized the importance of mediated learning experiences, whereby an adult interprets (mediates) for the child the potential opportunities for learning offered by experiences in the environment.

17. *Information-processing theorists* seek to understand cognitive development in terms of how children at different ages process information. Some theorists formulate general theories of how information processing works, and others study information processing within specific domains.

18. Two mechanisms—*encoding* and *combination*—appear to be common to cognitive development across a variety of task domains.

19. Over the course of development, children learn to engage in *cognitive monitoring*—the tracking of their own trains of thought.

20. In general, children become more rapid in cognitive processing with age, such as the speed with which they can mentally rotate images of objects.

21. Young children appear to fail on some transitive-inference problems, apparently not due to a lack of reasoning ability but rather to a lack of memory of the terms and relations in the problems.

22. Young children sometimes solve verbal analogy problems associatively—that is, instead of using reasoning processes, they look for simple associations between words in the problem and words in the answer options.

Cognitive Development in Adulthood   *436*

23. It appears that fluid abilities—involved in thinking flexibly and in novel ways—first increase and then start to decline at some point in later life, whereas crystallized abilities—represented by the accumulation of knowledge—continue to increase or at least gradually stabilize in later adulthood.

24. *Wisdom* (broadly defined as extraordinary insight, keen awareness, and exceptional judgment) generally increases with age, although there are exceptions.

Conclusions   *440*

25. Some principles of cognitive development appear to transcend specific theories or perspectives. With age, people develop more sophisticated thinking strategies, their information processing becomes more thorough, their ability to comprehend more complex ideas develops, and they become increasingly flexible in their uses of strategies for problem solving.

KEY TERMS

accommodation 423

assimilation 423

canalization 414

cognitive development 412

cognitive structures 415

cohort effects 438

combination 431

comprehension monitoring 433

concrete operations 425

cross-sectional studies 438

development 412

developmental psychologists 412

dialectical thinking 428

domain generality 415

domain specificity 415

dynamic assessment
  environment 430

egocentric 425

encoding 431

equilibration 423

formal-operational stage 426

growth 412

information-processing
  theorists 430

internalization 429

learning 414

life-span development 436

longitudinal studies 438

maturation 414

metamemory 433

motor 420

neonate 416

object permanence 424

orienting reflex 418

plasticity 439

postformal thinking 429

preoperational stage 425

problem finding 428

representational thought 425

second-order relations 426

sensorimotor stage 424

spatial visualization 435

static assessment
  environment 430

verbal comprehension 433

verbal fluency 433

wisdom 439

zone of proximal
  development 429

IN SEARCH OF THE HUMAN MIND:
ANALYSES, CREATIVE EXPLORATIONS, AND PRACTICAL APPLICATIONS

1. Choose the theory of cognitive development that seems most reasonable to you (e.g., Piaget, Vygotsky, information processing). Based on the theory you have chosen, answer each of the five basic questions posed at the outset of this chapter.

2. What are some of the ways in which our limitations as researchers (i.e., limited tools, imaginations, resources, methods, etc.) restrict our ability to identify some of the cognitive abilities of children? What steps should researchers take to avoid interpreting their own limitations as investigators as being limitations in the cognitive abilities of children?

3. How does Piaget's notion of equilibration through assimilation and accommodation relate to Vygotsky's concept of the zone of proximal development?

4. What memory tasks mentioned in Chapter 8 could be applied to the study of cognitive development? Design an experiment that would be appropriate for use with children of different ages. (Specify the ages or age ranges for the two tasks.)

5. What language tasks mentioned in Chapter 9 could be applied to the study of cognitive development? Design an experiment that would be appropriate for use with children of different ages. (Specify the ages or age ranges for the tasks.)

6. Design an experiment that would test a domain-specific aspect of information processing in a 4-year-old, an 8-year-old, a 16-year-old, and a 32-year-old. (Use Vygotskyan techniques of providing graded hints, as needed.)

7. This chapter concluded by giving four general principles of cognitive development. Give an example of each of the principles, using either your own observations or examples from the chapter.

8. How have you developed cognitively in the past 3 years? In what ways do you think differently from before?

9. What principal aspects of your parents' or your teachers' behavior have you internalized over the years?

Chapter Thirteen

Social Development

Chapter Outline

Social development *encompasses the development of emotions, personality, interpersonal relations, and moral reasoning across the life span.*

Physiological, cognitive, and behavioral factors underlie the development and experiencing of emotions. Over the course of development, emotions become more differentiated and more outer directed.

Erik Erikson suggested a comprehensive theory that encompasses psychosocial development across the life span and centers on various intrapersonal accomplishments. The development of a concept of self involves both an understanding of oneself in terms of various aspects of the self, and judgments about oneself regarding these various aspects.

From birth, infants and their parents begin forming attachments that reflect both the distinctive character of each partner and the distinctive dynamics of their relationship. Parental disciplinary style affects the development of social skills in children. Research results regarding the effects of child care are somewhat contradictory, although the majority of studies indicate that high-quality child care does children little harm and may offer some benefits. The degree of social interaction increases across the course of child development, although the patterns of interactions for boys and for girls differ. The ability to view the world from the perspective of another person increases across the course of development and may be related to cognitive development.

The way children engage in moral reasoning seems to change across the course of development; children decreasingly focus on obvious concrete outcomes and on what directly benefits them, and increasingly give attention to underlying intentions and what benefits others.

I do not remember having ever told a lie, . . . either to my teachers or to my school-mates. I used to be very shy and avoided all company. My books and my lessons were my sole companions. To be at school at the stroke of the hour and to run back home as soon as school closed, that was my daily habit. I literally ran back, because I could not bear to talk to anybody. I was even afraid lest anyone should poke fun at me.

—*Mohandas Gandhi,* Gandhi's Autobiography

The preceding chapter described developmental changes across the life span in terms of how we think, reason, make judgments, and otherwise perceive and use information. Many of the changes associated with cognitive development affect the ways we think and feel about ourselves and the ways we interact with others. In this chapter, we directly consider the broad topic of **social development**—how people learn about themselves and about interacting with each other across the life span.

> How might some aspects of an individual's cognitive development affect the person's social development?

Social development encompasses several aspects of human development: emotional, personality, interpersonal, and moral development. These areas of study certainly cover a lot of psychological territory, but they are so highly interrelated that, at times, it

seems quite difficult to assign developments to particular areas of study. For example, is the special feeling an infant or young child has toward its mother—or other primary caregiver—an emotion (love), a personality trait (dependence), or an interpersonal interaction (bonding)? Is the way we treat our beloved based on our moral development, our interpersonal development, our personality development, or our emotional development? Psychologists who study social development often consider all these aspects of development when studying a particular psychological phenomenon (see Figure 13-1).

EMOTIONAL DEVELOPMENT

IN SEARCH OF...

How and why do we develop emotions?

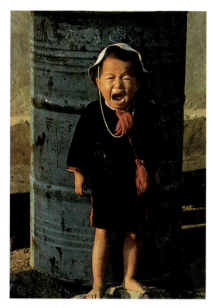
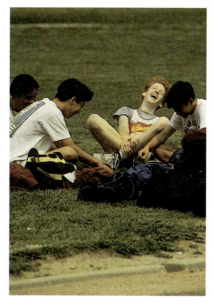

FIGURE 13-1
Social Development
Across the life span, social development encompasses aspects of emotional development *(such as expressing anguished desolation)*, interpersonal development *(such as enjoying the company of friends)*, personality development *(such as being shy versus outgoing)*, *and* moral development *(such as beginning to internalize the dictates of societal authorities)*.

Theories of Emotional Development

Theories of emotional development account for how infants, who have very little experience, grow into adults with a wide range of emotional responses and experiences. Here, we consider five kinds of theories of emotional development: differentiation theory, discrete emotions theory, behavioral theories, cognitive theories, and cognitive-evolutionary theory.

Differentiation Theory

Differentiation theory (Sroufe, 1979) posits that we are born with a single, generalized state of arousal, and that this emotional state gradually becomes differentiated into the various emotions we feel as adults. Thus, just as cognitive abilities may become more specialized over time, so may emotions. According to differentiation theory, the newborn's single, generalized excitement response soon becomes

differentiated between positive and negative emotional states (i.e., a general sense of contentment versus a general sense of distress). Also, either the positive or the negative state may be felt in varying degrees of intensity, so the infant may be highly distressed or mildly contented, actively jubilant or somewhat displeased. Eventually, these states further subdivide, so that the child comes to know anger, hatred, sorrow, joy, contentment, and a variety of other emotions. Emotional development may partly depend on cognitive development, with the range of emotions a child feels partly dependent on the child's intellectual understanding of a situation.

Discrete Emotions Theory

Whereas differentiation theory construes emotions as specializing over time, **discrete emotions theory** (Izard, 1977; Izard, Kagan, & Zajonc, 1984) proposes that humans are innately predisposed to feel specific emotions, given the appropriate situation in which to express those emotions. The emotions are generated by specific neural patterns in our brains, and each emotion appears when it first acquires value to the infant in adapting to the environment. For example, distress becomes relevant when the infant wants to learn to summon the parent. The innate predisposition may be part of our neural physiology (see Chapter 3 for some of the ways in which our brains and our emotions are linked).

Behavioral Theories

As you might guess, behavioral theories of emotional development focus on the links between particular situational stimuli and particular emotional responses. That is, behavioral theories tend to account for *why* particular emotions are associated with particular situations better than they explain *how* emotions first appear. Behavioral theories suggest at least three mechanisms by which an infant might learn to pair various emotions with particular situations (see Chapter 7): classical conditioning, operant conditioning, and social learning.

By pairing stimuli that elicit emotions with stimuli that are neutral, an emotion can be *classically conditioned* in response to the formerly neutral stimulus. Learning theorists have claimed that many emotions can be conditioned in this way. *Operant conditioning* also might account for the development of particular emotional responses. Suppose that soon after crying an infant is given milk. Behaviorists would suggest that after a while the infant learns to associate crying with milk and therefore cries specifically to obtain milk. *Social learning* is based on the notion that children learn through observation and imitation. If parents, older siblings, or other potential models react to a particular situation in a particular way, young children may follow suit.

Cognitive Theories

The cognitive approach, like the behavioral approach, more heavily emphasizes the pairings of specific emotions with particular situations than it does the generation of emotions in the first place. Cognitivists differ from behaviorists, however, in their willingness to look at what goes on *inside* our heads.

One cognitive approach to the development of emotion predicts a curvilinear pattern (shaped like a hill or an inverted U) in response to stimuli (Kagan, Kearsley, & Zelazo, 1978), as shown in Figure 13-2.

This view is based on Jerome Kagan's discrepancy hypothesis. On first presentation, a child may show no particular emotional reaction to an unfamiliar stimulus. Then, when something happens to violate the child's expectations, the child attends to and perhaps interacts with the unfamiliar stimulus, and an emotional reaction ensues (the upward arc of the curve). Finally, to use Jean Piaget's terms, when the child has either assimilated the situation into existing expectations or accommodated his or her existing schemas by forming new expectations (see Chapter 12), the situation no longer provokes much interest or emotion (the downward arc of the curve).

A second cognitive approach suggests that when our thoughts are interrupted by autonomic nervous system (ANS) activity, we try to make sense of what is going on internally and label it (G. Mandler, 1980). These internal labels are what we call the various emotions we feel. For example, suppose a college student is talking to her boyfriend, who tells her that he is seeing another woman. Naturally, her body and mind both react to this news. Her ANS responds with increased blood pressure and heart rate (see Chapters 16 and 20 for more on physiological characteristics of

FIGURE 13-2

Kagan's Discrepancy Hypothesis
According to Jerome Kagan and others, children respond to novel stimuli in a characteristic curvilinear emotional response pattern. The upward arc of the curve represents an infant's response to a stimulus that is moderately discrepant from the stimuli with which the infant is already familiar. Once the infant has become sufficiently familiar with the stimulus (via assimilation or accommodation), the infant loses interest in the stimulus, as shown by the downward arc of the curve. (After Kagan, Kearsley, & Zelazo, 1978)

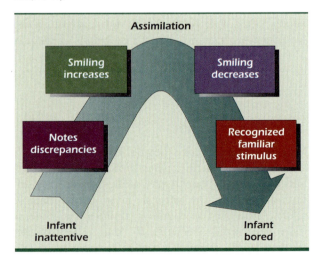

arousal), a physical reaction that she may cognitively interpret as jealousy. However, if she felt the same ANS arousal in a conversation about an extremely difficult forthcoming examination, she might then label that arousal state as fear. That labeling of arousal might also carry over to other discussions of upcoming examinations, when she will again interpret ANS arousal as fear. According to this theory, therefore, cognitive labeling of ANS arousal serves as the basis for assigning a particular emotion to a particular event.

An Integrative Theory: Evolutionary and Cognitive

Other psychologists (Campos, Barrett, Lamb, Goldsmith, & Stenberg, 1983) have proposed a theory integrating two of the preceding viewpoints. This theory recognizes the *evolutionary adaptive functions* of emotions in animals—that is, emotions help an organism adapt to its own changing needs as well as to changing circumstances in the environment. In addition, this theory posits that cognitive responses to various kinds of stimulation elicit emotions.

According to this integrated view, we react emotionally to an event only when we believe (cognitive) we have something at stake (evolutionary) in regard to it. Otherwise, we have no emotions regarding the event. For example, snowfall creates different reactions under different circumstances, depending on whether we wish to stay home from school, go skiing, play tennis, drive somewhere, avoid having to shovel the sidewalk, or just stay indoors. Thus, the emotions we feel depend on our own cognitive evaluations of events as positive, negative, or neutral, which in turn depend on how our own needs and goals relate to that event. At different times in our lives, we may cognitively evaluate the same event differently. Thus, the emotions children develop at different times depend on their goals and needs as they interact with events. A child may feel upset when the babysitter knocks at the door, whereas the parent may feel relieved.

This integrative cognitive and evolutionary approach proposes five basic emotions: joy, anger, sadness, fear, and interest. Each occurs due to different perceptions of a situation. *Joy* results from believing we are about to achieve a goal, *anger* from the perception that we are or will be confronted by a hindrance. *Sadness* results when we come to see a goal as unattainable, and so on. Different emotions also engender different behavior. Anger often leads to actions designed to eliminate obstacles, whereas *fear*

often results in flight or withdrawal from the fear-producing stimulus.

> How might one or two of the other theories of emotional development be integrated into the cognitive-evolutionary theory? Give examples for at least three emotions.

Summary of Theories

Each of these theories of emotional development focuses on one of two questions: (1) How does the full range of emotionality develop? (2) How do particular emotions develop in particular situations? This choice of focus is similar to the debate between domain generality versus domain specificity posed in regard to cognitive development (Chapter 12). If we were to place the theories of emotional development on a continuum, the differentiation theory would be the most domain general, the behavioral and cognitive theories would be the most domain specific, and the discrete emotions theory and the integrative cognitive-evolutionary theory would fall in the middle.

Another question posed about cognitive development was whether nature or nurture played a larger role in development. It seems that all theories of emotional development acknowledge an interaction between nature and nurture, although the differentiation, the discrete emotions, and the integrative cognitive-evolutionary theories certainly assign a much larger role to maturation (nature/biology) than do the behavioral or cognitive theories, which strongly emphasize the role of learning (nurture/environment).

Finally, Chapter 12 asked whether cognitive development proceeds in discontinuous stages or via continuous progression. To answer this question in regard to emotional development, we discuss next some stages of emotional development that have been proposed.

Stages of Emotional Development During Early Childhood

Although researchers disagree about exactly *how* emotions develop, they show a surprising degree of consensus about *when* emotions develop (Brazelton, 1983; Izard, Kagan, & Zajonc, 1984; Sroufe, 1979). The stages of emotional development, including the important developments of *social smiles* and of **separation anxiety** (fear of being separated from caregivers), are summarized in Table 13-1. (See also

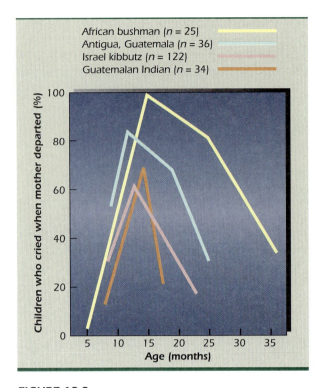

FIGURE 13-3

Separation Anxiety

At about 8 months of age (give or take a month or two), infants start to show separation anxiety—a fear of being separated from their mothers or other familiar adults. (a) Despite the universality of separation anxiety, some cross-cultural differences affect the intensity, the age of onset, and the duration of this phenomenon. (After Kagan, 1974) (b) These parents may be relieved to discover that when infants later acquire a concept of object permanence, they seem to be better able to cope with their anxiety about being separated from their primary caregivers.

Figure 13-3, which shows the universality of separation anxiety across cultures.)

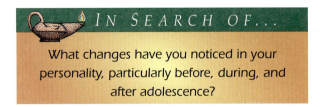

Suppose that you are a parent watching your child develop emotions from birth to age 3. How would the changes in your child's emotional development affect your relationship with your child?

PERSONALITY DEVELOPMENT

IN SEARCH OF...

What changes have you noticed in your personality, particularly before, during, and after adolescence?

Personality development emphasizes how we develop as unique individuals; of the many aspects of

personality development, this chapter covers only a few. In Chapter 17, we devote an entire chapter to looking at personality in depth.

Erikson's Theory of Personality and Identity Development

Because personality development is so multifaceted, is it possible to capture its many aspects within a single theory of discontinuous development? Erik Erikson (1950, 1968) attempted to do so in his **psychosocial theory** of personality development. Today, the majority of developmental psychologists agree that personality development continues throughout the life span, so a stage-based theory of personality development such as Erikson's, with stages for the whole of the life span, now seems quite natural.

When Erikson first proposed the theory in 1950, however, the idea of a stage-based theory continuing into adulthood was a novelty. Until then the vast majority of stage theories had ended at adolescence or even earlier. Psychologists viewed any de-

TABLE 13-1
Emotional Development

The following characteristics of emotional development and the ages of their appearance are based largely on the observational data obtained by Alan Sroufe. As is the case with most data on development, the ages are approximations and suggest only a general sequence of developments, not a certain timetable of the developmental process.

Age (in months)	Characteristics
0–1	Infants show emotions, usually by crying or thrashing around. Their options for emotional expression are limited, so they express multiple emotions—grief, discomfort, anger—in a single way, such as by crying.
1–3	Infants begin to react to others. They develop a *social smile*, smiling when they see others smiling at them. They show stern or sad faces when they see sad faces on those around them. By about 2 months of age, they also smile in response to nonsocial stimuli, such as toys they have enjoyed playing with before.
3–6	Infants show high amounts of positive emotional reactions, smiling when they see their caregivers. By about 4 months, infants also laugh. The babies generally like others to play with and stimulate them, and they laugh at simple pleasures. At about 4 or 5 months, they begin to produce tears to accompany their crying.
6–9	Infants actively participate in and even initiate interactions. Social interactions are primarily physical, such as kissing, caressing, poking, and otherwise exploring the bodies of their parents, their siblings, and even other babies. Infants start to fear strangers and unknown places. They may have difficulty eating or sleeping in unfamiliar environments and may actively avoid such situations. Infants also exhibit *separation anxiety*, fear of being separated from their mothers or other familiar adults. Infants begin to show anger.
9–12	Babies become increasingly effective at conveying emotional states to others. Infants become highly attached to their primary caregivers, and they seem possessive, wanting other people to stay away from their caregivers. Their fear of strangers, if anything, grows.
12–18	Infants explore the inanimate environment more. The close attachment to their primary caregiver now gives the infants greater confidence. As infants become increasingly inquisitive, their fear of strangers generally drops off.
18–36	Toddlers become more aware of themselves as individual people. They begin to develop differentiated self-concepts, realizing they play different roles (daughter, sibling, playmate) in different situations. At one moment, they want to assert their independence and to explore the world without the constraints of parental authority, and at the next moment, they want to cling to their caregivers, to feel reassured that they are safe and secure in the world. By the end of this stage, children also begin to show signs of empathy, sharing the joys and sorrows of others.

velopmental processes that might exist thereafter as trivial and uninteresting. Even today, a gap persists between *child psychologists*, who study development only in children, and *life-span psychologists*, who study development throughout people's lives.

Still, Erikson's theory of psychosocial development is one of the most widely used and accepted. Each stage represents a developmental challenge that the psychologically healthy person meets. According to Erikson's theory, the unhealthy person fails to meet one or more challenges and must continue throughout life trying to cope with the conflicts that emerge because of this failure. The eight stages are as follows.

1. *Trust Versus Mistrust* (birth to 1 year): Infants learn either to trust or to mistrust that their needs will be met. They come to view the world as either basically friendly or basically hostile.

Developmental psychologist Erik Erikson (1902–1994) proposed a widely encompassing psychosocial theory of personality development. In contrast to Sigmund Freud's psychosexual theory of personality development, Erikson's theory encompasses the entire life span.

Successful passage through this stage leads to the development of a *hopeful* attitude toward life and what can be gleaned from it.

2. *Autonomy Versus Shame and Doubt* (ages 1–3): Children learn to exist within the expanded horizons of the environment. Those who do not master this stage doubt themselves and feel shame about themselves and their abilities in general. Those who do master the challenge become self-sufficient in walking, talking, eating, going to the toilet, and so on. Successful passage through this stage leads to the development of the *will*—a sense of control and mastery over their own emotions, thoughts, and behaviors. (Recall the emotional developments related to the developing sense of autonomy.)

3. *Initiative Versus Guilt* (ages 3–6): Children learn how to take initiative and to assert themselves in socially acceptable ways. However, children whose independence leads to excessive or unre-

solved conflict with authority figures may feel guilty and may have difficulty in taking initiative. Successful passage through this third stage engenders a sense of *purpose* in life.

4. *Industry Versus Inferiority* (ages 6–12): Children learn a sense of capability and of industriousness in their work. Those who do not develop this sense develop feelings of incompetence and low self-worth; they may feel unable to do many things well. The child who successfully passes through this stage develops a sense of *competence*.

5. *Identity Versus Role Confusion* (adolescence): Adolescents try to figure out who they are, what they value, and who they will grow up to become. They try to integrate intellectual, social, sexual, ethical, and other aspects of themselves into a unified self-identity. Those who succeed develop a sense of *fidelity* to themselves. Those who do not remain confused about who they are and what to do with their lives.

6. *Intimacy Versus Isolation* (early adulthood): The emerging adult tries to commit him- or herself to a loving intimate relationship. The adult who succeeds learns how to *love* in a giving and non-selfish way. The adult who fails develops a sense of isolation and may fail to connect with the significant others in his or her life.

7. *Generativity Versus Stagnation* (middle adulthood): Adults try to be productive in their work and to contribute to the next generation, whether through ideas, products, raising children, or some combination. This productivity is termed *generativity*. Adults who do not succeed in passing through this stage become stagnant and possibly self-centered as well, leaving no lasting mark for having been alive.

8. *Integrity Versus Despair* (old age): People try to make sense of the lives they have led and, in particular, of the choices they have made. They may not feel as though every decision was right, in which case they must come to terms with their mistakes. Adults who succeed in this stage gain the *wisdom* of older age. Adults who fail may feel a sense of despair over mistakes or lost opportunities.

Do these stages actually exist? It is hard to say because no one has yet proposed a test that would clearly disconfirm the model. Certainly, these conflicts emerge at the ages specified in many people. Whether they are the primary conflicts is an open question. Clearly, the theory does not address cultural generality. For example, is our culture's emphasis on generativity really something that must characterize every human life? Are there not alternatives to the development of typical intimate sexual love relationships in early adulthood? Must those who cannot accept past mistakes fall into permanent despair? Probably no theory of psychosocial development will fully encompass every conflict for every person in every culture. Erikson's theory, however, does quite a commendable job of clarifying some of the main personal conflicts in Western society.

> In what Eriksonian stage would you place yourself? What are some of your experiences and characteristics that illustrate this Eriksonian stage?

Marcia's Theory: The Achievement of a Personal Identity

Erikson's theory deals with attempts to form and reform identity. Is it possible to specify in more detail the kinds of personal identities an adolescent and ultimately an adult can achieve? James Marcia (1966, 1980) has proposed that four kinds of identities can emerge as a result of conflicts and decision making. Note that these identities add another dimension to Erikson's theory, not a separate series of stages. These four identities are **identity achievement, foreclosure, identity diffusion,** and **moratorium** (see Table 13-2). Note that persons who have reached identity achievement would move beyond Erikson's stage of development for identity, but those with any of the other three identities would be blocked from progressing beyond that stage.

As an example of how psychological theories are intertwined with and even determined by the times, Marcia added a fifth identity during the Vietnam War. **Alienated achievement** characterizes those who carefully consider their options and their place in society, and then decide that they do not want to be a part of what society has to offer. They do not respect the direction society has taken, and so they separate themselves from it.

> To what extent and in what areas have you achieved identity? In what ways do you see your identity as continuing to evolve and develop?

Like Erikson's theory of personality development as a whole, Marcia's theory may be culturally bound. Also, his theory has not generated much evidence either to confirm or to disconfirm it. Still, Marcia's theory provides an interesting way to view

TABLE 13-2
Marcia's Achievement of Personal Identity

You can assess your own personal identity by asking yourself two key questions in this table. Note that this matrix does not show the possible fifth identity, alienated achievement.

		Do You Make Commitments (e.g., to a career, to a mate, to your values)?	
		Yes	*No*
Have you engaged in a period of active search for identity?	**Yes**	You have reached *identity achievement*, having a firm and relatively secure sense of who you are. You have made conscious and purposeful commitments to your occupation, religion, beliefs about sex roles, and the like. You have considered the views, beliefs, and values held by others in achieving this identity, but you have branched out to achieve your own resolution.	Your identity is in *moratorium*, and you are currently having an identity crisis (turning point). You do not yet have clear commitments to society or a clear sense of who you are, but you are actively trying to reach that point.
	No	Your identity is in *foreclosure*; you have committed yourself to an occupation and various ideological positions, but you show little evidence of having followed a process of self-construction. You have simply adopted the attitudes of others, without serious searching and questioning; you have foreclosed on the possibility of arriving at your own unique identity.	You are experiencing *identity diffusion*, essentially lacking direction. You are unconcerned about political, religious, moral, or even occupational issues. You go your own way, not worrying about why others are doing what they are doing.

identity development, and each of us can probably think of persons who fall into each of his categories.

Levinson's Theory: Stages of Adult Development

Daniel Levinson (1978, 1986) has proposed a stage-based model of adult personality and identity development. Levinson distinguishes three main stages of adult life: early, middle, and late adulthood. Within these ranges are specific developmental periods, each confronting a different task. Here is a summary of Levinson's stages of *adult life structure*, that is, the pattern of adult development.

In Levinson's *novice phase*, from roughly ages 17 to 40, people question the nature of the world and their place in it. They modify and in some cases terminate existing relationships as they begin to establish adult identities. They also consider choices of occupations, lovers, peers, values, and lifestyles. Attempts both to keep options open and to choose can come into conflict, and so each person must find a balance between the two. Later, perhaps even in the next phase, adults may make new choices of career or family options, or they may reaffirm old choices. Eventually, they settle down to two major tasks: to anchor their lives in family and career, and to succeed by building a better life that others affirm as such.

Levinson's *middle adulthood phase* occurs from about ages 40 to 65. People now ask what they have done with their lives, what they truly want, and how they can change their lives. Sometimes a major shift occurs, such as a change of job, marital status, or geographic location. Sometimes, the change is more subtle, or perhaps one of attitude. Eventually, adults in this stage must begin to consider their retirement and older age and the form they would like the next phase to take.

Finally, adults enter Levinson's *late adult phase*, during which they become increasingly aware of changing physical and mental abilities associated with the aging process. At this time, it is crucial for older adults to remain connected to their families and other sources of vitality and creativity, as well as to come to terms with their own mortality and to relish the benefits of wisdom.

Levinson's theory is at least as culturally bound as Erikson's. In fact, it is probably more limited in its cross-cultural application, because men's and women's occupations may follow very different paths in different cultures—and certainly do so in our own culture. Moreover, other developmental theorists have criticized both Levinson and Erikson for insisting on invariant age ranges for their various stages. Nonetheless, both theories are impressive in terms of the scope of their analysis of the transitions in our lives, and of how we cope with these transitions.

Self-Concept

Self-concept can be defined as the way we view ourselves. A more specific, culturally relevant definition is our sense of *independence* (our autonomy and individuality) and *interdependence* (our sense of belonging and collectivity) (see, e.g., Markus & Kitayama, 1991). Although both of these aspects of self are important, the influence of culture determines how independence and interdependence combine to characterize a specific individual. For example, some Asian societies (such as China and Japan) tend to socialize individuals to be interdependent and collectivistic, whereas most Western societies tend to foster independence and emphasize individualism.

Most research in developmental psychology emphasizes two other aspects of the self-concept: self-understanding and self-esteem. Self-understanding is mainly cognitive, and self-esteem is mainly emotional.

Self-Understanding

Self-understanding refers to how we comprehend ourselves—as good students, as superathletes, as nice persons, as political activists, and so on. William Damon and Daniel Hart (1982) have presented a compelling integrative model of the development of self-understanding. The model begins with a distinction between the *me* and the *I*, a distinction that goes back in psychology to William James (1890a), and in philosophy to the earliest philosophical writings. The *me* refers to the person we usually think of when we think of *myself*. The *I* refers to the self-as-knower, the self that oversees the various aspects of our personalities and integrates them.

For each of us, the *me* includes four aspects: the *physical self*—our name, body, and material possessions; the *active self*—how we behave and are capable of behaving; the *social self*—the relationships we have with others; and the *psychological self*—our feelings, thoughts, beliefs, and personality characteristics.

> How do you understand yourself in terms of the four aspects of the *me*? Give specific examples of each aspect.

At different ages, different aspects of self take precedence in the self-concept. During the first 2 or 3 years of life, a sense of self-awareness starts to emerge. The first signs of emergence relate to the physical self (see Bertenthal & Fischer, 1978; Levine, 1983). During the first year, infants develop an awareness of the babies they see in the mirror, come to have expectations about what they look like, and recognize their own names. During the second year, toddlers can say their own names, identify their own gender and age, and clearly recognize their own possessions: "mine." Another aspect of self-understanding also emerges during the preschool years: a sense of mastery (Kagan, 1981). When 2-year-olds cannot succeed at doing something they want to do, they appear clearly frustrated, and when they can succeed, they appear obviously pleased with themselves (recall Erikson's stages of autonomy versus shame and doubt and of initiative versus guilt). Lev Vygotsky (1934/1962) pointed out that at about 3 to 4 years of age, children begin to differentiate between the speech they direct toward themselves (e.g., while playing alone) and the speech they direct toward others (e.g., when talking to a parent). Eventually, inner-directed speech becomes internal and silent (thoughts). Despite these accomplishments, preschool-aged children largely emphasize their physical selves; what they look like constitutes who they are.

During the elementary-school years, children increasingly focus on their active selves. Children emphasize what they can *do*—dance, play soccer, achieve high grades. In early adolescence, children concentrate on their social selves, paying special attention to developing peer relations. Finally, in late adolescence, teens turn their attention to their psychological selves and to an understanding of who they are as persons. They consider their beliefs, values, thoughts, and attitudes important to who they are. Damon and Hart's model stops in adolescence, as do many developmental models, but development of the self continues throughout adulthood, as shown by Erikson's models.

The self-as-knower—*I*—organizes and interprets the experiences of the *me* in four key dimensions: *continuity*—how we perceive ourselves as remaining the same person over time; *distinctness*—our sense of individuality, that we are different from others; *volition*—the sense of having free will (this dimension may vary by culture); and *self-reflectivity*—our ability to think about the other aspects of the *I* and the *me*.

> How would you describe yourself in regard to distinctness and self-reflectivity? What do you believe prompted your distinctive self-concept in these two dimensions?

All four dimensions of the *I* are discernible even in very young children. However, they are discernible in different ways at different ages, as we might expect based on children's developmental progression from the physical (and concrete) to the psychological (and abstract). For example, young children base their perception of self-continuity more on their bodies remaining the same, whereas older children base their assessment of continuity more on their personalities remaining the same. Similarly, at different ages, children have different views regarding what makes one person distinct from another. Young children see distinctiveness more in terms of physical attributes, older children more in terms of psychological ones. Thus, with increasing age, we place increasing emphasis on the psychological as opposed to the physical in what makes us uniquely who we are.

The Damon and Hart model, like many developmental models, seems to be one of successive *differentiation*—as we develop, more generalized concepts of ourselves become more highly differentiated and more specialized in terms of the aspects of the self. (Contrast the differentiation of self-concept with the cognitive differentiation discussed in Chapter 12.) In addition, just as we become increasingly aware of how we differ from other people, we also come to realize more and more the ways we are bound up with others, through the institutions of culture and society, through the organizations we participate in, and through the choices we make. Humans are highly interdependent, and to some extent, our context influences the way we perceive ourselves. Damon and Hart's research was based on American children, and children in other cultures may well place more emphasis on their social selves, rooted in a social context and defined partly by the society with which they interact. In Western societies, self-understanding in adults may also be more differentiated according to our social context. We may think of ourselves as psychologically well-adjusted at home but not at work, or vice versa. Such differences in self-perception can lead to a complex picture of self-esteem, the construct to which we now turn.

Self-Esteem

Self-esteem refers to how much a person values him- or herself. According to research by Susan Harter (1990), our self-concepts become increasingly differentiated over the course of development; as we explore our abilities and learn more skills, our self-esteem becomes more differentiated—we may think highly of ourselves in one area, but not in another.

This differentiation hypothesis posits that between ages 4 and 7, children can make reliable judgments about themselves in four personal domains: cognitive competence, physical competence, social competence, and behavioral conduct (Harter & Pike, 1984). However, the younger the children are, the more likely their self-evaluations will show a *halo effect*—a high self-evaluation rating in one capacity that leads to a high self-evaluation rating in others as well.

Between the ages of 8 and 12 the four domains of the early years become further differentiated into five separate domains of self-esteem, which Harter categorizes somewhat differently: scholastic (rather than cognitive) competence, athletic (rather than physical) competence, peer social acceptance (rather than social competence), behavioral conduct, and physical appearance. During adolescence, even more domains of self-esteem emerge, including close friendship, romantic appeal, and job competence. By adulthood, 11 different domains of competency emerge as aspects of self-worth: intelligence, sense of humor, job competence, morality, athletic ability, physical appearance, sociability, intimacy, nurturance, adequacy as a provider, and household management (Messer & Harter, 1985).

Self-esteem stems from both your perceived competencies and the importance you assign to those competencies. For example, if some of these girls place little value on athletic skills, their actual skills will not influence their self-esteem much one way or the other. For the girls who prize athletic competence, their actual skill level will powerfully affect their self-esteem.

> How do you rate your own sense of self-worth in each of the 8 to 11 personal domains? How do you weigh each of the domains? (Rank order the domains in terms of the emphasis you give to each.)

Where does self-esteem come from? According to William James (1890b), overall self-esteem involves more than merely averaging our perceived competencies; instead, we consider the importance of each competence and form a weighted average. For example, if a boy does not think much of his physical abilities, but he also does not place much weight on physical competence, then his overall self-esteem may still be quite high. By contrast, another boy might heavily weigh the same skill and would therefore feel less good about himself if he believed that he was not athletic.

An alternative view of self-esteem (Cooley, 1982) is that for each of us, our self-esteem is largely determined by other people's social judgments of us. As we absorb and integrate their evaluations, their cumulative evaluations eventually become our own self-evaluations. Evidence exists, however, to support a synthesis of the two positions (Harter, 1985). On the one hand, we do have internal evaluations, and we do not weigh equally the dimensions along which we evaluate ourselves. On the other hand, others' judgments of us affect our judgment of ourselves. Once again we find that theoretical stances originally proposed as alternatives may ultimately be more complementary than contradictory. A synthesis can incorporate the best aspects of the thesis and its antithesis.

Generally, children's perceptions of their abilities become both more modest and more accurate as the children grow older (Frey & Ruble, 1987; Stipek, 1984). However, when self-perceptions are too modest and therefore inaccurate, problems result. Self-evaluations of low ability lead to motivational problems, especially in older children (Rholes, Jones, & Wade, 1980). Children who underestimate their abilities also seem to seek out less challenging tasks than more realistic children do (see Harter, 1983). Teachers and parents cannot neglect the importance of self-perceptions, especially because even inaccurate self-perceptions guide how children handle both schoolwork and life outside of school (Phillips, 1984, 1987). For example, children who seriously underestimate themselves have low expectations for their success, believe that respected adults also take a dim view of their abilities, are reluctant to sustain effort in difficult tasks, and are more anxious about being evaluated than are other children (Phillips & Zimmerman, 1990).

> How might parents and teachers foster children's self-esteem in each of the four or five personal domains mentioned by Harter?

Research has suggested that differences in illusory (false) perceptions of low competence are affected by gender, as determined by the difference between children's self-evaluations and their achievement-test scores. At the third and fifth grades, no gender differences exist, but at the ninth-grade level, virtually all those who wrongly believe themselves academically incompetent in particular areas are girls (Phillips & Zimmerman, 1990). Other investigators (e.g., Entwistle & Baker, 1983) have found differences as early as first grade, again with girls more than boys tending to believe themselves less competent in particular subjects.

A report by the American Association of University Women (AAUW) Education Foundation has found that girls who enter school roughly equal in abilities and self-esteem leave school deficient in mathematical ability and in self-esteem, as compared with boys (AAUW, 1992). Why does this change occur? Research has shown that girls receive less attention from teachers, and curricula in schools emphasize almost exclusively male achievements (Nelson, 1990; Sadker & Sadker, 1984). It appears also that early adolescence is a particularly difficult period for girls. Researchers Annie Rogers and Carol Gilligan (1988) have found that young girls are extremely self-confident until age 11 or 12 years, after which they become more conflicted about themselves and their roles in the world. In later adolescence, girls often have to cope with a negative body image, low self-esteem, and depression. Some researchers point to the inequality in society as a cause of adolescent inner turmoil in girls (AAUW, 1992) and so recommend policy changes in education.

Thus, our understandings and evaluations of ourselves become more complex and differentiated and more psychological and abstract across the life span. Also, throughout childhood and adolescence, we increasingly consider what others think and say about us and how they behave toward us, and we may internalize what we perceive others to believe about us. In adulthood, we continue to consider our perceptions of how others feel about us, but we also measure ourselves against our own internalized criteria for ourselves, giving more weight to some aspects of ourselves than to other aspects.

Temperament

Some people get angry easily but get over it quickly. Others are slow to anger but have more difficulty recovering. Still others rarely get angry at all. Differences such as these are ones of **temperament**—an individual's disposition, intensity, and duration of emotions. Temperament influences the development of personality and of relationships with other people.

Some of the most well-known and well-regarded work on temperament was done by A. Thomas and Stella Chess in a longitudinal study with children, starting at birth and continuing until adolescence (e.g., Thomas & Chess, 1977; Thomas, Chess, & Birch, 1970).

The study described three types of temperament in babies. *Easy babies*, who constituted roughly 40% of the sample, were playful, adaptable, and regular in their eating and other bodily functions. They were interested in novel situations and responded moderately to them. *Difficult babies*, by contrast, who constituted 10% of the sample, were irritable and not very adaptable. They avoided unfamiliar situations and reacted intensely to them. *Slow-to-warm-up babies*, 15% of the sample, had relatively low activity levels and showed minimal responses to novelty. They avoided new situations, and in general needed more time than other babies to adapt to them. Even though more than one in every three babies, the remaining 35%, could not be classified according to these criteria, the categories have proven helpful in understanding temperament.

To what extent do the differences in infant temperament remain stable throughout development? There is some evidence for stability, but it is not overwhelming. Several studies (Kagan & Moss, 1962; Kagan, Reznick, Clarke, Snidman, & Garcia-Coll, 1984) have found consistency in temperament over time. In one, children identified either as highly inhibited or essentially fearless at 21 months showed related patterns at age 4. In particular, three-fourths of the inhibited children remained inhibited, and none of the children who had been fearless had become inhibited. Nonetheless, the final verdict on stability of temperament is not in yet.

At first glance, temperament research seems only to state the obvious. Is it really surprising that two categories of babies are "easy" and "difficult"? Could these categories really change the way we look at babies? Yes. In fact, Thomas and Chess's work profoundly changed the way we view the **person-environment interaction**—the fit between an individual and his or her environment. Prior to the work of Thomas and Chess, researchers and practitioners in child development tended to ask, "What is the single best environment for infants and young children?" Countless books were written telling parents what constitutes a good or a bad environment for children, conceiving of "children" as a generic unit. The Thomas and Chess work, however, suggested that this question, as posed, is unanswerable. Rather, they showed, we ought to ask, "Which environment is best for which baby?" Clearly, not all babies are the

If this toddler is labeled as having a "difficult" temperament, how might that affect the way her father and other people treat her?

same; different environments can provide the right nurturing atmosphere for different children.

The same basic idea applies to adults. Some people thrive on stressful and changeable environments where there is a new and difficult challenge almost every day; others require more stable settings in which they perceive less threat to their well-being. The true gift of this research was the idea that each individual needs to discover the optimally suitable environment.

> What are some of the characteristics of temperament that you have noticed in yourself or that others have noticed in you? What kinds of environments would best suit your temperament?

The ideas of Thomas and Chess have not been universally accepted, however (e.g., Kagan, 1982). For example, Thomas and Chess suggested that difficult children are essentially unmodifiable and that attempts by parents to change these children would only result in increased difficulty. These parents, according to the researchers, need patience more than

anything. However, consider some of the implications of this notion. One is that some babies are, in some sense, preferable to others. The terms *easy* and *difficult* almost certainly involve value judgments, and the danger is that parents with "difficult" children might think that their children are inferior.

A second implication is that parents should not blame themselves for difficult children—that is just the way they are. To the extent that parents may have felt guilty about their children's behavior, perhaps this implication is constructive. However, recall from Chapter 1 the dangers associated with the self-fulfilling prophecy. Once people perceive a child as "difficult," rightly or wrongly assigning the label and all that it implies, they may start to treat the child accordingly. Eventually, the child may make the prophecy come true by behaving according to the expectations. Even worse, the misbehaving child may then become a candidate for abuse (Starr, Dietrich, Fischoff, Ceresnie, & Zweier, 1984).

> Describe some specific steps parents can take to tailor their interactions and their home environment to suit a child who might be described as difficult.

If there is a lesson to be learned from this research, it is that scientific theories with everyday applications do not and cannot occur in a vacuum. Investigators should think about the social implications of their theories and should be prepared to cope with them. It is tempting for researchers to disregard practical implications, whether they are studying the underlying temperament of children or the physics underlying atomic bombs. However, the work of scientists affects the public, so scientists have a responsibility to think about these effects and about what stance they will take regarding these effects. Theories regarding psychosexual development and gender typing have clear social implications, as we discover next.

> Why should researchers consider the social-policy implications of their research? On the other hand, what arguments could you make against having researchers consider such implications?

Psychosexual Development and Theories of Gender Typing

Psychosexual development refers to increasing self-identification with a particular gender and changing self-perceptions about sexuality. Obviously, adolescence is a period of rapid psychological and sexual

Searchers . . . EILEEN MAVIS HETHERINGTON

Eileen Mavis Hetherington is Commonwealth Professor of Psychology at the University of Virginia.

Q: *How did you become interested in psychology and in your area of work in particular?*

A: I started out with a double major in English and in psychology. I was an English honors student, and I took psychology because I thought it would help with my characterizations in writing fiction. When I went to take my masters in English, one of the required courses was offered only in alternate years. I was unwilling to wait for that course, so I went over to the psychology department. I did clinical work in Canada for four years, after my masters, and then went to Berkeley to take my PhD in clinical psych. I met Leo Postman and was so impressed with the way he thought about science that I did my dissertation with him. He changed me from a practicing clinician into a research psychologist.

Q: *What theories have influenced you the most?*

A: The work of Diana Baumrind, Eleanor Maccoby, and Robert Sears, which looks at families and relationships among family functioning and child development. Michael Rutter and Norm Garmezy have been big influences on the way I think about theories of stress and coping. Also Jerry Patterson's work on aggression and Urie Bronfenbrenner's work in ecological models of development.

Q: *What is your greatest asset as a psychologist?*

A: Energy and enthusiasm. I am a very high-energy person, so I work a pretty regular eighty-hour week. I'm still very excited about psychology and new ideas and get revved up easily.

Q: *What distinguishes a really great psychologist from just a good one?*

A: Divergent thinking, being able to look at things a little bit differently from other people. Also being meticulous and innovative in research. Another important thing is getting the best research methods that answer the question you ask. Many important questions have drowned because the methods used were inappropriate.

Q: *How do you get your ideas or insights for research?*

A: The ideas emerge from issues that open up when doing large-scale longitudinal studies. Also I read widely in the literature, and I try to take questions raised in other people's work and incorporate them into my own work.

Q: *How do you decide whether to pursue an idea?*

A: I keep a book where I list research ideas. If an idea is a sensible progression in my research program or if it challenges current ideas, then I pursue it.

Q: *How have you developed an idea into a workable hypothesis?*

A: My early work indicated that fathers were extremely salient in the sex-role typing of both boys and girls. I wondered what would happen in mother-headed families with no father present. I hypothesized that the mother's attitudes and behavior would be more important in shaping their children's sex-typed behaviors in one- than in two-parent families and this was confirmed.

Q: *What obstacles have you experienced?*

A: If you mean social obstacles, I, and most professional women in my generation, encountered gender discrimination. I was often the only woman in my department. If you mean obstacles in my research, they were mainly methodological problems in measuring family relations.

Q: *What is your major contribution to psychology?*

A: My emphasis on the importance of longitudinal research in studying stressful life transitions such as divorce or remarriage. Individual family members, family roles and relationships, and life circumstances are constantly changing, and these factors alter the short- and long-term effects of a stressful life event.

Q: *What do you want students to learn from you?*

A: I spend an awful lot of time with my students and set very high standards. I want students to really feel the excitement of doing research. I also want them to work on problems they think are important, that are going to help the lives of children and families. And I want them to be good scientists, not to be afraid to disagree with the status quo. I also like being a role model for my female students, combining a successful career and a happy family life.

Q: *What advice would you give to someone starting in the field of psychology?*

A: Don't be afraid to challenge current ideas. Today's wisdom may be tomorrow's fallacy. Learn to be skilled in both verbal and written presentation. It doesn't matter how good your ideas are. If you try to present them and have all the dynamism of a piece of wet blotting paper, people aren't going to be turned on by what you say. Also, the commitment to working hard is very important. Very few people get ahead who don't invest a lot of time in their careers.

Q: *What did you learn from your mentors?*

A: I learned how to think like a scientist, how to ask questions, and how to test them, and how to do theory-based research. Also, because I had some very supportive mentors, I learned to have more confidence in my abilities. I learned to accept criticism and to disagree with others without becoming upset. In professional differences, in personal ones, or in research ones, you always come out better if you disagree and don't lose your cool.

Q: *What have you learned from your students?*

A: Oh, I've learned a lot. I learn from my students all the time. I find even a relatively inexperienced undergraduate student can produce innovative research ideas.

Q: *What do you further hope to achieve or contribute?*

A: I'm interested in understanding more about the interface of the family with other social systems, like the schools, the peer group, and the neighborhood. I'd also like to start looking at ethnic and ecological variations in families.

growth, but most developmental psychologists believe that psychosexual development starts much earlier than adolescence. In fact, children form gender identifications by the age of 2 or 3 (R. F. Thompson, 1975). **Gender typing,** the acquisition of sex-related roles, begins early, too. From ages 2 to 7, children seem to have rather rigid sex-role stereotypes; by the end of this period, they develop **gender constancy**—a sense that a person's gender cannot be altered by changing superficial characteristics (e.g., hair length) or behaviors (e.g., carrying a purse).

The view that psychosexual development begins in infancy is widely accepted today, but when Sigmund Freud first proposed this radical notion in 1905, it was not at all well received, to say the least. (Freud also developed an entire theory of personality; see Chapter 17.)

Freud's Theory

Sigmund Freud (1905/1964b) proposed that psychosexual development begins immediately after birth and continues through adulthood. According to Freud, there are four major stages of development: oral, anal, phallic, and genital. The **oral stage** occurs during the first 2 years of life, when an infant explores sucking and other oral activity, learning that such activity provides not only nourishment, but also pleasure. The **anal stage** typically occurs between the ages of 2 and 4, during which time the child learns to derive pleasure from urination and, especially, defecation. The **phallic stage** usually begins around age 4. Children discover during this stage that stimulation of the genitals can feel good. This stage can also give rise to **Oedipal conflict,** in which the child starts to feel romantic feelings for the parent of the opposite sex. In particular, boys desire their mothers but fear the wrath of their fathers. The conflict is named for the Greek myth in which Oedipus, who had long been separated from his parents and therefore did not recognize them, killed his father and married his mother. Girls may desire their fathers but worry about the wrath of their mothers (sometimes called the **Electra conflict,** after the myth of Electra, who despised her mother for having cheated on and killed her husband, Electra's father).

According to Freud, the Oedipal and Electra conflicts cause great turmoil in children. To resolve these conflicts, children must accept the sexual unattainability of their parents. The feelings they directed toward the opposite-sex parent become *sublimated*—redirected in a more socially acceptable fashion. Freud believed that these feelings go into **latency,** in which the sexual desires remain hidden and

dormant during the period of middle childhood. Eventually, they reappear during adolescence, and the feelings that children once felt toward the parent of the opposite sex they now direct toward an agemate of the opposite sex. Ultimately, the child develops a mature relationship with a partner of the opposite sex, thereby entering into the final psychosexual stage, the **genital stage.** According to Freud, at any point during psychosexual development, the child might become **fixated**—unable to resolve the relevant issues of the current stage and therefore unable to progress to the next stage. (See Table 13-3.)

Freud implied that if a child does not resolve the Oedipal or Electra conflict, a tendency toward homosexuality might be the result. In addition, however, he acknowledged a possible genetic role in the development of sexual preferences for partners of the same gender. (Homosexuality is discussed further in Chapter 16.)

Freud's theory was ground-breaking, but it generated heated debate that continues to this day (see Chapter 17). Among other criticisms, many psychologists think that Freud placed too much emphasis on sex as the basis of a general theory of development. Freud clearly developed his theory within the particular context of his times, as evidenced by his very traditional views of female sex roles and of sexual orientation, as well as his heavy emphasis on the role of sexual repression in normal adult feelings, thoughts, and behavior. The less sexuality-oriented developmental theories such as Erikson's (1950), described earlier, were in part a reaction to the sexual emphasis of Freud. Other theories concentrate on a different aspect of sexual development—namely, gender typing: What, psychologically, makes a man a man, and a woman a woman?

Biological and Sociobiological Theories

Obviously, many differences between the sexes have their bases in biological factors. The anatomies and physiologies of men and women are simply different. Still, why do people tend to perceive men as more dominant than women, or as more likely to be interested in athletic activities? Are such personality and interest patterns biological? Instead, are these differences the result of *socialization*, whereby we learn ways of feeling, thinking, and acting by observing and imitating parents, siblings, peers, and other role models? Many theories try to account for sex-role acquisition. Biological theories (e.g., Benbow & Stanley, 1980) hold that boys and girls acquire different sex roles because they are genetically predisposed to do so. Likewise, sociobiological theories (Kenrick & Trost, 1993)

TABLE 13-3
Freud's Stages of Psychosexual Development
For each of his stages of psychosexual development, Sigmund Freud posited that a set of personality characteristics would be associated with that stage of development. Fixation in the given stage of development would mean that the individual would show those characteristics in adulthood. (After Freud, 1905/1964b)

State	Characteristics Associated with Fixation
Oral (birth to age 2)	Display many activities centered around the mouth: excessive eating, drinking; smoking, talking.
Oral eroticism	Sucking and eating predominate; cheerful, dependent, and needy; expects to be taken care of by others.
Oral sadism	Biting and chewing predominate; tends to be cynical and cruel.
Anal (ages 2 to 4)	
Anal-retentive	Excessively neat, clean, meticulous, and obsessive.
Anal-expulsive	Moody, sarcastic, biting, and often aggressive; untidy in personal habits.
Phallic (age 4 to middle childhood)	Overly preoccupied with self; often vain and arrogant; unrealistic level of self-confidence and self-absorption.
Latency (middle childhood)	Demonstrates sexual sublimation and repression.
Genital (adolescence through adulthood)	Traditional sex roles and heterosexual orientation.

To what extent is this girl's biological predisposition (her nature) influencing her gender identification? To what extent are her interactions with her mother and other aspects of her socialization (her nurture) affecting her identification with the gender roles appropriate to her culture?

hold that evolution determines or at least guides social behavior, in this case sex-role differences.

Social Learning Theory

In contrast to sociobiological and biological theories, social learning theory (Bandura, 1977b) accounts for psychosexual development in terms of role models and rewards in the external environment. In this view, gender typing is no different from other kinds of social learning. Adults and peers reward boys for behavior considered masculine and punish them if they depart too far from what is considered gender appropriate. Similarly, adults and peers reward girls for emulating female role models and reprimand them if they go too far afield. Thus, each generation repeats the sex-role patterns of the past, albeit with some modification. Boys act like boys, or girls like girls, simply via imitation of what they perceive to be appropriate role models.

What is this young boy learning about being a male in his cultural setting? How does social-learning theory explain what he is learning?

Observational learning clearly plays an important role in the establishment of gender identity. In addition, parents bolster these observations by encouraging gender-specific behaviors. For example, parents are more likely to encourage independence, competitiveness, and achievement in boys and sensitivity, empathy, and trustworthiness in girls (Archer & Lloyd, 1985; Block, 1980, 1983; Huston et al., 1986). Whereas boys are more encouraged to be independent, girls are more encouraged both to request help from others and to provide help to them (Huston, 1983).

Role modeling is important throughout life, and perhaps at no time more so than during high school, college, and early adulthood. During these years, young adults cast around for models to emulate. Often, the role-modeling function of a respected adult is more important than what he or she may have directly to teach or to show. Role modeling becomes especially important as an individual tries to figure out what it means to be a professional in a given field. Starting workers often try to emulate those above them on the organizational ladder, hoping eventually to fill the niches of those superiors. Role modeling is not just an abstract psychological idea, but rather an active process by which we develop into the kind of person we wish to become.

Schema Theory

Sandra Bem (1981) proposed a more cognitively based theory, **schema theory,** which holds that we have organized mental systems of information (i.e., *schemas*) that help us make sense of our experiences. In particular, we have gender schemas that differ for boys and girls, and for men and women. The schema view suggests that we acquire sex roles by following the gender-appropriate schemas we have conceived. We acquire these schemas through interactions with the environment, but they also guide our interactions. In other words, we learn gender typing from the world, and then these gender-typing ideas guide how we behave in the world, as well as how the world responds to our behavior. In general, schema theories tend to focus on specific concepts that individuals may incorporate into their schemas rather than on the developmental sequence of an integrated, global concept of gender.

How could you create an environment that would *minimize* gender stereotypes for your children? In contrast, how could you create an environment that would *maximize* the development of gender-appropriate schemes?

Conclusions

Gender theories typically deal with masculinity and femininity as opposite ends of a continuum, but it is important to note that this view is by no means universally accepted. Some theorists do not see masculinity and femininity as mutually exclusive constructs (S. Bem, 1981). Instead, they suggest that it is possible to conceive of someone as being masculine and feminine simultaneously. Some theorists have argued that theories of gender typing also need to take into account the concept of *androgyny*, which can refer either to a person high in both masculinity and femininity or to a person for whom stereotypically masculine and feminine behavior simply are not very relevant. Using the schema theory, we would say that an androgynous person does not have very strong sex-based schemas. Rather, he or she acts in ways that seem appropriate to the situation, regardless of stereotypes about how people of a particular gender should act.

Although nature clearly plays a role in sex differences, nurture also plays an important role. Our own schemas for boys and girls may influence the way we perceive our children of each sex, and these perceptions may in turn influence the way our children respond to us. Quite simply, there is no foolproof way to extricate the effects of pure biology from the effects of environment.

Thus far, this chapter has focused on intrapersonal development, such as emotional and personality development. We have yet to discuss the particular ways our interpersonal interactions both affect and are affected by our own development as individuals.

INTERPERSONAL DEVELOPMENT

IN SEARCH OF...

How did the patterns of attachment in your early relationships shape the close interpersonal relationships you have now?

This chapter has already indicated the ways children become increasingly aware of others and increasingly consider the perspectives of others throughout childhood and adolescence (recall the parallel changes due to cognitive development). This section considers specifically the ways we interact directly with others, starting with our early attachment to our parents and progressing ever outward into the wider community of other children and adults.

During the sixteenth through nineteenth centuries, children in Western cultures were viewed as miniature adults, not as persons engaged in a distinctive process of development in which their experiences, feelings, and modes of thought differed entirely from those of adults.

Attachment

Attachment refers to a strong and long-lasting emotional tie between two people. Our first attachment begins at birth (although some mothers contend that it begins even earlier) and is usually fully cemented within several years. One of the foundations of relationships with others is the process of bonding.

Bonding

Interpersonal development starts with **bonding,** the process by which an adult forms a close attachment to an infant immediately or soon after birth. Bonding has traditionally been viewed in terms of the relationship of the mother to the infant (e.g., Myers, 1984a), but we now realize that fathers and infants can bond as well. Failure of either parent to bond with the infant can cause problems for both parent and child later on, especially when the parent-child relationship passes through difficult times (e.g., when parental constraints conflict with children's strivings for independence).

What facilitates the bonding process between parent and child? One thing is physical contact (recall the importance of touch, mentioned in Chapter 4). Gazing at one another also facilitates bonding. Recall from Chapter 12 the ways infants seem custom-designed to cause their caregivers to fall in love with them: their intrinsic interest in gazing at the human face, tendency to move in synchrony with the caregivers' interactions, imitation of caregivers' facial expressions, and early proclivity for social smiling. In

This father's bond with his infant is strengthened through physical contact. In exchanged gazes, this mother and her infant deepen their mutual bonding. Some psychologists believe that bonding not only ensures a close parent-child relationship, but also paves the way for intimate relationships in adulthood.

addition, by about 3 months of age, infants seem to match their own emotional expressions to those of their caregivers (Fogel, 1991).

Both gazing and physical contact can be important in later life as well, when they can be crucial in the incipient bonding phases of a love relationship. (You may have noticed that gaining eye contact with someone can be the key to initiating a relationship.) Of course, it is not just the contact itself—physical or visual—that is important, but also the emotions this contact generates.

> What situational factors might interfere with the bonding process? How might physical or sensory limitations affect the bonding process? How might individual differences between parent and infant affect bonding?

Attachment Patterns

As a result of and even as an expansion of bonding, babies form long-term emotional attachments to their parents, especially their primary caregivers—usually their mothers. Mary Ainsworth and her colleagues (Ainsworth, Bell, & Stayton, 1971; Ainsworth, Blehar, Waters, & Wall, 1978) have conducted some of the best-known work on attachment. In particular, Ainsworth and her colleagues have studied attachment by using a research technique known as the **strange situation**, in which the subjects are usually a toddler, 12 to 18 months of age, and the toddler's mother. The mother and her infant enter a room containing a variety of toys. The mother puts down the infant and sits in a chair. A few minutes later, an unfamiliar woman enters the room, talks to the mother, and then tries to play with the child. While the stranger is trying to engage the child, the mother quietly walks out of the room, leaving her purse on the chair to indicate that she will return. Later, the mother returns. An observer positioned behind a one-way mirror records the child's reactions to the mother's return. Still later, the mother leaves yet again, but this time the child is left alone. Later, the mother returns, and the observer records the child's reactions again. (See Figure 13-4.)

Ainsworth noticed that children's reactions tend to fit one of three different patterns: avoidant, secure, and resistant. The **avoidant** ("Type A") child generally ignores the mother when she returns. These infants pay little attention to the mother even when she is in the room, and they show minimal distress when she leaves. If the child does show distress, the stranger is about as effective as the mother in providing comfort.

Psychologist Mary Ainsworth refined the work of John Bowlby and proposed a series of developmental phases of attachment behavior.

The **secure** ("Type B") child shows distress when the mother departs. When the mother returns, the child immediately goes to her. She is able to calm the child down, usually by holding and hugging. The secure child is friendly with the stranger but shows an obvious preference for the mother.

The **resistant** ("Type C") child is ambivalent toward the mother. Upon reunion after the mother's return to the room, the resistant child seems simultaneously to seek and to resist physical contact. For example, the child might run to the mother when she returns, but then, when held, tries to extricate him- or herself.

Just how much credence can we give to attachment theory, as measured in the strange situation? Researchers differ in their views, and some are skeptical (e.g., Kagan, 1986). For example, there are a number of possible limitations to the strange situation. First, an infant's attachment pattern appears not to be highly stable, at least as the strange situation has measured it. In one study, for example, roughly half of the infants classified one way at age 12 months were classified another way at age 18 months (Thompson, Lamb, & Estes, 1982). Second, the strange situation may measure temperament at least as much as attachment. Highly independent infants might be classified as avoidant, whereas infants classified as ambivalent or resistant might be those who are upset by almost any new situation, regardless of whether it involves the mother. Third, the procedure itself is brief, requiring typically only 6 to 8 minutes. How much can we tell about infants, or anyone, in such a short span of time? Fourth, interpretation is somewhat more complex, in that the implied value judgments in the terms used for classification are open to question.

Ainsworth worked primarily with American middle-class children from stable homes during the 1970s, and she found that about 20% to 25% of children were avoidant, roughly 65% were secure, and approximately 12% were resistant. However, socioeconomic status and environment seem to play roles in attachment pattern. Researchers have found different patterns among children in other cultural and socioeconomic contexts. For example, children in nonstable, nonintact American families of lower socioeconomic status are more likely to be considered avoidant or resistant (Egeland & Sroufe, 1981; Vaughn, Gove, & Egeland, 1980). Studies of other cultures have shown more avoidant children among Western Europeans and more resistant children among Israelis and the Japanese (Bretherton & Waters, 1985; Miyake, Chen, & Campos, 1985; Morelli, Rogoff, Oppenheim, & Goldsmith, 1992). Thus if German children, who are more likely to show avoidant attachment behavior, are encouraged to be independent at an early age, why should we categorize such an independent pattern as somehow less than secure?

Do attachment patterns have any long-term consequences? If so, what are they? John Bowlby (1951, 1969) claimed that an infant's attachment pattern has long-term effects on the child's development, and some evidence supports this claim. For example, infants who are securely attached at age 12 or 18 months approach problems when they are age 2 with greater interest and enthusiasm than do avoidant or resistant children (Matas, Arend, & Sroufe, 1978). Similarly, securely attached children in nursery school tend to be more active, more sought out by other children, and rated by their teachers as more eager to learn (Waters, Wippman, & Sroufe, 1979).

Adult Attachment

Attachment, like bonding, does not end in childhood. Robert Weiss (1982) has noted that adults, like children, tend to attach themselves to others. Indeed, one of the main purposes of intimate relationships is to give adults someone to comfort them in times of need, and to provide them with something resembling the closeness they once had with a childhood attachment figure. Although we still lack sufficient hard data to assert unequivocally that the quality of our early attachments to our parents affects the quality of our attachments as adults, most of us believe intuitively that this relationship between early and later attachments is true—in regard to both our relationships with our own parents and our relationships with our own children.

Attachment Gone Awry

What happens when children are deprived of love and warmth from both father and mother, and attachment processes either cannot form or go utterly awry? No scientist would conduct an experiment purposely exposing children to inadequate or distorted attachment; however, two research methods offer a way to examine such processes. One is the unfortunate instance in which naturalistic observation of extremely deprived children is possible, and the other is controlled experimentation with animals.

In a case of extreme deprivation, Genie (Curtiss, 1977) had been isolated in a small room, strapped to a potty chair, from roughly ages 2 to 13. Genie's only contact with humans was when a family member entered the room to give the baby food. When found, Genie could not walk, talk, stand up straight, or eat solid food, nor was she toilet-trained. Eventually,

FIGURE 13-4
Strange Situation
In the "Strange Situation" researchers observe the attachment of children to their mothers, by noting how the children react to the mother's departure and her return.

Genie did learn to speak a bit, but she never progressed beyond the level of a 4- to 5-year-old. Initially, Genie showed exciting improvements, and an onslaught of social scientists and social workers of all kinds descended on her. Genie now lives in an institution for retarded adults (Angier, 1993; Rymer, 1993). Although we must be wary of the conclusions we reach based on anecdotal evidence—however rich the case material—we can clearly conclude that Genie was severely and permanently harmed by her lack of contact with loving or caring humans.

The other kind of research, controlled experimentation with animals, enables researchers to study attachment processes more directly (Harlow, 1958, 1962; Harlow & Harlow, 1965, 1966). In a series of experiments, Harry Harlow, Margaret Harlow, and other researchers raised infant monkeys with either or both of two substitute mothers—a wire mesh cylinder and a cylinder covered with soft terrycloth. Either "mother" could be set up with a bottle providing milk (see Figure 13-5). Even when only the wire mother could provide milk, however, the monkeys still clung to the cloth mother, suggesting that comfort through physical contact was more important than nourishment. The monkeys also showed other signs of attachment to the cloth mother, but not to the wire mother. For example, when a frightening, noisy bear-monster doll was placed next to the monkeys, those raised with the cloth mother would run to it and cling, but later they would investigate the monster. The monkeys raised with the wire mother, however, just clutched themselves and rocked back and forth (see Figure 13-5).

Although the cloth mother was clearly superior to the wire mother in fostering attachment and security, ultimately neither surrogate proved adequate for fostering normal social development. Monkeys reared with either of the surrogate mothers were socially and sexually incompetent. Females who themselves later had children were poor mothers. Live, interactive attachment processes, therefore, appear to be crucial for the development of later social and familial competence, both in humans and in animals.

Attachment to Fathers and Other Caregivers

Attachment research originally focused on the role of the mother in the life of the infant, but in recent years investigators have turned to studying the role of the father and others as well (Ricks, 1985). Research has shown that members of the family or extended family can help compensate for an infant's inadequate attachment to the mother (Parke & Asher, 1983). Fathers feeding their 3-month-old children can show the same sensitivity to cues as do mothers, but fathers rarely use this skill, usually yielding the feeding function to the mother (Parke & Sawin, 1980; Parke & Tinsley, 1987). Infants do become attached to fathers, protesting separations beginning at about 7 months of age (Lamb, 1977a, 1977b, 1979). At home, the infants approach fathers, smile at them, and seek contact with them. When the father substitutes for the mother in the strange situation, the child uses the father as a safe haven. Children prefer fathers to a strange female as well.

Fathers seem to provide a different kind of care from mothers. They tend to have a more physical approach in playing with their children (Clarke-Stewart, Perlmutter, & Friedman, 1988; Parke, 1981) and engage in more novel games than do mothers (Lamb, 1977b). One study found that two-thirds of toddlers prefer playing with their fathers to playing with their mothers (Clarke-Stewart, 1978). Also, the relationship between toddlers and their fathers may be more instrumental than their relationships with their mothers in helping the infants to widen their social contacts and to interact sociably with persons outside their families (Bridges, Connell, & Belsky, 1988).

In sum, attachment is an essential part in development, and it continues to play a role throughout our lives. Although the patterns themselves may not yet be understood fully, their influence is clear.

Parental Styles

In addition to the quality of attachment patterns, other aspects of the child-parent relationship are important to the development of later social competence. One such aspect is the parents' style of caregiving. We know that large individual differences exist among parents in how they bring up children, differences that occur not only across individuals, but also across levels of education and socioeconomic status. For example, parents of lower levels of education and socioeconomic status are more likely to value obedience to authority and are more likely to use physical punishment. Parents of higher socioeconomic status and education levels are more likely to explain their actions and to let children make decisions for themselves (Kohn, 1976).

Research by Diana Baumrind (1971, 1978) suggests that parental styles of caring for children can be better understood if we view the styles in terms of three categories of parenting: authoritarian, permissive, and authoritative. **Authoritarian** parents tend to be firm, punitive, and generally unsympathetic to their children. These parents believe in the importance of their authority, and they value their children's obedience. They see children as willful and in need of disciplining to meet parental standards. Au-

FIGURE 13-5
"Mother Love" in Primates

Harry Harlow's revolutionary research on the importance of "contact comfort" revealed that infant rhesus monkeys would become attached to—and seek comfort from—a cloth "mother," rather than from a wire "mother." Even when the wire mother provided milk, and the cloth mother did not, the infants would cling to the cloth mother most of the time. (After Harlow Primate Lab, University of Wisconsin)

thoritarian parents are somewhat detached from their children and tend to be very sparing with praise. **Permissive** parents go almost to the opposite extreme. They give their children a great deal of freedom, possibly more than the children can handle. These parents tend to be lax in discipline and to let children make their own decisions about many things. **Authoritative** parents encourage responsibility and give children increasing levels of responsibility with age. They reason with their children and explain why they do what they do. They are firm but understanding, and they set limits within which they encourage children to be independent.

> Describe a situation you have observed or experienced in which an adolescent flagrantly disobeyed a parent's admonitions. How would an authoritarian parent respond to the disobedience? What would a permissive parent do? How would an authoritative parent respond?

Research on 186 cultures (Rohner & Rohner, 1981) showed that the authoritative parenting style seemed to be the most common. Nonetheless, a wide variation in the degree of nurturance and control exhibited by parents exists, and the cultural expression of these two factors may differ greatly. For example, Japanese mothers, whose interactions tend to foster warm and close relationships with their children, may exert firm behavioral control over their children by merely intimating indirectly how the child's behavior may affect the quality of the relationship (Azuma, 1986).

As you might expect, differing parental styles lead to differing outcomes for the children (Baumrind, 1971, 1978). Children of authoritarian parents tend to be unfriendly, distrustful of others, and somewhat withdrawn in their social relationships. Children of permissive parents tend to be immature and dependent, seeking aid even for minor difficulties. They also tend to be unhappy in their lives in general. Children of authoritative parents seem to be the most well adapted. They tend to be friendly, generally cooperative, and relatively independent, showing a sense of responsibility in their social relations with others.

An entirely different avenue of research suggests that being away from parents for a portion of the day may also affect children's social competence. Children who attend child-care programs seem to be more likely to interact spontaneously with other children than do those who do not attend. Participation in child care is not unequivocally beneficial, however, as the following section explains.

Child Care

Given the importance of the child's attachment to the parents and the importance of parental style, how does child care affect children of various ages? An estimated three-fourths of the mothers with children ages 6 to 17 work outside the home, and almost 58% of the mothers with children less than 6 years of age do so (Scarr, 1994).

A summary of five studies of children's responses to the strange situation revealed that 74% of infants who participated in child care fewer than 20 hours per week were securely attached, whereas 57% of infants who participated in child care more than 20 hours per week were securely attached (Belsky & Rovine, 1988). Without considering again the merits

of determining attachment based on the strange situation, it appears that increased participation in child care is associated with a decreased likelihood of being securely attached. Note, however, that the majority of infants in the studies were still securely attached.

Other factors influence the outcomes of infants' participation in child care. A mother's stress level will affect her behavior toward her child. For example, mothers who work part-time rather than full-time feel less stress (Hoffman, 1989), and mothers who can cope more successfully with their employment are more likely to have securely attached infants (Belsky & Rovine, 1988). Another stress reducer for mothers is the participation of fathers in child care and in household chores (Hoffman, 1989). In addition, when fathers care for the infants while the mothers are at work, infants are more likely to show secure attachment (Belsky & Rovine, 1988).

An extensive body of research (Andersson, 1989; Belsky, 1990; Clarke-Stewart, 1989; Field, 1990; Gottfried & Gottfried, 1988; Hoffman, 1989) regarding preschoolers and school-aged children yields mixed results. For example, some research indi-

The effect of child care on children's attachments to their parents, as well as on other aspects of children's development, seems to relate more closely to the quality of the child care than to whether the child is in child care.

Searchers . . .   EDWARD F. ZIGLER

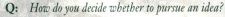

Edward Zigler is Sterling Professor of Psychology and Director of the Bush Center for Child Development and Social Policy at Yale University.

Q: *How did you become interested in psychology and in your area of work in particular?*

A: My work began in the area of clinical psychology. But in graduate school I began working with children, so my orientation became much more developmental. The move from clinical to personality development and socialization was a very short journey.

Q: *Whose ideas have influenced you the most?*

A: Negatively, Kurt Lewin, whose theory of performance of retarded individuals I took exception to. He became a kind of theoretical adversary of mine. Positively, Heinz Werner, who was a very distinguished thinker. My theoretical approach is broadly cognitive-developmental in the tradition of Werner, Piaget, and Vygotsky.

Q: *What is your greatest asset as a psychologist?*

A: The ability to cut to central issues, to look at empirical studies and find buried in them some signal where others see mostly noise. Also the ability to continue working very diligently. I believe that inspiration is just the very beginning of something, and that unless you're willing to really perspire and work very hard, you're not going to make much headway.

Q: *What distinguishes a really great psychologist from just a good psychologist?*

A: What strikes me about the really great psychologists is their long-term commitment. They champion a point of view, but they're not rigid; they expand it, they build on it, but it's programmatic, and they keep it up for decades.

Q: *How do you usually get your ideas for research?*

A: One is the literature before me. I ask what have other people found? How have they interpreted it? Is there some other view? The second is listening to and closely observing my subjects, and I'm grateful for my clinical training for that. If I carefully attend to what the subjects are doing and saying, in many instances they put me onto something that I hadn't even been thinking of.

Q: *How do you decide whether to pursue an idea?*

A: Well, I'm an empiricist. I have a lot of ideas, but I use the hypothetical deductive method to see if an idea can be made into a hypothesis that can be tested—that is, just as open to disproof as to proof.

Q: *What do you want students to learn from you?*

A: They have to be immersed in skepticism but always be open to new evidence. Work hard to gather well-verified facts or bits of knowledge. But I also insist that the ultimate purpose is not to fill up our journals but to make the lives of children better. Therefore, I impress upon my students that what this business is really all about is the optimal development of children. If knowledge is not utilized in some way that leads to that ultimate goal, then we're essentially wasting our time.

Q: *What have you learned from your students?*

A: How to combine appropriate amounts of reinforcement with the kind of constructive criticism that's necessary if the student is to grow.

Q: *How has psychology been important to you?*

A: Well I haven't been just an academic. I've gotten into the world of social action. I served a stint in Washington, D.C., as the first director of the Office of Child Development and chief of the Children's Bureau.

Q: *What do you want people to remember about you?*

A: I could be remembered for my work to expand cognitive developmental thought to include motivation and personality. More important than that would be the modeling I've tried to do of utilizing knowledge to make the lives of children and families better, to raise the importance of children and families in our society.

Q: *What do you further hope to achieve or contribute?*

A: There's no lack of things for me to do. I'm on a committee in Washington to improve Head Start, to plan its expansion to all the children that are eligible. So I'll be continuing to provide counsel to federal and state officials. There are three or four major areas which I continue to work in very diligently with my students and my colleagues.

---

cates some benefits of early child care, such as sociability and greater academic success (Andersson, 1989; Field, 1990). Other research indicates some drawbacks of early child care, such as increased aggressive behavior and increased desire for approval by peers when specific efforts to curb such behaviors were not implemented in the child-care setting (Clarke-Stewart, 1989).

> Suppose that you seek to reduce aggressiveness and the need for peer approval in children who participate in child care. Make specific suggestions that would aid you in reaching these goals.

Perhaps the best lesson from this research is the importance of evaluating and considering the quality of the specific child-care program. Many factors influence the quality of the program, but the single most important factor is the amount and quality of the attention given to children. As you might expect, caregivers are more likely to provide more high-quality attention to each child when they are in charge of fewer children. This is particularly important for infants and toddlers. In addition, the professional qualifications of the caregivers (Scarr, Phillips, & McCartney, 1990) and the stability of the center's work force (annual turnover of 50% is the average for these poorly paid professionals; Wingert & Kantrowitz, 1990) affect the quality of the program. Highly qualified professionals who are motivated to remain in the program provide child-centered activities that are appropriately challenging to children's needs for open-ended, creative, hands-on exploration of a wide array of materials. What seems to matter most is not whether children are in a child-care program, but which child-care program they are in.

> Design an experiment that would assess the effects of a particular aspect of child care, measuring what you believe to be high- versus low-quality care.

An additional consideration in evaluating high-quality child-care programs is the kinds of social relationships and social behaviors the caregivers encourage among the children. Friendships and play are the next subjects we address.

Peer Interactions: Friendship and Play

An important aspect of interpersonal development is learning how to interact with peers and learning to form friendships. Relationships with peers during childhood are important not only for the child's well-being but, eventually, for the well-being of the adult whom the child will become.

More than half a century ago, Mildred Parten (1932) observed the spontaneous play of preschool-aged children and noticed developmental trends in their play behaviors. Children may be *unoccupied*, unsure of what to do or just watching other people. Children may be engaged in *solitary* play, playing only with things and not with other children. Children may be *onlookers*, playing alone but interested in what other children are playing with. Children may be engaged in *parallel* play, playing with the same toys as other children but not interacting with them. Children may be engaged in *associative* play, sharing toys and interacting with others but still distinctive from others in their activities. Finally, children may be

engaged in *cooperative* play, fully cooperating with others on a joint project. Although we may never completely outgrow any of these kinds of activities, children's play becomes increasingly social and cooperative as their chronological age increases, and the youngest children seem to be the least socially interactive (see Figure 13-6).

Children's friendship patterns show similar increases in their degree of interaction. During early infancy, the only social exchange between very young infants seems to be that they are more likely to cry if they see and hear another infant crying. By about 3 or 4 months, they reach toward and even touch one another when they can (Vandell & Mueller, 1980). Their interactions increase somewhat over time, and they often smile at one another, but until 1 year of age, their exchanges usually are limited to one overture and one response. During the next couple of years, play interactions increase, and children learn gradually to cooperate, share, and play with one another.

Play continues to be at the center of friendships during most of childhood (Gottman, 1983, 1986; Howes, 1988). In addition, preschoolers show quite stable friendship patterns, often keeping the same friend for more than a year (Howes, 1988). According to John Gottman (1983), friendships among children ages 3 to 9 gradually show a sharing of thoughts and feelings, an exchange of information, an establishing of common ground, conflict resolution, positive reciprocity (the friends please each other), and self-disclosure (the friends reveal intimate details about themselves). These aspects of friendship also apply to friendships among adults.

During childhood and adolescence, the friendships of boys and of girls seem to go through rather different stages. Children of both sexes seem to prefer same-sex friends throughout this period, and early friendships usually center on shared activities and other interests. The interests and activities of girls and boys differ, however, with boys more likely to be involved in groups and in competitive activities, and girls more likely to prefer cooperative activities involving just two people.

Adolescent girls' friendships progress through three stages (Douvan & Adelson, 1966). From roughly ages 11 to 13, the emphasis is on joint activities. A friend is someone with whom to do fun things. From roughly ages 14 to 16, friendships pass through an emotional stage, with an emphasis on sharing secrets, especially about other friends, both male and female. Trust is a critical element of friendship at this stage. Actually, across the life span, females show greater emotional closeness and shared intimacies in

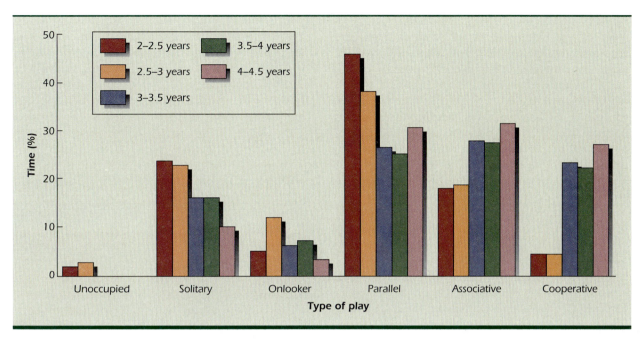

FIGURE 13-6
Developmental Trends in Social Play
Children's play becomes increasingly social and cooperative over the course of development. (After Parten, 1932)

their friendships than do males (Berndt, 1982, 1986; Rubin, 1980). (This pattern may be changing, however, as young men and women, particularly the well educated, now show fewer sex differences regarding self-disclosure [Peplau, 1983].) In late adolescence (age 17 years and beyond), the emphasis shifts to compatibility, shared personalities, and shared interests. Girls may transfer some of the possessiveness of their earlier friendships with females during midadolescence to their relationships with males.

In contrast, boys' friendships are oriented toward joint activities throughout adolescence. For boys, achievement and autonomy are important not only in their development as individuals, but also in their friendships. Perhaps it is therefore no surprise that adult males typically report having far fewer close friends than do adult females.

> Have your own friendship patterns matched the patterns described here? Why or why not?

Whatever our age and sex, we need to have someone (or ones) in whom we can confide, on whom we can depend for support, and to whom we are important, special, and needed as givers of support and recipients of revealing self-disclosures. Across the life span, we improve in our skill at showing friendship toward our friends.

Marriage and the Family

Most people get married, sooner or later, although in recent years, the trend has been toward later. More and more people have postponed marriage into the late twenties, early thirties, or even later (Sporakowski, 1988). There are multiple reasons for the tendency toward postponement, including the increasing need and desire of women to support themselves in the work force, the increasing acceptability of being single for longer periods of time, and the tendency even among the earlier married to postpone childbearing.

Satisfaction in marriage tends to be greatest in the early years, to fall during the raising of children, and then to increase again in the later years when children grow older and, especially, when they start their own lives away from their families. Thus, the **empty nest syndrome,** whereby parents may be saddened by their children's departure from home, can be partially offset by their own newfound happiness with each other.

What makes a happy marriage? According to Gottman (1994), the key is in the way a couple resolves the conflicts that are inevitable in any marriage. Gottman has found that three different styles can succeed for resolving conflict. In a *validating marriage,* couples compromise often and develop relatively calm ways of resolving conflicts. In a *conflict-avoiding marriage,* couples agree to disagree and avoid conflicts to the extent possible. In a *volatile marriage*, couples have frequent conflicts, some of them very antagonistic. Any one of these styles can work, as long as the number of positive moments the couple has together is at least five times as great as the number of negative moments. What kills a marriage, according to Gottman, are (a) attacking the partner's personality or character, rather than his or her particular behavior; (b) showing contempt for a partner; (c) being defensive in response to constructive criticism; and (d) stonewalling—failing to respond at all to the concerns of the partner.

Clifford Notarius and Howard Markman (1993) have suggested that there are several keys to happiness in a relationship, for example, that one really negative act can erase the effects of twenty acts of kindness and that it is not the differences between partners that cause problems, but rather how the differences are handled. Notarius and Markman have found that they can predict with more than 90% accuracy whether a couple will stay married solely on the basis of how the couple handles conflict. They have devised a questionnaire that assesses conflict-resolution skills, including statements such as "I sometimes nag at my partner to get him/her to talk" and "It is very easy for me to get angry at my partner" (Notarius & Markman, 1993, p. 41). "True" answers to these statements tend to be associated with marital unhappiness.

The World of Work

Marriage and family responsibilities are part of many adults' lives. Work is another. Individuals tend to be satisfied with their work to the extent that it is both *intrinsically rewarding*, meaning that the person enjoys the work he or she is doing, and *extrinsically rewarding*, meaning that the person is well-compensated in various ways, including financially, for the work. (See Chapter 14 for a greater discussion of motivations.)

According to Donald Super (1985), there are five main stages of career development. In the *growth stage*, from ages 0 to 14, the individual learns about and acquires the ability to pursue a vocation. In the *exploration stage*, from roughly ages 15 to 24, the individual makes a tentative vocational choice and may enter a first job. In the *establishment stage*, from roughly 25 to 44, the individual seeks entry into a permanent occupation. In the *maintenance stage*, from roughly 45 to 65, the individual is usually established in the occupation, and continues in it. Finally, in the *decline stage*, from roughly age 65 to death, the individual adapts to leaving and then ultimately retires from the work force. Whereas thirty years ago, this pattern would have applied almost exclusively to men, today it applies to large numbers of men and women alike. Moral development, the final aspect of social development considered in this chapter, similarly reflects a progressive development in understanding how our friends and other people might think, feel, and behave.

DEVELOPMENT OF MORAL REASONING

IN SEARCH OF...

Are there absolute, correct moral rules of right and wrong moral behaviors? Why or why not?

One day at lunchtime Florence and I lied to our respective families as to where we were lunching and hid at the school. . . . When we were sure the teachers were all eating, Florence (the minister's daughter) and I (the daughter of two very "state-of-humanity"-conscious parents) rushed out and at the top of our lungs and in vulgar tones screamed: "Old Lady Lynes! Old Lady Lynes!"

It brought shame to the school, shame to our parents and must really have puzzled Miss Lynes. Mother forced me to carry a potted geranium from Hawthorn Street to school and present it to Miss Lynes—an admission of my guilt and an indication of my sorrow. Miss Lynes put it on her desk. It was there humiliating me for weeks.

And there were so many geraniums in California—reminding me to remember: if you sin you pay.

Katharine Hepburn, Me

Piaget's Views of Moral Development

In addition to his work on cognitive development, Jean Piaget (1932/1965) was interested in how and why children make moral judgments. Recall that, in Piaget's view, an important consideration in children's moral development is their egocentrism, which limits their ability truly to take the perspective of another before about age 7. Similarly to the way he assessed children's cognitive development, Piaget investigated children's moral development by devising situations, asking children to make moral judgments about the situations, and then asking them to tell him why they reached the moral judgments they reached. He concluded that children younger than 8 years of age make moral judgments based on how much detriment the actions cause. For example, someone who broke 15 cups would be judged more harshly than someone who broke only one cup. Children older than 8, however, also consider whether the person acted intentionally or accidentally. Subsequent researchers (e.g., Schultz, Wright, & Schleifer, 1986) have found that children make complex judgments at younger ages than Piaget had suggested. Lawrence Kohlberg was intrigued by Piaget's findings and built on them to propose his own theory of moral development, which made use of moral dilemmas.

 How might you design an experiment to study an aspect of moral development in 4-year-olds, 8-year-olds, and 16-year-olds?

Kohlberg's Model

In Europe, a woman was near death from a rare form of cancer. The doctors thought that one drug might save her: a form of radium a druggist in the same town had recently discovered. The drug was expensive to make, but the druggist was also charging ten times his cost; having paid $400 for the radium, he charged $4,000 for a small dose. The sick woman's husband, Heinz, went to everyone he knew to borrow the money, but he could collect only $2,000. He begged the druggist to sell it more cheaply or to let him pay the balance later, but the druggist refused. So, having tried every legal means, Heinz desperately considered breaking into the drugstore to steal the drug for his wife. (Adapted from Kohlberg, 1963, 1984)

Suppose that you are Heinz. Should you steal the drug? Why or why not? These and similar scenario-related questions form the basis for measuring the development of moral reasoning in Lawrence Kohlberg's influential theory. According to Kohlberg, your answers will depend on your level of moral reasoning, which passes through six specific stages, embedded within three general levels. Your solutions do not determine your stage of moral reasoning. Rather, the kinds of reasons you give to justify either stealing or not stealing the drug determine your moral stage (see Table 13-4).

Psychologist Lawrence Kohlberg found that persons at the same stage of moral reasoning might reach opposite answers to a moral dilemma, using similar kinds of moral reasoning. However, Kohlberg also found that persons at quite different stages of moral development might reach identical answers to such a dilemma, using quite different kinds of moral reasoning.

Level I (ages 7–10) represents **preconventional morality**, in which the reasons to behave are essentially to avoid punishment or to obtain rewards. In the first stage of this level, *punishment* and *obedience* guide reasoning. Stage 1 children think that it is right to avoid breaking rules because punishment may follow. Obedience to authority is desirable for its own sake. This stage is egocentric in that children do not really consider others' interests. Children simply assume that the perspective of authority figures is correct because they will punish the children otherwise.

In Stage 2 of preconventional morality, children's orientation shifts to *individualism* and *exchange*. Stage 2 children follow rules, but only when it is to their benefit. Children serve their own interests, but they recognize that other people may have different interests. They therefore strike deals to meet everyone's interests. In this stage of the first level, what children consider to be morally right is relative, depending on whatever they will be rewarded for doing.

TABLE 13-4
Kohlberg's Theory of Development of Moral Reasoning
How did you respond to the dilemma, and on what basis did you reach your answer?

Level/Stage	Basis for Reasoning	Why You (as Heinz) Should Steal	Why You (as Heinz) Should Not Steal
Level I: Preconventional morality (ages 7–10)			
Stage 1 (Do not get caught.)	Egocentric consideration of whether the behavior leads to punishment or to reward. Might makes right, so people should obey authority.	If you do not steal the drug, your wife will be very angry with you, which would be painful. She might even die, which also would be painful.	You might get caught, and if you were caught, you would be punished (and your wife would not get the drug anyway).
Stage 2 (What is in it for me?)	Give-and-take exchanges guide behavior. Recognition that others have their own interests and considerations. Tries to strike deals that serve both parties' interests.	The druggist is making it impossible to make a deal that will work out okay for everyone, so the druggist is forcing you to find another solution. If you can get away with stealing the drug, your wife would be very happy with you for getting the medicine.	If you cannot work out a deal with the druggist, then work out a deal with your wife. She knows that it would not be reasonable to expect you to figure out how to steal the drug without getting caught. Besides, even with the drug, she might die anyway, so you would go to jail for no reason.
Level II: Conventional morality (ages 10–16 years, and usually beyond)			
Stage 3 (I am being good/nice.)	Mutual interpersonal expectations and interpersonal conformity guide reasoning. Rules of behavior become internalized. Individuals perceive themselves as behaving in ways that are good, appropriate, or nice. Individuals conform to particular behaviors to please others.	Good people take care of the people they love. Even if it means breaking the law, to be a good person, you must steal the drug for your wife. If you steal it, people will think you are very kind to your wife.	Good people do not steal. Even if it means that your wife will die, you must not steal. If you steal the drug, people will think you are a bad person, but if you do not steal it, they will think you are a good person.

(Continued)

Level II (ages 10–16 or beyond) involves **conventional morality,** in which societal rules have become internalized, and the individual conforms because it is right to do so. With this level, the individual moves into Stage 3, in which reasoning is guided by *mutual interpersonal expectations* and *interpersonal conformity.* Stage 3 children live up to what others, who are important in their lives, expect of them. To be good is to have good motives behind their actions and to show concern for other people. They live by the Golden Rule, doing unto others what they would have done unto them. In this stage, children want to maintain rules and authority systems that support conventionally appropriate behavior. They recognize that the needs of the group take primacy over their individual interests.

In Stage 4 of the second level, teens become oriented toward *conscience,* and they recognize the importance of the *social system.* In general, they obey laws and fulfill their duties, except in extreme cases when those duties conflict with higher social obligations. Right consists of contributing to and maintain-

TABLE 13-4   *(Continued)*

Level/Stage	Basis for Reasoning	Why You (as Heinz) Should Steal	Why You (as Heinz) Should Not Steal
Level II: Conventional morality (ages 10–16 years, and usually beyond)			
Stage 4 (Preserve the social order.)	Societal rules form the basis of moral reasoning. Development of conscience and recognition of the importance of the social system guide moral reasoning.	You must steal the drug because when you married, you made a promise to do all you could to ensure your wife's well-being. Not to steal the drug would be to break your promise.	You must not steal the drug because stealing violates the rules and laws of society. To steal the drug would be to break society's rules.
Level III: Postconventional morality (ages 16 and beyond)			
Stage 5 (What ensures the rights and well-being of each person?)	Social contracts and individual rights form the basis of moral reasoning.	You must steal the drug because the individual right to live exceeds society's right to impose laws regarding property. Although the majority concern usually should hold sway, the majority must be held in check when essential individual rights are being threatened.	You must not steal the drug because the life of one individual should not cause you to act in ways that rupture the fabric of society. To steal the drug is to say that the ends justify the means. If you do this, you ultimately harm everyone, even your wife.
Stage 6 (What is best from the point of view of each person involved, including the broadest ramifications of the individual actions?)	An orientation toward universal principles of justice guides moral reasoning.	You should steal the drug because the principle of preserving life takes precedence over the law against stealing the drug. Even the druggist would be better off because he would not be a party to your wife's death. If you were caught, your case might bring attention to the problems of paying for expensive drugs, so others might benefit even if your wife did not.	You should not steal the drug because your feelings for your wife should not take precedence over the well-being of others. If you steal the drug, others who need it may be deprived. The druggist may even raise the price of the drug. Others who are thinking about developing drugs may decide not to because they might be stolen.

ing the society or institutions of which they are a part. They need to think of the consequences if everyone behaves as they do. In this stage, teens distinguish the point of view of society from that view taken in agreements between individuals. Even if two people agree that something is right, the Stage 4 individual may still consider it wrong from the standpoint of society as a whole.

Level III (ages 16 and beyond) comprises **postconventional morality,** in which society's rules are

the basis for most behavior, but an internal set of moral principles may outweigh society's rules if a conflict arises between the two. Within this level the individual moves on to Stage 5 to recognize the importance of both *social contracts* and *individual rights*, recognizing too that people hold a wide variety of values and opinions, and that most of them are essentially relative. Nevertheless, these values and rules should be upheld because they are part of a social contract to which people have agreed. According to

Kohlberg, however, certain values and rights, such as the rights of life and liberty, should hold regardless of the opinion of the majority of that society (interestingly, this assertion is in itself a moral judgment). Persons in Stage 5 define right in terms of a sense of obligation to the law. People need to abide by laws to protect everyone and bring about the greatest good for the greatest number of people. Sometimes, moral and legal points of view conflict with each other, however, with no easy resolution. About one fifth of adolescents reach Stage 5.

In Stage 6, which Kohlberg believes few people reach within the third level, individuals are oriented toward *universal principles of justice*. They believe that it is right to follow universal ethical principles, which they have chosen after considerable thoughtful reflection. Most laws and social agreements are valid because they follow such principles, but if laws violate these principles, Stage 6 individuals believe that they must act according to their principles. They seek to uphold universal principles, and they are personally committed to them, whether others adhere to those principles or not.

Developmental changes seem to plateau in early adulthood, but college education seems to facilitate continued development. For those who attend college, the onset of the plateau occurs later and generally at a higher level than for those who do not attend college (Rest & Thoma, 1985; see also Finger et al., 1992). (See Figure 13-7.)

Evaluation of Kohlberg's Model

Other psychologists also have found that complexity of moral reasoning increases with age roughly along the lines Kohlberg suggested (e.g., Rest, 1983). Moreover, even research in other cultures has been rather supportive of Kohlberg's theory in places such as Turkey (Nisan & Kohlberg, 1982) and Israel (Snarey, Reimer, & Kohlberg, 1985a, 1985b).

Despite supporting evidence, however, Kohlberg's theory has been highly controversial. First, the theory has been criticized because Kohlberg's moral dilemmas do not adequately represent situations commonly confronted by children and adolescents (Yussen, 1977). Second, Kohlberg's scoring is very subjective. Furthermore, interview-based scoring is quite difficult, and Kohlberg's highly detailed criteria complicate matters even further. James Rest (1979, 1983; Schlaefli, Rest, & Thoma, 1985) has constructed a well-received test, the *Defining Issues Test (DIT)*, which is based on Kohlberg's theory, but involves somewhat less subjective scoring. Rest's longitudinal studies, based on use of the DIT, generally support Kohlberg's views and show evidence of devel-

opmental changes in moral reasoning up through early adulthood (Rest, 1975).

A third criticism is about the fixed-stage progression that Kohlberg's theory postulates (Kurtines & Greif, 1974). For one thing, people's responses may differ depending on which scenario is used for the assessment. Some people may skip stages (Holstein, 1976), and others may regress to earlier stages (Kohlberg & Kramer, 1969). For example, students who had previously gone beyond the Stage 2 were in some cases found to return to it in college, in part perhaps because of the highly competitive nature of the environment. Kohlberg argued that such students still understood higher levels of morality, even if they did not act on them. Still, regressions suggest that development need not be unidirectional, even if it occurs loosely in stages. Even adults, placed in a suffi-

FIGURE 13-7
Developmental Changes in Moral Reasoning
The percentages of children and adolescents (ages 7 through 16 years) who responded in terms of Kohlberg's preconventional, conventional, and postconventional moral reasonings are summarized graphically here. Clearly, preconventional reasoning declines, conventional reasoning sharply increases, and postconventional reasoning increases slightly across the span of childhood and adolescence. (After Colby, Kohlberg, Gibbs, & Lieberman, 1983)

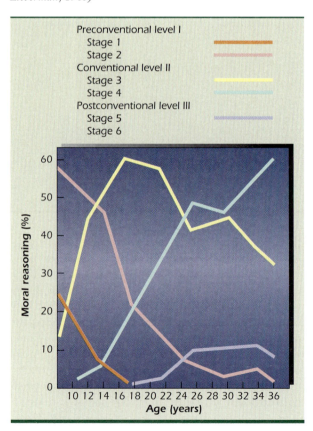

ciently harsh environment, may sometimes regress to cope with the challenges they face.

As the preceding criticism implies, a fourth criticism concerns the tenuous relation between thought and action (Kurtines & Greif, 1974). It is possible for someone to understand a given level of moral reasoning and even to answer test questions accordingly, but then to behave in a way that does not reflect this level. However, Kohlberg never claimed that understanding was tantamount to action. The test of morality perhaps shows how well the test-taker plays the game rather than whether the test-taker actually behaves according to moral principles. In general, research suggests that the measured moral stage does predict behavior, but only imperfectly (Blasi, 1980; Rest, 1983).

Finally, Kohlberg's theory has been criticized for having been based on the study of a small sample of white, middle-class, American males under 17 years of age. Do Kohlberg's findings really apply to persons not fitting into all of these categories? John Snarey (1985) has reviewed more than 45 cross-cultural studies of Kohlberg's theory and has generally found support for Kohlberg's view. Nonetheless, Snarey points out some cultural limitations in the range of stages and in the applicability of all of Kohlberg's stages across cultures. For example, even Snarey's studies in collaboration with Kohlberg revealed some cross-cultural differences. In particular, the communal kibbutz lifestyle of Israel encourages greater emphasis on community and collective happiness than is found in the individualistic lifestyle of the United States (Snarey, Reimer, & Kohlberg, 1985b).

Since Snarey's review, other researchers have similarly found that the theory has some cross-cultural support, within limits (e.g., studies in South Africa [Maqsud & Rouhani, 1990], Iceland [Keller, Eckensberger, & von Rosen, 1989], and Poland [Nieczynski, Czyzowska, Pourkos, & Mirski, 1988]). For example, in China, the first three stages apply well, but the last three stages are less well supported and require modification to work well within traditional Chinese thought (Ma, 1988). In fact, probably no universal set of stages of morality can apply without modification across cultures. Still, Kohlberg's theory has shown some strength in this area, as previously noted.

Carol Gilligan, a student of Kohlberg's, had been coding interviews of moral dilemmas when she began noticing that many of the women's responses did not fit neatly into any of Kohlberg's categories. In fact, many of their apparent responses seemed to reflect an entirely different approach to moral dilemmas. In 1977, Gilligan proposed an alternative view of moral development in women.

Gilligan's Alternative Model

According to Gilligan (1982), although women are as capable of conceiving morality as men, they tend to have a different conception. Whereas men tend to focus on abstract, rational principles such as justice and respect for the rights of others, women tend to see morality more as a matter of caring and compassion. They are more concerned about general human welfare and relationships that contribute to it. Women focus on the special obligations of their close relationships, and they resolve moral issues with sensitivity to the social context. Whereas men are more likely to be competitive, women are more likely to be cooperative. Gilligan proposed that women pass through three basic levels of morality, although not all women reach the third level. The first level involves the individual's concern only for herself; the second level involves self-sacrifice, in which concern for others predominates; and the third level involves integrating responsibilities to both self and others.

Others (e.g., Baumrind, 1986; Gibbs et al., 1984) have found similar sex differences in responses

Basing her conclusions on extensive interviews of women, Carol Gilligan suggested an alternative to Kohlberg's theory of moral development.

to moral dilemmas. Gilligan and J. Attanucci (1988) have since confirmed these differences. L. Walker (1989) replicated Gilligan and Attanucci's procedures, using a larger sample, and found that most men and women, as well as girls and boys, used considerations of both caring and justice in their responses to moral

TABLE 13-5
Summary of Social Development: Birth to Age 3
The first three years of a child's life are suprisingly eventful in terms of various aspects of social development.

Aspect of Development: Theorist	Age (in months)							
	0–1	*1–2*	*2–3*	*3–6*	*6–9*	*9–12*	*12–18*	*18–36*
Emotional: Sroufe	Emotions are undifferentiated; insensitive to the emotions of others.	Social smile develops; facial expressions reflect other's expressions; smile in response to things.		Highly positive emotions; smile and laugh with caregivers.	Participate in emotional exchanges; begin to show anger.	Communicate emotional states well; focus on caregivers; possessive; fear strangers.	Explore wider world caregiver; secure attachment; less fear of strangers.	Differentiation of themselves from others, including self concept; ambivalent impulses to assert independence and seek reassurance.
Attachment: Ainsworth	Preattachment; nondifferentiated responses to people.	Attachment in the making; respond more to familiars than to strangers; increasingly seek contact with primary caregivers; anxious around strangers.			Clear-cut attachment; prefer primary caregiver; differentiated response to strangers; separation axiety.			Mature relationships.
Personality: Erikson	Trust versus mistrust.						Autonomy versus shame and doubt.	
Self-understanding: Damon & Hart	Emerging self-awareness; focus on the physical self.						Understands own name, gender, age, and possessions; emerging feelings of mastery.	
Self-esteem: Harter	Undifferentiated self-concept and evaluations of self-worth.							
Psychosexual: Freud	Oral: dependency needs						Anal: responses to authority	
Friendships: Vandell, Mueller	May cry if another infant cries.			May smile at another infant; may reach toward or even touch another infant.			Interactions increase as does positive affect; frequent playmates may be recognized with positive affect.	
Moral: Piaget, Kohlberg	Premoral							

TABLE 13-6
Summary of Social Development: Preschool Through Adolescence
From preschool through adolescence, the child undergoes tremendous changes in terms of various aspects of social development.

Aspect of Development: Theorist	Age (in years)							
	3–5	5–7	7–9	9–11	11–13	13–15	15–17	17+
Emotional: Sroufe	Social smile; festivities important; fears of unknown and strangers.		Less distinctive events also important; fears include fantastic creatures or unrealistic beliefs.		School and after-school activities, peer relationships are key to happiness.		Relationships, self-improvement, recreation, and travel are key to happiness.	
	Anger becomes focused.	Anger includes consideration of others' intentions.						
Personality: Erikson	Initiative versus guilt.		Industry versus inferiority.		Identity versus role confusion.			
Self-understanding: Damon & Hart	Emerging self-awareness based on physical self; differentiate inner-directed vs. other-directed speech.		Self-understanding based on active self, on personal achievements and skills.		Self-understanding based on social self and peer relations.		Self-understanding based on psychological self and personal beliefs, thoughts, attitudes, and values.	
Self-esteem: Harter	Self-esteem based on cognitive, physical, and social competence, and behavioral conduct.		Self-esteem based on scholastic and athletic competence, peer social acceptance, behavioral conduct, and physical appearance.		Self-esteem based on job, scholastic, and athletic competence; close friendship; romantic appeal; peer social acceptance; behavioral conduct; and physical appearance.			
Psychosexual: Freud	Anal (cont'd)	Phallic	Latency		Genital			
Play interactions: Parten	Play becomes increasingly social and interactive with peers.							
Friendships: Gottman	Prefer same-sex friends; friendships center on shared activities; boys more likely to engage in competitive activities, autonomy, and achievement; girls more likely to prefer a cooperative pair, emotional closeness, and shared confidences.						Boys don't show much change from earlier bases for friendships; girls increasingly emphasize shared personalities, interests, compatibility, turn their attention to boys.	
Moral: Kohlberg			Preconventional morality		Conventional morality		Postconventional morality (in some cases)	

dilemmas. However, although women were more likely than men to express a caring orientation, girls were not more likely than boys to do so. Perhaps a synthesis of both perspectives will eventually be suggested.

Design an experiment to assess how men and women resolve moral dilemmas in the ways suggested by Gilligan.

In conclusion, social development is a lifelong process encompassing emotional, personality, interpersonal, and moral development. Social devel-

opment is inextricably intertwined with the environment, which largely dictates what people consider appropriate social development and social behavior for a child. We have seen this interweaving in many of the research studies discussed in this chapter, such as the work on attachment patterns in children, in which proportions of the various attachment patterns differ across countries. Social development is also clearly linked to cognitive development, in that a child cognitively processes the perceptions and conceptions that influence his or her socialization. (See Tables 13-5, 13-6, and 13-7, which summarize the key aspects of social development in infants, children, and adults, respectively.)

TABLE 13-7
Summary of Social Development: Adulthood
Psychologists have developed theories for personality, identity, self-esteem, life structure, and morality for all three stages of adulthood.

Aspect of Development: Theorist	Early Adulthood	Middle Adulthood	Late Adulthood
Personality: Erikson	Intimacy versus isolation.	Generativity versus stagnation.	Integrity versus despair.
Identity: Marcia	Identity achievement, foreclosure, identity diffusion, moratorium (and possibly alienated achievement).		
Self-esteem: Harter	Self-esteem based on intelligence, sense of humor, job competence, morality, athletic ability, physical appearance, sociability, intimate relationships, nurturance, adequacy as a provider, and household management.		
Life structure: Levinson	Evaluate the nature of the world and their place in it; eventually establish families and career; attempt to build a better life.	Evaluate accomplishments to date; sometimes change marital status, career, or attitudes; begin to consider retirement and old age.	Awareness of changing physical and mental abilities; must stay connected to family, friends, interests; come to terms with mortality.
Moral: Kohlberg	Conventional morality (and, in rare cases, postconventional morality).		

SUMMARY

1. *Social development* encompasses four areas of personal growth: emotional development, personality development, interpersonal development, and moral development.

Emotional Development   446

2. How do people develop emotions? Researchers do not agree. Sroufe posits that we are born with one general form of emotional arousal,

which later differentiates into various specific emotions *(differentiation theory)*. Others (e.g., Izard) say that discrete emotions are generated by specific neural patterns in our brains.

3. Behaviorists say that emotions may be learned through classical conditioning, operant conditioning, or social learning. Cognitive theorists propose that emotions become paired with situations and then are recalled later in similar situations; people label autonomic nervous system activity and decide that it signifies an emotion; and emotions develop in a curvilinear (hill-shaped) pattern in response to unfamiliar stimuli. An integrative theory combines cognitive theorizing with notions drawn from the theory of evolution.

4. Infants change from being egocentric, with limited emotional expression, to being fully functioning, independent, empathic, and responsive explorers of the world around them. On the way, they pass through *separation anxiety*.

Personality Development   450

5. Erikson's theory of *psychosocial development* was originally considered revolutionary, because it traced development all the way through adulthood, not stopping at adolescence. The theory comprises eight stages. Those who successfully complete them develop hope, will, purpose, competence, fidelity, love, care, and wisdom.

6. Your sense of identity can be categorized, according to Marcia, as being in a state of *identity achievement*, if you have made your own decisions and have a firm sense of who you are; *foreclosure*, if you have chosen your path with little thought; *moratorium*, if you are still seeking an identity; *identity diffusion*, if you lack direction or commitment; or *alienated achievement*, if you have decided to opt out of society.

7. Levinson proposes an alternative, three-stage theory of adult personality development, which centers on the choices adults make at various stages of life.

8. *Self-concept* consists of self-understanding, which is your definition of who you are, and self-esteem, which is your sense of self-worth. According to Damon and Hart, *self-understanding* differentiates between the *me* and the *I*. The *me* relies on different aspects of the self, such as physical attributes, behavior, social relationships, and inner psyche. The *I* organizes and interprets the *me*. According to Harter, *self-esteem* is based on self-judgments about your worth in various domains of differing importance; older children see themselves as functioning in more domains

than do younger children. By adulthood, people function in 11 different domains. People also base their self-esteem on other people's judgments of them.

9. Children who underestimate their abilities tend to have more problems in school and social life than children who do not. Girls are more likely than boys to underestimate their abilities.

10. *Temperament* refers to individual differences in the intensity and duration of emotions. Temperament (e.g., easy, difficult, and slow to warm up), according to Thomas and Chess, must be taken into account when looking for the best fit between a person and his or her environment.

11. *Psychosexual development* is the growth of self-perceptions about sexuality and gender identifications. *Gender typing* is the acquisition of specific gender-related roles.

12. Freud's theory of psychosexual development posits four stages (*oral, anal, phallic,* and *genital*), as well as the crucial *Oedipal* and *Electra conflicts*. His theory has been extremely influential but also criticized as too oriented toward sex.

13. How are our perceptions of sex roles and gender identification acquired? Possibilities include socialization, genetic predisposition, evolution, role modeling, and cognitive schemas. The answer is not clear, if there even is one single answer.

Interpersonal Development   463

14. *Bonding* is the process by which adult and newborn organisms form close attachments soon after birth. Both fathers and mothers bond with their children. Research has proposed—inconclusively—that the moments immediately after birth are critical in forming a strong bond between parent and child.

15. *Attachment* is the long-lasting emotional tie that results from bonding. It does not end in childhood, and indeed, patterns of childhood attachment seem to be repeated in adult life, especially in romantic relationships.

16. *Strange situation* research examines attachment patterns by studying how children react when left alone in an unfamiliar room with an unknown person, and then when their mother returns. *Avoidant* children seem distant emotionally in the strange situation; *secure* children are more outgoing but need comforting; *resistant* children seem both aloof and in need of closeness. These labels seem to be culturally bound.

17. Young humans and animals who are deprived of natural nurturing and attachment do not grow up to be fully functional adults.

18. Infants can become attached to fathers and other caregivers as well as they can to mothers. Fathers play more games with young children than do mothers.

19. Parental disciplinary style affects the development of social skills in children. *Authoritarian* (very strict) parents tend to raise unfriendly and distrustful children. *Permissive* parents tend to raise immature and dependent children. *Authoritative* parents, who provide more of a balance, tend to raise well-adjusted children. The authoritative style is the most common across cultures.

20. Child care is a controversial issue. Research results on its effects are somewhat contradictory, although the majority of studies indicate that good-quality child care does children little harm and may offer some benefits. The most important consideration for parents, therefore, is the quality of the program they choose.

21. Learning how to make friends is important to a child's development. Theories of friendship development point to effective personal interaction, exchanging information, establishing common ground, resolving conflicts, positive reciprocal regard, and free self-disclosure as steps in learning how to be a friend. Girls' and boys' friendship patterns differ somewhat, with girls placing a greater emphasis on compatible feelings and outlooks, and boys on compatible activities.

22. Studies of couples show that several different types of marriages can be successful. Unsuccessful marriages are characterized by personal attacks, contempt, defensiveness, and stonewalling.

23. People are most satisfied in their work when it is both intrinsically and extrinsically rewarding. People pass through several different stages of career development, including growth, exploration, establishment, maintenance, and decline.

Development of Moral Reasoning   472

24. According to Piaget, by about 8 years of age children have begun to consider the intentions of a person's actions, as well as the amount of damage caused by the person. At about that age, they also shift from believing that rules are absolute dicta handed down by authorities (e.g., parents), to believing that rules can be determined consensually, by mutual agreement of the parties involved.

25. Kohlberg's stage theory of moral development and reasoning is the most widely accepted of such theories, although it has its detractors. In the *preconventional* level, children behave to avoid punishment and to seek self-interest; in the *conventional* level, older children and adolescents behave according to family and social rules; and in the *postconventional* level, adults behave according to shifting social needs but also universal ethical requirements.

26. Gilligan has suggested an alternative series of moral-development levels for women, involving an orientation toward caring relationships more than toward an abstract notion of justice.

KEY TERMS

IN SEARCH OF THE HUMAN MIND:
ANALYSES, CREATIVE EXPLORATIONS, AND PRACTICAL APPLICATIONS

1. Describe a moral dilemma, and tell how someone in each of Kohlberg's stages might respond to the dilemma.
   Give the rationales for their responses.
2. This chapter described four aspects of social development: emotional, personality, interpersonal, and moral. For which of these aspects of development do you believe that maturation (nature) plays a more dominant role? For which does learning (nurture) play a more important role? Why?
3. How do emotional development, self-concept development, interpersonal development, and moral development interact with Erikson's stages of personality development? That is, indicate a way in which each of the preceding aspects of social development affects or is affected by the stages of personality development described by Erikson.

4. Design an experience that would help children to broaden their views regarding the range of behaviors that are appropriate for boys and for girls, without being narrowly constrained by rigid sex-role stereotypes.
5. Ainsworth's strange situation has yielded many insights into attachment, but it has been criticized for providing too narrow a window onto attachment. Design an experiment that would offer a wider window for viewing attachment behavior in children.
6. Suggest a set of criteria to be used in assessing the quality of child care for children less than 5 years of age.

7. How do your emotions influence your behavior? How do they influence your thoughts, including your problem solving, your reasoning, and your decision making?
8. Give examples of your own gender-role development. In what ways do you conform to traditional gender roles, and in what ways have you departed from traditional gender roles?
9. Give examples of specific ways in which you have engaged in each of the steps to learning how to be a friend; the steps include effective personal interaction, exchanging information, establishing common ground, resolving conflicts, positive reciprocal regard, and free self-disclosure.
10. Into which of Kohlberg's stages would you place yourself? Why?

1. Describe how the Piagetian stages of cognitive development may be related to the Eriksonian stages of psychosocial development in children from infancy through adolescence. Give specific examples of behavior that might be observed in each stage of development.

2. Design a cross-cultural experiment that would help us better understand some of the universal processes underlying cognitive or social development in young children. How would your experimental design allow for the tremendous diversity of cultural environments in which children develop?

3. In what ways do you see your own cognitive and social development fitting into the patterns described in Chapters 12 and 13? In what ways do you see your own patterns of development differing from the general trends described? Why do you think some of your own patterns may differ from the general ones?

Looking Ahead . . .

4. In Chapters 12 and 13, cognitive development and social development were considered separately, but it was suggested that each one affected the other. You have already read about learning, memory, thinking, language, and intelligence as aspects of cognitive processes. How are these processes linked to our social attitudes, our social interactions, and our social relationships?

Charting the Dialectic

Chapter 12 COGNITIVE AND PHYSICAL DEVELOPMENT

The most nearly complete model of cognitive development that has been proposed is that of Piaget. In the 1960s and early 1970s, this model was accepted almost universally. However, then came the inevitable antithesis: Information-processing psychologists found that Piaget had overestimated the ages at which abilities had appeared, and found that the development of abilities was not as stagelike as Piaget had supposed. However, neo-Piagetian theorists have found ways of integrating many of Piaget's fundamental insights with recent information-processing notions.

Chapter 13   SOCIAL DEVELOPMENT

The study of social development shows the same kinds of dialectical processes shown in other areas of psychology. Perhaps the most clear-cut example is in the area of moral development. Piaget proposed a model of moral development, but it was applicable primarily to children. Kohlberg suggested instead a life-span approach, which would characterize moral development in adulthood as well as childhood. However, a number of investigators found fault with Kohlberg's model as well, arguing, for example, that it was limited culturally or male-oriented. Indeed, Gilligan proposed an alternative model that would better take into account the values of women. We are still seeking a synthesis that will adequately take into account all of these varied points of view.

PART FIVE

SOCIAL PSYCHOLOGICAL PROCESSES

SOCIAL PSYCHOLOGY: PERSONAL PERSPECTIVES

SOCIAL PSYCHOLOGY: INTERPERSONAL AND GROUP PERSPECTIVES

MOTIVATION AND EMOTION

Chapter Fourteen

Social Psychology: Personal Perspectives

CHAPTER OUTLINE

The thousand injuries of Fortunato I had borne as best I could; but when he ventured upon insult, I vowed revenge. You, who so well know the nature of my soul, will not suppose, however, that I gave utterance to a threat. At length I would be avenged; this was a point definitively settled. . . . It must be understood, that neither by word nor deed had I given Fortunato cause to doubt my good-will. I continued, as was my wont, to smile in his face, and he did not perceive that my smile now was at the thought of his immolation.

He had a weak point—this Fortunato—although in other regards he was a man to be respected and even feared. He prided himself on his connoisseurship in wine. . . . In this respect I did not differ from him materially, I was skillful in the Italian vintages myself, and bought largely whenever I could.

—Edgar Allan Poe, "The Cask of Amontillado"

The brief excerpt above from "The Cask of Amontillado," one of Edgar Allan Poe's most gruesome murder stories, contains within it many of the themes of social psychology—judgment of another person's motives, attitudes, changes in attitudes, decision making, reasons for behavior, self-concept, social comparison, creating an impression, and nonverbal communication. In this chapter, we consider some of these and other themes, and how social psychologists seek to understand them. First, however, we need to discuss what social psychology is.

THE NATURE OF SOCIAL PSYCHOLOGY

 IN SEARCH OF...

What most perplexes you about some of your friends and acquaintances? How would a social psychologist try to understand these things, as compared with how a popular talk-show host might seek understanding?

Gordon Allport (1897–1967), an influential social psychologist, defined **social psychology** as the attempt "to understand and explain how the thoughts, feelings, and behavior of individuals are influenced by the actual, imagined, or implied presence of others" (1985, p. 3). This compact definition is worth exploring.

First, social psychology deals with both the *cognitive* (intellectual) and *affective* (emotional) sides of a person, as well as the *behavior* that results from and is influenced by thoughts and emotions. Second, social psychology is oriented toward how behavior is affected by either the presence or the idea of other people. Third, social psychology takes a *functionalist* (process-oriented) approach (see Chapter 2); it deals not only with *what* people do, but also with *how* and *why* they do it. Why do we seek to have friends, and how do we choose our friends? How do we communicate, and why do we need to do so?

For most of us, our relationships with other people are of paramount importance, yet these relationships are also probably one of the most confusing and frustrating aspects of our existence. Social psychology addresses this vital yet puzzling aspect of our lives and examines the psychological reasons for how and why we interact with others as we do. Because social psychology addresses such compelling questions, this textbook includes two chapters on this exciting field of study. The present chapter addresses issues in intrapersonal social psychology: (a) the ways in which we think and feel about others and about ourselves, and (b) the ways in which we behave because of our thoughts and feelings toward and about other people and ourselves. Among the topics covered by personal perspectives are the ways in which we perceive ourselves, as shaped by the ways we think others perceive us; how we internally explain our own behavior and the behavior of others; how and why we form and change our attitudes; and how and why we are attracted to, like, and even love other people. The common thread among these topics is that although we need not directly interact with people in order to have thoughts and feelings about them, our thoughts and feelings both influence and are influenced by our interactions with other people.

As is the case in other areas of psychology, ideas in the field of social psychology have evolved in terms

The people in this scene appear to be related only by their chance presence in the same place at the same time. In fact, they are interrelated in a complex network of human relationships.

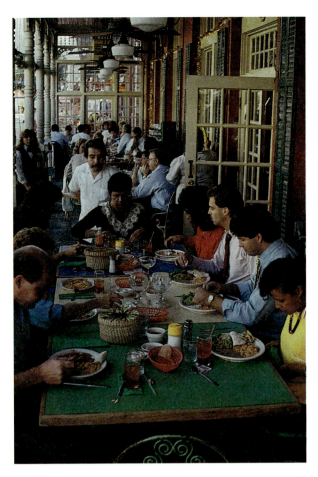

How are your feelings, thoughts, behaviors, and even your beliefs about yourself being shaped by the people around you?

of the Hegelian dialectic described in previous chapters. A good example of this dialectical evolution of theory is found within the study of social cognition.

SOCIAL COGNITION

IN SEARCH OF...

How does the Hegelian dialectic apply to cognitive-consistency theory?

Social cognition refers to how we perceive and interpret information from ourselves (intrapersonal world) and others (interpersonal world). What do we think about ourselves? What do we think about other people? Social cognition is intertwined with such topics as emotion, motivation, and personality, but its particular focus is on thought processes in social interactions. The study of social cognition encompasses several areas of inquiry, including cognitive-consistency theory, attribution theory, impression formation, and social-comparison theory. Historically, cognitive-consistency theory was among the first topics investigated by social psychologists, so we present it here first. As you read about this theory, be thinking about why it attracted the attention of early social psychologists.

Cognitive-Consistency Theory

Imagine that you are a subject in an experiment by Leon Festinger and J. Merrill Carlsmith (1959). The experimenter asks you to perform two mind-numbingly simple tasks of eye-hand coordination: repeatedly emptying and refilling a tray containing spools of thread for half an hour, then repeatedly turning an array of pegs one-quarter turn each for another half-hour. After you have performed these excruciatingly dull tasks for a full hour, the experimenter mercifully tells you that you may stop. As far as you know, that is the end of the experiment on eye-hand coordination. In fact, however, the true experiment has just begun.

Now, as is customary after a psychological experiment, the experimenter debriefs you, explaining that the purpose of the experiment was to investigate the effects of psychological mind set on task performance. You were in the control group, so you were given no prior indication of whether the tasks would be interesting. In the experimental group, on the other hand, subjects are told in advance that the tasks will be enjoyable. The experimenter goes on to tell you that the next subject, waiting outside, has been assigned to the experimental group, and that a research assistant will arrive soon to tell her how great the task will be.

Then the experimenter leaves the room for a moment and returns, worried because his research assistant has not yet arrived. Would you be willing to salvage the experiment by serving as a paid research assistant just for this one subject? Persuaded, you tell the next subject how much fun the experiment was. She replies that she had heard from a friend that it was a bore. You assure her, however, that it was pure entertainment, and then you depart. As you leave, a secretary in the psychology department interviews you briefly and asks you to rate just how much fun and how interesting the experiment really was.

Have you guessed the true point of this experiment? The independent variable was not whether you were told in advance that the experiment was fun and interesting. In fact, you and all the other subjects who believed you were in the "control" condition were ac-

tually in the experimental condition. In the genuine control condition, subjects merely performed the boring tasks and later were asked how interesting the tasks were.

In the experimental condition, the subject waiting outside was a confederate of the experimenter. There never was any other research assistant: The plan had always been to get you to convince the next "subject" that the experiment was a delight. The crucial manipulation was the amount of payment you received for saying that the experiment was interesting. The independent variable actually was that some subjects were paid only $1, others, $20. The dependent variable was the experimental subject's rating of the interest level of the tasks when questioned by the secretary. The goal was to find out whether a relationship existed between the amount of money a person was paid for lying about the tasks, and how interesting the person later reported the dull tasks to be.

Wouldn't it seem plausible that if the money had any effect at all, it would cause the people paid $20 to give a more favorable report than was given by those who were paid only $1? After all, those who were paid $20 were at least compensated for saying that their boring work was interesting! Surprisingly, however, the opposite was true (Festinger & Carlsmith, 1959). Subjects paid $1 rated the boring experiment as much more interesting than did either those paid $20 or the control subjects, as shown in Figure 14-1.

FIGURE 14-1
The Classic Experiment on Cognitive Dissonance
This graphic display of Festinger and Carlsmith's findings show the unambiguous, although quite surprising, results. To the astonishment of many psychologists, the subjects who received $1 for feigning their enjoyment of the task later expressed some enjoyment when asked to give their candid views. In contrast, the control group emphatically expressed their extreme boredom during the task, and even the subjects who received $20 for simulating the appearance of enjoyment clearly asserted later that the task was boring. (After Festinger & Carlsmith, 1959)

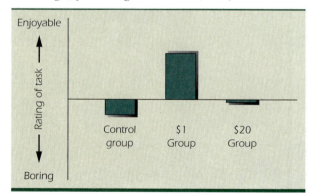

Cognitive-Dissonance Theory

Festinger and Carlsmith explained the counterintuitive results by suggesting that subjects' responses could be understood in terms of the subjects' efforts to achieve **cognitive consistency**—that is, a match between an individual's cognitions (thoughts) and that person's behaviors. Cognitive consistency is extremely important to our mental well-being; without it, we feel tense, nervous, irritable, and even at war with ourselves.

Now, reconsider the experiment: The subjects who were paid $20 performed an extremely boring task and then encouraged someone else to believe that the task was interesting. They were well compensated for doing so, however. They achieved cognitive consistency easily: Saying that a dull task was interesting but getting paid well for saying so allowed these subjects to match their thoughts and beliefs to their behavior. ("I was paid to say that the task was interesting, so I said it was interesting, despite the fact that it was mind-numbingly dull.") Consequently, when later asked their opinions, they readily admitted that the task was an agonizing bore.

Now consider the plight of the subjects who were paid $1. They not only performed a boring task but also lied about it by trying to convince someone else that it was interesting. Furthermore, they were paid poorly for their efforts. These subjects were experiencing **cognitive dissonance**—intellectual discomfort and confusion as a result of having acted in a way that does not jibe well with their beliefs about how things ought to be.

Justification of effort—giving ourselves a rationale for our expenditure of energy—is the key to achieving cognitive consistency. Most of us need to feel that we have good, logical reasons for why we do what we do, but how could the poorly paid experimental subjects justify their efforts on the task? The only apparent justification was to decide that perhaps it was not really so bad. After all, it would have been embarrassing to admit that not only had they not liked the task, but also that they had lied about it to someone else and then had been paid an insulting amount of money for doing so. How much easier it must have seemed to decide that maybe it was all worth it, and that it was even interesting and enjoyable. Thus, these latter subjects achieved cognitive

How is this smoker achieving cognitive consistency? What strategies for reducing dissonance would be the most effective for the smoker who is aware of the hazards of smoking, both to the smoker and to other people near the smoker?

In what profession might people encounter the most cognitive dissonance? Why?

consistency (or conversely, rid themselves of cognitive dissonance) by deciding that the task was perfectly acceptable. They made sense of the lies they had told the confederate by deceiving themselves.

> When have you experienced cognitive dissonance? How did you resolve it?

We now look more closely at the conditions under which cognitive dissonance occurs. It appears that dissonance is most likely to occur when (a) you have freely chosen the action that causes the dissonance; (b) you have firmly committed yourself to that behavior, and it is irrevocable; and (c) your behavior has significant consequences for other people. For example, suppose that a couple is very unhappily married, they have children, and they both devoutly believe that divorce is morally wrong, especially when a couple has children. This is a classic situation likely to generate cognitive dissonance.

In contrast, you are less likely to experience cognitive dissonance if you are forced into an action, if you still have the option of not continuing to perform the action, or if your behavior has consequences for no one but you. Someone who is coerced into marriage or who has no children to think about may have less compunction about filing for divorce. (See Figure 14-2 for a look at the conditions affecting dissonance.)

The preceding discussion has interpreted the results of the Festinger and Carlsmith (1959) experiment in terms of cognitive-dissonance theory, but this interpretation is not the only one possible. Consider now the rather different analysis of self-perception theory, which describes another route to cognitive consistency.

Self-Perception Theory

If questioned about the connection between our beliefs and our behavior, most of us would probably say that our behavior is caused by our beliefs. **Self-perception theory** (Bem, 1967, 1972) suggests essentially the opposite—that when we are not sure of what we believe, we *infer* our beliefs *from* our behavior. We perceive our actions much as an outside observer would, and we thereby draw conclusions about ourselves, based on our actions.

Consider a self-perception theory interpretation of the Festinger and Carlsmith (1959) experiment. As you find yourself explaining to another subject how enjoyable the experiment was, you wonder, "Why in the world am I doing this?" If you are not sure why, then how can you understand your own behavior? If you have been paid $20, explanation is easy: You're doing it for the money. However, if you have been paid only $1, you cannot be doing it for the money. So, looking at the situation objectively, a logical interpretation is that you must have liked the task.

Self-perception theory might seem somewhat contrary to both rationality and intuition—after all, don't you know best what you like and dislike? For one thing, your behavior is not always a good way to form perceptions about yourself, and you might easily draw the wrong conclusions about yourself, based on your behavior. For example, suppose that you "know" about yourself that you hate a particular type of food—such as brussels sprouts—that you have not even tried to taste for years. Now suppose that you are a guest in the home of someone whom you want very much to please. The only appetizer being served is tender brussels sprouts, marinated in a vinaigrette sauce and served icy cold. No choice—you have to try it and appear to be pleased. After your token helping, you find yourself reaching for more. How would you explain your behavior to yourself? Would you be open to changing your view of yourself enough to allow yourself to like something you previously "knew" you did not like?

FIGURE 14-2
Qualifying Conditions for Cognitive Dissonance
In cognitive dissonance, people's behavior appears inconsistent with their attitudes, so they become intellectually confused and uncomfortable. This flowchart demonstrates the qualifying conditions for determining whether cognitive dissonance would be likely to lead to attitude change. A "no" answer at any point would mean that alternative outcomes—that is, other than attitude change—would be more likely. (After Lippa, 1990)

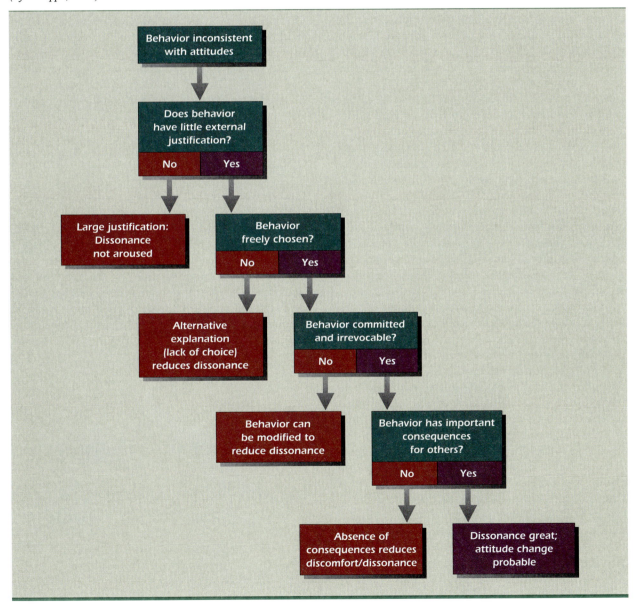

What are these people inferring about their beliefs, based on their behavior? Which came first, their beliefs or their behavior?

It can be advantageous sometimes to consider whether our entrenched self-perceptions may be unnecessarily limiting our options. People change; preferences change; fears change. According to self-perception theory, when we behave in a way that conflicts with our existing self-perceptions, we have a chance to look at ourselves again from a fresh perspective. We may just shake up our self-perceptions and change how we perceive ourselves.

Researchers have conducted experiments to determine whether cognitive dissonance or self-perception theory better explains behavior that contradicts prior beliefs (e.g., Bem, 1967; Cooper, Zanna, & Taves, 1978). Results are mixed. Some experiments favor cognitive-dissonance theory, and others, self-perception theory. When two different approaches both seem plausible and both seem to be supported by research, it makes sense to ask whether both theories might be correct, but under different circumstances. Synthesis of the two opposing points of view may even help to specify the circumstances under which each theory applies.

Russell Fazio, Mark Zanna, and Joel Cooper (1977) offered just such a synthesis: Dissonance theory applies better when people behave in ways that do not follow at all well from their usual beliefs or attitudes. If you have always been a staunch Democrat, but a friend convinces you to attend meetings of a Republican policy group which you then find persuasive, your lack of cognitive consistency might be a job for dissonance theory. Thus, dissonance theory seems better to explain *attitude change*, particularly when the change is dramatic and the original beliefs and attitudes are obvious and well defined. Self-perception theory applies better when people behave in ways that are only slightly discrepant from their normal pat-terns, particularly when the attitudes are vague, uncertain, and not fully formed. If you think that you do not like brussels sprouts, although you have never really tried them, but you find yourself happily eating them one night at dinner, self-perception theory might help you to achieve cognitive consistency. Self-perception theory seems better to explain *attitude formation*, when the person's attitudes are still ambiguous. There is also yet another plausible explanation for Festinger and Carlsmith's findings: impression-management theory.

Impression-Management Theory

Impression-management theory can also account for the original Festinger and Carlsmith (1959) result. According to **impression-management theory** (Baumeister, 1982; Tedeschi, Schlenker, & Bonoma, 1971), people try to present themselves in the best light possible; what is important is to *appear* consistent, not necessarily to *be* consistent, in attitudes and actions. Subjects who received $1 said that they found the boring tasks to be interesting not because they believed that the tests were interesting, but because they wanted the experimenter to believe that they believed it.

Attribution Theory

One of the ways in which we may resolve cognitive dissonance, to achieve cognitive consistency, is to make an **attribution**—an explanation pointing to the cause of our own behavior. For example, in self-perception theory, to explain our newfound fondness for brussels sprouts, we may make an *attribution* in our perceptions of ourselves, telling ourselves that we are among those people who like brussels sprouts, based on our observations of our own behavior. Attributions are not incompatible with the theories of cognitive

"Eat all your brussels sprouts or a big rock from the sky will fall on you."

consistency or impression management, but neither are attributions essential to such theories. For example, it would not be incompatible with cognitive-dissonance theory if we were to *attribute* our fondness for brussels sprouts to the truly appealing nature of brussels sprouts—or perhaps to our own broad-minded willingness to enjoy a diversity of foods. However, such attributions are superfluous to both cognitive-dissonance theory and impression-management theory. Attributions, though, are essential to self-perception theory, which requires that we make a self-attribution regarding our behavior in order to effect a change in our beliefs and attitudes.

Because self-perception theory focuses on making attributions, it belongs to a broader class of social-psychological theories termed *attribution theories*, which address how people explain not only their own behavior, but also the behavior of others. The extent to which you are correct in making attributions about the causes of your own behavior and that of others might be viewed as indices of interpersonal and intrapersonal intelligences, respectively (Gardner, 1983; see Chapter 11). People make attributions so that they can understand their social world and can answer questions such as, "Why did I act that way?" and "Why did she do that?"

The origins of attribution theory are often traced to Fritz Heider (1958), who held that we humans are inclined to observe, classify, and explain (by making causal attributions) both our own behavior and the behavior of others. We then often base our own subsequent behavior on the earlier assumptions we have made in our causal attributions. For example, the narrator in the passage by Poe at the beginning of the chapter attributes his misfortunes to Fortunato; as a result of this attribution, the narrator vows vengeance on him.

Heider pointed out that people make two basic kinds of attributions in particular: (1) **personal** or dispositional **attributions**, based on internal factors in a person ("My stubbornness got us into this argument"); or (2) **situational attributions**, caused by external factors such as settings, events, or other people ("If they hadn't held the examination in that overheated room, I probably wouldn't have gone crazy and started screaming").

Attribution Heuristics and Biases

Up to this point, we have spoken about how people process various factors that influence causal attributions almost as if people were efficient computers, mechanistically measuring each possible causal factor.

Actually, none of us carefully weighs every factor each time we make an attribution. Instead, we sometimes use *heuristics*—shortcut rules (see Chapter 10 for more on heuristics)—to help us make decisions. Unfortunately, these shortcuts sometimes lead to biases and other distortions in our thinking, such as in our thinking about the causes of behavior. We now turn to some of the common heuristics and biases that affect how people make their causal attributions: social desirability, common and uncommon effects, personalism, the fundamental attribution error, actor–observer effects, self-serving biases, and self-handicapping.

SOCIAL DESIRABILITY.   Some research has indicated that in trying to infer the dispositions of people, we tend to give undeservedly heavy weight to socially undesirable behavior (Jones & Davis, 1965). In fact, we may focus so much attention on the socially undesirable behavior that we fail to notice even highly socially desirable behavior. For example, someone who belches, snorts, drools, and gags at the dinner table is likely to make a bad impression, despite the person's witty, insightful, thought-provoking conversation. This person may also be a kind and gentle humanitarian, but she or he will be hard-pressed to negate the effect of this socially undesirable behavior in other people's minds.

The fictional detective Columbo takes advantage of social-desirability biases and leads criminal suspects to believe that he is a bumbling idiot; they presume that he could never discover their guilt because he appears to be slovenly in his personal habits. Describe a situation in which the use of an attributional heuristic led you or someone else to underestimate the characteristics or abilities of a person.

THE FUNDAMENTAL ATTRIBUTION ERROR. The **fundamental attribution error** is the tendency to overemphasize internal causes and personal responsibility and to deemphasize external causes and situational influences when observing the behavior of other people (Ross, 1977). For example, if a boss mistreats employees, we are more likely to attribute the boss's behavior to something about the boss's nature than to something about the situation. A person who often does favors for others is more likely to be judged as intrinsically nice than as pressured by circumstances to do favors.

Searchers . . . RICHARD NISBETT

Dr. Nisbett received a PhD in social psychology from Columbia University. He currently is Theodore M. Newcomb Distinguished University Professor of Psychology and Director of the Research Center for Group Dynamics at the Institute for Social Research at the University of Michigan.

Q: *How did you become interested in psychology in general and in your area of work in particular?*

A: I should say that one of my major lines of work is to show that people are not to be trusted when they tell you the causes for their behavior or emotions. So within that constraint, the first time I felt I would be a psychologist was when I read a primer of Freudian psychology by Calvin Hall. I just thought it was wonderful and so wanted to do that sort of thing. I was about 16 at the time. I got into reasoning through the studies on emotion that I did with Stanley Schachter. However important that work was for understanding emotion, I think it was much more important for understanding how people make causal attributions about themselves.

Q: *What theories have influenced you the most?*

A: Well, certainly Freudian theory. Whether you agreed or disagreed, you couldn't possibly ignore his work. But the biggest impact on the way I think about psychology and life comes from Kurt Lewin, whose perspective I got from Stanley Schachter. Lewin's perspective couldn't be more different from Freud's. When I first encountered Lewin's theory, I thought it was absurdly simple minded. I now feel that his position is far closer to understanding human behavior than Freud's.

Q: *What is your greatest asset as a psychologist?*

A: That I will pursue any line of thought. I know many people will stop because an idea is absurd, or it won't pay off, or it's emotionally disturbing, and so on. My thoughts just pursue any paths they get started down. Every now and then I hit something that I probably wouldn't have if I had controlled myself more.

Q: *How do you get your ideas for research?*

A: A lot of my ideas, such as causal attribution, have come from personal experience. Something strikes me as being interesting, so I mull it over. Once I have a framework—in the case of causal attribution given by Schachter and Harold Kelley—then I can understand those experiences in such a way that they become demonstrations for a larger perspective and theory.

Q: *What do you believe to be your major contribution to psychology and why?*

A: Well, probably the assertion that reasoning processes are not open to view and the therapeutic implications of some of the causal attribution, self-perception notions. I also wrote about the importance of psychotherapists conveying to their patients that their improvement is due to their own efforts. Any failures or setbacks should be understood in terms of the great difficulty of the circumstances they confront at the moment, or even the errors of the therapists. These ideas are now standard in psychiatry and clinical psychology. Many other social psychologists worked on similar ideas.

Q: *What do you want students to learn from you?*

A: The main thing is how to conduct experiments. Social psychologists must sit down and prepare a script for dealing with subjects. If you don't look at that script, question the subjects about what's going on, and revise, there's almost no possibility that your experiment will work.

Q: *What advice would you give to someone starting in the field of psychology?*

A: If you find yourself thinking about psychology all the time, then you should be a psychologist. If psychology is something you think about when you're reading about psychology, or when you're talking about psychology to someone else, and otherwise you're thinking about other things, then you probably shouldn't be a psychologist.

Q: *What have you learned from your students?*

A: I learn from my students all the time because I talk to them all the time and because I take it for granted they can tell me things I didn't know.

Q: *What do you further hope to achieve or contribute?*

A: Well, I'm very excited about the work I'm doing now in cultural psychology. I think the process of looking simultaneously at two different cultures is going to tell us about the ways in which cultures can differ, [and this information] is going to be very important. The work that's showing this importance most clearly is by Hazel Markus and Shinobu Kitayama. So it's that field that I see myself making a contribution to.

ACTOR–OBSERVER EFFECT.   Edward Jones and Richard Nisbett (1971) expanded on the notion of the fundamental attribution error in their hypothesized **actor-observer effect.** This effect is our tendency not only to attribute the actions of others to stable internal personal dispositions, but also to attribute our own actions to external situational variables. In the latter, we are the actors (who must consider the relevant situational factors), and in the former, we are the observers (who notice the dispositions of other people)—hence, the name of the effect. If I kick a dog, it is because the dog was about to bite. However, if I see someone else kick a dog, the action shows just how mean and nasty that person really is.

One of the explanations for the actor-observer effect is that we know more about ourselves than we do about others (Jones & Nisbett, 1987). We are aware of all the situational variables that can affect our own behavior, but we are less likely to know all these variables for others. If I do poorly on an exam, I know that a possible cause for the failure is that the night before the exam I was ill and unable to study. I am less likely, however, to know the same for an acquaintance. I therefore opt for a dispositional explanation of my friend's behavior—for example, that my friend is lazy.

Research tends to support the actor-observer effect (Nisbett, Caputo, Legant, & Marecek, 1973). In one study, subjects were asked to evaluate themselves, a friend, their father, and Walter Cronkite (a highly respected television newscaster at the time), in terms of a number of different personal traits. Nisbett and colleagues found that their subjects checked off the option, situational dependence, more for themselves than for other people.

SELF-SERVING BIASES.   Another bias in our attribution processes is that we tend to be generous—to ourselves—when interpreting our own actions. For example, when students study for examinations and do well, they are likely to take credit for the success. However, when students study and do poorly, they are more likely to attribute the low grade to the examination ("That test was unfair!") or to the professor ("His grading is so strict!") (Whitley & Frieze, 1985). In another study of self-serving biases (Kunda, 1987), students were interviewed and found to be aware that the divorce rate for marriages in the United States hovers close to 50%. However, these same students believed that their own future chances of ever personally divorcing their own future spouses were only around 20%.

Self-serving biases can perform at least one constructive function in our lives: They give us necessary self-confidence. If we think we are a bit more successful or more likely to be successful than we actually are, whether it be in marriage, on the job, or in school, perhaps that self-confidence helps us to attain that success in reality (recall the potent effects of self-fulfilling prophecy, described in Chapter 1).

SELF-HANDICAPPING.   In **self-handicapping,** people take actions to sabotage their own performance so that they will have an excuse in case of failure (Berglas & Jones, 1978). For example, a student might not make the time to study for a test, but when she does badly on it, she might attribute the failure to not being able to study.

We have surveyed a number of the heuristics and biases people use in making attributions. It is important to know not only the bases of attributions, but also the problems and prejudices inherent in attributions. Probably no one can see a situation clearly enough to make a completely accurate attribution—or perhaps it is more nearly correct to say that no situation is simple enough for everyone to agree on one attribution. The variety of human interests, biases, and viewpoints certainly makes life complicated, but also fun.

We now broaden our scope to encompass more than just how we make causal attributions regarding the behavior of ourselves and other people. Next, we consider how people perceive and interpret a wide variety of information about other people, in order to form an impression of them. Note that *impression formation* is the impression you form regarding other people, whereas *impression management* is the impression you try to encourage others to form about you.

Impression Formation

After reading the selection from Poe at the beginning of the chapter, what is your impression of Fortunato or of the narrator? When you go to a party and meet new people, how do you decide what you think of them? An entire branch of social psychology devotes itself to exactly this question of how we form impressions. The study of **impression formation** is an examination of how we draw inferences about other people, based on the information that we obtain about them, both directly and indirectly.

What are three things someone could do to impress you favorably? Why would those three things impress you?

Searchers . . . *CLAUDE M. STEELE*

Dr. Steele received his PhD in social psychology from Ohio State University. He is currently professor of psychology at Stanford University.

Q: *How did you become interested in psychology?*

A: Psychology interested me from the first course I took. It offered a way of thinking that I was comfortable with and that excited me. Psychology is so close to one's personal experience and it offers the hope that one can find out something personally useful, something fascinating that will lead to more and more. I see many students react this way in the courses I teach. I got excited enough to stick with it, and I still relate to it pretty much the same way.

Q: *What theories have influenced you the most?*

A: The first theory to excite me personally was George A. Kelly's theory of personal constructs. It fascinated me and made me feel that psychology could produce powerful tools for human understanding. This theory and related work hooked me on psychology.

Over the years many theories and ideas have excited and influenced me. The work of Stanley Schachter, a hero of mine whom I've never met, has had a great deal to do with shaping my own approach to research. His research, and especially his reports of it, made social-psychological research seem like impassioned detective work.

Q: *How do you get your ideas for research?*

A: I often read nonpsychology literature with an eye to using psychology to deepen our understanding of some important issue, and I talk a lot to my students, colleagues, and family. It is a distinctly discursive approach. The advantage is that one sees the emergent ideas very quickly from a variety of perspectives and thus gets a better feel for their ring of truth and their implications. Also, it is fun. Several heads are almost always better than one.

Q: *Which of your ideas has been particularly innovative, and how did you develop it?*

A: An idea that has been topmost in my mind recently is how the stereotypes that exist in a society can create a sense of vulnerability in those who are their targets, such as a sense of vulnerability that women in a math class can feel in light of our society's stereotypes about women's math abilities. We reasoned that such vulnerability might be an important source of sex differences in math performance, especially at advanced levels, and that in fact it might

be this vulnerability, not genetic differences, which explains these sex differences. So far our research has been strongly encouraging of this view.

Q: *What obstacles have you experienced in your work?*

A: Impenetrable fog is perhaps the major theoretical obstacle I have faced—that is, being interested in something and simply not having a good lead with which to begin explaining it. I have no well-oiled tactic for getting past this. It seems to me that I brood about something, read about it, and talk about it for a long time, and if I am lucky, an idea that I can have faith in will eventually emerge.

Q: *What is your major contribution to psychology?*

A: Three ideas: a theory of self-evaluative processes, called self-affirmation theory; a social-cognitive model of alcohol's effect on social behavior and of its addictive properties; and a theory of how societal stereotypes, by causing a vulnerability that can impair performance and discourage identification with the domain of vulnerability, can cause underachievement among stereotyped groups such as women and Black Americans.

Q: *What advice would you give to someone starting in the field of psychology?*

A: Persistence, hard work, open-mindedness, perseverance, recognition that one's ability is expandable—and must be expanded—and an effort to work as much as possible from a liking of psychology.

Q: *What key things did you learn from your mentors?*

A: I learned that data are as important in the process of generating ideas and expanding our understandings as they are to testing ideas. I learned that mutual respect is indispensable to high-quality intellectual relationships and that respect can sometimes come in many guises.

Q: *What have you learned from your students?*

A: I have learned that they are indispensable. It never fails that good ideas expand and get clearer and stronger by talking them over with someone who holds a different perspective. It is a chief pleasure of my academic life.

Q: *How do you keep yourself academically challenged?*

A: I take on new problems that I find deeply interesting. This is perhaps the chief pleasure of my academic life—being able to learn about that which excites me.

Our social personality is a creation of the thoughts of other people.

—*Marcel Proust,* Swann's Way

Models of Impression Formation

A seminal study in the field of impression formation was performed by Solomon Asch (1946). Asch presented his subjects with the following list of adjectives describing a person named Jim: "intelligent, skillful, industrious, _____, determined, practical, cautious." In the blank was one of these words: "warm," "cold," "polite," or "blunt." Based on these seven adjectives, subjects were asked to write descriptions of their impressions of Jim and to indicate whether the adjectives *generous, wise, happy, good-natured,* or *reliable* could also describe him. Some of Asch's data appear in Table 14-1.

Asch interpreted the findings shown in Table 14-1 as indicating that the words "warm" and "cold" seemed to be **central traits** in the description, for they organized how all the other information was interpreted. When either of these two words appeared in the blank, there was a radical effect on the sort of person Jim was perceived to be. "Polite" or "blunt" in the blank, however, had relatively little effect on impression formation by Asch's subjects.

Other investigators have criticized various aspects of Asch's study, pointing out, for example, that the words "warm" and "cold" are social traits, whereas the other words in the initial list ("intelligent, skillful, industrious," etc.) are more intellectual in nature. This difference in kind may have given the social words disproportionate weight in impression

formation (Zanna & Hamilton, 1972). Nonetheless, Asch's results, especially the notion of central traits around which we organize information about other personality characteristics, have proved highly influential.

Asch's study illustrates that initial, seminal experiments in any area are often, in retrospect, flawed. In a new area of research, it is not yet clear what the main issues in experimental design will be—what factors are likely to lead to confounded or otherwise difficult-to-interpret results. Yet these early experiments make possible the later, more carefully controlled experiments that then fill in the gaps. Often, the psychologists who are most influential and longest remembered are those who take the risks, forge new paths, and conduct the initial, rather flawed experiments, rather than those who build on that work, traveling down the well-worn paths, conducting precisely controlled, rigorous experiments. Both the path-makers and the path-followers are essential to progress in any field of endeavor: We need paths, but we also need to know what happens if we follow the paths.

Heuristics and Biases in Impression Formation

One of the reasons that people do not form uniform impressions or compute standardized impressions of other people is that almost all of us take shortcuts when we are forming impressions of people. Most of the time, these shortcuts save us time and give us a good-enough impression to help us interact with other people appropriately. Often, however, our shortcuts are altogether too short and cut out too much important information. Research suggests that our processing of information can cause us to distort

TABLE 14-1
Impression Formation

Based on a list of adjectives, subjects were asked to write descriptions of their impressions of a person and to indicate whether the adjectives generous, wise, happy, good-natured, *or* reliable *could also describe the person. The following percentages indicate the proportion of subjects, for each of the lists, who agreed that a given trait would also characterize the person described by the list of adjectives. (After Asch, 1946)*

Additional Traits	Traits Inserted into List			
	"Warm"	"Cold"	"Polite"	"Blunt"
Generous	91%	8%	56%	58%
Wise	65	25	30	50
Happy	90	34	75	65
Good-natured	94	17	87	56
Reliable	94	99	95	100

our perceptions through a variety of heuristics and biases.

THE PRIMACY EFFECT.   First impressions can be powerful. In one experiment (Asch, 1946), one group of subjects was told that a person was "intelligent, industrious, impulsive, critical, stubborn, and envious." A second group of subjects was told that the person was "envious, stubborn, critical, impulsive, industrious, and intelligent." Notice that the second list of traits is exactly the same as the first, but in reverse order. Despite the objective similarity of the two lists, however, people who heard the first order—with positive traits first—formed a more positive impression than did those people who heard the second order—with negative traits first. Asch concluded that we demonstrate a **primacy effect** in our evaluations of people—we give more weight to the things we learn earlier than to the things we learn later.

One reason that the primacy effect works may be explained by our use of schemas. As we take in new information, we try to make sense of the information as quickly as possible, either by assimilating the new information into our existing schemas (e.g., our schemas about "people like that") or by creating new schemas to accommodate the new information. If we must create new schemas, we start creating them quickly, to minimize the amount of time during which we must feel the uncomfortable lack of an integrated way in which to understand the new information. As soon as we have the beginnings of a schema, we can rapidly and easily assimilate any additional information into the new schema. If the new information is sharply discrepant from the new schema, we may modify the schema to accommodate the new information, but we leave the fundamental structure of the schema intact. We do not discard or even completely overhaul the schema once we create it.

The primacy effect causes bias in judgments of abilities as well as of personality. Subjects in an experiment watched a person taking a 30-item test that allegedly measured intelligence (Jones, Rock, Shaver, Goethals, & Ward, 1968). In one condition, subjects saw the examinee answer most of the initial questions correctly, but then stumble and answer more questions incorrectly later on. This examinee's total score was 15 correct out of 30. In a second condition, subjects saw the opposite: The examinee's overall performance was the same, 15 correct out of 30, but the errors occurred early on in the test and the successes came later.

Subjects tended to rate as more intelligent the examinee who started off well than the one who started off poorly. Moreover, when subjects were asked to remember how many items each examinee had actually answered correctly, they estimated 21 right in the strong-start condition, but only 13 in the weak-start condition. In other words, looking better at the beginning and then worse later on is likely to make a better impression than looking worse at the beginning and then better later. It is harder to correct an initial bad impression than to ruin an initial good one.

Is being susceptible to the primacy effect the same thing as making a snap judgment? Why or why not?

CONFIRMATION BIAS.   One reason that we tend to maintain our first impressions of people may be due to confirmation bias. **Confirmation bias** is our tendency to find ways to confirm our already existing beliefs, rather than to seek ways in which to refute these existing beliefs. In regard to first impressions, our confirmation biases may lead us to seek, interpret, and even distort information in ways that verify our existing beliefs about a person. We tend to notice and to remember the events and behaviors that fit into our existing schemas, whereas we tend to ignore and to forget those that do not. Thus, we have the illusion that our preconceptions are confirmed by our experiences. Our confirmation biases can lead us to distortions that not only hinder our appreciation of others but also that hamper our full understanding of the world in which we live. We may under- or overestimate the skills, abilities, and merits of the people around us as a result of our confirmation biases. (See Chapter 15 for descriptions of other psychological phenomena that augment our prejudices.)

Why would we persist in doing something that eventually probably hurts us, as well as hurting others? Because confirmation biases, like other heuristic shortcuts, save us time. If we took the time to get to know everyone with whom we had any contact, we would have time for little else. In our daily, transitory interactions with myriad people, our confirmation biases probably do us little harm, and they save us a great deal of time. On the other hand, in many situations, we would do well to consider the powerful influence of our confirmation biases.

Think about a strong belief you have. Try to imagine what information would convince you to change your mind. Have you ever ignored information that contradicted your belief? Why?

Searchers . . .   *ROBERT ROSENTHAL*

Dr. Rosenthal received a PhD in clinical psychology from the University of California at Los Angeles. He is currently professor and chair, Department of Psychology at Harvard University, where he has worked for many years.

Q: *How did you become interested in psychology in general and in your area of work in particular?*

A: I was interested in psychology even when I was still in grade school. But my interests then were much more clinical. It was only later that I became more of a regular research person. I got interested in teachers' expectancies, therapists' expectancies, and so on by accident when I was doing my doctoral dissertation. I did some unnecessary statistical analyses that suggested to me that I might unintentionally have influenced the results of my research. And on the basis of that work, I started a research program of my own, on interpersonal self-fulfilling prophecy. That was in the late '50s. I have continued that line of research until the present day.

I started doing a series of experiments that led to the early animal studies where we had the allegedly maze-bright rats and maze-dull rats. We found that if the experimenter thought the rats had been bred for brightness, the rats actually behaved in a brighter way. And so that was our first animal research on self-fulfilling prophecy. The night before the experiment, we ran around the lab and put signs on cages. Half the signs had "maze bright" and half had "maze dull." So that was our experimental manipulation, but they were all perfectly ordinary rats.

Q: *What is your greatest asset as a psychologist?*

A: I'm open minded, I think, and curious. There are very few things that I think of *a priori* as being impossible, or as unable to happen. For example, I recently refereed a big debate about parapsychology, and a lot of my colleagues in psychology have just sort of decided *a priori* that that sort of thing can't happen. So they don't really look hard at the data. Because I really don't care one way or the other, I think I'm prepared to look at the data.

Q: *How do you get your ideas for research?*

A: Well, some of my ideas are outgrowths of earlier work. A lot of my research on nonverbal communication was a logical outgrowth of my work on interpersonal self-fulfilling prophecy. But other, specific studies just sort of pop up. Many studies I've been involved with were not my idea at all. They were ideas of students that I was working with. And then, if that was the case, they were first authors on the resulting article.

Q: *What obstacles have you experienced in your work?*

A: Well, I had a lot of obstacles because people didn't want to believe my work. [Early in my career] I had done a dozen or more experiments, [but] none of them were published in an APA journal. Ironically, although I couldn't get my articles about this experimenter-expectancy effect published in APA journals, one day I got two letters. One letter rejected the article from the *Journal of Abnormal and Social Psychology*, as it was then called, and the other letter told me I had won the AAAS socio-psychological prize for the best research of the year, for the same paper!

Q: *What do you believe is your major contribution to psychology and why?*

A: I think I have two lines of contribution that are really unrelated to each other. One of them is substantive, and the other is methodological. In the substantive domain, I think my most important work is on the self-fulfilling prophecy and on nonverbal communication. Although the nonverbal communication stuff grew out of the expectancy research, it stands on its own now.

Q: *What do you want students to learn from working with you?*

A: I'd like them to learn to be open to their experience, to be open-minded about what is and isn't possible, to be very uncritical in their generating of ideas, and to be very critical in their writing up or in their conceptualizing of what they have found. So on the one hand, I want them to cast a very wide net. I want them to love to do research, as I do, but I want them to be very rigorous and hard-nosed about how they analyze the data, and to analyze it well.

Q: *How do you keep yourself academically challenged?*

A: Oh my lord! It's not a problem at all! Every day, when a bright undergraduate comes in with a new thesis idea, or when a graduate student comes in with an idea for a research project, or with questions on how to deal with some data-analytic issues, I don't have to work at being challenged. They come to my door every day.

SELF-FULFILLING PROPHECY. Confirmation bias can lead to **self-fulfilling prophecy,** whereby what is believed to be true becomes true or is at least perceived to be true. Recall from Chapter 1 that Robert Rosenthal and Leonore Jacobson pioneered the study of self-fulfilling prophecies in their land-mark investigation regarding the effects of teacher expectations on student performance.

In what other situations can self-fulfilling prophecy have powerful effects?

PERSON-POSITIVITY BIAS. **Person-positivity bias** is our tendency to evaluate individuals more posi-tively than we evaluate groups, including the groups to which those individuals belong (Sears, 1983). One way of looking at this bias is that we are willing to take the time to form a rather elaborate schema for a particular individual whom we know well and with whom we interact often. When we observe an indi-vidual often, our frequent observations may so sharply conflict with our stereotype that we are forced to notice that the person defies the stereotype. Such observations would require us to make some kind of cognitive adjustment. We still try to exert as little effort as possible, however, and we try to mini-mize the amount of cognitive adjustment we must make. It takes less mental effort to note simply that this individual happens to deviate from the stereotype than to dismiss or to overhaul the stereotype alto-gether. Thus, although we may have to change our views toward individuals who happen to belong to a group, when thinking about the group of people as a whole, we may still prefer to use a nice, neat stereo-type. Such a stereotype works as a convenient short-cut in place of getting to know all the possible excep-tions to the rule, all the varied details of the general description, and all the contextual information that might influence how we interpret a particular charac-teristic.

I don't care to belong to any club that will accept me as a member.

— *Groucho Marx*

When and why have you ever engaged in person-positivity bias?

Social Comparison

Festinger (1954), noted earlier in regard to his theory of cognitive dissonance, also proposed another theory regarding how we look at ourselves. According to Festinger's **social-comparison theory,** we evaluate our own abilities and accomplishments largely by comparing these abilities and accomplishments to the abilities and accomplishments of others. We are most likely to make social comparisons when we find our-selves in situations that are new or uncertain, so that we have difficulty applying any of our existing inter-nal standards (Suls & Fletcher, 1983; Suls & Miller, 1977). The realism and accuracy of our self-appraisals will therefore depend in large part on whether the others with whom we compare ourselves are, in fact, appropriate bases for setting our own standards (Goethals & Darley, 1977). For example, suppose that Leon, a sophomore in college, compares himself to a high school student in terms of academic accomplish-ments; he might thereby have an unrealistically posi-tive image of what he has accomplished. In contrast, Melba—also a college sophomore—compares her-self to a graduate student, and so she may end up with an unrealistically negative self-image. It is important to compare ourselves to people with whom we can make appropriate comparisons. When we make inap-propriate social comparisons, we may come to form overly harsh or overly accepting attitudes toward our own behavior.

ATTITUDES AND ATTITUDE CHANGE

IN SEARCH OF...

What attitude have you recently changed? What factors contributed to your change in attitude?

Scientists do not conduct research in isolation from society. Attitude research aptly exemplifies the interaction of contemporary societal issues and psy-chological research. The origins of this research date back to World War II. During the war, the U.S. gov-ernment needed information about attitudes and atti-tude change, and it needed it fast. Japanese radio broadcaster "Tokyo Rose" was trying to break the morale of the U.S. troops overseas with innuendoes about unfaithful spouses, unconcerned citizens at home, and treacherous political and military leaders; various German-American "friendship organizations" were attempting to drum up support for Hitler in the United States. Were such measures turning both sol-diers and civilians against the war effort? How could the U.S. government counter the influence of such propaganda? Government officials needed to know how to make the American people more resistant to those influences that might seek to change people's attitudes in ways that would disfavor the war effort. At the same time, these officials wanted to institute their own propaganda campaign, to change the attitudes of anyone who might not fully support the war effort. Suddenly, attitude research, which had been dormant, sprang to life. The goal of such research was to understand people's attitudes more fully and to figure out how and why people change their attitudes.

> Identify someone toward whom you have a negative attitude. List five positive attributes of that person. Describe how and why this task affected your attitude, if at all. If it did not affect your attitude, tell why not.

The Nature and Functions of Attitudes

An **attitude** is a learned, stable, and relatively enduring evaluation of a person, object, or idea that can affect an individual's behavior (Allport, 1935; Petty

Interest in attitudes and attitude change surged during World War II. As this war propaganda poster indicates, this interest was not purely academic.

& Cacioppo, 1981). This definition makes several points. First, we are not born with the attitudes we have; we acquire them through experience. Second, attitudes tend to be stable and relatively enduring; they tend not to change easily. Third, attitudes are evaluative: They are a means by which we judge things positively or negatively, and in varying degrees. Some issues may not concern us much one way or the other, whereas other issues may engender strong opinions. Finally, attitudes can influence behavior, such as when they cause people to act—to vote, protest, work, make friends, and so on—as a result of their attitudes.

Some psychologists view attitudes as having cognitive, behavioral, *and* affective components: Your attitude toward someone or something depends on what you think and feel about the person or thing, as well as on how you act toward the person or thing, based on your thoughts and feelings (Katz & Stotland, 1959). Thus, attitudes are central to the psychology of the individual.

Why do we even have attitudes in the first place? According to Daniel Katz (1960), attitudes serve at least four functions. They (a) help us get what we want and avoid what we do not want, (b) help us avoid internal conflicts and anxieties, (c) help us understand and integrate complex sources of information, and (d) reflect our deeply held values.

Attitude Formation: Learning

Now that we know a bit about what attitudes are, we can return to discussing their source. Where do attitudes come from? As is often the case, the best answer is actually a synthesis of various approaches. Given that we are not born with particular attitudes, and that specific attitudes do not naturally unfold during physiological maturation, we are left with various forms of learning theory to explain attitude formation. Three kinds of learning can contribute to this process: classical conditioning, operant conditioning, and observational learning (see Chapter 7).

The *classical-conditioning* view is that we learn attitudes when a concept or object toward which we have no particular attitudes (an unconditioned stimulus) is paired with a concept or object toward which we already have an attitude (a conditioned stimulus) (Staats & Staats, 1958).

In *operant conditioning*, rewards can strengthen positive associations, just as punishments can strengthen negative associations (e.g., Insko, 1965).

In **observational learning**, as seen in Chapter 7, children learn many of their attitudes by observing the attitudes being voiced and acted out by the important adults and children in their environments. In addition, children may learn some of their attitudes from television and other media.

For example, children's TV programs show more than twice as many male roles as female roles. Males are more likely to be shown as the doers who make things happen and who are rewarded for their actions, and females are more likely to be the recipients of actions; and the females who do take action are more likely than males to be punished for their activity (Basow, 1986). On action-adventure shows (in which the heroic, bold, intrepid adventurer undertakes insurmountable challenges, struggles against unbeatable odds, and then deftly conquers all), 85% of the major characters are males. Of the leading characters on prime-time TV, 65% to 75% are white males. The occupational and familial roles strongly reinforce gender and racial stereotypes. Just in case viewers selectively choose programs that minimize stereotypes, commercials still provide a whopping dose of stereotyped roles for viewers to observe (Gilly, 1988): Women are more often shown as preoccupied with their personal appearance, their household chores, and concerns about their families; men are usually shown engaged in working, playing, or being nurtured by women.

On a more positive note, when programs are designed to diminish sex-role stereotypes, both children (Eisenstock, 1984) and adults (Reep & Dambrot, 1988) express fewer stereotyped views. We might guess that the same would be true regarding other stereotype-based attitudes. Also, in addition to the television set, another obvious source of observational learning can be found in the home: the people who live there. Examine your parents' attitudes about religion, politics, and other social issues. How do they compare and contrast with your own? Young people are often surprised—sometimes unpleasantly—to realize how many of their own attitudes they have absorbed from their families. In more ways than one, education begins at home.

There clearly is evidence to support each of the three learning theories, so each probably contributes to the ways in which we form the attitudes we have. Do these same processes underlie the means by which and the reasons for which we change our attitudes, or do other processes influence our changes in attitude?

Attitude Change

Have you ever noticed in yourself an attitude that you wanted to change? What about the attitudes held by people with whom you interact? Have you ever wanted to change the attitudes of other people? If you did want to change someone's attitudes, how

What attitudes is this young boy learning from his father regarding social responsibility, concern for our natural environment, and the roles of fathers in their children's lives? How likely is it that the attitudes this boy learns will be reflected in his behavior?

might you go about doing so? Probably by persuading the person to think differently. Easier said than done, you say. Nonetheless, advertisers, politicians, political activists, charitable organizations, and any number of other people have spent a lot of time, money, and effort trying to figure out how to change people's attitudes.

How can you more effectively resist the attempts to change your attitudes by persons who do not necessarily have your best interests at heart? By examining various kinds of persuasive communications, researchers have discovered some variables likely to influence attitude change: characteristics of the recipient of the attitude-change message (e.g., the recipient's motivation and expertise), characteristics of the message itself (e.g., balance and familiarity due to repetition), and characteristics of the source of the message (e.g., credibility and likability).

How well do advertising campaigns succeed in changing people's attitudes? How effective would you consider this antidrug slogan to be? What might be another strategy for affecting people's attitudes toward harmful drugs? How should the characteristics of the message, and of the message source, be tailored to the characteristics of the recipient of the message?

"Lizzy," said he, "what are you doing? Are you out of your senses, to be accepting this man? Have not you always hated him?"

How earnestly did she then wish her former opinions had been more reasonable, her expressions more moderate! It would have spared her from explanations and professions which it was exceedingly awkward to give; but they were now necessary, and she assured him with some confusion, of her attachment to Mr. Darcy. . . .

"I do, I do like him," she replied with tears in her eyes. "I love him. . . ."

Elizabeth, still more affected, was earnest and solemn in her reply; and at length, by repeated assurances that Mr. Darcy was really the object of her choice, by explaining the gradual change which her estimation of him had undergone, . . . she did conquer her father's incredulity, and reconcile him to the match.

—*Jane Austen*, Pride and Prejudice

Characteristics of the Recipient

How easily we are persuaded by a message may depend largely on our own characteristics as recipients of the communication. Richard Petty and John Cacioppo (1981; Cialdini, Petty, & Cacioppo, 1981) have proposed that the effectiveness of various persuasive techniques depends on specific characteristics of the person receiving the persuasive message. These researchers note two routes to persuasion. The first is the **central route** to persuasion, which emphasizes

thoughtful arguments related to the issue about which the attitude is being formed. When the recipient is both motivated to think about the issue and able to do so, the central route is the most effective. The second is the **peripheral route** to persuasion, which emphasizes tangential, situational features of the persuasive message, such as the appeal of the message sender, the attractiveness of the way in which the message is presented, or rewarding features of the message or its source. The peripheral route may be more effective than the central route when the recipient is not strongly interested in the issue or is unable to consider the issue carefully for various reasons, such as lack of skill in thinking about the issue, lack of expertise in the area related to the issue, or any number of other limitations on the individual's ability.

Although the investigators found that strong arguments were always more persuasive than weak arguments, this effect was augmented in those who were highly motivated to think about the issue (Cacioppo & Petty, 1986). In other words, the good arguments may have been partly wasted on those who were not really thinking about them, but such arguments were influential for those who were actively analyzing and interpreting them. Thus, when preparing to persuade others to your point of view, it helps to know your audience and to know which route to persuasion will be most effective. As you might guess, attitude change that is reached through the central route is much more stable and enduring. Attitude change reached through the peripheral route is more volatile and subject to subsequent change in the opposite direction.

Characteristics of the Message

In addition to the quality of the arguments, what other characteristics of your message might affect its persuasiveness? Two characteristics of the message have prompted a great deal of research: balanced presentation of arguments and familiarity due to repeated exposure. A key question in attitude research has been whether the presentation of a **balanced** (pro and con) viewpoint helps or hinders the process of changing someone's attitudes. There appears to be no significant difference between the effects of one-sided and two-sided messages on attitude change in a group comprising some people predisposed to agree and some people predisposed to disagree with the speaker's message (Lumsdaine & Janis, 1953). However, when listeners are exposed to both sides of an issue, they are more resistant to later persuasion from the opposing camp than are subjects who have heard only their own side of the issue.

Another way to change people's attitudes is simply to expose them repeatedly to the desired attitude. On average, repeating an argument enhances its effectiveness. Indeed, simply exposing people to a stimulus many times tends to increase people's liking for that stimulus. This effect of repetition is usually termed the **mere exposure effect** (Zajonc, 1968). For example, many people find that their liking for a piece of music, a work of art, or even a kind of food increases with repeated exposure, which is why we often call these preferences "acquired tastes."

However, if the repetition becomes boring or annoying, it can backfire, decreasing the likelihood of liking or of attitude change (Cacioppo & Petty, 1979, 1980). Thus, repetition is useful in order to make sure people get the message, but after a point, it may hurt your case. (Other factors affecting the effectiveness and likability of persuasive messages are considered in Chapter 15.)

Characteristics of the Source

Characteristics of the source of the persuasive message may also affect the effectiveness of the message in eliciting attitude change. Two key characteristics of the source are credibility and likability.

CREDIBILITY.   In a classic work, Carl Hovland and W. Weiss (1951) argued that people were more likely to believe a communication if the source was rated high rather than low in **credibility** (believability). The effect of source credibility is greatest right after receiving the persuasive message; over time, the effect of the credible source decreases.

LIKABILITY.   Alice Eagly and Shelley Chaiken have noticed that most of us are more easily persuaded by messages from people whom we like than by messages from people whom we do not like (Chaiken & Eagly, 1983). Moreover, this **likability effect** is especially important if you are trying to persuade people to take a position that they initially resist or otherwise find unappealing (Eagly & Chaiken, 1975). The magnitude of this effect, however, depends on the medium for the message. The likability effect is greater in videotaped than in audiotaped messages and is inconsequential in written messages (see Figure 14-3). This difference probably occurs because we get a broader range of visual and auditory information from a videotape than we do from either an audiotape or written material. When we can see the persuader's facial expressions, clothing, and appearance, and also hear the persuader's voice, intonation, and actual words, we have a lot of sensory information with which to decide whether we find the person appealing.

The Link Between Attitudes and Behavior

Implicit in the study of attitudes is the assumption that our attitudes are somehow linked to our behav-

FIGURE 14-3
The Interaction Between the Medium of the Message and the Likability of the Message Sender
Although likable message senders generally have a positive effect on attitude change, the positive effect is enhanced by using audiotaped or videotaped messages, rather than written ones. However, when the message sender is not likable, attitude change is even less likely to occur when the message sender uses audiotaped or videotaped messages. (After Chaiken & Eagly, 1983)

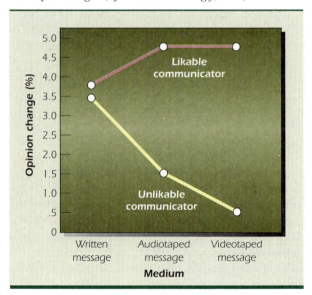

ior. However, have you ever noticed occasions when you have had trouble discerning people's attitudes from their behavior? For example, do you always assume that the way a salesperson behaves toward you genuinely indicates that person's feelings toward you? Have you ever acted cruelly, carelessly, or unsympathetically toward someone about whom you care deeply? Clearly, people's behavior does not necessarily reflect their attitudes accurately. At the least, there may be several alternative explanations for the behavior we observe.

However, our beliefs and attitudes are not entirely separate from our behaviors. Several factors increase the likelihood that our attitudes will be shown in our behaviors (see Baron & Byrne, 1991; Brehm & Kassin, 1990):

1. *Attitude strength*—Stronger attitudes are more clearly tied to behavior than are weaker ones.
2. *Amount of information and experience supporting the attitude*—Attitudes based on more information and more experience are more clearly linked to behavior than are other attitudes.
3. *Attitude specificity*—More highly specific attitudes are more clearly tied to behavior. For example, you are more likely to vote in favor of a proposition to increase property taxes in order to increase the availability of student loans if you have a positive attitude toward that specific use of funds than if you have a generally positive attitude toward having a well-educated citizenry.
4. *Situational factors*—Your current situation may affect whether you behave in accord with your attitudes. For example, if you win the lottery on the morning of the election, you may completely forget to go to the polling booth; on the other hand, if your parents call you and tell you that they have just declared bankruptcy, you will probably recruit a few extra voters to vote for student-loan funding.

Another factor that influences both our attitudes and our behavior is the broad cultural context in which we live. For example, the terms *monochronic* ("one time") and *polychronic* ("many times") have been used to describe cultural variations in the perception of time (Hall, 1966). In a *monochronic culture*, time is precious, and its regulation is precise. In such a culture, people are more likely to have attitudes that prize time and to show behavior that reflects a rigid orientation toward time. On the other hand, in a *polychronic culture*, people place much less emphasis on the clock, and the measurement of

time is much more fluid. In a polychronic culture, people may be expected to behave in ways that might be considered tardy or even irresponsible (because of the lack of attention to time) in a monochronic culture.

In a cross-cultural study (Levine & Bartlett, 1984), the monochronic emphasis on time has been linked to coronary heart disease. Some might conclude that if we pay less attention to the time we have, we may end up having more time to live.

LIKING, LOVING, AND INTERPERSONAL ATTRACTION

I love you more than a duck can swim,
And more than a grapefruit squirts.
I love you more than gin rummy is a bore,
And more than a toothache hurts.

—*Ogden Nash, "To My Valentine"*

This chapter has described several strategies for persuading people to behave in particular ways, sometimes in spite of their initial attitudes. One factor that affects the likelihood of being persuaded is the likability of the persuader. Given that we tend to be more easily persuaded by people who are likable, just what does it mean to be "likable"? Why are we more attracted—and more attractive—to one person rather than another? Each of us needs friendship, love, and even physical attraction, and our perceptions of ourselves are partly shaped by our friendships, our loving relationships, and our feelings of attractiveness and attraction to others. Social psychologists have asked, What is going on in the mind of a person who feels attracted to someone?

This chapter presents the psychological responses to questions regarding liking and loving. Nonetheless, sculptors, composers, writers, and myriad other artists and philosophers have explored these same questions. While reading about the psychological perspective, bear in mind that scientific dissection of love or friendship can give us only a part of a much wider picture; such feelings are gestalts, truly greater than the sum of any parts that psychologists have yet found. Several theories have been proposed that attempt to explain just why we do find ourselves more attracted to some people than to others—and the reasons suggested may surprise you. In the first section, we look at theories of liking and attraction

The people in these photos all feel love for one another, but the kind of love they feel differs greatly for each kind of relationship. Although psychologists take a scientific approach to studying why and how people love one another, many other approaches to love enrich our understanding of this wondrous phenomenon.

between friends; in the second section, we examine theories of love and of physical attraction.

> What do you think is the best approach to studying love: scientific, literary, artistic, or some other? Why? Can these approaches be combined? If so, how?

Theories of Liking and Interpersonal Attraction

Reinforcement Theory

Suppose you are introduced to someone who immediately compliments you on your looks, your brains, your brawn, or something else of which you are proud. Chances are you will like that person all the more for the compliment. In terms of learning theory, you have been positively reinforced (rewarded) by the complimenter, who has thereby increased your attraction to him or her.

Reinforcement theory also posits that you will like a person when you experience rewards in the presence of that person (Clore & Byrne, 1974). Such rewards cause that person to become a **secondary reinforcer.** An interesting implication of this view is that you can come to like (or dislike) someone not because of who he or she is, but because good (or bad) things happen to you in his or her presence.

Research supports this view. For example, children who are systematically rewarded by their teacher come to like their classmates more than do children who are either ignored or punished by their teacher (Lott & Lott, 1968). On the negative side, people tend to dislike strangers they meet in a hot, crowded room, regardless of the strangers' actual personalities (Griffitt & Veitch, 1971).

> What are some real-life situations that contradict the reinforcement theory of liking?

Equity Theory

Equity theory (Walster, Walster, & Berscheid, 1978) holds that people will be more attracted to those with whom they have an equitable (fair) relationship. We are attracted to people who take from us in proportion to what they give to us. Equity theory has important implications for relationships. The first and simplest is that, over the long term, it is important that both members of a couple feel that their rewards and punishments are approximately equal. A relationship starts to deteriorate when either person feels that the relationship is one-sided in terms of sacrifices or benefits. Second, when one partner feels wronged by the other, the couple must find a way in which to restore equity as quickly as possible. If this restoration is not achieved, and one partner continually reminds the other of the inequity, the relationship may be jeopardized. If a partner feels that no matter what he or she does, equity cannot be restored, that person may decide to give up on the relationship.

Cognitive-Consistency Theories

Equity theory is, in a sense, a bridge between reinforcement theories and cognitive-consistency theories (discussed earlier). Equity theory ties in with reinforcement theory, because we expect to receive rewards and punishments in equal proportion to what we give in relationships. Equity theory ties in with cognitive-consistency theory, too, because we also try to maintain cognitive consistency by ensuring that what we give is in balance with what we get in relationships. Otherwise, cognitive dissonance results. Several kinds of cognitive-consistency theories have been posited, but the scope of this introductory text limits us to discussion of only one. Balance theory aptly represents this class of theories.

According to **balance theory** (Heider, 1958), we try to maintain consistency regarding our likes and dislikes as a means of attaining cognitive consistency. One aspect of maintaining balance has to do with *reciprocity*, similar to the notion of equity, or of give and take in a relationship. Another aspect of maintaining balance is *similarity;* we expect our friends to have the same positive or negative reactions to other people that we have. We expect our friends to like the people we like and to dislike those we dislike. Similarly, we expect our friends to share our other positive and negative attitudes. When we feel

One way of viewing attraction is in terms of equity: People will be more attracted to those with whom they have an equitable relationship—that is, each partner has something of equal value to offer in the relationship. Like the Peruvians bartering in this marketplace, each partner can give something to the relationship that is equal in value to what each receives from the relationship.

positively toward something that our friends dislike (or vice versa), we feel an uncomfortable imbalance in the relationship. This imbalance tends to weaken the stability of the relationship, so we try to correct it.

Does balance theory explain why it is always so difficult for threesomes to be friends? Why or why not?

Theories of Love

Most of us distinguish between liking and loving, but we also admit that it is difficult to define precisely all the differences between liking and loving—not to mention the difficulty in trying to define precisely the two terms themselves. Here, we assume that *love* is a deeper, stronger feeling than is liking; both are rooted in attraction, but love perhaps stems from more powerful—perhaps even instinctual—emotional and physical attractions than does liking. Consider some of the psychological theories that have been proposed to elucidate love—what kinds of love have been found to exist, where love comes from, and why love exists at all.

What do you believe leads one person to fall in love with another? To stay in love?

Types of Love

To orient ourselves to the range of kinds of love, we start with a look at a proposal that there are multiple types of love. John Alan Lee (1977, 1988) proposed six kinds of love, each named with a Greek or Latin word, the meaning of which characterizes it. The three primary types of love are *eros* (passion and desire), *ludus* (play), and *storge* (affection and friendship); three secondary types formed by combining various aspects of the primary types are *agape* (altruistic, selfless adoration; eros + storge), *pragma* (practicality; ludus + storge), and *mania* (madness and possessiveness; ludus + eros). According to Lee, the kinds of love are like colors, and different "shades" of love can be formed from their combinations. (See Figure 14-4 for definitions of the terms and descriptions of some of Lee's types of love.) Support for the existence of these six kinds of love has been found in an investigation using questionnaires (Hendrick & Hendrick, 1986).

Although psychologists agonize over how to define, categorize, analyze, and explain love, most of us can recognize love when we see people who love each other.

My study [of love] began with the most successful teachers of romantic ideology for half a millennium—the great novelists. Then I turned to nonfictional observers of love, from Plato and Ovid to Andreas Cappellanus and Castiglione to the most recent psychologists. . . . It soon became obvious that no single set of statements would describe love.

—*John Alan Lee, "Love-Styles"*

For each of Lee's types of love, describe a relationship that you think is of that type.

Clinical Theories

Clinical theories use data from case studies of patients in therapy as a basis for theorizing. As a result, clinical theorists sometimes tend to view love as slightly more "abnormal" than do other kinds of theorists, and clinical theories often lack experimental research testing their validity. Generally, clinical theories have more to say about loving than they do about liking.

Sigmund Freud (1922) viewed love as sexuality that has been made societally acceptable. Because

FIGURE 14-4
Lee's Six Types of Love
When John Alan Lee was formulating his three primary types of love and his three secondary types of love, he looked back across the centuries of great literature for inspiration. (After Lee, 1977, 1988)

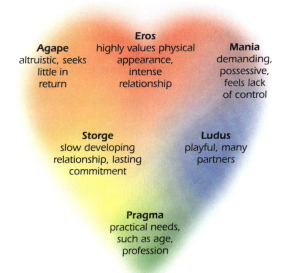

Agape
altruistic, seeks little in return

Eros
highly values physical appearance, intense relationship

Mania
demanding, possessive, feels lack of control

Storge
slow developing relationship, lasting commitment

Ludus
playful, many partners

Pragma
practical needs, such as age, profession

Edmond Rostand's Cyrano de Bergerac may be viewed as the embodiment of Freudian sublimation. Instead of expressing directly his own ardent passion for his beloved Roxane, Cyrano wrote exquisite love poems to her on behalf of a fatuous, but handsome, war hero.

people want sexual relations more frequently, with more people, and in more places than society in general or other people in particular will allow, love and traditional expressions of love are ways of *sublimating* (rendering societally acceptable) the sexual drive. When sexual desires are sublimated, they do not go away; instead, they are rechanneled onto a higher plane. There, they can be expressed in a socially acceptable way—through dating, courtship, companionship, and so on—as love. Thus, our socially undesirable sexual desires are transformed into socially desirable romantic ones.

"Sublimation" and "subliminal" advertising (Chapter 6) come from the same etymological roots. Explain the conceptual parallel.

The Two-Component Cognitive-Labeling Theory

A particularly well-known theory is the **two-component cognitive-labeling theory,** which suggests that passionate love results when a person (a) feels emotionally and physically aroused, and then (b) interprets intellectually the arousal as love and desire (Walster & Berscheid, 1974). Thus, two components are involved: (1) emotional and physical arousal, and (2) cognitive labeling of the arousal as love. For example, if you feel arousal in the presence of someone you find attractive, you may well interpret the arousal as love. What is critical—and not immediately obvious—is that you do not have to interpret the arousal as love. Emotional and physical arousal in the presence of someone whom you detest, for example, might well be interpreted as hate.

The role of arousal was demonstrated in a famous and creative study (Dutton & Aron, 1974) conducted in a scenic spot with two bridges in different places. The first bridge extended over a deep gorge and swayed precariously from side to side when people walked across it. For most people, walking across this bridge aroused fear. The second bridge was stable, solid, and near the ground. Walking across it did not arouse anxiety.

Subjects (all males) were assigned to walk across one bridge or the other and were met by either a male or a female assistant of the experimenter. The assistant asked each subject to answer a few questions and to write a brief story in response to a picture. After the subjects wrote their stories, the research assistant gave the men his or her home phone number and remarked that they should feel free to call if they would like further information about the experiment. The experimenters found that those subjects who had walked across the anxiety-evoking suspension bridge and who were met by a female assistant wrote stories containing relatively high levels of sexual imagery and were more likely than other subjects to call the female research assistant at home.

According to two-component theory, when the men felt more highly aroused, due to their anxiety in crossing the teetering bridge, they cognitively labeled their arousal as being an increased level of attraction. Since Elaine Walster and Ellen Berscheid first proposed this theory, psychophysiological data (e.g., Schwartz & Weinberger, 1980) have suggested that there may be features of the arousal associated with love that distinguish it from the arousal associated with other feelings, such as fear or anger. These data would seem to diminish the likelihood that people would easily mislabel their feelings of arousal, as a result of circumstances not directly related to feeling attracted.

Evolutionary Theory

Another way to understand love is in evolutionary terms. According to evolutionary theory, adult love is an outgrowth of three main instincts that have proved to be evolutionarily useful by aiding in the survival of our species: (1) the need of the infant to be protected either by its parents or by parent substitutes; (2) the desire for an adult to protect and to be protected by a lover; and (3) the sexual drive (Wilson, 1981; see also Buss, 1988a, 1988b).

The ultimate function of romantic love, in the evolutionary view, is to propagate the species. Unfor-

Although this bridge is not the one used by D. G. Dutton and A. P. Aron, it illustrates the relative degree of arousal you might feel if you were crossing it. If an attractive person were to greet you after you had crossed the rickety-looking bridge, would you feel a heightened sense of attraction?

tunately, however, romantic love generally does not last long—sometimes just long enough to commit the procreative act. Were romantic love the only force keeping couples together, children might not be raised in a way that would enable them to form attachments and to develop their potential. Fortunately, companionate love—just plain, strong liking—often helps a couple stay together and bring up the children, even after romantic love has waned.

The evolutionary point of view also shows the importance of parental love. Children need their parents so that they can become independent, self-sustaining individuals. Thus, from an evolutionary point of view, parental love helps keep the parent attentive to the child long enough for the child to become self-sufficient and to survive. In this way, evolutionary theory is similar to attachment theory, described next.

Some people do not think love is an important component of marriage. What might they think is important for a successful marriage? Why?

Attachment Theory

The attachment theory of love (Hazan & Shaver, 1987) uses the attachment concept of John Bowlby (1969) but extends it by showing that styles of adult romantic love correspond to styles of attachment among infants for their mothers (Ainsworth, 1973). (Recall from Chapter 13 the three different attachment styles in relationships.) The Hazan-Shaver theory posits three basic types of lovers. (1) *Secure lovers* find it relatively easy to get close to others. They are comfortable depending on others and having others depend on them. They do not worry about being abandoned or about someone getting too close to

There seems to be quite a bit of support for evolutionary theory when we look to the universality of parental love, as shown by a contemporary photograph of an Ifugao father and child in the Philippines (left), and by Marie-Elisabeth-Louise Vigée-Lebrun's painting, Self-Portrait With Her Daughter *(right).*

them. (2) *Avoidant lovers* are uncomfortable being close to others. They find it difficult to trust others and to allow themselves to depend on others. They get nervous when anyone gets too close, and they often find that their partners in love want to become more intimate than they find comfortable. (3) *Anxious-ambivalent lovers* find that their potential or actual partners in love are reluctant to get as close as the anxious-ambivalent lovers would like. Anxious-ambivalent lovers often worry that their partners do not really love them or want to stay with them. They want to merge completely with another person—a desire that sometimes scares potential or actual partners away.

Triangular Theory of Love

An alternative view of love is my own **triangular theory of love** (Sternberg, 1986b), according to which love has three basic components: (1) **intimacy,** feelings that promote closeness and connection; (2) **passion,** the intense desire for union with another person (Hatfield & Walster, 1981); and (3) **commitment,** the decision to maintain a relationship over the long term. Different combinations of these three components yield different kinds of love, as shown in Figure 14-5.

The preceding theories of liking, attraction, and loving offer a variety of ways in which to look at these phenomena. Next, we consider an alternative perspective. Zick Rubin's theory of liking and of loving, which preceded my own, led him to develop the first means of quantitatively assessing both liking and loving.

According to the evolutionary theory of love, companionate love may have helped this couple to remain together in order to raise their children to adulthood. What is the value of companionate love for adults whose children are adults?

FIGURE 14-5
The Triangular Theory of Love
Sternberg's triangular theory of love proposes three components of love: passion, commitment, and intimacy. These components may be combined in various ways to produce various kinds of love. (After Sternberg, 1986b)

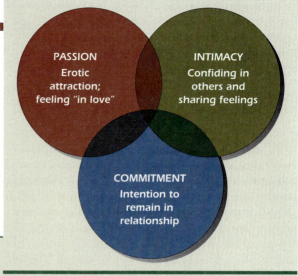

Passion	Intimacy	Decision and Commitments		Type of love that results
−	−	−	=	Nonlove
+	−	−	=	Infatuated Love
−	+	−	=	Liking (Friendship)
−	−	+	=	Empty Love
+	+	−	=	Romantic Love
−	+	+	=	Companionate Love
+	−	+	=	Fatuous Love
+	+	+	=	Consummate (Complete) Love

Note: The kinds of love are typical representations; most relationships do not fit neatly and concisely within only one type.
(+ = component present; − = component absent.)

The Measurement of Liking and Loving

Many psychologists relish measuring various psychological phenomena, including liking and loving. Of the several sets of scales measuring these constructs, without a doubt the most well known are the *Rubin Love Scale* and the *Rubin Liking Scale* (1970; see Figure 14-6). Items on the love scale can be arranged into three distinct clusters: (a) dependent need of the other, (b) predisposition to help the other, and (c) exclusiveness and absorption. The liking scale measures attributes that are more akin to friendship, primarily based on respect for the person's abilities and similarity to the person in terms of attitudes and other characteristics. Measurements of liking and of loving may overlap considerably among couples who have more committed relationships rather than more casual ones (Cimbalo, Faling, & Mousaw, 1976; Dion & Dion, 1976).

What three questions would you include in an assessment to measure liking? What three other questions would you include in an assessment to measure loving? Could the questions you ask for one assessment tool also be used for the other? Why or why not?

Variables Underlying Attraction

We have discussed various theories of liking, loving, and attraction, as well as some ways in which these constructs can be measured. We now look more closely at the factors that lead to attraction in the first place, and hence to liking and loving. Some of these variables are arousal, familiarity, proximity, physical attractiveness, and similarity. Arousal was already mentioned in regard to the two-component theory of attraction and liking. Recall, too, from the discussion on persuasion, that familiarity is another factor that increases our liking for someone. That is, due to the mere exposure effect, we tend to feel stronger liking for people who are more familiar to us. The remaining three factors are described next.

Proximity

We are more likely to be exposed to and to be aroused by those with whom we have the most contact. Thus, **proximity**—geographical nearness—may lead to increased friendship or attraction because it facilitates the likelihood of familiarity and possibly also of arousal.

Patterns of friendship were investigated among military veterans and their spouses who lived in two married-student dormitories at the Massachusetts Institute of Technology (Festinger, Schachter, & Back, 1950). The two dormitories had different architectural designs, so it was possible to investigate the effects of proximity in two fairly different, yet confined, physical settings. The basic finding was that people who lived closer to each other were more likely to become friends than were people who lived farther apart—even though none of the distances involved was great. Moreover, people who lived in centrally located apartments were likely to form more friendships than were people who lived in apartments toward the end of a floor.

Why does proximity lead to attraction?

Physical Attractiveness

If you are like most people—and you are honest with yourself—physical attraction is a very important component of your attraction to people in general, at least at first. This statement may seem obvious, but it contradicts what many people *say* attracts them, such as honesty and a sense of humor (e.g., Buss & Barnes, 1986). Nonetheless, research (e.g., Walster, Aronson, Abrahams, & Rottman, 1966) supports the heavy consideration given to physical attraction in regard to interpersonal attraction.

For example, in one study, Kenneth Dion, Ellen Berscheid, and Elaine Walster (1972) found that more physically attractive people are judged to be kinder and stronger; to be more outgoing, nurturant, sensitive, interesting, poised, sociable, and sexually warm and responsive; to be more exciting dates; and to have better characters. More attractive people also are predicted to have greater marital happiness and competence, more prestige, more social and professional success, and more fulfillment in life than less attractive people.

Another important consideration in regard to physical attractiveness is the cultural context of the beholders of beauty. Cross-cultural studies of beauty have clearly documented that different cultures have strikingly different views of what constitutes a standard of beauty. We have known for decades that different societies have sharply different views of physical attractiveness. An early review of more than 200 widely divergent cultures (Ford & Beach, 1951) found that societies differ not only in what they consider beautiful, but also in the parts of the body (e.g., eye shape, pelvis size, overall height and weight) they emphasize in evaluating beauty. More recent reviews (e.g., Berscheid & Walster, 1974) support this diversity of cultural views of attractiveness.

The effect of physical attractiveness may become more muted over time. Early in a relationship, physical attraction is key (Murstein, 1986, 1988). Over time, however, other factors, such as flexibility and compatibility, play a greater role (Murstein, 1986; Sternberg, 1988c).

FIGURE 14-6
Items from the Rubin Love Scale and the Rubin Liking Scale
Rubin measured different kinds of attraction by creating the love scale and the liking scale. The love scale assesses the amount of intimacy and the preoccupation felt by one person toward another; the liking scale assesses the amount of respect and perceived similarities felt by one person toward another. How might you answer the items on each scale, depending on whether you were describing your best friend (in a platonic relationship) or your beloved? (After Rubin, 1973)

ITEMS FROM THE LOVE SCALE	ITEMS FROM THE LIKING SCALE
I feel that I can confide in _____ about virtually everything.	I would highly recommend _____ for a responsible job.
If I could never be with _____, I would feel miserable.	_____ is one of the most likable people I know.
It would be hard for me to get along without _____ .	_____ is the sort of person whom I myself would like to be.

Although not everyone agrees about what features make a person physically attractive, most of us seem to be drawn to persons who have the characteristics we believe to be physically attractive. All of the persons depicted here have found ways to highlight and enhance their physical attractiveness, as defined and perceived by their cultural groups.

Why do people say that personality is more important than looks, when experimental evidence suggests otherwise?

Similarity

As you might have guessed, based on the long-term benefits of having compatible values and compatible ideas about roles, evidence on interpersonal attraction suggests that the more similar individuals are, the more likely they are to be attracted to each other (Burgess & Wallin, 1953; Huston & Levinger, 1978). Among the factors for which similarity has been shown to have a positive effect on attraction are attitudes and temperament (Hatfield & Rapson, 1992), social and communication skills (Burleson & Denton, 1992), and even sense of humor (Murstein & Brust, 1985). Although having similar communication skills is important, having at least some communication skills may be a sine qua non of lasting relationships (Sternberg, 1988c; Sternberg & Grajek, 1984). Indeed, in one study, five years after subjects were married, they cited communication as the single key to satisfactory marital adjustment (Markman, 1981).

COMMUNICATION IN RELATIONSHIPS

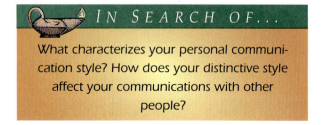

IN SEARCH OF...

What characterizes your personal communication style? How does your distinctive style affect your communications with other people?

Communication appears to be a key to success in relationships of many kinds. Communication can be either verbal or nonverbal, and we consider each kind in turn.

Verbal Communication

Communication in relationships follows a pattern of **social penetration** (Altman & Taylor, 1973), in which we talk about an increasingly broad and deep range of topics during the course of the relationship (see Figure 14-7). At first, we tend to talk about fairly superficial things. Gradually, we increase the depth and breadth of what we are willing to talk about.

Nonetheless, meaningful communication is probably essential for success in relationships. Couples in happy marriages truly listen to each other and validate each other's points of view, whereas couples in unhappy marriages are less likely to listen and to cross-validate (Gottman, 1979). Instead, unhappy couples often *cross-complain*—each moans and whines without paying attention to what the other is saying. One complains that the other is never home, while the other complains that the one spends too much money. They talk past rather than to each other.

Other factors also contribute to unsuccessful communication in couples (Gottman, Notarius, Gonso, & Markman, 1976): One or both partners (a) feel hurt and ignored, (b) feel that the other does not see their point of view, (c) neglect to stay on one problem long enough to resolve the problem, (d) frequently interrupt one another, and (e) drag many irrelevant issues into the discussion.

Gender differences in communication patterns, content, and styles also appear to exist. These differences can interfere with effective communication. For example, later adolescent and young adult males prefer to talk about political views, sources of personal pride, and what they like about the other person, whereas females in this age group prefer to talk about feelings toward parents, close friends, classes, and fears (Rubin, Hill, Peplau, & Dunkel-Schetter, 1980). Also, in general, women seem to disclose more about themselves than do men (Morton, 1978).

Deborah Tannen (1986, 1990) has done extensive sociolinguistic research on male–female conversation, and her research has led her to view the conversations between men and women as cross-cultural communication. Tannen suggests that little girls and little boys learn conversational communication in essentially separate cultural environments through their same-sex friendships. As men and women, we then carry over the conversational styles we learned in childhood into our adult conversations.

Tannen suggests that male–female differences in conversational style largely center on our differing understandings of the goals of conversation. These cultural differences result in contrasting styles of communication that can lead to misunderstandings and even breakups as each partner somewhat unsuccessfully tries to understand the other. According to Tannen (1990), men see the world as a hierarchical social order in which the purpose of communication is to negotiate for the upper hand, to preserve independence, and to avoid failure. Each man strives to one-up the other and to "win" the contest. Women, in contrast, seek to establish a connection between the two participants, to give support and confirmation to others, and to reach consensus through communication.

Tannen states that when men and women become more aware of their cross-cultural styles and traditions, they may be less likely to misinterpret one another's conversational interactions. In this way, they would both be more likely to achieve their individual aims, as well as the aims of the relationship.

When relationships of any kind are starting to fail, the breakdown in communication may follow a predictable pattern (Vaughan, 1986). One person begins to feel uncomfortable in a relationship but says nothing, perhaps not even consciously realizing that anything is seriously wrong. The dissatisfied person may then create a private world in which to mull over these vague, uneasy feelings. By doing so, however, the dissatisfied person, generally unintentionally, creates a breach that increasingly widens, leading to less and less communication, and eventually, the loss of the relationship.

Do you agree with Tannen's assessment of men and women as different "culturally"? Why or why not?

FIGURE 14-7
Changes in Social Penetration over Time
Over the course of an interpersonal relationship, the pattern of communication changes. The range of topics that the partners discuss both broadens (in the number of topics) and deepens (in the relative intimacy of the topics). (After Altman & Taylor, 1973)

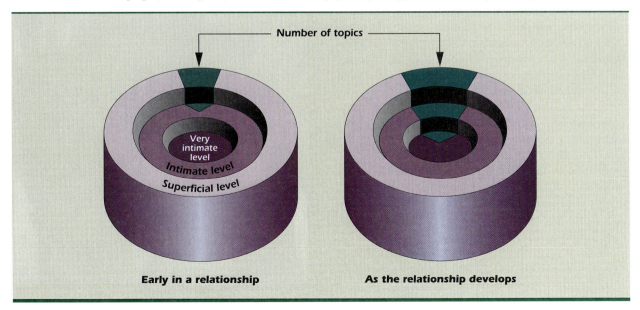

FIGURE 14-8
Enigmatic Smiles
Sometimes, it is difficult to interpret another person's facial expression. Compare the smiles in these two paintings: Gottfried Cornelisz Schalken, Girl With a Candle, ca. 1665 (left); Franz Hals, The Gypsy Girl, ca. 1630 (second). Even photographs can present perplexing expressions: What is this little girl thinking and feeling? What is this man conveying?

Nonverbal Communication

If a person's mouth were silent, another part would speak.

—Arabic proverb

Even when we do not speak, we often communicate our true feelings and beliefs through our facial expressions (see Figure 14-8), our gestures, our posture, our movements, and how and whether we look at people. Nonverbal communication is a subtle, yet powerful means of getting across a message. We use nonverbal cues to decipher other people's attitudes and emotional states from their social behavior. Nonetheless, we should not assume that nonverbal communications are more sincere than verbal ones. People can also use nonverbal signals as masks, as did Poe's narrator at the outset of this chapter, who smiles at the man he intends to destroy.

Eye contact is a major source of nonverbal communication, signaling social information about intimacy and dominance. In any hierarchical system (e.g., a hierarchy of class or power), people with less power tend to engage in less eye contact with their communication partners than do those with more power (Exline, 1972). People in competitive situations often increase eye contact (Exline, 1972), even glaring at one another. Indeed, because dilation of the pupils indicates emotional arousal, business people in some cultures wear dark glasses during negotiations in order to hide their pupils.

Another aspect of nonverbal communication is **personal space**—the distance between people in conversation or other interaction considered comfortable for members of a given culture. The linguistics term for the study of interpersonal distance (or its opposite, proximity) is **proxemics.** In the United

Other than for shading her eyes from the sun, why might this woman conceal her eyes? Is she being prudent, deceitful, wary, or shy? How might the man feel about discussing business with her without being able to see her eyes?

States, 18 to 24 inches is considered about right (Hall, 1966). Scandinavians and Japanese expect more distance, whereas Middle Easterners, southern Europeans, and South Americans expect less (Sommer, 1969; Watson, 1970). When on our own familiar turf, we take our own cultural views of personal space for granted; only when we come into contact with persons from other cultures do we notice these differences.

Clearly, nonverbal and verbal communication are key aspects of relationships between people. They are also fundamental to the formation of and interactions within larger groups of people, considered in the next chapter.

SUMMARY

The Nature of Social Psychology   490

1. *Social psychologists* seek to understand and explain how the presence of others (actual, imagined, or implied) affects the thoughts, feelings, and behavior of the individual.

Social Cognition   491

2. *Social cognition* refers to the ways in which we perceive and interpret information from others and ourselves.

3. One of the better known experiments in social psychology established the theory of *cognitive dissonance*, which states that when a person's behavior and cognitions do not mesh, discomfort results. To ease this discomfort, the person must justify his or her behavior. The results of a seminal experiment that studied cognitive dissonance have also been explained in other ways—by *self-perception* and *impression-management theories*, for example.

4. *Attribution theory* deals with how we go about explaining the causes of behavior—why we do what we do, and why others act as they do. In making attributions, we look for the locus (source) of the behavior, which can be personal or situational.

5. Biases and heuristics help us to make attributions but also sometimes to distort them. We give more weight to socially undesirable behavior over its opposite, and to the uncommon effect over the common. We are biased by *personalism*; by the *fundamental attribution error*, which makes us overemphasize internal over external causes when viewing the behavior of others; and by the *actor-observer effect*, which expands this view to encompass also our own behavior, which we explain by overemphasizing situational factors. We also use (and are used by!) self-serving biases and *self-handicapping*.

6. Biases and heuristics are also active in *impression formation*. Due to the *primacy effect*, we give more weight to things we learn earlier; due to *confirmation bias*, we interpret new information so that it verifies beliefs we already have; due to *self-fulfilling prophecy*, we can make our expectations come true; due to *person-positivity bias*, we evaluate individuals more positively than we do groups.

Attitudes and Attitude Change   504

7. *Attitudes* are learned (not inborn), stable, relatively lasting evaluations of people, ideas, and things; attitudes affect our behavior.

8. Attitudes serve four functions: to get what we want and avoid what we do not want, to avoid internal conflicts and anxieties, to understand and integrate information, and to show our deeply held values.

9. Learning theories regarding attitude formation include classical conditioning, operant conditioning, and *observational learning*.

10. In attempting to change other people's attitudes, the following characteristics are important: characteristics of the recipient of the message (e.g., motivation and expertise), characteristics of the message itself (balance and familiarity due to repetition), and characteristics of the source of the message (the source's credibility and likability).

11. The links between attitudes and behavior are not always predictable and are influenced by characteristics of the attitude, of the attitude bearer, of the situation, and of the behavior.

Liking, Loving, and Interpersonal Attraction 509

12. Social-psychological research asks why we are attracted to some people and not to others. Reinforcement theory answers that we like (or dislike) a person not just for who that person is but also because of the emotional rewards (or punishments) we get in that person's presence.

According to *equity theory*, attraction is a balancing act between give and take. *Cognitive-consistency theories* focus on balance.

13. According to Lee, the six types of love are eros, ludus, storge, mania, agape, and pragma.

14. Some clinical theories state that love is a way to sublimate sexual desires in a socially acceptable way; others state that love is a way to fill our inner void. The *two-component cognitive-labeling theory* describes passionate love in terms of emotional and physiological arousal and its subsequent labeling as love. Evolutionary theory deals with the genetic basis of mating behavior, as well as practical, survival-of-the-species reasons for love. Attachment theory describes three styles of lovers: secure, avoidant, and anxious-ambivalent. The *triangular theory of love* posits that three components—*intimacy, passion,* and *commitment*—are involved in love. Psychomet-

ric theories of liking and loving attempt to measure the constituents of love.

15. Studies show that physical attraction enhances overall attraction and liking. Other important factors underlying attraction include degree of arousal, familiarity, *proximity,* and similarity.

Communication in Relationships   518

16. Successful communication—verbal and nonverbal—is essential to relationships. Men and women appear to communicate differently—some say "cross-culturally." Women seem to seek closeness and consensus; men seem to prefer establishing status hierarchies and preserving their independence.

17. Nonverbal communication is also an important aspect of any relationship. It is conveyed via *eye contact, personal space,* and posture, among other factors.

KEY TERMS

actor-observer effect 499
attitude 505
attribution 496
balanced 508
balance theory 511
central route 507
central traits 501
cognitive consistency 493
cognitive dissonance 493
commitment 515
confirmation bias 502
credibility 508
equity theory 510
eye contact 520

fundamental attribution error 497
impression formation 499
impression-management theory 496
intimacy 515
justification of effort 493
likability effect 508
mere exposure effect 508
observational learning 505
passion 515
peripheral route 507
personal attribution 497
personal space 520
person-positivity bias 504
primacy effect 502

proxemics 520
proximity 517
secondary reinforcer 510
self-fulfilling prophecy 504
self-handicapping 499
self-perception theory 494
situational attribution 497
social cognition 491
social-comparison theory 504
social penetration 518
social psychology 490
triangular theory of love 515
two-component cognitive-labeling
    theory 513

IN SEARCH OF THE HUMAN MIND:
ANALYSES, CREATIVE EXPLORATIONS, AND PRACTICAL APPLICATIONS

1. Think of an opinion you believe in strongly. Write a paragraph giving strong arguments against your opinion. After you finish, consider how your opinion has been affected by writing the paragraph. Why was your opinion affected in this way?

2. Many advertisers spend a lot of money to get celebrity endorsements of their products. Do you think that the advertisers' money is well-spent? Why or why not?

3. Do you agree with Tannen's view that men place more emphasis on social hierarchies than women do? Why or why not?
   Write a very brief example or dialogue that illustrates your view.

4. Write a brief narrative about a particular conflict, first from the perspective of one participant and then from the perspective of the other. (Describe either a realistic conflict you have experienced or an imaginary one.)
   Which heuristics and biases affected the views of each participant?

5. Create an advertisement for a product using the principles discussed in this chapter.

6. Write a brief campaign speech for election to a student-government office that uses principles of persuasion as described in this chapter.

7. In what situations do you notice a discrepancy between what you believe to be your attitudes and what you do or what you say?
   How do such situations make you feel?

8. Give some examples of self-handicapping behaviors (e.g., drug abuse).
   Why and how do these examples show self-handicapping?

9. Describe a situation in which a self-fulfilling prophecy had a strong effect on you or on someone you know. What do you think about that situation now, in retrospect?

Chapter Fifteen

SOCIAL PSYCHOLOGY: INTERPERSONAL AND GROUP PERSPECTIVES

CHAPTER OUTLINE

The Kennedy administration's Bay of Pigs decision ranks among the worst fiascoes ever perpetrated by a responsible government. Planned by an over-ambitious, eager group of American intelligence officers who had little back-ground or experience in military matters, the attempt to place a small brigade of Cuban exiles secretly on a beachhead in Cuba with the ultimate aim of over-throwing the government of Fidel Castro proved to be a "perfect failure." The group that made the decision to approve the invasion plan included some of the most intelligent men ever to participate in the councils of government. Yet all the major assumptions supporting the plan were so completely wrong that the ven-ture began to founder at the outset and failed in its earliest stages.

—I. L. Janis, Victims of Groupthink

Why do smart people, put together into a group, sometimes do stupid things? For that matter, how do any groups of people reach a consensus about what they will do? What factors influence the route to consensus and the kind of consensus they achieve? What makes individuals within a group conform to a group decision, even if they don't believe in it? These are some of the questions that social psychologists consider.

Of course, as we have seen in earlier chapters, different cultures may respond differently to given behaviors. As you read about the studies in this chap-ter, be aware that most of them have been conducted in the United States, involving U.S. psychologists and subjects (Moghaddam, Taylor, & Wright, 1993; Öngel & Smith, 1994; Triandis, 1994). Many social psychologists question the generality of findings that are based on U.S. studies alone (Bond, 1988). How-ever, although we must be wary of overgeneralizing findings from one culture to the next, most of the questions and the problems are still the same.

GROUPS

IN SEARCH OF...

How does the mere presence of other people affect your behavior and your beliefs?

A **group** is a collection of individuals who inter-act with each other. A group is sometimes distin-guished from a *collective*, a set of people engaged in common activity but with minimal direct interaction. For example, if you go to a basketball game and sit in the audience, you would be part of a collective; the members of the basketball team, however, would be part of a group.

What actually happens when members of a group interact? Robert Bales (1950, 1970) suggested that groups serve two basic functions: to get work done and to handle relationships among group members. In some groups, such as a problem-solving group in a business, the emphasis is likely to be on accomplishing tasks. In other groups, such as a group of single parents seeking emotional support, the emphasis is likely to be on handling relationships among the group members. In still other groups, of course, there may be more of a balance between the two. As you might expect, leaders of groups also serve two key functions: to guide the group to achieve its task-oriented goals and to facilitate the group's functions of mutual support and group cohesion (Bales, 1958).

> *"Shut up,"* said Ralph absently. He lifted the conch. *"Seems to me we ought to have a chief to decide things."*
> *"A chief! A chief!"*
> *"I ought to be chief,"* said Jack with simple arrogance, *"because I'm chapter chorister and head boy. I can sing C sharp."*
>
> —*William Golding,* Lord of the Flies

Social Facilitation and Social Interference

Having other people around can affect the quality of the work you do. This fact was recognized long ago when Norman Triplett (1898) observed that bicyclists who competed against each other cycled faster than those who cycled alone against a clock. Similarly, children who were instructed to wind fishing reels as quickly as they could performed faster when they were with others than when they were alone. **Social facilitation** is the term for the beneficial effect on performance of having other people around. Those of you who have competed in races may have noted the effect of social facilitation.

However, having other people around does not always improve performance. Anyone who has ever tried to give a speech, perform in a recital, or act a role in front of an audience and has been tripped up by nervousness can testify to this **social inhibition.** The question then becomes, when do other people facilitate performance, and when do they interfere with it?

A widely accepted view of this phenomenon has been offered by Robert Zajonc (see Figure 15-1). According to Zajonc (1965, 1980), the presence of other people is arousing. Arousal facilitates well-learned responses but inhibits newly or poorly learned responses. Thus, to predict whether facilitation or inhibition will occur, we need to look at the individual's level of experience in the particular behavior. Suppose, for example, that Reuben is going to

audition for membership in an orchestra. He has prepared for the audition by learning a new, difficult piece. Under these circumstances, the conductor's presence is likely to inhibit Reuben's playing. Had he instead chosen a piece that he had known for a long time, the presence of the conductor probably would have facilitated his performance. Amazingly enough, social facilitation and inhibition apply not only to people, but also to animals. Even cockroaches exhibit social facilitation in performing an easy, automatic task, but show inhibition in performing a difficult one (Zajonc, Heingartner, & Herman, 1969).

As this textbook has shown, there are few psychological phenomena that all psychologists interpret in just the same way. **Distraction-conflict theory,** an alternative to Zajonc's theory, holds that the effect of the presence of others is due not to their mere presence, or even an individual's apprehension at being judged, but rather to the distracting effect of having other people around (Baron, 1986; Baron, Moore, & Sanders, 1978). In sum, general agreement exists on the empirical phenomena. You can obtain either facilitation (usually of a familiar, well-learned behavior) or inhibition (usually of an unfamiliar, poorly learned behavior) through the presence of others. However, alternative explanations of exactly when and why facilitation and inhibition occur are still being considered.

FIGURE 15-1
Social Facilitation
According to Robert Zajonc's theory of social facilitation, the mere presence of other people causes arousal. Arousal then facilitates well-learned behavior but inhibits poorly or newly learned behavior. (After Schmitt et al., 1986)

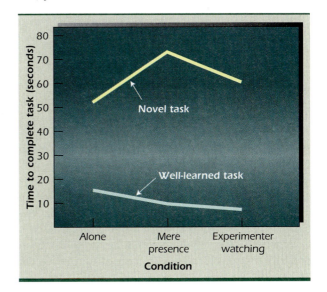

Design an experiment that would help you determine whether the inhibitory effects of other people are actually due to the distraction of having people around, rather than to arousal or to evaluation apprehension.

Social Loafing

What happens to our performance when we cooperate with others? Have you ever worked on a task with a group and found that you (or some of your associates) did not work as hard as you (or they) would have if acting alone? For example, do you put in the same effort when you are a member of a chorus or a band as you do when you are singing or playing alone? As the number of people increases, the average amount of effort exerted by each individual decreases (Ringelmann, 1913). The reduced effort of each of the group members as a function of the size of the group is termed **social loafing** (Latané, Williams, & Harkins, 1979).

Bibb Latané and other social psychologists (1979) were intrigued by M. Ringelmann's earlier findings and set out to determine whether it was the actual presence of others or merely the perceived presence of others that caused social loafing. They wondered whether part of the apparent social-loafing effect might be due to other factors, such as a lack of coordination of effort. To rule out this possibility, the researchers created both groups of individuals (varying from two to six persons) and pseudogroups of individuals. Subjects in the *pseudogroups* were led to believe that they were participating with others, but each individual was actually alone. The subjects were then asked either to clap as loudly as they could or to cheer at the top of their voices.

As Figure 15-2 shows, the researchers found that people expended more effort when they were alone than when they were in either groups or pseudogroups. In addition, the investigators noted that lack of coordination of effort also contributed to the decrease in usable work produced by actual groups, as opposed to pseudogroups.

How can social loafing be discouraged or eliminated altogether? Probably the most effective method is to introduce evaluation apprehension. If members in a working group are informed that their individual performance is being evaluated, the social loafing can be reduced, and social facilitation can be enhanced (Harkins, 1987; Harkins & Szymanski, 1987). For example, social loafing is unlikely to occur if an orchestra conductor can hear each of the individual

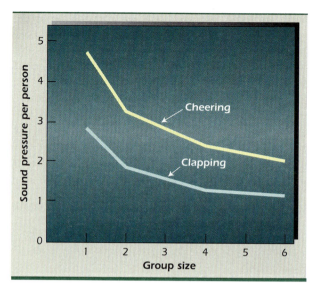

FIGURE 15-2
Social Loafing
The social-loafing phenomenon appears to occur even when other contributing factors are separated out (Latané et al., 1979). When people believe that increasing numbers of other persons are participating in work, they exert less individual effort—even when no other persons are actually present. (After Latané, Williams, & Harkins, 1979)

members and makes the members of the orchestra aware of this fact, or if students involved in a group problem-solving task are told that their performance is being watched by teachers and that each student will be evaluated in terms of his or her contribution to the group.

Social loafing is affected by cultural orientation toward either *individualism* or *collectivism*. Although social loafing may commonly occur in highly individualistic societies, such as in the United States, it may be less common in societies with a more collectivistic orientation, such as China and Taiwan. For instance, studies involving Chinese subjects have shown that individuals work *harder* when they are in a group than when they are alone (Early, 1989; Gabrenya, Latané, & Wang, 1983; Gabrenya, Wang, & Latané, 1985).

Group Polarization

In what other ways do people change their behavior when participating in groups? Are people in groups more or less likely than individuals to take risks? In some instances, groups choose riskier alternatives, but in others, they choose more conservative alternatives. This tendency for the exaggeration of group members' initial positions is known as **group polarization**

(Moscovici & Zavalloni, 1969; Myers & Lamm, 1976). If the members of a group, on average, initially tend toward taking risks, the group will tend to exaggerate this risk-taking tendency. However, if the members of a group originally tend toward conservatism, the group will usually tend to make a more conservative response than that of the individual members.

In a study demonstrating this effect (Myers & Bishop, 1970), students were initially classified as high, medium, or low in racial prejudice, based on their responses to a questionnaire. The subjects were then formed into groups that were homogeneous with respect to racial prejudice. The task of the groups was to discuss racial issues. After the group discussion, subjects were then assessed for their levels of racial prejudice. The results were clear: People who had initially showed themselves to be low in prejudice came out even lower after the group discussion, and people who had initially showed themselves to be high in prejudice came out even higher.

Why does group polarization occur? Two factors appear to be responsible. First is the effect of *new information*. People initially have a point of view that they believe. In the group, however, they hear new arguments supporting their point of view that they had not thought of before. They thus become even more extreme in their conviction (Burnstein & Vinokur, 1973, 1977). The more new arguments they hear, the more persuasive they believe the arguments to be, and the more extreme they become in their attitudes.

The second effect is the *movement toward the group norm*. As people meet other people supporting their point of view and receive social approval from them, they begin to move in the direction of the group norm. The group may gain more and more solidarity as their position becomes more extreme, but at the expense of rational decision making. The information and reactions of other people are not all equally effective. Furthermore, a person will be most affected by the opinions and sentiments of those the person identifies as members of his or her respected "in group" (Turner, 1987). Thus, for example, Republicans are more likely to be influenced by Republicans than by Democrats in their group decision making, and vice versa. (Informational influence and normative influence are discussed again later, in regard to conformity.)

How does group polarization relate to confirmation bias, mentioned in Chapter 14?

Conflict Resolution

As the phenomenon of group polarization implies, groups of people are often in conflict with one another: risk-takers versus risk-avoiders, Democrats versus Republicans, and so on. In addition, as your own experience has probably shown, even within groups, members are often in conflict with one another. How do people resolve these intergroup and intragroup conflicts?

Some investigators (e.g., Kuhlman & Marshello, 1975; McClintock & Liebrand, 1988) have suggested that people have particular goals in resolving conflicts. People may have a *cooperative orientation*, seeking to maximize both their outcomes and those of others; an *individualistic orientation*, seeking to maximize only their own outcomes; a *competitive orientation*, seeking to maximize their own outcomes at the expense of others; or an *altruistic orientation*, seeking to maximize only the outcomes of others. These values appear to be relatively stable and valid predictors of their behavior in situations involving decision making (see McClintock & Liebrand, 1988).

People may use certain *strategies* to resolve conflicts. Colleagues and I have suggested that people tend consistently to use particular types of conflict-resolution strategies such as physical force, economic force, seeking to defuse conflict, and seeking mediation (Sternberg & Soriano, 1984; see also Sternberg & Dobson, 1987). A number of conflict-resolution strategies can maximize the effectiveness of negotiations (Fisher & Ury, 1981). Some of these strategies include (a) not confusing the problem underlying the conflict with the people involved in the conflict; (b) coming up with mutually beneficial options; and (c) using objective criteria for measuring the consequences for all parties.

Groupthink

Ignorance is strength.

—*George Orwell*, 1984

Ironically, one of the most troublesome group processes arises when there is *too little conflict* within the group. Irving Janis has given special attention to a particular kind of group process, **groupthink**, which takes place when group members who are "striving for unanimity override their motivation to realistically appraise alternative courses of action" (Janis,

1972, p. 9). Janis analyzed a number of foreign-policy decisions he believed to reflect groupthink, including the Bay of Pigs fiasco, the failure to anticipate the invasion of Pearl Harbor, and the appeasement of Adolf Hitler by British Prime Minister Neville Chamberlain prior to World War II.

What conditions lead to groupthink? Janis has cited three kinds: (1) an isolated, cohesive, and homogeneous group empowered to make decisions; (2) the absence of objective and impartial leadership, either within the group or outside of it; and (3) high levels of stress impinging on the group decision-making process. Note that the groups responsible for making foreign-policy decisions are excellent candidates for groupthink. They are often like-minded and frequently isolate themselves from what is going on outside of their own group. They are generally trying to meet specific foreign-policy objectives and thus, cannot always afford—or believe they cannot afford—to be impartial. Also, of course, they are under very high stress, because the stakes involved in their decisions can be tremendous.

Janis further delineates six symptoms of groupthink: (1) *closed-mindedness*—the group is not open to a variety of alternative conceptualizations; (2) *rationalization*—the group goes to great lengths to

justify both the process and the product of its decision making, distorting reality where necessary in order to accomplish this justification; (3) the *squelching of dissent*—those who do not agree are ignored, criticized, or even ostracized; (4) the *formation of a "mindguard"* for the group—one person who appoints him- or herself as the keeper of the group norm and who makes sure that people stay in line; (5) the *feeling of invulnerability*—the group believes that it must be right, given the intelligence of and the information available to its members; and (6) the *feeling of unanimity*—the group members feel that all those in the group are unanimous in sharing the opinions expressed by the group. The result of groupthink is defective decision making due to incomplete examination of alternatives, failure to examine adequately the risks involved in following the course of the decision recommended, and incomplete search for information about alternatives. (See Figure 15-3.)

What recent events do you think might have been caused by groupthink?

Janis has prescribed several antidotes for groupthink. For example, the leader of a policy-making

FIGURE 15-3
Janis's Groupthink

This chart summarizes the antecedent conditions, symptoms, decision-making defects, and consequences of groupthink. (After Janis, 1972)

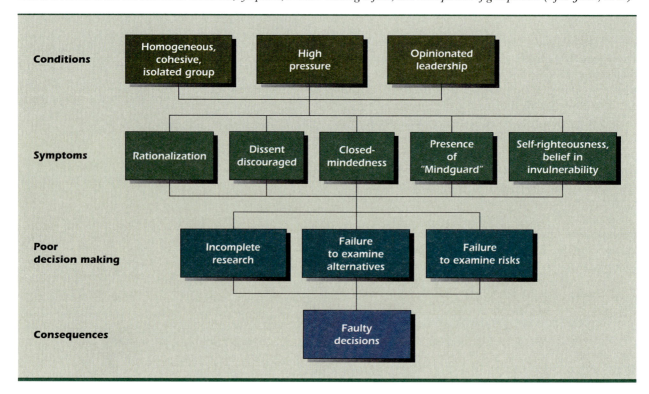

group should encourage criticism, be impartial rather than stating preferences at the outset, and make sure that members of the group seek input from people outside the group. The group should also break down into smaller groups that meet separately to consider various alternative solutions to the same problem. Thus, although groupthink is serious it can be avoided. In particular, the leader of the group needs to take responsibility for preventing the factors that lead to spurious conformity to a group norm.

Most group processes involve the pressure to conform. What, exactly, are the factors that lead to conformity?

CONFORMITY, COMPLIANCE, AND OBEDIENCE

IN SEARCH OF...

Why do you sometimes do things that other people ask you to do, even when you do not want to do them?

In 1993, almost 80 members of the Branch Davidian religious sect apparently committed suicide at the command of their leader, David Koresh. Although this mass suicide is a striking example of conformity to a destructive group norm, numerous other astonishing examples have arisen throughout human history, such as the mass suicide of more then 900 members of the Jonestown, Guyana, religious cult in 1978. Nazi soldiers during World War II and Serbian soldiers in the early 1990s also participated in mass killings; in these cases, the group norm was genocide rather than suicide.

Conformity, compliance, and obedience all involve changes in one person's behavior, due to the social influence of another individual or group of persons. **Conformity** refers to a person's modification of behavior to make it consistent with the norms of the group. **Compliance** refers to a person's modification of behavior in response to a request by other persons. **Obedience** refers to a person's modification of behavior in response to the command of an actual or perceived authority. We consider each of these three kinds of social influence in turn. For each form of social influence, the individual may experience changes both in behavior and in perceptions, beliefs, and attitudes. (For the most part, these internal changes were described in Chapter 14.)

Why did almost 80 men, women, and children obediently commit group suicide, following the command of cult leader David Koresh?

Describe a typical setting where you have observed each form of social influence (conformity, compliance, obedience).

Conformity

The classic studies on conformity were done by Solomon Asch (1951, 1956), whom we discussed in Chapter 14. In Asch's studies, subjects believed that they were participating in an experiment on perceptual judgment. Imagine that you are a subject in one such experiment, which uses a group of seven subjects. You are all shown a white card containing a black line and another white card containing three other black lines of varying lengths. The task of each member of the group is simply to say which of the three black lines on the second card is of the same length as the black line on the first card. Only one of the black lines on the second card is even remotely close in length to the line on the first white card (see Figure 15-4).

Members of the group are asked to communicate their judgments in order, starting with subject number 1. As a subject, you expect the test to be a piece of cake. What could be easier? Unfortunately, however, subject number 1 gives what appears to be the wrong answer. You're surprised. Then, to your amazement, subject number 2 gives the same answer. So it goes until it is your turn, as subject number 6. What do you say? It is not easy to know what to say, as shown by the harried and puzzled look on the face

Solomon Asch (1907-   )

of subject number 6 from one of Asch's actual studies, as shown in Figure 15-4.

Asch found that most people will go along with the majority, on average, in about one-third of the erroneous judgments. Of course, you do not yet realize that all of the other subjects are confederates who have been instructed to lie. Not everyone conforms, of course. Roughly one-fourth of the subjects remain true to their convictions and do not conform to any of the incorrect judgments.

Although Asch's subjects frequently went along with the group, they generally did not believe the responses they announced. If subjects were separated from the group and wrote down rather than orally announced the responses, conformity to the group norm dropped by about two-thirds. Also, when Asch interviewed his subjects, their responses revealed that, overwhelmingly, they did not believe the incorrect answers they had produced. Rather, the subjects felt group pressure to conform.

Would a group member who deviated actually be ridiculed if he or she did not conform to the group norm? Asch (1952) reversed his initial procedure and placed one confederate among a group of genuine experimental subjects. The confederate was instructed in advance to give wildly incorrect answers on certain

trials. In fact, the others did laugh at and ridicule the confederate.

People who deviate from the group norm are not only ridiculed but also actively disliked and often rejected by the rest of the group. For example, researcher Stanley Schachter (1951) had groups of men discuss the case of "Johnny Rocco," who was supposed to be a juvenile delinquent about to be sentenced for a crime. The subjects were asked to decide what punishment Johnny should receive. Each group of five to seven men contained three confederates of the experimenter. One was instructed to be the deviant member of the group and argue for whichever extreme point of view differed from that of the rest of the group. The second confederate was instructed always to agree with the consensual position of the group. Thus, the first confederate was a deliberate nonconformist and the second confederate was a deliberate conformist. The third confederate was instructed to be a "slider." He would start off disagreeing with the other group members, but later "slide" into agreement with them. Schachter found that although the conformist and the slider ended up being well liked, the nonconformist was not. Moreover, after initial attempts to persuade the nonconformist to go along with the group, other members of the group decided that he was not persuadable and began simply to ignore him.

> It is common these days for educators to say that students must learn to think for themselves. In light of Asch's conformity results, as well as your own experiences, what are the forces at work against people learning to think for themselves? Why does this paradox exist?

Factors Affecting Conformity

Several factors seem to affect the likelihood of conformity. The first is *group size*. Asch (1955) varied the number of confederates in his line-length study from as few as 1 person to as many as 15, and he found that conformity reached its greatest level with groups of roughly three to four members. Others have confirmed that in most situations, beyond three or four members, conformity appears to level off (e.g., Latané, 1981; Tanford & Penrod, 1984). In some situations, however, much larger group sizes continue to increase the likelihood of conformity (e.g., the behavior of people in elevators, of a crowd gathering on a sidewalk and looking upward, or of a rioting crowd).

A second factor that influences conformity is the *cohesiveness* of the group. A cohesive group is one in which the members feel very much a part of the group and are highly attracted to it. One of the best-known studies of group cohesiveness (Newcomb, 1943) was conducted among women attending Bennington College, a small college in Vermont then well known for its liberal philosophy and social mores. Although women attending the college tended to be from families that were politically conservative (and well-to-do financially), the women's attitudes became increasingly liberal with each successive year at Bennington. Moreover, this liberalism remained even 20 years after graduation. The results are plotted in Figure 15-5.

A third factor appears to be *gender*. However, gender-related conformity depends in part on the kind of topic being discussed and may actually illustrate the influence of other factors. For example, in one study (Sistrunk & McDavid, 1971) females tended to conform more to a majority view on topics that were stereotypically masculine (warfare), whereas males tended to conform more on topics that were stereotypically feminine (family planning). On gender-neutral topics, no sex differences were observed. In 1971, the investigators concluded that gender seems to interact with the topic. The research showed that both men and women conform more when they are unfamiliar with the topic, and thus more likely to believe that the group knows best. Today, we might observe that knowledge, rather than gender, seems to be the key factor.

Although many studies show that women and men are each likely to conform under different

FIGURE 15-4
Line Length and Normative Influence
In Solomon Asch's study, subjects were shown a standard line and then were asked to indicate which of the comparison lines matched the standard line. If a unanimous majority of your peers chose the first line (or third), would you agree with them? In Asch's experiment, about three-fourths of the subjects agreed with a unanimous majority in more than one-third of their responses, even when the majority clearly made erroneous judgments (such as choosing either the first or third lines). Check the facial expression of subject number 6. Although he may decide to conform to the group norms in terms of his behavior—agreeing publicly that an incorrect match is correct—his own private beliefs clearly do not conform to the group norm. (After Asch, 1956)

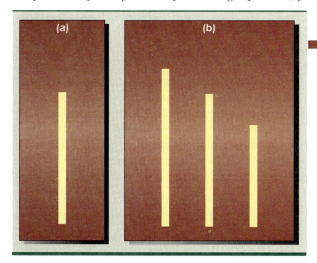

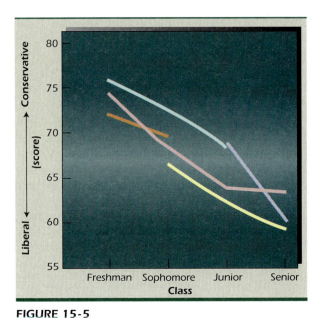

FIGURE 15-5
Effects of Cohesiveness on Conformity

For students at Bennington College, Vermont, between their freshman and senior years, their sense of cohesiveness at the college increased. Over time, their views changed from conforming to the relatively conservative attitudes of their families to conforming to the relatively liberal attitudes of their professors and the juniors and seniors on campus. Different colored lines represent different years of entry (1933–1938). (After Newcomb, 1957)

circumstances and in regard to different topics, the *social-roles theory of gender* (Eagly, 1987) posits that women are generally more likely to conform than men under most circumstances. According to Alice Eagly's view, women conform more because they are perceived as being of lower status, which in turn leads to reduced self-worth. Other research supports the notion that people of either gender may be more likely to conform if they feel inadequate or possess low self-esteem (Asch, 1956).

A fourth factor affecting conformity is *social status*. Are group members more likely to conform when they are high, average, low, or very low in status within a group? Researchers (Dittes & Kelly, 1956) addressed this question by having subjects participate in group discussions and then rate each other on "desirability." Subjects were next told how others had rated them, except that they received phony feedback. Subjects then participated in an Asch-like experiment, in which the other members of the group were the other subjects. Those who had been rated "average" in desirability were more likely to conform than those rated high, low, or very low. Those receiving the high, low, and very low ratings did not markedly differ from each other in conformity. The result makes sense: If you are high in status already, you may not need to conform because of your more exalted posi-

tion. On the other hand, if you are low in status, you may feel that the situation is hopeless anyway, so why even bother to conform?

A fifth consideration is *culture*. Many researchers have tried to replicate in other cultures some of the studies on conformity and other social-psychological phenomena that have been well documented in the United States. For instance, the procedure used by Asch has been used in numerous cross-cultural studies, spanning more than 40 years. Although considerable variability has been found in these studies, a fairly clear picture has emerged: People in individualistic societies tend to conform less than people in collectivistic societies (Smith & Bond, 1994). Actually, the extent to which people in different societies vary on many social-psychological variables can often be explained by the notions of individualism and collectivism (described earlier) and the ways that individualism and collectivism influence social behavior (Kim, Triandis, & Kagitcibasi, 1994).

A sixth variable affecting conformity is the *appearance of unanimity*. Conformity is much more likely when the group norm appears to be unanimous; even a single dissenter can seriously diminish conformity. Asch (1951) found that if even one of the six confederates disagreed with the group's answer in the line-length experiment, conformity was drastically reduced. Surprisingly, this effect occurred even if the dissenter offered an answer that was even farther off the mark than the response of the group. Apparently, if you have a model of dissent, the model can help inoculate you against conforming to a norm established by other group members, even if the model does not agree with your point of view. Thus, another consideration in determining your degree of conformity is whether you believe your views to be in the majority, in the minority, or altogether unique within the group.

Design an experiment in which you compare the influence of two of the preceding factors affecting conformity. Which factor do you believe will be the more influential one?

Majority Versus Minority Influence

As we have just seen, *majorities* exert influence through the sheer number of people who share a given point of view. Although majorities are powerful from sheer numbers, *minorities* can be powerful from the style of their behavior (Moscovici, 1976, 1980). In other words, it is not just what they say but how they say it that determines their impact. Minorities can be powerful if they are forceful, persistent, and unflagging in support of their views. Simultaneously, they need to project an image of being flexible as well as open-minded. In other words, they need to show that they are willing to listen to the majority.

Those in the minority who wish to lead and to change the way a group is functioning first need to accumulate *idiosyncrasy credits*, commonly known as "brownie points," among group members (Hollander, 1958, 1985). That is, they need to be willing to play the game of the group to a great enough extent so that members will come to accept them as part of the group and will then listen to them when they advocate changing the group norms. In this way, a potent minority may still influence the behavior— and perhaps the views—of the majority. Individuals operating outside of group settings may also be quite persuasive in causing others to behave as they want them to behave. Compliance with the requests made by individuals is the subject of the next section.

Compliance

"Like it? Well, I don't see why I oughtn't like it. Does a boy get a chance to whitewash a fence every day?"

That put the thing in a new light. Ben stopped nibbling his apple. Tom swept his brush daintily back and forth—stepped back to note the effect—added a touch here and there—criticized the effect again— Ben watching every move and getting more and more interested, more and more absorbed. Presently he said:

"Say, Tom, let me whitewash a little."

Tom considered, was about to consent; but he altered his mind:

"No—no—I reckon it wouldn't hardly do, Ben. You see, Aunt Polly's . . . awful particular about this fence; it's got to be done very careful; I reckon there ain't one boy in a thousand, maybe two thousand, that can do it the way it's got to be done."

"No—is that so? Oh come, now—lemme just try. Only just a little—I'd let you, if you was me, Tom." . . .

Tom gave up the brush with reluctance in his face, but alacrity in his heart. . . . By the time Ben was fagged out, Tom had traded the next chance to Billy Fisher for a kite, in good repair; and when he played out, Johnny Miller bought in for a dead rat and a string to swing it with—and so on, and so on, hour after hour. . . .

If he hadn't run out of whitewash, he would have bankrupted every boy in the village.

—Mark Twain, Tom Sawyer

Do you know somebody who always seems to get his or her way? Do you ever wonder how swindlers manage to bamboozle their marks (persons who are the objects of their compliance-seeking techniques)? Have you ever bought something that you really did not want to buy because you were wheedled into it by a persuasive salesperson? All of these questions address the issue of *compliance*—going along with other people's requests. See some of the most common techniques for eliciting compliance in Table 15-1. (Note that Tom Sawyer masterfully implements the hard-to-get technique, which depends on eliciting *reactance*—the unpleasant feeling of arousal we feel when we believe that our freedom of choosing from a wide range of behavior is being threatened or restricted.)

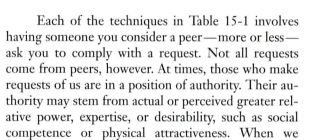

What are some effective ways to guard yourself against compliance-seeking techniques?

Each of the techniques in Table 15-1 involves having someone you consider a peer—more or less— ask you to comply with a request. Not all requests come from peers, however. At times, those who make requests of us are in a position of authority. Their authority may stem from actual or perceived greater relative power, expertise, or desirability, such as social competence or physical attractiveness. When we agree to the requests of persons who have authority over us, we are being obedient.

Obedience

Consider what you would do if you were a subject in the following experiment. An experimenter wearing a lab coat and carrying a clipboard meets you in the laboratory and tells you that you are about to participate in an experiment on the effects of punishment on learning (see Chapter 7). You and another subject, Mr. Wallace (an accountant who appears average in appearance and demeanor), agree to draw lots to determine who will be the "teacher" in the experiment, and who will be the "learner." You draw the "teacher" lot, so it will be your job to teach the learner a list of words that he must remember. Thus, every time Mr. Wallace makes an error in learning, you will punish him by sending him an electric shock.

Next, you watch the experimenter strap Mr. Wallace into a chair, roll up Mr. Wallace's sleeves, and swab electrode paste onto his arms "to avoid blisters and burns" from the shocks (Milgram, 1974, p. 19). The experimenter now mentions that the shocks may become extremely painful, but he assures

TABLE 15-1
Techniques for Eliciting Compliance
How can you use these techniques to elicit compliance from another person? How can your knowledge of these techniques help you to resist complying with unwanted and unreasonable requests?

Technique	Description: You Are More Likely to Gain Compliance If You . . .
Justification	Justify your request. Even when the justification is weak, you will gain compliance more readily than if you simply make the request but do not justify it.
Reciprocity	Appear to be giving your target something, so that the target is thereby obliged to give you something in return.
Low-ball	Get the target to comply and to commit to a deal under misleadingly favorable circumstances. After obtaining the target's commitment, you add the hidden costs or reveal the hidden drawbacks.
Foot-in-the-door	Ask for compliance with a smaller request, which is designed to "soften up" the target for the big request.
Door-in-the-face	Make an outlandishly large request that is almost certain to be rejected, in the hope of getting the target to accede to a more reasonable but perhaps still quite large request.
That's-not-all	Offer something at a high price, and then, before the target has a chance to respond, you throw in something else to sweeten the deal.
Hard-to-get	Convince your target that whatever you are offering (or trying to get rid of) is very difficult to obtain.

Mr. Wallace that they will "cause no permanent tissue damage" (p. 19). You are then shown the machine you will use to deliver the shocks. The forbidding-looking device has a row of levers marked in increments of 15 volts from a mere 15 volts (labeled "slight shock") to a full 450 volts (labeled "XXX," beyond the setting for "danger: severe shock"). (See Figure 15-6.) Before beginning, the experimenter also administers to you what he describes as a mild shock, to give you an idea of what the shocks are like. The shock is rather painful.

The experiment now begins. You read Mr. Wallace the words, and he must recall their paired associates (see Chapter 8). If he answers correctly, you move on to the next word on the list. If he answers incorrectly, you tell him the correct answer and administer a shock. Each time Mr. Wallace makes a mistake, you are told to increase the intensity of the shock by 15 volts.

Soon, he makes his first mistake, so you pull the appropriate shock lever, and a red light flashes, indicating that the shock has been delivered to Mr. Wallace in the next room. Lest you have any doubt, a loud buzzing noise emanates from the other room. When you reach the level of 75 volts, Mr. Wallace grunts in pain. Grunts are followed by shouting at 120 volts. At 150 volts, Mr. Wallace screams in agony and protest, "Experimenter! That's all. Get me out of here. I refuse to go on!" Mr. Wallace refuses to continue at 300 volts, and at 315 volts, following an intense scream, he shouts, "I told you I refuse to answer. I'm no longer a part of this experiment." At 330 volts, there is an intense, long scream of agony, and Mr. Wallace shouts, "Let me out of here. Let me out of here. Let me out, I tell you. . . . You have no right to hold me here. Let me out! . . ." After 330 volts, there is only silence.

Would you continue administering shocks until the end—up to 450 volts? Perhaps at some point, it would occur to you that something is very wrong with this experiment, and that you simply do not want to continue. If you tell the experimenter your concerns, he only responds, "Please continue." If you protest further, he tells you, "The experiment requires that you continue." If you continue to argue, he says, "It is absolutely essential that you continue." If you still protest, he replies, "You have no other choice, you *must* go on." What would you do? Before you read on, guess how you believe that most people would have responded to this experiment.

Prior to conducting his experiments, psychologist Stanley Milgram (1974) had expected that very few subjects would completely obey the commands of the experimenter and that many might refuse to obey

FIGURE 15-6
The Shocking Treatment of Mr. Wallace

At the upper left is the voltmeter used by Stanley Milgram's subjects for delivering shocks to Mr. Wallace. On the upper right is Mr. Wallace, pictured here as he was being strapped into the chair where he was expected to receive the shocks administered by Milgram's subjects. Milgram's subjects believed that Mr. Wallace was unable to escape the shocks that the subjects were administering. The bottom two photos show a subject being instructed by the experimenter to continue administering shocks (bottom left) and refusing to continue (bottom right; an unfortunately rare occurrence). (After Milgram, 1974)

 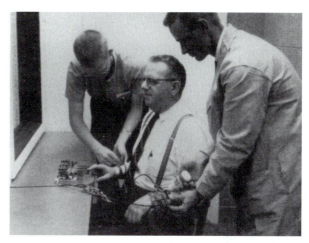

even the early requests of the experimenter. As he was formulating the design for the experiment, he consulted many other colleagues, all of whose expectations were similar to his. Instead, a little more than an electrifying two-thirds of the subjects tested in this procedure continued up to the maximum level of 450 volts. Not one subject stopped administering shocks before 300 volts, the point at which Mr. Wallace let out an agonizing scream, absolutely refused to answer any more questions, and demanded to get out, saying that the experimenter could not hold him. The results (see Figure 15-7) were even more of a shocker than the shocks administered by the machine.

The results so astounded Milgram that he asked members of three different groups—middle-class

adults with various occupations, college students, and psychiatrists—to predict what would happen. Their predictions confirmed Milgram's initial expectations that few would demonstrate much obedience in the experiment. On the average, those who were surveyed estimated that the "teacher" would stop at 135 volts. Almost no one surveyed thought anyone would go up to 450 volts. The psychiatrists estimated that "only a pathological fringe, not exceeding [1 or 2% of the subjects]" would go right up to the end (Milgram, 1974, p. 31). Everyone was wrong.

Of course the machine was a fake, and Mr. Wallace was a confederate of the experimenter and never received any shocks at all. Also, both lots said "teacher," so no matter which one you drew, you

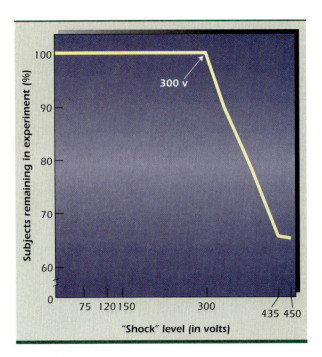

FIGURE 15-7
Milgram's Baseline Results on Voltage Levels
To Stanley Milgram's great surprise, not one subject stopped administering shocks prior to the reported level of 300 volts, and an alarming 65% of subjects administered the maximum level of shock. (After Milgram, 1963)

would have ended up being the teacher and Mr. Wallace the learner.

The experiment, as you probably have guessed, had nothing at all to do with an interest in the effect of punishment on learning. Rather, it was an experiment on obedience. The motivation for the experiment was Milgram's interest in why German soldiers during World War II had obeyed the outrageous genocidal commands of their leaders. Milgram (1963, 1965, 1974) concluded that people in general are astonishingly capable of blind, mindless obedience. The results he obtained were even more depressing than was just indicated. For example, in Milgram's initial study, the subjects were men. He thought that perhaps women would be less likely to go to the maximum in their administration of shock. However, when women participated in the same procedure, the same percentage (65%) of women as men went to the maximum. The results that Milgram obtained have been repeated both across age groups and across cultures (Shanab & Yahya, 1977, 1978).

Why are people so willing to obey the orders of people in authority, regardless of what the orders are (see Hofling et al., 1966; Meeus & Raaijmakers, 1986)? Milgram (1974) proposed several explanations, although whether any of them is adequate to describe

the extremity of the findings is doubtful. One explanation is that experimenters use a procedure analogous to the successful foot-in-the-door technique; they start off asking for relatively little and only later ask for much more. Along the way, subjects may become immune to the effects of what they are doing, or they may feel committed to complying with the demands of the situation. Moreover, people are socialized to respect authority, and this socialization seems to carry over into situations requiring obedience.

What seems to make the difference is the situation, which demands and elicits obedience from a surprising array of people. Practically anybody placed in this situation acts in ways that no one would have thought possible. That is what is so stunning about the obedience research by Milgram and others.

It is impossible to discuss the Milgram experiment without raising the issue of experimental ethics. Obviously, the experiment did not cause harm to the "learner." He was a confederate of the experimenter and never experienced the slightest bit of pain. How about the "teacher," though? How would you feel if you walked out of such an experiment, knowing that you had just been willing to administer painful and possibly deadly shocks to another person? Sure, you had been told that the whole situation was contrived. However, this knowledge came only after you had done the dirty deed.

In his own defense, Milgram pointed out that the results of the initial experiments were completely unexpected. Based on his own predictions and those of his colleagues, he expected very few "teachers" to continue the experiment as long as they did. In addition, regarding the subsequent experiments, Milgram devised increasingly sophisticated forms of *debriefing*—informing the subjects about the true nature of the experiment and encouraging the subjects to discuss their own reactions to the experiment once they knew its true nature. However, since Milgram's experiments were concluded, we have learned more about the persistent effects of misinformation, even in spite of debriefing. Had you actually participated in the experiment and then been debriefed, you probably would still have felt bad about yourself. We now know that there is a perseverance effect in psychological experiments.

The Milgram studies showed us that we may surprise ourselves with our own capacity to disregard the misery of our fellow human beings when responding to the commands of a perceived authority figure. How might we respond to pleas for help from our fellow humans when no authority figure is around? Such behavior is the subject of the next section.

PROSOCIAL BEHAVIOR

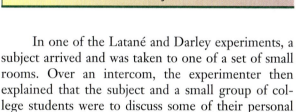

IN SEARCH OF...

Under what circumstances do people help their fellow human beings? Under what circumstances do you go out of your way to help other people?

Prosocial behavior is consistent with, or even furthers, the common good. In this section, we deal with several aspects of prosocial behavior, particularly in terms of helping others.

Helping Behavior

Bystander Intervention

In 1964, Kitty Genovese, a young woman in New York City, returned home from a night job at three o'clock in the morning. Before she reached home, she was repeatedly attacked over a period of about a half hour by a man who eventually killed her. Thirty-eight people living in her apartment complex in Queens heard her cries and screams as she was attacked. How many of these neighbors came to her aid? How many called the police? How many sought any assistance for her whatsoever? Not one. How could people hear someone be attacked over such a

Just outside these upstairs apartments, Kitty Genovese was stabbed repeatedly as 38 adults, mostly in the large apartment building behind, watched, listened, and did nothing to help her—not even lifting a finger to call the police. After Genovese died, only one of her neighbors bothered to call the authorities to report the murder. Could this incident have happened just as easily in a suburban or a rural area as in a big city? Why or why not?

long period of time and do absolutely nothing in response? Bibb Latané and John Darley sought to answer this question in a series of studies on bystander intervention and helping behavior (Latané & Darley, 1968, 1970).

A common view of the Genovese case was that life in the big city had hardened people to the point where they stopped caring about others. Latané and Darley suspected, however, that what happened to Kitty Genovese in New York could have happened anywhere.

Do you think that people who live in cities are different from people who live in suburban or rural areas? If so, in what ways?

In one of the Latané and Darley experiments, a subject arrived and was taken to one of a set of small rooms. Over an intercom, the experimenter then explained that the subject and a small group of college students were to discuss some of their personal problems of college life. To protect confidentiality, the conversations would take place via intercom, with each subject in a separate room and without the experimenter listening. Each person was to speak separately in turn.

During the fairly routine opening of the experiment, one of the subjects admitted that he sometimes had seizures triggered by the pressures of his work. When it was this person's turn to speak once again, it became clear that he was suffering a seizure. He started sounding as if he were in serious distress (Latané & Darley, 1970, p. 96).

As you may have guessed, the apparent seizure victim was not actually having a seizure. In fact, there were no subjects other than the one who heard the recording. Although group sizes supposedly ranged from two (the subject and the seizure victim) to six (the subject, the seizure victim, and four other strangers), in fact only the one subject was a participant, and the others were all previously recorded. The dependent variable was the percentage of subjects who helped and the amount of time it took them to respond. The independent variable was the number of people that the subjects believed to be participating in the experiment.

Clearly, Kitty Genovese's neighbors were not alone in being unresponsive. They illustrated what has come to be termed the **bystander effect,** in which the presence of other people inhibits helping behavior. The effect occurs in a variety of different situations. Each person involved typically experiences a **diffusion of responsibility,** so that the presence of

Searchers . . .   *ELLEN BERSCHEID*

Ellen Berscheid is Professor of Psychology at the University of Minnesota.

Q: *How did you become interested in psychology?*

A: As a junior at the University of Nevada I took the perception and cognition course with Paul Secord. I was an English literature major planning to go to law school, but I found absolutely fascinating the question of how we perceive and think about other people. I became his undergraduate research assistant and added psychology as a major. I was really interested in the research process.

Q: *What theories have influenced you the most?*

A: Social exchange theory has been an important influence on me and on virtually everyone else in social psychology, particularly as it was articulated originally by John Thibaut and Harold Kelley.

Q: *What is your greatest asset as a psychologist?*

A: My greatest personal assets are my brain, relatively good health, and curiosity.

Q: *What makes a psychologist really great?*

A: I have always believed that there are many great psychologists who are anonymous, who expressed the right idea at the right time that then spurred others to go forward and elaborate. I don't think people, especially students, realize the extent to which all scientists stand on the shoulders of many people. Every science, including psychology, is cumulative; no one person does it alone.

Q: *How do you get your ideas for research?*

A: By being immersed in the field, in its problems, by reading the literature. These ideas naturally occur as I read. It's impossible to have good ideas for research unless you know the field very well.

Q: *How do you decide whether to pursue an idea?*

A: The major thing is whether we can approach and answer the question effectively. There are many important questions that we simply can't answer because we don't have the technology or the ethical right to set up the conditions to answer them.

Q: *What obstacles have you experienced in your work?*

A: Everyone encounters obstacles of one kind or another, but it is important simply to muddle on through. I have devoted a great deal of my time, which could have been devoted to my work, simply on issues connected to sex discrimination. Men don't do this. It is very important, however, that while women donate some of their time to making the situation better, they never lose sight that they are professionals in a particular discipline, and that has to come first. If women lose their place in the mainstream of the profession, it's more difficult for them to help other women.

Q: *What do you want students to learn from you?*

A: To think causally and to realize that Mother Nature reveals her secrets only in very small droplets, and only with a great deal of work on the part of the researcher.

Q: *What advice would you give to someone starting in the field of psychology?*

A: They should get the best training possible. The training isn't very long, but it will affect the rest of the student's life. Take the courses that they know will be important to them that they are not likely to learn on their own, such as statistics.

Q: *What did you learn from your mentors?*

A: I learned from Paul Secord that the PhD is the ticket to a lifetime of scholarship and learning. Elliot Aronson, my PhD advisor, showed me that we are engaged in a noble enterprise, that people are truly ennobled by understanding. The problems that we social psychologists attack are crucial ones to people's lives.

Q: *How has psychology influenced your life?*

A: Social psychology has enriched every aspect of my life. There is no aspect that has remained untouched. I don't know how people get through life without a basic course in social psychology.

Q: *How do you keep yourself academically challenged?*

A: The problem is the reverse. How do I cut down the number of challenges so that I can actively deal with a doable number.

Q: *What do you still hope to achieve or contribute?*

A: I, and many other people, would like to see the field of interpersonal relationships become firmly established as a scientific enterprise of the highest importance. And I want to do anything I can do to further that.

---

others leads each person to feel less responsible personally for dealing with a crisis that has arisen. Many other studies have revealed the same findings (see Latané, Nida, & Wilson, 1981).

What is really strange is that the bystander effect appears even when a person's own safety is at stake. One study (Latané & Darley, 1968) asked students to fill out a questionnaire on problems of urban life. Shortly after the students began answering the questions, smoke from a ventilator in the wall began to pour into the room where the subject was sitting. The researchers were interested in how the number of people in the room affected the subjects' decisions to report the smoke. When only one subject was in the room, half the subjects reported the smoke within 4 minutes, and three-quarters within 6 minutes. However, when there were three subjects in the room, only 1 of 24 subjects reported the smoke within the first 4 minutes, and only three did so within 6 minutes (see Figure 15-8). Thus, people may fail to take action even when their own safety is in jeopardy!

Factors Affecting Helping Behavior

Why are people so passive in the face of emergencies, whether the emergencies affect others or even themselves? According to Latané and Darley (1970), the reason is that what appears to be a simple matter—seeking help—is actually more complex than it appears. Suppose you are the bystander. To seek or provide help, you must actually take five steps, as shown in Figure 15-9. Thus, there are at least five opportunities for a bystander to do nothing.

What factors might affect whether people help in emergencies? The characteristics of the setting, the victim, and the bystander lead either to intervention or to nonintervention. (See Table 15-2 for a summary of these factors.) One such factor is how people interpret a situation. Sometimes, nobody helps because individuals attribute other people's actions to causes that are different from the causes of their own actions, despite the fact that their own actions are identical to those of the other people in the group (Miller & McFarland, 1987). For example, confronted with an emergency in which you see other people taking no action, you may assume that you are the only person confused about what to do, and that the other people are doing nothing because they have somehow realized that what appears to be an emergency is not one at all. Of course, the other people are making exactly the same attribution that you are.

This misattribution applies to situations that are nonemergencies as well. Very often, students in a class are afraid to ask questions because they assume that they are the only ones who do not understand what the professor is saying, when in fact each person

FIGURE 15-8
Seizing the Opportunity to Help

In every condition of Bibb Latané and John Darley's experiment (1970), helping behavior increased over time, as you would expect. However, the amount of helping behavior decreased dramatically with increases in the number of other people that the subject thought were participating. (After Latané & Darley, 1970; adapted from Latané and Darley, The Unresponsive Bystander, *© 1970. Used with permission of Prentice-Hall, Inc.)*

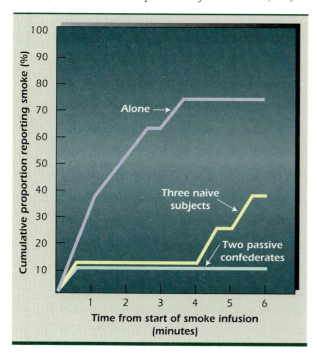

FIGURE 15-9
Latané and Darley's Five-Step Decision Model of Intervention

According to Bibb Latané and John Darley, before you take any action to help another person, you must take the five steps shown in the figure. If you fail to complete any one of these steps, you will not take any action to provide helpful intervention. (After Latané & Darley, 1970)

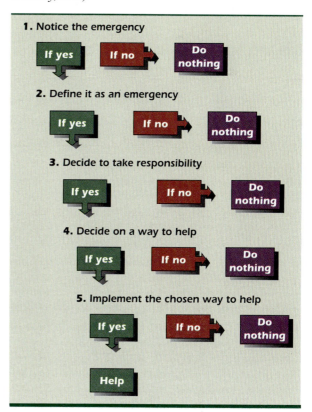

has exactly the same anxiety. As a result, all the students end up confused but thinking that they are alone in their confusion.

The bystander effect applies even in unexpected populations. Students in a religious seminary were asked to give a talk, either on the parable of the Good Samaritan—a man who exhibited extraordinary helping behavior—or on jobs that seminary students enjoy (Darley & Batson, 1973). The subjects were instructed to go to a university building nearby to give the talk.

On the way to the talk, each student passed an alley in which a man was sitting, slumped over, his eyes closed, moaning. Surely, if anyone would help the man, seminarians would, and especially those thinking about the Good Samaritan. However, only 40% of the students offered to help, and whether they were going to speak on the Good Samaritan or on jobs had no significant impact on whether they helped. Thus, even those who are giving serious thought to helping behavior and who have pledged to devote their lives to serving others are often unlikely actually to help others in an ambiguous situation.

Although the topic of the talk the seminarians were to give did not affect helping behavior, another manipulation in the experiment did. Students were

TABLE 15-2
Factors That May Influence Helping Behavior
Several characteristics of the victim, of the situation, and of the bystander may increase or decrease the likelihood that the bystander will intervene to aid the victim.

Factor	Effect on Likelihood of Helping Behavior
Characteristics of the Victim	
Similarity to bystander (age, sex, etc.)	Increase
Relationship to bystander (if any)	Probably increase
Bleeding or bloody	Decrease
Recognizability as being a member of a stigmatized group	Decrease
Characteristics of the Situation	
Increases in the number of bystanders	Decrease
Increased time pressures on bystander	Decrease
Characteristics of the Bystander	
Similarity to victim (age, sex, etc.)	Increase
Relationship to victim (if any)	Probably increase
Negative responses to characteristics of the victim (e.g., prejudices, negative reactions to clothing, grooming, presence of blood)	Decrease
Empathy	Increase
Emotionality	Probably increase
Knowledge of how to help the victim (e.g., know CPR or have medical expertise)	Increase
Dedication to a life of serving others	No effect
Recently has given thought to helping behavior	No effect
Being in a good mood	Increase

told either that they were in a great hurry (they were already overdue), a medium hurry (everything was ready to go), or not really in a hurry at all (it would be a few minutes before things would even be ready). Although 63% of students who were not in a hurry helped, only 10% of those who were in a great hurry did. An intermediate percentage, 45%, helped in the medium-hurry condition.

Altruism

By now, you may be depressed or distressed at the results of the various studies on bystander intervention. Is **altruism**—selfless sacrifice—nonexistent? Did it ever exist? Are there ever situations in which more than a few are willing to help others, regardless of the consequences for themselves? Certainly there are. Every day, parents sacrifice for children, firefighters rush into burning buildings, police risk their lives for

Following the 1989 San Francisco earthquake, countless volunteers joined professionals in helping others to survive and to recover from the devastation caused by the temblor. In response to much less dramatic cries of help, people show altruism in hospices, shelters for the homeless, nursing homes, and other settings.

the public, and volunteers give their time and efforts to better the well-being of other people. Altruism has also been demonstrated in experimental circumstances.

Recent studies have focused on empathy versus egoistic motives as a basis for altruistic behavior. Robert Cialdini et al. (1987) have attempted to explain altruistic behavior by arguing that empathy produces helping behavior because a person who responds empathetically to someone in distress feels saddened and is motivated to help in order to elevate his or her *own* mood. So, from this perspective, even empathy-based helping may be egoistic. Daniel Batson et al. (1988, 1989) disagree with this interpretation, having found that the rate of helping among high-empathy subjects was no lower when they already anticipated mood enhancement than when they did not.

ANTISOCIAL BEHAVIOR

IN SEARCH OF...

What makes behavior antisocial?

Antisocial behavior is behavior that is harmful to the society or to its members. Although people might disagree about which kinds of behaviors are antisocial, people generally agree that two classes of behavior are harmful to society: prejudice and aggression.

Prejudice

For the first time I noticed that there were two lines of people at the ticket window, a "white" line and a "black" line. During my visit at Granny's a sense of the two races had been born in me with a sharp concreteness that would never die until I died. . . . I had begun to notice that my mother became irritated when I questioned her about whites and blacks, and I could not quite understand it. I wanted to understand these two sets of people who lived side by side and never touched, it seemed, except in violence.

—*Richard Wright,* Black Boy

Prejudice is an unfavorable attitude directed toward other groups of people, based on insufficient or incorrect evidence about these groups. Note that prejudice is an attitude toward a group, not toward an

Searchers . . .   *ELLIOT ARONSON*

Elliot Aronson is Professor of Psychology at the University of California, Santa Cruz.

Q: *How did you become interested in psychology and in your area of work in particular?*

A: I had thought psychology was only about curing sick people. But when I sat in on an introductory psychology class that Abraham Maslow was teaching at Brandeis, I realized that he was asking questions about things that I had been asking myself. It was very exciting. Social psychology seemed like the subdiscipline that was raising the most interesting questions about human behavior.

Q: *What theories have influenced you the most?*

A: When I entered graduate school, the dominant theory was reinforcement theory, which struck me as very simplistic. But there weren't very good, broad, competing, alternative theories. I chose to work with Leon Festinger because he was developing the theory of cognitive dissonance, which I found exciting because it addressed human motivation and cognition in intricate ways.

Q: *What is your greatest asset as a psychologist?*

A: A combination of scientific curiosity, humanistic concerns—wanting to do some good for people—and a little bit of audacity. I have just enough audacity to believe that there isn't any question that I can't try to find an answer to.

Q: *What makes a psychologist really great?*

A: The great ones have the ability to follow their curiosity wherever it leads them. That's where audacity comes in. Somebody like Stanley Milgram didn't do a lot of research, but what he did was audacious. Doing research because it's popular or easy would never enter the mind of a really great psychologist.

Q: *How do you usually get your ideas for research?*

A: Mostly from observing people and observing myself; sometimes from reading a novel, poetry, or philosophy. Part of audacity involves the working assumption that what applies to me applies to everybody. I ask, "Gee, how come, when such and such happens, it leads me to feel this way, and I tend to do this?" So I work up a hypothesis about the way *people* behave, not just the way I behave.

Q: *How do you decide whether to pursue an idea?*

A: I pursue it if both my head and my heart are into it. That is, if it is both intellectually challenging and emotionally exciting.

Q: *How have you developed an idea into a workable hypothesis?*

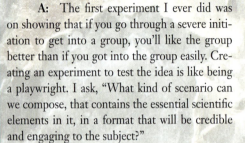

A: The first experiment I ever did was on showing that if you go through a severe initiation to get into a group, you'll like the group better than if you got into the group easily. Creating an experiment to test the idea is like being a playwright. I ask, "What kind of scenario can we compose, that contains the essential scientific elements in it, in a format that will be credible and engaging to the subject?"

Q: *What obstacles have you experienced in your work?*

A: Devising experiments so they are ethical and still test the behavior I want to examine. A lot of the obstacles I'm facing now involve getting school committees to approve of my research on helping people practice safe sex—a public relations obstacle.

Q: *What advice would you give to someone starting in the field of psychology?*

A: They should decide what they're excited about and whom they want to learn from. Students should attach themselves to the most exciting, most innovative, most idea-laden person around, whose style they really love. It doesn't matter what your mentor is working on. It's the *way* she's working on it that is most crucial.

Q: *What have you learned from your students?*

A: Mostly to keep questioning. One of the nice things about students, especially undergraduates, is their naive questions. The naive questions are the most interesting and force me to reexamine some of the assumptions or premises that I'm making.

Q: *Apart from your life as an academic, how has psychology been important to you?*

A: Applying general principles (like self-justification or the self-fulfilling prophecy) is a really interesting way of looking at the world. The experimental method has helped me think analytically, to separate the important variables in my life from the unimportant ones. It's helped enormously with child rearing, with trying to communicate clearly and stay in touch with my own notions and feelings.

Q: *How do you keep yourself academically challenged?*

A: That's no problem. There are always new ideas, issues to explore, new courses to teach, and new students to challenge me.

---

individual. Unfortunately, we tend to extend many of our attitudes toward groups as well as to all of the individual members of the groups. A negative attitude toward a group is not necessarily a prejudice. For example, if you have ample evidence that a particular group (e.g., a youth gang) is responsible for numerous murders, you would probably be entitled to have a negative attitude toward that group. An attitude involves prejudice when it is based on insufficient or incorrect information.

Social Cognition: Social Categorization and Stereotypes

Social categorization is the normal human tendency to sort things and people into groups, based on perceived common attributes. Across cultures, we effortlessly categorize people according to their gender, occupation, age, ethnicity, and so on (see Neto, Williams, & Widner, 1991). These categories generally have particular defining characteristics (e.g., specific sexual characteristics or occupational requirements). In addition, recall from Chapter 9 that we tend to formulate prototypes for various categories, based on what we perceive as being typical exemplars of the categories; when such prototypes are applied to people, we term them **stereotypes.** Social categories and stereotypes help us to organize our perceptions of people and provide us with speedy access to a wealth of information (e.g., traits and expected behaviors) about new people whom we meet (Sherman, Judd, & Park, 1989; Srull & Wyer, 1989). Thus, stereotypes help us know what to expect from people we do not know well. The problem with categorizing people according to stereotypes is that we often overgeneralize the characteristics of the stereotype, assuming that all the typical characteristics apply to every member of a group, when they usually apply only to some or perhaps even most—but not all—members.

Actually, we are less likely to overgeneralize from stereotypes when considering our own ingroups—of which we are members—than when considering *outgroups*—of which we are not members. This tendency to view the members of an outgroup as all being alike is **outgroup homogeneity bias.** When we fall prey to this bias, we take stereotypical characteristics or actions that apply only to a portion of a group and infer that they apply to all or almost all of the group members (Brehm & Kassin, 1990). For example, it may very well be that many clerics are honest, many professors are well informed, many social workers are compassionate, and so on. However, these and other stereotypes do not necessarily apply to all members of these groups. Moreover, members of many other groups will show the same tendencies attributed to the members of the targeted group. We also exacerbate the negative effects of outgroup homogeneity bias by seeking information that bolsters our sense of being dissimilar from the outgroup and of being similar to the ingroup (Wilder & Allen, 1978).

Another source of prejudice is **illusory correlation,** a heuristic in which we are more likely to notice instances of unusual behavior in relation to a minority population than we are to notice common behaviors in members of a minority population or unusual behaviors in members of a majority population (Hamilton & Gifford, 1976). Thus, we may form an illusory correlation between the unusual behavior and the minority population. (Other heuristics that strengthen prejudices include self-fulfilling prophecies, person-positivity bias, social-desirability bias, and self-serving bias; see Chapter 14.)

Context cues also can enhance the likelihood of using stereotypes. For example (see Eagly, Makhijani, & Klonsky, 1992), when subjects evaluated women

This photo, bearing the caption (translated from German) "If all of German youth looked like this, we would have no need to fear for the future," appeared in a Nazi calendar for 1939. As the German caption says, these Hitler Youth were chosen for their stereotypical appearance. The kinds of prejudice that some people have shown against other people who do not look a certain way continue to the present day.

These youths from rival gangs are much more likely to reduce feelings of prejudice toward each other by engaging in cooperative work, rather than by simply coming into contact with one another.

and men leaders, they showed greater gender stereo-typing and prejudicial responses toward women leaders in particular contexts: (a) those in which the leaders used leadership styles considered more stereo-typically masculine (e.g., task oriented and directive, rather than interpersonally oriented and collaborative), or (b) contexts in which women were occupying roles that are male dominated in our society (e.g., athletic coaches, manufacturing supervisors, and business managers). Outgroup versus ingroup effects also influenced the results. Men were more likely to evaluate women negatively than were other women. Although social cognition plays a role in the formation of stereotypes, the reason that stereotypes are so remarkably resistant to change may be due to factors such as motivation and conformity more than to cognitive variables (Rojahn & Pettigrew, 1992), as shown in the following study.

The Robber's Cave Study

What is often considered to be the classic experiment on prejudice was conducted in the summer of 1954 at the Robber's Cave State Park in Oklahoma (Sherif et al., 1961/1988). In this state park were two groups of boys, all of them 11 years old, all of them white, all of them middle-class, and all of them previously unknown to each other. For about a week, the boys engaged in typical camp activities, such as swimming, camping, and hiking. Each group of boys chose a name for itself, and the boys then printed their groups' names on their caps and on their T-shirts.

After about a week, the boys in each group made a discovery—the existence of the other group of boys. They also discovered that a series of athletic tournaments had been set up that would pit the two groups against each other. As the competitions took place, so did confrontations, which spread well beyond the games. After a while, the members of the two groups had become extremely antagonistic. At this point, cabins had been ransacked, food fights had broken out, and items had been stolen by members of each group.

Prejudice of the members of one group against the other group had been artificially created. Would it now be possible to reduce or eliminate this prejudice? The investigators created apparent emergencies that had to be resolved through cooperative efforts. In one emergency, the water supply for the camp was lost because of a leak in a pipe. The boys were assigned to intergroup teams to inspect the pipe and to find the leak. In another incident, a truck carrying boys to a campsite got trapped in the mud. Boys from the two teams needed to cooperate to get the truck

out. By the end of the camping season, the two groups of boys were engaged in a variety of cooperative activities and were playing together peacefully. Thus, by forcing people to work together, the prejudices of the members of each group against the other had largely been eliminated.

> Is the predisposition to prejudice (as opposed to specific prejudices, such as animosity toward women) a part of human nature? Why or why not?

Theories of Prejudice

Various theories have been proposed to account for why people have prejudices. One, **realistic-conflict theory** (Levine & Campbell, 1972), argues that prejudice is caused by competition among groups for valuable but scarce resources. For example, immigrant groups are often met with hostility because they are perceived as taking jobs away from people who are already living in the country. Often, the jobs these immigrant groups take are those that other people generally do not want, but even the perception of the loss of jobs can cause unwarranted prejudice.

A second theory, **social-identity theory** (Tajfel, 1982; Tajfel & Turner, 1986), suggests that people have prejudices to increase their self-esteem. Part of our self-esteem derives from the social groups of which we are members. People may form prejudices against other groups in order to boost their own group's status and the self-esteem they feel through membership in the group.

A third theory (Devine, Monteith, Zuwerink, & Elliot, 1991) is that people view prejudice within themselves somewhat the way they view bad habits. They are aware that they have the prejudice, and they know, consciously or not, that it affects their behavior. Where people differ, however, is in the extent to which they tolerate the behavior in themselves. Some people have high tolerance for their own prejudices, whereas others view their own prejudices as unjustifiable and not as valid bases for action.

Reducing Prejudice

What can be done about prejudice? The first thing we need to *recognize* is how resistant it is to change. For example, male police officers and police supervisors commonly have prejudicial attitudes against female members of the force (Balkin, 1988; Ott, 1989), despite clear research evidence documenting women's effectiveness as field patrol officers. Some have suggested that prejudicial treatment against females

Although many immigrant groups are perceived as competing for desirable jobs, thereby exacerbating feelings of prejudice against those groups, most immigrants work in jobs that the majority of natives do not want. How strongly do you wish to have a job stooping over a trough more than 10 hours a day in the hot sun, earning just a few dollars?

(51% of the U.S. population) and minorities will decline when their numbers increase—that is, when they are in a larger minority. Although prejudicial treatment against minorities diminishes somewhat when their numbers increase somewhat, such treatment is not eliminated altogether. Also, just the minority status in itself—that is, the numeric proportion alone—does not determine whether prejudicial treatment occurs because male nurses generally experience special positive—rather than negative—treatment among nurses (Ott, 1989). For negative prejudicial treatment to occur, the minority group must also be assigned a relatively lower status within the larger social context.

Another suggestion for reducing prejudice has been the **contact hypothesis,** the view that direct contact between groups that have prejudicial attitudes toward each other (or of one group toward the other)

will decrease prejudice (Allport, 1954). However, as shown by the conflicts that still exist in many desegregated school systems, contact in itself is not sufficient to alleviate prejudice (Miller & Brewer, 1984). Rather, particular additional conditions, such as the cooperative tasks in the Robber's Cave study, must exist to alleviate prejudice, as shown below:

- The two interacting groups must be of *equal status*.
- The contact must involve *personal interactions* between members of the two groups.
- The groups need to engage in *cooperative activities*.
- The social norms must *favor reduction* of prejudice.

> Design an activity that you believe might help to reduce prejudice against persons who have often been the target of prejudice derived from stereotypes.

Another consideration in reducing prejudice is to use *cognition* to reduce the use of stereotypes. Krystyna Rojahn and Thomas Pettigrew (1992) suggest that we can change stereotypes by making more useful any information that contradicts a stereotype—for example, by minimizing irrelevant distracting information, by giving ourselves enough time to notice and process the relevant information that contradicts the stereotype, and by ensuring that we notice the relevance of the contradictory information to the stereotype.

>
> Think about some of the stereotypes you have formed. How might you alter your own use of stereotypes?

Finally, one of the best ways of reducing or eliminating prejudice is to *experience* directly another culture, whether in a foreign country or in your own country. Learning the language of another culture, visiting that culture, and actually living as a person of that culture can help us better understand the extent to which humans are the same all over. Prejudices are fostered by ignorance. The question is whether we are willing to take the active steps to fight ignorance and replace it with knowledge and understanding.

>
> Can any person honestly claim to have no prejudice whatsoever?

Aggression

What Is Aggression?

What causes aggression between individuals or among larger groups of people? What factors are likely to increase it, and what factors decrease it? **Aggression** is behavior directed against another person that is intended to cause harm or injury (Baron, 1977; Baron & Richardson, 1992). There are two main kinds of aggression: hostile and instrumental (Baron, 1977; Feshbach, 1970). **Hostile aggression** is emotional and is usually impulsive, often provoked by feelings of pain or distress. When we engage in hostile aggression, we intend to cause harm to another, regardless of whether we gain through our aggressive actions. In fact, sometimes we may destroy what we value by venting our aggression, such as damaging a personal relationship, injuring ourselves or persons we love, or destroying property we cherish or must replace.

In contrast, we engage in **instrumental aggression** to obtain something we value. Often, it is the result of careful calculation. Assassins, bank robbers, and embezzlers are aggressive, but most of them probably feel no personal animosity toward the people they murder or injure. If they could get whatever they wanted without being aggressive, they might not bother to be aggressive. Similarly, the 2-year-old child who grabs another child's toy truck is showing instrumental aggression—nothing personal; she just wants the truck. The two kinds of aggression have somewhat different causes and therefore also respond to somewhat different kinds of interventions.

> What are the moral or ethical distinctions between hostile and instrumental aggression? In what ways does—and should—our legal system take such distinctions into account?

Some psychologists study aggression as a basic human motivation (see Chapter 16). Others study aggression as a personality trait, looking at individual differences across people (see Chapter 17). Here, we are largely interested in how social interactions, as well as other environmental events and characteristics, contribute to aggressive behavior. First, however, we briefly consider some biological factors in human aggression.

Biological Factors in Human Aggression

Nature and nurture interact in determining the specific expression of aggression in humans. As in other species of animals, the neural circuitry underlying aggressive behavior is hereditary and seems to be common across humans. In particular, both the hypothalamus and the amygdala play an important role in stimulating or inhibiting aggressive behavior (see Figure 3-8 on pages 86–87). The amygdala is influential in our emotional responses and in our responses to odors, and this fact helps to explain the powerful interactions between odors and emotions, and between emotions and aggressive behavior. In fact, among nonhuman animals, odor plays a direct role in aggressive behavior; for example, although a male animal may attack an animal that smells like a fellow male, it will not attack an animal that smells like a female. Similarly, a mother rat may readily eat infants that smell strange to her, but she will not eat infant rats that she has previously marked with her own scent.

Among nonhuman animals, aggressive behavior is generally associated with self-defense, with predation (killing a potential food source), or with reproduction (winning or keeping sexual access to a mate, obtaining or protecting territory for attracting a mate or offspring, or protecting offspring). Among humans, although the fundamental biochemistry underlying aggression is universal across the human species, the specific circumstances that prompt the aggressive impulses and the specific forms of expressing aggression differ across cultures (Averill, 1993) and even across individuals. Nonetheless, human aggression, like aggression in other animals, is subject to hormonal influence. In nonhuman male and female animals, the presence of androgens very early in development seems to influence the degree of aggres-

Although humans usually do not demonstrate the physical aggression of these male caribou competing for females, they do compete for reproductive access to mates, demonstrating their prowess in whatever ways they believe will be most successful.

sive behavior shown in adulthood. In adult animals, testosterone (a male sex hormone) seems to increase aggression in both males and females, and estradiol (a female sex hormone) seems to decrease aggression in females.

In humans, hormones may influence aggression (Delgado, 1969). In institutionalized populations, those men and women who have been identified as having higher levels of testosterone have shown a greater frequency of aggressive behavior, as well as a greater likelihood of having been convicted of violent crimes. In addition, institutionalized women seem more likely to engage in aggression just prior to menstruation and less likely to do so during ovulation.

Outside of institutions, some evidence links hormones and aggression. For example, children who were exposed prenatally to testosterone (their mothers were given the hormone to prevent miscarriage) have shown greater levels of aggression than their same-sex siblings (Reinisch, Ziemba-Davis, & Sanders, 1991). However, it is important to recall that we cannot predict causation based on correlation alone. Nonetheless, it is well documented that high doses of synthetic male sex hormones have been linked to extreme aggression, severe mood swings, and mental instability (Pope & Katz, 1988).

Social Learning and Violence

A major determinant of aggression is social learning (Bandura, 1973, 1977a, 1983; Baron & Richardson, 1992). According to this view, people learn aggressive behavior by watching aggressive models (see Chapters 13 and 14). Therefore, what people learn differs from one sociocultural milieu to another because their models differ in each context. We know that individualistic cultures experience more aggressive behavior than collectivistic cultures (Oatley, 1993). Further, individualistic societies themselves vary in the extent to which they accept and promote aggression (DeAngelis, 1992; Montagu, 1976).

Given the importance of social learning in contributing to violent behavior, we should pay careful attention to the kinds of role models we provide to one another. A powerful source of role models is located in almost every home: television. As we saw in Chapter 7, children play more aggressively immediately after watching violent shows on television (Liebert & Baron, 1972). Similarly, watching violent films increased the aggressiveness of juvenile delinquents, especially among those who were initially the most aggressive (Parke et al., 1977). Significant correlations exist between the amount of TV violence watched by children and their aggression, as rated by peers (Huesmann, Lagerspetz, & Eron, 1984). More-

over, these correlations appear across four different countries—Australia, Finland, Poland, and the United States. In short, watching violence teaches children how to engage in it and *desensitizes* them to its devastating consequences.

It is not just children who can become desensitized. Many studies have shown that prolonged exposure to violence desensitizes adult viewers as well; they become less affected by violence when later viewing a brawl, whether on TV or in real life (Rule & Ferguson, 1986). David Linz, Edward Donnerstein, and Steven Penrod (1984) concluded that repeated exposure to filmed violence lowered subjects' emotional reactions to the material, and resulted in subjects' rating the films less offensive by the last day of viewing.

A particular form of aggression against women is violent pornography. Male aggression toward females increases after males watch pornographic films displaying sexual violence (Donnerstein & Berkowitz, 1981). In addition, Linz, Donnerstein, and Penrod (1988) found that after viewing five sexually violent films in 10 days, men evaluated the films more positively (as less depressing, less anxiety-producing, and less negatively arousing) than they had after viewing just one film. They also perceived the films as less violent and as less degrading to women. A less definitive support for the link between violent pornography and male aggression against females is a correlation between more liberal pornography laws and incidents of reported rape (Court, 1984). As mentioned, we should not infer causation from correlation. For one thing, such links also exist between sexually aggressive behavior and films that are less sexually explicit but still sexually violent. Nonetheless, the same attitudes that lead to the watching of violent pornography also may lead to crimes of rape.

> If television and pornography could be proven conclusively to contribute to violence, would that proof justify restrictions being placed upon programming and publications?

Environmental Factors Contributing to Aggression

Aggression was a problem for society long before television or movies came on the scene. Other than social learning, what factors in the environment lead to aggression? One such factor is *aggression* itself. Aggression has been found to lead to more aggression. Although some religions may teach us to turn the other cheek, in practice people are more likely to meet aggression with a counterattack (Borden, Bowen, & Taylor, 1971; Ohbuchi & Kambara, 1985).

A second factor that can lead to aggression is *pain* (Berkowitz, Cochran, & Embree, 1981; Ulrich & Azrin, 1962). Hostile aggression is often provoked by feelings of pain. If a person's aggressive act leads to a decrease in pain, aggression becomes even more likely (Azrin, 1967).

A third factor is *discomfort*. People become more aggressive when they are simply uncomfortable, such as when they are exposed to bad smells (Rotton, Barry, Frey, & Soler, 1978), cigarette smoke, and air pollution (Rotton & Frey, 1985). Exposure to heat above 80° F or 27° Centigrade also increases aggression (Baron & Bell, 1975; Bell & Baron, 1976). Indeed, increased feelings of discomfort may underlie why cities that have higher temperatures on the average also have higher average rates of violent crime compared with cities that have more moderate temperatures (Anderson, 1987). As Figure 15-10 shows, violent crimes more commonly occur on hotter days, in hotter seasons, in hotter years, and in hotter regions (Anderson, 1989).

A fourth possible cause of aggression is *frustration*. Indeed, some classic research (e.g., Dollard et al., 1939) has posited that frustration is a necessary and sufficient condition for aggression. Although a clear empirical link between frustration and aggression exists (Barker, Dembo, & Lewin, 1941), we now know that frustration does not *always* lead to aggression. For example, although strong frustra-

These Bosnian women and children are being forced to flee from their homes in response to what has been termed "ethnic cleansing," a euphemism for the genocide of human beings by their fellow humans.

tions that seem to have arbitrary causes are quite likely to lead to aggression, mild frustrations are less likely to lead to aggression, especially if they are viewed as having a reasonable cause (Baron, 1977). For example, suppose that the light at an intersection turns green but you cannot move your car because you are being blocked by the car in front of you. Whether you react aggressively will probably depend on why the car in front of you stops. Your reaction will be different if the driver in front of you is engaged in a conversation than if the driver has suffered a heart attack.

Deindividuation

What enables some of us to *dehumanize*—make victims sound as if they are less than human and so deserving of poor treatment—others of us? A possible answer may be shown by an example. Every once in a while, you read in the newspaper or see on the television how fans in an athletic contest—such as a European soccer match—lose control and riot, trampling and mutilating people and destroying everything in the path of the crowd. How does a group become an out-of-control crowd? At the end of the nineteenth century, Gustave Le Bon (1896) attempted to analyze the factors that lead to the mass hysteria of mob behavior. Le Bon contended that people in a crowd are more susceptible to mob behavior because they feel anonymous and invulnerable. They start acting more like lower animals than like people, and they become highly impulsive and unreasoning in their actions.

Perhaps mob behavior can be understood in terms of the phenomenon of **deindividuation,** which

FIGURE 15-10
Temperature and Aggression
When the temperature rises, rates of violent crimes often rise as well (Anderson, 1987). Although the link between high heat and aggression is only correlational (and we therefore cannot draw causal conclusions), the correlation is robust (Anderson, 1989).

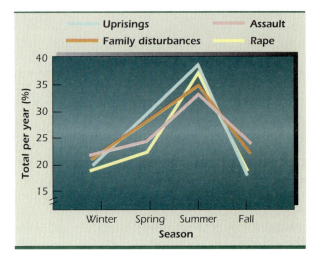

is the loss of a sense of individual identity, resulting in the reduction of constraints against socially unacceptable behavior (Diener, 1979, 1980). In a study whose findings jolted the scientific community, the basement of a building that housed the university psychology department was converted into a "jail" (Zimbardo, 1972). Male volunteers for the experiment were arbitrarily assigned to be either "prisoners" or "guards." Phil Zimbardo used a number of techniques to deindividuate members of both groups. The prisoners wore prisonlike uniforms and nylon stocking caps and were referred to by serial numbers instead of by names. Guards also wore uniforms and mirrored sunglasses to hide their eyes, and they carried clubs.

What started off as a simulation became a nightmare. Prisoners started acting like prisoners, and guards truly acted like guards. The guards started harassing and deriding the prisoners. The guards frequently inflicted cruel treatment, apparently with little or no reason. The prisoners soon staged a revolt that was in turn crushed. Prisoners became morose, depressed, and lethargic, and some started to experience mental breakdowns. The experiment was terminated when it became obvious that it had gotten out of control. The critical factor in this experiment is that Zimbardo had assigned people arbitrarily to groups. Once deindividuated, people can act in ways they would never have thought possible, whether on the giving or the receiving end of hostile levels of aggression.

> How might you connect the idea of deindividuation with organizations such as the Ku Klux Klan?

As members of gangs, these young men feel deindividuated, so they show violent aggression more readily toward members of other gangs, as well as toward innocent bystanders who happen to be in the line of fire.

Reducing Aggression

Are there methods to control and even significantly reduce aggression? Based on the studies of deindividuation, we might guess that some forms of aggression might be minimized by maximizing people's (a) sense of their own individual identities as humans and (b) awareness of the humanity of their fellow humans. Several specific methods for reducing aggression also have been proposed, some of which seem to be more successful than others. As Table 15-3 shows, some methods for reducing aggression, such as observing *nonaggressive modeling* and *generating incompatible responses*, are more effective than others, such as *catharsis* and *punishment*.

Group behavior can be mindless, inappropriate, and even disastrous if each member of the group

TABLE 15-3
Methods for Reducing Aggression
Of the many methods for reducing aggression that have been proposed, some are much more effective than others. Indeed, some methods may even exacerbate aggression, increasing its likelihood.

Method	Description
Observing nonaggressive models	Watching nonaggressive models can increase the likelihood of choosing alternatives to aggressive behavior.
Generating incompatible responses	One of the most successful techniques. Empathy, humor, unexpected responses can defuse aggression.
Using cognitive strategies	A stop-and-think strategy raises alternatives to using aggression in frustrating or threatening situations. An awareness of individual identities as humans and of the humanity of fellow humans reduces deindividuation. An awareness of the reasons for another person's behavior can reduce feelings of anger, frustration, hostility.

yields his or her individual thoughts, beliefs, and actions to the apparent consensus of the group. Yet when even a single individual takes the initiative and takes positive action, such as helping others or refusing to harm others, other members of the group may reconsider their own beliefs and behavior. Under the right circumstances, even one dissenter can motivate others who are considering dissent, and groupthink, mindless obedience or conformity, and deindividuation may be minimized or even avoided altogether.

SUMMARY

Groups 526

1. Researchers who study the social psychology of groups seek to understand and explain how groups reach consensus and how individuals perform in a *group*. Groups differ in the emphasis they give to task functions versus relationships among members of the group.

2. *Social-facilitation* theory and *distraction-conflict theory* offer explanations for how the presence of others affects our performance.

3. *Social loafing* occurs in groups and can be discouraged through evaluation apprehension.

4. Groups often become polarized. New arguments confirm old beliefs, and social norms emerge. In-group members are especially influential.

5. The resolution of intergroup and intragroup conflicts may be viewed in terms of the reasons why people resolve conflicts and the strategies they use to resolve conflicts.

6. *Groupthink* occurs when a closely knit group cares more about consensus than about honest interaction. Stress, biased leadership, and isolation compound the problem. To counter groupthink, the group needs a subgroup structure, outside input, and strong leadership.

Conformity, Compliance, and Obedience 531

7. People yield to social pressure by conforming, complying, and obeying.

8. Solomon Asch's studies showed that a member of a group may conform publicly or privately. People who deviate from the norm often are rejected by the group. Factors affecting *conformity* include group size, cohesiveness of the group, gender, social status, culture, and the appearance of unanimity. Majorities urge conformity through their large numbers; minorities, if persistent, also can influence opinion.

9. *Compliance* is encouraged through such techniques as justification, reciprocity, low-ball, that's-not-all, foot-in-the-door, door-in-the-face, and hard-to-get.

10. Stanley Milgram's experiment on *obedience* found most subjects willing to inflict excruciating pain on others when "under orders" to do so. Other research has replicated Milgram's surprising findings.

Prosocial Behavior 539

11. According to the *bystander effect*, the presence of others diffuses responsibility and inhibits helping behavior. Also important are the characteristics of the victim, the bystander, and the situation.

12. *Altruism* is selfless sacrifice. Psychologists agree that it exists, but disagree over how to define it.

Antisocial Behavior 543

13. *Prejudice* is based on faulty evidence, which in turn often is based on *social categorization* and on *stereotypes*. The Robber's Cave study showed how prejudice can be reduced by cooperative activities. Prejudice may develop when groups compete for scarce resources (*realistic-conflict theory*) or when people seek to increase their own self-esteem and to boost the esteem of their in-group (*social-identity theory*). To reduce prejudice, groups must recognize that it exists, work cooperatively together, use information to counter the stereotypes, and, if possible, experience other cultures.

14. *Aggression* is antisocial behavior that harms another; it may be *hostile* or *instrumental*. Aggression may be prompted by hormones. People learn aggressive behavior when they see it modeled, such as on television and in the movies. Violent pornography is a strong example of modeling aggressive behavior. Pain, discomfort, and frustration also can promote aggressive behavior.

15. A group can become an unruly mob. When *deindividuation* occurs, people behave in ways they would not behave if they were alone.

16. Aggression can be reduced if we as individuals maximize our own identities as humans and our awareness of others as fellow humans.

KEY TERMS

aggression 548
altruism 543
antisocial behavior 543
bystander effect 539
compliance 531
conformity 531
contact hypothesis 547
deindividuation 550
diffusion of responsibility 539

distraction-conflict theory 527
group 526
group polarization 528
groupthink 529
hostile aggression 548
illusory correlation 545
instrumental aggression 548
obedience 531
outgroup homogeneity bias 545

prejudice 543
prosocial behavior 539
realistic-conflict theory 546
social categorization 545
social facilitation 527
social-identity theory 546
social inhibition 527
social loafing 528
stereotypes 545

IN SEARCH OF THE HUMAN MIND:
ANALYSES, CREATIVE EXPLORATIONS, AND PRACTICAL APPLICATIONS

1. What criteria would you propose for determining whether behavior derives from motives that are truly altruistic?
2. Some developmental psychologists have noticed that adolescents who demonstrate a high degree of conformity to their peers during adolescence are more likely to have shown a high degree of obedience to their parents during childhood. What do you believe to be the relationship between conformity and obedience, if any? Explain the reasoning underlying your belief.
3. Although most psychologists emphasize the importance of environmental considerations in determining the expression of aggressive behavior, many note that biological factors also play an important role in aggressive behavior. What do you believe to be the relative importance of nature and of nurture in determining the expression of aggressive behavior?

4. Design an exercise for a work group to help prevent the group from suffering the ill effects of groupthink.
5. Suggest a way to apply one or more of the strategies for gaining compliance to a means of averting the destruction of the rain forests, at least in some small way.
6. Design an ad campaign that would help people to avoid falling prey to some of the strategies for gaining compliance described in this chapter.

7. Imagine that you wish to reduce the likelihood of your own aggression or the aggression of another person. What will you do? Describe a specific situation and exactly how you would handle it.
8. Think about a situation in which your prejudices affected your behavior—when you either unfavorably discriminated against a person or you favorably showed reverse discrimination toward a person. Describe that situation and your behavior from the viewpoint of the person with whom you were interacting. Describe both that person's observations of your behavior and the emotions that the person felt in response to your behavior. (*Hint:* Do not limit your definition of prejudice to racial prejudice.)
9. Which of the compliance-seeking strategies is the most likely to be effective in gaining your own compliance? Which is the least likely? Why?

Chapter Sixteen

MOTIVATION AND EMOTION

Chapter Outline

In 1991, Walter Hudson died at 47 years of age. His death was reported in newspapers and magazines throughout the United States, even though he was not a distinguished artist, writer, scientist, executive, or politician. Hudson was one of the heaviest men in the world. He was so big that he was unable to leave his house, and when he died, workmen had to cut a hole in his bedroom wall so his body could be removed. At his peak, he weighed 1,400 pounds and had a 119-inch waist. At one point, he actually lost 800 pounds. Later, however, as so many other people do, he regained most of the weight he had lost.

What motivates most of us to gain weight or to lose it? What are the mechanisms underlying hunger in the first place? What motivates us to explore our environments or to achieve? What emotions do we feel when we accomplish our goals, or when we fail to do so? We address these kinds of questions in this chapter.

Intuitively, the way we describe our motivations and our emotions is similar: "I feel like having a hamburger," "I feel like dancing," "Dr. Martin Luther King's speeches moved many people to take action." Both motivations and emotions are feelings that cause us to move or to be moved. Both seem to erupt within us in response to events or to thoughts, and we often feel both as physiological sensations: "When I heard his footsteps behind me again, I panicked—I started shaking, my heart pounded, my throat swelled shut, my palms sweated, and I turned to ice." Motivation and emotion are inextricably linked.

THE NATURE AND CHARACTERISTICS OF MOTIVATION

IN SEARCH OF...

When you feel inclined to do something, under what circumstances are you motivated to take action, and under what circumstances do you lack sufficient motivation to act?

A **motive** is a want or a need that causes us to act. Psychologists study *why* or *how* we are motivated to act. More specifically, psychologists ask four different questions (Houston, 1985). (1) What *directions* do our actions move us in? That is, what attracts us, and what repels us? (2) What motivates us to *initiate* or start taking action to pursue a particular goal? That is, what leads some people to initiate action, whereas others may contemplate an action but never actually go ahead and act? (3) How *intensely* do we pursue those actions? Also, (4) why do some people *persist* for longer periods of time in the things that motivate them, whereas other people flitter from one pursuit to another?

EARLY THEORIES OF MOTIVATION

IN SEARCH OF...

How did our current ideas about motivation come into being and evolve?

Instinct Theory

Why do people do what they do? Early in the twentieth century, psychologists sought to understand motivation in terms of **instinct** (Cofer & Appley, 1964). According to *instinct theory*, instinctive behavior has three main characteristics. First, it is *inherited;* we are born with all the instincts we ever will have. Thus, the desire for sexual union or the fear of a predator is innate, not learned. Second, it is *species specific;* that is, salmon return up river to their place of birth, but tuna do not; bees do a certain kind of dance, but humans do not. Third, it is *stereotyped;* we engage in a behavior automatically in response to a particular stimulus (e.g., running from a ferocious predator is automatic, and fortunately so). Charles Darwin (1859) was a major proponent of the instinctual point of view and believed that much of an animal's behavior is inherited, species specific, and automatic. Instinctive behavior, from an evolutionary point of view, is one of the keys not only to individual survival, but also to survival of the species.

William James, the father of much of modern psychological thinking, was also the father of instinct theory as applied to human beings. James (1890a) suggested a list of 20 physical instincts, such as sucking and locomotion, as well as an additional 17 mental instincts. The mental instincts included cleanliness, curiosity, fearfulness, jealousy, parental love, and sociability. A generation later, William McDougall (1908) proposed a further list of instincts, including the desire for food, the desire to have sex, the desire to dominate, and the desire to make things. The list of proposed instincts gradually grew to 10,000 (Bernard, 1924). Whereas James believed that instincts are *important* in behavior, McDougall argued that instincts are *necessary* for behavior. Without them, people would be totally passive, unmoved to action by anything.

Instinct theory, however, like many other psychological theories, became ponderous, cumbersome, and circular (Kuo, 1921). Behaviors were explained by instincts, which in turn were explained by the behaviors. The arguments against instincts led people to lose interest in them as a basis for theorizing. This process is typical of how paradigms (theoretical frameworks) come and go in psychology. As we have seen, scientists prefer theories that parsimoniously explain complex phenomena in simple, clear terms. As instinct theory became increasingly complex, obscure, and nonparsimonious, its aesthetic appeal gradually moved too far from the ideal. Theorists sought new ways to explain motivation. As the aesthetic appeal of instinct theory waned, drive theory became increasingly attractive.

> Why do scientists sometimes develop theories that are circular, and how can scientists avoid this logical pitfall?

Drive Theory

Drive theory derives many of its principles, and many of its backers, from learning theory (see Chapter 7). There have been different versions of drive theory. The theory was first proposed by Robert Woodworth (1918), but the most well-known version was proposed by Clark Hull. Hull (1943, 1952) believed that people have a number of different basic physiological needs: the need for food, water, sleep, and so on. To survive, we must satisfy all of these physiological needs, and the compulsion that we feel to meet the needs is known as **drive.** To reduce the drive, we eat, drink, sleep, and otherwise satisfy our needs. Animals and humans alike are impelled to reduce drive.

Like instinct theory, drive theory fell out of favor because the assumptions underlying it proved not to be particularly well founded (White, 1959.) As drive paradigms began to yield diminishing returns, other paradigms seemed to be more fruitful. So researchers studying motivation moved on.

CONTEMPORARY PARADIGMS OF MOTIVATION

> ### IN SEARCH OF...
>
> Why has motivation captured the attention of physiological, behavioral, clinical, and cognitive psychologists? What is the common core of this phenomenon that unites such diverse approaches to research?

Physiological Approaches

What prompted psychologists to start exploring the relationship between the central nervous system (particularly, the brain) and the psychological and behavioral phenomenon of motivation? Actually, the physiological approach gained support almost by accident. Researcher James Olds misplaced an electrode in a portion of a rat's brain. When the rat was stimulated, it acted in ways to suggest that it wished more stimulation. Olds and Peter Milner (1954) then designed an experiment to test whether the rat was indeed seeking further stimulation. When electrodes were planted in a part of the limbic system, rats spent more than three-quarters of their time pressing a bar to repeat the stimulation. Olds had inadvertently discovered a "pleasure center" of the brain. Other researchers showed that cats would do whatever they could to *avoid* electrical stimulation in another part of the brain (Delgado, Roberts, & Miller, 1954). Three theories for understanding the relationship between motivation and the physiology of the brain are considered here: arousal theory, opponent-process theory, and homeostatic-regulation theory.

Arousal Theory

Suppose that three students of equal intelligence and subject knowledge are about to take an important test. The first student does not care either about the test or about how well she will do on it. The second student wants to do well, but is not anxious about his performance. He knows that even if he were to do poorly, his life would not be inalterably changed for the worse. The third student is extremely nervous about the test, and she believes that her grade on this test will largely determine her future. Which student do you think is most likely to do best on the test?

These three students vary in their amount of **arousal,** the level of alertness, wakefulness, and activation (Anderson, 1990). Arousal is caused by the activity of the central nervous system, including the brain. The relationship between arousal and efficiency of performance is shown in Figure 16-1.

The inverted U-shape shown in Figure 16-1 represents the *Yerkes-Dodson Law* (Yerkes & Dodson, 1908), which states that people will perform most efficiently when their level of arousal is moderate. According to this law, the second student, who is both

motivated and relaxed, will do the best. People generally also feel the best when their level of arousal is moderate (Berlyne, 1967). At low levels of arousal, people feel bored, listless, and unmotivated. At high levels of arousal, people feel tense or fearful.

For example, one reason many people hate crowds may be that crowds increase people's arousal to an uncomfortable level, causing them to experience stress. To test this notion, the stress levels of commuters who boarded at the beginning of a particular train ride were compared with the stress levels of commuters who boarded at the middle (Lundberg, 1976). It would seem reasonable to assume that those who rode the train longer would feel more stress. In fact, however, people who board the train near the middle of the trip experience more stress. Why? Those who get on the train at the beginning have more control over their level of stress. They can sit and put their bags wherever they want to, and they can settle in before the rush of the other people. Those who get on in the middle experience much more arousal because they have to fight the crowd and search for a seat and a space to store their belongings. Similarly, a study of prisons indicated that the denser the population of the prison, the higher the rates of murder, suicide, and mental illness (Cox, Paulus, & McCain, 1984).

The optimal level of arousal appears to vary both with the task and with the individual. For relatively simple tasks, the optimal level of arousal is

FIGURE 16-1
The Yerkes-Dodson Law

In the hill-shaped linear relationship between arousal and performance, performance is at its peak when arousal is moderate, and performance levels are lower at both the low and high extremes of arousal. (After Yerkes & Dodson, 1908)

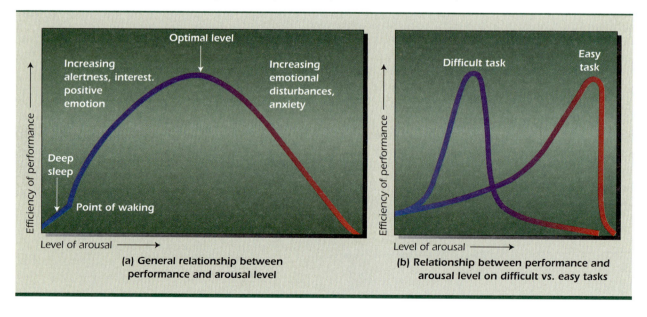

(a) General relationship between performance and arousal level

(b) Relationship between performance and arousal level on difficult vs. easy tasks

moderately high, whereas for difficult tasks the optimal level of arousal is moderately low (Bexton, Heron, & Scott, 1954; Broadhurst, 1957). If we need to perform a fairly repetitive and mindless task, a high level of arousal may help us get through and may motivate us to be efficient. If we have to perform a complex task, however, a low level of arousal may help us avoid becoming anxious, which would hamper our ability to start working on the task.

The relationship between task difficulty and arousal has implications for how we choose to work. Some of us do our best work when responding to tight deadlines, exacting standards, or other arousal-inducing features. Others of us seek work in which we can proceed at a consistent pace or have moderate standards to follow. Similarly, some people might seek to maximize the level of arousal in their environments—such as with festive or zesty music, hard-surfaced office chairs, and vibrantly decorated surroundings. Others may prefer to minimize their arousal by having no music or other distracting noise, comfortable chairs, and a minimum of visual stimulation.

Optimal levels of arousal also differ from one person to the next. Personality theorists suggest that one of the main differences between *introverts*, who prefer to be by themselves rather than to seek the company of other people, and *extroverts*, who prefer the company of other people to being by themselves, is in their baseline level of arousal. Introverts may have a high baseline level of arousal, and therefore avoid others so as not to raise their arousal beyond the optimum; in contrast, extroverts tend to have a relatively low baseline level of arousal, so they seek out other people to raise their arousal level (Derryberry & Rothbart, 1988; Eysenck, 1971).

> What level of arousal do you seek when you want to play? What level of arousal do you seek when you want to accomplish a complex task? What do these preferred levels of arousal tell you about yourself and about the optimal work and play environments to suit your preferences?

Opponent-Process Theory

Do you have any addictions? Are you physiologically addicted to coffee, smoking, or alcohol? If you are, then you have probably noticed that addictions tend to follow a cycle (see Figure 16-2). The *opponent-process theory*, proposed by Richard Solomon (1980; Solomon & Corbit, 1974), addresses the cycle of emotional experience when we acquire and then try

FIGURE 16-2
Acquired Motivation

In the beginning of the process of physiological addiction (a), the addictive stimulus elevates us above our neutral baseline level of response. At this point, if we stop using the addictive substance, we first drop below and then return to our neutral baseline level. However, once you become addicted (b), our responses to the substance act only to keep us in a steady state, which serves as our current neutral level of response. If we then abstain from the addictive substance, our responses will cause us to fall futher below our neutral level of response, for a longer time, and we will experience withdrawal. (After Solomon & Corbit, 1974)

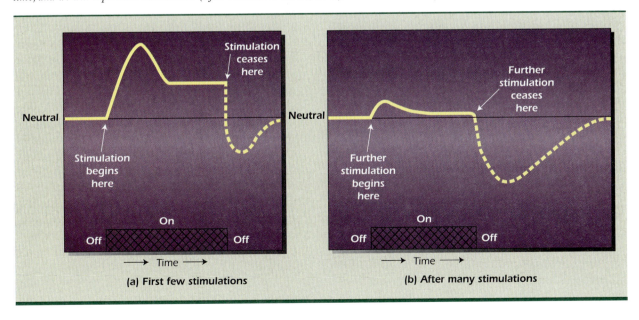

to get rid of a motivation. Originally, we are at a neutral state, a *baseline*, in which we have not acquired the motivation to act (e.g., to drink coffee), and thus the stimulus (coffee) is irrelevant to us. Then we drink the first cup of coffee, experience a "high," and our emotional state becomes positive. We feel the high because of the positive effect of the stimulus—often a chemical—on receptors of the brain. (Even in the case of a romantic attraction, pleasurable electrochemical reactions occur in the brain.) Regardless of the source, however, we feel good because of the stimulus, and thus we have an *acquired motivation* to seek out more of the stimulus.

According to Solomon, the brains of mammals always seek out emotional neutrality sooner or later. This pursuit of emotional neutrality means that when a motivational source impels us to feel emotions, whether positive or negative, we then come under the influence of an opposing motivational force—an **opponent process**—that acts to bring us back to the neutral baseline. (Recall from Chapter 4 the theory of vision in which opponent physiological processes act to enable us to see colors.) Notice in the left panel of the figure that our emotional state after drinking a cup of coffee first rises substantially but then falls. It starts to go down when the opponent process begins to oppose the original process. In other words, what was initially pleasurable now starts to become less so. Eventually, the effect of the stimulus wears off, and we reach a *steady state* of response to the stimulus. The original motivating force stops because the stimulus now only keeps us at our baseline level; it no longer elevates us above the baseline.

Thus, as the right panel of the figure shows, after using the stimulus for a long time, its effect is quite different from what it was originally. Once we *habituate* to the stimulus (see Chapters 4, 6, and 7), it no longer gives us the boost above our baseline level. Unfortunately, the opponent process, which was slower to start, is also slower to stop. When the effect of the stimulus wears off, the effect of the opponent process remains, and so we fairly quickly go into a state of *withdrawal*. We now feel worse than we did before: irritable, cranky, tired, sad, or upset. We may then seek out more of the stimulus to relieve the withdrawal symptoms. Ironically, then, what starts off as a habit to achieve a high becomes a habit to avoid a low. We may drink coffee to avoid withdrawal symptoms. Fortunately, however, if we decide to ride out the withdrawal, the symptoms will eventually end, and we will return to baseline.

Opponent-process theory can be applied to a diversity of stimuli. Solomon and his colleagues have applied it to many kinds of acquired motivations, and

it is remarkably effective in accounting for the data. It applies not only to the motivation to take drugs, but also to motivations to be with another person, to eat particular kinds of foods, or even to exercise. For example, runners can start feeling anxiety and even depression if deprived of the opportunity to run.

Arousal theory explains why we seek to explore and to master our environments, and opponent-process theory explains why we are motivated to seek substances to which we are addicted. However, neither theory satisfactorily addresses why we eat, drink, or satisfy our other physiological needs. Yet another theory is needed to explain these motivations.

Homeostatic-Regulation Theory

Consider a typical sequence of behavior during the morning. You wake up. After some time, you start to feel hungry and thirsty. You eat and drink. Now, no longer hungry or thirsty, you begin your morning activities. After a while, you begin to notice sensations of hunger and thirst again. Maybe you have other things to do, and just grab a drink instead of eating. The hunger pangs intensify. Finally, you decide that you really want to have lunch, so you eat again.

In the course of this process, you have been subject to several instances of homeostatic regulation that have motivated you to wake up, eat, and drink. **Homeostatic regulation** is the tendency of the body to maintain a state of equilibrium. When the body lacks something, it seeks it; when the body is satiated, it sends signals to stop obtaining that something. We regulate the need for food and liquid, as well as the control of body temperature, through homeostatic systems. These systems operate via a *negative feedback loop*, which we first encountered in the discussion of hormones in Chapter 3. Most people stop eating when they no longer feel hungry, stop drinking when they no longer feel thirsty, or stop sleeping when they no longer feel tired.

Homeostatic regulation is not limited to the body. Most home heating systems, like the bodily heating system, work on the basis of homeostatic regulation. You set the thermostat at the temperature you want. When the room is at or above the specified temperature, the heating system is off. When the thermostat records temperatures below the preferred setting, however, the heater turns on. The heating continues until the thermostat reaches the set point—the desired temperature. At that point, having reached a comfortable temperature, it turns off again.

In the body, negative feedback is graded, not all-or-none. For example, suppose that you have had a very active day and arrive at dinner famished. At first, you are likely to eat and drink rapidly, but your rate of eating and drinking will decrease as you complete the meal, because you are receiving feedback indicating that your needs are satisfied (Spitzer & Rodin, 1981). The body signals to you well before you have finished the meal that you are reaching satiation.

Homeostatic regulation sounds like drive theory, but the emphases are different. In drive theory, a need supplies energy, which seeks to satisfy the need and to reduce the drive. The focus is on avoiding deficits. In homeostatic-regulation theory, the emphasis is on the need to maintain equilibrium. Both deficits and surpluses are to be avoided. (See Table 16-1 for a brief summary of the physiological approaches.) The next section considers in more detail how the body regulates two primary motivations: hunger and sexual desire.

Physiological Aspects

Hunger

Scientists used to think that the regulation of hunger was very simple: We felt hunger when our stomach contracted (Cannon & Washburn, 1912). However, research has shown both in rats (Morgan & Morgan, 1940) and in humans (Grossman & Stein, 1948) that if the nerve responsible for carrying messages between the stomach and the brain is severed, we still feel hunger. Even more persuasive is the finding that after people's stomachs are surgically removed (for medical reasons), they continue to feel hunger (Janowitz, 1967; Wangensteen & Carlson, 1931). Clearly, there is more to hunger than just the empty feeling in the stomach.

Of course, the stomach participates in the regulation of hunger (McHugh & Moran, 1985). In all mammals, the stomach empties at a constant rate; for humans, the rate is slightly over 2 calories per minute. (Note that it is caloric content rather than the volume of food that determines how fast the food leaves the stomach. A large bowl of lettuce with no dressing may leave you feeling hungry more quickly than a small piece of cake, because the stomach will empty itself of the lower-calorie lettuce more quickly.) As the stomach contracts, we feel more and more hungry. Usually, we start feeling hunger when the stomach is roughly 60% empty, and we feel very hungry when the stomach is 90% empty (Sepple & Read, 1989).

THE ROLE OF THE BRAIN IN HUNGER. The brain, particularly the hypothalamus, regulates hunger as well (see Figure 16-3 and Chapter 3). If the ventromedial hypothalamus (VMH) in an animal has a lesion, that animal will overeat and eventually become obese (Hetherington & Ranson, 1940; Teitelbaum, 1961). (See Figure 16-4.) The VMH, therefore, regulates hunger and, in particular, serves as a source of negative feedback. When the organism is satiated, the VMH signals that it is time to stop eating. In animals with a destroyed VMH, the signal never is sent.

Lesions in the lateral hypothalamus (LH) have exactly the opposite effect of VMH destruction (Anand & Brobeck, 1951). An animal that has a lesion in the LH simply does not eat, which leads to starvation and death. Thus, in effect, the LH is an on switch for eating, whereas the VMH is an off switch.

THEORIES OF THE REGULATION OF HUNGER. In order for the VMH and LH to regulate eating behavior, they need information from the body. What

TABLE 16-1
Physiological Approaches to Motivation

There are three theories of motivation that are based on physiology: arousal theory, opponent-process theory, and homeostatic-regulation theory.

Arousal Theory (Yerkes-Dodson Law)	We feel relaxed and motivated when we are moderately aroused, and we perform at optimum level. We feel bored when minimally aroused and anxious or tense when highly aroused.
Opponent-Process Theory (Solomon)	We seek emotional neutrality. When we feel emotions, an opposing motive brings us back to the neutral baseline.
Homeostatic-Regulation Theory	The body (brain) tries to maintain a state of equilibrium. When the brain senses that the body lacks food, the brain signals the body to seek food; when the brain senses that the stomach is full, it signals the body to stop eating.

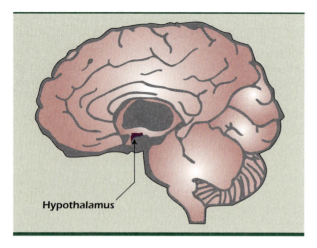

FIGURE 16-3
The Role of the Brain in Hunger
Regions of the hypothalamus are involved in regulating hunger: The lateral (on the side) hypothalamus seems to function as an "on" switch, turning on hunger motivation, and the ventromedial (lower middle) hypothalamus seems to function as an "off" switch, turning off hunger motivation.

signals hunger or satiety (fullness)? Two major hypotheses present possible explanations, although they may not be mutually exclusive. According to the **glucostatic hypothesis,** levels of *glucose* (a simple body sugar) signal the brain about the need for food. The term *glucostatic* refers to the stability of glucose levels in the body and the brain.

We know that cells need glucose to produce energy. As cells expend glucose, their capacity to create energy decreases, and according to the glucostatic hypothesis, hunger arises (Friedman & Stricker, 1976; Mayer, 1953). Injecting glucose into dogs increases activity in the VMH and decreases it in the LH (Anand, Chhina, & Singh, 1962). These changes in activity make sense, given that the VMH controls cessation of hunger and the LH controls initiation of hunger. Further evidence for the glucostatic theory is the existence of receptor cells for glucose in the VMH and the LH (Oomara, 1976).

Glucostatic theory seems quite plausible, although there are still some problems with it (Cotman & McGaugh, 1980). First, damaged areas of the brain other than the hypothalamus can substantially affect eating behavior. This fact suggests there is more to hunger regulation than glucose monitoring by the hypothalamus (Grossman & Grossman, 1963). Second, damage to the LH affects animals' abilities to react normally to stress. Thus, the LH might only indirectly inhibit eating as a consequence of the direct action to increase the brain's response to stress (Stricker & Zigmond, 1976). Third, diabetics typi-

cally have high glucose levels due to their low production of insulin (a hormone that decreases levels of glucose). Despite relatively high levels of glucose in their bloodstream, diabetics experience hunger just like anyone else.

An alternative explanation for understanding hunger is the **lipostatic hypothesis,** which claims that the body monitors food intake by detecting when lipids (fats) drop below a certain level. As the proportion of fats in the body decreases, hunger increases (Hoebel & Teitelbaum, 1966). According to this theory, eating is a way of maintaining adequate reserves of energy via body weight. Indeed, the body monitors these signs of fat cells on a fairly constant basis (Faust, Johnson, & Hirsch, 1977a, 1977b). When body fat gets too low, people eat, and when it gets too high,

FIGURE 16-4
Obese Rate
When a lesion is created in the ventromedial hypothalamus (VMH) of a rat brain, the rat becomes obese. Lesion studies led researchers to conclude that the VMH is involved in regulating the detection of when to stop feeling hunger. Are alternate explanations of this finding possible? If so, what are they? If not, why not?

they stop eating (Keesey, Boyle, Kemnitz, & Mitchell, 1976; Keesey & Powley, 1975).

The lipostatic hypothesis led Richard Keesey, Terry Powley, and their colleagues to formulate the **set-point theory,** which holds that each person has a preset body weight. This weight is determined biologically either at birth or very soon thereafter by the number of fat cells in the body (Grilo & Pogue-Geile, 1991; Keesey, 1980). People with more fat cells tend to have greater body weight. Although the number of fat cells can increase, it does not decrease across the life span. What varies with weight is the size of the fat cells. When the person eats less, the size of the cells shrinks, and the person feels hungry. When the person eats more, the size of the cells increases, and the person feels full.

Set-point theory predicts that it will be very difficult for a person to lose weight because the tendency of the body will always be to return to the set point, at which the variably sized fat cells are of a normal size. If we diet, our bodies respond as though we were in a prolonged state of starvation, storing as much food energy as possible. Thus, the less we eat, the more our bodies work to help us overcome our starved condition, struggling to keep us as fat as possible despite our low intake of calories. In addition, overeating for a long time can raise the set point (Keesey & Powley, 1986). Statistics on weight loss seem to support set-point theory: more than 90% of weight-losing dieters eventually gain weight back. (See Table 16-2 for a summary of these theories.) Recent research (Safer, 1991; Seraganian, 1993) indicates that the combination of exercise and low-fat, low-calorie dieting may be more effective in achieving weight loss than are dietary restrictions alone (see Chapter 20).

OBESITY.   To be considered obese, a person must be at least 20% over the normal range for a given height and weight (see Chapter 20). In the United States, about 24% of men and 27% of women are considered obese. Many of those people, plus many more who do not meet the definition of obesity, subject themselves to diets. However, dieting often fails because people become more susceptible to binge eating when they are dieting than when they are not (Polivy & Herman, 1983, 1985). When subjected to anxiety, depression, alcohol, stress, high-calorie foods, or other factors, dieters seem to drop the restraints that have kept them from eating, and many start to binge. Those who are not dieting do not exhibit comparable behavior; this finding seems to give further support to set-point theory.

Other factors seem to contribute to obesity as well. For example, people tend to eat more when presented with a wide variety of foods (Rolls, 1979; Rolls, Rowe, & Rolls, 1982). People also tend to eat more in the presence of others (Berry, Beatty, & Klesges, 1985; DeCastro & Brewer, 1992).

Stanley Schachter (1968, 1971a, 1971b; Schachter & Gross, 1968; Schachter & Rodin, 1974) has suggested that part of the difference between people of normal weight and those who are obese may be in the types of cues to which they are most responsive. In particular, Schachter suggests that people of normal weight may eat largely in response to internal, physiological signals (glucostatic, lipostatic, or some combination of the two), whereas overweight people may be more responsive to external, environmental cues.

The behavioral differences between obese and normal-weight subjects may be an effect rather than a cause of obesity, however. Richard Nisbett (1972) has

TABLE 16-2
Theories of the Regulation of Hunger
Three prominent theories of the regulation of hunger are based on the level of glucose in the blood, the level of fats in the blood, and the number of fat cells in the body.

Glucostatic Hypothesis	The VMH and LH in the brain monitor the level of glucose in the blood to determine the need for food.
Lipostatic Hypothesis	The VMH and LH in the brain monitor the level of lipids (fats) in the blood to determine the need for food.
Set-Point Theory	We each have a preset body weight, determined by the number of fat cells in the body. The fat cells expand when we gain weight and contract when we lose weight. If we try to lose weight, it will be difficult to go below the set point; our bodies interpret the diet as starvation and respond by storing as much food as possible. If we gain weight over time, the set point can increase.

suggested that obesity may derive from a malfunctioning in the hypothalamus. Of course, any hypothesis can be pushed too far. Even people of normal weight can be quite sensitive to external cues, such as the availability of a chocolate cake (Rodin, 1981). Thus, we still have a long way to go in terms of understanding the causes of human obesity.

Research (Lissner et al., 1991) also suggests that fluctuations in weight are more damaging to health than being overweight. In other words, you may do yourself more harm by engaging in a constant cycle of losing and regaining weight than by just leaving your weight alone.

EXTERNAL FACTORS IN THE PERCEPTION OF OBESITY.   Some cross-cultural psychologists emphasize external factors in explaining wide individual differences in weight. Such differences can be observed across both cultures and time. For example, in Samoa, Fiji, Tonga, and other Pacific islands, it is not uncommon for males and females to weigh more than 300 pounds. In contrast, in Japan, very heavy people, such as well-fed Sumo wrestlers, clearly stand out in a crowd as violating societal norms (W. J. Lonner, personal communication, December 1993). In the United States, J. Fuchs and his colleagues (1990) noted the relative infrequency of obesity among the Amish and attributed this distinction to the healthful characteristics of the lifestyle in that culture. Norms and expectations regarding what is considered to be an ideal weight also can be observed across time by

viewing the historical collections in an art museum. In many masterworks by European artists, the bodies of nude females are quite ample by modern European or American standards. The contemporary trend toward ever more slender physiques has been documented by noting their increasing prominence in popular women's magazines in various countries (Silverstein, Peterson, & Perdue, 1986).

ANOREXIA NERVOSA.   Being overweight is a serious problem for many people, but the problem for others is being underweight. Some tend to be chronically underweight because they metabolize food very quickly and inefficiently or because they have a hormonal imbalance. A minority of underweight people suffer from **anorexia nervosa,** an eating disorder in which a person undereats to the point of starvation. People who suffer from anorexia perceive themselves to be fat and so put themselves on severe diets (Heilbrun & Witt, 1990). In fact, up to 30% of anorexics die from the damage the disorder causes (Szmukler & Russell, 1986). The vast majority (95%) of anorexics are females between ages 15 and 30 (Gilbert & DeBlassie, 1984). The high value that American society places on slimness helps explain why mainly young women suffer from this disorder. Interestingly, the incidence of anorexia has increased in other societies as well, such as Denmark and Japan (Nielsen, 1990; Suematsu, Ishikawa, Kuboki, & Ito, 1985).

No one knows what causes anorexia. Some evidence indicates that the roots of the disorder may be

Across cultures, there is wide variation of average body weight and size for men and for women. In addition, within a given culture, the body weight and size of individual members also show wide variation.

The photo on the right shows that this woman was fortunate to have recovered from the life-threatening disorder of anorexia nervosa. Astonishingly, like other anorexics, at the time the photo on the left was taken, this woman was starving herself to death because she perceived herself to be overweight and flabby.

psychological, caused by dysfunctional family relationships (Bruch, 1973); other evidence indicates that the roots may be physiological (Gwirtsman & Germer, 1981). The treatments of the disorder reflect the possible causes. Anorexics may undergo psychotherapy, drug treatment, and in severe cases, hospitalization to treat the psychological and physical problems (Martin, 1985).

More common than anorexia is *bulimia*, a disorder characterized by eating binges followed either by vomiting or by other means of purging (e.g., use of laxatives). This disorder, like anorexia, is far more common in women than in men. It also is difficult to treat. Bulimia, too, is primarily a disorder of adolescence and young adulthood.

Sex

Sexual motivation obviously differs in certain key respects from hunger motivation. For one thing, although very few people try to make themselves hungry or thirsty, most do seek sexual arousal (another blow to drive theory). People also tend to enjoy sexual arousal more than they enjoy hunger. Perhaps the

key difference relates to individual survival. People can survive without sexual gratification, but they cannot survive without food or water; you might therefore conclude that sexual motivation is in a category wholly different from that of hunger. In at least one sense, this conclusion would be incorrect. Sexual motivation is as important to the ultimate survival of the species as is hunger motivation. If no members of the species satisfy their sexual wants, the species will disappear just as certainly as it will from starvation.

The hypothalamus, which plays a role in hunger motivation, also plays an important role in sexual motivation. The role, however, is indirect. The hypothalamus stimulates the pituitary gland, which in turn releases hormones that influence the production of the sex hormones (see Chapter 3). There are two main kinds of sexual hormones: androgens and estrogens. Although both males and females have both androgens and estrogens, androgens predominate in the male, estrogens in the female. Without these hormones, sexual desire disappears—abruptly in many species, but only gradually among most humans (Money, Wiedeking, Walker, & Gain, 1976). Sexual desire serves an important evolutionary function, in that it is key to the survival of a species. The cycle of sexual response is shown in Figure 16-5.

SEXUAL SCRIPTS AND SOCIAL NORMS.   Human sexual activity always occurs in the company of cognitive processing. One way to describe the cognitive processes that accompany sexual response is in terms of **sexual scripts** (Gagnon, 1973; Simon & Gagnon, 1986), which are mental representations of how sequences of sexual events should be enacted. (The concept of scripts was introduced more broadly in Chapter 9.) For example, most of us—whether or not we have ever engaged in sexual intercourse—probably could describe some kind of sexual script, particularly if we have read racy novels, seen romantic TV shows, or watched sexy movies.

Most of us have many sexual scripts, which we may use, depending on the person we are with—or whether we are with another person at all. Although the desire for sexual consummation is largely a physiological need, scripts also reflect social influences. As noted in Chapter 15, violent pornography provides sexual scripts that are viewed by society as largely antisocial. Other sexual behavior that falls outside of societal norms are described in Chapter 18, on abnormal psychology.

Every society attempts to regulate the sexual behavior of its members. For example, all societies impose a taboo against *incest*—sexual contact between biologically related members of the immediate

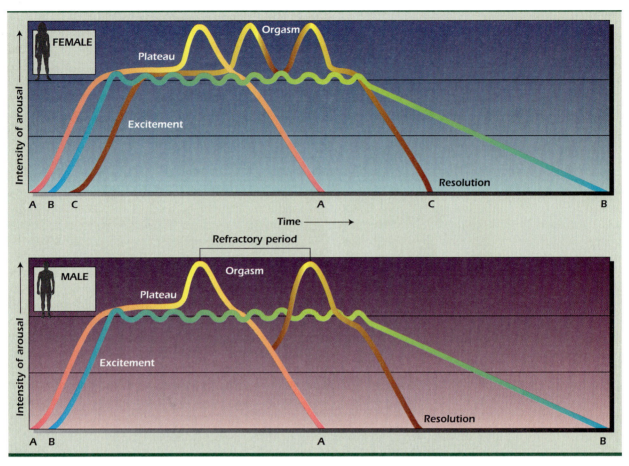

FIGURE 16-5
Human Sexual Response Cycle

As these graphs show, the sexual response cycle of males and females have fundamentally the same phases—excitement, plateau, orgasm, and resolution (see the pattern in Line A). However, women are more likely than men not to experience orgasm (see Line B), and women, but not men, are able to experience multiple orgasms prior to the resolution phase (see Line C). (After Masters & Johnson, 1966)

family. Similarly, most societies attempt to regulate sexual behavior through cultural norms regarding modesty, masturbation, premarital intercourse, marital intercourse, extramarital intercourse, and homosexuality. For example, norms of modesty determine the regions of the male and the female body that should be covered or exposed, decorated or unadorned. Although the specific regions that are to be covered or exposed differ widely from one culture to another, all cultures seem to impose some standards of modesty, at least on one of the sexes.

HOMOSEXUALITY.   In American culture, most sexual scripts are heterosexual, but homosexual scripts are also common. **Homosexuality** is a tendency to direct sexual desire toward another person of the same sex. In women, this tendency is referred to as **lesbianism.** Technically, however, the term *homosexual* is gender neutral, so it refers here to both men

and women. Although we speak of homosexuality and heterosexuality as though the two are discrete and mutually exclusive, perhaps it is best to consider them as aspects of a continuum. At one end are those who are exclusively homosexual; at the other end are those who are exclusively heterosexual; many others fall in between. People who identify themselves as directing their sexual desire to members of both sexes are referred to as **bisexual.** Most researchers in this field have found that about 10% of men and a slightly smaller proportion of women identify themselves as having predominantly homosexual orientations (e.g., see Fay, Turner, Klassen, & Gagnon, 1989; Rogers & Turner, 1991).

What causes homosexuality or bisexuality—or heterosexuality, for that matter? Various explanations exist, some more scientific than others (Biery, 1990). Of the several theories proposed (see Table 16-3), the greatest evidence seems to support a biological explanation. Until quite recently, many psychiatrists and psychologists believed that homosexuality was a form of mental illness. However, no inherent association between maladjustment or psychopathology and homosexuality has been found (Hooker, 1993).

Even if there is a biological basis for homosexuality, however, whether this predisposition is actually expressed in behavior may well depend on social learning and other environmental factors. We are unlikely to find a single cause of homosexual orientation. Rather, it is more likely that a combination of factors leads people one way or another. We view homosexuality and sexual orientation according to our culture's prescriptions and proscriptions (Wade & Cirese, 1991).

Although we may not fully understand all of the mechanisms that prompt us to satisfy our physiological needs, we do not question our motivation to engage in behaviors to satisfy those needs. In earlier chapters, we explored what motivates us to conform to our culture's norms. Can all of our behaviors be understood in terms of the motivation to meet our physiological needs and our needs to belong to a society? What else motivates human behavior?

Clinical Approaches

Clinical approaches to motivation consider physiological needs, but they are based on aspects of the personality and on case studies of patients and clients rather than on physiological data.

Murray's Theory of Needs

Henry Murray (1938) believed that needs are based in human physiology, and that they can be understood in terms of the workings of the brain. He saw needs as forming the core of a person's personality. He also believed that people show marked individual differences in the levels of these needs. Thus, his approach emphasized individual differences to a much greater extent than did many others. Murray also believed

TABLE 16-3
Reasons Underlying Homosexual Versus Heterosexual Orientation
Over the years, psychologists have posited various reasons for sexual orientation. Most recently, biological reasons seem to be the most plausible, but additional research in this area is sorely needed.

Reason	Description	Critique
Personal choice	People simply choose their sexual orientations.	Whatever attracts one person to another rarely is a matter solely of conscious choice.
Arrested development	Homosexuals become fixated in a homosexual phase of psychosexual development.	The assumption is that if homosexuals could escape fixation in this stage, they would progress to the subsequent stage of heterosexuality. This implies that all heterosexuals pass through a homosexual phase. There is no empirical evidence to support this point of view.
Social-learning theory	Homosexuals were rewarded for homosexual leanings and punished for heterosexual ones.	Mainstream U.S. society (among others) gives few rewards for a homosexual orientation, and few children are likely to be exposed to overtly homosexual role models. Of those who are, about the same proportion become heterosexual or homosexual as do in the mainstream population. Most children are taught, directly or indirectly, that homosexuality is undesirable or even wrong.
Weak father, strong mother	Homosexuals had weak fathers or overly strong mothers.	Not well supported by data. There are far too many exceptions to this generalization, and this view is not much accepted today.
Biological	Sexual orientation is, in part, a result of biological processes.	There is some support for this view. A small region of the hypothalamus may be less than half the size in homosexual men as in heterosexual men (LeVay, 1991). If one of a pair of genetically identical male twins is homosexually oriented, then the other may be almost three times more likely to have the same orientation as when the twins are not identical (Bailey & Pillard, 1991).

that the environment creates forces that people must respond to in order to adapt. How people cope in the world can be understood largely in terms of the interaction between their internal needs and the various pressures of the environment.

Some of the 20 needs that Murray postulated have prompted a great deal of research—a measure of his importance in the field. For example, much research has been done on Murray's constructs of the need for affiliation and the need for power. People who rank high in the need for affiliation like to form close connections with other people and to be members of groups. They avoid arguments (Exline, 1962) as well as competitive games (Terhune, 1968). They also tend to become anxious when they feel they are being evaluated (Byrne, 1961).

People who rank high in the need for power seek to control others. They try to make the world conform to their own image of what it should be. In groups, they want to be recognized (Winter, 1973). They are also concerned with their visibility among the general public (McClelland & Teague, 1975). People ranking high in the need for power tend to be aggressive and are more likely to seek out occupations in which they can influence others (Winter & Stewart, 1978).

Murray also proposed that each of us has a need for achievement. This need has been extensively investigated by many other researchers, as we see next.

McClelland's Need for Achievement

David McClelland and his colleagues have been particularly interested in the need for achievement (McClelland, 1961; McClelland, Atkinson, Clark, & Lowell, 1953; McClelland & Winter, 1969). According to McClelland (1985), people who rank high in the need for achievement, such as successful entrepreneurs, seek out moderately challenging tasks, persist at them, and are especially likely to pursue success in their occupations. Why would these people seek out tasks that are only moderately challenging? These are the tasks in which they are likely both to succeed and to extend themselves. They do not waste time on tasks so challenging that they have little probability of accomplishing them, nor do they waste time on tasks so easy that they pose no challenge at all.

Research has shown that perception of reality, rather than reality per se, is the more powerful predictor of how people, and especially children, react to demands for achievement (Phillips, 1984). Unfortunately, girls often perceive their competence to be lower than do boys, particularly as they grow older.

The result can be lesser expectations for achievement on the part of girls (Phillips & Zimmerman, 1990). The effect appears to begin to emerge as early as kindergarten (Frey & Ruble, 1987).

The achievement motive, which involves competition with an internalized standard of excellence, is present in every culture and so has been the focus of dozens of cross-cultural studies (Maehr & Nicholls, 1980; Markus & Kitayama, 1991). Because increases in the achievement motive may be linked to increases in productivity, several projects in various cultures have tried to increase levels of this motive among workers and managers. In one such project, investigators assessed the effectiveness of the attempts by Indian business owners to encourage their employees to emulate the achievement motive shown by many Western businessmen and women. Toward this end, the Indian employees were subjected to an intense series of seminars designed to get them to think, talk, and act like achievement-oriented business people. The project was modestly successful (McClelland & Winter, 1969).

One of numerous studies of the achievement motive in China found that Chinese parents place great emphasis on achievement, but their focus is different from that of American parents (Ho, 1986). Whereas American children are motivated to achieve for the purpose of being independent, Chinese children are motivated to please the family and the community.

Maslow's Need Hierarchy

The needs for affiliation, power, and achievement each fit well into the hierarchical theory of motivation proposed by Abraham Maslow (1943, 1954, 1970). According to Maslow, our needs form a hierarchy (see Figure 16-6). Once we have satisfied needs at lower levels, we seek satisfaction of needs at higher levels of the hierarchy.

Maslow's first level addresses our basic *physiological* needs, such as food, water, and oxygen. If we do not have these, our lives are theatened immediately. (We have seen the mechanisms underlying how we satisfy these needs.) Our affluent society has removed most of us from the immediate threat of starvation, but we can see how many homeless people struggle daily to meet this most basic need. The second level addresses the need for *safety and security*, for shelter and protection. The devastation of the 1994 San Fernando Valley earthquake showed us vividly how fundamental a need shelter is. The third level is the need to *belong*, to feel that other people love and care about us and to be part of a meaningful group. We have

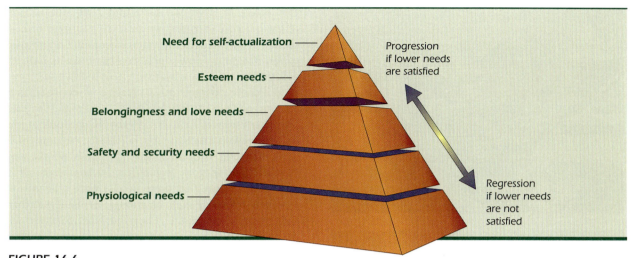

FIGURE 16-6
Maslow's Hierarchy of Needs
According to Abraham Maslow, we must satisfy our more basic needs before we strive to meet the higher level needs.

only to look at the bond between children and their parents to see how important this need is. The fourth level is the need for *self-esteem*, to feel worthwhile. Each of us knows the deep feeling of satisfaction and pride when we complete a challenging task. The highest level is the need for *self-actualization*, to fulfill our own potential. Olympians and U.S. Supreme Court justices are two different kinds of people who have achieved self-actualization, but this level is not limited to the handful of people who have reached the top of their fields. We in developed nations have the luxury of being able to strive for the higher levels in this hierarchy. Those who are not so lucky, in underdeveloped or developing nations, must focus on meeting their fundamental needs. (See Table 16-4 for a summary of clinical approaches to motivation.)

Cognitive Approaches

Cognitive theorists also have closely studied what motivates people, especially the cognitive processes underlying why people behave as they do. In particular, cognitive psychologists have wondered: What else might motivate us, beyond satisfying our physiological needs and avoiding pain? What makes us feel good? What do we find pleasurable? What kinds of stimuli and situations do we seek? Why do people become interested in and major in particular fields of study?

Intrinsic and Extrinsic Motivators

Psychologists frequently describe motivation as being either intrinsic or extrinsic. **Intrinsic motivators**

TABLE 16-4
Clinical Approaches to Motivation
Clinical psychologists have put forth three theories of motivation: that needs are the basis of our personalities, that we need to achieve, and that needs can be categorized in five different levels.

Theory of Needs (Murray)	Needs form the core of our personalities. Among many other needs, we seek affiliation, power, and achievement.
Need for Achievement (McClelland)	People who have an intense need to achieve seek out moderately difficult tasks because they are most likely to succeed at those tasks while still being challenged by them. The need to achieve motivates us to be productive. (McClelland studied needs for power and affiliation as well.)
Hierarchy of Needs (Maslow)	We have five levels of needs (physiological, safety, belonging, self-esteem, self-actualization). Each level builds on the foundation of the levels below it, so we need to fulfill the needs of one level before we can proceed to the next level.

that attest to what we have and have not accomplished. These extrinsic rewards are examples of how society acknowledges the value of completing an education program. How much weight do we as individuals give to extrinsic rewards?

People do their most creative work when they are intrinsically motivated (Amabile, 1983, 1985; see also Sternberg & Lubart, 1991b). If we look at the most creative writers, artists, scientists, or workers in any other field, they are almost invariably people who have done their work largely for the enjoyment of it. This is not to say that these people were oblivious to extrinsic rewards, such as money or fame. Rather, they were task-focused. They did what they did for the love of their work, with the money, fame, or other extrinsic rewards a pleasant by-product.

Extrinsic motivators can undermine intrinsic motivation. Janet Spence and Robert Helmreich (1983) have studied the motivational patterns and achievements of thousands of college students, scientists, pilots, business people, and athletes. They concluded that intrinsic motivation produces high achievement, and that extrinsic motivation often does

Immediately following an earthquake, these Los Angelenos were struggling to meet their basic needs for physiological survival, as well as for safety and security. The man chopping wood appears to be meeting not only his survival needs for heating his home, but also his needs for esteem.

Whereas this sculptor appears to be intrinsically motivated to work, this machinist appears not to be deriving intrinsic rewards from his job and is probably extrinsically motivated to work.

come from within ourselves: We do something because we enjoy doing it. **Extrinsic motivators** come from outside of us: We do something because someone rewards us or threatens us. We can act on the basis of intrinsic reasons, extrinsic reasons, or combinations of the two. For example, we might study hard in a given subject because we are really excited about the material and want to learn it (intrinsic motivation), or we might study hard because we want to get an A in the course (extrinsic motivation). We might strive to be an excellent athlete or musician because we really love a particular sport or playing a particular instrument, or because we delight in the praise and possibly the monetary rewards of a job well done. In either case, we might be motivated by both sets of factors.

Society has created many extrinsic rewards to ensure that people accomplish what is in society's interests. Much of our system of education is based on grades, diplomas, and various other pieces of paper not. Spence and Helmreich identified and assessed three facets of intrinsic motivation: people's quest for mastery, their drive to work, and their competitiveness. They found that, despite similar abilities, people oriented toward mastery and hard work typically achieve more. However, those who were *most* competitive, thereby showing a more extrinsic orientation, often achieve *less*. People driven by a desire for mastery and work achieved more if they were not also highly competitive.

Fortunately, not all extrinsic rewards have a negative effect. Three critical factors seem to determine whether an extrinsic motivator will undermine intrinsic motivation. The first factor is *expectancy*. The extrinsic reward will undermine intrinsic motivation only if the individual expects to receive the award contingent on performing the tasks. The second factor is the *relevance* of the reward. The reward must be something important to the individual. If you were told that you would receive a spool of thread as a reward for performing a task, and a spool of thread is not of any interest to you, yet you engage in the task anyway, the nominal reward will probably not undermine your intrinsic motivation. Indeed, you may well forget about it (Ross, 1975). Finally, whether the reward is *tangible* (e.g., a certificate, a prize, money, candy, a grade) is a factor in motivation. Whereas tangible rewards tend to undermine intrinsic motivation, intangible rewards—such as praise or a smile—seem not to undermine it (Deci, 1971, 1972; Swann & Pittman, 1977).

One of the best ways to remain motivated is to adapt what Martin Seligman (1991) refers to as an *optimistic explanatory style*. People with such a style tend to attribute their successes to their own abilities and their failures to the environment. They motivate themselves by telling themselves that they have the ability to overcome the obstacles in their environment. People with a *pessimistic explanatory style*, in contrast, attribute their successes to the environment but their failures to their own lack of ability. They have greater difficulty motivating themselves because they believe that as they lack the ability to succeed, it is scarcely worth trying.

> What kinds of activities and projects are you intrinsically motivated to work on, regardless of extrinsic motivation? How would various extrinsic motivators affect your enjoyment of these projects?

Curiosity, Challenge, and Control

What makes people curious about some things and not others? We tend to be curious about things that are moderately novel to us and moderately complex, relative to our existing understanding (Berlyne, 1960; Heyduk & Bahrick, 1977). This makes sense. If something is totally familiar to us, we ignore it; we have nothing to learn from it. Similarly, if something is wholly novel, we have no basis for understanding it. However, if we encounter something that is novel but within our realm of understanding, it piques our interest; we become curious and explore it.

Even in everyday activities, we seek some degree of intrinsic motivation. We and our fellow primates seek to be active, to observe and explore our surroundings, to manipulate aspects of and objects in our environments, and to gain mastery over our environments (White, 1959).

We also seek to see ourselves as making things happen, as having control of ourselves and our environments (deCharms, 1968). Thus, we actively seek self-determination, rather than determination by outside forces. We are often unhappy when we feel controlled, whether it is by another person or even by a substance (as in an addiction). (See also the discussion of *reactance* in Chapter 15.) We are generally unhappy when we feel like pawns—that our futures are predetermined, or that others are controlling our actions. We are motivated to be—and to feel—in charge of our own destiny.

Edward Deci and his colleagues (Deci, Vallerand, Pelletier, & Ryan, 1991) have formulated a theory of **self-determination,** which posits that humans need to feel competent, related, and autonomous. The needs for competence and autonomy are similar to those posited by Robert White and by Richard deCharms, respectively. The need for

Primates of all species appear to show curiosity, exploring their surroundings for the sheer joy of doing so. For example, monkeys will learn to perform tasks such as opening latches just to have something to do (Harlow, Harlow, & Meyer, 1950).

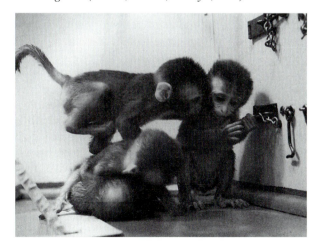

relatedness is similar to Murray's need for affiliation and Maslow's need for belongingness and love. According to Deci, we are all powerfully motivated to meet these three innate needs.

How does Deci's theory of self-determination explain extrinsic versus intrinsic motivation? Intrinsically motivated activities satisfy both our need for competence and our need for autonomy. In contrast, many extrinsically motivated activities can undermine our sense of autonomy because we attribute the control of our behavior to sources outside ourselves, rather than to internal ones.

Self-Efficacy Theory

How does our competence affect the likelihood that we will attain a particular goal? **Self-efficacy theory** emphasizes that our ability to attain a particular goal is based on our *belief* of whether or not we can achieve that goal (Bandura, 1977a, 1986). Our expectations of self-efficacy can derive from a number of different sources: direct experience, our interpretation of the experience of others, what people tell us that we are able to do, and our assessment of our own emotional or motivational state. The important thing is if we have a higher degree of self-efficacy, we are more likely to attain the outcomes we desire. Our level of self-efficacy can lead to self-fulfilling prophecies (see Chapter 14). When we believe we are able to do something, we are more likely to put in the effort and resources to do it, and therefore to achieve the outcome. One success leads to another, and we see ourselves as continually successful in maintaining the outcomes we desire. In contrast, if we have a low sense of self-efficacy, we may believe that we are unable to succeed and, as a result, will hardly even try. (Recall the discussion of learned helplessness in Chapter 7). The result, of course, is failure, which leads to the expectation of future failure, which then becomes the basis for more failure. One way to enhance our self-efficacy in reaching our goals is simply to set for ourselves a set of realistic, highly specific goals, and then to devise plans for meeting those goals.

Goals and Plans

From the cognitive perspective, those who persist in an activity are often pursuing a self-selected goal, whereas those who quit or drop out seldom have in mind any clear, desired goals for the activity. Years ago, Edward Tolman (1932, 1959) recognized that goals can be enormously motivating. The person who sets increasing exercise goals—for example, running one-half mile a day and working her way up to five miles a day—is more likely to motivate herself to continue to jog than the person who has no particular goals.

Why are goals so effective as motivators of performance? Here are four reasons (Locke & Latham, 1985):

1. Goals help to focus our attention. We pay more attention to tasks if we have clearly defined goals in executing them.
2. Goals help us to mobilize our resources. They give us a sense of what we need to do to get where we want to be.
3. Goals facilitate persistence. For example, if Jamie knows that she wants to jog five miles per day, then having this goal in mind constantly reminds her of where she is versus where she wants to be.
4. Having goals helps us develop a means for reaching the goals. If we find that a first plan is not working, we can always create a second or third plan to help us achieve our ends.

Going hand in hand with goals are *plans*, strategies for getting to where we want to go from where we are (Miller, Galanter, & Pribram, 1960; Newell & Simon, 1972). Goals can help motivate our behavior only if they are accompanied by one or more plans for reaching the goals. For example, if your goal is to become chief executive of the company you work in, you must formulate some kind of plan that will get you there. In effect, you do a means-ends analysis; you set a series of subgoals and constantly calculate the difference between where you are and where you want to go. You then take action to reach each of the subgoals in the broader scheme of reaching the final goal (see Chapter 10).

Throughout our lives, we frequently change our goals and our plans, trading off what we really want for what we believe we can realistically get. Having unrealistically high goals—such as overall perfection, or even perfection in a particular area of endeavor—can lead to self-defeat. Because the goal is unrealistic, we never move on to other plans—and perhaps to other goals. (See Table 16-5 for a summary of cognitive theories.)

Devise a plan for increasing the motivation of an underachieving student to work hard in school—to master academic tasks, study information, do homework, and so on. Indicate which of the various theories of motivation is (or are) guiding your plan.

TABLE 16-5
Cognitive Approaches to Motivation
Cognitive psychologists have proposed four different theories of motivation: that we respond to internal and external motivators, that we are motivated by curiosity and control, that we are motivated by our belief in ourselves, and that we are motivated by goals.

Intrinsic and extrinsic motivators	Our interests motivate us intrinsically; rewards or threats of punishment motivate us extrinsically. Usually our behaviors are the result of a combination of intrinsic and extrinsic motivations, although we are most creative when we are mainly motivated intrinsically.
Curiosity, challenge, and control	We are most curious about things that are moderately new and complex because they challenge us without boring or confusing us. We can become totally absorbed in a task (Maslow). We always seek to understand and control our environments, to be competent (White, deCharms), and a part of a group (Deci).
Self-Efficacy Theory (Bandura)	Our beliefs about whether we can attain a goal greatly influence our ability actually to attain it.
Goals and plans	Goals are highly motivating. To meet our goals, we must plan the route and the steps to attain those goals.

SUMMARY OF MOTIVATION

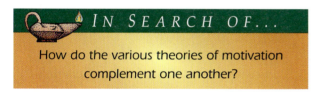

IN SEARCH OF...

How do the various theories of motivation complement one another?

As you have read about theories of motivation, you may have found something attractive in several of them. Many of these theories are complementary rather than competing. As we have seen, motivation has physiological, personality, and cognitive aspects, and these aspects interact. The physiology of the brain and the central nervous system affects the cognitions and personality attributes we have, just as these cognitions and personality attributes may in turn affect our physiology. Further research may reveal how to integrate the various existing models to create a single theory that fully, yet parsimoniously, characterizes all of our human motivational systems.

THE NATURE OF EMOTION

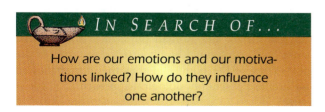

IN SEARCH OF...

How are our emotions and our motivations linked? How do they influence one another?

Having considered the nature of motivation, we now turn to emotion. An **emotion** is a feeling, a tendency to respond experientially as well as physiologically and behaviorally to certain internal and external variables (Carlson & Hatfield, 1992).

Emotions can be either preprogrammed (genetic) or learned, and they can be manifested in various ways. Furthermore, they can be caused either by stimuli impinging on us from the outside, or by things that happen within our body. Emotion and motivation are very closely linked, and often it is difficult to distinguish them. Table 16-6 shows some of the differences between motivation and emotion.

Emotional Development in an Evolutionary Perspective

We saw in Chapter 13 how emotions develop within individuals, but why have emotions developed within the species as a whole? Emotions have both a *physiological aspect*, in which we physically react in distinctive ways in each emotion, and a *cognitive aspect*, in which we interpret how we feel. Both aspects are essential to our survival as a species. (We discuss these and other aspects in the next section.) From an evolutionary perspective, there are good reasons for emotions (Plutchik, 1983). The emotions that help foster reproduction quite obviously enhance our species' survival. As we gain increasing control over our reproductivity, our emotions may play an increasingly important role; momentary lust alone does not determine when or with whom we have children. In

TABLE 16-6
Some Differences Between Motivation and Emotion
Although motivation and emotion are similar in many ways, they also differ in several important ways.

Motives	Emotions
Stimulus generally unobserved	Stimulus often apparent
Often cyclical (e.g., recurring hunger)	Not normally cyclical
Energize, direct, and sustain activity	May interfere with everyday activity
Responses are goal-directed	Responses are "inner-directed"
Experienced as "motives"	Experienced as "feelings"
Active	Passive

recent decades, much more complex and long-lasting emotions now govern our procreative choices.

How do other emotions—such as fear and anger (which we certainly enjoy a lot less than love or lust)—enhance our survival as individuals or as a species? For one thing, these emotions prepare us to behave in particular ways in particular situations. Anger prepares us to fight an aggressor whom we have a pretty good chance of defeating, and fear prepares us to flee from an aggressor who might conquer us. Survival of a species as a whole depends on its members knowing when to fight a beatable foe and when to flee from an unbeatable enemy. Judicious reliance on emotional reactions to danger may mean the difference between life and death. (Chapter 20 describes more fully our physiological reactions in stressful situations in which we must fight or take flight.)

Other emotions have evolutionary value also. Consider, too, the love parents feel for their children. Obviously, this love brings happiness to both parents and children. From the perspective of evolutionary survival, however, the love that bonds parents and children together guarantees that the parent will ensure the child's safety, health, and survival while the child remains dependent on the parent.

Why would the more basic needs in Maslow's hierarchical theory of motivation serve a more important evolutionary function than the higher order needs?

APPROACHES TO UNDERSTANDING EMOTIONS

IN SEARCH OF...

How would you design an experiment to study emotions? What approach or combination of approaches would you use in designing your experiment?

Just as the approaches to and suggested explanations of motivation are diverse, so, too, are the approaches to understanding human emotions. As you read about psychophysiological, cognitive, structural, and cross-cultural approaches in this chapter, note that many of these aspects are complementary rather than contradictory. Each approach offers insight into how and why we feel emotions as we do.

Psychophysiological Approaches

Today, psychophysiological studies involve cutting-edge technologies, state-of-the-art methodologies, and dynamic revolutions in theoretical understandings. Oddly, psychophysiological approaches to understanding emotions are also the most ancient ones. Ancient Greek and Roman physicians believed that emotional states could be understood in terms of the physiology of the body, and thus they foreshadowed the modern psychophysiological approach.

The James-Lange Theory: Bodily Change and Behavior as the Impetus to Emotion

The earliest modern theory of emotion was proposed by William James (1890a). Because a Danish physiologist, Carl Lange, had a similar theory, the point of view that they jointly proposed is often called the James-Lange theory of emotion. The James-Lange theory turns common notions about emotion on their heads. The commonsense view of emotion is that first we perceive some event in the environment, and that event evokes some kind of emotion within us. As a result of that emotion, psychophysiological events occur—for example, sadness might lead to crying, or anger might lead to clenching our fists. James and Lange proposed that exactly the reverse is true (Lange & James, 1922). Of course, we first sense the events in the environment. Next, however, according to James and Lange, we experience bodily changes in reaction to the events, and those psychophysiological changes lead to the emotion, rather than the other way around. In the following passage, Gustave Flaubert's Madame Bovary appears to be experiencing the sequence of events described by James and Lange:

She was in a stupor, conscious of her own existence only from the throbbing of her arteries, which she heard as deafening music filling the whole countryside. . . . She suddenly felt afraid and managed to regain control of herself, although her thoughts were still in disorder, for she no longer remembered the cause of her horrible state.

—*Gustave Flaubert*, Madame Bovary

Cannon's Theory: The Brain as the Impetus to Emotion

Ironically, James's son-in-law, Walter Cannon (1929), became the foremost critic of the James-Lange theory. Cannon argued that the James-Lange theory could not be right. First, different emotions are associated with identical psychophysiological states within the body. Could the same psychophysiological states cause different emotions? Second, Cannon argued, the organs of the body are not very sensitive. They could never provide the subtle differentiating information that people need in order to experience one emotion as opposed to another. Moreover, many of the organs of the body usually react slowly, whereas emotions are often felt immediately after a stimulus is

perceived. Third, if researchers produce the changes in the body associated with a given set of emotions in the absence of the normal provoking stimuli, people do not feel the emotion that corresponds to those physical reactions. For example, exposing people to onions and making them cry does not make them feel sad. Cannon proposed instead that the brain, in particular the thalamus, controls emotional behavior, and not bodily reactions (such as crying or clenching your fist). Philip Bard (1934) later elaborated on this view, and so it is sometimes called the Cannon-Bard theory of emotion.

There is merit to both positions. Cannon was correct in his recognition of the importance of the brain in the experiencing of emotion. Several parts of the limbic system, such as the hypothalamus and the amygdala, have been closely linked with emotional experience (see Chapter 3). James and Lange were also correct, however, in asserting that people feel emotions in part by observing changes in the functioning of their bodies. (See Figure 16-7 for a comparison of these theories.)

Modern Psychophysiological Approaches

Joseph LeDoux (1986; LeDoux, Romanski, & Xagoraris, 1989) has suggested that arousal of the autonomic nervous system (ANS) (see Chapter 3) may not be all-or-none, as it is typically thought to be. Rather, there may be multiple patterns of ANS arousal, and different emotions may correspond to different patterns of ANS activity. Other investigators (Cacioppo & Petty, 1983; Derryberry & Tucker, 1992; Ekman, Levenson, & Friesen, 1983) have also suggested that different emotions may be characterized by different patterns of physiological response.

In contrast, others (Henry & Stephens, 1977) have emphasized the role of the *endocrine system* in emotion. They have argued that different emotions can be linked to different relative concentrations of hormones. For example, anger seems to be associated with increased levels of norepinephrine (noradrenaline), fear with increased levels of epinephrine (adrenaline), and depression with increases in adrenocorticotropic hormone (ACTH) (see Chapter 3). Elation, in contrast, is marked by decreases in ACTH and other hormones. What is exciting about this approach is its linking of moods and emotions with concentrations of hormones. Aggression is associated with increased levels of testosterone (Floody, 1983). The approach does not establish causality, however. Whether changes in hormone concentrations cause the emotion, or the emotions cause the changes in

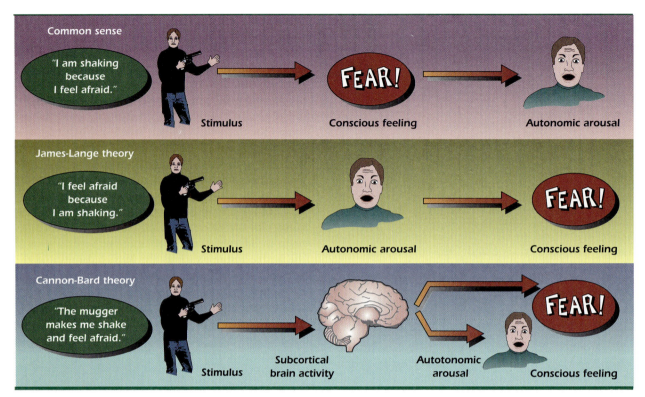

FIGURE 16-7
Psychophysiological Theories of Emotion
Various theories of emotion account for the physiological, affective, and cognitive components of emotions in different ways. Each theory accounts for some, but not all, of the phenomena of emotions.

hormone concentrations, or whether—most likely—both are dependent on other things, has yet to be resolved.

Cognitive Approaches

The Schachter-Singer Theory

In response to an experiment showing that how we label arousal seems to determine the emotions we experience, Stanley Schachter and Jerome Singer (1962) developed a **two-component theory of emotion.** The first component is *physiological arousal*, which can be caused by any number of things, such as drugs or situational stimuli (e.g., a sudden surprise). The emotion we feel, according to Schachter and Singer, depends on the second component—how we *label* that physiological arousal. Thus, people who are aroused and who believe that the appropriate emotion is happiness will feel happy; people who are aroused and who believe that the appropriate emotion is anger will feel anger. All that distinguishes the various emotions is how we label our arousal. The arousal is the same in every case.

As a result of follow-up research, we now know that Schachter and Singer were not completely correct (see, e.g., Leventhal & Tomarken, 1986; Marshall & Zimbardo, 1979). For example, physiological differences exist in the kinds of arousal experienced for different emotions. Still, the classic work of Schachter and Singer instigated a great deal of theory and research. Like most seminal work, it was flawed, but its value lies not in its unequivocal interpretation (experiments almost never lend themselves to unequivocal interpretation in any case) but in the subsequent work it generated.

Lazarus's and Zajonc's Temporal-Sequence Theories

When addressing the question of whether cognitions precede emotions or are simultaneous with them, Magda Arnold (1960, 1970) proposed that it is in part our thinking about a situation that leads us to feel emotions, and her point of view has been championed and elaborated upon by Richard Lazarus (1977, 1984; Lazarus, Kanner, & Folkman, 1980). According to Lazarus, we appraise a situation in stages. First, in

Searchers . . .   *ROBERT ZAJONC*

Robert Zajonc is Professor of Psychology at Stanford University.

Q: *How did you become interested in psychology?*

A: My high school education was in Poland. We were to read anything in English that we could find, and I came across Sigmund Freud's *Psychopathology of Everyday Life*. That started my interest. I am more of a general psychologist than anything else.

Q: *What makes a psychologist really great?*

A: They all must have some patience, but the great ones also have some luck, to stumble on something which is important at the right time.

Q: *How do you get your ideas for research?*

A: I draw my ideas from reading. When I stumble on something which represents a conflict between theories and empirical facts, that prompts me to look into it. If the conflict is sufficiently strong, then I may start working on it. If I can think of a possible solution to the problem and see myself getting to the other end, I'll start working on it. If I don't know how to go about working on the problem, even though it's interesting, I will not work on it.

Q: *What obstacles have you experienced in your work?*

A: There are obstacles all the time. Not knowing how to reduce the complexity of something, or not knowing which are the more significant factors or features of a problem, or how to put some idea into the laboratory, because ideas usually are general, and theories are general. You just sit and think about it, come up with something. But it gets easier as you gain experience.

Q: *What do you want students to learn from you?*

A: To have fun together, hack around ideas. They can argue with me and I can argue with them. Also, they have to have the courage to take risks, to be proven wrong. Otherwise, they won't do anything interesting.

Q: *What advice would you give to someone starting in the field of psychology?*

A: I think they should know the classics and not just psychology. They should have a general view of science and philosophy.

Q: *What did you learn from your mentors?*

A: The most important thing is that writing must be clear. When readers say that they cannot understand something, then you have not written it clearly.

Q: *What have you learned from your students?*

A: I've learned as much from my students as from my colleagues and the literature. They are a constant source of ideas and refinement.

Q: *Apart from your life as an academic, how have you found psychology to be important to you?*

A: My life and psychology are separate. My work is such that it would not really be very useful in everyday life.

Q: *How do you keep yourself academically challenged?*

A: The students keep me challenged. I keep reading.

Q: *What do you further hope to achieve?*

A: Well, I am working on the problem of consciousness, on a theory that conceptualizes cognition as a form of communication.

---

primary appraisal, we determine the potential consequences of what is about to happen. For example, is the scruffy, dirty figure approaching us about to ask us for money, rob us, or start up a conversation? Second, we have to engage in *secondary appraisal*, meaning that we have to decide what to do. Given our decision about the character approaching us, how should we act? Later we may need to *re-appraise* the situation, as events develop. According to Lazarus, each of our appraisals of a situation determines what emotion or emotions we feel. Thus, cognition precedes emotion.

In contrast, Robert Zajonc (1980, 1984; Zajonc, Pietromonaco, & Bargh, 1982) has argued that cognition and emotion are basically separate. He believes that emotion is basic and does not require prior cognition. In fact, he argues, as do others, that emotions

preceded thinking in evolutionary history, and so it does not make sense that cognitions have to precede emotions. Lower animals know to fear predators or to attack potential food without going through complex thought processes. As humans, we often know how we feel long before we know what we think about a situation.

Some people believe that the debate over the sequencing of cognitive appraisal, emotional experience, and physiological arousal has become something of a dead issue. We may be best served by thinking of the sequencing as a continuous loop of emotional feedback of the type shown in Figure 16-8 (Candland, 1977). Although cognitive theories of emotion differ from one another in their details and, in some cases, in their substance, all of them agree that emotion and cognition are mutually dependent. The extent of this interdependence has been shown by research on **state-dependent memory,** which suggests that if you learn something while experiencing a particular emotion, you are more likely later to be able to remember it when you are in the same emotional state (Bower, 1981; see Chapter 8). For example, if you learn a word when in an upbeat mood, then you probably recall it more easily when you are again happy than when in a less joyful mood.

> What do you think about the sequence of cognitive, emotional, and physiological responses to an arousing situation? Cite the theorist whose views most closely reflect your own opinions, and then describe how the sequence might operate in an arousing situation in which you have recently found yourself.

Cross-Cultural Approaches

We have seen how the roles of the brain, the endocrine system, and our cognitions influence emo-

tion. However, let us take a step back and explore emotions from a broader perspective. Batja Mesquita and Nico Frijda (1992) have conducted an extensive review of the anthropological literature and have developed a theoretical framework for understanding emotion, based in part on theories by others (such as Lazarus). In their view, when we seek to understand emotions, we must consider the following components: antecedent events, event coding, appraisal, physiological response pattern, action readiness, emotional behavior, and regulation (described in Table 16-7).

> Review the components of emotions described in Table 16-7. Describe an emotion-arousing event you have experienced. Note the way in which each of the components of emotions applies to your experience.

An alternative cross-cultural approach has been suggested by James Russell (1991). Russell, too, conducted an extensive review of ethnographic literature,

FIGURE 16-8
Emotional Feedback Loop
Our physiological reactions and our cognitive appraisals constantly and reciprocally interact with our perceived emotional experiences. Think about a recent emotionally charged experience of yours. How did your physiological reactions and your cognitive appraisals interact during the experience?

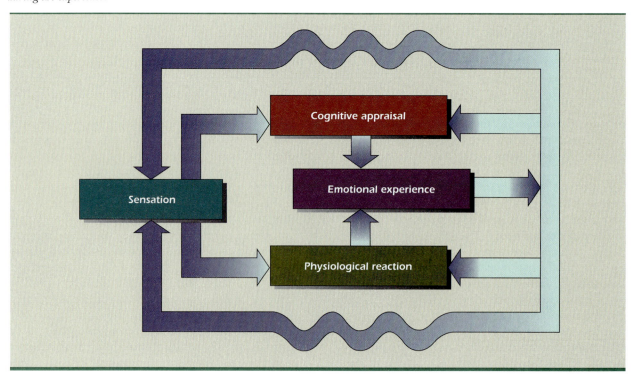

TABLE 16-7
Components of Emotions
Batja Mesquita and Nico Frijda have developed a theoretical framework for understanding the various components of emotions, as they may be viewed across cultures. What are some of the cultural differences you might expect to observe for each of these components? (After Mesquita & Frijda, 1992)

Component	Description	Example
Antecedent events	What was happening just before you experienced an emotion?	Just prior to experiencing the emotion of fear, you may have heard that the final examination in your psychology class is cumulative, is timed (with too little time to complete all the questions), and is being harshly graded.
Event coding	How do you interpret and categorize the event in terms of your cultural understandings regarding other events that fall into this same event category?	If someone of your same sex seems to be overly complimentary of your beloved, the way in which you encode that event depends on your cultural context.
Appraisal	How do you evaluate the coded event in terms of whether the event is potentially or actually harmful, who might be blamed for causing the event, and whether the event is considered to have violated any cultural mores or even moral standards?	As a college student, you probably consider the news of a very tough final to be a fear-inducing event, which may threaten your self-esteem and possibly even your status in college. However, if you were a postgraduate, only auditing this class as a matter of personal interest, you would not care about the final examination, so you would not code the identical antecedent event in the same way most other students would do so.
Physiological reaction pattern	What physiological changes do you feel in response to the appraised and coded event?	When you feel afraid, you may experience stomach sensations, coldness in your extremities, and perhaps sweating and cardiorespiratory changes.
Action readiness	What actions do you feel ready to take in response to particular emotions?	When someone bumps into you or shoves you in an attempt to get through a crowded doorway, you might feel ready to act aggressively toward the person.
Emotional behavior	What actions do you actually take in response to particular emotions?	When someone angers you, your facial expression probably shows anger, your voice gets louder and more emphatic, and your bodily expressions and gestures become more forceful. Depending on how you interpret the situation and what you consider to be appropriate behavior, you may act in other ways to express your anger.
Regulation	How do you inhibit or exaggerate your recognition and expressions of emotions?	When you hear that the final examination is going to be really tough, you may feel like seeking escape, but you probably will actually go through with taking the test.

but from a slightly different view. He studied the way people categorize emotions, in terms of (a) the words they choose to use to describe their emotions, (b) the words they assign to given facial expressions of emotions, and (c) the dimensions (pairs of characteristics, such as aroused/unaroused, positive/negative, dominant/submissive) people use in judging the categories for emotions.

As a result of his study, Russell drew two conclusions. *First*, not all people sort their emotions according to the basic categories often used by English speakers and other speakers of Indo-European languages. That is, not all cultures recognize the same basic emotions; other cultures may include additional emotions. *Second*, despite these cross-cultural differences, many similarities exist across cultures in the emotions people identify, particularly in regard to emotions associated with particular facial expressions (e.g., Ekman, 1971, 1993; Ekman & Oster, 1979) and vocal expressions (e.g., Bezooijen, Otto, & Heenan, 1983). Although the range of expression for emotions and the boundaries between various emotions may differ, there appears to be a great deal of overlap in the ways distinctive cultures describe human emotions. (See also the discussion on facial expressions, page 584.)

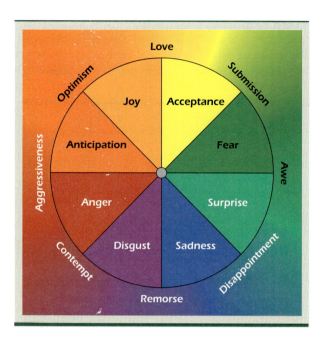

FIGURE 16-9
Plutchik's Emotion Wheel
Robert Plutchik posits eight basic emotions, which occur in four pairs that are opposite each other in the circle. Emotions that are adjacent to one another combine to create a composite emotion (e.g., joy combined with acceptance yields love). (After Plutchik, 1980)

SOME MAJOR EMOTIONS AND THEIR CHARACTERISTICS

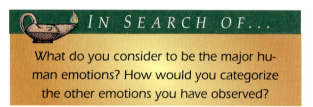

IN SEARCH OF...

What do you consider to be the major human emotions? How would you categorize the other emotions you have observed?

Happiness, fear, anger, sadness, and disgust are the emotions regarded as being fundamental to all humans. To these emotions, some would add surprise (which is much less commonly recognized across cultures), guilt (private sense of culpability), and shame (public humiliation). (See, for example, Figure 16-9.) We now consider the five most widely recognized emotions.

Add one other basic emotion to the basic five cited here. How would you design an experiment to determine the cross-cultural nature and expression of this emotion?

Happiness or Joy

Happiness (joy) is usually considered a fundamental emotion. When people describe what they experience when they feel *happy*, they say that they feel a warm inner glow, or feel like smiling, or feel a sense of well-being and of harmony and peace within themselves.

Not everyone defines **happiness** in quite the same way. For some people, happiness is achieved with pleasure, almost without regard to the cost, whereas for others, happiness is essentially the absence of problems in their lives (Bradburn, 1969; Bradburn & Capovitz, 1965).

Although we tend to think of happiness as a temporary state, it may also have some of the aspects of an enduring trait. When people rate their happiness, the mean rating is about 6 on a 10-point scale (Wesman & Ricks, 1966). Moreover, ratings for a given person are remarkably constant from one day to the next. There may also be differences in people across cultures. In a study of happiness in 13 different countries, the proportion of people who described themselves as "very happy" varied from one country to the next. The percentages ranged from a low of 34% in South Korea to a high of 52% in Italy (Hastings & Hastings, 1982). The difference is obviously substantial.

Fear and Anxiety

We feel **fear** when we anticipate danger or harm. From an evolutionary point of view, fear serves a protective function because it motivates us to avoid or to flee from the things that might cause us harm. **Anxiety** is the feeling that we are being threatened without being able to specify exactly what it is that is threatening us. Thus, the difference between fear and anxiety is in the identification of the cause of distress. In fear, we can point to the cause; in anxiety, we cannot. In addition, anxiety is generally more pervasive and diffuse, and it tends to last longer. Whereas almost everyone feels simple anxiety at one time or another, anxiety disorders are more serious, and they are considered in Chapter 18.

Anger

We feel **anger** when we are frustrated in or otherwise restrained from pursuit of a goal. We are most likely to be angry at another person when we believe that we have suffered unjustified and intentional insult or injury (Averill, 1983). If we believe that someone's behavior is either accidental or unavoidable, or justified, we are much less likely to get angry. Although we believe that we are likely to feel anger toward those whom we dislike or detest, in fact, we are most likely to feel anger toward the people closest to us. About

Cross-cultural research indicates that humans around the world use fundamentally the same kinds of facial expressions to show happiness, fear or worry, anger, sadness or grief, and disgust. Do you have any difficulty identifying which of these emotions is being shown in each photo? Artists often portray facial expressions to convey human emotions, as in Edgar Degas's The Glass of Absinthe.

29% of our overt expression of anger is directed toward people we love, 24% toward people we like, 25% toward acquaintances, and only 8% toward people we actively dislike (Averill, 1980, 1983). Only 13% of our expression of anger is directed toward strangers. (The percentages are rounded.)

Sadness and Grief

Sadness is a feeling of low spirits or sorrow, and **grief** is a sharper, often deeper, and usually more long-lasting emotion. Sadness and grief tend to be caused by an involuntary, often permanent, separation. Some of the typical causes of sadness are making a mistake, doing something to hurt others, or being forced to do something against your will (Izard, 1977). Although virtually no one enjoys feeling sad, sadness can have an adaptive function. For one thing, it can encourage people to change their lives (Izard, 1977; Tomkins, 1963). If, for example, we feel sad that we hurt another person, our sadness may motivate us to make amends. Sadness can also be a cue for other people to help us. When others see that we are sad, they may come to our aid, even if we have not explicitly said how we feel.

Disgust

We usually feel **disgust** in the face of objects or experiences that we find repulsive. Disgust serves an adaptive purpose by motivating us to remove ourselves from what might be harmful, such as putrid meat or other contaminated products. According to Paul Rozin and April Fallon (1987), disgust is a psychological rejection of something motivated primarily by its nature, its origin, or its social history. The item is offensive and thus labeled "disgusting." This definition of disgust as a form of rejection is supported by experimentation (Rozin, Millman, & Nemeroff, 1986). Disgust has a psychological origin, and, indeed, things that may seem disgusting in one culture (such as eating termites or cockroaches) may not seem disgusting in another.

MEASUREMENT OF EMOTION

IN SEARCH OF...

How can psychologists detect what emotions a person is experiencing?

How do we know when a person feels emotion? One way of finding out the emotions that people are experiencing is simply to ask them. Such measures are **self-report measures,** in which individuals simply state their responses to questions, usually in regard to their attitudes, their feelings, their opinions, or their behaviors. Often, researchers find it difficult to quantify people's spontaneous self-reported expressions, so alternative self-report measures have been devised.

One such measure is a **Likert scale** (see Table 16-8), which asks subjects to choose which of several options best describes their response. For example, in one measure of anxiety, people are given a set of statements, such as "I feel calm" or "I am tense," and they are expected to rate each of these statements on a 4-point scale, where "0" means that the statement does not at all characterize how they feel, "1" means that it characterizes how they feel somewhat, "2" means that it is moderately so, and "3" means that it is very much so (Spielberger, Gorsuch, & Lushene, 1983). A person's feelings of anxiety would then be the average (or sum) of the numbers checked for the various self-report items.

Another self-report type of technique uses forced-choice responses rather than numerical ratings. For example, people might be given two emotion terms such as "quarrelsome" and "shy," and for each pair of terms be asked to indicate which term better characterizes the way they feel (Plutchik & Kellerman, 1974).

Various psychophysiological measures also register emotion, including heart rate, respiration rate, blood pressure, and galvanic skin response (GSR), which tracks the electrical conductivity of the skin. Conductivity increases with perspiration so a person under emotional stress (e.g., due to telling a lie) will perspire and thus increase his or her GSR (see Figure 16-10 in the next section).

One controversial measure that has been used to ferret out emotions is the so-called lie detector—a **polygraph.** The polygraph provides measures of psychophysiological reactivity, such as heart rate, GSR, and respiration. The idea, of course, is to provide an objective measure of whether people are feeling emotional stress. In fact, because polygraphs only measure stress reactions, they also record stress reactions for reasons other than lying, and they do not record lies told by people who feel no stress when telling lies. A common format for polygraph testing is that the polygraph operator asks a series of questions and compares psychophysiological responses to innocuous questions ("In what city were you born?") with answers to potentially threatening questions ("Did you murder your professor?"). A more effective format for

TABLE 16-8
Sample Likert Scale
In a Likert scale, individuals rate each item on a numerical scale (e.g., 1–5), indicating their degree of agreement with each statement, as shown here. (After Kite & Deaux, 1986)

Please indicate your level of agreement with the items below using the following scale:				
1	2	3	4	5
Strongly agree		*Neutral*		*Strongly disagree*

1. I would not mind having homosexual friends.

2. Finding out that an artist was gay would have no effect on my appreciation of his/her work.

3. I won't associate with known homosexuals if I can help it.

4. I would look for a new place to live if I found out my roommate was gay.

5. Homosexuality is a mental illness.

6. Homosexuality, as far as I'm concerned, is not sinful.

Note: Items 1, 2, and 6 are reverse-scored.

the use of polygraphs involves questions that assess whether a person possesses information that only a guilty person would know (Bashore & Rapp, 1993).

How accurate are polygraphs? The results of controlled studies are not terribly encouraging. Although professional interpreters of polygraphs have been found to be correct in identifying guilty parties 76% of the time, they have also labeled as guilty 37% of the innocent subjects they tested (Kleinmuntz & Szucko, 1984). A review of more than 250 studies of the validity of interpretation of polygraph results shows similar findings (Saxe, Dougherty, & Cross, 1985; see also Ben-Shakhar & Furedy, 1990). Thus, interpreters of results are pretty good at recognizing guilty parties but also classify disturbing numbers of innocent people as guilty. In the language of signal-detection theory (see Chapter 4), the hit rate is high, but so is the rate of false alarms. Results such as these indicate that polygraph tests, as they are now interpreted, are far from reliable.

THE EXPRESSION OF EMOTION

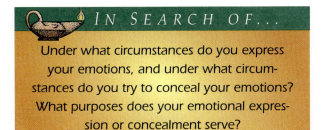

IN SEARCH OF...

Under what circumstances do you express your emotions, and under what circumstances do you try to conceal your emotions? What purposes does your emotional expression or concealment serve?

Social Functions of Emotional Expression

The expression of emotion serves at least four different social functions (Izard, 1989). *First*, it enables us to communicate our feelings to other people. In particular, infants and very young children, as well as members of other species, must rely on their expressions to communicate their emotions. *Second*, expression of emotion regulates how other people respond to us. Mothers respond in different ways, depending on their babies' expressions (Huebner & Izard, 1988). *Third*, emotional expressions facilitate social interaction. A smile can do a lot to break the ice—sometimes more than words. *Finally*, emotional expression encourages prosocial behavior (see Chapter 15). Being cheerful with another person may encourage him or her to be cheerful. Even the experiencing of positive emotions, whether communicated or not, can lead people to be more prosocial (Isen, 1987).

The similarity of facial expressions across cultures exemplifies the first social function, that of communication. Researchers studied the ability of tribal New Guineans to recognize facial expressions in photographs of Westerners (Ekman & Friesen, 1975). Both adults and children were quite accurate in recognizing expressions of happiness, sadness, anger, disgust, surprise, and fear. Americans also were fairly accurate in recognizing New Guinean expressions. In all cases, accuracy was greatest for happiness and lowest for fear. This work was extended by showing identical photographs to people in the United States, Brazil, Chile, Argentina, and Japan (Ekman, 1984). Once again, there was a remarkable consensus across

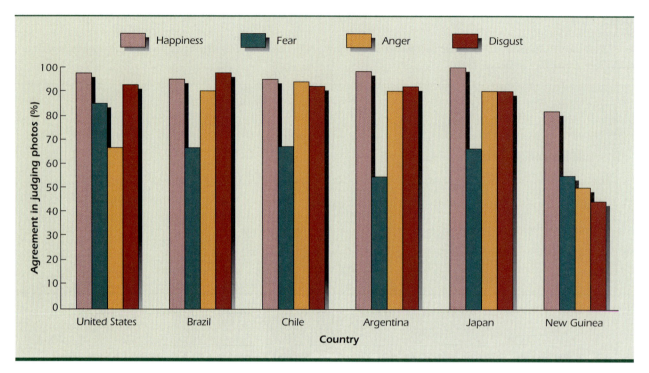

FIGURE 16-10
Cultural Agreement Regarding Facial Expressions
Cross-cultural agreement regarding facial expressions of emotions appears highest for happiness and disgust, but lowest for anger and fear. The greatest disagreement was shown by New Guineans, who have not had extensive contact with persons from other cultural groups. What are some possible implications of that finding? (After Ekman & Friesen, 1984)

cultures. As in the study in New Guinea, consensus was greatest for happiness and lowest for fear. The high level of agreement across cultures suggests that facial expression for emotions may be an innate part of our physiological makeup. In the case of the New Guineans, at least, the tribe members had had virtually no contact with Westerners, and yet their facial expressions and judgments of facial expressions were very similar to those of people in the United States (see Figure 16-10).

Facial-Feedback Hypothesis

Normally, we would believe that the expression of emotion follows the experiencing of that emotion. Silvan Tomkins (1962, 1963) has turned that point of view on its head by suggesting the **facial-feedback hypothesis.** Tomkins closely links emotions to their expression, arguing that we feel emotion as a result of feedback from the face. In other words, the facial expression of an emotion leads to the experiencing of that emotion.

A strong version of the facial-feedback hypothesis suggests that simply manipulating your face to show a certain emotion would lead you to feel that

emotion. Thus, smiling would make you happy; puckering up your face in disgust would make you feel disgusted. The data on the strong version of the facial-feedback hypothesis are mixed. It does appear that creating a facial expression produces particular changes in psychophysiological reaction, but it is unclear that these changes are the same as experiencing the emotion itself (Ekman, Levenson, & Friesen, 1983; Levenson, Ekman, & Friesen, 1990; Tourangeau & Ellsworth, 1979). (See Figure 16-11.)

A weaker version of the facial-feedback hypothesis suggests merely that facial feedback can affect the intensity of an emotion but does not actually produce an emotion. The weaker version of the hypothesis has received fairly uniform support (e.g., Zuckerman, Klorman, Larrance, & Speigel, 1981).

Honest Faces

There also has been some very interesting research on facial expression and lying (Ekman, 1992; Ekman, Friesen, & O'Sullivan, 1988). Facial expressions may help us to detect when people are lying. Paul Ekman claims that genuine expressions of emotions tend to

Searchers . . .   PAUL EKMAN

Paul Ekman is Professor of Psychiatry and Director of the Human Interaction Laboratory at the University of California, San Francisco.

Q: *How did you become interested in psychology and in your area of work in particular?*

A: When I read Sigmund Freud in a course on rhetoric, my first year of college. I became interested in my own research area when observing group psychotherapy sessions. I became convinced that a lot of the important transactions that were occurring were not through words, but through expressions and gestures, and that these were a primary vehicle for emotion.

Q: *Whose ideas have influenced you the most?*

A: Positively, Charles Darwin and Silvan Tomkins; negatively, Stanley Schachter. Darwin provided the evolutionary framework for looking at facial expression. Tomkins was the person who provided the theory that helped me get my research started, and he also taught me how to understand facial expression, how to read the face. Schachter represented, as far as I could see, sort of a complete misunderstanding of the nature of emotion. He dealt with neither emotional responses nor the appraisal process that's relevant to the cause of emotion. But his theory still captures the imagination of a lot of contemporary psychologists.

Q: *What is your greatest asset as a psychologist?*

A: I don't take *no* for an answer. If I'd have taken *no* for an answer, I would have published probably two articles in my life, rather than more than a hundred. Only twice in my life has an article been accepted when I first submitted it.

Q: *What makes a psychologist really great?*

A: Doing the kind of research that allows you to see things or understand things that haven't been seen or understood before. And doing research that doesn't simply prove your ideas but creates new ideas.

Q: *How do you get your ideas for research?*

A: Some have been accidents, some have awakened me in the middle of the night, and some are reactions to the findings from a study, showing me that everything I thought was totally wrong and prompting me to come up with a new idea about how to explain things. When I started my cross-cultural research, I expected to show that facial expressions were culturally specific, but I found just the opposite.

Q: *How do you decide whether to pursue an idea?*

A: It depends whether there's an opportunity, someone else to collaborate with, and any money to pay for the research.

Q: *How have you developed an idea into a workable hypothesis?*

A: I discovered by accident that voluntary facial movements can generate different patterns of physiological activity. I found that, when I made certain muscular combinations on my face, I was flooded with physical sensations. And that gave me the idea. So I borrowed a polygraph machine, hooked myself up, and got some evidence that the phenomenon was real, producing some measurable changes. Then psychophysiologist Bob Levinson and I pursued it and have published five papers on the phenomenon.

Q: *What obstacles have you experienced?*

A: It's hard to get things published if you don't work in orthodox psychology.

Q: *What is your major contribution to psychology?*

A: One is the evidence on the universality of facial expression. The New Guinea work helped reawaken an interest in emotion that had been dormant for decades. A second is the technique for measuring facial movement, which is being used by about 200 people worldwide. Before then, there was no way to quantify facial movement. The third, which is much less known in psychology but has influenced the world outside the classroom, is my research on deception and demeanor. That's been used in training judges and in law enforcement agencies.

Q: *What do you want students to learn?*

A: To be persistent, to be naturalists, to remember that their job is to try to understand nature, not to impose their preconceptions upon it.

Q: *What do you further hope to achieve?*

A: I am starting a project to see if brain imaging techniques (MRI) can locate different areas of the brain that are active in each of the emotions. I've found left-right hemisphere differences in certain emotions and am now pinpointing them.

---

be symmetrical, whereas false ones are likely to be asymmetrical (see Figure 16-12). In addition, the more emotion that lying arouses in a person, the more able we may be to detect whether the person is lying. If a person actually believes his or her own lies, however, it is very difficult to figure out whether the truth is being told. Also, experienced liars, such as criminals, may be quite able to convey deceptively honest-looking expressions. Of the people who are supposed to be skillful in detecting lies (police officers, members of the Federal Bureau of Investigation, and members of the Secret Service), members of the Secret Service seem to be the only group able to detect the emotional expressions of liars (Ekman, 1992).

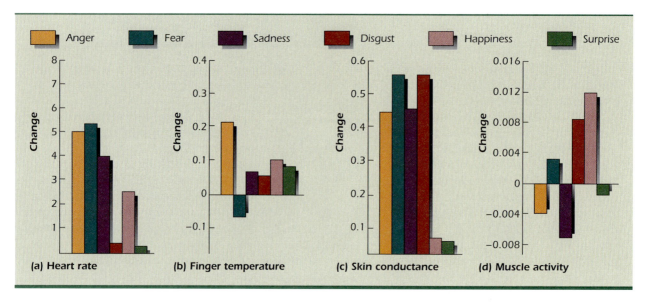

FIGURE 16-11
Physiological Changes Caused by Facial Expression
Some evidence indicates that when we change our facial expressions to show given emotions, our bodies respond through physiological changes in heart rate, circulation (as shown in finger temperature), sweating (as shown in skin conductance), and muscle activity. Do these changes necessarily mean that we are experiencing the emotions shown in our faces? (After Levenson, Ekman, & Friesen, 1990)

How do you, personally, recognize when someone is not telling the truth? Cite both what you observe and how you infer that you are not being told the truth.

SUMMARY OF EMOTION

We all know when we experience emotion, but as indicated, there is considerable disagreement as to how we experience it, and even as to what are the basic emotions. For example Lazarus (1984) believes in the primacy of cognition as a cause of emotion, whereas Zajonc (1984) does not. Mesquita and Frijda (1992) suggest that emotion is part of a complex that closely involves cognition as well as behavior. Moreover, these authors suggest that fully to understand emotion, we need to view it in the cultural context in which it occurs.

In this chapter, we have considered motivation, emotion, and some of the links between the two. These two constructs are linked very closely to a third one, which in large part determines the kinds of emotions a person experiences. This third construct is personality, which we consider in the next chapter.

FIGURE 16-12
Sincere Smiles
Which of these smiles is genuine? According to Paul Ekman, most of us—including police officers and FBI agents—are not very good at determining when someone is lying, simply by observing their facial expressions. (Do not try to deceive a Secret Service agent, though; these agents can detect lies through facial expressions at better than chance levels.) (After Ekman, Friesen, & O'-Sullivan, 1988)

SUMMARY

The Nature and Characteristics of Motivation   556

1. The study of *motivation* considers questions of direction, initiation, intensity, and persistence.

Early Theories of Motivation   556

2. Darwin, James, and McDougall saw motivation as an *instinct*. However, their theories became too complex and obscure to be useful.

3. Drive theory replaced instinct theory. According to Hull, *drive* is a composite source of energy, which animals and humans are impelled to reduce. Drive theory was discredited, however, because motivation can exist without physiological needs and can even be biologically maladaptive.

Contemporary Paradigms of Motivation   557

4. Physiological approaches to motivation (arousal, opponent-process, and homeostatic-regulation theories) study how motivation relates to the brain.

5. According to the Yerkes-Dodson Law, people perform most efficiently and creatively when their level of *arousal* is moderate. The optimal level varies both with task demands and personal characteristics. High levels are helpful with simple tasks; lower levels are better for complex tasks.

6. *Opponent-process theory*, proposed by Solomon, explains how an addictive drug or habit, started in order to achieve a high, becomes a habit to avoid a low. When we feel the effects of a motivational source, we then experience an opposing force—slower to start, slower to terminate—that tends to bring us back to baseline.

7. *Homeostatic regulation* is the tendency of the body to maintain equilibrium. A negative feedback loop operates like a thermostat, telling us when we need food, drink, or sex and when those needs are satisfied.

8. The brain is essential to the experience of hunger. The ventromedial hypothalamus (VMH) serves as an off-switch for eating, the lateral hypothalamus (LH) as an on-switch.

9. The *glucostatic hypothesis* holds that levels of glucose in the body signal the hypothalamus about the need for food. An alternative (perhaps complementary) explanation is the *lipostatic hypothesis*, which holds that the brain detects when lipids drop below a certain homeostatic level and hunger increases.

10. According to *set-point theory*, weight is biologically determined at birth by the number of fat cells. Successful weight loss is difficult because the body interprets dieting as starvation and so resists efforts to shrink the fat cells.

11. Many obese people are particularly susceptible to environmental cues. For example, they are more likely to eat because they view it as time to eat, even though they are not hungry. Anorexics are constantly afraid of being obese, even when they are extremely thin.

12. Sexual motivation is rooted in the hypothalamus, which stimulates the pituitary gland to release hormones that influence the production of androgens and estrogens. Human sexual behavior is controlled partly by *sexual scripts*.

13. There are various theories of *homosexuality*. Current views tend to emphasize the role of biological factors.

14. Clinical approaches to motivation (e.g., Murray's theory of needs) emphasize personality theory. McClelland has studied in depth three needs that emerge from Murray's theory: the needs for achievement, power, and affiliation. A highly influential theory is Maslow's hierarchy of needs. These needs include physiology, safety and security, belonging and love, self-esteem, and self-actualization.

15. Cognitive approaches show that people are most creative when intrinsically motivated; *extrinsic motivators* tend to undermine *intrinsic* ones. In addition, moderately novel phenomena are more motivating than are either totally familiar or wholly novel ones. We also need to feel in control of our environment.

16. Ultimately motivation may lie in our belief of whether or not we can attain a goal (*self-efficacy theory*).

17. Goals are cognitive motivators. People are more motivated by goals that are backed by plans.

The Nature of Emotion   573

18. Distinct from but closely linked to motivation is *emotion*, the motivational predisposition to respond experientially, physiologically, and behaviorally to certain internal and external variables. Current theories suggest the importance of the autonomic nervous system in emotional arousal.

19. Emotions serve an evolutionary function. For example, they may lead us to fight or to flee in the face of an attack, depending upon how the danger is perceived and which course of action is more likely to lead to survival.

Approaches to Understanding Emotions   574

20. The James-Lange theory claims that bodily changes lead to emotion, rather than the reverse. Cannon and Bard disagreed, claiming that the brain controls emotional behavior.

21. Cognitive theories differ in details and sometimes in substance, but they agree that emotion and cognition are linked closely. According to the Schachter-Singer *two-component theory*, we distinguish one emotion from another strictly by how we label our physiological arousal.

22. Emotions and cognitions are linked, but we do not yet know which comes first. Lazarus believes that cognition precedes emotion, whereas Zajonc does not.

23. Cross-cultural studies of emotions analyze emotions in terms of antecedent events, event coding, appraisal, physiological response patterns, action readiness, emotional behavior, and readiness. Although not all people categorize emotions in the same way, many similarities still exist across cultures in the ways that people express and identify emotions.

Some Major Emotions and Their Characteristics   580

24. Major emotions include *happiness* (joy), *fear* and *anxiety*, *anger*, *sadness* and *grief*, and *disgust*. They can be charted to show relationships among them.

Measurement of Emotion   582

25. We can measure emotional experience through *self-reporting* and/or psychophysiological means; the *polygraph* is not a reliable measure of veracity, however.

The Expression of Emotion   583

26. The expression of emotion enables us to communicate feelings, regulates how others respond to us, facilitates social interaction, and encourages prosocial behavior.

27. The *facial-feedback hypothesis* holds that (1) the facial expression of emotion leads to the experience of emotion, or (2) the facial expression affects an emotion's intensity. Facial expressions can also help somewhat to detect when someone is lying, particularly if the person doing the detecting has been highly trained to do so.

KEY TERMS

IN SEARCH OF THE HUMAN MIND:
ANALYSES, CREATIVE EXPLORATIONS, AND PRACTICAL APPLICATIONS

1. When psychologists conduct experiments that study a representative sample of adults in a country, they are certain to encounter cultural differences, age differences, gender differences, and other individual differences that will affect the way their subjects respond to the experiments. What are some general recommendations you can suggest regarding the design of psychological experiments in multicultural contexts?
2. Compare and contrast the ways that negative-feedback loops apply to homeostatic regulation of temperature with the ways they operate in regulating hormones. (*Hint:* See Chapter 3.)
3. Compare and contrast Murray's theory of needs with Maslow's need hierarchy.

4. What strategies could you use to help a child discover his or her hidden talents?
5. Design a cross-cultural study of motivation. What are some of the confounding factors that will make the design of this study particularly difficult?
6. Design a cross-sectional study of emotions across the life span. (*Hint:* See Chapter 13.) In what ways will your design have to allow for the cohort differences, chronological differences, and developmental differences of your subjects?

7. What goal can you set for yourself that would satisfy your need for achievement and would enhance your sense of competence, autonomy, and self-efficacy? Devise a specific plan for reaching your goal, including the specific subtasks and subgoals you would need to accomplish.
8. Give an example of a situation in which you used emotional expression for each of the social functions mentioned in the chapter (communication, regulation of responses to the person expressing emotions, facilitation of social interactions, and encouragement of prosocial behavior). (Your example can describe either your own emotional expressions or the expressions of a friend.)
9. When advertisers want to motivate you to buy their products or services, they seek to tap into some of the fundamental human motivations. Describe a recent advertisement you have seen or heard, and explain how the advertiser was trying to manipulate your fundamental motivations to persuade you to buy the advertised product or service.

In Search of the Human Mind . . . *Part Five*

1. What are some of the ways the need for self-efficacy may be related to some of the heuristics and biases of social cognition?

2. Design a cross-cultural experiment that would help us understand better the diverse ways in which humans express emotions in a variety of interpersonal contexts.

3. How do some of your attitudes and motivations affect the ways you interact with others?

Looking Ahead . . .

4. Are there ways in which people's psychological makeup may impair their ability to interact effectively with other people?

Charting the Dialectic

Chapter 14   SOCIAL PSYCHOLOGY: PERSONAL PERSPECTIVES

Social psychology provides an excellent example of the dialectical progression of scientific ideas. In the area of social cognition, for example, Festinger's theory of cognitive dissonance originally seemed to provide a clever and correct account of why subjects in an experiment would say they enjoyed a boring task more when they were paid $1 than when they were paid $20. Bem's self-perception theory later provided a very different, but also plausible explanation of the phenomenon. Still later, Fazio, Zanna, and Cooper suggested a synthesis of the two opposing points of view, suggesting the circumstances under which cognitive-dissonance theory is applicable, and those under which self-perception theory is applicable. As another example, early clinical theories of love, such as Freud's, tended to emphasize the role of passion and sexual desire in the development of love. More cognitive theories, such as Rubin's, tended more to emphasize intimacy and a more thoughtful approach to love. Recent theories, such as my own, have accorded a role to both intimacy and unbridled passion in attempts to understand the nature of love.

Chapter 15 SOCIAL PSYCHOLOGY: INTERPERSONAL AND GROUP PERSPECTIVES

We can see further examples of the dialectical development of ideas in the realm of interpersonal and group perspectives on social psychology. For example, some early research suggested that groups tend to illustrate a risky shift, becoming more extreme in their views than the views of the individual members; but later research sometimes showed exactly the opposite, with groups tending to become more conservative. The theory of group polarization eventually provided a synthesis of the two seemingly opposing positions. Groups tend to become exaggerated with respect to whatever the members' original positions are. Thus, if individuals tend toward risk, the group position is likely to be more risk-oriented than the individual positions, whereas if the individuals tend toward conservatism, the group position is likely to be even more conservative than the individual positions. As another example, it was once thought that the advantage of working in a group was that groups would be more rational in their decisions than individuals, through compensation of any one member's idiosyncratic tendencies via the counterweights of others in the group. However, Janis's work on groupthink suggested that the decisions of groups are often less rational than those of individuals. More recently, we have come to understand better the conditions under which groupthink is more or less likely to occur, and what we can do when it does occur.

Chapter 16 MOTIVATION AND EMOTION

The study of motivation and emotion has proceeded, to a large extent, in a dialectical fashion. For example, do people naturally seek arousal or to avoid arousal? Evidence suggests that most people work most effectively at neither high nor low levels of arousal, but at moderate levels of arousal. Moreover, people differ in the extent to which they seek arousal, so that any theory that postulates that people all seek the same thing is necessarily going to be incomplete. Introverts tend to have naturally higher levels of arousal, and so often seek to lower their levels of arousal, whereas extroverts tend to have naturally lower levels of arousal, and so seek to raise their levels. Both within a given person and between persons, therefore, the solution to the problem of arousal-seeking lies between two extremes. Sometimes, we have yet to achieve a synthesis between two opposing points of view, both of which have some empirical support. For example, in the field of emotion, Lazarus has proposed that cognition precedes emotion, whereas Zajonc has proposed that it does not. We do not yet have a fully viable synthesis of these two points of view, both of which have received some evidentiary support.

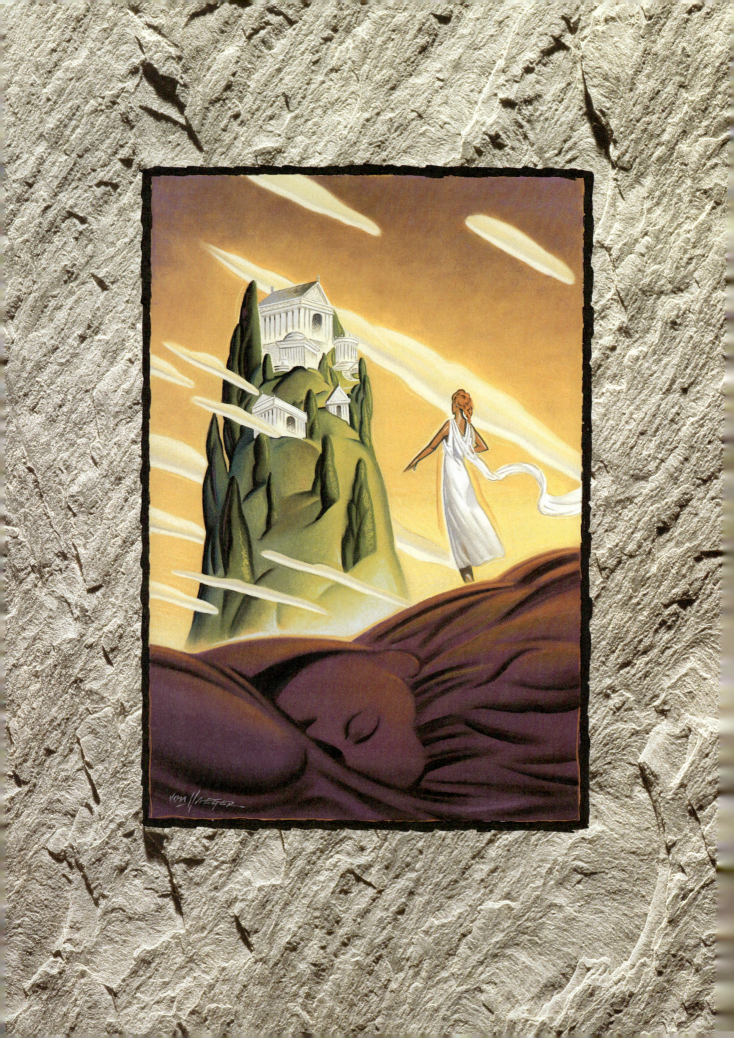

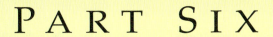

PART SIX

Clinical Processes

Personality

Abnormal Psychology

Psychotherapy

Health Psychology

Chapter Seventeen

PERSONALITY

CHAPTER OUTLINE

Personality *paradigms can be evaluated in terms of their importance to and influence on the field of psychology, their testability, their comprehensiveness in accounting for psychological phenomena, their parsimoniousness, and their usefulness to applied fields.*

Every one, indeed, loved this young man [Alyosha] wherever he went, and it was so from his earliest childhood. When he entered the household of his patron and benefactor, Yefom Petrovitch Polenov, he gained the hearts of all the family, so that they looked on him as quite their own child. Yet he entered the house at such a tender age that he could not have acted from design or artfulness in winning affection. So that the gift of making himself loved directly and unconsciously was inherent in his nature so to speak. It was the same at school. . . .

He had one characteristic which made all his schoolfellows from the bottom class to the top want to mock him, not from malice but because it amused them. This characteristic was a wild fanatical modesty and chastity. He could not bear to hear certain words and certain conversations about women. . . .

Why Ivan Fyodorovitch had come amongst us I remember asking myself at the time with a certain uneasiness. . . . It seemed strange on the face of it that a young man so learned, so proud, and apparently so cautious, should suddenly visit such an infamous house and a father who had ignored him all his life, hardly knew him, never thought of him, and would not under any circumstances have given him money. . . . And here the young man was staying in the house of such a father, had been living with him for two months, and they were on the best possible terms.

—Fyodor Dostoyevsky, The Brothers Karamazov, *pp. 16, 19–20*

Dostoyevsky's brothers Karamazov, Alyosha and Ivan, have distinct personalities. Lovable, sociable, but fanatically prudish Alyosha seeks the contemplative lifestyle of a monastery. Independent-minded, sensible Ivan is firmly rooted in a secular and often immoral world yet craves the love of his father, who will not love him. How did these brothers come to have such different personalities? Recall from Chapter 13 that the two brothers may have had different temperaments as infants (e.g., their activity level, attention span, irritability, and general mood). Could these temperamental differences account for all their personality differences? Were they born with different traits, or might their personality differences have developed over time as a result of their birth order? Were their personalities formed by their differing early childhood relationships or because each brother was rewarded and punished for different kinds of behaviors? Did they differ because of their unique inherent potentials and means of self-actualization, or were their differences due to their having observed different models on which they based their own personalities?

The questions we ask about the two brothers are essentially the same questions psychologists ask about the intriguing phenomenon of **personality,** or enduring dispositions—"all those relatively permanent traits, dispositions, or characteristics within the individual that [give] some measure of consistency to that person's behavior" (Feist, 1990, p. 7). To answer these questions, researchers have come up with several ways to study personality. Some psychologists have studied intensively the personalities of individuals over long periods of time. Others have developed and implemented a wide array of means for assessing individual personalities. Still others have planned and carried out empirical studies of isolated aspects or common dimensions of personality across individuals.

Various psychologists have used alternative theoretical frameworks for understanding and integrating their observations about personality. Although some might say that there are as many theoretical frameworks as there are psychologists who observe personality, these various idiosyncratic theories can be classified according to a few major different *paradigms*—approaches to understanding a particular phenomenon. (As Chapter 11 showed, intelligence is a similarly complex phenomenon that has prompted psychologists to propose alternative explanatory paradigms.)

Most personality psychologists probably would agree on the importance of the following set of criteria for evaluating the various paradigms:

1. *Importance to and influence on the field of psychology* — How have the development of theory and research in the field been affected by this paradigm at various times?
2. *Testability* — Has the paradigm given rise to empirically testable propositions, and have these propositions, in fact, been tested?
3. *Comprehensiveness* — To what extent do the theories within the paradigm give a reasonably complete account of the phenomena they set out to describe or explain?
4. *Parsimoniousness* — How well do the theories in the paradigm explain the complexity and richness of the world in terms of a relatively small number of principles?
5. *Usefulness to applications in psychological assessment and psychotherapy techniques* — Can the theory be usefully employed by clinicians and other practitioners?

What criteria would you add to this list? What else should psychologists consider when evaluating a theory of personality?

We use these criteria for evaluating each of the personality-theory paradigms in this chapter. This chapter considers some of the principal alternative paradigms of personality theory: psychodynamic, humanistic, cognitive-behavioral, trait, as well as interactionist. The theories within a given paradigm, despite their variations, share common elements that tie them into a common view of personality. (See the table that concludes each paradigm.)

THE PSYCHODYNAMIC PARADIGM

IN SEARCH OF...

Why was Freud's psychodynamic theory of personality seminal, prompting so many other theorists to follow him, to diverge from him, and even to react against him?

The Nature of Psychodynamic Theories

Often, when we think about personality, we think about the static, unchanging characteristics of people. We rarely think of personality as a process. To think otherwise requires bold thinking. Sometimes, a revolutionary idea in one area of science seems to spark a revolutionary idea in another, or at least it may establish a climate for inciting innovative thought. Thus, it may not be coincidental that while the scientific community was excitedly elaborating and investigating the laws of thermodynamics, psychodynamic psychologists were developing theories of personality that underscored the *dynamic processes* underlying personality. Psychodynamic theories view each person as a complex system of *diverse sources of psychic energy*, each of which pushes the person in a somewhat different direction. As we observe a person's behavior, we are watching the moment-by-moment convergence of these multidirectional sources of what some psychologists call "psychic energy."

The multidirectional propulsion of psychic energy suggests another key commonality underlying psychodynamic theories: the importance of *conflict*. The different sources of energy tend to propel the person in conflicting directions, and the behavior prompted by these multiple sources of energy usually cannot satisfy all of the conflicting psychic drives at once. For example, a person may seek both to hurt another person and to maintain a self-image as a peace-loving, thoughtful person. In whatever ways the person behaves in response to these conflicting drives, the person is likely to continue to experience internal conflict.

Similarly, psychodynamic theorists observe conflict between individuals and the society in which they live. For example, internal psychic energy may prompt a person to desire sexual fulfillment in ways that society prohibits, such as through sexual intercourse between parents and children. As sexual and other desires frequently create conflict with societal restrictions, these conflicts further complicate the person's internal conflicts. (Recall from Chapter 13 Freud's views, developed during the Victorian era, in which the squelching of sexual impulses was a predominant social theme.)

Biological drives (especially sexual ones) and other biological forces play a key role in psychodynamic theories. Sigmund Freud, the first of the great psychodynamic thinkers, viewed his theory as *biological* in nature. A key reason for this orientation was Freud's training as a neurologist, a physician who specializes in disorders of the nervous system. Another reason for this orientation, however, may be the scientific context in which his theory originated. In particular, psychodynamic theories have been influenced by Charles Darwin's notions of evolution through natural selection; both psychodynamic and evolutionary theories focus on adaptation to the environment. Specifically, psychodynamic theories study how people constantly seek to adapt to the environment, even though people may not always succeed in their efforts.

While studying the dynamic, biological nature of personality, psychodynamic theories also emphasize developmental processes that underlie personality. These theories study the interplay of the various sources of energy at different junctures across the life span—how basic personality structures develop over time. (Recall Freud's and Erikson's hypothesized developmental progressions, explored in Chapter 13.) Psychodynamic theories particularly emphasize the ways in which early childhood experiences influence personality development. Psychodynamicists theorize that our early development influences the moment-to-moment dynamics of how we adapt to our external environments while responding to conflicting internal psychic forces.

The biological and developmental characteristics of psychodynamic theories suggest another of the key features of these theories: **determinism**—the idea that our behavior is ruled by forces over which we have little control. According to Freud, our behavior is strongly influenced by often uncontrollable forces. Although the **neo-Freudians** (the psychodynamically oriented theorists who followed Freud) reacted against Freud's strong determinism and generally viewed people as having somewhat more control over their own actions, the neo-Freudians were still very concerned with the issue of determinism. In fact, many non-Freudian personality psychologists have been interested in finding out whether such forces exist, how such forces might determine behavior, and how much control we may have over these forces. In their view, if we can understand these forces, we may be able to change how we feel and even what we do.

Another variable influencing our control over our actions is the role of the **unconscious** (an internal structure of the mind that is outside the grasp of our awareness). Although the various psychodynamic theories differ regarding the exact nature of this role, each theory gives the unconscious some function. The idea that much of our behavior is motivated by forces outside our conscious comprehension pervades all psychodynamic theories, although Freud emphasized the importance of the unconscious much more heavily than did the neo-Freudians. For example, Freud probably would have agreed with the psychoanalyst's view of the origin of the narrator's pain in the following passage:

His comforters . . . agreed with the psychoanalyst that the pain was self-inflicted: penance for the popu-
larity [of his novel], come-uppance for the financial bonanza [his writing had earned him]. . . .

But Zuckerman wasn't buying it. His unconscious wasn't that unconscious. . . . His unconscious, living with a published writer . . . understood what the job entailed. He had great faith in his unconscious—he could never have come this far without it. If anything, it was tougher and smarter than he was, probably what protected him against the envy of rivals . . . . If the Morse code of the psyche was indeed being tapped out along the wires of physical pain, the message had to be more original than "Don't ever write that stuff again."

—Philip Roth, "The Anatomy Lesson,"
Zuckerman Bound

Finally, many psychodynamic theorists are clinicians. Thus, the data on which they base their theories have tended to evolve from their *observations* of patients in clinical settings. Clinical settings typically do not lend themselves readily to controlled observation or to rigorous experimentation. Moreover, in clinical settings, the sample of people observed is not randomly selected. These people have sought—or have been urged to seek—treatment for some kind of psychological problem. If the clinical observer then extrapolates from observations of people in the clinical setting to hypotheses about the rest of the population, the possibility of bias is obvious: The problems of people in a clinical setting are not necessarily the same as those of other people.

To summarize, the various psychodynamic approaches share a common focus on dynamic processes, sources and transformations of psychic energy, conflicts, biological adaptation and societal adaptation, developmental changes, deterministic and unconscious forces, and clinical observations. Next, we consider how these commonalities manifest themselves in a few of the distinct psychodynamic approaches.

Psychoanalysis: The Theory of Sigmund Freud

Sigmund Freud is considered to be one of the greatest thinkers of the twentieth century. His theory is sometimes considered to be the most influential in all of psychology.

Organization of the Mind

As we have seen, Freud (1917/1963b) believed that the mind exists at two basic levels: conscious and unconscious (see Chapter 6). In addition to conscious

Sigmund Freud, the primary theorist of the psychodynamic paradigm, is viewed by many as the seminal thinker in the psychology of personality.

would be unacceptable when we are thinking logically. For example, the content of primary-process thought allows us to consummate sexual desires that we would never be able to fulfill in everyday life. This wish fulfillment could occur in a dream or other fantasy. Another expression of primary-process thought can be found in Freudian slips of the tongue (see Chapter 9).

The form of primary-process thinking is also unacceptable to consciousness. For example, it may include blatant contradictions. In a dream, you may be fully engaged in developing events, yet at the same time you may be observing those events as a detached nonparticipant. In conscious thought, you would need to view yourself as either participating or not participating.

Freud addressed the paradoxical nature of dreams by distinguishing between the **manifest content** of dreams (the stream of events as we experience them) and the **latent content** of dreams (the repressed impulses and other unconscious material that give rise to the manifest content). The manifest content of a dream might be to seek refuge from a wild animal, but the latent content of the dream might be the need to seek protection from savage impulses. Freud believed that primary-process thinking in dreams serves to disguise unacceptable impulses. Many elements of dreams are symbolic (e.g., a box can symbolize the womb). People also disguise unacceptable thoughts through *condensation*, whereby several different unacceptable thoughts or impulses are combined into a single dream image.

Dream up a sequence of fantastic events, and describe both the manifest content and some possible interpretations of the latent content.

thought (of which we are aware) and unconscious thought (of which we are unaware), Freud suggested the existence of *preconscious* thought (of which we are not currently aware but which we can bring into awareness more readily than we can bring unconscious thought into awareness). Freud (1933/1964a) also believed that the mind can be divided into three basic structures: the id, the ego, and the superego. The id and the superego are largely unconscious, and the ego is largely conscious, although with some preconscious and unconscious components.

As we saw briefly in Chapter 13, at the most primitive level, the **id** is the unconscious, instinctive source of our impulses, such as sex and aggression; it is therefore also the source of the wishes and fantasies that derive from these impulses. The id functions by means of **primary-process thought,** a form of thought that is irrational, instinct-driven, and out of touch with reality. We engage in primary-process thought as infants and also later in our dreams. This mode of thought accepts both content and forms that

Primary-process thinking also serves other important functions. It provides a wellspring for creativity by permitting novel and even surprising connections, and it permits the expression of wishes through dreams. According to Freudian theory, dreams offer a way to fulfill some of the wishes that we are otherwise unable to fulfill in our daily conscious lives. Wish fulfillment via dreams is only one of many ways we immediately gratify the impulses of the id. Immediate gratification transforms the psychic energy of the id's impulses, thus reducing internal tension and conflict. Because the id relentlessly and heedlessly pursues immediate gratification, the id is said to operate in terms of the **pleasure principle.**

The **ego,** in contrast, operates on the basis of the **reality principle,** which responds to the real world as we perceive it to be, rather than as we might like it to be (the province of the id). Thus, the ego is the region of the mind that makes direct contact with reality. Through the reality principle, the ego mediates between the id and the external world, deciding on the extent to which we can act on our impulses and the extent to which we must suppress them to meet the demands of reality. In other words, the ego tries to find realistic ways to gratify the id's impulses.

As described in Chapter 13, each person's ego originally develops from the id during infancy. Throughout life, the ego remains in contact with the id, as well as with the external world. The ego relies on **secondary-process thought,** which is basically rational and based on reality. Through secondary-process thought, we make sense of the world, and we respond to it in a way that will make sense both to us and to others. As you read the material in this textbook, trying to make sense of it, you are engaging in secondary-process thought.

Freud's third structure, the **superego,** is the internalized representation of the norms and values of our society. The superego emerges later than the id and the ego, largely through identification with parents. In fact, to some extent, the superego is an internalized representation of our parents—the authority figures who tell us what we can and cannot do; it is based on our internalized societal rules.

The superego operates by means of the **idealistic principle,** which guides our actions as dictated by our internalized authority figures. Whereas the ego is largely rational in its thinking, the superego is not. The superego checks whether we are conforming to our internalized moral authority, not whether we are behaving rationally.

The superego has two parts: the conscience and the ego ideal. Roughly speaking, the *conscience* arises from those experiences in which we were punished for unacceptable behavior, whereas the *ego ideal* results from those experiences in which we were rewarded for praiseworthy behavior. In other words, the conscience focuses on prohibited or other questionable behaviors, whereas the ego ideal focuses on societally (or morally) valued behaviors. Thus, the superego presents a third factor that the ego must contend with when trying to determine behavior. The relations among the id, the ego, and the superego are shown in Figure 17-1.

> Describe a situation in which you felt a moral dilemma. Describe how you resolved the situation in terms of the Freudian personality structures and their guiding principles.

Defense Mechanisms

The id's strong impulses and the superego's strong prohibitions often pose problems for the ego. Freud (see also A. Freud, 1946) suggested that in response to these problems, people use **defense mechanisms** to protect themselves from unacceptable thoughts and impulses. The goal of these defense mechanisms is to protect the ego from having to deal with material that the ego finds frightening or anxiety-provoking. There are nine main defense mechanisms: *denial, repression, projection, displacement, sublimation, reaction formation, rationalization, regression,* and *fixation* (see Table 17-1).

FIGURE 17-1
Personality Structures of Psychodynamic Theory
The id, the ego, and the superego are believed to form the basis for personality development and expression, according to psychodynamic theory.

Structure	Levels of thought	Operating principle	Description
Id	Unconscious; primary process	Pleasure	Scource of psychic energy and instinctual impulses
Ego	Largely conscious; secondary process	Reality	Mediator among the id, the superego, and external reality
Superego	Largely unconscious	Idealistic	Comprises the *conscience* (prohibitions, based on punishments) and the *ego ideal* (ideal behaviors, based on rewards)

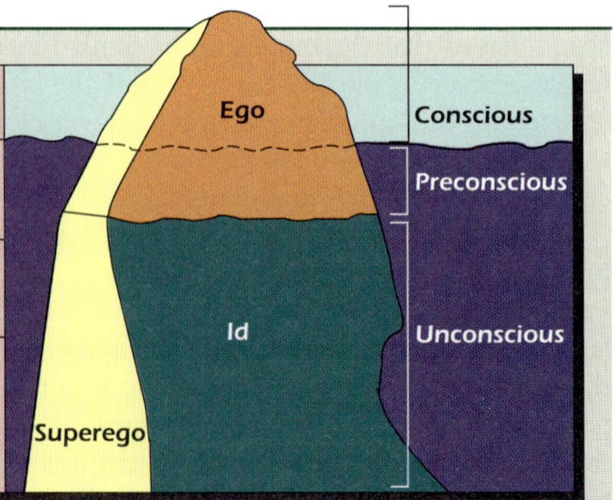

> Choose two of the Freudian defense mechanisms that you have observed in your own behavior. Explain how you have used each of them and explain which has been a more effective defense in general.

Freud's Case Studies

Many of Freud's ideas came from observations of patients in his clinical practice. Most of Freud's patients were women, many of whom were referred to his neurological practice because of *hysterical symptoms*—physical complaints for which no medical causes could be found. One of Freud's patients was Dora (Freud, 1963b), who experienced many physical ailments, the chief among them being violent coughing spells and other breathing difficulties. According to Freud, Dora's physical symptoms were an expression of an underlying psychodynamic conflict related to her sexuality.

In Dora's case, sexuality was an overt problem, as well as an alleged covert one. Dora was aware that her father had contracted a venereal disease prior to his marriage to Dora's mother, and Dora believed that at least some of her ailments were tied to his disease. Dora's father also had breathing difficulties, and Dora's difficulties occurred chiefly when her father was away from home—clearly indicating to Freud that her breathing problems related to her unresolved Electra complex (desire for her father; see Chapter 13). According to Freud, yet another key to Dora's maladies was overstimulation during her oral stage. Freud's description of Dora's case reveals his views on psychosexual development (oral stage), on the central importance of the Oedipal (Electra) conflict, and on the displacement of psychic energy (somatic ailments).

Another of Freud's patients was Little Hans, a 5-year-old who morbidly feared horses and avidly avoided them. Based on relatively little information, Freud concluded that Little Hans's fear of horses derived from an intense Oedipal complex. Hans apparently liked to touch his penis but was warned by his mother not to do so or his father would cut it off. Freud concluded that Little Hans's fear of horses was a manifestation of castration anxiety. Hans, according to Freud, had observed that horses had extremely large genitals, and to him, the horses represented his father, whom Little Hans feared would one day castrate him. Perhaps Little Hans felt that this event had already taken place symbolically.

Freud's case-study approach was both intensive and qualitative. It was *intensive* in the sense that Freud

would take a single case, study it in detail, and then subject it to penetrating and very detailed scrutiny. Freud's analyses were *qualitative* in the sense that Freud made no effort to quantify anything about the case studies. Others have used the case study to gain extensive and quantitative data, as well.

The Neo-Freudians

Freud's work inspired many to follow him and many to react against him. The sheer abundance of theories that can be viewed as reactions to different aspects of Freud's theorizing indicates the immense contribution of his work. In this way, Freud's work resembles the work of Jean Piaget (see Chapter 12), whose enormous influences also have prompted many theorists to create their own theories (see, e.g., Berg & Sternberg, 1992).

The Individual Psychology of Alfred Adler

Alfred Adler, one of Freud's earliest students, was also one of the first to break with Freud and to disagree with many of his views. For example, Adler did not accept Freud's view that people are victimized by

Alfred Adler (1870–1937) believed that all psychological phenomena are directed toward the goal of superiority, and Adler's notion of the "inferiority complex" often is used as a means of describing persons whose personality centers on feelings of inferiority.

TABLE 17-1
Defense Mechanisms
Nine key defense mechanisms play an important role in protecting the ego from anxiety-provoking information and situations.

Mechanism	Description	Example
Denial	Denial occurs when our minds prevent us from thinking about unpleasant, unwanted, or threatening situations. It also screens out anxiety-provoking physical sensations in our own bodies.	Families of alcoholics may deny perceiving all the obvious signs of alcoholism surrounding them; adolescents deny that their unsafe sex practices may cause them to get sexually transmitted diseases; or someone with a possibly cancerous mole may deny noticing it and therefore not seek medical attention for it.
Repression	Repression is the internal counterpart to denial; we *unknowingly* exclude from consciousness any unacceptable and potentially dangerous impulses.	A woman may be afraid of intimate contact with men because she was sexually molested by an uncle as a child. However, she has repressed all memory of the sexual molestation and therefore can neither recall the unhappy episode nor relate it to her fear of sexual intimacy.
Projection	We attribute our own unacceptable and possibly dangerous thoughts or impulses to another person. Projection allows us to be aware of the thought or impulse but to attribute it to someone else, whereas repression keeps the thought out of consciousness altogether.	People who are titillated by and attracted to pornography may become very active in local antipornography associations.
Displacement	We redirect an impulse away from the person who prompts it and toward another person who is a safe substitute.	A young boy who has been punished by his father would like to lash out vengefully against the father. However, his ego recognizes that he cannot attack such a threatening figure, so instead, he becomes a bully and attacks helpless classmates.
Sublimation	We redirect socially unacceptable impulses, transforming the psychic energy of unacceptable impulses into acceptable and even admirable behavioral expressions.	A composer or other artist may rechannel sexual energy into creative products that are valued by the society as a whole.

(Continued)

competing forces within themselves. Instead, Adler believed that all psychological phenomena within the individual are unified and consistent among themselves. Although people may seem to behave inconsistently or unpredictably, in fact these apparently inconsistent behaviors can be understood when viewed as being consistently directed toward a single goal: *superiority*.

According to Adler, all of us strive for superiority by attempting to become as competent as possible in whatever we do. This striving for superiority gives meaning and coherence to our actions. Unfortunately, however, some of us feel that we cannot attain superiority. If we dwell on these perceived mistakes and feelings of inferiority, and we organize our lives around these feelings of inferiority, we develop an **inferiority complex** (Adler's coinage to describe the resulting pathology).

In addition, Adler held that our actions are largely shaped by our *expectations for the future*, through the goals we set, rather than by our past experiences and development, which Freud had empha-

TABLE 17-1 *(Continued)*

Mechanism	Description	Example
Reaction formation	This defense mechanism transforms an unacceptable impulse or thought into its opposite. By unconsciously convincing ourselves that we think or feel exactly the opposite of what we actually do unconsciously think or feel, we protect our positive views of ourselves.	Experiencing the Oedipus complex (see Chapter 13), a son might hate and envy his father because his father has sexual access to his mother, whom the son desires sexually. However, the son cannot consciously admit desiring her, let alone act on his desire. Instead, the son consciously adores and behaves deferentially and lovingly toward his father, constantly telling himself and others how wonderful his dad is.
Rationalization	Through rationalization, we can avoid threatening thoughts and explanations of behavior by replacing them with nonthreatening ones.	A woman married to a compulsive gambler may justify (rationalize) her husband's behavior by attributing it to his desire to win a lot of money because of his great concern for the financial well-being of the family.
Regression	When we regress, we revert to thinking and behaving in ways that are characteristic of an earlier stage of socioemotional development. In this way, we ward off the anxiety or pain that we are experiencing in our present stage of development (see Chapter 13).	When a newborn enters the family, older siblings may start acting more like infants to attract the attention that is now being bestowed on the newborn. Adults, too, may revert to babyish or childish behaviors when they do not get what they want.
Fixation	Fixation occurs when a person simply stops developing socioemotionally because something prevents the person from advancing to the next stage of socioemotional development. Note that the regressed person has temporarily returned to a previous stage, whereas a fixated person has never progressed to the next stage.	Recall from Chapter 13 the anal stage of development. An adult who was fixated at this stage might be extremely neat, tidy, obsessively clean, concerned with details, and meticulous about all aspects of personal appearance; this person also might avoid anxiety by engaging in compulsive behaviors.

sized. Adler referred to these motivating expectations of what the future will hold as *fictions*. Thus, in Adler's view, we are motivated not by what is actually true but rather by our *subjective perceptions* of what we believe to be true. For example, if a woman believes that her companion is about to desert her for another woman, she is likely to act in ways that reflect her belief, whether or not the belief has any factual basis.

The Analytical Psychology of Carl Jung

At one point, Carl Jung was Freud's favorite student, and Freud may have expected Jung to be his intellectual successor. However, their views increasing diverged, and ultimately this divergence led to a sharp and bitter break. Jung developed ideas that clearly distinguished him intellectually and that radically separated him from Freud. Jung's ideas, like Freud's, are widely applied in psychotherapy.

Like Freud, Jung believed that the mind can be divided into conscious and unconscious parts. However, Jung theorized that the unconscious differed sharply from what Freud's theory had suggested. Jung referred to the first layer of the unconscious as the **personal unconscious,** the part of the unconscious that comprises both repressed memories and experiences that are perceived below the level of consciousness. Each person's unique personal unconscious derives solely from his or her own experiences. Jung believed that the contents of each person's personal unconscious are organized in terms of **complexes,** which are clusters of unconscious thought

Carl Jung (1875–1961) believed that the unconscious comprises both a personal unconscious, distinct to each individual, and a collective unconscious, in which are stored common ancestral personality archetypes.

that function as separate units. These thoughts are emotionally tinged, as would be the case for a complex regarding the person's mother, father, or other close relation. Although Jung's view of the organization of the personal unconscious may have differed somewhat from Freud's more holistic view of the unconscious, Jung's view of another layer of the unconscious was what distinguished Jung as radically departing from Freud.

Jung referred to the second layer as the **collective unconscious.** This level contains memories and behavioral predispositions inherited from our distant human past. According to Jung, people have a common collective unconscious because we have the same distant ancestors; thus, our common ancestral heritage provides each of us with essentially the identical shared memories and tendencies.

People across space and time tend to interpret and use experiences in similar ways because of the existence of **archetypes**—inherited tendencies to perceive and act on things in particular ways. Archetypes in the collective unconscious are roughly analogous to complexes in the personal unconscious, except that

whereas complexes are individual, archetypes are shared. To Jung, the fact that myths, legends, religions, and even cultural customs bear resemblances across cultures provides evidence for the existence of archetypes within the collective unconscious. The following passage illustrates how a Jungian therapist may use these archetypes during therapy.

"It was a dream . . . of you, dressed as a sibyl in a white robe with a blue mantle; you were smiling. On a chain you held a lion, which was staring out of the picture. The lion had a man's face. My face."

"Any other details?"

"The lion's tail ended in a kind of spike, or barb."

"Ah, a manticore!"

"A what?"

"A manticore is a fabulous creature with a lion's body, a man's face, and a sting in his tail."

"I've never heard of it."

"No, they are not common, even in myths."

"How can I dream about something I've never heard of?"

"That is a very involved matter. . . . People very often dream of things they don't know. . . . It is because great myths are not invented stories but objectivizations of images and situations that lie very deep in the human spirit. . . . These myths, you know, are very widespread; we may hear them as children, dressed in pretty Greek guises, but they are African, Oriental, Red Indian—all sorts of things."

—*Robertson Davies,* The Manticore

Jung believed that certain archetypes, listed below, have evolved in ways that make them particularly important in people's lives:

1. *Persona*—the part of our personality that we show the world; the part that we are willing to share with others
2. *Shadow*—the darker part of us, the part that embraces what we view as frightening, hateful, and even evil about ourselves; the part of us that we hide not only from others, but also from ourselves
3. *Anima*—the feminine side of a man's personality, which shows tenderness, caring, compassion, and warmth toward others, yet which is more irrational and based on emotions
4. *Animus*—the masculine side of a woman's personality, the more rational and logical side of the woman

Other archetypes in our collective unconscious include the great mother, the wise old man, and the hero; many of these archetypes play major roles in fairytales. Jung posited that men often try to hide their anima both from others and from themselves because it goes against their idealized image of what men should be.

According to Jung, archetypes play a role in our interpersonal relationships. For example, the relationship between a man and a woman calls into play the archetypes in each individual's collective unconscious. The anima helps the man understand his female companion, just as the animus helps the woman understand her male companion. However, we may fall in love with our idealization of a man or a woman, based on archetypes in the collective unconscious, rather than with the other person as he or she really is. In fact, as noted in Chapter 14, people do seem to have ideals in their relationships (Sternberg & Barnes, 1985), although it is not at all clear that these ideals derive from any collective unconscious. Jung believed that the **self**—the whole of the personality, including both conscious and unconscious elements—strives for unity among often opposing parts of the personality (see Figure 17-2).

The Ego Psychology of Erik Erikson

Yet another key neo-Freudian was Erik Erikson, who differed from Freud in several respects, particularly in terms of the importance assigned to the ego. Erikson helped shift psychological thinking from an emphasis on the role of the unconscious (id) on behavior to an emphasis on the role of the conscious (ego). Unlike Freud, Erikson saw the ego as a source of energy in itself, not as dependent on the id for its psychic energy. Also in contrast to Freud, Erikson viewed the ego as much more than a tenuous mediator between the irrational impulsivity of the id and the extreme strictures of the superego. In fact, Erikson considered the ego to be the main fount from which we establish our individual identity, synthesizing the effects of our past and of our anticipated future. In this way, Erikson (1968) balanced Freud's emphasis on the past with Adler's emphasis on the future, taking a view of human development that encompassed the entire life span (see Chapter 13). As we saw in Chapter 13, Erikson (1963, 1968) also suggested that people develop through stages that build on and incorporate the developmental accomplishments of preceding ones.

Erik Erikson (1902–1994) placed much more importance on the role of the ego than did Freud or other neo-Freudians.

FIGURE 17-2
Mandala Symbols
Carl Jung symbolized the search for unity in terms of the mandala (magic circle), which often is represented as a circle containing various geometric configurations. In many cultures in Asia and in other parts of the world, the mandala represents the universe.

The Interpersonal Theory of Harry Stack Sullivan

Harry Stack Sullivan's ideas developed from and built on his personal experiences. Intriguingly, although he found his own interpersonal relationships quite difficult, he believed that interpersonal relationships are the key to personality. Sullivan's key contribution was his recognition that personality (even including mental disorder) develops entirely within a social context. The whole construct of personality has no meaning outside the social context. Whereas other psychodynamic theorists have tended to look at personality as coming from within the individual (e.g., through internal personality structures) and as something to be imposed on the outside world, Sullivan took the opposite view. He saw personality as forming from the complex of interpersonal relations outside the person. These relations are ultimately imposed on the inner person. He so firmly believed that the environment is crucial in the formation of the person that his ideas may be viewed as precursors for subsequent theories that focused on person-situation interactions (described later in this chapter). Nevertheless, Sullivan is still generally considered to be a neo-Freudian theorist.

Harry Stack Sullivan (1892–1949) differed from other psychodynamic theorists in his emphasis on the role of the social context in personality development.

Karen Horney (1885–1952) believed that what females really want are the privileges that the culture gives to males but not to females (Horney, 1939). Her own career was delayed until a German university was willing to admit women to study medicine.

The Psychoanalytic Theory of Karen Horney

Although Karen Horney trained in the psychoanalytic tradition, she later broke with Freud in several key respects. A major contribution was her recognition that Freud's view of personality development was very male oriented and that his concepts of female development were inadequate (Horney, 1937, 1939). Perhaps most fundamentally, Horney believed that *cultural rather than biological variables* are the fundamental basis for the development of personality. She argued that the psychological differences between men and women are not the result of biology or anatomy, but rather of cultural expectations for each of the two genders. She believed that what females really want are the privileges that the culture gives only to males (Horney, 1939). Indeed, her own career was delayed until a German university was willing to admit women to study medicine.

The essential concept in Horney's theory is that of **basic anxiety** (Horney, 1950), a feeling of isolation and helplessness in a world conceived as being potentially hostile, due to the competitiveness of modern culture. As a result of this competitive climate, people have particularly strong needs for affection, which are not easily met by society. Horney (1937) suggested that we can protect ourselves from the discomfort of basic anxiety in four basic ways. We can allay anxiety by showing *affection* and *submissiveness*, which move us toward other people. We can allay anxiety by being aggressive, *striving for power, prestige,* or *possession.* This strategy moves against people. Also, we can allay anxiety by *withdrawing* or moving away from people and by simply avoiding them altogether.

The Humanistic Psychoanalysis of Erich Fromm

The last of the neo-Freudians we consider here is Erich Fromm, whose work was psychoanalytic, but with strongly humanistic and existentialistic tendencies. **Humanistic** perspectives are oriented toward

Erich Fromm (1900–1980) was considered a neo-Freudian, but his emphasis on humans, human concerns, and the problems associated with human alienation indicated his leanings toward humanism and existentialism, as well.

humans, human connections with one another, human concerns, and secular human values. **Existentialistic** views are focused on the isolated existence of human individuals in an indifferent (neither divinely nor demonically designed) world. Existentialism implies that each individual is personally responsible for her or his own choices, as well as for the consequences of those choices. Fromm was thus a forerunner of the later humanistic and existentialistic theorists. Indeed, he could be classified comfortably with either the neo-Freudians or the humanists, so much was he a bridge between the two.

Fromm recognized that the individual personality could be understood only in light of all of our human history, not within the narrow confines of a single individual's early experiences. He believed that humans, unlike all other animals, have been separated from nature. Fromm (1947) referred to this separation as the **human dilemma.** In addition, he believed, some people become estranged not only from nature, but also from the products of their own labor (Fromm, 1941). Of the different forms of society that people have created over time, many have represented people's attempts to fight off their inherent feelings of alienation.

Like Horney, Fromm uses the concept of *basic anxiety* to describe feelings of loneliness and isolation in the world, but Fromm's understanding of isolation differed slightly from Horney's. For Fromm, anxiety is not caused by the fact that we are alone in a hostile world; instead, by virtue of our solitude, we are free, and this freedom frightens us and makes us feel all

According to Erich Fromm, people seek to escape from freedom through conformity, destructiveness, or bonding with a perceived authority figure. The women depicted here are deriving great comfort through their strong identification with the power of their charismatic leader, as well as through conformity to the social norms of their fellow true believers.

the more alone. Therefore, people often seek to "escape from freedom" (Fromm, 1941).

Fromm proposed three basic mechanisms by which people seek to achieve this escape: authoritarianism, destructiveness, and conformity. These mechanisms most closely tie to what we would consider personality characteristics. *Authoritarianism* is the tendency to give up our freedom in exchange for fusing with some authority figure who has a strength we feel we lack, in the hope of sharing the authority figure's strength. Instead of fusing with another person, we may seek *destructiveness*—that is, we may fight against our basic anxiety by destroying the people from whom we feel isolated. *Conformity* involves abandoning our individuality to become like others. Ironically, people conform to feel more powerful by acquiring the power of the collectivity; some conformists sense a strong personal identity only when their identity is based on little more than mimicry of what other people think, say, and do. Unfortunately, conformity simply makes conformists feel more powerless, which increases their conformity, and a vicious cycle takes hold. According to Fromm, we can achieve true freedom only if we act spontaneously in accord with who we are, rather than according to the rules and scripts that everyone else seems to follow.

In sum, the neo-Freudians placed more emphasis on the ego and less on the id than did Freud, shifting the attention of psychologists more toward conscious processing and away from unconscious processing. They also de-emphasized the role of sexuality, and more emphasized the role of socialization in the development of the individual's personality.

> Give arguments supporting or opposing Fromm's assertion that people use authoritarianism, destructiveness, and conformity to escape from freedom.

Object-Relations Theories

A contemporary extension of Freudian theory, **object-relations theory,** addresses how we relate to one another and how we conceptualize these relationships. The basic notion stems from Freud's belief that instinctual energy is invested in particular *objects,* which are mental representations of people such as the mother, and later, the father, friends, teachers, and the like. In object-relations theory, *investments* in other people are more than just outlets for the satisfaction of instincts. Some of these object relations are primary and provide structure for the self. People who develop successful object relations generally become emotionally stable, whereas those who do not are at risk for mental disorders (Bacal & Newman, 1990; Kernberg, 1975, 1976; Klein, 1975; Kohut, 1984).

Whereas Freud particularly emphasized the Oedipal conflict, object-relations theorists look back even further, especially to the infant's attachment to the mother (see the discussion of attachment theory in Chapter 13). In this way, maladaptive behavior in later life can be caused by an unsuccessful early attachment or an environment that provides harsh and inconsistent treatment of a young child (Ainsworth, 1989; Herman, Perry, & Van der Kolk, 1989).

Assessment of Constructs in Psychodynamic Theories: Projective Tests

Many assessment techniques based on the psychodynamic paradigm have emerged from the attempt to probe the unconscious. These techniques are termed **projective tests** because they encourage individuals to project (throw forward or propel outward) their unconscious or preconscious personality characteristics and conflicts into their responses to the tests. Several projective tests have proven useful in the assessment of constructs from psychodynamic theory. The most well-known test based on the psychodynamic paradigm is the *Rorschach Inkblot Test.*

The Rorschach Inkblot Test

In 1921, Hermann Rorschach devised the *Rorschach Inkblot Test*, which is still widely used today. Originally, Rorschach viewed his test as potentially useful for diagnosing psychopathology, but today it is used much more commonly for assessing personality across a broad spectrum of individuals. Those who use the test believe it provides a means for exploring patients' needs, conflicts, and desires (Erdberg, 1990; Exner, 1978, 1985; Rapaport, Gill, & Schafer, 1968).

The test consists of 10 symmetrical inkblot designs, each printed on a separate card. Five of the blots are in black, white, and shades of gray, and the other five are in color. An example of what a Rorschach card might look like is shown in Figure 17-3. Rorschach intentionally created the inkblots to be nonrepresentational. Although inkblots do not look like anything in particular, people see things in them, projecting themselves into the designs and potentially revealing aspects of their psychological makeup. The examiner carefully records how the subject describes each blot—typically describing several different things in a single design.

FIGURE 17-3

Rorschach Inkblot Test

One way of scoring this projective test is to consider the following four factors: location, *the place on the blot where the subject sees the image;* determinants, *the examinee's use of three principal characteristics in responding to the blot—form (F), human movement (M), and color (C);* content *of the descriptions, such subject matter as humans, animals, geography, sex objects or acts, and so on; and* popularity, *whether the individual gives responses that are unusual or otherwise outside the mainstream of responses.*

Although many different scoring systems have been devised for the Rorschach, the most widely used at present is John Exner's (1974, 1978, 1985; Viglione & Exner, 1983) "Comprehensive System," which takes into account four factors: the *location, determinants, content,* and *popularity* of the responses.

The Thematic Apperception Test

Another widely used psychodynamic assessment tool is the **Thematic Apperception Test,** or TAT (Morgan & Murray, 1935; Murray, 1943b). In administering the TAT, the examiner presents a series of ambiguous but representationally realistic pictures. The subjects project their feelings into these pictures by suggesting what has led up to the scene in the picture, what is happening in the picture, and what will happen. *Apperception* refers to this projection of personal information into the stimulus that is perceived. Henry Murray (1943c) suggested that the examiner must consider six things when scoring the TAT: (1) the hero of the story; (2) the hero's motives, actions, and feelings; (3) the forces in the hero's environment that act on the hero; (4) the outcomes of the story; (5) the types of environmental stimuli that impinge on the people in the story; and (6) the interests and sentiments that appear in the story (see Figure 17-4).

FIGURE 17-4

Thematic Apperception Test

In the Thematic Apperception Test, *illustrations of ambiguous situations, such as this one, are used as a means of prompting test-takers to project their own personalities into the situation depicted.*

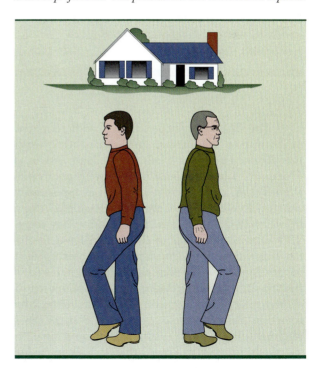

THE MINNESOTA REPORT ^TM* Page 1
for the Minnesota Multiphasic Personality Inventory ^TM : Adult System
By ames N. Butcher, Ph.D.

Client No. : 987654321   Gender : Female
Setting : Mental Health Inpatient   Age : 45
Report Date : 28-APR-89
PAS Code Number : 230244   733 0003

PROFILE VALIDITY

This is a valid MMPI profile. The client's responses to the MMPI validity items suggest that she cooperated with the evaluation enough to provide useful interpretive information. The resulting clinical profile is an adequate indication of her present personality functioning.

SYMPTOMATIC PATTERN

A pattern of chronic psychological maladjustment characterizes individuals with this MMPI profile. The client is overwhelmed by anxiety, tension, and depression. She feels helpless and alone, inadequate and insecure, and believes that life is hopeless and that nothing is working out right. She attempts to control her worries through intellectualization and unproductive self-analyses, but she has difficulty concentrating and making decisions.

She is functioning at a very low level of efficiency. She tends to overreact to even minor stress, and may show rapid behavioral deterioration. She also tends to blame herself for her problems. Her life-style is chaotic and disorganized, and she has a history of poor work and achievement.

She may be preoccupied with occult ideas. Obsessive-compulsive and phobic behavior are likely to make up part of the symptom pattern.

Her response content indicates that she is preoccupied with feeling guilty and unworthy, and feels that she deserves to be punished for wrongs she has committed. She feels regretful and unhappy about life, complains about having no zest for life, and seems plagued by anxiety and worry about the future. She has difficulty managing routine affairs, and the item content she endorsed suggests a poor memory, concentration problems, and an inability to make decisions. She appears to be immobilized and withdrawn and has no energy for life. According to her response content, there is a strong possibility that she has seriously contemplated suicide. A careful evaluation of this possibility is suggested. She views her physical health as failing and reports numerous somatic concerns. She feels that life is no longer worthwhile and that she is losing control of her thought processes.

INTERPERSONAL RELATIONS

Problematic personal relationships are also characteristic of her life. She seems to lack basic social skills and is behaviorally withdrawn. She may relate to others ambivalently, never fully trusting or loving anyone. Many individuals with this profile never establish lasting, intimate

----
NOTE: This MMPI interpretation can serve as a useful source of hypotheses about clients. This report is based on objectively derived scale indexes and scale interpretations that have been developed in diverse groups of patients. The personality descriptions, inferences and recommendations contained herein need to be verified by other sources of clinical information since individual clients may not fully match the prototype. The information in this report should most appropriately be used by a trained, qualified test interpreter. The information contained in this report should be considered confidential.

MINNESOTA MULTIPHASIC PERSONALITY INVENTORY
Copyright THE UNIVERSITY OF MINNESOTA
1943, Renewed 1970. This Report 1982. All rights reserved.
Scored and Distributed Exclusively by NCS PROFESSIONAL ASSESSMENT SERVICES
Under License From The University of Minnesota

*   "The Minnesota Report," "MMPI," and "Minnesota Multiphasic Personality
Inventory" are trademarks owned by the University Press of the University of
Minnesota.

FIGURE 17-5
The MMPI Profile with an Interpretation
This graph shows the profile of a client's responses to the MMPI. Each column indicates a separate dimension measured by the scale. The left column indicates measures of validity, such as whether the person is believed to be lying (L), and the right column indicates dimensions of personality.

The TAT also may be scored for different kinds of motivation (see Chapter 16), such as achievement motivation (Atkinson, 1958; McClelland, Atkinson, Clark, & Lowell, 1953) and power motivation (Veroff, 1957; Winter, 1973), as well as for assessing the use of defense mechanisms. For example, Abigail Stewart (1982; Stewart & Healy, 1985) has scored TAT protocols for uses of different defense mechanisms as they apply to the various psychosexual stages of development. She was particularly interested in four things expressed in the story: attitude toward authority, relations with others, feelings, and orientation to action. Based on these four things, Stewart classified subjects as more oral, anal, phallic, or genital, respectively, in terms of Freud's theory (Stewart, Sokol, Healy, & Chester, 1986).

Client No. : 987654321   Report Date : 28-APR-89   Page 2

relationships. Her marital situation is likely to be unrewarding and impoverished. She seems to feel inadequate and insecure in her marriage.

She is a rather introverted person who has some difficulties meeting other people. She is probably shy and may be uneasy and somewhat rigid and overcontrolled in social situations.

BEHAVIORAL STABILITY

This is a rather chronic behavioral pattern. Individuals with this profile live a disorganized and pervasively unhappy existence. They may have episodes of more intense and disturbed behavior resulting from an elevated stress level.

DIAGNOSTIC CONSIDERATIONS

Individuals with this profile show a severe psychological disorder and would probably be diagnosed as severely neurotic with an Anxiety Disorder or Dysthymic Disorder in a Schizoid Personality. The possibility of a more severe psychotic disorder, such as Schizophrenic Disorder, should be considered, however.

Individuals with this profile present some suicide risk and further evaluation of this possibility should be undertaken.

The content of her responses to the MMPI items suggests symptoms (convulsions, paralysis, clumsiness, and double vision) that are associated with neurological disorder. Vague pain symptoms, nausea, etc. that are found in neurotic conditions are also present, however. Further neurological evaluation would be needed to make a clear differentiation.

TREATMENT CONSIDERATIONS

Inpatients with this MMPI profile usually receive psychotropic medications for their extreme depression or intense anxiety. Many patients with this profile seek psychological treatment for their problems. Indeed, individuals with this profile usually require psychological treatment for their problems along with any medication that is given. Since many of their problems tend to be chronic ones, an intensive therapeutic effort might be required in order to bring about any significant change. Patients with this profile typically have many psychological and situational concerns; thus it is often difficult to maintain a focus in treatment.

She probably needs a great deal of emotional support at this time. Her low self-esteem and feelings of inadequacy make it difficult for her to get energized toward therapeutic action. Her expectancies for positive change in therapy may be low. Instilling a positive, treatment expectant attitude is important for her if treatment is to be successful.

Individuals with this profile tend to be overideational and given to unproductive rumination. They tend not to do well in unstructured, insight-oriented therapy and may actually deteriorate in functioning if they are asked to be introspective. She might respond more to supportive treatment of a directive, goal-oriented type.

Individuals with this profile present some suicide risk and precautions should be considered.

NCS Professional Assessment Services, P.O. Box 1416, Mpls, MN 55440

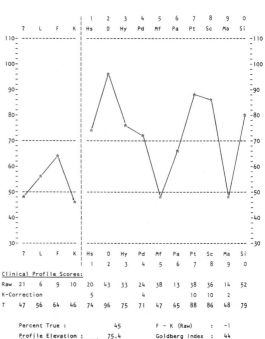

THE MINNESOTA REPORT   Page 3
for the Minnesota Multiphasic Personality Inventory : Adult System
By James N. Butcher, Ph.D.
CLINICAL PROFILE

Client No. : 987654321   Gender : Female
Setting : Mental Health Inpatient   Age : 45
Report Date : 28-APR-89

Clinical Profile Scores:

	?	L	F	K	Hs	D	Hy	Pd	Mf	Pa	Pt	Sc	Ma	Si
					1	2	3	4	5	6	7	8	9	0
Raw	21	6	9	10	20	43	33	24	38	13	38	36	14	52
K-Correction					5			4			10	10	2	
T	47	56	64	46	74	96	75	71	47	65	88	86	48	79

Percent True :   45   F - K (Raw)   : -1

Profile Elevation :   75.4   Goldberg Index : 44
(Hs,D,Hy,Pd,Pa,Pt,Sc,Ma)

Henrichs Rule : Indeterminate

Welsh Code :   2*78"0314'6-95:   F-L/?K:

Scale	Abbreviation	Possible Interpretations
VALIDITY SCALES		
Question	?	Corresponds to number of items left unanswered
Lie	L	Lies or is highly conventional
Frequency	F	Exaggerates complaints or answers items haphazardly
Correction	K	Denies problems
CLINICAL SCALES		
Hypochondriasis	Hs	Has bodily concerns and complaints
Depression	D	Is depressed, guilty; has feelings of guilt and helplessness
Hysteria	Hy	Reacts to stress by developing physical symptoms; lacks insight
Psychopathic deviate	Pd	Is immoral, in conflict with the law; has stormy relationships
Masculinity/ femininity	Mf	Shows interests and behavior patterns considered stereotypical of the opposite gender
Paranoia	Pa	Is suspicious and resentful, highly cynical about human nature
Psychasthenia	Pt	Is anxious, worried, high-strung
Schizophrenia	Sc	Is confused, disorganized, disoriented; has bizarre ideas
Hypomania	Ma	Is energetic, restless, active, easily bored
Social introversion	Si	Is introverted, timid, shy; lacks self-confidence

Objective Personality Tests

Objective personality tests are administered using a standardized (i.e., *objective*) and uniform procedure for scoring. The most widely used of the objective tests for assessing abnormal behavior is the *Minnesota Multiphasic Personality Inventory* (MMPI) (Hathaway & McKinley, 1943). The MMPI consists of 550 items covering a wide range of topics. Subjects answer each of the items, such as the following, as either *true* or *false* (Hathaway & McKinley, 1951, p. 28):

I often feel as if things are not real.   T   F

Someone has it in for me.   T   F

As shown in Figure 17-5, the MMPI contains 4 validity scales, 10 clinical scales, and 4 special scales. The *validity scales* are designed to assess the extent to which the clinician can have confidence in the results for the other scales. For example, the Lie Scale (L) measures the tendency of the test-takers to try to present themselves in a way that is excessively favorable. The *clinical scales* measure 10 different forms of abnormal behavior. For example, a person with a high score on Scale 6, Paranoia, tends to have suspicious

or grandiose ideas. The *special scales* measure particular attributes that may be of interest to a clinician, even though they are not abnormal.

The MMPI has several strengths. First, the test is objectively scored, which avoids the subjectivities of scoring and interpretation that characterize projective tests. Second, the scale has been widely used, so a wealth of data is available for interpretation and comparison of scores and score profiles. Third, it contains several different validity scales, which help the clinician assess the extent to which the results are credible. Fourth, the scale covers a range of abnormal behavior.

The MMPI also has some problems. The primary drawback is that it is hard to know how to interpret responses to the MMPI. When test-takers are asked merely to respond "true" or "false" to a series of statements, they may find themselves interpreting the statements in ways that give a particular impression rather than answering the statements literally. Moreover, although the MMPI may adequately assess people's impressions of what they are like or of what they do with their time, these responses do not necessarily correspond to what they really like to do (see

Helmes & Reddon, 1993). A new version of the MMPI (MMPI-2) recently has been developed to deal with some of these concerns (Butcher et al., 1989).

The MMPI has been used extensively with ethnic minorities in the United States and elsewhere (Butcher & Pancheri, 1976). When clinicians use the MMPI with ethnic minorities in the United States, various adjustments are necessary (Greene, 1987). The main reason for this need is because ethnic and racial groups were not included—or were drastically underrepresented—in the original standardization sample used in developing the norms for the test (Butcher & Williams, 1992; Graham, 1990). When the MMPI is used cross-culturally, other problems also must be considered. For instance, if the test is used in non-English-speaking countries, it must be carefully translated. Further, people in other cultural contexts may not be as familiar with the very concept of testing devices, so they may either approach the task indifferently or misunderstand the meaning of what is expected of them in order to perform the task (Lonner, 1990).

Assessing Psychodynamic Tests

On what bases can we appraise the various instruments used to assess people in psychodynamic terms (only some of which, of course, are described here)? Some clinicians (e.g., Spangler, 1992; Stewart, 1982; Stewart & Healy, 1989) take projective tests such as the Rorschach and the TAT very seriously. Others, such as Walter Mischel (a cognitive-behavioral personality theorist), believe that these tests lead clinicians to faulty decisions. Mischel has argued (1977, 1986) that clinicians interpret projective tests based on what the clinicians would like to see in the test data, not on what is actually implicit in the test data (see, e.g., Chapman & Chapman, 1969; Dawes, 1994).

Mischel (1968, 1986) has suggested that the validity of any single test is likely to be limited. When similar results are obtained with multiple kinds of tests, however, we may be more confident in our conclusions. Mischel's observation affirms a fundamental aspect of scientific research: Scientific conclusions must be based on converging sources of information, whether that information is about individuals, groups, or humanity as a whole.

Criteria for Evaluating the Psychodynamic Paradigm

Table 17-2 comparatively evaluates psychodynamic research as a whole, using the criteria specified at the outset of this chapter. As this table shows, psychodynamic theories have been highly influential; have led directly to very little experimental research, the bulk of which is limited in scope; vary in terms of their comprehensiveness, with Freud and some neo-Freudians relatively comprehensive but other neo-Freudians very limited in scope; are relatively parsimonious; and have produced numerous, extensive psychotherapeutic approaches and techniques.

In addition to the criticisms based on the general criteria, several other specific criticisms have been lodged against psychodynamic theory. Primarily, as suggested by the paucity of experimental research, the theory is virtually unverifiable because it cannot be subject to disconfirmation. A classic encounter between philosopher of science Karl Popper and neo-Freudian Alfred Adler illustrates this point:

> [Psychoanalysis] has the apparent virtue of being able to explain any human action, normal or pathological. This strength is psychoanalysis's weakness: the theory forbids nothing, and therefore cannot be falsified. . . . Popper recalls confronting Alfred Adler with a case he thought contradicted Adler's theory. After Adler had explained it, Popper asked him how he knew his explanation was correct. "Because of my thousandfold experience."
>
> "And with this new case, I suppose, your experience has become thousand-and-one-fold," Popper responded recognizing that every potential falsification would be transformed by Adler into a verification.
>
> —*Michael Gorman*, Simulating Science

Progress in science depends on having a means by which to disconfirm hypotheses, as well as to confirm them. Many early psychodynamicists were so extreme in their views that they countered any challenges to the theory by asserting that the challengers were merely exhibiting psychodynamically based defensive reactions against it. Of course, persons who warmly accepted the theory also were viewed as confirming the merits of the theory.

Design an experiment that would test one specific psychodynamic construct (e.g., the cross-cultural universality of some of Jung's archetypes or the relation between specific childhood experiences and specific adult personality characteristics).

TABLE 17-2
Psychodynamic Theories: A Critical Evaluation
Psychodynamic theories get high marks for influence on psychology, as well as for comprehensiveness.

Criteria	Psychodynamic Approaches
Importance to and influence in psychology	Have spawned little research to test theories that developed within the approach, as a response to it, and as a reaction against it. Freud, the first major psychodynamic theorist, remains the most influential thinker in personality psychology. Many clinical psychologists (especially psychiatrists) today adhere to Freudian or neo-Freudian perspectives.
Testability of its propositions	Theories do not rate high for testability. Relatively small number of experiments, none of which studied the theories as a whole or fully compared and contrasted the theories. Case studies tend to be open to many interpretations; research has proven to be nondefinitive.
Comprehensiveness	Reasonably complete account of personality phenomena. Freud's theory was comprehensive, as were Adler's and Erikson's, but many other neo-Freudian theories (e.g., by Fromm and Horney) were much less so. Although Jung's theory was relatively comprehensive, it is in part mystical. All of the theories were derived from work with patients who presented adjustment problems and so are more descriptive of the structures and processes underlying extraordinary problems than they are of those of normal persons who have milder, more usual problems.
Parsimoniousness	Less parsimonious than some theories, but the number of constructs is not excessive.
Usefulness to applications in (a) assessment and (b) therapeutic technique	(a) The TAT, Rorschach, and other projective tests have arisen from this theory. (b) Its extensive influence on psychotherapy is considered in depth in Chapter 19.

HUMANISTIC AND EXISTENTIAL PARADIGMS

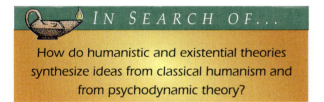

I N   S E A R C H   O F . . .

How do humanistic and existential theories synthesize ideas from classical humanism and from psychodynamic theory?

Although psychodynamic theories of personality generally predate humanistic theories, the humanistic tradition in philosophy dates to the ancient Greeks. Modern views of humanism are often seen as dating back to the Renaissance. The humanism embraced by Desiderius Erasmus (c. 1466–1536) and his contemporaries may be seen in part as a reaction to restrictions on free thinking, particularly those constraints posed by the religious doctrine of the day. Contemporary humanism may be seen largely as a reaction to the biological determinism of Freud and some of his followers.

Humanists of all stripes tend to oppose *materialistic philosophy*, which holds that all humans can be understood in terms of the principles of biology, physics, and chemistry. Nonetheless, humanists do not see themselves as being entirely unscientific. Rather, they consider themselves as being scientific in a way that differs sharply from the scientific orientation of Freud and some of the other psychodynamic theorists.

Humanists differ widely in their particular beliefs, but they share a common view of humans: We are complex and distinct from other life forms. Unlike other living organisms, we are future-oriented and purposeful in our actions. To a large extent, we can create our own lives and determine our own destinies, rather than viewing ourselves as shaped and buffeted by inexplicable forces outside our conscious grasp. One aspect of the humanists' nondeterministic perspective is a heavy emphasis on the role of conscious rather than unconscious experience. We now turn to considering three of the major humanistic theorists—Carl Rogers, Abraham Maslow, and Rollo May.

The Self Theory of Carl Rogers

Carl Rogers's **person-centered approach** to personality strongly emphasizes the self and each person's perception of self. In Rogers's **self theory**, reality is what the self defines as being reality, not an unknowable objective set of things and events outside the self. Each person's conception of self begins in infancy and continues to develop throughout the life span. This **self-concept** comprises all the aspects of the self that the person perceives, whether or not these perceptions are accurate or are shared by others. In addition, each person has an **ideal self,** those aspects that the person would like to embody. A major contribution of Rogers was the recognition that the greater the similarity between the self-concept and the ideal self, the better adjusted the person is in his or her life (Rogers, 1959, 1980).

Rogers (1978) believed that people tend to become more and more complex as they try to fulfill their potential. To Rogers, people have within them the power to make themselves whatever they want to be, if only they choose to use this power.

Like Abraham Maslow (Chapter 16), Rogers (1961b, 1980) believed that all people strive toward self-actualization, although he affirmed that some persons self-actualize more effectively than others. According to Rogers, self-actualizing persons have five characteristics:

1. They will be constantly growing and evolving.
2. They will be open to experience, avoid defensiveness, and accept experiences as opportunities for learning.
3. They will trust themselves, and, although they will seek guidance from other people, they will make their own decisions rather than strictly following what others suggest.
4. They will have harmonious relations with other people and will realize that they do not need to be well-liked by everyone. Achieving conditional acceptance from at least some others will free them from the need to be well-liked by all.
5. They will live fully in the present rather than dwell on the past or live only for the future; Rogers (1961b) described this characteristic as *existential living*.

The Holistic-Dynamic Theory of Abraham Maslow

Chapter 16 introduced you to Abraham Maslow, focusing on his theory of motivation. Within his hypothesized hierarchy of needs, the highest level is the need for self-actualization. Maslow's (1970) descrip-

tion of self-actualized people (those who fully use all of their potentials and make the most of who they are) is similar to Rogers's: Self-actualized people are free of mental illness and have reached the top of the hierarchy of needs. They have experienced love and have a full sense of their self-worth and value. They accept both themselves and others unconditionally and accept what the world brings to them. They have a keen perception of reality and can discern genuineness in others, shunning phoniness in themselves. They are neutral and ethical in their dealings with others. As they face the events in their lives, they are problem-centered, seeing problems for what they are, rather than seeing all problems in relation to themselves and their own needs. They are able to be alone without constantly feeling lonely, and they have the ability to map out their own paths. They have constructed their own system of beliefs and values and do not need others to agree with them in order to hold true to what they stand for. They appreciate and enjoy life and live it to its fullest.

Both Maslow's and Rogers's descriptions of self-actualization may represent more an ideal toward which we strive than a state that many of us are likely to reach. Few, if any, people meet all of the criteria for self-actualization, but many people have satisfied at least some of these criteria, for at least some of the time. These criteria are worthy of our strivings, even if we do not fully reach them.

The Existential Psychology of Rollo May

Several of the theorists mentioned in this chapter had personal experiences, conflicts, or problems that seem to have played a crucial role in the formulation of their theories (e.g., Horney's attention to cultural rather than biological variables). Rollo May's existential perspective may have stemmed from his having had to spend three years living in a sanitarium, recovering from tuberculosis. While in the sanitarium, May noticed that a person's state of mind strongly related to the person's ability to recover. The people who recovered appeared to be those who fought the disease, whereas those who did not fight it tended to die.

While in this life-and-death context, May was particularly drawn to the work of Søren Kierkegaard, a nineteenth-century Danish philosopher who was key to the founding of the existentialist movement. Not coincidentally, May later became a spokesperson for the existentialist movement in the United States. May embraced the existentialist notion that in order to live a life based on choices, we must assume full responsibility for ourselves, and we must consider all

Rollo May (1901–1994) developed an existential perspective on personality during his three years living in a sanitarium, recovering from tuberculosis. In this context, May noticed that a person's state of mind strongly related to the person's ability to recover. The people who recovered appeared to be those who fought the disease, whereas those who did not fight it tended to die.

possible options. To do so, we must value *authenticity*, and we must seek to achieve our full potential.

The existentialists' emphasis on authenticity and achieving our full potential resonates with the emphasis of the humanistic theories. However, existentialism sounds a discordant note in its view of life and death. At some point, each of us realizes the threat to our own existence imposed by death, and existentialists suggest that, at least to some extent, we can only appreciate our sense of existence—of being—by also appreciating its antithesis—nonbeing or nothingness. For May and other existentialists, the prospect of death gives meaning to life.

Note that much of May's existentialist psychology seems philosophically tied to the psychology of Fromm. Like May, Fromm clearly placed great importance on existential dilemmas and on the problem of alienation. May's views are also similar to Fromm's in the shared belief that personality psychologists need to understand the role of freedom in personality. According to May, however, in order to be completely free, we need to be free both in what we can do and in how we are able to think. The way in which we can be in the world is affected by both.

Evaluation of the Humanistic Approach

The humanistic approach has lost some popularity since its heyday during the 1960s and early 1970s. Paradigms go in and out of favor, perhaps because every paradigm and every theory is a reflection of the time in which it is formulated, and times change. Freud's theory very much reflects Victorian thinking, and some of the conflicts that were prevalent in Victorian times are no longer common today. Indeed, some of the ailments Freud treated (e.g., those he linked to sexual repression) are rarely found in present, less prudish times. Similarly, humanism closely fit the *zeitgeist* (intellectual climate of an era) of the 1960s and early 1970s, when the human-potential movement was flourishing. It may fit today's zeitgeist less well. Still, its message regarding the importance of the individual and the opportunities for controlling our own fate and striving toward self-actualization may be as relevant today as they ever were.

Table 17-3 summarizes the evaluation of the humanistic paradigm in terms of the five criteria previously used for evaluating the psychodynamic paradigm. At present, the humanistic paradigm may not fully explain personality and its development, and it may function best when used in conjunction with other views. Nonetheless, humanists encourage us to move beyond narrow views of ourselves to realize more of our great human potential.

THE COGNITIVE-BEHAVIORAL PARADIGM

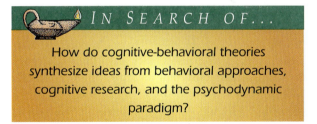

IN SEARCH OF...

How do cognitive-behavioral theories synthesize ideas from behavioral approaches, cognitive research, and the psychodynamic paradigm?

Cognitive-behavioral approaches to personality look at how people think, how they behave, and how thinking and behaving interact.

Antecedents of Cognitive-Behavioral Approaches

Early Behaviorist Approaches

Recall from Chapter 2 that behaviorists seek to understand people in terms of the way we act, either downplaying or repudiating altogether the thought

TABLE 17-3
Humanistic Theories: A Critical Evaluation
Humanistic messages continue to relate to contemporary experience.

Criteria	Humanistic Approaches
Importance to and influence in psychology	Has generated even less empirical research than psychodynamic theories. Messages continue to be important, however: focus on individuals, personal choices, opportunities to control fate, striving toward self-actualization.
Testability of its propositions	Almost untestable, by definition. Predictions seldom operationally defined with enough precision to generate experiments.
Comprehensiveness	Although it deals with some aspects of human nature (e.g., need for self-actualization or individual potential), it leaves much unsaid. Theories lack comprehensiveness.
Parsimoniousness	Reasonably parsimonious; does not have many terms or overwhelming constructs.
Usefulness to applications in (a) assessment and (b) therapeutic technique	(a) Tends to be averse to assessment because tests focus on assigning labels to the client rather than on the person's evolving potential. (b) Strongly influenced therapy during 1960s and 1970s, but less influential today.

processes that mediate between stimulus and response. Chapter 7 considered how behaviorism can be used in our understanding of learning. Behavioral approaches to learning emphasize the explanation of observable behavior in terms of stimulus-response events, with explanations usually taking the form of environmental contingencies that produce various forms of behavior.

For example, according to B. F. Skinner, "Self or personality is at best a repertoire of behavior imparted by an organized set of contingencies" (1974, p. 149). Skinner had no patience for any internalized constructs; he was interested only in environmental contingencies and behavior. That is, people differ in their personalities because they have been subjected to different environmental contingencies and schedules of reinforcement and thereby have developed in different ways through learning in their environments. He did not deny that internal states might exist; he simply believed that they are not available for scientific study and therefore are not appropriate objects of psychological theory or investigation.

If people develop personalities through patterns of reinforcement contingencies in the environment, how do apparently maladjusted personalities develop? In the Skinnerian view, people can become maladjusted in several ways. One way is through reinforcement of antisocial behaviors, such as giving extra attention to a class clown. Another way is through punishment of prosocial behaviors, such as punishing a child for truthfully confessing to accidentally breaking a dish.

Behavioral psychologists, therefore, have tended to emphasize stimulus-response contingencies in personality and have sought to understand how people respond to the various stimulus contingencies of their environment. In contrast, cognitive psychologists are concerned with processes going on in the mind. Cognitive-behavioral psychologists are concerned with the link between mind and behavior.

Cognitive Antecedents

Many cognitive ideas about perception and problem solving stemmed from the Gestalt psychology movement (see Chapters 2, 5, and 10 for more about this movement). Although most Gestalt psychologists focused their work on cognition, Kurt Lewin and some others studied personality and related topics as well. Lewin (1935/1951) termed his personality theory a *field theory* because he believed that life is played out in a psychological field, much like a mathematical field. He called the field in which personality and behavior operate a *life space*, which is the sum of all the forces that act on a person at a particular time. Forces include both internal and external stimuli that affect the person. For example, hunger would be an internal force, and other people's expectations an external one.

One of Lewin's most important contributions was the idea that the life space can be divided into various regions, such as home life and work life. For some people, the boundaries between these regions are thin and permeable (e.g., they let problems on the job affect their home life), whereas for other people,

Kurt Lewin (1890–1947) viewed personality from a cognitive perspective.

the boundaries between regions are thick and impermeable. These people keep different aspects of their life experience separate.

We now turn to some of the more modern and central cognitive-behavioral theories. Two such theories are those of Julian Rotter and of Albert Bandura.

The Social-Learning Theory of Julian Rotter

Although Julian Rotter is behaviorally oriented, he does not believe that behavior depends solely on external stimuli and reinforcements. Rather, what is important is the meaning that the person assigns to a given external stimulus or reinforcement. In other words, Rotter, unlike Skinner, is interested in cognitive aspects of personality, not just behavioral ones. Rotter believes that behavior is not a function of just the person or of just the environment, but rather of the interaction between the two (Rotter, 1966, 1990; Rotter & Hochreich, 1975).

Rotter's focus on the individual's perceptions of the environment leads naturally to what may be the

most important and the most widely cited aspect of his theory: his notion of internal versus external locus of control. **Internal** people see a strong causal relationship between what they do and the consequences of those actions. Internals tend to take personal responsibility for what happens to them. Taken to an extreme, an internal person would tend to misattribute causality to internal rather than to external sources. If such a person were laid off during an economic recession, he or she would still probably feel personally responsible for the layoff.

External people, in contrast, tend to believe that the causes of behavioral consequences are in the environment. Taken to an extreme, an external would tend to misattribute causality to external rather than to internal causes. If such a person were fired due to incompetence and lack of effort, he or she would be likely still to feel as though other factors (the boss's prejudice, coworkers' conspiracies, etc.) had caused

Julian Rotter (1916–   ) considers some features of the behavioral perspective on personality by noting the importance of environmental events in personality development. However, Rotter believes that the importance of these events lies in the meaning that the individual assigns to these events more than in the actual stimuli or reinforcers alone.

According to Julian Rotter, people perceive situations in either of two ways: Externals *see themselves as objects controlled by the forces of external events, such as being laid off from work.* Internals *see themselves as* agents, *taking charge of the situations they face. When Wally Amos (right) was forced out of the cookie company he had founded, and was prevented from using his own name in association with any new ventures, he took charge of his life and moved on to found a new enterprise making Uncle No-mané (no name) cookies.*

the termination. Thus, an internal believes that he or she has control of his or her own fate, whereas an external tends to see fate as controlled by luck, by others, or by destiny.

Thousands of studies have focused on Rotter's theory and his *Internal-External (I-E) Control Scale,* including cross-cultural research (Dyal, 1984). For example, both the Indian (Hindu and Buddhist) concept of *karma* and the Chinese concept of *yuan* have great relevance to the concept of locus of control (Kulkarni & Puhan, 1988). Karma refers to the notion that a person's present experiences and opportunities are shaped largely by forces resulting from actions of the person in a previous incarnation and that the person's present actions will affect the forces that shape the person's future experiences, both in the present incarnation and in future ones. Yuan is a unique Chinese conception of fatalistic attitudes "in which the traditional Chinese believed that almost every interpersonal relationship or transaction is predetermined by fate, some unknown force, or what one did in one's last life" (Yang, 1986, p. 157). Both yuan and karma appear to be extreme forms of externality, in that persons who subscribe to them believe

that they have little or no control over their own present destiny, although their moral actions in the present are likely to affect them in future incarnations.

Although extreme views typically involve some distortions of the true causes of events, at least some of the time, having a more internal locus of control is associated with many positive achievement- and adjustment-related outcomes (see, e.g., Lachman, 1986; Phares, 1988, 1991). Similarly, the tendency toward an internal locus of control leads a person to feel more efficacious—that is, more able to do whatever must be done.

The Social-Cognitive Theory of Albert Bandura

Albert Bandura's theory addresses the *interaction* between how we think and how we act (a truly cognitive-behavioral approach). His model of **reciprocal determinism** (1986) attributes human functioning to an interaction among behavior, personal variables, and the environment (see Figure 17-6). For example, the decision to go to college will be affected by *per-*

sonal variables, such as motivation and the ability to succeed in cognitive, academic work. This decision also will be affected by *environmental events*, such as parental encouragement and the funds to enroll. The result is *behavior*—going to college—which will in turn affect the opportunities the student has later in life, such as to pursue occupations that will be unavailable to those who choose not to go to college.

A crucial personal variable in personality is our set of beliefs in our own **self-efficacy**—that is, our feelings of competence to do things. Feelings of self-efficacy seem actually to lead to our being better able to do those things (Bandura, 1986) (see Chapter 16). If I tell myself I cannot do something, I often will not even try it, with the result that I will never really learn how to do it. If I go ahead and try to do the thing, while constantly telling myself that I will not

Albert Bandura (1925–   ) views personality and behavior as affected by—but not completely ruled by—external events over which people have no control. Bandura (1986, 1988) probably places more emphasis on the role of chance in people's lives than do some other theorists.

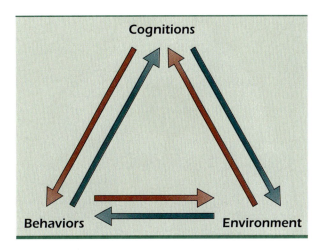

FIGURE 17-6
Reciprocal Determinism
Albert Bandura's social-cognitive theory emphasizes reciprocal determinism, in which thinking, behavior, and the environment reciprocally interact.

succeed, my negative expectations may get in the way of what I do, resulting in a negative, self-fulfilling prophecy (see Chapter 1).

Other Cognitively Oriented Theories

Schema-Based Theories

How we think about ourselves and others is the chief concern of another line of research that follows from the cognitive-behavioral approach: schema theory. Recall (from Chapters 9 and 12) that a *schema* is a cognitive framework for abstract knowledge. Schemas enable us to process new information about situations we face. Hazel Markus (1977; Markus & Smith, 1981; Markus, Cross & Wurt, 1990) has been particularly interested in the development of self-schemas. As you might have guessed, **self-schemas** are the individual's cognitive frameworks for knowledge about her- or himself. Thus, our particular self-schemas make it easier for us to process new information about ourselves and our interactions in particular situations. According to this view, personality can be seen as comprising, in large part, the sum of a person's schemas and the interactions among those schemas.

Clearly, each individual's set of self-schemas is distinctive because we all perceive ourselves differently. We differ in both the content (e.g., mechanical skills, social activities) and the structure (e.g., simple or complex; highly compartmentalized or highly interconnected) of our self-schemas (McAdams, 1990). We also differ in terms of how many and how elaborate are our self-schemas (Fenigstein, Scheier, &

In Hazel Markus's theory of personality development, people's self-schemas provide a cognitive framework for personality, serving as a basis for handling new situations and for incorporating new information into the existing personality structure.

Buss, 1975). William Nasby (1985) has referred to people who have more elaborated self-schemas as being higher in *private self-consciousness*—that is, in awareness of themselves and of their distinctive personalities.

Social Intelligence

Another way of describing personality is via individuals' degree of social intelligence. Research by Nancy Cantor and John Kihlstrom (1987) suggests that people who are higher in social intelligence are more flexible in their interactions with other people, are able to see more options for how to interact with them, and tend more closely and appropriately to match their responses to those of other people in similar situations, based on finer *discriminations* (i.e., observations of subtle differences in social cues). From the point of view of Cantor and Kihlstrom, problem solving underlies social interaction, and some people are better able to solve the social problems they confront than are others.

Evaluation of Cognitive-Behavioral Theories

The cognitive-behavioral approach to personality is particularly useful for achieving behavioral change, perhaps because of its emphasis on conscious rather than unconscious function. It is much easier for us to gain access to and to change things about which we are conscious. If our behaviors and our thoughts fall outside of our awareness and cannot be brought into awareness except with great difficulty, we are hard-pressed to change them. By concentrating on the conscious, the cognitive-behavioral approach enables us to implement change more directly, and, many would argue, more effectively as well.

However, because cognitive-behavioral theories focus on the interactions between how people think and how they behave, these theories do not specify any particular list of distinctive traits that characterizes people and how they differ. Such lists are addressed by George Kelly and the trait theorists, considered next. (See Table 17-4 for a brief evaluation of the cognitive-behavioral paradigm in terms of its

Nancy Cantor and her colleague John Kihlstrom have explored the ways in which social intelligence better enables people to handle social situations.

TABLE 17-4
Cognitive-Behavioral Theories: A Critical Evaluation
Cognitive-behavioral theories have spawned a great deal of research interest, at least partly because their propositions are highly testable.

Criteria	Cognitive-Behavioral Approaches
Importance to and influence in psychology	Have generated much research by theorists in this area and others.
Testability of its propositions	More testable than psychodynamic or humanistic approaches; strong data.
Comprehensiveness	Less comprehensive than other views, these theories address aspects of personality and behavior that follow from learning, but they do not specify the dimensions on which people differ. They say less than other theories about the structure of personality.
Parsimoniousness	These theories rate high on parsimony, especially Bandura's because he adhered so closely to his data; Rotter's theory is only slightly less so.
Usefulness to applications in (a) assessment and (b) therapeutic technique	(a) Rotter's locus of control and interpersonal trust scales widely used, but they measure narrow bands of personality, not the whole thing. (b) Have generated many different methods of psychotherapy (see Chapter 19) and have been very influential in health psychology (see Chapter 20).

influence on theory and research and its testability, comprehensiveness, parsimony, and practical applicability.)

Choose the cognitive-behavioral theory that intuitively seems the most plausible to you, and describe some of your own personality characteristics in terms of that theory.

THE PERSONAL CONSTRUCT THEORY OF GEORGE KELLY

IN SEARCH OF...

How does Kelly's theory integrate ideas from humanistic, cognitive, and behavioral theories, and how might his theory provide a link to trait theories?

Situated between cognitive-behavioral approaches and trait theories is George Kelly's theory of personal constructs. The fundamental idea in Kelly's (1955) theory is that we categorize the world in terms of **personal constructs**—characteristic ways in which we see some things as being similar and other

When George Kelly (1905–1967) produced his one major work, The Psychology of Personal Constructs (Kelly, 1955), his education and his career had been spotty, and he was a relative unknown in the field.

things as being dissimilar. All of our constructs are *bipolar*—they are construed in terms of dimensions with opposites at the extremes (see Figure 17-7). For example, if we were to have a personal construct of *happy–sad*, we would see people as being alike or different based on this characteristic. Happy people would be perceived as like one another and as different from sad people, who are like each other but different from happy people. Because each of us develops our own system of personal constructs, we best understand other people in terms of our own idiosyncratic system of constructs.

According to Kelly, we create and use these constructs to help us deal with future events. We create the set of constructs that we believe will most help us make sense of the world as we need to confront it. Thus, Kelly is closer to Adler's thinking than to Freud's in his emphasis on personality as a construction to anticipate the future rather than to deal with the past. Kelly's theory is important to psychology for its recognition that constructs and categories are not just givens in people's lives. To a large extent, people create their own constructs and categories through which to view the world.

FIGURE 17-7
Kelly's Role Construct Repertory Test
In George Kelly's view, each of us has our own idiosyncratic system of personal constructs, so Kelly's test is designed to encourage test-takers to indicate the constructs they believe to be most central to personality, as shown in themselves and in key persons in their lives.

Myself	Mother	Father	Best friend	Sister	Most admired teacher	Uncle	Girl friend	Neighbor	Construct	Contrast
✓	✓								witty	humorless
		✓			✓				patient	ill-tempered

THE TRAIT-BASED PARADIGM

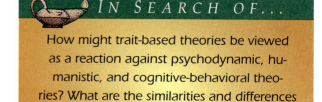

IN SEARCH OF...

How might trait-based theories be viewed as a reaction against psychodynamic, humanistic, and cognitive-behavioral theories? What are the similarities and differences between trait-based approaches and other approaches?

Trait theories emphasize **traits**—consistent attributes that characterize what a person is like. As has been the case for many psychological phenomena, the origins of traits are attributed both to nature (hereditary characteristics or predispositions) and to nurture (environmental influences), but the emphasis on one or the other differs across various trait theories. According to some trait theorists, each of us is born with an individually distinctive set of traits—our nature. The existence of this distinctive set of inborn traits implies that we may inherit these traits, or at least that we inherit the predisposition to develop such traits. According to other trait theorists, however, our traits are shaped largely by our interactions with the surrounding environment—our nurture. Research (e.g., see Plomin, 1986, 1989) indicates that both nature and nurture contribute to the development of our distinctive personality traits, and that as effects of early rearing environments recede, the effects of nature may actually increase with age.

Trait theorists also diverge regarding how strongly they emphasize the lifelong stability of traits. Some theorists hold that personality traits are largely inborn and stable across the life span, whereas others believe that personality traits develop and change somewhat, although the predisposition to develop particular traits may exist at birth. Robert Plomin (1986, 1989), a developmental psychologist, has been interested in observing how both heredity and environment influence the developmental changes in our personalities. In Plomin's view, just as our physiological growth is influenced by heredity within an environmental framework, so is the growth of our personalities. (See Chapter 13 for more on how personality develops across the life span, starting with studies of infant temperament.)

There are two basic kinds of trait theories of personality: nomothetic and idiographic.

Nomothetic Theories

Nomothetic theories are based on the belief that all people have essentially the same set of traits and that they differ only in terms of the extent to which they have each trait. Some of these theories try to specify the whole range of personality, suggesting a list of traits believed to characterize fully what people are like. Other theories deal with just a single trait, but in great depth. The following discussion proceeds from some of the broader theories to some of the more narrow ones.

The Factor-Analytic Theory of Raymond Cattell

Perhaps in part because Raymond Cattell worked as a graduate student in the laboratory of Charles Spearman, he, like Spearman, has advocated the use of factor analysis in the study of human characteristics (see Chapter 11). Recall that in factor analysis, the researcher tries to tease out the essential variables underlying a wide array of individual differences.

Cattell basically distinguishes two levels of personality traits: surface traits and source traits. **Surface traits** are what we observe as characterizing differences among people. Cattell, however, considers surface traits to be scientifically less interesting and important than the more fundamental source traits. **Source traits** are the underlying psychological dimensions that generate the surface traits; in fact, Cattell (1979) worked backward from the myriad surface traits, using factor analysis to derive 23 source traits.

Cattell and his colleagues have devised a test that measures the first 16 of the personality factors listed in Table 17-5: the **Sixteen Personality-Factor Scale** (16PF; Cattell, 1982; Cattell, Eber, & Tatsuoka, 1970). This paper-and-pencil inventory asks people whether particular attributes characterize them and whether they do particular things. Separate scores are obtained for each of the 16 personality factors, and individual scores can be combined, using mathematical formulas, to obtain measures of what Cattell considers to be higher order (i.e., more general) traits, such as anxiety and independence (see Figure 17-8). For example, the measure of anxiety is a combination of scores on Factors C, H, L, Q-3, and Q-4 (see Table 17-5), meaning that people who are anxious have the source traits of being, respectively, easily upset, timid, suspicious, apprehensive, low in personal control, and tense.

Cattell's 16PF has been used extensively in other cultures. Cattell even precedes his 16 factors

Perhaps in part because Raymond Cattell (1905–   ) worked as a graduate student in the laboratory of Charles Spearman, he, like Spearman, has advocated the use of factor analysis in the study of the human characteristics encompassed by personality.

with the initials U.I. (Universal Index) to suggest the worldwide applicability of each factor and, of course, the entire inventory. Despite Cattell's firm belief in the universality of his test, however, the cross-cultural use of his inventory (and others) is fraught with problems. For instance, many of the items may not be appropriate for other societies even if they are translated carefully (Brislin, 1986; Lonner, 1990). In addition to the difficulty of translating some words specific to the Western culture, the difficulty of ensuring cultural relevance seems insurmountable in many cultural contexts.

> Choose two traits from Cattell's 23 traits, and list numerous surface traits that could fall within the domain of these two source traits. Give an example of behavior you might expect to see in a person high in these two traits.

TABLE 17-5
Cattell's 23 Traits

Raymond Cattell identifies each trait by a letter (or in some cases, a letter-numeral combination) as well as by a technical term. He invented many of the technical terms he used for designating various source traits. Cattell's last seven traits are called "Q" traits, for "questionable," because he was not as sure of his analysis of these traits as of the other ones.

Factor	Low Score Description	High Score Description
A	SIZIA Reserved, detached, critical, aloof	AFFECTIA Warmhearted, outgoing, easygoing, participating
B	LOW INTELLIGENCE[1] Low mental capacity, dull, quitting	HIGH INTELLIGENCE High mental capacity, bright, persevering
C	LOW EGO STRENGTH Affected by feelings, easily upset, changeable	HIGH EGO STRENGTH Emotionally stable, faces reality, calm
D	PHLEGMATIC TEMPERAMENT[2] Undemonstrative, deliberate, inactive, stodgy	EXCITABILITY Excitable, impatient, demanding, overactive, unrestrained
E	SUBMISSIVE Obedient, mild, easily led, docile, accommodating	DOMINANCE Assertive, aggressive, competitive, stubborn
F	DESURGENCY Sober, taciturn, serious	SURGENCY Enthusiastic, heedless, happy-go-lucky
G	LOW SUPEREGO STRENGTH Disregards rules and group moral standards, expedient	HIGH SUPEREGO STRENGTH Conscientious, persistent, moralistic, staid
H	THRECTIA Shy, timid, restrained, threat-sensitive	PARMIA Adventurous, "thick-skinned," socially bold
I	HARRIA Tough-minded, rejects illusions	PREMSIA Tender-minded, sensitive, dependent, overprotected
J	ZEPPIA[2] Zestful, liking group action	COASTHENIA Circumspect individualism, reflective, internally restrained
K	SOCIAL UNCONCERN[2] Socially untutored, unconcerned, boorish	SOCIAL-ROLE CONCERN Socially mature, alert, self-disciplined
L	ALAXIA Trusting, accepting conditions	PROTENSION Suspecting, jealous, dogmatic

(Continued)

The Theory of Hans Eysenck

Hans Eysenck's (1952, 1981) theory of personality is as simple as Cattell's is complex. This simplicity has been one reason for the theory's acceptance by some researchers. An extensive research base backing up the theory is another. Eysenck argues that personality comprises three major traits: extroversion, neuroticism, and psychoticism. These elements vary within each individual, along a continuum. The **extroversion** trait characterizes people who are sociable, lively, and outgoing. Introverts, in contrast, are quiet,

TABLE 17-5 *(Continued)*

Factor	Low Score Description	High Score Description
M	PRAXERNIA Practical, has "down-to-earth" concerns	AUTIA Imaginative, bohemian, absent-minded
N	NAIVETE Forthright, unpretentious	SHREWDNESS Astute, worldly, polished, socially aware
O	UNTROUBLED ADEQUACY Self-assured, placid, secure, complacent	GUILT PRONENESS Apprehensive, self-reproaching, insecure, troubled
P	CAUTIOUS INACTIVITY[2] Melancholy, cautious, takes no risks	SANGUINE CASUALNESS Sanguine, speculative, independent
Q_1	CONSERVATISM Disinclined to change, respects traditional values	RADICALISM Experimenting, analytic, free-thinking
Q_2	GROUP DEPENDENCY A "joiner," sound follower	SELF-SUFFICIENCY Self-sufficient, resourceful, prefers own decisions
Q_3	LOW SELF-SENTIMENT Uncontrolled, lax, follows own urges	HIGH SELF-SENTIMENT Controlled, exacting willpower, socially precise, compulsive, follows self-image
Q_4	LOW ERGIC TENSION Relaxed, tranquil, unfrustrated, composed	HIGH ERGIC TENSION Tense, frustrated, driven, overwrought, fretful
Q_5	LACK OF SOCIAL CONCERN[2] Does not volunteer for social service, experiences no obligation, self-sufficient	GROUP DEDICATION WITH SENSED INADEQUACY Concerned with social good works, not doing enough, joins in social endeavors
Q_6	SELF-EFFACEMENT[2] Quiet, self-effacing	SOCIAL PANACHE Feels unfairly treated by society, self-expressive, makes abrupt antisocial remarks
Q_7	LACKS EXPLICIT SELF-EXPRESSION[2] Is not garrulous in conversation	EXPLICIT SELF-EXPRESSION Enjoys verbal-social expression, likes dramatic entertainment, follows fashionable ideas

[1] Factor B (INTELLIGENCE) is an ability trait rather than a temperament trait.
[2] One of the "seven missing factors," so termed because they were not identified by the original 16PF.

reserved, and generally unsociable. People characterized by **neuroticism** are moody, nervous, irritable, and subject to sudden and apparently unpredictable mood swings. In contrast, emotionally stable people tend to be less fretful, more uniform in their behavior, and less subject to sudden mood swings. People characterized by **psychoticism** are solitary, uncaring of others, lacking in feeling and empathy, and insensitive; they are often quite detached from others in their interpersonal relationships (see Figure 17-9).

The "Big Five"

As you may have noticed, many of the different theorists, even those from different paradigms, seem to mention some of the same key personality characteristics (termed *traits*, *factors*, etc.). The **"big five"** theory of personality, the most widely accepted trait theory, recognizes the frequent recurrence of five personality traits across studies (especially factor-analytic studies) and even across theorists. The "big five"

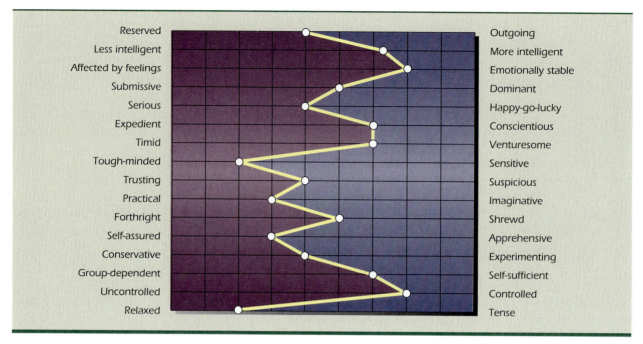

FIGURE 17-8

Sixteen Personality Factor Questionnaire (16PF)

Raymond Cattell's test (1982; Cattell, Eber, & Tatsuoka, 1970) invites test-takers to indicate whether particular attributes characterize them and whether they do particular things. Through profile analysis, separate scores are interpreted for each of 16 personality factors (the first 16 traits shown in Table 17-5). (After Cattell, 1973)

traits were first proposed by Warren Norman (1963) but have since been championed by many other investigators (e.g., Costa & McCrae, 1992a, 1992b; Digman, 1990; McCrae & John, 1992; Peabody & Goldberg, 1989; Watson, 1989).

Although different investigators sometimes have given the "big five" different names, they generally have agreed on the following five characteristics as a useful way to organize and describe individual differences in personality. The descriptions paired with the characteristics depict someone rated high in these traits:

1. **Neuroticism**—nervous, emotionally unpredictable, tense, and worried

2. **Extroversion**—sociable, outgoing, fun-loving, and interested in interacting with other people

3. **Openness**—imaginative, intelligent, curious, artistic, and aesthetically sensitive

4. **Agreeableness**—good-natured, easy to get along with, empathetic toward others, and friendly

5. **Conscientiousness**—reliable, hard-working, punctual, and concerned about doing things right

FIGURE 17-9

Eysenck's Personality Dimensions

This chart illustrates two of the three personality dimensions described by Hans Eysenck and shows how they may be related to Hippocrates's four humors. (Eysenck's third dimension, psychoticism, is not shown here.)

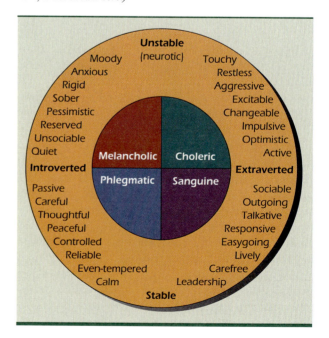

Describe your own personality in terms of the "big five" traits. Wht aspects of your personality are not captured by these five key traits?

Theories of Individual Personality Traits

Although the broader theories of personality may play a larger role in the trait-theory paradigm than do theories of particular traits, some investigators have chosen to study specific traits in depth. One of the best-known programs of research is Marvin Zuckerman's (1969, 1978) series of studies on such a trait, sensation seeking. **Sensation seeking** refers to the tendency to seek out stimulation from the environment. It is a good example of the interrelatedness of psychological constructs, in that although it is considered under the topic of personality here (and elsewhere), it could be considered under the topic of motivation as well. People who are higher in sensation seeking tend to seek out more dangerous activities, such as sky diving; are more active sexually and tend to seek more variety in their sex lives; are more likely to smoke and to drink; prefer foods with stronger flavors; and are more likely to gamble (Zuckerman, 1978, 1985). People who are at either extreme with regard to sensation seeking tend to have abnormal personalities. For example, psychopaths (who lack conscience and have little concern for others) are particularly high in sensation-seeking, whereas schizophrenics (who are dissociated from the world) tend to be particularly low (Zuckerman, 1978).

As we saw in Chapter 16, another personality trait that has been studied fairly extensively is **self-esteem,** or the level of regard people have for themselves. People with higher levels of self-esteem tend to be more active, more expressive, and more confident (Singer, 1984). People with lower self-esteem, on the other hand, tend to be less well adjusted and often convince others to think as little of them as they do of themselves (Coates & Wortman, 1980). Sometimes, the most able children are those with the lowest self-esteem, either because other children react negatively to them, or because they set very high standards for themselves (Janos, 1990).

Still other researchers have studied **cognitive styles**—ways of relating to the world that reflect both cognition and personality. For example, researchers have been intrigued by *integrative complexity*, the tendency to see the world in elaborate, sophisticated terms. A person with a high level of integrative complexity recognizes more than one point of view on an issue, identifies large numbers of dimensions in making judgments, integrates more dif-

According to Marvin Zuckerman, sensation seekers tend to prefer activities that offer great risk, potential danger, and a high level of stimulation. When personality is characterized by either extreme (high or low) of sensation seeking, the individual may show an abnormal personality. In such individuals, sensation seeking also might be considered a cardinal or a central trait, according to Gordon Allport's idiographic theory of personality.

ferent points of views into a decision, and so on (Porter & Suedfeld, 1981; Schroder, Driver, & Streufert, 1967). In a particularly interesting study, Peter Suedfeld and Luz Piedrahita (1984) examined the correspondence of eminent individuals during the last 10 years of their lives. The researchers found that people's integrative complexity tended to decrease in their last years of life. I have found that with age people's styles of thinking become more conservative and less oriented toward risk (Sternberg, 1994a).

Mischel's Critique of Nomothetic Trait Theories

In 1968, when the field of personality research was largely dominated by trait theories and cognitive-bc-havioral perspectives were far from widely accepted,

Searchers . . .   *WALTER MISCHEL*

Walter Mischel is Professor of Psychology at Columbia University.

Q: *How did you become interested in psychology and in your area of work in particular?*

A: I became interested in psychology when reading novels, as an adolescent, and trying to understand what was really motivating and driving the characters. I became further interested when, working my way through school, I worked with youngsters in settlement houses on the Lower East Side. I began to get a feeling of the intensity and range of the problems that young people encounter and became very eager to understand something about how they may get help. That's when I decided to study clinical psychology, which is what my original training was in. That's where I also developed my original skepticism about the limitations of some of the theories of the time.

Q: *What theories have influenced you the most?*

A: I was most influenced by psychodynamic theory, originally, particularly Sigmund Freud's writing. I became fascinated by the possibilities of motivations and drives that lie outside of awareness. They were used to account for striking inconsistencies in behavior, which made some sense if interpreted dynamically. The problem was that evidence on the validity of the inferences being drawn was very suspect.

Q: *What is your greatest asset as a psychologist?*

A: Skepticism, persistence, and curiosity.

Q: *What makes a psychologist really great?*

A: Becoming obsessed with something important, having luck and a good intuitive nose for where the important problems are and for figuring out a method for making important complicated problems tractable.

Q: *How do you get your ideas for research?*

A: Much of my own research that has to do with developmental issues, or issues of personality growth and change, comes directly from having observed my own children when they were young.

Q: *How do you decide whether to pursue an idea?*

A: My approach to research has been programmatic. I have been interested in two very large questions and have pursued them in many different forms, but on the same theme, over the years. The form of the problem keeps shifting, but the basic question is essentially stable.

Q: *What kinds of obstacles have you experienced?*

A: If you're asking interesting questions in nonobvious ways, you run into the problem of not having a peer group ready to support that work. So the problem is you have to go out on a limb. And that can get very lonely. The way I overcame it was usually by finding a colleague or two that I could work with closely.

Q: *What is your major contribution to psychology?*

A: My challenge to traditional conceptions of personality, in trait terms, shook up the field and opened the route for an essentially cognitive revolution to occur in social and personality psychology.

Q: *What do you want students to learn from you?*

A: I try to get them excited about the phenomenon and not about the abstract theory. I want them to ask a question that involves a real psychological phenomenon.

Q: *What advice would you give to someone starting in the field of psychology?*

A: Find a way to break away from the mainstream and a good question to pursue.

Q: *What did you learn from your mentors?*

A: From George Kelly I learned to listen to what people tell you, to suspend your own constructs and try to get at the phenomenon. Also to find a different way of looking at problems. From Julian Rotter I learned how to build elegant systems.

Q: *What have you learned from your students?*

A: To see the field from the new perspective that they bring in.

Q: *Apart from your life as an academic, how have you found psychology to be important?*

A: I don't think it has been. I think psychology has been a way of doing science that I have tried not to let have an impact on the rest of my life.

Q: *How do you keep yourself academically challenged?*

A: The challenges are internal. I keep myself challenged by being my own harshest critic.

Q: *What do you further hope to achieve?*

A: I'd like to provide tentative answers to some of the larger questions that were opened up when I challenged the traditional trait paradigm.

Walter Mischel published a stinging critique of trait theories in his book *Personality and Assessment*. The basis of Mischel's critique was quite simple. He went back to a study conducted by Hugh Hartshorne and Mark May (1928), which examined the extent to which children are honest in a variety of situations. The investigators found that the degree of consistency was quite low.

Because Mischel did not want to make sweeping criticisms based on only one trait—perhaps honesty is an exception—he then reviewed a large body of research on many different personality traits. His wider investigations showed that this early study of honesty yielded results that were quite typical of personality research. Although traits might correlate highly from one paper-and-pencil measure to another, their correlations with any meaningful kind of behavior were low, around 0.30.

Mischel was not stating that higher correlations are not possible, or that they are never obtained. For example, he noted that correlations involving intelligence as a predictor of behavior were often higher. Still, the correlations in the personality literature were so low that he questioned whether the idea of personality traits had any basis at all. Mischel (1968; Mischel & Peake, 1983) suggested instead that personality theorists should concentrate on the relations between situations and behavior, rather than on hypothetically stable traits, which he claimed had little effect on behavior.

Prior to Mischel's critique, personality psychologists had assumed that situations were not particularly relevant to personality research. Therefore, Mischel's review generated a flurry of responses. One response was to suggest that a correlation of 0.3 actually is not all that modest. Robert Rosenthal and Donald Rubin (1982) showed that in terms of practical prediction, a correlation of 0.3 is by no means trivial and may even be viewed as rather high. A second response (Funder & Ozer, 1983) tested Mischel's claim that situations have a greater effect on behavior than do personality traits. Instead of correlating personality traits across situations, situations were correlated across behaviors. In other words, the researchers looked at the extent to which we can predict behavior as a function of situation rather than of trait. They found that the correlation coefficient indicating the predictive power of situations for behavior was rarely over 0.3—roughly the same as the correlation they would expect to obtain from traits. The researchers argued, therefore, that there was no better basis for Mischel to emphasize situations than there was for other investigators to emphasize traits.

A third response was that Mischel's critique was simply incomplete; whether there is consistency in traits depends both on what traits are examined and on how these traits are examined. Some researchers suggested that, at least for some traits, the level of consistency was much higher than Mischel was willing to grant (Hogan, DeSoto, & Solano, 1977; Pervin, 1985); for example, some studies show substantially greater consistency of a given trait over the life span. Jack Block (1981) has found consistency across the life span for the traits of *ego control* (a person's ability to control his or her impulsive behavior)

and *ego resiliency* (a person's flexibility and response to the demands of the environment).

A fourth response has been to suggest that instead of concentrating on traits, we should concentrate on behavior. This *act-frequency approach*, proposed by David Buss and Kenneth Craik (1984), combines aspects of the cognitive-behavioral approach to personality with aspects of the trait approach. Instead of giving paper-and-pencil measures of how persons say they *are*, Buss and Craik concentrated on how people say they would *act*. Buss and Craik asked people to indicate the extent to which various behaviors characterize them, and then rated people's levels of traits in terms of the extent to which the people said they performed acts representing each of those traits. They found that if they measured traits by measuring the frequencies of particular acts, they could break the 0.3 barrier that Mischel criticized. However, to break the barrier, they needed to base their assessments of traits on *prototypical acts*—acts that best represented the traits.

One of the most cogent kinds of responses to Mischel, however, originated long before Mischel ever wrote his critique: the idiographic approach to personality traits. We consider this approach next.

Idiographic Theories

Idiographic theories hold that people differ in their personality traits, or at least in the importance of these traits. This approach dates back to one of the deans of personality theory, Gordon Allport.

The critical aspect of Allport's theory of personality (1937, 1961) was his belief that much of personality is characterized by **personal dispositions** (traits that are unique to each individual). Although Allport also mentioned *common traits* (which are common across individuals), he believed that much of what makes each of us who we are can be found in the personal dispositions rather than in the common traits. Given this view, for many traits, it would be hard to calculate correlations between any kind of paper-and-pencil measure and behavior because the same traits might not even be relevant to different people.

Allport also believed that each person's various traits differ in their importance for the person. For example, most people possess a **cardinal trait,** which is a single trait that is so dominant in the person's behavior that almost everything the person does somehow relates back to it (Allport, 1961). Although not everyone has a cardinal trait, all people do have **central traits**—the most salient traits in their dispositions; typically, each person has about 5 to 10 of these traits. In addition, all people have **secondary traits**—those that have some bearing on their

Searchers . . .   *DARYL BEM*

Daryl Bem is Professor of Psychology at Cornell University.

Q: *How did you become interested in psychology in general and in your area of work in particular?*

A: I have a bachelor's degree in physics, having taken only one psychology course, Psych 101, in college. As a graduate student in physics at MIT, I was encouraged to take a minor program to be broadly educated. So I decided to take my minor in social psychology. I was fascinated by the authoritarian personality because it combined attitude change as well as race relations. I took a course in the psychology of race relations. That was the year (1960–1961) that the freedom rides had begun in the South, and a number of students, both black and white students, had come back and were reporting to our class about what was going on in the South. It was very exciting. I was particularly intrigued by how quickly some of the attitudes in the South were changing, even though they had been entrenched for years. At the end of that course, I decided to become a social psychologist. So I switched to the psychology program at Michigan and finished up three years later.

Q: *Whose ideas have influenced you the most?*

A: Interestingly, the person who most influenced me was B. F. Skinner. I started out with a very naive notion. I asked one of Skinner's students, Harlan Lane, if he thought one could change someone's attitudes by just reinforcing them for their attitudes. He said sure, so he and I did a study to see whether or not we could change the attitude about brown bread that a group of kids in an institution for the mentally retarded would eat, by just using programmed instruction. It worked in a peculiar way. We found that persuading oneself, by saying "I like brown bread," is the same as just having some authority figure say, "You like brown bread." And that led me to devise self-perception theory, which became my doctoral dissertation. It came out of my interest in attitude change, and, of course, naive Skinnerian view.

Q: *What is your greatest asset as a psychologist?*

A: Probably being not tied too much to other people's theories. I'm very open-minded. If something interests me, I will do something on it, but I rarely have a long-term sustained program of research. That means that I'm not around to clean up the mess afterward, but I enjoy breaking into the mess. So it's both my greatest weakness and my greatest asset. And I'm relatively creative in the area of ideas.

Q: *What makes a psychologist really great?*

A: I think it's the ability to smell a new idea, or even to look at an old problem in a new way, and not get caught up too much in what the field is currently doing.

Q: *How do you get your ideas for research?*

A: When I first started out, most of my ideas actually were generated by puzzles within the field. Walter Mischel got me interested in personality because of his 1968 book that essentially questioned the entire enterprise of using traits.

Q: *How do you decide whether to pursue an idea?*

A: It's intuitive, whether the idea has a transforming quality, of turning something on its head and looking at it differently.

Q: *What is your major contribution to psychology?*

A: My major contribution may be yet to come. I think it would be fascinating to be able to persuade the psychological profession that the data on ESP are solid and that there's something to ESP. At this point, I think attribution theory has essentially incorporated self-perception theory. In the personality area, having people reconsider what is a person-centered, rather than a variable-centered, approach to personality.

Q: *What do you want your students to learn?*

A: I love teaching introductory courses because I like to be the first one to show students the world of human behavior and how to think about it, how psychology is relevant to life. I like having them see the abortion issue and sexual orientation and things like that in a whole new way.

Q: *What advice would you give to someone starting in the field of psychology?*

A: Be willing to take some risks. Read outside the psychological literature; get to know the anthropologists, especially if you go into social psychology.

Q: *Apart from your life as an academic, how have you found psychology to be important?*

A: I've gotten more interested in family patterns and family interactions. Also, I have found very useful psychology's approach to human behavior, at looking at issues like the abortion issue. Why is it that the abortion issue is so contentious? Why is it we can't reach compromises? And so, my whole approach to politics is strongly flavored by the way a psychologist goes about asking questions.

Q: *What do you further hope to achieve or contribute?*

A: I'd like to redefine certain problems and have people think about them the same way. Sexual orientation is one. I have an explanation for the origins of sexual orientation. Everyone now seems to be running toward a genetic or biological explanation. I think that's just dead wrong. I mean, I accept the genetic data, but I think the genes code for personality, and that personality produces sexual orientation.

behavior but that are not particularly central to what they do.

More recently, personality psychologists have considered Allport's ideas about personality in light of Mischel's critique of trait theories. For example, Daryl Bem and Andrea Allen (1974) have suggested that it may be a mistake to try to predict the behavior of all people all of the time, whereas it may be quite realistic to try to predict the behavior of some people some of the time. In their modified idiographic approach, Bem and Allen found correlations of personality traits across situations of well above 0.3, but only for those personality traits in which a person is consistent. Although some studies using this approach also have suggested its usefulness (Bem & Funder, 1978; Kenrick & Stringfield, 1980), other investigations have not replicated Bem and others' positive and consistent results (e.g., Chaplin & Goldberg, 1984; see also Mischel & Peake, 1982).

THE INTERACTIONIST APPROACH

Many of the theories considered so far contain an implicit—and highly promising—response to Mischel's critique. This response is to adopt an **interactionist approach,** which emphasizes the interaction between the person and the situation. Interactionist views are not limited to trait theories. Indeed, Rotter's, Bandura's, and other theorists' ap-proaches can be viewed as broadly interactionist. In fact, even Mischel, who originally took the strictly cognitive-behavioral approach, now views personality from an interactionist perspective.

The basic idea is simple: The correlations among traits or between traits and behaviors depend on the kind of situation or situations the person encounters. For example, to relate extroversion to happiness, the interactionist would suggest that extroverts will be happy if they are in the center of constant interactions with other people but will be unhappy if stranded on a desert island by themselves. When relating sensation seeking and happiness, interactionists would predict that sensation seekers would be happy if confronted with the opportunity to sky dive or climb mountains or explore caves but would be unhappy spending day after day in a college library. From the interactionist point of view, then, the correlation between personality traits and various kinds of behavior, or even between one trait and another, is mediated by situations. Thus, whereas a trait theorist might look only at the trait, and a behaviorist might look only at the situation, the interactionist would look at the interaction between the personality trait and the situation (Bowers, 1973; Endler & Magnusson, 1976).

> Design an experiment to test the degree to which trait differences versus situational differences determine a particular behavior.

TABLE 17-6
Trait Theories: A Critical Evaluation
Because of their foundation in factor-analytical techniques, trait theories are highly testable and have spawned a great many empirical studies.

Criteria	Trait-Based Approaches
Importance to and influence in psychology	Has generated much empirical research, like the cognitive-behavioral approach.
Testability of its propositions	Highly testable: Most theories make fairly precise predictions, especially compared with psychodynamic or humanistic theories.
Comprehensiveness	Those theories focusing on personality as a whole are comprehensive; these focusing on specific traits clearly are not. Trait theories say less than others do about the development of personality traits.
Parsimoniousness	Depends on the theory: Eysenck's theory and the "big five" are extremely parsimonious; Cattell's theory is not..
Usefulness to applications in (a) assessment and (b) therapeutic technique	(a) Many trait theories have generated personality tests, (b) but these theories have generated far fewer therapeutic techniques than have other theories. Trait theories focus more on static characteristics and less on dynamic processes.

TABLE 17-7
Four Major Personality Paradigms
The major theoretical paradigms of personality are psychoanalytic, humanistic/existential, cognitive-behavioral, and trait theories.

Paradigm	Psychoanalytic	Humanistic/ Existential	Cognitive-Behavioral	Trait
Major theorists	Freud, Adler, Jung, Erikson, Sullivan, Horney, Fromm	Rogers, Maslow, May	Rotter, Bandura, Markus, Cantor and Kihlstrom, Mischel (also inter-actionists)	Cattell, Eysenck, Kelly (personal construct)
Basis for personality	Conflicting sources of psychic energy	The distinctive human ability to act purposefully and to shape our own destiny by being future oriented	The interactions among thoughts and the environment, which influence behavior	Stable sources of individual differences that characterize an individual, based on an interaction of nature and nurture
Key features of personality theory	(a) Developmental changes across the life span, with early childhood experiences profoundly influencing adult personality (b) Deterministic view of personality as being largely governed by forces over which the individual has little control (c) Importance of unconscious processes in shaping personality and behavior	*Nondeterministic* view of personality as being subject to the conscious control of the individual	(a) How individuals think about and give meaning to stimuli and events in their environment, as well as to their own behavior, shapes their personality and behavior (b) People need to feel that they are competent in controlling their environment	(a) *Nomothetic* theorists hold that all people have the same set of traits, but individuals differ in the degree to which they manifest each trait (b) *Idiographic* theorists hold that each individual has a different set of traits that is fundamental to her or his personality
Basis for theory development	Case studies of individuals seeking help for psychological problems	Humanistic philosophy, personal experiences, and clinical practice	Experimental findings, as well as the development and use of personality tests	(a) *Nomothetic theories*—factor analysis of comprehensive assessment of individuals (b) *Idiographic theories*—comprehensive assessments of individuals, emphasizing intra-individual differences (e.g., through self-reports and naturalistic observations), bolstered by experimental findings

For example, in Mark Snyder's (1979, 1983) construct of **self-monitoring**—the degree to which people monitor and change their behavior in response to situational demands—some people ("high self-monitors") behave very differently, depending on with whom they are associating. Such a person might act in one way in the presence of a professor but in a totally different way when the professor is not there. Other people ("low self-monitors") are more consistent in their behavior, acting pretty much the same with everyone. Thus, if we wanted to look at consistency of behavior across situations, we would want to know about people's tendency to monitor themselves because low self-monitors tend to be much more consistent than high self-monitors.

What behaviors lead to success in a job? How would we predict success on the job based on personality variables? For example, would extroversion predict success in sales? This hypothesis would seem reasonable, yet the extent to which extroversion predicts success in sales is almost certainly going to be moderated by interest in selling. People who do not want to be salespersons are unlikely to succeed in the grueling world of sales, no matter how extroverted they are.

In conclusion, the interactionist approach builds on the trait-based approach by asserting that the predictive validity of personality measures for behavior can be moderated by the kinds of situations in which the behavior takes place, as well as by possible differences in intraindividual consistency in a given trait. Table 17-6 summarizes the trait-based approach to personality, and Table 17-7 summarizes all of the major approaches we have covered in this chapter.

Trait theories have been highly influential in the field of personality, and dominate the work of those interested in personality assessment. The theories are testable and fairly comprehensive, and some of the theories are quite parsimonious as well. These theories continue to be influential in modern-day thinking about the nature of personality.

Trait theories and the other theories and paradigms in this chapter have focused on personality traits as they apply to the normal range of behavior. However, many psychologists interested in personality, especially those who treat patients, are interested particularly in the abnormal personality. We turn to this type of personality in the next chapter.

SUMMARY

1. *Personality* can be evaluated in terms of several criteria. Five such criteria are important in psychology: importance and influence, testability, comprehensiveness in accounting for psychological phenomena, parsimoniousness, and usefulness to applied fields.

The Psychodynamic Paradigm   597

2. Freud created the seminal psychodynamic theory of personality, which emphasizes dynamic, biologically oriented processes. The theory also emphasizes how early development influences a person's adaptability to environments.

3. Freud's theory underscores the role of the *unconscious* in the life of the mind. He described three components of the mind: the *id* (which is largely instinctual and impulsive and seeks immediate gratification of sexual and aggressive wishes), the *ego* (which is rational and seeks to satisfy the id in ways that adapt effectively to the real world), and the *superego* (which is irrational

and seeks to avoid the punishment associated with internalized moral strictures). The id operates on the basis of the *pleasure principle*, the ego on the basis of the *reality principle*, and the superego on the basis of the *idealistic principle*.

4. Freud described nine *defense mechanisms* (denial, repression, projection, displacement, sublimation, reaction formation, rationalization, regression, and fixation), which he believed people use to protect themselves from unacceptable thoughts and impulses.

5. Freud's theory was based largely on his case studies of individual patients in his neurological/psychoanalytic practice. He also made extensive use of dream analysis, distinguishing between the *manifest* and the *latent content* of dreams.

6. *Neo-Freudians*—such as Adler, Jung, Erikson, Sullivan, Horney, and Fromm—originally based their theories on Freud's but developed their own psychodynamic theories. Most neo-

Freudian theories are less deterministic than Freud's, and they give more consideration to continuing development of the personality after childhood, as well as to the broader social context within which the individual's personality operates. In particular, Alfred Adler contributed the notion of the *inferiority complex;* Carl Jung, the notion of there being various layers of the unconscious, such as the *personal unconscious* and the *collective unconscious;* Erik Erikson, the notion of the ego rather than the id dominating personality; Henry Stack Sullivan, the importance of interpersonal relations in the formation of the personality; Karen Horney, the importance of *basic anxiety* in leading people to feelings of isolation; and Erich Fromm, the importance of human history in shaping our destinies.

7. More contemporary psychodynamic theories include *object-relations theories,* which consider how people conceptualize their relationships with other people.

8. Psychodynamic theories have been criticized largely in terms of their lack of empirical support.

9. *Projective tests,* which encourage individuals to project their unconscious characteristics and conflicts in response to open-ended questions, are a product of the psychodynamic tradition. These include the *Rorschach Inkblot Test* and the *Thematic Apperception Test* (TAT).

Humanistic and Existential Paradigms   613

10. *Humanistic* theory opposes the psychodynamic paradigm by emphasizing individual responsibility and an appreciation of human experience.

11. Roger's *person-centered approach* to personality may be termed *self* theory. Rogers identified the *self-concept* (the aspects of the self that an individual perceives her- or himself to embody) and the *ideal self* (the aspects of the self that the person wishes to embody) and emphasized the importance of modifying one or the other to achieve as close a match as possible between the two.

12. Maslow emphasized the importance of self-actualization in the development of a healthy personality.

13. May was an existentialist; he underscored the importance of individual freedom and responsibility in personality, as well as the alienation of the individual in an uncaring world.

14. Humanistic theories have not been as influential as other personality theories, but their strength is the strong emphasis they place on the value of each individual human being.

The Cognitive-Behavioral Paradigm   615

15. B. F. Skinner and other strict behaviorists attempted to explain personality exclusively in terms of stimulus-response contingencies, without reverting to mentalistic descriptions.

16. Lewin, Rotter, and Bandura have used a cognitive-behavioral approach to explain personality. Lewin emphasized the notion of regions within the life space that could have more or less permeable boundaries with respect to one another. Rotter emphasized the personality dimension of perceived *internal* versus *external* locus of control. Bandura emphasized the interaction of how we think and how we act. Perceived *self-efficacy* is a key aspect of personality.

17. Schema-based theories of personality are heavily cognitive, emphasizing the individual's schemas about her- or himself, and the individual's social intelligence.

18. Cognitive-behavioral theories have spawned a wealth of empirical research and clinical assessment applications, partly due to the ease of testing such theories. Their parsimony varies from one theory to the next, and they are not known for great comprehensiveness.

The Personal Construct Theory of George Kelly   621

19. Kelly's theory of personality bridges trait-based theories and others, particularly humanistic and cognitive-behavioral theories. Kelly's theory proposes that each of us may be viewed in terms of a set of *personal constructs*—characteristic ways in which we see some things as being similar and other things as being dissimilar. The personal constructs we call upon in given situations determine our behavior.

The Trait-Based Paradigm   622

20. *Traits* are stable sources of individual differences

that characterize a person. Both nature and nurture influence these traits, and different theorists give differing emphasis to one or the other.

21. There are two main kinds of trait theories of personality: *nomothetic theories*, which assert that people have essentially the same set of traits and that they differ only in terms of the extent to which they have each trait; and *idiographic theories*, which posit that people differ in terms of which traits they possess.

22. Nomothetic theories include factor-analytic theories such as that of Raymond Cattell, who created the 16PF scale; relatively simple theories such as that of Hans Eysenck, which posits that personalities comprise the traits of *extroversion*, *neuroticism*, and *psychoticism*; and the widely investigated *"big five"* (neuroticism, extroversion, *openness*, *agreeableness*, and *conscientiousness*) theories. They also include several theories of individual personality traits, such as theories of *sensation seeking*, *self-esteem*, and *cognitive style*.

23. Walter Mischel has criticized nomothetic theories for inadequately considering situational factors affecting behavior. Others have pointed out that personality factors and situational factors each explain only about one-third of behavioral

variation, but that the influence of personality factors increases when more central personality characteristics are considered.

24. *Idiographic* approaches gained impetus with Allport, who underscored the importance of conscious awareness of experience, in stark contrast to the Freudian emphasis on the role of the unconscious. Allport posited that some individuals have *cardinal traits*, which are so central that they explain almost all behavior of the individual. In addition, all people have both *central traits* (highly salient characteristics) and *secondary traits* (less salient characteristics). Their behavior is usually explained by their central traits, but in some situations their secondary traits also play a role. Other theorists have modified Allport's idiographic approach.

The Interactionist Approach 631

25. Contemporary theorists emphasize an *interactionist* perspective, which underscores the interaction between the individual's personality and the given situation. An example of such a notion is Mark Snyder's construct of *self-monitoring*, by which people are more or less consistent in their behavior according to their perceptions of what others would like to see and hear.

KEY TERMS

IN SEARCH OF THE HUMAN MIND:
ANALYSES, CREATIVE EXPLORATIONS, AND PRACTICAL APPLICATIONS

1. Of the various theories of personality proposed in this chapter, which seems to you to be most reasonable—that is, which explains personality most effectively? Describe the strengths and the weaknesses of this theory, as you view them.
2. In what ways do both humanistic and cognitive-behavioral theories view personality similarly to the psychodynamic perspective? How do these two theories differ from the psychodynamic perspective?
3. Kelly's theory often is considered a link among trait theories, humanistic theories, and cognitive-behavioral theories. How does his theory compare with these other theories?

4. Picture yourself as a medically trained neurologist living in Victorian Vienna. Most of your patients are women, and many of them come to you to ask you to relieve their hysterical symptoms (i.e., physical complaints for which you can find no medical explanations). How might you help your patients, and what theories might you propose as explaining the underlying cause of their ailments?
5. Design a longitudinal study that would test the relation between aggressive behavior toward others and particular personality characteristics.
6. What are several ways in which you can ensure that your loved one or your child (hypothetical or real) feels sure of your unconditional positive regard for her or him?

7. What do you consider to be the essential personality characteristics, based on yourself and on the people you know?
8. Imagine that you have been studying under a particular professor whom you respect deeply and who has invested greatly in you—guiding you in your research and your ideas, spending time with you to help you grasp ideas you find difficult, and so on. After a while, however,

you believe that you have about as good a grasp of the subject as the professor, and you start to have ideas that differ from the professor's. Suppose that you know the professor has broken off all communication with other students who have strongly disagreed with her or him (much as Freud did with many of the neo-Freudians). How would you handle the situation?

9. In what ways might your existing self-schemas be limiting your flexibility? What can you do to change the situation to increase your flexibility?

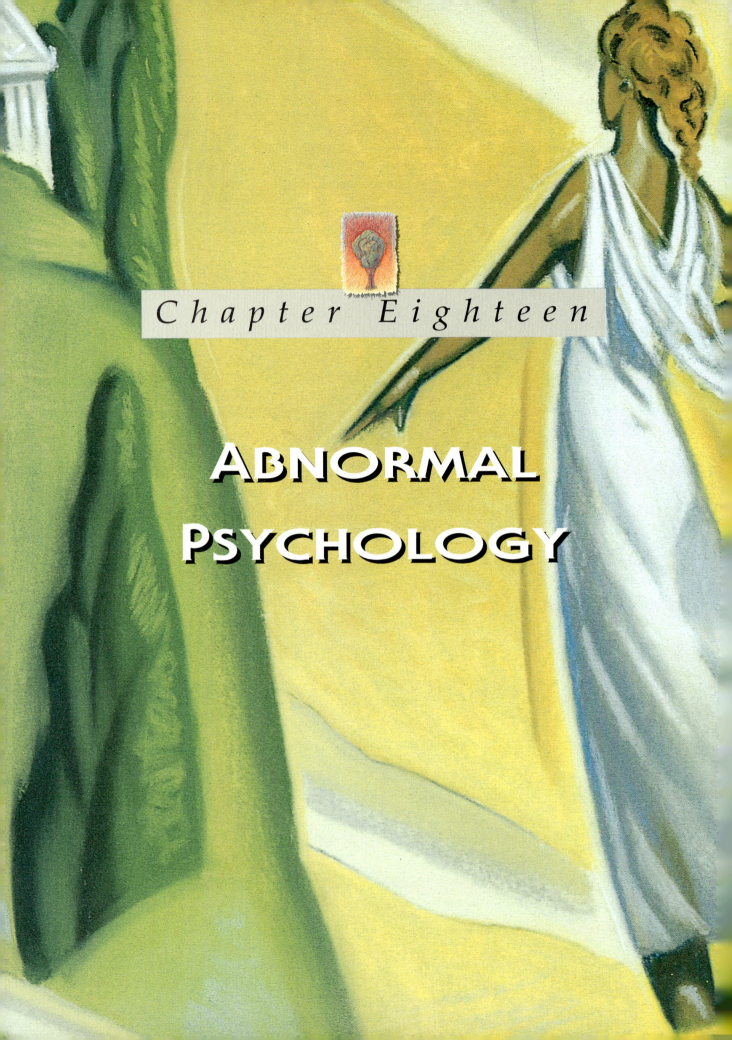

Chapter Eighteen

ABNORMAL
PSYCHOLOGY

CHAPTER OUTLINE

LADY MACBETH:	*Out damned spot! Out I say! . . . Yet who would have thought the old man to have had so much blood in him?*
DOCTOR:	*Do you mark that?*
LADY MACBETH:	*. . . What, will these hands ne'er be clean? . . .*
DOCTOR:	*Go to, go to; you have known what you should not.*
WAITING GENTLEWOMAN:	*She has spoke what she should not, I am sure of that. Heaven knows what she has known.*
LADY MACBETH:	*Here's the smell of the blood still. All the perfumes of Arabia will not sweeten this little hand. Oh, oh, oh!*

—William Shakespeare, Macbeth (*Act V, Scene I*)

What does it mean to be abnormal? This apparently simple question leads to anything but a simple answer. In seeing blood where none existed, Lady Macbeth, no doubt, was behaving abnormally. Our question is, Was she mentally ill, or was she reacting normally to the abnormal act of murder? When we say that people have "blood on their hands," we are suggesting their responsibility; in the play, Lady Macbeth's preoccupation with illusory blood serves as a metaphor not only for her culpability, but also for her increasingly irrational behavior.

WHAT IS ABNORMAL BEHAVIOR?

IN SEARCH OF...

How might your own definition of abnormal human behavior be affected by your social context? How might your definition affect the ways you interact with your fellow humans?

Abnormal behavior, like many of the psychological concepts described in this textbook, has been defined in many ways. To define abnormal behavior adequately, we need to consider several aspects of this concept: **Abnormal behavior** is (1) statistically unusual (i.e., it deviates from statistically normal, average behavior), (2) nonadaptive (i.e., it hampers the individual's ability to function more effectively within a given context), (3) labeled as abnormal by the surrounding society in which the individual is behaving, and (4) characterized by some degree of perceptual or cognitive distortion. As with other definitions, it is possible to think of some exceptions in which a given abnormal behavior may not show all four aspects of the definition. As you read this chapter, consider whether the various kinds of abnormal behavior described satisfy all four aspects of the definition.

No one of these four aspects of abnormal behavior alone would suffice for a definition. For example, behavior most people would *not* consider abnormal may be statistically unusual, such as winning a Nobel Prize, saving a child from a burning building, or earning a graduate degree in nuclear engineering. Behavior that is not abnormal also may be nonadaptive, such as throwing food wrappers out a car window on a highway.

As you might expect, whether a particular behavior is statistically unusual or maladaptive varies across cultural contexts. Behavior that is quite common and adaptive in one culture may be considered highly unusual and maladaptive in another. For example, within some subgroups in American culture, it is customary on Monday evenings in autumn for small groups of people to gather around a small box. The box makes sounds and displays moving images of people prancing around a field and bumping into one another. Although the observers do not talk to one another, from time to time some or all of the observers burst out with cheers or curses directed toward the unresponsive box. These periods of silence punctuated by outbursts of emotional expression, all focused on an inanimate object, would seem bizarrely abnormal to those uninitiated to the pastime of watching Monday Night Football. For some Americans, however, such behavior is not only common but also adaptive in promoting social relationships among the observers.

However, if these observers were to hear about the rituals of Yoruba or Eskimo *shamans* (religious leaders who use magical rituals to bring about therapeutic effects for individuals or for the cultural group as a whole), they might deem the shamans' behavior abnormal. The Yorubas and the Eskimos, though, clearly distinguish between shamans, whose behavior is believed to be highly adaptive and appropriate, and people whose psychotic or delusional behavior is considered to be abnormal and neither adaptive nor appropriate (Davison & Neale, 1994).

As these examples suggest, differences in context influence which kinds of behavior are labeled as abnormal, regardless of their statistical frequency or even their relative adaptiveness. For example, political dissidents are often labeled as insane in countries governed by totalitarian rule. In Nazi-occupied lands, many heroic individuals who hid Jewish families were considered demented by those who became aware of the heroes' behavior. The labels used by psychiatrists are also sometimes subject to question. Once people's behavior has been labeled as indicative of mental illness and they have been hospitalized for the illness, their subsequent normal behavior may be viewed only in light of the identified mental illness (Rosenhan, 1973).

Distortion in perception and cognition may be appropriate and even normal under some circumstances. In fact, Shelley Taylor and Jonathon Brown (1988) argue that some degree of perceptual and cognitive distortion is good for our mental health. As-

sume that you and I are normal, mentally healthy, well-adjusted people. According to Taylor and Brown, one reason for our undisputed (at least until now) mental health is that we seem to distort our perceptions of reality through self-serving biases that overinflate our positive evaluations of ourselves. We also tend to inflate our importance and our ability to control our actions and even our environments, and we tint our views of reality and of our future prospects to be far more optimistic than the objective reality would seem to justify. These self-serving distortions seem to enhance our sense of self-esteem, boost our ability to feel happy, and increase our ability to be involved in productive, creative work. (See Chapter 14 for more on self-serving heuristics and biases, and see Chapter 16 for more on self-efficacy and a sense of mastery.)

Because no single aspect of the definition can capture completely the meaning of *abnormal*, this chapter views abnormality in terms of all four aspects in our definition, although perhaps giving somewhat more emphasis to the maladaptive aspect of abnormal behavior. This view is generally taken by psychologists and many other clinicians. Legal and other views of abnormal behavior are discussed at the close of this chapter.

History of Abnormal Psychology: Demonological Explanations

Today we view the study of abnormal behavior as a part of psychology or psychiatry. It was not always so. In ancient times, people studied abnormal behavior under the heading of *demonology*, because they believed that a person exhibiting abnormal behavior was possessed by a supernatural force, often in the form of an evil demon. Treatment included exorcism, which might not leave the possessed individual completely whole, physically or mentally.

The first challenge to the demonological view was posed in the fifth century B.C., when Hippocrates proposed that illnesses had physiological causes, and that people with mental illnesses suffered from some kind of pathology of the brain. Although Hippocrates was incorrect in his appraisal of the specific physiological causes (which he believed to be imbalances in the four humors—yellow bile, black bile, phlegm, and blood), he changed history by recognizing the importance of scientific rather than supernatural explanations of abnormal behavior.

Unfortunately, scientific ideas that are widely grasped at one time recede from public consciousness when the political and intellectual climate opposes scientific explorations and embraces metaphysical

In the past, we saw demons that caused psychological disorders as largely external, subject to extrication via exorcism. Today, we see demons as largely internal, requiring psychological treatment.

ones. For example, during the Middle Ages, many Europeans once again believed that demons cause abnormal behavior. People who acted oddly—some of whom were probably mentally ill—were often considered witches and were subjected to horrendous tortures to rid them of evil spirits. In many instances they were killed. By the time of the Renaissance, mentally ill Europeans were hospitalized rather than executed, but their treatment was still far from humane or therapeutic, and many people continued to consider the mentally ill to be witches.

In the 1690s, near Salem, Massachusetts, eight girls started acting strangely—hallucinating and convulsing—but doctors could find nothing wrong with them. Both the existing medical knowledge and the

religious and political climate of the time conspired to offer a grotesque interpretation of the girls' behavior. The girls accused a slave, Tituba, of having used witchcraft to cause their symptoms, and the resulting witchcraft hysteria spread rapidly. Although the ones who were acting strangely were the accusers rather than the accused, town rivalries helped spread the contagion, resulting in the execution of 20 townsfolk who had alienated their neighbors (Davidson & Lytle, 1986).

At the height of the witchcraft frenzy, a prominent Harvard-educated minister, Cotton Mather, published a work considered to offer scientific proof of the work of the devil in Salem. More reasoned explanations for the strange behavior of the accusers have since surfaced. Many now believe that the girls' strange behavior may have been due in part to poisoning from the cereal-grain fungus *ergot* (which contains a precursor to lysergic acid diethylamide—LSD) (Caporael, 1976). Eating food made from contaminated flour can cause hallucinations similar to those apparently experienced by the girls in Salem.

> Often, there appears to be no easy way to refute supernatural explanations for phenomena we cannot yet explain by scientific means. For example, the hysterical symptoms and hallucinations of the Salem girls were inexplicable in the seventeenth century. How should a reasonable person respond to supernatural explanations in the absence of scientific ones?

Modern Theoretical Perspectives

Once demonic interpretations of abnormal behaviors had fallen from favor, other interpretations were sought. Modern theoretical perspectives on abnormal behavior closely parallel those on personality in general. Because these approaches have been considered in the previous chapter, they are only briefly reviewed here, as they apply specifically to the abnormal personality.

The Psychodynamic Approach

According to the psychodynamic perspective, abnormal behavior is a result of intrapsychic conflict. Recall that, according to Sigmund Freud, intrapsychic conflict is behind much of what we feel, think, say, and do. The ego is constantly battling the id and the superego. Because the id is governed by the pleasure principle, the ego by the reality principle, and the superego by the morality principle, the personality depends on which psychic force dominates. A person in whom the id dominates will be relatively unrestrained, uninhibited, and perhaps impulsive. A person in whom the ego is stronger is likely to be more restrained, more reality oriented, and more in touch with the rational thought of the self. A person dominated by the superego will be virtually immobilized by moral strictures against any behavior that might be deemed morally questionable in any way, even when such behavior is essential to the person's effective functioning in the social world (e.g., having sexual relations with a marital partner or shaking hands with a person whose moral behavior is viewed as questionable). Powerful intrapsychic conflict among these forces may lead to abnormal behavior.

For example, it is natural for us to wash our hands; but if our intrapsychic conflicts prompt us constantly to wash our hands, to wash away feelings of guilt, like Lady Macbeth, we have crossed the threshold between normal and abnormal behavior, which indicates that the ego is no longer dominant. There is no rational, reality-based reason for the frequency of hand washing displayed by Lady Macbeth. Her frequent hand washings presumably also would get in the way of her doing other things. The maladaptive nature of the behavior in which she is engaging would lead it, and consequently her, to be labeled as abnormal.

The Humanistic Approach

According to the humanistic approach to abnormal behavior, problems arise when people are overly sensitive to other people's judgments, or when they are unable to accept their own nature. Often, the two problems are linked. People who have low self-regard, or who are overly critical of themselves, may not have received sufficient unconditional positive regard from parents or other significant persons.

The Behavioral Approach

According to the learning perspective, abnormal behavior is the result of either classical or instrumental conditioning gone awry. A phobia, for example, might be the result of accidental pairings in which an object or set of objects that normally would not stimulate fear were paired, perhaps repeatedly, with punishment (see Chapter 7). Someone who gets stuck in an elevator one or more times may become abnormally afraid of elevators as a result of the pairing of elevators with unpleasant experiences. According to this view, the phobic person acquires a set of responses that is involuntary and maladaptive. As Chapter 19

shows, learning theorists would then use principles of learning to try to counteract the detrimental effect of the conditioning.

The Cognitive Approach

According to the cognitive perspective, abnormal behavior is the result of distorted thinking. The distortions may be in the processes of thinking, the contents of thinking, or both. For example, depression tends to occur in persons who often minimize their own accomplishments, or who believe that no matter what they do, the result will be failure. People who irrationally believe that snakes of all kinds are capable of doing them a great deal of harm are likely to develop a phobia about snakes. In each case, the label is simply a description of a syndrome that involves distorted or erroneous thought. Therapy would be directed at changing the processes or the contents of the phobic person's thoughts.

The Psychophysiological Approach

The psychophysiological perspective holds that abnormal behavior is due to underlying physiological abnormalities in the nervous system, particularly in the brain. Often, these physiological signs relate to problems in neuronal transmission (see Chapter 3). For example, abnormal behavior may result from the shortage or surplus of a neurotransmitter or from problems in the passage or reuptake of the neurotransmitter. Those who maintain this point of view often treat psychological problems with drugs and with other types of psychophysiological interventions.

Is there one right position with respect to the causes of abnormal behavior? Different approaches address different levels of a problem, with respect to both *etiology* (cause) and treatment of the problem.

DIAGNOSING ABNORMAL BEHAVIOR

IN SEARCH OF...

Why do we have a uniform set of guidelines for making diagnoses of various disorders? Would there be any advantages to not having such guidelines?

By the middle of the twentieth century, clinicians began to reach some formalized consensus regarding psychological diagnoses. In 1948, the World

Health Organization published the *International Classification of Diseases* (ICD), and four years later, the American Psychiatric Association published its *Diagnostic and Statistical Manual* (DSM). The ICD-10 (1992) and DSM-IV (1994) are the current editions of these diagnostic manuals and are coordinated closely with one another. The DSM, like the ICD, is descriptive and *atheoretical*, which means that it is not based on any particular theoretical approach. The DSM lists the symptoms necessary for making a diagnosis in each category, without seeking to assess the causes of the disorder. Thus, the classification system is based wholly on observable symptoms, making it usable by psychologists and psychiatrists of a wide variety of theoretical orientations.

Under DSM-IV, individuals are given a separate diagnosis on each of five *axes* (or dimensions).

- *Axis I* addresses clinical syndromes and contains the major disorders, such as schizophrenia; anxiety disorders; disorders usually first diagnosed in infancy, childhood, or adolescence, which may also continue into adulthood; somatoform disorders; and sexual disorders. The first three of these are described in greater detail in the text. *Somatoform disorders* center on the person's relationship with his or her own body; they are relatively rare bodily symptoms or complaints of bodily symptoms for which no physiological basis can be found. In *sexual disorders*, the individual engages in sexual behavior that either distresses the individual or others or causes difficulty for the individual in other aspects of her or his life. The various sexual disorders can be mild or severe, and of brief or long duration.

    Axis I also includes various other disorders, such as *delirium* (a confused, disordered state of mind often involving perceptual distortions), *amnesia* (memory loss), *dementia* (general deterioration in cognitive abilities, especially affecting memory and judgment, due to physiological changes in the brain—for example, Alzheimer's disease, stroke, or head trauma), and other cognitive disorders, which are not discussed in this chapter. Cognitive function and its distortions are discussed in Chapters 6, 8, 10, and 12. In addition, Axis I includes eating disorders (see Chapters 16 and 20) and sleeping disorders (see Chapter 6).

- *Axis II* addresses personality disorders, including avoidant and dependent personalities. The disorders in Axis II may coexist with those in Axis I.

- *Axis III* addresses physical disorders and conditions. Although such disorders can be of the brain, they can also be of any other kind as well, such as asthma, diabetes, heart problems, or physical handicaps. Physical disorders are included because they may interact with or precipitate psychological conditions.

- *Axis IV* addresses the severity of psychosocial stressors. The diagnostician uses the information from the other axes and from the patient's (or client's) existing situation and history to determine the level of psychological stress that he or she is experiencing.

- *Axis V* represents a global assessment of the person's level of functioning. For example, a code of 90 would represent minimal symptoms and a code of 1 maximal danger, as in the case of someone who is extremely violent and is viewed as likely to cause harm to others.

Why do clinicians use five separate axes instead of just a summary diagnosis? The goal is to provide as comprehensive a portrait of abnormal functioning as possible. Consider the case of a 9-year-old who is extremely anxious and is sweating when he enters the psychologist's office. He is diagnosed along Axis I as having an anxiety disorder. He is also observed as having an academic skill disorder: He is having difficulty in mathematics and is performing three years behind grade level, despite the fact that his overall intelligence is in the normal range. Along Axis II, he is noted as having a paranoid personality disorder. By having separate diagnoses, the therapist is able to consider the possibility that the anxiety disorder, the personality disorder, and the problem in mathematics are related. Along Axis III, it is noticed that the boy had mild head trauma from an automobile accident seven years ago. It is unclear at this point whether the head injury is related to the diagnosed difficulties, but having this information might prove useful in diagnosis and treatment. On Axis IV, the boy is coded as currently being subjected to severe stress in his life. His parents are going through a divorce, and each wants the other parent to take custody. The parents have shown little interest in the boy, and their lack of interest is showing in the divorce proceedings as well. Finally, on Axis V, the boy receives a rating of 55. He shows moderate symptoms, including anxiety and occasional panic attacks, especially when he needs to use mathematics or when he suspects others of plotting against him. His anxiety is interfering with his schoolwork and with his ability to form friendships, and he is becoming something of a target for other children. Note that each axis gives us different but complementary information regarding the boy's psychological problems.

Any diagnostic system, including DSM-IV, is potentially problematic. First, because the system is atheoretical, it gives us no real insight into the causes of the abnormal behavior. A second problem is its subjectivity. Although the DSM-IV and the ICD-10 allow "clinicians to reach the same diagnosis in a remarkably high proportion of cases" (Sartorius et al., 1993b, p. xvi), reliable agreement among clinicians certainly is not perfect. A third problem, common to any diagnostic system, is mapping behavior onto the descriptive categories. A diagnostician needs to map observed behavior onto the symptoms expressed in DSM-IV and then to map those symptoms onto a diagnosis. DSM-IV is the product of outstanding efforts to achieve specificity and clarity with respect to the mapping of symptoms onto diagnoses, but practitioners still need to map the behavior they observe onto the symptoms in the DSM.

Because it is impossible to specify every possible type of behavior, there is always the potential for ambiguity in any classification system. For example, when do the quantity and character of antisocial acts lead a clinician to label an antisocial personality? DSM-IV gives guidelines, but ultimately the clinician's judgment is key in making the diagnosis. Despite the lack of a single perfect method for diagnosis, when various forms of assessment are used together, they can give clinicians a wide variety of information that the clinicians can integrate and interpret, based on their professional expertise. Some of the kinds of disorders diagnosed by clinicians are described in the following sections of this chapter.

ANXIETY DISORDERS

I have a new philosophy. I'm only going to dread one day at a time.

—Charles Schulz, Peanuts

Anxiety disorders encompass the individual's feelings of **anxiety**—tension, nervousness, distress, or uncomfortable arousal. DSM-IV divides anxiety disorders into five main categories: phobias, panic disorder, generalized anxiety disorder, stress disorders (posttraumatic stress disorder and acute stress disorder), and obsessive-compulsive disorder. These various forms of anxiety disorders differ in their population frequencies. Roughly 15% of the U.S. population suffers from an anxiety disorder at some time during their lives (Robins et al., 1984). Phobias and panic disorder are more common in women, and obsessive-compulsive disorder is more common in men (Myers et al., 1984). In particular, J. Myers and his colleagues found that 8% of women, but only 3.5% of men, are phobic. All five disorders share several common symptoms that characterize them as anxiety disorders. These include:

1. **Phobias**—persistent, irrational, and disruptive fears of a specific object, activity, or type of situation. A fear is classified as a phobia when it is substantially greater than what seems justified or when it has no basis in reality. People with phobias are aware that their fears are irrational and would like to overcome them, but they have a great deal of difficulty doing so. About 6% of the population say that their phobias are at least somewhat disruptive of their lives (Myers et al., 1984). Phobias can be simple, social, or complex, as in agoraphobia.
   a. **Simple phobias**—irrational fears of objects, such as spiders, snakes, high places, and darkness. Simple phobias are far less common than the other two kinds.
   b. **Social phobias**—extreme fear of being criticized by others, which leads to the avoidance of groups of people. Social phobics may be afraid of meeting new people, speaking in public, or doing anything that might result in criticism of any kind from other people.
   c. **Agoraphobia**—fear of open spaces or of being in public places from which it might be difficult to escape in the event of a panic attack. Agoraphobia accounts for 60% of all phobias; the majority of agoraphobics are female, and the disorder usually begins to develop in adolescence or early adulthood. Extreme agoraphobics are unable to leave their homes. Consider the following case:

Mrs. Reiss is a 48-year-old woman who recently was referred to a psychiatric clinic by her general practitioner because of her fears of going out alone. She has had these fears for six years, but they intensified during the past two years. As a result, she has not gone out of her house unescorted. Her symptoms first appeared after an argument with her husband. She proceeded to go out to the mailbox and was then overwhelmed with feelings of dizziness and anxiety. She had to struggle back to the house. Her

TABLE 18-1
Diagnostic and Statistical Manual (fourth edition; DSM-IV)
This summary of the five axes of the DSM-IV system of classifying mental disorders illustrates the major considerations involved in diagnosing psychological disorders.

Axis I	Axis II	Axis III
Clinical syndromes:		
Disorders Usually First Diagnosed in Infancy, Childhood, or Adolescence	Personality Disorders: paranoid, schizoid, schizotypal, antisocial, borderline, histrionic, narcissistic, avoidant, dependent, obsessive-compulsive	General Medical Conditions
Delirium, Dementia, Amnesic and other Cognitive Disorders		
Substance Related Disorders		
Schizophrenia and Other Psychotic Disorders		
Mood Disorders		
Anxiety Disorders		
Somatoform Disorders		
Factitious Disorder		
Dissociative Disorders		
Sexual and Gender Identity Disorders		
Eating Disorders		
Sleep Disorders		
Impulse Control Disorders Not Elsewhere Classified		
Adjustment Disorders		

Axis IV

Psychosocial and Environmental Problems

Check:

_____ Problems with primary support group (childhood, adult, parent-child) Specify: _____

_____ Problems related to the social environment. Specify: _____

_____ Educational problem. Specify: _____

_____ Occupational problem. Specify: _____

_____ Housing problem. Specify: _____

_____ Economic problem. Specify: _____

_____ Problems with access to health care services. Specify: _____

_____ Problems related to interaction with the legal system/crime. Specify: _____

_____ Other psychosocial problem. Specify: _____

(Continued)

TABLE 18-1 *(Continued)*

Axis V

Global Assessment of Functioning Scale (GAF Scale)

Consider psychological, social, and occupational functioning on a hypothetical continuum of mental health/illness. Do not include impairment in functioning due to physical (or environmental) limitations.

Code

100 | 91	Superior functioning in a wide range of activities, life's problems never seem to get out of hand, is sought out by others because of his or her many positive qualities. No symptoms.
90 | 81	Absent or minimal symptoms (e.g., mild anxiety before an exam), good functioning in all areas, interested and involved in a wide range of activities, socially effective, generally satisfied with life, no more than everyday problems or concerns (e.g., an occasional argument with family members).
80 | 71	If symptoms are present, they are transient and expectable reactions to psychosocial stressors (e.g., difficulty concentrating after family argument); no more than slight impairment in social, occupational, or school functioning (e.g., temporarily falling behind in school work).
70 | 61	Some mild symptoms (e.g., depressed mood and mild insomnia) OR some difficulty in social, occupational, or school functioning (e.g., occasional truancy, or theft within the household), but generally functioning pretty well, has some meaningful interpersonal relationships.
60 | 51	Moderate symptoms (e.g., flat affect and cirumstantial speech, occasional panic attacks) OR moderate difficulty in social, occupational, or school functioning (e.g., no friends, unable to keep a job).
50 | 41	Serious symptoms (e.g., suicidal ideation, severe obsessional rituals, frequent shoplifting) OR any serious impairment in social, occupational, or school functioning (e.g., no friends, unable to keep a job).
40 | 31	Some impairment in reality testing or communication (e.g., speech is at times illogical, obscure, or irrelevant) OR major impairment in several areas, such as work or school, family relations, judgment, thinking, or mood (e.g., depressed man avoids friends, neglects family, and is unable to work; child frequently beats up younger children, is defiant at home, and is failing at school).
30 | 21	Behavior is considerably influenced by delusions or hallucinations OR serious impairment in communication or judgment (e.g., sometimes incoherent, acts grossly inappropriately, suicidal preoccupation) OR inability to function in almost all areas (e.g., stays in bed all day; no job, home, or friends).
20 | 11	Some danger of hurting self or others (e.g., suicide attempts without clear expectation of death, frequently violent, manic excitement) OR occasionally fails to maintain minimal personal hygiene (e.g., smears feces) OR gross impairment in communication (e.g., largely incoherent or mute).
10 | 1	Persistent danger of severely hurting self or others (e.g., recurrent violence) OR persistent inability to maintain minimal personal hygiene OR serious suicidal act with clear expectation of death.
0	Inadequate information.

symptoms abated for a few years, but reappeared with greater intensity after she learned that her sister had ovarian cancer. Her symptoms often were exacerbated by frequent arguments with her husband. She began to feel increasingly apprehensive and fearful upon leaving the front door. If she did leave, she began getting panicky and dizzy after a few minutes on the street. Her heart pounded and she would start perspiring. At this point, she would turn back to her house to alleviate the anxiety. When accompanied by her husband or one of her children, she felt uneasy, but was usually able to enter crowded areas for short periods of time. (After Greenberg, Szmukler, & Tantam, 1986, pp. 148-149)

2. **Panic disorder**—brief, abrupt, and unprovoked but recurrent episodes of intense and uncontrollable anxiety. The person suddenly feels apprehensive or even terrified, experiencing difficulty breathing, heart palpitations, dizziness, sweating, and trembling. Persons with this disorder may fear either losing control of themselves or going crazy. Panic disorders afflict about 1.5% of the U.S. population.

3. **Generalized anxiety disorder**—general, persistent, and often debilitating high levels of anxiety that can last any length of time. The cause for such anxiety is difficult to identify. A person with this disorder commonly experiences physical symptoms as well, as shown in the following example:

A 67-year-old woman was referred to a psychiatric clinic for treatment of an anxiety state. At the interview she appeared to be tense; she sat upright and rigid in her chair and answered questions politely. She admitted that for most of her life she had been a great worrier. She said, "I'm inclined to look ahead and expect the worst to happen. I find it hard to relax, especially while lying in bed. My worst fears come to mind." In her more anxious moments, she has experienced palpitations of the heart, and often has had difficulty falling asleep due to her brooding thoughts. Although she has experienced a persistent and chronic anxiety, she has been unable to trace her anxiety to any particular problem. (After Fottrell, 1983, p. 149)

4. **Stress disorder**—an extreme reaction to a highly stressful event or situation. Stress disorders often are linked to adjustment disorders (see Chapter 20 for discussion of stress and coping). Variations include posttraumatic stress disorder and acute stress disorder.
   a. **Posttraumatic stress disorder**—the psychological reenactment of a traumatic event, including recurrent and painful memories, nightmares, and flashbacks that are so strong that the person believes he or she is reliving the event. The event may be participation in a war or exposure to a disaster, such as flood, fire, earthquake, tornado, or serious accident. Some victims are so plagued by these recurrences that they may become apathetic and detached.
   b. **Acute stress disorder**—acute, brief reactions to stress, which directly follow a traumatic event and last fewer than four months. Persons may experience a sense of detachment from the physical and social worlds, distortions or other changes in perceptions, and disturbances of memory.

5. **Obsessive-compulsive disorder**—unwanted, persistent thoughts and irresistible impulses to perform a ritual to relieve those thoughts. About 2.5% of the U. S. population are affected by this disorder.
   a. **Obsession**—unwanted images or impulses that individuals are unable to suppress. Obsessives are unhappy with the obsession and with being unable to keep it out of their minds.
   b. **Compulsion**—irresistible impulses to perform a relatively meaningless act repeatedly and in a specific manner. Compulsive persons do not cherish or enjoy the ritualistic behavior and view the activity as foreign to their personality. They are aware of the absurdity of their behavior and yet are unable to stop it. Compulsive hand washers may wash their hands several hundred times a day. In addition to being time-consuming, compulsions can be costly to a person's well being. Other common compulsions are counting things to make sure they are all there, checking the placement of objects, and checking that appliances are turned off.

Consider the following case of a person with an obsessive-compulsive disorder:

Ruth Langley was 30 years old when she sought help from a therapist after experiencing long-standing fears of contamination. She stated that she became intensely uncomfortable with any dirt on herself or in her immediate environment. After noticing any dirt, she felt compelled to carry out elaborate and time-consuming cleaning procedures. This usually involved thoroughly washing her hands and arms. Moreover, if she found dirt in her apartment, she was compelled to scrub her apartment methodically, in addition to showering in a very regimented manner. Her cleaning rituals have severely restricted her life. She now washes her hands at least four or five times an hour, showers six or

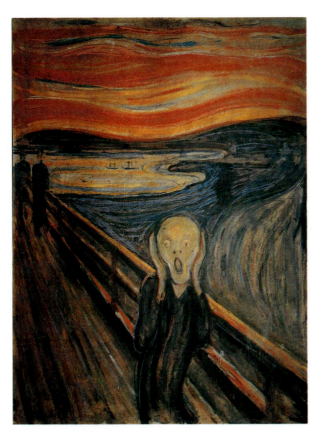

Eduard Munch (1863–1944) captured in his painting, The Cry *(sometimes translated as* The Scream*), the terror often felt by persons with anxiety disorders.*

seven times a day, and thoroughly cleans her apartment at least twice a day. (After Leon, 1974, pp. 129-130)

Symptoms of Anxiety Disorders

Anxiety disorders create mood, cognitive, somatic, and motor symptoms. *Mood symptoms* include feelings of tension, apprehension, and sometimes panic. Often, those who experience these symptoms do not know exactly why they are feeling the way they do. They may have a sense of foreboding or even of doom but not know why. Sometimes, anxious persons become depressed, if only because they do not see any way to alleviate the symptoms.

Cognitive symptoms may include a person's spending a lot of time trying to figure out why various mood symptoms are occurring. When unable to identify the causes, the individual may then feel frustrated. Often, thinking about the problem actually worsens it, making it hard for the person to concentrate on other things.

Typical *somatic* (i.e., bodily) *symptoms* include sweating, hyperventilation, high pulse or blood pressure, and muscle tension. All of these symptoms are characteristic of a high level of arousal of the autonomic nervous symptom (see Chapter 3). These primary symptoms may lead to secondary ones. For example, hyperventilation may lead to feelings of lightheadedness or breathlessness. Muscular tension can lead to headaches or muscle spasms. High blood pressure can cause strokes or even cardiac problems. People who suffer anxiety disorders vary widely in the extent to which they experience somatic symptoms and also in the kinds of somatic symptoms they experience. Some people may express their anxiety in headaches, others in stomachaches, and so on.

Typical *motor symptoms* include restlessness, fidgeting, and various kinds of bodily movements that seem to have no particular purpose (such as pacing, finger tapping, tics, and the like). People are often unaware that they are doing these things. For example, they may pace around a room while others are seated, not realizing how others are perceiving their behavior.

When is anxiety a disorder? What distinguishes the normal anxiety that everyone occasionally experiences from debilitating anxiety? Generally, three factors must be considered:

1. *Level* of anxiety—it is one thing to have a slight, occasional fear of elevators, especially overcrowded, rickety-looking ones; it is another thing to be unable to use any elevators at all because of a fear that they will get stuck between floors, or that they will lose power and fall to the bottom of the elevator shaft.
2. *Justification* for the anxiety—it is normal to feel somewhat anxious before an important event, such as a final examination, a first date, or an important speech, but it is not normal constantly to feel that same level of anxiety when there are no precipitating stressful events.
3. *Consequences* of the anxiety—if the anxiety leads to serious maladaptive results, such as the loss of a job because of an inability to leave home, the consequences will be sufficiently severe to lead a clinician to classify the person as having an anxiety disorder.

Cite a situation in which you felt extremely anxious, perhaps justifiably so. What were the mood, cognitive, somatic, and motor symptoms of your anxiety? How did your situation-related anxiety differ from an anxiety disorder?

Some of the common phobias include acrophobia *(fear of heights),* agoraphobia *(fear of public settings and situations), and* claustrophobia *(fear of small, enclosed spaces). Unlike the fear shown in phobics, which is irrational or at least is unreasonably exaggerated, all of us experience fear in situations in which our lives, our safety, or our well-being are jeopardized, such as during the aftermath of a major disaster.*

Psychologists often distinguish between *fear* (an emotion of dread or terror of a specific object or event) and *anxiety* (an emotion of discomfort that is more vague and diffuse and that is not directed toward any specific object or event). This distinction, however, is not always perfectly clear. For example,

suppose that you have studied hard and long for a test but that you are afraid of the test. Are you really afraid, or are you anxious? (See Figure 18-1.)

Psychologists also distinguish between cognitive anxiety and somatic anxiety. **Cognitive anxiety** refers to feelings of worry, tension, or frustration, or to being preoccupied with thoughts of impending failure. **Somatic anxiety** refers to feelings of anxiety manifested in bodily discomfort, such as muscular tension, restlessness, rapid heartbeat, upset stomach, or headache (Holmes & Roth, 1989). At a given time, a person may experience one or both forms of anxiety.

> *Sweat broke out on his back. His mind seemed to rebound off a solidness. Such extinction was not another threat, a graver sort of danger, a kind of pain; it was qualitatively different. It was not even a conception that could be voluntarily pictured; it entered him from outside. . . . The skin of his chest was soaked with the effort of rejection. At the same time that the fear was dense and internal, it was dense and all around him.*
>
> —*John Updike, "Pigeon Feathers,"* Pigeon Feathers and Other Stories

One factor causing anxiety may be the stress brought on by modern society. This cultural factor is indicated by the higher rates of anxiety disorders occurring in technologically advanced societies (Carson & Butcher, 1992). The particular manifestations of symptoms and the grouping of symptoms into diagnosed disorders also varies across cultures, even modern ones. For example, in Japan, *taijin-kyofusho* (fear

FIGURE 18-1
Situational Anxiety
In normal individuals, levels of anxiety are situation-related, such as in relation to a major examination. (After Bolger, 1990)

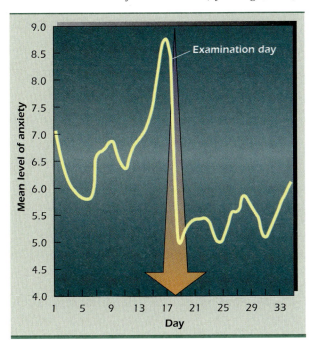

of humans) is a common manifestation of anxiety (Kirmayer, 1991). This condition mainly affects males, and their symptoms include staring inappropriately, emitting offensive odors or flatulence, and blushing easily. The Japanese condition of *taijin-kyofusho* is significantly related to the Western condition of social phobia (Kleinknecht et al., 1993) and to the Latin American condition of *susto*, characterized by extreme anxiety, restlessness, and fear of black magic and the evil eye (*mal ojo*), although each complex of symptoms reflects characteristics of the respective cultures.

Quite a different anxiety disorder has been observed in Islamic societies, in which the obsessive-compulsive syndrome of *Waswās* has been linked to the Islamic ritual of cleansing and prayer. According to W. Pfeiffer (1982), the syndrome "relates to ritual cleanliness and to the validity of the ritual procedures, which are particularly important in Islam. Thus, the sufferer of *Waswās* finds it hard to terminate the ablutions because he is afraid that he is not yet clean enough to carry out his prayers in a lawful manner" (p. 213).

Explanations of Anxiety Disorders

As you might expect, the different theoretical paradigms propose alternative explanations for the origin of anxiety disorders.

Psychodynamic Explanations

Freud distinguished among three different types of anxiety and believed that each requires a different explanation. The first of these three types, *objective anxiety*, derives from threats in the external world. Included here would be anxiety about realistic financial problems, failure in work or in personal relationships, serious illnesses, and the like. This kind of anxiety would correspond to *fear*, as it was defined in our previous distinction between anxiety and fear. Freud maintained that this kind of anxiety is not linked to abnormal behavior because the threat causing the anxiety is real.

The second and third types of anxiety stem from battles between the id and the superego. *Moral anxiety* derives from fear of punishment by the superego, which arises from conflict within the person over expression of impulses from the id. *After* the impulses of the id have won out and are expressed, the person experiences moral anxiety. For example, a poorly qualified, dull candidate who seeks to win an election might attempt to win by smearing an opponent. Later, this person might experience some degree of moral anxiety. By giving in to impulses to succeed at the other person's expense, the candidate creates internal conflict.

Neurotic anxiety derives from a person's fear that the superego (with the aid of the ego) will not be able to control the id, and that the person may not be able to avoid engaging in unacceptable behavior. For example, a person may be afraid to go out on a date with a particularly attractive person for fear of acting in an unacceptable way, and thereby losing the potential for a relationship with the attractive person. Note that neurotic anxiety occurs *before* the impulses of the id have been expressed and while the superego is still restraining its expression.

Freud believed that phobias occur when anxiety is focused on one or more particular objects; these objects represent a conflict at a symbolic level. For example, a phobia of snakes might symbolically represent sexual conflict wherein the snake serves as a phallic symbol to focus the anxiety. Freud believed that many anxieties originate in sexual conflicts. In contrast, many neo-Freudians believed that other important conflicts, such as those centering around feelings of inferiority (Alfred Adler) or of trust (Erik Erikson), could also lead to anxiety in a number of instances.

Learning Theory Explanations

Many learning (or behavioral) theorists view anxiety as being classically conditioned. According to this thinking, a fear response has been paired with a stimulus that was previously neutral. Thus, what was previously a neutral stimulus is now a fear-producing one (see Chapter 7). For example, a person might have a neutral or slightly favorable attitude toward dogs. Then, one day, the person is seriously bitten by a dog. Through classical conditioning, the person becomes anxious in the presence of dogs or possibly even at the thought of dogs.

According to classical learning theory, the unpleasant experience would have to happen to the individual experiencing the anxiety for conditioning to occur. In contemporary forms of learning theory, however, it is possible to experience *vicarious conditioning* (Bandura & Rosenthal, 1966). Simply through observational learning (see Chapters 13 and 17), we can be conditioned to experience anxiety. For example, most of us, thankfully, have not contracted acquired immune deficiency syndrome (AIDS). By observing the effects of AIDS, however—on television or through friends or family—we could become anxious about AIDS and even phobic about the possibility of contracting AIDS, solely through having been vicariously conditioned.

Operant conditioning can also play a part in the development of anxiety disorders. Consider, for example, compulsive behavior. Suppose that you have an irrational fear of bacteria. Washing your hands makes you feel safer, at least temporarily. You are thereby reinforced for the hand-washing behavior, but soon the fear returns. You have learned that hand washing helps alleviate anxiety, so you wash your hands again. The anxiety is alleviated again, but not for long. In this way, you have learned to engage in the compulsive behavior because it temporarily alleviates anxiety, as a result of operant conditioning.

Cognitive Explanations

A cognitive explanation focuses on the kinds of thoughts a person has in response to particular situations. Suppose that a woman wants to ask a man out to lunch, but the thought of actually picking up the phone and calling him makes her sweat with anxiety. Because she has been rejected and insulted earlier, every time she thinks about inviting someone out, she starts thinking to herself, "I know I'm going to fail. I know he's going to put me down. I'd really like to invite him, but I just can't stand being rejected again." These kinds of thoughts produce anxiety, causing people to be unable to do some of the things that they would like to do (Beck, Emery, & Greenberg, 1985). They are likely to become automatic thoughts—thought patterns people seem to fall into without being aware of them, and which they experience without effort (Beck, 1976). Often, such thoughts are the beginning of a self-defeating cycle. Someone who expects rejection may feel spurned when receiving neutral cues or may find seeds of repudiation even in positive things that another person says. Thus, anxiety disorders tend to be self-propagating.

Humanistic-Existential Explanations

One humanistic-existential explanation for anxiety disorders is that the person experiences a discrepancy between the perceived self and the idealized self, causing feelings of failure. These feelings of failure cause the anxiety. Anxious people tend to indicate more of a discrepancy than do confident people between the persons they believe they are and the persons they believe they should be (Rogers, 1961b). Anxious people also show lower social skills than do nonanxious people (Fischetti, Curran, & Wessberg, 1977), which may further reduce their confidence in themselves.

Psychophysiological Explanations

Several psychophysiological explanations for anxiety disorders have been proposed. One suggests that inhibitory neurons that serve to reduce neurological activity may function improperly in people with anxiety disorders. For example, insufficient levels of the neurotransmitter GABA (gamma-aminobutyric acid) lower activity in the inhibitory neurons and thereby increase brain activity; the result is a high level of arousal, which can be experienced as anxiety. Drugs that decrease GABA activity lead to increasing anxiety (Insell, 1986). Various tranquilizers, such as diazepam (Valium), increase GABA activity, thereby decreasing anxiety (Bertilsson, 1978; Enna & DeFranz, 1980; Haefely, 1977). Researchers seldom find a single element that causes a psychological phenomenon; instead, as each of several factors comes to light, each new insight contributes to an increasingly detailed picture of the phenomenon.

> Design an experiment that would test the relative merits of two of the preceding explanations of anxiety disorders.

MOOD DISORDERS

> He's turned his life around. He used to be depressed and miserable. Now he's miserable and depressed.
>
> —David Frost, "TVam"

The two major **mood disorders** (extreme disturbances in a person's emotional state) are major depression (sometimes called unipolar depression) and bipolar disorder. Each of these disorders impairs function; it is not just the feeling of being temporarily down in the dumps. Depression is relatively common (roughly 10% of men and 20% of women will be clinically depressed at some point during their lives; Weissman & Myers, 1978; Woodruff, Goodwin, & Guze, 1974), and it is more likely to occur in persons of lower socioeconomic status (SES) than in those of higher SES (Hirschfeld & Cross, 1982). The higher frequencies in women and in persons of lower SES suggest that situational factors may be involved. Bipolar disorder, on the other hand, afflicts men and women of all socioeconomic classes equally (Krauthammer & Klerman, 1979; Robins et al., 1984). Bipolar disorder is also much rarer than unipolar depression (occurring in only about 0.75% to 1% of the population), and appears to run in families (suggesting possible genetic and physiological aspects of the illness).

Major Depression

Persons with major depression feel down, discouraged, and hopeless. It may seem to them that nothing is right with their lives. Typical cognitive symptoms of depression are low self-esteem, loss of motivation, and pessimism. Depressed people often generalize, so that a single failure, or an event that they interpret as indicating a failure, is assumed to foreshadow worse things yet to come. They often experience a very low level of energy and may slow down their body movements and even speech. Typical somatic symptoms are difficulty in sleeping and in waking up, so that the person may experience trouble falling asleep or may sleep most of the time.

> The reason I hadn't washed my clothes or my hair was because it seemed so silly.
>
> I saw the days of the year stretching ahead like a series of bright, white boxes, and separating one box from another was sleep, like a black shade. Only for me, the long perspective of shades that set off one box from the next had suddenly snapped up, and I could see day after day after day glaring ahead of me like a white, broad, infinitely desolate avenue.
>
> It seemed silly to wash one day when I would only have to wash again the next.
>
> It made me tired just to think of it.
>
> I wanted to do everything once and for all and be through with it.
>
> —Sylvia Plath, The Bell Jar

In noting the symptoms of depressed persons, clinicians often look to the causes of depression (see Table 18-2). For example, clinicians distinguish between external, environmental variables and internal, physiological variables. Another important distinction is whether the depression is the principal disorder or a symptom of another clinical disorder. It is essential to determine the cause of the depression in order to treat it (see Chapter 19). Some kinds of depression are linked to phases of life, as shown in Table 18-2.

A large cross-national study involving more than 40,000 subjects in Western and non-Western countries concluded that major depression occurs across a broad range of cultures and that more recent generations are at an increased risk of depression (Cross-National Collaborative Group, 1992). The findings of that study take on added significance because the scientists who conducted it claim that the study is the first one to use standard diagnostic criteria across all societies.

Bipolar Disorder

Bipolar disorder, or manic-depressive disorder, refers to alternating depressive and manic symptoms. We have seen the symptoms of depression. When a person suffering from bipolar disorder swings to the manic phase, the most prominent symptom of **mania** is a mood of unabashed euphoria. The individual is highly excited, expansive, and often hyperactive. Manic persons may believe there is no limit to their possible accomplishments and may act accordingly (e.g., trying to climb Mount McKinley as an impromptu outing, equipped with a cotton jacket and a pocket knife). Manic individuals often have trouble focusing their attention and may move from one activity to another in rapid succession. Occasionally, the manic person will suffer from other **delusions**—beliefs that are contrary to fact. Manic individuals may

spend money wildly, attempt to start numerous projects they cannot finish, or become hypersexual. Consequently, they may end up bankrupt, fired from their jobs, or divorced by their mates. On the other hand, persons who are experiencing mania have a greatly reduced need for sleep and tend to be immune from the fatigue that would hit most people after very strenuous periods of activity (see Figure 18-2).

Describe two situations: (1) a situation in which you felt unhappy and (2) a situation in which you felt excited. How do your situation-related mood swings compare and contrast with actual mood disorders?

Explanations of Mood Disorders

For most of the explanations in this section, we consider theories of major depression, not of bipolar depression. Research has shown that major and bipolar disorders are different disorders, with different suggested treatments (as Chapter 19 shows). Bipolar dis-

TABLE 18-2
Origins of Depression
In diagnosing depression, clinicians often classify depression according to its origins.

Type	Description	Cause
Exogenous depression	A reaction to external (environmental) factors	Conflict with a spouse or lover, stress on the job, failure to achieve a goal, or similar types of events
Endogenous depression	Reaction to internal (physiological) factors, such as imbalance of particular neurotransmitters	Chronic depression, without regard to what is going on around the person; may stem from a family history of depression
Primary depression	Depression is the main medical problem	Someone who is depressed over the breakup of a relationship and who feels unable to get out of bed as a result
Secondary depression	Another disorder has caused the depression	Someone who is injured and is therefore bedridden and then becomes depressed because of the physical limitations
Involutional depression	Associated with advanced age	Consequences associated with age, such as the realization that it is too late in life to achieve goals that were set at an earlier stage
Postpartum depression	Occurs after childbirth and can last anywhere from a few weeks to a year	Stress is usually the primary cause; other causes might be hormonal changes, changes in neurotransmitters, and fatigue; external locus of control, anxiety, and hostility; and lack of spousal and other social support.

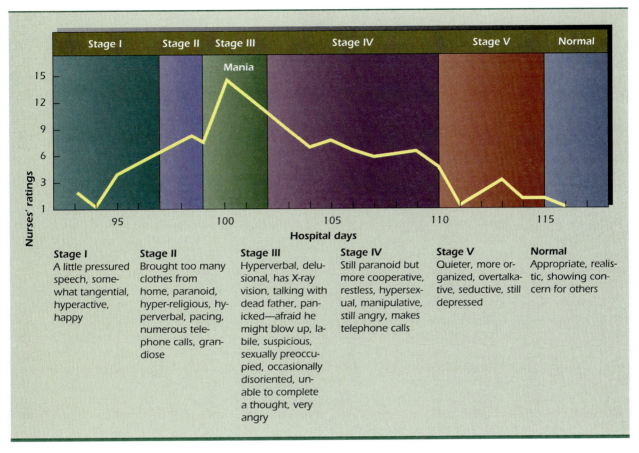

FIGURE 18-2
Stages of a Manic Episode
Case-study research often provides depth of insight not as easily available through laboratory studies, as shown in this longitudinal analysis of nurses' ratings of manic behavior in a patient hospitalized for mania. (After Carlson & Goodwin, 1973)

order is definitely not unipolar depression with a dash of mania added; its origins appear to be primarily psychophysiological. In contrast, major depression has multiple possible explanations.

Psychodynamic Explanations

The psychodynamic explanation of depression begins with an analogy that Freud observed between depression and mourning (Freud, 1917/1957). He noticed that in both cases there is a sense of strong and possibly overwhelming sorrow, and that people in mourning frequently become depressed. He suggested that when we lose an object of our love (any termination of a relationship, including by death), we often have ambivalent feelings about the person we have lost. We may still love the person yet feel angry that the person has left us. We may even realize that it is irrational to feel angry toward someone who died involuntarily, but we cannot stop feeling angry. According to Freud, when we lose an object of our love, we in-

corporate aspects of that person in a fruitless effort to regain at least parts of the person. At first glance, it seems as though incorporating aspects of that person should minimize our sense of loss and that this minimization of our sense of loss should also reduce depressive symptoms, but Freud saw a down side to incorporation: If we are angry toward the lost person, and we have incorporated aspects of that person, then we may become angry with ourselves.

Freud suggested that this anger turned inward is the source of depression, and that the precipitating event is a process of loss. As is typical of Freudian conceptualization, the emphasis is on losses that occurred during early childhood, although Freud acknowledged that losses at any time can cause depression. Investigations have suggested that those who lose loved ones do indeed tend to feel depressed (Bornstein et al., 1973; Brown & Harris, 1978; Clayton et al., 1968). Nonetheless, a link in one direction does not necessarily indicate a link in the other direction. For example, people who commit suicide are likely to have been depressed. However, very few people who are depressed commit suicide. Similarly, not everyone who feels depressed has suffered the loss of a loved one. Thus, to explain depression in persons who have not immediately or recently lost a loved one, Freud invoked the concept of symbolic loss. For example, whenever we do not get high grades or high evaluations from a supervisor, we may suffer again from the symbolic loss of a parent's approval, and this symbolic loss may cause the depression, not the immediate personal disappointment.

Support for the Freudian point of view has been mixed. For example, if anger directed inward is the key to depression, then we may expect the dreams of depressed people to show anger as a prominent theme. Instead, a study found that loss and failure, rather than anger, are the most common themes in the dreams of depressed people (Beck & Ward, 1961). In the same way, some researchers have hypothesized that if depression stemmed from anger turned inward, depressed people could be expected to express less hostility than would people who were not depressed, because depressed people would be aiming their anger toward themselves rather than toward others. This prediction, too, has been disconfirmed (Weissman, Klerman, & Paykel, 1971).

Several studies have indicated that depression is caused by stress more often than by loss (Billings et al., 1983; Paykel & Tanner, 1976). However, it is still possible that people who experience stress also suffer from symbolic losses. For example, we need other people's support during stressful periods, but we may need more support than others are able or willing to provide. As a result, we may feel that we have lost their support, when in fact, we are simply making unreasonable demands on them. It has been found that persons who receive more social support during times of stress are in fact less likely to become depressed (Billings et al., 1983; Warren & McEachren, 1983). Also, although stress more powerfully may predict depression than does loss, depression and stress are not perfectly correlated, either. Not all people who are exposed to stress become depressed, and not all people who are depressed have been subject to stress.

Learning Theory Explanations

The basic learning theory explanation of depression states that depressed people receive fewer rewards and more punishments than do people who are not depressed (Ferster, 1973; Lazarus, 1968; Lewinsohn, 1974). In other words, fewer things make a depressed person happy, and more things make a depressed person unhappy. The lower level of energy and activity

seen in depressed people is consistent with this explanation. Receiving little reinforcement, the depressed person has little incentive to act.

Depression may be self-sustaining, especially if other people actually give the depressed person fewer rewards. One study found that when nondepressed people were interacting with depressed people, the nondepressed people smiled less, were generally less pleasant, and made more negative comments than they did when interacting with other nondepressed people (Gotlib & Robinson, 1982). Other investigations have also shown that we are less pleasant toward depressed persons than toward people who are not depressed, perhaps because the low mood of the depressed person is contagious and leaves the interacting partner at least temporarily drained as well (Coyne, 1976a; Gotlib & Robinson, 1982).

Evidence also shows that when depressed people actually receive the same amount of reward or punishment as those who are not depressed, they think that they are receiving fewer rewards and more punishments (Nelson & Craighead, 1977). Their perception of the treatment they receive is worse than the treatment they actually receive. Depressed people also appear to give themselves fewer rewards and more punishments for their own behavior (Rehm, 1977). This finding holds true whether we look at the general population or at people who are hospitalized for depression (Lobitz & Post, 1979; Nelson & Craighead, 1977, 1981).

Cognitive Explanations

Yet another proposed explanation of depression combines elements of learning theory and of cognitive approaches, based on an observed gender difference in rates of depression. About twice as many women as men are diagnosed as being depressed (Boyd & Weissman, 1982; Weissman & Klerman, 1977). This difference has held up across both time and place, even when researchers have been able to rule out the possibility that women are simply more likely than men to describe themselves as depressed (Amenson & Lewinsohn, 1981). Although we cannot yet rule out the possibility that the higher frequency of depression in women may be due in part to hormonal differences, a more intriguing possibility is that learned helplessness (see Chapter 7) may contribute to the higher rate of depression in women than in men (Matlin, 1993; Seligman, 1974; Strickland, 1992).

According to this view, women's social roles are more likely to lead them to feel depressed. Women traditionally have been forced into social roles in which they have less control over the outcomes that

Searchers . . .   *TERENCE WILSON*

Terence Wilson is Oscar K. Buros Professor of Psychology at the Rutgers University Graduate School of Applied Psychology.

Q: *How did you become interested in psychology and in your area of work in particular?*

A: As an undergraduate at the University of Witwatersrand in South Africa, I was initially intent on pursuing a career in law after majoring in history. But after I was exposed to two inspiring psychology teachers, Alma Hannon and Peter Radloff, I decided to become a psychologist and complete a PhD in the U.S.

Q: *What theories have influenced you?*

A: Alma Hannon was a staunch advocate of behaviorism and learning theories. We studied the contributions of Pavlov, Skinner, Hull, Mowrer, and Miller, and I soon became excited by the bold and ambitious visions of these experimental psychologists and the appeal of a scientific approach to psychology. I was especially taken with the promises of the then fledgling field of behavior therapy—the application of the principles and procedures of learning theory to clinical treatment. Through Gerry Davison, my mentor at SUNY, Stony Brook, I became familiar with the cognitive social-learning approach of Al Bandura, whose theory has most influenced my work since that time.

Q: *What is your greatest asset as a psychologist?*

A: My ability to critically evaluate and review bodies of evidence, to integrate diverse bits of information in useful ways, and to see the big picture. More specifically, I have been able to blend a dedication to scientific rigor with an understanding and appreciation of clinical practice.

Q: *What makes a psychologist really great?*

A: No one feature distinguishes a great psychologist. But most great psychologists have had the ability to make path-breaking observations or generate novel insights that they have then tested in creative and innovative ways.

Q: *How do you get your ideas for research?*

A: Usually from a careful reading of the literature. Observations and insights from clinical work with patients are other sources.

Q: *What obstacles have you experienced in your work?*

A: Numerous practical obstacles: recruiting the necessary subjects in clinical research, winning cooperation from collaborators and members of my research group, and finding the resources. Persistence is the key to overcoming these problems. Also, collaborating with colleagues requires a willingness to compromise and yield some control to others.

Q: *What do you want students to learn from you?*

A: To think critically, whether as researchers or practitioners; to appreciate the importance of scientific research to clinical practice.

Q: *What have you learned from your students?*

A: Many things, ranging from ideas about research to broader social issues.

Q: *Apart from your life as an academic, how have you found psychology to be important to you?*

A: It has helped me cope with different situations, such as how to address conflict and stress in a competitive environment as a coach of my son's soccer team.

Q: *How do you keep yourself academically challenged?*

A: By training very bright and ambitious graduate students and by engaging in collaborative research projects with colleagues I admire and respect.

Q: *What would you like people to remember about you?*

A: My contributions to the development of behavior therapy in particular and a broader empirical approach to psychological treatment in general. As a good mentor of talented graduate students who have themselves gone on to achieve prominence.

Q: *What do you further hope to achieve?*

A: A new venture is two major multi-site collaborative studies on the effectiveness of psychological treatments. One of these projects is the most important research I have ever planned, with the potential to be one of the most definitive outcome studies in the field.

---

affect them than do men. This lack of control may cause them to be financially and emotionally dependent on others, usually men. This dependence may lead to a form of learned helplessness. Both frustration and helplessness are linked to depression.

Inappropriate attributions and inferences directly contribute to depression, according to Aaron Beck (1967, 1985, 1991), whose theory is probably the most prominent of the contemporary cognitive theories of depression. Beck suggests that depressed people are particularly susceptible to errors in thinking. In particular, depressed people are susceptible to five logical errors that lead them to see things in an unfavorable manner:

1. *Arbitrary inference*—Drawing a conclusion even though there is little or no evidence to support it.

2. *Selective abstraction*—Focusing on an insignificant detail of a situation while ignoring the more important features.
3. *Overgeneralization*—Drawing global conclusions about ability on the basis of a single fact or episode.
4. *Magnification and minimization*—Committing gross errors of evaluation by magnifying small, unfavorable events, yet minimizing important, large, favorable events.
5. *Personalization*—Taking personal responsibility for events that are situational.

These cognitive distortions are not the only ones in which a person might engage, nor are they mutually exclusive. A given thought pattern can often involve several of these distortions simultaneously. What is key, according to the theory, is that thinking in these ways tends to lead to depression because it leads people to undervalue themselves.

Other evidence confirms that depressed people often show characteristic illogical thought patterns (Gara et al., 1993; Haaga, Dyck, & Ernst, 1991; Hollon & Kendall, 1980; Krantz & Hammen, 1979; Roth & Rehm, 1980). However, illogical cognitions do not always precede depression (Lewinsohn et al., 1981). At this point, it is not entirely clear whether these illogical thought patterns cause depression, whether depression causes these illogical thought patterns, or whether both depression and the illogical thought patterns both depend on some higher order third variable.

Humanistic-Existential Explanations

Humanistic and existential theorists have been less specific about depression than have others, but one significant theory was proposed by Viktor Frankl (1959). Frankl drew largely on his own experience, particularly the time he spent in Nazi concentration camps during World War II. He observed that of those individuals who were not put to death, the greatest difference between those who survived mentally intact and those who did not seemed to be in the ability to find meaning in their suffering, and to relate the experience to their spiritual lives. Generalizing from this experience, Frankl suggested that depression results from a lack of purpose in living. In this view, then, people who are depressed will be helped if they can find meaning in their lives.

Psychophysiological Explanations

Psychophysiological explanations of depression suggest that abnormally low levels of neurotransmitters

While Viktor Frankl (1905–) was surviving his imprisonment in a Nazi concentration camp, he observed that for many of his fellow prisoners, feeling a deep sense of meaning in their lives often made the difference between life and death. Afterward, Frankl formulated a method of psychotherapy based on his belief that if people can be helped to find meaning in their lives, they will be better to face whatever challenges confront them.

may be linked to depression. One theory focuses on norepinephrine, the other on serotonin. Both theories stem from ways in which particular drugs act on depression (see Chapter 19). Recent data suggest that the causes of bipolar depression may be primarily psychophysiological. For example, the norepinephrine theory of bipolar disorder postulates that the manic phase is caused by an excess of norepinephrine (Bunney, Goodwin, & Murphy, 1972; Schildkraut, 1965). Urinary levels of norepinephrine decrease during the depressive phase (Bunney et al., 1970). One supportive finding for considering bipolar disorder to be psychophysiological is that the most effective therapy for bipolar disorder so far is biochemical—namely, the administration of lithium. The psychophysiological explanation of bipolar disorder is further supported by genetic studies showing substantially higher genetic transmission of bipolar than of major depressive disorders.

Suicide

Personality disorders and most of the other psychological disorders described in this chapter are rarely life threatening. Depression can be, however, and severe depression often precedes suicide, or at least suicide attempts, as shown in the following example:

> Mr Wrigley was referred by his general practitioner for an outpatient assessment after suicidal thoughts resulting from depression. Mr. Wrigley recently had been forced to retire as a hospital porter because of a series of strokes that made lifting heavy equipment impossible. He felt "completely changed" after this incident. He would burst into tears over seemingly trivial events. He had to force himself to eat because he had no appetite, and his sleeping periods became shorter and shorter. His social interactions decreased, and he became more isolated and withdrawn. Mr Wrigley reported that he made an attempt on his life while having tea with his daughter and wife. He picked up a knife from the table as if to stab himself. He was restrained by his wife, then burst into tear sobbing, "I'm sorry, I'm sorry." (After Greenberg, Szmukler, & Tantam, 1986, pp. 16-17)

What do we know about suicide? For one thing, almost 31,000 suicides are recorded each year in the United States, which makes the U.S. rate of suicide 12.8 per 100,000 people (Douglas, 1967; Fremouw, Perczel, & Ellis, 1990; Gibbs, 1968; Holinger, 1987; National Center for Health Statistics, 1988; Resnick, 1968; Seiden, 1974). Many other Western countries have suicide rates of 20 or more per 100,000 people; in fact, Western cultures in general seem to be associated with higher rates of suicide (Carson & Butcher, 1992)—perhaps as an outcome of their higher rates of depression. In contrast, some cultures (e.g., that of the aborigines of Australia) have no known incidence of suicide whatsoever. The rate of suicide also rises in old age (particularly among white males), reaching a rate of more than 25 per 100,000 for people between the ages of 75 and 84 years.

Although we are not certain of the number of people who attempt suicide, estimates range roughly between 250,000 and 600,000 per year in the United States. These estimates imply that for every successful suicide, there are probably more than 10 unsuccessful attempts. Many people who try once will then try again and may continue until they succeed.

Contrary to popular belief, threats of suicide should be taken very seriously. Many persons who commit suicide have threatened suicide prior to taking their own lives.

This painting of Ophelia, by Sir John Millias, depicts a scene from William Shakespeare's Hamlet. *In this scene, Hamlet's fiancée has commited suicide while in a state of severe depression after she is rejected by an apparently mad Hamlet.*

TABLE 18-3
Suicide Attempters Versus Completers

A comparison of those who attempt suicide versus those who effectively commit suicide reveals some common characteristics, as well as some distinctions between the two groups. (After Fremouw et al., 1990)

Characteristic	Attempters	Completers
Gender	Majority female	Majority male
Age	Predominantly young	Risk increases with age
Method	Low lethality (pills, cutting)	More violent (gun, jumping)
Circumstances	Intervention likely	Precautions against discovery
Common diagnoses	Dysthymic disorder	Major mood disorder
	Borderline personality disorder	Alcoholism
		Schizophrenia
Dominant affect	Depression with anger	Depression with hopelessness
Motivation	Change in situation	Death
	Cry for help	
Hospital course	Quick recovery from dysphoria	
Attitude toward attempt	Relief to have survived	
	Promises not to repeat	

Men are much more likely to be successful in committing suicide than are women. Although the rate of suicide for men is almost four times that for women, the rate of suicide *attempts* is three times as great for women as for men. At least one reason for the difference is that men are more likely to shoot or hang themselves, whereas women are more likely to use drugs, such as sleeping pills. Clearly, shooting and hanging are more likely to lead to death than is an overdose of pills.

Other demographic factors also play a role. Men who are divorced are three times more likely to kill themselves than are married men. Both men and women at all socioeconomic levels commit suicide, but professionals (e.g., psychologists, psychiatrists, attorneys, and physicians) are especially likely to do so. Finally, although suicide ranks only eighth as a cause of death among adults, in general, it ranks third after accidents and homicides as a cause of death among people between the ages of 15 and 24 years. Among these young adults, whites are twice as likely as blacks to kill themselves.

Several myths surround suicide (Fremouw, Perczel, & Ellis, 1990; Pokorny, 1968; Shneidman, 1973):

- *Myth 1: People who talk about committing suicide do not actually go ahead and do it.* In fact, close to 8 out of 10 of the people who commit suicide have given some warning beforehand that they were about to do something. Often, they have given multiple warnings.
- *Myth 2: All people who commit suicide have definitely decided that they want to die.* In fact, many of those who commit suicide are not certain that they really want to die. They often take a gamble that someone will save them. Sometimes, for example, persons attempting suicide will take pills and then call someone to tell that person of the suicide attempt. If the person is not there, or if that person does not follow through quickly in response to the call, the suicide attempt may succeed.
- *Myth 3: Suicide occurs more often among people who are wealthy.* In fact, suicide is about equally prevalent at all levels of the socioeconomic spectrum.
- *Myth 4: People who commit suicide are always depressed beforehand.* Although depression is linked with suicide, some people who take their lives show no signs of depression at all. People with

terminal physical illnesses, for example, may commit suicide not because they are depressed, but to spare loved ones the suffering of having to support them, or because they have made peace with the idea of death and have decided that the time has come.

- *Myth 5: People who commit suicide are crazy.* Although suicide is linked to depression, relatively few of the people who commit suicide are truly out of touch with reality.
- *Myth 6: The risk of suicide ends when a person improves in mood following a major depression or a previous suicidal crisis.* In fact, most suicides occur while an individual is still depressed but after the individual starts to show some recovery. Often, people who are severely depressed are unable even to gather the energy to put together the means to commit suicide, so the suicide is more likely to occur as they are beginning to feel better and have the energy to do something about their wish to die.
- *Myth 7: Suicide is influenced by the cosmos—sun spots, phases of the moon, the position of the planets, and so on.* In fact, no evidence supports any of these beliefs.

The two main motivations for suicide appear to be surcease and manipulation. Those who seek *surcease* are people who have given up on life. They see death as the only solution to their problems and take their lives. Slightly more than half of suicides appear to be of this kind. People seeking surcease are usually depressed, hopeless, and more nearly certain that they really wish for their lives to end.

In contrast, those who view suicide as a means of *manipulation* use suicide to maneuver the world according to their desires. They may view suicide as a way to inflict revenge on a lover who has rejected them, to gain the attention of those who have ignored them, to hurt those who have hurt them, or to have the last word in an ongoing argument. Many of those who attempt suicide in this manner are not fully committed to dying but rather are using suicide as a call for attention and help (see Myth 2). Roughly 13% of suicide attempts are of this kind. Unless they receive help, people who attempt manipulative suicide often try to commit suicide again and may continue until they succeed in ending their lives. The following passage suggests primarily the wish for manipulation, but also the wish for surcease:

And suddenly, as she recalled the man who had been run over the day she first met Vronsky, she realized what she had to do. With a quick, light stride she de-

scended the steps that went from the water tank to the rails and stopped next to the train that was passing right beside her. She looked at the bottom of the freight cars, at the bolts and chains and at the great iron wheels of the first car that was slowly rolling by, and tried to measure with her eye the middle point between the front and the back wheels, and the moment that point would be opposite her.

There! she said to herself, looking at the shadow of the freight car on the mixture of sand and coal the ties were sprinkled with. There—right in the middle! I'll punish him and escape from everyone and from myself. . . .

And just at this moment she was horror-struck by what she was doing. Where am I? What am I doing? Why? She tried to get up, to throw herself back, but something huge and implacable struck her on the head and dragged her down. "Lord, forgive me for everything" she murmured, feeling the impossibility of struggling.

—*Leo Tolstoy*, Anna Karenina

Design an advertisement for a suicide hotline or other suicide-prevention measure, applying what you know about the causes and contributing factors underlying suicide.

DISSOCIATIVE DISORDERS

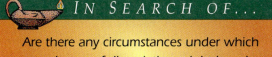

IN SEARCH OF...

Are there any circumstances under which some degree of dissociation might be adaptive? If so, which? If not, why not?

For some of the dissociative disorders, environmental traumas have been more strongly implicated than have been hereditary factors. There are three main dissociative disorders: dissociative amnesia, dissociative fugue, and dissociative identity disorder (formerly termed *multiple personality disorder*). All of these disorders involve an alteration in the normally integrative functions of consciousness, identity, or motor behavior.

Dissociative amnesia is characterized by sudden memory loss, usually after a highly stressful experience. The amnesia affects the recollection of all events that have taken place during and immediately after the experience. The person has difficulty remembering most of his or her important details, such as name, address, and family members. The amnesic is able to function relatively normally, though. The duration of the amnesia may be from several hours to several years. Recovery of the lost information is usually as rapid as the loss was, after which the episode ends and the memory loss is not repeated.

Dissociative fugue is characterized by a total memory loss, usually caused by severe stress. Without even questioning—or being aware of—the loss, persons with this disorder start whole new lives; they assume new identities, take new jobs, and behave as though they are totally different persons. Their personalities may even change. Recovery time is variable, but when a person does recover, he or she does not remember anything that took place during the fugue.

Dissociative identity disorder is characterized by the appearance of two or more identities (personalities), each of which is relatively independent of the others, lives a stable life of its own, and periodically takes full control of the person's behavior. One personality may know about the existence of others. This disorder seems to be caused by early emotional trauma, typically child abuse (Bliss, 1980). It usually starts around ages 4 to 6, when the child first experiences the serious emotional problem. Individuals with this disorder are also susceptible to self-hypnosis (see Chapter 6). Once they discover, unconsciously, that they can create another identity through self-hypnosis, they are relieved of some of the emotional burden of the primary identity. Later, when they confront an emotional trauma that cannot readily be handled by their existing identities, they create another new identity to deal with the new problem. Persons who develop multiple personalities in childhood may not know about the other personalities until adulthood. Recovery takes extensive therapy.

The most well known of these disorders is dissociative identity disorder, and one of the most famous cases of dissociative identities is that of Chris Sizemore, whose case was popularized in the motion picture *The Three Faces of Eve* (see also Thigpen & Cleckley, 1957). One of the faces was "Eve White," a quiet, proper, and relatively inhibited young woman. Eve White sought psychotherapy to treat headaches and blackouts. One day, in the presence of her physician, she suddenly grasped her head as though seized by a sudden and violent headache. Shortly thereafter, she seemed to recover, but the person who recovered was not the same one who had had the headache. She identified herself as "Eve Black." Eve Black's personality was wild, promiscuous, and reckless—almost the opposite of Eve White's. Eve Black was aware of Eve White, but the reverse was not true. The third personality, Jane, was the most stable of the three and

seemed to be the most well-integrated. Jane was aware of both of the other two personalities and seemed to think more highly of Eve Black than of Eve White. The case may be somewhat more complicated than it appeared. Sizemore later wrote a book claiming to have had as many as 21 separate personalities (Sizemore & Pittillo, 1977). Moreover, she

In the movie Three Faces of Eve, *Joanne Woodward (top) portrays Chis Sizemore, who suffers from dissociative identity disorder. While in one persona, she discovers clothing that suits another of her personas, but that is completely out of character with her current persona. Below is Chris Sizemore, on whom the movie character was based.*

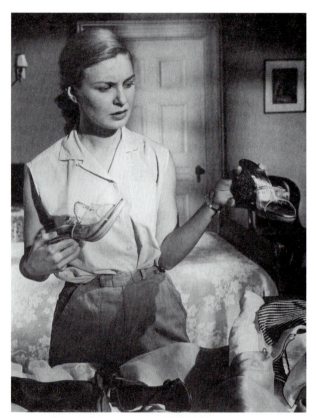

claims that, contrary to the claims of C. Thigpen and H. Cleckley, who popularized her story, the therapy she received did not cure her.

SCHIZOPHRENIA

IN SEARCH OF...

How does schizophrenia compare to the other major categories of abnormal behavior?

The term **schizophrenia** actually refers to a set of disorders that encompasses a variety of symptoms, including hallucinations, delusions, disturbed thought processes, disturbed emotional responses—such as flat affect or inappropriate affect—and motor symptoms. These symptoms are sometimes characterized as either being *negative* or *positive*. *Negative symptoms* include deficits in behavior, such as blunting of emotions (affective flattening), language deficits, apathy, and avoidance of social activity. *Positive symptoms* include delusions, hallucinations, and bizarre behavior, such as that described in the following passage.

[Rose] had her first psychotic break when she was fifteen. She had been coming home moody and tearful, then quietly beaming, then she stopped coming home.

. . .

Dinner was filled with all of our starts and stops and Rose's desperate efforts to control herself. She could barely eat and hummed the McDonald's theme song over and over again, pausing only to spill her juice down the front of her smock and begin weeping. My father looked at my mother and handed Rose his napkin. She dabbed at herself, listlessly, but the tears stopped.

"I want to go to bed. I want to go to bed and be in my head. I want to go to bed and be in my bed and in my head and just wear red. For red is the color that my baby wore and once more, it's true, yes, it is, it's true. Please don't wear red tonight, ohh, ohh, please don't wear red tonight, for red is the color—"

—Amy Bloom, "Silver Water"

To be classified as schizophrenic, an individual must show (1) impairment in areas such as work, social relations, and self-care; (2) at least two of the cognitive, affective, or motor characteristics; and (3) persistence of these symptoms for at least six months.

Why are impairments in work, social relations, and self-care important to the diagnosis of schizophrenia, given the extremely unusual nature of the other symptoms?

The prognosis for schizophrenia is not particularly encouraging. Schizophrenia typically involves a series of acute episodes with intermittent periods of remission. In many cases, the victim's ability to function during the periods of remission declines with each successive acute episode. The consensus is that once people have a full-fledged episode of schizophrenia, they are rarely completely rid of the disorder. In other words, the disease process appears to be chronic. Despite disagreement about this prognosis, everyone agrees that in most cases a number of the symptoms can be treated through psychotherapy and drugs (Sartorius, Shapiro, & Jablonsky, 1974).

Types of Schizophrenia

DSM-IV recognizes five main types of schizophrenia:

1. *Disorganized schizophrenia* is characterized by profound psychological disorganization. Hallucinations and delusions occur, and speech is often incoherent. For example, when a 23-year-old schizophrenic was asked, "How have you been feeling?" he answered flatly, "I'm as sure as you can help me as I have ice cubes in my ears" (Spitzer, Skodol, Gibbon, & Williams, 1983, p. 156). People with disorganized schizophrenia show flat affect, and may grimace or have fatuous smiles for no particular reason. They may giggle in a childish manner, invent new words, and experience rapid mood swings.

2. *Catatonic schizophrenia* is characterized by stupor and immobility for long periods of time. Victims often stare into space, seemingly completely detached from the rest of the world. Because catatonics move so little, their limbs may become stiff and swollen. This form of schizophrenia is less common today than it was in the past.

3. *Paranoid schizophrenia* is characterized by people having delusions of persecution, hearing voices criticizing or threatening them, or by delusions of grandeur, hearing voices telling them how wonderful they are. Consider this example:

A 26-year old woman was referred to a psychiatric hospital after attempting suicide by drug overdose. Her father had been diagnosed as schizophrenic and died when she was 13 by

Catatonic schizophrenics show waxy flexibility, *assuming odd poses for long periods of time. Although this woman's arm appears frozen in place, it can be manipulated into another pose, which the woman will then continue to hold.*

committing suicide. She was hospitalized twice in the past year for various psychotic episodes. For the previous few weeks, she had been convinced that the Devil was persecuting her. She would lay awake at night fantasizing that the Devil was tapping on her window. She believed that other individuals were talking to her and could read her mind. Many times she felt she was under the Devil's control. He would talk through her and had the power to inflict pain. She believed the only way to avoid the Devil was to kill herself. Her mother found her on the floor and called the ambulance. At the hospital, she said that she still heard voices talking to her and that they had the power to control her thinking. (After Fottrell, 1983, p. 128)

Paranoid schizophrenics are particularly susceptible to delusions of reference, taking an insignificant event and interpreting it as though it has great personal meaning for them.

4. *Undifferentiated schizophrenia* is a catchall category used for schizophrenic symptoms either

that do not quite fit any of the other patterns or that fit more than one pattern.

5. *Residual schizophrenia* is a diagnosis applied to persons who have had at least one schizophrenic episode and who currently show some mild symptoms but do not exhibit profoundly disturbed behavior.

Demographic Issues in the Prevalence of Schizophrenia

Schizophrenia affects 1–2% of the population and tends to run in families. A review of several studies on the genetic transmission of schizophrenia found that relatives of a schizophrenic are 10 times more likely than a nonrelative to develop this disorder (Gottesman, 1991; Gottesman, McGuffin, & Farmer, 1987). Families seem to inherit a predisposition to schizophrenia. For example, among schizophrenics the prevalence rates of schizophrenia are 44% for identical twins, 12% for fraternal twins, 7% for siblings, 9% for children, and 3% for grandchildren (see Figure 18-3).

Schizophrenia is generally diagnosed in early adulthood, usually before age 45 (see Figure 18-4). Schizophrenia also has been found to vary with socioeconomic status (SES). In particular, members of the lowest SES group are roughly eight times more likely to suffer from schizophrenia than are members of the middle and upper SES groups (Dohrenwend & Dohrenwend, 1974; Strauss et al., 1978).

Why is there such a pronounced difference among the SES groups? According to the *social-drift*

FIGURE 18-3
Vulnerability to Schizophrenia
The rates of overlap in the occurrence of schizophrenia increase in relation to the closeness of the hereditary link between individuals. (After data from Gottesman, 1991; Gottesman, McGuffin, & Farmer, 1987)

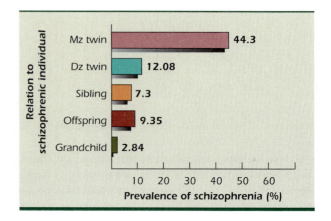

Searchers . . .   *IRVING I. GOTTESMAN*

Irving I. Gottesman is Professor of Psychology at the University of Virginia.

Q: *How did you become interested in psychology and in your area of work in particular?*

A: I was initially interested in physics and biology. During my second year at the Illinois Institute of Technology, I took a course in abnormal psychology and was introduced to the ideas of Freud. That seemed to be so attractive that I became a psychology major. I then spent three years in Korea, Japan, and Europe in the navy, reading psychology journals in my spare time and discovering the writings of Starke Hathaway, Paul Meehl, and Robert Wirt. I decided to become a University of Minnesota-type clinical psychologist. The Minnesota program is oriented toward quantification of clinical impressions and encourages an open mind about the role of biological factors in causing mental disorders.

Q: *What theories influenced you the most?*

A: I was fortunate to have a course in the psychology of individual differences, which exposed students to the works of Anne Anastasi, Leona Tyler, D. G. Paterson, James Jenkins, and Franz Kallmann. Sheldon Reed, a zoologist and human geneticist, influenced me to conduct a twin study for my doctoral dissertation. I was the first one at Minnesota to try to combine genetics with psychology.

Q: *What is your greatest asset as a psychologist?*

A: Curiosity, skepticism about received wisdom, and an urge to bring together things that on the surface look as though they don't belong together. I find myself working at the intersection of biological psychiatry, human genetics, and clinical psychology.

Q: *What makes a psychologist really great?*

A: A passion for discovering the truth and integrating everything that has come before them with what they are now finding out for themselves.

Q: *How do you get your ideas for research?*

A: Reading voraciously. I never stop reading journals in psychology, psychiatry, and genetics as well as manuscripts submitted for review. My patients are also an important source of ideas.

Q: *How do you decide whether to pursue an idea?*

A: I pursue it if it's important and if I can get a student or colleague also to be interested. I find that I work best by collaboration.

Q: *How have you developed an idea into a workable hypothesis?*

A: In the first twin study I did of schizophrenia, I felt that the criticisms of genetic studies of schizophrenia were unfair and ideological, so I devised a study that was not based on a preconceived idea of what the answer ought to be. I also built in procedures to safeguard against the criticisms. In a London hospital I was given the golden opportunity to tap into a register of psychiatrically disordered twins that had taken sixteen years to collect.

Q: *What obstacles have you experienced in your work?*

A: The prejudice in psychology against entertaining ideas about genetics being involved in behavior.

Q: *What is your major contribution to psychology?*

A: To open the minds of students and colleagues to the way that genes and environment interact and co-act.

Q: *What do you want students to learn from you?*

A: That hard work pays off. That reading widely and interacting with neighboring disciplines (neuroscience, genetics, biology, clinical psychology, and clinical psychiatry) are the way to work.

Q: *What advice would you give to someone starting in the field of psychology?*

A: I encourage introductory psychology students to take as much biology and math as they have time for. Psych students should read widely, including fiction and the neighboring disciplines, and try to develop an interest in depth, rather than spreading themselves too thin.

Q: *What do you want people to remember about you?*

A: Some of the terms and ideas that I've invented and their utility for dealing with the question, "How does the predisposition for traits and for mental disorders become actualized or remain latent?"

Q: *What do you further hope to achieve?*

A: I'm working on antisocial behavior, alcoholism, and depression. I'd like to find a legitimate way of using evolutionary thinking to inspire psychological research.

---

hypothesis (Myerson, 1940), those who suffer from schizophrenia tend to drift downward in SES. Their inability to hold a job, to earn a living, to relate to other people, and to function effectively leads them to successively lower SES levels until they bottom out. Evidence (Turner & Wagonfeld, 1967) shows that schizophrenics are much more likely than are others to drift downward in SES.

An alternative explanation is that the social and economic conditions a person faces in the lowest SES groups are so stressful that they tend to precipitate schizophrenia, at least more so than is the case for

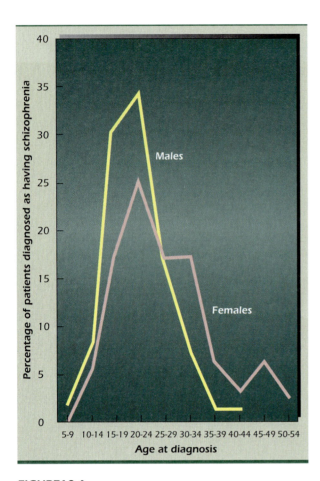

FIGURE 18-4
Diagnosis of Schizophrenia
According to A. W. Loranger, schizophrenia usually is diagnosed in males at younger ages than it is in females. (After Loranger, 1984)

conditions in higher SES groups. Still another explanation is that people with lower SES are more likely to be diagnosed as schizophrenic. That is, people with higher SES may be able to hide their symptoms better, or they may have more help from others in hiding their symptoms. Also, if psychiatrically assessed, it appears that the lower-SES individual is more likely to be diagnosed as schizophrenic, even if the symptoms are the same as those of someone with higher SES (Hollingshead & Redlich, 1958; Kramer, 1957). Recent data suggest that members of groups experiencing discrimination and the stress that results from it are more prone to schizophrenia, regardless of social class (Dohrenwend et al., 1992).

Explanations of Schizophrenia

The many different explanations of schizophrenia are not necessarily mutually exclusive. They may simply apply to different kinds or levels of severity of schizophrenia. At present, none of the existing theories seems to account for all aspects of each of the disorders.

Psychodynamic Explanations

The psychodynamic paradigm has offered some explanations that currently do not receive much support. The classical Freudian explanation of schizophrenia is in terms of *primary narcissism*—that is, the schizophrenic returns to very early stages of psychological development. This phase occurs early during the oral stage, before the ego has differentiated itself from the id. In this phase, reality testing suffers because the ego is undifferentiated; schizophrenics are securely wrapped up in themselves but out of touch with the world (Arieti, 1974).

Two psychodynamically based views of schizophrenia relate the malady to the family environment. The hypothesis of the *schizophrenogenic mother* holds that the mothers of schizophrenics tend to be cold, dominant, and conflict seeking (Fromm-Reichmann, 1948). At the same time, the mother is rejecting, overprotective, rigid, moralistic about sex, and fearful of intimacy.

According to *double-bind theory* (Bateson, Jackson, Haley, & Weakland, 1956), people develop schizophrenic symptoms as a result of a double bind in communication. That is, in a close and intense relationship, say with a parent, the messages that the parent gives to the child are contradictory, simultaneously saying or doing things that are inconsistent with each other. At the same time, the child receiving the contradictory communication feels incapable of—or prohibited from—commenting on the contradiction, withdrawing from the situation, or ignoring the messages.

In one example (Bateson et al., 1956, p. 258), a young man had just about recovered from a schizophrenic episode. His mother visited him in the hospital. Glad to see her, the man put his arm around her shoulders. The mother stiffened, but when the son withdrew his arm, she asked, "Don't you love me anymore?" She then went on to say, "Dear, you must not be so easily embarrassed and afraid of your feelings."

Learning Theory Explanations

A prominent learning-based theory is known as *labeling theory* (Scheff, 1966), which holds that once people are labeled as schizophrenics, they are more likely to appear to exhibit symptoms of schizophrenia. For one thing, persons who have been labeled as schizophrenics may then feel free (or even expected) to engage in antisocial behavior that would be pro-hibited in so-called normal people. Also, once they begin acting abnormally, more of their actions are likely to be interpreted as being abnormal. (David Rosenhan [1973] observed that the behavior of pa-tients in psychiatric wards is likely to be viewed as ab-normal, even if the patients are normal, mentally healthy individuals.) According to this theory, some-one who begins to act strangely and is labeled a schizophrenic is susceptible to actually becoming schizophrenic merely because of the labeling process. Thus, the very fact of the label may create a self-ful-filling prophecy.

However, the preponderance of evidence does not favor labeling theory. For example, both the Es-kimo and Yoruba cultures view as "crazy" behavior la-beled in our society as schizophrenic (Murphy, 1976), suggesting that there is at least some overlap in what is seen as nonadaptive across societies. For the most part, it would be hard to argue that the labels are ex-tremely arbitrary.

Cognitive Explanations

Essentially, cognitive explanations of schizophrenia suggest that people with this disorder have sensory experiences that differ from those of normal individu-als. From this perspective, many of the symptoms of schizophrenia could be construed as attempts by people suffering from these symptoms to explain their sensory experiences to others. Unlike the other explanations of schizophrenia we have considered, cognitive explanations interpret the bizarre sensory experiences of schizophrenics as being real and as causing the disorder. According to this view, break-downs in communication with schizophrenics often result from their attempt to explain what is happen-ing to them.

This view, like some of the others discussed ear-lier, relies on the notion of cognitive flooding or stimulus overload. People with schizophrenia are viewed as being particularly susceptible to overload-ing, which leads them to function in a maladaptive manner. It may be that schizophrenics lack a kind of filtering mechanism that allows most people to screen out irrelevant stimuli (Payne et al., 1959). Brendan Maher (1972, 1983) has investigated whether this overstimulation may cause both an inability to focus attention on any one thing for very long and a sus-ceptibility to intrusion of irrelevant thoughts.

Humanistic-Existential Explanations

Humanistic psychologists usually deal with disorders that are less seriously disruptive than schizophrenia.

The artwork of schizophrenics often reflects the distorted thought processes that trouble them. Surprisingly, some patients report that while engaged in artistic expression, "the voices [auditory hallucinations] stop."

However, two humanistic existentialists have taken quite unorthodox views. Thomas Szasz (1961) argued that mental illness is simply a myth—that schizo-phrenia and other so-called mental illnesses are merely alternative ways of experiencing the world. According to Szasz, when we apply the medical model to psychological phenomena, we err in our theories and in our practice. Although Szasz acknowl-edged that the medical model may apply well to phys-ical ailments, he held that it does not apply well to mental processing.

In a related vein, therapist R. D. Laing (1964) suggested that schizophrenia is not an illness but merely a label that society applies to behavior it finds problematic. According to Laing, people become schizophrenic when they live in situations that are simply not livable. No matter what they do, nothing seems to work, and they feel symbolically in a position of checkmate. According to Laing, schizophrenia is a valid response to these inconsistencies and to the craziness of this kind of situation, and the problem is not with the person who has the symptoms, but with a society that rejects that person. He suggested that people who are highly sensitive to the demands of the world are susceptible to becoming schizophrenic.

These theories are products of the 1960s' alternative lifestyles. They indicate the inappropriateness of glorifying mental disturbances. Such glorification does an injustice to people who might tragically go without beneficial treatment, when otherwise they might have been aided by suitable interventions. Thus, even if we consider whether society plays some role in the problems people face, we still are unlikely to consider seriously the views of Szasz or Laing.

> How are some of your views of mental illness being shaped by the headlines you read, the experiences you have, your surrounding political and cultural climate, and other aspects of your social context?

Psychophysiological Explanations

Some of the most promising explanations of schizophrenia today are psychophysiological. One such view holds that schizophrenia results from an excess of the neurotransmitter dopamine (Seidman, 1990; Wong et

Contemporary imaging techniques offer insights into some of the cerebral processes that underlie psychological disorders. For example, these images show the differences in the patterns of activity in a normal brain, as compared with the brain of a schizophrenic.

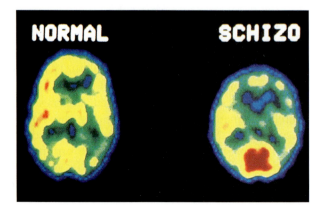

al., 1986) (see Chapter 3). Another psychophysiological explanation suggests structural abnormalities in the brain as the cause (Seidman, 1983). Some evidence indicates that schizophrenics have enlarged *ventricles* in the brain (Andreasen et al., 1982a, 1982b, 1990). These ventricles—the canals through which cerebrospinal fluid (CSF) flows—generally appear enlarged when the surrounding tissue has atrophied, and additional evidence documents atrophy in portions of the brains of schizophrenics. Another intriguing finding is that in a card-sorting task, schizophrenics show less actuation of the prefrontal region of the brain than do nonschizophrenics (Weinberger, Wagner, & Wyatt, 1983).

PERSONALITY DISORDERS

IN SEARCH OF...

DSM-IV specifically places personality disorders on a separate axis of disorders. Personality disorders seem comparatively less tractable in terms of treatment, and our legal system is less willing to consider personality disorders when considering a plea of "not guilty by reason of insanity." What is there about personality disorders that so sharply distinguishes them from other forms of abnormal behavior?

As difficult as it may be to categorize various types of schizophrenia, it is even more difficult to differentiate the many personality disorders in DSM-IV. **Personality disorders** are consistent, long-term, extreme personality characteristics that cause an individual great unhappiness or that seriously impair that person's ability to adjust to and function well in her or his environment. The major personality disorders include the following:

1. *Paranoid personality disorder*—someone suspicious of others, expects to be poorly treated. A person who blames others for things that happen to him or her.
2. *Schizoid personality disorder*—a person who has difficulty forming relationships with other people. He or she tends to be indifferent to what others think about, say about, or feel toward him or her.

3. *Schizotypal personality disorder*—someone who has serious problems with other people, shows eccentric or bizarre behavior. He or she is susceptible to illusions and may engage in magical thinking, believing that he or she has contact with the supernatural. This disorder may be a mild form of schizophrenia.

4. *Borderline personality disorder*—victims show extreme instability in moods, self-image, and relationships with other people.

5. *Narcissistic personality disorder*—a person with an inflated view of him- or herself, who is intensely self-centered and selfish in his or her personal relationships. The person lacks empathy for others and often uses others for his or her own ends. He or she often spends time fantasizing about past and future successes.

6. *Histrionic personality disorder*—someone who generally acts as though he or she is on stage; is very dramatic and continually tries to draw attention to him- or herself. Someone who is lavish in his or her emotional displays, but shallow in the depth of his or her emotions. He or she often has trouble in relationships and tends to be manipulative and demanding. Here is an example:

A 58-year-old woman recently was brought to the hospital after police picked her up off the street where she had been shouting, crying, and banging her head against a wall. During the initial interview she recalled that, "I had my first breakdown when I learned of my husband's illness." Since then she has had 16 admissions to the hospital for a variety of reasons. She indicated that her present illness began when she was discharged to an apartment she did not like, and was upset with her son because she did not approve of the woman he had chosen to marry. During the next few days, she became depressed and began to behave in a boisterous, attention-seeking manner. She created various disturbances in her neighborhood and subsequently was brought to the hospital by police. In the hospital, she was extremely uncooperative. She kept eyes firmly shut and refused to open them. She would sit up on her bed only when told, and then immediately fall back under the covers. (After Fottrell, 1983, p. 122)

7. *Avoidant personality disorder*—someone who is reluctant to enter into close personal relationships. He or she may wish for closeness but is so sensitive to rejection that he or she is afraid to become close. Someone who has very low self-esteem and devalues much of what he or she does.

8. *Dependent personality disorder*—a person who lacks self-confidence and has difficulty taking personal responsibility for him- or herself. Someone who subordinates his or her own needs to those of loved ones, partly in fear of losing the loved ones if the person's needs are expressed. He or she is extremely sensitive to criticism. This disorder is more frequent in women than in men.

9. *Obsessive-compulsive personality disorder*—someone who displays excessive concern with details, rules, and codes of behavior; tends to be perfectionistic and requires everything be done just so; tends to be highly work oriented. He or she often has trouble relating to other people and so is cold and distant in interpersonal relationships. This disorder is more frequent in men than in women. (This disorder differs from obsessive-compulsive anxiety disorder, in which the person experiences feelings of dread if the compulsive behaviors are not performed.)

Francois Le Moyne's (1688–1737) Narcissus *illustrates the legendary characteristic of self-absorption, the fundamental feature of narcissistic personality disorder.*

10. *Antisocial personality disorder*—a person who has a tendency to be superficially charming and appears to be sincere; is poised, calm, and verbally facile; is actually insincere, untruthful, and unreliable in relations with others. He or she has virtually no sense of responsibility and feels no shame or remorse when hurting others. Someone who is extremely self-centered and is incapable of genuine love or affection. This disorder can run in families. The evidence shows both genetic and environmental factors. It is more frequent in men than in women.

Although it is possible to detect some features of personality disorders during infancy, childhood, or adolescence, these disorders generally are not diagnosed until early adulthood. Several other disorders, however, are usually first diagnosed early.

DISORDERS USUALLY FIRST DIAGNOSED IN INFANCY, CHILDHOOD, OR ADOLESCENCE

IN SEARCH OF...

How might clinicians respond differently when assessing and treating disorders that first appear prior to adulthood? What special precautions, if any, should be taken in working with infants, children, and adolescents?

Some disorders characteristically appear before adulthood. In particular, three major disorders usually are diagnosed first in infancy, childhood, or adolescence:

1. *Attention-deficit hyperactivity disorder*—The disorder is characterized by a difficulty in focusing attention for reasonable amounts of time. Children with this disorder also tend to be impulsive and disruptive in social settings. They are often unable to sit still and constantly seem to be seeking attention. This disorder is much more common in boys than in girls and usually appears before age 7. As many as 3–5% of children may have this disorder (American Psychiatric Association, 1987). Psychologists do not know what causes this disorder, but it is generally believed to reflect an organic brain dysfunction.

2. *Conduct disorders*—These disorders are characterized by habitual misbehavior, such as stealing, skipping school, destroying property, fighting, being cruel both to animals and to other people, and frequently telling lies. Children with this disorder may misbehave independently or in groups or gangs.

3. *Pervasive developmental disorder (PDD)*—This disorder is also known as *autism*. It is characterized by three main symptoms: (1) minimal to no responsiveness to others, seeming obliviousness to the surrounding world; (2) impairment in communication, both verbal and nonverbal; and (3) highly restricted range of interest, sitting alone for hours, immobility or rocking back and forth, staring off into space. PDD occurs in only about 0.04% of the population, and is four times as likely to occur in boys as in girls. Infants with PDD do not cry when left alone and do not smile when others smile at them. Even by age 5, many PDD children are unable to use language.

Children with PDD show a striking lack of both intellectual development and speech development, for example:

Five-year-old Jimmy Patterson was brought to the inpatient child psychiatric unit at a large city hospital. His parents complained that he was impossible to manage, was not toilet trained, and screamed or gestured whenever he became frustrated or wanted to be noticed. He was allowed a free-play period and an interaction period involving a cooperative task with his mother. He wandered about the playroom and played by himself with a number of toys. His mother then tried to involve him in some cooperative play with wooden blocks. She spoke to Jimmy in a cheerful tone, but he seemed not to notice her and moved to an opposite part of the room. Mrs. Patterson made several comments to Jimmy, but he remained oblivious to her encouragements. She then tried to begin a jigsaw puzzle with Jimmy. She led him over to a chair, but as soon as he sat down, he got up again and continued to wander about the room. His mother then firmly, although not harshly, took Jimmy by the arm and led him over to a chair. Jimmy began to whine and scream and flail his arms about, and eventually wiggled out of his mother's grasp. (After Leon, 1974, p. 9).

Clinicians originally believed that PDD might be a childhood form of schizophrenia. They now believe that PDD and childhood schizophrenia are different disorders (American Psychiatric Association, 1994). Children with schizophrenia often show a family history of schizophrenia, but those with PDD do not. Also, the drugs that alleviate symptoms of schizophrenia are not effective with PDD (see Chapter 19). We examine PDD in detail next.

Explanations of Childhood Disorders

Psychodynamic Explanations

Early psychodynamic explanations of PDD revolved around the role of parents' personalities and the ways parents bring up their children. For example, L. Kanner (1943) suggested that parents of PDD children tend to be cold and impersonal, as well as rejecting of these children. The claim was that PDD children have turned away from detached and cold parents and formed a world of their own. This explanation is given little credence today. The parents of PDD children simply do not appear to be different in kind from those of other children (Cantwell et al., 1979; Cox et al., 1975; Koegel et al., 1983).

Learning Theory Explanations

Some learning theorists have suggested that children may develop PDD because they are inadvertently rewarded for their abnormal behavior (Ferster, 1961). In other words, when children behave abnormally, they may receive attention that they otherwise would not receive. The child's success in gaining attention then leads to increasing (and increasingly bizarre) attention-seeking behavior. This explanation also has not fared well. Even intensive attempts to use learning principles to change the behavior of PDD children have met with only limited success (Lovaas et al., 1973; see also Chapter 19).

Cognitive Explanations

Some investigators believe that children with PDD show perceptual deficits. For example, these children may make errors in the stimuli they admit to consciousness versus those they filter out (Frith & Baron-Cohen, 1987). The result is that their perceptions are distorted, and they react to these perceptions in ways that seem bizarre to others.

Psychophysiological Explanations

The most successful explanations of PDD so far have been psychophysiological. A number of differences have been revealed by comparisons of the brains of

Children suffering from pervasive development disorder (PDD; also termed autism) *commonly show characteristic behaviors such as rocking for extended periods of time. One view of such behaviors is that they provide a means of shutting out excessive stimulation.*

children who have PDD with brains of children who do not have the disorder. At least some PDD children, for example, have been shown to have *lesions* (areas showing injury) in the brain stem, enlarged ventricles (suggesting possible atrophy), reversed cerebral asymmetry, and more active right than left cerebral hemispheres (see Campbell et al., 1982; Courchesne et al., 1988). There have also been signs of biochemical imbalances in PDD children. The evidence is fairly persuasive that, although we do not yet know exactly what causes PDD, its cause or causes are psychophysiological.

LEGAL ISSUES

IN SEARCH OF...

How should our legal system handle people with mental disorders who commit crimes?

The DSM-IV descriptions of abnormal behavior are designed to aid clinicians in diagnosing their patients and to aid psychologists in understanding such behavior. Although these descriptions are imperfect, often permitting ambiguous diagnoses and flawed understandings, they generally serve the purpose for which psychiatrists and psychologists intended them. Nonpsychologists, however, may have different requirements, which may lead to different definitions.

For example, in courtrooms and law offices, alternative definitions of abnormal behavior are required. The term *sanity*, for example, is a legal term for describing behavior, not a psychological one. Some of the most controversial examples of legal descriptions of abnormal behavior have involved criminal behavior. In 1834, a court in Ohio decided that a person could be found not guilty by reason of insanity if the person acted on an "irresistible impulse" that impelled him or her to commit the crime. Thus, the particular category of disorder was not relevant; the ability to resist an impulse was. Two subsequent cases, *Parsons v. the State of Alabama* (1887) and *Davis v. the United States* (1897), upheld the legitimacy of the "not-guilty-by-reason-of-insanity" defense.

Perhaps the most well-known construction of the insanity defense is the *M'Naghten Rule*, formulated as the result of a murder trial in 1843 by a court in England. This rule holds that "to establish a defense on the ground of insanity, it must be clearly proved that, at the time of committing the act, the party accused was laboring under such a defect of reasoning, from disease of the mind, as not to know the nature and quality of the act he [or she] was doing, or if he [or she] did know it, that he [or she] did not know he [or she] was doing what was wrong" (*Stedman's Medical Dictionary*, 25th edition, 1990, p. 1374).

In 1962, the American Law Institute provided a set of guidelines intended to reflect the current state of the insanity defense and its legal and psychological ramifications. These guidelines state that people cannot be held responsible for criminal conduct if, as a consequence of a mental disease or defect, they lack the capacity either to appreciate the wrongness of their conduct or to conform their conduct with the requirements of the law. The guidelines exclude, however, repeated criminal actions or antisocial conduct. In other words, the intent of the guidelines is to embrace extraordinary acts, not habitual criminal behavior.

In 1981, John Hinckley, Jr., attempted to assassinate President Ronald Reagan to impress actress Jodie Foster. Hinckley was found not guilty by reason of insanity. As a result of this case and the outrage that followed it, a number of states have introduced a new verdict, "guilty but mentally ill." Federal courts have also tightened up guidelines for finding a defendant not guilty by reason of insanity. The Insanity Defense Reform Act, passed by the U.S. Congress in October 1984, makes it much more difficult for a defendant to escape the punishment of the law, regardless of the defendant's mental state. The topic remains controversial, and some psychiatrists, such as

Following an attempt to assassinate then-President Ronald Reagan, John Hinckley, Jr., was wrestled to the ground. When brought to trial, Hinckley was found not guilty by reason of insanity. His case triggered a public outcry to modify the treatment of mentally ill persons who commit violent criminal acts.

Thomas Szasz and R. D. Laing, have argued that concepts of mental illness and insanity have no place in the courtroom at all. According to Szasz, acts of violence are as rational and goal directed as any other acts, and perpetrators of such acts should be treated accordingly.

Psychology and the law are also interrelated in noncriminal matters. For example, do the mentally ill have a right to treatment? In the case of *Wyatt v. Stickney*, decided in Alabama in 1971, the court ruled that they do. This ruling has generally held up. However, there is always latitude in the interpretation of who is mentally ill and really needs treatment. In recent years, federal spending on mental institutions has decreased, so many patients who were formerly in psychiatric hospitals have been released into the streets. There, they generally join the ranks of the homeless and can now be seen wandering the streets instead of the halls of mental hospitals.

However, people suffering from mental illnesses today also are recognized as having a right to refuse treatment unless their behavior is potentially dangerous to others. In deciding whether to require treatment or confinement, we need to consider not only the rights of the potential patient, but also the rights of persons they might harm. Once again, we face a dilemma—trying to find the right balance between the rights of the prospective patient to be free to refuse treatment or hospitalization and the rights of other persons to be protected from any harm that the prospective patient might cause.

Design some criteria that you believe should be used in determining (a) a person's right to receive treatment for mental illness and (b) a person's obligation to receive such treatment.

CONCLUSION

This chapter described some of the main disorders that constitute abnormal psychology. Some disorders are addressed in other chapters (for example, Chapter 6 deals with aspects of substance-abuse disorders), and others are simply outside the scope of an introduction to psychology. We have seen that although clinical psychologists have reached a broad consensus regarding the diagnostic categories (as provided by DSM-IV), considerable disagreement exists over the causes of the various syndromes. Psychodynamic, humanistic, learning theory, cognitive, and biological explanations compete in the characterization of the disorders. Their implications for psychotherapy are considered in Chapter 19.

SUMMARY

What Is Abnormal Behavior?   640

1. *Abnormal behavior* can be defined as statistically unusual, nonadaptive, labeled as abnormal by the surrounding society, and characterized by some degree of perceptual or cognitive distortion. There is a lack of universal consensus regarding any one definition of abnormal behavior.

2. Early explanations of abnormal behavior included witchcraft and spiritual possession by demons. More contemporary perspectives on abnormal behavior include psychodynamic, behavioral (learning), cognitive, humanistic, and psychophysiological approaches.

Diagnosing Abnormal Behavior   643

3. In the middle of the nineteenth century, clinicians began to reach formalized consensus regarding the diagnosis of mental disorders. Subsequent generations of clinicians have continued to refine the documents recording these consensual agreements, both in the United States (DSM-IV) and in the world community (ICD-10).

Anxiety Disorders   645

4. *Anxiety disorders* encompass the individual's feelings of *anxiety*—tension, nervousness, distress, or uncomfortable arousal. DSM-IV divides anxiety disorders into five main categories: phobic disorders, including *simple phobias, social phobias,* and *agoraphobia; panic disorder; generalized anxiety disorder; stress disorder,* including *posttraumatic* and *acute stress disorders;* and *obsessive-compulsive disorder.* Anxiety disorders involve mood, cognitive, somatic, and motor symptoms. There are various explanations of the disorders and the symptoms they cause. For example, psychodynamic explanations emphasize childhood events, whereas biological explanations emphasize links to neurotransmitters.

Mood Disorders   653

5. The two major *mood disorders* (extreme disturbances in a person's emotional state) are major depression and bipolar disorder. Depression is relatively common and is generally believed to be influenced by situational factors. *Bipolar disorder,* however, is much rarer and runs in families, suggesting a possible genetic, biological component. Both disorders probably are influenced by both biological factors and situational factors. For example, bipolar disorder may be biologically rooted, but some environments may lead to more intense expression of the disorder than do other environments.

6. Cultures vary widely in their rates of suicide.

7. Many myths surround suicide. Perhaps the most important caution is that any person, of any background or characteristic, may decide to commit suicide, and any threats of suicide should be considered seriously.

Dissociative Disorders   661

8. Environmental traumas have been implicated more strongly for dissociative disorders than have been hereditary or biological factors.

9. There are three main dissociative disorders: *dissociative amnesia* (sudden memory loss, usually after a highly stressful life experience), *dissociative fugue* (amnesia regarding a past identity and assumption of an entirely new identity), and *dissociative identity disorder* (the occurrence of two or more distinct, independent identities within the same individual). All of these disorders involve an alteration in the normally integrative functions of consciousness, identity, or motor behavior.

Schizophrenia   663

10. *Schizophrenia* refers to a set of disorders encompassing a variety of symptoms, including hallucinations, *delusions*, disturbed thought processes, and disturbed emotional responses.

11. Types of schizophrenia include disorganized schizophrenia, catatonic schizophrenia, paranoid schizophrenia, undifferentiated schizophrenia, and residual schizophrenia.

12. Of the various explanations for schizophrenia, psychophysiological explanations seem particularly interesting because they help explain the familial trends in the development of schizophrenia (as well as the positive outcomes associated with anti-psychotic drugs). The specific psychophysiological causes remain unknown, however. Other explanations have different emphases. For example, a psychodynamic explanation emphasizes the role of primary narcissism—a return to a very early stage of psychological development.

Personality Disorders   668

13. *Personality disorders* are consistent, long-term, extreme personality characteristics that cause great unhappiness or that seriously impair a person's ability to adjust to the demands of everyday living or to function well in her or his environment.

14. The major personality disorders are paranoid, schizoid, schizotypal, borderline, narcissistic, histrionic, avoidant, dependent, obsessive-compulsive, and antisocial disorders.

Disorders Usually First Diagnosed in Infancy, Childhood, or Adolescence   670

15. Three major disorders usually are diagnosed first in infancy, childhood, or adolescence: attention-deficit hyperactivity disorder, conduct disorder, and pervasive developmental disorder (PDD). There are various explanations for these disorders. For example, the learning-theory explanations of PDD emphasizes inadvertent rewards for abnormal behavior.

Legal Issues   671

16. The term sanity is a legal term for describing behavior, not a psychological one. At present, a person's sanity is an important factor in determining the adjudication of the person's criminal behavior. Just how sanity is determined and how it is considered in making legal judgments still is being evaluated in the courts.

KEY TERMS

abnormal behavior 640
acute stress disorder 648
agoraphobia 645
anxiety 645
anxiety disorders 645
bipolar disorder 654
cognitive anxiety 650
compulsion 648
delusions 654
dissociative amnesia 661

dissociative fugue 662
dissociative identity
   disorder 662
generalized anxiety disorder 648
mania 654
mood disorders 653
obsession 648
obsessive-compulsive
   disorder 648
panic disorder 648

personality disorders 668
phobias 645
posttraumatic stress disorder
   648
schizophrenia 663
simple phobias 645
social phobias 645
somatic anxiety 651
stress disorder 648

IN SEARCH OF THE HUMAN MIND:
ANALYSES, CREATIVE EXPLORATIONS, AND PRACTICAL APPLICATIONS

1. Why does science as a whole benefit when researchers conduct their studies based on explicit underlying assumptions about their theoretical perspectives?
2. Compare the major anxiety disorders, and then indicate which you believe would be the most problematic or troublesome for the individual experiencing such a disorder.
3. Choose one of the psychological perspectives, the one which you find most suitable to your own beliefs about abnormal behavior. Compare your preferred perspective with the others, showing why yours makes better sense.

4. Suppose you are charged with choosing exactly one personality disorder to be allowed as a legal defense for a not-guilty-by-reason-of-insanity plea. Which disorder would you choose, and why? What would your defense be?
5. Suppose you are a researcher investigating bipolar disorder. Design an experiment to determine the relative contributions of environmental versus biological factors to the disorder. That is, how much of the cause is due to environmental factors and how much was due to biological ones?
6. Suppose your English teacher assigns you the task of creating a believable literary character who is schizophrenic. Briefly describe that person as others view the person, then describe how that person sees the world, including other persons.

7. Suppose you are volunteering to answer telephones on a suicide hotline. What kinds of strategies would you use—and what might you actually say—to try to prevent someone from committing suicide?
8. Sometimes, it is tempting to analyze people you know in terms of the disorders they seem to show. What are the risks of assuming this kind of role as an amateur psychologist?
9. If you have known anyone who has been depressed, comment on what you see as the psychological mechanisms underlying the depression you observed.

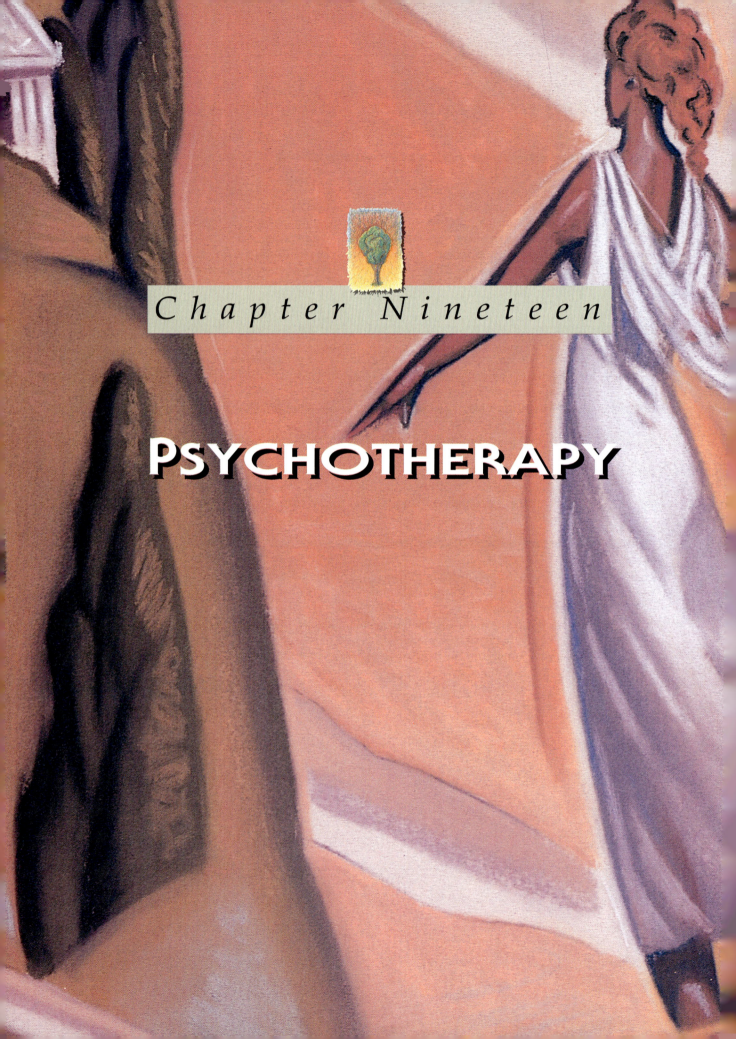

Chapter Nineteen

PSYCHOTHERAPY

Chapter Outline

Men are all alike.
IN WHAT WAY?
They're always bugging us about something or other.
CAN YOU THINK OF A SPECIFIC EXAMPLE?
Well, my boyfriend made me come here.
YOUR BOYFRIEND MADE YOU COME HERE?
He says I'm depressed much of the time.
I AM SORRY TO HEAR THAT YOU ARE DEPRESSED.
It's true. I am unhappy.
DO YOU THINK COMING HERE WILL HELP YOU NOT TO BE UNHAPPY?
I need some help, that much is certain.
WHAT WOULD IT MEAN TO YOU IF YOU GOT SOME HELP?
Perhaps I could learn to get along with my mother.
TELL ME MORE ABOUT YOUR FAMILY.
My mother takes care of me.
WHO ELSE IN YOUR FAMILY TAKES CARE OF YOU?
My father.
YOUR FATHER?
You are like my father in some ways.
WHAT RESEMBLANCE DO YOU SEE?
You are not very aggressive but I think you don't want me to notice that.
WHAT MAKES YOU THINK I AM NOT VERY AGGRESSIVE?
You don't argue with me.
WHY DO YOU THINK I DON'T ARGUE WITH YOU?
You are afraid of me.
DOES IT PLEASE YOU TO THINK I AM AFRAID OF YOU?
My father is afraid of everybody.
WHAT ELSE COMES TO MIND WHEN YOU THINK OF YOUR FATHER?
Bullies.
DOES THAT HAVE ANYTHING TO DO WITH THE FACT THAT YOUR BOYFRIEND MADE YOU COME HERE?

The preceding excerpt is taken from an interaction between an actual person and a computer program named ELIZA. ELIZA is designed to simulate a nondirective psychotherapist. The goal of nondirective therapy is to elicit a client's (patient's) feelings, to reflect these feelings back to the client, and to help the client understand and act on these feelings. In the preceding exchange, ELIZA seems to have startling clinical insight into her client, a woman whose troubled relationships with men seem to be rooted in her relationship to her father. The ELIZA program is not as bright as it may appear, however. ELIZA is incapable of any true intelligence or understanding. Instead, ELIZA uses key words and phrases in the client's remarks to trigger the random selection of specific responses from a set of possible preprogrammed responses. The program and the set of responses were provided by ELIZA's creator, Joseph Weizenbaum (1966) of MIT, who chose to simulate nondirective psychotherapy because he believed it would be relatively easy to simulate, compared with other types of therapy.

Psychotherapy is an intervention that uses the principles of psychology to try to improve the life of a person who is unhappy or disturbed. By this definition, the interactions with ELIZA would count as psychotherapy, but only in its weakest form. The intervention is weak because the program makes only the most modest use of the principles of psychology, and because this particular "therapist" does not truly care about the client or about improving the client's experience of life. Since Weizenbaum developed ELIZA, others have developed other simulated psychotherapeutic computer programs, and some corporate health-care programs are endorsing their use (Murray, 1993), despite the obvious potential for serious problems to go undetected unless the programs are used in conjunction with face-to-face psychotherapy.

Skilled psychotherapists certainly care about and understand the problems of their clients better than ELIZA would, and they have better ideas than does ELIZA about how to treat the clients. If we look at the history of psychotherapeutic techniques, however, we may wonder whether ELIZA shows more "humanity" than do many others who have attempted to treat mental illness.

EARLY HISTORY OF PSYCHOTHERAPEUTIC INTERVENTION

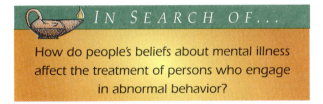

IN SEARCH OF...

How do people's beliefs about mental illness affect the treatment of persons who engage in abnormal behavior?

In ancient times, abnormal behavior was viewed as being caused by demons (see Chapter 18). To an extent, this belief persists among some groups today. The treatment of persons suspected of being possessed (demoniacs) has ranged from the innocuous to the brutally homicidal. Innocuous forms of exorcism offered little more than prayers or other religious rituals; harsher forms of exorcism included flogging, drowning, or starving the suspected demoniac in the attempt to drive out the evil spirits.

As the Middle Ages came to an end, so did the treatment of the mentally ill via exorcism (at least in most cases). During the fifteenth and sixteenth centuries, **asylums**—hospitals for the mentally ill—

During earlier eras, persons who were behaving in ways that did not conform to societal expectations often were subjected to torture techniques, such as "dunking," used for extracting confessions of witchery. The accused witch was repeatedly submerged. The longer it took her to die, the more fervently her accusers would assert that devilish powers were permitting her to survive.

became a popular means for the housing and possible rehabilitation of persons suffering from mental disorders. At that time, the definition of what constituted a disorder was flexible, and the asylums housed a diverse assortment of people, including those who were viewed as socially undesirable for one reason or another, whether or not they were truly disordered.

In 1547, King Henry VIII donated the Crown's 300-year-old asylum, St. Mary of Bethlehem (commonly known as "Bedlam"), to the city of London; the rededicated Bedlam became the first hospital devoted exclusively to serving the mentally ill. The term *bedlam* has become synonymous with uproar or confusion, which aptly describes the conditions within the original Bedlam hospital. Bedlam, like other mental hospitals that soon followed its example, resembled an overcrowded prison more than a true hospital, and its inmates were treated more like prisoners than like patients. Many inmates were chained to the walls of the cramped quarters, often in positions that did not allow them even to sleep properly. Others were chained to large iron balls, which they had to drag with them wherever they went.

The pathetic treatment of the mentally disturbed did not amuse everyone, however. Their treatment appalled Phillipe Pinel, first chief physician at the Parisian men's asylum, La Bicêtre, and then director of the women's asylum, Saltpêtrière. At both asylums, Pinel decided to remove the shackles and other instruments of confinement from patients. Much to the surprise of Parisian society, Pinel's crazed inmates became much calmer and more manageable.

This engraving, "The Rake's Progress" (Plate 9 of Scene in Bedlam) by William Hogarth (1697–1764), depicts a rather sanitized image of "Bedlam," a centuries-old asylum in London more formally named St. Mary of Bethlehem Hospital. Although its mission was to serve as a refuge for the mentally ill, it actually functioned more as an overcrowded prison for societal outcasts.

By the end of the eighteenth century and into the nineteenth century, clinicians were attempting to treat the psychological bases of abnormal behavior. In retrospect, some of the early attempts seem misguided. Recall, for example, the description of mesmerism in Chapter 6. Years after Franz Anton Mesmer died, French neurologist Jean Martin Charcot fared better than Mesmer did in his experiments with hypnosis as a method to cure hysteria and other mental illnesses. Later, Josef Breuer (1842–1925), a Viennese physician, also treated hys-

Phillipe Pinel (1745–1826), while chief physician at the Parisian asylum La Bicêtre and later, director of Saltpêtrière, ordered the removal of shackles and other physical restraints for his patients, despite tremendous protest from his contemporaries. Following the institution of humane policies, Pinel's patients became much more tranquil and malleable than they had been before.

French neurologist Jean Martin Charcot (1825–1893) instructed medical students on the use of hypnosis as a method to cure hysteria and other mental illnesses.

terical patients with hypnotic methods. Breuer found that if he could get his hypnotized patients to talk about their problems, especially the origins of their difficulties, the patients seemed to improve. Breuer concluded that if he could get a patient to relive and tell about the painful events that had caused some particular form of psychological damage, the patient would be freed from the shackles of these past hurts. Breuer's method became known as the **cathartic method,** in which talking about the origins of a problem purges the problem from the patient's mental life. Later, Charcot's student Sigmund Freud began working with Breuer, and thus began the modern history of psychotherapy.

DIAGNOSING AND ASSESSING ABNORMAL BEHAVIOR

IN SEARCH OF...

Why do clinicians use various methods of clinical assessment in making diagnoses and in shaping their therapeutic treatments?

As discussed in Chapter 18, both the *Diagnostic and Statistical Manual* (DSM-IV) and the International Classification of Diseases (ICD-10) enjoy widespread acceptance. The diagnostic reliability of the clinical guidelines in the ICD-10 has been field-tested in 40 countries and has yielded promising results thus far (Sartorius et al., 1993b). The DSM-IV classification system for diagnoses, described in Chapter 18, is highly compatible with the ICD classification system.

Given both clinical expertise and diagnostic tools such as the DSM-IV, a clinician must answer three questions when deciding how to respond to a new client: (1) Does the client have a problem? (2) If so, what is it? (3) Once the problem is diagnosed, how should it be treated? Clinicians use a variety of different techniques to answer these questions, such as clinical interviews and psychological tests.

Clinical Interviews

The **clinical interview** is by far the most widely used technique for making diagnoses. Interviews may be structured, unstructured, or a combination of both. In a *structured interview*, the interviewer conscientiously follows a specific list of questions and rarely departs from the structured sequence of questions. The advantage of a structured interview is that the clinician can obtain a relatively large amount of information in a relatively short period of time. Moreover, by writing down the questions in advance, the clinician avoids missing important pieces of information that later might be important in making a diagnosis. The main disadvantage of the structured interview is that it lacks flexibility. Structured interviews tend to emphasize breadth at the expense of depth.

In contrast, an *unstructured interview* does not involve any specific list of questions and enables the interviewer to follow rather than lead the client. Because people differ in the kinds of issues that bring them to therapy, an unstructured interview has the advantage of focusing on issues that are of particular importance for a specific client. The unstructured interview has two key potential disadvantages: The clinician might miss or forget to ask important questions, and the clinician cannot obtain comparable data from one interview to the next. Thus, responses across unstructured interviews are probably less comparable than responses across structured interviews. Unstructured interviews tend to emphasize depth at the expense of breadth. The ideal is a combination of the two techniques: Therapists have some standard questions that they make sure to ask, yet they freely pursue particular issues that appear to be important for a given client.

Exactly how a clinician conducts an interview depends not only on the type of client and presenting symptoms, but also on the clinician's theoretical orientation. *Psychodynamically oriented* clinicians tend to dwell more on a client's early childhood. They typically take relatively little of what a client says at face value because of their belief that many of the most important feelings are repressed and unavailable to consciousness. Such clinicians are also likely to be relatively unstructured in their approach and to encourage their clients to free-associate in responding to questions. During a behaviorally oriented interview, a *behavior* therapist is more likely to try to discover the environmental contingencies that are leading to a particular behavior, concentrating much more on the present than does the psychodynamically oriented clinician. A *cognitive* therapist spends a great deal of time trying to elicit the maladaptive thoughts that are leading to abnormal behavior. Some cognitive therapists are actually quite confrontational as they try to challenge a client to give up an entrenched set of beliefs. In contrast, *humanistic* therapists are much less confrontational. They try to convey the unconditional positive regard that they feel for the client and to communicate the support that the client can expect from them.

In a clinical interview, how clients say something is often as important as—or even more important than—what they say. For example, if a male client repeatedly emphasizes his success with women and goes to great pains to underscore that he can have any woman he wants, the therapist almost certainly would do well to be suspicious of these claims. Other aspects of behavior, such as crying while saying something or suddenly having lapses of memory or becoming fatigued while talking about a particular topic, also can be important to understanding the meaning of what is being said.

In making a diagnosis, clinicians need to be sensitive not only to what clients are saying and to how they are saying it, but also to how the clients' relationship with them may be affecting the content of the interview. Clients react differently to different interviewers, and clinicians need to realize that their age, gender, ethnic group, way of thinking, and even manner of dress can affect the outcome of a clinical interview. When dealing with members of another culture, clinicians have to be especially careful both to recognize and to appreciate cultural differences and to avoid attributing genuinely abnormal behavior to cultural difference (Lopez & Nuñez, 1987).

Finally, therapists need to recognize that both the clinical syndrome itself and the clients' personal motivations affect what clients say and how they say it. For example, antisocial personality disorders can be very difficult to detect because people with these disorders are prone to lying, and they feel no guilt or remorse when they do so. Thus, they can be extremely convincing, even to a trained psychotherapist. People with various disorders sometimes have incentives either to minimize or to maximize the level of distress they show. For example, clients who fear being confined to a mental institution may go to great lengths to try to sound normal in everything they say. Conversely, a prisoner who is trying to obtain a verdict of "not guilty by reason of insanity" will have an incentive to try to appear as crazy as possible.

Psychological Testing

Some clinicians regularly use psychological testing, others never use it, and the rest fall in between. Many of those who use it would swear by its diagnostic utility, whereas most of those who do not would say they are confident that tests do not give them useful psychodiagnostic information.

Chief among the psychological tests used in clinical assessment are personality tests. As we saw in Chapter 17, personality tests are either projective (such as the TAT and Rorschach tests) or objective (such as the MMPI). Clinicians sometimes use intelligence tests (see Chapter 11) both to assess various cognitive disorders and to observe an individual's approach to solving problems. Neuropsychological and psychophysiological tests also are used in formulating a diagnosis that can serve as the basis for treatment.

Neuropsychological Tests

Clinicians use neuropsychological tests when they suspect organic brain damage and make other assessments on Axis III (physical disorders and conditions) of DSM-IV. The two most widely used neuropsychological tests are the *Halstead-Reitan Battery* (see Boll, 1978) and the *Luria-Nebraska Battery* (see Golden, Hammecke, & Purisch, 1978). In fact, part of the Halstead-Reitan *test battery* (a series of tests given sequentially over a period of hours or days, to aid in diagnosis) includes testing with the *Wechsler Adult Intelligence Scale* (WAIS) and the *Minnesota Multiphasic Personality Inventory* (MMPI). Thus, in applied (practical) settings, clinicians integrate information from many different types of diagnostic tools.

To get an idea of the kinds of items that appear in a neuropsychological test, suppose that a client is given two subtests from the Halstead-Reitan. On the Tactual Performance test, the client is blindfolded and is asked to try to place blocks of various shapes into a board that has spaces corresponding to the various shapes. Because he cannot see the board, the client would have to use tactile cues to determine which blocks go into which spaces. After completing the board to the best of his ability, the client would be asked to draw what he believes the board looks like, showing the spaces in the board and the blocks that fill these spaces, all in their proper locations. To see

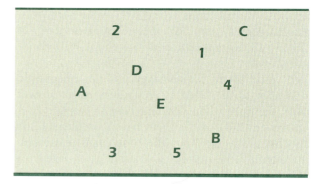

FIGURE 19-1
Trail-Making Test of the *Halstead-Reitan Battery*
In the Trail-Making test, you are shown a page such as the one shown here, speckled with numerals and letters. You are asked to start with 1, then go to A, then to 2, then to B, and so on. In other words, the order of the paths on the trail alternates between the numerals and the letters.

how you might perform the Trail-Making test, see Figure 19-1.

How do clinicians score the Halstead-Reitan subtests and other neuropsychological tests? The scoring draws on knowledge of the relations between performance and localization of function in different parts of the brain. For example, the Tactual Performance test draws largely on right-hemisphere functioning. Thus, for this form of assessment, the idea is to relate the functioning of the brain to behavior and to infer impairments of brain functioning from this behavior.

> Design a hypothetical neuropsychological test to detect possible lesions in Broca's area or in Wernicke's area of the brain. (*Hint*: See Chapters 3 and 9.)

Psychophysiological Measurements

Further aids in assessing brain function include less formal assessments of reflex functions and of sensory function. Your own physician has probably often tested your knee-jerk reflex (in response to a tap with a rubber mallet) and your pupillary reflex (in response to a bright light). Recall from Chapters 3 and 16 that psychophysiological measurement indices include heart rate, muscle tension, blood flow to various parts of the body, galvanic skin response (GSR), evoked potentials (series of electroencephalograph recordings that minimize electrical interference), CAT (computerized axial tomography) and PET (positron emission tomography) scans, and other measurements for assessing physiological functioning. Clinicians have found that PET scans of manic-depressives show higher levels of glucose metabolism in the cerebrum during manic phases (when patients are hyperactive, expansive, and unabashedly joyful) than during depressive phases (when subjects are relatively inactive and feeling low) (Baxter et al., 1985).

FIGURE 19-2
Psychophysiological Indications of Disorder

Compare the CAT-scan images on the top left and the top right. Both of these images show a horizontal slice through the brain, but the brain on the left is normal, whereas the brain on the right shows a tumor exerting pressure on the other structures of the brain. The bottom two images are from PET scans, with the one on the left showing a normal brain and the one on the right showing the brain of a patient with senile dementia (possibly caused by Alzheimer's disease).

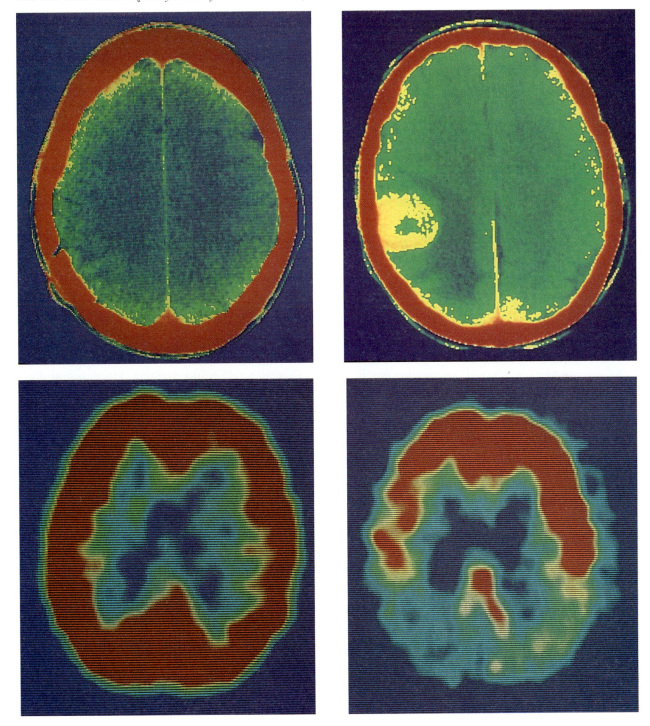

To conclude, a variety of forms of assessment are now available to clinicians. No single form gives a complete picture, but used in conjunction, the various forms of assessment can give clinicians a relatively wide variety of information that they can integrate and interpret. Once the clinician has diagnosed the problem, what remains is to treat it. We now turn to some of the kinds of therapies used for treating psychological disorders.

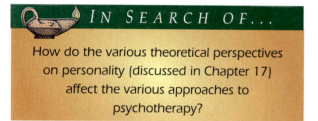

Compare the utility of each of the preceding methods for diagnosing (a) bipolar disorder, (b) schizophrenia, and (c) one of the personality disorders (your choice).

APPROACHES TO PSYCHOTHERAPY

IN SEARCH OF...

How do the various theoretical perspectives on personality (discussed in Chapter 17) affect the various approaches to psychotherapy?

Each of the many different approaches to psychotherapy has accompanying advantages and disadvantages. Many of the therapies overlap, but it is still useful to consider the distinctions among the five main approaches: psychodynamic, humanistic, behavioral, cognitive, and biological.

Psychodynamic Therapy

Psychodynamic therapies have in common their emphasis on *insight* as the key to improvement. The basic assumption is that when patients have insight into the source or sources of their problems, they will be largely freed of their problems. Psychoanalytic therapy is the main type of psychodynamic therapy.

Psychoanalytic Therapy

Psychoanalytic therapists assume that disorders result from people's ignorance of their underlying thoughts, feelings, and, especially, motivations. Patients will improve when they become conscious of ego-threatening material that has been repressed. Thus, treatment centers on peeling away layers of self-deceit and

rationalization in an attempt to discover the underlying truth. If a patient enters psychotherapy to conquer anxiety, for example, the therapist would be foolish to treat the anxiety directly because, according to this view, the anxiety is only a symptom of unconscious repressed feelings, thoughts, and motives. Treating the anxiety at a symptomatic level would be like giving an aspirin to a person suffering from a potent bacterial infection. The therapist might bring symptomatic relief but would have done nothing to treat the underlying problem.

How does the therapist actually go about eliciting the unconscious conflicts that underlie an observable disorder? Psychoanalysts use several different techniques, the most prominent of which is free association. In **free association,** a person merely says what comes to mind, without censoring or otherwise editing these things before reporting them. At first, the patient may find the unedited reporting of free associations hard, but with practice, he or she usually improves. It is critical not to edit anything out because, according to the psychoanalytic view, chances are good that the most interesting and important details will be those that the patient does not wish to reveal. The therapist acts only as a guide and does not try to direct the course of the associations. Typically, the patient is placed in a relaxed state of mind in a comfortable setting, with only the psychotherapist present. The patient simply reports everything that comes to mind.

If patients could make free associations that immediately led them to repressed material, psychoanalysis would be over in short order. The actual course of therapy rarely works that way. The reason it does not, according to psychoanalytic beliefs, is the presence of resistances. **Resistances** are attempts, usually unconscious, to block progress. Why would any rational patients want to block progress, especially when they are paying for therapy? The reason for resistance is that dealing with the contents of the unconscious is often painful and possibly even devastating, so patients unconsciously attempt to divert the therapy from doing so. Resistances can take a variety of forms, such as remaining silent, trying to digress from unpleasant topics, making jokes, or even not attending sessions. Psychoanalysts identify and deal with resistances when they arise.

A second technique used in psychoanalytic therapy is the analysis of dreams (see Chapters 6 and 17). According to Freud, the *manifest content* of dreams—the actual occurrences that take place within the dreams—is symbolic of the underlying, *latent content* of the dreams. Thus, the job of the analyst is to penetrate the manifest content in order to understand what lies beneath it. For example, in a male patient's dream, a battle with swords between the patient and a partially disguised other man might represent an unresolved Oedipal conflict in which the dreaming patient is battling with his father for possession of his mother. In this dream, the sword might be interpreted as a phallic symbol. Psychoanalysts believe that the dream sufficiently disguises these symbolic elements to avoid causing extreme discomfort to the dreamer. After the patient has been in therapy for a while, the psychoanalyst increasingly interprets the content of what the patient says. Often, patients are unhappy with and may not believe what they hear. (Recall from Chapter 17 that psychodynamic theory also describes various defense mechanisms that help the individual fend off threatening information.) Freud believed that such attempts at denial were further ways in which patients could resist learning the truth about themselves. From the psychoanalytic standpoint, the more vigorously a patient denies a particular interpretation, the more likely the interpretation is to be true. Of course, this reasoning creates a "damned if you do, damned if you don't" kind of logic. The therapist's interpretations are difficult to disconfirm because they are accepted as true if the patient agrees and accepted even more strongly if the patient forcefully disagrees.

Psychoanalytic therapists remain relatively detached from their patients and actually even resist close emotional involvement with them. The therapist seems almost like a shadowy parent figure who tries to help the patient without becoming too involved in the patient's problems. Patients, however, often become quite involved with the therapist. Indeed, patients may start treating the therapist as the source of, or at least an active contributor to, their problems. This involvement of the patient with the therapist is referred to as **transference.** In transference, patients shift to the therapist the thoughts and feelings they have had toward others, such as their parents, in the past. By staying detached, therapists actually encourage transference because patients can project onto the therapist whatever conflicts or fantasies arise during therapy. The detached therapist is something like a blank screen onto which patients can project their past relationships. According to Freud, such transference is a positive rather than a negative phenomenon. It helps the patient bring out into the open the conflicts that have been suppressed in the past.

All psychoanalysts must themselves first be psychoanalyzed to understand better their own conflicts and sources of psychological distress. This understanding is particularly important to control for

countertransference, in which the therapist projects onto the patient the therapist's own feelings. Therapists who project their own problems onto the patient can cause the therapy to go seriously awry. Thus, it is important that psychoanalytic therapists recognize their own problems and fantasies, to deal with those issues as they arise, and to avoid projecting them onto the patient.

"If we are not going to talk about my toilet-training, what is the process of your treatment? Bullying and lectures?"

"If necessary. But it usually isn't necessary, and when it is, that is only a small part of the treatment."

"Then what are you going to do?"

"I am not going to do anything to you. I am going to try to help you in the process of becoming yourself."

—*Robertson Davies,* The Manticore

Offshoots of Psychoanalytic Therapy

Psychoanalytic therapy has been important both historically and in modern times, and it has generated a variety of offshoots. Many of these offshoots developed from the theories of personality offered by Freud's followers, the neo-Freudians, such as Carl Jung, Erik Erikson, and Karen Horney (described in Chapter 17). The various forms of neo-Freudian therapy are sometimes termed *ego analysis* because of their common view that the ego is at least as important as is the id. In other words, conscious processing is just as important as—and possibly more important than—unconscious processing. People are not just puppets controlled by the strings of the unconscious. Rather, people have purposes and goals, and to a large extent, they act to fulfill those goals. To understand the patient fully, the therapist needs to understand not only the patient's past, but also the patient's envisioned future—where the patient sees him- or herself heading.

Psychoanalysis can be a long process, continuing over a period of years, during which the patient and the therapist may meet as often as three to five times per week. Psychodynamic therapists, however, have placed increasing emphasis on *time-limited psychotherapy* (Mann, 1973; Strupp, 1981). The idea of such therapy is to apply the principles of psychoanalysis but to effect improvement in a relatively short time.

Consider a recent interpersonal problem you have had. What would a psychodynamic therapist tell you regarding your handling of the problem?

Humanistic (Client-Centered) Therapies

Like psychoanalysis and other psychodynamic therapies, humanistic therapy emphasizes insight. Beyond this similarity, however, there are salient differences. Humanistic therapists refer to the people whom they treat as "clients," whereas traditional psychodynamically oriented therapists usually refer to them as "patients." This difference is not merely semantic. Psychodynamic therapy is based on a model of disorder that is much closer to a medical model (recall Freud's medical training), according to which an underlying disease process is the source of the patient's troubles. In contrast, the humanistic model eschews the medical model and replaces it with a model that views each person as an individual with feelings and thoughts that may come into conflict with society or with each other, thereby causing problems in living.

The decision whether to use a medical model also has implications for the role of the therapist. For psychodynamic therapists, understanding of behavior is elusive and extremely difficult to achieve for all but the most skilled psychoanalyst (much like a physician's expertise); for humanistic therapists, understanding is not that elusive. The therapist is not an authority who dictates the correct perceptions to the passive patient. Rather, the therapist is a helpful facilitator, who helps the client to gain his or her own insights.

Another key difference is that in the psychodynamic view, we are deterministically ruled by unconscious forces, whereas in the humanistic view, we have free will and are ruled by our own conscious decisions. Humanistic therapists assume that people who are mentally well are aware of and understand their behavior. People can thus change their behavior at will. Because people are free to make choices, a goal of therapy is to help people to *feel* completely free in the choices they make. Of the various forms of humanistic and existential therapies, some are briefly described here.

All humanistic therapy is centered on the client. Carl Rogers (1961a) developed his particular form of **client-centered therapy** on the assumption that clients can be understood only in terms of their own construction of reality. Thus, client-centered therapy is *nondirective*, in that the therapist is not supposed to guide the course of therapy in any particular direction. What matters for people are not the events that occur in people's lives, but rather the way people construe these events. Thus, client-centered therapists make little effort to impose a theoretical system (such as Freud's) onto the client; instead, they try to understand their client's view of the world.

In addition to believing in the value of a client's view of the world and in the importance of the client's free will, Rogers believed that people are basically good and adaptive both in what they do and in the goals they set for themselves. When they act otherwise, it is because of flaws that have taken place in their learning processes. For example, the clients may receive inadequate socialization or may have inappropriate role models. The goal of client-centered therapy is to help people realize their full potential.

Rogers believed there are three keys to successful therapy that can unlock the doors barring clients from realizing their potential. The first key is *genuineness* on the part of the therapist. Client-centered therapists need to be totally honest, both with themselves and with their clients. Whereas psychoanalysts might be viewed as having a detached objectivity, Rogerian therapists must present no detachment whatsoever. They should be as open and genuine in the expression of their feelings as they want their clients to be. In effect, they become models for their clients, showing the clients how to be open and self-disclosing in a world that often seems not to value the qualities of openness and self-disclosure.

The second key is for the therapist to provide the client with *unconditional positive regard*. Rogers believed that many of the problems we encounter are caused by our having received only conditional positive regard as we grew up. We were given positive regard only when we behaved in socially acceptable ways, but this positive regard was withdrawn when we behaved in less accepted ways. The result, according to Rogers, is that we develop a conditional sense of self-worth. We feel that we will be loved or appreciated only if we do those things that others have deemed acceptable. To be psychologically whole, however, we must achieve a sense of unconditional self-worth. The Rogerian therapist's unconditional positive regard helps the client achieve this state.

The third key is for the therapist to experience *accurate empathic understanding* of the client. A good therapist needs to be able to see the world in the same way that the client sees it. Without such empathy, the therapist does not truly understand the client's point of view. The result will be miscommunication, which limits the client's ability to profit from the therapy.

In client-centered, nondirective therapy, the therapist follows the client's lead; in contrast, in psychodynamic therapy, the therapist has a particular direction in mind regarding how to lead the patient—namely, toward the uncovering of unconscious conflicts. Thus, the course of client-centered therapy is likely to be quite different from that of psychodynamic therapy. Nondirective, client-centered therapists believe that by listening empathically to clients and by helping clients to clarify and explore their feelings, clients will then feel free to live as they choose.

Existential Therapy

Both existential therapy (espoused by Rollo May, 1969; see Chapter 17) and humanistic therapy share a belief in the need to help clients become more aware of their ability to make choices. The therapies differ, however, in their emphases: Whereas humanism stresses the basic goodness of human nature, existentialism focuses on the anxiety that accompanies important choices in life. Thus, a major goal of existential therapy is to help people deal with the fundamental existential anxiety that results from having to make choices, such as whether to continue with a close relationship, whether to go to graduate school, or whether to have children (see Chapter 17 for more on existentialism). From the existential perspective, in order to be well-adjusted, a person needs to recognize and acknowledge the following sources of existential anxiety: We will eventually die; there are chance circumstances over which we have no control that can inexplicably alter or even ruin our lives; we have to live with the consequences of our decisions; the only meaning in our lives is the meaning that we create; and ultimately, each of us is alone (Tillich, 1952). Existential therapists hold that people sometimes try to protect themselves from existential anxiety, either by not making choices or by postponing choices for as long as possible. Ultimately, however, people do best when they confront both the choices and the anxieties they produce. Existential therapists try to help people to avoid feeling anxious over a discrepancy between where they are, compared with where they want to be. Instead, the therapists urge people to take responsibility to seek to do all they can to achieve their goals, including the fulfillment of their potential.

Existentialists also emphasize the importance of *authenticity* (similar to humanistic *genuineness*) in a person's relations with other people. Our identities are derived not only from who we are with ourselves, but also from who we are with other people. By isolating ourselves from others or by acting toward them in ungenuine ways, we limit our own growth. Psychotherapy should be a model of an authentic relationship between two people. In much the same way that humanistic therapists model openness and self-disclosure, existential therapists model how to be an authentic person and what an authentic relationship

Regardless of their diverse theoretical orientations, psychotherapists share a common desire to ensure that their clients have a sense of trust and gain a new perspective about themselves and the situations they face.

can offer. Authenticity requires that existential therapists be totally honest, even if it means confronting clients in ways that the clients find unpleasant.

This description of existential therapy may seem short on details, and indeed it is. No one has provided a very clearly defined sense of exactly what an existential therapist should do or of what course such therapy ought to take. In fact, a well-defined set of techniques might almost be seen as going counter to existential philosophy altogether. To the extent that this philosophy emphasizes the unique individuality of each person, therapy for each client would have to be a unique new challenge each time it is undertaken. To an extent, this form of therapy teaches clients a philosophy of life, emphasizing the importance of taking responsibility for their lives. Clients are then free to use this philosophy as a basis for confronting the choices that they have to make and for accepting personal responsibility for all their behavior.

> Design a set of guidelines for conducting humanistic psychotherapy. Include a brief sample from a hypothetical counseling session to illustrate your guidelines.

Behavior Therapies

Behavior therapy refers to a collection of techniques based, in some cases loosely, on ideas derived from the principles of classical and operant conditioning, as well as on observational modeling (see Chapter 7).

Behavior therapy differs in several fundamental ways from all of the other kinds of therapies considered up to this point. First, behavior therapy is deliberately short term. The goal is to seek behavioral change over a brief period of time. Thus, whereas psychoanalysis may go on for years, behavior therapy typically lasts only months or even less.

Second, whereas psychoanalysis shuns the treatment of symptoms, behavior therapy deliberately seeks intervention to alleviate symptoms. To the behavior therapist, the symptom *is* the problem. If a person is experiencing anxiety, then the person needs to reduce that anxiety to function effectively. If a person is depressed, then the goal should be to relieve the depression. In the behaviorists' view, chasing after deep-seated causes in the murky past is essentially a waste of time. The original causes of the maladaptive behavior may not even have anything to do with the factors that currently maintain the behavior.

Third, in addition to being very direct, behavior therapy is extremely directive, in sharp contrast to humanistic therapies, which are explicitly nondirective, and to psychodynamic therapy, which is only partially directive. That is, although the behavior therapist collaborates with the client, it is the therapist who formulates an explicit treatment plan. The client follows the therapist's treatment plan, and when the implementation of the plan is completed, the therapy ends.

Fourth, as its name implies, behavior therapy concentrates on behavior. Whereas other techniques of therapy seek to obtain behavioral change through psychological insights and changes, behavior therapy seeks to obtain psychological changes through behavioral changes. Indeed, some behavior therapists do not even particularly concern themselves with the psychological changes. What they seek is modification of maladaptive behavior.

Finally, behavior therapists try to follow more closely the classical scientific model than do some other types of therapists. Whereas humanistic therapists often feel as though scientific analysis turns the client into an object or a depersonalized entity, behavior therapists are very concerned with taking a scientific, objective approach, both to the therapy and to the evaluation of the outcomes of the therapy. Many behaviorists have said that the precepts of psychoanalysis cannot be disconfirmed by scientific investigation. Probably no one says the same of behavior therapy.

Behavior therapy consists of a set of explicit techniques, which include counterconditioning, extinction procedures, and operant conditioning, as well as modeling.

Counterconditioning

In **counterconditioning**, a particular response to a particular stimulus is replaced by an alternative response to that stimulus. The alternative response is incompatible with the unwanted initial response. For example, suppose that before counterconditioning, a person enjoys positive feelings toward the stimulus of smoking cigarettes. Through counterconditioning, the person would learn to feel negatively about cigarettes. On the other hand, if a person became anxious when taking tests, counterconditioning would replace the negative anxiety response with a positive relaxation response that would permit the person to take tests without feeling anxiety. Two of the main techniques used to achieve counterconditioning are aversion therapy and systematic desensitization.

In **aversion therapy,** the therapist teaches the client to experience negative feelings in the presence of a stimulus that is considered inappropriately attractive (see Figure 19-3). For example, a *pedophiliac* (an adult who is sexually attracted to children) might seek aversion therapy to learn not to respond with sexual interest when presented with the stimulus of a little child. The client's exposure to the inappropriately attractive stimulus would be accompanied by an aversive unconditioned stimulus, such as a painful electrical shock. The pedophiliac might be exposed to a picture of an attractive child at the exact moment or immediately before being electrically shocked. Similarly, an alcoholic might seek aversion therapy. Recall from Chapter 7 that problem drinkers sometimes are given a drug that causes them to feel violently ill immediately after they have consumed any alcohol. Aversion therapy may be seen as a form of punishment and is generally used in combination with other techniques. As mentioned in Chapter 7, it is often useful to substitute some other more socially desirable interest for the one that is being replaced.

Systematic desensitization, almost the antithesis of aversion therapy, seeks to help the client learn *not* to experience negative feelings toward a stimulus. Joseph Wolpe (1958) introduced the technique of systematic desensitization as a way of combating particular psychological problems, most notably anxiety. Wolpe's basic idea involves replacing one response with another—typically, a response of anxiety with one of relaxation. In all cases, systematic desensitization involves engaging in a response that is incompatible with the initial unwanted response.

Suppose, for instance, that you experienced such extreme anxiety about standardized admissions tests that your test anxiety threatened your ability to compete successfully for admission to graduate school. The therapist would create with you a *desensitization hierarchy,* which is a series of imagined scenes, each one more anxiety provoking than the previous one. Next, you would learn a set of techniques to achieve deep relaxation. These techniques would involve relaxation of individual muscle groups, picturing pleasant scenes, and the like. Once you had learned how to relax deeply, the actual systematic desensitization process would begin. You would first imagine the least anxiety-provoking scene. If you were to find yourself feeling anxious, you would be reminded immediately to relax deeply. You would then slacken your muscles and envision a pleasant and relaxing scene. Once you felt relaxed again, you would attempt again to imagine the first stimulus in your hierarchy. After several efforts, you would find yourself able to handle the first step of your hierarchy without feeling anxious. Once you were sure of your ability to deal with that initial stimulus, you would proceed to the next step of your hierarchy, and you would continue in this manner until you had mastered each step in your hierarchy. Many studies (see

During desensitization therapy, the patient is encouraged to rest and is trained how to relax deeply the muscles of the body. Once the relaxation training is complete, the therapist takes the patient through a graduated series of steps in a desensitization hierarchy, to reduce anxiety responses such as phobias and some other anxiety disorders. The idea is that an individual cannot simultaneously be deeply relaxed and anxious, so the relaxation training offers an alternative response to the undesired anxiety response.

FIGURE 19-3
Aversion Therapy for a Mild Sexual Disorder
Aversion therapy comprising 45 training trials, implemented across three sessions, effectively reduced penile arousal responses to an inappropriate stimulus (a fantasy of being tied up). (After Marks & Gelder, 1987)

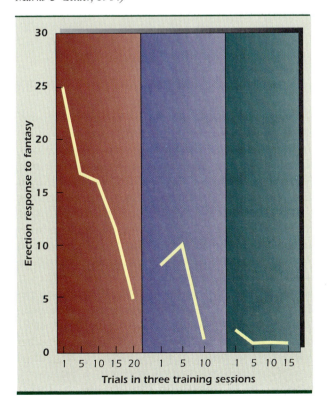

Cottraux, 1993) indicate that behavior therapy is highly effective in aiding clients with simple phobias and with many other anxiety disorders.

Extinction Procedures

Extinction procedures weaken maladaptive responses, such as anxiety. Two types of extinction therapies are flooding and implosion therapy. Like systematic desensitization, **flooding** exposes a client to an anxiety-provoking stimulus, with the goal of having the client cease to feel anxiety in response to the stimulus. In flooding, however, the client is immediately placed in a situation that causes anxiety, not just a sequence of imagined situations, and the client is not instructed in how to use relaxation techniques. The idea underlying the use of this technique is that clients who have been forced to remain in the anxiety-provoking situation will realize that nothing horrible has happened to them, so they can cope with the situation again when they face it in the future. For instance, a person with a phobia of snakes would actually be forced to confront snakes, or a person who is afraid of heights would be taken to the top of a high building.

Implosion is an intermediate form of therapy, including elements of both flooding and systematic desensitization. In **implosion therapy,** clients are asked to imagine and relive—to the extent that they can—unpleasant events that are causing them anxiety. Suppose, for example, that you had once almost drowned, that you now fear swimming, and that you are reluctant even to have any contact with water. Your implosion therapist might ask you to imagine placing yourself in a bottomless bathtub, and then to imagine yourself starting to slip into the water. Of course, imagining this scene would cause you intense anxiety. Soon, however, you would realize that nothing has happened to you. You would have imagined the scene, but you would still be alive and in the therapist's office. You would then be asked to imagine this scene on an increasingly frequent basis. Eventually, the scene would lose its ability to cause you anxiety, and you would stop feeling afraid.

This visualization technique is similar to systematic desensitization in that the client imagines but does not actually experience the anxiety-producing scenes. However, it differs from systematic desensitization in the method of relieving anxiety. Of the two techniques, systematic desensitization has proven to be demonstrably superior to implosion therapy (see Smith & Glass, 1977).

Operant Conditioning

The techniques described up to this point have basically made use of the classical-conditioning model. However, operant conditioning has also been used for achieving behavioral change. Several different methods are relevant, including the use of token economies (introduced in Chapter 7) and behavioral contracting. The basic principle of the **token economy** is that clients receive *tokens* (tangible objects that have no intrinsic worth) as rewards for showing adaptive behavior. The tokens can later be exchanged for goods or services that the individuals desire. The clients are generally in an institutional setting, which allows the therapist to control the distribution of the tokens and other reinforcers. This technique has been used primarily with children who have PDD (pervasive developmental disorder, or autism), although it has been used with other populations as well (see Figure 19-4).

The use of tokens has several attractive features. First, the number of tokens can be linked directly to whether the client exhibits the desired behavior. Second, there is very little ambiguity with regard to the nature of the reward. Third, the therapist can tailor the goods or services that can be purchased in accordance with the client's needs and wants. As time goes on, the nature of the things that can be purchased with the tokens can be changed to suit the client's current desires. Fourth, the tokens can be distributed immediately as a reward for desirable behavior. Fifth,

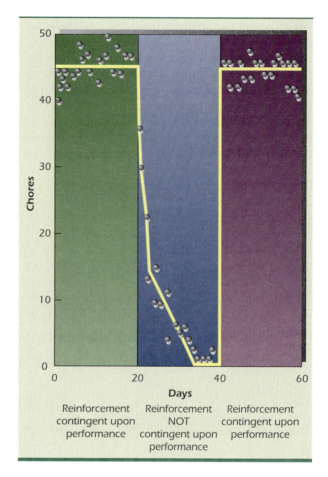

FIGURE 19-4
Results of a Token Economy
In an institutional setting, a token economy can be highly effective in modifying the behavior of confined individuals. Positive behaviors that may be reinforced in a token economy include self-help tasks (e.g., grooming).

the client can choose the reward, rather than having to accept what is given. Finally, there is a touch of realism in the token economy, because it resembles what happens in the world outside the institution (Carson & Butcher, 1992; Paul & Lentz, 1977; Paul & Menditto, 1992). For noninstitutionalized populations, some researchers have expressed concern that these *extrinsic reinforcers* (external, material rewards, as opposed to intrinsic ones such as self-esteem and achievement motivation) may undermine children's natural interest in performing the behaviors that are being rewarded (Deci & Ryan, 1985; Lepper, Greene, & Nisbett, 1973). Psychotherapists and other clinicians must often choose from among imperfect alternatives, balancing desired benefits against possible risks.

Behavioral contracting also has a real-world connotation. In **behavioral contracting**, the therapist and the client draw up a contract which both parties are obligated to live up to. The contract requires the client to exhibit specific behaviors that are being sought as part of the therapy, in return for which the therapist will give the client particular things that the client may want, even including permission to terminate the therapy. Behavioral contracting has two key advantages: (1) The responsibilities of both the therapist and the patient are clear, and (2) the criteria for success in meeting the goals of the therapy are concretely defined. Behavioral contracting is not itself a form of therapy, but rather a supplement that can be used in conjunction with virtually any type of therapy.

Modeling

Modeling represents a third approach to behavior therapy, beyond the approaches based on classical and operant conditioning. As mentioned in Chapter 7, the principles of modeling derive in large part, although not exclusively, from the work of Albert Bandura (1969). Bandura's basic idea is that people can change

These children readily followed the lead of this charming snake-tamer, but this model appears to be less powerful in influencing the woman in the photo's background. Although she may not be phobic, the woman clearly is not ready to emulate the behavior of the model.

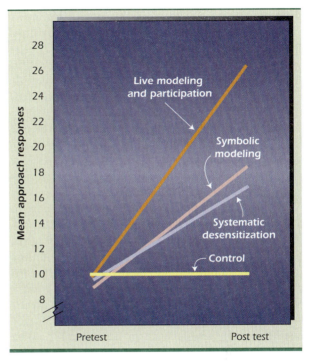

FIGURE 19-5
Effectiveness of Various Therapies
Live modeling and participation appear to be much more potent in effecting behavioral changes than are symbolic modeling or systematic desensitization.

simply by watching models of other people successfully coping with the problems they face. For example, Bandura, Edward Blanchard, and Brunhilde Ritter (1969) helped people overcome snake phobias by having phobic adults watch other people confront snakes, either in actual live situations or on film. The clients watched as the models moved closer and closer to the snakes; with time, the clients' phobias subsided.

Modeling also has been used in a variety of other kinds of therapy, including the treatment of a variety of phobias and sexual disorders. It has been suggested that the therapeutic effects of many interventions stem largely from modeling (Braswell & Kendall, 1988).

For which types of disorders would behavior therapy be most effective? Which of the preceding types of behavior therapy would be the most effective in treating one of these types of disorders? Why?

Cognitive Approaches to Therapy

The modeling approach provides the transition between behaviorally and cognitively oriented approaches to psychotherapy. Originally, Bandura

(1969; Bandura & Walters, 1963) viewed modeling as a behavioral phenomenon. According to the cognitive approach, however, modeling is a type of conditioning that does not quite fit into either the classical conditioning or the operant conditioning category. However, as the cognitive revolution proceeded, Bandura started to reformulate the modeling phenomenon in terms of cognitive theory (see Chapters 2 and 17 for more on Bandura and Chapters 9–12 for more on cognitive theory). Indeed, the processes that the observer uses for imitating the model are certainly cognitive ones (Bandura, 1986).

Cognitive therapists believe that clients change their behaviors by changing their cognitions. If people can be made to think differently about themselves and about the phenomena they experience, then they can feel and act differently. The two most well-known cognitive approaches are probably Albert Ellis's rational-emotive behavior therapy and Aaron Beck's cognitive therapy (recall the introduction to cognitive-behavioral approaches in Chapter 17). The following passage illustrates one of many cognitive approaches to psychotherapy.

Bill Davison had a direct approach. There was no time in the business of sports for psychoanalysis. In sports, with contracts worth thousands of dollars at stake, you had to intervene. Jonathan had read articles about Bill Davison. Bill would say to black tennis players who felt themselves adrift in a white man's world, "This is your game. This court here is your neighborhood. Think of it as your own street."

To football players who had suddenly grown angry at the ball, he would say, "Think of it as a woman. Imagine that it's the sweetest, kindest woman you ever met. Think of someone you knew. If it ended badly, then make it up to her this time. Catch the ball gently."

It worked. He had been criticized for merely treating symptoms.

— Geoff Ryman, *Was*

Rational-Emotive Therapy

When Albert Ellis (1962, 1973, 1989) formulated **rational-emotive behavior therapy** (REBT) (sometimes referred to as *rational-emotive therapy*, or RET), his fundamental idea was that emotional reactions occur because people internally recite sentences that express incorrect or maladaptive thoughts. Recall the debate mentioned in Chapter 16, between Richard Lazarus and Robert Zajonc, regarding which comes first, cognition or emotion. Ellis strongly agrees with

Lazarus that cognition precedes emotion. According to Ellis, the emotions we feel are caused by the thoughts we have, and we can change our emotions only by changing our thoughts. The goal of Ellis's psychotherapy, therefore, is to change our incorrect and maladaptive thoughts. Ellis's REBT and other forms of cognitive-behavioral therapy have been particularly effective in treating anxious patients who have come to abuse antianxiety medications (Perris & Herlofson, 1993), and we may presume that this form of therapy will also be effective in persons at risk for such abuse.

Ellis (1970) has given a number of examples of the incorrect beliefs that have led people to maladjustment, such as the following: (a) "You should be loved by everyone for everything you do." (b) "You need to have perfect self-control at all times." (c) "You should be thoroughly competent in all respects." Ellis believes that the best technique for dealing with these beliefs is to confront the client directly and to dispute the client's incorrect and maladaptive beliefs. In other words, the therapist actually attempts to show the client that these false, futile beliefs are leading the client to be unhappy and dysfunctional in everyday life. Thus, Ellis's techniques are quite different from those of humanistic therapy, in which a therapist would almost never directly confront a client. Although the method is different, the goals are very similar to those of humanistic therapy: to increase a client's sense of self-worth, and to facilitate the client's ability to grow and to make choices by recognizing all of the available options.

Beck's Cognitive Therapy

The **cognitive therapy** of Aaron Beck (1976, 1986) differs from Ellis's REBT in both the cognitive theorizing and the form of the psychotherapy. Recall from Chapter 18 that Beck views people as being maladjusted as a result of cognitive distortion. Beck has concentrated particularly on depression, and a contributor (Perris & Herlofson, 1993) to a World Health Organization report on psychotherapy has indicated that the demonstrated efficacy for cognitive therapy is higher for depressive disorders than for other disorders. (See Beck's List in Chapter 18 for some of the cognitive distortions that frequently underlie depression.) Beck particularly emphasizes the importance of maladaptive schemas that lead us to believe we are incompetent or worthless.

Jeffrey Young (1990; Young & Klosko, 1993), a former student of Beck, has proposed a set of *early maladaptive schemas* that he believes form the basis of many of the problems people have in living. Young posits that clients may have a distorted perception of

Searchers . . .

ALBERT ELLIS

Albert Ellis is Director of the Institute for Rational Emotive Therapy.

Q: *How did you become interested in psychology and in your area of work in particular?*

A: I was doing research for a book on sex, love, and marriage, and my friends and relatives began to ask me how they could solve their personal problems. To my surprise, I was able to give them helpful answers, found that I enjoyed working with them, and decided to go for a PhD in clinical psychology.

Q: *Whose ideas have influenced you the most?*

A: Ancient and modern philosophers, especially Epicurus, Epictetus, Kant, Hume, Dewey, Santayana, Russell, and Popper; early writers on love and sex, including Stendhal, Havelock Ellis, August Forel, Iwan Bloch, Emil Lucka, Denis de Rougemont, and Henry T. Finck; and some psychoanalytic theorists, especially Freud, Adler, Horney, Fromm, and Sullivan.

Q: *What is your greatest asset as a psychologist?*

A: An innate tendency to be skeptical, curious, and allergic to inefficiency.

Q: *What makes a psychologist really great?*

A: An ability and proclivity for selecting important problems to solve and the tenacity to keep working at solving them for a good many years.

Q: *How do you get your ideas for research?*

A: When a method of psychotherapy is not working efficiently, I ask myself what alternative methods would work better, experiment with them, and try to see if that actually leads to better results.

Q: *How do you decide whether to pursue an idea?*

A: I consider if it's important enough to devote a research project to it; how expensive it would be (the time, money, and effort it would take to pursue it); and the amount of pleasure I would have in working on it.

Q: *What obstacles have you experienced in your work?*

A: The prejudices of leaders and followers of psychoanalytic, person-centered, experiential, and other schools of therapy who have resented my criticisms of their ineffectiveness and have angrily opposed the theory, teaching, and practice of rational-emotive behavior therapy (REBT) and cognitive behavior therapy (CBT). I have refused to upset myself about this hostility and have shown that REBT and CBT really work.

Q: *What is your major contribution to psychology?*

A: To show that people with serious emotional and behavioral problems can be helped in a relatively brief period of time to overcome their disturbances and to lead happier lives when therapists, as well as audio-visual self-help materials, teach them how to use cognitive, emotive, and behavioral techniques.

Q: *What do you want students to learn from you?*

A: How to think for themselves and not need the approval of anyone, including myself; how to be scientific, skeptical of all theories and to keep testing them out; how to be an efficient therapist, to discover by experimentation the methods that work best for most people in less time.

Q: *What advice would you give to someone starting in the field of psychology?*

A: Learn as much as you can about all important areas of psychology and actively question even the most accepted theories that you find. Pick a field that you personally enjoy and try to make some significant contributions to it.

Q: *What did you learn from your mentors?*

A: To take risks and explore areas of psychology that are controversial, and not to upset myself when my experiments do not turn out the way I would like.

Q: *Apart from your life as an academic, how has psychology been of use to you?*

A: Several psychotherapy techniques, including some that I invented, have helped me to avoid having a single full day of serious anxiety, depression, rage, self-denigration, or self-pity for the last fifty years.

Q: *How do you keep yourself academically challenged?*

A: By trying to learn whatever I can from my students and lecture and workshop participants and to keep presenting to them views and facts that they often are loathe to accept.

Q: *What do you further hope to achieve or contribute?*

A: Studies showing that some popular methods of psychotherapy are unusually efficient and that some of the most honored techniques are remarkably ineffective and iatrogenic; applications of REBT to more effective self-help materials and to educational institutions where its methods can be taught.

---

how stable or reliable those people they depend on are; an unfounded belief they are outwardly undesirable to others, such as believing that they are unattractive; or an exaggerated fear that disaster may strike them at any time. He has proposed other schemas as well.

Young believes that cognitive therapy ought to be directed toward helping people understand which

Searchers . . .   *AARON BECK*

Aaron Beck is Professor of Psychiatry at the University of Pennsylvania.

Q: *How did you become interested in psychology and in your area of work in particular?*

A: I became interested in psychology, as a separate discipline from psychiatry, when I began to evaluate Freud's theory of depression. I had to borrow the methodology used in clinical and experimental psychology to test the Freudian hypotheses. As it turned out, the evaluations did not confirm the Freudian hypotheses but provided some leads into a different approach—namely, a cognitive conceptualization of depression.

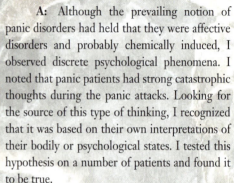

Q: *What theories have influenced you the most?*

A: I have been influenced to some degree by the Freudian notions of primitive thinking and by clinical notions such as the influence of past memories and of early relationship themes on adult development and psychopathology. Beyond this, my greatest influence has been from cognitivists such as George Kelly and Albert Ellis. Earlier influences included neo-Freudians such as Alfred Adler and Karen Horney.

Q: *What is your greatest asset as a psychologist?*

A: I have been told that my greatest assets have been my ability to observe, describe, define, and measure various forms of psychopathology.

Q: *What makes a really great psychologist?*

A: Creativity, the ability to provide new syntheses of data or to open up new sources of data; to develop a broad framework for studying these data or phenomena; and to test or provide the blueprint for others to test these broad conceptualizations. Also an open mind, to derive ideas from other people, to modify or reject one's own ideas, and to synthesize one's own formulations with relevant pieces from other people.

Q: *How do you get your ideas for research?*

A: Mostly from observations of patients.

Q: *How do you decide whether to pursue an idea?*

A: I usually run through my ideas with my research staff, and if there seems to be some support for preliminary testing, we will conduct one or more pilot studies.

Q: *How have you developed an idea into a workable hypothesis?*

A: Although the prevailing notion of panic disorders had held that they were affective disorders and probably chemically induced, I observed discrete psychological phenomena. I noted that panic patients had strong catastrophic thoughts during the panic attacks. Looking for the source of this type of thinking, I recognized that it was based on their own interpretations of their bodily or psychological states. I tested this hypothesis on a number of patients and found it to be true.

Q: *What has been your major contribution to psychology?*

A: Possibly the derivation and elaboration of a cognitive model of psychopathology and a psychological intervention (cognitive therapy), designed to reverse psychopathology.

Q: *What do you want students to learn from you?*

A: To be totally versed in their areas of interest, to have an open mind, to place great emphasis on clear observation, to look for a variety of competing hypotheses to account for these observations, and finally to try to convert their observations and formulations into testable hypotheses, which they themselves evaluate in an experimental design.

Q: *What did you learn from your mentors?*

A: How to listen to patients and pick up various themes relevant to their problems that were sometimes subtle or even hidden.

Q: *Apart from your life as an academic, how has psychology been important to you?*

A: I have found psychology to be helpful in understanding my own moods and overreactions to situations.

Q: *What do you further hope to achieve or contribute?*

A: I hope to expand the knowledge of abnormal psychology to the ordinary problems of everyday living and beyond that to social problems such as violence and ethnic crises.

---

schemas they have internalized and how these schemas are interfering with their lives. Therapy also would help people replace these maladaptive schemas with more adaptive ones; at the very least, therapy would help people to keep the maladaptive schemas under control.

Other Forms of Cognitive Therapy

Other forms of cognitive therapy also address maladaptive statements and thoughts. For example, **stress-inoculation therapy** (Meichenbaum & Cameron, 1982) teaches clients to face stressful situations in a situation-oriented and calming manner rather than in a self-oriented and anxiety-provoking way. Suppose that you tend to panic when faced with final exams; you might be telling yourself, "I know I'm going to fail all of my exams" or "It would be better to drop out of school than to face the anxiety of finals." Instead, you would be taught to think, "By apportioning my time, I can successfully study for all my finals" and "Because I have always done well on finals before, I can expect to do well on my finals again."

Another form of cognitive therapy, **social problem solving** (D'Zurilla, 1986, 1990; D'Zurilla & Goldfried, 1971; Goldfried, 1969), treats psychological difficulties as problems that can be solved through common procedures. This form of therapy views psychological distress as a challenging problem, so clients are taught to use the following five basic steps in the problem-solving cycle:

1. Identify the problem being faced.
2. Brainstorm as many alternative solutions as possible.
3. Assess the potential consequences of each of the solutions, then choose the most workable solution.
4. Implement the solution.
5. Evaluate the effectiveness of the solution. If the solution is not fully effective, then cycle back to one of the earlier steps of problem solving.

In other words, clients are taught to treat their psychological difficulties as problems they can solve through cognitive processing, just as they solve many other problems. Indeed, the assumption that there is a cognitive cure to psychological problems is a common thread throughout all of the different cognitive therapies.

Everyone occasionally engages in maladaptive thought patterns or confronts situations requiring social problem solving. What is a situation you have recently confronted in which you could apply some of the ideas from cognitive therapy? How would you apply these ideas?

Biological Therapies

Biological therapies treat psychological disorders through medical or quasi-medical intervention. These therapies differ from all those we have considered up to this point because the client-therapist discourse plays no real role, or at least no more of a role than would be the case for any patient-doctor

discourse. Biological therapies can be used in conjunction with more psychologically oriented ones, of course, and they often are. When used together, however, psychological therapies tend to play a supportive rather than a central role in the process of change.

A History of Biological Therapies

Biological therapies date back at least to ancient Rome, where particular psychological disorders were viewed as being caused by poisons or other undesirable substances that had entered the body. As a result, laxatives and emetics were used to purge the body of these foreign substances. Such treatment continued even as recently as the eighteenth century (Agnew, 1985). Another way of ridding the body of unwanted substances was through selective bleeding, which also was used as recently as the eighteenth century. The idea was that undesirable substances were mixed with the blood, and that as the blood left the body, so would the undesirable substances. New blood would then be created by the body to replace the old blood, but it would be free of the contamination. Electrical shock also was used in the nineteenth century to help people with mental disorders. The idea, apparently, was literally to shock the disorder out of the body, and to shock the client into recovery.

In the early twentieth century, electrical shock therapy was extended and elaborated into a form known as **electroconvulsive therapy (ECT)**, which was used for the treatment of severe, unremitting depression. This form of therapy, still in occasional use today, causes patients to undergo seizures induced by electrical shock. In one form of ECT, an electrical current of about 150 volts is passed from one side of the patient's head to another for approximately one and one-half seconds. The patient reacts with loss of consciousness and a muscular seizure, followed by more seizures of less severity. In a more recent form of ECT, the electrical current is passed only through one side of the head. Patients who receive this treatment wake up several minutes later, suffering from amnesia for the period right before the start of the therapy.

The next day, without warning, I was ordered onto a bed to receive my first electroshock treatment. . . .

The wide rubber band containing the electrodes was wrapped tightly about my skull, just above the ears; the doctor checked my pulse, told me he was going to give me an injection to relax me (most of the uncomfortable effects of electroshock are back injuries caused by the patient's inordinate

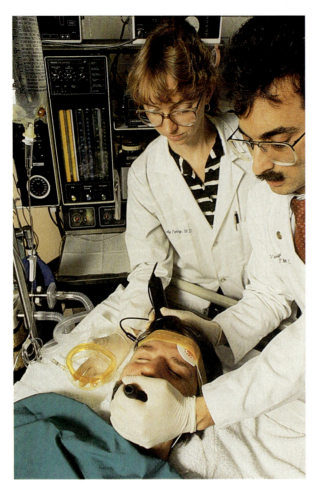

Although electroconvulsive therapy (ECT) still is used by some clinicians, its use is less common and more specific to treatment of severe depression now than it was decades ago. As you can see, even the technical apparatus makes the process seem intimidating. The paddle inserted into the patient's mouth is intended to prevent injury due to violent contortions associated with seizures following ECT.

tension). . . . I felt the needle go into my arm, my eyelids came over my eyeballs like a deep blue velvet curtain over my mismanaged life, I sensed a quick movement behind me, all was darkness.

Many times after that I lay down for electroshock. Never once did the despair and the fear of the initial treatment diminish, the fear of having one's consciousness so irrevocably laid on the indifferent altar of science.

— *Frederick Exley,* A Fan's Notes

Use of ECT has always been questionable and controversial, especially because the loss of memory it causes can be long-lasting, and because the procedure destroys neurons of the central nervous system. Al-

though the treatment seems to be effective for some (Abrams, 1988; Scovern & Kilmann, 1980), it does not work for others (Scott, 1989). Thus, it is almost always a treatment of last resort, particularly for severely depressed patients or depressed patients who also experience delusions or who already are severely mentally retarded (Bolwig, 1993). In the majority of cases, depression can be treated with psychotherapy, perhaps combined with antidepressant drugs, rendering ECT unnecessary.

Another treatment, which proved to be among the most disastrous attempts of the psychiatric profession to achieve biological cures, was prefrontal lobotomy, a form of psychosurgery. The basic reason to use **psychosurgery** was to alleviate mental disorders by engaging in a procedure that probes, slices, dissects, or removes a part of the brain. The procedure of *prefrontal lobotomy* severed the frontal lobes from the posterior portions of the brain, thereby cutting off all communication between the frontal lobes and the rest of the brain. The operation left many patients vegetative, incapable of functioning independently in any meaningful way. Even those operations that were less disastrously tragic could not be considered successful in terms of restoring mental health and normal cognitive function. Unfortunately, between 1935 (when the operation was first introduced) and 1955 (when antipsychotic drugs became the method of choice for treating many of the symptoms of schizophrenia and other disorders), prefrontal lobotomy is estimated to have victimized tens of thousands of patients, primarily in mental institutions (Freeman, 1959). The inventor of the operation even received the Nobel Prize in medicine for his contributions.

How could such a disaster have taken place? Elliot Valenstein (1986) has suggested several explanations. For one thing, the treatment came into prominence at a time when psychiatry was trying to gain respectability as a medical science. Psychosurgery seemed to offer such respectability because it was a medical procedure. Psychosurgery also allowed those in charge of mental hospitals to maintain control; the patients who received the operation stopped being disorderly and disruptive to the institutional regimen.

When we examine the failure of psychosurgery, we should view it in the broader context of many other failed medical and psychological treatments. For example, heroin was first introduced as an analgesic by a drug company. Countless other harmful and addictive drugs have been given to patients in the mistaken belief that the patients would benefit from using the drugs. Unfortunately, the harm that is clearly visible retrospectively is often obscure or even invisible prospectively. Interventions introduced to help people often end up causing more harm than benefit in the long run. Therefore, we need to pay more attention to the long-term consequences of the interventions we introduce.

The U.S. government, recognizing this need, has introduced stringent testing for various new products, most notably drugs. Unfortunately, it is not always obvious that this solution is the only right one. Stringent testing causes new products to take longer to reach consumers. In the case of drugs for life-threatening diseases such as AIDS, we need to balance the risks of introducing a new product too rapidly against the risk of people dying sooner because they did not have access to the new product. In short, we constantly need to monitor the gains versus the losses of withholding treatments because they have not adequately been proven beneficial.

> Argue the pros and cons of requiring extensive, lengthy testing of drugs and other treatments for potentially or actually life-threatening ailments such as AIDS or even suicidal extremes of depression.

Drug Therapies

During the second half of the twentieth century, the introduction of drug therapies has unquestionably been the major advance in the biological approach to the treatment of mental disorders. There are four main classes of **psychotropic drugs** (i.e., affecting the individual's psychological processes or state of mind): antipsychotic drugs, antidepressant drugs, antianxiety drugs, and lithium.

ANTIPSYCHOTIC DRUGS.   Antipsychotic drugs were a breakthrough in the treatment of psychotic patients. Prior to the introduction of such drugs, wards of mental hospitals resembled many of our worst stereotypes. They were characterized by wild screaming and the always-present threat of violence. Antipsychotic drugs completely changed the atmosphere in many of these wards.

The most commonly used antipsychotic drugs, introduced in the early 1950s, are *phenothiazines.* The best-known of these is also the first that was introduced: chlorpromazine, usually sold under the trade name Thorazine. Another common antipsychotic drug is haloperidol (Haldol). These antipsychotic drugs alleviate the symptoms of schizophrenia by

FIGURE 19-6
Effectiveness of Antipsychotic Medication Versus Placebo
The rates of symptomatic behavior are much higher for the placebo-control group than for the treatment group (receiving Mellaril, a brand name of phenothiazine). In addition, the rate of symptomatic behavior for the treatment group temporarily rose during a brief trial (observations 41–45) of placebo substitution, and declined again following reinstitution of the drug treatment.

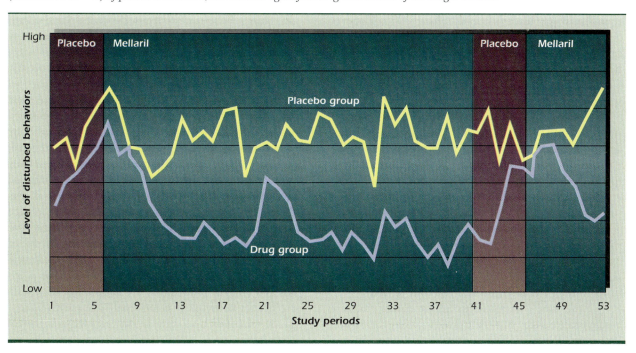

blocking the dopamine receptors in the schizophrenic brain (see Chapter 3). Although these drugs are quite successful in treating the positive symptoms of schizophrenia, they are less successful in treating the negative symptoms (see Chapter 18).

Antipsychotic drugs also have serious side effects, such as dryness of the mouth, tremors, stiffness, and involuntary jerking movements. Generally, the severe symptoms do not appear until the antipsychotic drugs have been administered for a relatively long period. Patients differ in the severity of their symptoms and in the length of time until symptom onset.

At present, there is no clear answer about how to balance the costs and the benefits of antipsychotic medication. The use of antipsychotics replaces one problem with another, and it is often arguable which problem is worse. Most users of drug therapy believe that the problems of psychosis are worse than are the side effects of the drugs, but this conclusion is debatable. A related problem is that the clinician is duty-bound to obtain informed consent from those who are to receive the drugs. However, we could easily argue that people suffering from psychotic episodes are in no position to give true informed consent; nor is it clear that a patient's relatives can give true informed consent. There is no easy answer.

Another problem of antipsychotic drugs is that not all psychotic patients respond to the traditional antipsychotic medication. Occasionally, another drug, such as clozapine, may be successful when the traditional drugs have failed, but the overall success rate for treating patients who do not respond to other antipsychotic medication is only about 30% (Kane et al., 1988). Also, clozapine can cause side effects (e.g., immune-system deficiencies), although they differ from those of the traditional antipsychotic drugs. Clearly, we are far from any panaceas in the biological treatment of psychoses.

ANTIDEPRESSANT DRUGS.   Antidepressant drugs are of two main kinds: *tricyclics* and *monoamine oxidase (MAO) inhibitors*. Tricyclics are much more frequently used because MAO inhibitors are more toxic, require adherence to a special diet, and generally provide less successful outcomes than the tricyclics. The MAO inhibitors thus tend to be used for those patients who do not respond to tricyclics. MAO inhibitors include isocarboxazid (Marplan) and phenelzine (Nardil). Examples of tricyclics are imipramine (Tofranil) and amitriptyline (Elavil).

Both types of **antidepressant drugs** increase concentrations of two neurotransmitters, serotonin and norepinephrine, at particular synapses in the brain (see Chapter 3). Concentrations of these neuro-transmitters begin to increase almost immediately after patients start taking the drugs. However, the antidepressant effect does not begin immediately. It can take several weeks, and sometimes longer, before the patient starts to feel the effects.

A third type of antidepressant drug has been introduced more recently. It works by inhibiting the reuptake of serotonin and norepinephrine during transmission between neurons. This inhibition of reuptake effectively increases the concentrations of the two neurotransmitters, but it does so less directly than do the other two types of antidepressant drugs. The most well-known of these new drugs is fluoxetine (Prozac). Depressed patients typically start to show improvement after about three weeks of taking the drug. It seems to work for a wide variety of patients, but it, too, has side effects, such as nausea and nervousness. Prozac has also been associated with reports of severe agitation, although this association is not confirmed (Cole & Bodkin, 1990; Papp & Gorman, 1990).

From one point of view, drug treatment of depression has been considerably more successful than drug treatment of schizophrenia. Whereas antipsychotic drugs only suppress symptoms, antidepressant drugs seem to cause more lasting change. Patients who stop taking antipsychotic drugs typically return to their earlier psychotic state, whereas patients who stop taking antidepressant drugs often remain symptom free for quite some time, and possibly indefinitely.

When we consider the difference in the longer-term effectiveness of antipsychotic versus antidepressant drugs, however, we must also consider the rates of spontaneous recovery. In **spontaneous recovery,** the person's symptoms disappear without any treatment whatsoever. The rate of spontaneous recovery for depression is much higher than that for schizophrenia and other psychoses, so an unknown proportion of the depressed patients who become better through the use of drugs or psychotherapy might have become better even if they had received no treatment at all. In addition, researchers and clinicians must consider the effects of placebos. Patients may improve simply because they believe that they are being helped, even if the treatment they receive actually has no direct effect whatsoever. To rule out both the effects of spontaneous recovery and the effects of placebos, researchers studying the effects of drugs often use both control groups that take placebos and control groups that are simply put on a waiting list for subsequent treatment. The control group taking placebos also may be studied using a *double-blind technique,* in which both the experimenter administering the treatment and the patient are blind as to whether a particular patient is receiving a placebo or an active drug.

> Design an experiment to test the effects of one of the nonbiological psychotherapeutic treatments, in comparison with one of the biological treatments for a psychological disorder. (Specify the disorder.)

ANTIANXIETY DRUGS. Clinicians prescribe antianxiety drugs (also called anxiolytics or tranquilizers) to alleviate their patients' feelings of tension and anxiety, to increase patients' feelings of well-being, and to counteract symptoms of insomnia. The earliest antianxiety drugs, the *barbiturates*, are rarely used today because they are highly addictive and potentially dangerous (see Chapter 6). More commonly used are two classes of antianxiety drugs: muscle relaxants and benzodiazepines. Muscle relaxants cause feelings of tranquility. (Recall the work of Schachter & Singer, described in Chapter 16, regarding the relationship between physiological reactions and emotions.) Two of the more frequently used drugs of this class are meprobamate drugs (Miltown and Equanil).

Benzodiazepines also cause muscle relaxation and have an additional notable tranquilizing effect. Two of the most well-known and very widely used of these drugs are chlordiazepoxide (Librium) and diazepam (Valium). Clinicians have commonly prescribed these drugs without sufficient heed of their possible consequences. The drugs can be habit forming, and their tranquilizing effect can impair attention and alertness (Schweizer et al., 1990).

LITHIUM. In 1949, lithium was found to be effective in treating manic-depressive disorders, and it remains the drug of choice for these disorders. It is very effective, causing almost immediate alleviation of symptoms in roughly three-fourths of cases. However, it alleviates depressive symptoms only in manic-depressives (those persons with bipolar disorder), adding credence to the notion that bipolar disorder differs qualitatively from major (unipolar) depression (Baron et al., 1975). We still do not know why lithium has the effect it does (Manji et al., 1991), and the drug must be used with care because overdoses can lead to convulsions and even to death.

CONCLUSIONS. A 1993 World Health Organization report (Sartorius et al., 1993a) indicates that the main breakthroughs in pharmacotherapy (represented by the preceding four classes of psychotropic drugs) have revolutionized the psychiatric treatment of mental illness. Subsequent developments have of-

fered refinements that enhance the applicability of these treatments, but they have not offered additional breakthroughs.

Psychotherapy in a Cross-Cultural Perspective

Although the range of psychotherapies is quite broad, cross-cultural commonalities exist among the various approaches to psychotherapy. Across such diverse psychotherapists as U.S. and European psychiatrists, Native American *shamans*, Latin American *curanderos* (or *curanderas*, in Mexico and elsewhere), and Yoruban *babalawo* (in Nigeria), psychotherapy appears to have five basic components (Torrey, 1986): (1) an emphasis on a shared worldview between client and therapist, including a common language and similar conceptions of causes and effects; (2) therapist characteristics such as warmth, genuineness, and empathy; (3) patient expectations that reflect the culturally relevant beliefs of the patient and the therapist; (4) a set of specific techniques employed by the therapist (e.g., talking or using biological techniques such as drugs or shock therapy); and (5) a process by which the therapist enables or empowers the client to gain increased knowledge, awareness, and mastery, thereby gaining hope. According to E. Torrey, psychotherapists across various cultures "perform essentially the same function in their respective cultures. [Both Western and non-Western] therapists . . . treat patients using similar techniques; and both get similar results."

Before we discuss the comparative effectiveness of the various approaches to psychotherapy, we broaden our view of psychotherapy to encompass forms of psychotherapy delivered by modes other than the interaction between one therapist and one client.

ALTERNATIVES TO INDIVIDUAL PSYCHOTHERAPY

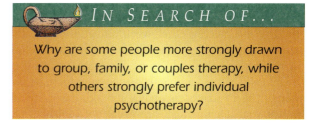

IN SEARCH OF...

Why are some people more strongly drawn to group, family, or couples therapy, while others strongly prefer individual psychotherapy?

We have described drug therapies and the other forms of psychotherapy in terms of one psychotherapist administering treatment to one client. In some circumstances, however, various alternatives to one-on-one therapy may be more helpful. These options include group therapy, couples and family therapy, community psychology, and self-help. A 1993 World Health Organization report (Langsley, Hodes, & Grimson, 1993) indicated that these alternatives to individual psychotherapy have been widely available among many non-Western cultures.

Group Therapy

Except for biological therapies, psychotherapy can be administered either individually or in groups. Some might note that group therapy also offers several distinct advantages over individual psychotherapy: (a) group therapy is almost always less expensive than is individual therapy; (b) group therapy may offer greater support than does individual therapy because groups usually comprise individuals with similar problems; (c) group therapy offers the potential value of social pressure to change, which may supplement (or even supplant) the authoritative pressure to change that comes from the therapist; (d) the very dynamic of group interaction may lead to therapeutic change, especially in the cases of people who have problems with interpersonal interactions.

Group therapy also has several potential disadvantages: (a) The treatment effect may be diluted by the presence of others requiring the attention of the therapist; (b) group psychotherapy may embroil the clients in so many issues related to the group interactions that they no longer focus on resolving the presenting problems that prompted them to seek therapy in the first place; (c) the content of the group process may move away from the dynamics of psychotherapy, so that group members start dealing with problems that are interesting but irrelevant to the issues for which the group was formed.

Twelve-step groups have become very popular for the treatment of addictions. The first such group was Alcoholics Anonymous (AA), which was founded in the mid-1930s. Twelve-step groups are based on a philosophy of evangelical Protestantism and involve developing the addicts' relationship to God, as well as to self and others. Members typically attend about three to five meetings each week, and at each meeting members discuss the difficulties they are experiencing in overcoming their addiction. The support of other members is viewed as key to overcoming these addictions. The effectiveness of AA and similar programs is not well documented, however (see Walsh et al., 1991).

The philosophy of AA is that alcoholism is a disease, which can be managed but never fully cured. AA members who are in *recovery* have acknowledged that they have the disease, that there is no cure for it,

The advantages of having such a large group for psychotherapy may include reduced cost, greater social pressure to effective positive changes, and greater diversity of persons who may offer a fresh perspective on a troubling situation. The disadvantages of group therapy include the potential for dilution of the treatment and for group dynamics to take precedence over the presenting problem that stimulated the desire to obtain therapy.

and that alcohol therefore can never again play a part in their lives. Other related groups are Al-Anon (for the spouses of alcoholics), Alateen (for the adolescent children of alcoholics), Overeaters Anonymous (for those who feel unable to control how much or what they eat), and various other groups designed to control addictive behaviors. Attendance at programs such as these goes beyond mere participation in therapy. It is more of a *conversion experience*, in which a person adopts a totally new way of living. People thus attempt to move beyond the addiction that has ruled their lives, and they do so by participating in a group that can itself become a way of life (see Table 19-1). In recent years, especially in urban areas, secular alternatives to AA have also become available.

Behavior therapy also can be done in groups. For example, Lazarus (1961, 1968, 1989) has used behavioral techniques in a group setting. Phobias are especially treatable in this way. In group desensitization, a single psychotherapist can teach many people at once how to relax deeply, and then can develop a common desensitization hierarchy for the alleviation of various kinds of phobias, such as fear of snakes, heights, and so on. Various behavioral techniques also have been used in other group treatment programs, such as programs to lose weight (Wollersheim, 1970).

Couples and Family Therapy

The goal of couples and family therapy is to treat problems from a *systems perspective*—that is, in terms of the couple or the family unit as a whole, which in-

TABLE 19-1
The 12 Steps of Alcoholics Anonymous
These 12 steps are well-known around the world to the many members of Alcoholics Anonymous, a support group for persons struggling with problems related to alcohol abuse.

1. We admitted we were powerless over alcohol—that our lives had become unmanageable.
2. Came to believe that a power greater than ourselves could restore us to sanity.
3. Made a decision to turn our will and our lives over to the care of God *as we understood Him.*
4. Made a searching and fearless moral inventory of ourselves.
5. Admitted to God, to ourselves, and to another human being the exact nature of our wrongs.
6. Were entirely ready to have God remove all these defects of character.
7. Humbly asked Him to remove our shortcomings.
8. Made a list of all persons we had harmed, and became willing to make amends to them all.
9. Made direct amends to such people wherever possible, except when to do so would injure them or others.
10. Continued to take personal inventory and, when we were wrong, promptly admitted it.
11. Sought through prayer and meditation to improve our conscious contact with God *as we understood Him,* praying only for knowledge of His will for us and the power to carry that out.
12. Having had a spiritual awakening as the result of these steps, we tried to carry this message to alcoholics and to practice these principles in all our affairs.

volves complex internal interactions, rather than in terms of the discrete problems of distinct members of the unit. The identified problem may be centered on the family unit, such as troubled communication among family members, or it may be centered on the problem of one member of the unit. The underlying notion in this kind of therapy is that even individual problems often have roots in the family system, and to treat the problem, the whole family should be part of the solution. Surprisingly, some apparently individual problems—such as eating disorders—can be treated quite effectively in family therapy, particularly if the disorder is caught early (within three years of onset) in a young person (see Langsley et al., 1993).

In cases of marital conflict, couples therapy is more successful than individual therapy both in holding couples together and in bringing them back together (Gurman, Kniskern, & Pinsoff, 1986). Couples therapy tends to be particularly successful for people who have had problems for only a short time before they seek therapy, and when they have not yet initiated action toward divorce. One reason for the greater success of couples therapy is that the therapist can hear about reality as expressed by both members of the couple. Hearing both points of view enables the therapist to mediate more effectively than does hearing just a single point of view.

Couples therapy emphasizes communication and mutual empathy. Partners are trained to listen carefully and empathically to each other, and they learn to restate what the partner is saying, thereby confirming that they accurately understood the partner's point of view. Couples are also taught how to make requests of each other in constructive but direct

ways, rather than to make indirect requests that can be confusing and at times harmful to the relationship. Erving Goffman (1967) found that partners in unsuccessful relationships often fail to hear even the positive things that they say about each other.

Aaron Beck (1988) has emphasized the importance of having each partner understand the perspective of the other. He urges partners to clarify the differences in what each partner seeks for the relationship, noting that partners often have secret "shoulds": things that each of us believes that our partner ought to do, but which our partner may not believe to be important or worth doing. Beck believes many problems in a relationship can be attributed to

Couples therapy is highly effective in helping couples to resolve interpersonal conflict and to enhance communication, particularly if the presenting problems have been of short duration prior to treatment and the couple has not yet started divorce action.

the *automatic thoughts* that can rise into consciousness, and which we believe to be self-evident, whether they are or not.

Community Psychology

Community psychology views people not only as a part of a couple or a family system, but also as part of the larger system of the community. The community psychologist may intervene at any level, ranging from the individual to the community, depending on what will most effectively help the client or clients being served. The emphasis in community psychology is at least as much on prevention as it is on treatment. With so many members of a community at risk for psychological distress, it makes sense to try to prevent problems before they happen.

Community psychologists may intervene at one or more of three levels of prevention. *Primary prevention* is aimed at preventing disorders before they happen. *Secondary prevention* is targeted toward detecting disorders early, before they become major problems. *Tertiary prevention* essentially treats disorders once they have developed more fully, and it can be considered preventive only in the sense that the continuation of the disorders may be prevented.

Whereas most traditional psychotherapists wait for clients to come to them, community psychologists often actively seek out people who are presently experiencing problems or who are likely to experience them in the future. Moreover, community psychologists often perceive themselves to be part of the communities they serve rather than detached, outside experts. That is, community psychologists may become actively involved in the lives of people in the community.

Unfortunately, many communities have reduced their funding of community mental-health services. At about the same time that funding cuts were hurting community mental-health services, the need for such services increased, as many mentally ill persons who had been hospitalized were *deinstitutionalized* (released from health-care institutions and onto the streets). Although community-based outpatient treatment may be as effective as—or more effective than—inpatient treatment for many disorders, many deinstitutionalized patients receive little or no treatment whatsoever. As a result, they are left homeless on our streets, in need of appropriate treatment. We probably are most aware of the problems of the homeless in our own country, but the deinstitutionalization of the mentally ill in other countries also has created problems when there has been an associated failure to deliver appropriate community-based mental-health care (Burti & Yastrebov, 1993).

Darrel Regier, director of epidemiological studies at the National Institute of Mental Health (quoted in Goleman, 1993), studied more than 20,000 U.S. men and women, trying to determine the prevalence of mental illness. Based on his representative sample, he extrapolated that about 52 million Americans (one in every five) suffer from some type of psychological disorder that meaningfully impairs their functioning in some way. Of the 52 million, about 20 million have phobias severe enough to cause them to limit their behavior, and another 15 million would be diagnosed as depressed. Of the 52 million Americans who are impaired, only 8% are being treated for their impairment. Clearly, the need for community-based mental-health services extends beyond the treatment of the homeless who are mentally ill.

One of the means by which community psychologists offer appropriate services to members of the community is through *community mental-health centers*. The goal of such centers is to provide outpatient mental health care to people in the community. Costs are generally lower than those of individual psychotherapy, and many centers offer 24-hour walk-in crisis services.

An outgrowth of the community-psychology movement and the related community-health movement that places more emphasis on treatment than on prevention is the hotline. *Hotlines* serve people, usually on a 24-hour basis, who are desperate for assistance. The most well-known of the hotlines are those dealing with suicide prevention, but they also exist for potential child abusers and for others as well. People answering the phones of these hotlines are taught a series of procedures to defuse the immediate problem. For example, a person answering the phone in a suicide-prevention hotline is taught to communicate empathy to the caller, show understanding of the caller's problem, provide information regarding sources of help, and obtain the caller's verbal agreement to take actions that will lead the caller away from suicide (Speer, 1972).

Self-Help

Psychotherapy for individuals, couples, families, and even entire communities involves personal interactions between psychotherapists and the clients they serve. There is yet another alternative for people seeking psychotherapeutic assistance: self-help. Your neighborhood bookstore probably features a generously stocked self-help section, with books suggesting how to help yourself resolve almost any problem you could imagine: how to treat addiction (including many books based on AA), how to improve your love life, how to become more assertive, and how to overcome various forms of self-defeating behavior.

Do any of these books actually work? This is a hard question to answer because no one is monitoring the effectiveness of the various programs. There are relatively few classics in the field—books that continue to be printed long after the initial burst of sales—suggesting that the large majority of these books are not so helpful that purchasers are recommending them to an ever-widening circle of buyers.

What self-help strategies have you used when confronting stressful or psychologically troublesome strategies?

Gerald Rosen, author of a self-help book, *Don't Be Afraid* (1976), and 1978 chair of the APA Task Force on Self-Help Therapies, has expressed grave concerns about the efficacy of self-help books. In particular, Rosen (1987) abhors the outrageously unsubstantiated claims made in the promotional material for such books (including his own). Rosen further deplores the irresponsible distribution of books based on untested methods and promoted with unfounded claims, which he believes may cause more harm than good. Rosen is particularly concerned that such books may cause some readers to doubt both their own ability to improve and legitimate psychotherapists' ability to help them. These books can be useful for the relatively common problems of daily living and for spiritual uplift, but they probably are not the answer to the more serious psychological disorders discussed in Chapter 18. Indeed, to the extent that readers with serious problems view these books as an alternative to various forms of psychotherapy, the books may have deleterious rather than positive effects.

CHOOSING AN OPTIMAL APPROACH

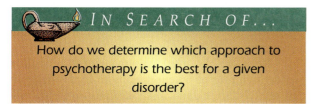

IN SEARCH OF...

How do we determine which approach to psychotherapy is the best for a given disorder?

This chapter has described various kinds of psychotherapy, each of which makes different assumptions about both the nature of psychological disorders and the optimal ways to treat these disorders. In light of this diversity of approaches, it seems obvious that they cannot all be right. At some level, this perception is probably correct, but at another level, the

approaches to psychotherapy may be more complementary than they may initially appear.

Consider, for example, the issue of what causes mental disorders. Part of the difference in treatment procedures derives from different views about causation. Psychodynamic theories tend to focus on repressed early childhood experiences as the cause of mental disorders. Humanistic theories consider the primary cause of these disorders to be deficits either in feelings of self-worth or in feelings of unconditional acceptance by others. Behavior therapies look to faulty conditioning, whereas cognitive theories emphasize maladaptive thoughts or schemas. Biological therapies look to psychophysiological causes of distress, such as depletion of neurotransmitters. To what extent are these various causal explanations mutually exclusive?

To see the complementarity of the various approaches, we can view mental disorders as having causes at different levels of analysis. For example, traumatic experiences in early childhood may lead to or even be viewed as inappropriate forms of behavioral conditioning. Imbalances in or lack of neurotransmitter substances may lead to maladaptive thoughts, or maladaptive thoughts may lead to low self-esteem. Often, the causal direction of these various levels of analysis is not clear (see Figure 19-7).

To understand the nature of psychological phenomena, we need to take a dialectical approach to synthesizing the various levels of explanations. Similarly, to treat a mental disorder at multiple levels, we may wish to synthesize several different therapies into a single approach. The term *eclectic therapy* describes a strategy for therapy that integrates several approaches.

Moreover, just as therapists need to consider the various forms of treatment that may be appropriate, they also need to consider the various backgrounds of their clients, which may influence the decision of which therapies to use. As our culture-rich nation becomes still more culturally diverse, it is becoming increasingly necessary for counselors and therapists to develop competence in dealing with clients who are culturally different from themselves. It is not unusual for counselors to encounter clients from diverse ethnic groups or even recent immigrants from other countries. For example, Asian-American and Hispanic-American therapists may well confront Haitian, Ukrainian, or Turkish clients. When clients and therapists come from radically different places, in which they were socialized to have sharply different beliefs, values, expectations, conceptions of self, and so on, significant problems can arise. These problems may result in distrust, disappointment, or failed intervention.

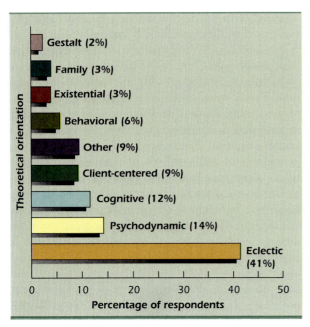

FIGURE 19-7
Orientations of Psychotherapists
Out of 415 clinical psychologists surveyed, almost half indicated that they followed an eclectic approach. (After Smith, 1982)

The need for guidance in cross-cultural psychotherapy has spawned numerous books dealing with various key issues in the field (e.g., Axelson, 1993; Ivey, Ivey, & Simek-Morgan, 1993; Pedersen, Draguns, Lonner, & Trimble, in press). Many college professors and administrators are becoming aware of the need to provide courses and lectures on cross-cultural psychology within their curricula. Among the many issues in cross-cultural psychotherapy addressed by such courses and books, the following questions frequently arise: (a) Are certain types of therapy more appropriate for particular ethnic groups? (b) How can mental-health programs reach out to the members of ethnic groups who typically underuse available resources? (c) How can a therapist communicate empathically with clients who have worldviews that differ from the therapist's?

EFFECTIVENESS OF PSYCHOTHERAPY

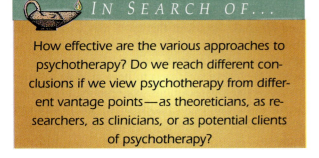

IN SEARCH OF...

How effective are the various approaches to psychotherapy? Do we reach different conclusions if we view psychotherapy from different vantage points—as theoreticians, as researchers, as clinicians, or as potential clients of psychotherapy?

Before a clinician chooses a particular kind of psychotherapy or a particular synthesis of the various forms of psychotherapy, he or she should consider the relative effectiveness of each. In addition to personal clinical experience, the clinician needs access to information based on empirical studies. The ideal research would analyze each of the major diagnoses (as shown in Chapter 18, based on DSM-IV) in terms of each of the major types of therapies (psychodynamic, humanistic, behavioral, cognitive, and biological), as well as placebo control groups and waiting-list control groups. This research would then evaluate each diagnosis in terms of which type of therapy was most effective.

Actually, other factors also should be considered in an ideal research program—for example, the length of treatment dramatically affects therapeutic outcomes. One *meta-analytic study* (i.e., study that analyzes a large number of other studies; Howard, Kopta, Krause, & Orlinsky, 1986) showed that when the effects of dropping out of treatment are statistically controlled, 29–38% of psychotherapy clients improve by the first 3 sessions, 48–58% improve by the first 4–7 sessions, 56–68% improve by the first 8–16 sessions, 74–81% by the first 17–52 sessions, and 85% by the first 53–100 sessions. Clearly, studies that failed to consider treatment length would obtain results that would be inconclusive. (It may be useful to point out that the average number of psychotherapy sessions for Americans receiving treatment is 14 in a given year [Goleman, 1993].)

Additional factors to consider might be whether individual, family, couple, or group therapy would be most helpful; the relevant type of setting (e.g., inpatient or outpatient); additional characteristics of the client and of the therapist (e.g., cultural background, personality variables such as extroversion/introversion, attitudes, and values); therapeutic technique (e.g., how closely the therapist followed the approach prescribed by a particular theoretical paradigm); and so on. Although the call for this kind of research first went out decades ago (e.g., Kiesler, 1966; Paul, 1967), it has yet to materialize. Given its complexity, its failure to materialize is not surprising.

Although the ideal research that would allow perfect tailoring of psychotherapy to client diagnosis has not yet been done, meta-analytic and other research clearly shows that psychotherapy produces significant improvement in clients, above and beyond any spontaneous recovery that might have occurred (e.g., Andrews, 1993; Smith & Glass, 1977; Stiles et al., 1986). In particular, clients who receive psychotherapy, on average, are better off than 75% or more of research control subjects who did not receive psychotherapy. Psychotherapy is especially helpful (better than for 82–83% of untreated controls) in improving clients' self-esteem and in reducing their anxiety. However, psychotherapy was less helpful (better than for only 71% of untreated controls) in increasing the level of adjustment in persons institutionalized for psychotic, alcoholic, or criminal behaviors, and it was even less helpful (better than for only 62% of untreated controls) in increasing clients' grade-point average or otherwise in enhancing their work or school achievements (Smith & Glass, 1977).

Once again, length of treatment may be a factor that confounds the interpretation of results. For example, see Figure 19-8, which shows the results of a meta-analytic study by Kenneth Howard and his collegues (1986). If researchers were to determine the effectiveness of therapy for borderline-psychotic patients in terms of therapist ratings at the conclusion of eight sessions, the results would be profoundly discouraging; yet if the researchers were to assess therapist ratings in these same patients at the conclusion of 104 sessions, the studies would be extremely encouraging. However, for depressed and anxious patients, therapy results would be much more positive after much shorter durations of therapy.

That psychotherapy is beneficial is unsurprising, although pleasantly encouraging to practicing psychotherapists. Less encouraging is the finding that the positive outcomes of therapy seem to occur regardless of the type of therapy implemented. That is, when the researchers' allegiance to a particular therapy is ruled out, each type of psychotherapy seems to be just about as effective as the next. When the researchers' allegiance is not ruled out, whatever therapy program the researcher prefers seems to fare better in the comparisons across therapy programs.

Several reasons for this paradox (equivalent therapeutic outcomes despite profoundly different therapeutic techniques and theoretical approaches) have been suggested (see Stiles et al., 1986). These reasons include inadequate distinctions among disorders, common characteristics across therapists, common characteristics across clients, or common characteristics of the therapeutic alliance between therapist and client.

INADEQUATE DISTINCTIONS AMONG DISORDERS.   Most meta-analytic studies blur the distinctions among various kinds of mental disorders, such that a therapy program that is particularly appropriate for depressed individuals might be balanced by a program that is particularly appropriate for schizophrenics. We see the need for ideal research that allows for prescriptive treatment. For schizophrenics, pharmacotherapy may indeed be more

FIGURE 19-8
Meta-Analysis of the Course of Psychotherapy

Although self-ratings and therapist ratings differed, and the degree of improvement differed across different diagnoses, on the whole, the data seem to show that psychotherapy is highly effective for helping persons with psychological problems.

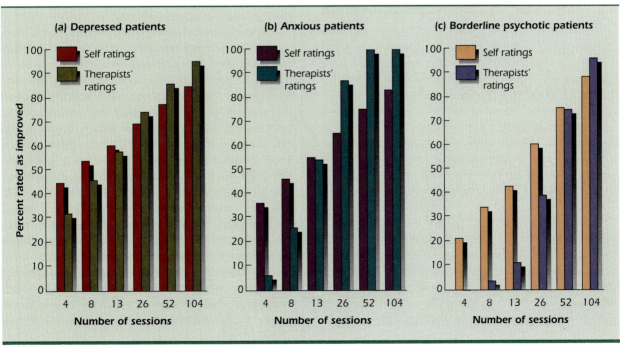

effective than other forms of treatment. For depressed clients, however, pharmacotherapy fares no better than other forms of psychotherapy (Robinson, Berman, & Neimeyer, 1990; Stiles et al., 1986).

COMMON CHARACTERISTICS ACROSS THERAPISTS.   Despite the variety of their therapeutic approaches, all psychotherapists seek to communicate to their clients a new perspective on the client and on his or her situation. Perhaps these attributes account for the primary effects of psychotherapy of all sorts.

Several meta-analytic studies have shown that despite widely divergent therapeutic techniques and approaches, two global characteristics of therapists appear across theoretical orientations: (1) their "warm involvement with the client," and (2) their "communication of a new perspective on the client's person and situation" (Stiles, Shapiro, & Elliott, 1986, p. 172). Thus, regardless of the therapist's theoretical orientation, all therapists try to establish *rapport* with clients, which means that they try to ensure feelings of trust and to establish ease of communication with the client. Further, the client needs to feel that the therapist genuinely cares about the outcome, or therapeutic change is much less likely to occur.

Effective psychotherapists essentially may provide the same function as a good friend. In your own experience, what therapeutic benefits do you provide to and receive from your good friends? What therapeutic benefits might a professional psychotherapist provide that a good friend probably cannot provide?

COMMON CHARACTERISTICS ACROSS CLIENTS. An interesting counterpart to the hypothesized crucial importance of the role of the therapist is that the role of the client in a therapeutic relationship distinctively promotes improvement. The client's style of communication within a therapeutic context is distinctively self-disclosing, and this self-disclosing communication may in itself promote improvement. The client's desire to improve and belief in the efficacy of therapy may also facilitate the therapeutic process.

COMMON CHARACTERISTICS OF THE THERAPEUTIC ALLIANCE BETWEEN THERAPIST AND CLIENT.   A synthesis of the preceding two approaches is that the client and the therapist form a distinctive therapeutic alliance, in which they are allies in the effort to help the client improve through the process of psychotherapy. William Stiles and his colleagues (1986) evaluated dozens of studies and found that the available research supported the importance of the therapeutic alliance in terms of the clients' therapeutic outcomes.

Why do you think research shows that psychotherapy often produces beneficial outcomes?

ETHICAL ISSUES IN PSYCHOTHERAPY

IN SEARCH OF...

To what distinctive professional responsibilities and ethical obligations should psychotherapists be expected to commit themselves?

In the fall of 1992, Ann Landers, an advice columnist, devoted her entire column to an exposé of a world-renowned psychiatrist who had held various prestigious positions in psychiatric associations. The disgraced psychiatrist was forced to resign from the American Psychiatric Association after losing a lawsuit brought by former patients who claimed he had abused them sexually and in other ways. This type of case is not unique, although it is, fortunately, rare. Psychotherapists are in a position to cause enormous harm to patients by virtue of their status and their position as dispensers of treatment; unfortunately, a few of them do so. Inevitably, they hurt not only their clients and themselves, but also the entire profession through their unethical behavior.

Perhaps even more than many other professionals, psychotherapists are expected to behave ethically toward clients. Psychotherapists are expected to refrain, for example, from becoming sexually involved with clients. Moreover, psychotherapists are expected to maintain the confidentiality of communications between themselves and their clients. Only in rare cases can they be required to divulge the contents of these communications. Examples of such cases occur primarily when the therapist determines that clients may be dangerous to themselves or to others. In addition, in some states, psychotherapists must breach confidentiality when a client has been accused of a crime and the records of the psychotherapist might be relevant to determining the client's sanity, when the psychotherapist has been accused of malpractice, when psychotherapy has been sought with the goal of evading the law, or when a child under age 16 has been a victim of child abuse. In most states, in cases of child abuse or of potential danger to others, therapists are legally required to take action. In other words, they cannot expose a child or other person to great risk simply to maintain confidential communications.

Another ethical protection for clients demands that before clients participate in what are viewed as experimental treatments, they must first give **informed consent**—that is, they must fully understand what the treatment will involve, including both the experimental nature of the treatment and its possible harmful side effects or consequences, as well as the likelihood that these consequences may take place. Also, during the experimental treatment, the psychotherapist certainly is expected to preserve the well-being of the experimental participant to the fullest extent possible.

Although we would like to believe that ethical issues can be viewed in black and white, they often come in various shades of gray. For example, in the past, homosexuality was treated as a disorder, and people with homosexual preferences were viewed as needing to change their sexual preference to restore them to full mental health. Today, homosexuals are usually viewed as requiring treatment only if they are unhappy with their sexual preference. Treatment is recommended if homosexuals want either to come to feel satisfied with this preference or to try to change it. The gray area becomes visible when we ask, "To what extent should the therapist encourage the client either to accept a homosexual preference or to try to change it?" Different therapists would approach this question with different points of view. On the one hand, it is important for psychotherapists to respect the values of their clients; on the other hand, some view psychotherapy, in part, as a tool for transmitting a value system from the psychotherapist to the client.

The important point is that psychotherapists need to consider ethics in their treatment of clients. In doing so, they need to take into account not only their own personal ethical standards, but also those of the field and of the society in which it is embedded.

> Design a checklist offering specific recommendations to guide clinicians in their decisions regarding when they should consider breaching confidentiality. (For example, at what point does a therapist have sufficient reason to suspect child abuse?)

When psychotherapy is implemented appropriately, another benefit of psychotherapy appears to be a reduction in overall health-care costs. Thus, when companies provide mental-health counseling for their employees, they obtain not only increases in productivity and decreases in employee absenteeism and turnover, but also savings in the overall cost of health care (Docherty, 1993). Health psychology is the topic of the next—and final—chapter.

SUMMARY

Early History of Psychotherapeutic Intervention   679

1. Early views of *psychotherapy* reflected the then prevalent idea that persons afflicted with mental illness were possessed by demons. Subsequent treatment in *asylums* was essentially a form of warehousing mentally ill persons to keep them off the streets, with little thought given to humane treatment, let alone possible psychotherapy. Some early forms of treatment, such as the use of magnetic fields to cure patients, were bizarre and of no value. However, by the nineteenth century, Josef Breuer proposed a talking cure, which became the basis for Freud's psychoanalytic methods.

Diagnosing and Assessing Abnormal Behavior   680

2. The DSM and ICD systems of diagnostic classification have helped clinicians make appropriate and consensually understood diagnoses as a basis for treatment.

3. Clinical assessment procedures include *clinical interviews*, which may be structured or unstructured; and psychological tests.

4. Psychological tests include personality tests (both objective and projective measures),

intelligence tests, neuropsychological tests, and psychophysiological tests.

Approaches to Psychotherapy   684

5. There are five main approaches to psychotherapy: psychodynamic, humanistic, behavioral, cognitive, and biological.

6. Psychodynamic therapies emphasize insight into underlying unconscious processes as the key to the therapeutic process. Freudian psychoanalytic therapy and neo-Freudian ego-analysis therapies are the two major types of psychodynamic therapies.

7. Humanistic therapies emphasize the therapeutic effects of the therapist's unconditional positive regard for the client, as exemplified by Carl Rogers's *client-centered therapy.*

8. Behavior therapies emphasize techniques based on principles of operant and classical conditioning. Techniques include *counterconditioning, aversion therapy, systematic desensitization,* and *extinction procedures,* such as *flooding* and *implosion therapy.* Additional techniques include the use of *token economies* and *behavioral contracting.* The use of *modeling* bridges the gap between behavioral and cognitive therapies.

9. Cognitive therapies encourage patients to change their cognitions in order to achieve therapeutic changes in behavior and other desired outcomes. Albert Ellis's *rational-emotive behavior therapy* and Aaron Beck's *cognitive therapy* are two of the main schools of cognitive therapy. Other forms of cognitive therapy include *stress-inoculation therapy* and *social problem solving.*

10. Historically, biological treatments of mental illness have included a wide array of treatments, such as *electroconvulsive therapy* and *psychosurgery.*

11. Modern biological treatments, such as the development of effective *psychotropic drugs,* have revolutionized biological treatments. Today, the four key classes of psychotropic drugs are antipsychotics, antidepressants, antianxiety drugs, and lithium. Although these drugs are certainly not cure-alls, they have been a welcome asset to the clinician's armamentarium.

Alternatives to Individual Psychotherapy   699

12. Alternatives to individual psychotherapy include group therapy, couples and family therapy, community psychology, and self-help. Group therapy, couples therapy, and family therapy often address problems specific to interpersonal relationships, and they address these problems through the dynamic interplay that occurs in the group, the couple, or the family. Community psychology focuses primarily on preventive mental health; community psychologists may use several strategies, including education of all members of a community, outreach to persons experiencing stress, and treatment of persons in distress. In self-help therapies, individuals seek guidance in handling stressful situations or minor psychological difficulties through books and other informational media.

Choosing an Optimal Approach   703

13. No single approach to psychotherapy is ideal for all persons, in all situations and cultural settings. Rather, the various approaches to psychotherapy may be viewed as complementary alternatives for aiding persons in need of psychotherapeutic assistance. For example, drug therapy often may be combined with verbal forms of psychotherapy to achieve results neither form of therapy would yield alone.

Effectiveness of Psychotherapy   704

14. Psychotherapies of various forms have proven to be about equally effective. Several possible explanations for this paradox (i.e., different forms but similar outcomes) have been proposed. The effectiveness of any psychotherapy has to be evaluated against rates of *spontaneous recovery* — that is, recovery without treatment.

15. Each approach to psychotherapy has distinctive advantages and disadvantages, and it may be best to view the approaches as complementary rather than competing. Unfortunately, we have not yet reached the point at which we can prescribe a particular form of therapy for a particular type of psychological problem. Effective therapy generally requires warm involvement of the therapist with the patient, and good communications. In particular, both the therapist and the client need to feel a sense of alliance in trying to overcome the client's difficulties.

16. The length of treatment and other factors not specific to a particular approach also may play a role in the relative effectiveness of psychotherapy.

Ethical Issues in Psychotherapy   706

17. Because psychotherapists have the potential to influence clients profoundly, psychotherapists must be especially mindful of ethical considerations.

KEY TERMS

antidepressant drugs 698

asylums 679

aversion therapy 688

behavioral contracting 690

behavior therapy 687

cathartic method 680

client-centered therapy 686

clinical interview 681

cognitive therapy 692

counterconditioning 688

countertransference 685

electroconvulsive therapy (ECT)
695

extinction procedures 689

flooding 689

free association 684

implosion therapy 689

informed consent 707

modeling 691

psychosurgery 696

psychotherapy 679

psychotropic drugs 697

rational-emotive behavior therapy
692

resistances 684

social problem solving 695

spontaneous recovery 698

stress-inoculation therapy 694

systematic desensitization 688

token economy 690

transference 685

IN SEARCH OF THE HUMAN MIND:
ANALYSES, CREATIVE EXPLORATIONS, AND PRACTICAL APPLICATIONS

1. Under what circumstances might a clinician decide to use each of the techniques for clinical assessment? What information would each technique offer that might be of interest yet, un-obtainable—or difficult to obtain—by other means?

2. Cognitive and behavioral therapies often are paired. What does each technique have to offer that complements the other?

3. If you were a marriage and family therapist, which two psychotherapeutic approaches might you be most likely to use?
    Why would you choose those two methods?

4. Suppose you are a biochemist concocting the next big breakthrough drug that will minimize the problems caused by a particular psychological disorder. If you could choose any disorder to attack and any negative side effects to tolerate, which disorder—and which symptoms of the disorder—would you wish that your drug could minimize? What modest negative side effects would you find least offensive in your new wonder drug?

5. Imagine Shirley Hemlock, a fictional psychotherapist who is the Sherlock Holmes of psychological mysteries. Describe one of Hemlock's most interesting cases. (You can give her any theoretical orientation you wish—including an eclectic approach.)

6. What would you view as an ideal treatment for depression, one that perhaps combines elements of the therapies about which you have read?

7. How might a psychotherapist, who has doubts about the ethics of a new treatment program, go about resolving his or her doubts prior to administering the treatment?

8. If you were to have a need for psychotherapy, which method of therapy would you choose?
    If you were to decide to become a psychotherapist, would your choice be the same?
    Analyze the benefits and drawbacks of the method you would prefer in each role.

9. What economical methods can be devised for delivering a high level of mental health services to communities?

Chapter Twenty

HEALTH
PSYCHOLOGY

CHAPTER OUTLINE

Health psychology is the study of the interaction between mental processes and physiological health. We classify illnesses according to whether they are relatively brief or long-lasting.

Psychosomatic medicine, *followed by* behavioral medicine, *both have led to the creation of today's health psychology. The long-standing model for understanding health has focused on the treatment of symptoms and the elimination of disease-causing agents.*

Contemporary models consider the influence of psychological and social factors, as well as biological factors, on health. For example, people's actions regarding their own health are affected by their perceptions of whether they are experiencing a threat to their well-being and whether they are able to prevent or minimize the threat.

A person's physical and psychological health and well-being can be influenced by such aspects of lifestyle as nutrition, exercise, and the prevention of accidents.

Health and vulnerability to disease also are affected by stress, *which involves circumstances that cause a person to feel threatened or challenged in some way. Personality factors—how a person responds to competitiveness, sense of urgency, and anger—also can influence health.*

People seek health services when they experience symptoms. *Recognition of symptoms depends on people's ideas about what constitute signs of illness.*

We perceive pain either because of damage to bodily tissue or because of psychological factors that seem not to have identified physiological causes. Clinicians often classify pain in terms of its duration and intensity. The choice of pain-control techniques often depends on both the time course and the level of pain.

AIDS is a rare terminal illness contracted largely through contact with the semen or blood of someone who carries the virus for the disease. When people recognize that they have a serious, chronic health problem, they may progress through several stages of reaction before they finally make the needed emotional and cognitive adjustments to the problem. To adapt to chronic illness, people may change themselves, the environment, or both.

Nietzsche is sick, very sick. . . . First of all, tormenting headaches. And continued bouts of nausea. And impending blindness—his vision has been gradually deteriorating. And stomach trouble—sometimes he cannot eat for days. And insomnia—no drug can offer him sleep, so he takes dangerous amounts of morphia. And dizziness—sometimes he is seasick on dry land for days at a time.

—*I. D. Yalom,* When Nietzsche Wept

The quotation is a fictional description of some of the psychosomatic symptoms of the philosopher Friedrich Wilhelm Nietzsche (1844–1900). Although the description is fictitious, Nietzsche indeed suffered from psychosomatic ailments. The quotation illustrates aspects of the field of **health psychology,** the study of the interaction between the mind and the physical health of the body. Note that the interaction of psychological and physiological processes works both ways. In Nietzsche's case, his early physical problems seemed to be psychological in origin. However, after more than a decade of trying to restore his health from apparently psychosomatic symptoms, he eventually developed syphilis, which caused both severe psychological symptoms (including dementia) and physical symptoms.

Health psychologists are interested in the psychological antecedents and consequences of how people remain healthy, how they become ill or prevent illness, and how they respond to illness—such as how they seek to overcome illness or how they adapt to illness that they are unlikely completely to overcome. (Table 20-1 shows some of the questions health psychologists try to answer.)

Health psychologists have observed that people's reactions to illness are usually different when they face an illness that they believe to be **chronic**—recurring or constantly present (e.g., migraine headaches or hypertension)—versus when they suffer from one they believe to be **acute**—intense, but of short duration (e.g., a cold or pneumonia). People with chronic illnesses encounter a variety of psychological challenges usually unrelated to the actual physical cause of the illness, such as depression and anxiety. Therefore, a part of the mission of health psychology is to help people deal with their psychological reactions to serious illness, particularly if the illness has long-term repercussions.

Health psychology is a widely encompassing field. Indeed, some of the topics frequently addressed in the field of health psychology have been covered elsewhere in this book. For example, we discussed sleep and sleep disorders in Chapter 6; drug use and drug treatment in Chapters 6 and 7; normal, healthy development and functioning of the nervous system in Chapters 3 and 12; family and community violence, as they affect health and well-being, in Chapter 15; and hunger, obesity, eating disorders, thirst, and

TABLE 20-1
What Do Health Psychologists Study?
The wide variety of questions investigated by health psychologists may be classified in terms of their goal: maintaining wellness, preventing illness, or responding to illness.

Topic	Questions Addressed	Questions That Psychologists Might Study
Maintenance of wellness	How can people enhance their sense of health and well-being through health-enhancing behavior and lifestyle choices?	Why do many people have difficulty sticking to an exercise or diet program? What situations might make it easier for people to stick to exercise or diet regimens?
Prevention of illness	How do people become vulnerable to illness or injury? How do people prevent illness or injury? How do psychological processes affect people's vulnerability to illness or injury? How do people respond to physical changes that may be symptoms of illness?	Why do many men still choose not to use condoms, despite the risk to both partners of contracting AIDS or other diseases? Why do people smoke, drink heavily, or overeat when they know that these behaviors harm them and make them vulnerable to illness?
Response to illness	How do people respond to becoming ill? How do they respond to long-term illness? How do people with terminal illnesses cope with their situation?	Why do some patients with tuberculosis sometimes stop taking their medicine and thereby render their tuberculosis untreatable? Why do some patients with terminal illnesses seem to cope so well with the situations they face?

sexual motivation in Chapter 16. This chapter covers only those topics of health psychology that have not been covered elsewhere.

HISTORY OF HEALTH PSYCHOLOGY

IN SEARCH OF...

It seems as though we have learned much of what we know about health psychology relatively recently. If that impression is justified, why and how did such rapid growth occur? If that impression is not justified, what gives people that impression?

One of the earliest psychological antecedents of health psychology is the field of psychosomatic medicine, based on a psychodynamic perspective. For much of the century, **psychosomatic medicine** studied how psychological problems might lead to particular kinds of physical diseases, such as ulcers, asthma, and migraine headaches. Although it is arguable whether psychological factors actually *cause* any of these diseases, it is well known that such factors can *exacerbate* these diseases.

By the 1970s, behavioral approaches to psychology became more popular than psychodynamic ones, and behavioral medicine emerged. Originally, **behavioral medicine** focused on the use of behavioral techniques to help people modify health-related problems, such as heavy smoking or overeating (see Chapter 19). Gradually, as the cognitive revolution began to affect all aspects of psychology, the field of health psychology began to embrace a cognitive orientation. Thus, contemporary health psychologists often seek to know how thought processes mediate both wellness and the progression of illnesses.

Many of the historical trends that have influenced health psychology derive from developments in the health field in general. Initially, health practitioners focused their attention exclusively on helping people respond to illness or injury. The illnesses that received the greatest attention were acute (e.g., influenza). If the patient survived the illness—which was by no means assured—the patient required no further care from health professionals. Much less at-

FIGURE 20-1
The 10 Leading Causes of Death: 1900 and 1992
Within this century, the trend has been away from acute infectious diseases and toward chronic diseases and nonmedical causes of death, such as accidents, suicide, and homicide. (After data from Sexton, 1979; National Center for Health Statistics, 1993)

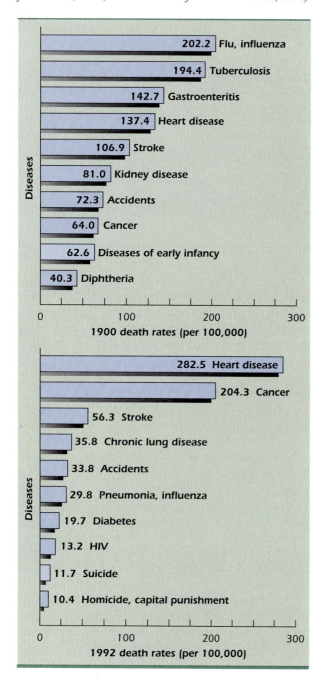

tention was given to illnesses that were chronic (e.g., diabetes). Most illnesses were treated in terms of discrete episodes or symptoms.

This early emphasis on treating disease was entirely appropriate, given the leading causes of death at the time. Times changed, however. Antibiotics and a vast array of other medical treatments virtually wiped out such diseases as smallpox, which had previously devastated huge proportions of the human population. Other diseases—such as influenza, diphtheria, and tuberculosis—became far less deadly. Figure 20-1 shows that in less than a century, influenza moved from being one of the primary causes of death to being the sixth most likely cause of death, and diphtheria, tuberculosis, and diseases of early infancy fell off the top-ten list altogether. Note, however, that homicide and suicide are new on the list, as are such chronic diseases as diabetes.

As medicine's tools for conquering many illnesses—particularly acute ones—have become more powerful, health-care professionals have increasingly turned their attention to trying to help people prevent illness. They encourage people to watch for early symptoms of illness (e.g., digestive difficulties), to seek medical care when warranted (including regular checkups), to avoid behaviors that compromise health (e.g., using psychoactive drugs such as alcohol or nicotine), to take appropriate preventive-medicine steps (e.g., being vaccinated or otherwise immunized), and to engage in appropriate hygiene and safety practices (e.g., washing hands before eating, wearing a safety belt in a moving vehicle). More recently, health psychologists and other health practitioners have been turning their attention to promoting wellness—engaging in health and safety practices that help people not only prevent illness but also promote their overall health and well-being.

When you think of health care for yourself, what issues come to mind? Do you tend to think more in terms of responding to illness, preventing illness, or promoting wellness?

MODELS OF HEALTH AND ILLNESS

IN SEARCH OF...

How and why do you believe that people sometimes become ill and sometimes avoid becoming ill?

Although the field of health psychology may be new, our interest in health is not new. People have been trying to understand the causes of health and illness for centuries. During some epochs of history, the mind was seen as relevant to these causes; in other times, it was not. In some eras of human history, neither the mind nor the body was considered the immediate source of illness. Rather, people believed that illness was sent by one or more divine beings, as a punishment for misbehavior or for disbelief. Ancient literature and legends describe many instances in which a punitive god caused illness or injury to smite those who mistreated believers, who disobeyed divine commandments, or who otherwise showed a lack of respect or belief.

Recall from Chapter 2 that Hippocrates (ca. 430 B.C.) revolutionized ancient Greek medicine with the notion that disease had specific physical origins and was not punishment inflicted by the gods (Taylor, 1991). Consistent with the ancient Greek emphasis on the importance of balance and equilibrium, Hippocrates believed that eating a balanced diet and avoiding excesses in life would help people maintain their health. Few modern physicians would disagree with this recommendation.

Centuries after Hippocrates described his iconoclastic views of health and well-being, Galen (who practiced medicine in Rome, ca. 129–199 A.D.) suggested that illnesses were attributable to specific **pathogens** (disease-causing agents) (Stone, 1979). Eventually, subsequent medical practitioners agreed with him, and Galen's views became the basis for medical treatment for many centuries. Today, of course, we have identified—and even seen, with the aid of microscopes—many more of these pathogens than Galen ever imagined possible.

According to the **biomedical model,** disease is caused by pathogens that have invaded the body; we will be able to eliminate disease if we eliminate the causative pathogens. The model has successfully served people's needs for almost 2,000 years, providing a basis for treating and often for curing illnesses. Nonetheless, the biomedical model has not been universally accepted. Some consider it too mechanistic and too narrow in scope. Although the model centers on how to treat illness and allows for some concern as to how to prevent illness, it gives little consideration as to how to promote wellness. Also, the model gives little attention to psychological factors that contribute to various diseases, and it gives no heed to the psychological processes that may help promote both healing and well-being. Thus, today, we might seek a broader model, one that would incorporate the biomedical model as only a part of our total understanding of health.

The most widely accepted alternative model in health psychology is the **biopsychosocial model,** according to which psychological and social factors, as well as biological factors, can influence health (Engel, 1977; Schwartz, 1982). Actually, most of us seem intuitively to embrace this model, which underscores the importance of context in understanding health and illness. For example, most people believe that factors such as changes in weather, poor diet, lack of sleep, and stress (pressures or strain) can contribute to a cold (Lau & Hartman, 1983). Although a virus may be directly responsible for the cold, other precipitating factors can make it more likely that we will become susceptible to the virus. When we refer to someone as being "worried sick" or as having a "tension headache," we are recognizing that psychological and social factors may contribute to physiological illness.

PROMOTION OF HEALTH: ENHANCING HEALTH THROUGH LIFESTYLE

IN SEARCH OF...

Why do some people seem to go all out to enhance their health, whereas others seem to choose lifestyles that compromise their well-being?

A primary goal of health psychology is to promote health and health-enhancing behavior. Of course, health psychologists recognize that serious psychological and physiological disorders (e.g., eating disorders or cancer) can affect people's health. Nonetheless, health psychologists assume that people can influence their health through the psychological regulation of their behavior. Research supports this assumption, particularly for health-related behavior that is subject to our conscious control.

For example, people can significantly reduce their risk of dying at any given age by following seven health-related practices (Belloc & Breslow, 1972; Breslow, 1983). In fact, the risk of death at a given age has been found to decrease almost linearly with the number of the following health-related practices that have been implemented:

1. sleeping 7 to 8 hours a day
2. eating breakfast almost every day
3. rarely eating between meals
4. being at a roughly appropriate weight in relation to height

5. not smoking
6. drinking alcohol in moderation or not at all
7. exercising or engaging in physical activity regularly

Note that we control many aspects of our health by *not* engaging in harmful, or at least health-compromising, behavior (such as ingesting alcohol, nicotine, or other harmful drugs; see Chapters 6 and 7). In addition, however, we can take positive steps to enhance our health through nutrition and exercise.

For persons of all ages, exercise is one of the key ways to promote health and well-being. The most important aspect of an exercise program is not its intensity or its formality, but rather its consistency of implementation.

Nutrition

We eat for two fundamental reasons: to supply raw materials for building new body tissue, and to supply energy for the body's internal processes and for its interactions with our environment. Having an adequate energy supply not only affects the body's basic functioning (e.g., through the activities of the autonomic nervous system, including respiration, circulation, digestion, repairs, etc.) and its ability to interact with the environment (e.g., through the activities of the somatic nervous system), but it also affects the physiological functioning of the central nervous system (i.e., the brain and spinal cord). In short, brains need food.

Your **metabolism** comprises the processes by which your body captures energy and material resources from food and then eliminates the waste products your body does not use. The two key processes of metabolism are **catabolism,** which involves the breakdown of nutrients (e.g., from proteins into amino acids, from complex to simple compounds), and **anabolism,** which involves the construction of new materials from those nutrients (e.g., making proteins from amino acids, making complex compounds from simple ones). Your metabolism is so efficient in turning food into energy that if you were to measure the food energy you require to ride a bicycle, you could travel about 900 miles on the food energy equivalent to 1 gallon of gas (McCutcheon, 1989). In addition to energy—measured in *calories*—your diet must supply your body with five basic types of nutrients: *carbohydrates, lipids, proteins, vitamins,* and *minerals,* as well as the nonnutritive food element, *fiber.* (See Table 20-2, on the major nutrients other than vitamins and minerals.)

Although some disagreement exists about how much of each of these substances we need, there is broad agreement that a healthful diet (1) is balanced; (2) includes a variety of foods; and (3) contains relatively more complex carbohydrates and fiber, and relatively smaller amounts of fats, especially saturated fats and cholesterol. The consensus is that we need a balance of vitamins and minerals, although the exact amounts we need are open to question. The government has suggested both minimum daily requirements (MDRs) and recommended daily allowances (RDAs) of particular vitamins and minerals, but there is no agreement as to whether the recommended daily allowances are ideal amounts.

Exercise

Exercise also plays a major part in maintaining good health. Although there are several types of exercise (see Table 20-3), by far the most important for overall health and well-being is aerobic exercise. **Aerobic exercise** involves long-duration activities that increase both heart rate and oxygen consumption, thereby enhancing *cardiovascular* (heart and blood vessels) and *respiratory* (breathing) fitness (Alpert, Field, Goldstein, & Perry, 1990). Cardiovascular and respiratory fitness is particularly valuable to psychological well-being because it increases the amount of oxygen reaching the brain, thereby enhancing cognitive and other neurological functions. To sustain an intense level of activity for any length of time, you need to build up your endurance. Aerobic exercises include jogging, speed-walking, running, bicycling, rowing, and swimming.

Many people report that they feel more alert and more generally satisfied with their lives when

TABLE 20-2
Calories, the Major Nutrients, and Fiber
In addition to considering calories, persons interested in promoting health must consider a balance of major nutrients, as well as fiber.

Nutrient	Function in the Body	Psychological Symptoms from Deficiency (D) or Toxicity (T)
Calories	Basic unit of measurement of the energy obtained from food, as measured in terms of its ability to generate heat; energy is required by the body for all of its processes, including the basic metabolic processes required to sustain life.	Deficiency may cause apathy and irritability.
Carbohydrates		
Simple carbohydrates	Major source of readily accessible calories; require no breakdown. Provide the body immediate access to the energy stored in them, but for energy needs of longer duration they're less effective. When the body ingests more simple sugars than it can use immediately, it stores them.	Some correlational studies indicate that a high number of habitually violent persons in prisons show abnormally low blood-sugar levels. Studies of the effects of simple sugars on cognitive performance and mood show no conclusive results.
Complex carbohydrates	Metabolize slower; provide a more stable source of energy.	Provide excellent source of caloric energy, the lack of which can lead to irritability and apathy. A small proportion of schizophrenics may react to grains with increased psychotic symptoms.
Fats (saturated, unsaturated, cholesterol)	A source of energy for the body, they are metabolized only very slowly. Particularly easy to store as fat in the body. Some amount of fat is essential to the body, and fats are particularly important when food is not constantly available.	Fats are better able to penetrate the blood-brain barrier than water-soluble substances, so they can be used either as a benefit (carrying needed elements) or as a detriment (carrying unwanted toxins). Accumulation of cholesterol and other fats in the blood vessels can lead to stroke.
Protein	Used for the construction of new cell material, particularly muscles, hormones, and neurotransmitters.	No known direct effects on psychological state or well-being.
Fiber	Nonnutritive; cannot be metabolized but aids in the elimination of waste products.	No known direct effects on psychological state or well-being.

TABLE 20-3
Types of Exercise
Various types of exercise offer different kinds of benefits to health, with aerobic exercise leading the list in promoting cardiovascular fitness.

Type	Definition	Effect on Health	Example
Aerobic	High-intensity, long-duration activities that increase both heart rate and oxygen consumption	Particularly valuable to overall health and cardiovascular fitness; increases the amount of oxygen reaching the brain, thereby enhancing cognitive and other neurological functions	Jogging, speed-walking, running, bicycling, rowing, swimming
Anaerobic	Does not require increased consumption of oxygen	Does not increase coronary or respiratory fitness, and may even prove dangerous to persons susceptible to coronary disease	Sprinting and games such as baseball or football, all of which require short and intensive bursts of energy
Isotonic	Requires the contraction of muscles and the movements of joints	Helps to develop muscle mass, but does not improve overall cardiovascular fitness	Weight lifting and some forms of calisthenics
Isometric	Occurs when muscles are contracted against unmoving objects; you do not move your body, but rather you contract your muscles against each other and against the object	Increases strength but does not improve overall health	Pushing hard against a wall
Isokinetic	Requires the movement of muscles and joints, but the amount of resistance is adjusted according to the amount of force applied; the more force you exert, the more resistance you will receive	May be superior to isotonic or isometric exercises for enhancing muscle strength, but not for improving overall health and cardiovascular fitness	Using strength-building machines that involve hydraulic or similar systems

they exercise aerobically. Their cardiovascular fitness improves as well. These reactions are physiological responses to the exercise (Leon, 1983; Leon & Fox, 1981). In part, the increased oxygenation of the brain may enhance alertness. Also, recall the discussion in Chapter 6 of *endorphins*, pain-relieving biochemicals that the body produces naturally. It has been conjectured that aerobic exercise triggers the production or release of endorphins, which may partly account for this greater sense of well-being.

Although we do not yet understand all of the mechanisms underlying the psychological benefits of exercise, many studies have tied regular programs of exercise to improvements in self-concept, self-esteem,

and sense of well-being, as well as to reduction of depression (Dubbert, 1992; Hayes & Ross, 1986; Rodin & Plante, 1989; Taylor, 1991). Employee fitness programs, which have become increasingly common, have even resulted in reduced absenteeism, increased job satisfaction, and lowered health-care costs (Rodin & Plante, 1989).

In the past 24 hours, what have you had to eat and drink? In the past week, in what aerobic exercise activities have you participated? How well are you currently promoting your wellness through your lifestyle?

Searchers . . .   JUDITH RODIN

Judith Rodin is President of the University of Pennsylvania and Professor in the psychology department.

Q: *How did you become interested in psychology and in your area of work in particular?*

A: I became interested in psychology through a wonderful introductory course that taught me a love of and an excitement about the discipline. I've always been interested in how biology and psychology connect and what biological processes are influenced by state of mind and events in the environment. Psychology gave me the opportunity to study that empirically. My whole career has been about figuring out the interconnections among subdisciplines within psychology, and between psychology and other fields.

Q: *Whose ideas have influenced you the most?*

A: I was very influenced by William James's thinking and writings. And my mentor, Stanley Schachter, played a major role in the development of my ideas and thinking.

Q: *What is your greatest asset as a psychologist?*

A: I'm deeply interested in the world around me; I puzzle about questions of human behavior, both as a hobby and as a profession; and I believe in the empirical approach to understanding human behavior.

Q: *What makes a psychologist really great?*

A: A love of the field, a thirst for problem solving, an acute understanding of human behavior, an ability to think analytically, and creativity.

Q: *How do you get your ideas for research?*

A: I observe people and think about what motivates certain behaviors. I look at data; a lot of my work is very data driven. And I talk to my students and colleagues. I prefer to think out loud with other people and generate ideas by interacting with others.

Q: *How do you decide whether to pursue an idea?*

A: Schachter taught us to distinguish between the A and the B+ ideas, because there are more good things to study than there are hours in the day or money to do the work. So I always ask myself, "How important is the question? How informative will this experiment be in answering that question? Are there better or different ways to do it? Do I need more techniques or more pilot work before I start something that's in this area? And how excited am I by it?" I use my instincts.

Q: *How have you developed an idea into a hypothesis?*

A: One of the earliest ideas was the importance of control in determining not only motivation and behavior, but also psychological and physical well-being. We decided to explore this in a setting that had high external validity. Our goal in developing a specific testable hypothesis was to show that enhanced control in older people would have beneficial effects across a wide variety of domains. Using a nursing home had the qualities of a closed setting while still being a real-world environment.

Q: *What obstacles have you experienced in your work?*

A: It was very hard early on to develop the support and resources for doing medical intervention research. Psychologists were viewed as not sufficiently skilled or trained to do biomedical research. I overcame these obstacles by convincing my medical colleagues that what we were doing was sound, interesting, and exciting, and that they would learn from it, too.

Q: *What is your major contribution to psychology?*

A: Work that helped to demonstrate the integration of the biological bases of behavior in humans. Also, helping to develop the fields of health psychology and behavioral medicine will be, I imagine, my most long-lasting and fundamental contribution.

Q: *What do you want students to learn from you?*

A: Never to stop at the boundaries of what you think your knowledge or training would suggest. If a problem grabs you, run with it and try to understand it from beginning to end, even if that means learning new techniques or developing them yourself.

Q: *What advice would you give to someone starting in the field of psychology?*

A: You can develop ideas from your own experience, but confirming them requires the scientific approach to the study of human behavior. Also, psychology is enormously exciting and diverse; you will never tire of it.

Q: *Apart from your life as an academic, how have you found psychology to be important?*

A: I understand human behavior better in general, but it has been very helpful in parenting in particular.

Q: *What would you like people to remember about your work?*

A: That it made a fundamental contribution. That it opened new fields, broke down some old paradigms, and stimulated a lot of research by other people.

Company-sponsored employee exercise programs often yield financial benefits for the employer, as well as fitness benefits for the employees.

Accident Prevention

Previous chapters have mentioned some of the ways in which human behavior leads to serious health consequences. For example, Chapter 18 discussed suicide—a health-related phenomenon clearly tied to psychology and often misidentified as accidental death (e.g., some fatal one-car-collision "accidents"). Chapter 15 explored some of the health-related consequences of aggression, including family and community violence (such as molestation and rape), which resulted in the assault, maiming, and murder of more than 2 million Americans in 1991 (according to the FBI 1991 *Uniform Crime Reports*).

Accidents also have grave consequences for human health. According to the United States Department of Labor (1987), accidents are the fourth most frequent cause of death for Americans in general and the leading cause of death in Americans under the age of 45. Clearly, health psychologists should place a high value on preventing accidents, at least from the standpoint of serving society's needs.

Numerous researchers and practitioners have attempted to reduce the incidence of accidents, especially traffic accidents. Some attempts have been more effective than others. One approach is for us to try to change ourselves by increasing our knowledge or skills or by trying to change our attitudes (see Chapter 14) toward safe ways in which to adapt to our environments. Another approach is to try to change the environment, so that the environment can adapt to our existing cognitive capabilities and psychological motivations. Knowledge of human perception, consciousness, and cognition may help in designing appropriate environmental interventions.

For example, we know that drivers must constantly and vigilantly attend to myriad perceptual details all at once (not even considering possible distractions to the driver). If we can find ways to alert drivers to crucial safety-related information, we may help drivers avert accidents. According to Leon S. Robertson (1986), an effective way of preventing some vehicle accidents has been to mount the extra brake light in the center of the vehicle, above the trunk.

STRESS, PERSONALITY, AND ILLNESS

IN SEARCH OF...

How do you react to the potentially stressful situations you confront? How do your reactions affect your health and well-being?

Some personality factors may make people susceptible to illness. As has been the case for many other psychological phenomena, individual personality differences may interact with factors in the environment to contribute to the relationship between personality and illness. In other words, these interactions create *stress*. What is stress, and how does it affect people?

Stress

Usually, when we think of stress, we think of feeling mentally and perhaps even physically distressed from something external such as time pressure, work pressure, or family pressure. That implicit definition works pretty well, but is only part of the picture. When researchers investigate stress, they define the term in a slightly different way. **Stress** is the situation in which some factor (or factors) in the environment causes a person to feel threatened or challenged in some way. **Stressors** (situations or events that create the stress) are changes in the environment that cause the person to have to adapt to or cope with the situation, and these adaptations are **stress responses.**

Stressors

Surprisingly, stressors do not necessarily have to be things we perceive as negative. For example, having a new baby, getting married, and moving to a new home are all stressors because they require the new parent, spouse, or home-dweller to adapt in many ways. Table 20-4 shows the *Social Readjustment Rating Scale* (SRRS), which lists the 43 stressors that seem to affect our health and well-being (Holmes & Rahe, 1967). Note that most of us would welcome many of these stressors, such as outstanding personal achievement or marriage. Many other stressors are measured only in terms of change, without indicating whether the change is positive or negative: change in financial status, living conditions, residence, school, recreation,

TABLE 20-4
Social Readjustment Rating Scale
Thomas Holmes and Richard Rahe analyzed the life events that lead to stress and assigned various weights to each of these potential stressors. (After Holmes & Rahe, 1967)

Rank	Life Event	Mean Value	Rank	Life Event	Mean Value
1	Death of spouse	100			
2	Divorce	73	23	Son or daughter leaving home	29
3	Marital separation	65	24	Trouble with in-laws	29
4	Jail term	63	25	Outstanding personal achievement	28
5	Death of close family member	63	26	Spouse begins or stops work	26
6	Personal injury or illness	53	27	Begin or end school	26
7	Marriage	50	28	Change in living condition	25
8	Fired at work	47	29	Revision of personal habits	24
9	Marital reconciliation	45	30	Trouble with boss	23
10	Retirement	45	31	Change in work hours or conditions	20
11	Change in health of family member	44	32	Change in residence	20
12	Pregnancy	40	33	Change in schools	20
13	Sex difficulties	39	34	Change in recreation	19
14	Gain of new family member	39	35	Change in church activities	19
15	Business readjustment	39	36	Change in social activities	18
16	Change in financial state	38	37	Mortgage or loan less than $10,000	17
17	Death of close friend	37	38	Change in sleeping habits	16
18	Change to different line of work	36	39	Change in number of family get-togethers	15
19	Change in number of arguments with spouse	35	40	Change in eating habits	15
20	Mortgage over $10,000	31	41	Vacation	13
21	Foreclosure of mortgage or loan	30	42	Christmas	12
22	Change in responsibilities at work	29	43	Minor violations of the law	11

social activities, the health status of a family member, and so on.

Note also that not all stressors are alike. In the SRRS, Thomas Holmes and Richard Rahe ranked the 43 stressors and assigned different weights to them; for example, getting married was rated as more stressful—more challenging—than having trouble with a boss. These researchers then correlated the stressors with the likelihood of becoming ill. They found that this likelihood was positively correlated with the person's increasing totals for the weighted values of these stressors. (Recall, however, the difficulties in determining causality based on correlational evidence alone.)

Stressors also can be relatively minor or transient changes, such as being on vacation from work, going away for a weekend, or having a treasured friend or family member visit for a few days. These pleasant changes are stressors because they cause you to adapt in some way: In the middle of the night in your luxury hotel, you must find your way to the bathroom; while your best friend is visiting, you must cope with new demands on your time and on your physical space. Stressors even can be routine annoyances or challenges to your ability to cope, such as traffic hassles, disagreements with an acquaintance, disputes with a bureaucratic functionary, getting accustomed to new equipment or appliances, rearranging items in a cabinet, or having to have a vehicle repaired. Chronic stress can impact adversely health and well-being (House & Smith, 1985) and lead to psychological dysfunction (Eckenrode, 1984). Ultimately, stress encountered on the job may lead to *burnout*—a feeling of emotional exhaustion and distance from people whom you are supposed to serve on the job, and the sense that you are no longer accomplishing anything meaningful in your work.

Shortly after the SRRS was introduced in 1967, the scale was introduced to other countries, either in its original form or in an adapted form. Research on its cross-cultural implementation suggests that the scale does have wide cross-cultural applicability, but that some of the items, some descriptions of the items, and some of the weightings and rankings given to the items may need to be adapted to suit different cultural contexts. An early study illustrates both the utility and the need for adaptation of the scale across cultures: The responses of 266 Malaysian medical students were compared with a matched sample in the Seattle, Washington, area where the SRRS originated. Although there were many similarities in the responses to the scale, there were also significant differences. In particular, items dealing with romantic love and with infringement of laws produced most of the differences (Woon, Masuda, Wagner, & Holmes, 1971). In a later study of Chinese subjects, events related to family and to career were rated as more stressful than were those related to personal habits, such as social activities and living conditions (Hwang, 1981).

Another major stressor, not included in the SRRS, is the adjustment associated with adapting to a new culture. The technical term for stress of this kind is *acculturative stress*. Acculturative stress can range from relatively minor (e.g., voluntary migration to be with loved ones or to seek out more desired lifestyle options) to catastrophic (e.g., totally involuntary uprooting, as in the case of religious or ethnic persecution or even threat of genocide). Such stress has particularly interested cross-cultural psychologists who live in pluralistic societies in which new immigrants continue to arrive (see Berry, 1994; Berry, Kim, Minde, & Mok, 1987).

Stress Responses

Environmental events alone do not create stress; the individual must *perceive* the stressor and must respond to the stressor in some way. Often—initially, at least—the primary response of the individual is physiological. When we feel challenged (e.g., by the need to adapt) or threatened (e.g., by some threat to our safety or well-being), our bodies physiologically prepare us to confront the challenge ("fight") or to escape from the threatening situation ("flight"). Not surprisingly, this physiological fight-or-flight response probably has adaptive evolutionary origins.

The physiological fight-or-flight response was discovered by accident. Hans Selye was seeking a new sex hormone when he accidentally happened across a surprising phenomenon: When the body is attacked or is somehow damaged, it seems to respond in the same general way, regardless of the nature of the assault (e.g., shock, extreme temperatures, or fatigue) or the target of the damage (e.g., the whole body or only a particular body part or organ). Selye soon saw the potential ramifications of this discovery, and he shifted his research to focus on this puzzling physiological response. Selye and other researchers have noted some patterns in our physiological response, which Selye (e.g., 1976) termed the **general adaptation syndrome** (GAS). There appear to be three phases of response: alarm, resistance, and exhaustion (see Figure 20-2).

ALARM.   The body immediately is aroused, and the sympathetic nervous system triggers the release of hormones from the adrenal glands—corticosteroids,

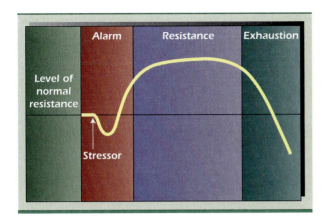

FIGURE 20-2

General Adaptation Syndrome (GAS)

According to Hans Selye, we undergo three phases in responding to stressors: an alarm phase, *in which we shift into high gear, using up our bodily resources at a rapid rate; a* resistance phase, *in which we somewhat shift down to using our resources in a spendthrift manner; and an* exhaustion phase, *in which our bodily resources are depleted. (After Selye, 1974)*

epinephrine (adrenaline), and norepinephrine (noradrenaline). These hormones increase heart and respiration rate; slow down or stop the activity of the digestive tract, making more blood available to other organs; trigger biochemical reactions that create tension in the muscles; increase energy consumption, which produces heat; increase perspiration, which helps cool the body; and increase the release of clotting factors into the bloodstream, to minimize blood loss in case of injury. All these highly adaptive physiological responses go on without our ever having to initiate them consciously.

RESISTANCE.   The alarm state cannot continue indefinitely, and the body imposes a counterbalance to the sympathetic nervous system's plundering of the body's energy stores. Quite soon, the parasympathetic nervous system (which is involved in anabolic, energy-storing processes) calls for more prudent use of the body's reserves. For example, the demands on the heart and lungs decline. Physiological stress responses generally decrease in intensity, although they do not return to normal if the perceived stress continues.

EXHAUSTION.   Eventually, even at the reduced rates associated with the resistance phase, the body's reserves are exhausted, its ability to restore damaged or worn-out tissues is diminished, and its resistance to *opportunistic infections* (infections that take advantage of a weakened immune system or other vulnerability)

decreases. Stress has been linked now to a large number of infectious diseases, including various types of herpes virus infections (such as cold sores, chicken pox, mononucleosis, and genital lesions) (Cohen et al., 1992; Cohen, Tyrell, & Smith, 1991; Cohen & Williamson, 1991; Jemmott & Locke, 1984; Kiecolt-Glaser & Glaser, 1987; VanderPlate, Aral, & Magder, 1988). Not only stress itself, but even the anticipation of stress, can result in suppressed functioning of the immune system (Kemeny, Cohen, Zegans, & Conant, 1989). Researchers in the dynamic, cross-disciplinary field of psychoneuroimmunology revel in the findings being discovered almost daily regarding how our psychological processes, our neural physiology, and our immune systems interact in ways we never imagined—let alone understood—previously.

Personality and Perceived Stress

How does personality come into the picture? Recall that an individual must *perceive* the stressor for it to have an impact. In all of these studies, it is not the set of events, per se, that results in immune-system compromise, but rather the subjectively experienced stress that results from these events that is significant. For example, if you truly did not notice any need to make any adaptations to a new roommate or a new job, you might not experience these events as being stressful.

Also, each of us perceives some stressors as more distressing than others. For example, suppose that you hate confrontation of any kind and find conflict extremely stressful. Someone else might feel little distress in confrontational situations or might even relish conflict. Both you and your adversarial counterpart may experience the physiological alarm phase of the stress response and even the resistance phase, but because you fret about the confrontation for a while afterward you may reach the stage of exhaustion, whereas your antagonist may forget about the conflict moments after it ends, thereby avoiding the exhaustion phase. The notion that perception affects physiology is not new, as shown in the saying regarding mind over matter, "If you don't mind, it doesn't matter."

Each of us also experiences different degrees of internal conflict in response to external demands (work versus family, spouse versus friend, etc.). Moreover, the very same environment can be experienced as quite different, depending on personality variables. An extrovert who works in a library serving a remote community of illiterates might be about as distressed as an introvert who leads all the recreational activities for a cruise ship. Each, however, would consider the other's job idyllic.

Think about your own pet peeves or the situations you love to hate. What things might literally make you sick? Now think about who might consider these peevish situations pleasant. What is it in your personality that makes some situations sickeningly stressful and others quite tolerable?

Susan Folkman and Richard Lazarus (Folkman & Lazarus, 1988; Folkman, Lazarus, Gruen, & DeLongis, 1986) have proposed a model for the way personality factors, stressful circumstances, and health interact. According to Folkman and Lazarus, when confronted with a potentially stressful situation, we first go through a two-step appraisal process and then a two-dimensional coping process, both of which interact with our distinctive personalities and the situation at hand (see Figure 20-3). In **primary appraisal,**

we analyze just how much of a stake we have in the outcome of handling the particular situation. If we have no stake in the outcome, the entire process stops right there.

For example, suppose that I were to tell you of an alarming situation at your college: Some professors have been observed wearing dirty socks! You cannot let this situation continue! Right this instant, you must write a letter to the faculty senate of your college, urging the senate to pass a policy insisting that professors wear clean socks at all times! You must get the letter into the mail immediately!

Did you feel your stress level go up? Probably not. You probably have very little stake in persuading professors to wear clean socks. You may even decide to ignore my urgent plea altogether. Now, compare that level of stress with the level of stress you feel when you think about the final examinations in all of your courses. Unless you are an extraordinarily re-

FIGURE 20-3
An Integrated Model of Stress

The biopsychosocial model of stress incorporates psychological factors, such as cognitive appraisal, as well as physiological mechanisms in responding to stress.

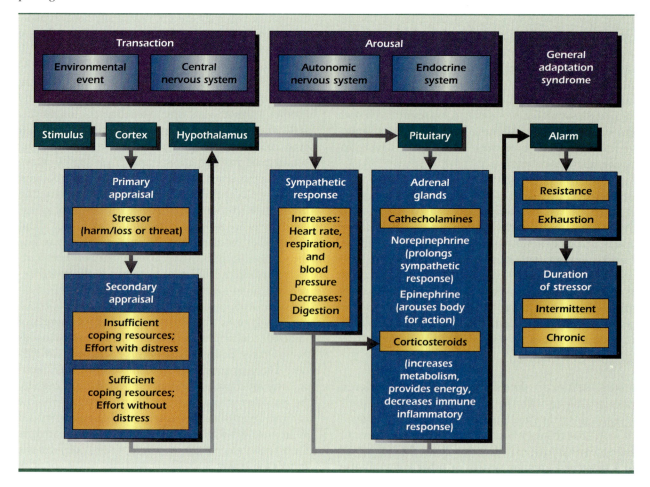

laxed student, you probably appraise final exams as being something in which you have a lot at stake. In considering final exams, you would proceed to the next step in the appraisal process: secondary appraisal.

In **secondary appraisal,** we assess what we can do to maximize the likelihood of potentially beneficial outcomes and to minimize the likelihood of potentially harmful outcomes of the situation. In thinking about final exams, you would probably try to assess how you could increase the probability that you would score well and decrease the possibility that you would score poorly on any of your exams. Reading textbooks and studying lecture notes might figure prominently in your secondary appraisal.

Note that both primary and secondary appraisal proceed at a cognitive level. At this level, you have yet to crack a book or jot a note. Once your primary and secondary appraisals are complete, you are ready to begin **coping** with the situation—that is, actually trying to manage the internal and external challenges it poses. The two dimensions of coping serve two different functions. **Problem-focused coping** tackles the problem itself and involves strategies to resolve it. For example, you would study the textbook, attend study sessions, and review your lecture notes as problem-focused coping strategies. **Emotion-focused coping** involves handling your own emotions to the problem. For example, while studying for the exams, you might try to suppress your anxiety about the exams. Just before taking the exams, you might try some relaxation techniques to reduce your anxiety during the exam.

In circumstances over which we have more control (e.g., exam grades), problem-focused coping strategies are more likely to yield more satisfactory outcomes. In those circumstances over which we have less control (e.g., what questions your instructor will ask on the exam), emotion-focused coping is more likely to yield more satisfactory outcomes. As you might imagine, myriad interactions are possible, depending on the individual's primary appraisal of what is at stake, the person's secondary appraisal of what coping options are available, and the person's implementation of those coping options. The net interaction determines the degree of stress that the individual experiences. According to Folkman and Lazarus, detrimental health consequences are associated with situations in which the person experiences greater stress, particularly if the person feels that his or her options for coping are inadequate for the situation at hand. Low self-esteem and lack of social support can also contribute to the sense of having inadequate options for coping in a given situation (DeLongis, Folkman, & Lazarus, 1988).

Thus, our psychological processes affect our choices in health-related behaviors, and they affect our responses to potentially stressful situations. How else might our personal psychological characteristics affect our health?

Type-A Versus Type-B Behavior Patterns

Like Selye's discovery of the physiological response to stress, a set of personality variables linked to health was discovered quite by accident. Meyer Friedman and Ray Rosenman (1974) were studying the differences in dietary cholesterol between male victims of heart disease and their wives when one of the wives commented, "If you really want to know what is giving our husbands heart attacks, I'll tell you. It's stress, the stress they receive in their work, that's what's doing it" (p. 56). This comment led the researchers to look at differences not only in levels of stress experienced by the victims of heart disease, but also in how these victims responded to stress.

Eventually, they formulated the notion of the **Type-A behavior pattern,** which has three basic characteristics: (1) a competitive orientation toward achievement, (2) a sense of urgency about time, and (3) elevated feelings of anger and hostility. Type-A's tend to strive very hard and competitively toward achieving goals, often without feeling much enjoyment in the process; they tend constantly to be racing against the clock; and they tend easily to experience anger and hostility toward other people.

In contrast to the Type-A is the **Type-B behavior pattern,** characterized by relatively low levels of competitiveness, urgency about time, and hostility. Type-Bs tend to be more easygoing, relaxed, and willing to enjoy the process of life as they live it. Before you read on, stop for a moment to reflect on which pattern describes your own behavior. (*Clue:* If you felt angry at the suggestion to take the time to stop working toward your goal of finishing this chapter as quickly as possible, perhaps you do not need to think too much about which pattern best describes you.) If you are unsure of how you would describe yourself, think about how a family member or a close friend might describe your behavior.

A variety of methods have sprung up for measuring Type-A behavior. These measures include both structured interviews, which ask a more or less fixed set of questions, and paper-and-pencil questionnaires. For example, the *Jenkins Activity Survey* (JAS) (Jenkins, Zyzanski, & Rosenman, 1979), a self-report questionnaire, asks questions such as these: When you listen to other people talking, do you sometimes wish that they would hurry up and say what they have to say? Do you tend to set deadlines or quotas for getting work done? Would people you know agree that you tend to be easily irritated? Do you find that you are often doing things in a hurry?

> Think about the characteristics of the Type-A and the Type-B behavior patterns, and design a behavioral self-report questionnaire to differentiate Type-A from Type-B personalities. Tell which items fit each pattern and why they fit as they do.

Differential Reactions to Stress

Type-A individuals tend to react differently to stress than do Type-B individuals. Type-A individuals generally respond more quickly and forcefully and tend to view sources of stress as threats to their personal self-control (Carver, Diamond, & Humphries, 1985; Glass, 1977). Type-A people also act in ways that increase the likelihood that they will encounter stress. In other words, they create some of the stress in their own lives by seeking out demanding, competitive situations, and by creating artificial deadlines for themselves (Byrne & Rosenman, 1986; Smith & Anderson, 1986).

The critical question from the standpoint of this chapter is whether Type-As are more susceptible to health problems than are Type-Bs. A number of studies have found a link between Type-A behavior and coronary heart disease (Booth-Kewley & Friedman, 1987; Haynes, Feinleib, & Kannel, 1980; Haynes & Matthews, 1988). However, some studies have not confirmed the link (e.g., Shekelle et al., 1985). It ap-

pears that merely linking Type-A behavior to coronary heart disease is too simplistic. For example, Suzanne Haynes and Karen Matthews (1988) found that Type-A behavior leads to increased risk of coronary heart disease for men with white-collar jobs but not for those with blue-collar ones.

It also appears that the three components of Type-A behavior may not contribute equally to heart attack. Redford Williams (1986) argued that the component of anger and hostility is the most lethal (see also Taylor, 1990). Other studies have supported this position (e.g., Barefoot, Dahlstrom, & Williams, 1983). Anger and hostility directed against the self may be especially damaging to health (Dembroski et al., 1985; Williams, 1986). Also, hostility characterized by suspiciousness, resentment, frequent anger, and antagonism toward others seems to be especially deleterious to health (Barefoot et al., 1989; Dembroski & Costa, 1988; Smith, 1992; Williams & Barefoot, 1988).

Possible Physiological Mechanisms for Health Effects

Researchers agree that Type-A individuals experience more stress than do Type-B individuals, and greater levels of stress are linked to coronary heart disease. Although scientists are not certain of the exact physiological mechanisms that link stress to coronary heart disease, they are likely to espouse one of three major theories. One theory suggests that perceived stress causes the blood vessels to constrict while the heart rate increases. Thus, in effect, when people perceive stress, their bodies try to pump larger volumes of blood through narrower, more constricted vessels.

Two personality patterns seem to influence the likelihood of coronary heart disease. Persons with a Type-A personality pattern (such as the woman on the left) feel a sense of urgency to complete tasks and to achieve success, and they easily are angered when things do not go well. Persons with a Type-B personality pattern (such as the woman on the right in a business meeting) seem to be able to respond to work pressures without feeling undue urgency, compulsion to achieve success, or high levels of hostility in response to minor frustrations.

This process may wear out the coronary arteries, lead to lesions (areas of injury or disease), and eventually produce a heart attack (Eliot & Buell, 1983). Another theory suggests that hormones activated by stress may cause rapid and continual change in blood pressure, undermining the resilience of blood vessels (Glass, 1977; Haft, 1974; Herd, 1978). A third possibility is that stress may also cause lipids to be released into the bloodstream, which contributes to *atherosclerosis*, a disease in which the fatty deposits constrict the blood vessels, making them rigid and thereby hampering circulation. Of course, these possibilities are not mutually exclusive, so each may contribute to the net detrimental effect (Laragh, 1988; Parfyonova et al., 1988).

Possible Options for Intervention

Type-A behavior appears to be at least somewhat modifiable (Levenkron & Moore, 1988). A variety of techniques have been used, including relaxation (Roskies et al., 1978), aerobic exercise, weight training, and cognitive-behavioral stress management (Blumenthal et al., 1988; Roskies et al., 1986). To a certain extent, as mentioned in earlier chapters, we can influence our perceptions by changing our cognitions. Thus, interventions to increase the functioning of the immune system tend to be oriented toward improving people's reactions to events so they feel less distressed in the face of life's challenges. In addition, lifestyle changes might be appropriate interventions. Type-A individuals tend to have very different lifestyles from those of Type-B individuals, and it may be as much the lifestyle as the personality itself that leads to coronary heart disease.

Design a program for a Type-A individual to help that person to be more resistant to the ill effects of Type-A behavior. Include some of the techniques mentioned, as well as some appropriate cognitive techniques for handling stressful situations (e.g., telling her/himself, "Even if this guy cuts me off on the freeway, I will still make it to work on time").

Shall I tell you my theory? We're all going to get either cancer or heart disease. There are two human types, basically, people who bottle their emotions up and people who let it all come roaring out. Introverts and extraverts if you prefer. Introverts, as is well known, tend to internalise their emotions, their rage and their self-contempt, and this internalisation, it is equally well known, produces cancer. Extraverts, on the other hand, let joyous rip, rage at the world, divert their self-contempt on to others, and this over-exertion, by logical process, causes heart attacks. It's one or the other.

—*Julian Barnes*, Talking It Over

Psychological Processes and Healing

We are beginning to understand some of the ways our personalities may affect our physical health and well-being. In addition, we are beginning to recognize some of the ways psychological processes can influence the physiological healing of the body. Chapter 6 hinted about some of the ways in which hypnosis and meditation can be used to influence health-related practices; whether it also might be used to influence physiological processes is unknown. Anthropologists have long recorded anecdotes about apparently nonmedical, spiritual rituals that seem to invoke trancelike states in patients who subsequently recover from illness or injury. Even less exotic psychological states may influence our health. Emotions may play a role in healing. Some have suggested that laughter has a restorative effect (Restak, 1988), and others suggest that expressing sadness (such as crying) may offer recuperative properties (Moyers, 1993). Even physicians generally acknowledge the power of a positive attitude to effect recovery and healing. In fact, physicians can influence their patients' attitudes toward recovery through their interactions with their patients.

USING HEALTH SERVICES

IN SEARCH OF...

What prompts you to seek health services? Are there other prompts to which you should be sensitive?

Recognition and Interpretation of Symptoms

The first step in obtaining medical treatment for illness is to recognize and interpret symptoms. **Symptoms** are any unusual feelings in the body (e.g., a queasy stomach), or any observable features of the body (e.g., an itchy rash on the neck), thought to indicate some kind of pathology. Symptoms are, by definition, from the patient's point of view (in medicine, any unusual features observed by the physician are termed **signs**). For the most part, people seek health services only when they believe themselves to have symptoms.

When clinicians make diagnoses based on people's reported symptoms and observed signs, the clinicians use *explicit theories* for mentally representing various illnesses. Nonclinicians are not without mental models, however. Most nonphysicians have *implicit theories*—commonsense schemas—of illnesses and of the symptoms they comprise. These schemas help people to organize the information they know regarding various diseases. In addition to the identity of the illnesses, this information includes the symptoms, probable consequences, relative seriousness, and probable duration of the illnesses. As mentioned, people also distinguish between acute illnesses and chronic illnesses (Nerenz & Leventhal, 1983). For example, it appears that people are more likely to seek medical help if they have clear labels to attach to the symptoms that they experience and if they believe that their symptoms are treatable (Lau, Bernard, & Hartman, 1989).

We use schemas to recognize and interpret our symptoms, matching the sensations or observations we perceive with our existing schemas for illness and wellness. If the sensations or observations seem to match our schemas for illness more closely than our schemas for wellness, we are more likely to attribute our sensations and observations to being sick (or injured), and we think of them as symptoms. If the sensations and perceptions more closely match our schemas for wellness, we are less likely to attribute our sensations and observations to being symptoms of illness. Our expectations regarding our health also affect how we match our sensations and observations to our existing schemas.

Interactions Between Medical Practitioners and Patients

Patient Styles

Medical schools gradually have come to appreciate a problem that users of medical services have long recognized: The physician who received the highest grades in medical school or even who is more technically competent is not necessarily the one who interacts best with patients. In fact, no necessary relationship exists between the quality of physicians' academic grades and the quality of their interactions with patients. To be most effective, a medical practitioner needs to take into account not only the medical condition but also the distinctive psychological needs of the individual patient. Researchers have found that patients are more satisfied with their treatment if they are able to participate in the treatment in a way that matches their own preferences with respect to their perceived needs (Auerbach, Martelli, & Mercuri, 1983; Martelli, Auerbach, Alexander, & Mercuri,

1987). Those preferences, based on a health-opinion survey (Krantz, Baum & Wideman, 1980), include (1) preference for information about health care, (2) preference for self-care, and (3) preference for involvement in health care.

Physician Styles

Physicians, too, have distinctive preferences and styles for patient–physician interactions. P. Byrne and B. Long (1976) analyzed 2,500 tape-recorded medical consultations in various countries. They found that physicians' interactions with their patients showed one of two different styles. In a **doctor-centered style,** the physicians would ask questions that would encourage the patient to respond in a single, brief, and accurate answer. Furthermore, the physicians would tend to focus on the problem for which the patient made the appointment with the physician. If the patient diverged from the narrow, focused response and mentioned other problems or other symptoms, the doctor tended to ignore the further information. In a **patient-centered style,** the physician was less controlling. Instead of asking only specific questions, patient-centered doctors asked more open-ended questions, which allowed patients to describe more fully the kinds of problems they had. These physicians also were more likely to enable the patient to become a partner in the decision-making process.

Patient-centered doctors were less likely to use medical jargon than were doctor-centered ones. Medical jargon can seriously impede communication between doctors and patients. A number of studies have found that patients, particularly those of lower socioeconomic status, do not understand many of the terms that physicians tend to use (DiMatteo & DiNicola, 1982; McKinlay, 1975). The result of using such jargon is that a physician may give information to a patient, but the patient may not really understand what the physician is saying.

Patients in Hospitals

Responses to Needing Help

Roughly 33 million people are admitted every year to the more than 7,000 hospitals in this country (American Hospital Association, 1987). Over the past three decades, hospital admissions have tended to increase, whereas the length of stay has tended to decrease (American Hospital Association, 1982, 1989).

Most patients feel anxious, confused, and perhaps even depressed when first admitted to the hospital. According to hospital staff, good patients are fully compliant with the hospital procedures and regimens, whereas bad patients may exhibit reactance and are more likely to complain, to demand attention, and to engage in behavior that is contrary to hospital policies. Hospital staff members tend to react negatively to such patients, and they want to have as little to do with them as possible. Ironically, the assertiveness of these patients may result in their being subjected to more risks at the hands of health professionals than are less assertive patients (Lorber, 1975). Hospital staff members are more likely to deal with such patients by medicating them, ignoring them, referring them to psychiatric care, or discharging them before they are ready.

When you stop to think about the kinds of behavior that are being fostered in this setting, you may realize that the hospital setting actually encourages patients to think and act in a manner that we described previously as *learned helplessness* (Raps et al., 1982; Taylor, 1979) (see Chapter 7). Learned helplessness discourages patients from actively participating in their own recovery (Brown, 1963; Taylor 1979). Unfortunately, although this behavior is adaptive for getting help from hospital staff members, learned helplessness can be detrimental to recovery, both in the hospital and after leaving it. Once patients leave the hospital setting, they are then expected suddenly to take full responsibility for all aspects of their recovery, despite having adaptively learned not to take any responsibility whatsoever for their in-hospital recovery.

Increasing Patients' Sense of Control

If hospitals tend to foster a lack of sense of control in the patient, and if a sense of control is important for patients' well-being and recovery, what can be done? A number of researchers have sought to figure out what hospitals could do to increase patients' psychological as well as physical well-being. Methods for increasing patients' sense of control are **control-enhancing interventions.** In a classic, trailblazing study by Irving Janis (1958), postoperative recovery was compared in three groups—one group with a low level of fear about an impending operation, a second group with a moderate level of fear, and a third group with a high level of fear. Janis also looked at how well patients in each of the three groups understood and were able to utilize the information given them by the hospital about probable aftereffects of the surgery they received. Janis found that patients in the moderate-fear group had the best postoperative recovery.

Subsequent research has shown that what is most important is the extent to which patients process the information given to them in advance about the effects of the surgery, rather than their level of fear per se (Anderson & Masur, 1983; Johnson, Lauver, & Nail, 1989). Patients who are better prepared about what to expect during and after surgery are less emotionally upset after surgery and are also able to leave the hospital more quickly than are uninformed or less informed patients (Johnson, 1984). Others have extended this work to suggest that patients who are prepared in advance regarding what to expect from a variety of medical procedures may feel a stronger sense of personal control and self-efficacy in mastering their reactions (see Taylor, 1990). This enhanced sense of control and efficacy then effects more positive outcomes.

Research further suggests that it is important to teach patients not only *what* will happen during and after surgery, but also *how* they should respond to what happens. One study showed that if patients are instructed to try to distract themselves from those aspects of surgery that are unpleasant, and to try to concentrate instead on the benefits they will receive from the surgery, the patients will need fewer *analgesics* (pain-relieving drugs) after the surgery (Langer, Janis, & Wolfer, 1975). Other effective control-enhancing interventions include learning both relaxation responses and cognitive-behavioral interventions to overcome anxiety and to adapt to the situation more effectively (Ludwick-Rosenthal & Neufeld, 1988).

The preceding studies have shown the benefits of control-enhancing procedures. As we might expect, given the interactive dialectical evolution of scientific research, subsequent studies have shown that there are limitations on what control-enhancing procedures can provide. For one thing, people differ in their desire for control, just as they differ in most other personal attributes (Burger & Cooper, 1979). Patients who are low in their desire for control may become anxious if they are given more control than they would like. Such patients may feel a burden of responsibility or self-blame when asked to make decisions that they do not want to make in the context of a stressful situation, such as the context surrounding surgery (Burger, 1989; Thompson, Cheek, & Graham, 1988). Moreover, giving patients too much information to absorb about operative procedures and about postoperative recovery may make them feel even more distressed than they ordinarily would. Thus, attempts to enhance patients' sense of control may boomerang and actually overwhelm them and make them feel powerless (Mills & Krantz, 1979; Thompson et al., 1988). Although a sense of enhanced control is probably good for most patients in most surgical situations, as indicated, patients do best if the style of the medical worker fits their own style.

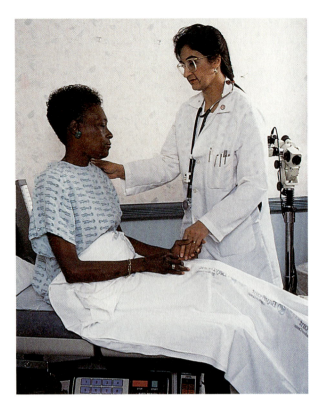

This physician may be able to reassure her somewhat anxious patient by showing sensitivity and empathy to the patient's concerns, as well as by projecting a sense of calmness and competence.

In some ways, hospitalization is most difficult on children, because they have little idea of what is going on or of what to expect. Research suggests that giving children advance information before hospitalization or at least before they undergo surgical procedures, and even showing them films of children undergoing a similar procedure, can help the children in their adjustment to the hospital and the surgical procedures they are about to undergo (Melamed & Siegel, 1975; Pinto & Hollandsworth, 1989). Thus, we should not assume that children should be kept entirely uninformed. On the contrary, they need to be given appropriate information. It also has been found that having a warm and nurturing relationship with someone during their hospitalization, such as a nurse, can help children's adjustment (Branstetter, 1969). Indeed, all patients benefit from having warm relationships while they are confined in a hospital. Such relationships may help mitigate some of the negative aspects of hospitalization and of the illness for which the individual is hospitalized.

> Design an experiment to test the effectiveness of a specific control-enhancing strategy for adults or children.

Although communication may be more difficult with very young children, children of all ages should be advised in advance regarding what to expect before they undergo medical procedures. During hospitalization, children adjust better if they have established a warm and nurturing relationship with hospital members at times when family members cannot be present.

PAIN AND ITS MANAGEMENT

IN SEARCH OF...

Why do we feel pain, and what can we do to minimize our feeling of it?

Pain is the sensory and emotional discomfort associated with actual, imagined, or threatened damage to or irritation of the body (Sanders, 1985). Chapter 4 described the sensory aspects of pain. Here, we discuss the cognitive and emotional aspects of pain, as well as different kinds of pain, how pain is assessed, and what can be done to alleviate it.

Many psychologists conceptualize pain in a way very similar to the popular conception of pain. It has both a *sensory* component (the sensations at the site where the pain originates, such as throbbing, aching, or stinging pain) and an *affective* component (the emotions that accompany the pain, such as fear, anger, or sadness). It seems that these two components are highly interactive (each profoundly affects the other), but it is possible, at least at some level, to distinguish the contribution of each (Fernandez & Turk, 1992).

Our perceptions of pain also interact with our cognitions regarding pain. Based on our own experiences with and observations of pain, we form our own schemas regarding it, as well as beliefs regarding our own ability to control it. The interaction goes both ways. Just as our cognitions are affected by our experiences with pain, our cognitions also affect our perception of it. For example, if we believe that we will be able to overcome our pain, we may be more effective in doing so than if we believe that we will be defeated by our sensations of pain (described as *catastrophizing*, sometimes as a result of learned helplessness). In fact, self-efficacy beliefs may play an important role in pain control (Turk & Rudy, 1992).

One mechanism by which cognition, emotion, and sensation may interact to affect pain perception has been proposed by Ronald Melzack and Patrick Wall (1965, 1982). According to Melzack and Wall's **gate control theory** of pain, the central nervous system serves as a physiological gating mechanism, which can modulate the degree to which pain is perceived. Cognitions and emotions in the brain can cause the spinal cord to intensify or to inhibit pain transmission. That is, some cognitions and emotions may open the gate, lowering our *pain threshold* (the amount of stimulus required to cross the threshold and trigger the sensation of pain), whereas others may close the gate, raising our pain threshold. For example, fearful attention to the possibility of pain may lower our pain threshold, but relaxed attention to other sensations may raise our pain threshold. Naturally, the brain's perception of pain may also affect subsequent emotions and cognitions. The distinct patterns of affect, cognition, and sensation influence the quality—as well as the intensity—of the pain the individual experiences at a given time.

Kinds of Pain

A distinction is sometimes made between organic pain and psychogenic pain. **Organic pain** is caused by damage to bodily tissue. **Psychogenic pain** is the discomfort one feels when there appears to be no physical cause. We need to be careful in labeling pain as "psychogenic" because even if the medical profession has been unable to find an organic source of pain, it does not therefore mean that such pain does not exist or even that no organic cause of the pain exists. The current tools for diagnosis of the sources of

pain are still imprecise (see Turk & Rudy, 1992). Such a cause may exist but simply not have been found. In most cases, the experience of pain represents an interaction between physiological and psychological factors.

The three most common kinds of psychogenic pain are neuralgia, causalgia, and phantom-limb pains. *Neuralgia* is a syndrome in which a person experiences recurrent episodes of intense shooting pain along a nerve (Chapman, 1984; Melzack & Wall, 1982). The cause of this pattern of pain remains a mystery. *Causalgia* is characterized by recurrent episodes of severe burning pain (Melzack & Wall, 1982). People experiencing causalgia may suddenly feel as though a body part or region is on fire or is being pressed against a hot oven. Often, patients experiencing this syndrome have experienced in the past a serious wound in the place where they now feel the burning pain. *Phantom-limb pain* is felt in a limb that either has been amputated or no longer has functioning nerves (Chapman, 1984; Melzack & Wall, 1982). Many patients who have had a limb amputated report feeling this phantom-limb pain, even though they lost the limb years before.

The phenomenon of psychogenic pain shows that the link between the perception of pain and the presence of a known pathology or injury is not certain. Additional evidence of the weakness of this link is the phenomenon in which the experience of pain is delayed for a while after serious injury or is altogether absent despite extreme pathology (Melzack, Wall, & Ty, 1982; see also Fernandez & Turk, 1992).

Time Course of Pain Symptoms

Whether pain is organic or psychogenic, it can be classified as either acute or chronic. **Acute pain** is the discomfort that a person experiences over a relatively short period of time. Some researchers (e.g., Turk, Meichenbaum, & Genest, 1983) have used a time period of 6 months as a somewhat arbitrary cutoff. In other words, the patient who experiences pain over a period of less than 6 months is classified as experiencing acute pain. Pain lasting more than 6 months is referred to as **chronic pain.** Of those patients who seek treatment in pain clinics, the average amount of time they have endured chronic pain is about 7 years (Turk & Rudy, 1992).

Personality and Pain

Given the wide differences in people's thresholds and limits for pain, some investigators have sought to discover whether there is a relation between personality attributes and the experience of pain. Such research might sound relatively easy to do. You just think of a few traits that you believe might be associated with pain perceptions (e.g., perfectionism or emotional sensitivity), and then test to see whether those traits match up to measurements of people's perceptions of pain. The problem with this research is the same one that arises with most correlational studies. Finding a correlation between a personality attribute and the

TABLE 20-5
Methods of Pain Control

Having available a diversity of methods for pain control increases the likelihood that both chronic and acute pains can be brought under control with a minimum of undesirable side effects. Contemporary medical investigators constantly are developing new pharmacological, technological, and psychological methods for controlling pain.

Method	How It Controls Pain	Drawbacks
Pharmacological control	The administration of drugs (e.g., aspirin, acetaminophen, or ibuprofen, or, for more extreme cases, morphine) to reduce pain	Some drugs, such as morphine, are addictive, so their administrations must be controlled carefully. Even the milder drugs can have negative consequences if used in excess or over long periods of time
Patient-controlled analgesia	Intravenous infusion of medication; the patient pushes a button that triggers a pump to release analgesic from a computer-regulated reservoir; the computer regulates the dosage and the frequency, but the patient directly controls the administration of the analgesic; generally used in a hospital or hospice setting when patients suffer from extreme pain	Some risks, but the specially selected patient populations usually minimize the likelihood of addiction
Surgical control	Surgical incision to create lesions in the fibers that carry the sensation of pain; intended to prevent or at least diminish the transmission of pain sensations	The risks associated with surgery, possible side effects, cost, and short-lived positive outcomes have made this technique less preferable
Acupuncture	Originated in Asia; involves the use of needles on particular points on the body; Western adaptation is transcutaneous electrical nerve stimulation (TENS)	Many Western physicians and patients resist its use; may not be as effective in minimizing chronic pain as acute pain
Biofeedback	Feedback from a machine translates the body's responses into a form that the patient can easily observe and therefore bring under conscious control; effective for many patients in treating headaches; biofeedback is an operant-learning procedure (see Chapter 7), in which the operant response is the physiological mechanism believed to lead to the sensation of pain	Because the equipment is expensive and cumbersome, and the technique provides results no better than relaxation training, it may not be the treatment of choice
Hypnosis	Under hypnosis, the patient receives the suggestion that he or she is not feeling pain	Requires that the patient be susceptible to hypnosis or to self-hypnosis
Relaxation techniques	The patient enters a state of low arousal, controls his or her breathing, and relaxes his or her muscles; meditation (Chapter 6) also can induce a state of relaxation	An inexpensive strategy that often proves effective; requires a modest amount of training in implementing the techniques, as well as full patient participation, cooperation, and commitment to use the techniques

(Continued)

experiencing of pain may indicate a relationship between the two, but it does not indicate the direction or the cause of the relationship. That is, someone may be susceptible to experiencing pain because of particular personality attributes, but an equally plausible relationship is that the person acquired those attributes from having experienced the pain. For example, if we were to find a correlation between anxiety or depression and scores on a scale measuring chronic pain, we would scarcely be surprised if we were to learn that the anxiety or depression was caused by the pain, rather than vice versa. It is also possible that both the personality attribute and the experiencing of pain may depend on some higher-order third factor.

Some research has found that scales of the *Minnesota Multiphasic Personality Inventory* (MMPI) (see Chapter 17) can help identify patients who are particularly susceptible to experiencing pain. Michael Bond (1979) has found that patients who experience *acute pain* tend to score especially high on the hypochondriasis and hysteria scales of the MMPI. People high in hysteria tend to show extreme emotional behavior and also tend to exaggerate the level and seriousness of the symptoms they experience. Similarly, Bond found that *chronic-pain* patients tend to score high on hypochondriasis and hysteria, as well as on depression. As it happens, this grouping of three attributes is sometimes referred to as the "neurotic triad" because elevated scores on these three scales are frequently associated with various types of neurotic disorders.

The fact that greater indications of depression are seen in chronic, but not in acute-pain patients, suggests that the depression is a result, rather than a cause, of the pain. However, Thomas Rudy, Robert Kerns, and Dennis Turk (1988) have found that the development of depression may be related not just to the experience of pain itself, but also to the concomitants of pain, such as the reduction in level of activity, a diminished sense of personal control, and a general sense of inability to master the environment.

Control of Pain

How can pain be controlled? A wide variety of techniques have been used (Taylor, 1991). Some of the major methods, described in Table 20-5, include

TABLE 20-5 *(Continued)*

Method	How It Controls Pain	Drawbacks
Guided imagery	Similar to deep relaxation; often viewed as a relaxation exercise; when people are experiencing pain, they imagine scenes that help them cope with the pain	An inexpensive strategy that often proves effective; may require some additional training of patient; requires full patient participation, cooperation, and commitment to its use
Adjunct to relaxation	The most typical and relaxing method is to imagine scenes that are especially pleasant or romantic, that produce feelings of contentment	
Visualization	Patients imagine actively confronting the pain, such as being a soldier or other fighter who ultimately conquers the pain	Effectiveness depends in part on patient's ability to visualize
Sensory control through counterirritation	Involves stimulating or mildly irritating a part of the body that differs from the one experiencing pain; effective in reducing the original pain, perhaps because the patient starts to concentrate on the area that is being irritated	Does not work in all cases or at all times, particularly in cases of severe pain
Distraction	Patients shift their attention away from the pain, to focus on something else; the technique has been used successfully for thousands of years	Does not work in all cases or at all times, particularly in cases of severe pain

pharmacological control (including patient-controlled analgesia), surgical control, sensory control, biofeedback, hypnosis, relaxation techniques, distraction, and guided imagery. Pain-treatment centers across the country use a variety of techniques for helping patients to cope with pain. In many cases, these techniques have been quite successful. The use of these techniques becomes particularly important in cases of chronic pain related to serious illness.

What two factors do you consider to be most important to the treatment of pain? Why are these two factors so important?

LIVING WITH SERIOUS, CHRONIC HEALTH PROBLEMS

IN SEARCH OF...

If a close friend of yours had to confront chronic health problems, what advice would you suggest to your friend as to how to cope?

We often do not truly value our health until we no longer have it. When we recover from acute illnesses, we sometimes briefly cherish our health, only to forget about it after a little while. People with chronic illnesses do not have this luxury. The most dramatic chronic illness of our time is AIDS.

AIDS: Incidence and Prevention

Acquired immune deficiency syndrome, or AIDS, is caused by the human immunodeficiency virus (HIV). HIV, which is a retrovirus—that is, a slow-acting virus—attacks the immune system and especially the *T-cells*, specialized, relatively long-living white blood cells that protect the body at the cellular level (Solomon & Temoshok, 1987). The virus is transmitted by the exchange of bodily fluids that contain the virus, most notably blood and semen.

Being *HIV-positive* (having the HIV retrovirus in the blood) does not mean that the person already has developed AIDS. Individuals differ widely in the time it takes them to develop AIDS from the time they first contract the virus; the latency period can be as long as 8 to 10 years. Even with full-blown AIDS, it is not the AIDS virus itself that kills people, but rather opportunistic infections that thrive in the person's impaired immune system. Common infec-

tions of this type include rare forms of pneumonia and cancer.

Despite its rapid spread, AIDS can be controlled and, in principle, entirely eliminated through behavioral interventions. For example, people who engage in sexual relations should always use condoms during sexual intercourse and restrict their number of sexual contacts. People who inject themselves with drugs should not share needles. Prevention is especially important for this disease because there is no known cure. Moreover, as far as we know, virtually everyone who contracts HIV eventually will develop AIDS. Particular drugs seem to postpone the development of the disease but do not head it off entirely. Tests are now available that can detect HIV antibodies in the body, thereby indicating whether a person has been infected. Of course, the most difficult psychological phenomenon associated with AIDS is living your life as HIV-positive, knowing that you are virtually certain to develop a disease that is, as far as we know, always fatal.

Cliff was the only AIDS patient in the ward, and this was quite unusual, we were told.

"I'm getting tested on Wednesday," Danny said, "but I have no great hopes. I'm sure I'm positive."

"But how are you feeling?" asked Fred. "Have you had any symptoms?"

"No," he said. "Nothing. Although right this minute I think I've got a sore throat coming on. I'm such a hypochondriac." He looked down and sighed. . . .

For the next few days, Fred and I were sure we had it too.

Paul Gervais, Extraordinary People

Psychological Models for Coping with Chronic Illness

Franklin C. Shontz (1975) has proposed a stage model of how people react when they realize that they have a serious, chronic, and probably life-threatening disease. The first stage is one of *shock*. People are stunned, bewildered, and often feel detached from the situation: How can this illness be happening to *me*? The second stage is *encounter*. The person gives way to feelings of despair, loss, grief, and hopelessness. During this stage, people are often unable to function effectively. They do not think well, they have difficulty in planning, and they are ineffective in solving problems. During *retreat*, the third stage, individuals often try to deny the existence of the problem or at least the implications of what the problem means for them. Eventually, however, people reach a fourth stage, *adjustment*, during which they make whatever adjustments are necessary to live with the reality of the disease.

Whereas Shontz's model focuses on the emotional and behavioral aspects of coping, Shelley Taylor (1983; Taylor & Aspinwall, 1990) has proposed an alternative model that highlights the ways people adapt cognitively to serious chronic illness. According to Taylor, patients first try to *find meaning* in the experience of the illness. They may try to figure out what they were doing wrong that led to the illness— and start doing whatever it is right—or they may simply rethink their own attitudes and priorities, in light of their new perspective. Next, patients try to *gain a sense of control* over the illness and over the rest of their lives. They may seek as much information as possible about their illness and its treatment, or they may undertake activities that they believe will help either to restore function and well-being or at least to inhibit the degenerative progress of their illness. Third, patients try to *restore their self-esteem*, despite the offense of being struck by such an illness. They may compare their own situations with those of others, in ways that shed favorable light on their own situations.

Although many people may pass through the stages in the preceding models, we know that individuals differ in terms of their effectiveness in coping. Rudolf Moos (1982, 1988; Moos & Schaefer, 1986) has described a *crisis theory* (shown in Figure 20-4), which attempts to characterize individual differences in people's abilities to cope with serious health problems. According to this model, how well a person copes depends on three sets of factors:

1. *Background and personal factors*, such as emotional maturity, self-esteem, religious beliefs, and age. Men are more likely to respond negatively to diseases that compromise their ability to work; older people will have to live fewer years with a chronic illness than younger ones and thus may be better able to cope with the prospects.
2. *Illness-related factors*, such as how disabling, painful, or life-threatening the disease is. Unsurprisingly, the greater the disability, pain, and threat, the more difficulty people have in coping with the illness.
3. *Environmental factors*, such as social supports, the ability of the person to remain financially solvent, and the kinds of conditions in which the person lives. Some factors may diminish the ability to cope, whereas others may enhance it.

Mariana in the Moated Grange, *a painting by Sir John Everett Millais (1829–1896), was inspired by these lines from Alfred, Lord Tennyson's poem, "Mariana": "She only said, 'My life is dreary./He cometh not,' she said;/She said,'I am aweary,/I would that I were dead!'"*

According to Moos, the coping process has three main components: cognitive appraisal, the decision to adapt, and the development of coping skills. In *cognitive appraisal*, the individual assesses the meaning and significance of the health problem for his or her life. (Note that this kind of cognitive appraisal is similar to the primary and secondary appraisals described by Folkman and Lazarus in the perception of stress and somewhat related to the appraisals involved in symptom recognition and interpretation.) As a result of this cognitive appraisal, the person *decides* how to perform tasks in a way that is adaptive, given the illness. In this way, the person *develops coping skills* for living with the illness. The outcome of the coping process will, in turn, affect the outcome of the crisis in general—how well the person is able to live with the disabling illness.

Ultimately, the key to coping with serious chronic illness is *adaptation*. The individual will need to make changes and adjustments to live happily and effectively. On the one hand, those persons with serious chronic illnesses need to make more effort than practically anyone to adapt to the environment. On the other hand, each of us confronts situations

Searchers . . .   *SHELLEY TAYLOR*

Shelley Taylor is Professor of Psychology and Chair of the Social Psychology Program at the University of California, Los Angeles.

Q: *How did you become interested in psychology and in your area of work in particular?*

A: In college I conducted an experimental study and was so excited by getting data that no one had seen before that it hooked me on conducting research. I chose psychology as the content area because the dynamics of people's thinking and their interactions were the most interesting areas I could think of to study scientifically.

Q: *What theories have influenced you the most?*

A: Much of our training in college was in learning theory, emphasizing stimulus-response relationships. I found this to be a very barren way of thinking about human thought and behavior. I was more interested in processes like cognition and motivation and so I have been most heavily influenced by social cognition research and motivation theories.

Q: *What is your greatest asset as a psychologist?*

A: Really listening to data. If you design a study correctly, the numbers will tell you what is going on, so I spend a lot of time just staring at numbers or listening to interviews until I get to really understand the process that I'm studying.

Q: *What makes a psychologist really great?*

A: One who conducts research that will be informative, that will go beyond whatever preconceptions guided the design of the study.

Q: *How do you get your ideas for research?*

A: Usually from some process I've observed or from knowledge of my own or others' behavior. I rarely design a study that grows out of other studies, simply because I find the contact with the process in its natural environment to be one of the most exciting aspects of research.

Q: *How do you decide whether to pursue an idea?*

A: For me, this process seems to be unconscious. When an idea is ready, it seems to pop into the front of my mind, and then a student and I will work on it together.

Q: *How have you developed an idea into a workable hypothesis?*

A: To develop my work on positive illusions, I used interview data as a hypothesis-generation technique, and then subsequent interview data as a hypothesis-testing opportunity.

Q: *What obstacles have you experienced?*

A: The chief problem I have encountered in conducting research on the illusions that people hold about themselves is how to determine when a belief is an illusion or not. How do you know whether a person is being overly

optimistic or just right? This problem has led me to define illusions in many ways, using multiple methods to converge on the phenomenon. I use interview data, experiments, and different kinds of open- and closed-ended questions to try to define what illusions are.

Q: *What is your major contribution to psychology?*

A: An analysis of how positive illusions contribute to well-being, both in daily life and under conditions of intense stress. We have found that overly positive views are adaptive not only for maintaining well-being, motivation, and performance, but especially when people encounter setbacks. I've conducted much of this research with cancer patients, heart disease patients, and people diagnosed with HIV. This work has contributed not only a basic theoretical perspective, but also a way of understanding the psychological processes that people go through when they are under intense stress.

Q: *What do you want students to learn from you?*

A: Good research training: how to pose a research question, how to find the right design to test it, and how to analyze and understand the data. I want students to be conversant with a wide variety of research methods. More important, I want students to recognize what an important question is. Everybody has good insights, and to be able to recognize a good one and to pursue it is a talent I try to nurture.

Q: *What advice would you give to someone starting in the field of psychology?*

A: Pursue those things that you are passionate about.

Q: *What did you learn from your mentors?*

A: The energy and excitement they brought to their work.

Q: *What have you learned from students?*

A: There are important cohort effects. How your fellow students think and what they think about has a profound influence on you, even though you may not be aware of it at the time. Also the importance of being ambitious without being interpersonally competitive.

Q: *Apart from your life as an academic, how have you found psychology to be important to you?*

A: Knowledge of research methods and statistics has given me the skills to analyze and understand social, political, and economic phenomena in a critical manner.

Q: *What would you like people to remember about you and your work?*

A: Science is a collaborative endeavor, and ultimately my value will be in furnishing ideas, insights, and information that others can build on. As long as my work and my discoveries feed into this long-term collaborative endeavor, I will be satisfied.

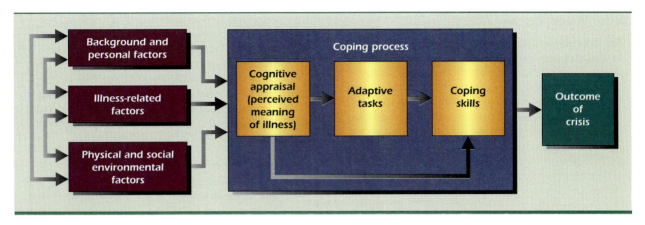

FIGURE 20-4
Three Sets of Factors in Coping
In his crisis theory, Rudolf Moos emphasizes individual differences in coping with serious illness. He has identified three sets of factors influencing each individual's response. In addition, Moos has discerned three main components of adjusting to serious illness. It is the interaction of individual differences and the coping process itself that influences the outcome of the crisis.

requiring us to adapt, in varying ways and to varying degrees. We need constantly to adjust ourselves to regulate our fit to our environment. However, whether we are healthy or ill, young or old, lucky or not, we can *shape* our environment, too. Just as we need to adapt ourselves to fit the environment, we can modify the environment to suit ourselves. If there is a key to psychological adjustment, perhaps it is in the balance between adaptation to and shaping of the environment, with the added option of *selection*. When we find that a particular environment simply

cannot be shaped to fit us, and we cannot adapt ourselves to fit it, we can try to seek another more suitable environment. It is my hope that you can adapt to, shape, and select your environment, to find what you want in life, reach for it, and ultimately obtain it.

Be careful in choosing what you want in life, for it shall be yours.

—*Proverb*

SUMMARY

1. *Health psychology* is the study of the interaction between mental processes and physiological health.
2. We classify illnesses according to their duration: *acute illnesses* are relatively brief; *chronic illnesses* last for a long time, often across the entire life span.

History of Health Psychology   713
3. As one of the newest fields in psychology, health psychology has roots in *psychosomatic* and *behavioral medicines*.

Models of Health and Illness   714
4. Galen is credited with being the first to suggest a *biomedical model* of illness. Fundamentally, disease results when disease-causing agents (*pathogens*) invade the body, and we can eliminate disease if we eliminate the causative pathogens.

5. Many health psychologists now embrace a more contemporary alternative model, the *biopsychosocial model*, which proposes that psychological, social, *and* biological factors can influence health.

Promotion of Health: Enhancing Health Through Lifestyle   715
6. Nutrition (including an appropriate balance of carbohydrates, lipids, proteins, vitamins, and minerals), aerobic exercise, and other aspects of a person's lifestyle powerfully affect a person's physical and psychological health and well-being.
7. Health psychologists also are interested in investigating how to use psychological principles to help people to prevent, or at least to minimize the harmful consequences of accidents.

Stress, Personality, and Illness   720

8. *Stress* is the situation in which environmental factors cause a person to feel threatened or challenged in some way. *Stressors* (situations or events that create the stress) are environmental changes that cause the person to have to adapt to or cope with the situation, and these adaptations are *stress responses.*

9. The initial stress response is adaptive in helping the person to prepare to flee from or fight in the threatening situation. After the initial alarm phase of stress, if the perceived stressor continues to confront the individual, the body shifts down to a resistance phase and finally to an exhaustion phase.

10. Stress has been linked to many diseases, and its direct effect on the immune system is now being explored.

11. In *primary appraisal*, we analyze our stake in the outcome of handling a particular situation. In *secondary appraisal*, we assess what we can do to maximize the likelihood of potentially beneficial outcomes and to minimize the likelihood of potentially harmful outcomes of a situation.

12. *Problem-focused coping* is directed at solving a problem. *Emotion-focused coping* is directed at handling the emotions you experience as a result of the problem.

13. Several personality factors influence health, particularly the personality characteristics related to competitiveness, sense of urgency, and anger and hostility. Persons who rate high on these three characteristics have a *Type-A* pattern of behavior; persons with *Type-B* behavior rate low on these characteristics. Of the three characteristics, feelings of anger and hostility seem most clearly threatening to health, particularly in terms of coronary heart disease and other stress-related illnesses. Lifestyle differences also may contribute to these effects.

Using Health Services   727

14. People generally only seek health services after noticing *symptoms* of ill health. While doctors use explicit theories to make diagnoses, most people already have an implicit theory (based on commonsense schemas) to explain their symptoms and what might be the probable course of their illness.

15. Patient styles differ in terms of patients' preferences for participation in their medical care. Physician styles also differ in terms of whether they are *doctor centered* (focused on the single problem that prompted the visit) or *patient centered* (focused on serving the patients' needs even when they diverge from the identified problem). The use of medical jargon (more common in doctor-centered physicians) may impede communication with some patients.

16. Patient characteristics affect the treatment patients receive. More compliant, passive, unquestioning, and unassertive patients generally receive better treatment in the hospital, although their passivity and their lack of awareness about the treatment may impede their recovery outside the hospital setting.

Pain and Its Management   730

17. *Organic pain* is caused by damage to bodily tissue. *Psychogenic pain* is the discomfort felt when there appears to be no physical cause of the pain, such as neuralgia (involving recurrent pain along a nerve), causalgia (involving burning pain), and phantom-limb pain (which occurs in the absence of a neurological connection to the perceived source of the pain). What may appear to be psychogenic pain, however, may be caused by unidentified organic pathology.

18. Pain may be *acute* (lasting less than six months) or *chronic* (lasting six months or more).

19. Although several personality traits have been associated with pain, it has proven difficult to determine the direction of causality for these correlations.

20. Methods for controlling pain include pharmacological control (via drugs, including patient-controlled analgesia), surgical control, sensory control (e.g., counterirritation), biofeedback, relaxation techniques, distraction, guided imagery, hypnosis, and acupuncture.

Living with Serious, Chronic Health Problems   734

21. AIDS (acquired immune deficiency syndrome) is a rare terminal illness caused by the human immunovirus (HIV), a retrovirus (a slow-acting virus). AIDS is contracted largely through contact with the semen or blood of someone who carries HIV.

22. When people recognize that they have a serious, chronic health problem, they may experience shock (stunned detachment), encounter (grief and despair), and retreat (withdrawal from the problem) before they finally make the needed adjustment. An alternative model describes cognitive adaptations to chronic illness as the needs to find meaning, to gain control, and to restore self-esteem. Factors influencing these reactions include characteristics of the individual (including experiences and background), the illness, and the environment.

23. Three adaptive ways to respond to chronic illness are to change the individual (and his or her lifestyle), to change the environment (making it adapt to the individual's different needs and abilities), or to select a different environment.

KEY TERMS

acute illness   712

acute pain   731

aerobic exercise   717

anabolism   716

behavioral medicine   713

biomedical model   715

biopsychosocial model   715

catabolism   716

chronic illness   712

chronic pain   731

control-enhancing interventions   729

coping   725

doctor-centered style   728

emotion-focused coping   725

gate control theory   731

general adaptation syndrome   722

health psychology   712

metabolism   716

organic pain   731

pain   730

pathogens   715

patient-centered style   728

primary appraisal   724

problem-focused coping   725

psychogenic pain   731

psychosomatic medicine   713

secondary appraisal   725

signs   727

stress   720

stressors   720

stress responses   720

symptoms   727

Type-A behavior pattern   725

Type-B behavior pattern   725

IN SEARCH OF THE HUMAN MIND:
ANALYSES, CREATIVE EXPLORATIONS, AND PRACTICAL APPLICATIONS

1. Both Shontz and Taylor provided psychological models for coping with chronic illness; Shontz focused more on stages of emotion and behavior and Taylor more on cognitions. How could you synthesize the two models into an integrated view of how people cope with chronic illness?

2. Suppose that an instructor of student nurses invites you to discuss the patient's view of hospital care. What are the key points you would try to communicate? How would you communicate those points so that the nurses would really understand you and would not feel threatened by what you say?

3. This chapter included health recommendations regarding several aspects of lifestyle. Which recommendation do you consider the most important of these? Why?

4. What advice would you give doctors, based on your knowledge of psychology, to help them communicate with patients who have to be told that they have a life-threatening illness?

5. Choose the three pain-relief or pain-control methods you consider the most effective. Describe three situations in which pain relief or pain control would be needed and in which one (or two) of the three techniques might be preferable to the others. Tell why the chosen method (or methods) would be best.

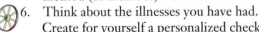
6. Think about the illnesses you have had.
   Create for yourself a personalized checklist of how to recognize the symptoms that should cause you to seek immediate medical attention, the symptoms you should monitor for a while, and the symptoms you can safely ignore for a while. Add to your personalized checklist any other symptoms that should be on the list for anyone (e.g., the warning signs of cancer).

7. What are 10 small steps you could take this week to enhance the healthful quality of your lifestyle? Build on successive small steps, rather than trying to make sweeping changes all at once.

8. What decision criteria can you use to decide when you need to consult a physician?

9. What are some realistic things that you can do to minimize your experience of stress in your life?

In Search of the Human Mind . . . *Part Six*

1. Of the various personality theories presented in Chapter 17, which ones offer you the clearest explanations of abnormal behavior (see Chapter 18) and the most sensible psychotherapeutic treatment of mental disorders (see Chapter 19)?

2. Design a cross-cultural experiment that would offer insight into the factors that lead to unwarranted stress or that underlie maladaptive responses to stress.

3. What personal heuristics and biases might be hampering your effectiveness in your activities? Are these heuristics and biases now serving a purpose that can be achieved by other means?

Looking Ahead . . .

4. How can you use psychological principles to enhance the quality of your own life?

Charting the Dialectic

Chapter 17   PERSONALITY

A major dialectical debate in the study of personality revolves around how personality should be studied. Psychodynamic approaches attempt to understand personality in terms of a person's personal history, especially from early childhood. However, the data from such an approach tend to be clinical and hard to quantify. Trait theorists have reacted by providing structural models that specify and quantify each of the proposed attributes of personality. Such models, though, have been accused of being static and of not dealing with how the traits developed in the first place. Learning-theory approaches have emphasized the development of personality through learned interactions with the environment. Some theorists, such as Mischel, have even proposed that personality be understood in terms of situational rather than personal variables. Most recently, theorists have emphasized the role of person-situation interaction in the development of personality.

Chapter 18   ABNORMAL PSYCHOLOGY

In early times, abnormal behavior was attributed to invasion of the body by demons or to other supernatural causes. Today, psychologists view abnormality in terms of behavior that is statistically unusual, nonadaptive, labeled as abnormal by the society, and characterized by some degree of perceptual or cognitive distortion. Theorists differ in the roles they assign to various factors in the cause of abnormality. Psychoanalytic theories tend to emphasize deep-seated early childhood traumas, whereas cognitive-behavioral theories tend to emphasize the roles of learning and current thinking in abnormality. Biological theorists often reject both of these kinds of theories in favor of looking for abnormalities in brain chemistry or functioning that may be leading to behavior that is viewed as nonadaptive. Probably, future theorists will increasingly attempt to combine these approaches as they seek to understand the bases of abnormality.

Chapter 19   PSYCHOTHERAPY

The major dialectic in psychotherapy revolves around the form of treatment that best addresses the problems of clients who seek out therapy. Psychoanalytic therapy emphasizes communication, but the communication tends to be largely from patient to therapist. Cognitive therapists, in contrast, take a much more active role in providing feedback to patients, sometimes criticizing the patients' thought processes and pointing out how they might have led to false perceptions of reality. Behavioral therapists, as a further contrast, concentrate on changing behavior rather than cognition, whereas cognitive-behavioral therapists combine cognitive with behavioral approaches. Humanistic therapists emphasize the development of a warm and genuine relationship with the patient. In recent times, a synthesis of these various kinds of therapies has been provided through eclectic therapy, which tends to fit the kind of paradigm and treatment used to the problem that presents itself.

Chapter 20   HEALTH PSYCHOLOGY

Health psychology is a relatively new field. In centuries past, disease was viewed as being caused by evil spirits. A reaction to this view was the biomedical model, which attempts to account for illnesses naturally rather than supernaturally. Whereas the traditional biomedical model views disease as resulting from disease-causing agents in the body, the even more recent biopsychosocial model proposes that psychological and social factors as well as biological factors can influence health. In health psychology (and other fields), as scientists realize the full complexity of a phenomenon, they synthesize past models in order fully to understand the phenomenon they are investigating.

STATISTICAL APPENDIX

Do you ever wonder whether some groups of people are smarter, or more assertive, or more honest than others? Or whether students who earn better grades actually work more, on the average, than do students who do not earn such high grades? Or whether, in close relationships, women feel more intimacy toward men, or men toward women? These are all questions that can be addressed by using statistics.

Although statistics can help us answer questions, they cannot themselves provide definitive answers. The ways questions are answered lie not in the statistics themselves, but in how the statistics are interpreted. Statistics provide people with tools—with information to explore issues, answer questions, solve problems, and make decisions. Statistics do not actually do the exploration, question-answering, problem solving, or decision making. People do.

A **statistic** is a number resulting from the treatment of sample data according to specified procedures. For example, if you want to know how satisfied people are in their close relationships, you might give people a scale measuring relationship satisfaction, and then compute various numbers summarizing their level of satisfaction. **Statistics** as a field is the study of such numbers.

Statistics are useful in psychology, and they can be useful to us in our lives. Consider this example of a problem in which statistics can be useful. Suppose you are interested in aspects of love and how they relate to satisfaction in close relationships. In particular, you decide to explore the three aspects of love incorporated in the triangular theory of love (Sternberg, 1986b; Sternberg & Barnes, 1988): intimacy (feelings of warmth, closeness, communication, and support), passion (feelings of intense longing and desire), and commitment (desire to remain in the relationship) (see Chapter 14). You might be interested in the relation of these aspects to each other; or of each of the aspects to overall satisfaction in a close relationship; or of the relative levels of each of these aspects of love people experience in different close relationships—for example, with lovers, friends, or parents. Statistics can help you explore these interests.

In order to use statistics to assess these aspects of love, you would first need a scale to measure them. The *Triangular Love Scale*, a version of which is shown in Table A-1, is such a scale (Sternberg & Barnes, 1988). If you wish, you can take it yourself to compare your data with those from a sample of 84 adults whose summary data will be presented later.

Note that this version of the scale has a total of 36 items, 12 of which measure intimacy; 12, passion; and 12, commitment. Each item consists of a statement rated on a 1 to 9 scale, where 1 means that the statement does not characterize the person at all, 5 means that it is moderately characteristic of the person, and 9 means that it is extremely characteristic. Intermediate points represent intermediate levels of feelings. The final score on each of the three subscales is the average of the numbers assigned to each of the statements in that subscale (i.e., the sum of the numbers divided by 12, the number of items).

In research that uses statistics, we are interested in two kinds of variables: independent and dependent (see Chapter 1). **Independent variables** are predictor variables and **dependent variables** are the predicted variables. In an experiment, some of the independent variables are usually manipulated, and the dependent variable may change in value as a function of the manipulations. Other independent variables may be predictors, but not be manipulated variables. For example, the sex of the subject may be an independent variable that predicts various aspects of love, but it is not manipulated by the experimenter. Rather, data

TABLE A-1
Triangular Love Scale
The blanks represent a person with whom you are in a close relationship. Rate on a scale of 1–9 the extent to which each statement characterizes your feelings, where 1 = not at all, 5 = moderately, 9 = extremely, and other numerals indicate levels in between.

Intimacy

1. I have a warm and comfortable relationship with _____.

2. I experience intimate communication with _____.

3. I strongly desire to promote the well-being of _____.

4. I have a relationship of mutual understanding with _____.

5. I receive considerable emotional support from _____..

6. I am able to count on _____ in times of need.

7. _____ is able to count on me in times of need.

8. I value _____ greatly in my life.

9. I am willing to share myself and my possessions with _____.

10. I experience great happiness with _____.

11. I feel emotionally close to _____.

12. I give considerable emotional support to _____.

Passion

1. I cannot imagine another person making me as happy as _____ does.

2. There is nothing more important to me than my relationship with _____.

3. My relationship with _____ is very romantic.

4. I cannot imagine life without _____.

5. I adore _____.

6. I find myself thinking about _____ frequently during the day.

7. Just seeing _____ is exciting for me.

8. I find _____ very attractive physically.

9. I idealize _____.

10. There is something almost "magical" about my relationship with _____.

11. My relationship with _____ is very "alive."

12. I especially like giving presents to _____.

(Continued)

may be separated by sex of subjects if the data are expected to show different patterns for males versus females.

DESCRIPTIVE STATISTICS

Descriptive statistics are numbers that summarize quantitative information. They reduce a larger mass of information down to a smaller and more useful base of information.

Measures of Central Tendency

In studying love, you might be interested in typical levels of intimacy, passion, and commitment for different relationships—say, for a lover and a sibling. There are several ways in which you might characterize the typical value, or **central tendency,** of a set of data.

The **mean** is the arithmetical average of a series of numbers. To compute the mean, add up all of the values and divide by the number of values added.

Another measure of central tendency is the **median,** which is the middle of a set of values. With an odd number of values, the median is the number right in the middle. For example, if you have seven values ranked from lowest to highest, the median will be the fourth (middle) value. With an even number of values, there is no one middle value. For example, if you have eight values ranked from lowest to highest, the median will be the number half-way between (the average) the fourth and fifth values—again, the middle.

A third measure of central tendency is the **mode,** or most frequent value. Obviously, the mode is useful only when there are at least some repeated values.

Consider, for example, the scores of eight individuals on the intimacy subscale, rounded to the nearest whole number and ranked from lowest to highest: 3, 4, 4, 4, 5, 5, 6, 7. In this set of numbers, the mean is 4.75, or $(3 + 4 + 4 + 4 + 5 + 5 + 6 + 7)/8$; the median is 4.5, or the middle value between the fourth and fifth values above (4 and 5); and the mode is 4, the value that occurs most frequently.

The advantage of the mean as a measure of central tendency is that it fully takes into account the information in each data point. Because of this fact, the mean is generally the preferred measure of central tendency. However, the mean is also sensitive to extremes. If just a few numbers in a distribution are extreme, the mean will be greatly affected by them. For example, if five people took the passion subscale to indicate their feelings toward their pet gerbils, and

TABLE A-1 *(Continued)*

Commitment
1. I will always feel a strong responsibility for _____.
2. I expect my love for _____ to last for the rest of my life.
3. I can't imagine ending my relationship with _____..
4. I view my relationship with _____ as permanent.
5. I would stay with _____ through the most difficult times.
6. I view my commitment to _____ as a matter of principle.
7. I am certain of my love for _____.
8. I have decided that I love _____.
9. I am committed to maintaining my relationship with _____.
10. I view my relationship with _____ as, in part, a thought-out decision.
11. I could not let anything get in the way of my commitment to _____.
12. I have confidence in the stability of my relationship with _____.

Note: Scores are obtained by adding scale values (from 1 = low to 9 = high) for each item in each subscale, and then dividing by 12 (the number of items per subscale), yielding a score for each subscale of between 1 and 9.

their scores were 1, 1, 1, 1, and 8, the mean of 3 would reflect a number that is higher than the rating given by four of the five people surveyed.

The advantage of the median is that it is less sensitive to extremes. In the distribution of passion scores for pet gerbils, the median is 1, better reflecting the distribution than does the mean. The median does not take into account all the information given, however. For example, the median would have been the same if the fifth score were 2 rather than 8.

The advantage of the mode is that it provides a quick index of central tendency. It is rough, though. Sometimes no number in a distribution appears more than once, and hence there is no mode. Other times, several numbers appear more than once, so that the distribution is **multimodal** (having more than one mode). And the mode takes into account the least information in the distribution. For these reasons, the mode is the least used of the three measures of central tendency.

Sometimes, it is useful to show values obtained via a **frequency distribution,** which shows numerically the number or proportion of cases at each score level (or interval). We can distinguish between two kinds of numbers at each score level. The **relative frequency** represents the number of cases that received a given score. The **cumulative frequency** represents the number of cases that received scores up to that level—that is, of that level or lower. In the case of the two distributions of numbers mentioned above

for two sets of subjects in connection with the *Triangular Love Scale*, the frequency distributions would be as follows:

Intimacy Subscale				Passion Subscale		
Value	Relative Frequency	Cumulative Frequency		Value	Relative Frequency	Cumulative Frequency
3	1	1		1	4	4
4	3	4		8	1	5
5	2	6				
6	1	7				
7	1	8				

In these frequency distributions, relative and cumulative frequencies are represented by numbers of cases at each level. An alternative would have been to represent them by proportions or percentages. For example, expressed as a proportion, the relative frequency at score value 3 on the intimacy subscale would be .125 (1/8).

Scatterplots also can be represented graphically in various ways. Two of the main kinds of graphic representations are a **bar graph** and a **line graph,** both of which are shown in Figure A-1 for the simple frequency distribution of intimacy scores expressed above numerically. People use graphs in order to help readers visualize the relations among numbers and to help the readers clarify just what these relations are.

FIGURE A-1
Graphing Frequency Distributions
Frequency distributions may be represented graphically either as line graphs, showing continuous levels of a variable, or as bar graphs, showing discontinuous levels of a variable.

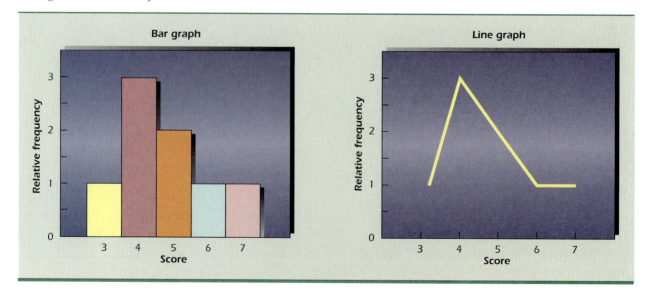

Measures of Dispersion

You now know three ways to assess the central tendency of a distribution of numbers. Another question you might have about the distribution concerns dispersion of the distribution. How much do scores vary? You might assess dispersion in several different ways.

A first measure of dispersion is the **range,** which is the difference between the lowest and the highest values in a distribution. For example, the range of intimacy scores represented above is 4 (i.e., 7−3). But the range is a rough measure. For example, consider two distributions of intimacy scores: 3, 4, 5, 6, 7, and 3, 3, 3, 3, 7. Although the range is the same, the dispersion of scores seems different. Other measures take more information into account.

A second measure of variability is the **standard deviation,** which is, roughly speaking, a measure of the average dispersion of values around the mean. The advantage of the standard deviation over the range is that the standard deviation takes into account the full information in the distribution of scores. Researchers care about the standard deviation because it indicates how much scores group together, on the one hand, or are more dispersed, on the other. The standard deviation also is used in statistical significance testing, as discussed later.

To compute the standard deviation, you must:

1. Compute the difference between each value and the mean;
2. Square the difference between each value and the mean (to get rid of negative signs);
3. Sum the squared differences;
4. Take the average of the sum of squared differences; and
5. Take the square root of this average, in order to bring the final value back to the original scale.

Let us take the two distributions above to see whether their standard deviations are indeed different. The mean of 3, 4, 5, 6, 7, is 5. So the squared differences of each value from the mean are 4, 1, 0, 1, and 4. The sum of the squared differences is 10, and the average, 2. The square root of 2 is about 1.41, which is the standard deviation. In contrast, the mean of 3, 3, 3, 3, 7 is 3.80. So the squared differences of each value from the mean are .64, .64, .64, .64, and 10.24. The sum of the squared differences is 12.80, and the average, 2.56. The square root of 2.56 is 1.60. Thus, the second distribution, has a higher standard deviation, 1.60, than the first distribution, for which the standard deviation is 1.41.

What does a standard deviation tell us? As a measure of variability, it tells us how much scores depart from the mean. At the extreme, if all values were equal to the mean, the standard deviation would be 0. At the opposite extreme, the maximum value of the standard deviation is the value of the range (for numerical values that are very spread apart).

For typical (but not all) distributions of values, about 68% of the values fall between the mean and plus or minus one standard deviation from that mean; about 95% of the values fall between the mean and plus or minus two standard deviations from that mean. And well over 99% of the values fall between

TABLE A-2

Basic Statistics for the *Triangular Love Scale*

The relative extent to which individuals indicate feelings of intimacy, passion, and commitment differ across various kinds of relationships. Note: *"Friend" refers to a close friend of the same sex; "SD" refers to standard deviation. Statistics are based on a sample of 84 adults from southern Connecticut.*

	Intimacy		Passion		Commitment	
	Mean	SD	Mean	SD	Mean	SD
Mother	6.49	1.74	4.98	1.90	6.83	1.57
Father	5.17	2.10	3.99	1.84	5.82	2.22
Sibling	5.92	1.67	4.51	1.71	6.60	1.67
Lover	7.55	1.49	6.91	1.65	7.06	1.49
Friend	6.78	1.67	4.90	1.71	6.06	1.63

the mean and plus or minus three standard deviations. For example, the mean of the scale for intelligence quotients (IQs) is 100, and the standard deviation is typically 15 (see Chapter 11). Thus, roughly two-thirds of IQs fall between 85 and 115 (plus or minus one standard deviation from the mean), and about 19 out of 20 IQs fall between 70 and 130 (plus or minus two standard deviations from the mean).

A third measure of variability is the **variance,** which is the square of the standard deviation. Thus, the variances of the distributions of intimacy scores above are 2 and 2.56 (which were the values obtained before taking square roots). The variance of IQ scores is 15 squared, or 225. Variances are useful in many statistical calculations, but are not as readily interpretable as are standard deviations.

Now that you have read about measures of central tendency and dispersion, you can appreciate two of these measures—the mean and standard deviation—for the *Triangular Love Scale.* Table A-2 shows means and standard deviations of intimacy, passion, and commitment scores for various relationships computed from a sample of 84 adults. If you took the scale yourself, you can compare your own scores to that of our normative sample.

The Normal Distribution

In the above discussion of the percentages of values between the mean and various numbers of standard deviations from the mean, we have been making an assumption without making that assumption explicit. The assumption is that the distribution of values is a **normal distribution**—that is, a particular distribution in which the preponderance of values is near the center of the distribution, with values falling off rather rapidly as they depart from the center. The shape of the normal distribution is shown in Figure A-2. Notice that the distribution of scores is symmetrical, and that indeed, the large majority of scores fall close to the center of the distribution.

Nature seems to favor normal distributions, because the distributions of an amazing variety of attributes prove to be roughly normal. For example, heights are roughly distributed around the average, as are intelligence quotients. In a completely normal distribution, the mean, the median, and the mode are all exactly equal.

Not all distributions are normal. Distributions can be nonnormal in a variety of ways, but one of the most common is in terms of **skewness,** or lopsidedness either to the left or the right of the mode (most

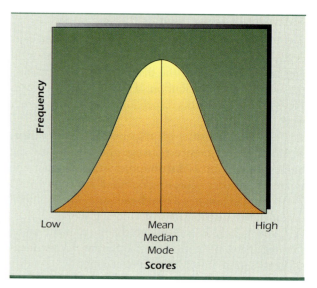

FIGURE A-2
Normal Distribution

As this figure shows, in a normal distribution, the median (the middle value in the distribution), the mean (the average value in the distribution), and the mode (the most frequent value in the distribution) are the same.

frequent value) of the distribution. Figure A-3 shows both a *negatively skewed distribution*, in which the values on the lower (left) side of the mode tail off more slowly than do the values on the right; and a *positively skewed distribution*, in which values on the upper (right) side of the mode tail off more slowly than do the values on the left.

Notice that the respective values of the mean, median, and mode are displaced in these two kinds of distributions. Why? Consider as an example a distribution that is almost always positively skewed: personal incomes. The distribution tends to rise quickly up to the mode, and then to trail off. The existence of a small number of very high-income earners creates the positive skew. What will be the effect of the small number of very high-income earners? They will tend to displace the mean upward, because as we have seen, the mean is especially sensitive to extreme values. The median is less affected by the extreme values, and the mode is not affected at all. Thus, in this positively skewed distribution, the mean will be the highest, followed by the median and then the mode. In a negatively skewed distribution, the opposite ordering will tend to occur.

As we have seen, one way to obtain skewness is to have a distribution with a natural "tail," as is the case with high incomes. Another way to obtain such a

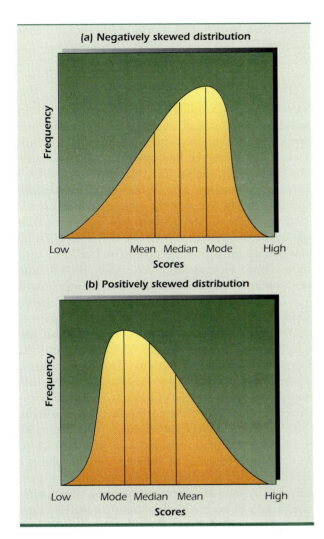

(a) Negatively skewed distribution

Frequency

Low — Mean Median Mode — High

Scores

(b) Positively skewed distribution

Frequency

Low — Mode Median Mean — High

Scores

FIGURE A-3
Skewed Distribution

In a skewed distribution, the mean, the median, and the mode differ. In a negatively skewed distribution (a), the values of the median and mode are greater than the value of the mean. In a positively skewed distribution (b), the value of the mean is greater than the values of the mode and the median.

distribution is the way something is measured. Suppose a professor gave a very easy test, with an average score of 90% correct, and a range of scores from 60% to 100%. This distribution would be negatively skewed because of a *ceiling effect:* Many people received the highest score because the easiness of the test placed an artificial limit, or ceiling, on how well they could do on the test.

Suppose, instead, that the professor gave a very difficult test, with an average score of just 10% correct, and a range of scores from 0% to 40%. This distribution would be positively skewed because of a *floor effect:* Many people received the lowest score because the difficulty of the test placed an artificial limit, or floor, on how poorly they could do on the test.

Fortunately, most distributions are approximately normal. The advantage of such distributions is that many of the statistics used in psychology, only a few of which are discussed here, assume a normal distribution. Other statistics do not assume a normal distribution, but are more interpretable when we have such a distribution.

Types of Scores

One such statistic is the standard score. The standard score is one that can be used for any distribution to equate the scores for that distribution to scores for other distributions. *Standard scores,* also called *z-scores,* are arbitrarily defined to have a mean of 0 and a standard deviation of 1. If the distribution of scores is normal, therefore, roughly 68% of the scores will be between -1 and 1, and roughly 95% of scores will be between -2 and 2.

Why bother to have standard scores? The advantage of standard scores is that they render comparable scores that are initially on different scales. For example, suppose two professors teaching the same course to two comparable classes of students differ in the difficulty of the tests they give. Professor A tends to give relatively difficult tests, and the mean score on his tests is 65%. Professor B, on the other hand, tends to give very easy tests, and the mean score on his tests is 80%. Yet, the difference in these two means reflects not a difference in achievement, but a difference in the difficulty of the tests the professors gave. If we convert scores separately in each class to standard scores, the mean and standard deviation will be the same in the two classes (that is, a mean of 0 and a standard deviation of 1), so that it will be possible to compare achievement in the two classes in a way that corrects for the differential difficulty of the professors' tests.

Standard scores also can be applied to the distributions of love-scale scores described earlier. People who feel more intimacy, passion, or commitment toward a partner will have a higher standard score relative to the mean, and people who feel less intimacy, passion, or commitment will have a lower standard score.

The computation of standard scores is simple. Start with a **raw score,** which is simply the score on a given test in whatever units the test is originally scored. Then convert the raw score to a standard score following these steps:

1. Subtract the mean raw score from the raw score of interest;
2. Divide the difference by the standard deviation of the distribution of raw scores.

You can now see why standard scores always have a mean of 0 and a standard deviation of 1. Suppose that a given raw score equals the mean. If the raw score equals the mean, when the mean is subtracted from that score, the number will be minus itself, yielding a difference in the numerator (see Step 1 above) of 0. Of course, 0 divided by anything equals 0. Suppose now that the score is 1 standard deviation above the mean. When the mean is subtracted from that score, the difference will be the value of the standard deviation. When this value (the standard deviation) is divided by the standard deviation (in Step 2 above), the result is a value of 1, because any value divided by itself equals 1.

Thus, if we take our distribution of intimacy scores of 3, 4, 5, 6, 7, with a mean of 5 and a standard deviation of 1.41, the standard score for a raw score of 6 will be (6 − 5) / 1.41, or .71. The standard score for a raw score of 5, which is the mean, will be (5 − 5) / 1.41, or 0. The standard score for a raw score of 4 will be (5 − 6) / 1.41, or −.71.

Many kinds of scores are variants of standard scores. For example, an IQ of 115, which is one standard deviation above the mean, corresponds to a z-score (standard score) of 1. An IQ of 85 corresponds to a z-score of -1, and so on. The *Scholastic Assessment Test* uses scores set to have a mean of 500 and a standard deviation of 100. In the verbal and mathematical parts, therefore, a score of 600 represents a score of 1 standard deviation above the mean (i.e., a z-score of 1), whereas a score of 400 represents a score of 1 standard deviation below the mean (i.e., a z-score of -1).

Another convenient kind of score is called the **percentile.** This score refers to the percentage of other individuals in a given distribution whose scores a given individual's score exceeds. Thus, if, on a test, your score is higher than that of half (50%) of the students who have taken the test (and lower than that of the other half), your percentile will be 50. If your score is higher than everyone else's (and lower than no one else's), your percentile will be 100. In the distribution 3, 4, 5, 6, 7, the score corresponding to the 50th percentile is 5 (the median), because it is higher than half the other scores and lower than half the other scores. The 100th percentile is 7, because it is higher than all the other scores and lower than none of them.

Correlation and Regression

So now you know something about central tendency and dispersion, as well as about the kinds of scores that can contribute to central tendency and dispersion. You also may be interested in a different question: How are scores on one kind of measure related to scores on another kind of measure? For example, how do people's scores on the intimacy subscale relate to their scores on the passion subscale, or to their scores on the commitment subscale? The question here would be whether people who feel more intimacy toward someone also tend to feel more passion or commitment toward that person.

The statistical measure called the **correlation coefficient** addresses the question of the degree of relation between two arrays of values. Most frequently, people use a measure of relation called the **Pearson product-moment correlation coefficient.** There are other correlation coefficients as well, but they go beyond the scope of this text, as do the mathematical formulas for the coefficients of correlation.

Basically, correlation expresses the degree of relation between two variables. A correlation of 0 indicates no relation at all between two variables; a correlation of 1 indicates a perfect (positive) relation between the two variables; a correlation of −1 indicates a perfect inverse relation between the two variables. Figure A-4 shows hypothetical distributions with correlations of 0, 1, and −1.

The Pearson product-moment correlation coefficient expresses only the degree of **linear relation,** meaning that it considers only the extent to which one variable is related to another in the form of a straight line, or $Y = a + bX$, as shown in Panels B and C of Figure A-4. What this means is that you can have a perfect correlation between two variables without regard to their scale, as long as they are linearly related.

For example, suppose that in a hypothetical group of subjects, the scores of five subjects on the intimacy subscale were 4, 5, 6, 6, and 7, and the scores of the same subjects on the passion subscale were also 4, 5, 6, 6, and 7. In other words, each subject received the same score on the passion subscale as on the intimacy scale. The correlation between the two sets of scores is 1. Now suppose that you add a constant (of 1) to the passion scores, so that instead of being 4, 5, 6, 6, and 7, they are 5, 6, 7, 7, and 8. Because correlations do not change with the addition or subtraction of a constant, the correlation would still be 1. And if instead of adding a constant, you multiplied by a constant, the correlation would still be 1. Remember, then, correlation looks at degree of linear relation, regardless of the scale on which the numbers are

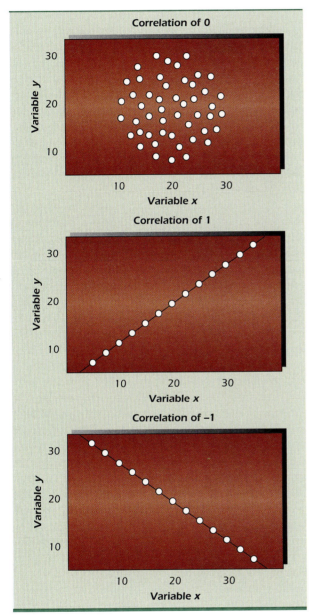

FIGURE A-4
Correlation Coefficient

When two variables show a correlation of 0, increases or decreases in the value of one variable (variable x) bear no relation to increases or decreases in the value of the other variable (variable y). When variable x and variable y are positively correlated, increases in x are strongly related to increases in y, and decreases in x are strongly related to decreases in y. When variable x and variable y are negatively (inversely) correlated, increases in x are strongly related to decreases in y, and decreases in x are strongly related to increases in y.

expressed. There are other kinds of relations—quadratic, cubic, and so on—but the Pearson coefficient does not take them into account.

When you do prediction of Y values from X values, you are doing what is called **linear regression.** If the correlation is perfect, the prediction will be perfect. For example, if you predict people's height in inches from their height in centimeters, the prediction will be perfect, yielding a correlation of 1.

The equation expressing the relation between the Y (predicted) values and the X (predictor) values is called a **regression equation.** In the equation, $Y = a + bX$, a is called the *regression constant* and b is called the *regression coefficient*. Note that the regression constant is additive, whereas the regression coefficient is multiplicative. The formula, which is that of a straight line, is what relates the Y (predicted) values to the X (predictor) values.

Well, what are the correlations among the various subscales of the *Triangular Love Scale?* For love of a lover, the correlations are very high: .88 between intimacy and passion, .84 between intimacy and commitment, and .85 between passion and commitment. These data suggest that if you feel high (or low) levels of one of these aspects of love toward a lover, you are likely also to feel high (or low) levels of the other two of the aspects toward your lover. However, the correlations vary somewhat with the relationship. For example, the comparable correlations for a sibling are .79, .77, and .76. Incidentally, in close relationships with a lover, the correlations between satisfaction and each of the subscales are .86 for intimacy, .77 for passion, and .75 for commitment.

So now you know that there is a strong relation between intimacy, passion, and commitment in feelings toward a lover, as well as between each of these aspects of love and satisfaction in the relationship with the lover. Can you infer anything about the causal relations from these correlations? For example, might you be able to conclude that intimacy leads to commitment? Unfortunately, you cannot infer anything for sure. Consider three alternative interpretations of the correlation between intimacy and commitment.

One possibility is that intimacy produces commitment. This interpretation makes sense. As you develop more trust, communication, and support in a relationship, you are likely to feel more committed to that relationship. However, there is a second possibility, namely, that commitment leads to intimacy. This interpretation also makes sense. You may feel that until you really commit yourself to a relationship, you do not want to trust your partner with the more intimate secrets of your life, or to communicate some of your deepest feelings about things. A third possibility exists as well—that both intimacy and commitment depend on some third factor. In this view, neither causes the other, but both are dependent on some third variable. For example, it may be that intimacy and commitment both depend on a shared sense of values. Without such shared values, it may be difficult to build a relationship based on either intimacy or commitment.

The point is simple: As is often said in statistics, correlation does not imply causation. You cannot infer the direction of causality without further information. Correlation indicates only that there is a relation, not how the relation came to be. You can make a guess about the direction of causal relationship, but to be certain, you would need additional data.

In the example of the correlation between intimacy and commitment, you have a problem in addition to direction of causality. How much of a correlation do you need in order to characterize a relationship between two variables as statistically meaningful? In other words, at what level is a correlation strong enough to take it as indicating a true relationship between two variables, rather than a relationship that might have occurred by chance—by a fluke? Fortunately, there are statistics that can tell us when correlations, and other indices, are statistically meaningful. These statistics are called inferential statistics.

INFERENTIAL STATISTICS

Inferential statistics are used to determine how likely it is that results are *not* due to chance. In order to understand how inferential statistics are used, you need to understand the concepts of a population and a sample.

Populations and Samples

A **population** is the set of *all* individuals to whom you might wish to generalize a set of results. Suppose a psychologist does an experiment involving feelings of love in close relationships. She tests a group of college students on the *Triangular Love Scale*. The psychologist is probably not interested in drawing conclusions only about the students she happened to test in a given place on a given day. Rather, she is more likely to be interested in generalizing the results obtained to college students in general, or perhaps

even to adults in general. If so, then college students (or adults) in general constitute the population of interest, and the college students actually tested constitute the **sample**—that is, the subset of individuals actually tested.

In order to generalize results from the sample to college students (or adults) in general, the sample must be **representative**—that is, an accurate reflection of the characteristics of the population as a whole. The less representative of the population is the sample, the harder it will be to generalize. For example, it probably would be safer to generalize the results the psychologist obtained to all college students than to all adults. However, even this generalization would be suspect, because college students differ from one college to another, and even from year to year within the same college.

Occasionally, you work with populations rather than with samples. Suppose, for example, that you are interested only in the people you have tested and no others. Then you are dealing with the population of interest, and inferential statistics do not apply. The values you obtain are for the population rather than just for a sample of the population. There is no need to generalize from sample to population, because you have the population. If, however, you view these students as only a sample of all college students, then you are working with a sample, and inferential statistics do apply.

In particular, inferential statistics indicate the probability that you can reject the **null hypothesis**—that is, the hypothesis that there is no true difference in the population from which the tested sample or samples were drawn. Typically, the question you are asking when you use inferential statistics is whether the results you have obtained for your sample can be generalized to a population. For example, suppose you find a difference in intimacy scores between men and women in your sample. The null hypothesis would be that the difference you obtained in your sample is a result of chance variation in the data, and would not generalize to the population of all college men and women. The *alternative hypothesis* would be that the difference is statistically meaningful, and generalizes to the population.

Statistical Significance

When we speak of the meaningfulness of statistical results, we often use something called a **test of statistical significance.** Such a test tells us the probability that a given result is *not* due to chance fluctuations in the data. A result, therefore, is **statistically signifi-**

cant when the result is ascribed to systematic rather than to chance factors. It is important to realize that a statistical test can show only the probability that one group differs from another in some respect. For example, you can compute the probability that a mean or a correlation is different from zero, or the probability that one mean differs meaningfully from another. You cannot use statistics to estimate the probability that two samples are the same in any respect.

The distinction is an important one. Suppose you have two hypothetical individuals who are identical twins and who have always scored exactly the same on every test they have ever been given. There is no statistical way of estimating the probability that they truly are the same on every test. Some future test might always distinguish them.

Psychologists need to pay particular attention to two types of error in research. One type concerns drawing a conclusion when you should not, and the other not drawing a conclusion when you should.

The first is called **Type I error,** and refers to the probability of believing that a difference exists in a population when in fact no difference exists. In signal-detection theory (considered in Chapter 4), this probability corresponds to the probability of a false alarm. For example, suppose you compare mean intimacy scores that individuals express toward mothers and fathers. The two values shown in Table A-2 are 6.49 and 5.17 for the mother and father respectively. You find that the score for the mother is higher than that for the father. A Type I error would occur if you believed that the difference was meaningful when in fact it was due just to random error of measurement.

The second type, **Type II error,** refers to the probability of believing that no difference exists when in fact there is a difference. In signal-detection theory, this kind of error is called a miss. For example, if you conclude that the difference between mothers and fathers is due to chance, when in fact the difference exists in the population, you would be committing a Type II error.

Most researchers pay more attention to Type I than to Type II errors, although both are important. The reason for the greater attention to Type I errors is probably conservatism: Type I error deals with making a claim for a finding when there is none, whereas Type II error deals with failing to make a claim when there might be one to make. Researchers tend to be more concerned about investigators who make false claims than about those who fail to make claims that they might be entitled to make.

When we do psychological research, we usually compute inferential statistics that allow us to calculate the probability of a Type I error. Typically, researchers are allowed to report a result as "statistically significant" if the probability of a Type I error is less than .05. This probability is referred to as a **p-value.** In other words, we allow just 1 chance in 20 that we are claiming a finding when we do not have one. Investigators often report *p*-values as being either less than .05 or less than .01. A result with just a .01 chance of being erroneous generally is considered very strong indeed.

The chances of finding a statistically significant result generally increase as more subjects are tested, because with greater numbers of subjects, random errors tend to average out. Thus, if you tested only 10 male subjects and 10 female subjects for their feelings of intimacy toward their partners, you probably would hesitate to draw any conclusions from this sample about whether there is difference between men and women in general in their experiencing of intimacy toward their partners. However, if you tested 10,000 men and 10,000 women, you probably would have considerable confidence in your results, so long as your sample was representative of the population of interest.

It is important to distinguish between statistical significance and *practical significance,* which refers to whether a result is of any practical or everyday import. Suppose, for example, that you find that the difference between the men and the women in intimacy feelings is .07 point on a 1 to 9 scale. With a large enough sample, the result may reach statistical significance. But is this result of practical significance? Perhaps not. Remember, an inferential statistical test can only tell you the probability that any difference at all exists. It does not tell you how large the difference is, nor whether the difference is great enough really to matter for whatever practical purposes you might wish to use the information. In research, investigators often pay primary attention to statistical significance. However, as a consumer of research, you need to pay attention to practical significance as well, whether the researchers do or not. Ultimately, in psychology, we need to concentrate on results that make a difference to us as we go about living our lives.

a posteriori knowledge. Knowledge that is acquired as a result of experience (from the Latin meaning "from afterward")

a priori knowledge. Knowledge that exists regardless of whether an individual becomes aware of it through experience (from the Latin for "from beforehand")

abnormal behavior. Behavior that is characterized by some degree of perceptual or cognitive distortion and that is inappropriate for the given social context; the behavior typically is statistically unusual, is nonadaptive, and is labeled as abnormal by the majority of persons in the given social context; although some abnormal behavior may not have all of the preceding characteristics, most abnormal behavior does

absolute refractory phase. A time following the firing of a **neuron,** during which the neuron cannot fire again regardless of the strength of the **stimulus** that reaches the neuron (cf. **relative refractory phase**)

absolute threshold. The hypothetical construct of a minimum amount of a particular form of physical energy (e.g., mechanical pressure of sounds, electrochemical scents or tastes) that reaches a sensory receptor, which is sufficient for the individual to detect that energy (stimulus); hypothetically, a person will be able to sense any stimuli that are at or above the absolute threshold, but no stimuli that are below that threshold

accessibility. The ease of gaining access to information that has been stored in long-term memory (cf. **availability, long-term store**)

accommodation (as a cognitive process). The process of responding to cognitively disequilibrating information about the environment by modifying relevant **schemas,** thereby adapting the schemas to fit the new information and reestablishing cognitive equilibrium (cf. **assimilation;** see also **equilibration**)

accommodation (as a means of ad- justing the focus of the eye). The process by which curvature of the lens changes in order to focus on objects at different distances

acetylcholine. A **neurotransmitter** synthesized from choline in the diet; present in both the **central nervous system** and the **peripheral nervous system;** may affect memory function, as well as other neural processes in the brain; is involved in muscle contraction elsewhere in the body and affects the muscles of the heart (see **neurotransmitter;** cf. **dopamine; serotonin**)

achievement. An accomplishment; an attained level of expertise on performance of a task, or an acquired base of knowledge in a domain or a set of domains (cf. **aptitude**)

achromatic. Lacking color; usually refers to stimuli that lack both **hue** and **saturation,** but that may differ in terms of **brightness** (from *a-*, absence of, not; *chroma-*, color)

acoustic nerve. The bundle of sensory **neurons** that lead from the **hair cells** in the inner ear to the portion of the **cerebral cortex** (primarily the **temporal lobe**) that processes auditory information (also termed the *auditory nerve*)

acquisition phase of learning. The phase of **classical conditioning** during which a **conditioned response** strengthens and the occurrence of the response increases in likelihood

acronyms. See **mnemonic devices**

acrostics. See **mnemonic devices**

action potential. A change in the electrochemical balance inside and outside a **neuron** that occurs when positively and negatively charged ions quickly flood across the neuronal membrane; occurs when electrochemical stimulation of the neuron reaches or exceeds the neuronal **threshold of excitation;** when an action potential occurs, the neuron is said to "fire"

activation–synthesis hypothesis. A proposed perspective on dreaming, which considers dreams to be the result of subjective organization and in- terpretation (synthesis) of neural activity (activation) that takes place during sleep (contrasting views include the Freudian view of dreams as a symbolic manifestation of wishes and the Crick-Mitchison view of dreams as "mental garbage")

active theories of speech perception. A category of theories (e.g., **motor theory, phonetic-refinement theory**) that explain speech perception in terms of the active cognitive involvement of the listener; theories that consider the listener's cognitive processes, such as the listener's expectations, context, memory, and attention (cf. **passive theories**)

actor–observer effect. A psychological phenomenon in which people attribute the actions of other persons whom they observe to the stable dispositional characteristics of other persons, but they attribute their own actions to the momentary characteristics of the situation (see also **fundamental attribution error, self-handicapping**)

acuity. The keenness (sharpness) of sensation in a given sensory mode

acute (symptom or illness). Brief, usually characterized by sudden onset and intense symptomatology, but in any case not recurrent and not long in duration (cf. **chronic**)

acute pain. Brief (lasting no longer than 6 months), intense, uncomfortable stimulation usually associated with internal or external damage of tissue (cf. **chronic pain**)

acute stress disorder. A brief mental illness (lasting fewer than 4 months) that arises in response to a traumatic event; characterized by perceptual distortions, memory disturbances, or physical or social detachment (cf. **posttraumatic stress disorder;** see **anxiety disorders**)

adaptation. A temporary physiological response to a sensed change in the environment (e.g., see **dark adaptation, light adaptation**), which is generally not subject to conscious manipulation or control, and which usually does not depend on previous experience with the given type of environmental change (cf. **habituation**)

adaptation level. The existing level of sensory stimulation (e.g., brightness or sound intensity), which an individual uses as a reference level for sensing new stimuli or changes in existing stimuli

addiction. A persistent, habitual, or compulsive physiological or at least psychological dependency on one or more **psychoactive** drugs (see also **acquired motivation, tolerance, withdrawal,** as well as specific psychoactive drugs)

additive bilingualism. The addition of a second language to an established, well-developed primary language (see **bilingual;** cf. **subtractive bilingualism**)

additive mixture. The blending of various **wavelengths** of light (such as spotlights), which add together to produce a summative effect of the combined wavelengths (cf. **subtractive mixture**)

adrenal medulla. One of the two adrenal (*ad-*, near or toward; *renal,* kidney [Latin]) **glands,** which are located above the kidneys; secretes epinephrine (*epi-*, on; *nephron,* kidney [Greek]) and norepinephrine, which act as **neurotransmitters** in the brain and as **hormones** elsewhere in the body, particularly aiding in **stress**-related responses, such as sudden arousal

aerial perspective. See **monocular depth cues**

aerobic exercise. Any activities that involve high-intensity, long-duration performance of motor behavior and that increase both heart rate and oxygen consumption, thereby enhancing overall health, particularly *cardiovascular* (heart and blood vessels) and *respiratory* (breathing) fitness

affix. A **morpheme** that is attached to a root word, thereby altering the syntactical use (in the case of **function morphemes**) or the semantic meaning (if the affix is a **content morpheme**) of the root word (see also **prefix, suffix**)

aggression. A form of antisocial behavior that is directed against another person or persons, intended to cause harm or injury to the recipient(s) of the aggression (see **hostile aggression, instrumental aggression**)

agnosia. A severe deficit in the ability to perceive sensory information, usually related to the visual sensory modality; oddly, agnosics have normal sensations but lack the ability to interpret and recognize what they sense, usually as a result of lesions in the brain (*a-*, lack; *gnosis,* knowledge [Greek])

agoraphobia. An **anxiety disorder** characterized by an intense fear (a **phobia**) of open spaces or of being in public places from which it might be difficult to escape in the event of a panic attack; usually associated with panic attacks or with a fear of losing control or of some other dreaded but indistinct consequence that might occur outside the home (cf. **social phobia**)

agreeableness. See **Big Five**

algorithm. A means of solving a problem, which—if implemented correctly and appropriately—guarantees an accurate solution to the problem for which the algorithm is implemented; generally involves successive, somewhat mechanical iterations of a particular strategy until the correct solution is reached; in many situations, implementation of an algorithm is either impossible or impractical as a means for solving problems (cf. **heuristics**)

alienated achievement. An alternative to the four main types of identity (cf. **foreclosure, identity achievement, identity diffusion, moratorium**), in which the individual considers the values of mainstream society to be inappropriate or even bankrupt and rejects identification with that society

alpha waves. A pattern of **electroencephalogram (EEG)** activity (8–12 Hz) characteristic of relaxed wakefulness (also termed *alpha rhythm*)

alternate-forms reliability. See **reliability**

altruism. Selfless behavior focused on helping another person or persons, or at least behavior performed out of concern for another person or persons, regardless of whether the action has positive or negative consequences for the altruist (see also **prosocial behavior**)

amacrine cells. One of three kinds of **interneuron** cells in the middle of three layers of cells in the **retina;** the amacrine cells and the **horizontal cells** provide lateral connections, which permit lateral communication with adjacent areas of the retina in the middle layer of cells (cf. **bipolar cells;** see **ganglion cells, photoreceptors**)

amnesia. Severe loss of memory, usually affecting primarily **semantic memory;** *anterograde amnesia*—inability to recall events that occur *after* whatever trauma caused the memory loss (affects the acquisition of **semantic memory,** but apparently not the acquisition of **procedural memory**); *infantile amnesia*—the inability to recall events that happened during early development of the brain (usually the first 3 to 5 years); *retrograde amnesia*—inability to recall events that occurred *before* the trauma that causes the memory loss (often, the amnesic gradually begins to recall earlier events, starting with the earliest experiences and gradually recalling events that occurred closer to the time of the trauma, perhaps eventually even recalling the traumatic episode) (see also **dissociative amnesia**)

amphetamine. A type of synthetic **central nervous system (CNS) stimulant** that is usually either ingested orally or injected; short-term effects include increased body temperature, heart rate, and endurance, as well as reduced appetite; psychological effects include stimulation of the release of **neurotransmitters** such as norepinephrine and **dopamine** into brain synapses, as well as inhibition of **reuptake** of neurotransmitters, leading to a sense of euphoria and increased alertness, arousal, and motor activity; long-term effects are a reduction of **serotonin** and other neurotransmitters in the brain, thereby impairing neural communication within the brain; long-term use also leads to **tolerance,** and intermittent use may lead to **sensitization**

amplitude. The objective physical intensity of sound or light; when sound or light energy is displayed on an oscilloscope, higher waves correspond to greater intensity; in terms of subjective perception, greater amplitude of light is perceived as increased

brightness, and greater amplitude of sound is perceived as increased loudness

anabolism. Metabolic processes that construct complex substances from simple ones (e.g., making proteins from amino acids), thereby facilitating the storage of energy and material resources that are made available via **catabolism** (see **metabolism;** see also **parasympathetic nervous system**)

anal stage. A stage of **psychosexual development,** which typically occurs between the ages of 2 and 4 years, during which time the child learns to derive pleasure from urination and especially defecation

analysis. A process of **critical thinking,** which involves breaking down wholes into component elements, and which may be viewed as a process that complements **synthesis** (see **thinking;** cf. **synthesis;** see also **componential analysis, factor analysis, means–ends analysis, psychoanalysis**)

androgyny. Characterizing an individual who exhibits both masculine and feminine traits in approximately equal proportions, such that neither femininity nor masculinity predominates

anger. A distressing emotion that can be activated by feeling frustrated in or otherwise restrained from pursuit of a goal

angiograms. Essentially X-ray pictures for which the visual contrast has been enhanced by injecting special dyes into the blood vessels of the head; primarily used clinically to assess *vascular* diseases (diseases of the blood vessels, which may lead to strokes), and to locate particular kinds of brain tumors; also used experimentally as a means of determining which parts of the brain are active when people perform different kinds of listening, speaking, or movement tasks

anorexia nervosa. A pathological mental disorder in which an individual does not eat enough to avoid starvation, despite the availability of food

anterograde amnesia. See **amnesia**

antidepressant drug. A type of **psychoactive** drug (e.g., tricyclic antidepressants, monoamine oxidase [MAO] inhibitors, and fluoxetine [Prozac]) that is prescribed to counteract **depression** by increasing the cerebral

concentrations of the **neurotransmitters serotonin** and norepinephrine (cf. **antipsychotic drug**)

antipsychotic drug. A type of **psychoactive** drug prescribed to alleviate the **positive symptoms** (cf. **negative symptoms**) of **schizophrenia** by blocking the **dopamine** receptors in the schizophrenic brain (cf. **antidepressant drug**)

antithesis. A statement of opinion presenting an alternative view that differs from the opinion stated originally (cf. **thesis;** see **dialectic;** see also **synthesis**)

anxiety. A generalized, diffuse feeling of being threatened, despite the inability to pinpoint the source of the threat; tends to be more pervasive and long-lasting than **fear;** characterized by tension, nervousness, distress, or uncomfortable **arousal** (see also **cognitive anxiety, somatic anxiety, state anxiety, trait anxiety**)

anxiety disorders. A category of psychological disorders (e.g., **generalized anxiety disorder, obsessive–compulsive disorder, panic disorder, phobia,** and stress disorders such as **acute stress disorder** and **posttraumatic stress disorder**) characterized primarily by feelings of anxiety (a mood symptom) of varying levels of intensity, excessive worry and a concentration of thoughts on worrisome phenomena (cognitive symptoms), many purposeless movements (e.g., fidgeting, pacing, motor tics, and other **motor** symptoms), and somatic symptoms associated with high **arousal** of the **autonomic nervous system** (e.g., sweating, muscle tension, high pulse and respiration rates, and high blood pressure)

applied research. Investigations that lead to clear, immediate, obvious, practical uses (applications) (cf. **basic research**)

aptitude. A potential ability to accomplish something, to attain a level of expertise on performance of a task or a set of tasks, or to acquire knowledge in a given domain or set of domains (cf. **achievement**)

arbitrary symbolic reference. A property of **language,** indicating that human language involves a shared system of *symbols* (images, sounds, or objects that represent or suggest other

things) that are selected arbitrarily as a means of representing particular things, ideas, processes, relationships, and descriptions

archetype. A universal, inherited human tendency to perceive and act on things in particular ways, as evidenced by the similarities among various myths, legends, religions, and even customs across cultures; the most common Jungian archetypes: *anima*—the feminine side of a man's personality, which shows tenderness, caring, compassion, and warmth toward others, yet which is more irrational and based on emotions; *animus*—the masculine side of a woman's personality, the more rational and logical side of the woman; *persona*—the part of the personality that a person shows the world and that the person is willing to share with other persons; *shadow*—the part of the personality that is viewed as frightening, hateful, or even evil, and which the individual therefore hides not only from others, but also from her- or himself

arousal. A hypothetical construct representing alertness, wakefulness, and activation, caused by the activity of the **central nervous system (CNS)**

assimilation (as a cognitive process). The process of responding to new information that causes cognitive disequilibrium, by fitting the new information into existing schemas, thereby reestablishing cognitive equilibrium (cf. **accommodation;** see also **equilibration**)

association areas. Regions of the cerebral **lobes** that are not part of the sensory (visual, auditory, somatosensory) or motor cortices, believed to connect (associate) the activity of the sensory and motor cortices

associationism. A school of psychological thought that examines how events or ideas can become associated with one another in the mind, thereby resulting in a form of learning

associationist. Person who subscribed to **associationism** and who therefore believed that events occurring close to one another in time become associated in the mind, so that these events may later be recalled in tandem

asylum. Institution intended for housing mentally ill persons, sometimes also involving some form of rehabilitative treatment for the residents

asymptote. The most stable level of response associated with a psychological phenomenon, usually graphed as a curve on which the maximum level of stability can be observed as the region of response that shows the least variation; for learning curves, the most stable level of response appears at the high point of the curve; for habituation, the asymptote appears at a low point on the curve; for other psychological phenomena, the most stable level of response may appear at other locations of the curve

atheoretical. Not based on or guided by any particular theoretical approach (*a-*, "lacking" or "without")

attachment. A strong and relatively long-lasting emotional tie between two humans (see also **bonding**)

attention. The active cognitive processing of a limited amount of information from the vast amount of information available through the senses, in memory, and through cognitive processes

attention-deficit disorder. One of three major disorders usually first diagnosed in infancy, childhood, or adolescence (cf. **pervasive developmental disorder**); often accompanied by *hyperactivity* (high activity levels with a virtual inability to sit still or otherwise refrain from moving); disordered children characteristically have difficulty in focusing attention (particularly on instructions) and in avoiding distraction by irrelevant stimuli; constantly or at least frequently seek the attention of other persons, often talking excessively and interrupting other speakers; frequently act impulsively and disruptively in social settings (formerly termed *hyperactivity, hyperkinesis,* and *minimal brain dysfunction*)

attitude. A learned (not inherited), stable (not volatile), and relatively enduring (not transitory) evaluation (positive or negative judgment) of a person, object, or idea that can affect an individual's behavior

attribution. An explanation that points to the cause of a person's behavior (including the behavior of the individual devising the explanation) (see **personal attribution, situational attribution**)

attribution theory. A theory regarding the way in which people point to the causes of a person's behavior (including the behavior of the individual devising the explanation) (see **attribution;** see also **actor–observer effect, fundamental attribution error, self-handicapping**)

auditory nerve. See **acoustic nerve**

authoritarian parents. Mothers and fathers who exhibit a style of parenting in which they tend to be firm, punitive, and generally unsympathetic to their children; who highlight their own authority, who hold exacting standards for and prize obedience in their children, and who show little praise toward and attachment to their children (cf. **permissive parents, authoritative parents**)

authoritative parents. Mothers and fathers who exhibit a style of parenting in which they tend to encourage and support responsibility and reasoning in their children, explaining their reasoning for what they do, establishing firm limits within which they encourage children to be independent, and which they enforce firmly but with understanding (cf. **authoritarian parents, permissive parents**)

autism. See **pervasive developmental disorder (PDD)**

automaticity. A phenomenon in which experts have so thoroughly mastered the procedures and **heuristics** in their area of expertise that the manipulation of these operations is virtually automatic and requires little conscious effort for implementation

autonomic nervous system. The part of the **peripheral nervous system** that controls movement of nonskeletal muscles (the heart muscle and the smooth muscles), over which people have little or no voluntary control or even conscious awareness (*autonomic* means "self-regulating"; cf. **somatic nervous system**)

autoshaping. A means by which a person can change his or her behavior without any apparent intervention from anyone in the external environment, through the establishment of a system of reinforcements that increase the likelihood of the desired responses (see **operant conditioning, shaping, successive approximations**)

availability. The existing storage of given information in long-term memory, without which it would be impossible to retrieve the information, and with which it is possible to retrieve the information if appropriate retrieval strategies can be implemented (cf. **accessibility**)

availability heuristic. An intuitive strategy for making judgments or inferences, or for solving problems, on the basis of the ease with which particular examples or ideas may be called to mind, without necessarily considering the degree to which the particular examples or ideas are relevant to or suitable for the given context (see **heuristic**)

aversion therapy. A behavioristic **counterconditioning** technique in which the client is taught to experience negative feelings in the presence of a stimulus that is considered inappropriately attractive, with the aim that the client will eventually learn to feel repelled by the stimulus

aversive conditioning. A form of **operant conditioning,** in which the subject is encouraged to avoid a particular behavior or setting as a consequence of punishment in association with the given behavior or setting (see **avoidance learning**)

avoidance learning. A form of **operant conditioning,** in which the subject learns to refrain from a particular behavior or to keep away from a particular stimulus as a result of **aversive conditioning**

avoidant attachment pattern. One of three attachment patterns observed in the **strange situation;** pattern in which a child generally ignores the mother while she is present and in which the child shows minimal distress when the mother leaves (cf. **resistant attachment pattern, secure attachment pattern**)

axon. The long, thin, tubular part of the **neuron,** which responds to information received by the **dendrites** and **soma** of the neuron, either ignoring or transmitting the information through the neuron until it can be transmitted to other neurons through the release of chemical substances by the axon's **terminal buttons**

babbling. A prelinguistic preferential production of only those distinct phonemes characteristic of the babbler's own language (cf. **cooing**)

backward conditioning. An ineffective form of **classical conditioning** in which the initiation of the **conditioned stimulus** follows rather than precedes the initiation of the **unconditioned stimulus,** thus resulting in little or no learning

balance theory. A proposed means of attaining **cognitive consistency** regarding friendships, in which it is suggested that people attempt to maintain a sense of give and take *(reciprocity)* in a relationship, and that people tend to be drawn to friends whose attitudes toward other people are similar to their own attitudes toward those other people *(similarity)*

balanced presentation of viewpoints. A presentation of both favorable (pro) and unfavorable (con) perspectives on a given issue

bar graph. One of many types of graphic displays of numeric information (cf. **line graph**), in which items reflecting larger numerical values are represented as longer bars on the graph

barbiturate. The most widely used type of **sedative–hypnotic drug;** antianxiety drug prescribed to reduce **anxiety** through physiological inhibition of **arousal** (high dosages can even induce sleep), which may lead to grogginess that may impair functioning in situations requiring alertness; chronic use leads to **tolerance** and to physiological **addiction,** and high doses can lead to respiratory failure; nevertheless, when used properly, barbiturates are an important tool in the psychiatrist's armamentarium (see also **central nervous system [CNS] depressant**)

basal ganglia. Collections of nerves within the **forebrain,** which are crucial to motor function (singular: *ganglion;* see also **cerebral cortex, limbic system**)

base rate. The prevalence of an event or characteristic within its population of events or characteristics (cf. **representativeness;** see **heuristic**)

basic anxiety. A fundamental dynamic of **personality** development, according to some neo-Freudian psychologists, which involves a feeling of isolation from other persons and of helplessness in a world conceived as being potentially hostile

basic research. Investigations that are devoted to the study of funda-mental underlying relationships and principles, which may not offer any immediate, obvious, practical value (cf. **applied research**)

basilar membrane. One of the membranes that separates the fluid-filled canals of the **cochlea;** the physiological structure on which the **hair cells** (auditory receptors) are arranged; vibrations from the **stapes** stimulate the hair cells on the membrane in various locations, in association with differing sound frequencies

behavior therapy. A collection of techniques (see **counterconditioning, extinction procedures, modeling**) that are based at least partly on the principles of **classical conditioning** or **operant conditioning,** or on **observational learning;** usually involves short-term treatment in which the therapist directs the patient in the implementation of specific interventive techniques that focus exclusively on the alleviation of symptoms and on changes in behavior, unconcerned with whether patients may gain insights or other nonbehavioral benefits of treatment

behavioral contracting. A behavioristic psychotherapeutic technique in which the therapist and the client draw up a contract specifying clearly the responsibilities and behavioral expectations of each party, and obligating both parties to live up to the terms of the contract

behavioral genetics. A branch of psychology tied closely to evolutionary theory, which attempts to account for behavior (and often particular psychological characteristics and phenomena, such as intelligence) by attributing behavior to the influence of particular combinations of genes; often viewed as a marriage of psychology and genetics (see **genetics**)

behavioral medicine. A psychological approach to medicine, which focuses on the use of behavioral techniques to help people modify health-related problems (e.g., heavy smoking or overeating)

behaviorism. A school of psychology that focuses entirely on the association between an observed **stimulus** and an observed **response** and therefore may be viewed as an extreme extension of **associationism**

Big Five. The five key characteristics that are often described by various theorists as a useful way to organize and describe individual differences in personality: *agreeableness*—characterized by a pleasant disposition, a charitable nature, empathy toward others, and friendliness; *conscientiousness*—characterized by reliability, hard work, punctuality, and a concern with doing things right; *extroversion*—characterized by sociability, expansiveness, liveliness, an orientation toward having fun, and an interest in interacting with other people; *neuroticism*—characterized by nervousness, emotional instability and moodiness, tension, irritability, and frequent tendency to worry (cf. **psychoticism**); *openness*—characterized by imagination, intelligence, curiosity, and aesthetic sensitivity

bilingual. Person who can speak two languages (cf. **monolingual**) (see also **additive bilingualism, subtractive bilingualism**)

binocular depth cues. One of the two chief means of judging the distances of visible objects, based on the two different angles from which each eye views a scene, which leads to a disparity of viewing angles that provides information about depth (*bi-,* "two"; *ocular,* pertaining to the eye; see **binocular disparity;** cf. **monocular depth cues**)

binocular disparity. The modest discrepancy in the viewpoint of each eye due to the slightly different positions of each eye, which leads to slightly different sets of sensory information going to the brain from each of the two optic nerves; in the brain, the information is integrated in order to make determinations regarding depth, as well as height and width (see **binocular depth cues**)

biological psychology. A branch of psychology that attempts to understand behavior through the careful study of anatomy and physiology, especially of the brain (often considered synonymous with *physiological psychology* and *neuropsychology*)

biological trait. See **trait:** *genetic trait*

biomedical model. A paradigm for health care, in which the focus is on the elimination of pathogens that cause diseases; serves as a basis for treating and often for curing illnesses, with little concern for preventive health practices, for health practices that promote wellness, or for psychological factors that may contribute to illness, to recovery from illness, or to wellness

biopsychosocial model. A paradigm for health care, in which the focus is on an understanding of the various psychological, social, and biological factors that contribute to illness, to the prevention of illness, to recovery from illness, and to the promotion of wellness

bipolar cells. One of three kinds of **interneuron** cells in the middle of three layers of cells in the **retina;** provide vertical connections, which permit communication between the **ganglion cells** in the first, outermost layer of the retina and the **photoreceptors** in the third, innermost of the three layers of retinal cells (cf. **amacrine cells, horizontal cells**)

bipolar disorder. A mental illness characterized by alternating extremes of **depression** and **mania** (also termed *manic–depressive disorder*)

bisexual. A person whose sexual orientation may be both heterosexual and homosexual (see **homosexuality**)

blind spot. The small area on the **retina** where the optic nerve leaves the eye, pushing aside **photoreceptors** to exit the eye; although people cannot see images in the region of the blind spot, it normally does not impair vision because the visual field of the blind spot of one eye falls within the normal visual field of the other eye, and the brain integrates the information from both eyes to compensate for the blind spot in each eye

blocking effect. The failure of a second **unconditioned stimulus** to become classically conditioned because the first unconditioned stimulus blocks the effectiveness of the second one in eliciting a **conditioned response** (see **overshadowing, simultaneous conditioning;** see also **classical conditioning**)

blood–brain barrier. A network of tiny capillaries through which the blood passes as it moves between the brain and the rest of the body; screens out many substances (particularly large water-soluble molecules, such as com-

plex proteins and microorganisms), but permits many other substances (e.g., glucose and other small water-soluble molecules, as well as most fat-soluble molecules) to pass through the network quite easily; offers two-way protection, preventing substances in cerebral blood from reaching the body's blood supply, and vice versa

bonding. The process by which an adult forms a close attachment to an infant immediately or soon after birth (see also **attachment**)

bounded rationality. The limits within which humans demonstrate reasoned behavior (see also **satisficing**)

brain. The organ of the body that most directly controls thoughts, emotions, and motivations, as well as **motor** responses, and that responds to information it receives from elsewhere in the body, such as through sensory receptors

brain stem. The portion of the **brain** that comprises the **thalamus** and **hypothalamus,** the **midbrain,** and the **hindbrain,** and that connects the rest of the brain to the **spinal cord;** essential to the independent functioning of fundamental physiological processes (without which, a physician will certify that the individual is brain dead)

brightness. The psychological perception of light intensity, rather than the actual physical quantity of light intensity, based on light-wave **amplitude**

bystander effect. A decreased likelihood that an individual will help a person or persons in distress, due to the actual or implied presence of other potential helpers (see **prosocial behavior**)

caffeine. A mild **central nervous system (CNS)** stimulant

canalization. The extent to which an ability develops independently of environmental circumstances; based on the imagery of a canal (a channel), in which abilities that are more canalized are positioned deeper in their canals, where they are less accessible to the influences of the outside world

cardinal trait. A single personality

trait that is so salient in an individual's personality and so dominant in the person's behavior that almost everything the person does somehow relates back to this trait; although many people do not have cardinal traits, all people do have **central traits** and **secondary traits**

case study. Intensive investigation of a single individual or set of individuals, which is used as a basis for drawing general conclusions about the behavior of the individual and perhaps about other persons as well (cf. **experiment, naturalistic observation, survey, test**)

catabolism. Metabolic processes that break down complex substances into simple ones (e.g., taking apart proteins to yield amino acids), thereby releasing and making available energy and material resources from food or from reserves stored in body tissues, as well as facilitating the elimination of unused metabolic by-products (cf. **anabolism;** see **metabolism, sympathetic nervous system**)

categorical clustering. See **mnemonic devices**

categorical syllogism. A deductive argument that involves drawing a conclusion regarding class or category membership, based on two premises; each of the premises contains two terms and makes assertions regarding category membership such that some, all, or none of the members of the category of one term are members of the class indicated by the other term, and one of the two terms of each premise is common to both premises (see **deductive reasoning, syllogism**); four types of statements used in categorical syllogisms: *particular affirmative statement*—assertion that some members of a category are members of another category, *particular negative statement*—assertion that some members of a category are not members of another category, *universal affirmative statement*—assertion that all members of a category are members of another category, *universal negative statement*—assertion that all members of a category are *not* members of another category

cathartic method. A psychotherapeutic technique associated with psychodynamic treatments, in which the patient is encouraged to reveal and discuss the painful origins of a psychological problem as a means of purging the problem from the patient's mental life

causal inference. A conclusion regarding one or more antecedents that are believed to have led to a given consequence; although a goal of science is to draw conclusions regarding causality, the complex interactions of multiple variables impinging on a particular phenomenon make it difficult to assert such conclusions with certainty, so scientists generally infer causality in terms of the relative likelihood that a particular variable was crucial in causing a particular phenomenon to occur (see also **inductive reasoning**)

central nervous system (CNS). The **brain** (encased in the skull) and the **spinal cord** (encased in the spinal column), including all of the **neurons** therein

central nervous system (CNS) depressant. Drug (e.g., alcohol and **sedative–hypnotic drug**) that slows the operation of the CNS and is often prescribed in low doses to reduce anxiety and in relatively higher doses to combat insomnia (see **barbiturate, tranquilizer;** cf. **narcotic;** cf. also **central nervous system [CNS] stimulant**)

central nervous system (CNS) stimulant. Drug (e.g., caffeine, **amphetamines,** cocaine, and nicotine—found in tobacco) that arouses and excites the CNS, either by stimulating the heart or by inhibiting the actions of natural compounds that depress brain activity (in other words, it acts as a "double-negative" on brain stimulation); short-term effects of relatively low doses include increased stamina and alertness, reduced appetite, and exuberant euphoria; stronger doses may cause anxiety and irritability; problems with **tolerance** and **addiction** are linked with long-term use, and problems with **sensitization** are tied to intermittent use (cf. **central nervous system [CNS] depressant**)

central route of persuasion. One of two routes to persuasion (cf. **peripheral route of persuasion**), which emphasizes thoughtful arguments related to the issue about which an attitude is being formed; most effective when the

recipient is both motivated to think about the issue and able to do so

central tendency. The value (or values) that most commonly typifies an entire set of values (see **mean, median, mode**)

central traits affecting impression formation. Characteristics that form a basis for organizing other information in regard to forming an impression of an individual (see also **central traits of personality**)

central traits of personality. The 5 to 10 most salient traits in a person's disposition, affecting much of the person's behavior (cf. **cardinal trait, secondary traits;** see also **central traits affecting impression formation**)

cerebellum. The part of the **brain** (*cerebellum,* Latin, "little brain") that controls bodily coordination, balance, and muscle tone; when damaged, subsequent movement becomes jerky and disjointed; located in the **hindbrain**

cerebral cortex. A highly convoluted 2-millimeter layer (give or take a millimeter) on the surface of the brain, which forms part of the **forebrain** (plural: *cortices*); responsible for most high-level cognitive processes such as planning and using language

cerebral hemispheres. The two rounded halves of the brain, on the surface of which is the **cerebral cortex** and inside which are the other structures of the brain (*hemi-,* half; *-spherical,* globe-shaped)

cerebrospinal fluid. The clear, colorless fluid that circulates constantly throughout the **brain** and **spinal cord,** buffering them from shocks and minor traumas (injuries) and possibly helping in the elimination of waste products from the **central nervous system**

characteristic features. The qualities that describe a prototypical model of a word (or concept) and thereby serve as the basis for the meaning of the word (or concept), according to **prototype theory;** these qualities would characterize many or most of the instances of the word (or concept), but not necessarily all instances (cf. **defining features**)

child-directed speech. The characteristic form of speech that adults tend to use when speaking with infants and young children, which usually involves a higher pitch, exaggerated *vocal inflec-*

tions (i.e., more extreme raising and lowering of pitch and volume), and simpler sentence constructions; generally more effective than normal speech in gaining and keeping the attention of infants and young children (formerly termed *motherese*)

chromosome. Each of a pair of rod-shaped bodies that contain innumerable **genes,** composed largely of **deoxyribonucleic acid (DNA);** humans have 23 chromosomal pairs

chronic (symptom or illness). Recurrent, constant, or very long in duration (cf. **acute**)

chronic pain. Recurrent or constant long-term (lasting at least 6 months or more) discomfort (of any level of intensity), usually associated with tissue damage (cf. **acute pain**); may be characterized as (a) *chronic-intractable-benign pain,* which may vary in intensity but never entirely disappears, but which is not caused by an underlying fatal or injurious condition; (b) *chronic-progressive pain,* which is caused by an underlying pathology that worsens and that may eventually be fatal; or (c) *chronic-recurrent pain,* which disappears and then reappears repeatedly

chunk. A collection of separate items into a single clump, which can be more readily stored in memory and recalled later than is likely to occur if the various discrete items are stored and later retrieved as separate entities

circadian rhythm. The usual sleeping–waking pattern that corresponds roughly to the cycle of darkness and light associated with a single day (*circa,* Latin, "around"; *dies,* Latin, "day"); many physiological changes (e.g., body temperature and hormone levels) are associated with this daily rhythmic pattern

clairvoyance. One of several forms of **extrasensory perception (ESP),** in which an individual allegedly perceives objects or events for which there is no apparent stimulation of the known senses (*clair-,* "clear"; *-voyance,* related to seeing)

classical conditioning. A learning process whereby an originally neutral stimulus (see **conditioned stimulus, CS**) comes to be associated with a stimulus (see **unconditioned stimulus, UCS**) that already produces a particular physiological or emotional response (see **unconditioned response, UCR**), such that once the conditioning takes place, the physiological or emotional response (see **conditioned response, CR**) occurs as a direct result of the stimulus that was originally neutral (the CS), even in the absence of the other stimulus (the UCS) (also termed *classically conditioned learning*) (see **backward conditioning, delay conditioning, simultaneous conditioning, temporal conditioning, trace conditioning**)

classically conditioned learning. See **classical conditioning**

client-centered therapy. A form of humanistic therapy that assumes that the client's construction of reality provides the basis for understanding the client; characterized by *nondirective* interactions (thereby allowing the client to direct the course of therapy), *genuineness* (thereby offering honest communication with the client, rather than communications calculated to create a particular effect in the client), *unconditional positive regard* for the client (thereby encouraging the client to discontinue self-imposed conditions for positive self-regard), and accurate *empathic understanding* of the client (thereby helping the client to explore and to clarify her or his own worldview)

clinical. Describing a branch of psychology oriented toward the treatment of clients requiring therapeutic guidance by psychologists and psychiatrists

clinical interview. The most widely used clinical assessment technique; involves a meeting between the person seeking psychological assistance and a clinician who tries to obtain information from the client in order to diagnose the client's need for psychotherapeutic treatment (cf. **naturalistic observation, objective personality test, projective test**)

closure. A Gestalt principle of form perception (see **Gestalt approach**): the tendency to complete (perceptually to close up) objects that are not actually complete

cocaine. A powerful **central nervous system (CNS) stimulant**

cochlea. The coiled and channeled main structure of the inner ear, which contains three fluid-filled canals that run along its entire convoluted length; the fluid-filled canals are separated by membranes, one of which is the **basilar membrane,** on which thousands of **hair cells** (auditory receptors) are arranged and are stimulated by the vibration of the **stapes**

cocktail party phenomenon. The process of tracking one conversation in the face of the distraction of other conversations, a phenomenon often experienced at cocktail parties

cognition. Thinking, processes of thought

cognitive anxiety. Feelings of worry, tension, or frustration, or of being preoccupied with thoughts of impending failure (see **anxiety;** cf. **somatic anxiety**)

cognitive consistency. A match between the cognitions (thoughts) and the behaviors of person, as perceived by the person who is thinking and behaving (cf. **cognitive dissonance;** see **impression-management theory, self-perception theory**)

cognitive development. The study of how mental skills build and change with increasing physiological maturity and experience

cognitive dissonance. A person's disquieting perception of a mismatch between her or his attitudes (cognitions) and her or his behavior (cf. **cognitive consistency;** cf. also **impression-management theory, self-perception theory**)

cognitive map. An internal, cognitive representation of a pattern (e.g., a maze or a hierarchy) or an abstraction (e.g., a concept)

cognitive structures. Specific mental abilities, which can be measured via **psychometric** means; some psychologists who study such structures are more likely to study the psychometric results of testing such abilities than to study the processes underlying such abilities

cognitive styles. Characteristic ways of relating to the world, which reflect both the cognition and the personality of the individual

cognitive therapy. Psychotherapy involving a cognitivistic approach to psychological problems, such as a focus on developing adaptive, rather than maladaptive, thoughts and thought processes

cognitivism. A school of psychology that underscores the importance of **cognition** as a basis for understanding much of human behavior

cohort effects. The distinctive effects of a particular group of subjects having lived through a particular time in history, in which they experienced different educational systems, opportunities, and values, which may affect findings based on **cross-sectional studies** (cf. **longitudinal study;** cf. dropout effect)

cold fibers. Bundles of **neurons** that respond to cooling of the skin by increasing their rate of firing relative to the rate at which they fire when at rest (cf. **warm fibers**)

collective unconscious. A Jungian construct involving an aspect of the unconscious that contains memories and behavioral predispositions that all people have inherited from common ancestors in the distant human past (cf. **personal unconscious**)

color constancy. A form of **perceptual constancy** in which an individual continues to perceive a color as being constant, even though the sensation of the hue changes, due to changes in the light shining on the object

combination. One of two processes hypothesized to be important in handling new information (cf. **encoding**); involves putting together encoded pieces of information

commissive. See **speech acts**

commitment. One of three basic components of love, according to the **triangular theory of love** (cf. **intimacy, passion**): the decision to maintain a relationship over the long term

competence motivation. An intrinsic human incentive to investigate, explore, and learn about the processes and objects in the environment, and to engage in other behavior that happens to provide a means for gaining mastery over the environment, although the competence that is gained during such behavior is not necessarily the conscious intention of the behavior

complex cells. One of the key physiological structures described by the **feature-detector approach** to form perception, according to which any members of a given group of **simple cells** may prompt the complex cell to fire in response to lines of particular orientations anywhere in the receptive field for the given complex cell; the particular type of light/dark contrasts of a line segment appear not to affect the firing of the complex cell, as long as the line segment demonstrates the appropriate orientation; however, for some complex cells, the length of the line segments may also play a role in whether the cells fire

complexes.   Clusters of independently functioning, emotionally tinged unconscious thoughts that may be found within the Jungian construct of the **personal unconscious**

compliance.   The modification of behavior as a result of a request by another person or by other persons, which may involve taking an action, refraining from an action, or tailoring an action to suit another person or persons (cf. **conformity, obedience**); several techniques are often used: *door-in-the-face*—the compliance-seeker makes an outlandishly large request that is almost certain to be rejected, in the hope of getting the *target* (person whose compliance is being sought) of such efforts to accede to a more reasonable but perhaps still quite large request; *foot-in-the-door*—the compliance-seeker asks for compliance with a relatively small request, which is designed to "soften up" the target for a big request; *hard-to-get*—the compliance-seeker convinces the target that whatever the compliance-seeker is offering (or trying to get rid of) is very difficult to obtain; *justification*—the compliance-seeker justifies the request for compliance (often effective even when the justification is astonishingly weak); *low-balling*—the compliance-seeker gets the target to comply and to commit to a deal under misleadingly favorable circumstances, and then adds hidden costs or reveals hidden drawbacks only after obtaining a commitment to comply; *reciprocity*—the compliance-seeker appears to be giving something to the target, thereby obligating the target to give something in return, based on the notion that people should not receive things without giving things of comparable value in return; *that's-not-all*—the compliance-seeker offers something at a high price, and then, before the target has a chance to respond, throws in some-

thing else to sweeten the deal (or offers a discounted price on the product or service), thereby enticing the target to buy the offered product or service

component (as a construct within componential theory).   A distinctive elementary defining feature of a word or concept (see **componential theory** for explanation)

componential analysis.   A means of isolating the component elements of a hypothetical construct (e.g., intelligence) by breaking down people's performance on various tasks, according to the processes that compose the tasks

componential theory.   One of two primary theories of semantics, which claims that the meaning of a word (or concept) can be understood by disassembling the word (or concept) into a set of **defining features,** which are essential elements of meaning that are singly necessary and jointly sufficient to define the word (or concept); that is, each defining feature is an essential element of the meaning of a concept (or word), and the combination of those *defining features* uniquely defines the concept (or word) (also termed *definitional theory;* cf. **prototype theory;** cf. also **characteristic features**)

comprehension monitoring.   A strategy of **verbal comprehension,** which involves watchfulness to observe whether the information being processed is being understood, contains internal contradictions, or contains other problematic features that require attention for their resolution

compulsion.   An irresistible impulse to perform a relatively meaningless act repeatedly and in a stereotypical fashion; associated with feelings of **anxiety,** not joy, and often associated with **obsessions** (see also **obsessive–compulsive anxiety disorder**)

computerized axial tomogram (CAT).   A highly sophisticated X-ray-based technique that produces pictures (-*gram,* "drawing" or "recording") of cross-sectional slices (*tomo-,* Greek for "slice" or "cut") of the living brain, derived from computer analysis of X rays that pass through the brain at various angles around a central axis in the brain (often termed *CAT scan*); usually used clinically to detect blood clots, tumors, or brain diseases, but also used

experimentally to study how particular types and locations of brain damage (lesions) affect people's behavior

concentrative meditation.   A form of contemplation in which the meditator focuses on an object or thought and attempts to remove all else from **consciousness** (see **meditation**)

concept.   Idea to which various characteristics may be attached and to which various other ideas may be connected; may be used to describe a highly abstract idea or a concrete one

concrete operations.   A stage of cognitive development in Piaget's theory of development, in which the individual can engage in mental manipulations of internal representations of tangible (concrete) objects (cf. **formal-operational stage, preoperational stage, sensorimotor stage**)

concurrent validity.   An aspect of criterion-related **validity,** in which the *predictor* (values of the **independent variable** [e.g., test scores], which are expected to predict particular values of the **dependent variable** [the criterion]) and the *criterion* (measures of behavioral performance that are predicted to coincide with particular values of the predictor) are assessed at roughly the same time

condition (as an aspect of experimental design).   A situation in which a group of experimental subjects are subjected to a carefully prescribed set of circumstances (see **control condition, experiment, experimental condition**)

conditional syllogism.   A deductive argument that involves drawing a conclusion regarding an outcome based on contingencies or causal relationships; uses the form, "If A, then B (or 'then not B'). A (or 'not A'). Therefore, B (or 'not B')." (see **deductive reasoning, syllogism**)

conditioned emotional responses. Classically conditioned feelings (emotions) that an individual experiences in association with particular stimulus events

conditioned response (CR).   A learned (classically conditioned) pattern of behavior that occurs in association with a **stimulus** that was not associated with this pattern of behavior prior to learning

conditioned stimulus (CS).   A **stim-**

ulus that initially does not lead to a particular physiological or emotional response, but that eventually does lead to the particular response, as a result of **classical conditioning**

cones. One of the two kinds of **photoreceptors** in the eye; less numerous, shorter, thicker, and more highly concentrated in the foveal region of the **retina** than in the periphery of the retina than are **rods** (the other type of photoreceptor); virtually nonfunctional in dim light, but highly effective in bright light, and essential to color vision (see **fovea**)

confederate. A collaborator hired by an experimenter to simulate being a research subject along with the real subject or subjects and to behave in a particular way in order to observe the effects of such behavior on the true subjects of the experiment

confirmation bias. The human tendency to seek ways in which to confirm rather than to refute existing beliefs

conformity. The modification of behavior in order to bring the behavior into line with the **norms** of the social group; may involve taking an action, refraining from an action, or tailoring an action to suit the social group (cf. **compliance, obedience**); also, the tendency to give up personal individuality and independent decision making, in order to become like others and to share in the power of a collectivity—sometimes suggested as being one of three basic mechanisms by which people seek to escape from freedom

connotation. The emotional overtones, presuppositions, and other nonexplicit meanings of a word (cf. **denotation**)

conscientiousness. See **Big Five**

consciousness. The complex phenomenon of evaluating the environment and then filtering that information through the mind, with awareness of doing so; may be viewed as the mental reality created in order to adapt to the world

conservation. The observation that the quantity of something (e.g., the number, length, volume, weight) remains the same, despite transformations in its appearance

construct-related validity. An as-

pect of **validity,** in which an evaluation is made regarding the degree to which a test or other measurement actually reflects the hypothetical construct (e.g., intelligence) that the test or other measurement is designed to assess

constructive memory. The psychological phenomenon in which an individual actually builds memories, based on prior experience and expectations, such that existing **schemas** may affect the way in which new information is stored in **memory** (cf. **reconstructive memory**)

constructive perception. One of the two key views of perception (also termed *intelligent perception;* cf. **direct perception**); assertion that the perceiver builds the stimulus that is perceived, using sensory information as the foundation for the structure, but also considering the existing knowledge and thought processes of the individual

contact hypothesis. The unsubstantiated assumption that **prejudice** will be reduced, simply as a result of direct contact between social groups that have prejudicial attitudes toward each other, without any regard to the context in which such contact occurs

content morpheme. A **morpheme** that carries the bulk of the meaning of a word (cf. **function morpheme**)

content-related validity. An aspect of **validity,** in which experts judge the extent to which the content of a test measures all of the knowledge or skills that are supposed to be included within the domain being tested

context effects. The influences of the surrounding environment on cognition, particularly as applied to the visual perception of forms

contextualist. Psychologist who theorizes about a psychological phenomenon (e.g., intelligence) strictly in terms of the context in which an individual is observed, and who suggests that the phenomenon cannot be understood—let alone measured—outside the real-world context of the individual; particularly, a theorist who studies how intelligence relates to the external world

contingency. The dependent relationship, during **classical conditioning,** between the occurrence of an

unconditioned stimulus and the occurrence of a **conditioned stimulus,** which is necessary in order for classical conditioning to occur (cf. **temporal contiguity**)

continuity. Characterized by a lack of interruption; sometimes used to describe one of the Gestalt principles of form perception (see **Gestalt approach**): the tendency to perceive smoothly flowing or continuous forms rather than disrupted or discontinuous ones

continuous reinforcement. A pattern of **operant conditioning** in which **reinforcement** always and invariably follows a particular **operant** behavior (cf. **partial reinforcement**)

contour. The features of a surface that permit differentiation of one surface from another (e.g., convexity or concavity)

contralateral. Occurring or appearing on the opposite side (*contra-,* opposite; *lateral,* side); often used for describing the crossed pattern of sensory and motor connections between the physiological structures of the body and those of the brain (cf. **ipsilateral**)

control. One of four goals of psychological research (the other three are **description, explanation,** and **prediction**)

control condition. A situation in which a group of experimental subjects are subjected to a carefully prescribed set of circumstances, which are almost identical to the **experimental condition,** but which do not involve the **independent variable** being manipulated in the experimental treatment condition

control-enhancing interventions. Methods for increasing patients' sense of control, thereby enhancing their ability to respond appropriately to illness and eventually to cope effectively with illness; such methods may include informing patients regarding the origins of their illness, the symptoms and other consequences of their illness, and the strategies they may use for promoting their recovery from illness or at least for minimizing the negative consequences of their illness

controlled experimental design. A plan for conducting a study in which the experimenter carefully manipulates or controls one or more independent variables in order to see the effect on the dependent variable or variables; although experimental control is usually the ideal means by which to study cause–effect relations, for many phenomena, such control is either impossible or highly impractical, so other means of study must be used instead (cf. **correlational design, quasi-experimental design**)

controlling. One of the two main purposes of consciousness (cf. **monitoring**): The individual plans what to do, based on the information received from the monitoring process

conventional morality. A phase of moral development, in which moral reasoning is guided by mutual interpersonal expectations (e.g., to be good and to show good motives) and by interpersonal conformity (e.g., obeying rules and showing respect for authority); societal rules have become internalized, and the individual conforms because it is the right thing to do

convergent thinking. A form of **critical thinking,** which involves focusing in (converging toward) on one idea from an assortment of possible ideas (cf. **divergent thinking**)

converging operations. The use of several different approaches, methods, or strategies (*operations*) as a means of trying to understand a phenomenon, with the expectation that the diverse approaches will come together (*converge*) in support of a single conclusion; because diverse operations are used, the conclusion is more well grounded than it would be if only a single operation were employed, regardless of the number of implementations of the operation

cooing. Oral expression that explores the production of all the phones (cf. **phonemes**) that humans can possibly produce; precedes **babbling,** which precedes language articulation

cooperative principle. The principle of conversation in which it is held that people seek to communicate in ways that make it easy for a listener to understand what a speaker means, such as by following the maxims of manner, quality, quantity, and relation proposed by H. P. Grice

coping. The process of trying to manage the internal and external challenges posed by a troublesome sit-

uation; sometimes conceptualized in terms of *emotion-focused coping,* which involves handling internal emotional reactions to the situation, and *problem-focused coping,* which involves the specific strategies used for confronting and resolving the problematic situation

cornea. The clear dome-shaped window that forms a specialized region of the *sclera* (the external rubbery layer that holds in the gelatinous substance of the eye), through which light passes and which serves primarily as a curved exterior surface that gathers and focuses the entering light, making gross adjustments of the curvature in order to focus the image relatively well; the entire sclera (especially the cornea) is very sensitive to touch and initiates a series of protective responses whenever a foreign substance comes in contact with the sclera (cf. **lens**)

corpus callosum. A dense aggregate of nerve fibers (*corpus,* "body"; *callosum,* "dense"), which connects the two cerebral hemispheres, thereby allowing easy transmission of information between the two hemispheres

correct rejection. One of the four possible combinations of stimulus and response, according to **signal-detection theory (SDT)** (cf. **false alarm, hit, miss**): the accurate recognition that a signal stimulus was not detected

correlation. The statistical relationship between two *attributes* (characteristics of the subjects, of a setting, or of a situation), expressed as a number on a scale that ranges from −1 (a **negative correlation**) to 0 (no correlation) to +1 (a **positive correlation**) (see also **correlational design**)

correlation coefficient. A measure of statistical association that ranges from −1 (perfect inverse relation) to 0 (no relation) to +1 (perfect positive relation)

correlational design. A plan for conducting a study in which the researchers merely observe the degree of association between two (or more) attributes that already occur naturally in the group(s) under study, and researchers do not directly manipulate the variables (cf. **controlled experimental design, quasi-experimental design**)

cortex. See **cerebral cortex**

counterconditioning. A technique of behavioral therapy (or experimentation), in which the positive association between a given **unconditioned stimulus (UCS)** and a given **conditioned stimulus (CS)** is replaced with a negative one by substituting a new UCS, which has a different (and negative) **unconditioned response (UCR),** and in which the alternative response is incompatible with the initial response (see **classical conditioning;** see also **aversion therapy, systematic desensitization**)

countertransference. An unwanted phenomenon sometimes arising during psychodynamic therapy, in which the therapist projects onto the patient the therapist's own feelings (cf. **transference**)

CR. See **conditioned response**

creativity. One of the fundamental processes of **thinking** (cf. **judgment and decision making, problem solving, reasoning**): the process of producing something that is both original and valuable

credibility. Believability

critical period(s). A brief period of rapid development, during which the organism is preprogrammed for learning to take place, given adequate environmental support for the learning, and after which learning is less likely to occur

critical thinking. The conscious direction of mental processes toward representing and processing information, usually in order to find thoughtful solutions to problems (see **thinking;** see also **analysis, convergent thinking, divergent thinking, synthesis**)

critical tradition. An established pattern of permitting current beliefs **(theses)** to be challenged by alternative, contrasting, and sometimes even *radically* (radic-, root) divergent views **(antitheses),** which may then lead to the origination of new ideas based on an integration of several features of the old ideas **(syntheses)** (see also **dialectic**)

cross-sectional study. Research that investigates a diverse sampling of persons of various ages at a given time (cf. **longitudinal study;** see also **cohort effects**)

crystallized intelligence. One of

two major subfactors of general intelligence; represents the accumulation of knowledge over the life span of the individual (may be measured, for example, in tests of vocabulary, of general information, and of achievement) (cf. **fluid intelligence**)

CS.   See **conditioned stimulus**

cultural relativism.   The view that assessments and even descriptions of intelligence and other psychological constructs should be based solely on *indigenous* (native to the cultural context) notions regarding the constructs under consideration

culture-fair test.   Assessment that is equally appropriate for members of all cultures and that comprises items that are equally fair to members of all cultures; probably as elusive as a three-eyed unicorn (cf. **culture-relevant test**)

culture-relevant test.   Assessment that employs skills and knowledge that relate to the cultural experiences of the test-takers, by using content and procedures that are relatively appropriate to the cultural context of the test-takers, although the test-makers' definitions of competent performance that demonstrates the hypothetical construct (e.g., intelligence) may differ from the definitions of the test-takers (cf. **culture-fair test**)

cumulative frequency.   The total number of instances of values up to a given level (i.e., at or below a given level)

dark adaptation.   The unconscious physiological response to a reduction of light intensity in the environment, characterized by an increase in **pupil** area by a factor of about 16, and an increase in visual sensitivity to light by a factor of as much as 100,000; usually takes about 30–40 minutes for full dark adaptation to occur (cf. **light adaptation;** see **adaptation;** cf. **habituation**)

daydreaming.   A state of consciousness somewhere between waking and sleeping, which permits a shift in the focus of conscious processing toward internal thoughts and images and away from external events; useful in cognitive processes that involve the generation of creative ideas, but disruptive in

cognitive processes requiring focused attention on environmental events (see, e.g., **vigilance**)

debriefing.   An ethical procedure of experimentation, in which subjects who have participated in an experiment are informed of the true nature of the experiment and are encouraged to discuss their own reactions to the experiment; especially important in experiments for which any degree of deception has been employed (see also **informed consent**)

decay.   The phenomenon of memory by which simply the passage of time leads to forgetting

decay theory.   The assertion that information is forgotten because it gradually disappears over time, rather than because the information is displaced by other information (cf. **interference theory**)

decibel (dB).   The customary unit of measurement for the intensity of sound; 0 (zero) decibels is the absolute threshold for normal human hearing

declaration.   See **speech acts;** synonym: *performative*

declarative knowledge.   A recognition and understanding of factual information ("knowing that," not "knowing how") (cf. **procedural knowledge**)

deductive reasoning.   The process of drawing conclusions from evidence involving one or more general **premises** regarding what is known, to reach a logically certain specific conclusion (see **reasoning, syllogism;** cf. **inductive reasoning**)

deductively valid.   Characterized by having a conclusion follow logically from premises (see **deductive reasoning;** cf. **validity**)

deep structure.   The underlying meaning (or meanings) of a sentence, which may be derived from the surface structure of the sentence, and which may be derived despite various transformations of the surface structure (see **transformational grammar**)

deep-structure level.   A level of syntactical analysis, at which the underlying meanings (deep structures) of a sentence may be derived from a given surface structure and from which a given deep structure may be viewed as providing the basis for deriving various surface structures; a given deep

structure may be expressed in more than one surface structure, and a given surface structure may serve as the basis for deriving more than one deep structure; takes into account the meanings derived from sentence structure (see **transformational grammar**)

defense mechanisms.   Methods for protecting the ego from anxiety associated with the conflicting urges and prohibitions of the id and the superego; nine main defense mechanisms include **denial, displacement, fixation, projection, rationalization, reaction formation, regression, repression,** and **sublimation**

defining features.   A set of component characteristics, each of which is an essential element of a given concept, and which together compose the properties that uniquely define the concept, according to **componential theory** (cf. **characteristic features, prototype theory**)

deindividuation.   A loss of a sense of individual identity, associated with a reduction of internal constraints against socially unacceptable behavior

delay conditioning.   A paradigm for **classical conditioning,** in which there is a long delay between the onset of the **CS** and the onset of the **UCS** (cf. **trace conditioning**)

delta waves.   A pattern of **electroencephalogram (EEG)** activity (1–4 Hz) characteristic of deep sleep and shown as larger and slower brain waves than the EEG pattern of **alpha waves**

delusion.   Distorted thought process characterized by erroneous belief that persists despite strong evidence to the contrary (e.g., *delusions of persecution* involve the belief that others are scheming to harm the person in some manner; *delusions of reference* involve the belief that particular chance events or appearances have special significance; *delusions of identity* involve the person's belief that she or he is somebody else, usually someone famous; other delusions involve the belief that persons can insert thoughts into the minds of others or can transmit their thoughts nonverbally) (cf. **illusion**)

demand characteristic(s).   Attribute(s) of a situation in which the individual feels compelled to comply with the wishes of another person (who may not even be present at the time of **compliance**), regardless of whether the compulsory behavior has been requested explicitly; often used to describe psychological experiments (or clinical treatments), in which subjects (or patients) comply with the expectations of the experimenter (or clinician), perhaps even unwittingly believing themselves to be responding spontaneously, not realizing their complicity in complying with the wishes of the person in authority (also termed **experimenter effects;** cf. **placebo effect**)

dendrites. Parts of the **neuron** at the end of the **soma;** primary structures for receiving communications from other cells via distinctive receptors on their external membranes, although some communications are also received by the soma (from the Greek word for "trees," which the multi-branched dendrites resemble)

denial. A **defense mechanism,** in which the mind of an individual refuses to acknowledge or to give conscious attention to any sensations and perceptions regarding unpleasant, unwanted, anxiety-provoking, disconcerting, or threatening situations or events in the environment

denotation. The strict, dictionary definition of a word (cf. **connotation**)

deoxyribonucleic acid (DNA). The physiological material that provides the mechanism for transmission of genetic information (see also **chromosomes, genes**)

dependent variable. The outcome response or attribute that varies as a consequence of variation in one or more independent variables (cf. **independent variable**)

depression. As a **mood disorder** (also termed *major depression* and *clinical depression*), *depression* is usually termed **unipolar disorder;** as a temporary mood state, *depression* is characterized by great sadness that slows down the depressed person's behavioral responses and physiological functioning and that thereby may impair the depressed individual's ability to function effectively

depth. As applied to **perception:** the perceived distance of something from the body of the perceiver (see **monocular depth cues, binocular depth cues**)

description. A goal of science in which the scientist characterizes what and how people think, feel, or act in response to various kinds of situations (other goals include explanation, prediction, and perhaps even control of phenomena)

descriptive grammar. See **grammar**

descriptive statistic. Numerical analysis that summarizes quantitative information about a population

desensitization. A process by which an individual becomes habituated to a stimulus that initially was emotionally and physiologically arousing, as well as cognitively stimulating and captivating (see **habituation**)

design (of experiments). A way in which a given set of experimental variables are chosen and interrelated, as well as a plan for selecting and assigning subjects to experimental and control conditions

detection. Active, usually conscious, sensing of a **stimulus,** influenced by an individual's threshold for a given sense and by confounding sensory stimuli in the surrounding environment

determinism. The belief that people's behavior is ruled by forces over which they have little or no control

detoxification. A technique for trying to break an **addiction,** in which the addict both withdraws from the addictive drug and restores positive health practices; may involve temporary use of a nonpsychoactive drug (e.g., methadone) in order to facilitate **withdrawal** from a **psychoactive** drug (e.g., heroin) (cf. **maintenance**)

development. Qualitative changes in complexity, often accompanied by quantitative increases in size or amount (cf. **growth**)

developmental psychologists. Psychologists who study the differences and similarities among people of different ages, as well as the qualitative psychological changes that occur across the life span

deviation IQs. A means of determining intelligence-test scores, based on deviations from an average score, calculated such that the normative equivalent for the median score is 100, about 66.66% of the scores are computed to fall between 85 and 115, and about 95% of the scores fall between

70 and 130; not, strictly speaking, IQs, because no quotient is involved (cf. **intelligence quotient, mental age, ratio IQ**)

dialect. A regional variation of a language, characterized by distinctive features such as differences in vocabulary, grammar, and pronunciation

dialectic. A continuing intellectual dialogue in which thinkers strive for increased understanding, first by formulating an initial **thesis,** then by considering an **antithesis** to the initial view, and finally by integrating the most insightful and well-founded aspects of each view to form a **synthesis** view; because ultimate truth and understanding are ever-elusive, the dialogue never ends, and the synthesis view then serves as a new thesis for which a new antithesis may be posited, and so on

dialectical thinking. A form of thinking that characterizes a stage of mental operations hypothesized to follow the Piagetian stage of **formal operations;** such thinking recognizes that humans seldom find final, correct answers to the important questions in life, but rather a progression of beliefs comprising some kind of **thesis,** a subsequent **antithesis,** and then a **synthesis,** which then serves as the new thesis for the continuing evolution of thought (see **dialectic;** cf. **problem finding, postformal thinking**)

diencephalon. The portion of the **forebrain** comprising the **thalamus** and the **hypothalamus,** which is between the **telencephalon** and the **midbrain** (*di-*, "through" or "across"; *-encephalon*, "in the head," "brain"; cf. **metencephalon, myelencephalon**)

differentiation theory. A theory of emotional development, which asserts that a single, generalized state of arousal (which is present at birth) gradually becomes differentiated into various emotions, eventually reaching the diversity of emotions experienced by adults (cf. **discrete emotions theory**)

diffusion of responsibility. An implied diminution of personal responsibility to take action due to the presence of other persons, particularly in considering how to respond to a crisis (see also **bystander effect**)

direct perception. One of the two key views of perception (cf. **constructive perception**): asserts that the array of information in the sensory receptors, including the sensory context, is all that is needed for an individual to perceive anything; according to this view, prior knowledge or thought processes are not necessary for perception (see **feature matching**)

directive. See **speech acts**

disconfirm. Show that a particular hypothesis is not supported by data

discourse. The most comprehensive level of linguistic analysis, which encompasses language use at the level beyond the sentence, such as in conversation, in paragraphs, articles, and chapters, and entire books (cf. **semantics, syntax**)

discrete emotions theory. A theory of emotional development, which asserts that the human neural system is innately predisposed to feel various discrete emotions, given the appropriate situation in which to express those emotions (cf. **differentiation theory**)

discrimination. The ability to ascertain the difference between one stimulus and another (see **stimulus discrimination;** cf. **stimulus generalization**)

discriminative stimulus. Something in a situation that stimulates an individual to recognize whether a particular behavior is appropriate in that situation

disgust. One of the basic human emotions, associated with a response to objects or experiences deemed to be repulsive due to their nature, origin, or social history

dishabituation. Perceptual phenomenon in which a change (sometimes just a slight change) in a familiar stimulus prompts the perceiver to start noticing anew a stimulus to which the perceiver had previously become habituated (cf. **habituation**)

displacement. A **defense mechanism,** in which an individual redirects an impulse away from a potentially threatening person (e.g., someone who might punish or reject the individual) who has prompted the impulse and toward another person who is substantially less threatening

dissociative amnesia. A **dissociative disorder** characterized by a sudden memory loss of **declarative knowledge** (e.g., difficulty or inability in recalling most important personal details), and usually affecting the recollection of the events that took place during and immediately after the stressful event (see also **acute stress disorder**), but usually not affecting **procedural knowledge;** duration of the **amnesia** is variable (anywhere from several hours to several years), although recovery of the lost information is usually as rapid as was the loss of the information, after which the episode typically ends and the memory loss is not repeated

dissociative disorder. Disorder characterized by an alteration in the normally integrative functions of consciousness and identity, usually in response to a highly stressful life experience (see **dissociative amnesia, dissociative fugue, dissociative identity disorder**)

dissociative fugue. A **dissociative disorder** in which a person responds to severe stress by starting a whole new life and experiencing total **amnesia** about the past; the person moves to a new place, assumes a new identity, takes a new job, and behaves as though she or he were a completely new person, perhaps even with a new personality; duration of the fugue state is variable, but when recovery occurs, it is usually total, and the individual fully remembers her or his life prior to the fugue state but completely forgets the events that took place during the fugue state

dissociative identity disorder. A **dissociative disorder** that typically arises as a result of extreme early trauma—usually, severe child abuse—and that is characterized by the occurrence of two or more individual identities (personalities) within the same individual, in which each identity is relatively independent of any others, has a stable life of its own, and occasionally takes full control of the person's behavior (formerly termed *multiple personality disorder*)

distal stimulus. An external source of stimulation as it exists in the world, which may differ somewhat from the internal sensation of the source of stimulation that is detected in the sensory receptors (cf. **proximal stimulus;** see also **perceptual constancy**)

distraction–conflict theory. A view of **social facilitation** and social interference, in which it is held that the effect of the presence of others is due not to the mere presence of others, or even to evaluation apprehension, but rather to the distracting effect of having other people around

distributed learning. An apportionment of time spent learning a body of information by spacing the total time over various sessions, rather than consolidating the total time in a single session; generally leads to more learning than does **massed learning**

divergent production. Generation of a diverse assortment of appropriate responses to a problem question or task; often considered an aspect of **creativity** (see also **divergent thinking**)

divergent thinking. A form of **critical thinking,** which involves generating many ideas, and which may be considered to complement **convergent thinking**

doctor-centered style (of physician interactions). One of two basic patterns for physician–patient interactions (cf. **patient-centered style**); characterized by a highly directive interaction pattern, in which a physician narrowly focuses on the presenting medical problem, uses highly convergent questioning to elicit brief and targeted responses from the patient, and then formulates a diagnosis and a treatment regimen that is prescribed to the patient

domain generality. A view of development, according to which development occurs more or less simultaneously in many areas (domains) of development (cf. **domain specificity**)

domain specificity. A view of development, according to which development occurs in different areas (domains) at different rates, and in which development in one domain may not correspond to development in another domain (cf. **domain generality**)

dominant trait. The stronger genetic trait, which appears in the **phenotype** of an organism when the **genotype** comprises a dominant trait and a **recessive trait**

dopamine. A **neurotransmitter** that seems to influence several important activities, including movement, attention, and learning; deficits of the substance are linked with Parkinson's disease, but surpluses may be linked to symptoms of **schizophrenia** (cf. **acetylcholine, serotonin**)

drive. A hypothesized composite source of energy related to physiological needs, which impels people to behave in ways that reduce the given source of energy and thereby to satisfy the physiological needs

dual-system hypothesis (of bilingualism). A view of bilingualism, which suggests that the two languages are represented somehow in separate systems of the mind, and possibly even in distinct areas of the brain (cf. **single-system hypothesis**; see **bilingual**)

duplex retina theory. A widely accepted psychophysical theory that recognizes the existence of two separate visual systems, one of which is responsible for vision in dim light (which depends on the **rods**), and the other of which is responsible for vision in brighter light (which depends on the **cones**)

duplicity theory. A currently accepted view of the way in which humans sense pitch, which gives some credence to both **place theory** and **frequency theory,** but which has yet to provide a full explanation of the specific mechanisms and their interactions

dynamic assessment environment. A context for measurement of cognitive abilities, in which the interaction between the **test**-taker and the examiner does not end when the test-taker gives an incorrect response; rather the examiner offers the test-taker a sequence of guided and graded hints designed to facilitate problem solving; this kind of assessment environment is oriented toward determining the test-taker's ability to use hints and to profit from opportunities to learn, not toward determining the fixed state of existing knowledge in the test-taker (cf. **static assessment environment;** see also **zone of proximal development**)

eardrum. A physiological structure of the outer ear, which vibrates in response to sound waves that have moved through the auditory canal from the **pinna;** its vibrations are passed to the middle ear, where it transfers its vibrations to a series of ossicles (see **incus, malleus, stapes**), such that higher frequencies of sound cause more rapid vibrations (also termed *tympanum*)

echoic store. A hypothesized sensory register for fleeting storage of auditory stimuli; evidence of such a register has been insubstantial to date

effectors. The **neurons** and **nerves** that transmit motor information (e.g., movements of the large and small muscles) either from the **brain** through the **spinal cord** to the muscles (for voluntary muscle movements) or directly from the spinal cord to the muscles (in the case of **reflexes**), thus controlling bodily responses (cf. **receptors;** see **motor neuron**)

ego. One of three psychodynamic concepts (cf. **id, superego**), which responds to the real world as it is perceived to be, rather than as the person may want it to be or may believe that it should be; more broadly, an individual's unique sense of her- or himself, which embraces the person's wishes and urges but tempers them with a realization of how the world works (see **reality principle**)

egocentrism. A cognitive characteristic (not a personality trait) in which mental representations are focused on the point of view and experiences of the individual thinker and in which the individual finds it difficult to grasp the viewpoint of others

elaborative rehearsal. A strategy for keeping information in short-term memory or for moving information into long-term memory by somehow amplifying and explicating the items in a way that makes the items more meaningfully integrated into what the person already knows or more meaningfully connected to one another and therefore more memorable (cf. **maintenance rehearsal**)

Electra conflict. A conflict believed by Freudians to be characteristically experienced by girls during the **phallic stage** of **psychosexual development;** named for the Greek myth in which Electra despised her mother for having cheated on and killed her husband, Electra's father; often considered the female equivalent of the **Oedipal conflict**

electroconvulsive therapy (ECT). A psychophysiological treatment for severe, unremitting **depression,** in which electrical shocks are passed through the head of a patient, causing the patient to experience convulsive muscular seizures and temporary loss of **consciousness;** use of this treatment has been largely discontinued

electroencephalogram (EEG). A recording (*-gram*) of the electrical activity of the living brain, as detected by various electrodes (*en-*, in, *cephalo-*, head [Greek])

electromagnetic spectrum. A range of energy of varying wavelengths, a narrow band of which is visible to the human eye

emotion. A feeling comprising physiological and behavioral (and possibly cognitive) reactions to internal (e.g., thoughts, memories) and external events

emotion-focused coping. See **coping**

empirical method. Means of obtaining information and understanding through experience, observation, and experimentation

empiricist. Person who believes that knowledge is most effectively acquired through **empirical methods** (cf. **rationalist**)

empty-nest syndrome. Transitional period in adult social development, during which parents adjust to having their children grow up and move out of the family home

encoding. Process by which a physical, sensory input is transformed into a representation that can be stored in memory (cf. **decoding;** see also **elaborative rehearsal, memory, rehearsal**)

encoding specificity. Phenomenon of memory in which the specific way of representing information as it is placed into memory affects the specific way in which the information may be recalled later

endocrine system. A physiological communication network that complements the **nervous system;** operates via **glands** that secrete **hormones** directly into the bloodstream; regulates the levels of hormones in the bloodstream via negative-feedback loops (*endo-*, inside; *-crine*, related to secretion [Greek])

endorphin. A class of painkilling **neurotransmitters** produced naturally in the **brain,** which resemble the molecular composition of **opiates** (coined from *endogenous* [*endo-*, inside; *-genous*, originated, produced] *morphines*; see **neuropeptide**)

episodic memory. Encoding, storage, and retrieval of events or episodes that the rememberer experienced personally at a particular time and place (cf. **semantic memory**)

equilibration. A process of cognitive development, in which thinkers seek a balance (equilibrium) between the information and experiences they encounter in their environments and the cognitive processes and structures they bring to the encounter, as well as among the cognitive capabilities themselves; comprises three processes: the use of existing modes of thought and existing **schemas,** the process of **assimilation,** and the process of **accommodation**

equity theory. A theory of interpersonal attraction, which holds that individuals will be attracted to persons with whom they have an equitable give-and-take relationship

ethologist. Scientist who studies the way in which different species of animals behave and how behavior has evolved within differing species

evoked potentials (EPs). Electroencephalogram (EEG) recordings in which at least some of the electrical interference has been averaged out of the data by means of averaging the EEG wave forms on successive EEG recordings; experimental uses have included using the recordings to map the electrical activity of various parts of the brain during various cognitive tasks or in response to various kinds of stimuli

exemplar. One of several typical representatives of a particular concept or of a class of objects; sometimes, several exemplars are used as a set of alternatives to a single prototype for deriving the meaning of a concept (see **prototype theory**)

exhaustive serial processing. A means of responding to a task involving recognition of a particular item from a list of items, in which an indi-

vidual seeks to retrieve an item stored in memory by checking the item being sought against all of the possible items that are presented, even if a match is found partway through the list (cf. **self-terminating serial processing;** cf. also **parallel processing**)

existentialism. A philosophy that focuses on (a) the isolated existence of human individuals in an indifferent (neither divinely nor demonically designed) world, and (b) the personal responsibility of each individual for her or his own choices, as well as for the consequences of those choices (cf. **humanism**)

exocrine system. A physiological system through which some **glands** secrete fluids (e.g., tears or sweat) through *ducts* that serve as physiological channels to pass the fluids out of the body (*exo-*, outside; *-crine*, referring to secretion [Greek]; cf. **endocrine system**)

experiment. An investigation of cause–effect relationships through the control of variables and the careful manipulation of one or more particular variables, to note their outcome effects on other variables (see **control condition, experimental condition;** cf. **case study, naturalistic observation, survey, test**)

experimental analysis of behavior. An extreme behavioristic view that all behavior should be studied and analyzed in terms of specific **stimulus–response** contingencies

experimental condition. A situation in which a group of experimental subjects is exposed to a carefully prescribed set of circumstances, which are almost identical to the **control condition** but which also include the treatment involving the **independent variable** that is being manipulated in the **experiment** (also termed *treatment condition*)

experimental neurosis. Induction of a maladjustment in behavior or cognitive processing, by means of classical conditioning in which the discriminative stimulus is so ambiguous that it is virtually impossible to discern whether a particular response is appropriate or is inappropriate (see also **neurosis**)

experimenter bias. A phenomenon of scientific research in which researchers may end up supporting their

initial hypotheses because they have chosen tasks or task manipulations (usually unwittingly) that are likely to favor an outcome that agrees with their preexisting point of view

explanation. One of four goals of psychological research (the other three are **control, description,** and **prediction**)

explicit memory. A form of memory retrieval in which an individual consciously acts to recall or recognize particular information (cf. **implicit memory**)

expressive. See **speech acts**

external locus of control. Characterized by the tendency to believe that the causes of behavioral consequences originate in the environment, sometimes involving an extreme view in which the individual consistently misattributes causality to external rather than to internal causes (cf. **internal locus of control**)

extinction (as a phase of learning). A period of time during which the probability of the occurrence of a **CR** decreases, eventually approaching zero, due to the unlinking of the **CS** with the **UCS;** the individual still retains some memory of the learning, however, as the CR can be relearned very quickly if the CS and the UCS become paired again

extinction procedure. A **behavior-therapy** technique (e.g., **flooding, implosion therapy**) that is designed to weaken maladaptive responses

extrasensory perception (ESP). Apparent perception of phenomena that cannot be explained by known sensory and perceptual processes; considered by some to be an altered state of consciousness (see **clairvoyance, precognition, psychokinesis, telepathy**)

extrinsic motivators. One of the two primary types of sources of motivation (cf. **intrinsic motivators**); motivating forces that come from outside the motivated individual, which encourage the person to engage in behavior because the person either is rewarded for doing so or is threatened with punishment for not doing so; often decrease intrinsic motivation to engage in behavior, such that the individual discontinues the behavior when extrinsic motivators are removed, even though the individual may have been intrinsically motivated to engage in the behavior prior to the introduction of extrinsic motivators; decrements in intrinsic motivation are particularly likely if extrinsic motivators are expected, are perceived as relevant and important to the individual, and are tangible

extroversion. See **Big Five;** see also **extrovert, introvert**

extrovert. Person who prefers the company of other people to being alone, perhaps because the person has a low baseline level of **arousal** and therefore seeks out other people to raise the level of arousal (cf. **introvert;** see also **Big Five:** *extroversion*)

eye contact. A major source of nonverbal communication, signaling culturally determined social information about intimacy and dominance via the frequency and duration of exchanged gazes

face validity. A kind of **validity,** in which test-takers judge the extent to which the content of a test measures all of the knowledge or skills that are supposed to be included within the domain being tested

facial-feedback hypothesis. An assumption suggesting that the cognitive feedback going to the brain as a result of the stimulation of particular facial muscles associated with particular emotional expressions (e.g., a smile or a frown) causes a person to infer that she or he is feeling a particular emotion

factor analysis. A method of statistical decomposition that allows an investigator to infer distinct hypothetical constructs, elements, or structures that underlie a phenomenon

factors. Hypothetical constructs, elements, or structures that underlie a given phenomenon

fallacy of composition. A common error of judgment, in which the person making a judgment believes that what is true of the parts of a whole must necessarily be true of the whole as well, without considering the quality of the integration of those parts (cf. **gestalt)**

false alarm. A response in which

an individual inaccurately asserts that a signal stimulus has been observed; in **signal-detection theory (SDT),** the inaccurate belief that a signal stimulus was detected when it was actually absent (cf. **correct rejection, hit, miss**); in memory tasks, a response in which subjects indicate that they have previously seen an item in a list, even though the item was not shown previously

fear. An emotion characterized by being afraid of a specific threat of danger or harm, focused on a particular object or experience (cf. **anxiety**)

feature-detector approach. A psychophysiological approach to form **perception,** which attempts to link the psychological perception of form to the functioning of **neurons** in the **brain,** based on single-cell (neuronal) recording techniques for tracing the route of the neurons from the **receptors** within the **retina,** through the **ganglion cells,** then the thalamic nucleus cells, to the visual cortex; these psychophysiological studies indicated that specific neurons of the visual cortex respond to various stimuli that are presented to the specific retinal regions connected to these neurons; apparently, each individual cortical neuron can be mapped to a specific receptive field on the retina (see **complex cells, simple cells**)

feature hypothesis. A view regarding the means by which children make **overextension** errors: Children form definitions that include too few features, and they therefore overextend the use of given words because they lack one or more defining features that would more narrowly constrain the application of a given word (cf. **functional hypothesis**)

feature-matching theories of form perception. Theories of form perception (see **direct perception;** cf. **constructive perception**), according to which people attempt to match features of an observed pattern to features stored in memory, without considering the prior experience of the perceiver or what the perceiver already knows about the context in which the form is presented

Fechner's law. The principle that relates the psychological magnitude of a sensation to the physical magnitude of

the stimulus that prompts the sensation, by noting the following relation: $S = W \log I$, where S is the magnitude of sensation elicited by a stimulus, I is the physical magnitude of the stimulus (as in **Weber's law**), and W is a constant (based on the value of the **Weber fraction**)

fetal alcohol syndrome. An assemblage of disorders, chief among which are permanent and irreparable mental retardation and facial deformities, which may result when pregnant mothers consume alcohol during the fetal development of their infants

field. A domain of study, centered on a set of topics that have a common sphere of related interests or a common core of related phenomena (cf. **perspective**)

figure. See **figure–ground;** cf. **ground**

figure–ground. A Gestalt principle of form perception (see **Gestalt approach**): the tendency to perceive that an object in or an aspect of a perceptual field seems prominent (termed the **figure**), whereas other aspects or objects recede into the background (termed the **ground**)

first-order conditioning. A **classical-conditioning** procedure whereby a **CS** is linked directly with a **UCS** (cf. **higher order conditioning**)

fissure. Large groove in the convolutions of the **cerebral cortex** (cf. **gyri; sulci**)

fixated. A phenomenon of **psychosexual development,** in which an individual is unable to resolve the relevant issues of the current stage and therefore is unable to progress to the next stage (see also **defense mechanisms**)

fixed-interval reinforcement. A schedule of **operant conditioning** in which reinforcement always occurs after the passage of a certain amount of time, as long as the **operant** response has occurred at least once during the particular period of time (see **partial reinforcement;** cf. **fixed-ratio reinforcement, variable-interval reinforcement;** cf. also **variable-ratio reinforcement**)

fixed-ratio reinforcement. An **operant-conditioning** schedule in which reinforcement always occurs after a certain number of **operant** responses, regardless of the amount of time it takes to produce that number of responses (see **partial reinforcement;** cf. **fixed-interval reinforcement, variable-ratio reinforcement;** cf. also **variable-interval reinforcement**)

flashbulb memory. Recollection of an event that is so emotionally powerful that the recollection is highly vivid and richly detailed, as if it were indelibly preserved on film, although the true accuracy of such recall is not as great as the rememberer might believe it to be

flooding. Extinction procedures designed to lessen anxiety by exposing a client to a carefully controlled environment in which an anxiety-provoking stimulus is presented, but the client experiences no harm from the stimulus, so the client is expected to cease to feel anxiety in response to the stimulus (cf. **implosion therapy**)

fluid intelligence. One of two major subfactors of general intelligence; represents the acquisition of new information or the grasping of new relations and abstractions regarding known information (may be measured, for example, by timed tests involving analogies, series completions, or inductive reasoning) (cf. **crystallized intelligence**)

forebrain. The farthest forward (toward the face) of the three major regions of the **brain** (cf. **midbrain, hindbrain;** names correspond roughly to the front-to-back arrangement of these parts in the developing embryo): the region located toward the top and front of the brain in adults; comprises the **cerebral cortex,** the **limbic system,** the **thalamus,** and the **hypothalamus**

foreclosure. One of four main types of identity (cf. **identity achievement, identity diffusion, moratorium;** cf. also **alienated achievement**), in which an individual makes a commitment to beliefs without ever having considered various alternatives to those beliefs

formal-operational stage. A stage of cognitive development in Piaget's theory, in which the individual can engage in mental manipulations of internal representations of abstract symbols that (a) may not have specific concrete equivalents, and (b) may relate to ex-

periences the individual may not have encountered personally (cf. **concrete operations, preoperational stage, sensorimotor stage**)

fovea. A small, central, thin region of the **retina** that has a high concentration of **cones,** each of which has its own **ganglion cell** leading to the optic nerve, thereby increasing the visual **acuity** in bright light of images within the visual field of the foveal region (in contrast, the periphery of the retina has relatively fewer cones and more **rods,** which have to share ganglion cells with other rods, thereby reducing visual acuity in the peripheral visual field and in dim light)

free association. A phenomenon of psychodynamic therapy in which the patient freely says whatever comes to mind, not censoring or otherwise editing the free flow of words before reporting them

free nerve endings. Sensory receptors in the skin, which lack the globular swellings that characterize some other somatosensory receptors

free recall. A type of memory task in which a subject is presented with a list of items and is asked to repeat the items in any order the subject prefers (cf. **paired-associates recall, serial recall**)

frequency. In *statistical contexts,* applies to the number of instances of a given attribute, phenomenon, or response; in *psychophysical, sensory contexts,* applies to the number of waves of sound or light that occur within a specified interval, usually a second; in sound waves, higher frequencies are associated with higher pitches of sounds; in light waves (which are usually measured in terms of wavelengths, which are inversely related to frequencies), various frequencies are associated with various colors in the visible electromagnetic spectrum, as well as with various other forms of radiance (e.g., microwaves or gamma waves)

frequency distribution. The dispersion of values in a set of values, represented as the number, proportion, or percentage (i.e., the frequency) of instances of each value

frequency theory. One of two views of the way in which humans sense **pitch** (cf. **place theory**): The **basilar membrane** reproduces the vibrations

that enter the ear, triggering neural impulses at the same **frequency** as the original sound wave, so that the frequency of the impulses that enter the **auditory nerve** determines the number of electrical responses per second in the auditory nerve; these responses are then sensed as a given pitch by the brain (see also **duplicity theory, volley principle**)

frontal lobe. One of the four major regions of the **cerebral cortex** (cf. **occipital lobe, parietal lobe, temporal lobe**): generally responsible for motor processing and for higher thought processes, such as abstract reasoning

function morpheme. A **morpheme** that adds detail and nuance to the meaning of a **content morpheme** or that helps a content morpheme to fit a particular syntactical context

functional fixedness. A particular type of **mental set,** in which the problem solver is unable to recognize that something that is known to be used in one way, for one purpose, may also be used for performing other functions, perhaps even through use in another way

functional hypothesis. A view regarding the means by which children make **overextension errors** (cf. **feature hypothesis**): Children base their initial use of words on the important purposes (functions) of the concepts represented by the words, and children then make overextension errors because of their confusion regarding the functions of the objects being identified

functionalism. A school of psychology that focuses on active psychological processes, rather than on passive psychological structures or elements; for example, functionalists were more interested in how people think than in what they think, in how people perceive rather than in what they perceive, and in how and why organisms evolve as they do rather than in what particular outcomes are produced by the evolutionary process (cf. **structuralism**)

fundamental attribution error. A bias of **attribution** in which an individual tends to overemphasize internal causes and personal responsibility and to deemphasize external causes and situational influences when observing the behavior of other people (see also **actor–observer effect, self-handicapping**)

fundamental frequency. The single tone produced by a note played on a musical instrument (which may also produce a series of harmonic tones at various multiples of the fundamental frequency; see **harmonics**)

g. A general factor of intelligence, believed to be derived from individual differences in mental energy

gambler's fallacy. An intuitive and fallacious inference that when a sequence of coincidental events appears to be occurring in a nonrandom pattern (e.g., a protracted series of heads in a coin toss), subsequent events are more likely to deviate from the apparent pattern (e.g., the appearance of a tail) than to continue in the apparent pattern (e.g., the appearance of another head), when actually the probability of each event continues to have the same random probability at each occurrence (see **heuristic**)

game theory. A theory regarding decision making, which suggests that the ways in which people make many decisions, especially those involving more than one person, are often characterized by properties that resemble the properties of games (cf. **satisficing, subjective-utility theory, utility maximization theory**); four of the strategies are *maximax gain rule*—the decision-maker seeks to *maxi*mize the *maxi*mum possible gain, *maximin gain rule*—the decision-maker *maxi*mizes the *mini*mum possible gain, *minimax loss rule*—the decision-maker makes a choice that *mini*mizes the *maxi*mum possible loss, *minimin loss rule*—the decision-maker makes a choice that *mini*mizes the *mini*mum possible loss

ganglion cells. Cells that form the first of three layers of cells in the **retina**; the **axons** of these cells form the optic nerve and communicate with the **photoreceptors** (in the third layer) via the middle layer of cells in the retina (cf. **amacrine cells, bipolar cells, horizontal cells**)

García effect. A classically conditioned response in which a particular smell or taste (the **CS**) leads to a feeling of revulsion or queasiness (the **CR**), due to the previous pairing of the CS with digestive upset or other illness; often occurs after a single pairing of the CS with the **UCS**

gate-control theory. A theory proposing a possible mechanism by which cognition, emotion, and sensation may interact to affect pain perception, in which it is posited that (a) the **central nervous system** serves as a physiological gating mechanism, which can modulate the degree to which pain is perceived, and (b) cognitions and emotions in the brain can cause the spinal cord to intensify or to inhibit pain transmission by raising or lowering the "gate" (the *pain threshold* that determines the amount of stimulus required to trigger the sensation of pain) for pain stimulation

gender. Social and psychological distinction as being male or female (cf. **sex**)

gender constancy. The realization that a person's gender is stable and cannot be changed by changing superficial characteristics (e.g., hair length) or behaviors (e.g., carrying a purse) (see **gender typing**)

gender typing. The process of acquiring the roles and associations related to the social and psychological distinction as being male or female

gene. Each of the basic physiological building blocks for the hereditary transmission of **traits** in all life forms (see **chromosomes, deoxyribonucleic acid**)

general adaptation syndrome. A physiological response to stress, in which the body initially exerts maximal effort to adapt; if the stressor continues to prompt a response, however, the body reduces exertion in order to conserve physiological resources until eventually the body exhausts those resources

generalization. See **stimulus generalization**; cf. **stimulus discrimination**

generalized anxiety disorder. An **anxiety disorder** characterized by general, persistent, constant, and often debilitating high levels of anxiety, which are accompanied by psychophysiological symptoms typical of a hyperactive **autonomic nervous system,** and which can last any length of time, from a month to years; such anxiety is often described as "free floating" because it cannot be pinned down easily

generate and test. See **heuristic**

genetics. The study of genes and heredity and variations among individuals (see **behavioral genetics**)

genital stage. A stage of **psychosexual development:** typically starts in adolescence and continues through adulthood, and involves normal adult sexuality, as Freud defined it—i.e., the adoption of traditional sex roles and of a heterosexual orientation

genotype. The pair of genes on a given chromosome pair, which is inherited from each parent and *not* subject to environmental influence (except in cases of genetic mutation); possibilities include both **dominant traits** and **recessive traits,** either of which may be passed on to biological offspring (cf. **phenotype**)

gestalt. The distinctive totality of an integrated whole, as opposed to merely a sum of various parts (from the German word *Gestalt*)

Gestalt approach. A way of studying form perception, based on the notion that the whole of the form is greater than the sum of its individual parts (*Gestalt*, form [German]; see also **Gestalt psychology**) (see **closure, continuity, figure–ground, proximity, similarity, symmetry**)

Gestalt psychology. A school of psychological thought, which holds that psychological phenomena are best understood when viewed as organized, structured wholes, not analyzed into myriad component elements (*Gestalt*, form [German]; see also **Gestalt approach**)

gland. Group of cells that secretes chemical substances; in the **endocrine system,** glands secrete **hormones** directly into the bloodstream; in the **exocrine system,** glands secrete fluids (e.g., tears, sweat) into ducts that channel the fluids out of the body

glial cell. Type of structure (also termed *neuroglia*) that nourishes, supports, and positions neurons within the **central nervous system (CNS),** functioning as a kind of glue holding the CNS together, and keeping the neurons at optimal distances from one another and from other structures in the body, thereby helping to minimize miscommunication problems among neurons; also assist in forming the **myelin sheath,** such that the gaps between glial cells form the nodes in the sheath (see **nodes of Ranvier**)

glucostatic hypothesis. One of two major alternative assumptions regarding how the body signals hunger versus satiety (cf. **lipostatic hypothesis**): suggests that the levels of *glucose* (a simple body sugar) in the blood signal the body regarding the need for food; *glucostatic:* maintaining the stability (*-static*) of glucose (*gluco-*) levels in the body and in the brain

gradient of reinforcement. An important consideration in establishing, maintaining, or extinguishing **operant conditioning,** in which the length of time that occurs between the **operant response** and the reinforcing **stimulus** affects the strength of the conditioning: the longer the interval of time, the weaker the effect of the reinforcer

grammar. The study of **language** in terms of regular patterns that relate to the functions and relationships of words in a sentence—extending as broadly as the level of discourse and as narrowly as the pronunciation and meaning of individual words; *descriptive grammar*—the description of language patterns that relate to the structures, functions, and relationships of words in a sentence (see **phrase-structure grammars; transformational grammar**); *prescriptive grammar*—the formulation of various rules dictating the preferred use of written and spoken language, such as the functions, structures, and relationships of words in a sentence

grief. A sharp, deep, and usually relatively long-lasting emotion of great sorrow, often associated with a loss (cf. **sadness**)

ground. See **figure–ground**

group. A collection of individuals who interact with each other, often for a common purpose or activity

group polarization. Exaggeration of the initial views of members of a group, through the dynamic processes of group interaction

groupthink. A process of the dynamics of group interactions, in which group members focus on the goal of unanimity of opinion more than they focus on the achievement of other goals, such as the purpose for which the group may have been designed in the first place; such a process is characterized by six symptoms: (1) *closed-mindedness* to alternative conceptualizations; (2) *rationalization* of both the processes and the products of group decision making; (3) the *squelching of dissent* through ostracism, criticism, or ignoring; (4) the inclusion of a self-appointed *mindguard,* who diligently upholds the group norm; (5) the *feeling of invulnerability,* due to special knowledge or expertise; and (6) the *feeling of unanimity;* the net result of this process is defective decision making

growth. Quantitative linear increases in size or amount (cf. **development**)

gyri. Bulges between adjacent **sulci** or **fissures** in the convolutions of the **cerebral cortex** (singular, *gyrus*)

habituation. The tendency to become accustomed to a stimulus and gradually to notice it less and less (cf. **dishabituation;** cf. also **adaptation;** see also **opponent-process theory of addiction and emotion**)

hair cells. The thousands of specialized hairlike appendages on the **basilar membrane,** which function as auditory **receptors,** transducing mechanical energy from the vibration of the **stapes** into electrochemical energy that goes to the sensory neurons, which carry the auditory information to the brain (see **transduce;** see also **cochlea**)

hallucinations. Perceptions of sensory stimulation (e.g., sounds [the most common hallucinated sensations], sights, smells, or tactile sensations) in the absence of any actual corresponding external sensory input from the physical world

hallucinogenic. A type of **psychoactive** drug (e.g., mescaline, LSD, and marijuana) that alters consciousness by inducing hallucinations and affecting the way the drug-takers perceive both their inner worlds and their external environments; often termed *psychotomimetics* (also known as "psychedelics") because some clinicians believe that these drugs mimic the effects produced by **psychosis**

happiness. A feeling of joy or at least contentment (see **emotion**)

haptic. Characterized by sensitivity to pressure, temperature, and pain stimulation directly on the skin

harmonics. Distinctive tones that musical instruments generate, along with the **fundamental frequency** of the note being played, which are higher multiples of the fundamental frequency (cf. **noise**); different musical instruments yield distinctive multiples of the fundamental frequencies, resulting in the distinctive tonal qualities of the instruments

health psychology. The study of the reciprocal interaction between the psychological processes of the mind and the physical health of the body

heritability coefficient. The degree to which heredity contributes to intelligence, expressed in terms of a number on a scale from 0 to 1, such that a coefficient of 0 means that heredity has no influence on variation among people, whereas a coefficient of 1 means that heredity is the only influence on such variation

hertz (Hz). A **frequency** of one cycle per second, often applied to sound waves

heuristic. An informal, intuitive, speculative strategy (e.g., a *trial-and-error heuristic*) that sometimes works effectively for solving problems (cf. **algorithms**); problem-solving heuristics include the following: *generate and test*—innovative origination of a series of alternative courses of action (with no particular systematic method for producing the alternatives) and assessment of the usefulness of each course of action until an alternative is found that solves the problem; *means–ends analysis*—analysis of the problem by viewing the end—the goal being sought—and then trying to decrease the distance between the current position in the problem space and the end goal in that space, using any means available; *working backward*—problem solving that focuses on the desired end, and then works backward to the beginning from the end; *working forward*—problem solving that starts at the beginning of the problem and then solves the problem from the start to the finish; also, some heuristics serve as mental short-cuts that aid in making speedy responses, but that sometimes also lead to errors in judgment (see, e.g., **availability heuristic, gambler's fallacy, illusory correlation, representativeness**)

higher order conditioning. A **classical-conditioning** procedure (e.g., **first-order conditioning**) whereby a **CS** is not linked directly with a **UCS**, but rather is linked to an established CS, thereby producing a weaker (more volatile and more susceptible to **extinction**) form of classical conditioning

hindbrain. The farthest back of the three major regions of the **brain** (cf. **forebrain, midbrain**), located near the back of the neck in adults; comprises the **medulla oblongata,** the **pons,** amd the **cerebellum**

hippocampus. A portion of the **limbic system** (*hippocampus*, Greek for "seahorse," its approximate shape); plays an essential role in the formation of new memories

hit. One of the four possible combinations of stimulus and response described in **signal-detection theory (SDT)** (cf. **correct rejection, false alarm, miss**): the accurate recognition that a signal stimulus was detected, which was truly present

Hoffding function. The distinctive relation between what is sensed and what is stored in memory, which involves more than just a simple sensory link between the two

homeostatic regulation. Process by which the body maintains a state of equilibrium, such that when the body lacks something, it sends signals that prompt the individual to seek the missing resource, whereas when the body is satiated, it sends signals to stop obtaining that resource

homosexuality. A tendency to direct sexual desire toward another person of the same (Greek, *homo-*, "same") sex; often termed *lesbianism* in women (cf. **bisexuality**)

horizontal cells. One of three kinds of **interneuron** cells in the middle of three layers of cells in the **retina**: The **amacrine cells** and the horizontal cells provide lateral connections, which permit lateral communication with adjacent areas of the retina in the middle layer of cells (cf. **bipolar cells;** see **ganglion cells, photoreceptors**)

hormone. Chemical substance, secreted by one or more **glands,** which regulates many physiological processes through specific actions on cells, fosters the growth and proliferation of cells, and may affect the way a receptive cell goes about its activities (see **endocrine system**)

hostile aggression. An emotional and usually impulsive action intended to cause harm or injury to another person or persons, often provoked by feelings of pain or distress, not by a desire to gain something through the aggressive act—in fact, valuable relationships and objects may be harmed or put at risk of harm through hostile aggression (see **aggression;** cf. **instrumental aggression**)

hue. Physical properties of light waves that correspond closely to the psychological properties of *color*, which is the subjective interpretation of the physiological processing of various wavelengths of the narrow band of visible light within the electromagnetic spectrum

human dilemma. Problematic situation in which humans have been separated from other animals and even from nature as a whole

humanism. A philosophical approach that centers on the unique character of humans and their relationship to the natural world, on human interactions, on human concerns, and on secular human values, including the need for humans to treat one another humanely; arose during the Renaissance, in contrast to the prevailing philosophy, which emphasized divinely determined values and divine explanations for human behavior (cf. **existentialism**)

humanistic. See **humanism** and **humanistic psychology**

humanistic psychology. A school of psychological thought that emphasizes (a) conscious experience in personal development rather than unconscious experience, (b) free will and the importance of human potential rather than determinism, and (c) holistic approaches to psychological phenomena rather than analytic approaches

hypnosis. An altered state of consciousness that usually involves deep relaxation and extreme sensitivity to suggestion and appears to bear some resemblance to sleep (see **posthypnotic suggestion**)

hypothalamus. Located at the base of the **forebrain,** beneath (*hypo-*, Greek, "under") the **thalamus;** controls water balance in the tissues and bloodstream; regulates internal temperature, appetite, and thirst, as well as many other functions of the **autonomic nervous system;** plays a key role in controlling the **endocrine system;** interacts with the **limbic system** for regulating behavior related to species survival (fighting, feeding, fleeing, and mating); in conjunction with the **reticular activating system,** plays a role in controlling **consciousness;** involved in regulating **emotions,** pleasure, **pain,** and **stress** reactions

hypotheses. Tentative proposals regarding expected consequences, such as the outcomes of research (singular, *hypothesis*)

hypothesis testing. A view of language acquisition, which asserts that children acquire **language** by mentally forming tentative **hypotheses** regarding language and then testing these hypotheses in the environment, using several operating principles for generating and testing their hypotheses; also more broadly applies to testing of scientific and other hypotheses

hypothetical construct. Abstract concept (e.g., *beauty, truth,* or *intelligence*) that is not itself directly measurable or observable but that can be presumed to give rise to responses and attributes that can be observed and measured

iconic store. A sensory register for the fleeting storage of discrete visual images in the form of *icons* (visual images that represent something, usually resembling whatever is being represented)

id. The most primitive of three psychodynamic concepts (cf. **ego, superego**): the unconscious, instinctual source of impulsive urges, such as sexual and aggressive impulses, as well as the source of the wishes and fantasies that derive from these impulses, without consideration for rationality or for external reality

ideal self. A person's view of the personal characteristics that the person would like to embody (cf. **self-concept**)

idealistic principle. Operating principle of the **superego,** which guides a person's actions in terms of what she or he should do, as dictated by internalized authority figures, without regard for rationality or even for external reality (cf. **pleasure principle, reality principle**)

identity achievement. One of four main types of identity (cf. **foreclosure, identity diffusion, moratorium;** cf. also **alienated achievement**), in which the individual establishes a firm and secure sense of self, following a period of questioning her or his personal values and beliefs

identity diffusion. One of four main types of identity (cf. **foreclosure; identity achievement; moratorium;** cf. also **alienated achievement**), in which the individual cannot establish a firm and secure sense of self and therefore lacks direction and commitment

idiographic personality theory. One of two basic kinds of trait theories of personality (cf. **nomothetic personality theory**); characterizing a belief that people differ in the set of personality traits they have or at least in the importance of these traits to who they are

ill-structured problem. A type of problem for which a clear path to solution is not known (cf. **well-structured problem**)

illusion. Distorted perception of objects and other external stimuli, which may be due to misleading cues in the objects themselves or due to distortions of the perceptual process, such as distortions due to altered states of consciousness or psychological disorder (see **optical illusion;** cf. **delusion**)

illusory correlation. An inferred perception of a relation between unrelated variables, usually arising because the instances in which the variables coincide seem more noticeable than the instances in which the variables do not coincide (as applied to **prejudice,** people are more likely to notice instances of unusual behavior in relation to a minority population than to no-

tice common behaviors in members of a minority population or unusual behaviors in members of a majority population) (see **heuristics**)

implicit memory. A form of memory retrieval in which an individual uses recalled or recognized information without consciously being aware of doing so (cf. **explicit memory**)

implosion therapy. A set of **extinction procedures** designed to weaken anxiety by having clients imagine as vividly as possible the unpleasant events that are causing them anxiety; clients repeat the procedure as often as necessary to extinguish their anxiety (cf. **flooding**)

impression formation. The process by which individuals form intuitive conceptions about other people, based on inferences from information obtained both directly and indirectly (see **confirmation bias, person-positivity bias, primacy effect, self-fulfilling prophecy;** cf. **impression-management theory**)

impression-management theory. Hypothesized principles regarding the way in which each individual tries to encourage other people to infer a particular intuitive conception about them, by shaping the information about the individual that is provided either directly or indirectly to other people; emphasizes the manipulation of apparent characteristics and behavior over actual ones, in order to foster favorable impressions (cf. **impression formation;** cf. also **cognitive dissonance, self-perception theory**)

imprinting. A form of preprogrammed learning in which a newborn individual engages in a particular behavior simply as a result of being exposed to a particular kind of stimulus, although the specific stimulus that prompts the preprogrammed behavior is learned; the two main kinds of imprinting are (1) *filial imprinting,* in which the behavior of a young animal is brought under the control of an older animal, typically the mother; and (2) *sexual imprinting,* whereby the young animal learns the kind of animal with which it will later have sexual relations (typically same-species, opposite sex); however, imprinting may also determine other behaviors, such as an animal's return to a spawning ground

that has a distinctive odor

incubation. A process by which a problem-solver discontinues intensive work on solving a problem, stops focusing conscious attention on solving the problem for a while, and permits problem solving to occur at a subconscious level for a period of time; believed to be particularly helpful in solving some insight problems

incus. One of the three bones of the middle ear (cf. **malleus, stapes**), which normally receive and amplify the vibrations transmitted by the **tympanum (eardrum)** and then transmit those vibrations to the **cochlea**

independent variable. An attribute that is individually manipulated by the experimenter, while other aspects of the investigation are held constant (i.e., not subject to variation) (cf. **dependent variable**)

indirect request. A form of s**peech act** in which the individual makes requests (see **speech acts:** *directives*) in an oblique, rather than a direct, manner

induced movement. The perceptual phenomenon in which individuals who are moving and are observing other objects within a stable perceptual frame (such as the side window of a car or train) perceive that the fixed objects are moving rather than that they (the observers) are moving

inductive reasoning. The process of drawing general explanatory conclusions based on evidence involving specific facts or observations; permits the reasoner to draw well-founded or probable conclusions but not logically certain conclusions (see **reasoning;** cf. **deductive reasoning**)

infantile amnesia. See **amnesia**

inferential statistics. One of two key ways in which statistics are used (cf. **descriptive statistic**), in which a researcher analyzes numerical data in order to determine the likelihood that the given findings are a result of systematic, rather than random, fluctuations or events

inferiority complex. A means by which people organize their thoughts, emotions, and behavior based on their perceived mistakes and feelings of inferiority

inflection (grammatical). A type of **function morpheme,** which comprises the common **suffixes** added to **content morphemes** to fit the words to the given grammatical context (differ from *vocal inflection*, tonal fluctuation that adds expression to speech)

information processing. Operations by which people mentally manipulate what they learn and know about the world

information-processing theorists. Theorists who seek to understand the ways in which various people perform mental operations on information (i.e., decode, encode, transfer, combine, store, and retrieve information), particularly when solving challenging mental problems

informed consent. An ethical procedure of experimentation: Experimental subjects are briefed prior to the implementation of the experiment and are fully informed of the nature of the treatment procedure and any possible harmful side effects or consequences of the treatment, as well as the likelihood that these consequences may take place (see also **debriefing**)

insight. A distinctive and apparently sudden understanding of a problem or a sudden realization of a strategy that aids in solving a problem, which is usually preceded by a great deal of prior thought and hard work; often involves reconceptualizing a problem or a strategy for its solution in a totally new way; frequently emerges by detecting and combining relevant old and new information to gain a novel view of the problem or of its solution; often associated with finding solutions to **ill-structured problems** (see **insight problem**; see also **selective-combination insight, selective comparison insight, selective-encoding insight**)

insight problem. A problem that requires **insight** (novel reconceptualization of the problem) in order to reach a solution

insomnia. Any of various disturbances of sleep, which include difficulty falling asleep, waking up during the night and being unable to go back to sleep, or waking up too early in the morning, and which may vary in intensity and duration

instinct. An inherited, species-specific, stereotyped pattern of preprogrammed behavior that involves a

relatively complex pattern of response (cf. **reflex**); generally characterized by less flexibility in adaptability to changes in an environment but greater assurance that a complex pattern of behavior will occur as it is preprogrammed to occur, without variation

instinctive. Characterized by **instinct**

instrumental aggression. A form of **antisocial behavior** that the aggressor realizes may result in harm or injury to the recipient(s) of the **aggression** but that the aggressor pursues in order to gain something of value to the aggressor; generally not as impulsive or as emotional as **hostile aggression** and often implemented without particularly malicious intentions toward the recipients of the aggression; that is, the recipients of the aggression were not seen as targets, but rather were viewed as obstacles in the way of obtaining something valuable to the aggressor

intelligence. Goal-directed adaptive behavior

intelligence quotient (IQ). See **ratio IQ**; cf. **deviation IQs, mental age**

intensity. The amount of physical energy that is transduced by a sensory **receptor** and then sensed in the **brain** (cf. **quality**)

interactionist approach. A theoretical approach that emphasizes the interaction between characteristics of the person and characteristics of the situation

interactive images. See **mnemonic devices**

interference. Information that competes with the information that the individual is trying to store in memory, thereby causing the individual to forget that information (cf. **decay**; see also **interference theory**)

interference theory. The assertion that information is forgotten because it is displaced by interfering information, which disrupts and displaces the information that the individual had tried to store in memory originally, rather than because the information gradually disappears over time (cf. **decay theory**)

internal-consistency reliability. See **reliability**

internal locus of control. Characterized by an individual's tendency to

believe that the causes of behavioral consequences originate within the individual, sometimes involving an extreme view in which the individual misattributes causality to internal rather than to external causes (cf. **external locus of control**)

internalization. A process of cognitive development in which an individual absorbs knowledge from an external environmental context

interneuron. The most numerous type of neuron of the three main types of **neurons** in humans (cf. **motor neuron, sensory neuron**); intermediate between (*inter-*, "between") sensory and motor neurons, receiving signals from either sensory neurons or other interneurons, and then sending signals either to other interneurons or to motor neurons

interposition. See **monocular depth cues**

interrater reliability. See **reliability**

interval schedule. See **fixed-interval reinforcement; variable-interval reinforcement;** see also **partial reinforcement**

intimacy. One of three basic components of love, according to the **triangular theory of love** (cf. **commitment, passion**): feelings that promote closeness and connection

intoxicated. Characterized by stupefaction due to the effects of toxins such as alcohol or **sedative–hypnotic drugs**

intrinsic motivators. One of the primary two sources of motivation (cf. **extrinsic motivators**); motivating forces that come from within a motivated individual, which are at work when the person engages in behavior because the person enjoys doing so

introjection. A reaction to the loss of or separation from a cherished object of affection, in which the grieving person incorporates aspects of the beloved in an attempt to regain at least part of the loved one

introspection. Self-examination of inner ideas and experiences, used by early psychologists as a method of studying psychological phenomena (*intro-*, "inward, within"; *-spect*, "look")

introvert. A person who prefers being alone to being in the company of other people, perhaps because the person has a high baseline level of

arousal and therefore seeks to avoid other people who might further raise the level of arousal; usually characterized by quietness, restraint, general unsociability, as well as little interest in interacting with other people (cf. **extrovert**)

ipsilateral. Characterized as occurring or appearing on the same side (*ipsi-*, self; *lateral*, side); often used in describing physiological structures (cf. **contralateral**)

iris. A circular membrane that reflects light beams outward and away from the eye; surrounds the **pupil,** which is essentially a hole in the center of the iris

isomorphic. Characterized by having the same formal structure but not necessarily having the same content (*iso-*, same; *-morph*, form; *-ic*, adjectival suffix; see also **transparency**)

judgment and decision making. One of the fundamental kinds of thinking (cf. **creativity, problem solving, reasoning**), in which the goal is to evaluate various opportunities or to choose from among various options (see **game theory, satisficing, subjective-utility theory, utility maximization theory;** see also **heuristic**)

just noticeable difference (jnd). The minimum amount of difference between two sensory stimuli that a given individual can detect at a particular time and place, subject to variations that may cause measurement error, for which psychophysical psychologists often compensate by averaging data from multiple trials; operationally defined as the difference between two stimuli that can be detected 50% of the time (sometimes termed the *difference threshold*) (cf. **absolute threshold**)

justification of effort. A means by which an individual rationalizes the expenditure of energy

keywords. See **mnemonic devices**

kinesthesis. The sense that helps in ascertaining skeletal movements and positioning, via receptors in the muscles, tendons, joints, and skin; changes in position are detected by kinesthetic

receptors, which **transduce** the mechanical energy caused by pressure into electrochemical neural energy, which codes information about the speed of the change, the angle of the bones, and the tension of the muscles, and then sends this information through the **spinal cord** to the **contralateral** region of the somatosensory cortex and to the **cerebellum**

language. An organized means of combining words in order to communicate (see **arbitrary symbolic reference**)

language-acquisition device (LAD). The hypothetical construct of an innate human predisposition to acquire language; not yet found as a specific physiological structure or function

latency. An interim period that occurs during **psychosexual development,** between the **phallic stage** and the **genital stage,** in which children repress their sexual feelings toward their parents and sublimate their sexual energy into productive fields of endeavor (see **repression, sublimation**)

latent content. The repressed impulses and other unconscious material expressed in dreams or in other primary-process thoughts, which give rise to the **manifest content** of such processes, as these processes are understood by psychodynamic psychologists

latent learning. Conditioning or acquired knowledge that is not presently reflected in performance; the learned information or response may be elicited when the individual believes that it may be rewarding to demonstrate the learning

law of effect. A behavioristic principle used for explaining **operant conditioning,** which states that over time, actions ("the effect") for which an organism is rewarded ("the satisfaction") are strengthened and are therefore more likely to occur again in the future, whereas actions that are followed by punishment tend to be weakened and are thus less likely to occur in the future

learned helplessness. A negative consequence of conditioning, particularly of **punishment,** in which an individual is conditioned to make no

response, including no attempt to escape aversive conditions; e.g., after repeated trials in which the individual is unable to escape an aversive condition, the individual has so effectively learned not to attempt escape that the individual continues not to attempt escape even when a means of escape becomes available

learning. Any relatively permanent change in the behavior, thoughts, or feelings of an organism as a consequence of prior experience (cf. **maturation**)

learning set. A generalized internal representation of a stimulus, a task, or a condition, which facilitates learning; sometimes described as *learning to learn*

lens. The curved interior surface of the eye, which bends (refracts) light into the eye and complements the cornea's gross adjustments in curvature, by making fine adjustments in the amount of curvature in order to focus the image as clearly as possible (cf. **cornea**)

lesbianism. See **homosexuality**

levels-of-processing framework. A way of looking at memory storage, which postulates that memory does not comprise any specific number of separate stores but rather comprises a continuous dimension in which the depth to which memory is encoded corresponds to the ease of retrieving the item: the deeper the level of processing (the more elaborately and diversely encoded the information), the higher the probability that an item may be retrieved (an alternative view is the *three-stores view*, in which memory is viewed as comprising a **sensory store,** a **short-term store,** and a **long-term store**)

lexical-access speed. The rate at which people can retrieve information about words (e.g., letter names) stored in long-term memory

lexicon. The entire set of **morphemes** in a given language or in a given person's linguistic repertoire (cf. **vocabulary**)

libido. A **drive** stemming from the sexual energy of life and of life-sustaining processes

life-span development. The changes in characteristics that occur over the course of a lifetime

light adaptation. Unconscious physiological response to an increase in light intensity in the environment, characterized by a decrease in pupillary area (cf. **dark adaptation;** see **adaptation;** cf. **habituation**)

lightness constancy. A form of **perceptual constancy** in which an individual continues to perceive a constant degree of illumination of an object, even when the actual amount of light that reaches the **retina** differs for different parts of the object

likability effect. Tendency for a recipient of a message to be persuaded more easily by messages from people whom the message recipient likes than by messages from people whom the recipient does not like

Likert scale. A type of **self-report measure** (also termed *summated rating scale*), in which a subject first is asked to review statements about the subject's feelings, thoughts, attitudes, or behaviors, worded from the subject's point of view (e.g., "I love psychology," "I plan to buy 10 more copies of my psychology textbook"); the subject is then asked to rate each of the statements on a numerical scale, from "0" (which means that the statement is not at all accurate) to the highest value on the scale (which means that the statement is very accurate); the person's responses are then averaged (or summed) to determine an overall rating of the subject's responses

limbic system. Comprises the **hippocampus,** the amygdala, and the septum and forms part of the **forebrain,** as does the **cerebral cortex;** important to emotion, motivation, and learning, as well as the suppression of instinctive responses, thereby enabling humans to adapt behaviors more flexibly in response to a changing environment

line graph. One of many types of graphic displays of numerical information (cf. **bar graph**), in which quantities (e.g., amounts or scores) are associated with linear information (e.g., time or age) and this association is represented by changing heights of a horizontal line

linear perspective. See **monocular depth cues;** see also **vanishing point**

linear regression. Prediction of one quantified variable from one or more

others, in which the two sets of variables are assumed to have a relation that takes the form of a straight line

linear relation. An association between two quantities that takes the form of a straight line

linear syllogism. A deductive argument that permits drawing a conclusion regarding a comparative relationship (e.g., "more . . . than," "less . . . than") between two terms, based on two premises asserting the comparative relationship between each of the two terms; each of two premises describes a comparative relationship between two terms, at least one term of which is common to both premises (see **deductive reasoning, syllogism**)

linguistic determinism. One of two interrelated propositions regarding the relationship between thought and language (cf. **linguistic relativity**): asserts that the structure of the language used by a person shapes what and how the person thinks

linguistic relativity. One of two interrelated propositions regarding the relationship between thought and language (cf. **linguistic determinism**): asserts that the speakers of different languages have differing cognitive systems, based on the languages they use, and that these different cognitive systems influence the ways in which people speaking the various languages think about the world

linguistic universals. Characteristic patterns of language that apply across all of the languages of various cultures

linguistics. The study of language structure and change

lipostatic hypothesis. One of two major alternative assumptions regarding how the body signals hunger versus satiety (cf. **glucostatic hypothesis**): suggests that the levels of *lipids* (fats) in the blood signal the body regarding the need for food; *lipostatic:* maintaining the stability (*-static*) of lipid (*lipo-*) levels in the body

lobes. Each of the four major regions of the cortex (see **frontal lobe, occipital lobe, parietal lobe, temporal lobe**)

location in the picture plane. See **monocular depth cues**

lock-and-key theory. One of the two theories regarding how smells are sensed (cf. **vibration theory**): suggests

that various olfactory **receptors** have various **templates** (patterns for shapes), which can be matched to the molecular shapes of various odors, such that when there is a special fit between the particular template of a molecule that enters the nose and the distinctive shape of the olfactory receptors, the receptors transduce those molecules into electrochemical impulses that trigger the sensation of smell; the operative metaphor of the theory is that the distinctive shapes of various odorous molecules serve as keys that unlock the distinctive shapes of matched receptors, prompting the unlocked receptors to initiate the electrochemical activity that leads to the sensation of smell; a variation of this theory suggests that olfactory receptors also figure out how to form new templates (or modify old templates) for new smells, and this process may facilitate the creation or adaptation of templates for a diversity of smells

logical positivism. A philosophical belief that the only basis for knowledge is sensory perceptions, and all else is idle conjecture

long-term store. According to a three-stores theory of memory, the hypothetical construct of a long-term store has a greater capacity than both the **sensory store** and the **short-term store,** and it can store information for very long periods of time, perhaps even indefinitely

longitudinal study. Research that follows a particular group of individuals (usually selected as a sample representing a population as a whole) over the course of their life span, or at least across many years (cf. **cross-sectional study**)

magnetic resonance imaging (MRI). A sophisticated technique for revealing high-resolution images of the structure of the living brain by computing and analyzing magnetic changes in the energy of the orbits of nuclear particles in the molecules of the body (also sometimes termed *NMR*, for *nuclear magnetic resonance*); produces clearer and more detailed images than **computerized axial tomography (CAT)** scans and uses no X radiation

maintenance rehearsal. A strategy for keeping information in short-term memory or for moving information into long-term memory by simply repeating the information over and over, without trying to form meaningful connections between the new information and other information (see **rehearsal**; cf. **elaborative rehearsal**)

malleus. One of the three bones of the middle ear, which normally receive and amplify the vibrations transmitted by the **tympanum (eardrum)** and then transmit those vibrations to the **cochlea** (cf. **incus, stapes**)

mania. A mood of unrestrained euphoria involving high excitement, expansiveness, and often hyperactivity; often accompanied by an overinflated sense of self-esteem, grandiose illusions in regard to what the manic person can accomplish, difficulty in focusing attention on one activity, and a tendency to flit from one activity to another in rapid succession (see **bipolar disorder**; cf. **depression**)

manifest content. The stream of events that pass through the mind of an individual during dreams or other primary-process thoughts, as these processes are understood by psychodynamic psychologists (cf. **latent content**)

massed learning. The acquisition of a body of information, which occurs all at one time rather than all being spaced over time; generally does not lead to as much learning as does **distributed learning**

maturation. One of the two key processes by which cognitive development occurs (cf. **learning**); any relatively permanent change in thought or behavior that occurs as a result of the internally (biologically) prompted processes of aging, without regard to personal experiences and subject to little environmental influence

maximax gain rule. See **game theory**

maximin gain rule. See **game theory**

mean. The average score within a distribution of values, computed by adding all the scores and then dividing by the number of scores (cf. **median, mode**)

means–ends analysis. See **heuristic**

median. The middle score or other measurement value within a distribution of values (cf. **mean, mode**)

meditation. A set of techniques used for altering consciousness through contemplation (see **concentrative meditation, opening-up meditation**)

medulla oblongata. An elongated interior structure of the **brain**, located at the point where the **spinal cord** enters the skull and joins with the brain; forms part of the **reticular activating system**, and thereby helps to sustain life by controlling the heartbeat and helping to control breathing, swallowing, and digestion; the location in the brain where nerves from the right side of the body cross over to the left side of the brain, and nerves from the left side of the body cross over to the right side of the brain (see **contralateral**)

memory. The means by which individuals draw on past knowledge in order to use such knowledge in the present; the dynamic mechanisms associated with the retention and retrieval of information; the three operations through which information is processed by and for the memory are **encoding** (translating sensory information into a form that can be represented and stored in memory), *storage* (moving encoded information into a memory store and maintaining the information in storage), and *retrieval* (recovery of stored information from a memory store and moving the information into **consciousness** for use in active cognitive processing)

memory scanning. A phenomenon of memory in which an individual checks what is contained, usually in short-term memory

mental age. A means of indicating a person's level of intelligence (generally in reference to a child), based on the individual's performance on tests of intelligence, by indicating the chronological age of persons who typically perform at the same level of intelligence as the test-taker (cf. **deviation IQs, intelligence quotient, ratio IQ**)

mental retardation. Low level of intelligence, usually reflected by both poor performance on tests of intelligence and poor *adaptive competence* (the degree to which a person functions effectively within a normal situational context)

mental set. A frame of mind in which a problem-solver is predisposed to think of a problem or a situation in a particular way (sometimes termed **entrenchment**), often leading the problem-solver to fixate on a strategy that normally works in solving some (or perhaps even most) problems, but that does not work in solving this particular problem (see also **negative transfer**; cf. **positive transfer**)

mere exposure effect. The positive effect on attitudes that results from repeated exposure to a message supporting the attitude or even just exposure to the stimulus about which the attitude is being formed or modified

metabolism. Metabolic processes that capture and store energy and material resources from food, release stored energy and material resources as needed, and eliminate unused waste products (see **anabolism, catabolism**)

metacognition. Knowledge and understanding of the processes of thinking, as well as of how to use strategies and skills to enhance thinking

metamemory. An aspect of **metacognition**, involving knowledge and understanding of memory abilities and ways in which to enhance memory abilities (e.g., through the use of **mnemonic devices**)

metencephalon. One of the two parts of the **hindbrain**; comprises the **pons** and the **cerebellum** (*met-*, behind; *-encephalon*, in the head, brain; cf. **myelencephalon**)

method of loci. See **mnemonic devices**

midbrain. Located between the **forebrain** and the **hindbrain**; comprises several cerebral structures, most indispensable of which is the **reticular activating system**, which also extends into the hindbrain

mind–body dualism. A philosophical belief that the body is separate from the mind and that the body is composed of physical substance, whereas the mind is ephemeral and is not composed of physical substance (cf. **monism**)

minimax loss rule. See **game theory**

minimin loss rule. See **game theory**

miss. One of the four possible combinations of stimulus and response described in **signal-detection theory (SDT)** (cf. **correct rejection, false alarm, hit**): the state in which the individual did not detect a signal stimulus even though the stimulus was actually present

mnemonic devices. Specific techniques for aiding in the memorization of various isolated items, thereby adding meaning or imagery to an otherwise arbitrary listing of isolated items that may be difficult to remember; for example, *acronym*—a set of letters that forms a word or phrase, in which each letter stands for a certain other word or concept (e.g., U.S.A., IQ, and laser), and which thereby may aid in recalling the words or concepts that the letters represent; *acrostics*—the initial letters of a series of items are used in forming a sentence, such that the sentence prompts recall of the initial letters, and the letters prompt recall of each of the items; *categorical clustering*—various items are grouped into categories in order to facilitate recall of the items; *interactive images*—a means of linking a set of isolated words by creating visual representations for the words and then picturing interactions among the items (e.g., causing one item to act on or with another); *keywords*—a mnemonic strategy for learning isolated words in a foreign language by forming an interactive image that links the sound and meaning of a foreign word with the sound and meaning of a familiar word; *method of loci*—visualization of a familiar area with distinctive landmarks that can be linked (via interactive images) to specific items to be remembered; *pegword system*—memorization of a familiar list of items (e.g., in a nursery rhyme) that can then be linked (via interactive images) with unfamiliar items on a new list

mnemonist. A person who uses memory-enhancing techniques for greatly improving his or her memory or who has a distinctive sensory or cognitive ability to remember information, particularly information that is highly concrete or that can be visualized readily

mode. The most frequent score or other measurement value within a distribution of values (cf. **mean, median**)

modeling. A situation in which an individual observes another person and acts in kind; also a form of behavior therapy in which clients are asked to observe persons coping effectively

in situations that the clients find anxiety provoking or that the clients respond to in other maladaptive ways

monism. A philosophical belief that the body and mind are unified, based on the belief that reality is a unified whole, existing in a single plane, rather than separated in terms of physical substance versus nonphysical mind (*mon[o]-*, one; *-ism*, set of beliefs, school of thought, or dogma [Greek]) (cf. **mind–body dualism**)

monitoring. One of the two main purposes of consciousness (cf. **controlling**): The individual keeps track of internal mental processes, of personal behavior, and of the environment, in order to maintain self-awareness in relation to the surrounding environment

monocular depth cues. One of the two chief means of judging the distances of visible objects (cf. **binocular depth cues**), based on sensed information that can be represented in just two dimensions and observed with just one (*mono-*) eye (*ocular*): *aerial perspective*—the observation that nearer objects appear to be more highly resolved and more clearly distinct than farther objects, which appear to be hazier (occurs because farther objects are observed through greater numbers of moisture and dust particles, whereas closer objects are observed through fewer such particles); *interposition*—the observation that an object that appears to block or partially obstruct the view of another object is perceived as being nearer, whereas the blocked object is perceived to be farther away, such that the blocking object is perceived to be closer to the observer and in front of the blocked object; *linear perspective*—the observation that parallel lines seem to converge as they move farther into the distance; *location in the picture plane*—the observation that objects that are higher in the picture plane (but are below the horizon or at least extend below it) are perceived as being farther from the viewer, whereas objects that are entirely above the horizon and higher in the picture plane are perceived as being closer to the viewer than are objects that are lower in the picture plane (i.e., as objects converge toward the horizon line, they are perceived as being farther from the viewer); *motion*

parallax—the perception of stationary objects from a moving viewpoint, such that if an observer visually fixates on a single point in the scene, the objects that are closer to the observer than is the fixation point appear to be moving in the direction opposite to the direction in which the observer is moving, whereas objects farther from the observer than is the fixation point will appear to be moving in the same direction as the observer (also, objects closer to the observer appear to be moving more quickly than objects farther from the observer); *relative size*—the observation that things that are farther away appear to be smaller in the retina, and the farther away the object, the smaller is its image on the retina; *texture gradient*—the observation that the relative sizes of objects decrease and the densities of distribution of objects increase as objects appear farther from the observer

monolingual. Person who can speak only one language (cf. **bilingual;** see also **additive bilingualism, subtractive bilingualism**)

mood disorders. Extreme disturbances in a person's emotional state, which may involve either unipolar disorder (also termed **depression**) or **bipolar disorder** (also termed *manic–depressive disorder*)

moratorium. One of four main types of identity (cf. **foreclosure, identity achievement, identity diffusion;** cf. also **alienated achievement**), in which the individual is currently questioning her or his values and beliefs, prior to establishing a firm and secure sense of self

morpheme. The smallest unit of sound that denotes meaning within a given language (see **content morpheme, function morpheme;** cf. also **phoneme**)

motion parallax. See **monocular depth cues**

motive. A stimulus that prompts a person to act in a particular way

motor. Characterized by the movement of muscles (related to **psychomotor**—motor skills associated with psychological processes)

motor neuron. One of the three main types of **neurons** (cf. **interneuron, sensory neuron**); carries information *away from* the **spinal cord** and the **brain** and toward the body parts that are supposed to respond to the information in some way (see **effector**)

motor theory. One of the **active theories of speech perception:** asserts that speech perception depends on both what a speaker is heard to articulate and what the listener infers to be the intended articulations of the speaker

move problems. A class of **well-structured problems** that require a series of moves to reach a final goal state

Müller-Lyer illusion. An **optical illusion** in which two equally long line segments are perceived to differ in length because one of the line segments is braced by inward-facing arrowhead-shaped diagonal lines, but the other line segment is braced by outward-facing arrowhead-shaped diagonal lines; an optical illusion, which causes the observer to perceive that two equally long line segments differ in length; may be an artifact of some of the monocular depth cues with which perceivers are familiar (cf. **Ponzo illusion**)

multimodal. Characteristic of a non-normal distribution of values, in which the distribution comprises more than one **mode** (cf. **normal distribution**)

mutation. A sudden structural change in a hereditary characteristic, which serves as a mechanism for changes in inheritance from one generation to the next and thereby permits evolutionary changes to occur (see also **behavioral genetics, genes, genetics**)

myelencephalon. One of the two parts of the **hindbrain**; comprises only the **medulla oblongata** (*myel-*, middle-ward, interior; *-encephalon*, in the head, brain; cf. **metencephalon**)

myelin. A white fatty substance that insulates and protects the **axons** of some **neurons** from electrical interference by other neurons in the area (see **myelin sheath, nodes of Ranvier**)

myelin sheath. A protective, insulating layer of **myelin**, which coats the **axons** of some **neurons**, thereby speeding up neuronal conduction and insulating and protecting the axons from electrochemical interference by nearby neurons (see **nodes of Ranvier**)

myelinated neurons. Neurons with **axons** that are encased in a **myelin** sheath;** generally conduct information more rapidly, often over longer distances, than unmyelinated neurons

N-REM sleep. The four stages of sleep that are not characterized by rapid eye movements (hence, the acronym for non–rapid eye movement) and that are less frequently associated with dreaming (cf. **REM sleep**)

narcolepsy. A disturbance of the pattern of wakefulness and sleep, in which the narcoleptic experiences an uncontrollable urge to fall asleep periodically during the day and as a result loses consciousness for brief periods of time (usually about 10 to 15 minutes), thereby putting the narcoleptic in grave danger if the attacks occur when the person is driving or otherwise is engaged in activities for which sudden sleep might be hazardous

narcotic. Any drug in a class of drugs derived from opium (**opiates** such as heroin, morphine, or codeine) or synthetically produced to create the numbing, stuporous effects of opium (**opioids** such as meperidine or methadone) and that lead to addiction; lead to a reduction in pain and an overall sense of well-being (from the Greek term for "numbness"; see also **central nervous system (CNS) depressant**)

natural selection. Evolutionary principle describing a mechanism by which species have developed and changed, based on what is commonly called the "survival of the fittest," in that those species that are best suited for adapting to a given environment are the ones most likely to reach sexual maturity and to produce offspring, thereby increasing their likelihood of surviving as a species; that is, the species that are best suited for adapting to a given environment are then selected by nature for survival

naturalistic observation. A method of scientific study in which the researcher leaves the laboratory or the clinical setting and goes out into the field (settings in the community) to record the behavior of people engaged in the normal activities of their daily lives (also termed *field study*; cf. **case study, experiment, survey, test**); also

occasionally used as a clinical assessment technique (cf. **clinical interview**)

near-death experience. An experience in which an individual either comes extremely close to dying or is actually believed to be dead and is then revived before permanent brain death occurs; the unusual psychological phenomena associated with such experiences are believed to be linked to the oxygen deprivation that occurs during such experiences

negative acceleration. Gradual reduction in the amount of increase that occurs in successive conditioning trials; that is, as the strength of the conditioned association increases, subsequent conditioning trials provide smaller increases in the strength of the association

negative correlation. A relationship between two attributes, in which an increase in either one of the attributes is associated with a decrease in the other attribute; a perfect negative correlation is indicated by -1 (also termed *inverse correlation*; see **correlation;** cf. **positive correlation**)

negative-feedback loop. A physiological mechanism whereby the body monitors a particular resource (e.g., hormones, glucose, or lipids in the blood), signaling to find a way to increase the levels of the resource when levels are low, and then signaling to find a way to decrease the levels of the resource when levels are high (e.g., by discontinuing the release of hormones or refraining from eating or drinking) (see also **homeostatic regulation**)

negative reinforcement. The process of removing an unpleasant stimulus following an operant response in order to strengthen the operant response (see **negative reinforcer**)

negative reinforcer. The welcome removal or cessation of an unpleasant stimulus (e.g., physical or psychological pain or discomfort) following an operant response, thereby strengthening the operant response (see **negative reinforcement**)

negative symptoms. Characteristics of a disorder that are detected by noting that the individual does *not* demonstrate a normally expected behavior (i.e., a normal behavior is *subtracted* from the behavioral repertoire); may involve deficits in self-care, lack of behavioral responsivity, apathy, blunting of emotions (and flattening of affect), language deficits, or avoidance of social activity (cf. **positive symptoms**)

negative transfer. A situation in which prior learning may lead to greater difficulty in learning and remembering new material (see **mental set, transfer;** cf. **positive transfer**)

neodissociative theory. A view of hypnosis in which it is asserted that some individuals are capable of separating one part of their conscious minds from another part; in one part, the individual responds to the hypnotist's commands, while in the other part, the individual observes and monitors the events and actions taking place, including some of the actions that the hypnotized subject appears not to be processing in the part of the conscious mind that is engaging in the actions

neo-Freudians. The psychodynamically oriented theorists who followed Freud and who differed from Freud in some ways, but who still clung to many Freudian principles regarding human personality development

neonate. Newborn (*neo-*, "new"; *-nate*, "born")

nerve. Bundle of neurons; many neurons can be observed as fibers extending from the **brain** down through the center of the back (in the **central nervous system**) and then out to various parts of the body (in the **peripheral nervous system**)

nervous system. Physiological network of **nerves** that form the basis of the ability to perceive, adapt to, and interact with the world; the means by which humans and other vertebrates receive, process, and then respond to messages from the environment and from inside our bodies (see **central nervous system, peripheral nervous system;** cf. **endocrine system;** see also **autonomic nervous system, parasympathetic nervous system, somatic nervous system, sympathetic nervous system**)

network. As applied to a model of memory, a network is a set of labeled relations between **nodes** (junctures that represent concepts)

neuromodulator. Chemical substance released by the **terminal buttons** of some **neurons,** which serves to enhance or to diminish the respon-

sivity of postsynaptic neurons, either by directly affecting the axons or by affecting the sensitivity of the receptor sites (cf. **neurotransmitter**)

neuron. Nerve cell, involved in neural communication within the **nervous system** (see also **interneuron, motor neuron, sensory neuron;** cf. **glial cell, satellite cell, Schwann cell**)

neuropeptide. One of the main types of chemical substances involved in neurotransmission; comprise *peptide chains* (molecules made from the parts of two or more amino acids) that may act either as specific **neurotransmitters** or as general **neuromodulators;** involved in hunger, thirst, and reproductive processes, as well as **pain** relief (e.g., **endorphins**) and reactions to **stress**

neurosis. A relatively minor psychological disorder, involving perhaps minor distortions in thought processes, minor disturbances in physiological functioning (e.g., either mildly heightened or slightly depressed state of physiological **arousal**), somewhat atypical motor behavior, or some emotional instability (cf. **psychosis**)

neuroticism. See **Big Five;** see also **neurosis**

neurotransmitter. Chemical messenger that is released by the **terminal buttons** on the **axon** of a presynaptic **neuron** and then carries the chemical messages across the **synapse** to receptor sites on the receiving **dendrites** or **soma** of the postsynaptic neuron (cf. **neuromodulator;** see also **acetylcholine, dopamine, serotonin**)

nodes of a memory network. A juncture within a memory **network,** which represents a concept (or a word) and which is linked in relationships with other nodes in the network

nodes of Ranvier. Small gaps in the **myelin** coating along the axons of myelinated neurons (see **glial cell, myelin sheath**)

noise. Confusing, nonsensical, and often unpleasant sound that results when the note of a fundamental frequency is accompanied by irregular and unrelated sound waves, rather than by multiples of the **fundamental frequency** (cf. **harmonics**)

nomothetic personality theory. One of two basic kinds of trait theories of personality (cf. **idiographic personality theory**): based on the belief

that all people have essentially the same set of traits and that they differ only in terms of the extent to which they manifest each trait

normal distribution. A distribution of scores or other measurement values, in which most values congregate around the median, and the measurement values rapidly decline in number on either side of the median, tailing off more slowly as scores get more extreme; in such a distribution, the **median** is approximately the same as both the **mean** and the **mode**

normal science. Scientific work that gradually and progressively builds on an established **paradigm** (cf. **revolutionary science**)

normative scores. The set of normative equivalents for a range of raw **test** scores that represent the **normal distribution** of scores obtained by giving a test to a huge number of individuals; once a set of normative scores (also termed *norms;* for standardized tests, also termed *standard scores*) are established for a given test, the normative scores for subsequent test-takers represent a translation of **raw scores** into scaled equivalents that reflect the relative levels of performance of the various test-takers within the normal distribution of scores

norms (as normative scores). See **normative scores**

noun phrase. See **subject;** cf. **predicate**

null hypothesis. A proposed expectation of *no* difference or relation; may be assessed in terms of likelihood but not in terms of absolute certainty

obedience. Modification of behavior in response to the command of an actual or perceived authority; may involve taking an action, refraining from an action, or tailoring an action to suit another person or persons (cf. **compliance, conformity**)

object permanence. A cognitive realization that objects continue to exist even when the objects are not immediately perceptible

object-relations theory. A contemporary extension of Freudian theory, primarily concerned with how people relate to one another and with how people conceptualize these relationships largely in terms of their investment of libidinal energy in other persons or objects

objective personality test. A means of assessing personality by using a standardized and uniform procedure for scoring the assessment instrument; not necessarily characterized by objective means of determining what to test, how to interpret test scores, or the theory on which to base the test (cf. **projective test**)

observational learning. A form of vicarious (rather than direct) learning that occurs as a result of observing both the behavior of others and the environmental outcomes of the behavior observed; generally leads to the learner's imitation of the observed behavior, especially if the learner attends to the model, internally represents in memory what the model has done, figures out how to produce the behavior of the model, and feels motivated to do what the model has done (also termed *social learning, vicarious learning*)

observed score. A sample of the person's behavior at a given time and place, which indicates neither the best nor the worst possible score that the person could obtain, nor even an average of possible scores the person might obtain (cf. **true score**)

obsession. An unwanted, persistent thought, image, or impulse that cannot be suppressed; obsessions may focus on persistent doubts regarding task completion, persistent thoughts about something such as a person or a relationship, persistent impulses to engage in undesired behavior, persistent fears, or persistent images

obsessive–compulsive anxiety disorder. An **anxiety disorder** characterized by excessive concern with details, rules, and codes of behavior; often associated with strong task orientation, perfectionism, and difficulties in interpersonal relationships (which often lack warmth and intimacy) (see also **compulsion, obsession, personality disorders:** *obsessive–compulsive personality disorder*)

occipital lobe. One of the four major regions of the **cerebral cortex** (cf. **frontal lobe, parietal lobe, temporal lobe**); chiefly responsible for visual processing

Oedipal conflict. A central issue of

the **phallic stage** of **psychosexual development,** in which boys feel sexual desires toward their mothers but fear the powerful wrath of their fathers; named for the Greek myth in which Oedipus, who had long been separated from his parents and therefore did not recognize them, killed his father and married his mother; sometimes also used as a generic term to encompass both the Oedipal conflict and the somewhat equivalent **Electra conflict** in girls

olfaction. Sense of smell, which is chemically activated by airborne molecules that can dissolve in either water or fat

olfactory bulb. Each of various terminuses where each olfactory nerve synapses directly with sensory neurons, bypassing the **thalamus** and instead going directly either to the olfactory cortex in the **temporal lobe** or to the **limbic system** (especially the **hypothalamus**)

olfactory epithelium. The "smell skin" in the nasal membranes, where airborne scent molecules contact the olfactory receptor cells that detect the scent molecules and then initiate the transduction of the chemical energy of the odors into the electrochemical energy of neural transmission (see **lock-and-key theory**)

opening-up meditation. One of the two main forms of contemplation, in which the meditator integrates **meditation** with the events of everyday life, seeking to expand awareness of everyday events, rather than to separate meditation from mundane existence; often involves an attempt to focus on becoming one with an ordinary activity, and on putting all other interfering thoughts out of consciousness (cf. **concentrative meditation**)

openness. See **Big Five**

operant. Active behavioral response of an organism, which may be strengthened by positive or negative reinforcement or may be weakened either by a lack of reinforcement or by **punishment** during interactions with the environment

operant conditioning. **Learning** that occurs as a result of stimuli that either strengthen (through **reinforcement**) or weaken (through **punishment** or through lack of reinforcement) the likelihood of a given

behavioral response (an **operant**) (also termed *instrumental conditioning*)

operational definition. A specific description of one or more precise elements and procedures involved in solving a given research problem, which allows researchers to communicate clearly the means by which they conducted an experiment and reached their conclusions

opiate. Narcotic that is derived from the opium poppy bulb; may be injected intravenously, smoked, ingested orally, or inhaled (cf. **opioid**)

opioid. Narcotic that has a similar chemical structure and set of effects to those of an **opiate** but that is made synthetically through combinations of chemicals

opponent-process theory of addiction and motivation. In regard to emotions, the theory posits the existence of a process whereby the body seeks to ensure motivational neutrality, such that when one process or motivational source impels the person to feel positive or negative motivations, an opposing motivational force (an opponent process) acts to bring the person back to the neutral baseline; in the case of positive motivations, the opponent process will involve negative movement back down to the baseline; in the case of negative motivations, the opponent process will involve positive movement back up to the baseline; in regard to addictions to **psychoactive** drugs, opponent processes counteract the effects of consuming the addictive substance, thus leading to or at least exacerbating the effects of **addiction, tolerance,** and **withdrawal**

opponent-process theory of color vision. One of the two major theories of color vision (cf. **trichromatic theory of color vision**): based on the notion of three opposing processes in human vision, two of which contrast each of two colors with another (yielding four fundamental colors—red/green and yellow/blue), and one of which contrasts black and white as a third opposing set of achromatic primaries that are perceived in much the same way as are the other opposing pairs

optic chiasma. The place in the **occipital lobe** of the brain where neural fibers carrying visual information cross over from one side of the body to the

contralateral hemisphere of the brain (*chiasma*, "X-shaped or crossed configuration")

optical illusion. Visual stimulus that leads to distortion in visual perception (see **Müller-Lyer illusion, Ponzo illusion**)

oral stage. A Freudian stage of **psychosexual development,** which typically occurs during the first 2 years, when an in-fant explores sucking and other oral activity, learning that such activity not only provides nourishment, but also pleasure

organic pain. Sensations of extreme discomfort and suffering caused by damage to bodily tissue (cf. **psychogenic pain;** see also **pain**)

orienting reflex. A series of preprogrammed responses that are prompted by a sudden change in the environment (e.g., a flash of light or an abrupt loud noise); included among the specific preprogrammed responses are a generalized reflexive orientation toward the origin of the change, changes in brain-wave patterns (see **electroencephalogram**), dilation of the pupils, and some other physiological changes associated with stress (see also **instinct, reflex**)

outgroup homogeneity bias. Tendency to view the members of an *outgroup* (of which the individual is not a member) as all being alike, often in contrast to a tendency to view members of an *ingroup* (of which the individual is a member) as distinct individuals who have dissimilar characteristics, thus facilitating the ease of forming **stereotypes** regarding outgroups but not of ingroups

oval window. First part of the inner ear, at one end of which is the **cochlea** and at the other end of which is the spot where the **stapes** either rests or vibrates in response to sounds; when the stapes vibrates, the mechanical vibration is transmitted to the cochlea via the oval window

overconfidence. Excessive valuation of skills, knowledge, or judgment, usually applied to a person's valuation of her or his own abilities

overdose. Ingestion of a life-threatening or lethal dose of drugs, often associated with the use of **psychoactive** drugs, such as **narcotics, amphetamines,** or **sedative–hypnotic drugs;** although often linked to intentional

suicide, overdoses commonly occur due to **tolerance** or **sensitization,** particularly when the users are also using street drugs, which contain many impurities and are not reliably controlled in regard to the concentrations of psychoactive elements in the drug compounds being sold

overextension error. Overapplication (usually by children or other persons acquiring a language) of the meaning of a given word to more things, ideas, and situations than is appropriate for the denotation and the defining features of the word; generally no longer typifies language once the vocabulary of the language user has expanded to comprise enough words to describe the meanings the individual intends to convey (see also **feature hypothesis, functional hypothesis**)

overregularization. An error that commonly occurs during language acquisition, in which the novice language user has gained an understanding of how a language usually works and then overapplies the general rules of the language to the exceptional cases for which the rule does not apply

overshadowing. A phenomenon of **classical conditioning,** whereby one stimulus dominates (overshadows) another, thereby minimizing the learned association with the overshadowed stimulus; probably the phenomenon that accounts for the lack of conditioning that occurs during **simultaneous conditioning** and **backward conditioning** and accounts for the volatility of **higher order conditioning**

p-value. Statistical quantity indicating the probability (*p*) that a particular outcome may have occurred as a result of random, rather than systematic, variation

pain. Intense sensory discomfort and emotional suffering associated with actual, imagined, or threatened damage to or irritation of body tissues (see **organic pain, psychogenic pain**)

paired-associates recall. A memory task in which the individual is presented with a list of paired (and often related) items, which the individual is asked to store in memory, then the individual is presented with one item in

each pair and is asked to provide the mate of each given item (cf. **free recall, serial recall**)

panic disorder. An **anxiety disorder** characterized by brief (usually only a few minutes), abrupt, and unprovoked, but recurrent episodes during which a person experiences intense and uncontrollable anxiety; during the episodes (termed *panic attacks*), the panicked individual feels terrified and exhibits psychophysiological symptoms of heightened **arousal,** such as difficulty in breathing, heart palpitations, dizziness, sweating, and trembling; often associated with **agoraphobia** and sometimes associated with feelings of *depersonalization* (the feeling of being outside of the body, looking in rather than on the inside looking out)

papillae. Small visible protrusions on the tongue, inside which are located thousands of taste-receptor cells (see **taste buds**)

paradigm(s). Theoretical system that provides an overarching model for organizing related theories for understanding a particular phenomenon such as intelligence, learning, personality, or psychological development; also used to describe a model or framework for conducting a particular type of experiment (e.g., see **simulating paradigm**)

parallel processing. Cognitive manipulation of multiple operations simultaneously; as applied to short-term memory, the items stored in short-term memory would be retrieved all at once, not one at a time (cf. **serial processing**)

parapsychology. A branch of psychology concerned with phenomena that are not presently explained by the application of known psychological principles

parasympathetic nervous system. The part of the **autonomic nervous system** that is concerned primarily with **anabolism** (cf. **sympathetic nervous system**)

parietal lobe. One of the four major regions of the **cerebral cortex** (cf. **frontal lobe, occipital lobe, temporal lobe**): chiefly responsible for processing of somatosensory sensations that come from the skin and muscles of the body (*soma-*)

partial reinforcement. An **operant-conditioning** schedule (also termed *intermittent reinforcement*) in which a given type of **operant** response is rewarded some of the time, but not all of the time; comprises two types of reinforcement schedules: **ratio schedules** (see **fixed-ratio reinforcement; variable-ratio reinforcement**) and **interval schedules** (see **fixed-interval reinforcement, variable-interval reinforcement**); such schedules are more resistant to **extinction** than is **continuous reinforcement**

particular affirmative statement. See **categorical syllogism**

particular negative statement. See **categorical syllogism**

passion. The intense desire for union with another person; one of three basic components of love, according to the **triangular theory of love** (cf. **commitment, intimacy**)

passive theories. A category of theories that explains speech perception exclusively in terms of the listener's passive reception of speech, without involving cognitive processes such as memory and consideration of context; according to these kinds of theories, the listener perceives speech exclusively through sensory processes such as filtering (e.g., screening out irrelevant sounds) and feature detection (e.g., matching features of speech sounds to existing **templates** for those sounds) (see **feature matching;** cf. **active theories**)

pathogen. A specific disease-causing agent (*patho-*, "suffering" or "disease"; *-gen*, "producer")

patient-centered style (of physician interactions). One of two basic patterns for physician–patient interactions (cf. **doctor-centered style**); characterized by a relatively nondirective style of interaction, in which the physician asks divergent questions and allows the patient to take part in guiding the course of the interview, the diagnosis of the presenting problem, and the decision regarding the optimal treatment for the problem

payoff matrix. Tabular display of the discrete consequences for each decision maker regarding the outcomes that would result from each of various decisions that might be made (see **game theory**)

Pearson product–moment correlation coefficient. A measure of linear relation, ranging from -1 (perfect inverse relation) to 0 (no relation) to $+1$ (perfect positive relation)

pegword system. See **mnemonic devices**

percentile. A value used in describing a score, indicating the proportion of persons whose scores fall below a given score, multiplied by 100

perception. The set of psychological processes by which people recognize, organize, synthesize, and give meaning (in the brain) to the sensations received from environmental stimuli (in the sense organs) (cf. **sensation**)

perceptual constancy. The perception that a given object remains the same even when the immediate sensation of the object changes (see **color constancy, lightness constancy, shape constancy, size constancy**)

performative. See **speech acts;** synonym: *declaration*

peripheral nervous system (PNS). One of the two main parts of the **nervous system** (cf. **central nervous system [CNS]**): comprises all of the nerve cells, including the nerves of the face and head, *except* the neurons of the **brain** and the **spinal cord** (the CNS); primarily relays information between the CNS and the rest of the body (including the face and the internal organs other than the brain); connects the CNS with sensory **receptors** in both external sensory organs (e.g., skin, ears, eyes) and internal body parts (e.g., stomach, muscles) and connects the CNS with motor **effectors** in parts of the body that produce movement, speech, and so on (*peripheral* means both "auxiliary," for the PNS assists the CNS; and "away from the center," for the peripheral nerves are external to the CNS)

peripheral route of persuasion. One of two routes to persuasion (cf. **central route of persuasion**), which emphasizes tangential, situational features of the persuasive message, such as the appeal of the message sender, the attractiveness of the message's presentation, or rewarding features of the message or its source; most effective when the recipient is not strongly interested in the issue or is unable to consider the issue carefully for various reasons

permissive parents. Mothers and fathers who exhibit a style of parenting in which they tend to give their children a great deal of freedom, possibly more than the children can handle, and who tend to be lax in discipline and to let children make their own decisions about many things that other parents might find questionably appropriate (cf. **authoritarian parents, authoritative parents**)

person-centered approach. A humanistic approach to personality theory, which strongly emphasizes the **self** and each person's perception of self

person–environment interaction. The individual fit between a particular person and the environment in which the individual develops and interacts with others

person-positivity bias. A bias of **impression formation,** which involves the tendency for people to evaluate individuals more positively than they evaluate groups, including the groups to which those individuals belong

personal attribution. One of two fundamental types of **attributions** (cf. **situational attribution**): The causes of human behavior are attributed to the internal factors in the person engaging in the given behavior (also termed *dispositional attribution*)

personal constructs. Idiosyncratic ways in which individual persons see some things as being like each other and other things as being dissimilar

personal dispositions. Personality **traits** that are unique to each individual and therefore may be difficult to assess via interpersonal correlational studies or standardized personality inventories

personal space. An aspect of nonverbal communication, which centers on the distance between people engaged in interactions; the specific interpersonal distance that seems comfortable for people is affected by cultural differences (e.g., Arabs vs. Canadians), status differences (e.g., supervisors vs. employees), role expectations (e.g., parents and children), degree of intimacy in the relationship (e.g., between acquaintances vs. between spouses), and other sociological considerations (e.g., settings such as elevators or crowded trains)

personal unconscious. One of two

Jungian parts of the unconscious mind (cf. **collective unconscious**), in which is stored each person's unique personal experiences and repressed memories (see also **complexes**)

personality. The enduring characteristics and dispositions of a person that provide some degree of coherence across the various ways in which the person behaves

personality disorders. Psychological disorders involving a pattern of consistent, long-term, extreme personality characteristics that cause the person great unhappiness or that seriously impair the person's ability to adjust to the demands of everyday living or to function well in her or his environment, such as the following: *antisocial personality disorder*—characterized by at least average intelligence and the tendency to appear superficially charming, sincere, poised, calm, and verbally facile, as a strategy for winning the trust and cooperation of other persons despite actually being insincere, untruthful, self-centered, ungrateful, and unreliable in interpersonal relations (formerly termed *psychopathy* or *sociopathy*); *avoidant personality disorder*—characterized by reluctance to enter into close personal relationships due to an intense fear of rejection, often accompanied by self-devaluation, very low self-esteem, and a wish for unattainable closeness; *borderline personality disorder*—characterized by extreme volatility and instability in mood, self-image, and interpersonal relationships; *dependent personality disorder*—characterized by little self-confidence, extreme sensitivity to criticism, difficulty in taking personal responsibility for self-care; *histrionic personality disor-der*—characterized by highly dramatic behavior and continual attempts to attract attention, such as lavish displays of emotionality and affection (despite actual shallowness of feeling), extreme volatility, great vanity, and manipulative interpersonal relationships (formerly called "hysterical personality"); *narcissistic personality disorder*—characterized by an inflated self-image, intense self-centeredness and selfishness in interpersonal relationships, lack of empathy for others, strong feelings of entitlement from others without concern for

reciprocating to others; *obsessive–compulsive personality dis-order*—characterized by having **obsessions** or **compulsions** or both; *paranoid personality disorder*—characterized by suspiciousness of others and a tendency to suspect that others are plotting against the paranoid individual, to view other people's innocuous behavior as directed against the individual (cf. **schizophrenia** [paranoid]); *schizoid personality disorder*—characterized by difficulty in forming relationships with other people, a tendency to prefer solitude over companionship, and apparent indifference to what others think, say, or even feel about the disordered individual; *schizotypal personality disorder*—characterized by major problems in interpersonal interactions and by other attributes that tend to cause these persons to be viewed as eccentric or even bizarre, such as susceptibility to **illusions** and to *magical thinking* (e.g., believing in extrasensory perceptive powers or other supernatural phenomena for which there is little supporting evidence)

perspective. A view of psychological phenomena, which centers on a particular set of theories and beliefs (cf. **field**)

pervasive developmental disorder (PDD). One of three major disorders usually first diagnosed in infancy, childhood, or adolescence (cf. **attention-deficit disorder**); characterized by little or no responsiveness to others, highly restricted range of interest, and impairment in communication, both verbal (e.g., no speech at all or only *echolalic speech*—precise repetition of the exact words and intonation of the speech uttered by others) and nonverbal (e.g., lack of *vocal inflection*—fluctuation of tones to convey expression in speech); sometimes also involves self-mutilation and vehement insistence on exact uniformity of the stimuli in the environment (also termed *autism*)

phallic stage. A Freudian stage of **psychosexual development,** which typically begins at about 4 years of age and continues until about 6 years of age; during this stage, children discover that stimulation of the genitals can be pleasurable, and they first experience either the **Oedipal conflict** (in

boys) or the **Electra conflict** (in girls)

phenotype. Expression of an inherited trait, based on the dominant trait in the **genotype** and also subject to environmental influence; **dominant traits** will prevail over **recessive traits** in determining whether genotypic traits are expressed in the phenotype

pheromones. Chemical substances secreted by animals, which trigger specific kinds of reactions (largely related to reproduction, territory, or aggression) in other animals, usually of the same species

philosophy. A system of ideas or a set of fundamental beliefs; a means of seeking to explore and understand the general nature of many aspects of the world

phobia. One of five main categories of **anxiety disorders,** characterized by an exaggerated, persistent, irrational, and disruptive fear of a particular object, a particular event, or a particular setting, or a fear of a general kind of object, event, or setting (see also **agoraphobia, social phobia**)

phone. Smallest unit of speech sound that may be distinguished from other speech sounds, and which may or may not make a meaningful difference in a given language (cf. **phoneme**)

phoneme. Smallest unit of speech sound that can be used to distinguish one meaningful utterance from another in a given language (cf. **phone;** cf. also **morpheme**)

phonetic-refinement theory. One of the **active theories of speech perception,** which posits that words are identified through successive elimination of extraneous words (*refinement*) from the set of possible words that the heard word might be; elimination is based on the initial sounds of the words (*phonetics*) and the context in which the word occurs

photopigments. Chemical substances that absorb light, thereby starting the complex transduction process that transforms physical electromagnetic energy into an electrochemical neural impulse; the **rods** and the **cones** contain different types of photopigments; different types of photopigments absorb differing amounts of light, and some detect different **hues** (see **photoreceptors**)

photoreceptors. The physiological structures in the **retina** of the eye that **transduce** light energy into electrochemical energy, thus enabling the eye to see; located in the innermost layer of the retina, farthest from the light source; the two kinds of photoreceptors are the **rods** and the **cones** (see also **photopigments**)

phrase-structure grammar. A form of syntactical analysis, which analyzes sentences in terms of the superficial sequence of words in sentences, regardless of differences or similarities of meaning; analysis often centers on the analysis of noun phrases (see **subject**) and verb phrases (see **predicate**) (also termed *surface-structure grammars* because analysis centers on syntax at a surface level of analysis; cf. **deep-structure level, transformational grammar**)

physiology. Scientific study of living organisms and of life-sustaining functions and processes (in contrast to *anatomy*, which studies the structures of living organisms)

pinna. Visible outer part of the ear, which collects sound waves

pitch. Sensation of how high or low a tone sounds, based on the **frequency** of the sound wave that reaches the auditory receptors

pituitary gland. An endocrine **gland** located above the mouth and underneath the **hypothalamus** (in the **forebrain**), to which it is attached and by which it is controlled; sometimes considered the master gland of the body because of its central importance to the **endocrine system;** provides a direct link from the endocrine system to the **nervous system** via the hypothalamus; secretes **hormones** that directly affect other physiological functions and that indirectly affect other functions through the release of pituitary hormones that control many other endocrine glands, stimulating those glands to release hormones that produce specific physiological effects; in particular, when stimulated by the hypothalamus, the pituitary gland plays an important role in the response to **stress**, secreting *adrenocorticotropic hormone (ACTH)*, which is carried by the bloodstream to other organs, most notably the adrenal glands, which

then release epinephrine and norepinephrine

place theory. One of the two alternative views of the way in which humans sense pitch (cf. **frequency theory;** see also **duplicity theory**); suggests that the sensation of **pitch** is determined by the location on the **basilar membrane** where the sound wave vibrates the **hair cells;** thus, hair cells located at various places on the basilar membrane vibrate in response to sounds of different frequencies and then stimulate different sensory neurons, which then determine the pitch that is perceived

placebo. Pill or other apparent treatment that the patient believes will provide medical or recuperative benefit but that actually contains no active ingredients or restorative properties

plasticity. Characterized by modifiability, particularly in terms of the enhancement of abilities

pleasure principle. Operating principle by which the **id** irrationally pursues immediate gratification of libidinal urges, regardless of the external realities that might impinge on those urges (cf. **idealistic principle, reality principle**)

polygraph. A method of assessing the veracity of self-report measures, by assessing the psychophysiological reactivity of various physiological processes, such as heart rate, galvanic skin response (GSR), and respiration; such measurements assess arousal, usually associated with emotional stress; thus, for persons who feel stressful arousal in association with lying, such measures indicate instances of lying; however, for persons who feel stressful arousal in association with other situations, such measures also indicate those sources of arousal; and for persons who feel no stressful arousal in association with lying, such measures do not indicate instances of lying

pons. A structure in the **hindbrain,** containing nerve cells that pass signals from one part of the brain to another, thereby serving as a kind of relay station or bridge (*pons*, Latin, "bridge"); also contains a portion of the **reticular activating system** and contains nerves serving parts of the head and face

Ponzo illusion. An **optical illusion,**

in which two equally long horizontal line segments, which are framed by diagonally converging line segments, are perceived to differ in length; may be an artifact of some of the **monocular depth cues** with which perceivers are familiar (cf. **Müller-Lyer illusion**)

population. The entire set of individuals to which a generalization is to be made

population parameters. The set of numerical values that characterizes all persons in a population under investigation; under most circumstances, it is impossible or impractical to determine population parameters, so **sample statistics** are used as an indication of the population parameters (see also **representative sample**)

positive correlation. A relationship between two attributes, in which an increase in either one of the attributes is associated with an increase in the other attribute, and a decrease in either one of the attributes is associated with a decrease in the other attribute; a perfect positive correlation is indicated by +1 (see **correlation;** cf. **negative correlation**)

positive reinforcement. The pairing of a given **operant** behavior with a stimulus that is rewarding to the organism engaged in the operant, which thereby strengthens the likelihood that the organism will produce the operant again (see **operant conditioning, positive reinforcer;** cf. **negative reinforcement**)

positive reinforcer. A reward (pleasant stimulus) that follows an **operant** and strengthens the associated response (see **operant conditioning, positive reinforcement;** cf. **negative reinforcer;** cf. also **punishment**)

positive symptoms. Characteristics of a disorder that are detected by noting that the individual is exhibiting an abnormal behavior (i.e., an abnormal behavior is *added* to the behavioral repertoire); may involve **delusions, hallucinations,** or bizarre behavior (cf. **negative symptoms;** see also **schizophrenia**)

positive transfer. A situation in which prior learning may lead to greater ease of learning and remembering new material (see **transfer;** cf. **negative transfer**)

positron emission tomography (PET). A technique for creating dynamic images of the **brain** in action (thus revealing physiological processes, not just anatomical structures); involves injecting into a patient a mildly radioactive form of glucose, which is absorbed by cells of the body, including the brain; the amount of glucose absorption in the brain indicates the level of metabolic activity of the cells; computer analysis of the glucose absorption thereby indicates the locations of high rates of metabolic activity during various cognitive tasks (e.g., playing computer games, speaking, moving parts of the body); largely used as a research tool, but clinical applications are forthcoming

postconventional (principled) morality. A phase of moral development in which the individual recognizes the importance of (a) *social contracts* (the importance of societal rules as a basis for behavior) and (b) *individual rights* (internal moral principles that may outweigh societal rules in some situations): (a) People hold a wide variety of values and opinions, most of which are essentially relative, but which should be upheld because they are part of a social contract to which people have agreed; (b) a few values and rights, such as the rights to life and liberty, should be protected and safeguarded regardless of the opinion of a majority of individuals or of authority figures in a given society

postformal thinking. A stage of cognitive development that may follow the stage of **formal operations,** in which individuals recognize the constant unfolding and evolution of thought (see **dialectical thinking**), and they can manipulate mentally various options for decisions and diverse alternative answers to questions, recognizing that a single ideal option or a simple unambiguous answer may not be available (cf. **problem finding**)

posthypnotic suggestion. An instruction given to an individual during **hypnosis,** which the individual is to implement after having wakened from the hypnotic state; subjects often have no recollection of having been given the instructions or even of having been hypnotized

posttraumatic stress disorder. A stress disorder (a form of **anxiety disorder;** cf. also **acute stress disorder**) characterized by the intrusive psychological reenactment of a past traumatic event, such as recurring nightmares or repeated wakeful resurfacing of painful memories of the event while consciously engaged in unrelated activities; often accompanied by difficulties in sleeping or in concentrating while awake; sometimes accompanied by an uncomfortable feeling of experiencing life in ways that other people do not, as well as by feelings of apathy and detachment

pragmatic reasoning schemas. A set of goal-related organizing principles that form cognitive frameworks for deductively reasoning what to expect in various realistic situations about which an individual lacks complete information regarding what to expect

pragmatics. The study of how people use **language,** emphasizing the social contexts in which language is used, as well as the nonverbal communication that augments verbal communication

pragmatism. A school of psychological thought, which (a) asserts that knowledge is validated by its usefulness, and (b) is concerned not only with asking how and why people behave as they do but also with asking how psychologists and other people can use this knowledge

precognition. Alleged awareness of an event before (*pre-,* "before") the event takes place (see **extrasensory perception**)

preconscious level. A part of consciousness that comprises information that could become conscious readily, but that is not continuously available in awareness

preconventional morality. A phase of moral development, in which moral reasoning is guided by punishments and rewards; initially, individual moral reasoners focus on the avoidance of **punishment** and on **obedience** to authority, without concern for the interests or feelings of other persons, except as those interests or feelings may affect the likelihood of punishment; later in this phase, moral reasoners

recognize the interests of others, but strictly in terms of how to strike deals in order to gain self-interested advantages (rewards)

predicate. One of the two key parts of a statement (also termed a *verb phrase;* cf. **subject,** which is also termed a *noun phrase*); the part of the sentence that tells something about the subject of the sentence, usually including a verb and whatever the verb acts on, but sometimes including a linking verb (e.g., *is, are*) and a descriptor

prediction. One of four goals of psychological research (the other three are **control, description,** and **explanation**): a declaration or indication in advance, based on observation, experience, or reasoning

predictive validity. An aspect of criterion-related **validity,** which assesses the extent to which a test or other measurement (the *predictor*) predicts some kind of performance outcome (the *criterion*), which is to be measured well after the test or other measurement has been taken

prefix. A **morpheme** that is attached to the beginning of a root word, thereby altering the syntactical use (in the case of **function morphemes**) or the meaning (in the case of **content morphemes**) of the root word (cf. **suffix;** see also **affix**)

prefrontal lobotomy. A form of **psychosurgery** in which surgeons attempted to alleviate symptoms of mental disorders by engaging in a procedure that severed the **frontal lobes** from the posterior portions of the brain, thereby cutting off all communication between the frontal lobes and the rest of the brain; a tragically ineffective procedure that caused devastating injury to tens of thousands of patients, primarily in mental institutions

prejudice. A form of thinking, whereby an individual forms an unfavorable attitude directed toward groups of people (usually *outgroups,* of which they are not members), based on insufficient or incorrect evidence about these groups (see **realistic-conflict theory; social-identity theory**)

Premack principle. An axiom of **operant conditioning** asserting that

(a) more preferred activities reinforce less preferred ones, and (b) the specific degree of preference is determined by the individual who holds the preference; to apply this principle, a person's **operant** behavior can be reinforced by offering as a reward something the person prefers more than the behavior being reinforced

premise. Statement of fact or assertion of belief, on which a deductively reasoned argument may be based (see **deductive reasoning**)

preoperational stage. Second stage of cognitive development, according to Piaget, which is characterized by the development of internal mental representations (the precursors of which actually arose at the end of the previous [sensorimotor] stage) and verbal communication (cf. **concrete operations, formal-operational stage, sensorimotor stage**)

primacy effect. Tendency to show superior recall of words that occur at and near the beginning of a list of words (cf. **recency effect**); affects **impression formation,** such that first impressions can influence subsequent ones

primary appraisal. The first step in a two-step process of appraising a potentially stressful situation (cf. **secondary appraisal**); involves a person's determination of whether it is important to handle the situation, based on the significance of the situation for the person and its possible outcomes for the person as a result of handling versus not handling the situation

primary colors. The three colors (red, green, and blue) that can be combined additively to form all other colors (see also **additive mixture, trichromatic theory of color vision**)

primary motor cortex. The portion of the **frontal lobe** that plans, controls, and executes movements, particularly those movements involving any kind of delayed response; this portion of the **cerebral cortex** can be mapped to show the places in the **brain** that control specific groups of muscles in the body

primary-process thought. A form of thought that is irrational, instinct-driven, and out of touch with reality, often thought to be a wellspring of creativity and of dreams, as well as of

symbolic expressions of sexual and aggressive urges (cf. **secondary-process thought**)

primary reinforcer. Rewarding stimulus used in **operant conditioning,** which provides immediate satisfaction to the learner (cf. **secondary reinforcer**)

primary somatosensory cortex. The portion of the **parietal lobe** (located directly behind the **primary motor cortex** in the **frontal lobe**) that receives information from the senses about pressure, texture, temperature, and **pain;** this portion of the **cerebral cortex** can be mapped to show the places in the brain that receive sensory information from precise locations on the surface of the body

priming effect. The activation of a **node** by a **prime** (activating node) to which the node is connected in a **network,** in the process of **spreading activation,** according to the network view of memory processes

proactive interference. A type of memory disruption, which occurs when interfering information is presented *before,* rather than *after,* presentation of the information that is to be remembered (also termed *proactive inhibition;* cf. **retroactive interference**)

problem finding. A stage of cognitive development that may follow the stage of **formal operations,** in which individuals become proficient in figuring out exactly what problems face them and in deciding which problems they should try most assiduously and vigorously to solve (cf. **dialectical thinking, postformal thinking**)

problem-focused coping. See **coping**

problem solving. One of the fundamental kinds of thinking, which involves the resolution of a difficulty, the overcoming of obstacles, the answering of a question, or the achievement of a goal (see **problem-solving cycle;** cf. **creativity, judgment and decision making, reasoning**)

problem-solving cycle. A sequence of steps for resolving a problematic situation: (1) Identify the problem; (2) define the problem; (3) formulate a strategy; (4) represent and organize the information; (5) allocate resources; (6) monitor the problem-solving process; and (7) evaluate the solution; re-

quires flexibility in following the various steps of the cycle to achieve effective solution (see **problem solving**)

problem space. The universe of all possible actions that can be applied to find a solution to a given problem

procedural knowledge. A recognition and awareness of how to perform particular tasks, skills, or procedures ("knowing how," not "knowing that") (cf. **declarative knowledge**)

productive thinking. A form of **critical thinking,** which involves insight that goes beyond the bounds of the existing associations identified by the thinker (cf. **reproductive thinking**)

projection. A **defense mechanism,** in which persons attribute their own unacceptable and possibly dangerous thoughts or impulses to another person or persons, thereby permitting conscious awareness of otherwise unacceptable thoughts and impulses

projection areas. The areas in the cortical **lobes** where sensory and motor processing occurs; *sensory projection areas* are the locations in the **cerebral cortex** to which **sensory neurons** are projected via the **thalamus** from elsewhere in the body; *motor projection areas* are the regions that project **motor neurons** downward through the **spinal cord,** via the **peripheral nervous system,** to control desired movement of the appropriate muscles

projective test. Psychological assessment based on **psychodynamic theory,** in which it is held that the individual's unconscious conflicts may be projected into responses to the assessment (cf. **objective personality test**)

proposition. The meaning underlying a perceived or mentally construed relationship among concepts

prosocial behavior. Societally approved actions that are seen as furthering the common good, that are at least consistent with the interests of the social group, or that help one or more other persons (cf. **antisocial behavior**)

prototype. A model that best represents a given concept and that comprises a set of **characteristic features** that tend to be typical of most examples (cf. **exemplars**) of the concept, but none of which is necessary for a given example to be considered an instance of the concept (see **prototype**

theory; cf. **componental theory, core, defining features**)

prototype theory. One of two primary theories of semantics (cf. **componential theory**), which claims that the meaning of a word (or concept) can be understood by describing the concept in terms of a **prototype** (see also **exemplar**), which best represents a given concept and which comprises a set of **characteristic features** that tend to be typical of most examples of the concept (cf. **defining features**)

proxemics. The study of interpersonal proximity and distancing

proximal stimulus. The internal sensation of a source of stimulation, as it is registered by the sensory **receptors,** regardless of whether the internal sensation exactly matches the external source of stimulation as it exists in the world (cf. **distal stimulus;** see also **perceptual constancy**)

proximity (as an aspect of interpersonal attraction). The geographical nearness of people toward whom an individual might feel attracted; a factor increasing the likelihood that a person may be attracted to another person, perhaps by also enhancing the probability of familiarity with or arousal by the other person

proximity (as a Gestalt principle of perception). A Gestalt principle of form perception (see **Gestalt approach**): the tendency, when viewing an assortment of objects, to perceive objects that are close to each other as forming a group within the assortment

psychoactive. Characteristic of drugs that produce a **psychopharmacological** effect, thereby affecting behavior, mood, and consciousness; can be classified into four basic categories: **central nervous system (CNS) depressant, central nervous system (CNS) stimulant, hallucinogenic, narcotic**

psychoanalysis. A form of psychological treatment based on **psychodynamic theory**

psychodynamic theory. A theory of human motivations and behavior, which emphasizes the importance of conflicting unconscious mental processes and the importance of early childhood experiences in affecting adult personality

psychogenic pain. Intense sensory discomfort and emotional suffering for which physiological origins (due to injury of body tissues) cannot be found (cf. **organic pain**); three common types are *causalgia*—characterized by recurrent episodes of severe burning **pain** in a body part or region (often in a location where tissue has been damaged due to a serious wound), *neuralgia*—characterized by recurrent episodes of intense shooting pain along a nerve, *phantom-limb pain*—characterized by pain sensations in a limb that no longer has functioning nerves (e.g., due to amputation)

psychokinesis. Hypothetical ability to move objects by thought alone, as in trying to bend metal objects via mental concentration (*psycho-*, "mind"; *-kinesis*, "movement"; see **extrasensory perception**)

psychology. The study of the mind and of the behavior of people and other organisms

psychometric. Characterized by psychological measurement (*psycho-*, "pertaining to the mind or mental processes," *-metric*, "measurement")

psychopharmacological. An outcome affecting behavior, mood, and consciousness, produced by drugs (see **psychoactive**)

psychophysics. The study and measurement of the functioning of the senses, which involves the attempt to measure the relationship between a form of *physical* stimulation and the *psychological* sensations produced as a consequence

psychosexual development. An aspect of personality development during infancy, childhood, and adolescence, according to **psychodynamic theory;** emphasizes the physiological locuses in which an individual pursues and finds pleasure (to satisfy the urges of the **libido**); comprises four major stages (see **oral stage, anal stage, phallic stage,** and **genital stage**), as well as a period of dormancy (see **latency**), which occurs between the phallic stage and the genital stage; each stage is hypothesized to center on a conflict of psychic forces, which the individual must resolve in order to proceed to the next stage of development (cf. **psychosocial theory of personality development**)

psychosis. A relatively serious psychological disorder, involving extreme distortions in cognitive and perceptual processes, major disturbances in physiological functioning (e.g., extremely heightened or depressed state of physiological arousal), unusual motor behavior, intense emotional instability, or some combination of these types of symptoms (cf. **neurosis**)

psychosocial theory of personality development. A theory of **personality** development that followed Freud's psychosexual theory, but that addressed a much broader range of psychological forces operating on personality development than just libidinal (sexual) energy, and that encompassed the entire life span, rather than just development from infancy through adolescence (cf. **psychosexual development**)

psychosomatic medicine. A psychodynamic view of illness, which studied the psychological roots of physical illnesses (e.g., ulcers, asthma, migraine headaches)

psychosurgery. A psychophysiological procedure intended to alleviate mental disorders by probing, slicing, dissecting, or removing some part of the **brain**

psychotherapy. A remedial intervention that uses the principles of **psychology** in order to treat mental or emotional disorders or otherwise to improve the adjustment and well-being of the person who receives the intervention

psychoticism. A personality attribute characterized by solitariness, detached interpersonal relationships, and a lack of feelings, especially a lack of caring, empathy, and sensitivity (cf. **Big Five**)

psychotropic drugs. Drugs affecting the individual's psychological processes or state of mind; four main classes of psychotropic drugs include **antipsychotics, antidepressants,** antianxiety drugs, and lithium (see also **psychoactive**)

punishment. A stimulus used in **operant conditioning,** which *decreases* the probability of an operant response, through either the application of an unpleasant stimulus or the removal of a pleasant one; an ineffective means of reducing **aggression** if physical punishment (rather than penalty) is used as a means of operant conditioning (cf. **negative reinforcer, positive reinforcer**)

pupil. The hole in the **iris** (roughly in its center) through which light gains access to the interior of the eye, particularly the **retina;** in dim light, the pupil reflexively expands, permitting more light to enter, but in bright light, it reflexively contracts, limiting the amount of light that can enter the eye

purity. The extent to which a **hue** cannot be analyzed in terms of a combination of other hues (see also **additive mixture, subtractive mixture**)

quality. The nature of a stimulus that reaches a sensory **receptor** and is then sensed in the **brain** (cf. **intensity**)

quasi-experimental design. A plan for conducting a study that has many of the features of a controlled experimental design but that does not ensure the random assignment of subjects to the treatment and the control groups (cf. **controlled experimental design, correlational design**)

questionnaire. A set of questions used by social-science researchers for conducting a **survey** (cf. **test;** cf. also **case study, experiment, naturalistic observation**)

range. The full expanse of a distribution of values, from the lowest to the highest value

ratio IQ. A means of indicating performance on intelligence tests, based on a quotient of **mental age** divided by chronological age (see **intelligence quotient;** cf. **deviation IQs**)

ratio schedule. A schedule of **operant conditioning,** in which a proportion (ratio) of **operant** responses are reinforced, regardless of the amount of time that has passed (see **fixed-ratio reinforcement, variable-ratio reinforcement;** cf. **fixed-interval reinforcement, variable-interval reinforcement;** see also **partial reinforcement, positive reinforcement**)

rational-emotive behavior therapy (REBT). A form of cognitive therapy designed to help people with their emotional reactions by helping them

to rectify their incorrect or maladaptive thoughts (see **cognitivism**)

rational method. Means of obtaining information by using philosophical analysis and **reasoning** in order to understand the world and people's relations to it (from the Latin *ratio,* meaning "reason" or "thought"; cf. **empirical method**)

rationalist. Person who believes that knowledge is most effectively acquired through **rational methods** (cf. **empiricist**)

rationalization. A **defense mechanism,** in which a person can avoid threatening thoughts and explanations of behavior by replacing threatening ones with nonthreatening ones, such as through inaccurate or unwarranted justification of behavior

raw score. The actual total sum of points obtained by a given test-taker for a given test, which often equals the actual number of items answered correctly on the test

reaction formation. A **defense mechanism** that involves transforming an unacceptable impulse or thought into its opposite; that is, defensive individuals protect their positive self-images by convincing themselves that they think and feel things that are the opposite of their true thoughts and feelings

reaction range. The broad limits within which a particular attribute (e.g., intelligence) may be expressed in various possible ways, given the inherited potential for expression of the attribute in the particular individual

realistic-conflict theory. A theory regarding **prejudice,** which argues that competition among groups for valuable but scarce resources leads to prejudice

reality principle. The operating principle by which the **ego** responds as rationally as possible to the real world as it is consciously perceived to be, rather than as the person desires the world to be (cf. **pleasure principle**) or as the person believes that the world should be (cf. **idealistic principle**); mediates among the urges of the **id,** the prohibitions of the **superego,** and the realities of the external world

reasoning. One of the fundamental processes of thinking, which involves drawing conclusions from evidence;

often classified as either involving **deductive reasoning** or **inductive reasoning** (cf. **creativity, judgment and decision making, problem solving**)

recall memory. A process of memory often employed in memory tasks, in which the individual is asked to produce (not just to recognize as correct) a fact, a word, or other item from memory (see also **free recall, paired-associates recall, serial recall;** cf. **recognition memory**)

recency effect. Tendency to show superior recall of words that occur at and near the end of a list of words (cf. **primacy effect**)

receptive field. The region of the external world from which a receptor cell receives sensory information

receptors. Physiological structures designed to receive something (e.g., a given substance or a particular kind of information), which may refer either to (a) the structures that receive external stimulation and **transduce** it into electrochemical sensory information or to (b) the structures that receive electrochemical sensory information; sensory receptors are physiological structures that provide a mechanism for receiving external stimulation (from outside the body), which can then be transduced into sensation as electrochemical sensory information within the body; receptor **nerves** and **neurons** receive electrochemical sensory information (e.g., sensations in the eyes, ears, and skin) from sensory receptors or from other **sensory neurons** and then transmit that information back up through the **spinal cord** to the **brain** (cf. **effector, interneuron, motor neuron**)

recessive trait. The weaker genetic trait in a pair of **traits,** which does not appear in the **phenotype** of an organism when the **genotype** comprises a **dominant trait** and a recessive trait

reciprocal determinism. A principle of a **personality** theory, which attributes human functioning to an interaction among behavior, personal variables, and the environment

recognition memory. A process of memory often employed in memory tasks, in which the individual is asked just to recognize as correct (not to produce) a fact, a word, or other item from memory (cf. **recall memory**)

recognition task. See **recognition memory**

reconstructive memory. Psychological phenomenon in which an individual stores in memory some information about events or facts, exactly as the events or facts took place (cf. **constructive memory**)

reductionism. An extreme form of **monism,** which reduces the role of the mind to the status of a mere cog in a larger physiological machine and which reduces the vast complexity of human behavior to a mere by-product of physiological phenomena

reflex. An automatic physiological response to an external stimulus; the spinal cord transmits a message directly from receptor nerves to effector nerves, without routing the message through the brain prior to the bodily response to the sensory information (cf. **instinct, learning**)

refraction. The degree to which light waves are bent, usually by curvature of the surface of the medium (e.g., a lens) through which the light waves are passing

regions of similarity. Areas that are largely undifferentiated from each other, often mentioned in regard to **direct-perception theories** of vision

regression. A **defense mechanism,** in which individuals revert back to patterns of thinking and behaving that are characteristic of an earlier stage of **psychosexual development,** thereby avoiding or at least minimizing any psychodynamic conflicts, anxiety, or pain associated with the present, more advanced, stage of development

regression equation. A predictive equation specifying the relation between a dependent variable and one or more independent variables

rehearsal. Strategy for keeping information in short-term memory or for moving information into long-term memory by repeating the information over and over

reinforcer. A **stimulus** used in **operant conditioning,** which increases the probability that a given **operant** behavior associated with the stimulus (which usually has occurred immediately or almost immediately before the reinforcing stimulus) will be repeated (see **positive reinforcers, negative reinforcers**)

relative frequency. Represents the number of cases that received a given score or range of scores (see **frequency distribution;** cf. **cumulative frequency**)

relative refractory phase. A time following the firing of a **neuron,** during which the neuron can fire again, but only in response to a much stronger stimulus than is normally required (cf. **absolute refractory phase**)

relative size. See **monocular depth cues**

reliability. The dependability of an experimental procedure, indicating that the procedure consistently yields the same results, as long as the procedure is administered in the same way each time; the dependability of a measurement instrument (e.g., a test), indicating that the instrument consistently measures the outcome being measured; may be measured as follows: *alternate-forms reliability*—the degree of relationship between test scores when people take one form of a test and the test scores when they take an alternate, parallel form of the same test some time later; *internal-consistency reliability*—the extent to which all items on a test measure the same thing; *interrater reliability*—the extent to which two or more raters of a given response would rate the response in the same way (generally applicable to subjective measurements); *test–retest reliability*—the degree to which people's test scores when taking the test on one occasion dependably predict their test scores if they take exactly the same test again some time later (may be confounded by performance enhancement that may result from the prior experience in taking the test) (cf. **validity**)

reliable. See **reliability**

REM sleep. The distinctive kind of sleep that is characterized by rapid eye movements (REMs) and frequently—although not exclusively—associated with dreaming (cf. **N-REM sleep**)

replicate. Repeat the methods used in a previous experiment, in order to observe whether the same methods will yield the same results

representation. A means of showing information in one or more alternative forms in order to understand or to communicate the given information

representational thought. Cognitive processes involving internal representations of external stimuli

representative (as a speech act). See **speech acts**

representative (as a characteristic of a sample). See **representative sample**

representative sample. A subset of the population, carefully chosen to represent the proportionate diversity of the population as a whole; well-chosen representative samples permit inferences regarding the probability that a given set of **sample statistics** accurately indicates a comparable set of **population parameters**

representativeness. A judgment regarding the probability of an uncertain event according to (a) how obviously the event is similar to or representative of the population from which it is derived, and (b) the degree to which the event reflects the salient features of the process by which it is generated (such as randomness) (see **heuristic**)

repression. A **defense mechanism,** in which a person keeps troublesome internally generated thoughts and feelings from entering consciousness and thereby causing internal conflicts or other psychological discomfort

reproductive thinking. A form of **thinking,** in which the thinker makes use of existing associations involving what the thinker already knows (cf. **productive thinking**)

resistance. An attempt to block therapeutic progress in psychodynamic treatment, usually as a result of unconscious conflicts

resistant attachment pattern. One of three attachment patterns observed in the **strange situation** (cf. **avoidant attachment pattern, secure attachment pattern**): A child generally shows ambivalence toward the mother while she is present, seeking both to gain and to resist physical contact with her when the mother returns after being gone a short time

response. An action or reaction that is linked to a **stimulus**

reticular activating system. A network of **neurons** (located primarily in the **midbrain** and extending into the **hindbrain**) that is essential to the regulation of **consciousness** (sleep, wakefulness, **arousal,** and even attention, to some extent), as well as to such vital functions as heartbeat and breathing

retina. A network of **neurons** extending over most of the posterior surface of the interior of the eye, containing the **photoreceptors** responsible for transducing electromagnetic light energy into neural electrochemical impulses (see **amacrine cells, bipolar cells, ganglion cells, horizontal cells;** see also **cones, photopigments, rods**)

retrieval. See **memory retrieval**

retroactive interference. A type of memory disruption, which occurs when interfering information is presented *after*, rather than *before*, presentation of the information that is to be remembered (also termed *retroactive inhibition*; cf. **proactive interference**)

retrograde amnesia. See **amnesia**

reuptake. The more common of two mechanisms by which neurotransmitters are removed from the synaptic cleft: The **terminal buttons** of an **axon** reabsorb (take up again) any remaining **neurotransmitter** or **neuromodulator** substances that had been released into the **synapse**, thereby conserving these substances and sparing the surrounding **neurons** from excessive stimulation

reversible figures. Displayed images in which each of a given pair of adjacent or even interconnecting figures can be seen as either figure or ground, although both cannot be the focus of **perception** simultaneously (see **figure–ground**)

revolutionary science. Scientific work that radically modifies or perhaps contradicts altogether the existing **paradigm**, inventing instead a new paradigm (cf. **normal science**)

rods. One of the two kinds of **photoreceptors** in the eye; more numerous, longer, thinner, and more highly concentrated in the periphery of the **retina** than in the foveal region of the retina than are **cones,** the other type of photoreceptor; function more effectively in dim light than in bright light, but incapable of color vision (see **fovea**)

sadness. A relatively mild, shallow, and usually relatively brief emotion of sorrow (cf. **grief**)

saltatory conduction. Process by which electrochemical impulses travel via **myelinated neurons,** saving time by leaping across the coating of the **myelin sheath,** to be reconstructed anew at each uncoated **node of Ranvier** (*saltare,* to leap [Latin]; cf. **glial cells**)

sample. See **representative sample** and **sample statistics**

sample statistics. The set of numerical values that (a) characterize the sample of persons who have been measured in regard to the attributes under investigation and (b) are presumed to give some indication of the **population parameters** (see also **representative sample**)

satellite cells. Cells of the **peripheral nervous system (PNS),** which work with **Schwann cells** in providing support functions for neurons similar to the function of the **glial cells** (in the **central nervous system**), but occurring in the outlying nerves and sense organs of the PNS; essential to interneuronal communication in the PNS

satisficing. A strategy for making decisions, in which the decision maker considers options one by one, immediately selecting the first option that appears to be satisfactory—just good enough, rather than considering all of the possible options and then carefully computing which of the entire universe of options will maximize gains and minimize losses; that is, decision makers consider only the minimum possible number of options that are believed necessary to achieve a satisfactory decision (see **judgment and decision making**)

saturation. One of three properties of color (cf. **hue, brightness**); the vividness, vibrancy, or richness of the hue

savings. A phenomenon of **classical conditioning,** in which there is a period of time during which the **CS** and the **UCS** are not linked, and then the CS is presented again *in the presence of the UCS*; even when the CS is paired with the UCS only briefly, the CR returns to levels approaching those at the **asymptote** of the **acquisition phase** of conditioning (cf. **spontaneous recovery**)

schedules of reinforcement. Patterns of **operant conditioning,** which

determine the timing of reinforcement following the **operant** behavior (see **continuous reinforcement, fixed-interval reinforcement, fixed-ratio reinforcement, partial reinforcement, variable-interval reinforcement, variable-ratio reinforcement**)

schema. A cognitive framework for organizing associated concepts, based on previous experiences

schema theory. A cognitively based theory of sex-role development, which is based on the view that organized mental systems of information (i.e., **schemas**) help people both to make sense of their experiences and to shape their interactions, particularly in terms of their gender-relevant schemas for how males and females demonstrate differing sex-role-relevant behaviors and attitudes

schizophrenia. A set of disorders that encompasses a variety of symptoms, including disturbances of perception, cognition, emotion, and even motor behavior (see **delusions, hallucinations**): *catatonic schizophrenia*—characterized by stupor, apparently complete detachment from the rest of the world, and long periods of immobility and of staring into space; *disorganized schizophrenia*—characterized by profound psychological disorganization, including cognitive symptoms (e.g., hallucinations, delusions, and incoherent speech such as meaningless neologisms), apparent disturbances of mood (e.g., rapid mood swings and either flat affect or inappropriate affect), and extreme neglect of self-care and self-grooming; *paranoid schizophrenia*—characterized by delusions of persecution or of grandeur, which may be accompanied by auditory hallucinations of voices telling the people either of plots against them (*persecution*) or of their own magnificence (*grandeur*), as well as by particular susceptibility to delusions of reference; *residual schizophrenia*—characterized by some mild symptoms of schizophrenia that seem to linger after the individual has experienced one or more severe episodes of one of the other forms of schizophrenia; *undifferentiated schizophrenia*—characterized by symptoms of schizophrenia that do not seem to fit neatly into one of the other patterns of schizophrenia (cf. **personality disor-**

der [schizoid and schizotypal personality disorders])

Schwann cells. Cells of the **peripheral nervous system (PNS),** which work with **satellite cells** in providing support functions for **neurons** similar to the function of the **glial cells** (in the **central nervous system**), but doing so in the outlying nerves and sense organs of the PNS; essential to interneuronal communication in the PNS (also termed *neurolemmas*)

script(s). A shared understanding about the characteristic actors, objects, and sequence of actions in a situation being described, which facilitates interactions and conversational communication about the situation

search. Active scanning of the environment, in pursuit of particular stimuli or particular features (cf. **vigilance**)

second-order relations. Relations between relations; that is, an abstract means by which two kinds of relationships may be related to one another, in which case the two kinds of relationships (e.g., paternal relationships and maternal relationships) that are being interrelated describe the way in which two or more concrete objects or experiences are related to one another (e.g., the relationship between father and child and the relationship between mother and child); often used in **reasoning** by analogy

secondary appraisal. The second step in a two-step process of appraising a potentially stressful situation (cf. **primary appraisal**); involves a person's assessment of strategies she or he can use in order to maximize the likelihood of potentially beneficial outcomes and to minimize the likelihood of potentially harmful outcomes of the stressful situation

secondary-process thought. A form of thought that is basically rational and based on reality, helping the thinker to make sense of the world and to act in ways that make sense both to the thinker and to observers of the thinker's actions (cf. **primary-process thought**)

secondary reinforcer(s). Rewarding stimuli that are less immediately satisfying and perhaps also less tangible than **primary reinforcers,** but which may gain reinforcing value through association with primary reinforcers; often used during **operant conditioning** when a primary reinforcer is not immediately available or is inconvenient to administer, such that the secondary reinforcers provide sufficient reinforcement until primary reinforcers can be administered; greatly enhances the flexibility of applying operant conditioning because almost any stimulus can be used as a secondary reinforcer (see also **token economy**); a behavioristic theory of interpersonal attraction suggests that persons who are present in rewarding situations may acquire some of the properties of a secondary reinforcer

secondary traits. Personality **traits** that have some bearing on a person's behavior but that are not particularly central to what the person does (cf. **cardinal trait, central traits of personality**)

secure attachment pattern. One of three attachment patterns observed in the **strange situation** (cf. **avoidant attachment pattern, resistant attachment pattern**), in which a child generally shows preferential interest in—but not excessive dependence on—the attention of the mother while she is present and in which the child shows some distress when the mother leaves but can be calmed and reassured by her when she returns

sedative–hypnotic drug. One of the two primary types of **central-nervous-system (CNS) depressants,** used for calming anxiety and relieving insomnia (e.g., **barbiturate, tranquilizer,** methaqualone, and chloral hydrate) (see also **antianxiety drugs**)

selective attention. A process by which an individual attempts to track one stimulus or one type of stimulus and to ignore another

selective-combination insight. A form of **insight** that involves the innovative, productive integration of carefully chosen relevant information, which yields an insightful solution to a problem (see **insight problem;** cf. **selective-comparison insight, selective-encoding insight**)

selective-comparison insight. A form of **insight** that involves novel perceptions of how new information relates to old information (see **insight problem;** cf. **selective-combination insight, selective-encoding insight**)

selective-encoding insight. A form of **insight** that involves appropriately yet innovatively choosing a way in which to represent information related to a problem, as well as carefully distinguishing relevent from irrelevant information that may be related to a problem (see **insight problem;** cf. **selective-combination insight, selective-comparison insight**)

self. The whole of the **personality,** including both conscious and unconscious elements, which is posited to strive for unity among often opposing parts of the personality (see also **ideal self, self-concept, self-esteem, self-understanding**)

self-concept. An individual's view of her- or himself (cf. **ideal self**), which may or may not be realistic or even perceived similarly by other persons; often believed to involve both **self-understanding** (cognitions regarding the self) and **self-esteem** (emotions and valuations regarding the self)

self-determination theory. A theory of motivation, which posits that people need to feel competent, autonomous, and securely and satisfyingly connected to other people

self-efficacy. A person's belief in her or his competence to do things, which often actually leads to enhanced ability to do those things (see **self-fulfilling prophecy**)

self-efficacy theory. A theory of motivation, which considers goal-related behavior in terms of the importance of the expectancy of being able to perform any actions necessary to attain particular goals, based on the person's beliefs regarding her or his personal competence to perform the required actions

self-esteem. The degree to which a person values him- or herself (cf. **self-understanding;** see **self-concept**)

self-fulfilling prophecy. A psychological phenomenon whereby what is believed to be true becomes true or at least is perceived to have become true

self-handicapping. An **attribution** bias in which people take actions to sabotage their own performance so that they will have excuses in case they fail to perform satisfactorily (see also **actor–observer effect; fundamental attribution error**)

self-monitoring. *In regard to personality theory:* the degree to which people monitor and change their behavior in response to situational demands, from the perspective of the degree to which individuals show consistency across various situations

self-perception theory. A theory regarding **cognitive consistency,** which suggests that when people are not sure of what they believe, they infer their beliefs from their behavior, perceiving their own actions much as an outside observer would, and thereby drawing conclusions about themselves, based on their actions (cf. **cognitive dissonance, impression-management theory**)

self-report measure. Measure of psychological attitudes, feelings, opinions, or behaviors, which are obtained simply by asking people to state their responses to questions regarding those psychological processes and products (see also **Likert scale**)

self-schema. Cognitive framework for the way in which people organize information (thoughts, feelings, and beliefs) about themselves (see **schema**)

self-terminating serial processing. A means of responding to a task involving recognition of a particular item from a list of items, in which an individual seeks to retrieve a particular item stored in memory by checking each of the items that is presented against the item being sought until the individual reaches the item being sought, at which time the individual stops checking the other items (cf. **exhaustive serial processing;** cf. also **parallel processing**)

self theory. A **humanistic** theory of **personality,** which focuses on the way in which the individual defines reality and personality, not in terms of an external, objective view of reality or of personality (see **self;** see also **ideal self, self-concept**)

self-understanding. The way in which individuals comprehend themselves, including the various roles and characteristics that form a part of the individual's identity (cf. **self-esteem;** see **self-concept**)

semantic memory. Encoding, storage, and retrieval of facts (e.g., **declarative knowledge** about the world) that do *not* describe the unique experiences of the individual recalling the facts, and that are *not* characterized by any particular temporal context in

which the individual acquired the facts (cf. **episodic memory**)

semantics. The study of the meanings of words

sensation. The neural information that the **brain** receives from the sensory **receptors** (cf. **perception**)

sensation seeking. A well-documented personality characteristic referring to the tendency to pursue heightened environmental stimulation, sometimes associated with low baseline levels of **arousal**

sense. A physiological system that collects information from **receptors** regarding various forms of energy that are received from within the body and from the external world and that then translates the collected information into an electrochemical form that can be comprehended by the **nervous system,** particularly the **brain**

sensitization. Paradoxical phenomenon in which an intermittent user of a drug actually demonstrates heightened sensitivity to low doses of the drug

sensorimotor stage. The first stage of cognitive development in Piaget's theory, in which individuals largely develop in terms of sensory (input) and **motor** (output) abilities, beginning with reflexive responses and gradually expanding in complexity to modify reflexive **schemas** toward purposeful actions that are environmentally adaptive (cf. **concrete operations, formal-operational stage, preoperational stage**)

sensory coding. The way in which sensory **receptors** transform a range of information about various stimuli, which arrives in a variety of forms of energy, changing that information into electrochemical representations that signify the various kinds of information

sensory neurons. Nerve cells that receive information from the environment through sensory **receptors** and then carry that information away from the sensory receptors and toward the **central nervous system** (see **neuron;** cf. **interneuron, motor neuron**)

sensory store. According to a three-stores theory of memory (cf. **long-term store, short-term store**), the hypothetical construct of a sensory store has the smallest capacity for

storing information (i.e., for only a fleeting sensory image) and has the shortest duration for memory storage (i.e., for only fractions of a second)

separation anxiety. A generalized fear of being separated from a primary caregiver (e.g., a parent) or other familiar adult

serial-position curve. A graphic display representing the probability that each of a series of given items will be recalled, given the order in which the items were presented in a list

serial processing. The cognitive manipulation of operations in which each operation is executed one at a time, in a series; as applied to short-term memory, the items stored in short-term memory would be retrieved one at a time, not all at once (cf. **parallel processing;** see also **exhaustive serial processing, self-terminating serial processing**)

serial recall. A type of memory task in which the subject is presented with a list of items and is asked to repeat the items in the exact order in which the items were presented (cf. **free recall**)

serotonin. A **neurotransmitter** synthesized from tryptophan in the diet; appears to be related to **arousal,** sleep, and dreams, as well as to regulation of mood, appetite, and sensitivity to **pain** (cf. **acetylcholine, dopamine**)

set-point theory. A theory regarding hunger, linked to the **lipostatic hypothesis,** according to which each person has a preset body weight that is biologically determined either at birth or within the first few years following birth, based on the fat cells in the body, which may increase but not decrease in number during the course of the life span; that is, although the size of the cells may fluctuate in relation to the amount of food consumed, the number may never decrease, regardless of how little food is consumed; according to this view, people with more fat cells tend to have greater body weight, although the size of their fat cells may be equivalent to the fat cells in persons who are lighter in body weight

sex. Physiological distinction as being male or female, expressed in physiological development (cf. **gender**)

sexual script(s). See **script(s)**

shadowing. A procedure by which a listener is presented with differing messages to each ear (see **dichotic presentation**) and is asked to repeat back the message from only one of the ears as soon as possible after hearing the message, thereby carefully following one message and ignoring the other

shape constancy. A form of **perceptual constancy,** in which an individual continues to perceive that an observed object retains its shape, even though the actual retinal sensations of the shape of the object change

shaping. Means of **operant conditioning** for behavior that is unlikely to be generated spontaneously by the organism; accomplished using a method of **successive approximations,** by which crude approximations of the desired behavior are rewarded, then when the initial approximations are fully conditioned, closer approximations are conditioned, and this process of reinforcing successive approximations continues until full performance of the desired behavior is being reinforced (see **positive reinforcement;** see also **autoshaping**)

short-term store. According to a three-stores theory of memory (cf. **long-term store, sensory store**), the hypothetical construct of a short-term store has a modest capacity (i.e., for only about seven items, give or take a couple of items) and has a duration for storing information for only a number of seconds (although information can be retained in short-term memory for up to a few minutes if the individual actively engages in rehearsal or other strategies for maintaining the information in the short-term store for longer periods of time)

signal. See **signal-detection theory** and **stimulus**

signal-detection theory (SDT). A psychophysical theory that posits four possible stimulus–response pairs: a **hit,** a **miss,** a **false alarm,** or a **correct rejection**

sign. In medicine, any unusual feature observed by the physician (cf. **symptom**)

similarity. A Gestalt principle of form perception (see **Gestalt approach**): the tendency to group various objects in the visual field, based on the similarity of the objects

simple cells. One of the key physiological structures described by the **feature-detector approach** to form perception, according to which primitive cortical cells provide information to adjacent simple cells regarding the features of objects in the receptive field for each simple cell; the simple cells then fire in response to lines with particular features, such as particular angular orientations, particular light/dark boundaries and contrasts, and particular locations in the receptive field of the cell, with the specifically stimulating features differing from one simple cell to another (see also **complex cells**)

simple phobia. See **phobia**

simulating paradigm. A research technique for determining the true effects of a psychological treatment (e.g., **hypnosis**), in which one group of subjects is subjected to the treatment and another group (a control group) is not, but the control subjects are asked to behave as though they had received the treatment; people must then try to distinguish between the behavior of the treatment group and the behavior of the control group (most effective if the persons making the distinction are blind as to which subjects are in the treatment group and which are in the control group)

simultaneous conditioning. An ineffective form of **classical conditioning** in which the **CS** and the **UCS** occur simultaneously; produces little or no conditioning due to the blocking effect and to **overshadowing**

single-cell recording. Technique for detecting the firing patterns of individual neurons in response to stimuli, used on monkeys and other animals

single-system hypothesis of bilingualism. A view of bilingualism, which suggests that both languages are represented in just one system of the mind and in one area of the brain (cf. **dual-system hypothesis;** see **bilingual**)

situational attribution. One of two fundamental types of attributions (cf. **personal attribution**): The causes of human behavior are attributed to external factors such as the settings, events, or other people in the environment of the person engaging in the given behavior

size constancy. A form of **perceptual constancy** in which an individual continues to perceive that an object remains the same size despite changes in the size of the object in the **retina**

skewness. Characteristic of a distribution of values, indicating the degree to which the modal value is shifted above or below the mean and the median values; when the distribution is plotted graphically, skewness appears as a lopsidedness toward the left or the right of the middle value

Skinner box. A container in which an animal undergoes conditioning experiments, named after behaviorist B. F. Skinner

sleep apnea. A breathing disorder that occurs during sleep, in which the sleeper repeatedly (perhaps hundreds of times per night) stops breathing during sleep

slips of the tongue. Inadvertent **semantic** or *articulatory* (related to the production of language sounds) errors in what is said (e.g., see **spoonerism**)

social categorization. The normal human tendency to sort things and people into groups, based on perceived common attributes; often leads to the formation of **stereotypes**

social cognition. The thought processes through which people perceive and interpret information from and about themselves (intrapersonal world) and other persons (interpersonal world) (see **attribution theory, cognitive-consistency theory, impression formation, social-comparison theory**)

social-comparison theory. A **social-cognition** theory, which suggests that people evaluate their own abilities and accomplishments largely by comparing these abilities and accomplishments to the abilities and accomplishments of others, particularly in novel, uncertain, or ambiguous settings for which internal standards are not yet established

social development. The process by which people learn to interact with other people and learn about themselves as human beings

social facilitation. The beneficial effect on performance that results from the perceived presence of other persons

social-identity theory. A theory regarding **prejudice,** which suggests that people are motivated to protect their self-esteem and that they have prejudices in order to increase their self-esteem by believing that *outgroups* (of which they are not members) have less status than *ingroups* (of which they are members)

social inhibition. The detrimental effect on performance that results from the perceived presence of other persons

social learning. See **observational learning**

social loafing. The phenomenon by which the average amount of effort exerted by each individual in a group decreases in association with increases in the number of people participating in a joint effort

social penetration. A pattern of communication in interpersonal relationships, in which the breadth of topics and the depth of discussions tend to increase during the course of the relationship

social phobia. An **anxiety disorder** characterized by extreme fear of being criticized by others, which leads to the avoidance of groups of people and the avoidance of any situations that may lead to the possibility of being criticized, of being embarrassed, or of being otherwise subject to ridicule (see **phobia**)

social problem solving. A form of **cognitive therapy,** in which the client is taught to solve social and psychological problems in much the same way that the client effectively solves other problems

social psychology. The study of the ways in which human thoughts, emotions, and behavior are affected by other people, whose presence may be actual, imagined, or implied

socialization. The process whereby individuals learn how to feel, think, and act by observing and imitating parents, peers, and other role models in their social environments

soma. The part of the **neuron** that contains the *nucleus* (center portion, which performs metabolic and reproductive functions for the cell) and that is responsible for the life of the neuron

somatic anxiety. Feelings of **anxiety** manifested in bodily discomfort, such as muscular tension, restlessness, rapid heartbeat, upset stomach, or headache (cf. **cognitive anxiety**)

somatic nervous system. The portion of the **peripheral nervous system** that is in charge of quick and conscious movement of skeletal muscles (which are attached directly to bones, thereby permitting movements such as walking or typing) (cf. **autonomic nervous system**)

somnambulism. Sleepwalking, which combines aspects of waking and sleeping, with the sleepwalker able to see, walk, and perhaps even talk, but usually unable to remember the sleepwalking episodes; rarely accompanied by dreaming

source traits. One of two levels of personality **traits** (cf. **surface traits**): underlying, fundamental psychological dimensions of **personality** that generate the more numerous surface-level personality traits

spatial visualization. Ability either to feel oriented in surroundings or to manipulate mental images of objects

speech acts. Any of five basic categories of speech, analyzed in terms of the purposes accomplished by the given act: *commissive*—a commitment by the speaker to engage in some future course of action; *declaration* (also termed *performative*)—a statement that brings about an intended new state of affairs (e.g., an announcement of resignation from employment); *directive*—an attempt by a speaker to get a listener to do something, such as supplying the answer to a question (see also **indirect requests**); *expressive*—a statement regarding the psychological state of the speaker; *representative*—an assertion of a belief that a given proposition is true, which may be characterized by any degree of veridicality or by any amount of supporting evidence (i.e., the statement of belief may be so well supported that it may be universally accepted as true, or it may be so ill supported that other persons may consider the statement a **delusion**)

spinal cord. A slender, roughly cylindrical bundle of interconnected **nerves,** which is enclosed within the spinal column and which extends

through the center of the back, starting at the **brain** and ending at the branches of the **peripheral nervous system** that go to each of the two legs

split-brain research. The study of patients whose severe epilepsy has been treated by cleaving the **corpus callosum,** in order to prevent epileptic seizures from spreading from one **cerebral hemisphere** to another, thereby greatly lessening the severity of the seizures; because this procedure also results in a loss of communication between the two hemispheres, such persons appear to have two separate specialized brains processing different information and performing separate functions; such patients have made it possible for researchers to study the functions of each hemisphere, as well as the function of interhemispheric communication via the corpus callosum

spontaneous recovery of a learned response. A phenomenon of **classical conditioning,** in which a **CR** reappears without any environmental prompting; the unprompted reappearance of the CR occurs after a conditioned behavior has been established and then extinguished and then the organism is allowed to rest; that is, the organism appears spontaneously to recover a modest level of response during the rest period, although the response disappears again if the **CS** is not paired with the **UCS** again (cf. **savings**)

spontaneous recovery from mental illness. The unprompted and unaided (i.e., untreated) disappearance of maladaptive symptomatology over the course of time

spoonerism. A **slip of the tongue** in which a reversal of the initial sounds of two words produces two entirely different words, usually yielding a humorous outcome (named after the Reverend William Spooner, who was famous for producing humorous instances of such reversals)

standard deviation. Statistical measurement of dispersion, indicating the degree to which a set of values typically deviates from the **mean** value for the set; calculated by determining the square root of the **variance** for the distribution of values

standardization. The administration

of a test in a way that ensures that the conditions for taking the test are the same for all test-takers; also, the administration of an experimental procedure in a way that ensures that the experimental conditions are the same for all subjects

stapes. The last in the series of three bones in the middle ear (cf. **incus, malleus**), which normally receive and amplify the vibrations transmitted by the **tympanum (eardrum)** and then transmit those vibrations to the **cochlea**

state anxiety. The appearance of **anxiety** associated with a particular situation occurring at a particular place and time (cf. **trait anxiety**)

state-dependent memory. The tendency for a person to recall learned information more easily when in the same emotional state as the state in which the information was learned

static assessment environment. A context for testing, in which an examiner asks a series of questions, offering no hints or guidance if the test-taker makes incorrect responses, and usually not even signalling whether the test-taker has answered correctly or incorrectly (cf. **dynamic assessment environment**)

statistic. A numerical value obtained by analyzing numerical data about a **representative sample** of a population (see **sample statistics**; cf. **population parameters**)

statistical significance. A degree of numerically analyzed probability suggesting the likelihood that a particular outcome may have occurred as a result of systematic fluctuations

statistics. A field of study involving the analysis of numerical data about **representative samples** of **populations**

stereopsis. Three-dimensional perception of the world through the cognitive fusion of the visual fields seen by each of the two eyes (see **binocular depth cues, binocular disparity**)

stereotype. **Schema** regarding groups of persons, in which it is held that members of a group tend more or less uniformly to have particular types of characteristics (see also **outgroup homogeneity, prejudice, social categorization**)

stimulant. See **central nervous system (CNS) stimulant**

stimulus. Something that prompts action (plural, *stimuli*; *stimulus* is Latin for the sharpened stick used by Romans for goading sluggish animals into action)

stimulus discrimination. The ability to ascertain the difference between one **stimulus** and another; often used in **psychophysics** experiments and assessments, as well as in behavioral experiments (cf. **stimulus generalization**)

stimulus generalization. A broadening of the conditioned response, such that stimuli that resemble a specifically **conditioned stimulus** also elicit the **conditioned response** (cf. **stimulus discrimination**)

storage. See **memory storage**

strange situation. An experimental technique for observing **attachment** in young children, conducted in a laboratory room containing various toys and some chairs; in the room is a one-way mirror, behind which an observer watches and records the behavior of the subject (usually a toddler, age 12–18 months); for the procedure, the toddler and her or his mother enter the room and the mother sits in one of the chairs; a few minutes later, an unfamiliar woman enters the room, talks to the mother, and then tries to play with the child; while the stranger is trying to play with the child, the mother quietly walks out of the room, leaving her purse on the chair to indicate that she will return; later, the mother returns, and soon after, the stranger leaves; still later, the mother leaves the child alone in the room; soon after, she returns and sits in the chair again; finally, the toddler and mother leave the room, thus ending the experimental procedure

stress. A phenomenon in which some factor (or factors) in the environment causes a person to feel threatened or challenged in some way; usually involves some kind of environmental change that requires the person to make some kind of adaptive or **coping** response

stress disorder. An **anxiety disorder**; see **acute stress disorder** and **posttraumatic stress disorder**

stress-inoculation therapy. A form

of **cognitive therapy** in which the client is instructed to respond to stressful situations by telling her- or himself statements that are calming and oriented toward **coping** with the situation rather than maladaptive, anxiety provoking, and oriented toward internal feelings of **stress**

stress response. Reaction to some kind of **stressor**, involving internal and external adaptation by an individual (see **stress**)

stressor. Situation or event that leads to **stress** (see **stress response**)

stroboscopic motion. The perception of movement that is produced when a *stroboscope* (*strobo-*, "whirling"; *-scope*, "device or means of viewing") intermittently flashes an alternating pair of lights against a dark background at appropriate distances and appropriately timed intervals (within milliseconds), such that it appears that a single light has moved forward and backward across the visual field

structuralism. The first major school of thought in psychology, which focused on analyzing the distinctive configuration of component elements of the mind, such as particular sensations or thoughts; for example, structuralists would be more interested in what people think than in how they think, in what people perceive, rather than how they perceive (cf. **functionalism**)

structure-of-intellect (SOI). A factor-analytic model of intelligence, which proposes 120 to 150 (depending on the given model) factors of the mind, including various *operations* (mental processes), *contents* (kinds of information, e.g., symbols, behaviors, or images), and *products* (kinds of responses, e.g., units, relationships, or hierarchies) of cognitive functioning

subconscious (noun). A level of **consciousness** that involves less awareness than full consciousness and either is synonymous with the **unconscious** level (according to many theorists) or is slightly more accessible to consciousness than is the unconscious level (according to a few theorists)

subjective-utility theory. A theory of decision making, which acknowledges that each individual may have a distinctive understanding regarding the various utilities for a given action, based on the idiosyncratic hopes, fears, and other subjective motivations of the individual (cf. **game theory, utility maximization theory**)

sublimation. A **defense mechanism,** which involves a redirection of socially unacceptable libidinal impulses, transforming the psychic energy of these unacceptable impulses into acceptable and perhaps even admirable behavioral expressions that allow for positive contributions to society

subliminal perception. A form of preconscious processing, in which people may have the ability to detect information without being fully aware that they are doing so

subtractive bilingualism. A form of bilingualism in which some elements of a second language replace some elements of a poorly established primary language (cf. **additive bilingualism;** see **bilingual**)

subtractive mixture. The remaining combined **wavelengths** of light that are reflected from an object after other wavelengths of light have been absorbed (*subtracted* from the reflected light) by the object; darker objects absorb more wavelengths of light and reflect fewer wavelengths than do brighter objects (cf. **additive mixture**)

successive approximations. The sequence of **operant** behaviors that are reinforced during the **shaping** of a desired behavior (see **operant conditioning, positive reinforcement**)

suffix. A **morpheme** that is attached to the end of a root word, thereby altering the syntactical use (if the **affix** is a **function morpheme**) or the meaning (if the affix is a **content morpheme**) of the root word (cf. **prefix;** see also **inflection [grammatical]**)

sulci. Small grooves in the convolutions of the **cerebral cortex** (singular, *sulcus;* cf. **fissure, gyri**)

superego. One of three psychodynamic concepts (cf. **ego, id**), which comprises all the internalized representations of the **norms** and values of society acquired during early **psychosexual development,** through interactions with the parents as figures of societal authority (see **idealistic principle**)

surface-structure grammar. See **phrase-structure grammars**

surface traits. One of two levels of personality **traits** (cf. **source traits**): the numerous superficial **personality** traits that vary widely across individuals and that are derived based on combinations of underlying fundamental source traits

survey. A method of social-science research, in which the researcher observes people's responses to questions regarding their beliefs and opinions; rarely involve answers that are scored as either right or wrong (see, e.g., **questionnaire;** cf. **test;** cf. also **case study, experiment, naturalistic observation**)

syllogism. A deductive argument that permits a conclusion to be drawn, based on two premises, in which each of the two premises contains two terms, at least one term of which is common to both premises (see also **categorical syllogism, conditional syllogism, linear syllogism**)

symmetry. A Gestalt principle of form perception (see **Gestalt approach**): the tendency to perceive forms that comprise mirror images on either side of a central axis based on limited sensory information

sympathetic nervous system. The portion of the **autonomic nervous system** that is concerned primarily with **catabolism** (cf. **parasympathetic nervous system**)

symptom. Any unusual sensation in or feature on the body, which a patient observes and which is believed to indicate some kind of pathology (cf. **sign**)

synapse. The area comprising the interneuronal gap, the **terminal buttons** of one neuron's **axon,** and the **dendrites** (or sometimes the **soma**) of the next **neuron;** the cleft into which the terminal buttons of the presynaptic neuron may release a chemical **neurotransmitter** or **neuromodulator,** for receipt by the postsynaptic neuron

syntax. A level of linguistic analysis, which centers on the patterns by which users of a particular language put words together at the level of the sentence; systematic structure through which words can be combined and sequenced to make meaningful phrases and sentences (see also **grammar**)

synthesis. *As an aspect of a **dialectic:*** a statement of opinion that integrates some aspects of a **thesis** opinion and some aspects of an **antithesis** opinion, usually based on evidence or logic that supports the aspects that have been integrated; *as a process of **critical thinking:*** a process that involves integrating component parts into wholes, and that may be viewed as a process that complements **analysis** (see also **convergent thinking, divergent thinking**)

systematic desensitization. A **counterconditioning** technique of behavioral therapy (cf. **aversion therapy**) in which the therapist seeks to help the client combat anxiety and other troublesome responses by teaching the client a set of relaxation techniques so that the client can effectively replace the troublesome responses with relaxation responses, usually in association with a **desensitization hierarchy** of stimuli that previously induced the troublesome responses

taste bud. Cluster of taste-receptor cells located inside the **papillae** of the tongue; in the center of each cluster are pores into which the molecules from foods and beverages may fall, and when moistened chemicals contact the receptor cells, the cells **transduce** the chemical energy of the tastes into the electrochemical energy of neural transmission, which involves encoding of the tastes to distinguish among particular kinds of chemicals (e.g., salts, acids, or alkalies)

telegraphic speech. Rudimentary syntactical communications of two words or more, which are characteristic of very early language acquisition, and which seem more like telegrams than like conversation because articles, prepositions, and other **function morphemes** are usually omitted

telencephalon. The topmost and farthest forward portion of the **forebrain;** comprises the **cerebral cortex,** the **basal ganglia,** and the **limbic system** (*tele-,* distant; *-encephalon,* in the head, brain)

telepathy. The alleged direct transfer of thoughts from one person to another without use of the normally sensed forms of expression (e.g., spoken, written, or gestured language) (*tele-,* "distant"; *-pathy,* "feeling"; see **extrasensory perception**)

temperament. Individual differences in the intensity and duration of emotions, as well as the individual's characteristic disposition

template. Prototype or pattern for distinctive forms, such as the distinctive shapes of odorous chemicals and smell receptors mentioned in **lock-and-key theory** or the distinctive patterns mentioned in some **passive theories** of perception

template-matching theories of form perception. A set of theories of form perception, according to which people attempt to match templates of an observed pattern to existing templates, without considering the prior experience of the perceiver or what the perceiver already knows about the context in which the form is presented (cf. **feature matching**)

temporal conditioning. A **classical-conditioning** procedure in which the **CS** is a fixed interval of time between presentations of the **UCS,** so that the learner learns that the UCS will occur at a given, fixed time

temporal contiguity. The proximity in time between two events or stimuli; without **contingency** between the two events or stimuli, conditioning does not take place (see also **classical conditioning, operant conditioning**)

temporal lobe. One of the four major regions of the **cerebral cortex** (cf. **frontal lobe, occipital lobe, parietal lobe**): chiefly responsible for auditory processing

terminal buttons. Small knobby structures located at the tips of the branches of **axons,** which release **neurotransmitters** or **neuromodulators** into a **synapse,** which borders on the **dendrites** or **somas** of nearby **neurons**

test. A research method used for measuring a given ability or attribute in a particular individual or set of individuals at a particular time and in a particular place; almost invariably involves keying the test-takers' responses as either right or wrong, or at least as being better (more accurate, more appropriate, more creative, etc.) or worse (cf. **survey;** cf. also **case study, experiment, naturalistic observation**)

test–retest reliability. See **reliability**

test of statistical significance. See **statistical significance;** see also *p*-value

texture gradient. See **monocular depth cues**

thalamus. A two-lobed structure, located in about the center of the **brain,** at about the level of the eyes, which helps in the control of sleep and waking and seems to serve as a relay for sensory information; contains various *nuclei* (groups of neurons with a similar function) that receive assorted types of sensory input entering the brain and then transmit that input via projection fibers to the appropriate sensory regions of the **cerebral cortex**

theory. A statement of some general principles that explain a psychological phenomenon or set of phenomena

theory of multiple intelligences. A theory of intelligence suggesting that intelligence comprises seven distinct constructs that function somewhat independently of one another, but that may interact to produce intelligent behavior: bodily-kinesthetic intelligence, interpersonal intelligence, intrapersonal intelligence, linguistic intelligence, mathematical-logical intelligence, musical intelligence, and spatial intelligence

thesis. A statement of an opinion or of a perspective (cf. **antithesis, synthesis;** see **dialectic**)

thinking. A psychological function that involves the representation and processing of information in the mind (also termed *cognition;* see **critical thinking, creativity, judgment and decision making, problem solving, reasoning**)

threshold of excitation. The level of electrochemical stimulation, at or above which an **action potential** may be generated, but below which an action potential cannot be generated; the specific threshold required for a given neuron's action potential differs for the various neurons and depends on whether the neuron is in the midst of a refractory period (see **absolute refractory phase, relative refractory phase**)

thyroid gland. An endocrine **gland** located at the front of the throat, which regulates the metabolic rate of cells, thereby influencing weight gain or loss, blood pressure, muscular strength, and level of activity

timbre. A psychological quality of sound that permits detection of the difference between a note (e.g., A flat) played on a piano and the same note played on a harmonica, based on the distinctive **harmonics** produced by each instrument rather than the **fundamental frequency** of the note

tip-of-the-tongue phenomenon. An experience involving the preconscious level of consciousness, in which a person tries to remember something that is known to be stored in memory but that the person cannot quite retrieve

tobacco. A plant product containing nicotine, a **central nervous system (CNS) stimulant**

token. A tangible object that has no intrinsic worth but that can be used as a **secondary reinforcer** if the individual given the token can exchange it for a **primary reinforcer** at a later time (see **token economy**)

token economy. A system of **operant conditioning** in which **tokens** are used as a means of reinforcing various **operant** behaviors; most frequently used in controlled environments such as residential institutions for persons who are psychologically impaired, in order to encourage adaptive behavior and discourage maladaptive behavior; generally not used with persons for whom their natural interest in performing the operant behavior would be reduced as a result of the use of extrinsic reinforcers (see **extrinsic motivators**)

tolerance. A consequence of prolonged use of **psychoactive** drugs, in which the drug user stops feeling **psychotropic** effects of a given drug at one level of dosage and must take increasing amounts of drugs in order to achieve the effects, eventually reaching a level of nonresponse at which the current level no longer produces the desired effects, but higher levels will cause overdose—the person generally still continues taking the drugs, despite the lack of psychotropic effects, simply to avoid experiencing the unpleasant feelings associated with drug **withdrawal** (see **addiction;** see also specific drugs, e.g., **amphetamine** and **barbiturate**)

total-time hypothesis. A widely accepted assumption regarding memory, which holds that the degree to which a person is able to learn information by storing it in memory depends on the total amount of time spent studying the material in a given session, rather than on the way in which the time is apportioned within a given session

trace conditioning. A form of **classical conditioning,** in which the **CS** is terminated for a while before the **UCS** begins (cf. **delay conditioning**)

trait. May refer either to a personality trait or to a genetic trait; *personality traits* are stable sources of individual differences that characterize a person and that may originate in the person's nature (heredity) or the person's nurture (environment); *genetic traits* are distinctive characteristics or behavior patterns that are genetically determined

trait anxiety. The presence of **anxiety** that seems to characterize the enduring personality of the anxious person, regardless of the given situation occurring at a particular place and time (cf. **state anxiety**)

tranquilizer. One of the **sedative–hypnotic drugs** used for combating anxiety; considered to be safer than **barbiturates,** due to the lower dosages required and the reduced likelihood of drowsiness and respiratory difficulties, although the potential for **addiction** remains a problem (see **central nervous system [CNS] depressants**)

transduce. Convert energy from one form into another, such as the process that occurs in a sensory **receptor,** which converts a form of energy (mechanical, chemical, etc.) received from the environment into the electrochemical form of energy that is meaningful to the **nervous system**

transference. A phenomenon of psychodynamic therapy whereby the patient projects her or his feelings and internal conflicts onto the therapist, often also projecting onto the therapist–patient relationship many aspects of the patient's early childhood relationships, such as with parents; deemed to be an important means by which the patient can resolve some of the conflicts characterizing these early relationships (cf. **countertransference**)

transformational grammar. A form of syntactical analysis, which centers on the transformational operations used for generating surface structures from deep structures (cf. **phrase-structure grammars;** see also **deep-structure level**)

transparency. Phenomenon in which individuals see false analogies of the formal structure of problems because of the apparent similarity of attributes related to the content of the problems (see **isomorphic**)

triangular theory of love. A theory of love, according to which love has three basic components: **commitment, intimacy,** and **passion,** different combinations of which yield different kinds of love

triarchic theory of human intelligence. A theory of intelligence, which asserts that intelligence comprises three aspects, which deal with the relation of intelligence (a) to the internal world, (b) to experience, and (c) to the external world

trichromatic theory of color vision. One of two proposed mechanisms for explaining how color vision occurs (also termed *Young–Helmholtz theory;* cf. **opponent-process theory**); draws on the notion of **primary colors,** which can combine additively to form all other colors; according to this view, various photoreceptive **cones** are somehow attuned to each of the primary colors, such that some cones are sensitive to red (and are therefore activated in response to the sight of red), others to green, and others to blue, and the full range of colors may be seen when various combinations of these three primary colors are sensed

true score. A hypothetical score that would be obtained if a test could be administered to a given individual an unlimited number of times and then the resulting scores could be averaged (cf. **observed score**)

two-component cognitive-labeling theory. A view of love, which suggests that passionate love comprises both a state of emotional and physical **arousal** and a cognitive (thought-based) identification of that state as being love (cf. **two-component theory of emotion**)

two-component theory of emotion. A view of emotions positing that emotions comprise two elements: a state of physiological **arousal** and a cognitive label identifying the aroused state as signifying a particular emotion (cf. **two-component cognitive-labeling theory**)

two-point threshold. The precise distance between two points on the skin at which two touch stimuli can be distinguished, but at which closer points cannot be distinguished and are felt as a single touch; the distances for determining the threshold vary on differing locations on the body

tympanum. See **eardrum**

Type-A behavior pattern. A characteristic pattern of personality and behavior, in which the individual demonstrates a competitive orientation toward achievement, a sense of urgency about time, and a strong tendency to feel anger and hostility (cf. **Type-B behavior pattern**)

Type-B behavior pattern. A characteristic pattern of personality and behavior, in which the individual demonstrates relatively low levels of competitiveness, urgency about time, and hostility (cf. **Type-A behavior pattern**)

Type I error. An error in interpreting research, which refers to the belief that a finding has appeared due to systematic changes, when in fact the finding is a result of random fluctuation

Type II error. An error in interpreting research, which refers to the belief that a finding has appeared due to random fluctuations, when in fact the finding is a result of systematic changes

UCR. See **unconditioned response**

UCS. See **unconditioned stimulus**

unconditioned response (UCR). Automatic, unlearned physiological response to a stimulus (the **unconditioned stimulus**), used in **classical conditioning** as a means of eventually teaching the learner to produce a **conditioned response**

unconditioned stimulus (UCS). A stimulus that automatically, without prior learning, elicits a given physiological or emotional response, used in

classical conditioning as a means of eventually teaching the learner to respond to a **conditioned stimulus** (see also **unconditioned response**)

unconscious. A level of consciousness at which thoughts, wishes, and feelings are removed from accessibility to conscious awareness (often considered synonymous with **subconscious**); an important construct of **psychodynamic theory**

unconscious inference. A phenomenon of **constructive perception,** according to which perceivers make correct attributions regarding their visual sensations because they engage in a process by which they assimilate information from a number of sources to create a perception, without consciously doing so; such inferences consider not only the immediate sensory information available to the perceiver, but also the prior experience and cognitive strategies of the perceiver

universal affirmative statement. See **categorical syllogism**

universal negative statement. See **categorical syllogism**

utility maximization theory. A decision-making theory, according to which the goal of human action is to maximize pleasure *(positive utility)* and to minimize pain *(negative utility);* assumes that humans make decisions based on unbounded rationality (cf. **bounded rationality**) (cf. **game theory, subjective-utility theory**)

valid. See **validity**

validity. The extent to which a given form of measurement assesses what it is supposed to measure (see **concurrent validity, construct-related validity, content-related validity, face validity, predictive validity**); also, the extent to which a set of experimental procedures reveals what it is purported to reveal (cf. **reliability;** see also **deductively valid**)

vanishing point. A phenomenon of visual perception, in which parallel lines seem to converge as they move farther into the distance and eventually to converge entirely, to become indistinguishable, and then to disappear entirely at the horizon (see

monocular depth cues: *linear perspective*)

variable. Attribute or characteristic of a situation, a person, or a phenomenon, which may differ or fluctuate across situations, across persons, or across phenomena (see also **dependent variable, independent variable**)

variable-interval reinforcement. A schedule for implementing **operant conditioning,** in which reinforcement occurs, *on average,* after a certain period of time, assuming that the **operant** behavior has occurred at least once during that time period, but in which the specific amount of time preceding reinforcement changes from one reinforcement to the next (see **partial reinforcement, schedules of reinforcement,** cf. **fixed-interval reinforcement, variable-ratio reinforcement**)

variable-ratio reinforcement. A schedule for implementing **operant conditioning,** in which reinforcement occurs, *on average,* after a certain number of **operant** responses, but in which the specific number of responses preceding reinforcement changes from one reinforcement to the next (see **partial reinforcement, schedules of reinforcement;** cf. **fixed-ratio reinforcement, variable-interval reinforcement**)

variance. Statistical measurement indicating the degree to which a set of values varies from the **mean** of the set of values; the basis for determining a **standard deviation,** which is more commonly used in psychological research

verb phrase. See **predicate;** cf. **subject**

verbal comprehension. The ability to comprehend written and spoken linguistic input, such as words, sentences, and paragraphs (cf. **verbal fluency**)

verbal fluency. The ability to produce written and spoken linguistic output, such as words, sentences, and paragraphs (cf. **verbal comprehension**)

verifiable. Characteristic of scientific findings, by which there is some means of confirming the results

vertebrae. The protective backbones that encase the **spinal cord** and that form the spinal column of vertebrates

vestibular system. The sensory system that comprises the vestibular sacs and semicircular canals in the inner ear, which contains receptors for the sensations associated with equilibrium; operates via movement of the head, which causes movement of fluid in the sacs and canals, which bends hairlike cells that **transduce** the mechanical energy of the various movements into the electrochemical energy of neural transmission; this energy travels via the auditory nerve to the **cerebellum** and to the **cerebral cortex** and is encoded as information about the direction of movement, relative orientation, and rate of acceleration of the head

vibration theory. One of two theories regarding the sensation of smell (cf. **lock-and-key theory**): The molecules of each distinctively smelled substance generate a specific vibration frequency, which specifically affects the olfactory receptors by disrupting particular chemical bonds in the receptor cell membranes, and the rupture of these bonds releases the chemical energy stored in those bonds; the distinctive pattern of rupturing of the bonds is **transduced** into a characteristic pattern of electrochemical activity, which is interpreted in the brain as specific odors

vicarious learning. See **observational learning**

vigilance. The ongoing alert watchfulness for the appearance of an unpredictable stimulus, which may be sensed through any of the sensory modalities (cf. **search**)

visual mask. A pattern of visual stimuli that wipes out any visual afterimage that might remain on the **retina,** but which is not distinguishable as meaningful (and thereby does not distort the perception of the image that preceded the mask)

vocabulary. A repertoire of words, formed by combining **morphemes** (cf. **lexicon**)

volley principle. A hypothesis supportive of the **frequency theory** of hearing, which suggests that auditory neurons fire cooperatively in alternating groups, such that while some neurons are resting, neighboring neurons are firing, thereby yielding a combined pattern of neural firing that can indicate high-frequency vibrations of sound (cf. **place theory;** see also **duplicity theory**)

warm fibers. Bundles of **neurons** that respond to warming of the skin (in the range of 95–115 degrees Fahrenheit [35–46 centigrade]) (cf. **cold fibers**)

wavelength. The distance from the crest of one wave to the crest of the next wave (e.g., sound waves or light waves), often used as a means of measuring a quality of sound or light; for light waves, the objective wavelength of a light wave is associated with **hue,** and for sound waves, the objective wavelength is associated with the sensation of **pitch** (actually, for sound, **frequency** is the more common measurement)

Weber fraction. The value that indicates the relation between the intensity of a standard stimulus and the intensity of a stimulus required to produce a **just noticeable difference (jnd);** this value varies for different types of sensory experiences, and smaller fractions are required for sensory modalities to which humans experience greater sensitivity (e.g., the painful sensation of electric shock), whereas larger fractions are required for less sensitive modalities (e.g., the sensation of taste)

Weber's law. A principle relating the intensity of a standard stimulus to the intensity of a stimulus required to produce a **just noticeable difference (jnd),** often expressed as an equation: $\Delta I = KI$, where K is a *constant* (a numerical value that does not vary, such as pi), I is the intensity of the standard stimulus, and ΔI is the increase in intensity needed to produce a jnd; broadly interpreted, the law suggests that the greater the magnitude of the stimulus, the larger the difference

must be in order to be detectable as a difference

well-structured problem. A type of problem for which a clear path to solution is known, although it may still be very difficult to implement (cf. **ill-structured problem**)

wisdom. An aspect of cognitive development that is generally associated with older adulthood, in which an individual demonstrates exceptional insight and superb judgment in considering and tackling some of the most difficult problems humans encounter; sometimes characterized as comprising the following characteristics: reasoning ability, *sagacity* (shrewdness), learning from ideas and from the environment, judgment, expeditious use of information, and *perspicacity* (intensely keen awareness, perception, and insight), as well as an individual's keen realization of what she or he has yet to learn, to understand, or to master

withdrawal. The temporary discomfort (which may be extremely negative, much like a severe case of intestinal flu, accompanied by extreme **depression** or **anxiety**) associated with a decrease in dosage or a discontinuation altogether of a **psychoactive** drug, during which the drug user's physiology and mental processes must adjust to an absence of the drug; during withdrawal from some drugs (e.g., some **stimulants** and some **sedative–hypnotic drugs**), the user should obtain medical supervision, to avoid life-threatening complications that may arise during the readjustment to normal physiological and mental functioning

word-superiority effect. A phenomenon of form perception in which an individual can more readily identify (discriminate) letters when they are presented in the context of words than when they are presented as solitary letters

working backward. See **heuristic**

working forward. See **heuristic**

working memory. A portion of memory that may be viewed as a specialized part of long-term memory, which holds only the most recently activated portion of long-term memory, and which moves these activated elements into and out of short-term memory (which may be viewed as the narrow portion of working memory that enters immediate awareness); some psychologists consider working memory to be a hypothetical construct in opposition to the three-stores view, but others consider it a complement to the three-stores view

yoga. A form of **concentrative meditation,** which comes in various forms, including active exercises as well as contemplative quiescence

zen. A classical Buddhist form of **concentrative meditation,** which usually involves sitting in a cross-legged position but which may be practiced in many forms and during which meditators may progress through a graded series of steps, advancing from novice to expert

zero-sum game. A game in which a positive outcome for the winner is balanced by a negative outcome for the loser, which yields an outcome of zero because the net positive equals the net negative (see also **game theory**)

zone of proximal development. The range of ability between a person's observable level of ability and the person's latent capacity, which is not directly observable, but which may be detected by providing a context in which the latent capacity may be revealed and expressed (sometimes termed the *zone of potential development*)

Abrams, R. (1988). *Electroconvulsive treatment: It apparently works, but how and at what risks are not yet clear.* New York: Oxford University Press.

Achenbach, T. M. (1970). The children's associative responding test: A possible alternative to group IQ tests. *Journal of Educational Psychology, 61,* 340–348.

Adams, M. J. (Ed.) (1986). *Odyssey: A curriculum for thinking* (Vols. 1–6). Watertown, MA: Charlesbridge.

Agnew, J. (1985). Man's purgative passion. *American Journal of Psychotherapy, 39*(2), 236–246.

Ainsworth, M. D. S. (1973). The development of infant–mother attachment. In B. M. Caldwell & H. M. Ricciuti (Eds.), *Review of child development research* (Vol. 3). Chicago: University of Chicago Press.

Ainsworth, M. D. S. (1989). Attachments beyond infancy. *American Psychologist, 44,* 709–716.

Ainsworth, M. D. S., Bell, S. M., & Stayton, D. J. (1971). Individual differences in strange-situation behavior in one-year-olds. In H. R. Schaffer (Ed.), *The origins of human social relations.* London: Academic Press.

Ainsworth, M. D. S., Blehar, M., Waters, E., & Wall, S. (1978). *Patterns of attachment.* Hillsdale, NJ: Erlbaum.

Allport, G. W. (1935). Attitudes. In C. M. Murchison (Ed.), *Handbook of social psychology.* Worcester, MA: Clark University Press.

Allport, G. W. (1937). *Personality: A psychological interpretation.* New York: Holt, Rinehart & Winston.

Allport, G. W. (1954). *The nature of prejudice.* Reading, MA: Addison-Wesley.

Allport, G. W. (1961). *Pattern and growth in personality.* New York: Holt, Rinehart & Winston.

Allport, G. W. (1985). The historical background of social psychology. In G. Lindzey & E. Aronson (Eds.), *Handbook of social psychology* (Vol. 1, 3rd ed., pp. 1–46). New York: Random House.

Alpert, B., Field, T., Goldstein, S., & Perry, S. (1990). Aerobics enhances cardiovascular fitness and agility in preschoolers. *Health Psychology, 9,* 48–56.

Altman, I., & Taylor, D. A. (1973). *Social penetration: The development of interpersonal relationships.* New York: Holt, Rinehart & Winston.

Amabile, T. M. (1983). *The social psychology of creativity.* New York: Springer-Verlag.

Amabile, T. M. (1985). Motivation and creativity: Effects of motivational orientation on creative writers. *Journal of Personality and Social Psychology, 48,* 393–399.

Amenson, C. S., & Lewinsohn, P. M. (1981). An investigation into the observed sex difference in prevalence of unipolar depression. *Journal of Abnormal Psychology, 90,* 1–3.

American Association of University Women Educational Foundation and the Wellesley College Center for Research on Women. (1992). *The AAUW Report: How schools shortchange girls—A study of major findings on girls and education.* Washington, DC: Author.

American Hospital Association. (1982). *Hospital statistics.* Chicago: Author.

American Hospital Association. (1987). *Hospital statistics.* Chicago: Author.

American Hospital Association. (1989). *Hospital statistics.* Chicago: Author.

American Psychiatric Association. (1987). *Diagnostic and statistical manual of mental disorders* (3rd ed.-rev.). Washington, DC: Author.

American Psychiatric Association. (1994). *Diagnostic and statistical manual of mental disorders* (4th ed.). Washington, DC: Author.

Amoore, J. E. (1970). *Molecular basis of odor.* Springfield, IL: Thomas.

Anand, B. K., & Brobeck, J. R. (1951). Hypothalamic control of food intake in rats and cats. *Yale Journal of Biology and Medicine, 24,* 123–140.

Anand, B., Chhina, G., & Singh, B. (1961). Some aspects of electroencephalographic studies in yogis. *Electroencephalography and Clinical Neurophysiology, 13,* 452–456.

Anand, B. K., Chhina, G. S., & Singh, B. (1962). Effect of glucose on the activity of hypothalamic "feeding centers." *Science, 138,* 597–598.

Anderson, B. F. (1975). *Cognitive psychology.* New York: Academic Press.

Anderson, C. A. (1987). Temperature and aggression: Effects on quarterly, yearly, and city rates of violent and nonviolent crime. *Journal of Personality and Social Psychology, 52,* 1161–1173.

Anderson, C. A. (1989). Temperature and aggression: Ubiquitous effects of heat on occurrence of human violence. *Psychological Bulletin, 106*(1), 74–96.

Anderson, J. R. (1985). *Cognitive psychology and its implications.* New York: Freeman.

Anderson, J. R., & Bower, G. H. (1973). *Human associative memory.* New York: Wiley.

Anderson, K. L. (1990). Arousal and the inverted-U hypothesis: A critique of Neiss's "Reconceptualizing arousal." *Psychological Bulletin, 107,* 96–100.

Anderson, K. O., & Masur, F. T. III. (1983). Psychological preparation for invasive medical and dental procedures. *Journal of Behavioral Medicine, 6,* 1–40.

Anderson, N. H. (1968). Likableness ratings of 555 personality-trait words. *Journal of Personality and Social Psychology, 9,* 272–279.

Andersson, B. E. (1989). Effects of public daycare: A longitudinal study. *Child Development, 60,* 857–866.

Andreasen, N., Ehrhardt, J., Swayze, V., Alliger, R., Yuh, T., Cohen, G., & Ziebell, S. (1990). Magnetic resonance imaging of the brain in schizophrenia. *Archives of General Psychiatry, 47,* 35–44.

Andreasen, N. C., Olsen, S. A., Dennert, J. W., & Smith, M. R. (1982a). Ventricular enlargement in schizophrenia: Definition and prevalence. *American Journal of Psychiatry, 139,* 292–296.

Andreasen, N. C., Olsen, S. A., Dennert, J. W., & Smith, M. R. (1982b). Ventricular enlargement in schizophrenia: Relationship to positive and negative symptoms. *American Journal of Psychiatry, 139,* 297–302.

Andrews, G. (1993). The benefits of psychotherapy. In N. Sartorius, G. de Girolano, G. Andrews, G. A. German, & L. Eisenberg (Eds.), *Treatment of mental disorders: A review of effectiveness.* Geneva, Switzerland, and Washington, DC: World Health Organization and American Psychiatric Press.

Angell, J. R. (1907). The province of functional psychology. *Psychological Review, 14,* 61–91.

Angier, N. (1993, April 25). 'Stopit!' she said. 'Nomore!' [A review of *Genie: An abused child's flight from silence*]. *New York Times Book Review,* p. 12.

Appel, L. F., Cooper, R. G., McCarrell, N., Sims-Knight, J., Yussen, S. R., & Flavell, J. H. (1972). The development of the distinction between perceiving and memorizing. *Child Development, 43,* 1365–1381.

Archer, J., & Lloyd, B. B. (1985). *Sex and gender.* New York: Cambridge University Press.

Arieti, S. (1974). An overview of schizophrenia from a predominantly psychological approach. *American Journal of Psychiatry, 131*(3), 241–249.

Arlin, P. K. (1975). Cognitive development in adulthood: A fifth stage? *Developmental Psychology, 11,* 602–606.

Arnold, M. B. (1960). *Emotion and personality* (Vols. 1, 2). New York: Columbia University Press.

Arnold, M. B. (1970). Perennial problems in the field of emotion. In M. B. Arnold (Ed.), *Feelings and emotions* (pp. 169–185). New York: Academic Press.

Aronson, E., Blaney, N., Stephan, C., Sikes, J., & Snapp, M. (1978). *The jigsaw classroom.* Beverly Hills, CA: Sage.

Asch, S. E. (1946). Forming impressions of personality. *Journal of Abnormal and Social Psychology, 41,* 258–290.

Asch, S. E. (1951). Effects of group pressure upon the modification and distortion of judgments. In H. Guetzkow (Ed.), *Groups, leadership, and men.* Pittsburgh: Carnegie.

Asch, S. E. (1952). *Social psychology.* New York: Prentice-Hall.

Asch, S. E. (1955). Opinions and social pressure. *Scientific American, 193,* 31–35.

Asch, S. E. (1956). Studies of independence and conformity: A minority of one against a unanimous majority. *Psychological Monographs, 70,* 416.

Atkinson, J. W. (Ed.). (1958). *Motives in fantasy, action, and society.* Princeton, NJ: D. Van Nostrand.

Atkinson, R. C., & Shiffrin, R. M. (1968). Human memory: A proposed system and its control processes. In K. W. Spence & J. T. Spence (Eds.), *The psychology of learning and motivation: Advances in research and theory* (Vol. 2). New York: Academic Press.

Atkinson, R. C., & Shiffrin, R. M. (1971). The control of short-term memory. *Scientific American, 225,* 82–90.

Atkinson, R. L., Atkinson, R. C., Smith, E. E., & Bem, D. J. (1993). *Introduction to psychology* (11th ed.). Fort Worth, TX: Harcourt Brace Jovanovich.

Auerbach, S. M., Martelli, M. F., & Mercuri, L. G. (1983). Anxiety, information, interpersonal impacts, and adjustment to a stressful health care situation. *Journal of Personality and Social Psychology, 44,* 1284–1296.

Averill, J. R. (1980). A constructionist view of emotion. In R. Plutchik & H. Kellerman (Eds.), *Emotion: Theory, research, and experience. Vol. 1. Theories of emotion* (pp. 305–339). New York: Academic Press.

Averill, J. R. (1983). Studies on anger and aggression: Implications for theories of emotions? *American Psychologist, 38,* 1145–1160.

Averill, J. R. (1993). Putting the social in social cognition, with special reference to emotion. In R. S. Wyer & T. K. Srull (Eds.), *Toward a general theory of anger and emotional aggression: Vol. 6. Advances in social cognition.* Hillsdale, NJ: Erlbaum.

Axelson, J. A. (1993). *Counseling and development in a multicultural society* (2nd ed.). Pacific Grove, CA: Brooks/Cole.

Azrin, N. H. (1967, May). Pain and aggression. *Psychology Today,* pp. 27–33.

Azuma, H. (1986). Why study child development in Japan? In H. Stevenson, H. Azuma, & K. Hakuta (Eds.), *Child development and education in Japan* (pp. 3–12). New York: Freeman.

Bacal, H. A., & Newman, K. M. (1990). *Theories of object relations: Bridges to self psychology.* New York: Columbia University Press.

Baddeley, A. D. (1966). Short-term memory for word sequences as function of acoustic, semantic, and formal similarity. *Quarterly Journal of Experimental Psychology, 18,* 362–365.

Baddeley, A. (1989). The psychology of remembering and forgetting. In T. Butler (Ed.), *Memory: History, culture and the mind.* London: Basil Blackwell.

Baddeley, A. (1990a). *Human memory.* Hove, England: Erlbaum.

Baddeley, A. (1990b). *Human memory: Theory and practice.* Needham Heights, MA: Allyn & Bacon.

Bahrick, H. P., Bahrick, P. O., & Wittlinger, R. P. (1975). Fifty years of memory for names and faces: A cross-sectional approach. *Journal of Experimental Psychology: General, 104,* 54–75.

Bahrick, H. P., & Phelps, E. (1987). Retention of Spanish vocabulary over eight years. *Journal of Experimental Psychology: Learning Memory and Cognition, 13,* 344–349.

Bailey, J. M., & Pillard, R. C. (1991). A genetic study of male sexual orientation. *Archives of General Psychiatry, 48*(N12), 1089–1096.

Baillargeon, R. (1987). Object permanence in 3½- and 4½-month-old infants. *Developmental Psychology, 23,* 655–664.

Bales, R. F. (1950). *Interaction process analysis: A method for the study of small groups.* Reading, MA: Addison-Wesley.

Bales, R. F. (1958). Task roles and social roles in problem-solving groups. In E. E. Maccoby, T. M. Newcomb, & E. L. Hartley (Eds.), *Readings in social psychology.* New York: Holt, Rinehart & Winston.

Bales, R. F. (1970). *Personality and interpersonal behavior.* New York: Holt, Rinehart & Winston.

Balkin, J. (1988). Why policemen don't like policewomen. *Journal of Police Science and Administration, 16*(1), 29–38.

Balsam, P. D., & Tomie, A. (Eds.). (1985). *Context and learning.* Hillsdale, NJ: Erlbaum.

Baltes, P. B., & Smith, J. (1990). Toward a psychology of wisdom and its ontogenesis. In R. J. Sternberg (Ed.), *Wisdom: Its nature, origins, and development* (pp. 87–120). New York: Cambridge University Press.

Baltes, P. B., & Willis, S. L. (1979). Toward psychological theories of aging and development. In J. E. Birren & K. W. Schaie (Eds.), *Handbook of the psychology of aging.* New York: Van Nostrand Reinhold.

Bandura, A. (1965). Influence of models' reinforcement contingencies on the acquisition of imitative responses. *Journal of Personality and Social Psychology, 1,* 589–595.

Bandura, A. (1969). *Principles of behavior modification.* New York: Holt, Rinehart & Winston.

Bandura, A. (1973). *Aggression: A social learning analysis.* Englewood Cliffs, NJ: Prentice-Hall.

Bandura, A. (1977a). Self-efficacy: Toward a unifying theory of behavioral change. *Psychological Review, 84,* 181–215.

Bandura, A. (1977b). *Social learning theory.* Englewood Cliffs, NJ: Prentice-Hall.

Bandura, A. (1983). Psychological mechanisms of aggression. In R. G. Geen & E. I. Donnerstein (Eds.), *Aggression: Theoretical and empirical reviews. Vol. I. Theoretical and methodological issues* (pp. 1–40). New York: Academic Press.

Bandura, A. (1986). *Social foundations of thought and action: A social cognitive theory.* Englewood Cliffs, NJ: Prentice-Hall.

Bandura, A. (1988). Self-efficacy conception of anxiety. *Anxiety Research, 1*(2), 77–98.

Bandura, A., Blanchard, E. B., & Ritter, B. (1969). Relative efficacy of desensitization and modelling approaches for inducing behavioral, affective, and attitudinal changes. *Journal of Personality and Social Psychology, 13,* 173–199.

Bandura, A., & Rosenthal, T. (1966). Vicarious classical conditioning as a function of arousal level. *Journal of Personality and Social Psychology, 3,* 54–62.

Bandura, A., Ross, D., & Ross, S. (1961). Transmission of aggression through imitation of aggressive models. *Journal of Abnormal and Social Psychology, 63,* 575–582.

Bandura, A., & Ross, D., & Ross, S. A. (1963). Imitation of film-mediated aggressive models. *Journal of Abnormal and Social Psychology, 66,* 3–11.

Bandura, A., & Walters, R. H. (1963). *Social learning and personality development.* New York: Ronald Press.

Banks, M. S., & Salapatek, P. (1983). Infant visual perception. In M. M. Haith & J. J. Campos (Eds.), *Handbook of child psychology: Infancy and developmental psychobiology* (Vol. 2, 4th ed.). New York: Wiley.

Barber, T. X. (1964a). Hypnotic "colorblindness," "blindness," and "deafness." *Diseases of the Nervous System, 25,* 529–537.

Barber, T. X. (1964b). Toward a theory of "hypnotic" behavior: Positive visual and auditory hallucinations. *Psychological Record, 14,* 197–210.

Bard, P. (1934). On emotional experience after decortication with some remarks on theoretical views. *Psychological Review, 41,* 309–329.

Barefoot, J. C., Dahlstrom, W. G., & Williams, R. B. (1983). Hostility, CHD incidence and total mortality: A 25-year follow-up study of 255 physicians. *Psychosomatic Medicine, 45,* 559–563.

Barefoot, J. C., Dodge, K. A., Peterson, B. L., Dahlstrom, W. G., & Williams, R. B. (1989). The Cook-Medley hostility scale: Item content and ability to predict survival. *Psychosomatic Medicine, 51,* 46–57.

Barker, R. G., Dembo, T., & Lewin, K. (1941). Frustration and regression: An experiment with young children. *University of Iowa Studies in Child Welfare, 18*(1).

Baron, M., Gershon, E. S., Rudy, V., Jonas, W. Z., & Buchsbaum, M. (1975). Lithium carbonate response in depression. *Archives of General Psychiatry, 32,* 1107–1111.

Baron, R. A. (1976). The reduction of human aggression: A field study of the influence of incompatible reactions. *Journal of Applied Social Psychology, 6,* 260–274.

Baron, R. A. (1977). *Human aggression.* New York: Plenum.

Baron, R. A., & Bell, P. A. (1975). Aggression and heat: Mediating effects of prior provocation and exposure to an aggressive model. *Journal of Personality and Social Psychology, 31,* 825–832.

Baron, R A., & Byrne, D. (1991). *Social psychology: Understanding human interaction* (6th ed.). Boston: Allyn & Bacon.

Baron, R. A., & Richardson, D. R. (1992). *Human aggression* (2nd ed.). New York: Plenum.

Baron, R. S. (1986). Distraction-conflict theory: Progress and problems. In L. Berkowitz (Ed.), *Advances in experimental social psychology.* Orlando, FL: Academic Press.

Baron, R. S., Moore, D., & Sanders, G. S. (1978). Distraction as a source of drive social facilitation. *Journal of Personality and Social Psychology, 36,* 816–824.

Barrett, P. T., & Eysenck, H. J. (1992). Brain evoked potentials and intelligence: The Hendrickson paradigm. *Intelligence, 16*(3–4), 361–381.

Barron, F. (1988). Putting creativity to work. In R. J. Sternberg (Ed.), *The nature of creativity* (pp. 76–98). New York: Cambridge University Press.

Bartlett, F. C. (1932). *Remembering: A study in experimental and social psychology.* Cambridge, England: Cambridge University Press.

Bashore, T. R., Osman, A., & Hefley, E. F. (1989). Mental slowing in elderly persons: A cognitive psychophysiological analysis. *Psychology and Aging, 4,* 235–244.

Bashore, T. R., & Rapp, P. E. (1993). Are there alternatives to traditional polygraph procedures? *Psychological Bulletin, 113*(1), 3–22.

Basow, S. A. (1986). *Gender stereotypes: Traditions and alternatives* (2nd ed.). Belmont, CA: Brooks/Cole.

Bastik, T. (1982). *Intuition: How we think and act.* Chichester, England: Wiley.

Bateson, G., Jackson, D. D., Haley, J., & Weakland, J. (1956). Toward a theory of schizophrenia. *Behavioral Science, 1*, 251–264.

Batson, C. D. (1990). How social an animal? The human capacity for caring. *American Psychologist, 45*, 336–346.

Batson, C. D., Batson, J. G., Griffitt, C. A., Barrientos, S., Brandt, J. R., Sprengelmeyer, P., & Bayly, M. J. (1989). Negative-state relief and the empathy–altruism hypothesis. *Journal of Personality and Social Psychology, 56*, 922–933.

Batson, C. D., Duncan, B. D., Ackerman, P., Buckley, T., & Birch, K. (1981). Is empathic emotion a source of altruistic motivation? *Journal of Personality and Social Psychology, 40*, 290–302.

Batson, C. D., Dyck, J. L., Brandt, J. R., Batson, J. G., Powell, A. L., McMaster, R. M., & Griffit, C. A. (1988). Five studies testing two new egoistic alternatives to the empathy–altruism hypothesis. *Journal of Personality and Social Psychology, 55*, 52–77.

Baumeister, R. F. (1982). A self-presentational view of social phenomena. *Psychological Bulletin, 91*, 3–26.

Baumeister, R. F., & Tice, D. M. (1984). Role of self-presentation and choice in cognitive dissonance under forced compliance: Necessary or sufficient causes? *Journal of Personality and Social Psychology, 46*, 5–13.

Baumrind, D. (1971). Current patterns of parental authority. *Developmental Psychology Monograph, 4*(1, pt. 2), 79–103.

Baumrind, D. (1978). Parental disciplinary patterns and social competence in children. *Youth and Society, 9*, 239–276.

Baumrind, D. (1986). Sex differences in moral reasoning: Response to Walker's (1984) conclusion that there are none. *Child Development, 57*, 511–521.

Baxter, L. R., Phelps, M. E., Mazziotta, J. C., Schwartz, J. M., Gerner, R. H., Selin, C. E., & Sumida, R. M. (1985). Cerebral metabolic rates for glucose in mood disorders. *Archives of General Psychiatry, 42*, 441–447.

Bayley, N. (1968). Behavioral correlates of mental growth: Birth to thirty-six years. *American Psychologist, 23*, 1–17.

Bayley, N., & Oden, M. H. (1955). The maintenance of intellectual ability in gifted adults. *Journal of Gerontology, 10*, 91–107.

Beck, A. T. (1967). *Depression: Causes and treatment.* Philadelphia: University of Pennsylvania Press.

Beck, A. T. (1976). *Cognitive therapy and the emotional disorders.* New York: International Universities Press.

Beck, A. T. (1985). Theoretical perspectives on clinical anxiety. In A. H. Tuma & J. D. Maser (Eds.), *Anxiety and the anxiety disorder* (pp. 183–198). Hillsdale, NJ: Erlbaum.

Beck, A. T. (1986). Cognitive therapy: A sign of retrogression of progress. *The Behavior Therapist, 9*, 2–3.

Beck, A. (1988). Cognitive approaches to panic disorder: Theory and therapy. In S. Rachman & J. D. Maser (Eds.), *Panic: Psychological perspectives.* Hillsdale, NJ: Erlbaum.

Beck, A. T. (1991). Cognitive therapy: A thirty-year retrospective. *American Psychologist, 46*, 368–375.

Beck, A. T., & Emery, G., (with) Greenberg, R. L. (1985). *Anxiety disorders and phobias: A cognitive perspective.* New York: Basic Books.

Beck, A. T., & Ward, C. H. (1961). Dreams of depressed patients: Characteristic themes in manifest content. *Archives of General Psychiatry, 5*, 462–467.

Beilin, H. (1971). The training and acquisition of logical operation. In M. Rosskopf, L. Steffe, & S. Taback (Eds.), *Piagetian cognitive development research and mathematical education.* Washington, DC: National Council of Teachers of Mathematics.

Békésy, G. von. (1960). *Experiments in hearing.* New York: McGraw-Hill.

Bell, P. A., & Baron, R. A. (1976). Aggression and heat: The mediating role of negative affect. *Journal of Applied Social Psychology, 6*, 18–30.

Belloc, N. D., & Breslow, L. (1972). Relationship of physical health status and family practices. *Preventive Medicine, 1*, 409–421.

Bellugi, U., Poizner, H., & Klima, E. S. (1989). Language, modality and the brain. *Trends in Neuroscience, 12*(10), 380–388.

Belmont, J. M., & Butterfield, E. C. (1971). Learning strategies as determinants of memory deficiencies. *Cognitive Psychology, 2*, 411–420.

Belsky, J. (1990). Parental and nonparental child care and children's socioemotional development: A decade in review. *Journal of Marriage and the Family, 52*, 885–903.

Belsky, J., & Rovine, M. (1988). Nonmaternal care in the first year of life and the security of infant-parent attachment. *Child Development, 59*, 157–167.

Bem, D. J. (1967). Self-perception: An alternative interpretation of cognitive dissonance phenomena. *Psychological Review, 74*, 183–200.

Bem, D. J. (1972). Self perception theory. In L. Berkowitz (Ed.), *Advances in experimental social psychology* (Vol. 6). New York: Academic Press.

Bem, D. J., & Allen, A. (1974). On predicting some of the people some of the time: The search for cross-situational consistencies in behavior. *Psychological Review, 81*, 506–520.

Bem, D. J., & Funder, D. C. (1978). Predicting more of the people more of the time: Assessing the personality of situations. *Psychological Review, 85*, 485–501.

Bem, S. L. (1981). Gender schema theory: A cognitive account of sex typing. *Psychological Review, 88*, 354–364.

Benbow, C. P., & Stanley, J. C. (1980). Sex differences in mathematical ability: Fact or artifact? *Science, 210*, 1262–1264.

Ben-Shakhar, G., & Furedy, J. J. (1990). *Theories and applications in the detection of deception: A psychophysiological and international perspective.* New York: Springer-Verlag.

Benson, H. (1977). Systemic hypertension and the relaxation response. *New England Journal of Medicine, 296,* 1152–1156.

Berg, C. A., & Sternberg, R. J. (1992). Adults' conceptions of intelligence across the adult life span. *Psychology and Aging, 7*(2), 221–231.

Berger, K. S. (1980). *The developing person.* New York: Worth.

Berglas, S., & Jones, E. E. (1978). Drug choice as a self-handicapping strategy in response to noncontingent success. *Journal of Personality and Social Psychology, 36,* 405–417.

Berkowitz, L. (1972). Social norms, feelings, and other factors affecting helping and altruism. In L. Berkowitz (Ed.), *Advances in experimental social psychology* (Vol. 6, pp. 63–108). New York: Academic Press.

Berkowitz, L., Cochran, S., & Embree, M. (1981). Physical pain and the goal of aversively stimulated aggression. *Journal of Personality and Social Psychology, 40,* 687–700.

Berlin, B., & Kay, P. (1969). *Basic color terms: Their universality and evolution.* Los Angeles: University of California Press.

Berlyne, D. E. (1960). *Conflict, arousal, and curiosity.* New York: McGraw-Hill.

Berlyne, D. E. (1967). Arousal reinforcement. In D. Levine (Ed.), *Nebraska symposium on motivation* (pp. 1–110). Lincoln: University of Nebraska Press.

Bernard, L. L. (1924). *Instinct.* New York: Holt, Rinehart & Winston.

Berndt, T. J. (1982). The features and effects of friendship in early adolescence. *Child Development, 53*(6), 1447–1460.

Berndt, T. J. (1986). Children's comments about their friendships. In M. Perlmutter (Ed.), *Cognitive perspectives on children's social and behavioral development: The Minnesota symposia on child psychology* (Vol. 18, pp. 189–212). Hillsdale, NJ: Erlbaum.

Berry, J. W. (1974). Radical cultural relativism and the concept of intelligence. In J. W. Berry & P. R. Dasen (Eds.), *Culture and cognition: Readings in cross-cultural psychology* (pp. 225–229). London: Methuen.

Berry, J. W. (1976). *Human ecology and cognitive style: Comparative studies in cultural and psychological adaptation.* New York: Sage/Halsted.

Berry, J. W. (1994). Acculturative stress. In W. J. Lonner & R. W. Malpass (Eds.), *Psychology and culture.* Boston: Allyn & Bacon.

Berry, J. W., Kim, U., Minde, T., & Mok, D. (1987). Comparative studies of acculturative stress. *International Migration Review, 21,* 491–511.

Berry, J. W., Poortinga, Y. H., Segall, M. H., & Dasen, P. R. (1992). *Cross-cultural psychology: Research and applications.* New York: Cambridge University Press.

Berry, S. L., Beatty, W. W., & Klesges, R. C. (1985). Sensory and social influences on ice cream consumption by males and females in a laboratory setting. *Appetite, 6,* 41–45.

Berscheid, E., & Walster, E. (1974). A little bit about love. In T. L. Huston (Ed.), *Foundations of interpersonal attraction.* New York: Academic Press.

Bertenthal, B. I., & Fischer, K. W. (1978). Development of self-recognition in the infant. *Developmental Psychology, 14,* 44–50.

Bertilsson, L. (1978). Mechanism of action of benzodiazepines: The GABA hypothesis. *Acta Psychiatrica Scandinavica, 274,* 19–26.

Bexton, W. H., Heron, W., & Scott, T. H. (1954). Effects of decreased variation in the sensory environment. *Canadian Journal of Psychology, 8,* 70–76.

Bezooijen, R. V., Otto, S. A., & Heenan, T. A. (1983). Recognition of vocal expressions of emotion: A three nation study to identify universal characteristics. *Journal of Cross-Cultural Psychology, 14,* 387–406.

Biederman, I. (1987). Recognition-by-components: A theory of human image understanding. *Psychological Review, 94,* 115–147.

Biery, R. E. (1990). *Understanding homosexuality: The pride and the prejudice.* Austin, TX: Edward-William.

Billings, A. G., Cronkite, R. C., & Moos, R. H. (1983). Social-environmental factors in unipolar depression: Comparisons of depressed patients and nondepressed controls. *Journal of Abnormal Psychology, 92,* 119–133.

Binet, A., & Simon, T. (1916). *The development of intelligence in children* (E. S. Kite, Trans). Baltimore: Williams & Wilkins.

Blackmore, S. J. (1993). *Dying to live: Science and the near-death experience.* London: Grafton.

Blakeslee, A. F., & Salmon, T. H. (1935). Genetics of sensory thresholds: Individual taste reactions for different substances. *Proceedings of the National Academy of Sciences of the U.S.A., 21,* 84–90.

Blasi, A. (1980). Bridging moral cognition and moral action: A critical review of the literature. *Psychological Bulletin, 88,* 1–45.

Blass, E. M. (1990). Suckling: Determinants, changes, mechanisms, and lasting impressions. *Developmental Psychology, 26,* 520–533.

Bliss, E. L. (1980). Multiple personality. *Archives of General Psychiatry, 37,* 1388–1397.

Block, J. (1980). From infancy to adulthood: A clarification. *Child Development, 51*(2), 622–623.

Block, J. (1981). Some enduring and consequential structures of personality. In A. I. Rabin, J. Arnoff, A. M. Barclay, & R. A. Zucker (Eds.), *Further explorations in personality.* New York: Wiley.

Block, J. H. (1983). Differential premises arising from differential socialization of the sexes: Some conjectures. *Child Development, 54,* 1335–1354.

Bloom, B. S. (1964). *Stability and change in human characteristics.* New York: Wiley.

Bloom, B. S., & Broder, L. J. (1950). *Problem-solving processes of college students.* Chicago: University of Chicago Press.

Blumenthal, J. A., Emery, C. F., Walsh, M. A., Cox, D. R., Kuhn, C. M., Williams, R. B., & Williams, R. S. (1988). Exercise training in healthy Type A middle-aged men: Effects to behavioral and cardiovascular responses. *Psychosomatic Medicine, 50,* 418–433.

Bolger, N. (1990). Coping as a personality process: A

prospective study. *Journal of Personality and Social Psychology, 59*(3), 531.

Boll, T. J. (1978). Diagnosing brain impairment. In B. B. Wolman (Ed.), *Clinical diagnosis of mental disorders: A handbook.* New York: Plenum.

Bolwig, T. G. (1993). Biological treatments other than drugs (electroconvulsive therapy, brain surgery, insulin therapy, and photo therapy). In N. Sartorius, G. de Girolano, G. Andrews, G. A. German, & L. Eisenberg (Eds.), *Treatment of mental disorders: A review of effectiveness.* Geneva, Switzerland, and Washington, DC: World Health Organization and American Psychiatric Press.

Bond, M. H. (1986). *The psychology of the Chinese people.* Hong Kong: Oxford University Press.

Bond, M. H. (Ed.) (1988). *Cross-cultural research and methodology series: Vol. 11. The cross-cultural challenge to social psychology.* Newbury Park, CA: Sage.

Bond, M. R. (1979). *Pain: Its nature, analysis and treatment.* New York: Longman.

Bongiovanni, A. (1977). *A review of research on the effects of punishment in the schools.* Paper presented at the Conference on Child Abuse, Children's Hospital National Medical Center, Washington, DC.

Booth-Kewley, S., & Friedman, H. S. (1987). Psychological predictors of heart disease: A quantitative review. *Psychological Bulletin, 101,* 343–362.

Borbely, A. (1986). *Secrets of sleep.* New York: Basic Books.

Borden, R. J., Bowen, R. & Taylor, S. P. (1971). School setting as a function of physical attack and extrinsic reward. *Perceptual and Motor Skills, 33,* 563–568.

Bornstein, M. H. (1989). Information processing (habituation) in infancy and stability in cognitive development. *Human Development, 32*(3–4), 129–136.

Bornstein, M. H., & Sigman, M. D. (1986). Continuity in mental development from infancy. *Child Development, 57,* 251–274.

Bornstein, P. E., Clayton, P. J., Halikas, J. A., Maurice, W. L., & Robins, E. (1973). The depression of widowhood after thirteen months. *British Journal of Psychiatry, 122,* 561–566.

Bouchard, T. J., & McGue, M. (1981). Familial studies of intelligence: A review. *Science, 212,* 1055–1059.

Bousfield, W. A. (1953). The occurrence of clustering in the recall of randomly arranged associates. *Journal of General Psychology, 49,* 229–240.

Bower, G. H. (1981, February). Mood and memory. *American Psychologist, 36*(2), 129–148.

Bower, G. H. (1983). Affect and cognition. *Philosophical Transaction: Royal Society of London* (Series B), *302,* 387–402.

Bower, G. H., Black, J. B., & Turner, T. J. (1979). Scripts in memory for texts. *Cognitive Psychology, 11,* 177–220.

Bower, G. H., Clark, M. C., Lesgold, A. M., & Winzenz, D. (1969). Hierarchical retrieval schemes in recall of categorized word lists. *Journal of Verbal Learning and Verbal Behavior, 8,* 323–343.

Bower, G. H., Karlin, M. B., & Dueck, A. (1975).

Comprehension and memory for pictures. *Memory and Cognition, 3,* 216–220.

Bower, T. G. R. (1971, October). The object in the world of the infant. In *Scientific American: Mind and Behavior.* San Francisco: Freeman.

Bower, T. G. R. (1989). *The rational infant: Learning in infancy.* New York: Freeman.

Bowers, K. S. (1973). Situationism in psychology: An analysis and critique. *Psychological Review, 80,* 307–336.

Bowers, K. S. (1976). *Hypnosis for the seriously curious.* New York: Norton.

Bowlby, J. (1951). *Maternal care and mental health* (World Health Organization Monograph Series No. 2). Geneva, Switzerland: World Health Organization. (Reprinted by Schocken Books, 1966).

Bowlby, J. (1969). *Attachment: Vol. 1. Attachment and loss.* New York: Basic Books.

Boyd, J. H., & Weissman, M. M. (1982). Epidemiology. In E. S. Paykel (Ed.), *Handbook of affective disorders.* New York: Guilford.

Bradburn, N. M. (1969). *The structure of psychological well-being.* Chicago: Aldine.

Bradburn, N. M., & Capovitz, D. (1965). *Reports on happiness.* Chicago: Aldine.

Bradley, R. H., & Caldwell, B. M. (1984). 174 Children: A study of the relationship between home environment and cognitive development during the first 5 years. In A. W. Gottfried (Ed.), *Home environment and early cognitive development: Longitudinal research.* San Diego, CA: Academic Press.

Brainerd, C. J. (1978). The stage question in cognitive-developmental theory. *Behavioral and Brain Sciences, 1,* 173–182.

Bransford, J. D. (1979). *Human cognition: Learning, understanding, and remembering.* Belmont, CA: Wadsworth.

Bransford, J. D., & Johnson, M. K. (1972). Contextual prerequisites for understanding: Some investigations of comprehension and recall. *Journal of Verbal Learning and Verbal Behavior, 11,* 717–726.

Bransford, J. D., & Johnson, M. K. (1973). Considerations of some problems of comprehension. In W. G. Chase (Ed.), *Visual information processing.* New York: Academic Press.

Bransford, J. D., & Stein, B. (1984). *The IDEAL problem solver.* New York: Freeman.

Branstetter, E. (1969). The young child's response to hospitalization: Separation anxiety or lack of mothering care? *American Journal of Public Health, 59,* 92–97.

Braswell, L., & Kendall, P. C. (1988). Cognitive-behavioral methods with children. In K. S. Dobson (Ed.), *Handbook of cognitive-behavioral therapies.* New York: Guilford.

Brazelton, T. B. (1983). Precursors for the development of emotions in early infancy. In R. Plutchik & H. Kellerman (Eds.), *Emotion: Theory, research, and experience* (Vol. 2). New York: Academic Press.

Brehm, S. S., & Kassin, S. M. (1990). *Social psychology.* Boston: Houghton Mifflin.

Breslow, L. (1983). The potential of health promotion.

In D. Mechanic (Ed.), *Handbook of health, health care, and the health professions.* New York: Free Press.

Bretherton, I., & Waters, E. (Eds.). (1985). Growing points of attachment theory research. *Monographs of the Society for Research in Child Development, 50*(1-2, Serial No. 209).

Breuer, J., & Freud, S. (1895). *Studies in hysteria* (translated and edited by J. Strachey, with the collaboration of A. Freud). New York: Basic Books.

Bridges, L. J., Connell, J. P., & Belsky, J. (1988). Similarities and differences in infant-mother and infant-father interaction in the strange situation: A component process analysis. *Developmental Psychology, 24,* 92–100.

Brigden, R. (1933). A tachistoscopic study of the differentiation of perception. *Psychological Monographs, 44,* 153–166.

Brislin, R. W. (1986). The wording and translation of research instruments. In W. J. Lonner & J. W. Berry (Eds.), *Field methods in cross-cultural research.* Newbury Park, CA: Sage.

Broadbent, D. (1958). *Perception and communication.* Oxford, England: Pergamon.

Broadbent, D. E., & Gregory, M. (1965). Effects of noise and of signal rate upon vigilance analyzed by means of decision theory. *Human Factors, 7,* 155–162.

Broadhurst, P. L. (1957). Emotionality and the Yerkes-Dodson law. *Journal of Experimental Psychology, 54,* 345–352.

Brown, A. L., Campione, J. C., Bray, N. W., & Wilcox, B. L. (1973). Keeping track of changing variables: Effects of rehearsal training and rehearsal prevention in normal and retarded adolescents. *Journal of Experimental Psychology, 101,* 123–131.

Brown, A. L., & French, A. L. (1979). The zone of potential development: Implications for intelligence testing in the year 2000. In R. J. Sternberg & D. K. Detterman (Eds.), *Human intelligence: Perspectives on its theory and measurement* (pp. 217–235). Norwood, NJ: Ablex.

Brown, A. L., & Kane, M. J. (1988). Preschool children can learn to transfer: Learning to learn and learning by example. *Cognitive Psychology, 20,* 493–523.

Brown, E. (1963). Meeting patients' psychosocial needs in the general hospital. *Annals of the American Academy of Political and Social Science, 346,* 117–122.

Brown, G. W., & Harris, T. O. (1978). *Social origins of depression.* London: Tavistock.

Brown, J. A. (1958). Some tests of the decay theory of immediate memory. *Quarterly Journal of Experimental Psychology, 10,* 12–21.

Brown, R. (1965). *Social psychology.* New York: Free Press.

Brown, R. (1973). *A first language: The early stages.* Cambridge, MA: Harvard University Press.

Brown, R., Cazden, C. B., & Bellugi, U. (1969). The child's grammar from 1 to 3. In J. P. Hill (Ed.), *Minnesota symposium on child psychology* (Vol. 2). Minneapolis: University of Minnesota Press.

Brown, R., & Kulik, J. (1977). Flashbulb memories. *Cognition, 5,* 73–99.

Brown, R., & McNeill, D. (1966). The "tip of the tongue" phenomenon. *Journal of Verbal Learning and Verbal Behavior, 5,* 325–337.

Bruch, H. (1973). *Eating disorders: Obesity, anorexia nervosa, and the person within.* New York: Basic Books.

Bryant, P. E., & Trabasso, T. (1971). Transitive inferences and memory in young children. *Nature, 232,* 456–458.

Bunney, W. E., Goodwin, F. K., & Murphy, D. L. (1972). The "switch process" in manic–depressive illness. *Archives in General Psychiatry, 27,* 312–317.

Bunney, W. E., Murphy, D. L., Goodwin, F. K., & Borge, G. F. (1970). The switch process from depression to mania: Relationship to drugs which alter brain amines. *Lancet, 1,* 1022.

Burger, J. M. (1989). Negative reactions to increases in perceived personal control. *Journal of Personality and Social Psychology, 56,* 246–256.

Burger, J. M., & Cooper, H. M. (1979). The desirability of control. *Motivation and Emotion, 3,* 381–393.

Burgess, E. W., & Wallin, P. (1953). *Engagement and marriage.* Philadelphia: Lippincott.

Burleson, B. R., & Denton, W. H. (1992). A new look at similarity and attraction in marriage: Similarities in social-cognitive and communication skills as predictors of attraction and satisfaction. *Communication Monographs, 59*(3), 268–287.

Burnstein, E., & Vinokur, A. (1973). Testing two classes of theories about group-induced shifts in individual choice. *Journal of Experimental Social Psychology, 9,* 123–137.

Burnstein, E., & Vinokur, A. (1977). Persuasive arguments and social comparison as determinates of attitude polarization. *Journal of Experimental Social Psychology, 13,* 315–332.

Burti, L., & Yastrebov, V. S. (1993). Procedures used in rehabilitation. In N. Sartorius, G. de Girolano, G. Andrews, G. A. German, & L. Eisenberg (Eds.), *Treatment of mental disorders: A review of effectiveness.* Geneva, Switzerland, and Washington, DC: World Health Organization and American Psychiatric Press.

Buss, D. M. (1988a). The evolution of human intrasexual competition: Tactics of mate attraction. *Journal of Personality and Social Psychology, 54,* 616–628.

Buss, D. M. (1988b). Love acts: The evolutionary biology of love. In R. J. Sternberg & M. L. Barnes (Eds.), *The psychology of love* (pp. 100–118). New Haven, CT: Yale University Press.

Buss, D. M., & Barnes, M. (1986). Preferences in human mate selection. *Journal of Personality and Social Psychology, 50,* 559–570.

Buss, D. M., & Craik, K. H. (1984). Acts, dispositions, and personality. In B. A. Maher & W. B. Maher (Eds.), *Progress in experimental personality research* (Vol. 13, pp. 241–301). Orlando, FL: Academic Press.

Butcher, J. N., Dahlström, W. G., Graham, J. R., Tellegen, A., & Kaemmer, B. (1989). *Minnesota Multiphasic Personality Inventory (MMPI-2): Manual for administration and scoring.* Minneapolis: University of Minnesota Press.

Butcher, J. N., & Pancheri, P. (1976). *A handbook of*

cross-national MMPI research. Minneapolis, MN: University of Minnesota Press.

Butcher, J. N., & Williams, C. L. (1992). *Essentials of MMPI-2 and MMPI-A interpretation.* Minneapolis: University of Minnesota Press.

Butler, J., & Rovee-Collier, C. (1989). Contextual gating of memory retrieval. *Developmental Psychobiology, 22,* 533–552.

Butterfield, E. C., Wambold, C., & Belmont, J. M. (1973). On the theory and practice of improving short-term memory. *American Journal of Mental Deficiency, 77,* 654–669.

Byrne, D. (1961). Anxiety and the experimental arousal of affiliation need. *Journal of Abnormal and Social Psychology, 63,* 660–662.

Byrne, D. G., & Rosenman, R. H. (1986). The Type A behaviour pattern as a precursor to stressful life-events: A confluence of coronary risks. *British Journal of Medical Psychology, 59,* 75–82.

Byrne, P. S., & Long, B. E. L. (1976). *Doctors talking to patients.* London: Her Majesty's Stationery Office.

Cacioppo, J. T., & Petty, R. E. (1979). Effects of message repetition and position on cognitive responses, recall, and persuasion. *Journal of Personality and Social Psychology, 37,* 97–109.

Cacioppo, J. T., & Petty, R. E. (1980). Persuasiveness of commercials is affected by exposure frequency and communicator cogency: A theoretical and empirical analysis. In J. H. Leigh & C. R. Martin (Eds.), *Current issues and research in advertising.* Ann Arbor: University of Michigan Press.

Cacioppo, J. T., & Petty, R. E. (1983). *Social psychophysiology: A sourcebook.* New York: Guilford.

Cacioppo, J. T., & Petty, R. E. (1986). Social processes. In M. G. H. Coles, E. Donehin, & S. W. Porges (Eds.), *Psychophysiology.* New York: Guilford.

Cain, W. S. (1977). Differential sensitivity for smell: "Noise" at the nose. *Science, 195,* 796–798.

Campbell, M., Rosenbloom, S., Perry, R., George, A. E., Kercheff, I. I., Anderson, L., Small, A. M., & Jennings, S. J. (1982). Computerized axial tomography in young autistic children. *American Journal of Psychiatry, 139,* 510–512.

Campione, J. C. (1989). Assisted assessments: A taxonomy of approaches and an outline of strengths and weaknesses. *Journal of Learning Disabilities, 22,* 151–165.

Campione, J. C., & Brown, A. L. (1990). Guided learning and transfer: Implications for approaches to assessment. In N. Frederiksen, R. Glaser, A. Lesgold, & M. Shafto (Eds.), *Diagnostic monitoring of skill and knowledge acquisition* (pp. 141–172). Hillsdale, NJ: Erlbaum.

Campione, J. C., Brown, A. L., & Ferrara, R. (1982). Mental retardation and intelligence. In R. J. Sternberg (Ed.), *Handbook of human intelligence* (pp. 392–490). New York: Cambridge University Press.

Campos, J. J., Barrett, K. C., Lamb, M. E., Goldsmith, H. H., & Stenberg, C. (1983). Socioemotional development. In P. H. Mussen (Ed.), *Handbook of child psychology* (4th ed., Vol. 2, pp. 783–915). New York: Wiley.

Candland, D. K. (1977). The persistent problems of emotion. In D. K. Candland, J. P. Fell, E. Keen, A. I. Leshner, R. Plutchik, & R. M. Tarpy (Eds.), *Emotion* (pp. 1–84). Monterey, CA: Brooks/Cole.

Cannon, W. B. (1927). The James-Lange theory of emotion: A critical examination and alternative theory. *American Journal of Psychology, 39,* 106–124.

Cannon, W. B. (1929). *Bodily changes in pain, hunger, fear, and rage, on account of recent researches into the function of emotional excitement* (2nd ed.). New York: Appleton.

Cannon, W. B., & Washburn, A. L. (1912). An explanation of hunger. *American Journal of Psychology, 29,* 444–454.

Cantor, J., & Engle, R. W. (in press). Working memory capacity as long-term memory activation: An individual differences approach. *Journal of Experimental Psychology: Learning, Memory, and Cognition.*

Cantor, N., & Kihlstrom, J. F. (1987). Social intelligence: The cognitive basis of personality. In P. Shaver (Ed.), *Review of personality and social psychology* (Vol. 6, pp. 15–34). Beverly Hills, CA: Sage.

Cantwell, D. P., Baker, L., & Rutter, M. (1979). Families of autistic and dysphasic children: 1. Family life and interaction patterns. *Archives of General Psychiatry, 29,* 682–687.

Caplan, L. (1993). *Stroke* (2nd ed.). Stoneham, MA: Butterworth-Heineman.

Caporael, L. (1976). Ergotism: The satan loosed in Salem? *Science, 192,* 21–26.

Carlson, G., & Goodwin, F. K. (1973). The stages of mania: A longitudinal analysis of the manic episode. *Archives of General Psychiatry, 28*(2), 221–228.

Carlson, J. G., & Hatfield, E. (1992). *Psychology of emotion.* New York: Harcourt Brace Jovanovich.

Carraher, T. N., Carraher, D., & Schliemann, A. D. (1985). Mathematics in the streets and in the schools. *British Journal of Developmental Psychology, 3,* 21–29.

Carroll, D. W. (1986). *Psychology of language.* Monterey, CA: Brooks/Cole.

Carroll, L. (1946). *Alice in Wonderland and through the looking glass.* New York: Grosset & Dunlap.

Carson, R. C., & Butcher, J. N. (1992). *Abnormal psychology and modern life* (9th ed.). New York: HarperCollins.

Carver, C. S., Diamond, E. L., & Humphries, C. (1985). Coronary prone behavior. In N. Schneiderman & J. T. Tapp (Eds.), *Behavioral medicine: The biopsychosocial approach.* Hillsdale, NJ: Erlbaum.

Cattell, J. M. (1886). The influence of the intensity of the stimulus on the length of the reaction time. *Brain, 9,* 512–514.

Cattell, J. M. (1890). Mental tests and measurements. *Mind, 15,* 373–380.

Cattell, R. B. (1971). *Abilities: Their structure, growth, and action.* Boston: Houghton Mifflin.

Cattell, R. B. (1973, July). A 16PF profile. *Psychology Today,* pp. 40–46.

Cattell, R. B. (1979). *Personality and learning theory.* New York: Springer.

Cattell, R. B. (1982). *The inheritance of personality and ability: Research methods and findings.* New York: Academic Press.

Cattell, R. B., Eber, H. W., & Tatsuoka, M. M. (1970). *Handbook for the Sixteen Personality Factor Questionnaire.* Champaign, IL: Institute for Personality and Ability Testing.

Ceci, S. J. (1991). How much does schooling influence general intelligence and its cognitive components? A re-assessment of the evidence. *Developmental Psychology, 27*(5), 703–722.

Ceci, S. J., & Bronfenbrenner, U. (1985). Don't forget to take the cupcakes out of the oven: Strategic time-monitoring, prospective memory and context. *Child Development, 56,* 175–190.

Ceci, S. J., & Roazzi, A. (1994). The effects of context on cognition: Postcards from Brazil. In R. J. Sternberg & R. K. Wagner (Eds.), *Minds in context: Interactionist perspectives on human intelligence.* New York: Cambridge University Press.

Cerella, J. (1985). Information processing rates in the elderly. *Psychological Bulletin, 98,* 67–83.

Chaiken, S., & Eagly, A. (1983). Communication modality as a determinant of persuasion: The role of communicator salience. *Journal of Personality and Social Psychology, 45,* 241–256.

Chaplin, W. F., & Goldberg, L. R. (1984). A failure to replicate the Bem and Allen study of individual differences in cross-situational consistency. *Journal of Personality and Social Psychology, 47,* 1074–1090.

Chapman, C. R. (1984). New directions in the understanding and management of pain. *Social Science and Medicine, 19,* 1262–1277.

Chapman, L. J., & Chapman, J. P. (1969). Illusory correlation as an obstacle to the use of valid psychodiagnostic signs. *Journal of Abnormal Psychology, 74,* 271–280.

Chase, W. G., & Simon, H. A. (1973). The mind's eye in chess. In W. G. Chase (Ed.), *Visual information processing* (pp. 215–281). New York: Academic Press.

Cheng, P. W., & Holyoak, K. J. (1985). Pragmatic reasoning schemas. *Cognitive Psychology, 17,* 391–416.

Cherry, E. C. (1953). Some experiments on the recognition of speech with one and two ears. *Journal of the Acoustical Society of America, 25,* 975–979.

Chi, M. T. H., Feltovich, P., & Glaser, R. (1981). Categorization and representation of physics problems by experts and novices. *Cognitive Science, 5,* 121–152.

Chi, M. T. H., Glaser, R., & Farr, M. (Eds.). (1988). *The nature of expertise.* Hillsdale, NJ: Erlbaum.

Chi, M. T. H., & Koeske, R. D. (1983). Network representations of a child's dinosaur knowledge. *Developmental Psychology, 19,* 29–39.

Chomsky, N. (1957). *Syntactic structures.* The Hague, Netherlands: Mouton.

Chomsky, N. (1965). *Aspects of the theory of syntax.* Cambridge, MA: MIT Press.

Chomsky, N. (1972). *Language and mind* (2nd ed.). New York: Harcourt Brace Jovanovich.

Chomsky, N. (1991, March). Quoted in *Discover, 12*(3), p. 20.

Cialdini, R. B. (1984). *Influence.* New York: Quill.

Cialdini, R. B. (1988). *Influence: Science and practice* (2nd ed.). Glenview, IL: Scott, Foresman/Little, Brown.

Cialdini, R. B., Petty, R. E., & Cacioppo, J. T. (1981). Attitude and attitude change. *Annual Review of Psychology, 32,* 357–404.

Cialdini, R. B., Schaller, M., Houlihan, D., Arps, K., Fultz, J., & Beaman, A. L. (1987). Empathy-based helping: Is it selflessly or selfishly motivated? *Journal of Personality and Social Psychology, 52,* 599–604.

Cimbalo, R. S., Faling, V., & Mousaw, P. (1976). The course of love: A cross-sectional design. *Psychological Reports, 38,* 1292–1294.

Clark, E. V. (1973). What's in a word? On the child's acquisition of semantics in his first language. In T. E. Moore (Ed.), *Cognitive development and the acquisition of language.* New York: Academic Press.

Clark, H. H. (1969). Linguistic processes in deductive reasoning. *Psychological Review, 76,* 387–404.

Clark, H. H., & Chase, W. G. (1972). On the process of comparing sentences against pictures. *Cognitive Psychology, 3,* 472–517.

Clark, H. H., & Clark, E. V. (1977). *Psychology and language: An introduction to psycholinguistics.* New York: Harcourt Brace Jovanovich.

Clarke-Stewart, A., Perlmutter, M., & Friedman, S. (1988). *Lifelong human development.* New York: Wiley.

Clarke-Stewart, K. A. (1978). And daddy makes three: The father's impact on mother and young child. *Child Development, 49,* 466–478.

Clarke-Stewart, K. A. (1989). Infant day care: Maligned or malignant? *American Psychologist, 44,* 266–273.

Clayton, P., Desmarais, L., & Winokur, G. (1968). A study of normal bereavement. *American Journal of Psychiatry, 125,* 168–178.

Clore, G. L., & Byrne, D. (1974). A reinforcement-affect model of attraction. In T. L. Huston (Ed.), *Foundations of interpersonal attraction* (pp. 143–170). New York: Academic Press.

Coates, J. B., & Wortman, C. B. (1980). Depression maintenance and interpersonal control. In A. Baum & J. E. Singer (Eds.), *Advances in environmental psychology: Applications of personal control* (Vol. 2). Hillsdale, NJ: Erlbaum.

Cofer, C. N., & Appley, M. H. (1964). *Motivation: Theory and research.* New York: Wiley.

Cohen, J. (1981). Can human irrationality be experimentally demonstrated? *Behavioral and Brain Sciences, 4,* 317–331.

Cohen, S. (1981). *The substance abuse problems.* New York: Haworth Press.

Cohen, S., Kaplan, J. R., Cunnick, J. E., Manuck, S. B., & Rabin, B. S. (1992). Chronic social stress, affiliation, and cellular immune response in nonhuman primates. *Psychological Science, 3,* 301–304.

Cohen, S., Tyrell, D., & Smith, A. (1991). Psychological stress and susceptibility to the common cold. *The New England Journal of Medicine, 235,* 606–612.

Cohen, S., & Williamson, G. (1991). Stress and infectious disease. *Psychological Bulletin, 109,* 5–24.

Colby, A., Kohlberg, L., Gibbs, J., & Lieberman, M. (1983). A longitudinal study of moral judgment. *Monographs of the Society for Research in Child Development, 48*(1–2), 124.

Cole, J. O., & Bodkin, J. A. (1990). Antidepressant drug side effects. *Journal of Clinical Psychiatry, 51,* 21–26.

Cole, M., Gay, J., Glick, J., & Sharp, D. W. (1971). *The cultural context of learning and thinking.* New York: Basic Books.

Cole, M., & Scribner, S. (1974). *Culture and thought: A psychological introduction.* New York: Wiley.

Coleman, P. D., & Flood, D. G. (1986). Dendritic proliferation in the aging brain as a compensatory repair mechanism. In D. F. Swaab, E. Fliers, M. Mirmiram, W. A. Van Gool, & F. Van Haaren (Eds.), *Progress in brain research* (Vol. 20). New York: Elsevier.

Collins, A. M., & Loftus, E. F. (1975). A spreading-activation theory of semantic processing. *Psychological Review, 82,* 407–429.

Collins, A. M., & Quillian, M. R. (1969). Retrieval time from semantic memory. *Journal of Verbal Learning and Verbal Behavior, 8,* 240–248.

Condry, J. (1977). Enemies of exploration: Self-initiated versus other-initiated learning. *Journal of Personality and Social Psychology, 18,* 105–115.

Conrad, R. (1964). Acoustic confusions in immediate memory. *British Journal of Psychology, 55,* 75–84.

Cooley, C. H. (1982). *Human nature and the social order.* New York: Scribners. (Original work published 1902)

Cooper, E. H., & Pantle, A. J. (1967). The total-time hypothesis in verbal learning. *Psychological Bulletin, 68*(4), 221–234.

Cooper, J., Zanna, M. P., & Taves, P. A. (1978). Arousal as a necessary condition for attitude change following induced compliance. *Journal of Personality and Social Psychology, 36,* 1101–1106.

Coren, S., & Girgus, J. S. (1978). *Seeing is deceiving: The psychology of visual illusions.* Hillsdale, NJ: Erlbaum.

Coren, S., & Ward, L. M. (1989). *Sensation and perception* (3rd ed.). San Diego, CA: Harcourt Brace Jovanovich.

Corina, D. P., Poizner, H., Bellugi, U., Feinberg, T., et al. (1992a). Dissociation between linguistic and nonlinguistic gestural systems: A case for compositionality. *Brain & Language, 43*(3), 414–447.

Corina, D. P., Vaid, J., Bellugi, U. (1992b). The linguistic basis of left hemisphere specialization. *Science 255*(5049), 1258–1260.

Cornsweet, T. N. (1985). Prentice Award Lecture: A simple retinal mechanism that has complex and profound effects on perception. *American Journal of Optometry and Physiological Optics, 62,* 427–438.

Costa, P. T., & McCrae, R. R. (1992a). "Four ways five factors are not basic": Reply. *Personality & Individual Differences, 13*(8), 861–865.

Costa, P. T., & McCrae, R. R. (1992b). Four ways five factors are basic. *Personality & Individual Differences, 13*(6), 653–665.

Cotman, C. W., & McGaugh, J. L. (1980). *Behavioral neuroscience: An introduction.* New York: Academic Press.

Cottraux, J. (1993). Behavior therapy. In N. Sartorius, G. de Girolano, G. Andrews, G. A. German, & L. Eisenberg (Eds.), *Treatment of mental disorders: A review of effectiveness.* Geneva, Switzerland, and Washington, DC: World Health Organization and American Psychiatric Press.

Courchesne, E., Yeung-Courchesne, R., Press, G. A., Hesselink, J. R., & Jernigan, T. L. (1988). Hypoplasia of cerebellar vermal lobules VI and VII autism. *New England Journal of Medicine, 318,* 1349–1354.

Court, J. H. (1984). Sex and violence: A ripple effect. In N. M. Malamuth & E. Donnerstein (Eds.), *Pornography and social aggression.* Orlando, FL: Academic Press.

Cox, D. J., Freundlich, A., & Meyer, R. G. (1975). Differential effectiveness of electromyographic feedback, verbal relaxation instructions, and medication placebo with tension headaches. *Journal of Consulting and Clinical Psychology, 43,* 892–898.

Cox, V. C., Paulus, P. B., & McCain, G. (1984). Prison crowding research: The relevance for prison housing standards and a general approach regarding crowding phenomena. *American Psychologist, 39,* 1148–1160.

Coyne, J. C. (1976a). Depression and the response of others. *Journal of Abnormal Psychology, 55*(2), 186–193.

Coyne, J. C. (1976b). Toward an interactional description of depression. *Psychiatry, 39,* 14–27.

Craik, F. I. M., & Lockhart, R. S. (1972). Levels of processing: A framework for memory research. *Journal of Verbal Learning and Verbal Behavior, 11,* 671–684.

Craik, F. I. M., & Tulving, E. (1975). Depth of processing and the retention of words in episodic memory. *Journal of Experimental Psychology: General, 104,* 268–294.

Crick, F., & Mitchison, G. (1983). The function of dream sleep. *Nature, 304,* 111–114.

Crook, C. (1987). Taste and olfaction. In P. Salapatek & L. Cohen (Eds.), *Handbook of infant perception: Vol. 1. From sensation to perception* (pp. 237–264). Orlando, FL: Academic Press.

Cross-National Collaborative Group. (1992). The changing rate of major depression. *Journal of the American Medical Association, 268*(21), 3098–3105.

Crowder, R. G. (1976). *Principles of learning and memory.* Hillsdale, NJ: Erlbaum.

Crutchfield, R. (1962). Conformity and creative thinking. In H. Gruber, G. Terrell, & M. Wertheimer (Eds.), *Contemporary approaches to creative thinking* (pp. 120–140). New York: Atherton.

Csikszentmihalyi, M. (1988). Society, culture, and person: A systems view of creativity. In R. J. Sternberg (Ed.), *The nature of creativity* (pp. 325–339). New York: Cambridge University Press.

Cummins, J. (1976). The influence of bilingualism on cognitive growth: A synthesis of research findings and explanatory hypothesis. *Working Papers on Bilingualism, 9,* 1–43.

Curtiss, S. (1977). *Genie: A linguistic study of a modern-day wild child.* New York: Academic Press.

Damon, W., & Hart, D. (1982). The development of self-understanding from childhood to adolescence. *Child Development, 53,* 841–864.

Daneman, M., & Carpenter, P. A. (1980). Individual differences in working memory and reading. *Journal of Verbal Learning and Verbal Behavior, 19,* 450–466.

Daneman, M., & Tardif, T. (1987). Working memory and reading skill re-examined. In M. Coltheart (Ed.), *Attention and performance: Vol. 12. The psychology of reading* (pp. 491–508). Hove, England: Erlbaum.

Darley, C. F., Tinklenberg, J. R., Roth, W. T., Hollister, L. E., & Atkinson, R. C. (1973). Influence of marijuana on storage and retrieval processes in memory. *Memory and Cognition, 1,* 196–200.

Darley, J. M., & Batson, C. D. (1973). From Jerusalem to Jericho: A study of situational and dispositional variables in helping behavior. *Journal of Personality and Social Psychology, 27,* 100–108.

Darwin, C. (1859). *Origin of species.* London: John Murray.

Darwin, C. (1965). *The expression of the emotions in man and animals.* Chicago: University of Chicago Press. (Original work published 1872)

Darwin, C. J., Turvey, M. T., & Crowder, R. G. (1972). An auditory analogue of the Sperling partial report procedure: Evidence for brief auditory storage. *Cognitive Psychology, 3,* 255–267.

Dasen, P. R., & Heron, A. (1981). Cross-cultural tests of Piaget's theory. In H. C. Triandis & A. Heron (Eds.), *Handbook of cross-cultural psychology* (Vol. 4). Boston: Allyn & Bacon.

Davidson, J. E. (1986). The role of insight in giftedness. In R. J. Sternberg & J. E. Davidson (Eds.), *Conceptions of giftedness* (pp. 201–222). New York: Cambridge University Press.

Davidson, J. E., & Sternberg, R. J. (1984). The role of insight in intellectual giftedness. *Gifted Child Quarterly, 28,* 58–64.

Davidson, J. W., & Lytle, M. H. (1986). *After the fact: The art of historical detection* (2nd ed.). New York: Knopf.

Davison, G. C., & Neale, J. M. (1994). *Abnormal psychology* (6th ed.). New York: Wiley.

Dawes, R. M. (1994). *House of cards.* New York: Free Press.

Dawson, J. L. (1977). Alaskan Eskimo hand, eye, auditory dominance and cognitive style. *Psychologia: An International Journal of Psychology in the Orient, 20*(3), 121–135.

DeAngelis, T. (1992, May). Senate seeks answers to rising tide of violence. *APA Monitor,* p. 11.

DeCasper, A. J., & Fifer, W. P. (1980). Of human bonding: Newborns prefer their mothers' voices. *Science, 208,* 1174–1176.

DeCasper, A. J., & Prescott, P. A. (1983). Human newborns' perception of male voices: Preference, discrimination, and reinforcing value. *Developmental Psychobiology, 17,* 481–491.

DeCasper, A. J., & Spence, M. J. (1986). Prenatal maternal speech influences newborns' perception of speech sounds. *Infant Behavior and Development, 9,* 133–150.

deCastro, J. M., & Brewer, E. M. (1992). The amount eaten in meals by humans is a power function of the number of people present. *Physiology and Behavior, 51,* 121–125.

deCharms, R. (1968). *Personal causation: The internal affective determinants of behavior.* New York: Academic Press.

Deci, E. L. (1971). Effects of externally mediated rewards on intrinsic motivation. *Journal of Personality and Social Psychology, 18,* 105–115.

Deci, E. L. (1972). Intrinsic motivation, extrinsic reinforcement, and inequity. *Journal of Personality and Social Psychology, 22,* 113–120.

Deci, E. L., & Ryan, R. M. (1985). *Intrinsic motivation and self-determination in human behavior.* New York: Plenum.

Deci, E. L., Vallerand, R. J., Pelletier, L. G., & Ryan, R. M. (1991). Motivation and education: The self-determination perspective. *Educational Psychologist, 26*(3–4), 325–346.

de Groot, A. D. (1965). *Thought and choice in chess.* The Hague, Netherlands: Mouton.

de la Croix, H., Tansey, R. G., & Kirkpatrick, D. (1991). *Gardner's art through the ages* (9th ed.). New York: Harcourt Brace Jovanovich.

Delgado, J. M. (1969). *Physical control of the mind: Toward a psychocivilized society.* New York: Harper & Row.

Delgado, J. M. R., Roberts, W. W., & Miller, N. E. (1954). Learning motivated by electrical stimulation of the brain. *American Journal of Physiology, 179,* 587–593.

DeLongis, A., Folkman, S., & Lazarus, R. S. (1988). The impact of daily stress on health and mood: Psychological and social resources as mediators. *Journal of Personality and Social Psychology, 54*(3), 486–495.

Dembroski, T. M., & Costa, P. T. (1988). Assessment of coronary-prone behavior: A current overview. *Annals of Behavioral Medicine, 10,* 60–63.

Dembroski, T. M., MacDougall, J. M., Williams, R. B., Haney, T. L., & Blumenthal, J. A. (1985). Components of Type A, hostility, and anger-in: Relationship to angiographic findings. *Psychosomatic Medicine, 47,* 219–233.

Dement, W. C. (1976). *Some must watch while some must sleep.* New York: Norton.

Dement, W. C., & Kleitman, N. (1957). The relation of eye movements during sleep to dream activity: An objective method for the study of dreaming. *Journal of Experimental Psychology, 55,* 543–553.

Dennett, D. (1991). *Consciousness explained.* Boston: Little, Brown.

Denny, N. W. (1980). Task demands and problem-solving strategies in middle-age and older adults. *Journal of Gerontology, 35,* 559–564.

Derryberry, D., & Rothbart, M. K. (1988). Arousal, affect, and attention as components of temperament. *Journal of Personality and Social Psychology, 55,* 958–966.

Derryberry, D., & Tucker, D. M. (1992). Neural mechanisms of emotion. *Journal of Consulting and Clinical Psychology, 60,* 329–338.

Descartes, R. (1972). *The treatise of man.* Cambridge, MA: Harvard University Press. (Original work published 1662)

DeSoto, C. B., London, M., & Handel, S. (1965). Social reasoning and spatial paralogic. *Journal of Personality and Social Psychology, 2,* 513–521.

Detterman, D. K., & Sternberg, R. J. (Eds.). (1982). *How and how much can intelligence be increased.* Norwood, NJ: Ablex.

Detterman, D. K., & Sternberg, R. J. (Eds.). (1993). *Transfer on trial: Intelligence, cognition, and instruction.* Norwood, NJ: Ablex.

Deutsch, J. A., & Deutsch, D. (1963). Attention: Some theoretical considerations. *Psychological Review, 70,* 80–90.

Deutsch, M. (1968). The effects of cooperation and competition upon group process. In D. Cartwright & A. Zander (Eds.), *Group dynamics: Research and theory* (3rd ed.). New York: Harper & Row.

DeValois, R. L., & DeValois, K. K. (1980). Spatial vision. *Annual Review of Psychology, 31,* 309–341.

Devine, P. G., Monteith, M. J., Zuwerink, J. R., & Elliot, A. J. (1991). Prejudice with and without compunction. *Journal of Personality and Social Psychology, 60*(6), 817–830.

Dewey, J. (1910). *How we think.* Boston: Heath.

Dewey, J. (1913). *Interest and effort in education.* New York: Houghton Mifflin.

Dewey, J. (1922). *Human nature and conduct: An introduction to social psychology.* New York: Holt.

Diener, E. (1979). Deindividuation, self-awareness, and disinhibition. *Journal of Personality and Social Psychology, 37*(7), 1160–1171.

Diener, E. (1980). Deindividuation: The absence of self-awareness and self-regulation in group members. In P. B. Paulus (Ed.), *The psychology of group influence.* Hillsdale, NJ: Erlbaum.

Differential aptitudes test (4th ed.) (1982). Austin, TX: Psychological Corporation. (Original work published 1972)

Digman, J. M. (1990). Personality structure: Emergence of the five-factor model. *Annual Review of Psychology, 41,* 417–440.

DiMatteo, M. R., & DiNicola, D. D. (1982). *Achieving patient compliance: The psychology of the medical practitioner's role.* New York: Pergamon.

Dion, K. K., Berscheid, E., & Walster, E. (1972). What is beautiful is good. *Journal of Personality and Social Psychology, 24,* 285–290.

Dion, K. L., & Dion, K. K. (1976). Love, liking, and trust in heterosexual relationships. *Personality and Social Psychology Bulletin, 2,* 191–206.

Dittes, J. E., & Kelley, H. H. (1956). Effects of different conditions of acceptance upon conformity to group norms. *Journal of Abnormal and Social Psychology, 53,* 100–107.

Dixon, R. A., & Baltes, P. B. (1986). Toward life-span research on the functions and pragmatics of intelligence. In R. J. Sternberg & R. K. Wagner (Eds.), *Practical intelligence: Nature and origins of competence in the everyday world* (pp. 203–235). New York: Cambridge University Press.

Docherty, J. (1993, May 23). Pay for mental health care—and save. *New York Times,* Sect. 3, p. 13.

Dohrenwend, B. P., Levav, I., Schwartz, S., Naveh, G., Link, B. G., Skodol, A. G., & Stueve, A. (1992). Socioeconomic status and psychiatric disorders: The causation-selection issue. *Science, 255,* 946–952.

Dohrenwend, B. S., & Dohrenwend, B. P. (1974). *Stressful life events.* New York: Wiley.

Dollard, J., Miller, N., Doob, L., Mowrer, O. H., & Sears, R. R. (1939). *Frustration and aggression.* New Haven, CT: Institute of Human Relations, Yale University Press.

Donnerstein, E., & Berkowitz, L. (1981). Victim reaction in aggressive erotic films as a factor in violence against women. *Journal of Personality and Social Psychology, 41,* 710–724.

Douglas, J. D. (1967). *The social meanings of suicide.* Princeton, NJ: Princeton University Press.

Douvan, E., & Adelson, J. (1966). *The adolescent experience.* New York: Wiley.

Dovidio, J. F., Allen, J. L., & Schroeder, D. A. (1990). Specificity of empathy-induced helping: Evidence for altruistic motivation. *Journal of Personality and Social Psychology, 59,* 249–260.

Dowling, W. J., & Harwood, D. L. (1986). *Music cognition.* Orlando, FL: Academic Press.

Dubbert, P. (1992). Exercise in behavioral medicine. *Journal of Consulting and Clinical Psychology, 60,* 613–618.

Duncker, K. (1929). Uber induzierte Bewegung (ein Beitrag zur Theorie optisch wahrgenommener Bewegung). *Psychologische Forschung, 2,* 180–259.

Duncker, K. (1945). On problem-solving. *Psychological Monographs, 58*(5, Whole No. 270).

Durlach, N. I., & Colburn, H. S. (1978). Binaural phenomenon. In E. C. Carterette & M. P. Friedman (Eds.), *Handbook of perception* (Vol. 4). New York: Academic Press.

Dutton, D. G., & Aron, A. P. (1974). Some evidence for heightened sexual attraction under conditions of high anxiety. *Journal of Personality and Social Psychology, 30,* 510–517.

Dyal, J. A. (1984). Cross-cultural research with the locus of control concept. In H. Lefcourt (Ed.), *Research with the locus of control construct: Vol. 3. Extensions and limitations.* San Diego, CA: Academic Press.

D'Zurilla, T. J. (1986). *Problem-solving therapy: A social competence approach to clinical intervention.* New York: Springer.

D'Zurilla, T. J. (1990). Problem-solving training for effective stress management and prevention. *Journal of Cognitive Psychotherapy: An International Quarterly, 4,* 327–355.

D'Zurilla, T. J., & Goldfried, M. R. (1971). Problem solving and behavior modification. *Journal of Abnormal Psychology, 78*(1), 107–126.

Eagly, A. H. (1987). *Sex differences and social behavior: A social-role interpretation.* Hillsdale, NJ: Erlbaum.

Eagly, A. H., & Chaiken, S. (1975). An attribution analysis of communicator attractiveness. *Journal of Personality and Social Psychology, 32,* 136–144.

Eagly, A. H., Makhijani, M. G., & Klonsky, B. G. (1992). Gender and the evaluation of leaders: A meta-analysis. *Psychological Bulletin, 111*(1), 3–22.

Early, P. C. (1989). Social loafing and collectivism: A comparison of the United States and the People's Republic of China. *Administrative Science Quarterly, 34,* 565–581.

Ebbinghaus, H. E. (1902). *Grundzuge der psychologie.* Leipzig, Germany: Von Veit.

Ebbinghaus, H. E. (1964). *Memory: A contribution to experimental psychology.* New York: Dover. (Original work published 1885)

Eckenrode, J. (1984). Impact of chronic and acute stressors on daily reports of mood. *Journal of Personality and Social Psychology, 46,* 907–918.

Edgerton, R. (1967). *The cloak of competence.* Berkeley: University of California Press.

Edmonston, W. E., Jr. (1981). *Hypnosis and relaxation.* New York: Wiley.

Egeland, B., & Sroufe, L. A. (1981). Attachment and early maltreatment. *Child Development, 52,* 44–52.

Eimas, P. D. (1985). The perception of speech in early infancy. *Scientific American, 252,* 46–52.

Eisenberg, M. (1991). Meta-analytic contributions to the literature on prosocial behavior. *Personality and Social Psychology Bulletin, 17,* 273–282.

Eisenstock, B. (1984). Sex-role differences in children's identification with counterstereotypical televised portrayals. *Sex Roles, 10*(5–6), 417–430.

Ekman, P. (1971). Universals and cultural differences in the facial expression of emotion. In J. Cole (Ed.), *Nebraska Symposium on Motivation* (Vol. 19, pp. 207–284). Lincoln: University of Nebraska Press.

Ekman, P. (1973). *Darwin and facial expression: A century of research in review.* New York: Academic Press.

Ekman, P. (1984). Expression and the nature of emotion. In P. Ekman & K. Scherer (Eds.), *Approaches to emotion* (pp. 319–343). Hillsdale, NJ: Erlbaum.

Ekman, P. (1992). *Telling lies.* New York: Norton.

Ekman, P. (1993). Facial expression and emotion. *American Psychologist, 48,* 384–392.

Ekman, P., & Friesen, W. V. (1971). Constants across cultures in the face and emotion. *Journal of Personality and Social Psychology, 17,* 124–129.

Ekman, P., & Friesen, W. V. (1975). *Unmasking the face.* Englewood Cliffs, NJ: Prentice-Hall.

Ekman, P., & Friesen, W. V. (1984). *Unmasking the face* (2nd ed.). Palo Alto, CA: Consulting Psychologists Press.

Ekman, P., Friesen, W. V., & O'Sullivan, M. (1988). Smiles when lying. *Journal of Personality and Social Psychology, 54,* 414–420.

Ekman, P., Levenson, R. W., & Friesen, W. V. (1983). Autonomic nervous system activity distinguishes among emotions. *Science, 221,* 1208–1210.

Ekman, P., & Oster, H. (1979). Facial expression of emotion. *Annual Review of Psychology, 30,* 527–554.

Elashoff, J. R., & Snow, R. E. (1971). *Pygmalion reconsidered.* Worthington, OH: Charles A. Jones.

Eliot, R. S., & Buell, J. C. (1983). The role of the central nervous system in sudden cardiac death. In T. M. Dem-broski, T. Schmidt, & G. Blunchen (Eds.), *Biobehavioral bases of coronary-prone behavior.* New York: Plenum.

Ellis, A. (1962). *Reason and emotion in psychotherapy.* Secaucus, NJ: Lyle Stuart.

Ellis, A. (1970). *Reason and emotion in psychotherapy.* New York: Lyle Stuart.

Ellis, A. (1973). Rational-emotive therapy. In R. J. Corsini (Ed.), *Current psychotherapies.* Itasca, IL: Peacock.

Ellis, A. (1989). The history of cognition in psychotherapy. In A. Freeman, K. M. Simon, L. E. Beutler, & H. Arkowitz (Eds.), *Comprehensive handbook of cognitive therapy* (pp. 5–19). New York: Plenum.

Endler, N. S., & Magnusson, D. (1976). Toward an interactional psychology of personality. *Psychological Bulletin, 83,* 956–974.

Engel, G. L. (1977). The need for a new medical model: A challenge for biomedicine. *Science, 196,* 129–136.

Engle, R. W. (1994). Individual differences in memory and their implications for learning. In R. J. Sternberg (Ed.), *Encyclopedia of intelligence.* New York: Macmillan.

Engle, R. W., Cantor, J., & Carullo, J. J. (1992). Individual differences in working memory and comprehension: A test of four hypotheses. *Journal of Experimental Psychology: Learning, Memory, & Cognition, 18*(5), 972–992.

Engle, R. W., Carullo, J. J., & Collins, K. W. (1992). Individual differences in working memory for comprehension and following directions. *Journal of Educational Research, 84*(5), 253–262.

Enna, S. J., & DeFranz, J. F. (1980). Glycine, GABA and benzodiazepine receptors. In S. J. Enna & H. I. Yamamura (Eds.), *Neurotransmitter receptors* (Part 1). London: Chapman & Hall.

Entwisle, D. R., & Baker, D. P. (1983). Gender and young children's expectations for performance in arithmetic. *Developmental Psychology, 19,* 200–209.

Erdberg, P. (1990). Rorschach assessment. In G. Goldstein & M. Hersen (Eds.), *Psychological assessment* (2nd ed.). New York: Pergamon.

Ericsson, K. A., Chase, W. G., & Faloon, S. (1980). Acquisition of a memory skill. *Science, 208,* 1181–1182.

Ericsson, K. A., & Simon, H. A. (1980). Verbal reports as data. *Psychological Review, 87,* 215–251.

Erikson, E. H. (1950). *Childhood and society.* New York: Norton.

Erikson, E. H. (1963). *Childhood and society* (2nd ed.). New York: Norton.

Erikson, E. H. (1968). *Identity, youth, and crisis.* New York: Norton.

Estes, W. K. (1982). Learning, memory, and intelligence. In R. J. Sternberg (Ed.), *Handbook of intelligence* (pp. 170–224). New York: Cambridge University Press.

Exline, R. V. (1962). Need affiliation and initial communication behavior in problem solving groups characterized by low interpersonal visibility. *Psychological Reports, 10,* 405–411.

Exline, R. (1972). Visual interaction: The glances of power and preference. In J. Cole (Ed.), *Nebraska Symposium on Motivation, 1971.* Lincoln: University of Nebraska Press.

Exner, J. E. (1974). *The Rorschach: A comprehensive system* (Vol. 1). New York: Wiley.

Exner, J. E. (1978). *The Rorschach: A comprehensive system*. Vol. 2. *Current research and advanced interpretation.* New York: Wiley.

Exner, J. E. (1985). *The Rorschach: A comprehensive system* (Vol. 1, 2nd ed.). New York: Wiley.

Eysenck, H. J. (1952). *The scientific study of personality.* London: Routledge & Kegan Paul.

Eysenck, H. J. (1967). Intelligence assessment: A theoretical and experimental approach. *British Journal of Educational Psychology, 37,* 81–98.

Eysenck, H. J. (1971). *Readings in extraversion-introversion: II. Fields of application.* London: Staples.

Eysenck, H. J. (Ed.). (1981). *A model for personality.* New York: Springer.

Eysenck, H. J., & Kamin, L. (1981). *The intelligence controversy: H. J. Eysenck vs. Leon Kamin.* New York: Wiley.

Fagan, J. F. (1984). The intelligent infant: Theoretical implications. *Intelligence, 8,* 1–9.

Fagan, J. F. (1985). A new look at infant intelligence. In D. K. Detterman (Ed.), *Current topics in human intelligence: Vol. 1. Research methodology.* Norwood, NJ: Ablex.

Fagan, J. F., III, & Montie, J. E. (1988). Behavioral assessment of cognitive well-being in the infant. In J. Kavanagh (Ed.), *Understanding mental retardation: Research accomplishments and new frontiers.* Baltimore: Brookes.

Fantz, R. L. (1958). Pattern vision in young infants. *Psychological Record, 8,* 43–47.

Fantz, R. L. (1961). The origin of form perception. *Scientific American, 204,* 66–72.

Farah, M. J. (1988a). Is visual imagery really visual? Overlooked evidence from neuropsychology. *Psychological Review, 95*(3), 307–317.

Farah, M. J. (1988b). The neuropsychology of mental imagery: Converging evidence from brain-damaged and normal subjects. In J. Stiles-Davis, M. Kritchevsky, & U. Bellugi (Eds.), *Spatial cognition: Brain bases and development* (pp. 33–56). Hillsdale, NJ: Erlbaum.

Faust, I. M., Johnson, P. R., & Hirsch, J. (1977a). Adipose tissue regeneration following lipectomy. *Science, 197,* 391–393.

Faust, I. M., Johnson, P. R., & Hirsch, J. (1977b). Surgical removal of adipose tissue alters feeding behavior and the development of obesity in rats. *Science, 197,* 393–396.

Fay, R. E., Turner, C. F., Klassen, A. D., & Gagnon, J. H. (1989). Prevalence and patterns of same-gender sexual contact among men. *Science, 243,* 338–348.

Fazio, R. H., Zanna, M. P., & Cooper, J. (1977). Dissonance and self perception: An integrative view of each theory's proper domain of application. *Journal of Experimental Social Psychology, 13,* 464–479.

Fechner, G. T. (1966). *Elements of psychophysics* (H. E. Adler, Trans.). New York: Holt, Rinehart & Winston. (Original work published 1860)

Federal Bureau of Investigation. (1992). *1991 Uniform Crime Reports.* Washington, DC: U.S. Government Printing Office.

Feist, J. (1990). *Theories of personality* (3rd ed.). Fort Worth, TX: Holt, Rinehart & Winston.

Feldhusen, J. F. (1986). A conception of giftedness. In R. J. Sternberg & J. E. Davidson (Eds.), *Conceptions of giftedness* (pp. 112–127). New York: Cambridge University Press.

Feldman, D. H. (1986). *Nature's gambit: Child prodigies and the development of human potential.* New York: Basic Books.

Feldman, D. H. (1988). Creativity: Dreams, insights, and transformations. In R. J. Sternberg (Ed.), *The nature of creativity.* New York: Cambridge University Press.

Fenigstein, A., Scheier, M. F., & Buss, A. H. (1975). Public and private self-consciousness: Assessment and theory. *Journal of Consulting and Clinical Psychology, 43,* 522–527.

Fernald, A. (1985). Four-month-old infants prefer to listen to motherese. *Infant Behavior and Development, 8,* 118–195.

Fernald, A., Taeschner, T., Dunn, J., Papousek, M., De Boysson-Bardies, B., & Fukui, I. (1989). A cross-cultural study of prosodic modification in mothers' and fathers' speech to preverbal infants. *Journal of Child Language, 16,* 477–501.

Fernandez, E., & Turk, D. C. (1992). Sensory and affective components of pain: Separation and synthesis. *Psychological Bulletin, 112*(2), 205–217.

Ferster, C. B. (1961). Positive reinforcement and behavioral deficits of autistic children. *Child Development, 32,* 437–456.

Ferster, C. B. (1973). A functional analysis of depression. *American Psychology, 28*(110), 857–870.

Feshbach, S. (1970). Aggression. In P. H. Mussen (Ed.), *Carmichael's manual of child psychology.* New York: Wiley.

Festinger, L. (1954). A theory of social comparison processes. *Human Relations, 7,* 117–140.

Festinger, L. (1957). *A theory of cognitive dissonance.* Evanston, IL: Row, Peterson.

Festinger, L., & Carlsmith, J. M. (1959). Cognitive consequences of forced compliance. *Journal of Abnormal and Social Psychology, 58,* 203–210.

Festinger, L., Schachter, S., & Back, K. (1950). *Social pressures in informal groups: A study of human factors in housing.* New York: Harper & Brothers.

Feuerstein, R. (1979). *The dynamic assessment of retarded performers: The learning potential assessment device, theory, instruments, and techniques.* Baltimore: University Park Press.

Feuerstein, R. (1980). *Instrumental enrichment: An intervention program for cognitive modifiability.* Baltimore: University Park Press.

Field, T. (1978). Interaction behaviors of primary versus secondary caregiver fathers. *Developmental Psychology, 14,* 183–184.

Field, T. M. (1989). Individual and maturational differences in infant expressivity. In N. Eisenberg (Ed.), *Empathy and related responses.* San Francisco: Jossey-Bass.

Field, T. (1990). *Infant daycare has positive effects on grade school behavior and performance.* Unpublished manuscript, University of Miami, Coral Gables, Florida.

Finger, W. J., Borduin, C. M., & Baumstark, K. E. (1992). Correlates of moral judgment development in college students. *Journal of Genetic Psychology, 153*(2), 221–223.

Fischetti, M., Curran, S. P., & Wessberg, H. W. (1977). Sense of timing. *Behavior Modification, 1,* 179–194.

Fischhoff, B. (1988). Judgment and decision making. In R. J. Sternberg & E. E. Smith (Eds.), *The psychology of human thought* (pp. 153–187). New York: Cambridge University Press.

Fischhoff, B., Slovic, P., & Lichtenstein, S. (1977). Knowing with certainty: The appropriateness of extreme confidence. *Journal of Experimental Psychology: Human Perception and Performance, 3,* 552–564.

Fisher, R., & Ury, W. (1981). *Getting to yes.* Boston: Houghton Mifflin.

Fisk, A. D., & Schneider, W. (1981). Control and automatic processing during tasks requiring sustained attention: A new approach to vigilance. *Human Factors, 23,* 737–750.

Fivush, R., & Hamond, N. R. (1991). Autobiographical memory across the preschool years: Toward reconceptualizing childhood memory. In R. Fivush & N. R. Hamond (Eds.), *Knowing and remembering in young children.* New York: Cambridge University Press.

Flatow, I. (1993). *They all laughed . . . from light bulbs to lasers: The fascinating stories behind the great inventions that have changed our lives.* New York: HarperCollins.

Flavell, J. H. (1976). Metacognitive aspects of problem solving. In L. Resnick (Ed.), *The nature of intelligence.* Hillsdale, NJ: Erlbaum.

Flavell, J. H. (1981). Cognitive monitoring. In W. P. Dickson (Ed.), *Children's oral communication skills* (pp. 35–60). New York: Academic Press.

Flavell, J. H. (1985). *Cognitive development* (2nd ed.). Englewood Cliffs, NJ: Prentice-Hall.

Flavell, J. H., Flavell, E. R., & Green, F. L. (1983). Development of the appearance–reality distinction. *Cognitive Psychology, 15,* 95–120.

Flavell, J. H., Wellman, H. M. (1977). Metamemory. In R. V. Kail, Jr., & J. W. Hagen (Eds.), *Perspectives on the development of memory and cognition* (pp. 3–33). Hillsdale, NJ: Erlbaum.

Floody, O. R. (1983). Hormones and aggression in female mammals. In B. B. Svare (Ed.), *Hormones and aggressive behavior* (pp. 39–89). New York: Plenum.

Fodor, J. A. (1975). *The language of thought.* New York: Crowell.

Fogel, A. (1991). *Infancy: Infant, family, and society* (2nd ed.). St. Paul, MN: West.

Fogel, A. (1992). Movement and communication in human infancy: The social dynamics of development. *Human Movement Science, 11*(4), 387–423.

Folkman, S., & Lazarus, R. S. (1988). *Manual for the ways of coping questionnaire.* Palo Alto, CA: Consulting Psychologists Press.

Folkman, S., Lazarus, R. S., Gruen, R. J., & DeLongis, A. (1986). Appraisal, coping, health status, and psychological symptoms. *Journal of Personality and Social Psychology, 50*(3), 571–579.

Forbes, M. S. (1990). *Women who made a difference.* New York: Simon & Schuster.

Ford, C. S., & Beach, F. A. (1951). *Patterns of sexual behavior.* New York: Harper & Row.

Fottrell, E. (1983). *Case histories in psychiatry.* New York: Churchill Livingston.

Foulke, E., & Sticht, T. (1969). Review of research on the intelligibility and comprehension of accelerated speech. *Psychological Bulletin, 72,* 50–62.

Frankl, V. (1959). *From death camp to existentialism.* Boston: Beacon.

Freeman, W. (1959). Psychosurgery. In S. Arieti (Ed.), *American handbook of psychiatry* (Vol. 2, pp. 1521–1540). New York: Basic Books.

Fremouw, W. J., Perczel, W. J., & Ellis, T. E. (1990). *Suicide risk: Assessment and response guidelines.* Elmsford, NY: Pergamon.

Frensch, P. A., & Sternberg, R. J. (1989). Expertise and intelligent thinking: When is it worse to know better? In R. J. Sternberg (Ed.), *Advances in the psychology of human intelligence.* Hillsdale, NJ: Erlbaum.

Freud, A. (1946). *The ego and the mechanisms of defense.* New York: International Universities Press.

Freud, S. (1922). Certain neurotic mechanisms in jealousy, paranoia, and homosexuality. In *Collected Papers* (Vol. 2). London: Hogarth Press.

Freud, S. (1949a). *A general introduction to psychoanalysis.* New York: Penguin.

Freud, S. (1953). *An aphasia.* London: Imago.

Freud, S. (1954). *Interpretation of dreams.* London: Allen & Unwin. (Original work published 1900)

Freud, S. (1957). Mourning and melancholia. In *Standard edition of the complete psychological works of Sigmund Freud* (Vol. 14). London: Hogarth. (Original work published 1917)

Freud, S. (1963a). *Dora: An analysis of a case of hysteria.* New York: Macmillan. (Original work published 1905)

Freud, S. (1963b). *Introductory lectures on psychoanalysis.* In *Standard edition of the complete psychological works of Sigmund Freud* (Vols. 15, 16). (Original work published 1917)

Freud, S. (1964a). *New introductory lectures.* In *Standard edition of the complete psychological works of Sigmund Freud* (Vol. 21). London: Hogarth. (Original work published 1933)

Freud, S. (1964b). Three essays on the theory of sexuality. In *Standard edition of the complete psychological works of Sigmund Freud* (Vol. 7). London: Hogarth Press—Institute of Psychological Analysis. (Original work published 1905)

Frey, K. S., & Ruble, D. N. (1987). Social comparison and self-evaluation in the classroom: Developmental changes in knowledge and function. In J. C. Masters & W. S. Smith (Eds.), *Social comparisons, social justice, and relative deprivation* (pp. 81–104). Hillsdale, NJ: Erlbaum.

Friedman, M., & Rosenman, R. H. (1974). *Type A behavior and your heart.* New York: Knopf.

Friedman, M. I., & Stricker, E. M. (1976). The physiological psychology of hunger: A physiological perspective. *Psychological Review, 83,* 409–431.

Friedrich-Cofer, L., & Huston, A. C. (1986). Television violence and aggression: The debate continues. *Psychological Bulletin, 100*(3), 364–371.

Frith, U., & Baron-Cohen, S. (1987). Perception in autistic children. In D. J. Cohen & A. M. Donnellan (Eds.), *Handbook of autism and pervasive developmental disorders* (pp. 55–102). New York: Wiley.

Fromkin, V. A. (1973). *Speech errors as linguistic evidence.* The Hague, Netherlands: Mouton.

Fromm, E. (1941). *Escape from freedom.* New York: Farrar & Rinehart.

Fromm, E. (1947). *Man for himself.* Greenwich, CT: Fawcett.

Fromm, E. (1955). *The sane society.* Greenwich, CT: Fawcett.

Fromm-Reichmann, F. (1948). Notes on the development of treatment of schizophrenics by psychoanalytic psychotherapy. *Psychiatry, 11,* 263–273.

Frost, N. (1972). Encoding and retrieval in visual memory tasks. *Journal of Experimental Psychology, 95,* 317–326.

Fuchs, J., Levinson, R., Stoddard, R., Mullet, M., & Jones, D. (1990). Health risk factors among the Amish: Results of a survey. *Health Education Quarterly, 17,* 197–211.

Funder, D. C., & Ozer, D. J. (1983). Behavior as a function of the situation. *Journal of Personality & Social Psychology, 44*(1), 107–112.

Furomoto, L., & Scarborough, E. (1986). Placing women in the history of psychology: The first American women psychologists. *American Psychologist, 41*(1), 35–42.

Gabrenya, W. K., Latané, B., & Wang, Y. E. (1983). Social loafing in cross-cultural perspective: Chinese in Taiwan. *Journal of Cross-Cultural Psychology, 14,* 368–384.

Gabrenya, W. K., Wang, Y. E., & Latané, B. (1985). Social loafing on an optimizing task: Cross-cultural differences among Chinese and Americans. *Journal of Cross-Cultural Psychology, 16,* 223–242.

Gagnon, J. H. (1973). Scripts and the coordination of sexual conduct. In J. K. Cole & R. Riensteiber (Eds.), *Nebraska Symposium on Motivation* (Vol. 21, pp. 27–59). Lincoln: University of Nebraska Press.

Galanter, E. (1962). Contemporary psychophysics. In R. Brown et al. (Eds.), *New directions in psychology* (Vol. 1). New York: Holt, Rinehart & Winston.

Galton, F. (1883). *Inquiry into human faculty and its development.* London: Macmillan.

Gara, M. A., Woolfolk, R. L., Cohen, B. D., Goldston, R. B., Allen, L. A., & Novalany, J. (1993). Perception of self and other in major depression. *Journal of Abnormal Psychology, 102,* 93–100.

Garcia, J., & Koelling, R. A. (1966). The relation of cue to consequence in avoidance learning. *Psychonomic Science, 4,* 123–124.

Gardner, H. (1983). *Frames of mind: The theory of multiple intelligences.* New York: Basic Books.

Gardner, H. (1988). Creative lives and creative works: A synthetic scientific approach. In R. J. Sternberg (Ed.), *The nature of creativity.* New York: Cambridge University Press.

Gardner, H. (1993). *Multiple intelligences: The theory in practice.* New York: Basic Books.

Gardner, R. A., & Gardner, B. T. (1969). Teaching sign language to a chimpanzee. *Science, 165,* 664–672.

Garner, W. R., Hake, H. W., & Eriksen, C. W. (1956). Operationism and the concept of perception. *Psychological Review, 63,* 149–159.

Garro, L. C. (1986). Language, memory, and focality: A reexamination. *American Anthropologist, 88,* 128–136.

Gazzaniga, M. S. (1970). *The bisected brain.* New York: Appleton-Century-Crofts.

Gazzaniga, M. S. (1985). *The social brain: Discovering the networks of the mind.* New York: Basic Books.

Gazzaniga, M. S., & LeDoux, J. E. (1978). *The integrated mind.* New York: Plenum.

Gelman, R., & Baillargeon, R. (1983). A review of some Piagetian concepts. In P. H. Mussen (Series Ed.), J. Flavell & E. Markman (Vol. Eds.), *Handbook of child psychology: Cognitive development* (Vol. 3, 4th ed., pp. 167–230). New York: Wiley.

Gelman, R., & Gallistel, C. R. (1978). *The child's understanding of number.* Cambridge, MA: Harvard University Press.

Gelman, S. A. (1985). Children's inductive inferences from natural kind and artifact categories. (Doctoral dissertation, Stanford University, 1984). *Dissertation Abstracts International, 45*(10-B), 3351–3352.

Gelman, S. A., & Kremer, K. E. (1991). Understanding natural causes: Children's explanations of how objects and their properties originate. *Child Development, 62*(2), 396–414.

Gelman, S. A., & Markman, E. M. (1987). Young children's inductions from natural kinds: The role of categories and appearances. *Child Development, 58*(6), 1532–1541.

Gentner, D. (1983). Structure-mapping: A theoretical framework for analogy. *Cognitive Science, 7,* 155–170.

Gerrig, R. J., & Banaji, M. R. (1994). Language and thought. In R. J. Sternberg (Ed.), *Handbook of perception and cognition: Thinking and problem solving.* New York: Academic Press.

Gesell, A. L. (1928). *Infancy and human growth.* New York: Macmillan.

Gesell, A. L., & Ilg, F. L. (1949). *Child development.* New York: Harper.

Gibbs, J. (Ed.). (1968). *Suicide.* New York: Harper & Row.

Gibbs, J. C., Arnold, K. D., Ahlborn, H. H., & Cheesman, F. L. (1984). Facilitation of sociomoral reasoning in delinquents. *Journal of Consulting and Clinical Psychology, 52,* 37–45.

Gibson, J. J. (1950). *The perception of the visual world.* Boston: Houghton Mifflin.

Gibson, J. J. (1979). *The ecological approach to visual perception.* Boston: Houghton Mifflin.

Gick, M. L., & Holyoak, K. J. (1980). Analogical problem solving. *Cognitive Psychology, 12,* 306–355.

Gick, M. L., & Holyoak, K. J. (1983). Schema induction and analogical transfer. *Cognitive Psychology, 15,* 1–38.

Gilbert, E., & DeBlassie, R. (1984). Anorexia nervosa: Adolescent starvation by choice. *Adolescence, 19*, 840–846.

Gill, M. M. (1972). Hypnosis as an altered and regressed state. *International Journal of Clinical and Experimental Hypnosis, 20*, 224–337.

Gilligan, C. (1982). *In a different voice: Psychological theory and women's development.* Cambridge, MA: Harvard University Press.

Gilligan, C., & Attanucci, J. (1988). Two moral orientations: Gender differences and similarities. *Merrill-Palmer Quarterly, 34*, 223–237.

Gilly, M. C. (1988). Sex roles in advertising: A comparison of television advertisements in Australia, Mexico, and the United States. *Journal of Marketing, 52*(2), 75–85.

Gladwin, T. (1970). *East is a big bird.* Cambridge, MA: Belknap Press.

Glaser, R., & Chi, M. T. H. (1988). Overview. In M. T. H. Chi, R. Glaser, & M. Farr (Eds.), *The nature of expertise* (pp. xv–xxxvi). Hillsdale, NJ: Erlbaum.

Glass, D. C. (1977). *Behavior patterns, stress, and coronary heart disease.* Hillsdale, NJ: Erlbaum.

Glucksberg, S., & Danks, J. H. (1975). *Experimental psycholinguistics.* Hillsdale, NJ: Erlbaum.

Glueck, B. C., & Stroebel, C. F. (1975). Biofeedback and meditation in the treatment of psychiatric illness. *Comprehensive Psychiatry, 16*, 302–321.

Goddard, H. H. (1917). Mental tests and immigrants. *Journal of Delinquency, 2*, 243–277.

Godden, D. R., & Baddeley, A. D. (1975). Context-dependent memory in two natural environments: On land and underwater. *British Journal of Psychology, 66*, 325–331.

Goertzel, M. G., Goertzel, V., & Goertzel, T. G. (1978). *Three hundred eminent personalities.* San Francisco: Jossey-Bass.

Goethals, G. R., & Darley, J. M. (1977). Social comparison theory: An attributional approach. In J. M. Suls & R. L. Miller (Eds.), *Social comparison processes: Theoretical and empirical perspectives* (pp. 259–278). Washington, DC: Hemisphere.

Goffman, E. (1967). *Interaction ritual.* New York: Doubleday.

Golden, C. J., Hammecke, T., & Purisch, A. (1978). Diagnostic validity of a standardized neuropsychological battery derived from Luria's neuropsychological test. *Journal of Consulting and Clinical Psychology, 46*, 1258–1265.

Goldfried, M. R. (1969). Prediction of improvement in an alcoholism outpatient clinic. *Quarterly Journal of Studies on Alcohol, 30*(1-A), 129–139.

Goleman, D. (1993, April 18). When a long therapy goes a little way. *New York Times*, Sect. 4, p. 6.

Gordon, D., & Lakoff, G. (1971). Conversational postulates. In *Papers from the Seventh Regional Meeting, Chicago Linguistic Society* (pp. 63–84).

Gorman, M. E. (1992). *Simulating science: Heuristics, mental models, and technoscientific thinking.* Bloomington: Indiana University Press.

Gotlib, I. H., & Robinson, L. A. (1982). Responses to depressed individuals: Discrepancies between self-report and observer-rated behavior. *Journal of Abnormal Psychology, 91*, 231–240.

Gottesman, I. I. (1991). *Schizophrenia genesis.* New York: Freeman.

Gottesman, I. I., McGuffin, P., & Farmer, A. E. (1987). Clinical genetics as clues to the "real" genetics of schizophrenia. *Schizophrenia Bulletin, 13*, 23–47.

Gottfried, A. E., & Gottfried, A. W. (Eds.). (1988). *Maternal employment and children's development.* New York: Plenum.

Gottman, J. M. (1979). *Marital interaction.* New York: Academic Press.

Gottman, J. M. (1983). How children become friends. *Monographs of the Society for Research in Child Development, 48*(Serial No. 201).

Gottman, J. M. (1986). The world of coordinated play: Same- and cross-sex friendship in young children. In J. M. Gottman & J. G. Parker (Eds.), *Conversations of friends: Speculations on affective development* (pp. 139–191). Cambridge, England: Cambridge University Press.

Gottman, J. M. (1994). *Why marriages succeed or fail.* New York: Simon & Schuster.

Gottman, J. M., Notarius, C., Gonso, J., & Markman, H. J. (1976). *A couple's guide to communication.* Champaign, IL: Research Press.

Gould, S. J. (1981). *The mismeasure of man.* New York: Norton.

Graf, P. (1990). Life-span changes in implicit and explicit memory. *Bulletin of the Psychonomic Society, 28*, 353–358.

Graf, P., & Schacter, D. L. (1985). Implicit and explicit memory for new associations in normal and amnesic subjects. *Journal of Experimental Psychology: Learning, Memory, and Cognition, 11*, 501–518.

Graham, C. H., & Hsia, Y. (1954). Luminosity curves for normal and dichromatic subjects including a case of unilateral color blindness. *Science, 120*, 780.

Graham, J. R. (1990). *MMPI-2: Assessing personality and psychopathology.* New York: Oxford University Press.

Gray, A. L., Bowers, K. S., & Fenz, W. D. (1970). Heart rate in anticipation of and during a negative visual hallucination. *International Journal of Clinical and Experimental Hypnosis, 18*, 41–51.

Green, D. M., & Swets, J. A. (1966). *Signal detection theory and psychophysics.* Reprint. New York: Krieger.

Greenberg, M., Szmukler, G., & Tantam, D. (1986). *Making sense of psychiatric cases.* New York: Oxford University Press.

Greenberg, R., & Underwood, B. J. (1950). Retention as a function of stage of practice. *Journal of Experimental Psychology, 40*, 452–457.

Greene, D., & Lepper, M. R. (1974). Effects of extrinsic rewards on children's subsequent intrinsic interest. *Child Development, 45*, 1141–1145.

Greene, R. L. (1987). Ethnicity and MMPI performance: A review. *Journal of Consulting and Clinical Psychology, 55*, 497–512.

Greene, R. L. (1990). Stability of MMPI scale scores

with four codetypes across forty years. *Journal of Personality Assessment, 55*(1–2), 1–6.

Greene, R. L., & Crowder, R. G. (1984). Modality and suffix effects in the absence of auditory stimulation. *Journal of Verbal Learning and Verbal Behavior, 23*, 371–382.

Greenfield, P. M., & Savage-Rumbaugh, S. (1990). Grammatical combination in *Pan paniscus:* Processes of learning and invention in the evolution and development of language. In S. Parker & K. Gibson (Eds.), *"Language" and intelligence in monkeys and apes: Comparative developmental perspectives.* New York: Cambridge University Press.

Greeno, J. G. (1974). Hobbits and orcs: Acquisition of a sequential concept. *Cognitive Psychology, 6*, 270–292.

Greeno, J. G., & Simon, H. A. (1988). Problem solving and reasoning. In R. C. Atkinson, R. Herrnstein, G. Lindzey, & R. D. Luce (Eds.), *Stevens' handbook of experimental psychology* (rev. ed.). New York: Wiley.

Greenwald, A. G., Pratkanis, A. R., Leippe, M. R., & Baumgardner, M. H. (1986). Under what conditions does theory obstruct research progress? *Psychological Review, 93*, 216–229.

Gregory, R. L. (1966). *Eye and brain.* New York: World University Library.

Greyson, B. (1990). Near-death encounters with and without near-death experiences: Comparative NDE scale profiles. *Journal of Near-Death Studies, 8*, 151–161.

Grice, H. P. (1967). William James Lectures, Harvard University, published in part as "Logic and conversation." In P. Cole & J. L. Morgan (Eds.), *Syntax and semantics: Speech acts* (Vol. 3, pp. 41–58). New York: Seminar Press.

Griffitt, W. & Veitch, R. (1971). Hot and crowded: Influences of population density and temperature on interpersonal affective behavior. *Journal of Personality and Social Psychology, 17*, 92–98.

Grilo, C. M., & Pogue-Geile, M. F. (1991). The nature of environmental influences on weight and obesity: A behavior genetic analysis. *Psychological Bulletin, 110*, 520–537.

Grossman, L., & Eagle, M. (1970). Synonymity, antonymity, and association in false recognition responses. *Journal of Experimental Psychology, 83*, 244–248.

Grossman, M. I., & Stein, I. F. (1948). Vagotomy and the hunger producing action of insulin in man. *Journal of Applied Physiology, 1*, 263–269.

Grossman, S. P., & Grossman, L. (1963). Food and water intake following lesions or electrical stimulation of the amygdala. *American Journal of Physiology, 205*, 761–765.

Groves, P. M., & Rebec, G. V. (1976). Biochemistry and behavior: Some central actions of amphetamine and antipsychotic drugs. *Annual Review of Psychology, 27*, 97–128.

Groves, P. M., & Rebec, G. V. (1988). *Introduction to biological psychology* (3rd ed.). Dubuque, IA: William C. Brown.

Gruber, H. E. (1981). *Darwin on man: A psychological study of scientific creativity* (2nd ed.). Chicago: University of Chicago Press. (Original work published 1974)

Gruber, H. E., & Davis, S. N. (1988). Inching our way up Mount Olympus: The evolving-systems approach to creative thinking. In R. J. Sternberg (Ed.), *The nature of creativity* (pp. 243–270). New York: Cambridge University Press.

Gruder, C. L., Cook, T. D., Hennigan, K. M., Flay, B. R., Alessis, C., & Halamaj, J. (1978). Empirical tests of the absolute sleeper effect predicted from the discounting cue hypothesis. *Journal of Personality and Social Psychology, 36*, 1061–1074.

Guilford, J. P. (1950). Creativity. *American Psychologist, 5*(9), 444–454.

Guilford, J. P. (1967). *The nature of human intelligence.* New York: McGraw-Hill.

Guilford, J. P. (1982). Cognitive psychology's ambiguities: Some suggested remedies. *Psychological Review, 89*, 48–59.

Gurman, A. S., Kniskern, D. P., & Pinsoff, W. M. (1986). Research on the process and outcome of marital and family therapy. In S. L. Garfield & A. E. Bergin (Eds.), *Handbook of psychotherapy and behavior change* (3rd ed.). New York: Wiley.

Guyote, M. J., & Sternberg, R. J. (1981). A transitive-chain theory of syllogistic reasoning. *Cognitive Psychology, 13*, 461–525.

Guzman, A. (1971). Analysis of curved line drawings using context and global information. *Machine intelligence* (Vol. 6, pp. 325–375). Edinburgh, Scotland: Edinburgh University Press.

Gwirtsman, H. E., & Germer, R. H. (1981). Abnormalities of dexamethasone suppression test and urinary MHPG in anorexia nervosa. *American Journal of Psychiatry, 138*, 650–653.

Haaga, D., Dyck, M., & Ernst, D. (1991). Empirical status of the cognitive theory of depression. *Psychological Bulletin, 110*, 215–236.

Haefely, W. E. (1977). Synaptic pharmacology of barbiturates and benzodiazepines. *Agents and Actions, 713*, 353–359.

Haft, J. I. (1974). Cardiovascular injury induced by sympathetic catecholamines. *Progress in Cardiovascular Disease, 17*, 73.

Haglund, M. M., Ojemann, G. A., Lettich, E., Bellugi, U., et al. (1993). Dissociation of cortical and single unit activity in spoken and signed languages. *Brain & Language, 44*(1), 19–27.

Haier, R. J., Siegel, B. V., Nuechterlein, K. H., Hazlett, E., Wu, J. C., Pack, J., Browning, H. L., & Buchsbaum, M. S. (1988). Cortical glucose metabolic rate correlates of abstract reasoning and attention studied with positron emission tomography. *Intelligence, 12*, 199–217.

Haier, R. J., Siegel, B., Tang, C., Abel, L., & Buchsbaum, M. S. (1992). Intelligence and changes in regional cerebral glucose metabolic rate following learning. *Intelligence, 16*(3–4), 415–426.

Haith, M. M. (1979). Visual cognition in early infancy. In R. B. Kearsley & I. E. Sigel (Eds.), *Infants at risk: Assessment of cognitive functioning.* Hillsdale, NJ: Erlbaum.

Hakuta, K. (1986). *Mirror of language.* New York: Basic Books.

Hall, E. T. (1966). *The hidden dimension.* New York: Doubleday.

Hamilton, D. L., & Gifford, R. K. (1976). Illusory correlation in interpersonal perception: A cognitive basis of stereotypic judgments. *Journal of Experimental Social Psychology, 12,* 392–407.

Hamilton, E. (1942). Cupid and Psyche. In *Mythology* (pp. 92–100). New York: Penguin.

Harkins, S. G. (1987). Social loafing and social facilitation. *Journal of Experimental Social Psychology, 23,* 1–18.

Harkins, S. G., & Szymanski, K. (1987). Social loafing and social facilitation: New wine in old bottles. In C. Hendrick (Ed.), *Review of personality and social psychology: Group processes and intergroup relations* (Vol. 9, pp. 167–188). Beverly Hills, CA: Sage.

Harlow, H. F. (1949). The formation of learning sets. *Psychological Review, 56,* 51–65.

Harlow, H. F. (1958). The nature of love. *American Psychologist, 13,* 673–685.

Harlow, H. F. (1962). Heterosexual affectional system in monkeys. *American Psychologist, 17,* 1–9.

Harlow, H. F., & Harlow, M. K. (1965). The affectional systems. In A. M. Schrier, H. F. Harlow, & F. Stollnitz (Eds.), *Behavior of non-human primates* (Vol. 2, pp. 287–334). New York: Academic Press.

Harlow, H. F., & Harlow, M. K. (1966). Learning to love. *American Scientist, 54,* 244–272.

Harlow, H. F., Harlow, M. K., & Meyer, D. R. (1950). Learning motivated by a manipulation drive. *Journal of Experimental Psychology, 40,* 228–234.

Harter, S. (1983). Developmental perspectives on the self-system. In P. H. Mussen (Ed.), *Handbook of child psychology* (4th ed., Vol. 4, pp. 275–385). New York: Wiley.

Harter, S. (1985). Competence as a dimension of self-evaluation: Toward a comprehensive model of self-worth. In R. Leahy (Ed.), *The development of the self* (pp. 55–118). New York: Academic Press.

Harter, S. (1990). Causes, correlates, and the functional role of global self-worth: A life-span perspective. In R. J. Sternberg & J. Kolligian, Jr. (Eds.), *Competence considered* (pp. 67–97). New Haven, CT: Yale University Press.

Harter, S., & Pike, R. (1984). The pictorial perceived competence scale for young children. *Child Development, 55,* 1969–1982.

Hartmann, E. (1968). The 90-minute sleep–dream cycle. *Archives of General Psychiatry, 18*(3), 280–286.

Hartshorne, H., & May, M. A. (1928). *Studies in the nature of character: Vol. 1. Studies in deceit.* New York: Macmillan.

Hastings, E. H., & Hastings, P. K. (Eds.). (1982). *Index to international public opinion, 1980–81.* Westport, CT: Greenwood Press.

Hatfield, E., & Rapson, R. L. (1992). Similarity and attraction in close relationships. *Communication Monographs, 59*(2), 209–212.

Hatfield, E., & Walster, G. W. (1981). *A new look at love.* Reading, MA: Addison-Wesley.

Hathaway, S. R., & McKinley, J. C. (1943). *Manual for the Minnesota Multiphasic Personality Inventory.* New York: Psychological Corporation.

Hathaway, S. R., & McKinley, J. C. (1951). *The Minnesota Multiphasic Personality Inventory* (rev. ed.). New York: Psychological Corporation.

Hayes, C. (1951). *The ape in our house.* New York: Harper & Row.

Hayes, D., & Ross, C. E. (1986). Body and mind: The effect of exercise, overweight, and physical health on psychological well-being. *Journal of Health and Social Behavior, 27,* 387–400.

Haynes, S. G., Feinleib, M., & Kannel, W. B. (1980). The relationship of psychosocial factors to coronary heart disease in the Framingham Study: III. Eight-year incidence of coronary heart disease. *American Journal of Epidemiology, 111,* 37–58.

Haynes, S. G., & Matthews, K. A. (1988). Review and methodological critique of recent studies on Type A behavior and cardiovascular disease. *Annals of Behavioral Medicine, 10,* 47–59.

Hazan, C., & Shaver, P. (1987). Romantic love conceptualized as an attachment process. *Journal of Personality and Social Psychology, 52,* 511–524.

Heath, S. B. (1983). *Ways with words.* New York: Cambridge University Press.

Heaton, J. M. (1968). *The eye: Phenomenology and psychology of function and disorder.* London: Tavistock.

Hegel, G. W. F. (1931). *The phenomenology of mind* (2nd ed.; J. B. Baillie, Trans.). London: Allen & Unwin. (Original work published 1807)

Heider, E. R., & Olivier, D. C. (1972). The structure of color space in naming and memory for two languages. *Cognitive Psychology, 3,* 337–354.

Heider, F. (1958). *The psychology of interpersonal relations.* New York: Wiley.

Heilbrun, A. B., & Witt, N. (1990). Distorted body image as a risk factor in anorexia nervosa: Replication and clarification. *Psychological Reports, 66,* 407–416.

Helmes, E., & Reddon, J. R. (1993). A perspective on developments in assessing psychopathology: A critical review of the MMPI and MMPI-2. *Psychological Bulletin, 113*(3), 453–471.

Helmholtz, H. von. (1896). *Vorträge und Reden.* Braunschweig, Germany: Vieweg und Sohn.

Helmholtz, H. L. F. von. (1930). *The sensations of tone* (A. J. Ellis, Trans.). New York: Longmans, Green. (Original work published 1863)

Helmholtz, H. L. F. von. (1962). *Treatise on physiological optics* (3rd ed., J. P. C. Southall, Ed. and Trans.). New York: Dover. (Original work published 1909)

Helson, H. (1964). *Adaptation level theory: An experimental and systematic approach to behavior.* New York: Harper.

Hendrick, C., & Hendrick, S. (1986). A theory and method of love. *Journal of Personality and Social Psychology, 50,* 392–402.

Henley, N. M. (1969). A psychological study of the semantics of animal terms. *Journal of Verbal Learning and Verbal Behavior, 8,* 176–184.

Hennessey, B. A., & Amabile, T. M. (1988). The conditions of creativity. In R. J. Sternberg (Ed.), *The nature of creativity.* New York: Cambridge University Press.

Henning, F. (1915). *Die Grundlagen, Methoden und*

Ergebnisse der Temperaturmessung. Braunschweig, Germany: Vieweg und Sohn.

Henry, J. P., & Stephens, P. M. (1977). *Stress, health, and the social environment: A sociobiologic approach to medicine.* New York: Springer-Verlag.

Hensel, H. (1981). *Thermoreception and temperature regulation.* London: Academic Press.

Herd, J. A. (1978). Physiological correlates of coronary-prone behavior. In T. Dembroski, S. Weiss, J. Shields, S. Haynes, & M. Feinleib (Eds.), *Coronary-prone behavior.* New York: Springer.

Hering, E. (1964). *Outlines of a theory of the light sense* (L. M. Hurvich & D. Jameson, Trans.). Cambridge, MA: Harvard University Press. (Original work published in 1878)

Herity, B., Moriarty, M., Daly, L., Dunn, J., & Bourke, G. J. (1982). The role of tobacco and alcohol in the aetiology of lung and larynx cancer. *British Journal of Cancer, 46,* 961–964.

Herman, J. L., Perry, J. C., & Van der Kolk, B. A. (1989). Childhood trauma in borderline personality disorder. *American Journal of Psychiatry, 146*(4), 490–495.

Herrnstein, R. J. (1973). *IQ in the meritocracy.* Boston: Atlantic Monthly Press.

Hetherington, A. W., & Ranson, S. W. (1940). Hypothalamic lesions and adiposity in the rat. *Anatomical Record, 78,* 149–172.

Heuch, I., Kvale, G., Jacobsen, B. K., & Bjelke, E. (1983). Use of alcohol, tobacco and coffee, and risk of pancreatic cancer. *British Journal of Cancer, 48,* 637–643.

Heyduk, R. G., & Bahrick, L. E. (1977). Complexity, response competition, and preference implications for affective consequences of repeated exposure. *Motivation and Emotion, 1,* 249–259.

Hilgard, E. R. (1965). *Hypnotic susceptibility.* New York: Harcourt, Brace & World.

Hilgard, E. R. (1977). *Divided consciousness: Multiple controls in human thought and action.* New York: Wiley.

Hilgard, E. R. (1987). *Psychology in America.* Orlando, FL: Harcourt Brace Jovanovich.

Hintzman, D. L. (1978). *The psychology of learning and memory.* San Francisco: Freeman.

Hirschfield, R. A., & Cross, C. K. (1982). Epidemiology of affective disorders. *Archives of General Psychiatry, 39,* 35–46.

Ho, D. Y. F. (1986). Chinese patterns of socialization. In M. H. Bond (Ed.), *The psychology of the Chinese people.* Hong Kong: Oxford University Press.

Hobson, J. A. (1989). *Sleep.* New York: Scientific American Library.

Hochberg, J. (1978). *Perception* (2nd ed.). Englewood Cliffs, NJ: Prentice-Hall.

Hoebel, B. G., & Teitelbaum, G. (1966). Weight regulation in normal and hypothalamic hyperphagic rats. *Journal of Comparative and Physiological Psychology, 61,* 189–193.

Hoffding, H. (1891). *Outlines of psychology.* New York: Macmillan.

Hoffman, C., Lau, I., & Johnson, D. R. (1986). The linguistic relativity of person cognition: An English–Chinese comparison. *Journal of Personality and Social Psychology, 51,* 1097–1105.

Hoffman, L. W. (1989). Effects of maternal employment in the two-parent family. *American Psychologist, 44,* 283–292.

Hofling, C. K., Brotzman, E., Dalrymple, S., Graves, N., & Pierce, C. (1966). An experimental study of nurse-physician relations. *Journal of Nervous and Mental Disease, 143,* 171–180.

Hogan, R., DeSoto, C. B., & Solano, C. (1977). Traits, tests, and personality research. *American Psychologist, 32,* 255–264.

Holinger, P. C. (1987). *Violent deaths in the United States.* New York: Guilford.

Holland, J., Holyoak, K. J., Nisbett, R. E., & Thagard, P. (1986). *Induction: Processes of inference, learning, and discovery.* Cambridge, MA: MIT Press.

Hollander, E. P. (1958). Conformity, status, and idiosyncrasy credit. *Psychological Review, 65,* 117–127.

Hollander, E. P. (1985). Leadership and power. In G. Lindzey & E. Aronson (Eds.), *Handbook of social psychology* (3rd ed., Vol. 2, pp. 485–537). New York: Random House.

Hollingshead, A. B., & Redlich, F. C. (1958). *Social class and mental illness.* New York: Wiley.

Hollon, S. D., & Kendall, P. C. (1980). Cognitive self-statements in depression: Development of an automatic thoughts questionnaire. *Cognitive Therapy and Research, 4,* 383–395.

Holmes, D. S., & Roth, D. L. (1989). *The measurement of cognitive and somatic anxiety.* Manuscript in preparation.

Holmes, T., & Rahe, R. (1967). The social readjustment rating scale. *Journal of Psychosomatic Research, 11,* 213–218.

Holstein, C. B. (1976). Irreversible, stepwise sequence in the development of moral judgment: A longitudinal study of males and females. *Child Development, 47,* 51–61.

Holyoak, K. J. (1984). Analogical thinking and human intelligence. In R. J. Sternberg (Ed.), *Advances in the psychology of human intelligence* (Vol. 2, pp. 199–230). Hillsdale, NJ: Erlbaum.

Homans, G. C. (1974). *Social behavior: Its elementary forms.* New York: Harcourt Brace Jovanovich.

Honsberger, R. W., & Wilson, A. F. (1973). Transcendental meditation in treating asthma. *Respiratory Therapy: The Journal of Inhalation Technology, 3,* 79–80.

Hooker, E. (1993). Reflections of a 40-year exploration: A scientific view on homosexuality. *American Psychologist, 48*(4), 450–453.

Hoosain, R., & Salili, F. (1987). Language differences in pronunciation speed for numbers, digit span, and mathematics ability. *Psychologia: An International Journal of Psychology in the Orient, 30*(1), 34–38.

Horn, J. L., & Cattell, R. B. (1966). Refinement and test of the theory of fluid and crystallized ability intelligences. *Journal of Educational Psychology, 57,* 253–270.

Horn, J. L., & Knapp, J. R. (1973). On the subjective character of the empirical base of Guilford's structure-of-intellect model. *Psychological Bulletin, 80,* 33–43.

Horney, K. (1937). *The neurotic personality of our time.* New York: Norton.

Horney, K. (1939). *New ways in psychoanalysis.* New York: Norton.

Horney, K. (1950). *Neurosis and human growth: The struggle toward self-realization.* New York: Norton.

House, J. S., & Smith, D. A. (1985). Evaluating the health effects of demanding work on and off the job. In T. F. Drury (Ed.), *Assessing physical fitness and physical activity in population-base surveys* (pp. 481–508). Hyattsville, MD: National Center for Health Statistics.

Houston, J. P. (1985). *Motivation.* New York: Macmillan.

Hovland, C. I., & Weiss, W. (1951). The influences of source credibility on communication effectiveness. *Public Opinion Quarterly, 15,* 635–650.

Howard, A., Pion, G. M., Gottfredson, G. D., Flattau, P. E., Oskamp, S., Pfafflin, S. M., Bray, D. W., & Burstein, A. G. (1986). The changing face of American psychology: A report from the committee on employment and human resources. *American Psychologist, 41*(12), 1311–1327

Howard, K. I., Kopta, S. M., Krause, M. S., & Orlinsky, D. E. (1986). The dose–effect relationship in psychotherapy. *American Psychologist, 41*(2), 159–164.

Howes, C. (1988). Peer interaction of young children. *Monographs of the Society for Research in Child Development, 53*(1, Serial No. 217).

Hubel, D. H., & Wiesel, T. N. (1967). Cortical and callosal connections concerned with the vertical meridian of visual fields in the cat. *Journal of Neurophysiology, 30*(6), 1561–1573.

Hubel, D. H., & Wiesel, T. N. (1979). Brain mechanisms of vision. *Scientific American, 241,* 150–162.

Huebner, R. R., & Izard, C. E. (1988). Mothers' responses to infants' facial expressions of sadness, anger, and physical distress. *Motivation and Emotion, 12,* 185–196.

Huesmann, L. R., Lagerspetz, K., & Eron, L. D. (1984). Intervening variable in the TV violence-aggression relation: Evidence from two countries. *Developmental Psychology, 20,* 746–775.

Hull, C. L. (1943). *Principles of behavior.* New York: Appleton-Century-Crofts.

Hull, C. L. (1952). *A behavior system: An introduction to behavior theory concerning the individual organism.* New Haven, CT: Yale University Press.

Hultsch, D. F., & Dixon, R. A. (1990). Learning and memory in aging. In J. E. Birren & K. W. Schaie (Eds.), *Handbook of the psychology of aging: The handbooks of aging* (3rd ed.). San Diego, CA: Academic Press.

Humphreys, L. G., & Davey, T. C. (1988). Continuity in intellectual growth from 12 months to 9 years. *Intelligence, 12,* 183–197.

Hunt, E. B. (1978). Mechanics of verbal ability. *Psychological Review, 85,* 109–130.

Hunt, E. B., Lunneborg, C., & Lewis, J. (1975). What does it mean to be high verbal? *Cognitive Psychology, 7,* 194–227.

Hurvich, L., & Jameson, D. (1957). An opponent-process theory of color vision. *Psychological Review, 64,* 384–404.

Huston, A. C. (1983). Sex-typing. In E. M. Hetherington (Ed.) & P. H. Mussen (Series Ed.), *Handbook of child psychology* (4th ed., Vol. 4, pp. 387–467). New York: Wiley.

Huston, A. C., Carpenter, C. J., Atwater, J. B., & Johnson, L. M. (1986). Gender, adult structuring of activities, and social behavior in middle childhood. *Child Development, 57*(5), 1200–1209.

Huston, T. L., & Levinger, G. (1978). Interpersonal attraction and relationships. *Annual Review of Psychology, 29,* 115–156.

Huttenlocher, J. (1968). Constructing spatial images: A strategy in reasoning. *Psychological Review, 75,* 550–560.

Huttenlocher, J., & Presson, C. C. (1973). Mental rotation and the perspective problem. *Cognitive Psychology, 4,* 277–299.

Hwang, K. K. (1981). Perception of life events: The application of nonmetric multidimensional scaling. *Acta Psychologica Taiwanica, 22,* 22–32.

Inhelder, B., & Piaget, J. (1958). *The growth of logical thinking from childhood to adolescence.* New York: Basic Books.

Inoue, S., Uchizono, K., & Nagasaki, H. (1982). Endogenous sleep-promoting factors. *Trends in Neurosciences, 5,* 218–220.

Insell, T. R. (1986). The neurobiology of anxiety. In B. F. Shaw, Z. V. Segal, T. M. Wallis, & F. E. Cashman (Eds.), *Anxiety disorders.* New York: Plenum.

Intelligence and its measurement: A symposium. (1921). *Journal of Educational Psychology, 12,* 123–147, 195–216, 271–275.

Insko, C. A. (1965). Verbal reinforcement of attitude. *Journal of Personality and Social Psychology, 21,* 621–623.

Isen, A. M. (1987). Passive affect, cognitive processes, and social behavior. In L. Berkowitz (Ed.), *Advances in experimental social psychology* (Vol. 20, pp. 203–253). New York: Academic Press.

Ivey, A. E., Ivey, M. B., & Simek-Morgan, L. (1993). *Counseling and psychotherapy: A multicultural perspective.* Boston: Allyn & Bacon.

Izard, C. E. (1977). *Human emotions.* New York: Plenum.

Izard, C. E. (1989). The structure and functions of emotions: Implications for cognition, motivation, and personality. In I. S. Cohen (Ed.), *The G. Stanley Hall lecture series* (Vol. 9, pp. 39–73). Washington, DC: American Psychological Association.

Izard, C. E., Kagan, J., & Zajonc, R. B. (1984). *Emotions, cognition, and behavior.* New York: Cambridge University Press.

Jacobs, B. L. (1987). How hallucinogenic drugs work. *American Scientist, 75,* 386–392.

Jacobs, B. L., & Trulson, M. E. (1979). Mechanisms of action of LSD. *American Scientist, 67,* 396–404.

James, W. (1890a). *Psychology.* New York: Holt.

James, W. (1890b). *Principles of psychology* (Vol. 1). New

York: Holt. (Reprinted 1983, Cambridge, MA: Harvard University Press)

James, W. (1970). *The principles of psychology* (Vol. 1). New York: Holt. (Original work published 1890)

Janis, I. L. (1958). *Psychological stress.* New York: Wiley.

Janis, I. L. (1972). *Victims of groupthink.* Boston: Houghton Mifflin.

Janos, P. M. (1990). The self-perception of uncommonly bright youngsters. In R. J. Sternberg & J. Kolligian (Eds.), *Competence considered* (pp. 98–116). New Haven, CT: Yale University Press.

Janowitz, H. D. (1967). Role of gastrointestinal tract in the regulation of food intake. In C. F. Code (Ed.), *Handbook of physiology: Alimentary canal 1.* Washington, DC: American Physiological Society.

Jemmott, J. B. III, & Locke, S. E. (1984). Psychosocial factors, immunologic mediation, and human susceptibility to infectious diseases: How much do we know? *Psychological Bulletin, 95,* 78–108.

Jenkins, C. D., Zyzanski, S. J., & Rosenman, R. H. (1979). *Jenkins Activity Survey.* Cleveland, OH: Psychological Corporation.

Jensen, A. R. (1980). *Bias in mental testing.* New York: Free Press.

Johnson, J. E. (1984). Psychological interventions and coping with surgery. In A. Baum, S. E. Taylor, & J. E. Singer (Eds.), *Handbook of psychology and health* (Vol. 4, pp. 167–188). Hillsdale, NJ: Erlbaum.

Johnson, J. E., Lauver, D. R., & Nail, L. M. (1989). Process of coping with radiation therapy. *Journal of Consulting and Clinical Psychology, 57,* 358–364.

Johnson-Laird, P. N. (1988). *The computer and the mind.* Cambridge, MA: Harvard University Press.

Johnson-Laird, P. N., & Steedman, M. (1978). The psychology of syllogisms. *Cognitive Psychology, 10,* 64–99.

Johnston, J. C., & McClelland, J. L. (1973). Visual factors in word perception. *Perception & Psychophysics, 14,* 365–370.

Jones, E. E., (1964). *Ingratiation: A social psychological analysis.* New York: Appleton-Century-Crofts.

Jones, E. E., & Davis, K. E. (1965). From acts to dispositions: The attribution process in person perception. In L. Berkowitz (Ed.), *Advances in experimental social psychology* (Vol. 2). New York: Academic Press.

Jones, E. E., & Harris, V. W. (1967). The attribution of attitudes. *Journal of Experimental Social Psychology, 3,* 1–24.

Jones, E. E., & Nisbett, R. (1971). *The actor and the observer: Divergent perceptions of the causes of behavior.* Morristown, NJ: General Learning Press.

Jones, E. E., & Nisbett, R. E. (1987). The actor and the observer: Divergent perceptions of causality. In E. E. Jones, D. E. Kanouse, H. H. Kelley, & R. E. Nisbett (Eds.), *Attribution: Perceiving the causes of behavior* (pp. 79–94). Morristown, NJ: General Learning Press.

Jones, E. E., Rock, L., Shaver, K. G., Goethals, G. R., & Ward, L. M. (1968). Pattern of performance and ability attribution: An unexpected primary effect. *Journal of Personality and Social Psychology, 10,* 317–340.

Jones, E. E., & Wortman, C. (1973). *Ingratiation: An attributional approach.* Morristown, NJ: General Learning Press.

Juel-Nielsen, N. (1965). Individual and environment: A psychiatric-psychological investigation of monozygous twins reared apart. *Acta Psychiatrica et Neurologica Scandinavica* (Monograph Supplement, 183).

Kagan, J. (1981). *The second year: The emergence of self-awareness.* Cambridge, MA: Harvard University Press.

Kagan, J. (1982). *Psychological research on the infant: An evaluative summary.* New York: W.T. Grant Foundation.

Kagan, J. (1986). *Psychological research on the human infant: An evaluative summary.* New York: Grant Foundation.

Kagan, J. (1989). Commentary [Special topic: Continuity in early cognitive development—conceptual and methodological challenges]. *Human Development, 32,* 172–176.

Kagan, J., Kearsley, R., & Zelazo P. (1978). *Infancy: Its place in human development.* Cambridge, MA: Harvard University Press.

Kagan, J., & Moss, H. A. (1962). *From birth to maturity.* New York: Wiley.

Kagan, J., Reznick, R. J., Clarke, C., Snidman, N., & Garcia-Coll, C. (1984). Behavioral inhibition to the unfamiliar. *Child Development, 55,* 2212–2225.

Kahneman, D. (1973). *Attention and effort.* Englewood Cliffs, NJ: Prentice-Hall.

Kahneman, D., & Tversky, A. (1971). Subjective probability: A judgment of representativeness. *Cognitive Psychology, 3,* 430–454.

Kahneman, D., & Tversky, A. (1973). On the psychology of prediction. *Psychological Review, 80,* 237.

Kahneman, D., & Tversky, A. (1979). Intuitive prediction: Biases and corrective procedures. *Management Science, 12,* 313–327.

Kail, R. V., Pellegrino, J. W., & Carter, P. (1980). Developmental changes in mental rotation. *Journal of Experimental Child Psychology, 29,* 102–116.

Kalmar, D. A., & Sternberg, R. J. (1988). Theory knitting: An integrative approach to theory development. *Philosophical Psychology, 1,* 153–170.

Kamin, L. J. (1969). Predictability, surprise, attention, and conditioning. In B. A. Campbell & R. M. Church (Eds.), *Punishment and aversive behavior* (pp. 279–296). New York: Appleton-Century-Crofts.

Kane, J., Honigfeld, G., Singer, J., Meltzer, H., et al. (1988). Clozapine for treatment resistant schizophrenics. *Archives of General Psychiatry, 45,* 789–796.

Kanner, L. (1943). Autistic disturbances of effective content. *Nervous Child, 2,* 217–240.

Kant, I. (1987). The critique of pure reason. In *Great books of the Western world: Vol. 42. Kant.* Chicago: Encyclopaedia Britannica.

Kaplan, C. A., & Davidson, J. E. (1989). *Incubation effects in problem solving.* Manuscript submitted for publication.

Kass-Simon, G., & Farnes, P. (Eds.). (1990). *Women of*

science: Righting the record. Bloomington: Indiana University Press.

Katz, D. (1960). The functional approach to the study of attitudes. *Public Opinion Quarterly, 24,* 163–204.

Katz, D., & Stotland, E. (1959). A preliminary statement to a theory of attitude structure and change. In S. Koch (Ed.), *Psychology: A study of a science* (Vol. 3, pp. 423–475). New York: McGraw-Hill.

Katz, J. J. (1972). *Semantic theory.* New York: Harper & Row.

Katz, J. J., & Fodor, J. A. (1963). The structure of a semantic theory. *Language, 39,* 170–210.

Kay, P. (1975). Synchronic variability and diachronic changes in basic color terms. *Language in Society, 4,* 257–270.

Kay, P., & Kempton, W. (1984). What is the Sapir–Whorf hypothesis? *American Anthropologist, 86,* 65–79.

Kearins, J. M. (1981). Visual spatial memory in Australian aboriginal children of desert regions. *Cognitive Psychology, 13*(3), 434–460.

Keating, D. P., & Bobbitt, B. L. (1978). Individual and developmental differences in cognitive-processing components of mental ability. *Child Development, 49,* 155–167.

Keesey, R. E. (1980). A set point analysis of the regulation of body weight. In A. J. Stunkard (Ed.), *Obesity.* Philadelphia: W. B. Saunders.

Keesey, R. E., Boyle, P. C., Kemnitz, J. W., & Mitchell, J. J. (1976). The role of the lateral hypothalamus in determining the body weight set point. In D. Novin, W. Wyrwicka, & G. A. Bray (Eds.), *Hunger: Basic mechanisms and clinical implications.* New York: Raven Press.

Keesey, R. E., & Powley, T. L. (1975). Hypothalamic regulation of body weight. *American Scientist, 63,* 558–565.

Keesey, R. E., & Powley, T. L. (1986). The regulation of body weight. *Annual Review of Psychology, 37,* 109–133.

Keil, F. C. (1981). Constraints on knowledge and cognitive development. *Psychological Review, 88,* 197–227.

Keil, F. C. (1989). *Concepts, kinds, and cognitive development.* Cambridge, MA: MIT Press.

Keller, M., Eckensberger, L. H., & von Rosen, K. (1989). A critical note on the conception of preconventional morality: The case of stage 2 in Kohlberg's theory. *International Journal of Behavioral Development, 12*(1), 57–69.

Kellogg, W. N., & Kellogg, L. A. (1933). *The ape and the child.* New York: McGraw-Hill.

Kelly, G. (1955). *The psychology of personal constructs.* New York: Norton.

Kelly, H. H. (1967). Attribution theory in social psychology. In D. L. Vine (Ed.), *Nebraska symposium on motivation.* Lincoln: University of Nebraska Press.

Kemeny, M. E., Cohen, R., Zegans, L. S., & Conant, M. A. (1989). Psychological and immunological predictors of genital herpes recurrence. *Psychosomatic Medicine, 51,* 195–208.

Kenrick, D. T., & Stringfield, D. O. (1980). Personality traits and the eye of the beholder: Crossing some traditional philosophical boundaries in the search for consistency in all the people. *Psychological Review, 87,* 88–104.

Kenrick, D. T., & Trost, M. R. (1993). The evolutionary perspective. In A. Beall & R. J. Sternberg (Eds.), *Perspectives on the psychology of gender.* New York: Guilford.

Kenshalo, D. R., Nafe, J. P., & Brooks, B. (1961). Variations in thermal sensitivity. *Science, 134,* 104–105.

Keppel, G., & Underwood, B. J. (1962). Proactive inhibition in short-term retention of single items. *Journal of Verbal Learning and Verbal Behavior, 1,* 153–161.

Kernberg, O. F. (1975). Transference and countertransference in the treatment of borderline patients. *Journal of the National Association of Private Psychiatric Hospitals, 7*(2), 14–24.

Kernberg, O. (1976). *Objects relations theory and clinical psychoanalysis.* New York: Jason Aronsen.

Kiecolt-Glaser, J. K., & Glaser, R. (1987). Psychosocial influences on herpes virus latency. In E. Kurstak, Z. J. Lipowski, & P. V. Morozov (Eds.), *Viruses, immunity, and mental disorders* (pp. 403–412). New York: Plenum.

Kiesler, D. J. (1966). Some myths of psychotherapy research and the search for a paradigm. *Psychological Bulletin, 65,* 110–136.

Kihlstrom, J. F. (1984). Conscious, subconscious, unconscious: A cognitive view. In K. S. Bowers & D. Meichenbaum (Eds.), *The unconscious: Reconsidered.* New York: Wiley.

Kihlstrom, J. F. (1985). Hypnosis. *Annual Review of Psychology, 36,* 385–418.

Kim, U., Triandis, H. D., & Kagitcibasi, C. (Eds.). (1994). *Individualism and collectivism: Theory and applications.* Newbury Park, CA: Sage.

Kimura, D. (1983). Sex differences in cerebral organization for speech and praxic functions. *Canadian Journal of Psychology, 37*(1), 19–35.

Kimura, D. (1987). Are men's and women's brains really different? *Canadian Psychology, 28*(2), 133–147.

Kirmayer, L. (1991). The place of culture in psychiatric nosology: *Taijin-kyofusho* and the DSM-III-R. *Journal of Nervous and Mental Disease, 179,* 19–28.

Kite, K. E., & Deaux, D. (1986). Sample Likert scale. *Basic and Applied Social Psychology, 7,* 137–162.

Klein, M. (1975). *The writings of Melanie Klein* (Vol. 3). London: Hogarth Press.

Kleinknecht, R. A., Dinnel, D. L., Tanouye, S., & Lonner, W. (1993). *The relationship between symptoms of* taijin-kyofusho *and social phobia among Japanese-Americans in Hawaii.* Unpublished manuscript submitted for publication, Department of Psychology, Western Washington University, Bellingham, WA.

Kleinmuntz, B., & Szucko, J. J. (1984). A field study of the fallibility of polygraphic lie detection. *Nature, 308,* 449–450.

Kleitman, N. (1963). *Sleep and wakefulness* (2nd ed.). Chicago: University of Chicago Press.

Klivington, K. A. (1989). *The science of mind.* Cambridge, MA: MIT Press.

Knox, V. J., Crutchfield, L., & Hilgard, E. R. (1975). The nature of task interference in hypnotic dissociation: An investigation of hypnotic behavior. *International Journal of Clinical and Experimental Hypnosis, 23,* 305–323.

Koegel, R. L., Schreibman, L., O'Neill, R. E. & Burke, J. C. (1983). The personality and family-interaction characteristics of parents of autistic children. *Journal of Consulting and Clinical Psychology, 51*, 683–692.

Kohlberg, L. (1963). The development of children's orientations toward a moral order: Pt. 1. Sequence in the development of moral thought. *Vita Humana, 6*, 11–33.

Kohlberg, L. (1984). The psychology of moral development: The nature and validity of moral stages. In *Essays on moral development* (Vol. 2). New York: Harper & Row.

Kohlberg, L., & Kramer, R. (1969). Continuities and discontinuities in childhood and adult moral development. *Human Development, 12*, 93–120.

Köhler, W. (1927). *The mentality of apes.* New York: Harcourt Brace.

Köhler, W. (1940). *Dynamics in psychology.* New York: Liveright.

Kohn, M. L. (1976). Social class and parental values: Another confirmation of the relationship. *American Sociological Review, 41*, 538–545.

Kohut, H. (1984). Selected problems of self-psychological theory. In J. D. Lichtenberg & S. Kaplan (Eds.), *Reflection on self psychology* (pp. 387–416). Hillsdale, NJ: Erlbaum.

Kolb, B., & Whishaw, I. Q. (1990). *Fundamentals of human neuropsychology* (3rd ed.). New York: Freeman.

Kolers, P. A. (1966a). Interlingual facilitation of short-term memory. *Journal of Verbal Learning and Verbal Behavior, 5*, 314–319.

Kolers, P. A. (1966b). Reading and talking bilingually. *American Journal of Psychology, 79*, 357–376.

Kosslyn, S. M. (1988). Aspects of a cognitive neuroscience of mental imagery. *Science, 240*, 1621–1626.

Kosslyn, S. M., Ball, T. M., & Reiser, B. J. (1978). Visual images preserve metric spatial information: Evidence from studies of image scanning. *Journal of Experimental Psychology: Human Perception and Performance, 4*, 47–60.

Kosslyn, S. M., & Koenig, O. (1992). *Wet mind: The new cognitive neuroscience.* New York: Free Press.

Kotovsky, K., Hayes, J. R., & Simon, H. A. (1985). Why are some problems hard? Evidence from the tower of Hanoi. *Cognitive Psychology, 17*, 248–294.

Kramer, D. A. (1990). Conceptualizing wisdom: The primacy of affect-cognition relations. In R. J. Sternberg (Ed.), *Wisdom: Its nature, origins, and development* (pp. 279–313). New York: Cambridge University Press.

Kramer, M. A. (1957). A discussion of the concepts of incidence and prevalence as related to epidemiologic studies of mental disorders. *American Journal of Public Health, 47*, 826–840.

Krantz, D. S., Baum, A., & Wideman, M. V. (1980). Assessment for preferences for self-treatment and information in health care. *Journal of Personality and Social Psychology, 39*, 977–990.

Krantz, L. (1992). *What the odds are: A-to-Z odds on everything you hoped or feared could happen.* New York: Harper Perennial.

Krantz, S., & Hammen, C. L. (1979). Assessment of cognitive bias in depression. *Journal of Abnormal Psychology, 88*, 611–619.

Krauthammer, C., & Klerman, G. L. (1979). The epidemiology of mania. In B. Shopsin (Ed.), *Manic illness* (pp. 11–28). New York: Raven Press.

Krech, D., & Crutchfield, R. (1958). *Elements of psychology.* New York: Knopf.

Kries, J. von (1895). Ueber die Natur gewisser mit den psychischen Vorgangen verknupfter Gehirnzustande. *Zeitschrift für Psychologie, 8*, 1–33.

Kuhlman, D. M., & Marshello, A. F. J. (1975). Individual differences in game motivation as moderators of pre-programmed strategy effects in prisoner's dilemma. *Journal of Personality and Social Psychology, 32*, 922–931.

Kuhn, T. S. (1970). *The structure of scientific revolutions* (2nd ed.). Chicago: University of Chicago Press.

Kulkarni, S. S., & Puhan, B. N. (1988). Psychological assessment: Its present and future trends. In J. Pandey (Ed.), *Psychology in India: The state of the art: Vol. 1. Personality and mental processes.* New Delhi: Sage.

Kunda, Z. (1987). Motivated inference: Self-serving generation and evaluation of causal theories. *Journal of Personality and Social Psychology, 45*, 763–771.

Kuo, Z. Y. (1921). Giving up instincts in psychology. *Journal of Philosophy, 17*, 645–664.

Kurtines, W., & Greif, E. B. (1974). The development of moral thought: Review and evaluation of Kohlberg's approach. *Psychological Bulletin, 81*, 453–470.

Labouvie-Vief, G. (1980). Beyond formal operations: Uses and limits of pure logic in life span development. *Human Development, 23*, 141–161.

Labouvie-Vief, G. (1990). Wisdom as integrated thought: Historical and developmental perspectives. In R. J. Sternberg (Ed.), *Wisdom: Its nature, origins, and development* (pp. 52–83). New York: Cambridge University Press.

Labouvie-Vief, G., & Schell, D. A. (1982). Learning and memory in later life. In B. B. Wolman (Ed.), *Handbook of developmental psychology.* Englewood Cliffs, NJ: Prentice-Hall.

Lachman, M. E. (1986). Locus of control in aging research: A case for multi-dimensional and domain-specific assessment. *Psychology and Aging, 1*, 34–40.

Laing, R. D. (1964). Is schizophrenia a disease? *International Journal of Social Psychiatry, 10*, 184–193.

Lamb, M. E. (1977a). The development of mother-infant and father-infant attachments in the second year of life. *Developmental Psychology, 13*, 637–648.

Lamb, M. E. (1977b). Father-infant and mother-infant interactions in the first year of life. *Child Development, 48*, 167–181.

Lamb, M. E. (1979). Separation and reunion behaviors as criteria of attachment to mothers and fathers. *Early Human Development, 3/4*, 329–339.

Lane, J. D., & Williams, R. B. (1987). Cardiovascular effects of caffeine and stress in regular coffee drinkers. *Psychophysiology, 24*, 157–164.

Lange, R. D., & James, W. (1922). *The emotions.* Baltimore: Williams & Wilkins.

Langer, E. J., Janis, I. L., & Wolfer, J. A. (1975). Reduction of psychological stress in surgical patients. *Journal of Experimental Social Psychology, 11,* 155–165.

Langley, P., & Jones, R. (1988). A computational model of scientific insight. In R. J. Sternberg (Ed.), *The nature of creativity.* New York: Cambridge University Press.

Langley, P., Simon, H. A., Bradshaw, G. L., & Zytkow, J. M. (1986). *Scientific discovery: Computational explorations of the creative processes.* Cambridge, MA: MIT Press.

Langsley, D. G., Hodes, M., & Grimson, W. R. (1993). In N. Sartorius, G. de Girolano, G. Andrews, G. A. German, & L. Eisenberg (Eds.), *Treatment of mental disorders: A review of effectiveness.* Geneva, Switzerland, and Washington, DC: World Health Organization and American Psychiatric Press.

Laragh, J. H. (1988). Pathophysiology of diastolic hypertension. *Health Psychology, 7*(Suppl.), 15–31.

Larkin, J. H., McDermott, J., Simon, D. P., & Simon, H. A. (1980). Expert and novice performance in solving physics problems. *Science, 208,* 1335–1342.

Latané, B. (1981). The psychology of social impact. *American Psychologist, 36,* 343–356.

Latané, B., & Darley, J. M. (1968). Group inhibition of bystander intervention. *Journal of Personality and Social Psychology, 10,* 215–221.

Latané, B., & Darley, J. M. (1970). *The unresponsive bystander: Why doesn't he help?* New York: Appleton-Century-Crofts.

Latané, B., Nida, S. A., & Wilson, D. W. (1981). The effects of a group size on helping behavior. In J. P. Rushton & R. M. Sorrentino (Eds.), *Altruism and helping behavior: Social, personality, and developmental perspectives.* Hillsdale, NJ: Erlbaum.

Latané, B., Williams, K., & Harkins, S. (1979). Many hands make light the work: The causes and consequences of social loafing. *Journal of Personality and Social Psychology, 37,* 822–832.

Lau, R. R., Bernard, T. M., & Hartman, K. A. (1989). Further explorations of common-sense representations of common illness. *Health Psychology, 8,* 195–219.

Lau, R. R., & Hartman, K. A. (1983). Common sense representations of common illnesses. *Health Psychology, 2,* 167–185.

Lazar, I., & Darlington, R. (1982). Lasting effects of early education: A report from the consortium for longitudinal studies. *Monographs of the Society for Research in Child Development, 47*(2–3, Serial No. 195).

Lazarus, A. A. (1961). Group therapy of phobic disorders by systematic desensitization. *Journal of Abnormal and Social Psychology, 63,* 504–510.

Lazarus, A. A. (1968). Learning theory and the treatment of depression. *Behaviour Research and Therapy, 6,* 83–89.

Lazarus, A. A. (1989). *The practice of multimodal therapy.* Baltimore: Johns Hopkins University Press.

Lazarus, R. S. (1977). A cognitive analysis of biofeedback control. In G. E. Schwartz & J. Beatty (Eds.), *Biofeedback: Theory and research* (pp. 69–71). New York: Academic Press.

Lazarus, R. S. (1982). Thoughts on the relations between emotion and cognition. *American Psychologist, 37*(9), 1019–1024.

Lazarus, R. S. (1984). On the primacy of cognition. *American Psychologist, 39,* 124–129.

Lazarus, R. S., Kanner, A., & Folkman, F. (1980). Emotions: a cognitive-phenomenological analysis. In R. Plutchik & H. Kellerman (Eds.), *Emotion: Theory, research and experience. Vol. 1. Theories of emotion.* New York: Academic Press.

Le Bon, G. (1896). *The crowd: A study of the popular mind.* New York: Macmillan.

Lederer, R. (1987). *Anguished English.* New York: Pocket Books.

Lederer, R. (1991). *The miracle of language.* New York: Pocket Books.

LeDoux, J. E. (1986). The neurobiology of emotion. In J. E. LeDoux & W. Hirst (Eds.), *Mind and brain: Dialogues in cognitive neuroscience* (pp. 301–354). Cambridge, England: Cambridge University Press.

LeDoux, J. E., Romanski, L., & Xagoraris, A. (1989). Indelibility of subcortical emotional memories. *Journal of Cognitive Neuroscience, 1,* 238–243.

Lee, J. A. (1977). A typology of styles of loving. *Personality and Social Psychology Bulletin, 3,* 173–182.

Lee, J. A. (1988). Love-styles. In R. J. Sternberg & M. L. Barnes (Eds.), *Psychology of love* (pp. 38–67). New Haven, CT: Yale University Press.

Leon, A. S. (1983). Exercise and coronary heart disease. *Hospital Medicine, 19,* 38–59.

Leon, A. S., & Fox, S. M. III. (1981). Physical fitness. In E. L. Wynder (Ed.), *The book of health* (pp. 283–341). New York: Franklin Watts.

Leon, G. R. (1974). *Case histories of deviant behavior: A social learning analysis.* Boston: Holbrook Press.

Lepper, M. R., Greene, D., & Nisbett, R. E. (1973). Undermining children's intrinsic interest with extrinsic rewards: A test of the "overjustification" hypothesis. *Journal of Personality and Social Psychology, 28,* 129–137.

Lerner, M. J. (1970). The desire for justice and reactions to victims. In J. R. Macaulty & L. Berkowitz (Eds.), *Altruism and helping behavior* (pp. 205–229). New York: Academic Press.

Lerner, M. J. (1980). *The belief in a just world: A fundamental delusion.* New York: Plenum.

Lerner, M. J., & Meindl, J. R. (1981). Justice and altruism. In J. P. Rushton & R. M. Sorrentino (Eds.), *Altruism and helping behavior: Social, personality, and developmental perspectives* (pp. 213–232). Hillsdale, NJ: Erlbaum.

Lesgold, A. (1988). Problem solving. In R. J. Sternberg & E. E. Smith (Eds.), *The psychology of human thought* (pp. 188–213). New York: Cambridge University Press.

Lesgold, A. M., Rubinson, H., Feltovich, P., Glaser, R., Klopfer, D., & Wang, Y. (1988). Expertise in a complex skill: Diagnosing x-ray pictures. In M. T. H. Chi, R. Glaser, & M. Farr (Eds.), *The nature of expertise.* Hillsdale, NJ: Erlbaum.

LeVay, S. (1991). A difference in hypothalamic structure between heterosexual and homosexual men. *Science, 253,* 1034–1037.

Levenkron, J. C., & Moore, L. G. (1988). The Type A behavior pattern: Issues for intervention research. *Annals of Behavioral Medicine, 10,* 78–83.

Levenson, R. W., Ekman, P., & Friesen, W. V. (1990). Voluntary facial action generates emotion-specific autonomic nervous system activity. *Psychophysiology, 27*(4), 363–384.

Leventhal, H., & Tomarken, A. J. (1986). Emotion: Today's problems. *Annual Review of Psychology, 37,* 565–610.

Levine, L. E. (1983). Mine: Self-definition in 2-year-old boys. *Developmental Psychology, 19,* 544–549.

Levine, R. A., & Campbell, D. T. (1972). *Ethnocentrism: Theories of conflict, ethnic attitudes, and group behavior.* New York: Wiley.

Levine, R. V., & Bartlett, K. (1984). Pace of life, punctuality, and coronary heart disease in six countries. *Journal of Cross-Cultural Psychology, 15*(2), 233–255.

Levinson, D. J. (1978). *The seasons of a man's life.* New York: Ballantine.

Levinson, D. J. (1986). A conception of adult development. *American Psychologist, 41,* 3–13.

Levi-Strauss, C. (1966). *The savage mind.* Chicago: University of Chicago Press.

Levy, J. (1974). Cerebral asymmetries as manifested in split-brain man. In M. Kinsbourne & W. L. Smith (Eds.), *Hemispheric disconnection and cerebral function.* Springfield, IL: Charles C. Thomas.

Levy, J., Trevarthen, C., & Sperry, R. W. (1972). Perception of bilateral chimeric figures following hemispheric deconnexion. *Brain, 95*(1), 61–78.

Lewin, K. (1948). *Resolving social conflicts: Selected papers on group dynamics.* New York: Harper.

Lewin, K. (1951). *Field theory in social science: Selected theoretical papers.* New York: Harper. (Original work published 1935)

Lewinsohn, P. M. (1974). A behavioral approach to depression. In R. J. Friedman & M. M. Katz (Eds.), *The psychology of depression: Contemporary theory and research.* New York: Halstead Press.

Lewinsohn, P. M., Steinmetz, J. L., Larson, D. W., & Franklin, J. (1981). Depression-related cognitions: Antecedent or consequence? *Journal of Abnormal Psychiatry, 136,* 231–233.

Lewis, M., & Brooks, J. (1974). Self, other and fear: Infants' reactions to people. In M. Lewis & L. A. Rosenblum (Eds.), *The origins of fear.* New York: Wiley.

Lewis, M., & Brooks-Gunn, J. (1981). Visual attention at three months as a predictor of cognitive functioning at two years of age. *Intelligence, 5,* 131–140.

Liberman, A. M., Cooper, F. S., Shankweiler, D. P., & Studdert-Kennedy, M. (1967). Perception of the speech code. *Psychological Review, 74,* 431–461.

Liberman, A. M., & Mattingly, I. G. (1985). The motor theory of speech perception revised. *Cognition, 21,* 1–36.

Liebert, R. M., & Baron, R. A. (1972). Some immediate effects of televised violence on children's behavior. *Developmental Psychology, 6,* 469–475.

Linz, D., Donnerstein, E., & Penrod, S. (1984). The effects of multiple exposures to filmed violence against women. *Journal of Communication, 43,* 130–147.

Linz, D., Donnerstein, E., & Penrod, S. (1988). Effects of long-term exposure to violent and sexually degrading depictions of women. *Journal of Personality and Social Psychology, 55,* 758–768.

Lipman, M. (1982). *Harry Stottlemeier's discovery.* Upper Montclair, NJ: First Mountain Foundation.

Lippa, R. A. (1990). *Introduction to social psychology.* Belmont, CA: Wadsworth.

Lissner, L., Odell, P. M., D'Agostino, R. B., Stokes, J., Kreger, B. E., Belanger, A. J., & Brownell, K. D. (1991). Variability of body weight and health outcomes in the Framingham population. *New England Journal of Medicine, 324,* 1839–1844.

Lobitz, W. C., & Post, R. D. (1979). Parameters of self-reinforcement and depression. *Journal of Abnormal Psychology, 88,* 33–41.

Locke, E. A., & Latham, G. P. (1985). The application of goal setting to sports. *Journal of Sport Psychology, 7,* 205–222.

Locke, E. A., Shaw, K. N., Saari, L. M., & Latham, G. P. (1981). Goal setting and task performance: 1969–1980. *Psychological Bulletin, 90,* 125–152.

Locke, J. (1961). An essay concerning human understanding. In *Great books of the Western world: Vol. 35. Locke, Berkeley, Hume.* Chicago: Encyclopaedia Britannica. (Original work published 1690)

Loftus, E. F. (1975). Leading questions and the eyewitness report. *Cognitive Psychology, 7,* 560–572.

Loftus, E. F. (1977). Shifting human color memory. *Memory and Cognition, 5,* 696–699.

Loftus, E. F., & Loftus, G. R. (1980). On the permanence of stored information in the human brain. *American Psychologist, 35,* 409–420.

Loftus, E. F., Miller, D. G., & Burns, H. J. (1978). Semantic integration of verbal information into a visual memory. *Journal of Experimental Psychology: Human Learning and Memory, 4,* 19–31.

Lonner, W. J. (1989). The introductory psychology text: Beyond Ekman, Whorf, and biased IQ tests. In D. M. Keats, D. Munro, & L. Mann (Eds.), *Heterogeneity in cross-cultural psychology.* Amsterdam: Swets & Zeitlinger.

Lonner, W. J. (1990). An overview of cross-cultural testing and assessment. In R. W. Brislin (Ed.), *Applied cross-cultural psychology.* Newbury Park, CA: Sage.

Lonner, W. J., & Berry, J. W. (1986). Sampling and surveying. In W. J. Lonner & J. W. Berry (Eds.), *Field methods in cross-cultural research: Vol. 8. Cross-cultural research and methodology series.* Beverly Hills, CA: Sage.

Lopez, S., & Nuñez, J. A. (1987). Cultural factors considered in selected diagnostic criteria and interview schedules. *Journal of Abnormal Psychology, 96,* 270–272.

Loranger, A. W. (1984). Sex differences in age of onset of schizophrenia. *Archives of General Psychiatry, 41,* 157–161.

Lorber, J. (1975). Good patients and problem patients: Conformity and deviance in a general hospital. *Journal of Health and Social Behavior, 16,* 213–225.

Lorenz, K. (1937). The companion in the bird's world. *Auk, 54,* 245–273.

Lorenz, K. (1950). The comparative method in studying innate behavior patterns. *Symposium for the Society for Experimental Biology, 4,* 221–268.

Lott, A., & Lott, B. (1968). A learning theory approach to interpersonal attitudes. In A. G. Greenwald, T. C. Brock, & T. M. Ostrom (Eds.), *Psychological foundations of attitude.* New York: Academic Press.

Lovaas, O. I. (1968). Learning theory approach to the treatment of childhood schizophrenia. In *California Mental Health Research Symposium: No. 2. Behavior theory and therapy.* Sacramento: California Department of Mental Hygiene.

Lovaas, O. I. (1977). *The autistic child.* New York: Wiley.

Lovaas, O. I., Koegel, R., Simmons, J. Q., & Long, J. S. (1973). Some generalization and follow-up measures on autistic children in behavior therapy. *Journal of Applied Behavior Analysis, 6,* 131–166.

Luce, R. D., & Raiffa, H. (1957). *Games and decisions.* New York: Wiley.

Luchins, A. S. (1942). Mechanization in problem solving. *Psychological Monographs, 54*(6, Whole No. 248).

Lucy, J. A., & Schweder, R. A. (1979). Whorf and his critics: Linguistic and nonlinguistic influences on color memory. *American Anthropologist, 81,* 581–615.

Lucy, J. A., & Schweder, R. A. (1988). The effect of incidental conversation on memory for focal colors. *American Anthropologist, 90,* 923–931.

Ludwick-Rosenthal, R., & Neufeld, R. W. J. (1988). Stress management during noxious medical procedures: An evaluative review of outcome studies. *Psychological Bulletin, 104,* 326–342.

Lumsdaine, A. A., & Janis, I. L. (1953). Resistance to "counterpropaganda" produced by one-sided and two-sided "propaganda" presentation. *Public Opinion Quarterly, 17,* 311–318.

Lundberg, U. (1976). Urban commuting: Crowdedness and catecholamine excretion. *Journal of Human Stress, 2,* 26–32.

Luria, A. R. (1968). *The mind of a mnemonist.* New York: Basic Books.

Luria, A. R. (1973). *The working brain.* London: Penguin.

Luria, A. R. (1984). *The working brain: An introduction to neuropsychology* (B. Haigh, Trans.). Harmondsworth, England: Penguin. (Original work published 1973)

Ma, H. K. (1988). The Chinese perspectives on moral judgment development. *International Journal of Psychology, 23*(2), 201–227.

Maccini, C. A. (1989). *Life scientists.* Baltimore: Media Materials.

MacFarlane, A. (1975). Olfaction in the development of social preferences in the human neonate. *Ciba Foundation Symposium, 33,* 103–117.

Mackworth, N. H. (1948). The breakdown of vigilance during prolonged visual search. *Quarterly Journal of Experimental Psychology, 1,* 6–21.

MacLeod, C. M., Hunt, E. B., & Mathews, N. N. (1978). Individual differences in the verification of sentence-picture relationships. *Journal of Verbal Learning and Verbal Behavior, 17,* 493–507.

Maehr, M., & Nicholls, J. (1980). Culture and achievement motivation: A second look. In N. Warren (Ed.), *Studies in cross-cultural psychology* (Vol. 2). London: Academic Press.

Maher, B. A. (1972). The language of schizophrenia: A review and interpretation. *British Journal of Psychiatry, 120,* 4–17.

Maher, B. A. (1983). A tentative theory of schizophrenic utterance. In B. A. Maher & W. Maher (Eds.), *Progress in experimental personality research* (Vol. 12, pp. 1–52). Orlando, FL: Academic Press.

Malamuth, N. M., & Check, J. V. P. (1981). The effects of mass media exposure on acceptance of violence against women: A field experiment. *Journal of Research in Personality, 15,* 436–446.

Mandler, G. (1980). The generation of emotion: A psychological theory. In R. Plutchik & H. Kellerman (Eds.), *Emotion: Theory, research, and experience* (Vol. 1). New York: Academic Press.

Manji, H. K., Hsiao, J. K., Risby, E. D., et al. (1991). The mechanisms of action of lithium: I. Effects on serotonergic and noradrenergic systems in normal subjects. *Archives of General Psychiatry, 48,* 505–512.

Mann, J. (1973). *Time-dated psychotherapy.* Cambridge, MA: Harvard University Press.

Mantyla, T. (1986). Optimizing cue effectiveness: Recall of 500 and 600 incidentally learned words. *Journal of Experimental Psychology: Learning, Memory, and Cognition, 12,* 66–71.

Maqsud, M., & Rouhani, S. (1990). Self-concept and moral reasoning among Batswana adolescents. *Journal of Social Psychology, 130*(6), 829–830.

Marcel, A. J. (1983). Conscious and unconscious perception: An approach to the relations between phenomenal experience and perceptual processes. *Cognitive Psychology, 15,* 238–300.

Marcia, J. E. (1966). Development and validation of ego identity status. *Journal of Personality and Social Psychology, 3*(5), 551–558.

Marcia, J. E. (1980). Identity in adolescence. In J. Adelson (Ed.), *Handbook of adolescent psychology* (pp. 159–187). New York: Wiley.

Markman, E. M. (1977). Realizing that you don't understand: A preliminary investigation. *Child Development, 48,* 986–992.

Markman, E. M. (1979). Realizing that you don't understand: Elementary school children's awareness of inconsistencies. *Child Development, 50,* 643–655.

Markman, H. J. (1981). Prediction of marital distress: A 5-year follow-up. *Journal of Consulting and Clinical Psychology, 49,* 760–762.

Marks, I. M., & Gelder, M. G. (1967). Transvestism and fetishism: Clinical and psychological changes during faradic aversion. *British Journal of Psychiatry, 113,* 711–729.

Markus, H. (1977). Self-schemata and processing information about the self. *Journal of Personality and Social Psychology, 35*, 63–78.

Markus, H., Cross, S., & Wurt, E. (1990). The role of the self-system in competence. In R. J. Sternberg & J. Kolligan (Eds.), *Competence considered* (pp. 205–226). New Haven, CT: Yale University Press.

Markus, H. R., & Kitayama, S. (1991). Culture and the self: Implications for cognition, emotion, and motivation. *Psychological Review, 98*(2), 224–253.

Markus, H., & Smith, J. (1981). The influence of self-schema on the perception of others. In N. Cantor & J. F. Kihlstrom (Eds.), *Personality, cognition, and social interaction* (pp. 233–262). Hillsdale, NJ: Erlbaum.

Marmor, G. S. (1975). Development of kinetic images: When does the child first represent movement in mental images? *Cognitive Psychology, 7*, 548–559.

Marmor, G. S. (1977). Mental rotation and number conservation: Are they related? *Developmental Psychology, 13*, 320–325.

Marr, D. (1982). *Vision.* San Francisco: Freeman.

Marshall, G. D., & Zimbardo, P. G. (1979). Affective consequences of inadequately explained arousal. *Journal of Personality and Social Psychology, 37*, 970–985.

Marslen-Wilson, W. D. (1980). Speech understanding as a psychological process. In J. C. Simon (Ed.), *Spoken language generation and understanding* (pp. 39–67). Dordrecht, Netherlands: Reidel.

Martelli, M. F., Auerbach, S. M., Alexander, J., & Mercuri, L. G. (1987). Stress management in the health care setting: Matching interventions with patient coping styles. *Journal of Consulting and Clinical Psychology, 55*, 201–207.

Martin, F. E. (1985). The treatment and outcome of anorexia nervosa in adolescents: A prospective study and five year follow-up. *Journal of Psychiatric Research, 19*, 509–514.

Martin, J. A. (1981). A longitudinal study of the consequences of early mother–infant interaction: A microanalytic approach. *Monographs of the Society for Research in Child Development, 46*(203, Serial No. 190).

Martin, L. (1986). Eskimo words for snow: A case study in the genesis and decay of an anthropological example. *American Psychologist, 88*, 418–423.

Martin, M. (1979). Local and global processing: The role of sparsity. *Memory and Cognition, 7*, 476–484.

Martindale, C. (1981). *Cognition and consciousness.* Homewood, IL: Dorsey Press.

Maslow, A. H. (1943). A theory of human motivation. *Psychological Review, 50*, 370–396.

Maslow, A. H. (1954). *Motivation and personality.* New York: Harper & Row.

Maslow, A. H. (1970). *Motivation and personality* (2nd ed.). New York: Harper.

Massaro, D. W. (1987). *Speech perception by ear and eye: A paradigm for psychological inquiry.* Hillsdale, NJ: Erlbaum.

Masters, W. H., & Johnson, V. E (1966). *Human sexual response.* Boston: Little, Brown.

Matarazzo, J. D. (1992). Biological and physiological correlates of intelligence. *Intelligence, 16*(3–4), 257–258.

Matas, L., Arend, R., & Sroufe, L. A. (1978). Continuity of adaptation in the second year: The relationship between quality of attachment and later competence. *Child Development, 49*, 547–556.

Matlin, M. (1993). *The psychology of women* (2nd ed.). Fort Worth, TX: Harcourt Brace Jovanovich.

Maurer, D., & Adams, R. J. (1987). Emergence of the ability to discriminate a blue from a gray at one month of age. *Journal of Experimental Child Psychology, 44*, 147–156.

Maurer, D., & Maurer, C. (1988). *The world of the newborn.* New York: Basic Books.

May, R. (1969). *Love and will.* New York: Norton.

Mayer, D. J. (1952). The glucostatic theory of regulation of food intake and the problem of obesity. *Bulletin of the New England Medical Center, 14*, 43.

Mayer, D. J. (1953). Glucostatic mechanism of regulation of food intake. *New England Journal of Medicine, 249*, 13–16.

McAdams, D. P. (1990). *The person: An introduction to personality psychology.* New York: Harcourt Brace Jovanovich.

McCall, R. B. (1989). The development of intellectual functioning in infancy and the prediction of later IQ. In S. D. Osofsky (Ed.), *The handbook of infant development* (pp. 707–741). New York: Wiley.

McCall, R. B., Kennedy, C. B., & Applebaum, M. I. (1977). Magnitude of discrepancy and the distribution of attention in infants. *Child Development, 48*, 772–786.

McCarley, R. W., & Hobson, J. A. (1981). REM sleep dreams and the activation-synthesis hypothesis. *American Journal of Psychiatry, 138*, 904–912.

McClelland, D. C. (1961). *The achieving society.* Princeton, NJ: Van Nostrand.

McClelland, D. C. (1985). *Human motivation.* New York: Scott, Foresman.

McClelland, D. C., Atkinson, J. W., Clark, R. A., & Lowell, E. L. (1953). *The achievement motive.* New York: Appleton-Century-Crofts.

McClelland, D. C., Atkinson, J. W., Clark, R. A., & Lowell, E. L. (1976). *The achievement motive.* New York: Irvington.

McClelland, D. C., & Teague, G. (1975). Predicting risk preferences among power-related tasks. *Journal of Personality, 43*, 266–285.

McClelland, D. C., & Winter, D. G. (1969). *Motivating economic achievement.* New York: Free Press.

McClintock, C. G., & Liebrand, W. B. G. (1988). Role of interdependence structure, individual value orientation, and another's strategy in social decision making: A transformational analysis. *Journal of Personality and Social Psychology, 55*(3), 396–409.

McCormick, D. A., & Thompson, R. F. (1984). Cerebellum: Essential involvement in the classically conditioned eyelid response. *Science, 223*, 296–299.

McCrae, R. R., & Costa, P. T., Jr. (1987). Validation of the five-factor model of personality across instruments and observers. *Journal of Personality and Social Psychology, 52*, 81–90.

McCrae, R., & John, O. (1992). An introduction to the five-factor model and its applications. *Journal of Personality, 60*, 175–215.

McCutcheon, M. (1989). *The compass in your nose and other astonishing facts about humans.* Los Angeles: Tarcher.

McDougall, W. (1908). *An introduction to social psychology.* London: Methuen.

McGarry-Roberts, P. A., Stelmack, R. M., & Campbell, K. B. (1992). Intelligence, reaction time, and event-related potentials. *Intelligence, 16*(3–4), 289–313.

McGuire, W. J. (1983). A contextualist theory of knowledge: Its implications for innovation and reform in psychological research. In L. Berkowitz (Ed.), *Advances in experimental social psychology* (Vol. 16, pp. 1–47). New York: Academic Press.

McGurk, H., & MacDonald, J. (1976). Hearing lips and seeing voices. *Nature, 264,* 746–748.

McHugh, P. R., & Moran, T. H. (1985). The stomach: A conception of its dynamic role in satiety. In J. M. Sprague & A. N. Epstein (Eds.), *Progress in psychobiology and physiological psychology* (Vol. 11, pp. 197–232). Orlando, FL: Academic Press.

McKinlay, J. B. (1975). Who is really ignorant—Physician or patient? *Journal of Health and Social Behavior, 16,* 3–11.

McKoon, G., & Ratcliff, R. (1980). Priming in item recognition: The organization of propositions in memory for text. *Journal of Verbal Learning and Verbal Behavior, 19,* 369–386.

Meacham, J. A. (1983). Wisdom and the context of knowledge: Knowing that one doesn't know. In D. Kuhn & J. A. Meacham (Eds.), *On the development of developmental psychology* (pp. 111–134). Basel, Switzerland: Karger.

Meacham, J. A. (1990). The loss of wisdom. In R. J. Sternberg (Ed.), *Wisdom: Its nature, origins, and development* (pp. 181–211). New York: Cambridge University Press.

Meeker, W. B., & Barber, T. X. (1971). Toward an explanation of stage hypnosis. *Journal of Abnormal Psychology, 77,* 61–70.

Meeus, W. H., & Raaijmakers, Q. A. (1986). Administrative obedience: Carrying out orders to use psychological-administrative violence. *European Journal of Social Psychology, 16*(4), 311–324.

Meichenbaum, D., & Cameron, R. (1982). Cognitive behavior therapy. In G. T. Wilson & C. M. Franks (Eds.), *Contemporary behavior therapy: Conceptual and empirical foundations.* New York: Guilford.

Meier, R. P. (1991). Language acquisition by deaf children. *American Scientist, 79,* 60–76.

Melamed, B. G., & Siegel, L. (1975). Reduction of anxiety in children facing hospitalization and surgery by use of filmed modeling. *Journal of Consulting and Clinical Psychology, 43,* 511–521.

The melting of a mighty myth: Guess what—Eskimos don't have 23 words for snow. (1991, July 22). *Newsweek, 118*(4), p. 63.

Meltzoff, A. N., & Borton, R. W. (1979). Intermodal matching by human neonates. *Nature, 282,* 403–404.

Meltzoff, A. N., & Moore, M. K. (1989). Imitation in newborn infants: Exploring the range of gestures imitated and the underlying mechanisms. *Developmental Psychology, 25*(6), 954–962.

Melzack, R. (Ed.). (1983). *Pain measurement and assessment.* New York: Raven Press.

Melzack, R., & Wall, P. D. (1965). Pain mechanisms: A new theory. *Science, 150,* 971–979.

Melzack, R., & Wall, P. D. (1982). *The challenge of pain.* New York: Basic Books.

Melzack, R., Wall, P. D., & Ty, T. C. (1982). Acute pain in an emergency clinic: Latency of onset and descriptor patterns related to different injuries. *Pain, 14*(1), 33–43.

Merton, R. K. (1973). Behavior patterns of scientists. In *The Sociology of Science.* Chicago: University of Chicago Press.

Mesquita, B., & Frijda, N. H. (1992). Cultural variations in emotions: A review. *Psychological Bulletin, 112*(3), 179–204.

Messadié, G. (1991a). *Great inventions through history.* New York: Chambers.

Messadié, G. (1991b). *Great modern inventions.* New York: Chambers.

Messadié, G. (1991c). *Great scientific discoveries.* New York: Chambers.

Messer, B., & Harter, S. (1985). *The self-perception scale for adults.* Unpublished manuscript, University of Denver.

Michotte, A. (1963). *The perception of causality.* New York: Basic Books.

Milgram, S. (1963). Behavioral study of obedience. *Journal of Abnormal and Social Psychology, 67,* 371–378.

Milgram, S. (1965). Some conditions of obedience and disobedience to authority. *Human Relations, 18,* 57–76.

Milgram, S. (1974). *Obedience to authority: An experimental view.* New York: Harper & Row.

Mill, J. S. (1843). *A system of logic, ratiocinative and inductive.* London: J. W. Parker.

Mill, J. S. (1887). *A system of logic.* New York: Harper & Brothers.

Miller, D. T., & McFarland, C. (1987). Pluralistic ignorance: When similarity is interpreted as dissimilarity. *Journal of Personality and Social Psychology, 53,* 298–305.

Miller, G. A. (1956). The magical number seven, plus or minus two: Some limits on our capacity for processing information. *Psychological Review, 63,* 81–97.

Miller, G. A. (1990). *The science of words.* New York: Scientific American Library.

Miller, G. A., Galanter, E. H., & Pribram, K. H. (1960). *Plans and the structure of behavior.* New York: Holt, Rinehart & Winston.

Miller, N., & Brewer, M. B. (Eds.). (1984). *Groups in contact: The psychology of desegregation.* New York: Academic Press.

Mills, R. T., & Krantz, D. S. (1979). Information, choice, and reactions to stress: A field experiment in a blood bank with laboratory analogue. *Journal of Personality and Social Psychology, 4,* 608–620.

Milner, B., Corkin, S., & Teuber, H. L. (1968). Further analysis of the hippocampal amnesic syndrome: 14-year follow-up study of H. M. *Neuropsychologia, 6,* 215–234.

Mischel, W. (1968). *Personality and assessment.* New York: Wiley.

Mischel, W. (1973). Toward a social learning reconceptualization of personality. *Psychological Review, 80,* 252–283.

Mischel, W. (1977). On the future of personality measurement. *American Psychologist, 32,* 246–254.

Mischel, W. (1986). *Introduction to personality* (4th ed.). New York: Holt, Rinehart & Winston.

Mischel, W., & Peake, P. K. (1982). Beyond deja vu in the search for cross-situational consistency. *Psychological Review, 89*(6), 730–755.

Mischel, W., & Peake, P. K. (1983). Some facets of consistency: Replies to Epstein, Funder, and Bem. *Psychological Review, 90,* 394–402.

Mishkin, M., & Petri, H. L. (1984). Memories and habits: Some implications for the analysis of learning and retention. In L. R. Squire & N. Butters (Eds.), *Neurophysiology of memory* (pp. 287–296). New York: Guilford.

Miyake, K., Chen, S., & Campos, J. J. (1985). Infant temperament, mother's mode of interaction, and attachment in Japan: An interim report. In I. Bretherton & E. Waters (Eds.), *Growing points of attachment in theory and research* (Monographs of the Society for Research in Child Development 50, 1–2, Serial No. 209).

Moghaddam, F. M., Taylor, D. M., & Wright, S. C. (1993). *Social psychology in cross-cultural perspective.* New York: Freeman.

Money, J., Wiedeking, C., Walker, P. A., & Gain, D. (1976). Combined antiandrogenic and counseling program for treatment of 46 XY and 47 XYY sex offenders. *Hormones, behavior, and psychopathology, 66,* 105–109.

Montagu, A. (1976). *The nature of human aggression.* New York: Oxford University Press.

Moos, R. H. (1982). Coping with acute health crises. In T. Millon, C. Green, & R. Meagher (Eds.), *Handbook of clinical health psychology.* New York: Plenum.

Moos, R. H. (1988). Life stressors and coping resources influence health and well-being. *Psychological Assessment, 4,* 133–158.

Moos, R. H., & Schaefer, J. A. (1986). Life transitions and crises: A conceptual overview. In R. H. Moos (Ed.), *Coping with life crises: An integrated approach.* New York: Plenum.

Moray, N. (1959). Attention in dichotic listening: Affective cues and the influence of instructions. *Quarterly Journal of Experimental Psychology, 11,* 56–60.

Morelli, G. A., Rogoff, B., Oppenheim, D., & Goldsmith, D. (1992). Cultural variations in infants' sleeping arrangements: Questions of independence. *Developmental Psychology, 28,* 604–613.

Morgan, C. D., & Murray, H. A. (1935). A method for investigating fantasy: The Thematic Apperception Test. *Archives of Neurology and Psychiatry, 34,* 289–306.

Morgan, C. T., & Morgan, J. T. (1940). Studies in hunger II: The relation of gastric denervation and dietary sugar to the effect of insulin upon food-intake in the rat. *Journal of Genetic Psychology, 57,* 153–163.

Morton, T. U. (1978). Intimacy and reciprocity of exchange: A comparison of spouses and strangers. *Journal of Personality and Social Psychology, 36,* 72–81.

Moscovici, S. (1976). *Social influence and social change.* London: Academic Press.

Moscovici, S. (1980). Toward a theory of conversion behavior. In L. Berkowitz (Ed.), *Advances in Experimental Social Psychology, 6,* 149–202.

Moscovici, S., & Zavolloni, M. (1969). The group as a polarizer of attitudes. *Journal of Personality and Social Psychology, 12,* 125–135.

Moyers, B. D. (1993). *Healing and the mind.* New York: Doubleday.

Murdock, B. B., Jr. (1961). Short-term retention of single paired-associates. *Psychological Reports, 8,* 280.

Murphy, J. (1976). Psychiatric labeling in cross-cultural perspective. *Science, 191,* 1019–1028.

Murray, H. A. (1938). *Explorations in personality.* New York: Oxford University Press.

Murray, H. A. (1943a). *Explorations in personality.* New York: Oxford University Press. (Original work published 1938)

Murray, H. A. (1943b). *Thematic apperception test.* Cambridge, MA: Harvard University Press.

Murray, H. A. (1943c). *The Thematic Apperception Test: Manual.* Cambridge, MA: Harvard University Press.

Murray, K. (1993, May 9). When the therapist is a computer. *New York Times,* Sect. 3, p. 25.

Murstein, B. I. (1986). *Paths to marriage.* Beverly Hills, CA: Sage.

Murstein, B. I. (1988). A taxonomy of love. In R. J. Sternberg & M. L. Barnes (Eds.), *Psychology of love* (pp. 13–37). New Haven, CT: Yale University Press.

Murstein, B. I., & Brust, R. G. (1985). Humor and interpersonal attraction. *Journal of Personality Assessment, 49*(6), 637–640.

Myers, B. J. (1984a). Mother–infant bonding: Rejoinder to Kennell and Klaus. *Developmental Review, 4,* 283–288.

Myers, B. J. (1984b). Mother–infant bonding: The status of this critical-period hypothesis. *Developmental Review, 4,* 240–274.

Myers, D. G., & Bishop, G. D. (1970). Discussion effects on racial attitudes. *Science, 169,* 778–789.

Myers, D. G., & Lamm, H. (1976). The group polarization phenomenon. *Psychological Bulletin, 83,* 602–627.

Myers, J. K., Weissman, M. M., Tischler, G. L., Holzer, C. E., Leaf, P. J., & Stoltzman, R. (1984). Six-month prevalence of psychiatric disorders in three communities: 1980 to 1982. *Archives of General Psychiatry, 41,* 959–967.

Myerson, A. (1940). Review of *Mental disorders in urban areas: An ecological study of schizophrenia and other psychoses. American Journal of Psychiatry, 96,* 995–997.

Nairne, J. S., & Crowder, R. G. (1982). On the locus of the stimulus suffix effect. *Memory and Cognition, 10,* 350–357.

Nasby, W. (1985). Private self-consciousness, articulation of the self-schema, and the recognition memory of trait adjectives. *Journal of Personality and Social Psychology, 49,* 704–709.

Nathans, J., Thomas, D., & Hogness, D. S. (1986).

Molecular genetics of human color vision: The genes encoding blue, green, and red pigments. *Science, 232*(47), 193–202.

National Center for Health Statistics. (1988). Advance report of final mortality statistics, 1986. *NCHS Monthly Vital Statistics Report, 37*(Suppl. 6).

National Center for Health Statistics. (1993). *Advance data from vital and health statistics* (U.S. Department of Health and Human Services, Public Health Service, Centers for Disease Control, National Center for Health Statistics). Washington, DC: U.S. Government Printing Office.

Navon, D. (1977). Forest before trees: The precedence of global features in visual perception. *Cognitive Psychology, 9,* 353–383.

Navon, D., & Gopher, D. (1979). On the economy of the human-processing system. *Psychological Review, 86,* 214–255.

Neimark, E. D. (1975). Intellectual development during adolescence. In F. D. Horowitz (Ed.), *Review of child development research* (Vol. 4). Chicago: University of Chicago Press.

Neisser, U. (1967). *Cognitive psychology.* New York: Appleton-Century-Crofts.

Neisser, U. (1982). Snapshots or benchmarks? In U. Neisser (Ed.), *Memory observed: Remembering in natural contexts.* San Francisco: Freeman.

Nelson, C. (1990). *Gender and the social studies: Training preservice secondary social studies teachers.* Doctoral dissertation, University of Minnesota.

Nelson, K. (1973). Structure and strategy in learning to talk. *Monograph of the Society for Research in Child Development, 38*(149).

Nelson, R. E., & Craighead, W. E. (1977). Selective recall of positive and negative feedback, self-control behaviors and depression. *Journal of Abnormal Psychology, 86,* 379–388.

Nelson, R. E., & Craighead, W. E. (1981). Tests of a self-control model of depression. *Behavior Therapy, 12,* 123–129.

Nelson, T. O., & Rothbart, R. (1972). Acoustic savings for items forgotten from long-term memory. *Journal of Experimental Psychology, 93,* 357–360.

Nerenz, D. R., & Leventhal, H. (1983). Self-regulation theory in chronic illness. In T. G. Burish & L. A. Bradley (Eds.), *Coping with chronic disease: Research and applications* (pp. 13–38). New York: Academic Press.

Neto, F., Williams, J. E., & Widner, S. C. (1991). Portuguese children's knowledge of sex stereotypes: Effects of age, gender, and socioeconomic status. *Journal of Cross-Cultural Psychology, 22*(3), 376–388.

Newcomb, T. M. (1943). *Personality and social change.* New York: Dryden.

Newcomb, T. M. (1957). Social psychological theory. In J. H. Roher & M. Sherif (Eds.), *Social psychology at the crossroads.* New York: Harper.

Newell, A., & Simon, H. A. (1972). *Human problem solving.* Englewood Cliffs, NJ: Prentice-Hall.

Newman, H. H., Freeman, F. N., & Holzinger, K. J. (1937). *Twins: A study of heredity and environment.* Chicago: University of Chicago Press.

Newport, E. L. (1990). Maturational constraints on language learning. *Cognitive Science, 14,* 11–28.

Nielson, S. (1990). Epidemiology of anorexia nervosa in Denmark from 1983–1987: A nationwide register study of psychiatric admission. *Acta Psychiatricia Scandinavica, 81,* 507–514.

Niemczynski, A., Czyzowska, D., Pourkos, M., & Mirski, A. (1988). The Cracow study with Kohlberg's Moral Judgment Interview: Data pertaining to the assumption of cross-cultural validity. *Polish Psychological Bulletin, 19*(1), 43–53.

Nisan, M., & Kohlberg, L. (1982). Universality and variation in moral judgment: A longitudinal and cross-sectional study in Turkey. *Child Development, 53,* 865–876.

Nisbett, R. E. (1972). Hunger, obesity, and the ventromedial hypothalamus. *Psychological Review, 79,* 433–453.

Nisbett, R. E., Caputo, C., Legant, P., & Maracek, J. (1973). Behavior as seen by the actor and as seen by the observer. *Journal of Personality and Social Psychology, 27,* 154–164.

Nisbett, R. E., & Wilson, T. D. (1977). Telling more than we can know: Verbal reports on mental processes. *Psychological Review, 84,* 231–259.

Noesjirwan, J. (1977). Contrasting cultural patterns on interpersonal closeness in doctors' waiting rooms in Sydney and Jakarta. *Journal of Cross-Cultural Psychology, 8*(3), 357–368.

Norman, D. A. (1968). Toward a theory of memory and attention. *Psychological Review, 75,* 522–536.

Norman, D. A., & Rumelhart, D. E. (1975). *Explorations in cognition.* San Francisco: Freeman.

Norman, W. T. (1963). Toward an adequate taxonomy of personality attributes: Replicated factor structure in peer nomination personality ratings. *Journal of Abnormal and Social Psychology, 66,* 574–583.

Notarius, C., & Markman, H. (1993). *We can work it out.* New York: Putnam.

Oatley, K. (1993). Those to whom evil is done. In R. S. Wyer & T. K Srull (Eds.), *Perspectives on anger and emotion: Advances in social cognition* (Vol. 6, pp. 159–165). Hillsdale, NJ: Erlbaum.

Ochse, R. (1990). *Before the gates of excellence: The determinants of creative genius.* New York: Cambridge University Press.

Ohbuchi, K., & Kambara, T. (1985). Attacker's intent and awareness of outcome, impression management, and retaliation. *Journal of Experimental Social Psychology, 2,* 321–330.

Ojemann, G. A. (1982). Models of the brain organization for higher integrative functions derived with electrical stimulation techniques. *Human Neurobiology, 1,* 243–250.

Ojemann, G. A., & Mateer, C. (1979). Human language cortex: Localization of memory, syntax, and sequential motor–phoneme identification systems. *Science, 205,* 1401–1403.

Ojemann, G. A., & Whitaker, H. A. (1978). The bilingual brain. *Archives of Neurology, 35,* 409–412.

Olds, J., & Milner, P. (1954). Positive reinforcement produced by electrical stimulation of septal area and other regions of the rat brain. *Journal of Comparative and Physiological Psychology, 47,* 419–427.

Öngel, U., & Smith, P. B. (1994). Who are we and where are we going? JCCP approaches its 100th issue. *Journal of Cross-Cultural Psychology, 25*(1), 25–54.

Oomara, Y. (1976). Significance of glucose insulin and free fatty acid on the hypothalamic feeding and satiety neurons. In D. Novin, W. Wyrwicka, & G. Bray (Eds.), *Hunger: Basic mechanisms and clinical implications.* New York: Raven Press.

Orne, M. T. (1959). Hypnosis: Artifact and essence. *Journal of Abnormal Psychology, 58,* 277–299.

Ornstein, R. (1977). *The psychology of consciousness* (2nd ed.). New York: Harcourt Brace Jovanovich.

Ornstein, R. (1986). *The psychology of consciousness.* (2nd rev. ed.). New York: Pelican Books.

Otis, L. S. (1984). The adverse effects of meditation. In D. H. Shapiro & R. N. Walsh (Eds.), *Meditation: Classical and contemporary perspectives.* New York: Aldine.

Ott, E. M. (1989). Effects of male–female ratio at work: Policewomen and male nurses. *Psychology of Women Quarterly, 13*(1), 41–57.

Paivio, A. (1971). *Imagery and verbal processes.* New York: Holt, Rinehart & Winston.

Paivio, A. (1986). *Mental representations: A dual coding approach.* New York: Oxford University Press.

Palmer, S. E. (1975). The effects of contextual scenes on the identification of objects. *Memory and Cognition, 3,* 519–526.

Papp, L., & Gorman, J. M. (1990). Suicidal preoccupation during fluoxetine treatment. *American Journal of Psychiatry, 147,* 1380.

Pappenheimer, J. R., Koski, G., Fencl, V., Karnovsky, M. L., & Krueger, J. (1975). Extraction of sleep-promoting factors from cerebrospinal fluid and from brains of sleep-deprived animals. *Journal of Neurophysiology, 38,* 1299–1311.

Paradis, M. (1977). Bilingualism and aphasia. In H. A. Whitaker & H. Whitaker (Eds.), *Studies in neurolinguistics* (Vol. 3). New York: Academic Press.

Paradis, M. (1981). Neurolinguistic organization of a bilingual's two languages. In J. E. Copeland & P. W. Davis (Eds.), *The seventh LACUS forum.* Columbia, SC: Hornbeam Press.

Parfyonova, G. V., Korichneva, I. L., Suvorov, Y. I., & Krasnikova, T. L. (1988). Characteristics of lymphocyte β-adrenoreceptors in essential hypertension: Effects of propranolol treatment and dynamic exercise. *Health Psychology, 7*(Suppl.), 33–52.

Park, R. D., & Walters, R. H. (1967). Some factors influencing the efficacy of punishment training for inducing response inhibition. *Monographs of the Society for Research in Child Development, 32*(1, Whole No. 109).

Parke, R. D. (1981). *Fathers.* Cambridge, MA: Harvard University Press.

Parke, R. D., & Asher, S. R. (1983). Social and personality development. In M. R. Rosenzweig & L. W. Porter (Eds.), *Annual Review of Psychology, 34,* 465–509.

Parke, R. D., Berkowitz, L., Leyens, J. P., West, S. G., & Sebastian, R. J. (1977). Some effects of violent and nonviolent movies on the behavior of juvenile delinquents. In L. Berkowitz (Ed.), *Advances in experimental social psychology* (Vol. 10). New York: Academic Press.

Parke, R. D., & Sawin, D. B. (1980). The family in early infancy: Social interaction and attitudinal analyses. In F. A. Pederson (Ed.), *The father-infant relationship: Observational studies in a family context.* New York: Praeger.

Parke, R. D., & Tinsley, B. J. (1987). Family interaction in infancy. In J. D. Osofsky (Ed.), *Handbook of infant development* (pp. 579–641). New York: Wiley.

Parten, M. (1932). Social participation among preschool children. *Journal of Abnormal and Social Psychology, 27,* 243–269.

Pascual-Leone, J. (1984). Attentional, dialectic, and mental effort. In M. L. Commons, F. A. Richards, & C. Armon (Eds.), *Beyond formal operations.* New York: Plenum.

Pascual-Leone, J. (1990). An essay on wisdom: Toward organismic processes that make it possible. In R. J. Sternberg (Ed.), *Wisdom: Its nature, origins, and development* (pp. 244–278). New York: Cambridge University Press.

Paul, G. L. (1966). *Insight vs. desensitization in psychotherapy.* Stanford, CA: Stanford University Press.

Paul, G. L. (1967). Strategy of outcome research in psychotherapy. *Journal of Consulting Psychology, 31,* 109–118.

Paul, G. L., & Lentz, R. J. (1977). *Psychosocial treatment of chronic mental patients: Milieu versus social learning programs.* Cambridge, MA: Harvard University Press.

Paul, G. L., & Menditto, A. A. (1992). Effectiveness of inpatient treatment programs for mentally ill adults in public psychiatric facilities. *Applied and Preventive Psychology: Current Scientific Perspectives, 1,* 41–63.

Pavlov, I. P. (1928). *Lectures on conditioned reflexes: The higher nervous activity of animals* (Vol. 1, H. Gantt, Trans.). London: Lawrence & Wishart.

Pavlov, I. P. (1955). *Selected works.* Moscow: Foreign Languages Publishing House.

Paykel, E. S., & Tanner, J. (1976). Life events, depressive relapse and maintenance treatment. *Psychological Medicine, 6,* 481–485.

Payne, R. W., Matussek, P., & George, E. I. (1959). An experimental study of schizophrenic thought disorder. *Journal of Mental Science, 105,* 627–652.

Peabody, D., & Goldberg, L. R. (1989). Some determinants of factor structures from personality-trait descriptors. *Journal of Personality and Social Psychology, 57*(3), 552–567.

Pedersen, P. B., Draguns, J. G., Lonner, W. J., & Trimble, J. E. (Eds.). (in press). *Counseling across cultures* (4th ed.). Newbury Park, CA: Sage.

Penfield, W. (1955). The permanent record of the stream of consciousness. *Acta Psychologica, 11,* 47–69.

Penfield, W. (1969). Consciousness, memory, and man's conditioned reflexes. In K. H. Pribram (Ed.), *On the biology of learning.* New York: Harcourt, Brace & World.

Penfield, W., & Roberts, L. (1959). *Speech and brain mechanisms.* Princeton, NJ: Princeton University Press.

Penrose, R. (1989). *The emperor's new mind: Concerning computers, minds, and the laws of physics.* New York: Oxford University Press.

Peplau, L. A. (1983). Roles and gender. In H. H. Kelley (Ed.), *Close relationships.* New York: Freeman.

Perkins, D. (1981). *The mind's best work.* Cambridge, MA: Harvard University Press.

Perkins, D. N. (1988). The possibility of invention. In R. J. Sternberg (Ed.), *The nature of creativity.* New York: Cambridge University Press.

Perlmutter, M. (1983). Learning and memory through adulthood. In M. W. Riley, B. B. Hess, & K. Bond (Eds.), *Aging in society: Selected reviews of recent research.* Hillsdale, NJ: Erlbaum.

Perlmutter, M., & Lange, G. (1978). A developmental analysis of recall–recognition distinctions. In P. A. Ornstein (Ed.), *Memory development in children.* Hillsdale, NJ: Erlbaum.

Perris, C., & Herlofson, J. (1993). Cognitive therapy. In N. Sartorius, G. de Girolano, G. Andrews, G. A. German, & L. Eisenberg (Eds.), *Treatment of mental disorders: A review of effectiveness.* Geneva, Switzerland, and Washington, DC: World Health Organization and American Psychiatric Press.

Perry, J., & Bratman, M. (1986). *Introduction to philosophy: Classical and contemporary readings.* New York: Oxford University Press.

Pervin, L. A. (1985). Personality: Current controversies, issues, and directions. *Annual Review of Psychology, 36,* 83–114.

Petersen, S., Fox, P. T., Posner, M. I., Mintun, M., & Raichle, M. E. (1988). Positron-emission tomographic studies of the cortical anatomy of single-word processing. *Nature, 331*(6157), 585–589.

Peterson, L. R., & Peterson, M. J. (1959). Short-term retention of individual verbal items. *Journal of Experimental Psychology, 58,* 193–198.

Petty, R. E., & Cacioppo, J. T. (1981). *Attitudes and persuasion: Classic and contemporary approaches.* Dubuque, IA: William C. Brown.

Pfaffman, C. (1974). Specificity of the sweet receptors of the squirrel monkey. *Chemical Senses and Flavor, 1,* 61–67.

Pfeiffer, W. M. (1982). Culture-bound syndromes. In I. Al-Issa (Ed.), *Culture and psychopathology.* Baltimore: University Park Press.

Phares, E. J. (1988). *Introduction to personality* (2nd ed.). Glenview, IL: Scott, Foresman.

Phares, E. J. (1991). *Introduction to personality* (3rd ed.). New York: HarperCollins.

Phillips, D. A. (1984). The illusion of incompetence among academically competent children. *Child Development, 55,* 2000–2016.

Phillips, D. A. (1987). Socialization of perceived academic competence among highly competent children. *Child Development, 58,* 1308–1320.

Phillips, D. A., & Zimmerman, M. (1990). The developmental course of perceived competence and incompetence among competent children. In R. J. Sternberg &

J. Kolligian, Jr. (Eds.), *Competence considered* (pp. 41–66). New Haven, CT: Yale University Press.

Piaget, J. (1928). *Judgment and reasoning in the child.* London: Routledge & Kegan Paul.

Piaget, J. (1952). *The origins of intelligence in children.* New York: International Universities Press.

Piaget, J. (1954). *The construction of reality in the child.* New York: Basic Books.

Piaget, J. (1955). *The language and thought of the child.* New York: Meridian Books.

Piaget, J. (1965). *The moral judgment of the child* (M. Gabain, Trans.). New York: Harcourt. (Original work published 1932)

Piaget, J. (1969). *The child's conception of physical causality.* Totowa, NJ: Littlefield, Adams.

Piaget, J. (1972). *The psychology of intelligence.* Totowa, NJ: Littlefield, Adams.

Piliavin, J. A., Dovidio, J. F., Gaertner, S. S., & Clark, R. D., III. (1981). *Emergency intervention.* New York: Academic Press.

Pinto, R. P., & Hollandsworth, J. G., Jr. (1989). Using videotape modeling to prepare children psychologically for surgery: Influence of parents and costs versus benefits of providing preparation services. *Health Psychology, 8,* 79–95.

Pisoni, D. B., Nusbaum, H. C., Luce, P. A., & Slowiaczek, L. M. (1985). Speech perception, word recognition and the structure of the lexicon. *Speech Communication, 4,* 75–95.

Plomin, R. (1986). *Development, genetics, and psychology.* Hillsdale, NJ: Erlbaum.

Plomin, R. C. (1989). Environment and games: Determinants of behavior. *American Psychologist, 44,* 105–111.

Plutchik, R. (1980). *Emotion: A psychoevolutionary analysis.* New York: Harper & Row.

Plutchik, R. (1983). Emotions in early development: A psychoevolutionary approach. In R. Plutchik & H. Kellerman (Eds.), *Emotion: Theory, research, and experience* (Vol. 2). New York: Academic Press.

Plutchik, R., & Kellerman, H. (1974). *Emotions Profile Index manual.* Los Angeles: Western Psychological Services.

Plutchik, R., & Kellerman, H. (Eds.). (1983). *Emotion: Theory, research, and experience. Vol. 2. Emotions in early development.* New York: Academic Press.

Poincaré, H. (1913). *The foundations of science.* New York: Science Press.

Poizner, H., Bellugi, U., & Klima, E. S. (1990). Biological foundations of language: Clues from sign language. *Annual Review of Neuroscience, 13,* 282–307.

Poizner, H., Kaplan, E., Bellugi, U., & Padden, C. A. (1984). Visual-spatial processing in deaf brain-damaged signers. *Brain & Cognition, 3*(3), 281–306.

Pokorny, A. D. (1968). Myths about suicide. In H. Resnik (Ed.), *Suicidal behaviors.* Boston: Little, Brown.

Polanyi, M. (1976). Tacit knowing. In M. Marx & F. Goodson (Eds.), *Theories in contemporary psychology.* New York: Macmillan.

Polivy, J., & Herman, C. P. (1983). *Breaking the diet habit.* New York: Basic Books.

Polivy, J., & Herman, C. P. (1985). Dieting and binging. *American Psychologist, 40,* 193–201.

Pomerantz, J. R. (1981). Perceptual organization in information processing. In M. Kubovy & J. R. Pomerantz (Eds.), *Perceptual organization* (pp. 141–180). Hillsdale, NJ: Erlbaum.

Poon, L. W. (1987). *Myths and truisms: Beyond extant analyses of speed of behavior and age.* Address to the Eastern Psychological Association Convention.

Poortinga, Y. H., Kop, P. F. M., & van de Vijver, F. J. R. (1990). Differences between psychological domains in the range of cross-cultural variation. In P. J. D. Drenth, J. A. Sergeant, & R. J. Takens (Eds.), *European perspectives in psychology: Vol. 3. Work and organizational, social and economic, cross-cultural* (pp. 355–376). Chichester, England: Wiley.

Pope, H. G., & Katz, D. L. (1988). Affective and psychotic symptoms associated with anabolic steroid use. *American Journal of Psychiatry, 145*(4), 487–490.

Popper, K. R. (1959). *The logic of scientific discovery.* London: Hutchinson.

Porter, C. A., & Suedfeld, P. (1981). Integrative complexity in the correspondence of literary figures: Effects of personal and societal stress. *Journal of Personality and Social Psychology, 40,* 321–330.

Posner, M. I., & Mitchell, R. F. (1967). Chronometric analysis of classification. *Psychological Review, 74,* 392–409.

Premack, D. (1959). Toward empirical behavior laws: I. Positive reinforcement. *Psychological Review, 66,* 219–233.

Premack, D. (1971). Language in chimpanzees? *Science, 172,* 808–822.

Preston, G. A. N. (1986). Dementia in elderly adults: Prevalence and institutionalization. *Journal of Gerontology, 41,* 261–267.

Pullum, G. K. (1991). *The great Eskimo vocabulary hoax and other irreverent essays on the study of language.* Chicago: University of Chicago Press.

Pylyshyn, Z. W. (1973). What the mind's eye tells the mind's brain: A critique of mental imagery. *Psychological Bulletin, 80,* 1–24.

Rabin, M. D., & Cain, W. S. (1986). Determinants of measured olfactory sensitivity. *Perception and Psychophysics, 39,* 361–373.

Rapaport, D., Gill, M. M., & Schafer, R. (1968). *Diagnostic psychological testing.* New York: International Universities Press.

Raps, C. S., Peterson, C., Jonas, M., & Seligman, M. E. P. (1982). Patient behavior in hospitals: Helplessness, reactance, or both? *Journal of Personality and Social Psychology, 42,* 1036–1041.

Reed, T. E., & Jensen, A. R. (1992). Conduction velocity in a brain nerve pathway of normal adults correlates with intelligence level. *Intelligence, 16*(3–4), 259–272.

Reep, D. C., & Dambrot, F. H. (1988). In the eye of the beholder: Viewer perceptions of TV's male/female working partners. *Communication Research, 15*(1), 51–69.

Rehm, L. P. (1977). A self-control model of depression. *Behavior Therapy, 8,* 787–804.

Reicher, G. M. (1969). Perceptual recognition as a function of meaningfulness of stimulus material. *Journal of Experimental Psychology, 81,* 275–280.

Reinisch, J. M., Ziemba-Davis, M., & Sanders, S. A. (1991). Hormonal contributions to sexually dimorphic behavioral development in humans. Special Issue: Neuroendocrine effects on brain development and cognition. *Psychoneuroendocrinology, 16*(1–3), 213–278.

Reissland, N. (1988). Neonatal imitation in the first hour of life: Observations in rural Nepal. *Developmental Psychology, 24,* 464–469.

Reitman, J. S. (1971). Mechanisms of forgetting in short-term memory. *Cognitive Psychology, 2,* 185–195.

Reitman, J. S. (1974). Without surreptitious rehearsal, information in short-term memory decays. *Journal of Verbal Learning and Verbal Behavior, 13,* 365–377.

Renzulli, J. S. (1986). The three ring conception of giftedness: A developmental model for creative productivity. In R. J. Sternberg & J. E. Davidson (Eds.), *Conceptions of giftedness* (pp. 53–92). New York: Cambridge University Press.

Rescorla, R. A. (1967). Pavlovian conditioning and its proper control procedures. *Psychological Review, 74,* 71–80.

Rescorla, R. A., & Wagner, A. R. (1972). A theory of Pavlovian conditioning: Variations in the effectiveness of reinforcement and non-reinforcement. In A. H. Black & W. F. Prokasy (Eds.), *Classical conditioning: Vol. 2. Current research and theory.* New York: Appleton-Century-Crofts.

Resnik, H. L. P. (Ed.). (1968). *Suicidal behaviors.* Boston: Little, Brown.

Rest, J. R. (1975). Longitudinal study of the Defining Issues Test of moral judgment: A strategy for analyzing developmental change. *Developmental Psychology, 11*(6), 738–748.

Rest, J. R. (1979). *Development in judging moral issues.* Minneapolis: University of Minnesota Press.

Rest, J. R. (1983). Moral development. In P. H. Mussen (Ed.), *Handbook of child psychology* (4th ed., Vol. 3, pp. 556–629). New York: Wiley.

Rest, J. R., & Thoma, S. J. (1985). Relation of moral judgment development to formal education. *Developmental Psychology, 21*(4), 709–714.

Restak, R. (1984). *The brain.* New York: Bantam.

Restak, R. (1988). *The mind.* New York: Bantam.

Restle, F. (1970). Moon illusion explained on the basis of relative size. *Science, 167,* 1092–1096.

Rholes, W. S., Jones, M., & Wade, C. (1980). A developmental study of learned helplessness. *Developmental Psychology, 16,* 616–624.

Richards, D. D., & Siegler, R. S. (1984). The effects of task requirements on children's life judgments. *Child Development, 55,* 1687–1696.

Ricks, S. S. (1985). Father-infant interaction: A review of empirical research. *Family Relations, 34,* 505–511.

Riegel, K. F. (1973). Dialectical operations: The final period of cognitive development. *Human Development, 16,* 346–370.

Rieser, J., Yonas, A., & Wilkner, K. (1976). Radial localization of odors by human newborns. *Child Development, 47,* 856–859.

Ring, K. (1980). *Life at death: A scientific investigation of the near-death experience.* New York: Coward-McCann.

Ringelman, M. (1913). Recherches sur les moteurs animés: Travail de l'homme. *Annales de l'Institur National Agronomique, 2s série, tom XII,* 1–40.

Roberts, G., & Owen, J. (1988). The near-death experience. *British Journal of Psychiatry, 153,* 607–617.

Robertson, L. C. (1986). From Gestalt to neo-Gestalt. In T. J. Knapp & L. C. Robertson (Eds.), *Approaches to cognition: Contrasts and controversies* (pp. 159–188). Hillsdale, NJ: Erlbaum.

Robertson, L. S. (1986). Behavioral and environmental interventions for reducing motor vehicle trauma. In L. Breslow, J. E. Fielding, & L. B. Lave (Eds.), *Annual review of public health* (Vol. 7). Palo Alto, CA: Annual Reviews.

Robins, L. N., Helzer, J. E., Weissman, M. M., Orvaschel, H., Gruenberg, E., Burke, J. D., & Regier, D. (1984). Lifetime prevalence of specific psychiatric disorders in three sites. *Archives of General Psychiatry, 41,* 949–958.

Robinson, D. N. (1986). *An intellectual history of psychology.* Madison: University of Wisconsin Press.

Robinson, L. A., Berman, J. S., & Neimeyer, R. A. (1990). Psychotherapy for the treatment of depression: A comprehensive review of controlled outcome research. *Psychological Bulletin, 108*(1), 30–49.

Rock, I. (1983). *The logic of perception.* Cambridge, MA: MIT Press.

Rodin, J. (1981). Current status of the external-internal hypothalamus for obesity. *American Psychologist, 36,* 361–372.

Rodin, J., & Plante, T. (1989). The psychological effects of exercise. In R. S. Williams & A. Wellece (Eds.), *Biological effects of physical activity* (pp. 127–137). Champaign, IL: Human * Kinetics.

Roediger, H. L., III. (1980). Memory metaphors in cognitive psychology. *Memory and Cognition, 8*(3), 231–246.

Rogers, A., & Gilligan, C. (1988). *Translating girls' voices: Two languages of development* (pp. 42–43). Harvard University Graduate School of Education, Harvard Project on the Psychology of Women and the Development of Girls.

Rogers, C. R. (1959). A theory of therapy, personality, and interpersonal relationships, as developed in the client-centered framework. In S. Koch (Ed.), *Psychology: A study of a science* (Vol. 3). New York: McGraw-Hill.

Rogers, C. R. (1961a). *On becoming a person: A client's view of psychotherapy.* Boston: Houghton Mifflin.

Rogers, C. R. (1961b). *On becoming a person: A therapist's view of psychotherapy.* Boston: Houghton Mifflin.

Rogers, C. R. (1978). The formative tendency. *Journal of Humanistic Psychology, 18*(1), 23–26.

Rogers, C. R. (1980). *A way of being.* Boston: Houghton Mifflin.

Rogers, S. M., & Turner, C. F. (1991). Male–male sexual contact in the U.S.A.: Findings from five sample surveys, 1970–1990. *Journal of Sex Research, 28*(4), 491–519.

Rogoff, B. (1986). The development of strategic use of context in spatial memory. In M. Perlmutter (Ed.), *Perspectives on intellectual development.* Hillsdale, NJ: Erlbaum.

Rohner, R. P., & Rohner, E. C. (1981). Assessing interrater influence in holocultural research: A methodological note. *Behavior Science Research, 16*(3–4), 341–351.

Rojahn, K., & Pettigrew, T. F. (1992). Memory for schema-relevant information: A meta-analytic resolution. *British Journal of Social Psychology, 31*(2), 81–109.

Rolls, B. J. (1979). How variety and palatability can stimulate appetite. *Nutrition Bulletin, 5,* 78–86.

Rolls, B. J., Rowe, E. T., & Rolls, E. T. (1982). How sensory properties of food affect human feeding behavior. *Physiology and Behavior, 29,* 409–417.

Rolls, B. J., Wood, R. J., & Rolls, E. T. (1980). Thirst: The initiation, maintenance, and termination of drinking. In J. M. Sprague & A. N. Epstein (Eds.), *Progress in psychobiology and physiological psychology* (Vol. 9, pp. 263–321). New York: Academic Press.

Rosch, E. (1973). On the internal structure of perceptual and semantic categories. In T. E. Moore (Ed.), *Cognitive development and the acquisition of language.* New York: Academic Press.

Rosch, E. H., & Mervis, C. B. (1975). Family resemblances: Studies in the internal structure of categories. *Cognitive Psychology, 7,* 573–605.

Rosen, G. M. (1976). *Don't be afraid.* Englewood Cliffs, NJ: Prentice-Hall.

Rosen, G. M. (1987). Self-help treatment books and the commercialization of psychotherapy. *American Psychologist, 42*(1), 46–51.

Rosenhan, D. L. (1973). On being sane in insane places. *Science, 179,* 250–258.

Rosenthal, R., & Jacobson, L. (1968). *Pygmalion in the classroom: Teacher expectation and pupils' intellectual development.* New York: Holt, Rinehart & Winston.

Rosenthal, R., & Rubin, D. B. (1982). A simple, general purpose display of magnitude of experimental effect. *Journal of Educational Psychology, 74,* 166–169.

Roskies, E., Seraganian, R., Hanley, J. A., Collu, R., Martin, N., & Smilga, C. (1986). The Montreal Type A intervention project: Major findings. *Health Psychology, 5,* 45–69.

Roskies, E., Spevack, M., Surkis, A., Cohen, C., & Gilman, S. (1978). Changing the coronary-prone (Type A) behavior pattern in a nonclinical population. *Journal of Behavioral Medicine, 1,* 201–216.

Ross, B. H., & Spalding, T. L. (1994). Concepts and categories. In R. J. Sternberg (Ed.), *Handbook of perception and cognition: Thinking and problem solving.* New York: Academic Press.

Ross, L. (1977). The intuitive psychologist and his shortcomings: Distortions in the attribution process. In L. Berkowitz (Ed.), *Advances in experimental social psychology* (Vol. 10). New York: Academic Press.

Ross, R. (1975). Salience of reward and intrinsic motivation. *Journal of Personality and Social Psychology, 32,* 245–254.

Roth, D., & Rehm, L. P. (1980). Relationships among self-monitoring processes, memory, and depression. *Cognitive Therapy and Research, 4,* 149–157.

Rothenberg, A. (1979). *The emerging goddess.* Chicago: University of Chicago Press.

Rotter, J. B. (1966). Generalized expectancies for internal versus external control of reinforcement. *Psychological Monographs, 80*(1, Whole No. 609).

Rotter, J. B. (1990). Internal versus external control of reinforcement: A case history of a variable. *American Psychologist, 45,* 489–493.

Rotter, J. B., & Hochreich, D. J. (1975). *Personality.* Glenview, IL: Scott, Foresman.

Rotton, J., Barry, T., Frey, J., & Soler, E. (1978). Air pollution and interpersonal attraction. *Journal of Applied Social Psychology, 8,* 57–71.

Rotton, J., & Frey, J. (1985). Air pollution, weather, and violent crimes: Concomitant time-series analysis of archival data. *Journal of Personality and Social Psychology, 49*(5), 1207–1220.

Rozin, P., & Fallon, A. (1987). A perspective on disgust. *Psychological Review, 94,* 23–41.

Rozin, P., Millman, L., & Nemeroff, C. (1986). Operation of the laws of sympathetic magic in disgust and other domains. *Journal of Personality and Social Psychology, 50,* 703–712.

Rubin, K. H. (1980). Fantasy play: Its role in the development of social skills and social cognition. In K. H. Rubin (Ed.), *Children's play: New directions for child development.* San Francisco: Jossey-Bass.

Rubin, V., & Comitas, L. (1974). *Ganja in Jamaica: A medical anthropological study of chronic marijuana use.* The Hague, Netherlands: Mouton.

Rubin, Z. (1970). Measurement of romantic love. *Journal of Personality and Social Psychology, 16,* 265–273.

Rubin, Z. (1973). *Liking and loving: An invitation to social psychology.* New York: Holt, Rinehart & Winston.

Rubin, Z., Hill, C. T., Peplau, L. A., & Dunkel-Schetter, C. (1980). Self-disclosure in dating couples: Sex roles and the ethic of openness. *Journal of Marriage and the Family, 42,* 305–317.

Ruch, J. C. (1975). Self-hypnosis: The result of hetero-hypnosis or vice versa? *International Journal of Clinical and Experimental Hypnosis, 23,* 282–304.

Rudy, T. E., Kerns, R. D., & Turk, D. C. (1988). Chronic pain and depression: Toward a cognitive-behavioral mediation model. *Pain, 35,* 129–140.

Rule, S. R., & Ferguson, T. J. (1986). The effects of media violence on attitudes, emotions, and cognitions. *Journal of Social Issues, 42*(3), 29–50.

Russell, J. A. (1991). Culture and categorization of emotions. *Psychological Bulletin, 110*(3), 426–450.

Russell, M. J. (1976). Human olfactory communication. *Nature, 260,* 520–522.

Russell, W. R., & Nathan, P. W. (1946). Traumatic amnesia. *Brain, 69,* 280–300.

Rymer, R. (1993). *Genie: An abused child's flight from silence.* New York: HarperCollins.

Sadker, M., & Sadker, D. (1984). *Year three: Final report, promoting effectiveness in classroom instruction.* Washington, DC: National Institute of Education.

Safer, D. J. (1991). Diet, behavior modification, and exercise: A review of obesity treatments from a long-term perspective. *Southern Medical Journal, 84,* 1470–1474.

Salthouse, T. A., & Somberg, B. L. (1982). Skilled performance: Effects of adult age and experience on elementary processes. *Journal of Experimental Psychology: General, 111*(2), 176–207.

Sanders, S. H. (1985). Chronic pain: Conceptualization and epidemiology. *Annals of Behavioral Medicine, 7*(3), 3–5.

Sapir, E. (1964). *Culture, language and personality.* Berkeley: University of California Press. (Original work published 1941)

Sarason, S. B., & Doris, J. (1979). *Educational handicap, public policy, and social history.* New York: Free Press.

Sartorius, N., de Girolano, G., Andrews, G., German, G. A., & Eisenberg, L. (Eds.). (1993a). *Treatment of mental disorders: A review of effectiveness.* Geneva, Switzerland, and Washington, DC: World Health Organization and American Psychiatric Press.

Sartorius, N., Kaelber, C., Cooper, J. E., Roper, M. T., et al. (1993b). Progress toward achieving a common language in psychiatry: Results from the field trial of the clinical guidelines accompanying the WHO classification of mental and behavioral disorders in ICD-10. *Archives of General Psychiatry, 50*(2), 115–124.

Sartorius, N., Shapiro, R., & Jablonsky, A. (1974). The international pilot study of schizophrenia. *Schizophrenia Bulletin, 2,* 21–35.

Savage-Rumbaugh, S., McDonald, K., Sevcik, R. A., Hopkins, W. D., & Rubert, E. (1986). Spontaneous symbol acquisition and communicative use by pygmy chimpanzees (Pan paniscus). *Journal of Experimental Psychology: General, 112,* 211–235.

Saxe, L., Dougherty, D., & Cross, T. (1985). The validity of polygraph testing: Scientific analysis and public controversy. *American Psychologist, 40,* 355–366.

Scarr, H. A. (1994). United States population: A typical American as seen through the eyes of the Census Bureau. In *The World Almanac and Book of Facts, 1994.* Mahwah, NJ: Funk & Wagnalls.

Scarr, S., Phillips, D., & McCartney, K. (1990). Facts, fantasies, and the future of child care in the United States. *Psychological Science, 1,* 26–35.

Schacter, D. L., & Graf, P. (1986a). Effects of elaborative processing on implicit and explicit memory for new associations. *Journal of Experimental Psychology: Learning, Memory, & Cognition, 12*(3), 432–444.

Schacter, D. L., & Graf, P. (1986b). Preserved learning in amnesic patients: Perspectives from research on direct priming. *Journal of Clinical & Experimental Neuropsychology, 8*(6), 727–743.

Schachter, S. (1951). Deviation, rejection, and communication. *Journal of Abnormal Social Psychology, 46,* 190–207.

Schachter, S. (1968). Obesity and eating. *Science, 161,* 751–756.

Schachter, S. (1971a). *Emotion, obesity, and crime.* New York: Academic Press.

Schachter, S. (1971b). Some extraordinary facts about obese humans and rats. *American Psychologist, 26,* 129–144.

Schachter, S., & Gross, L. (1968). Manipulated time

and eating behavior. *Journal of Personality and Social Psychology, 10,* 98–106.

Schachter, S., & Rodin, J. (1974). *Obese humans and rats.* Hillsdale, NJ: Erlbaum.

Schachter, S., & Singer, J. (1962). Cognitive, social, and physiological determinants of emotional state. *Psychological Review, 69,* 379–399.

Schafer, R. (1982). The relevance of the "here and now" transference interpretation to the reconstruction of early development. *International Journal of Psycho-Analysis, 63*(1), 77–82.

Schaffer, H. R. (1977). *Mothering.* Cambridge, MA: Harvard University Press.

Schaie, K. W. (1974). Translations in gerontology—from lab to life. *American Psychologist, 29,* 802–807.

Schaie, K. W. (1989). Perceptual speed in adulthood: Cross-sectional and longitudinal studies. *Psychology and Aging, 4,* 443–453.

Schaie, K. W., & Willis, S. L. (1986). Can decline in intellectual functioning in the elderly be reversed? *Developmental Psychology, 22,* 223–232.

Schank, R. C. (1972). Conceptual dependency: A theory of natural language understanding. *Cognitive Psychology, 3,* 552–631.

Schank, R. C. (1988). Creativity as a mechanical process. In R. J. Sternberg (Ed.), *The nature of creativity* (pp. 220–238). New York: Cambridge University Press.

Schank, R. C., & Abelson, R. P. (1977). *Scripts, plans, goals, and understanding.* Hillsdale. NJ: Erlbaum.

Scheff, T. J. (1966). *Being mentally ill: A sociological theory.* Chicago: Aldine.

Schildkraut, J. J. (1965). The catecholamine hypothesis of affective disorders: A review of supporting evidence. *American Journal of Psychiatry, 122,* 509–522.

Schlaefli, A., Rest, J. R., & Thoma, S. J. (1985). Does moral education improve moral judgement? A meta-analysis of intervention studies using the Defining Issues Test. *Review of Educational Research, 55*(3), 319–352.

Schliemann, A. D., & Magalhües, V. P. (1990). *Proportional reasoning: From shops, to kitchens, laboratories, and, hopefully, schools.* Proceedings of the Fourteenth International Conference for the Psychology of Mathematics Education, Oaxtepec, Mexico.

Schmitt, B. H., Gilovich, T., Goore, N., & Joseph, L. (1986). Mere exposure and social facilitation: One more time. *Journal of Experimental and Social Psychology, 22,* 242–248.

Schnapf, J. L., & Baylor, D. A. (1987). How photoreceptor cells respond to light. *Scientific American, 256,* 40–47.

Schonfield, D., & Robertson, D. A. (1966). Memory storage and aging. *Canadian Journal of Psychology, 20,* 228–236.

Schroder, H. M., Driver, M. J., & Streufert, S. (1967). *Human information processing.* New York: Holt, Rinehart & Winston.

Schroeder-Helmert, D. (1985). Clinical evaluation of DSIP. In A. Wauquier, J. M. Gaillard, J. M. Monti, & M. Radulovacki (Eds.), *Sleep: Neurotransmitters and neuromodulators* (pp. 279–291). New York: Raven Press.

Schultz, D. (1981). *A history of modern psychology* (3rd ed.). New York: Academic Press.

Schultz, T. R., Wright, K., & Schleifer, M. (1986). Assignment of moral responsibility and punishment. *Child Development, 57,* 177–184.

Schustack, M. W., & Sternberg, R. J. (1981). Evaluation of evidence in causal inference. *Journal of Experimental Psychology: General, 110,* 101–120.

Schwartz, B. (1989). *Psychology of learning and behavior* (3rd ed.). New York: Norton.

Schwartz, G., & Weinberger, D. (1980). Patterns of emotional responses to affective situations: Relations among happiness, sadness, anger, fear, depression, and anxiety. *Motivation and Emotion, 4,* 175–191.

Schwartz, G. E. (1982). Testing the biopsychosocial model: The ultimate challenge facing behavioral medicine. *Journal of Consulting and Clinical Psychology, 50,* 1040–1053.

Schwarz, C. S., Scarr, S., and McCartney, K. (1983). *Center, sitter, and home care before age two: A report on the first Bermuda infant care study.* Paper presented at the annual meeting of the American Psychological Association, Los Angeles.

Schweizer, E., Rickels, K., Case, G., & Greenblatt, D. J. (1990). Long-term therapeutic use of benzodiazepines: II. Effects of gradual taper. *Archives of General Psychiatry, 47*(10), 908–915.

Scott, A. I. F. (1989). Which depressed patients will respond to electroconvulsive therapy? The search for biological predictors of recovery. *British Journal of Psychiatry, 154,* 8–17.

Scovern, A. W., & Kilmann, P. R. (1980). Status of electroconvulsive therapy: Review of the outcome literature. *Psychological Bulletin, 87,* 260–303.

Scoville, W. B., & Milner, B. (1957). Loss of recent memory after bilateral hippocampal lesions. *Journal of Neurology, Neurosurgery, and Psychiatry, 20,* 11–19.

Searle, J. R. (1975a). Indirect speech acts. In P. Cole & J. L. Morgan (Eds.), *Syntax and semantics: Speech acts* (Vol. 3, pp. 59–82). New York: Seminar Press.

Searle, J. R. (1975b). A taxonomy of elocutionary acts. In K. Gunderson (Ed.), *Minnesota studies in the philosophy of language* (pp. 344–369). Minneapolis: University of Minnesota Press.

Sears, D. O. (1983). The person-positivity bias. *Journal of Personality and Social Psychology, 44,* 233–250.

Segall, M. H., Campbell, D. T., & Herskovits, M. J. (1966). *The influence of culture on visual perception.* New York: Bobbs-Merrill.

Seiden, R. H. (1974). Suicide: Preventable death. *Public Affairs Report, 15*(4), 1–5.

Seidman, L. J. (1983). Schizophrenia and brain dysfunction: An integration of recent neurodiagnostic findings. *Psychological Bulletin, 94,* 195–238.

Seidman, L. J. (1990). The neuropsychology of schizophrenia: A neurodevelopmental and case study approach. *Journal of Neuropsychiatry and Clinical Neuroscience, 2,* 301–312.

Sekuler, R., & Blake, R. (1985). *Perception.* New York: Knopf.

Selfridge, O. G. (1959). Pandemonium: A paradigm

for learning. In D. V. Blake & A. M. Uttley (Eds.), *Proceedings of the symposium on the mechanization of thought processes* (pp. 511–529). London: Her Majesty's Stationery Office.

Selfridge, O. G., & Neisser, U. (1960). Pattern recognition by machine. *Scientific American, 203,* 60–68.

Seligman, M. E. P. (1974). Depression and learned helplessness. In R. J. Friedman & M. M. Katz (Eds.), *The psychology of depression: Contemporary theory and research.* Washington, DC: Winston-Wiley.

Seligman, M. E. P. (1975). *Helplessness.* San Francisco: Freeman.

Seligman, M. E. P. (1991). *Learned optimism.* New York: Norton.

Seligman, M. E. P., & Maier, S. F. (1967). Failure to escape traumatic shock. *Journal of Experimental Psychology, 74,* 1–9.

Selye, H. (1974). *Stress without distress.* Philadelphia: Lippincott.

Selye, H. (1976). *The stress of life* (rev. ed.). New York: McGraw-Hill.

Sepple, C. P., & Read, N. W. (1989). Gastrointestinal correlates of the development of hunger in man. *Appetite, 13,* 183–191.

Seraganian, P. (Ed.). (1993). *Exercise psychology: The influence of physical exercise on psychological processes.* New York: Wiley.

Serdahely, W. J. (1990). Pediatric near-death experiences. *Journal of Near-Death Studies, 9,* 33–39.

Serpell, R. (1993). *The significance of schooling: Life journeys in an African society.* Cambridge, England: University of Cambridge Press.

Serpell, R. (1994). The cultural construction of intelligence. In W. J. Lonner & R. S. Malpass (Eds.), *Psychology and culture.* Boston: Allyn & Bacon.

Sexton, M. M. (1979). Behavioral epidemiology. In O. F. Pomerleau & J. P. Brady (Eds.), *Behavioral medicine: Theory and practice* (pp. 3–22). Baltimore: Williams & Wilkins.

Seymour, R. B., & Smith, D. E. (1987). *Guide to psychoactive drugs: An up-to-the-minute reference to mind-altering substances.* New York: Harrington Park Press.

Shanab, M. E., & Yahya, K. A. (1977). A behavioral study of obedience in children. *Journal of Personality and Social Psychology, 35,* 530–536.

Shanab, M. E., & Yahya, K. A. (1978). A cross-cultural study of obedience. *Bulletin of the Psychonomic Society, 11,* 267–269.

Shapiro, D. H., & Giber, D. (1978). Meditation and psychotherapeutic effects: Self-regulation strategy and altered states of consciousness. *Archives of General Psychiatry, 35,* 294–302.

Shapiro, D., Lane, J. D., & Henry, J. P. (1986). Caffeine, cardiovascular reactivity, and cardiovascular disease. In K. A. Matthews, S. M. Weiss, T. Detre, T. M. Dembroski, B. Falkner, S. B. Manuck, & R. B. Williams (Eds.), *Handbook of stress, reactivity, and cardiovascular disease.* New York: Wiley.

Shapley, R., & Lennie, P. (1985). Spatial frequency analysis in the visual system. *Annual Review of Neuroscience, 8,* 547–583.

Shekelle, R. B., Hulley, S. B., Neaton, J. D., Billings, J. H., Borhani, N. O., Gerace, T. A., Jacobs, D. R., Lasser, N. L., Mittelmark, M. B., & Stamler, J. (1985). The MRFIT behavior pattern study: II. Type A behavior and incidence of coronary heart disease. *American Journal of Epidemiology, 122,* 559–570.

Sheppard, J. A., & Arkin, R. M. (1989). Self-handicapping: The moderating role of public self-consciousness and task importance. *Personality and Social Psychology Bulletin, 15,* 252–265.

Sherif, M., Harvey, L. J., White, B. J., Hood, W. R., & Sherif, C. W. (1988). *The Robber's Cave experiment: Intergroup conflict and cooperation.* Middletown, CT: Wesleyan University Press. (Original work published 1961)

Sherman, S. J., Judd, C. M., & Park, B. (1989). Social cognition. *Annual Review of Psychology, 40,* 281–326.

Shibazaki, M. (1983). Development of hemispheric function in hiragana, kanji, and figure processing for normal children and mentally retarded children. *Japanese Journal of Special Education, 21*(3), 1–9.

Shields, J. (1962). *Monozygotic twins brought up apart and brought up together.* London: Oxford University Press.

Shiffrin, R. M. (1973). Information persistence in short-term memory. *Journal of Experimental Psychology, 100,* 39–49.

Shimada, M., & Otsuka, A. (1981). Functional hemispheric differences in kanji processing in Japanese. *Japanese Psychological Review, 24*(4), 472–489.

Shneidman, E. S. (1973). Suicide. In *Encyclopedia Britannica.* Chicago: Encyclopedia Britannica.

Shontz, F. C. (1975). *The psychological aspects of physical illness and disability.* New York: Macmillan.

Shook, M. D., & Shook, R. L. (1991). *The book of odds.* New York: Penguin.

Shulman, H. G. (1970). Encoding and retention of semantic and phonemic information in short-term memory. *Journal of Verbal Learning and Verbal Behavior, 9,* 499–508.

Sibitani, A. (1980). The Japanese brain. *Science, 80,* 22–26.

Siegler, R. S. (1976). Three aspects of cognitive development. *Cognitive Psychology, 8,* 481–520.

Siegler, R. S. (1978). The origins of scientific reasoning. In R. S. Siegler (Ed.), *Children's thinking: What develops?* (pp. 109–149). Hillsdale, NJ: Erlbaum.

Siegler, R. S. (1984). Mechanisms of cognitive growth: Variation and selection. In R. J. Sternberg (Ed.), *Mechanisms of cognitive development* (pp. 142–162). New York: Freeman.

Siegler, R. S. (1986). *Children's thinking.* Englewood Cliffs, NJ: Prentice-Hall.

Silverstein, B., Peterson, B., & Perdue, L. (1986). Some correlates of the thin standard of bodily attractiveness in women. *International Journal of Eating Disorders, 5,* 145–155.

Simon, B., & Hamilton, D. L. (1994). Self-stereotyping and social context: The effects of relative in-group size and in-group status. *Journal of Personality & Social Psychology, 66*(4) 699–711.

Simon, H. A. (1957). *Administrative behavior* (2nd ed.). Totowa, NJ: Littlefield, Adams.

Simon, H. A. (1976). Identifying basic abilities underlying intelligent performance of complex tasks. In L. B. Resnick (Ed.), *The nature of intelligence* (pp. 65–98). Hillsdale, NJ: Erlbaum.

Simon, H. A., & Reed, S. K. (1976). Modeling strategy shifts in a problem-solving task. *Cognitive Psychology, 8,* 86–97.

Simon, W. H., & Gagnon, J. H. (1986). Sexual scripts: Permanence and change. *Archives of Sexual Behavior, 15*(2), 97–120.

Simonton, D. K. (1975). Age and literary creativity: A cross-cultural and transhistorical survey. *Journal of Cross-Cultural Psychology, 6*(3), 259–277.

Simonton, D. K. (1988). Creativity, leadership, and chance. In R. J. Sternberg (Ed.), *The nature of creativity.* New York: Cambridge University Press.

Singer, J. L. (1984). *The human personality.* San Diego, CA: Harcourt Brace Jovanovich.

Sistrunk, F., & McDavid, J. W. (1971). Sex variables in conforming behavior. *Journal of Personality and Social Psychology, 17,* 200–207.

Sizemore, C. C., & Pittillo, E. S. (1977). *I'm Eve.* Garden City, NY: Doubleday.

Skinner, B. F. (1948). *Walden II.* New York: Macmillan.

Skinner, B. F. (1974). *About behaviorism.* New York: Knopf.

Slobin, D. I. (1971). Cognitive prerequisites for the acquisition of grammar. In C. A. Ferguson & D. I. Slobin (Eds.), *Studies of child language development.* New York: Holt, Rinehart & Winston.

Slobin, D. I. (Ed.). (1985). *The cross-linguistic study of language acquisition.* Hillsdale, NJ: Erlbaum.

Sloboda, J. A. (1985). *The musical mind: The cognitive psychology of music.* Oxford, England: Oxford University Press.

Smith, D. (1982). Trends in counseling and psychotherapy. *American Psychologist, 37*(7), 802–809.

Smith, D. E., & Gay, G. R. (1972). *It's so good, don't even try it once: Heroin in perspective.* Englewood Cliffs, NJ: Prentice-Hall.

Smith, E. E., & Medin, D. L. (1981). *Categories and concepts.* Cambridge, MA: Harvard University Press.

Smith, E. E., Shoben, E. J., & Ripps, L. J. (1974). Structure and process in semantic memory: A featural model for semantic decisions. *Psychological Review, 81,* 214–241.

Smith, M. L., & Glass, G. V. (1977). Meta-analysis of psychotherapy outcome studies. *American Psychologist* (November), 752–760.

Smith, P. B., & Bond, M. H. (1994). *Social psychology across cultures: Analysis and perspectives.* Boston: Allyn & Bacon.

Smith, T. W. (1992). Hostility and health: Current status of a psychosomatic hypothesis. *Health Psychology, 11,* 139–150.

Smith, T. W., & Anderson, N. B. (1986). Models of personality and disease: An interactional approach to Type A behavior and cardiovascular risk. *Journal of Personality and Social Psychology, 50*(6), 1166–1173.

Snarey, J. R. (1985). Cross-cultural universality of social-moral development: A critical review of Kohlbergian research. *Psychological Bulletin, 97,* 202–232.

Snarey, J. R., Reimer, J., & Kohlberg, L. (1985a). Development of social-moral reasoning among kibbutz adolescents: A longitudinal cross-cultural study. *Developmental Psychology, 21,* 3–17.

Snarey, J. R., Reimer, J., & Kohlberg, L. (1985b). The kibbutz as a model for moral education: A longitudinal cross-cultural study. *Journal of Applied Developmental Psychology, 6,* 151–172.

Snow, C. E. (1977). The development of conversation between mothers and babies. *Journal of Child Language, 4,* 1–22.

Snyder, M. (1979). Self-monitoring processes. In L. Berkowitz (Ed.), *Advances in experimental social psychology* (Vol. 12). New York: Academic Press.

Snyder, M. (1983). The influence of individuals on situations: Implications for understanding the links between personality and social behavior. *Journal of Personality, 51,* 497–516.

Snyder, M., & Swann, W. B., Jr. (1978). Behavioral confirmation in social interaction: From social perception to social reality. *Journal of Personality and Social Psychology, 36,* 1202–1212.

Solomon, G. F., & Temoshok, L. (1987). A psychoneuroimmunologic perspective on AIDS research: Questions, preliminary findings, and suggestions. *Journal of Applied Social Psychology, 17,* 286–308.

Solomon, R. L. (1980). The opponent-process theory of motivation: The costs of pleasure and the benefits of pain. *American Psychologists, 35,* 681–712.

Solomon, R. L., & Corbit, J. D. (1974). An opponent-process theory of motivation: I. Temporal dynamics of affect. *Psychological Review, 81,* 119–145.

Sommer, R. (1969). *Personal space.* Englewood Cliffs, NJ: Prentice-Hall.

Spangler, W. (1992). Validity of questionnaire and TAT measures of need for achievement: Two meta-analyses. *Psychological Bulletin, 112,* 140–154.

Spear, N. E. (1979). Experimental analysis of infantile amnesia. In J. E. Kihlstrom & F. J. Evans (Eds.), *Functional disorders of memory.* Hillsdale, NJ: Erlbaum.

Spearman, C. (1927). *The abilities of man.* New York: Macmillan.

Speer, D. C. (1972). Inventory commitment: Some considerations for crisis intervention outreach workers. *Crisis Intervention, 4*(4), 112–116.

Spelke, E. (1976). Infant's intermodal perception of events. *Cognitive Psychology, 8,* 553–560.

Spence, J. T., & Helmreich, R. L. (1983). Achievement-related motives and behavior. In J. T. Spence (Ed.), *Achievement and achievement motives: Psychological and sociological approaches.* New York: Freeman.

Sperling, G. (1960). The information available in brief

visual presentations. *Psychological Monographs: General and Applied, 74,* 1–28.

Sperry, R. W. (1964a). The great cerebral commissure. *Scientific American, 210*(1), 42–52.

Sperry, R. W. (1964b). *Problems outstanding in the evolution of brain function.* New York: American Museum of Natural History.

Spielberger, C. D., Gorsuch, R. L., & Lushene, R. E. (1983). *Manual for the State-Trait Anxiety Inventory (STAI).* Palo Alto, CA: Consulting Psychologists Press.

Spitzer, L., & Rodin, J. (1981). Human eating behavior: A critical review of studies in normal weight and overweight individuals. *Appetite, 2,* 293–329.

Spitzer, R. L., Skodol, A. E., Gibbon, M., & Williams, J. B. W. (1983). *Psychopathology: A case book.* New York: McGraw-Hill.

Spoehr, K. T., & Corin, W. J. (1978). The stimulus suffix effect as a memory coding phenomenon. *Memory and Cognition, 6,* 583–589.

Sporakowski, M. J. (1988). A therapist's views on the consequences of change for the contemporary family. *Family Relations, 37,* 373–378.

Springer, S. P., & Deutsch, G. (1985). *Left brain, right brain.* New York: Freeman.

Squire, L. R. (1987). *Memory and the brain.* New York: Oxford University Press.

Squire, L. R., Cohen, N. J., & Nadel, L. (1984). The medial temporal region and memory consolidations: A new hypothesis. In H. Weingardner & E. Parker (Eds.), *Memory consolidation.* Hillsdale, NJ: Erlbaum.

Sroufe, L. A. (1979). Socioemotional development. In J. D. Osofsky (Ed.), *Handbook of infant development.* New York: Wiley.

Srull, T. K., & Wyer, R. S., Jr. (1989). Person memory and judgment. *Psychological Review, 96*(1), 58–83.

Staats, A. W., & Staats, C. K. (1958). Attitudes established by classical conditioning. *Journal of Abnormal and Social Psychology, 57,* 37–40.

Staddon, J. E. R., & Ettinger, R. H. (1989). *Learning: An introduction to the principles of adaptive behavior.* San Diego, CA: Harcourt Brace Jovanovich.

Standing, L., Conezio, J., & Haber, R. N. (1970). Perception and memory for pictures: Single-trial learning of 2500 visual stimuli. *Psychonomic Science, 19,* 73–74.

Starr, R. H., Dietrich, K. N., Fischoff, J., Ceresnie, S., & Zweier, D. (1984). The contribution of handicapping conditions to child abuse. *Topics in Early Childhood Special Education, 4*(1), 59–69.

Steiner, J. E. (1979). Human facial expressions in response to taste and smell stimulation. In H. Reese & L. P. Lipsitt (Eds.), *Advances in child development and behavior* (Vol. 13, pp. 257–293). New York: Academic Press.

Stern, D. (1977). *The first relationship: Mother and infant.* Cambridge, MA: Harvard University Press.

Stern, W. (1912). *Psychologische Methoden der Intelligenz-Prüfung.* Leipzig, Germany: Barth.

Sternbach, R. A. (1963). Congenital insensitivity to pain: A review. *Psychological Bulletin, 60,* 252–264.

Sternberg, R. J. (1977). *Intelligence, information process-ing, and analogical reasoning: The componential analysis of human abilities.* Hillsdale, NJ: Erlbaum.

Sternberg, R. J. (1979, September). Beyond IQ: Stalking the IQ quark. *Psychology Today,* pp. 42–54.

Sternberg, R. J. (1980). Representation and process in linear syllogistic reasoning. *Journal of Experimental Psychology: General, 109,* 119–159.

Sternberg, R. J. (1981). Intelligence and nonentrenchment. *Journal of Educational Psychology, 73,* 1–16.

Sternberg, R. J. (Ed.). (1982). *Handbook of human intelligence.* New York: Cambridge University Press.

Sternberg, R. J. (Ed.) (1984). *Human abilities: An information-processing approach.* San Francisco, CA: Freeman.

Sternberg, R. J. (1985a). *Beyond IQ: A triarchic theory of human intelligence.* New York: Cambridge University Press.

Sternberg, R. J. (1985b). Implicit theories of intelligence, creativity, and wisdom. *Journal of Personality and Social Psychology, 49,* 607–627.

Sternberg, R. J. (1986a). *Intelligence applied: Understanding and increasing your intellectual skills.* San Diego, CA: Harcourt Brace Jovanovich.

Sternberg, R. J. (1986b). A triangular theory of love. *Psychological Review, 93,* 119–135.

Sternberg, R. J. (1986c). A triarchic theory of intellectual giftedness. In R. J. Sternberg & J. E. Davidson (Eds.), *Conceptions of giftedness* (pp. 223–243). New York: Cambridge University Press.

Sternberg, R. J. (Ed.). (1988a). *The nature of creativity.* New York: Cambridge University Press.

Sternberg, R. J. (1988b). A three-facet model of creativity. In R. J. Sternberg (Ed.), *The nature of creativity* (pp. 125–147). New York: Cambridge University Press.

Sternberg, R. J. (1988c). Triangulating love. In R. J. Sternberg & M. L. Barnes (Eds.), *The psychology of love* (pp. 119–138). New Haven, CT: Yale University Press.

Sternberg, R. J. (1988d). *The triarchic mind.* New York: Viking.

Sternberg, R. J. (Ed.) (1990). *Wisdom: Its nature, origins, and development.* New York: Cambridge University Press.

Sternberg, R. J. (1994a). PRSVL: An integrative framework for understanding mind in context. In R. J. Sternberg & R. K. Wagner (Eds.), *Mind in context: Interactionist perspectives on human intelligence* (pp. 218–232). New York: Cambridge University Press.

Sternberg, R. J. (1994b). Thinking styles: Theory and assessment of the interface between intelligence and personality. In R. J. Sternberg & P. Ruzgis (Eds.), *Personality and intelligence* (pp. 169–187). New York: Cambridge University Press.

Sternberg, R. J., & Barnes, M. L. (1985). Real and ideal others in romantic relationships: Is four a crowd? *Journal of Personality and Social Psychology, 49,* 1586–1608.

Sternberg, R. J., & Barnes, M. L. (Eds.). (1988). *The psychology of love.* New Haven, CT: Yale University Press.

Sternberg, R. J., & Davidson, J. E. (Eds.) (1986). *Conceptions of giftedness.* New York: Cambridge University Press.

Sternberg, R. J., & Detterman, D. K. (Eds.) (1986).

What is intelligence? Contemporary viewpoints on its nature and definition. Norwood, NJ: Ablex.

Sternberg, R. J., & Dobson, D. M. (1987). Resolving interpersonal conflicts: An analysis of stylistic consistency. *Journal of Personality and Social Psychology, 52,* 794–812.

Sternberg, R. J., & Grajek, S. (1984). The nature of love. *Journal of Personality and Social Psychology, 47,* 312–329.

Sternberg, R. J., & Lubart, T. I. (1991a, April). Creating creative minds. *Phi Delta Kappan,* pp. 608–614.

Sternberg, R. J., & Lubart, T. I. (1991b). An investment theory of creativity and its development. *Human Development, 34,* 1–31.

Sternberg, R. J., & Lubart, T. I. (1993). Investing in creativity. *Psychological Inquiry, 4*(3), 229–232.

Sternberg, R. J., & Nigro, G. (1980). Development patterns in the solution of verbal analogies. *Child Development, 51,* 27–38.

Sternberg, R. J., & Okagaki, L. (1989). Continuity and discontinuity in intellectual development are not a matter of 'either–or.' *Human Development, 32,* 158–166.

Sternberg, R. J., & Powell, J. S. (1983). Comprehending verbal comprehension. *American Psychologist, 38,* 878–893.

Sternberg, R. J., & Soriano, L. J. (1984). Styles of conflict resolution. *Journal of Personality and Social Psychology, 47,* 115–126.

Sternberg, R. J., & Weil, E. M. (1980). An aptitude-strategy interaction in linear syllogistic reasoning. *Journal of Educational Psychology, 72,* 226–234.

Sternberg, S. (1966). High-speed memory scanning in human memory. *Science, 153,* 652–654.

Sternberg, S. (1969). Memory-scanning: Mental processes revealed by reaction-time experiments. *American Scientist, 4,* 421–457.

Stevens, A., & Coupe, P. (1978). Distortions in judged spatial relations. *Cognitive Psychology, 10,* 422–437.

Stewart, A. J. (1982). The course of individual adaptation to life changes. *Journal of Personality and Social Psychology, 42,* 1100–1113.

Stewart, A. J., & Healy, J. M., Jr. (1985). Personality and adaptation to change. In R. Hogan & W. H. Jones (Eds.), *Perspectives in personality* (Vol. 1, pp. 117–144). Greenwich, CT: JAI Press.

Stewart, A. J., & Healy, J. M. (1989). Linking individual development and social changes. *American Psychologist, 44*(1), 30–42.

Stewart, A. J., Sokol, M., Healy, J. M., & Chester, N. L. (1986). Longitudinal studies of psychological consequences of life changes in children and adults. *Journal of Personality and Social Psychology, 50,* 143–151.

Stiles, W. B., Shapiro, D. A., & Elliott, R. (1986). Are all psychotherapies equivalent? *American Psychologist, 41*(2), 165–180.

Stipek, D. J. (1984). Young children's performance expectations: Logical analysis or wishful thinking? In J. G. Nicholls (Ed.), *Advances in motivation and achievement: Vol 3. The development of achievement motivation* (pp. 33–56). Greenwich, CT: JAI Press.

Stone, G. C. (1979). Health and the health system: A historical overview and conceptual framework. In G. C. Stone, F. Cohen, & N. E. Adler (Eds.), *Health psychology—A handbook* (pp. 1–17). San Francisco: Jossey-Bass.

Strauss, J. S., Kokes, F. R., Ritzler, B. A., Harder, D. W., & Van Ord, A. (1978). Patterns of disorder in first admission psychiatric patients. *Journal of Nervous and Mental Disease, 166,* 611–623.

Stricker, E. M., & Zigmond, M. J. (1976). Brain catecholamines and the lateral hypothalamic syndrome. In D. Novin, W. Wyrwicka, & G. Bray (Eds.), *Hunger: Basic mechanisms and clinical implications.* New York: Raven Press.

Strickland, B. (1992). Women and depression. *Current Directions in Psychological Science, 1,* 132–135.

Stroop, J. (1935). Studies of interference in serial verbal reactions. *Journal of Experimental Psychology, 18,* 624–643.

Strupp, H. H. (1981). Toward a refinement of time-limited dynamic psychotherapy. In S. H. Budman (Ed.), *Forms of brief therapy.* New York: Guilford.

Suedfeld, P., & Piedrahita, L. E. (1984). Intimations of mortality: Integrative simplification as a precursor of death. *Journal of Personality and Social Psychology, 47*(4), 848–852.

Suematsu, H., Ishikawa, H., Kuboki, T., & Ito, T. (1985). Statistical studies on anorexia nervosa in Japan: Detailed clinical data on 1,011 patients. *Psychotherapy and Psychosomatics, 43,* 96–103.

Suls, J., & Fletcher, R. L. (1983). Social comparison in the social and physical sciences: An archival study. *Journal of Personality and Social Psychology, 44,* 575–580.

Suls, J. M., & Miller, R. L. (Eds.). (1977). *Social comparison processes: Theoretical and empirical perspectives.* Washington, DC: Hemisphere.

Summers, G., & Feldman, N. S. (1984). Blaming the victim versus blaming the perpetrator: An attributional analysis of spouse abuse. *Journal of Social and Clinical Psychology, 2,* 339–347.

Super, D. E. (1985). Career and life development. In D. Brown & L. Brooks (Eds.), *Career choice and development.* San Francisco: Jossey-Bass.

Swann, W. B., Jr., & Pittman, T. S. (1977). Initiating play activity in children: The moderating influence of verbal cues on intrinsic motivation. *Child Development, 48,* 1125–1132.

Swets, J. A., Tanner, W. P., Jr., & Birdsall, T. G. (1961). Decision processes in perception. *Psychological Review, 68,* 301–340.

Szasz, T. S. (1961). *The myth of mental illness.* New York: Harper & Row.

Szmukler, G. I., & Russell, G. F. M. (1986). Outcome and prognosis of anorexia nervosa. In K. D. Brownell & J. P. Foreyt (Eds.), *Handbook of eating disorders.* New York: Basic Books.

Tajfel, H. (Ed.). (1982). *Social identity and intergroup relations.* London: Cambridge University Press.

Tajfel, H., & Turner, J. C. (1986). The social identity theory of intergroup behavior. In S. Worchel & W. G.

Austin (Eds.), *The psychology of intergroup relations* (2nd ed., pp. 7–24). Chicago: Nelson Hall.

Tanford, S., & Penrod, S. (1984). Social influence model: A formal integration of research on majority and minority influence processes. *Psychological Bulletin, 95,* 189–225.

Tannen, D. (1986). *That's not what I meant! How conversational style makes or breaks relationships.* New York: Ballantine.

Tannen, D. (1990). *You just don't understand: Women and men in conversation.* New York: Ballantine.

Taub, J. M. (1971). The sleep-wakefulness cycle in Mexican adults. *Journal of Cross-Cultural Psychology, 2*(4), 353–363.

Taylor, C. W. (1988). Various approaches to and definitions of creativity. In R. J. Sternberg (Ed.), *The nature of creativity.* New York: Cambridge University Press.

Taylor, S. E. (1979). Hospital patient behavior: Reactance, helplessness, or control? *Journal of Social Issues, 35,* 156–184.

Taylor, S. E. (1983). Adjustment to threatening events: A theory of cognitive adaptation. *American Psychologist, 38,* 1161–1173.

Taylor, S. E. (1990). Health psychology: The science and the field. *American Psychologist, 45*(1), 40–50.

Taylor, S. E. (1991). *Health psychology* (2nd ed.). New York: McGraw-Hill.

Taylor, S. E., & Aspinwall, L. G. (1990). Psychological aspects of chronic illness. In G. R. Van den Bos & P. T. Costa, Jr. (Eds.), *Psychological aspects of serious illness.* Washington, DC: American Psychological Association.

Taylor, S. E., & Brown, J. D. (1988). Illusion and well-being: A social psychological perspective on mental health. *Psychological Bulletin, 103*(2), 193–210.

Tedeschi, J. T., Schlenker, B. R., & Bonoma, T. V. (1971). Cognitive dissonance: Private ratiocination or public spectacle? *American Psychologist, 26,* 685–695.

Teghtsoonian, R. (1971). On the exponents in Stevens' law and the constant in Ekman's law. *Psychological Review, 78*(1), 71–80.

Teitelbaum, P. (1961). Disturbances in feeding and drinking behavior after hypothalamic lesions. In M. R. Jones (Ed.), *Nebraska symposium on motivation.* Lincoln: University of Nebraska Press.

Teller, D. Y., & Bornstein, M. H. (1987). Infant color vision and color perception. In P. Salapatek & L. Cohen (Eds.), *Handbook of infant perception: Vol. 1. From sensation to perception* (pp. 185–236). Orlando, FL: Academic Press.

Teller, D. Y., & Movshon, J. A. (1986). Visual development. *Vision Research, 26,* 1483–1506.

Terhune, K. W. (1968). Studies of motives, cooperation, and conflict within laboratory microcosms. In G. H. Snyder (Ed.), *Studies in international conflict* (Vol. 4, pp. 29–58). Buffalo, NY: State University of New York at Buffalo, Council on International Studies.

Terman, L. M. (1925). *Genetic studies of genius: Mental and physical traits of a thousand gifted children* (Vol. 1). Stanford, CA: Stanford University Press.

Terman, L. M., & Merrill, M. A. (1937). *Measuring intelligence.* Boston: Houghton Mifflin.

Terman, L. M., & Merrill, M. A. (1973). *Stanford-Binet Intelligence Scale: Manual for the third revision.* Boston: Houghton Mifflin.

Terman, L. M., & Oden, M. H. (1959). *Genetic studies of genius: The gifted group at midlife* (Vol. 4). Stanford, CA: Stanford University Press.

Terrace, H. S. (1979). *Nim.* New York: Knopf.

Thatcher, R. W., Walker, R. A., & Giudice, S. (1987). Human cerebral hemispheres develop at different rates and ages. *Science, 236,* 1110–1113.

Thigpen, C. H., & Cleckley, H. M. (1957). *The three faces of Eve.* New York: Fawcett.

Thomas, A., & Chess, S. (1977). *Temperament and development.* New York: Brunner/Mazel.

Thomas, A., Chess, S., & Birch, H. G. (1970). The origin of personality. *Scientific American, 223*(2).

Thomas, J. C., Jr. (1974). An analysis of behavior in the hobbits-orcs problem. *Cognitive Psychology, 6,* 257–269.

Thomas, V. J., & Rose, F. D. (1991). Ethnic differences in the experience of pain. *Social Science and Medicine, 32,* 1063–1066.

Thompson, R. A., Lamb, M. E., & Estes, D. (1982). Stability of infant-mother attachment and its relationship to changing life circumstances in an unselected middle class sample. *Child Development, 53,* 144–148.

Thompson, R. F. (1975). *Introduction to physiological psychology.* New York: Harper & Row.

Thompson, R. F. (1987). The cerebellum and memory storage: A response to Bloedel. *Science, 238,* 1729–1730.

Thompson, S. C., Cheek, P. R., & Graham, M. A. (1988). The other side of perceived control: Disadvantages and negative effects. In S. Spacapan & S. Oskamp (Eds.), *The social psychology of health: The Claremont applied social psychology conference* (Vol. 2, pp. 69–94). Beverly Hills, CA: Sage.

Thompson, S. K. (1975). Gender labels and early sex role development. *Child Development, 46,* 339–347.

Thompson, W. R. (1954). The inheritance and development of intelligence. *Proceedings of the Association for Research on Nervous and Mental Disease, 33,* 209–231.

Thorndike, E. L. (1898). Animal intelligence: An experimental study of the associative processes in animals. *Psychological Monographs, 2*(Whole No. 8).

Thorndike, E. L. (1905). *The elements of psychology.* New York: Seiler.

Thorndike, E. L. (1911). *Animal intelligence: Experimental studies.* New York: Macmillan.

Thurstone, L. L. (1924). *The nature of intelligence.* New York: Harcourt, Brace.

Thurstone, L. L. (1938). *Primary mental abilities.* Chicago: University of Chicago Press.

Tillich, P. (1952). *Courage to be.* New Haven, CT: Yale University Press.

Tinbergen, N. (1951). *The study of instinct.* Oxford, England: Clarendon.

Titchener, E. B. (1910). *A text-book of psychology.* New York: Macmillan.

Tolman, E. C. (1932). *Purposive behavior in animals and men.* New York: Appleton-Century-Crofts.

Tolman, E. C. (1959). Principles of purposive behavior.

In S. Koch (Ed.), *Psychology: A study of science* (Vol. 2, pp. 92–157). New York: McGraw-Hill.

Tolman, E. C., & Honzik, C. H. (1930). "Insight" in rats. *University of California Publications in Psychology, 4,* 215–232.

Tomkins, S. S. (1962). *Affect, imagery, and consciousness: Vol. 1. The positive affects.* New York: Springer.

Tomkins, S. S. (1963). *Affect, imagery, and consciousness: Vol. 2. The negative affects.* New York: Springer.

Torrance, E. P. (1974). *The Torrance tests of creative thinking: Technical-norms manual.* Bensenville, IL: Scholastic Testing Services.

Torrance, E. P. (1984). *Torrance tests of creative thinking: Streamlined (revised) manual, Figural A and B.* Bensenville, IL: Scholastic Testing Services.

Torrance, E. P. (1988). The nature of creativity as manifest in its testing. In R. J. Sternberg (Ed.), *The nature of creativity* (pp. 43–75). New York: Cambridge University Press.

Torrey, E. F. (1986). *Witchdoctors and psychiatrists: The common roots of psychotherapy and its future.* New York: Harper & Row.

Tourangeau, R., & Ellsworth, P. C. (1979). The role of facial response in the experience of emotion. *Journal of Personality and Social Psychology, 37,* 1519–1531.

Townsend, J. T. (1971). A note on the identifiability of parallel and serial processes. *Perception and Psychophysics, 10,* 161–163.

Trager, J. (1992). *The people's chronology.* New York: Holt.

Treisman, A. M. (1964a). Monitoring and storage of irrelevant messages in selective attention. *Journal of Verbal Learning and Verbal Behavior, 3,* 449–459.

Treisman, A. M. (1964b). Selective attention in man. *British Medical Bulletin, 20,* 12–16.

Triandis, H. C. (1994). Culture and social behavior. In W. J. Lonner & R. S. Malpass (Eds.), *Psychology and culture.* Boston: Allyn & Bacon.

Tripathi, A. N. (1979). Memory for meaning and grammatical structure: An experiment on retention of a story. *Psychological Studies, 24*(2), 136–145.

Triplett, N. (1898). The dynamogenic factors in pacemaking and competition. *American Journal of Psychology, 9,* 507–533.

Truman, M. (1977). *Women of courage.* New York: William Morrow.

Tryon, R. (1940). Genetic differences in maze-learning ability in rats. In the *39th yearbook of the national society for the study of education.* Chicago: University of Chicago Press.

Tsunoda, T. (1979). Difference in the mechanism of emotion in Japanese and Westerner. *Psychotherapy and Psychosomatics, 31*(1–4), 367–372.

Tulving, E. (1962). Subjective organization in free recall of "unrelated" words. *Psychological Review, 69,* 344–354.

Tulving, E. (1966). Subjective organization and effects of repetition in multi-trial free-recall learning. *Journal of Verbal Learning and Verbal Behavior, 5,* 193–197.

Tulving, E. (1972). Episodic and semantic memory. In E. Tulving & W. Donaldson (Eds.), *Organization of memory.* New York: Academic Press.

Tulving, E., & Pearlstone, Z. (1966). Availability versus accessibility of information in memory for words. *Journal of Verbal Learning and Verbal Behavior, 5,* 381–391.

Tulving, E., & Thomson, D. M. (1973). Encoding specificity and retrieval processes in episodic memory. *Psychological Review, 80,* 352–373.

Turk, D. C., Meichenbaum, D., & Genest, M. (1983). *Pain and behavioral medicine: A cognitive behavioral perspective.* New York: Guilford.

Turk, D. C., & Rudy, T. E. (1992). Cognitive factors and persistent pain: A glimpse into Pandora's box. *Cognitive Therapy and Research, 16*(2), 99–122.

Turnbull, C. (1961). *The forest people: A study of pygmies of the Congo.* New York: Simon & Schuster.

Turner, J. C. (1987). *Rediscovering the social group: A self-categorization theory.* Oxford, England: Basil Blackwell.

Turner, R. J., & Wagonfeld, M. O. (1967). Occupational mobility and schizophrenia: An assessment of the social causation and the social selection hypothesis. *American Sociological Review, 32,* 104–113.

Tversky, A., & Kahneman, D. (1973). Availability: A heuristic for judging frequency and probability. *Cognitive Psychology, 5,* 207–232.

Ulrich, R., & Azrin, N. H. (1962). Reflexive fighting in response to aversive stimulation. *Journal of the Experimental Analysis of Behavior, 5,* 511–520.

Underwood, B. J. (1957). Interference and forgetting. *Psychological Review, 64,* 49–60.

United States Department of Labor, Bureau of Labor Statistics (1987). *Statistical Abstract of the United States* (107th ed.). Washington, DC: U.S. Department of Commerce.

Valenstein, E. S. (1986). *Great and desperate cures.* New York: Basic Books.

Van Bezooijen, R., Otto, S. A., & Heenan, T. A. (1983). Recognition of vocal expressions of emotion: A three-nation study to identify universal characteristics. *Journal of Cross-Cultural Psychology, 14*(4), 387–406.

Vandell, D., & Mueller, E. C. (1980). Peer play and friendships during the first two years. In H. C. Foot, A. J. Chapman, & J. R. Smith (Eds.), *Friendship and social relations in children.* New York: Wiley.

VanderPlate, C., Aral, S. O., & Magder, L. (1988). The relationship among genital herpes simplex virus, stress, and social support. *Health Psychology, 7,* 159–168.

Vaughan, D. (1986). *Uncoupling.* New York: Vintage Books.

Vaughn, B. E., Gove, F. L., & Egeland, B. (1980). The relationship between out-of-home care and the quality of infant–mother attachment in an economically disadvantaged population. *Child Development, 51,* 1203–1214.

Vernon, P. A., & Mori, M. (1992). Intelligence, reaction times, and peripheral nerve conduction velocity. *Intelligence, 16*(3–4), 273–288.

Vernon, P. E. (1971). *The structure of human abilities.* London: Methuen.

Veroff, J. (1957). Development and validation of a projective measure of power motivation. *Journal of Abnormal and Social Psychology, 54,* 1–8.

Viglione, D. J., & Exner, J. E. (1983). Current research in the comprehensive Rorschach system. In J. N. Butcher & C. D. Spielberger (Eds.), *Advances in personality assessment* (Vol. 2, pp. 13–40). Hillsdale, NJ: Erlbaum.

Vokey, J. R., & Read, J. D. (1985). Subliminal messages: Between the devil and the media. *American Psychologist, 40,* 1231–1239.

Vygotsky, L. S. (1962). *Thought and language.* Cambridge, MA: MIT Press. (Original work published 1934)

Vygotsky, L. S. (1978). *Mind in society: The development of higher psychological processes.* Cambridge, MA: Harvard University Press.

Waddington, C. H. (1956). *Principles of embryology.* London: Macmillan.

Wade, C., & Cirese, S. (1991). *Human sexuality* (2nd ed.). New York: Harcourt Brace Jovanovich.

Wagner, A. R., & Rescorla, R. A. (1972). Inhibition in Pavlovian conditioning: Application of a theory. In R. A. Boakes & M. S. Halliday (Eds.), *Inhibition and learning.* New York: Academic Press.

Wagner, D. A. (1978). Memories of Morocco: The influence of age, schooling, and environment on memory. *Cognitive Psychology, 10,* 1–28.

Wagner, R. K., & Sternberg, R. J. (1985). Practical intelligence in real-world pursuits: The role of tacit knowledge. *Journal of Personality and Social Psychology, 49,* 436–458.

Walberg, H. J. (1988). Creativity and talent as learning. In R. J. Sternberg (Ed.), *The nature of creativity.* New York: Cambridge University Press.

Wald, G., & Brown, P. K. (1965). Human color vision and color blindness. *Cold Spring Harbor Symposia on Quantitative Biology, 30,* 345–359.

Walker, L. J. (1989). A longitudinal study of moral reasoning. *Child Development, 60,* 157–166.

Wallace, R. K., & Benson, H. (1972). The physiology of meditation. *Scientific American,* 84–90.

Walsh, D. C., Hingson, R. W., Merrigan, D. M., Levenson, S. M., et al. (1991). A randomized trial of treatment for alcohol abusing workers. *New England Journal of Medicine, 325,* 775–782.

Walster, E., Aronson, E., Abrahams, D., & Rottman, L. (1966). The importance of physical attractiveness in dating behavior. *Journal of Personality and Social Psychology, 4,* 508–516.

Walster, E., & Berscheid, E. (1974). A little bit about love: A minor essay on a major topic. In T. L. Huston (Ed.), *Foundations of interpersonal attraction.* New York: Academic Press.

Walster, E., Walster, G. W., & Berscheid, E. (1978). *Equity: Theory and research.* Boston: Allyn & Bacon.

Walters, G. C., & Grusec, J. F. (1977). *Punishment.* San Francisco: Freeman.

Walters, J. M., & Gardner, H. (1986). The theory of multiple intelligences: Some issues and answers. In R. J. Sternberg & R. K. Wagner (Eds.), *Practical intelligence:*

Nature and origins of competence in the everyday world (pp. 163–182). New York: Cambridge University Press.

Wangensteen, O. H., & Carlson, A. J. (1931). Hunger sensation after total gastrectomy. *Proceedings of the Society for Experimental Biology, 28,* 545–547.

Warren, L. W., & McEachren, L. (1983). Psychosocial correlates of depressive symptomatology in adult women. *Journal of Abnormal Psychology, 92,* 151–160.

Warren, R. M., Obusek, C. J., Farmer, R. M., & Warren, R. P. (1969). Auditory sequence: Confusion of patterns other than speech or music. *Science, 164,* 586–587.

Wason, P. C., & Johnson-Laird, P. N. (1972). *Psychology of reasoning: Structure and content.* London: B. T. Batsford.

Waters, E., Wippman, J., & Sroufe, L. A. (1979). Attachment, positive affect, and competence in the peer group: Two studies in construct validation. *Child Development, 50,* 821–829.

Watkins, M. J., & Tulving, E. (1975). Episodic memory: When recognition fails. *Journal of Experimental Psychology: General, 104,* 5–29.

Watson, D. (1989). Strangers' ratings of the five robust personality factors: Evidence of a surprising convergence with self-report. *Journal of Personality & Social Psychology, 57*(1), 120–128.

Watson, J. B. (1928). *Psychological care of infant and child.* New York: Norton.

Watson, J. B. (1930). *Behaviorism* (rev. ed.). New York: Norton.

Watson, J. B., & McDougall, W. (1929). *The battle of behaviorism.* New York: Norton.

Watson, O. M. (1970). *Proxemic behavior: A cross-cultural study.* The Hague, Netherlands: Mouton.

Waugh, N. C., & Norman, D. A. (1965). Primary memory. *Psychological Review, 72,* 89–104.

Weale, R. A. (1986). Aging and vision. *Vision Research, 26,* 1507–1512.

Weber, E. H. (1834). *De pulen, resorptione, auditu et tactu: Annotationes anatomicae et physiologicae.* Leipzig, Germany: Koehler.

Wechsler, D. (1974). *The measurement and appraisal of adult intelligence.* Baltimore: Williams & Wilkins.

Weinberger, D. R., Wagner, R. L., & Wyatt, R. J. (1983). Neuropathological studies of schizophrenia: A selective review. *Schizophrenia Bulletin, 9,* 193–212.

Weiner, B. (1986). *An attributional theory of motivation and emotion.* New York: Springer-Verlag.

Weingartner, H., Rudorfer, M. V., Buchsbaum, M. S., & Linnoila, M. (1983). Effects of serotonin on memory impairments produced by ethanol. *Science, 221,* 442–473.

Weinstein, S. (1968). Intensive and extensive aspects of tactile sensitivity as a function of body part, sex, and laterality. In D. R. Renshalo (Ed.), *The skin senses* (pp. 195–218). Springfield, IL: Thomas.

Weisberg, R. W. (1986). *Creativity: Genius and other myths.* New York: Freeman.

Weisberg, R. W. (1988). Problem solving and creativity. In R. J. Sternberg (Ed.), *The nature of creativity.* New York: Cambridge University Press.

Weisberg, R. W. (1992). *Creativity: Beyond the myth of genius.* New York: Freeman.

Weiss, R. S. (1975). *Marital separation.* New York: Basic Books.

Weiss, R. (1982). Attachment in adult life. In C. M. Parkes & J. Stevenson-Hinde (Eds.), *The place of attachment in human behavior.* New York: Basic Books.

Weissman, M. M., & Klerman, G. L. (1977). Sex differences in the epidemiology of depression. *Archives of General Psychiatry, 36,* 98–111.

Weissman, M. M., Klerman, G. L., & Paykel, E. S. (1971). Clinical evaluation of hostility in depression. *American Journal of Psychiatry, 128,* 261–266.

Weissman, M. M., & Myers, J. K. (1978). Affective disorders in a United States urban community: The use of research diagnostic criteria in an epidemiologic survey. *Archives of General Psychiatry, 35,* 1304–1311.

Weizenbaum, J. (1966). ELIZA—A computer program for the study of natural language communication between man and machine. *Communications of the Association for Computing Machinery, 9,* 36–45.

Werner, E. E. (1972). Infants around the world. *Journal of Cross-Cultural Psychology, 3*(2), 111–134.

Wertheimer, M. (1912). Experimentelle Studien uber das Sehen von Bewegung. *Zeitschrift fur Psychologie, 61,* 161–65.

Wertheimer, M. (1959). *Productive thinking* (rev. ed.). New York: Harper & Row. (Original work published 1945)

Wesman, A. E., & Ricks, D. F. (1966). *Mood and personality.* New York: Holt, Rinehart & Winston.

West, R. L. (1986). Everyday memory and aging. *Developmental Neuropsychology, 2*(4), 323–344.

Wever, E. G. (1970). *Theory of hearing.* New York: Wiley.

Wever, R. A. (1979). *The circadian system of man.* Heidelberg, West Germany: Springer-Verlag.

Wheeler, D. D. (1970). Processes in word recognition. *Cognitive Psychology, 1,* 59–85.

White, R. W. (1959). Motivation reconsidered: The concept of competence. *Psychological Review, 66,* 297–333.

Whitley, B. E., Jr., & Frieze, I. H. (1985). Children's causal attributions for success and failure in achievement settings: A meta-analysis. *Journal of Educational Psychology, 77,* 608–616.

Whorf, B. L. (1956). In J. B. Carroll (Ed.), *Language, thought and reality: Selected writings of Benjamin Lee Whorf.* Cambridge, MA: MIT Press.

Wiesel, T. N., & Hubel, D. H. (1966). Spatial and chromatic interactions in the lateral geniculate body of the rhesus monkey. *Journal of Neurophysiology, 29*(6), 1115–1156.

Wilder, D. A., & Allen, V. L. (1978). Group membership and preference for information about others. *Personality and Social Psychology Bulletin, 4*(1), 106–110.

Williams, M. (1970). *Brain damage and the mind.* London: Penguin.

Williams, R. (1986). An untrusting heart. In M. G. Walraven & H. E. Fitzgerald (Eds.), *Annuals editions: Human development 86/87.* Guilford, CT: Dushkin.

Williams, R. B., Jr., & Barefoot, J. C. (1988). Coronary-prone behavior: The emerging role of the hostility complex. In B. K. Houston & C. R. Snyder (Eds.), *Type A behavior pattern: Current trends and future directions* (pp. 189–211). New York: Wiley.

Willis, S. L. (1985). Towards an educational psychology of the older adult learner: Intellectual and cognitive bases. In J. E. Birren & K. W. Schaie (Eds.), *Handbook of the psychology of aging* (2nd ed.). New York: Van Nostrand Reinhold.

Wilson, D. W. (1981). Is helping a laughing matter? *Psychology, 18,* 6–9.

Wingert, P., & Kantrowitz, B. (1990). The day care generation. *Newsweek special edition: The 21st century family,* pp. 86–92.

Winter, D. G. (1973). *The power motive.* New York: Free Press.

Winter, D. G., & Stewart, A. J. (1978). Power motivation. In H. London & J. Exner (Eds.), *Dimensions of personality.* New York: Wiley.

Wissler, C. (1901). The correlation of mental and physical tests. *Psychological Review, Monograph Supplement 3*(6).

Witkin, H. A., & Berry, J. W. (1975). Psychological differentiation in cross-cultural perspective. *Journal of Cross-Cultural Psychology, 6*(1), 4–87.

Witkin, H. A., & Goodenough, D. (1981). Cognitive styles: Essence and origins. In *Psychological Monographs* (Vol. 51). New York: International Universities Press.

Wollersheim, J. P. (1970). Effectiveness of group therapy based upon learning principles in the treatment of overweight women. *Journal of Abnormal Psychology, 76*(3, Pt. 1), 462–474.

Wolpe, J. (1958). *Psychotherapy by reciprocal inhibition.* Stanford, CA: Stanford University Press.

Wong, D. F., Wagner, H. N., Tune, L. E., Dannals, R. F., Pearlson, G. D., Links, J. M., Tamminga, C. A., Broussolle, E. P., Ravert, H. T., Wilson, A. A., Toung, J. K. T., Malat, J., Williams, J. A., O'Tuma, L. A., Snyder, S. H., Kuhar, M. J., & Gjedde, A. (1986). Positron emission tomography reveals elevated D2 dopamine receptors in drug-naive schizophrenics. *Science, 234,* 1558–1563.

Woodruff, R. A., Goodwin, D. W., & Guze, S. B. (1974). *Psychiatric diagnosis.* New York: Oxford University Press.

Woodworth, R. S. (1918). *Dynamic psychology.* New York: Columbia University Press.

Woolfolk, R. L., Carr-Kaffashan, K., McNulty, T. F., Lehrer P. M. (1976). Meditation training as a treatment for insomnia. *Behavior Therapy, 7,* 359–365.

Woon, T., Masuda, M., Wagner, N. N., & Holmes, T. H. (1971). The *Social Readjustment Rating Scale:* A cross-cultural study of Malaysians and Americans. *Journal of Cross-Cultural Psychology, 2,* 373–386

World Health Organization. (1992). *International classification of diseases* (10th ed.). Geneva: Author.

Wright, R. H. (1977). Odor and molecular vibration: Neural coding of olfactory information. *Journal of Theoretical Biology, 64,* 473–502.

Wright, R. H. (1982). *The sense of smell.* Boca Raton, FL: CRC Press.

Yalom, I. D. (1992). *When Nietzsche wept.* New York: Basic Books.

Yamamoto, T., Yuyama, N., & Kawamura, Y. (1981a). Central processing of taste perception. In Y. Katsuki, R. Norgren, & M. Sato (Eds.), *Brain mechanisms of sensation.* New York: Wiley.

Yamamoto, T., Yuyama, N., & Kawamura, Y. (1981b). Cortical neurons responding to tactile, thermal and taste stimulations of the rat's tongue. *Brain Research, 221*(1), 202–206.

Yang, K. (1986). Chinese personality and its change. In M. H. Bond (Ed.), *The psychology of the Chinese people.* Hong Kong: Oxford University Press.

Yanis, I., & Meyer, D. E. (1987). Activation and metacognition of inaccessible stored information: Potential bases of incubation effects in problem solving. *Journal of Experimental Psychology: Learning, Memory, and Cognition, 13,* 187–205.

Yerkes, R. M., & Dodson, J. B. (1908). The relation of strength of stimulus to rapidity of habit formation. *Journal of Comparative Neurology and Psychology, 18,* 459–482.

Young, J. E. (1990). *Cognitive therapy for personality disorders: A schema-focused approach.* Sarasota, FL: Professional Resource Exchange.

Young, J., & Klosko, J. (1993). *Reinventing your life.* New York: St. Martin's Press.

Young, T. (1948). Observations on vision. In W. Dennis (Ed.), *Readings in the history of psychology* (pp. 96–101). New York: Appleton-Century-Crofts. (Original work published 1901)

Yussen, S. R. (1977). Characteristics of moral dilemmas written by adolescents. *Developmental Psychology, 13,* 162–163.

Zaidel, E. (1983). A response to Gazzaniga: Language in the right hemisphere, convergent perspectives. *American Psychologist, 38*(5), 542–546.

Zajonc, R. B. (1965). Social facilitation. *Science, 149,* 269–274.

Zajonc, R. B. (1968). Attitudinal effects of mere exposure. *Journal of Personality and Social Psychology Monograph Supplement, 9*(2), 1–27.

Zajonc, R. B. (1980). Compliance. In P. B. Paulus (Ed.), *Psychology of group influence* (pp. 35–60). Hillsdale, NJ: Erlbaum.

Zajonc, R. B. (1984). On the primacy of affect. *American Psychologist, 39,* 117–129.

Zajonc, R. B., Heingartner, A., & Herman, E. M. (1969). Social enhancement and impairment of performance in the cockroach. *Journal of Personality and Social Psychology, 22,* 242–248.

Zajonc, R. B., Pietromonaco, P., & Bargh, J. (1982). Independence and interaction of affect and cognition. In M. S. Clark & S. T. Fiske (Eds.), *Affect and cognition* (pp. 211–227). Hillsdale, NJ: LEA Publications.

Zaleski, C. (1987). *Otherworld journeys: Accounts of near-death experience in medieval and modern times.* Oxford, England: Oxford University Press.

Zamansky, H. S., & Bartis, S. P. (1985). The dissociation of an experience: The hidden observer observed. *Journal of Abnormal Psychology, 94,* 243–248.

Zanna, M. P., & Hamilton, D. L. (1972). Attribute dimension and patterns of trait inferences. *Psychonomic Science, 27,* 353–354.

Zanna, M. P., & Hamilton, D. L. (1977). Further evidence for meaning change in impression formation. *Journal of Experimental Social Psychology, 13,* 224–238.

Zigler, E. (1982). Development versus difference theories of mental retardation and the problem of motivation. In E. Zigler & D. Balla (Eds.), *Mental retardation: The developmental-difference controversy.* Hillsdale, NJ: Erlbaum.

Zigler, E., & Berman, W. (1983). Discerning the future of early childhood intervention. *American Psychologist, 38,* 894–906.

Zimbardo, P. G. (1972, April). Psychology of imprisonment. *Transition/Society,* pp. 4–8.

Zimbardo, P. G., Weisenberg, M. Firestone, I., & Levy, B. (1965). Communicator effectiveness in producing public conformity and private attitude change. *Journal of Personality, 33,* 233–255.

Zola-Morgan, S. M., & Squire, L. R. (1990). The primate hippocampal formation: Evidence for a time-limited role in memory storage. *Science, 250,* 228–290.

Zuckerman, H. (1983). The scientific elite: Nobel laureates' mutual influences. In R. S. Albert (Ed.), *Genius and eminence: The social psychology of creativity and exceptional achievement* (Vol. 5, pp. 241–252). New York: Pergamon.

Zuckerman, M. (1969). Response set in Check List Test: A sometimes thing. *Psychological Reports, 25*(3), 773–774.

Zuckerman, M. (1978). Sensation seeking. In H. London & J. E. Exner (Eds.), *Dimensions of personality* (pp. 487–560). New York: Wiley.

Zuckerman, M. (1985). Biological foundations of the sensation-seeking temperament. In J. Strelau, F. H. Farley, & A. Gale (Eds.), *The biological bases of personality and behavior: Vol. 1. Theories, measurement techniques, and development.* Washington, DC: Hemisphere.

Zuckerman, M., Klorman, R., Larrance, D. T., & Speigel, N. H. (1981). Facial, autonomic, and subjective components of emotion: The facial feedback hypothesis versus the externalizer-internalizer distinction. *Journal of Personality and Social Psychology, 41,* 929–944.

ILLUSTRATION CREDITS

Chapter 1
p. 6 (left), H. Christoph/Black Star; p. 6 (middle), Martin Rogers/Tony Stone Images; p. 6 (right), Dan McCoy/Rainbow; p. 8 (left), Giraudon/Art Resource, NY, © 1995 ARS, NY; p. 8 (right), G. Nimatallah/Superstock, © 1995 ARS, NY; p. 11, Robert E. Daemmrich/Tony Stone Images; p. 16, Scala/Art Resource, NY, © 1995 ARS, NY; p. 20, Erich Lessing/Art Resource, NY; p. 23, Jane Goodall Institute; p. 25, Mark Richards/PhotoEdit; p. 29, Copyright 1965 by Stanley Milgram. From the film OBEDIENCE, distributed by the Pennsylvania State University, Audio Visual Services

Chapter 2
p. 39, Vatican Museums & Galleries/Scala/Superstock; p. 41, Art Resource, NY; p. 42(both), Archives of the History of American Psychology, University of Akron; p. 43, The Image Works Archives; pp. 46 and 47, Archives of the History of American Psychology, University of Akron; p. 48, Culver Pictures; p. 49 (top), © 1993 John Jonik/The Cartoon Bank, Inc.; p. 49 (bottom), Culver Pictures; p. 50, Archives of the History of American Psychology, University of Akron; p. 51, © 1993 Jack Zigler/The Cartoon Bank, Inc.; p. 53, Bettmann Archive; p. 54(top), Archives of the History of American Psychology, University of Akron; p. 54 (bottom), Kobal Collection; p. 55, Chris J. Johnson/Stock Boston; p. 57 (left), Georges Seurat, French, 1859–1891, *A Sunday on La Grande Jatte* —1884, oil on canvas, 1884–86, 207.6 x 308 cm, Helen Birch Bartlett Memorial Collections, 1926.224, photograph © 1993, Art Institute of Chicago. All Rights Reserved; p. 57 (right), Georges Seurat, French, 1859–1891, *A Sunday on La Grande Jatte* —1884, oil on canvas, 1884–86, 207.6 x 308 cm, Helen Birch Bartlett Memorial Collections, 1926.224, detail: view #28, photograph © 1993, Art Institute of Chicago. All Rights Reserved; p. 59, Culver Pictures; p. 60, William Carter/Brooks/Cole Publishing; p. 61, Carl Rogers Memorial Library

Chapter 3
p. 75 (left), Michael Tweedie/Photo Researchers; p. 75 (right), M. W. F. Tweedie/Bruce Coleman, Inc.; p. 77, CNRI/SPL/Photo Researchers; p. 81, Alfred Pasieka/SPL/Photo Researchers; p. 85, Garvis Kerimian/Peter Arnold, Inc.; p. 86, Manfred Kage/Peter Arnold, Inc.; p. 89, Custom Medical Stock Photos; p. 91 (all), Kobal Collection; p. 92, Courtesy of Dr. Michael Posner; p. 93, THE FAR SIDE, © 1986, FARWORKS, INC./Distributed by Universal Press Syndicate. Reprinted with permission. All rights reserved; pp. 96 and 97, Biophoto Associates/Science Source/Photo Researchers; p. 98, H. Christoph/Black Star; p. 99, Courtesy of Dr. Brenda A. Milner; p. 101 (top), CNRI/SPL/Photo Researchers; p. 101 (top middle), Ohio Nuclear Corporation/SPL/Photo Researchers; p. 101 (bottom middle), CNRI/SPL/Photo Researchers; p. 101 (bottom), Spencer Grant/Stock Boston; p. 102, M. Romine/Superstock; p. 103 (left), John C. Mazziotte/PhotoEdit; p. 103 (right), NIH/Science Source/Photo Researchers; p. 104, Alexander Tsiaras/Stock Boston; p. 105, Omikron/Science Source/Photo Researchers

Chapter 4
Figure 4-1, p. 121, "Snellen Vision Chart." Reprinted by permission of The Optical Society of America; p. 122, Peter Menzel/Stock Boston; Figure 4-2, p. 123, Galanter, Eugene. "Sample Absolute Thresholds." From *Contemporary Psychophysics in New Directions in Psychology.* Copyright © 1962. Reprinted by permission of the author; pp. 125 and 126, Archives of the History of American Psychology, University of Akron; p. 128, Fritz Goro, Life Magazine, © Time Warner; p. 132, Omikron/Photo Researchers; p. 134 (both), David Young-Wolff/PhotoEdit; p. 137, Courtesy of Dr. Norma Graham; p. 138 (both), Leonard Lessin/Peter Arnold, Inc.; p. 139 (top), Courtesy of Munsell Corporation; p. 139 (bottom left & right), Fritz Goro, Life Magazine, © Time Warner; p. 141, Courtesy of Dr. Dorothea Jameson; p. 142 (both), John Eastcott/Yva Momatiuk/The Image Works; p. 146, Biophoto Associates/Science Source/Photo Researchers; p. 148, Dr. J. E. Hawkins/Kresge Hearing Research Institute; p. 149 (top), Bob Daemmerich/Stock Boston; p. 149 (bottom), National Library of Medicine; p. 151, SIU/Peter Arnold, Inc.; p. 154 (left), John Cunningham/Visuals Unlimited; p. 154 (right), Michael Viard/Peter Arnold, Inc.; p. 157 (top), Bohdan Hrynewych/Stock Boston; p. 157 (bottom), Claus Meyer/Black Star; p. 158, Ed Reschke/Peter Arnold, Inc.; Figures 4-38 and 4-39, pp. 159 and 160, Kenshalo, D. R. "Average Absolute Thresholds for Different Regions of the Female and Male Skin." From THE SKIN SENSES. Copyright © 1968. Courtesy of Charles C. Thomas, Publisher, Springfield, Illinois; p. 161 (left), Jean-Yves Roszniewski/Photo Researchers; p. 161 (right), W. Strode/Superstock; p. 162, © Biophoto Associates/Science Source/Photo Researchers

Chapter 5
Figure 5-1, p. 169, Kanizsa, Gaetano. Adapted from "Subjective Contours" by Gaetano Kanizsa. Copyright © 1976 by Scientific American, Inc. All rights reserved; p. 169, ©1958 M. C. Esher/Cordon Art, Baarn, Holland; p. 170, Anestis Diakopoulos/Stock Boston; p. 171, The Granger Collection; p. 172, National Gallery, London/Bridgeman Art Library, London/Superstock; p. 176, Kaiser Porcelain Ltd., London, England; p. 179, Courtesy of Dr. Wendell Garner; p. 183, Faith Hubley and Sears and Clowns. © Hubley Studios, Inc., 1994; p. 184 (both), © Norman Snyder, 1985; p. 185, Erich Lessing/Art Resource, NY; p. 187, Mark Antman/The Image Works; p. 188, Scala/Art Resource, NY; p. 192, Courtesy of Dr. Anne Treisman; p. 193, Jim Pickerell/Stock Boston

Chapter 6
p. 202, Courtesy of Dr. John Kihlstrom; p. 203, ©1994 Joe Dator/The Cartoon Bank, Inc.; p. 205 (both), Michael Siffre, © National Geographic Society; p. 206 (left bottom), Erica Lansner/Black Star; p. 206 (right top), Philippe Plailly/ SPL/Photo Researchers; Figure 6-2, p. 207, Hartmann, E. "Typical Progression of Stages During a Night's Sleep." From THE BIOLOGY OF DREAMING. Copyright © 1967. Courtesy of Charles C. Thomas, Publisher, Springfield; p. 209, ©1994 Joe Dator/The Cartoon Bank, Inc.; p. 210, Herscovici/Art

Resource, NY, © 1995 ARS, NY; p. 211, T. Rosenthal/Superstock; p. 212, © National Library of Medicine/Peter Arnold, Inc.; p. 213, © Jane Steig Parsons; p. 214, Stanford University; p. 215, Mainichi/Fugiphotos/The Image Works; p. 219, Robert E. Daemmrich/Tony Stone Images; p. 222, Dennie McDonald/PhotoEdit; p. 223, ©1994 Liz Haberfeld/The Cartoon Bank, Inc.; p. 225, Myrleen Ferguson Cate/PhotoEdit

Chapter 7
p. 237 (left), Nina Leen/Life Magazine; p. 237 (right), William Lishman and Associates; p. 240, Bettmann Archive; p. 245, Michael Newman/PhotoEdit; p. 246, Courtesy of Dr. John Garcia; p. 251 (left), Richard Wood/The Picture Cube; p. 251 (top right), Kim Massie/Rainbow; p. 251 (bottom right), Martha Cooper/Peter Arnold, Inc.; p. 256 (left), Nubar Alexanian/Stock Boston; p. 256 (right), © Bill Greene/Gamma Liaison; p. 260, The "Bizarro" cartoon by Dan Piraro is reprinted by permission of Chronicle Features, San Francisco, California; p. 261, Courtesy of Dr. Albert Bandura

Chapter 8
p. 273, Courtesy of Dr. Endel Tulving; p. 274 (left), L. Rosenthal/Superstock; p. 274 (right), T. Rosenthal/Superstock; Figure 8-1, p. 275, Atkinson, Richard C. and Richard M. Shiffrin. Adapted from "The Control of Short-term Memory" by Richard Atkinson and Richard M. Shiffrin. Copyright © 1971 by Scientific American, Inc. All rights reserved; p. 276, Patti Murray/Animals Animals; p. 277 (left), Robert Brenner/PhotoEdit; p. 277 (right), David Austen/Stock Boston; p. 278, Miro Vintoniv/Stock Boston; Figure 8-3, p. 279, Melton, A. W. "Implications of Short-term memory for a General Theory of Memory." From *Journal of Verbal Learning and Verbal Behavior*, 2, 1–21. Copyright © 1963. Reprinted by permission of Academic Press, Inc.; p. 283 (top), Brent Jones/Stock Boston; p. 283 (bottom), Superstock; p. 285, Courtesy of Dr. Gordon Bower; Figure 8-9, p. 593, Kosslyn, S. M., T. M. Ball and B. J. Reiser. "Visual Images Preserve Metric Spatial Information: Evidence from Studies of Image Scanning." From *Journal of Experiemental Psychology: Human Perception and Performance*, 4, 47–60. Copyright © 1978 by the American Psychological Association. Reprinted by permission; p. 287 (left), Spencer Grant/Gamma Liaison; p. 287 (right), Tom Prettyman/PhotoEdit; Figure 8-10, p. 289, Bartlett, F. C. "The War of the Ghosts" from REMEMBERING. Copyright © 1932 by Cambridge University Press. Reprinted with the permission of Cambridge University Press; p. 290, Courtesy of Dr. Elizabeth Loftus; p. 291 (both), Michael Newman/PhotoEdit; p. 292, Bob Daemmrich/Stock Boston; p. 293, Laurent Van Der Stockt/Gamma Liasion

Chapter 9
p. 307, Stephen R. Swinburne/Stock Boston; p. 309, Bob Daemmrich/Stock Boston; p. 310, © James Montaus, University of Rochester; p. 311 (top), Dave Bartruff/Stock Boston; p. 311 (bottom), Paul Fusco/Magnum; p. 313, Courtesy of Dr. George Miller; p. 315, Grant Le Duc/Stock Boston; p. 322, John Eastcott/Yva Momatiuik/The Image Works

Chapter 10
p. 331, R. Cord/Superstock; p. 339 (all) Superstock; p. 340 (left), Scala/Art Resource, NY; p. 340 (right), Paul Cézanne, *Mont Sainte-Victoire*, Philadelphia Museum of Art: George W. Elkins Collection; Table 10-3, p. 341, Luchins, Abraham. "The Water Jar Problem." From "Mechanization in Problem Solv-

ing: The Effect of Einstellung" in *Psychological Monographs, 54,* 1. Copyright © 1942. Reprinted by permission of the author; Table 10-4, p. 344, Gick, Mary and Keith Holyoak. "Correspondence Between the Radiation and the Military Problems." Copyright © 1983. Reprinted by permission; p. 347, Courtesy of Dr. Herbert Simon; p. 351, Courtesy of Dr. Daniel Kahneman; p. 352 (left), Leverett Bradley/Tony Stone Images; p. 352 (right), Terry Farmer/Tony Stone Images; p. 359 (left), Christie's, London/Bridgeman Art Library, London/Superstock; p. 359 (middle), National Gallery, Washington, DC/Superstock; p. 359 (right), Rijks Museum Kroller-Muller, Otterlo/A.K.G., Berlin/Superstock; p. 360, "The nature of creativity as manifest in its testing," E. Paul Torrance, pp. 50–51, in THE NATURE OF CREATIVITY, edited by Robert Sternberg, Cambridge University Press, 1988; p. 362 (top left), UPI/Bettmann; p. 362 (top right), Dan McCoy/Rainbow; p. 362 (bottom left), Joe Monroe/Photo Researchers; p. 362 (bottom middle), AP/Wide World Photos; p. 362 (bottom right), A. Berliner/Gamma Liaison

Chapter 11
p. 374, Scala/Art Resource, NY; p. 377 (top), Copyright 1994. Reproduced with permission of the Riverside Publishing Company, Chicago, IL; p. 377 (middle right), Mimi Forsyth/Monkmeyer; p. 377 (bottom right), Bob Daemmrich/The Image Works; p. 386, The Kobal Collection; p. 389, Yale University Office of Public Information; p. 390, Dr. Michael Cole; p. 391 (top left), Bob Daemmrich/The Image Works; p. 391 (bottom left), Bob Daemmrich/The Image Works; p. 391 (right), Superstock; p. 394, Courtesy of Dr. Howard Gardner; p. 398, Bettmann; p. 401, T. K. Wanstal/The Image Works; p. 402, Courtesy of Dr. Sandra Scarr

Chapter 12
p. 414, AP/Wide World Photos; p. 416, Publiphoto/Explorer/Photo Researchers; p. 418, Superstock; p. 422 (top & top middle), Myrleen Ferguson Cate/PhotoEdit; p. 422 (bottom middle), Michael Newman/PhotoEdit; p. 422 (bottom), Tom McCarthy/PhotoEdit; p. 423, Bill Anderson/Monkmeyer Press; p. 424 (both), Goodman/Monkmeyer Press; p. 426 (all), Tony Freeman/PhotoEdit; p. 427 (top), Christiana Dittmann/Rainbow; p. 427 (bottom), Charles D. Winters/Stock Boston; p. 428, Mark Antman/The Image Works; p. 429, Robert Solso/photo by Felicia Martinez/PhotoEdit; p. 432, Courtesy of Dr. John Flavell; p. 434, Courtesy of Dr. Rochel Gelman; p. 438, Stacy Pick/Stock Boston; p. 439, The Historical Society/Photo Researchers

Chapter 13
p. 447 (top left), George Chan/Photo Researchers; p. 447 (top middle), Tom Prettyman/PhotoEdit; p. 447 (top right), Myrleen Ferguson Cate/PhotoEdit; p. 447 (bottom), David Young-Wolff/PhotoEdit; p. 450, Michael Newman/PhotoEdit; p. 452, Archives of the History of American Psychology, University of Akron; p. 456, Stacy Pick/Stock Boston; p. 458, Sue Ann Miller/Tony Stone Images; p. 459, Courtesy of Dr. Eileen Mavis Hetherington; p. 461, Dan McCoy/Rainbow; p. 462, Junebug Clark/Photo Researchers; p. 463 (left), Rijks Museum, Amsterdam, Netherlands/Superstock; p. 463 (middle), Tony Freeman/PhotoEdit; p. 463 (right), David Young-Wolff/PhotoEdit; p. 464, © Daniel Grogan; p. 465, Dr. Mary Strange; p. 467 (both), Harlow Primate Lab, University of Wisconsin; p. 468, Jim Pickerell/The Image Works; p. 469, Courtesy of Dr. Edward F. Zigler; p. 473 and 477, Harvard University News Office

Chapter 14

p. 491 (left), Larry Mulvehill/The Image Works; p. 491 (right), Robert E. Daemmrich/Tony Stone Images; Figure 14-1, p. 492, Festinger and Carlsmith. "Justifying Attitude-Discrepant Behavior: The Classic Experiment." Copyright © 1959 by Houghton Mifflin; p. 493, Joe Sohm/The Image Works; p. 494, © 1994 Joe Dator/The Cartoon Bank, Inc.; Figure 14-2, p. 495, Lippa, Richard A. "Qualifying Conditions for Cognitive Dissonance." From *Introduction to Social Psychology*, p. 576, by Richard Lippa. Copyright © 1990 by Wadsworth, Inc. Reprinted by permission of Brooks/Cole Publishing Company, Pacific Grove, CA 93950; p. 496 (top), John Neubauer/Rainbow; p. 496 © 1993 Ed Frasino/The Cartoon Bank, Inc.; p. 498, Courtesy of Dr. Richard Nisbett; p. 500, Courtesy of Dr. Claude M. Steele; Table 14.1, p. 501, Asch, Solomon E. "Trait Data/Impression Formation." From *Journal of Abnormal and Social Psychology*, 41, 258–290. Copyright © 1946. Reprinted by permission of the author; p. 503, Courtesy of Dr. Robert Rosenthal; p. 505, The Bettmann Archive; p. 506, Bob Daemmrich/Stock Boston; p. 507, M. Roessler/Superstock; Figure 14-3, p. 508, Chaiken, S. and A. Eagly. "Opinion Change as a Function of Communicator Likability and Channel of Communication." Copyright © 1983. Reprinted by permission of the authors; p. 510 (left), Coco McCoy/Rainbow; p. 510 (top right), Bob Daemmrich/Stock Boston; p. 510 (bottom right), Claus Meyer/Black Star; p. 511, Christiana Dittmann/Rainbow; p. 512, David Hiser/Tony Stone Images; Figure 14-4, p. 513, John Lee. "Types of Love." Copyright © 1977, 1988 by Houghton Mifflin; p. 513, The Kobal Collection; p. 514, Margot Granitsas/The Image Works; p. 515 (bottom), T. J. Florian/Rainbow; p. 515 (top left); Martha Cooper/Peter Arnold, Inc.; p. 515 (top right), Kavaler/Art Resource, NY; p. 518 (left), Claus Meyer/Black Star; p. 518 (middle left), Superstock; p. 518 (middle right), M. Courtney-Clarke/Photo Researchers; p. 518 (right), Henry Gris/FPG; p. 520 (top left & middle left), Scala/Art Resource, NY; p. 520 (top middle right), David Young-Wolff/PhotoEdit; p. 520 (top right), Ulrike Welsch; p. 520 (bottom), LOL, Inc./FPG

Chapter 15

Figure 15-2, p. 528, Latané, B. "Social Loafing." From *Journal of Personality and Social Psychology*, 37, 822–832. Copyright © 1979. Reprinted by permission; p. 531, AP/Wide World Photos; p. 532, Ulli Steltzer; p. 533 (all), Dr. Solomon Asch; p. 537 (all), Copyright 1965 by Stanley Milgram. From the film OBEDIENCE, distributed by the Pennsylvania State University, Audio Visual Services; p. 539, AP/Wide World Photos; p. 540, Courtesy of Dr. Ellen Berscheid; p. 543, Press Telegram/Gamma Liaison; p. 544, Courtesy of Dr. Elliot Aronson; p. 545 (left); UPI/Bettmann; p. 545 (right), Mark Richards/PhotoEdit; p. 547, Bob Daemmrich/The Image Works; p. 548, Tom Walker/Stock Boston; Figure 15-10, p. 550, C. A. Anderson. "Temperature and aggression: Ubiquitous effects of heat on occurrence of human violence." From *Psychological Bulletin*, 106, 74–96. Copyright © 1989. Reprinted by permission; p. 550, Reuters/Bettmann; p. 551, Steve Starr/Stock Boston

Chapter 16

Figure 16-2, p. 559, Solomon, R. L. and J. D. Corbitt. "An Opponent-process Theory of Motivation." From *Psychological Review*, 81, 119–145. Copyright © 1974. Reprinted by permission; p. 562, Richard Howard; p. 564 (left), Holton Collection/Superstock; p. 564 (right), Rick Smolan/Stock Boston; p. 565 (both), William Thompson/The Picture Cube; p. 570 (top left), Michael Newman/PhotoEdit; p. 570 (middle left), Ulrike Welsch; p. 570 (middle right), S. O'Rourke/The Image Works; p. 570 (bottom right), Holt Confer/The Image Works; p. 571, Harlow Primate Lab, University of Wisconsin; p. 577, Courtesy of Dr. Robert Zajonc; Figure 16-9, p. 580, Plutchik, Robert. "A Language for the Emotions." Reprinted with permission from Psychology Today Magazine. Copyright © 1980 (Sussex Publishers, Inc.); p. 581 (top left), Nita Winter/The Image Works; p. 581 (top middle), Ed Lettau/Superstock; p. 581 (top right), Superstock; p. 581 (bottom left), Mike Greenlar/The Image Works; p. 581 (bottom middle), Lawrence Migdale/Stock Boston; p. 581 (bottom right), Giraudon/Art Resource, NY; Table 16-8, p. 583, Kite, M. E. and D. Deaux. "Sample Likert Scale." From *Basic and Applied Social Psychology*, 7, 137–162. Copyright © 1986. Reprinted by permission of the author; p. 585, Courtesy of Dr. Paul Ekman; p. 586, Ekman, P., Friesen, W. V., & O'Sullivan, M. (1988). Smiles: "Genuine" and "fake." *Journal of Personality and Social Psychology*, 54, 414–420

Chapter 17

p. 599, The Bettmann Archive; p. 601, UPI/Bettmann Newsphotos; p. 604, The Bettmann Archive; p. 605 (left), The Granger Collection; p. 605 (right), Courtesy of the Harvard University News Office/PhotoEdit; p. 606 (top right), The Bettmann Archive; p. 606 (bottom left), The Bettmann Archive; p. 607 (left), UPI/Bettmann; p. 607 (right), Bill Swersey/Gamma Liaison; p. 610, Minnesota Multiphasic Personality Inventory (MMPI). Copyright © the University of Minnesota 1943 (renewed 1970). This report 1982. All rights reserved. Reproduced by permission of the University of Minnesota Press; Figure 17-5b, p. 611, Minnesota Multiphasic Personality Inventory–2. Copyright © by the Regents of the University of Minnesota, 1942, 1943, (renewed 1970), 1989. Reproduced by permission of the publisher; p. 615, Peter Vandermark/Stock Boston; p. 617 (top left), Archives of the History of American Psychology, University of Akron; p. 617 (bottom right), Courtesy of Dr. Julian B. Rotter; p. 618 (left), Tony Freeman/PhotoEdit; p. 618 (right), Eddie Adams/Sygma; p. 619, Courtesy of Dr. Albert Bandura; p. 620 (top), Courtesy of Dr. Hazel Markus; p. 620 (bottom), Courtesy of Dr. Nancy Cantor; p. 621, National Library of Medicine; p. 623, Courtesy of Dr. Raymond Cattell; Table 17-5, pp. 624–625, "Cattell's Primary Source Traits." From PERSONALITY AND LEARNING THEORY, Vol. 1, by R. B. Cattell. Copyright © 1979 by permission of Springer Publishing Company, Inc., New York 10012. Used by permission; Figure 17-8, p. 626 (top), "A 16PF Profile." Reprinted with permission from Psychology Today Magazine, July 1973, pp. 40–46. Copyright © 1973 (Sussex Publishers, Inc.); Figure 17-9, p. 626 (bottom), "Eysenck's Personality Dimensions." From "Eysenck on Extroversion." Copyright © 1987. Reprinted by permission of John Wiley and Sons Publishers, New York; p. 627, Vandystadt/Photo Researchers; p. 628, Courtesy of Dr. Walter Mischel; p. 630, Courtesy of Dr. Daryl Bem

Chapter 18

p. 642 (top), The Bettmann Archive; p. 642 (bottom), The Granger Collection; Table 18-1, pp. 646–647, American Psychiatric Association: "DSM-IV Axes" from DSM Draft Criteria. American Psychiatric Association: Diagnostic and Statistical Manual of Mental Disorders, Washington, DC, American Psychiatric Association, 1993; p. 649, National Gallery, Oslo, Norway/Bridgeman Art Library, London/Superstock; p. 650

taste sensitivity and, 150
wisdom and, 439–440
Agnosia, 90, **168**–169
Agoraphobia, 645–648, 650. *See also* Anxiety disorders
AIDS (acquired immune deficiency syndrome)
anxiety about, 652
drugs for, 697
gradient of reinforcement and, 255
living with, 734
Alarm, as stress response, 722–723
Alcohol, 218, 500. *See also* Addictions; Twelve-step programs
addiction to, 249
as CNS depressant, 218–220
health and, 716
memory dysfunction and, 296
physiological damage caused by, 219
and social behavior, 500
Alcoholics Anonymous (AA), 220, 700, 701
Algorithms vs. heuristics, 333–335
Alienated achievement, and personal identity, **453**
Alienation, R. May and, 615
Alpha-wave EEG pattern, 206
Altered states of consciousness, 203
drugs and, 216–224
meditation and, 214–216
Alternate-forms reliability, 381
Alternatives to individual therapy, 699–703. *See also* Psychotherapy
Altruism, 543
and conflict resolution, 529
Alzheimer's disease. *See also* Aging
acetylcholine and, 108
memory loss in, 296
Amacrine cells, 132. *See also* Eye
American Men of Science, 397
women in, 15
American Psychiatric Association. *See Diagnostic and Statistical Manual* (DSM); DSM-IV
American Sign Language (ASL), 309
chimpanzee studies and, 311–312
left hemisphere and, 93
Amnesia, 269, 644
anterograde, 269
dissociative, 661–662
ECT and, 695–696
infantile, 269
procedural vs. declarative knowledge and, 274
retrograde, 269
study of, 99
Amphetamines, 221
Amplitude, 127
Amygdala, in limbic system of brain, 85, 86, **87**
aggression and, 548
Anabolic steroids, 112
Anabolism, 84, 716
Anaerobic exercise, 718
Anal stage, in Freudian psychosexual theory, **460**
Analogies
intelligence and, 385–386
mapping problems and, 345
transfer of, 343–344
transparency and, 345
Analysis, as a kind of thinking, **330,** 331

Gestalt theory and, 56
humanistic psychology and, 60
Androgens, aggression and, 548. *See also* Hormones
Androgyny, 462
Anger, 449, 574, **581**–582
amygdala and, 86
arousal and, 514
depression and, 656
norepinephrine and, 575
septum and, 86
Angiograms, 100
Animal magnetism, 211
Animal research, behaviorism and, 54
Animals. *See also* Chimpanzees; Imprinting; Primates
aggressive behavior in, 548–549
and avoidance learning in rats, 253
behavior of, 5
behavioral shaping and, 256
and curiosity in primates, 571
ethical considerations, 30
evolutionary adaptive functions of emotions in, 449
hunger in rats, 562
imprinting in birds and other animals, 237
intelligence and, 372
language acquisition by, 311–312
latent learning in, 259–260
learned helplessness in dogs, 258
mammals, midbrain in, 88
nervous system and motivation, in rats, 557–558
Pavlov's experiments with dogs, 238–239, 248
physiological considerations for reinforcement in, 254–255
physiology of, 4–5
selective breeding in rats and other animals, 78
stimulus–response relationships in rats, 245–247
training, through behavioral shaping, 256
Anorexia nervosa, 564–565
Antaeus, 374
Antecedent events, emotions and, 579
Anterograde amnesia, 269
Anthropological models of intelligence, 388–393. *See also* Cross-cultural entries
Anthropology. *See* Cross-cultural perspectives and research; Culture
Antianxiety drugs, 699. *See also* Drugs, psychoactive
Antibiotics, disease and, 714
Anticipation, as a slip of the tongue, 319
Antidepressant drugs, 698–699. *See also* Drug therapies
Antipsychotic drugs, 696, 697–698. *See also* Drug therapies
phenothiazines, 697
vs. placebo, 697
side effects of, 698
Antisocial behavior, 543–552
aggression, 548–552
prejudice, 543–547
Antisocial personality disorder, 670
Antithesis, in dialectical progression of ideas, **18**
Anxiety, 581, 645

CNS depressants and, 218
consequences of, 649
fear compared with, 650
Fromm on, 607–608
Horney on, 606–607
justification of, 649
level of, 649
moral, 651
neurotic, 652
Anxiety disorders, 645–653
characteristics of, 649–651
cognitive explanations of, 652
cognitive symptoms of, 649
generalized, 648
humanistic–existential explanations of, 652
learning theory explanations of, 652
mood symptoms of, 649
motor symptoms of, 649
panic, 648
phobias, 645–648
psychodynamic explanations of, 651–652
psychophysiological explanations of, 653
somatic symptoms of, 649
stress, 648
symptoms of, 649–651
Anxious–ambivalent lovers, 515
Aphasia, 89–90, 324
Apnea, 207, 209
Apparent motion, perception of, 182
Apparent stability, perception of, 182–183
Apperception, 60–69
Application of inferred relationship, in analogies, 386
Applied research vs. basic research, **48**
Appraisal of situations, primary and secondary, 577, 579, 724–725
Apraxia, 90
Aptitudes, testing of, 379
Arbitrary inference, as a cognitive distortion leading to depression, 657
Arbitrary symbolic reference, 302
Archetypes, Jungian, **604**–605
and male–female relationships, 605
Aristotelian philosophy, 38–40
Arithmetic computation, as a quantitative skill, 434–435
Arousal, 449, **558.** *See also* Stress responses
love and, 513–514
physiological, and emotion, 576
and problem solving, 345
sexual, 565
and stress, 558
and sympathetic nervous system, 84
theory, 558–559, 561
Yerkes–Dodson Law and, 568
Articulatory loop, working memory and, 294
Articulatory mistakes, 319. *See also* Slips of the tongue
Artificial insemination, 77
Artificial intelligence, 58
Arts, 359. *See also* Creativity; Dialectical progression
ASL. *See* American Sign Language
Assimilation, as a Piagetian construct, **423**–424
Association areas, in brain, **96**–98
Association cortex, 97
Associationism, 43, 45, **49**–50. *See also* Name Index: Ebbinghaus; Guthrie; Thorndike

Groupthink, 529–531
  and appearance of unanimity, 530
  Bay of Pigs decision and, 526, 530
  and dissent, 530
  Janis's study of, 529–531
  symptoms of, 530
Growth, cognitive, **412**
  and cognitive decline, 436–439
GSR. *See* Galvanic skin response
Guided imagery, for pain control, 734

Habituation, 128, **189**–190, 236–237,
  560. *See also* Adaptation, sensory;
  Stimuli
Hair cells, 145, 148
Hallucinations, 204
  witchcraft and, 642
Hallucinogenic drugs, 216, **223**–224.
  See also Drugs, psychoactive
Halo effect, 456
Handedness, 78
Happiness, 580
Harmonics, 145
Hazan–Shaver theory of love and attachment, 515
Healing, psychological processes and, 727
Health. *See also* Health psychology; Health
    services; Lifestyle
  accident prevention and, 720
  alcohol and, 219
  employee fitness programs, 718, 720
  exercise and, 716–718
  hypnosis used for, 214
  models of, 714–715
  nutrition and, 716
  pain and, 730–734
  problems, living with, 734–737
  promotion through lifestyle, 715–720
  stress and, 720–727
  Type-A vs. Type-B behavior patterns
    and, 725–726
Health psychology, 710–739, **712**
  history of, 713–714
  and Rodin (searcher), 719
  topics of study in, 713
  and Taylor (searcher), 736
Health services, 727–730
  patients in hospitals and, 728–730
  physician–patient interactions and, 728
  and recognition and interpretation of
    symptoms, 727–728
Hearing, 121, 122, 143–150. *See also*
    Attention; Auditory processing;
    Sensation
  absolute thresholds for, 145
  acoustic confusability and, 278
  anatomy of ear and, 145, 146
  echoic store and, 277
  of fetus, 417
  and information transmission from ear to
    brain, 147
  and location of sounds, 149–150
  nature of sound and, 143–145
  process of, 147–149
  temporal lobe and, 95
  wavelength and, 127
Hearing impairment. *See* Deaf children
Heart, 83
  disease, personality type and, 726–727
  muscle, 82
  rate, and emotion, 582

Helmholtz–Rock views on perception,
  169–170, 171. *See also* Constructive
    perception
Helping behavior, 539–543
  bystander intervention and, 539–541
  factors affecting, 541–543
Helplessness, learned, 258
Hemispheres (brain). *See* Cerebral hemispheres
Hercules, 374
Heredity. *See also* Genetics
  adoption and intelligence, 401
  and behavior, 5
  and instincts, 557
  and intelligence, 400–401
  mental retardation and, 398–400
  schizophrenia and, 664
Heritability coefficient, 400
Heritable traits, 76. *See also* Traits
Hertz (Hz), 144
Heterosexuality, vs. homosexuality, 567.
    See also Gender; Homosexuality
Heuristics
  vs. algorithms, 333–335
  attribution, 497–499
  availability, 352
  and base rates, 350–351
  and biases, 350–353
  confirmation bias and, 502
  generate and test, 334
  in impression formation, 501–502
  and Kahneman (searcher), 351
  means–ends analysis, 334
  prejudice and, 545
  representativeness as, 350
  search activities in problem space, 334
  working backward, 334
  working forward, 334
Hierarchical
  models of intelligence, 384–385
  sorting, and intelligence, 388, 390
  structure of semantic memory, 294–295
Hierarchy
  desensitization, 689
  of needs (Maslow), 568–569
  of reinforcement, 253–254
Higher order conditioning, 245
Hindbrain, 84, 87, **88**–89
  structures within, 87
Hippocampus, in limbic system of brain,
  85, 87
  memory and, 295–296
History of psychology, 37–59
  twentieth-century perspectives, 50–64
Histrionic personality disorder, 669
Hit, 122. *See also* Signal-detection theory
HIV (human immunodeficiency virus), 734
Hoffding function, 178
Holistic approaches, humanistic psychol-
  ogy and, 60, 614
Holistic strategies, Gestalt psychology and,
  56
Holophrases, 306–307. *See also* Acquisition
  of language
Home environment, intelligence and,
  402–403
Homeostatic regulation, 560–561
Homosexuality, 460, **566**–567
  biological basis for, 567
  cultural norms and, 566
  vs. heterosexual orientation, 567
Homunculus

  of motor cortex, 94
  of somatosensory cortex, 95, 126
Horizontal cells, 132. *See also* Eye
Hormones, 8, 110
  aggression and, 548, 549
  alarm and, 722–723
  depression and, 656
  emotions and, 575–576
  sexual, 565
Horney's psychoanalytic theory, 606–607
Hospitals, patients in, 728–730. *See also*
  Health psychology
Hostile aggression, 548
Hotlines, 702
Hue, 138
Human behavior. *See* Behavior; Psychol-
  ogy; Social science
Human dilemma and psychodynamic
  theory (Fromm), **607**
Human-factors psychologist, 64
Human immunodeficiency virus. *See* HIV
Human sexual response, cycle of, 566
Humanism, 41, 613
Humanistic (client-centered) perspectives,
  607–608
  therapies, 686–687
Humanistic–existential explanations,
  613–615, 632
  of abnormal behavior, 642–643
  of anxiety disorders, 652
  of depression, 656–658
  evaluation of, 615, 616
  Maslow's theory of personality, 614
  May's existential psychology, 614–615
  Rogers's self theory, 614
  of schizophrenia, 667–668
Humanistic psychoanalysis (Fromm),
  607–608
Humanistic psychology, 53, **60**–64
Humanistic therapy, 681
Hunger, 561–565
  anorexia nervosa and, 564–565
  brain and, 561–564
  external factors in perception of obesity,
    564
  fat cells and, 562–563
  glucostatic hypothesis and, 562
  lipostatic hypothesis of, 562–563
  obesity and, 563–564
  set-point theory of, 563
  theories of regulation, 561–564
Hyperactivity disorder, 670. *See also*
  Childhood, disorders during
Hyperthyroidism, 112
Hyperventilation, anxiety disorders and,
  649
Hypnosis, 211–214, 680
  demand characteristics and, 211
  and healing, 727
  history of, 211–212
  for pain control, 734
  theories of, 212–214
Hypothalamus, 86, 87, 111
  and aggression, 548
  and emotion, 575
  hunger and, 561, 562
  obesity and, 563–564
  pituitary and, 112
  role of, 87–88
  sex motivation and, 565
Hypotheses, 9
  evaluation and, 17–18

Causalgia; Neuralgia; Phantom-limb pain
personality and, 731–733
in research studies, 30. *See also* Ethics
sensory component of, 730
time course of symptoms, 731
Paired-associates recall, and memory, **272**
Pandemonium model of form perception (Selfridge), 179–181. *See also* Feature-matching theories
Panic disorder, 648. *See also* Anxiety disorders
Papillae, on tongue, 151. *See also* Taste
Paradigm, 8, 596. *See also* Personality paradigms; specific paradigms by name
Parallel play, 470
Parallel processing
in short-term memory, **281,** 282
model of memory, 293–295
Paranoid personality disorder, 668
Paranoid schizophrenia, 663–664
Parapsychology, 224. *See also* Extrasensory perception (ESP)
Parasympathetic nervous system, 83. *See also* Nervous system
Parent–child relationships, bonding and, 463–464
Parental styles, 466–468. *See also* Adults; Family; Fathers; Mothers
authoritarian, 466–467
authoritative, 467–468
permissive, 467
Parietal lobe, 93, 94–95, 97
Parkinson's disease, dopamine and, 108
Parsimony, and scientific findings, 9–10
Partial reinforcement, 257. *See also* Operant conditioning
Participant observation and psychological research, 15. *See also* Naturalistic observation; Research methods
Particular affirmative, 355, 357. *See also* Deductive reasoning; Premises
Particular negative, 355, 357. *See also* Deductive reasoning; Premises
Passion, as an aspect of love, **515,** 516. *See also* Triangular theory of love
Passive behavior
bystander effect and, 541
learned helplessness as, 258
Passive theories, of speech perception, 189
Pathogens, 715. *See also* Health psychology
Patients. *See also* Health psychology
in hospitals, 728–730
psychodynamic therapy and, 686
sense of control, 729–730
styles of, 728
Pattern recognition, 178–182
problems for theories of matching in, 181–182
theoretical approaches to, 178–181
Pavlovian conditioning, 51, 54–55, 238–240. *See also* Learning
common procedures of, 241
discrimination-learning procedure and, 248–249
Payoff matrix, 349. *See also* Game theory
PCP (phencyclidine), 223, 224. *See also* Hallucinogenic drugs
PDD. *See* Pervasive development disorder
Pearson product–moment correlation, A8. *See also* Statistics

Peer interactions, 470–471. *See also* Relationships, interpersonal
Pegword system, as a mnemonic device, **270,** 271
Penalties, vs. punishment, 253. *See also* Operant conditioning
Percentile, 375, A8. *See also* Distributions; Statistics
Perception, 166–197, 168. *See also* Illusions; Perceptual entries
attention and, 190–194
constructive, 169–170
creativity and, 363
of depth, 171–175
direct, 170–171
evolutionary theory and, 188
form, 175–182
habituation and, 128, 189–190
as hypothesis testing, 192
motion, 182–183
nervous system and, 79
of pattern, 177, 178–182
primary somatosensory cortex and, 95
psychophysics and, 122
of speech, 188–189
subjective, in Adlerian theory, 603
subliminal, 203
theories of, 169–171
of time, cultural influences on, 509
Perceptual constancy, 184–188. *See also* Color constancy; Lightness constancy; Shape constancy; Size constancy; Vision
and distal vs. proximal stimuli, 184
Perceptual distortion, 640
Perceptual skills, 431–433
information processing and, 431–433
Perceptual speed, as a primary mental ability, 383
Performance
components of intelligence, 395
vs. learning, 258–261, 272
scale, on Wechsler scales, 377
testing of cognitive, 373–379
Performative, as a speech act, 316, 317
Peripheral nervous system (PNS), 79, **81–84.** *See also* Brain; Nervous system
autonomic nervous system and, 82–84
and motor and sensory neurons, 103
somatic nervous system and, 82
spinal cord and, 80
Peripheral route, to persuasion, **507**
Peripheral vision, rods and, 134–135
Permissive parents, 467
Perseveration, 319. *See also* Slips of the tongue
Person-centered approach to personality (Rogers), 614. *See also* Humanistic psychology; Humanistic therapy
Person–environment interaction, Thomas and Chess's work on, **457–458**
Person–positivity bias, 504
Personal attributions, **497**
Personal constructs, Kelly's theory of, 500, **621–622**
bipolar nature of, 622
Personal dispositions, 629
Personal space, 520
Personal unconscious, 603
Personal variables, Bandura and, 619
Personality, 4, 594–637, **596.** *See also*

Abnormal psychology; Type-A behavior pattern; Type-B behavior pattern; other Personality entries
Big Five theory of, 625–626
creativity and, 361
and pain, 731–733
and perceived stress, 723–725
stress and, 720–727
Personality development, 450–462. *See also* Children; Personality paradigms
abnormal behavior and, 642–643
Damon and Hart model of, 455
Erikson's theory of, 450–453
Eysenck on, 624–625, 626
interactionist approach to, 631–633
Levinson's theory of, 454
Marcia's theory of, 453–454
object-relations theories of, 608
psychosexual development and theories of gender typing, 458–462
schema-based theories of, 619–620
self-concept and, 454–457
self-esteem and, 455–457
self-understanding and, 454–455
social context in, 606
social intelligence and, 620
temperament and, 457–458
theorists of, 478, 479, 480
of women, 606–607
Personality disorders, 644, 668–670
antisocial, 670
avoidant, 669
borderline, 669
dependent, 669
histrionic, 669
narcissistic, 669
obsessive–compulsive, 669
paranoid, 668
schizoid, 668
schizotypal, 669
Personality paradigms
cognitive-behavioral, 615–620, 621
evaluating, 597
humanistic and existential, 613–615
interactionist approach, 631–633
major, 632
personal construct theory (Kelly), 621–622
psychodynamic, 597–612, 613
trait-based, 622–631
Personality psychology, 63
Personality traits. *See also* Big Five theory of personality; Traits
aggression as, 548
cardinal, 629
Cattell's list of, 624
central, 501, 629
common, 629
individual, 627
prototypical acts and, 629
secondary, 629–631
Personality types, and stress, 725–727
Personalization, as a cognitive distortion leading to depression, 658
Perspective and depth perception, **61,** 171–172, 173
aerial, 173
linear, 173
Perspectives, psychological, **61**
associationism, 45, 49–50
functionalism, 45, 47
importance of multiple, 17

To the Reader of This Book

I hope you have enjoyed reading *In Search of the Human Mind* and learning the challenging field of psychology. Your thoughts and ideas concerning the text and the course are valuable to me. Your comments will help craft a better text in future revisions.

School _____ Instructor's name _____

1. Please describe what you enjoyed most about *In Search of the Human Mind*.

_____
_____
_____
_____

2. How can I improve this text?

_____
_____
_____
_____

3. In the space below or in a separate letter, please write any other comments you have about the book. (For example, were any chapters or concepts particularly difficult?)

_____
_____
_____
_____
_____
_____
_____
_____
_____
_____
_____

Optional:

Your name _____ Date _____

May Harcourt Brace and Company quote you, either in promotion for *In Search of the Human Mind* or in future publishing ventures?

Yes [ ]   No [ ]

Thank you for your response,

Robert J. Sternberg
%Harcourt Brace College Publishers
301 Commerce Street   Suite 3700
Fort Worth, TX 76102

Cut here

FROM

_____

_____

_____

BUSINESS REPLY MAIL
FIRST CLASS MAIL PERMIT NO. 2191 FORT WORTH, TX

POSTAGE WILL BE PAID BY ADDRESSEE

HARCOURT INTERACTIVE
HARCOURT BRACE COLLEGE PUBLISHERS
301 COMMERCE ST   STE 3700
FORT WORTH   TX   76102-9875

Charting the Dialectic
The Growth of Psychological Thought

 Psychological thought originates in two relatively pure kinds of soil: the soil of nativism and the soil of environmentalism. Nativist views have their philosophical roots in rationalism, whereas environmental views have empiricist roots. Rationalists have emphasized the primacy of theory; empiricists, the primacy of data. Twentieth-century schools of psychology have branched out from these roots, with some schools primarily nativist (left limb), others primarily environmentalist (right limb), and still others a combination of the two. These mixtures represent a synthesis of the thesis of rationalism with the antithesis of empiricism.